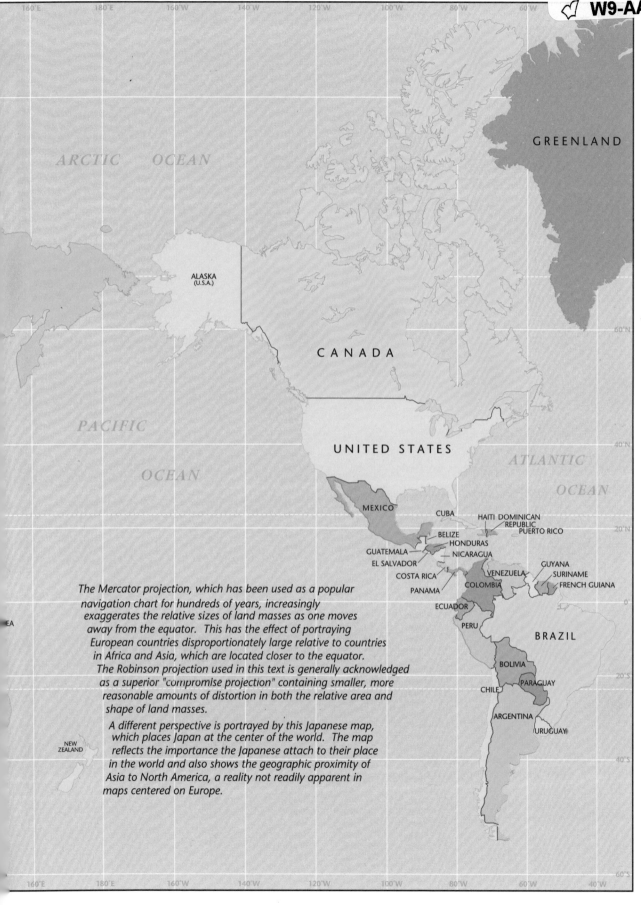

ARCTIC OCEAN

GREENLAND

ALASKA
(U.S.A.)

PACIFIC

CANADA

OCEAN

UNITED STATES

ATLANTIC

OCEAN

MEXICO

CUBA

HAITI DOMINICAN
REPUBLIC
PUERTO RICO

BELIZE
HONDURAS

GUATEMALA
NICARAGUA
EL SALVADOR

GUYANA
COSTA RICA
VENEZUELA
SURINAME
FRENCH GUIANA
PANAMA
COLOMBIA

ECUADOR

PERU

BRAZIL

BOLIVIA

PARAGUAY
CHILE

ARGENTINA

URUGUAY

NEW
ZEALAND

The Mercator projection, which has been used as a popular navigation chart for hundreds of years, increasingly exaggerates the relative sizes of land masses as one moves away from the equator. This has the effect of portraying European countries disproportionately large relative to countries in Africa and Asia, which are located closer to the equator. The Robinson projection used in this text is generally acknowledged as a superior "compromise projection" containing smaller, more reasonable amounts of distortion in both the relative area and shape of land masses.

A different perspective is portrayed by this Japanese map, which places Japan at the center of the world. The map reflects the importance the Japanese attach to their place in the world and also shows the geographic proximity of Asia to North America, a reality not readily apparent in maps centered on Europe.

Sociology

Sociology

FIFTH EDITION

BETH B. HESS

County College of Morris

ELIZABETH W. MARKSON

Boston University

PETER J. STEIN

William Paterson College

Allyn and Bacon

Boston ▪ London ▪ Toronto ▪ Sydney ▪ Tokyo ▪ Singapore

Executive Editor: Karen Hanson
Vice President, Publisher: Susan Badger
Executive Marketing Manager: Joyce Nilsen
Production Administrator: Marjorie Payne
Text Designer: Deborah Schneck
Cover Administrator: Linda Knowles
Composition Buyer: Linda Cox
Manufacturing Buyer: Megan Cochran

Hess, Beth B., 1928-
     Sociology / Beth B. Hess, Elizabeth W. Markson, Peter J. Stein. —
5th ed.
        p.   cm.
     Includes bibliographical references and indexes.
     ISBN 0-02-354621-2
     1. Sociology.   I. Markson, Elizabeth Warren.   II. Stein, Peter
J., 1937-   .   III. Title.
HM51.H46   1995
301–dc20.   94-1954
                                                              CIP

Photo Credits can be found on pages 661–662, which should be
considered extensions of the copyright page.

Printed in the United States of America
10 9 8 7 6 5 4 3 2 1   00 99 98 97 96 95

In Memoriam

This edition of *Sociology* is dedicated to the memory of our friend and colleague, Martin P. Levine, a man who combined a love of knowledge with a commitment to activism on behalf of others and who was taken from us much too soon.

About the Authors

Beth B. Hess is professor of sociology at County College of Morris, where she has taught introductory courses for over 25 years. A graduate of Radcliffe and Rutgers University, she joined the team assembled by Matilda White Riley to produce three volumes of *Aging and Society* (Russell Sage, 1968, 1970,  1972). She has published several book chapters and textbooks in the area of social gerontology, primarily four volumes of *Growing Old in America* (edited with Elizabeth W. Markson), and was elected a Fellow of the Gerontology Society of America in 1978. Most recently her work has focused on issues of concern to women, including two editions of *Controversy and Coalition: The New Feminist Movement* (Twayne, 1984, 1994), written with Myra Marx Ferree, and *Analysing Gender* (Sage, 1987), edited with Myra Marx Ferree. Beth Hess has also devoted much time and energy to professional organizations, serving as Chair of the Behavioral and Social Science Section of the Gerontological Society; as President of Sociologists for Women in Society; President of the Association for Humanist Sociology; as Vice President and President of the Eastern Sociological Society; Director and Vice President of the Society for the Study of Social Problems, and as Secretary of the American Sociological Association.

Elizabeth W. Markson is research associate professor of sociology and associate director, Gerontology Center, at Boston University. She is also adjunct associate professor of sociomedical sciences and community medicine at Boston University School of Medicine. Markson received her B.A. degree at Bryn Mawr  College, her Ph.D. in sociology from Yale University, and postgraduate training in family therapy at the Kantor Family Institute. She has worked in both applied and academic settings over the past 25 years and has contributed to various scholarly journals. Her books include *Older Women* (winner of the 1984 Books of the Year Award from the *American Journal of Nursing*), *Public Policies for an Aging Population* (with Gretchen Batra), and, most recently, *Growing Old in America* (with Beth B. Hess). She has been active in various professional organizations and has served on the executive boards of the Society for the Study of Social Problems and the Northeastern Gerontological Society, as well as being chair of the Youth, Aging, and Life Course, and Family Divisions of the Society for the Study of Social Problems.

Peter J. Stein is professor of sociology at William Paterson College. He received his B.A. at the City College of New York and his Ph.D. in sociology from Princeton University. Stein has taught a number of undergraduate and graduate courses over the past 25 years including Intro-  duction to Sociology, Marriage and the Family, Social Problems, Sociology of Adulthood, History of Social Theory, and Sociology of Sports. His published articles focus on work and family roles, corporate human resource policies, dual-earner couples, and single adults. His books include *Single; Single Life: Unmarried Adults in Social Context; The Family: Functions, Conflicts and Symbols* (with Judy Richman and Natalie Hannon); and *The Marriage Game: Understanding Marital Decision Making* (with Cathy Greenblat and Norman Washburne). He has also been active in various professional organizations and has served as vice president of the Eastern Sociological Society; chair of the Family Division of the Society for the Study of Social Problems; and as Council member of the Sex and Gender section of the American Sociological Association. He served as the chair of ASA's Committee on Teaching. Currently he is collaborating with a team of social scientists conducting research on corporate and union policies on eldercare in the U.S. and Canada.

Contents

8

Sexualities: Identity and Behavior   167

9

Social Stratification   191

10

Gendered Inequality   221

11

Minority Groups: Race, Religion, Ethnicity, and the Emerging American Mosaic   246

PART IV

INSTITUTIONAL SPHERES

12

Courtship, Marriage, and Family   274

13

Economic Systems and the Organization of Work   301

14

The Political System: Power, Politics, and Militarism   326

15

Education and Schooling   351

16

Belief Systems: Religions and Secular Ideologies   376

20

Human Ecology: Population and the Environment   475

21

Rural, Urban, and Suburban Life   497

22

Popular Culture, Mass Media, Popular Music, and Sports   521

Boxes

Sociologists at Work

Maps

Global

Regional

Domestic

Preface

Fifteen years ago we began work on the first edition of *Sociology* in the hopes of producing a textbook that was accessible to students and stimulating to instructors. Thanks to helpful feedback from colleagues and students, we have been able to refine this goal with each subsequent edition. Over time, we have honed our skills as textbook authors so that this Fifth Edition is much more focused than its predecessors. We have continually tried to simplify the presentation of complex ideas without sacrificing intellectual rigor—perhaps the most challenging task in textbook writing.

One of the strengths of earlier editions has been the treatment of gender, race, and class as elements of social structure, and the integration of these crucial variables into the substantive chapters as well as the chapters specifically focused on them. This approach continues to inform our thinking about and presentation of sociology.

And, as always, we use the most recent data and research findings available at the time of writing. The field changes rapidly, as do the needs of our students.

We bring to this task many decades of teaching in various settings, most recently at a community college, a four-year liberal arts state college, and a major research university. Throughout, our collaboration on these five editions of the text has strengthened our friendship and reinforced our commitment to the discipline.

DISTINCTIVE FEATURES OF SOCIOLOGY, FIFTH EDITION

Sociology, Fifth Edition, retains a number of highly praised features from previous editions which set it apart from other texts. All are designed to make the text as "user friendly" as possible.

- **Chapter Outlines.** Each chapter opens with a short outline of its contents. Students do not have to return to the Table of Contents for a quick overview of each chapter.
- **Chapter Openers.** Each chapter begins with a series of timely, interesting items and thought-provoking information. Intended to spark the interest of the reader, they introduce themes developed in the body of the chapter.
- **Marginal Definitions.** The universally praised glosses of key terms continue to reinforce concepts as they are presented in the body of the text. Students report that these highlighted definitions are very useful for chapter review. An alphabetical listing of all key terms appears in the Glossary at the end of the book.
- **Social Policy Issues.** Each chapter contains a social policy issue which helps students see how sociology relates to societal priorities and life choices. Because these issues are an integral part of the text, they are found within the core material rather than in separate boxes. Some of the policies examined include abortion, the war on drugs, workfare, health care, alternatives to prison, and religious conversion.
- **Sociologists at Work.** These autobiographical vignettes are written by sociologists explaining how their own experiences guided them to particular research topics and how they go about "doing sociology." The vignettes acquaint students with various styles of sociological research and show how different sociologists practice their craft. Some issues covered in the vignettes are AIDS research, Holocaust survivors, college athletes, environmental racism, the death penalty, the Civil Rights Movement, and social change in Russia.
- **Boxed Material.** Boxed case studies expand concepts and themes of the core material with the most recent research and up-to-date applications. Cross referencing clearly links the boxes to the text. This information has been completely reorganized to be more accessible to the students.
- **Summaries.** A numbered summary of important concepts at the end of each chapter helps students review the material.
- **Suggested Reading.** Each chapter includes a brief description of both current and classic books covering topics discussed within the chapter.
- **Colorful Illustrations: Photographs, Graphs, Charts, and Tables.** An extensive illustration program expands the learning process for students. A special effort has been made to illustrate the most recent social developments in the

United States and other countries. In this edition, a greater emphasis has been placed on global images. The photographs make the book more visually appealing, help students understand concepts presented, and to relate these to their own lives. Clear and lively charts, graphs, and tables present the most recent information available on societal trends.

- **Recent Sociological Studies and Research.** Because sociology is constantly revising and renewing itself, we have sought to blend classical insights with contemporary research. Our systematic review of all major sociological journals and publications ensures an accurate and up-to-date portrait of our discipline.

- **Inclusive Treatment of Gender, Race, and Social Class.** The crucial sociological concepts of gender, race, and social class are not only addressed in separate chapters but are integrated throughout the text as basic dimensions of social structure that affect all aspects of social life.

- **A Global Outlook.** Each chapter includes rich comparative material exploring cross-cultural diversity. We have included material from scores of different societies ranging from small, traditional bands to large developing and industrialized nations. Students will understand how the United States is influenced by world-wide trends and, in turn, how our social patterns and social policies affect other societies. The message of this global perspective is that to understand our society students must understand the place of the United States in the global order.

- **A Balanced Theoretical Approach.** The major sociological framework—functional, conflict, and interpretive analyses—are introduced in Chapter 1 and systematically applied throughout the text. Key concepts of other frameworks—humanist, feminist, and rational choice—are also used to help students understand how the theoretical models help us to comprehend social systems and social interaction.

- **Writing Style.** Each edition of *Sociology* has offered an engaging writing style that is welcome by both students and faculty. This new edition is even clearer. The theoretical and factual knowledge is presented simply and in most cases examples are provided so that students can more easily understand the material.

- **Appendix.** To help students who are taking their first sociology course, we have included an Appendix that focuses on the study of sociology at community colleges authored by Ann Sundgren of Tacoma Community College and on sociology and the Liberal Arts, written by Edward Kain of Southwestern University, both nationally recognized for their outstanding teaching. In the Appendix we also provide a listing of useful publications dealing with advanced training and careers in sociology, available to students from the American Sociological Association.

THE ORGANIZATION OF SOCIOLOGY, FIFTH EDITION

The text is divided into five parts. each of which develops a major sociological theme.

Part 1 defines and gives an overview of the study of society and its special subject matter; introduces the methods by which it is studied; and describes culture and social structure.

Chapter 1, *The Sociological Perspective* locates sociology in a historical context and discusses both classical and contemporary theorists and researchers. The chapter introduces the reader to the major conceptual models and concepts that serve as basic tools throughout the text. Chapter 2, *Doing Sociology,* moves from the question of *what* sociologists study to *how* they seek answers to these questions. We follow the research process from its origin in theory to evaluation of its findings. Scientific and nonscientific factors are identified, sources of information described, and ethical dilemmas discussed. A brief section on data analysis prepares students to read tables, graphs, and other figures.

In Chapter 3, *The Cultural Context,* we study *culture,* an integrated way of thinking, feeling, and acting that is created, maintained, and changed through human interaction. Chapter 4, *Social Structures: Systems, Groups, and Organizations,* introduces the concept of *social structure,* the patterned relationships through which culture is expressed. It is this regularity and predictability that permits humans to live together with some degree of order.

The four chapters of Part II cover the processes whereby individuals create worlds of meaning and patterns of behavior that meet their personal needs and permit the collectivity to survive over time. *The Social Self,* the subject of Chapter 5, examines the process of socialization, through which culture is transmitted and the self-concept is formed. In these ways society becomes a part of the self and people become active participants in their society.

Conformity, Deviance, and Social Control is the subject of Chapter 6, with special attention to the functions, dysfunctions, and social control of behaviors that violate the rules. We explore various explanations for deviance, including gambling, alcoholism, and mental illness. Chapter 7, *Aging and the Life Course,* focuses on the ways in which age categories and life stages are socially constructed. We examine the development of roles from infancy to old age with special emphasis on the elderly. In Chapter 8, we explore how one crucial aspect of self, sexuality, is socially constructed. The chapter is titled *Sexualities:*

Identity and Behaviors to convey the variety of experiences of both heterosexuals and homosexuals in contemporary America.

The three chapters in Part III describe how achieved characteristics such as skill and income and ascribed characteristics such as sex, race, religion, and ethnicity lead to judgments of social worth and unequal treatment within the society. Stratification systems are formed when people are placed in categories ranked from high to low on the basis of such traits. In most societies, stratification is the key element of social structure, shaping people's life chances and choices.

In Chapter 9, we discuss general principles of *Social Stratification*, the distribution of resources in our society, the consequences of structured inequality, and opportunities for social mobility. Chapter 10, *Gendered Inequality*, focuses on sex differences, socialization to gendered identities, inequality in terms of power, prestige, and property, and changes in gender relations. Chapter 11, *Minority Groups: Race, Religion, Ethnicity, and the Emerging American Mosaic,* focuses on the impact of race, religion, and ethnicity on social inequality. Historical and current experiences of racial and religious groups are examined including those of Native Americans, African-Americans, Asian-Americans, Latinos, Middle Easterners, as well as Protestants, Catholics, Jews, and Muslims.

The seven chapters of Part IV examine the major institutions that provide socially constructed norms and behaviors essential to the survival of individuals and societies. These institutional spheres center on the complex arenas of family life, economic activity, politics, education, belief systems, crime and punishment, and health and health care.

Structural differentiation is the process by which each activity becomes an increasingly complex part of the larger social system. Members of modern societies parcel out their days among the differentiated structures and the roles available to them.

Chapter 12, *Courtship, Marriage and the Family,* places the American family in cross-cultural and historical context and examines the family relationships with other institutions. The family is examined according to a set of socially constructed norms and behaviors that regulate the conduct of courtship, selection of marriage partners, relationships among family members, alternative life styles, inheritance of property, the circumstances under which a marriage can be ended, and remarriage.

Chapter 13, *Economic Systems and the Organization of Work,* examines components of economic systems, contemporary economies, the organization and experiences of work, the labor movement, unemployment and unemployment trends, and the organization of businesses.

Chapter 14, *The Political System: Power, Politics, and Militarism,* examines the concept of power, the structure of power in America, the origins and types of political systems, political socialization and participation in the United States, community action, and the structure and role of the military.

Chapter 15, *Education and Schooling,* reviews the historical role of education in the United States, its functions and dysfunctions, and its connections to other institutions. We also explore cross-cultural differences in education, the social system of the classroom, and the structure of higher education, and we review the current controversies over equality and inequality in American schools.

Chapter 16, *Belief Systems: Religions and Secular Ideologies,* reviews the reasons that belief systems which involve both faith and emotion can exist and how various systems have evolved over time. Traditional religions are discussed along with nontraditional belief systems, such as cults.

Chapter 17, *Law, Crime, and the Criminal Justice System,* focuses on the extent and variety of adult and juvenile criminal activity in the United States and the ways in which crime and criminals are controlled through the police, courts, jails, and prisons.

Chapter 18, *Health, Illness, and the Health Care System,* discusses health care as a prominent issue in the United States today. The major issue of concern to Americans is the absence of universal health care benefits. In this chapter, we focus on the definitions and distribution of health and illness in the United States and the organized social responses to control disease that have developed in American society.

The final five chapters deal explicitly with the processes and consequences of cultural and social change. Society is an ever changing collection of values, norms, and relationships.

Chapter 19 reviews the broad currents of *Modernization, Technology, and Social Change.* At all historical periods, cultures and social systems have been affected by contact with other societies, by conquest, by population pressures, and by the results of human inventiveness and curiosity. We include discussion of contemporary changes in Africa, Asia, and the former Soviet Union. Chapter 20, *Human Ecology: Population and the Environment,* focuses on population trends and the natural environment as these affect social life and are, in turn, affected by people's actions. Chapter 21, *Rural, Urban, and Suburban Life,* traces the causes and consequences of the movement of people from the countryside, villages, and farms into densely populated urban areas and global cities.

In Chapter 22, we look at *Popular Culture* in general and its specific manifestations in the mass media, popular music and sports. Chapter 23, *Collective Behavior and Social Movements* examines responses to historical change and organized efforts to to promote or resist specific changes.

CHANGES IN THE FIFTH EDITION

Each new edition of *Sociology* reflects changes in our discipline as well as domestic and global developments. After several years of hard work, guided by very useful feedback from faculty and students using the Fourth Edition (1991) and Fourth Edition Update (1993), we are confident that our new text will meet your expectations. We've summarized the changes in this newest edition.

Organizational Change

The major organizational change in the Fifth Edition reflects a shift of emphasis in our treatment of aging. As a result, we have moved this chapter from the unit on stratification to that on the self and socialization in a life course perspective. We continue the organization of the Fourth Edition Update yet each chapter has been substantially rewritten, many totally.

Other chapters have been completely reconceptualized as well as rewritten: Conformity, Deviance and Social Control; Aging and the Life Course; Sexualities; Minority Groups; Crime and the Criminal Justice System; Health and the Health Care System; Modernization and Social Changes; Human Ecology; and Rural, Urban, and Suburban Life. These changes reflect the trend in the field of sociology and in society to place greater emphasis on cross-cultural and multicultural materials.

We have recognized and expanded the material placed in boxes throughout the text, which is now color coded and labeled according to the type of information presented. This reorganization makes the material more easily recognized and understood by the students. *Sociology, Fifth Edition,* includes ninety boxes, many revised or completely new to this edition. The complete list of boxed material appears in the Table of Contents.

- **Sociology Around the World** boxes focus on global social diversity to help students appreciate other cultures and place their experience in perspective.
- **Research in Action** boxes illustrate how sociologists go about their craft conveying the excitement and practical effects of the research enterprise.
- **Sociology in Everyday Life** boxes report research involving aspects of ordinary experience that are illuminated by the sociological perspective.
- **Social Change** boxes examine global and national trends that will affect students in the 21st century.
- **Social Policy** boxes, which apply research and theory to crucial current political issues, have been updated and integrated within the text.

GLOBAL MAPS: LOOKING OUT. *Sociology, Fifth Edition,* includes a number of global maps highlighting cross-national developments. The maps allow students to locate countries or regions discussed in the text and to highlight international differences with respect to a number of social variables. This new feature also responds to the needs of colleagues who have had to carry bulky maps to classes to discuss developments in areas such as Bosnia-Herzegovina, Rwanda, India, Thailand, or Chechnya. The sociological maps also present data on economic and social development, education, relative equality or inequality within each country, labor force participation of women, accessibility to mass communication, the major global religions, the global spread of AIDS, and the proportion of the population living in urban areas. A complete list of the maps is in the Table of Contents.

While a number of global maps are available, we have chosen to use the Robinson projection which is generally acknowledged as the best compromise between the Eurocentric bias of the traditional Mercator projection and the Peters projection which distorts the shape of continents and some countries. The Robinson projection is widely used in American schools and colleges and has been adopted by the National Geographic Society as the best compromise between distortions of shape and size.

In addition to global maps, **regional maps** are used to locate specific countries, areas or groups within a country discussed in the body of the text. Among the nations identified on regional maps are countries of the Middle East, Nigeria, Brazil, India, Japan, Germany, and China.

NATIONAL MAPS: LOOKING IN. Maps of the United States are also included for the first time in this edition. These maps are intended to illustrate important domestic trends such as the geographical mobility of Americans, family income in the U.S., countries of origin for immigrants to the U.S., women with children in the labor force, the location of hate groups, and "binge" drinking on college campuses. The maps illustrate social trends and developments examined in the text.

SUPPLEMENTS

Sociology, Fifth Edition is supported by a complete learning package of instructional ancillaries. The supplements for this new edition have been fully updated, enlarged, and improved. For details on these and other items in the package, please contact your local Allyn and Bacon representative.

- **Annotated Instructor's Edition. (AIE)** The AIE has been developed by Peter Stein, and consists of the full student text with a built-in instructor's section, and an extensive set of helpful teaching annotations on virtually every page of the text. Included are summaries of each chapter, a listing of key concepts and ideas, discussion questions, in-class exercises, take-home projects, survey data from the National Opinion Research Center's (NORC) General Social Survey, summaries of recent research findings, information reflecting the impact of race, class, and gender, and notes on the in-text global and national maps. The material in the instructor's section is also available on disk, for both IBM-compatible and Macintosh computers.

- **Test Bank.** The Test Bank for this edition has been prepared by Beth Hess, and consists of approximately 2,500 test items, all carefully selected to test the full range of material in the new edition. It contains true-false, multiple-choice, and essay questions, with answers to all questions page-referenced to the text. The Test Bank is available in print and computerized, using EASATEST III, the best-selling state-of-the-art test generation software program. It is designed to operate on IBM (DOS and Windows), and Macintosh computers. Allyn and Bacon also provides call-in testing, a service that can have finished, ready-to-duplicate texts to you by mail or fax within 48 hours.

- **Study Guide.** As with previous editions, the Study Guide has been prepared by Ellen Rosengarten, a Professor at Sinclair Community College in Dayton, Ohio, who brings to the task substantial experience as a classroom instructor. The Study Guide provides chapter outlines, learning objectives, definitions, sample test questions, glossary terms, exercises, and other techniques to help students master sociology.

- **Videos.** The authors of the text in conjunction with CNN have developed as dynamic two-hour video that focuses on issues of race, class, and gender, both nationally and globally. These CNN segments have been selected to illustrate and expand issues covered in the text, and offer informative content and striking images that will spark classroom discussions. Notes on the usage of the videos in the classroom will accompany the tape. In addition, Allyn and Bacon offers a Video Library from which qualified adopters may select from a wide variety of high-quality videos from such sources as Films for the Humanities and Sciences, and Annenberg/CPB.

- **Transparencies.** A package of 100 color acetates accompanies the text. In addition, all maps found in the text are available in a supplementary color transparency package.

- **Maps 'N' Facts.** Adopters of this text are qualified to receive a copy of Maps 'N' Facts, a program from Broderbund Software. Six different types of maps, and extensive data sets allow the instructor great flexibility in analyzing issues on a regional or global basis.

- **America Online.** Upon adoption of this text, Allyn and Bacon will waive the America Online membership for the first two months. Use this introductory membership to acces a wide variety of interactive services and educational information, including a fast and easy getaway to the Internet. You'll also have access to College Online, a special section on American Online that gives you access to material specific to sociology and this text.

ACKNOWLEDGMENTS

The Hess-Markson-Stein team had the benefit of a very supportive Allyn and Bacon staff that successfully negotiated the complex transition of the text from Macmillan, the publisher of the first four editions. Karen Hanson, Executive Editor at Allyn and Bacon has contributed support, enthusiasm, and very useful advice throughout the project. The complex task of coordinating the many details involved in the production of the text was accomplished with great skill and care by Marjorie Payne, our production administrator. We appreciate her very hard work. Nancy Perry, our developmental editor for the fourth edition with Macmillan, played an important role in the earlier development of the fifth edition. Sarah Dunbar, Editorial Assistant, handled various details with great care and facilitated the completion of the project. While changes are never easy, the Allyn and Bacon staff, led by Bill Barke, President of the College Division, and Susan Badger, Vice-President, have made the transition easier and have made us feel welcome. We are grateful for their support.

We also want to acknowledge our debt to the many colleagues who reviewed *Sociology* for its fifth edition. Their guidance and suggestions proved to be very useful.

Michael R. Ball, *University of Wisconsin-Superior*
Janet Carlisle Bogdan, *Le Moyne College*
Suzanne Brandon, *College of St. Catherine*
Margo Capparelli, *Framingham State College*
Randall Clouse, *Montgomery County Community College*
Kelly R. Damphouse, *University of Alabama-Birmingham*
Ray Darville, *Stephen F. Austin State University*
Sandra French, *Indiana University Southeast*
James W. Grimm, *Western Kentucky University*
A. C. Higgins, *State University of New York-Albany*
Claus Meuller, *Hunter College of the City University of New York*
Howard L. Nixon II, *Appalachian State University*
James R. Palmer, *Edinboro University of Pennsylvania*
Priscilla S. Reinertsen, *University of New Hampshire*
Joyce Tang, *Queens College-City University of New York*
Bernard Turner, *Three Rivers Community College*
Joe Uris, *Clackamas Community College*

We also gratefully acknowledge our debt to the many colleagues who reviewed *Sociology* for previous editions. Their guidance and suggestions proved most valuable.

David P. Aday, Jr., *College of William and Mary*
William R. Aho, *Rhode Island College*
Robert Allegrucci, *Wichita State University*
Angelo A. Alonzo, *Ohio State University*
William R. Arnold, *University of Kansas*
Donald R. Bailey, *Francis Marion College*
Alan Bayer, *Virginia Polytechnic Institute*
Susanne Bleiburg-Seperson, *Dowling College*
Audie Blevins, *University of Wyoming*
Selma K. Brandow, *Trenton State College*
Janet Carlisle Bogdan, *Le Moyne College*
Ervin G. Bublitz, *Winona State University*
William Bruce Cameron, *University of South Florida*
Walter F. Carroll, *Bridgewater State College*
John B. Christiansen, *Gallaudet University*
Robert A. Clark, *Whitworth College*
John K. Cochran, *University of Oklahoma*
Gerry R. Cox, *Fort Hays State University*
John H. Curtis, *Valdosta State College*
M. Herbert Danzger, *Lehman College, CUNY*
Susan Dargan, *Framingham State College*
Ralph O. David, *Pittsburg State University*
David L. Decker, *California State University-San Bernadino*
William DiFazio, *St. John's University*
John R. Dugan, *Central Washington University*
Richard L. Dukes, *University of Colorado-Colorado Springs*
Isaac W. Eberstein, *Florida State University*
Jackie Eller, *Middle Tennessee State University*
J. Rex Enoch, *Memphis State University*
William Feigelman, *Nassau Community College*
Craig J. Forsyth, *University of Southwestern Louisiana*
Jesse J. Frankel, *Pace University*
Clyde W. Franklin, II, *Ohio State University*
Richard J. Gigliotti, *University of Akron*
Henry F. Gilmore, *Albany State University*
Judith Bograd Gordon, *University of New Haven*
Whitney Gordon, *Ball State University*
James W. Grimm, *Western Kentucky University*
Gerald J. Grzyb, *University of Wisconsin-Oshkosh*
Elaine J. Hall, *Kent State University*
Judith Hammond, *Memphis State University*
Donald W. Hastings, *University of Tennessee*
Jacqueline Hill, *Purdue University-Calumet*
Christine A. Hope, *College of Charleston*
Jeanne Humble, *Lexington Community College*
Gerald Hughes, *Northern Arizona University*
Anne S. Jenkins, *Cheyney University*
Daniel Johnson, *Virginia Commonwealth University*
Janis Johnson, *Immaculata College*
Ann Jones, *Northern Illinois University*
Dennis Kalob, *Loyola University*
Ali Kamali, *Upsala College*
Joseph A. Kotarba, *University of Houston*
Joan Krenzin, *Western Kentucky University*
Peter A. Kuo, *Chaminade University of Honolulu*
Michael Kupersanin, *Duquesne University*
Paul L. Leslie, *Greensboro College*
Barry B. Levine, *Florida International University*
Janet Huber Lowry, *Austin College*
Dale A. Lund, *University of Utah Gerontology Center*
Joan Luxenburg, *University of Central Oklahoma*
Mary Ann Maguire, *Tulane University*
Kooros M. Mahmoudi, *Northern Arizona University*

William T. Markham, *University of North Carolina-Greensboro*
Patricia Yancey Martin, *Florida State University*
Ron Matson, *Wichita State University*
C. Doyle McCarthy, *Fordham University*
Patricia McNamara, *University of New Mexico*
Ruth P. Miller, *John Carroll University*
Lynn D. Nelson, *Virginia Commonwealth University*
David O'Donnell, *Iowa State University*
John F. Owen, *Arizona State University*
Robert S. Palacio, *California State University-Fresno*
Philip J. Perricone, *Wake Forest University*
David M. Petersen, *Georgia State University*
Dretha M. Phillips, *Roanoke College*
Margaret E. Preble, *Thomas Nelson Community College*
Meredith D. Pugh, *Bowling Green University*
Claire M. Renzetti, *St. Joseph's University*
R. P. Rettig, *Central State University*
Pamela Richards, *University of Florida-Gainsville*
Ron Roberts, *University of Northern Iowa*
Edward Sabin, *Towson State University*
S. Frederick Seymour, *Northern Illinois University*
Henry M. Silvert, *Yeshiva University*
Ida Harper Simpson, *Duke University*
Paul Sites, *Kent State University*
H. Lovell Smith, *University of Maryland*
Rina Spano, *Caldwell College*
Steven Stack, *Wayne State College*
Suzanne Staggenborg, *Indiana University-Bloomington*
Charles E. Starnes, *Oregon State University*
Phillipa Stevens, *Marymount College*
Henry Stewart, *University of Richmond*
Don Swenson, *University of Notre Dame*
Nancy Thalnhofer, *Eastern Michigan University*
Robert Tillman, *Wheaton College*
Charles M. Tolbert, *II Florida State University*
Susan D. Toliver, *Iona College*
Steven L. Vassar, *Mankato State University*
Joseph Ventimiglia, *Memphis State University*
Bruce H. Wade, *Spelman College*
Edward J. Walsh, *Pennsylvania State University*
Sarah A. White, *J. Sargeant Reynolds Community College*
Timothy Wickham-Crowley, *Georgetown University*
Eric Woodrum, *North Carolina State University*
Diane Zablotsky, *University of North Carolina, Charlotte*

We wish to thank a number of sociologists at various colleges and universities and our colleagues at the County College of Morris, Boston University, and William Paterson College for their helpful comments and suggestions. Included in this supportive group are Ron Glassman, Vince Parrillo, Charley Flint, Rosanne Martorella, John Stimson, Suzanne Tardi, Mary Jane Baumgartner, Soon Man Rhim, Maboud Ansari, all at Wm. Paterson College, Celine Kraus at Kean College, Michael Kimmel at SUNY-Stony Brook, and Carla Howery at the ASA.

Additional thanks go to Joanne Walton for her research help and organizational skills, and steadfast responsiveness and support throughout the project, and to Fida Adely and Natalie Gerbacia for their creative input, dedicated work, and positive energy.

Sociology

1

The Sociological Perspective

The essence of the sociological perspective can be found in these three observations:

- A hippopotamus may stop eating but it will never go on a diet (Rosenberg, 1988).
- The seven-day week is a purely arbitrary construction, representing the triumph of the social over nature (Zerubavel, 1985).
- The basic assumption of sociology is that Robinson Crusoe is impossible (Wolfe, 1993).

That only humans can go on a diet, play games, transform sexual attraction into a love relationship, or organize days into weeks is based on one crucial difference between humans and animals: We can reflect on our actions and control our impulses and invent rules that govern our behavior in groups. We become fully human only through continued interaction with other people, and we maintain our humanity through group memberships. That is why there can be no Robinson Crusoe, a solitary person who keeps a grip on reality. Only humans can imagine how they look to others and think of things that are not visible; that is the difference between not eating and going on a diet. We are the creatures who have imposed order on the diversity of nature.

As we explain in Chapters 3 and 5, this flexibility and self-consciousness are the products of millions of years of evolution during which the powerful inner drives that trigger most animal behavior were brought under control of the uniquely complex human brain. Rather than being guided by genetic blueprints, the human mind is open to influences from the social environment. Indeed, the very name of our species is H*omo sapiens*, the "thinking people"; and as an added emphasis, the technical term for modern humans is H*omo sapiens sapiens*.

The content of this mind consists of ideas, feelings, and rules created by a set of people to bring order and predictability to their shared life. Precisely because H*omo sapiens* is born without prefixed social responses, we create words and rules that give shape to the chaos of the natural world. This is the significance of the seven-day week, an invention of the ancient Hebrews, later accepted by both Christians and Muslims. Although nothing in nature dictates a seven-day cycle, notice how quickly we adapt to its rhythm, feeling and acting differently depending on the day of the week. Note also the importance of a day off for relaxation, worship, and family activities—a day that refreshes the individual and unites families and communities. Yet each major religion has chosen a different day for its sabbath.

WHAT IS SOCIOLOGY?

Sociology is the study of human behavior as shaped by group life, including both collective forces (group constructions) and the ways in which people give meaning to their experiences (self-reflections). This means that the individual is *not* the appropriate unit of analysis for understanding behavior, because human beings do not—cannot—exist in isolation from others. To the contrary, humans have always lived in groups, or collectivities, where people are bound to one another by ties of feeling and obligation. Thus, we cannot predict how individuals will act in a group simply on the basis of what we know about each person. When we interact with others, we create a different level of reality—that of the collectivity, whether it be two people or 200. This larger unit has characteristics that refer only to the group and not to any specific member: a particular size, rules of behavior, a division of labor, a way of dealing with conflict, and so forth. These are the *social structures* that we examine throughout this text book.

> **Sociology** is the study of human behavior as shaped by collective life.

Just as we cannot predict the characteristics of a group based on the individuals who compose it—any more than we can see a cake in a collection of ingredients—so, too, is it impossible to predict the significance of an event or behavior without knowing the meanings created within that collectivity. What, for example, makes a baked good a birthday cake? The candles themselves are meaningless; they stand for something only because we, members of a particular collectivity, have decided that a candle marks the passage of a year and that it can transform an ordinary cake into a special treat. Similarly, all that we know and feel and believe is the product of our interactions with other people. In turn, our group memberships provide a sense of security and stability in daily life.

At the same time that our behavior is shaped by existing structures of thought and action we continually make changes in our social environment. It is precisely our unique human flexibility that allows us to invent new rules and adapt to novel challenges from the world around us. Because the social environment is continually modified by human actions, change is an inevitable accompaniment of collective life. Society is always *in process,* undergoing change, sometimes so slowly as to be barely noticeable and at other times so rapidly that existing structures cannot cope, and the collectivity disintegrates. Throughout this book, we are concerned with the constant tension between the forces of stability and change in human lives and social structures (Wrong, 1994). At the same

SOCIOLOGY IN EVERYDAY LIFE

Human Flexibility

Relative to body size, the human brain is larger than that of other animals, with more pathways and specialized parts that permit more complex cognitive processes. Although other animals can be taught to control some of their reactions, humans rely entirely on *learned* responses.

In a model of instinctual behavior, the organism (body) experiences the arousal of some deep drive (impulse) that then leads to a specific tension-reducing act, all as one unbroken chain of behavior, as the figure shows.

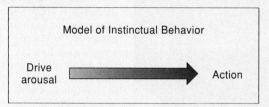

Model of Instinctual Behavior

Drive arousal → Action

A moment's thought should lead you to the conclusion that this is *not* how humans behave, or if they do, we remove them from the community, to prisons or asylums, precisely because they cannot control themselves.

Take, for example, the sex drive, often described as so powerful as to be irresistible. if this were so, we would spend our days as well as nights chasing one another. But we do not; we go to class, do homework, chat with friends, and act sexually only under certain very limited circumstances.

In a model of *human* behavior, then, the link between drive arousal and tension-reducing action is *mediated* (broken into) by the human mind, which both interprets what we are feeling and selects a response we have learned is acceptable.

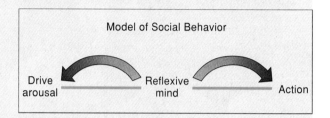

Model of Social Behavior

Drive arousal → Reflexive mind → Action

Notice, for example, that when your mind receives signals from your body indicating that your stomach is empty, you do not growl and begin nibbling the elbow of the student seated next to you or jump up and run to the cafeteria. You wait until class is over and decide when, where, and with what to relieve your hunger. You may even convince yourself that it's a good time to diet and you really are not so hungry after all.

---

time, we must remain aware of the power of people to resist and modify their social environment—a power that varies from society to society and for various groups within the society.

Sociology and the Other Social Sciences

Human behavior and group life can be studied from a number of perspectives in the *social* sciences (as distinguished from the natural sciences, such as biology or physics). Sociology differs from history, economics, and political science in that it is not focused exclusively on only one aspect of social structure. We examine the *totality* of collective experience, including a historical dimension, economic and political structures, and such other products of human interaction as beliefs and values, rules regulating sexuality and family life, patterns of learning, health care practices, and even music, art, and play.

This emphasis on the totality of collective life is shared with **social** or **cultural anthropology,** the study of relatively small, nonindustrial societies, or of a distinct subgroup within modern society such as urban teenagers. The anthropologist becomes intensely involved in the daily life of the people being observed, viewing their world from the inside, in all its richness and totality (see Chapter 3). The line between sociological and anthropological work is often blurred, as researchers borrow techniques and theories.

> **Social,** or **cultural, anthropology** is the study of total communities, typically nonmodern societies or unique subgroups in modern societies.

> Society is not a mere sum of individuals. Rather, the system formed by their association represents a specific reality which has its own characteristics. . . . The group thinks, feels, and acts quite differently from the way in which its members would were they isolated. If, then, we began with the individual, we shall be able to understand nothing of what takes place within the group.
>
> —EMILE DURKHEIM, 1895/1958, 103–4

Sociology is the study of human behavior as shaped by collective forces and the ways in which people give meaning to their experiences. People have always lived in groups or collectivities bound to each other by shared feelings and responsibilities.

The difference between sociology and **psychology,** however, is the most difficult to explain to introductory students. Americans tend to believe that their actions flow directly from personal needs or desires, as if people lived in a vacuum. The psychological perspective views behavior as largely determined by a person's emotional or mental states; that is, from *within* the organism. In contrast, the sociologist begins with the *situation* or context and views behavior as a response.

To illustrate the basic differences between these two approaches, let us take the example of the link that some researchers have found between low work motivation and living in poverty in the United States. From the psychological perspective, it has been argued that receiving welfare leads to a loss of the "work ethic" and a passive view of the world that reinforces the probability of remaining poor and dependent (Mead, 1992). One solution, therefore, would be to increase the motivation to work by reducing welfare benefits.

In contrast, the sociologist would argue that poverty in America today is largely due to low wages, limited job opportunities, and racial segregation, so that

> **Psychology** explains behavior in terms of a person's mental and emotional states.
>
> **Personal troubles** are private problems experienced directly by an individual.
>
> **Public issues** are factors outside one's personal control and are caused by crises in the larger system.

feelings of powerlessness and loss of work motivation are logical responses to the actual conditions of existence (Massey and Denton, 1993). The solution, then, is to raise wages above the poverty line and to keep employers from moving jobs out of areas with a high concentration of poor people. Positive attitudes will follow the changed circumstances.

Indeed, for most sociologists the link between attitudes and behavior is precisely the opposite of that which you have probably assumed up to now. Rather than acting out of a preexisting mind set, people respond to their specific situation and then find justifications for their behavior (Acock and Fuller, 1984; Matsueda, 1989).

The Sociological Imagination

The concept of "the sociological imagination" or level of reality is based on the distinction between "personal troubles" and "public issues" (Mills, 1959). **Personal troubles** refer to private matters of which a person is directly (often painfully) aware. **Public issues,** in contrast, stem from events outside one's control that ultimately affect daily life, such as business cycles, wars, or university policies.

To be out of work is to experience great personal trouble, but when large numbers of people are similarly affected, unemployment becomes a public issue, often leading to policy changes that relieve personal pain. Sociologists are particularly concerned with the process whereby private troubles are trans-

KATHRYN P. GAIANGUEST

Sociology, Social Change, and You

Kathryn P. Gaianguest (Ph.D., Indiana University) returned to academia in 1983 with a goal of teaching students how to apply their sociological knowledge in nonacademic work settings. She is an associate professor of sociology at the University of Maine, where she continues to combine teaching with social action initiatives. For example, she has presented policy-setting proposals to the Commission on Maine's Future and is involved in a community project to ensure education for homeless youths. She is past president of the Association for Humanist Sociology.

*M*any of you have come to this class in introductory sociology because it is required for your major, or because you are curious about sociology, or because it filled a slot in your schedule. As a class and as individuals you are diversified in your interest in, commitment to, and involvement with sociology. We can apply a sociological perspective to help us understand the effects of your diversity. For example, we can predict that this course will have different meanings for each of you—that some topics will be more relevant for some than for others, that some ideas will illuminate a personal relationship for one of you or give another of you a way to interpret issues that have been puzzling you in the past. Whatever meanings sociology will carry for you, I have a challenge for you as you begin your personal journey through this semester. At the end of each chapter and each exam, will you say, "That's behind me" and forget about this investment in your education? Or will you take something of sociology away with you to apply in your own life situations?

Throughout my career I have tried to combine sociological knowledge with active efforts for change in everyday life. After a few years of teaching, I moved into the public and private nonprofit sectors, where I practiced sociology for ten years: directing a statewide advocacy agency for children with special needs; planning and policy-making in state government (in mental health, mental retardation, corrections); directing off-campus learning for college students; and consulting for a public defender's office. During this time, I chose to "put sociology to work" and to build humanistically oriented relationships within institutions and communities.

The premise of a humanistic approach is that people can feel that they have control over their own lives. This approach led me to develop specific sociologically grounded proposals for social change such as (1) moving mental health patients from wards in an institution to five-person group homes in the community; (2) using evidence in a murder trial from the defendant's family life and community experiences to challenge the death penalty; (3) working with local grass-roots organizations to fight price-fixing by home heating oil distributors; (4) developing community self-help organizations to decrease dependency on large-scale, outside organizations; and (5) urging students to take some control over their own learning, including shared decision making in the requirements for the course and the method(s) of grading.

In all of these areas, my sociological knowledge has assisted me in understanding how change can happen. For example, in the case of the price-fixing, we knew that fighting the oil distributors in the courts would be beyond the financial means of this relatively poor community. But our analysis also told us that the community had two sources of power: (1) the numbers of people purchasing fuel (but feeling powerless as individuals) and (2) some independent oil companies within reasonable distance of the community. Once people agreed to purchase fuel collectively from a single source, it was economically possible for an independent oil company to offer a price lower than the local distributors'. The success of this cooperative action energized the community to search for new ways of empowering its members. So from this initial action, further social change emerged.

This semester you will read about how social organizations can strip people of their sense of control You will also learn about social structures—communities, schools, work environments, churches, and families, for example—that appear to meet our life-support needs yet that perpetuate inequality, conflict, and social injustices.

As someone who has combined sociology with many different aspects of work, I challenge you to ask the following questions as you read each chapter of this textbook, "So what?" and "What now?" Ask yourselves, "Can sociology be useful to me in the future? How can I *use* what I have learned throughout this semester in my family, at work, in my community? How can sociology help me make informed decisions about social change both at home and abroad?"

Just as each of you has a different attitude toward sociology coming into this course, so each of you can realize different applications of sociology to your lives, your relationships, and the world around you. From the examples I have given, you can see that sociology is not just scientific research but a living discipline. Put it to work for you in your everyday life and in areas where you seek social change.

While troubles are personal matters, issues develop from forces outside one's control. The increasing number of both underemployed and homeless Americans has forced the federal government to identify both underemployment and homelessness as public issues. Whose responsibility is it to ensure that those who need them have jobs, places to live, and food to eat?

2. An emphasis on the *context* of action, on the setting or situations that shape and channel individual decisions.
3. A recognition that people are also *active agents* in modifying their social environments.
4. Awareness of *meaning as a social product* rather than as something existing within an object or event.
5. A focus on the *collectivity* rather than on isolated individuals.

The sociological way of looking is based on the assumption that there is a *collective reality* that has its own structure and processes that can be studied in its own right. Our units of analysis are not persons but collectivities (Blau, 1964). There are several types of social unit: (1) an *aggregate*, a simple collection of individuals who are in the same place at the same time, such as students walking on campus; (2) a *category*, people who share a distinctive characteristic, such as redheads or Asian Americans; and (3) a *group*, people linked by shared goals and sense of unity, in direct or indirect contact over time. Such groups range from the dating couple to the entire student body. Group structure and processes are the subject of Chapter 4.

> The **sociological perspective** focuses on the totality of social life, the context of social interaction, meaning as a social product, the collectivity, and interaction among individuals.

formed into public issues, when people define their problems as due to outside forces rather than to personal failings.

The sociological imagination asks three questions: (1) How are activities patterned in the society? (2) Where is the society located in history? and (3) What kinds of people are produced in that society? Because the answers to these questions are different from one time and place to another, it is clear that the study of society cannot be based on the idea of an unchanging human nature or the automatic playing out of biological tendencies.

The Sociological Perspective

The **sociological perspective** or way of seeing involves the following:

1. A concern with the *totality* of social life and the links between various areas of activity such as the family and economy.

The government of the People's Republic of China has sought to replace the traditional value of large families with an "ideal" of one child per family. In fact, the public education campaign has helped reduce China's birthrate to the lowest among developing countries.

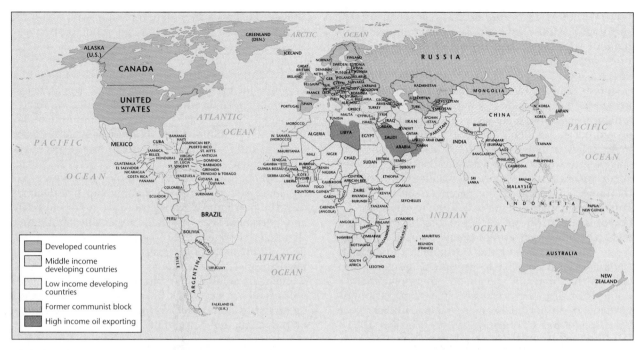

Global Differences in Economic and Social Development.
Sociology is concerned with global issues which will be explored throughout this text. Major differences exist between the developed or First World and the developing, or Third World, countries.

Characteristics of developed countries:

25% of world's people
80% of world's wealth
Average life expectancy 70 years
90% of the world's research and development
Formal education to sixteen years
Dominant trade and financial institutions

Characteristics of developing countries:

75% of world's people
20% of world's income
Average life expectancy 50 years
25% of children die before age 5
20% of people suffer from hunger and malnutrition
Only half of people receive any formal education

Source: Harper Collins World Atlas, 1994, p. 44. © Scott, Foresman, and Co., 10 East 53rd Street, New York, NY. 10022

Social Facts

As members of groups and **collectivities** make decisions, they produce patterned regularities that describe the whole rather than its separate parts. These patterns are called **social facts.** For example, although individual women bear children, the sum of these separate acts is a birthrate that describes the society as a whole. Birthrates are important evidence that humans are not primarily guided by biological drives; if such were the case, birthrates in the same society would not fluctuate with the condition of the economy or political policies. Nor would they vary by income or religion, or even time of the year. Can you guess why, in the United States, more children are born in late August and early September than any other time of the year—in both the South and the North (so it is not a matter of climate)? The Christmas and New Year holi-

day season in our society is associated with reunions and reconciliation, and if these meanings are expressed in physical closeness, is it any wonder that the birthrate peaks some nine months later?

And how can we explain the social fact that births also peak by day of the week, with over one-third as many babies born on Tuesday as on Sunday? Because this pattern emerged only recently and becomes more pronounced each year, we can guess that it has to do with modern health care practices, in this case the growing percentage of cesarean births—one in four in 1994—that can be timed for the convenience of physicians and hospital staff.

A **collectivity** is a set of people that can be as unconnected as an aggregate or as closely linked as a group.

Social facts are patterned regularities that describe the collectivity.

EMILE DURKHEIM ON SOCIAL FACTS.   The great French sociologist, Emile Durkheim, laid the groundwork for modern sociology when he stated that *social facts must be explained by other social facts*—by reference to social structure rather than individual bodies or minds. Durkheim (1897/1951) demonstrated this principle in his study of European suicide rates, which varied consistently over time from one country to another and which could not be explained by climate, religious beliefs, or race. In each country, the suicide rate was lower in Catholic than in Protestant areas, lower for married people than for unmarried of the same age, and lower for parents than for nonparents? The common factor, according to Durkheim, is **social integration,** the extent to which an individual feels part of a larger group. For all their strains, marriage, parenthood, and the communal emphasis of Catholicism (in contrast to Protestant individualism) are ties that bind one person to others. Durkheim's findings of the "preservative" value of social bonds have been supported by more recent studies (e.g., Pescosolido and Georgianna, 1989; Bearman 1991). But there are also cases in which being too closely integrated into the social unit can produce suicide, as when members of a religious group follow their leader into death.

Therefore, if we want to predict the likelihood of suicide, information on psychological states will be less useful than knowledge about enduring social ties. Even if every suicide left a note saying, "I'm so depressed, I can't go on living," we would still have to explain why such a feeling is more common among the unmarried, the unemployed, and the unchurched. Sociologists predict the **probability** of an event, and not what any given individual will do (that is the realm of psychology). We cannot, for example, identify the specific people who will jump off the Golden Gate Bridge, but we can predict what proportion of jumpers will be men or women, young or old, and will do so in April rather than in October.

Following Durkheim, let us examine the typical patterning of suicides in the United States by age, sex, and race, as shown in Figure 1-1. With slight variations, these patterns have been consistent for many years: women are less likely than men to commit suicide, and African Americans less likely than whites.

Social integration refers to the degree to which a person is a part of a larger group.

Probability refers to the statistical likelihood of a given event.

Reification is the logical fallacy of treating an abstract concept as a concrete object.

Subjective reality is developed through social interaction and refers to the ideas and feelings we have about ourselves and the world.

Suicide rates peak in midlife for white women, in the mid-thirties for African-American women, between ages 20 and 24 for African-American men, and at age 85 and over for white men. Obviously, such differences cannot be explained by biology, childhood experience, or mental illness. But if such social factors as stability in family and work relationships are related to suicide, we can see how these commitments are threatened or reinforced at different ages for men and women, and for whites and African Americans in the United States.

In Quebec, Canada, for example, the divorce rate has increased and church membership has declined over the past four decades, leading to a drop in births and a dramatic rise in suicides, especially among men (Krull and Trovato, 1994). Contrary to common wisdom, it appears that the loss of traditional integrating mechanisms has a stronger effect on men than on women. In general, age and sex patterns of suicide will vary by a country's level of economic development and its consequences for marriage, parenthood, employment, and community ties (Girard, 1993).

SOCIAL FACTS AND REIFICATION.   While recognizing social facts, we must be careful *not* to talk about "society" as if it were a person, All too often, one reads that "society does this" or "says that," but this is the logical fallacy of **reification** (from the Latin *res,* meaning "thing"), or making a concrete object out of an abstract concept. Societies are composed of people engaged in patterned behaviors, and we must always specify just who and what we are talking about when we speak of "society": who, under what circumstances, are doing what to whom.

SOCIAL FACTS AND SUBJECTIVE REALITY.   Thus far, we have discussed social facts as collective characteristics resulting from many individual acts. Another type of social fact is the *meaning* that people give to their shared experiences. People make sense of their experience through conversation with others. Together we define what is real or not real, good or bad, true or false. Notice how often you turn to friends for information about whether you are doing "the right thing." To be human is to be somewhat unsure, so that we must continually reinforce our own sense of what is real or true or beautiful with the impressions of others. In this way, the ideas and feelings that we carry in our heads—our **subjective reality**—are also products of social interaction. Such shared definitions are social facts just as much as the structural characteristics of the world around us. For example, take the meaning of money; how we think of "earnings" in contrast to an "allowance" or "pin money"—same dollars, very different meanings (Zelizer, 1994b).

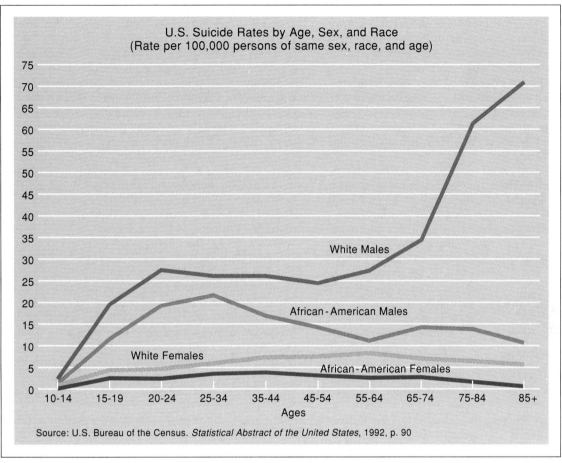

Figure 1-1   Suicide rates in the United States by age, sex, and race: 1991. (Rate per 100,000 persons of same sex, race, and age.

EARLY SOCIOLOGICAL THEORY

The Importance of Theory

The study of society begins with some general ideas of how social life is organized and how membership in various collectivities affects life choices and chances. A **theory** is a set of logically related statements that attempt to explain an entire class of events. Without a theory to guide us, pieces of information remain unconnected items that tell us little about larger patterns, as in the case of suicide rates.

This chapter would be easier to write—and much shorter—if a single theoretical framework covered all sociology. But sociologists have used a number of theoretical frameworks (or *models*) to explain the same sets of social facts. Each theory, by focusing on a limited segment of the larger social context, represents a special way of viewing the world.

In the remainder of this chapter, we will briefly examine the work of several major theorists, along with the guiding ideas and foundations of classic and contemporary sociology. These introductory comments on each theorist are rather short and selective, however, because their major contributions are discussed in detail throughout the book.

The Roots of Sociology

As early as the fourteenth century, the African Islamic historian Ibn Khaldun (1332–1406) claimed that social patterns obeyed laws similar to those that governed natural phenomena, and that society produced a distinctive level of reality worthy of study in its own right (Ansari, 1993). But the history of sociology has been written by Westerners, so that it is gener-

> A **theory** is a set of logically related statements that attempts to explain an entire class of events.

ally stated that sociology as the *systematic* study of human groups has its roots in late eighteenth-century Europe. This period, known as the Age of Enlightenment, followed the collapse of the old medieval order based on unquestioned obedience to royalty or religious authorities. In contrast to the "dark ages," the intellectual movement called the Enlightenment emphasized the ideals of progress, political and economic freedom, individualism, the scientific method, and a profound belief in the ability of human beings to solve social problems.

For many Enlightenment thinkers, faith in the divine was to be replaced by reliance on human reason and scientific analysis. The discovery of the individual and of society were major breakthroughs in intellectual history; new ideas were brought into the common language—democracy, self-consciousness, social system. And if all else could be rationally analyzed, why not society itself? Sociology thus emerges at a particular historical moment in response to a need for certain types of information, as does all knowledge. According to this view, called the **sociology of knowledge,** what we want to know and what we study are themselves social products, shaped by the historical context of thinkers (Mannheim, 1936). The theorists discussed in this chapter and their particular perspectives are all products of their own time and place.

> The **sociology of knowledge** is the study of the way in which the production of knowledge is shaped by the social context of thinkers.
>
> **Positivism** is based on the idea that science can be value free and objective.

ENTER SOCIOLOGY—COMTE (1798–1857) AND MARTINEAU (1802–1876). Auguste Comte, often called the founder of sociology, coined the word *sociology* from the Latin *socius* (companion, with others) and the Greek *logos* (reason, study of) to describe the new science of social life. The field of sociology would be distinguished by (1) its subject matter—society as something other than the sum of individual actions; and (2) its method—careful observation, objective measurement, and comparison. To the great question of the Enlightenment—"What shall be put in place of the old traditional order?"—Comte replied, "the scientific study of society and group life," by which he meant impartial, unbiased observation. The idea that science can be value free and objective is called **positivism.**

The ideal of objectivity, however, was often violated by Comte and others who assumed that their own values as educated modern men represented an eternal and timeless standard of truth. As a result, few women or nonEuropeans of that time could become educated or have their work taken seriously.

Nonetheless, as Comte began to envision this new field of study, two remarkable women had already embarked on the systematic study of society. Sophie Germain (1776–1831), a Frenchwoman and mathematician, had developed a philosophy of positivism and theory of stages of social development that was published a full decade before a similar work by Comte (Reinharz, 1993). An Englishwoman, Harriet Martineau, was making scientific observations of patterns of work and family life in England and the United States (Hoecker-Drysdale, 1992). Her book *Society in America,* is more theoretically integrated than the more famous study by another visitor, Alexis de Tocqueville. Yet Martineau remains best known not for her original work but as the English translator of August Comte.

In any event, the liberalizing trends of the Enlightenment, with their emphasis on individual freedom and economic justice, were soon challenged by the counter-Enlightenment and the restoration of traditional rulers. In this new intellectual atmosphere, the three "giants" of classical sociology—Marx, Durkheim, and Weber—attempted to preserve the Enlightenment vision of progress toward justice and equality (Hearn, 1985).

KARL MARX (1818–1883). As he observed the effects of the early stages of the Industrial Revolution in Europe in the middle of the nineteenth century, Marx was appalled by the miserable conditions of ordinary workers and by the vast inequality between the few who controlled economic and political power and the many who had only their labor to sell in a market crowded with other unorganized workers. For Marx, social order was always problematic (uncertain), because it was based on exploitation, which fueled the possibility of conflict.

As a child of the Enlightenment and its emphasis on science and reason, Marx developed a complex theory called *historical materialism,* based on the central importance of real-life (material) conditions rather than abstract ideas and spiritual forces in determining how people see the world and the social structures they create. The most fundamental material condition in any society was its *mode of production*—the things needed to produce goods and services, such as land, tools, knowledge, wealth, or factories. As Marx traced it through history, the mode of production seemed always to result in a few people having vast control over many others.

Although many of Marx's ideas are no longer as influential as in the past, and much of Marxism in practice has been discredited by the unfolding of recent history, several of his insights have had a profound and lasting impact on sociological theory and practice. Marx's influence on American sociologists was

Harriet Martineau (left) was one of many women who contributed to the development of sociology, although their contributions have only recently been recognized. While best known as the English translator of Comte, she developed a reputation for her early study of the United States including slavery, factory laws, and women's rights. Sophie Germain (right) created a philosophy of positivism and a theory of stages of social development.

especially strong in the 1970s, when many of today's faculty were graduate students, and his perspective continues to inform the field, though in somewhat changed form (Wright et al., 1992a). Four of Marx's contributions to social thought are referred to throughout this book: (1) the need to see society as a totality of interrelated parts, (2) the primary importance of the economic sector, (3) the social construc-

Karl Marx, pictured here at age 38, focused on the great inequality of power and wealth between owners and workers in early capitalist societies. His theories have had a profound influence on the social sciences and political movements for social change throughout the world.

tion of ideas, and (4) the importance of conflict in producing change (Wacquant, 1985).

Society as a Totality of Interrelated Parts.   As you will see in Chapter 4, the concept of society as a system composed of various areas of social activity is basic to the sociological perspective. Tracing the ever-changing links among educational, religious, political, economic, and family arrangements is a major preoccupation of theorists and researchers.

The Primary Importance of the Economic Sector. Of the many parts of a society, it is the economy and its resulting mode of production that shape the content of the other sectors. The relationship between owners and workers is the "base" out of which other patterns emerge—a "superstructure" of political, religious, family, and educational arrangements that maintain and reproduce the essential division between the few and the many.

The Social Construction of Ideas.   As with any other aspect of production, ideas and knowledge become resources controlled by the few. A Marxian analysis of our society today, for example, would show how the flow of information is controlled by the small circle of wealthy people who own and operate publishing companies, newspapers and magazines, and radio and television stations. In addition, the creators of ideas—professors and other intellectuals—come from the same background as the owners. As Marx put it, "the ideas of the ruling class are in every age the ruling ideas" of that society (1846/1976, 39). This concept of *ideological hegemony* (control over ideas) is discussed in Chapters 3 and 9.

Conflict and Change.   Because inequality leads to conflict, Marx saw history as a continual struggle between those who controlled the forces of production and the increasingly powerless masses. The struggle will end only when there is no longer a distinction between owners and workers, that is, when all members of the society share in the ownership of its resources. Although history has not worked out this way, you can probably understand the power that this vision still holds for those who live in extreme poverty. Although Marx saw history as determined by economic forces, he also believed in the importance of people's efforts to change the conditions of existence. People make history, he said, though not always as we please, given the dead weight of the past.

> **Social statistics** refer to official records and systematic observations from which social facts can be deduced.
>
> The **disenchantment of the world** occurs as science replaces faith and fantasy.

EMILE DURKHEIM (1858–1917).   In the tradition of Comte, Durkheim viewed society as a reality in its own right. Individual members of society are born, live, and die, but a certain common pattern to their experiences exists independently. Individual lives are played out in a society with a preexisting set of rules governing family life, for example, or economic activity. This is the social structure that Durkheim felt to be the proper object of sociological analysis.

Durkheim was very concerned with establishing sociology as a separate academic discipline, hence his emphasis on the uniqueness of society and the impossibility of reducing it to the study of individuals. Social facts, remember, must be explained with reference to other group-level characteristics. As a consequence, Durkheim was also a pioneer in the use of **social statistics** such as suicide rates.

As for beliefs and ideas, Durkheim saw these, too, as reflections of society, as a social reality shared by members of the group, and, therefore, as much a part of the social structure as any behavior. In later chapters, we will examine Durkheim's contributions to the study of family, work, religion, and crime.

MAX WEBER (1864–1920).   The concerns of Max Weber (pronounced "Vey-bear") were close to those of Marx in many ways. It was obvious by the end of World War I that a new type of society was emerging in Europe based on an industrial economy that would transform existing social structures in ways that could destroy as well as fulfill the promise of the Enlightenment.

Weber saw both the up- and downside of the modern age. As science uncovers the laws of nature, some of the wonder and mystery of existence is destroyed—Weber's **disenchantment of the world.** Far from liberating the human spirit, Weber saw that technology and modern organizations could become a new type of prison (an "iron cage") without the mystical faith that once helped people survive.

The range of Weber's work is evident in his subject matter. He shared Marx's focus on the big picture, the

Emile Durkheim developed some of the most important concepts in sociological theory by viewing society as a reality in its own right. He also helped establish sociology as a separate academic discipline.

Max Weber's extensive intellectual investigations spanned the diverse fields of sociology, economics, law, politics, history and the development of cities, music, and the world's major religions.

broad sweep of history, although Weber saw ideas and beliefs as having an independent influence on economic and political structures. Yet Weber was also insistent that social reality be understood in the terms of those experiencing it. He used the German word *Verstehen* ("insight" or "empathy") to refer to the ability to imagine how other people give meaning to their experiences.

American sociologists have been influenced by Weber's discussion of the place of one's own values and value judgments in sociological analysis. If sociology is to fulfill its claim to be a science of society, researchers must make an effort to be objective observers, without personal bias. But even if this were possible, would it be desirable? Weber, again, could see both sides: the necessity for value free research as well as the danger of being without any concern for the uses to which one's knowledge is put. But, like other classical theorists, Weber did not realize the extent to which his view of the world was shaped by his own background (Bologh, 1990).

GEORG SIMMEL (1858-1916).   The German sociologist Simmel, though a contemporary of Weber and Durkheim, was fascinated by a different set of concerns. His focus was the everyday world of human "sociability," the voluntary relationships that bind us together in patterns that have a particular shape and that require particular behaviors. Society, for Simmel, must be studied from the ground up, as the sum of responses to ordinary life events.

Simmel began with the basic elements of human interaction—playing games, eating meals, keeping secrets, forming friendships—and examined how the form of such activity affected the very content of the interaction: how the size of a group, for example, tends to produce a certain structure of relationships. Simmel resisted reducing social behavior to individual personality, even as he also avoided explanations based on broad abstractions such as "the economy." Rather, the world of sociability was a reality in its own right, an "interaction order" that is never fixed, always in process, and therefore always problematic. Simmel's influence on contemporary theory can be seen later in this chapter.

GEORGE HERBERT MEAD (1863-1931).   The American social psychologist George Herbert Mead also took the interaction level as his focus. It is through our conversations with others, claimed Mead, that we create meaning and agree on the rules that bring order to collective life. Because the reflexive mind allows us to imagine how we appear to other people, we can guide our behavior into acceptable patterns. Through such processes we come to learn who we are, that is, to develop a sense of self. Thus, both the outer struc-

ture of relationships and the inner structure of the self are products of the same interactions, continually being mutually created and re-created (Baldwin, 1986). As Mead put it, although all animals have an mind and a body, only humans have a mind and a self, the source and the consequence of our dependency on one another (Wolfe, 1993b). Many of these themes will reappear later in this chapter and in Chapter 5.

> *Verstehen* is the ability to see the world as it might be experienced by others.

MODERN SOCIAL THEORY

In the rest of this chapter we will briefly describe the three dominant perspectives in contemporary American sociology: (1) functional analysis, (2) the conflict model, and (3) the interpretive sociologies. We will also touch on several more recent theoretical trends: humanist social theory, feminist sociology, rational choice models, and postmodernism.

SOCIAL POLICY

Social Policy and Sociology

How valuable to government policymakers is the work of sociologists? Are there jobs in this area for sociology majors such as yourself? The answer to these questions, like so much else, is political: It depends on which party is in power. The policy objectives of Republican and Democratic administrations are very different, and each can pick and choose the research that supports its philosophical goals. For example, conservative Republicans have no difficulty finding scholars who claim that welfare programs increase the poverty rate, while liberal Democrats can muster ample evidence to the contrary.

Political considerations not only affect the influence of sociologists on government (public) policy; political control of research funding allows policymakers to influence what gets studied and who does it. In general, funding for sociological research is higher during Democratic than Republican administrations. This is so because contemporary sociology has the reputation of being somewhat radical because of its focus on social structure and specific problems such as race relations, crime, poverty, the decay of inner cities, and so forth. This focus tends to attract students who are idealistic enough to want to learn how to change the social systems that produce such problems.

But sociology has always been open to a variety of views, liberal and conservative, including highly racist and sexist views in leading sociological journals between 1895 and 1935 (Phelen, 1989).

Throughout this book, we will highlight many issues that have engaged sociologists on one side or the other, and sometimes on both. These are issues on which you, as an informed citizen, will be asked to vote throughout your life. Each social policy discussion will present specific questions to think about as you form your personal value system.

The Functional Perspective

The central focus of **functional analysis** is the relationship between two levels of social reality: the whole (the society, any group) and its parts (area of activity, members of the group). What do the parts contribute to the maintenance of the whole? How does the structure of the whole affect the parts? What are the feedback mechanisms that regulate change and adaptation among the parts? Success can be measured by collective survival over time.

At the level of society as a whole, the parts are what we call **institutional spheres:** the economy, political system, rules regulating marriage and family life, educational processes, and the beliefs and rituals that unify its members. The specific content of these spheres varies from one society to another and will change over time in any one society, but each essential task—each function— must be performed if the collectivity is to survive from one generation to another. The central question of functional analysis is this: What are the *consequences* of a given social pattern? How does it meet human needs and preserve the group as a whole? These points will be elaborated in Chapters 3 and 4, where we describe a functional model of social structure.

Functional analysis examines the relationship between the parts and the whole of a social system.

Institutional spheres are major areas of social activity.

Value consensus refers to an underlying agreement about the goals of a group or collectivity.

Manifest functions are open, stated, and intended goals.

Latent functions are unexpected and unintended consequences.

TALCOTT PARSONS (1902–1979).   The American sociologist Talcott Parsons is the best-known theorist of functional analysis. For over four decades, Parsons developed an extremely sophisticated conceptual model that we will only sketch briefly.

He began with the concept of a *social system* composed of interrelated parts, each of which must perform an essential function for the maintenance of the whole. The parts are linked by "exchanges" that make

task performance easier. For example, Parsons's (1955) functional analysis of the American family in the 1950s emphasizes the division of labor between husband and wife, which he saw as necessary for family stability and social order. This model portrays the husband as the family's representative to the outside world, whereas the wife provides emotional support to the family unit, preparing her husband for his daily duties in the workplace and training their children for eventually assuming similar tasks. In turn, the husband's job provides the income needed to maintain his family, while both husband and wife receive encouragement for their efforts from the religious and political systems. Furthermore, the children's education is highly supportive of the parents and of the existing social order. Thus, each part maintains the others and all combine to preserve the system over time—whether a family or an entire society.

The idea that the collectivity is held together by a basic harmony or balance among its parts ("functional relationships") is an important element of this perspective. Equally important is Parsons's claim that social order ultimately rests on value consensus among members of the group. **Value consensus** refers to an underlying agreement (*consensus* means to "think together") about the goals of the group or collectivity and the correct way to achieve those aims.

ROBERT K. MERTON (B. 1910) AND THE REFINEMENT OF FUNCTIONAL THEORY.   Merton's work focuses less on grand models than on "theories of the middle range," which are applications of functional analysis to a limited set of social patterns. Merton examines the *predictable impact* of social structure on human action: If this is how social systems operate, here are the logical alternatives for people located in that system.

For example, if immigrants need help in dealing with government agencies where no one speaks their language, the situation is ripe for politicians to help the powerless in return for their votes. This is a social system explanation for the rise of political machines in American cities between 1880 and 1920. It is an analysis that does not depend on personal characteristics of politicians or voters. The political machine was functional for the urban poor, and their loyalty was functional for the machine.

Merton made several refinements of functional analysis that will be used throughout this book. The first is the distinction between **manifest** and **latent functions.** Manifest function refers to "open, stated, or intended goals"; latent function refers to "unexpected and unintended consequences" (Merton, 1968). Every human act, every social pattern has more than one outcome, and many of these consequences will be unforeseen and undesired. In some cases, the unintended or latent consequences can undermine the manifest goals of policy, as when urban-renewal projects displace local communities and add

The functional perspective focuses on the relationship between society and its various institutional spheres, such as the economy, the political system, and education. Here is the Hong Kong stock exchange, a complex system in operation.

to the problems of the poor or when the military destroys villages to "save the inhabitants." Such *fatal remedies* (Sieber, 1981) characterize many policies undertaken to impose standards of morality, as when pregnant drug users are sentenced to jails where their medical needs are less likely to be met than on the outside (Hawk, 1992).

Recognition of multiple consequences leads also to the realization that not all behavioral patterns or aspects of social systems are functional; that is, they do not contribute to the maintenance of a society or group. Some patterns may actually reduce the capacity of a system to adapt and survive; these are, therefore, considered **dysfunctional.** When assessing functionality, the questions are, Does that behavior or structure help or hinder the system as a whole? and Are the goals of individuals and groups achieved?

But not all goals can be achieved, and one group's success may involve another group's failure. Therefore, the sociologist must identify *for whom or for what* the patterns or structures are functional. Clearly, a war could be functional for a society by reducing outside threats but highly dysfunctional for civilians whose homes are bombed. Defense contractors gain, consumer industries lose; generals win promotions, soldiers lose their lives.

CRITICISM OF FUNCTIONAL ANALYSIS.   Finding flaws in functional analysis has been a minor industry in academic sociology. Critics claim that the model is too broad and generalized and too removed from individual experience. A second target is the conservative

bias of the theory's emphasis on harmony and stability. In this view, disorder and conflict are seen as temporary surface problems in an otherwise healthy system and not as signals that the system itself may be deeply flawed.

Third, as Parsons's analysis of the American family suggests, what seemed clear in the 1950s is less so today. In the search for functionality, Parsons and others overlooked built-in sources of strain; and in the search for universal processes, they failed to appreciate specific historical contexts.

From the standpoint of the sociology of knowledge, it is not difficult to see why American sociologists working between 1945 and 1960 would have taken such an optimistic view of the society and its institutional spheres. These were years of great economic expansion, social stability, and what appeared to be widespread value consensus. This impression of harmony was shattered by the events of the 1960s, exposing the limitations of functional theory and bringing an alternative model and new generation of scholars into prominence.

> **Dysfunctional patterns** reduce the capacity of a system to adapt and survive.

Despite its shortcomings, functional analysis remains an important theoretical tool, illuminating many of the social patterns described throughout this book. Contemporary theorists are reworking Parsons's model to meet these criticisms and to incorporate insights from other perspectives (e.g., Alexander and Colomy, 1990).

The Conflict Perspective

As its name indicates, **conflict theory** focuses on disorder, disagreement, and open hostility among individuals and groups and on lack of harmony among system parts. From this point of view, struggle over power and resources is normal, and stability is the condition that requires explanation. Social systems are temporary and often fragile combinations of competing forces. Conflict can be minimized in periods of economic prosperity, such as the 1950s, but will be intensified during economic downturns, as in the 1930s and early 1990s.

From this perspective, sociologists examine (1) sources of tension among people and groups with different amounts of power, (2) techniques of conflict control, and (3) ways in which the powerful maintain and enlarge their influence. For example, a conflict perspective on the American family (Curtis, 1986) would focus on power inequality between parents and children and between husbands and wives, the strains this places on intimate relationships, and the subtle and not-so-subtle ways in which control is exercised—a far cry from Talcott Parsons's vision of a harmonious blending of complementary functions.

Conflict theory examines disagreement, hostility, and struggles over power and resources.

Macrosociology focuses on society as a whole or on social systems at a high level of abstraction.

Social order at any particular moment is the outcome of struggle among groups of unequal power rather than the result of blind forces of technology or other impersonal historical trends. The conflict question is, Who benefits from any given social arrangement? For example, where a functionalist would explain police violence as necessary to restore order, a conflict theorist would note that such violence is most often directed against the least powerful members of the society.

Both the functional and conflict models, however, share a tendency to examine social structure at a very abstract level ("modern society" or "the American family," for example), and to seek general rules about the nature of social systems. This emphasis is referred to as **macrosociology** (*macro,* meaning "large"). Macrolevel studies typically move from a general model of social structure back to everyday behavior—from the "out there" to the "down here." Although most often applied to large-scale social units, both conflict and functional analyses can be used to examine smaller groups such as a particular family or workplace or even the classroom. In fact, one interesting exercise would be to compare a functional analysis and a conflict analysis of your sociology classroom.

In contrast to macrosociological perspectives, many sociologists have followed the path of Simmel and Mead and examined human interaction at the personal, face-to-face level to see how people actually interpret their life and create meaning. This emphasis

The conflict perspective focuses on disorder, disagreement, and open hostility among individuals and groups and on lack of harmony among system parts. As the former Soviet Union disintegrated, various political and national groups have struggled for power. Here, old-line Communists clash with reformers in the streets of Moscow.

The Development of Sociology in the United States

The founders of American sociology were also products of their time and place. Many came from a strongly religious Protestant background, with its emphasis on individual responsibility and the obligation to do good deeds in this world; indeed, sociology found its most receptive audience among students at graduate schools of religion (Turner and Turner, 1990). They pursued a vision of science in the service of the public good, of unchanging laws of nature that would legitimize American individualism and its free-market economy (Ross, 1991).

The ideal of social betterment also drew many women to the field, especially to the University of Chicago's sociology program in the early years of this century: Jane Addams, Charlotte Perkins Gilman, Marion Talbot, Florence Kelley, Alice Paul, Elsie Clews Parsons, Leta Hollingworth, Alice Hamilton, Emily Greene Balch, and Sophonisba Breckinridge (Deegan, 1991; Fish, 1985; Reinharz, 1993). We list their names here because they are rarely mentioned in other books and because many were actually doing high-level "scientific" research (urban mapping, consumer surveys) when their male colleagues at Chicago were doing anthropological studies of criminals, boxers, hoboes, and other unusual urban types. But as sociology gradually became a recognized academic specialty and American universities sought to upgrade their prestige, women were discouraged from graduate departments of sociology.

In the 1930s and 1940s, the development of American sociology was influenced by the work of European scholars as well as by translations of Durkheim, Weber, and Marx. Uniquely American, however, was the enduring dominance of *positivism*, an emphasis on objective measurement of "facts," which has come to be associated with hard-headed "masculine" realism (Laslett, 1990). In contrast, the *humanistic* strain in American sociology—in which people's accounts of their own experience are the primary source of information—has come to be defined as softer, more feminine, and consequently, of lesser significance. The tension between a

Hull House, founded by Jane Addams in 1889, provided educational and social services to immigrants in the Chicago slums. Addams' work won her a Nobel Peace Prize in 1931.

focus on social structures "out there" and the "inner" reality of individuals is reflected in the variety of contemporary theories discussed in this chapter.

In addition, persistent racism in the United States created a form of educational segregation in which sociologists at historically black colleges and universities were and are perceived as less central to the profession than their counterparts at white institutions (Hudgins, 1994). A final distinction is the higher prestige of sociologist at major research universities compared with those at four- and two-year colleges who are primarily involved in teaching (Chapter 15).

on smaller, less abstract units of analysis is called **microsociology** (*micro,* meaning "small"), although it can also be used to explore and illuminate large-scale social systems (Collins, 1988).

The Interpretive Perspective

Microsociology is characterized by a diversity of approaches that share the assumption that sociological understanding begins with the study of *face-to-face interaction* (Denzin, 1992). These are called **interpretive** models because the focus is on how group members make sense of and give meaning to the events of daily life. This is sociology from the ground up—from the "interaction order" to larger social systems. In this section we will briefly describe three of these approaches: symbolic interaction, dramaturgy, and ethnomethodology — long terms but very recognizable subject matter, everyday life.

THE SYMBOLIC INTERACTION APPROACH. As described by Blumer (1969) and others, the **symbolic interaction** model is based on the two essential facts of

Microsociology focuses on smaller units of social systems, such as face-to-face interactions.

Interpretive sociology focuses on processes by which people make sense of daily life.

Symbolic interaction views social systems as products of interaction and the meanings that people give to their situations.

DONALD CUNNIGEN

African-American Sociologists and the Sociological Profession

After receiving his doctorate in sociology from Harvard University, Donald Cunnigen taught briefly at the University of Pennsylvania. He was a Pew Minority Postdoctoral Fellow at the Center for Afro-American Studies of Wesleyan University. Presently, he is a faculty member at the University of Rhode Island. He is completing a book on second-generation African-American sociologists.

W hen I entered Tougaloo College, a historically African-American institution, in the early 1970s to study sociology, I was shocked to discover that most of the department's faculty lacked knowledge of African-American contributions to the discipline. The predominantly white faculty, while extremely sensitive to racial issues, had limited exposure to African-

American scholarship as a result of their training in graduate departments where the basic perspective reflected the experience of white middle-class male intellectuals.

In my first theory course, the departmental emphasis nonwhite sociological scholarship became a critical experience for me. With the aggressiveness of an undergraduate trying to refine a sense of "black consciousness," I asked the instructor about African-American sociologists. He responded by acknowledging familiarity with only three names—E. Franklin Frazier, Charles S. Johnson, and W. E. B. DuBois—but had little to say about their work. I then decided to undertake an independent study of African-American sociologists to develop material for a formal course at the college, but Tougaloo's conservative academic dean refused to include a student-designed course in the regular curriculum.

Despite this experience, I continued my strong interest in the topic, and as a graduate student at Harvard, I compiled a bibliography of African-

American sociologists that allowed me to extend and deepen the undergraduate course I had developed at Tougaloo and to broaden my understanding of those who had gone before me.

I discovered four distinct periods in the African-American sociological tradition, each influenced by the broader social system at that period in time: (1) a founding generation (1895–1930); (2) a second generation (1931–59) concerned with fitting into the academic mainstream; (3) a third generation (1960–75) profoundly influenced by the Civil Rights Movement; and (4) the new scholars (1976 to the present). Each period reflected important social and intellectual influences on African-American sociologists.

The first generation trained and worked in an America that totally ignored African-American intellectuals. Scholars who had earned the doctorate, James R. Diggs, Richard R. Wright, W. E. B. DuBois, Isaac T. Brown, and George Edmund Hayes, along with brilliant students such as Walter R.

social life mentioned at the beginning of this chapter: (1) the reflexivity of human thought that allows us to communicate through *symbols* and (2) the need to be in continual association with others.

The questions addressed by symbolic interactionists are, How do people make sense of their experiences, influence one another, and define themselves? We interpret experience by talking to other people. The world "out there" is filtered through conversations and then reaffirmed by our actions. For example, the pattern of relationships called "the American family" exists only because individual women and men decided to get married, have children, and conduct themselves according to the expectations of others. But our idea of "the family" has changed dra-

matically over the past 200 years in terms of size, membership, the division of tasks, quality of interaction, and ultimate goals (see Chapter 12).

The social patterns that we think of as outside one's self and as limiting (constraining) our choices are themselves the product of chains of behavior at the microlevel, such as decisions about when to get married, how many children to have, and whether or not to join the labor force. In this approach, the rules of social order are never fixed, are always in a process of change, lending an element of flux and uncertainty to our life. We are not simple reactors to outside demands but active creators of meaning, although some people have greater power to impose their definitions of reality on the less powerful. Over time,

Chivers and Kelly Miller, were able to find employment primarily in African-American institutions of higher learning—Howard, Fisk, and Atlanta (now Clark-Atlanta). Their scholarship was unknown to all but a few in the white sociological community. They received little research support from their institutions and even less from the major foundations.

Second-generation African-American sociologists began their careers after 1930 and focused their research on the conditions immediately affecting the African-American community and the wider society. Their work was more sophisticated and better documented than that of the founders and several received recognition from the white sociological establishment. But they were not engaged in direct social action, and although able to participate more fully in mainstream professional organizations, they nonetheless formed their own Association of Negro Social Science Teachers.

This generation exemplifies the "dual consciousness" of African-American intellectuals of that period based on the conflict between the professional standards of objectivity to which they were trained and their personal commitment to a racially just society. Most were still located at the margins of academe (in government agencies and African-American institutions) but a few exceptional scholars, such as Charles Lawrence, Butler Jones, Hylan Lewis, and Ira deAugustine Reid found employment in white universities. The rest, despite such obvious talents as Horace

Cayton, St. Clair Drake, Anna Julian, Anna Grant, Preston Valien, and Mozell C. Hill remained excluded by the deep and widespread racism of both American society and its academic sphere.

Because many in this generation had been trained in a tradition that emphasized adaptation and assimilation into the dominant culture by minority groups, they also sought the same goal for themselves, to fit into the mold constructed by white sociology.

The next generation of African-American scholars came of age during the Civil Rights Movement of the 1960s, and many, such as Joyce Ladner, were participants in the movement. They formed the Caucus of Black Sociologists to challenge the racial exclusiveness of the major sociological organizations. With the assistance of white scholars who supported their goals they expanded the participation of African Americans in graduate sociology and in all aspects of professional life. The third generation also came from a broader spectrum of graduate schools, reflecting the expansion of social opportunities for African Americans in academia in general.

Third-generation scholars were no longer willing to accept the establishment version of the discipline, and they did not pursue their careers in primarily African-American schools. Many enjoyed the same career opportunities as white scholars while challenging the basis of white scholarship. Among the leaders of this generation were James E. Conyers,

Jacqueline J. Jackson, Lena Myers, Troy Duster, Alphonso Pinkney, Nathan Hare, LaFrances Rodgers-Rose, and Wilbur H. Watson.

The most recent, fourth, generation came to adulthood after the great wave of Civil Rights activism. They studied at a variety of institutions, and many were recipients of Minority Fellowships established by the American Sociological Association. As a group, they inherited the rich tradition of the three preceding generations, which led them to emphasize research on topics of immediate and crucial interest to the African-American experience and community, and to adopt a more radical position than that of earlier scholars. What they have developed is a unique perspective that enriches all of sociology, one that maintains the original concern of the discipline with social reform. The origins of American sociology were in the grand tradition of activism, not the sterile emphasis on ethical neutrality and bean-counting that characterize the field today.

While the future for African-American scholars appears very bright, the discipline has much room for improvement in increasing the numbers and financial support for minority graduate students; expanding opportunities for African-American faculty; and encouraging multicultural research on a society that is itself more racially and ethnically varied than ever before in our history. African-American scholars are now prepared to lead the way toward greater understanding of the America of the next century.

these meanings worked out through conversations at the microlevel take on a reality of their own at the macrolevel level of social structure. It is the *interplay* of individual consciousness and social structures that fascinates interpretive analysts (Becker and McCall, 1990) and social psychologists (Ridgeway, 1994).

Locating sociology in the details of everyday life, in ongoing interactions and encounters, is also the goal of the *dramaturgical analysis* of Erving Goffman (1959, 1983) and the *ethnomethodology* of Harold Garfinkel (1967).

DRAMATURGY. Goffman's work is called **dramaturgical** because social interaction is viewed as a series of little dramas in which actors present images of themselves, attempt to manipulate the reactions of other people (the audience), protect their identity, and develop rules that guide behavior in daily encounters. Just as an actor has a different script for each stage on which she or he appears, so does each of us play a different part as we

> The **dramaturgical view** sees social interaction as a series of minidramas.

move from one social setting to another in the course of a day. We play many different parts, depending on the context, and at each performance some aspect of our identity is at risk. Thus, social life is a series of challenges, with the outcome never fully predictable.

Drawing on the work of both Durkheim and Simmel, Goffman links the micro- and macrolevels

The field of sociology has only recently recognized the contributions of some of the early pioneers of the discipline. Among the first wave of African-American sociologists are W. E. B. DuBois, the first African-American male to receive a Ph.D. from Harvard University, and Anna Johnson Julian, the first African-American woman to receive a Ph.D. in Sociology in the United States (University of Pennsylvania in 1937). DuBois, a scholar and social critic, believed that social research should focus on current social problems, and he focused on the issue of race in the U.S. His classic study of Philadelphia's African-American community at the beginning of the 20th century was published as *The Philadelphia Negro: A Social Study* (1899). Anna Johnson Julian, who recently died at the age of 91, had been a life-long social activist, a teacher of sociology, a social worker, national President of the NAACP, and a member of the Executive Board of the United Nations Association.

through the concept of **frame analysis,** the study of those socially constructed rules that govern everyday encounters but that also exist apart from any given interaction. In other words, following Durkheim, there is a moral reality out there called "society" within which, following Simmel, individuals enact the rituals of daily life. Thus, our behavior is never fully determined by outside structures, but neither does it take place in a formless vacuum.

Examples of frame analysis include Goffman's own study of the interaction among surgeons and nurses in an operating room, where gender–power relations are symbolically re-created and where the life-and-death tensions of the moment are handled by joking among the medical team. You might try a dramaturgical-frame analysis of the ritual dramas played out in a college football game (Deegan, 1989). What are the not-so-hidden symbols of the uniforms or of what is not worn (the bare arms and belly of linemen are telling us something). Another example of frame analysis is the ritual drama of sin and redemption surrounding religious and political scandals, where

Frame analysis refers to the rules governing everyday encounters that also exist apart from specific interactions.

Ethnomethodology involves probing beneath the "taken-for-granted" reality.

the offender must publicly repent and be cleansed of evil before rehabilitation (T. R. Young, 1990).

ETHNOMETHODOLOGY. Uncertainty and excitement also characterize Garfinkel's **ethnomethodology,** a concept that refers both to the subject matter and the means for gaining information about it (Heritage, 1984). Because so much of what we do takes place without conscious awareness, the researcher must dig below the level of "taken-for-granted" reality to discover the basic meaning of social action. For example, when asked why men hold doors for women, most of our students say, "I was taught that it's a form of politeness or way of showing respect." These are taken-for-granted meanings. But suppose it was pointed out that because the other types of people for whom doors are held are children, the elderly, or the disabled—people thought to be incapable of managing for themselves—might not the deeper meaning of the custom be a reinforcement of women's powerlessness? If you were an ethnomethodologist you would test this possibility by conducting research on people's reactions to situations that upset the taken-for-granted reality, as when a woman holds open a door for a man to pass through (Richardson, 1974). How does he respond?

In this perspective, how people talk to one another and what they talk about are important objects of

Ethnomethodology in Action

What, for example, are the hidden, taken-for-granted meanings of the typical dating situation? The best way to find out is to break into these existing understandings by having the woman, at the end of the date, ask her partner how much she owes for her half of the evening's expenses or by having the man present his partner with a bill for her share of the tab. How does the other react? Why? Gradually, it will become clear that the date involves certain "understood" exchanges and that the person who pays has greater control over the terms of exchange. Contrast the definition of the situation in a traditional dating relationship to that for "going Dutch," when the partners agree in advance to share the costs.

---

analysis, because conversation both creates and is constrained by social structure (Boden and Zimmerman, 1991). On the one hand, our conversations are influenced by the context and its rules; but on the other hand, we can either reinforce or change those rules as we talk with one another. Even such a seemingly clear reality as one's sexual identity is continually being created and re-created through conversation and encounters. Sociologists differ, however, in the precise interpretation of one of Garfinkel's earliest essays, the study of "Agnes," a biological male who, as an adult, lived as a woman. But all agree that femininity and masculinity are socially constructed and symbolically accomplished.

All three major perspectives—functional, conflict, and interpretive—provide answers to one basic question, How is society possible? Each model helps us understand some aspects of social life, and each will be used throughout this book. In the study of unemployment, for example, a functionalist would explain unemployment rates in terms of whether or not a worker had the skills needed by employers and the solution as one of better job training. From the conflict perspective, unemployment rates reflect powerlessness and are the result of an employer's decision to close down or relocate to maximize profit. The solution is to create jobs where the workers live. In contrast, interpretive studies would examine the meaning of unemployment to the person and how it affects relationships with others. The differences are shown in Table 1–1.

NEW DIRECTIONS IN SOCIAL THEORY

In addition to the three dominant theoretical traditions, there are also several additional, relatively new models that have attracted considerable following. Paradoxically, however, the very diversity of perspectives has led to growing efforts to develop theories that integrate aspects of many different viewpoints and that provide a theoretical bridge between macro-

level and microlevel phenomena (Giddons, 1990; Huber, 1991; Ritzer, 1991). Let us examine three of these: humanist sociology, feminist sociology, and rational choice theory.

Humanist Sociology

Rejecting the positivist position that social science can—or should—be value free, **humanist sociology** is based on the belief that one should become actively engaged in social change. The professional goal of the sociologist should be to use the tools of sociology for the benefit of those deprived of full participation in the society rather than to build a personal reputation or to search for abstract knowledge.

Their concern for social justice rather than social order has led most humanist sociologists to the interpretive perspective, with its emphasis on the human capacity to resist and change social structures. A humanist sociology begins with the belief that we are free, reflexive individuals who, if fully informed, will choose to do the socially responsible thing (Scimecca, 1995). But because various collectivities control differing resources, the most powerful among them will be able to impose their meanings, creating oppressive structures that must then be actively resisted by the less powerful.

> **Humanist sociology** is based on the belief that sociologists must become actively involved in social change.

This tradition of research and thought is embodied in the Association for Humanist Sociology, founded in 1975, that has attracted a largely young and activist following deeply concerned with issues of inequality at all levels: between men and women, whites and minorities, owners and labor, and industrial nations and the less developed countries. Each article in the journal *Humanity & Society* begins with a "reflexive statement," in which authors inform the reader of their value positions and of how they came to study the particular topic. Most articles also conclude with specific policy proposals designed to improve the conditions of the less powerful.

TABLE 1-1   Models of Social Theory

	Functional Model	Conflict Model	Interpretive Model
Nature of Society	Integrated, interrelated social structures that together form a system	Competing groups and collectivities seeking to secure own ends	Interacting individuals, groups, and social networks
Basis of Interaction	Consensus on values; shared goals	Power, conflict, constraint	Shared meanings via shared symbols
Focus of Study	Social order and how society is maintained	Social change and conflict	Development of adaptation to group
Level	Social structure	Social structure	Interpersonal
Social Change	Orderly, moderate change	Change in power relationships and social structures	Changed meanings and symbols

Feminist Sociology

Concerns similar to those of the humanists have motivated *feminist* scholars who claim that positivism has produced a world view that separates the researcher from the objects of study and imposes a basically Western white male middle-class interpretation of reality onto the lives of others. Until recently, most research either left women out or assumed they shared the same perceptions as men or were somehow morally or mentally deficient if they held different views. Over the past two decades, feminist sociologists (both male and female) have filled the knowledge gap and confronted the biases in research and theory. Through **feminist sociology,** they direct attention to women's experience and to the importance of gender as an element of social structure.

Today women hold many of the highest offices in American sociological organizations, and feminist scholars have formed a professional society, Sociologists for Women in Society, and in 1987 launched a scholarly journal, *Gender & Society.* Although many feminist sociologists prefer interpretive techniques to give women their own voice, others have found macrosociological models equally important in tracing broad trends and explaining variations in the position of women across history and in different societies. What these scholars share, however, is a growing recognition of the importance of gender as an element of social structure rather than as a characteristic of individuals. Many claim that feminist sociology contains all the elements of a truly integrative theoretical model for sociology, combining analysis of macrolevel social structures *and* the microlevel encounters that maintain these structures (Hess, 1990). At the macrolevel, it weaves together functional and conflict approaches, and at the microlevel, it employs all the techniques developed by the interpretive theorists. Recent trends in gender theory and research will be discussed in Chapter 10.

Rational Choice Theory

In the current situation of theoretical flux in American sociology, it should not be surprising that a model based on an essentially economic view of behavior would emerge. **Exchange** and **rational choice** theories begin with the assumption that people tend to do that which brings the most benefits at the least cost (Homans, 1961; Coleman, 1992, 1993). Individuals, like corporations and other collective units, make rational choices among various alternatives based on judgments regarding the relative worth of what they can gain in contrast to what they must give up, but always within the constraints of available resources.

Theories based on an economic view of human behavior have always had great appeal to Americans, with their emphasis on rational calculations among individuals (see Chapter 3). By the same token, such models strike many critics as being essentially nonsociological by minimizing the societal-level context in which decisions are made. Neither decisions nor deciders act in a vacuum: There is a history to consider, there are usually other people involved, and there are always nonrational actions (Cook and Levi, 1991; Pescosolido, 1992; Risman and Ferree, 1995).

At the microsocial level, however, an exchange perspective can illuminate: Ask yourself what an individual expects to gain from a particular course of action and what that behavior costs in time and energy, in self-respect, and in other goals not pursued. We

Feminist sociology directs attention to women's experience and to the importance of gender as an element of social structure.

Exchange and **rational-choice** theories adopt an essentially economic model of cost and benefit to explain people's behaviors.

tend to do that which appears to bring rewards at least equal to what we have to spend to get them, and to avoid situations in which we risk more than we think we can afford. Perhaps this will explain why you have pursued certain romantic relationships and dropped others.

Reductionist Challenges to the Sociological Perspective

The sociological emphasis on the structural level of reality has been periodically challenged by **reductionism,** which attempts to explain social facts by reference to biology or individual behavior.

BIOLOGICAL DETERMINISM.   A common form of reductionism, **biological determinism,** involves the assumption that biological characteristics or inborn traits have a direct influence on human behavior, as is often observed among animals. Sociologists have difficulty accepting this view because it ignores the effects of social relationships and the uniquely human mind, as we detail in Chapters 3 and 4. Nonetheless, we cannot ignore totally the idea that biology sets some limits on human possibilities.

SOCIOBIOLOGY.   The most compelling modern theory of the inheritance of genetically determined behavior is **sociobiology** (Lumsden and Wilson, 1981). Just as Darwin traced the evolution of physical characteristics, sociobiologists suggest that certain social behaviors have become coded into the human genetic ground plan through the same process of selective survival. For example, a sociobiologist would argue that such traits as female nurturance and male sexual dominance maximize reproductive success. However, because most of the supporting evidence for these ideas have come from animal studies, the leap to human behavior remains highly debatable (Kitcher, 1985).

Supporters of this evolutionary model often ask why sociologists are so opposed to it (van den Berghe, 1990), and sociologists ask why theories of biological determinism enjoy such widespread acceptance by the general public. Why do Americans want to believe that their behavior is determined by forces over which they have no control? From the perspective of the sociology of knowledge this type of belief fits into the current climate of political and social conservatism in the United States. Sociobiology can be used to explain race and sex inequality as genetically determined and to justify protecting only one's own family rather than working for the welfare of others.

Yet even if the biological roots of human behavior could be accurately identified, this would explain only very general patterns such as the observation that women invest more time and energy in child rearing than do men. What interests us as social scientists however, are the wide variations in mother–child relationships from one society to another or from one time period to another. It is these differences that testify to the flexibility and creativity of people in society and that are the subject matter of this book.

There are currently several efforts to integrate biological and sociological factors in a cross-disciplinary model of behavior called "biosocial" or "biocultural" (Rossi, 1987; Lenski, 1985; Lopreato, 1990). For example, research on hormones and behavior have shown how each influences the other: Levels of testosterone, the male hormone, rise among men about to engage in competition, and rise even higher among the winners while declining among the losers (Mazur et al., 1992). In other words, hormonal changes are the outcome, not the cause, of social behavior. Indeed, as useful as a testosterone surge might be in a boxing bout, it is also associated with antisocial behavior and low intelligence, leading to troubled marriages and poor occupational achievement (Dabbs, 1992; Booth and Dabbs, 1993).

But whatever the direct effects of biology, each person lives in a unique web of relationships at a particular historical period that can modify any innate impulse. This is the essence of the sociological perspective. What possible differences in biological make-up, for example, can account for the fact that almost all running backs in professional football are black and all but a few quarterbacks are white? The answer does not lie in the genes or the brain or phases of the moon but, rather, in social structures.

> **Reductionism** involves reducing social life to individual behavior or biology.
>
> **Biological determinism** is based on the belief that genetic factors explain differences in human behavior.
>
> **Sociobiology** is the study of the inheritance of genetically determined behaviors.

Postmodern Social Thought

The goal of the Enlightenment—to use science to uncover the value-free truths that could promote social progress and free people from superstition, blind faith, and ignorance—remains largely unfulfilled. Indeed, it can be claimed that the only ones to benefit from this "modern" viewpoint were the leaders of Western industrial societies, who had the power to define "progress," "reality," and "normal" for everyone else. But by the late 1980s, many of these previously excluded voices—of women, people of color, non-Westerners, homosexuals—were challenging the basic intellectual foundation of modern thought; namely, that there was an underlying reality that could be discovered by the application of reason.

This new perspective has been called **postmodernism,** or deconstructionism, and owes much to European literary criticism. The basic point is that all claims to truth are suspect because they are based on the particular meaning given to words at that time and place. *It is the language that creates the reality,* and once concepts such as gender or normal sexuality are "deconstructed" (with every aspect of meaning thoroughly examined), we can see how the definition benefits some people and not others.

Postmodernism views all reality as constructed by language.

The potentially disruptive effects of postmodern thought can be seen in the titles of recent books and articles on the subject: "destabilizing theory" (Barrett and Phillips, 1992); "the twilight of the real," (Wakefield, 1990); "undoing the social" (Game, 1991); "the end of sociological theory" (Seidman, 1991); "the end of ideology" (Lemert, 1991). In essence, postmodernism can be seen as an *antitheory theory* and has drawn strong criticism from those who are engaged in the theoretical integration noted earlier in this chapter (Ritzer, 1990).

Given the especially fluid state of sociological theory today, it would be very difficult to present a single theoretical viewpoint in an introductory textbook. Rather, we have chosen to apply each of the various perspectives, including postmodernism, where we think it will deepen your understanding of behavior and society.

SUMMARY

1. This chapter defines the field of sociology and distinguishes it from other social sciences. Sociology is the study of human behavior as shaped by group life, including the collective forces that shape human behavior and the ways in which people give meaning to their experiences.

2. C. Wright Mills developed the concept of the sociological imagination by distinguishing between personal troubles, which are problems experienced directly by individuals, and public issues, which stem from factors outside one's control.

3. The sociological perspective focuses on the totality of social life, the context of human behavior, the group level of reality, and interaction among individuals.

4. Emile Durkheim identified social facts, which are patterned regularities of behavior that characterize the collectivity. Birth, death, and suicide rates are influenced by social structural factors.

5. Classical sociologists, including Harriet Martineau, Auguste Comte, Karl Marx, Max Weber, Emile Durkheim, Georg Simmel and George Herbert Mead, are introduced, and their major contributions are covered in the context of their historical periods and social locations.

6. Whereas Auguste Comte tried to uncover the basic laws of social life, Karl Marx understood history as the struggle to end the oppression of the powerless by the powerful. For Marx, the most fundamental material condition in any society was its mode of production and the struggle between owners and workers to control it. For Marx, historical change occurred through conflict.

7. Emile Durkheim, as did Comte, saw society as a reality in its own right, where individuals interact within a preexisting set of rules governing social life. The study of this social structure was, for Durkheim, the goal of sociology.

8. For Max Weber, the modern age held both the liberating potential of human reason as well as the possibility that technology and modern organizations could lead to a new "iron cage" without any of the faith that previously helped people survive.

9. The functional, conflict, and interpretive perspectives are described and compared.

10. The functional perspective focuses on the relationship between the parts and the whole of a social system. Talcott Parsons and Robert K. Merton are two major functional theorists.

11. The conflict perspective focuses on disagreements, hostility, and struggles over power and resources in a society. It focuses on who benefits from given social arrangements and how the powerful maintain their power.

12. The interpretive perspective, which includes symbolic interaction, dramaturgy, and ethnomethodology, focuses on how people interact with one another, how experiences are interpreted, and how people organize appropriate responses.

13. The functional and conflict perspectives examine social structure at an abstract level; this is referred to as *macrosociology.* The microsociology perspectives, such as the interpretive perspective, focus on smaller, interpersonal, and less abstract units of analysis.

14. Included among new directions in social theory are humanist sociology, feminist sociology, and rational choice theory.

15. Reductionist theories, most notably sociobiology, have challenged the sociological perspective.

16. Most recently, postmodernism, or deconstruction, has challenged the validity of how and by whom concepts are defined.

SUGGESTED READINGS

Collins, Randall, and Michael Makowsky. *The Discovery of Society,* 5th ed. New York: Random House, 1993. An articulate account of the historical and contemporary development of sociological theory, including analyses of the major contributions of Marx, Weber, Durkheim, Cooley, Mead, Parsons, and Merton.

Deegan, Mary Jo, ed. *Women in Sociology: A Bio-Bibliographical Sourcebook.* Westport, CT: Greenwood Press 1991. A valuable reference guide to the contributions and lives of the founding "sisters" of sociology, including international and American pioneers.

Durkheim, Emile. *The Elementary Forms of the Religious Life.* New York: Collier Books, 1961. A classic contribution to functionalism in which Durkheim shows how in the most traditional societies religion was a strong integrative force through its generation of common values and identification.

England, Paula, ed. *Theory on Gender/Feminism on Theory.* Hawthorne, NY: Aldine de Gruyter, 1993. A collection of original essays focusing both on the contribution of sociological theories to the understanding of gender inequality and the gender biases within sociological paradigms.

Hoecker-Drysdale, Susan. *Harriet Martineau: First Woman Sociologist.* New York: Berg, 1992. An excellent overview of the major accomplishments and primary writings of one of the founders of sociology.

Kennedy, Robert E., Jr. *Life Choices: Applying Sociology.* 2d ed. New York: Holt, Rinehart & Winston, 1989. This paperback illustrates the usefulness of studying sociology by focusing on some major life choices, including education, occupation, marriage, parenthood, housing, and retirement.

Levin, Jack. *Sociological Snapshots: Seeing Social Structure and Change in Everyday life.* Newbury Park, CA: Pine Forge Press, 1993. A contemporary collection of essays that introduce students to sociological thinking in such diverse areas as soap operas, foods, inequality, hate crimes, and aging.

Marx, Karl, and Friedrich Engels. *Manifesto of the Communist Party.* Original work published 1848. New York: International Publishers, 1983. A powerful call for social change, this revolutionary statement identifies the history of class struggles and predicts the overthrow of the ruling class by the working class.

Mills, C. Wright. *The Sociological Imagination.* New York: Oxford University Press, 1959. A classic work that applies the sociological imagination to a number of still-contemporary social issues.

Reinharz, Shulamit. *Feminist Methods in Social Research.* New York: Oxford University Press, 1992. An excellent source for understanding the development of feminist frameworks and methods over the last two decades. Selected as Outstanding Academic Book for 1992–1993 by *Choice.*

Scheff, Thomas J. *Microsociology: Discourse, Emotion, and Social Structure.* Chicago: The University of Chicago Press, 1993. An excellent synthesis that focuses on the social bond that unites macro- and microstructures of human interaction.

Weinberg, Meyer, ed. *W. E. B. DuBois: A Reader.* New York: Harper Collins, 1970. a collection of important essays on various aspects of African-American culture by a prominent sociologist of the early twentieth century.

2

Doing Sociology

- The National Rifle Association's (NRA) periodic survey of attitudes toward gun control contains the following question: "Do you support Federal legislation that would punish animal-rights extremists who harass law-abiding hunters in the field?"
- On the basis of responses to a questionnaire printed in TV *Guide*, presidential candidate Ross Perot claimed that 97 percent of the American public favored a $2 cut in federal spending for every dollar increase in taxes.
- Following a feature article in *Fortune* magazine on the "alarmingly high" rate at which women with MBAs were leaving corporate employment, applications from women to graduate schools of business declined sharply.
- Despite a complete lack of supporting evidence after two decades of research, many Americans continue to believe that natural childbirth creates a mystical bond between mother and child, with positive effects throughout their lives.

These four examples illustrate many of the uses and abuses of the research process. In each case, the way in which information was gathered and reported was deeply flawed. As you can easily see, the NRA question was worded in such a way as to encourage a "yes" response, using such emotionally tinged words as "extremists" and "law-abiding." Although the Perot questions also contained biased wording, the research can be criticized on the grounds that people who read TV *Guide* and who bother to return a questionnaire may not represent "the American public."

With respect to the fate of working women, especially those aiming for the top, the 1980s were filled with dire warnings about the dangers of placing career before marriage and motherhood. In the *Fortune* study, the author conveniently failed to mention how many male classmates had also "bailed out" of similar jobs, and did not discuss the working conditions that might make a woman executive prefer self-employment (Faludi, 1991).

The problem with the original mother–child bonding study was that it covered only 28 women who volunteered for the experiment and followed them for only a short period. Thus, there is no way of knowing how different they were from other mother–infant pairs, and the research could say nothing about long-term effects. Yet so powerful is the wish to believe that a mother holds the key to a child's development, that professionals as well as the general public still believe in bonding, even after the study was repudiated by the original researchers and never reproduced by other investigators (Eyer, 1992).

It is important, therefore, when trying to gather accurate information on beliefs and behaviors, that we ask unbiased questions of people who repre-sent the population of interest to us, and that we carefully examine our own fears and hopes. In this chapter, we discuss the need for research and the various techniques used by sociologists to gather *data* (the plural of *datum*, a single piece of information) and how this information is analyzed and reported. Issues of privacy and ethics are also examined.

WHY WE DO RESEARCH

Because so much of sociology deals with everyday experience, personal observation might seem to be the most accurate source of information. But as the case of the bonding study suggests, sometimes it is our ideas about what is natural or obviously true that must themselves be examined. In later chapters, you will find many examples of commonly accepted wisdom that are not supported by carefully designed research projects, including the following:

- Federal welfare programs encourage poor women to have additional children (Chapter 9).
- American schools reward children primarily on the basis of intellectual abilities (Chapter 15).
- Older people have been abandoned by their uncaring children (Chapter 7).
- Divorce rates continue to rise as more women enter the labor force (Chapter 12).
- Harsh punishments reduce the rate of street crime (Chapter 17).

Beliefs such as these often assume cause-and-effect relationships that seem so logical that they go unquestioned. But as you will find throughout this book, when the evidence is carefully examined, many of our so-called commonsense beliefs are simply inaccurate. We must also ask why people to continue to cling to certain ideas despite evidence to the contrary. Moreover, regardless of the accuracy of a given assumption, those who believe it will continue to act as if it were correct. This is the important sociological concept of the definition of the situation: *What people believe to be real is real in its consequences* (Thomas and Thomas, 1928; see Chapter 4). If, for example, a majority of Americans believe that welfare payments encourage childbearing, they will support cutting off benefits to single mothers, which has the very real consequence of reducing the quality of life of poor women and their children.

One important goal of sociological research is to gather the data needed to help us make wise policy choices. All too often, politicians and the public prefer to rely on generally accepted definitions of the situation, regardless of the research evidence. Nonetheless, sociologists continue to explore the social environment, examining how social facts are created and maintained, and how these change over time.

Movies provide good examples of how situations become defined and re-defined over time. The classic movie, *Casablanca*, set during World War II, explores the complexities of political causes, love, and friendships. In this scene Humphrey Bogart confronts Claude Rains, as Ingrid Bergman and Paul Henreid watch. Despite a previous romantic interest in Bergman, Bogart helps Bergman and Henreid, a member of the Resistance, to escape Occupied France. By the end of the movie, he and Rains have become good friends.

SUBJECTIVE AND OBJECTIVE WAYS OF KNOWING

We come to understand our world through both subjective and objective ways of knowing. **Subjective knowledge** is rooted in individual experience. Some understandings are a matter of *faith* ("God knows best"); others emerge from *personal observation* ("communities aren't as close as they used to be"); and still others are based on *intuition* ("I have a gut feeling"). For researchers in the interpretive tradition, the basic social process is precisely the way in which people arrive at these understandings through conversations with one another; how a common reality—the definition of the situation—is constructed from shared impressions (Mathisen, 1989).

This approach, however, tells us little about the broader context in which such conversations take place. The study of these outside constraints—the macrosystem—is typically undertaken by sociologists using more **objective** techniques of data gathering. Objectivity means that the observer is distanced from the object of study and assumed to be free of personal bias. The dominant trend in American sociology today is toward objective methods similar to those used in the natural sciences, a set of procedures and attitudes called *the scientific method,* as described later.

Subjective knowledge derives from an individual's own frame of reference.

Objective techniques of data gathering require the observer to be distanced from the object of study.

Yet many sociologists, especially humanist and feminist scholars working in the interpretive tradition, reject the goal of objectivity precisely because it distances the researcher from the lived experience of the people under study. These critics apply the sociology of knowledge approach to research methods as well as to theory; according to this view, what researchers decide to study and how they go about doing it is strongly influenced by their own upbringing and current goals, rather than some impartial, unbiased viewpoint (Cancian, 1992; Reinharz, 1992). The critics argue that because the scientific method reinforces the power of "experts" to interpret what people say and do, their research designs and findings until recently reflect a limited view of reality—the world as seen through the lens of the white male professional. For example, why is the study of complex organizations, using the most sophisticated statistics, given greater professional respect than the study of schoolchildren or unemployed coal miners?

In addition, the goal of pure objectivity has proved very difficult to achieve. The history of both natural and social sciences is one long tale of personality conflicts, turf wars, personal anxieties masked as the human condition, profound prejudice, intentional fraud, and even elementary errors (Laslett, 1990; Miller and Hersen, 1992; Harding, 1993). Nor is "expert knowledge" always superior to commonsense understanding (Pease, 1981). For example, over the past several decades, social scientists have solemnly announced the end of political passion, the decline of religious fervor, and the disappearance of nationalism in the modern world—all trends that are refuted daily

Sociological research involves objective observations, precise measurements, and full disclosure of research results. In light of the political history of the People's Republic of China, what questions do you think this researcher is allowed to ask? What questions would lead to his arrest?

in the headlines and about which the perceptions of ordinary citizens might have been more accurate than those of ivory-towered academicians.

Despite such criticisms, the reward system of American sociology—as exercised by its leading academic departments and professional publications—remains firmly rooted in the positivist tradition and the model of scientific objectivity.

The Scientific Method

The **scientific method** is a set of procedures for gathering information about the real world and for testing theory. These procedures are designed to minimize personal bias and maximize precise measurement, so that any researcher using the same techniques should uncover the same knowledge. In addition, all research findings must be open to criticism and correction. The three key elements are (1) objective observation, (2) precise measurement, and (3) full disclosure of methods and findings.

OBJECTIVITY.   Objectivity refers to both (1) the requirement that scientists be aware of possible influences of their own attitudes and expectations on their research and (2) the use of data-gathering techniques that lead to agreement about facts. Compared to natural scientists, who deal with nonhuman material, the social scientist must measure human behavior and attitudes that are always subject to change. Unlike boiling water, which registers the same temperature from one measurement to the next, people's beliefs and actions do not remain constant. Simply asking a question at one time can influence that person's answer to the same

question at a later time. If a researcher has asked your opinion of a breakfast cereal or presidential candidate, you must stop and think. The next time your opinion is sought, it will have been affected by your having thought about the topic earlier. People change in so many ways from one moment to the next, that measurement in sociology can never be as consistent or exact as in the natural sciences.

PRECISE MEASUREMENT.   The goal of objectivity is supported by measurement techniques that leave as little as possible to guesswork. Research *instruments,* such as questionnaires, checklists, and interview forms, allow different observers to obtain similar information.

Deciding *what* to measure is a major problem in most social research. Not everything we want to know about can be measured directly, especially such *abstract* (highly general) concepts as religiosity, satisfaction in marriage, or student conservatism. Something more concrete (countable) must be selected to stand for the abstraction. Concrete items that can be measured objectively are called **empirical referents.** The word *empirical* means "derived from experience and observation." Empirical referents can be feelings or behaviors. In the case of student conservatism, although you may have a clear idea of what constitutes "conservatism," this may not be quite the same as my idea. Therefore, we must agree on something both of us can measure accurately and similarly, such as peoples' responses to an attitude checklist or their actions in joining certain clubs. Figure 2-1 (page 30) diagrams these relationships.

When devising a research instrument—a questionnaire or observation checklist—there are two potential problems. One is the question of **reliability;** that is, does the instrument measure the empirical referent accurately? If both of us use the same data-gathering techniques on two different sets of respondents and come up with consistent findings, we can assume that our questions are tapping the same feelings or behaviors and that the instrument is reliable.

The other question is whether or not our selection of empirical referents is measuring what we claim it does. This is the problem of **validity.** If, for example, we found that students who join Young Republicans for Freedom also share similar attitudes toward homosexuality, welfare, and abortion rights, then our choice of questions appears to accurately reflect the abstraction "conservatism."

> The **scientific method** consists of objective observations, precise measurement, and full disclosure of results.
>
> **Empirical referents** are items that can be measured and counted.
>
> **Reliability** refers to whether the measuring instrument yields the same results on repeated trials.
>
> **Validity** refers to whether the measuring unit measures what it was designed to.

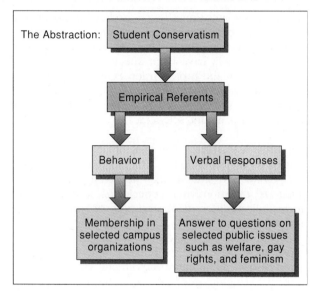

The Abstraction: Student Conservatism

Empirical Referents

Behavior

Verbal Responses

Membership in selected campus organizations

Answer to questions on selected public issues such as welfare, gay rights, and feminism

Figure 2-1 The relationship between an abstract concept and its empirical referents

Reliability and validity can never be ensured and can be judged only by other researchers. One way to test accuracy is to repeat the study. **Replication** involves using the same research instrument on different populations at various time periods.

FULL DISCLOSURE. It is a scientific duty to make one's research materials fully available to colleagues. Every published report must provide information on who was studied (the research subjects or respondents), what was measured and how (the empirical referents), the techniques of data analysis (statistical methods), and the findings. Researchers must be willing to provide additional information to those who might question the research design and its results or who seek to replicate the study. In this way, science acts as a check on itself; if findings cannot be replicated, the original research must be checked for flaws or its assumptions modified. This continual checking and modifying makes our knowledge cumulative.

Replication involves repeating a specific study often with different types of respondents in various settings and at other times.

Quantitative research uses the features of scientific objectivity, including complex statistical techniques.

Qualitative research relies primarily on interpretive description rather than statistics.

THE SCIENCE IN SOCIAL SCIENCE

Researchers have had varying success in using the scientific method to explore social life. Every study is somewhat flawed because of the essential changeabil-ity of human beings and the impossibility of total objectivity. These difficulties have led some sociologists to suggest that the use of the term *social scientist* implies an exactness that cannot be supported. Nonetheless, the royal road to fame and fortune in contemporary sociology is through **quantitative research,** ("number crunching") involving increasingly complex statistical techniques made possible by the computer revolution (Blalock, 1989).

Many sociologists prefer to be thought of as social scientists because science is associated with precision and accuracy. Think of all the television commercials that feature a man in a white coat pointing to a colorful chart showing that Brand X is 60 percent more powerful than its nearest competitor. Even though these "authorities" are actors, the impression of scientific support leads buyers to choose one detergent or car over another.

Furthermore, the use of statistics is associated with intellectual toughness (note how often we speak of "hard" facts) in contrast to ideas or impressions (referred to as "soft" data). Numbers are seen as masculine, verbal descriptions as feminine. Thus, **qualitative research** that depends on interpretive descriptions is frequently ignored and seldom published in the leading journals, even in the field of family studies, where feelings and emotions are of central concern (LaRossa and Wolf, 1985; Grant et al., 1987; Bakanic et al., 1987).

The choice of quantitative or qualitative methods is determined primarily by the topic under study, although most social phenomena could be approached either way. For example, although studies of complex organizations tend to be highly quantitative in contrast to research on popular culture, there are also qualitative studies of interaction patterns within an organization, as well as statistical analyses of Top-20 charts.

It should also be recognized that qualitative studies can be designed for great precision. Is a video-taped encounter any less real than a birthrate? At the same time, we cannot assume that qualitative methods automatically solve the problem of unequal power between researcher and subject or the issue of invading people's privacy to advance one's own career (Sprague and Zimmerman, 1992).

Sociology benefits from both types of data—from knowledge of the objective features of social structure as well as the subjective experiences of individuals. Indeed, the two are so closely intertwined that neither aspect can be fully understood without the other. Sociologists must consider the mutual influence of social organization at the macrolevel and the ways in which individual lives are organized at the microlevel (Thomas and Znaniecki, 1918-9/1984). Theories and methods that bridge these levels are only now being forged.

Issues related to quantitative and qualitative methods, as well as consideration of scientific and nonscientific factors in sociological research, will become

The choice of quantitative or qualitative methods is determined primarily by the phenomenon being studied, even though most topics can be studied by either approach.

clearer as we follow the research process from its beginning in theory to its final step in presentation of the data.

THE RESEARCH PROCESS

Five major steps make up the research process (see Figure 2-2 on page 32):

1. Select and frame the research question.
2. Choose the appropriate time frame, sample, and method.
3. Collect the data.
4. Analyze the data.
5. Draw conclusions and report the findings.

Each step involves choices, sometimes dictated by the researcher's conceptual model, and sometimes by practical considerations such as the availability of subjects, funding, and the time needed to do the work. Thus, many nonscientific elements affect the research process from the very beginning.

What to Study

Deciding what to study may be the most nonscientific step of all, for two reasons: (1) the researcher's own bias or interests and (2) the research agenda of funding sources. The more complex the research design, the more financial support is necessary for data gathering and analysis. Researchers are, therefore, increas-

ingly dependent on grants from foundations, private research firms, corporations, and government agencies. But this means that one studies what the funding organization wants to know. Even so, American scholars still enjoy great freedom in selecting research topics. In many countries today this is not the case; sociology is usually the first academic department to be closed down or brought under political control in a dictatorship, as in Nazi Germany, the former Soviet Union, or Iraq today.

As a mental exercise, ask yourself what aspect of social life you want to explore. Notice that this choice will be guided by your personal values and beliefs. Because sociologists are interested in the link between one social fact and another—between the nature of a job and the distribution of work-related stress disorders, for example—think of two social facts that you suspect are related. In our example, the two social facts are (1) characteristics of an occupation and (2) the probability of job-related stress, an abstraction that we will measure by empirical referents such as arguments with co-workers or family conflicts.

These social facts are called **variables.** A variable is a trait that differs from one person to another, or between men and women, adults and children, or from one time period to another, in contrast to a **constant,** which is a characteristic that does not change. For example, it is a constant that human beings must eat to stay alive, but what they eat, how often, with whom, and the meanings attached to food are all variables, changing from one society or time period to another and among subgroups within the same society.

Notice that when you thought about the variables you would like to study, and how they were related, you began with a theoretical model in your head, whether or not you realized it. A theory consists of a set of ideas about how variables are connected. "If the world works the way I think it does, then variable *X* should be linked to variable *Y* in a certain way." The theory guides you to make guesses about the relationship among variables. These kinds of guesses are called **hypotheses** (hypothesis in the singular). Because a hypothesis is a specific statement—"if variable *X* changes in a given direction, variable *Y* will also change in a predictable way"—it can be tested with data gathered by systematic observation, whether quantitative or qualitative. The relationship between one variable and another is called the **correlation.**

Variables are factors that differ from one person or collectivity to another or that change over time.

Constants are characteristics that do not change from one person or time to another.

Hypotheses are specific statements derived from a theory about relationships among variables.

Correlation refers to how change in one variable is associated with change in another variable.

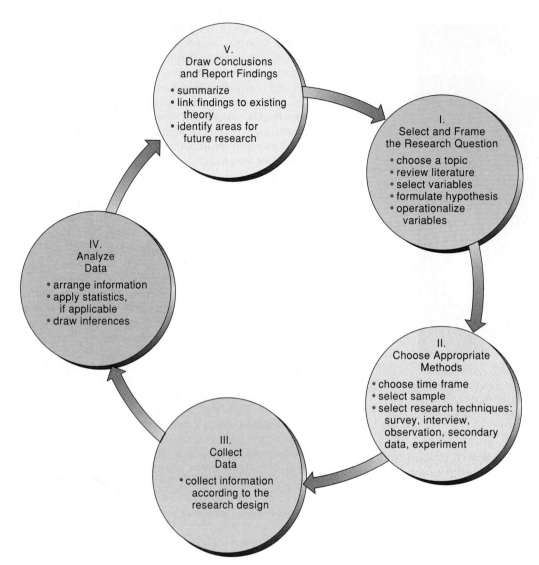

Figure 2-2   Steps in the research process

In the case of job stress, the functional model would suggest that people who take great risks should be highly rewarded. Therefore, the more responsible the job (variable X), the greater the likelihood of stress symptoms, from high blood pressure to a troubled marriage. An alternative hypothesis, derived from the conflict model, would suggest that powerlessness is more stressful than being in control, so that heavily supervised dead-end jobs would be associated with stress behaviors. Job responsibility is still variable X and the stress symptoms variable Y, but the hypotheses derived from theory predict dif-

Independent variables have the greatest impact, come first in the chain of events, are relatively fixed, and affect dependent variables.

Dependent variables are influenced by independent variables.

ferent outcomes. The occupational distribution of stress-related symptoms supports the conflict model; the more repetitive and supervised the job, the greater the likelihood of stress-related symptoms and behaviors. Therefore, you might predict that giving workers greater control over the pacing of their work would improve their physical health, raise morale, and enhance productivity.

Your theoretical framework also indicates which variable is most likely to produce change in the other; that is, the direction of the correlation. **Independent variables** are those assumed to be prior in a chain of events and to influence change in other variables. Typical independent variables in sociological research are age, sex, and race—characteristics that are given rather than chosen.

Dependent variables, in contrast, are assumed to be influenced by (to depend on) differences in the in-

Sociologists are interested in many aspects of social life—what people do for relaxation, how and why some people become street performers, how public spaces are used, how people respond to possible accidents. What questions interest you in this scene?

dependent variable. When, for example, the data show that American whites are more likely than African Americans to have a college degree, we conclude that race is the independent variable and education the dependent one. It would be difficult to argue that having a college degree changes a person's skin color.

When you select the empirical referents for the concepts of interest to you, this translation is called **operationalizing** the variables. For example, although you might think you have a clear definition of child abuse or unemployment, these are not easy to measure. What exactly is the line between a parent's idea of appropriate discipline and "abusive behavior?" How many weeks or months of nonwork equals "unemployment?"

Designing the Study

In general, the research question dictates the appropriate method for gathering data to test hypotheses. Much depends on whether the information must come from a large number of people or from a particular subgroup, on whether the topic is sensitive or not, and on whether follow-up studies will be needed to measure change, that is, the *time frame* of the study.

TIME FRAMES.   **Cross-sectional studies** take place at one time only and can be thought of as slices of life. They focus on how different kinds of people acted or responded at a given moment. The cross-sectional study is like a snapshot, capturing the events of a moment. But for information on process and changes—a moving picture, so to speak—we need several cross-sectional studies conducted at different times.

Panel or **longitudinal studies** follow a group of respondents over time. It is not always easy to keep track of people for long periods, and those who remain in the study could be quite different from those who drop out, thus reducing the accuracy of the findings.

SAMPLE SELECTION.   Your research topic will also determine the number and types of people you study. Sometimes, only a few key respondents will be sufficient, as in a study of motorcycle gangs. Other topics, such as attitudes on gun control, require a larger and more varied pool of respondents. For reasons of time and money, it may not be possible to observe or question the entire population of interest, so that you must select a subset, or **sample,** of the larger collectivity. If the sample is selected in a certain way, it can be considered to represent accurately the larger population from which it was drawn.

Random sampling occurs when all possible respondents have an equal chance of being selected. Within statistical limits, it will reflect the actual distribution of characteristics in the larger population. Common *random sampling* techniques include drawing numbers from a rotating drum or similar device, as used in a state lottery, and programming a computer to generate ten-digit telephone numbers. With a randomized sample, the researcher can generalize findings to the entire pool from which the sample was drawn. The larger the sample, the higher the probability that a similarly drawn sample would produce the same results.

In contrast, findings from a nonrandomized sample cannot be generalized to an entire population. In the example at the beginning of this chapter, for example, readers of *TV Guide* are not a mirror of all American adults, and the people who clipped out the questionnaire were not necessarily a representative sample of all *TV Guide* readers. The only scientifically legitimate claim that Ross Perot could have made was that 97

Operationalizing the variables involves translating an abstraction into something observable.

Cross-sectional studies take place at one time only.

Longitudinal studies follow a group of respondents over time.

A **sample** is a selection from the entire population of interest.

Random sampling occurs when all possible respondents have an equal chance of being chosen.

Lotteries are based on the process of random selection, which gives each player an equal chance of being selected. The probability of winning however, is very low. For example, your chances of winning the top cash prize in the Pennsylvania State lottery is about 1 in 10,000,000.

percent of *Guide* readers who returned the questionnaire agreed with the statement.

Having defined your research questions and chosen the appropriate time frame and sample, you must decide how to get the necessary information.

RESEARCH METHODS.   Sociological methods range from the most distant, such as a mailed questionnaire, to the most intimate, as when a researcher actually takes part in the events being studied.

Surveys.   The large-scale social **survey** (or **poll**) is used to yield data from a representative sample presented with a set of questions carefully designed to

> **Surveys** or **polls** yield information from a large group of respondents.

tap the relevant variables. Once the random sample has been selected, contact can be made by mail, phone, or personal visit, each of which has pros and cons in terms of cost, time, and response rate (Johnson et al., 1989). Personal visits, for example, are very costly but have the lowest rate of refusals, whereas mail questionnaires are inexpensive but produce few responses. Most survey research today is conducted by telephone, even though many people hang up immediately. Perhaps now, if your phone number is selected through the random digit dialing process, you will take pity on the

researcher who desperately needs your responses to ensure that the sample remains representative.

In any survey, the amount and quality of the data gathered will depend on a respondent's willingness to answer honestly, as well as on the reliability and validity of the instrument. In addition, the kinds of information that can be obtained by a mail or phone survey are limited. Despite these drawbacks, reams of information can be gathered from many people in a short time, and if the sample was randomly drawn, the findings can be generalized to the larger population.

Public opinion polling is a form of survey research used especially by politicians and market researchers to measure attitudes among the general population. Over the past four decades, techniques for sampling and data processing have become very sophisticated. You are probably most aware of this in the weeks before a national election, but the major private polling firms in the United States—Gallup, Roper, and Louis Harris—continually conduct polls on a variety of topics for a variety of clients. If the sample is randomly selected, a base of approximately 1,500–1,800 respondents can indeed reflect the views of tens of millions of American adults. You will notice that the findings are always presented with a range of error, for example, "give or take X percentage points," calculated by the laws of probability that apply to random samples. The larger the sample, the smaller the likelihood of error.

Problems and Pitfalls in Survey Research.   Despite the high level of technical skill that characterizes contemporary public opinion polls, a number of problems and pitfalls can reduce or distort the accuracy of the results. The most common of these problems is the "loaded question," which refers to wording designed to elicit a particular answer. For example, in June 1991, as Congress debated legislation to restrict access to abortion information, Planned Parenthood, an advocate of reproductive choice, published polling data showing that two-thirds of American adults opposed the ban on abortion counseling. Two weeks later, abortion opponents produced data from another national survey in which two-thirds supported the counseling restrictions! How could this be? The different results were a product of the wording of the questions and of the order in which they were asked (Clymer, 1991). An earlier question often influences the response to a later one, so that results of a survey can be manipulated for political ends.

Often, the wording of a question can act as a "red flag," designed to bring out a particular reaction. For example, a national survey in 1992 asked respondents whether they felt that the United States was spending too much, too little, or about the right amount on various programs (*New York Times/CBS News*, May 1992). As shown in Figure 2-3, when asked about "welfare," 44 percent said we were spending

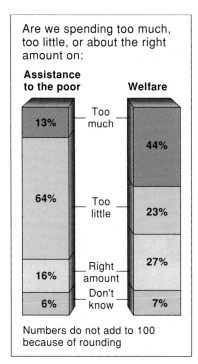

Are we spending too much, too little, or about the right amount on:

Assistance to the poor

Welfare

	Too much	
13%		44%
64%	Too little	23%
16%	Right amount	27%
6%	Don't know	7%

Numbers do not add to 100 because of rounding

Figure 2-3
The effect of wording on questionnaire responses

From: "Assistance to the poor/welfare," (from the *New York Times*/CBS Poll conducted May 6–8) July 5, 1992. Copyright © 1992 by The New York Times Company. Reprinted by permission.

views can tells us more than a telephone survey (De-Vault, 1991). As with phone interviews, however, the race or sex of the interviewer can influence respondents' answers (Williams and Heikes, 1993).

THE CASE STUDY. Because questionnaires and interviews tell us only what respondents are willing to reveal, they are typically limited to information on variables that do not probe deeply. But sociology is the study of collectivities, of group life, and of the social construction of meaning, none of which can be grasped adequately through survey research on individuals and data on the correlation among variables.

For many sociologists, the social world can be understood only through in-depth, descriptive **case studies** of particular groups, similar to the ethnographic or fieldwork approach by which anthropologists come to know the nature of social life in relatively small societies or of subgroups within a large, industrial society. As a powerful example of the qualitative, interpretive perspective, the case study is *holistic* in that the whole system under observation is seen as more than the sum of its parts, which is the essence of the sociological approach (Feagin et al., 1991; Ragin and Becker, 1992.)

Thus, although the leading journals in the field continue to reward quantitative, positivistic survey research, book publishers have found a receptive market for the naturalistic case study, such as an ethnography of the "teenage wasteland" of suburban New Jersey (Gaines, 1992a); an in-depth description of how a group of unemployed men who meet daily in a Chicago cafeteria maintain their dignity and self-discipline under difficult circumstances (Duneier, 1992); a longitudinal study of race relations in changing neighborhoods (E. Anderson, 1990); and the daily struggles of homeless women (Liebow, 1993).

OBSERVATION AND PARTICIPANT OBSERVATION. The case study is an example of research that depends primarily on observation. Survey and interview data tell us what people *say* they do, which is not necessarily what they actually do. Only direct observation can provide information on actual behavior, but observational studies are both time-consuming and necessarily limited in scope.

No observer can see everything. Each of us perceives selectively, tending to recognize what we expect to be there and overlooking the unexpected. Because the researcher must also be careful not to disrupt the activity being examined, observations are confined to places where he or she will be unnoticed or taken for granted. Otherwise, people might act as

Key informants are carefully selected cases providing information on processes not easily visible but having general application.

Case studies are in-depth descriptions of the social world of particular subgroups.

too much, but when asked about "assistance to the poor," only 13 percent said too much, while almost two-thirds thought the government spent too little. Because welfare *is* assistance to the poor, the questions actually tapped public reaction to the word "welfare." A similar poll found even stronger feelings in 1994 (*Time*, 1994).

Characteristics of the questioners can also affect responses. ABC News, for example, found that respondents gave different answers to the same questions on race relations when they thought they were talking to a white or to an African-American phone interviewer (Morin, 1989).

INTENSIVE INTERVIEWS. Sometimes, a large representative sample is not necessary, especially if one is conducting exploratory, or *pilot* research before designing a larger study or if one is seeking intimate information. In these circumstances, a small and nonrepresentative sample is sufficient. Nonrepresentative samples are also appropriate for studies that do not refer to the general public, such as research on influential members of a community. In this case only **key informants** need be interviewed.

In other research, the interview conversation itself becomes the research subject—what is said or unsaid, the unspoken understandings—providing an indepth view of one person's experience that illuminates the lives of others as well. This device is especially compatible with the goals of interpretive sociologists and feminist researchers. When trying to understand the meaning of preparing food for the family, for example, a small number of intensive inter-

The case study provides sociologists with in-depth descriptive information about an entire system. Sociologists keep field notes to record their observations, similar to the ethnographic or fieldwork approach used by anthropologists.

they wish to be seen rather than as they would without such self-consciousness.

Many of these observational barriers are reduced when the researcher can become part of the interaction under study, but **participant observation** has its hazards. It may take a long time before the participant observer is fully accepted. There is also the ethical question of furthering your career by using material gained from people you have asked to trust you. Researchers who have used this method typically "debrief" their subjects when the study is completed, asking them to read and comment on the material gathered. However, it is impossible to measure the extent to which the participant observer has subtly changed the group and its interactions.

In **participant observation**, the researcher becomes part of the interaction under study.

The classic participant observation study in American sociology was conducted by William Foote Whyte (1943/1984) over four decades ago in a working-class area of Boston. Whyte spent several years hanging out with the "Corner Boys," observing complex patterns of social relations in what other sociologists had written off as "disorganized slums." At first, Whyte told his subjects that he was writing a book about the history and customs of the area—which was not the full truth. As the research continued, Whyte became more open about what he was doing, but by then, he was accepted in the community.

Participant observation has been used most successfully in studying people and places not readily accessible to the general public, and in examining "from the inside" what might not be obvious to an outside observer. Recent participant observations have involved living among or working with office temporaries (Gottfried, 1991), domestic service workers (Hondagneu-Sotelo, 1994), day-haul farm laborers (Pfeffer, 1994), and homeless street people (Snow and Anderson, 1993). These studies are rich in the details of everyday life rather than in statistics.

Participatory Action Research. A more radical version of participant observation is currently being proposed by sociologists who feel that the distance between observed and observer can best be bridged by bringing the people under study into the research process as active agents in their own right (Whyte,

To find out what people actually do, anthropologists and sociologists observe everyday interaction. Margaret Mead, a well-known anthropologist, is shown here talking with one of her native respondents on Bali in the Pacific.

MARTIN P. LEVINE

The Making of an AIDS Sociologist

Courtesy of Cathy Stein Greenblat

Martin P. Levine was associate professor of sociology at Florida Atlantic University and a research associate at Memorial Sloan Kettering Cancer Center (New York). He helped organize and lead both the Sociologists AIDS Network and Lesbian and Gay Caucus and was an adviser to the Presidential Commission on the Human Immunodeficiency Virus Epidemic and the National Academy of Sciences' Panel on Monitoring the Social Impact of the AIDS Epidemic. He lectured widely and published on the sociology of AIDS, sexuality, and homosexuality. He died of AIDS in April 1993.

S ociologists have long recognized how social commitments can shape our work. Many of us feel that our professional lives should reflect activist sentiments. In my case, strongly held beliefs in social justice turned me into an AIDS sociologist.

My concern for social justice began early in life. Because I grew up in a poor, working-class family, in a tough inner-city neighborhood, I frequently observed instances of economic, ethnic, and sexual oppression. I saw how poverty prevented my father from obtaining needed dental care, how anti-Semitism led to attacks on my classmates in Hebrew school, and how prejudice fostered hateful slurs against my African-American, Puerto Rican, and gay friends. These incidents struck me as grossly unfair. How could a country as wealthy as ours let the health of some people suffer because they could not pay for medical treatments? And how could a nation as supposedly tolerant as ours permit hateful attacks on some of its citizens?

To right these wrongs, I became active in various social causes. In high school, I participated in the Civil Rights Movement; in college, I joined the Women's and Gay Liberation Movements. These experiences led me to question prevailing cultural assumptions about social injustice. At that time, many people believed that these inequities were biologically or psychologically determined: Poor people were shiftless and lazy, women and minorities were naturally inferior, and homosexuals suffered from a mental illness. In contrast, to student radicals, economic elites created poverty through unchecked pursuit of profits. To civil rights activists and feminists, the plight of minorities and women arose from cultural definitions of race and gender. And to gay liberationists, homosexuality was a healthy variant of human sexuality.

The validity of these beliefs became apparent in my undergraduate courses in sociology. My professors taught me about the relationship between the economic base of a society and its cultural order and about the relativity of racial categories, gender roles, and sexual variation. In particular, they showed me how the class interests of the rich reproduced inequality; how nature played an insignificant role in organizing the social position of the races and sexes; and how there was nothing inherently sick about homosexuality.

My decision to become a sociologist crystallized in these classes. I saw how my training as a sociologist could be used in the struggle for social justice. Subsequent experiences proved me right. Over my career, I repeatedly used my training for activist purposes. I chose to teach at a college that was committed to multicultural and multiracial education. The curriculum incorporated the experiences of all the peoples of the world, and its students came from diverse racial, ethnic, and class backgrounds. My time at school was mainly devoted to students who were traditionally denied access to

educational opportunities because of their race or social class. I helped them with their studies, offered them emotional support, and pushed them to finish school. At my urging several even applied and were admitted to law school. Others became criminal justice professionals.

My research on anti-gay violence and employment discrimination also reflects activist sentiments. Lesbian and gay activists have long maintained that there is widespread violence and job discrimination against gay men and women. However, the lack of systematic evidence on the extent of these problems stymied their efforts to redress the issues through legal remedies. Opponents typically argued that the lack of such evidence proved that the problems were insignificant, and thus there was no need for special protections.

I volunteered to see what was known about these issues and found concrete evidence of violence and employment discrimination against lesbians and gay men. In scientific studies on homosexuality, I incorporated this evidence into several published reports and articles, which were widely circulated within the movement.

This research played a role in the struggle to obtain lesbian and gay civil rights bills and protections. At legislative hearings across the nation, activists cited my findings and I testified before the U.S. House of Representatives.

My most recent work has focused on AIDS. The communities hit hardest by this epidemic—gay men, intravenous drug users, and poor African Americans and Latinos—were being denied adequate resources for fighting the disease. As a result, hundreds of thousands of people needlessly became infected or died, including scores of my friends and loved ones. There was no way I could ignore AIDS. I felt gay men, poor people, and racial minorities deserved social justice. Hence, I became an AIDS activist, educator, and researcher.

1991; Cancian, 1992). This point of view is embraced by humanist and feminist sociologists, as well as by researchers who work with relatively powerless populations. Rejecting the ideal of objective observer, they believe that part of their obligation as sociologists is to use their knowledge to empower the people they study. Not only does shared decision making raise the morale and self-respect of participants, but it also contributes to achieving collective goals.

Participatory action research (PAR) differs from participant observation in that the researcher does more than simply record events for later analysis but *actively* tries to change the social context. For example, on page 37, our colleague and friend, the late Martin Levine, tells how the acquired immune deficiency syndrome (AIDS) epidemic transformed him from an observer of sexual life-styles into a health care crusader. Marty used his sociological training in the service of others.

The U.S. government produces volumes of information every day providing much valuable data for sociological analysis.

Secondary analysis involves the use of data collected by others.

Official data are collected by government agencies.

Historical records such as documents, papers, and letters identify relationships among variables over time and space.

Comparative studies compare social patterns across different societies or time periods.

SECONDARY ANALYSIS. Surveys, interviews, case studies, and observations all generate original data—new information. Yet libraries and data banks are stocked with material that can be reused. **Secondary analysis** refers to the use of information already collected by others.

Official Data. The U.S. government alone produces volumes of information every day; in fact, the U.S. Government Printing Office is the world's largest publisher. Of special value to sociologists is the complete census of American households taken every ten years and the monthly or yearly random sample surveys of 60,000 selected households that yield data on unemployment, family characteristics, income distribution, voting behavior, and so forth. Throughout this textbook, we will depend heavily on information collected by the Bureau of the Census to describe contemporary trends. Although various administrations have tried to influence what the Bureau counts and when and how the data are presented, these publications remain our best source, despite political maneuvering.

Historical Records. Documents from the past are another source of secondary data. Letters, diaries, newspapers, books, and government records allow us to see what relationships among variables are relatively constant over time and which patterns undergo change. One of the classic sociological studies, *The Polish Peasant in Europe and America* (Thomas and Znaniecki, 1918–19/1984) was based largely on letters exchanged between family members who remained in Poland and those who emigrated to the United States.

Social historians are particularly attracted to records of wills, marriages, and property transfers that permit them to reconstruct the past of entire communities. From these documents, for example, we have learned that large multigeneration households were as rare in the eighteenth century as they are today in both the United States and western Europe (Demos, 1978).

Comparative Studies. A powerful method for testing the universality or variability of social patterns is to compare different societies as well as different time periods. Many **comparative studies** involve the reanalysis of ethnographic, largely qualitative material gathered by anthropologists from field trips to nonmodern societies. But increasing use is being made of cross-national case studies that bridge the gap between qualitative uniqueness and theoretical generality (Ragin, 1991). Comparative research has led to important revisions of standard sociological assumptions based on the history of Western societies—for example, the expectation that less developed countries would follow the same path to becoming modern industrial societies as did the nations of western Europe two centuries earlier. Economic development has not necessarily brought democratic rule or a decline in religious authority or greater equality for women. The boxed material entitled "Sociology around the World" suggests the many uses of census-type cross-cultural data.

Comparing Social Statistics

Sociologists learn about other societies through the work of anthropologists who study relatively small, simple societies, and through the data-gathering activities of organizations such as the United Nations and the World Bank. The Population Reference Bureau (PRB) is a private nonprofit educational organization that collects data from a variety of sources and prepares material for classroom use. The authors of this textbook rely heavily on PRB's publications for up-to-date comparisons across very different societies. The most useful PRB publication is its yearly "World Population Data Sheet," a huge chart that contains basic population information from every country on the globe, arranged by geographical area.

From the 1994 Data Sheet, we can compare birthrates in various countries, see what proportion of the population is under age 15 or over age 65, and find estimates of future population growth, among many other fascinating statistics. For example, fertility rates (the average number of children born to a woman during her lifetime) range from a high of 7.6 in the Arab na-tion of Yemen to a low of 1.2 in Spain (compared to 2.1 for the United States). In general, fertility rates are high in countries where women have least power and lowest in those in which women can attend college and keep their own earnings.

The wealthiest country in terms of value of its national production divided by number of citizens is Switzerland at $36,200, and the poorest is the African country of Mozambique at $60 (compared to $23,100 for the United States and $22,200 in the oil-rich United Arab Emirates). The most populous country is the People's Republic of China with 1.2 billion citizens, or one-fifth of the entire world's population. The smallest independent nations, with populations of around 100,000, are islands in the Caribbean such as Domenica, St. Lucia, and Grenada; the Marshall Islands in the South Pacific Ocean; and off the coast of Africa, the Seychelles, and São Tomé and Principe. You may purchase a copy of the "World Population Data Sheet" and other reasonably priced publications from PRB at 1875 Connecticut Avenue NW, Washington, DC 20009. You will find an endless stream of interesting information for term papers in a number of courses.

Content Analysis. Books, newspapers, magazines, videos and the like, are often used as source material for **content analysis,** which involves a systematic counting of the frequency of certain images, ideas, or words. These data permit hypothesis testing about social change, such as trends in images of female beauty (Wolf, 1991), African-American stereotypes (Wilkinson, 1984), conceptions of the "self" as reflected in self-help books (Thomson, 1992), or the effect of "labor-saving" devices (see the box on page 41).

Limitations of Secondary Analysis. Although the use of available data is time- and cost-effective, this method has a number of limitations.

> **Content analysis** counts the number of references to a given item in a sample of publications.

Maps are another source of data for secondary analysis, as is this graphic display of Americans on the move, by County, 1980–1990.

Source: American Demographics Desk Reference Series, no. 1, page 4. © American Demographics, Inc. 127 West State Street, P.O. Box 68, Ithaca, NY. 14851

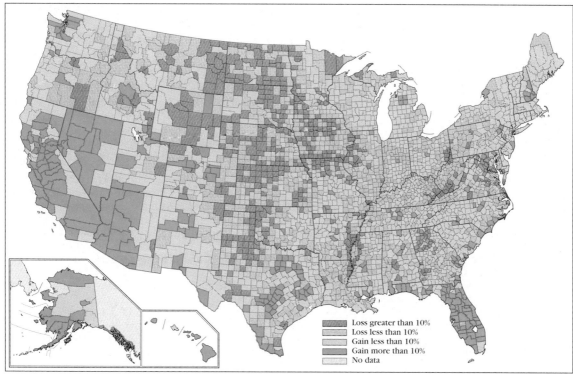

Loss greater than 10%
Loss less than 10%
Gain less than 10%
Gain more than 10%
No data

Comparison of different societies allows sociologists to test the universality of social patterns. Assumptions about paths to modernization, based on the history of Western societies, are being revised by studies of less developed countries such as The People's Republic of China.

Because the information was originally gathered for other purposes, the data may have gaps. Comparative studies, especially those done by anthropologists earlier in this century, are often marred by researcher bias. Nonetheless, a rich body of existing material is waiting to be mined by researchers with a lot of imagination and few resources for high-tech original data gathering and analysis.

EXPERIMENTS.   Of all social science methods, **experiments** are closest to the scientific ideal. The essence of the experimental design is *control over the variables,* which makes it the least appropriate and least used method for most so-

Experiments come closest to the scientific ideal of control over variables.

ciologists. In everyday life, such control over people or a situation is impossible. Furthermore, social behavior is always being modified by the interaction itself. Although experiments are useful in the study of small-group processes, most sociologists are concerned with issues not suitable for study in the laboratory. Nonetheless, experimental research conducted primarily by psychologists and social psychologists has produced some important insights for sociology (for example, the Milgram experiments described in Chapter 4, and the Zimbardo experiment discussed in Chapter 5).

The classic experiment has four stages.

1. In the first step, subjects are assigned to either an experimental (E) or control (C) group on the basis of random selection or some other tech-

---

SOCIAL CHANGE

Did the Vacuum Cleaner Set Her Free?

It is often assumed that the workload of American homemakers has been greatly lightened by the introduction of such household appliances as the washing machine, automatic dishwasher, sewing machine, and vacuum cleaner. Indeed, these appliances are frequently described as "labor-saving" devices. Yet all the available data indicate that while mechanization may have lessened the drudgery, it did not reduce the time spent on household tasks.

To explain this contradiction, Bonnie J. Fox (1990) conducted a content analysis of 70 years of advertisements for household goods in *Ladies Home Journal,* a

popular magazine for American housewives. The research found that the advertisements tended to focus on higher standards of household cleanliness and appearance rather than on the time-saving aspects of the product. The home was redefined as a showcase for a woman's unceasing efforts to achieve perfection, to be accomplished through purchasing the items featured in the advertisements.

Not only were standards of child care and household labor raised, but tasks that were once done by others outside the home, such as laundering or sewing, were now moved inside. Thus, for from liberating the American woman, the mechanized household bound her ever more closely to the home.

Raging flood waters brought devastation to people, property, and the environment in Missouri and Illinois in the summer of 1993. For sociologists, these events provide unique opportunities for field research on the disruption of the social order and how individuals, communities, and the government cope with disasters.

nique for ensuring that the two groups are as alike as possible.

2. All subjects are measured on the variable of interest, often an attitude—for example, feelings about AIDS patients—that the researchers think can be changed under certain circumstances.

3. The certain circumstance, or independent variable, is introduced to the E group only. In this example, it is a film intended to affect attitudes towards AIDS victims, the dependent variable.

4. Members of both E and C groups are then retested on AIDS attitudes to see if any change has occurred.

If the E group shows an increase in sympathy for AIDS patients, can we say that the film had an impact on attitudes? Not really. Only after comparing the E retest scores with those from the C group (alike in every respect except for not having seen the film) can we make any statement about the effects of the film. If C group also showed an increase in sympathy, it is likely that all subjects were influenced by the same outside event such as the AIDS-related death of a famous rock star.

Field Experiment. Once the researcher moves out of the laboratory, control over variables becomes almost impossible. Social psychologists, however, have developed the method of the **field experiment,** in which some aspects of the environment can be manipulated to influence the behavior of unaware ("naive") subjects. The television program *Candid Camera* is composed of field experiments that measure the reactions of naive subjects to an experimental situation. One of our favorites is the elevator that stops to pick up new passengers who see that everyone in the elevator is facing the rear. Without exception, all incoming passengers immediately face the rear, even though there is only one door to the elevator.

> **Field experiments** are conducted in the real world.

RESEARCH IN ACTION

"That's No Lady. That's My Wife!"

A classic field experiment in violence involved "spontaneous fights" staged by the researcher on public streets (Borofsky et al., 1971). There were four different scenarios: two women fighting, two men fighting, a woman beating a man, and a man beating a woman. The object was to observe bystander reaction. As you might expect, male bystanders were more willing than females to intervene, especially when two men or two women were fighting one another. Contrary to expectations, *none* of the male bystanders sought to stop the man who was beating a woman. At that time, the late

1960s, the experimenters thought that perhaps the "uniqueness" and "ridiculousness" of the sight may have inhibited the men from intervening. At the very least, they allowed the possibility that the bystanders obtained vicarious pleasure or hostile gratification from seeing a man hurt a woman.

When we have asked our own students why they thought the men did not stop the fight, the reason they gave most often was, very simply, "She is probably his wife." In other words, there is a generalized acceptance of the right of a man to use physical force on his wife, even in public.

More seriously, many field experiments deal with helping behavior. Although no psychological profile of "the helper" has yet emerged, the data show that *characteristics of the situation* rather than of the person are most important in determining how willing a bystander is to come to the assistance of someone in trouble (Amato, 1990). For example, the more people on the scene, the less likely is any one of them to offer assistance, and the more seriously hurt the "victim," the fewer the number of bystanders willing to help.

Natural Experiments. It is sometimes possible to study a population before and after some outside event changes their situation, for example, community reactions to chemical contamination (Aronoff and Gunter, 1992) or suicide rates following the highly publicized suicide of a famous person (Phillips et al., 1991). In these cases, the population itself is the control group, because it is assumed to be composed of the same people both before and after the introduction of the independent variable.

Evaluation Studies. Another "natural laboratory" has emerged from the growing field of **evaluation studies** that measure the effectiveness of different versions of a social program. The most studied program took place in the 1970s and consisted of four experimental conditions for increasing the income of poor families in Denver and Seattle to see if economic security would reduce rates of divorce and desertion. The findings from this experiment are still being debated (Cain and Wissoker, 1990; Hannan and Tuma, 1990). Some families were strengthened, but in other cases, the added income made it possible for a wife to leave an abusive relationship.

It has become routine to build in an evaluative component into funding for major social programs, such as those currently being designed to help welfare mothers become self-supporting and that also appear to be yielding contradictory results (Passell, 1993b; Chapter 9). The difficulty in evaluating such programs stems from the enormous number of variables that might have an effect, as well as the diversity of the populations being studied. All poor people are not alike, and income or job training are only two of the dozens of factors impinging on their life. Nonetheless, important information might be

Natural experiments involve measuring the same population before and after a natural event that is assumed to change the situation.

Evaluation studies involve testing different versions of social programs.

Statistics are numerical techniques for the classification and analysis of data.

A **percentage** indicates how many of a given item there are in every 100 cases.

Rates are the number of times a given event occurs in a population, on a base other than 100.

gained that will help policymakers reduce the negative impacts of poverty.

The major strengths and drawbacks of the data-gathering methods described in this section are summarized in Table 2-1.

ANALYZING THE DATA

Numbers alone rarely permit adequate testing of hypotheses. The many pieces of information must be arranged so that different sets of people or variables can be compared. Sociologists are trained in **statistics,** numerical techniques for the classification and analysis of data. The statistics impose order on a collection of facts.

As an introductory student, you are not expected to learn about most of these techniques. But as a citizen of a society that worships numbers, you should be able to understand and use some very basic statistics: percentages, rates, ratios, and other numbers that summarize a large body of data (measures of central tendency). In general, a grasp of research methods will help you evaluate the quality of information you will need for decisions in your career and personal life.

Percentages, Rates, and Ratios

PERCENTAGE. The most simple and most important statistic in this book is the **percentage,** or how many times a given item appears in every 100 cases. Percentages allow us to compare groups of different size. For example, although the population of Great Britain is much smaller than that of the United States, we can contrast the likelihood of living in or near a city in the two societies by counting how many of each hundred persons lives in an urban area; these percentages are comparable even though the populations vary in size. In this case, the smaller country has the larger percentage of city dwellers (92 percent versus 75 percent for the United States).

The term *proportion* can be used interchangeably with percentage. How easily can you tell which is the larger proportion: 25 of 300 cases or 30 of 400? The use of percentages simplifies the comparison: 8.3 percent versus 7.5 percent; the larger number, 30, is actually a smaller proportion of its total.

RATES. Like percentages, **rates** are the number of times a given item or event occurs in a population, but instead of 100, the base will be a larger number such as 1,000 or 100,000. Crime rates, for example, are typically based on the number of offenses for each 100,000 population. In the United States, in 1990, the homicide rate was 78 for each 100,000 persons living in Washington, D.C., compared to 3 per 100,000 residents of Omaha, Nebraska (U.S. Bureau of the Census, Statistical Abstract of the United States, 1993).

TABLE 2-1 Overview of Methods Used to Conduct Sociological Research

Method	Data source	Strengths	Drawbacks
Survey	Questionnaire Phone Mail In Person	Large random sample, easily generated, can be done quickly	Depends on honesty of respondent, questionnaires are restricted, "loaded" questions
Interview	Face-to-face	Can ask intimate questions Follow-up questions possible	Small sample, depends on honesty of respondent, researchers bias
Case study	In-depth analysis of one source	Rich detail	Researcher bias, limited in scope, unable to generalize
Participant observation	Active involvment in study	Rich detail, "inside" examination, can study groups and individuals	Time-consuming, limited in scope
Secondary Analysis			
Official records	Government publications	Large quantity of data, inexpensive, unobtrusive	Limited to what has been counted
Historical records	Documents, e.g., letters, diaries, newspapers	Reconstructs the past, unobtrusive	Limited to what others have preserved
Comparative studies	Cross-cultural analysis	Tests universality of cultural patterns, unobtrusive	Limited to what has been published
Content analysis	Counting frequency of images, ideas, or words	Can assess trends over time, unobtrusive	Time-consuming
Experiments			
Classic	Laboratory manipulation of variables	Maximum control, generalizable, easily replicated	Artificial
Field	Partial manipulation of variables	Some control, in-depth study of subject matter	Not always able to replicate, time-consuming
Natural	Before/after studies of social events	Real-life application, generalizable, unobtrusive	Limited to natural events
Evaluation studies	Before/after studies of social programs	Real-life application	Numerous variables complicate evaluation

RATIOS. A **ratio** compares one subpopulation with another, such as males to females, or infant deaths to live births. For example, the proportion of males to females, the *sex ratio,* varies with age. In the United States today, there are 104 males for every 100 females age 14 and under, but because male death rates are higher than those for women at any age, the ratio is down to 97/100 for people age 25–44. By age 85 and older, there are fewer than 40 men for every 100 women! The reasons for these ratios are discussed in Chapters 7 and 18.

Measures of Central Tendency

Three of the most common statistics are single numbers that summarize an entire set of data: **measures of central tendency.** These three important summary statistics are the *mean,* the *median,* and the *mode.* Most of you will have heard others speak of "mean test scores," "median income," or "modal family patterns," without knowing precisely what the terms mean. The three measures are very different, as the following example shows.

A group of 100 respondents has taken an "altruism" test to measure their willingness to help another person. The highest score is 10 and the lowest is zero. The 100 scores were distributed as shown in Table 2-2.

> A **ratio** compares one subpopulation to another.
>
> **Measures of central tendency** are single numbers that summarize an entire set of data.

TABLE 2-2   Altruism among College Students

Score	Number of Respondents with That Score
10	2
9	5
8	8
7	12
6	18
5	15
4	12
3	10
2	9
1	6
0	3
	$N = 100$

Total scores: *498*

MEAN.   The **mean** is an arithmetical average; in this case, 100 respondents had a total score of 498, for a *group mean* of 4.98 (the total scores divided by the number of respondents).

MEDIAN.   The **median** is the *midpoint* of a distribution of cases, with half of the cases above and half below that number. In the preceding example, the midpoint, or 50th case, comes in the score 5 category.

The **mean** is an average.

The **median** is the midpoint of an entire set of cases.

The **mode** is the single most common category of cases.

MODE.   The **mode** is the single most common category of cases: in this example, the largest number of respondents (18) had scores of 6. Therefore, 6 is the mode for this group.

If one wants to compare this set of respondents with any other group, only one measure of central tendency is needed, rather than the hundred individual scores.

REPORTING THE FINDINGS

To Tell or Not to Tell?

We have already mentioned the importance of full disclosure of research techniques, instruments, and findings. But suppose that you, the researcher, have data that you do not want to disclose, that you think might be used against groups with which you are in sympathy. Some researchers do not publish; others try to minimize negative outcomes by interpreting the findings as narrowly as possible.

There are a number of cases in which sociologists have published very controversial reports, for example, Daniel Patrick Moynihan (1965) on the African-American family and James Coleman (1975) on school desegregation. The Moynihan study was widely interpreted as blaming the educational and economic failures of many urban African-American males on their being raised in female-headed households. Coleman's report noted that court-enforced school desegregation, involving crosstown busing, was responsible for "white flight" to the suburbs. Both studies have been refuted by other sociologists, who have also raised the ethical issue of a more general responsibility of social scientists *not* to increase racism in our society.

The counterclaim that a researcher has an obligation, in the name of impartial science, to report findings even when they go against prevailing views, was forcefully made by Coleman (1989), who also noted that younger researchers are often afraid to publish data that might arouse hostility among colleagues. What would you do if your data could be used to support the positions of the American Nazi party?

For other sociologists, the problem is that they are doing research that offends or threatens the authorities (R. Lee, 1993), as seen in the case of Ric Scarce in the box, "The Hazards of Research."

Presenting the Data

Sociologists communicate with one another by publishing in professional journals, by reading papers at professional meetings, and by circulating copies of research papers among friends and colleagues. Major goals include linking one's own study to an existing body of theory and research and pointing out gaps in the knowledge base to generate new questions for further research. In this way, social sciences have tried to copy the natural sciences in creating a cumulative base of knowledge upon which most researchers can agree, but with only limited success (Spencer, 1987). Each new study appears to refute an earlier conclusion or to be open to a variety of theoretical interpretations, which may be due in part to the number of people doing social research today and in part to the vast scope of the field. Nonetheless, there is something that can be called contemporary sociology and that forms the content of this textbook.

The goal of sociological research is to *test* hypotheses, to see if the predicted correlations appear in the data. If so, the theoretical model is supported although never "proved," because there is always the possibility that new data will call the theory into question. And although a researcher should select the statistic that best reflects the data, it is very tempting to use those that best support the hypotheses on which the research was based.

Research findings are always subject to distortion and exaggeration on the part of the media, as seen in the items that began this chapter. In addition, untested correlations, if repeated often enough, come to

The Hazards of Research

For six months in 1993, Rik Scarce, a sociology graduate student, was forced to continue his studies from a jail cell in Spokane, Washington. His crime? Refusing to answer questions before a federal grand jury about his research on the animal rights movement. Some animal rights activists had raided an experimentation center, setting free the animals and damaging equipment. Although Scarce was not a suspect, the government thought he might have interviewed some of the participants in the raid and wanted him to testify about his confidential sources. He refused and was jailed.

Scarce claimed that a social science researcher had an ethical obligation to honor the promises of confidentiality made to informants. Otherwise, few people would talk about activities that might be embarrassing and/or illegal. The concept of academic freedom is based on the ideal of free inquiry, the unrestricted flow of information through which "truth" can be glimpsed. When government steps in and restricts this flow or uses such information to pursue its own ends, the research process is contaminated. In addition, the Code of Ethics of the American Sociological Association states that confidentiality *must* be maintained even when there is no legal protection and even at the risk of being jailed (Scarce, 1993; Monaghan, 1993).

An appeals court saw differently, upholding the district judge, and stating that researchers and reporters could be compelled to reveal the contents of confidential interviews. Fortunately for Ric Scarce, the federal law under which he was sentenced also says that such jailing must be used only to compel people to testify and not to punish them for refusing. Thus, when it became obvious that Scarce would not change his position, the judge was forced to release him.

Although Ric Scarce intends to continue his study of militant environmentalists, one wonders how many other sociologists have been warned off research on topics likely to bring them to the attention of law enforcement agencies.

---

be generally accepted, such as the belief that student grades have fallen because prayer is no longer permitted in public schools. But simply because two events occur at the same time does not prove that one causes the other; they could be unrelated or both the product of some third variable. No research has yet demonstrated that reciting prayers leads to higher grades, but it could be the case that children from very religious homes spend more time doing homework, which is then reflected in their grades.

On a lighter note, confusing correlation with cause-and-effect can be illustrated by the historical observation that birthrates are high in areas with a large number of storks. As it happens, both storks and high birthrates are found in rural areas in contrast to cities. Thus, storks and babies really do go together, but the correlation is produced by a third variable, place of residence.

> Nearly every sociological thesis proposes a new method, which, however, its author is very careful not to apply, so that sociology is the science with the greatest number of methods and the least results.
>
> —HENRI POINCARÉ (1908), 1952, 19–20.

We must also be careful not to fall into the trap of assuming that a correlation at the collective level also exists at the individual level. This problem is very common in popularized reports of research on sex differences. As you will see in Chapter 10, findings on sex differences refer to *group* means, for example, that on average boys are noisier than girls. In any large group, the boys may be twice as noisy as the girls, but this does not mean that each boy makes twice the noise of each girl. Yet most media reports of this research will strongly suggest that the difference exists in individuals rather than at the collective level.

Because sociologists are concerned with general patterns and probabilities, there will be many exceptions to each generalization. As a result, we tend to use words such as *most, typically, in general, often, perhaps,* and other terms that allow leeway in predictions. This usage is "probably" safer than talking in absolutes or giving the impression that the study of human behavior is more precise than it is now or ever has been.

> **Tables** consist of rows and columns of figures arranged to clarify relationships among variables.

Finally, data do not speak for themselves. Numbers become meaningful only when placed in a context. For example, the fact that the poverty rate in the United States in 1993 was 15 percent does not tell us whether this is "high" or "low" unless we have something with which to compare it, such as similar data from 1980 or from Canada.

Tables and Figures

Perhaps the most important part of a research report is the presentation of data in tables, charts, graphs, or diagrams.

READING TABLES.   A **table** consists of columns and rows of figures, arranged to clarify relationships

While the U.S. Census is intended to be an inventory of the entire population, some groups in the population, such as minorities, the poor, and the homeless, have usually been underrepresented. Because various federal support programs are directly tied to the number of people enumerated, municipalities have been concerned with inaccurate counts. Here a Census enumerator in Austin, Texas, questions two homeless men.

among variables. A glance at the table should, in most cases, convey information more readily than detailed descriptions. It would take several sentences to tell you what you should be able to read at a glance from Table 2-3.

Value neutrality, the claim that a researcher can be free of personal bias and judgment, is a foundation of the scientific method in the social sciences.

To interpret a table, start by carefully reading the title, the headings, and the footnotes. Only then will you understand the numbers in each part of the body of the table (called *cells*). In Table 2-3, for example, the title tells you that the cell numbers are the percentages in 1993 of people in the United States aged 65 and over who

TABLE 2-3   Marital Status of Persons 65 and Older, United States, 1993 (percent)

	Men	Women
Never married	4.4	4.4
Married	76.8	42.2
Widowed	14.3	47.6
Divorced	4.5	5.8

Source: U.S. Bureau of the Census, *Current Population Reports,* P20-478, 1994.

were either single, married, widowed, or divorced. The footnote in this case gives the source as the Bureau of the Census, based on the yearly household survey described on page 38.

The cells show the extreme difference between older men and women in the likelihood of their being married rather than widowed. Almost half of all elderly women are widowed, whereas over three-fourths of older men have a living wife. Once the cell data have been described, the researcher must explore their meanings. What explains these differences by sex? One clue is the higher death rates of males than of females of all ages (see Chapters 10 and 20). Another is that women typically marry men older than themselves. What differences do you think being married or widowed makes in terms of a person's standard of living in old age?

FIGURES AND GRAPHS.   Tables are only one way of presenting data. Graphics can be more powerful. Throughout this book, we shall use other techniques for displaying information. for example, data on marital status can be expressed either in *bar graphs* or in *pie-shaped diagrams* as shown in Figure 2-4.

SOCIOLOGY FOR WHAT AND WHOM? NONSCIENTIFIC AND ETHICAL CONSIDERATIONS

Although most researchers attempt to be objective and systematic in gathering information and analyzing the data, nonscientific factors intrude at each step of the research process. Such factors include (1) value judgments, (2) increasing reliance on outside funding, and (3) deception by both researchers and subjects.

Value Judgments

One of the foundations of the scientific method is its claim to be **value neutral,** that is, free of researcher bias and personal judgments. But value neutrality is itself a value-laden decision—*not* to accept responsibility for the uses to which one's findings are put. What if studies of the poor lead politicians to reduce assistance programs or research on Asian peasants is used by the military to destroy resistance movements? The potential conflict between the goals of objectivity and engagement that was a central concern of Max Weber continues to spark debate among sociologists. Can one do both good sociology and good deeds?

Funding Sources

Does it matter that today most large-scale research is funded by federal or state agencies, private foundations, major corporations, and even foreign govern-

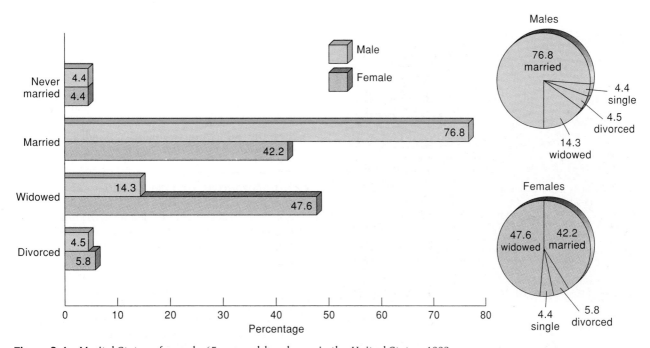

Figure 2-4   Marital Status of people 65 years old and over in the United States: 1993.

Source: U.S Bureau of the Census. "Marital Status and Living Arrangements: March, 1993." *Current Population Reports* P20-478. Washington, DC: Government Printing Office, 1994.

ments? There are enough recent examples to suggest that funders influence both what is studied and how the research findings are used.

Of particular concern is the recent increase in the number of drug and electronics companies awarding grants to universities and research laboratories to discover and test products, with the patents held by the profit-making corporation. In effect, the companies are using public resources for private gain. For example, in 1993, in return for $300,000 from a major drug manufacturer, a government-funded research laboratory agreed to give the company exclusive rights to certain products, as well as control over the scientists' contracts with other researchers (Hilts, 1993). This is a far cry from the scientific standards of open research and full disclosure.

Deception

Each research method contains some elements of deception. This is most obvious in experimental and observational studies in which it is important that the people being observed are unaware of the goals of the research. But even the simplest survey questionnaire invades the respondents' privacy for purposes that they do not know and of which they might not approve.

ETHICS IN EXPERIMENTS.   All experiments involve the manipulation of human subjects, either placing them in false situations or exposing some but not others to

a given stimulus. Suppose that you were testing a new program to reduce drug abuse. How would you justify random selection of some adolescents for the new program while leaving others untreated? Or giving the new treatment to those who have not requested it? You could ask for volunteers, but if all subjects were self-selected, the results would be biased.

Another dilemma revolves around how much the researchers need to tell to secure "informed consent" from research subjects. Many laboratory-type experiments today are conducted with "captive audiences" such as inmates of institutions and college students, who may risk losing parole or a lower grade if they refuse to take part in a research project. Other studies rely on volunteers who are paid for their time and who, therefore, might feel obligated to act in a certain way.

CORRECTING RESEARCH ABUSES AND MISUSES.   In response to questions raised by the misuses and abuses of the research process, most colleges and universities today have Human Subjects Review Committees that must approve all research on human beings being done by faculty or students. These procedures are designed to protect the privacy of respondents and to ensure that no harm will result from participation in the study. Weighing the costs and benefits to all the interested parties—sponsors, researchers, subjects, and the general public—is enormously complex (Bailey, 1988). Whose interests "ought" to count most is itself an ethical question.

Nonscientific factors intrude at each step of the research process. This is particularly true in countries run by repressive and military governments where citizens risk their lives by voicing opposition to existing regimes, such as those in many South American countries.

Government funding is typically regulated by "peer-review" panels of scholars who judge the quality of research proposals. Because peer-review panels are typically drawn from leading figures in a field, there is a tendency to approve projects that support existing conceptual models, as well as a temptation to help friends and colleagues (Chubin and Hackett, 1990). In addition, the peer panels can be stacked with people known to favor administration goals.

Despite such safeguards, fraud in scientific research appears to be much more widespread than previously thought (LaFollette, 1992). One large-scale study, funded by the National Science Foundation (a government agency) found that half of faculty members knew of some type of misconduct by their colleagues (Swazey et al., 1993). Acts of professional abuse ranged from misusing school resources and padding the budget to faking findings and withholding data from competing researchers.

RESPONDENT BIAS.   Not all deception is on the part of the researcher. It cannot simply be assumed that respondents and research subjects are always aware of, or wish to let others know, what they really think or do. Researchers may be deceived if they do not recognize the following problems (Douglas and Johnson, 1978):

1. *Misinformation.* Unintended falsehoods when respondents think that they know a "truth" that may not be correct. Examples include the misconceptions cited at the beginning of this chapter.
2. *Evasions.* Intentionally withholding information or turning the question aside.
3. *Lies.* Designed to mislead the questioner. Respondents often give false information about their age or occupation; politicians hide sources of campaign funds; advertisers skirt the truth as an occupational specialty; and even the Boy Scouts of America have padded membership counts for fund-raising purposes. These "dirty statistics" are often used to achieve what the subjects consider a higher goal.
4. *Fronts,* or *Shared Lies about Settings.* Massage parlors that claim to be health spas and banks that exist to "launder" money earned illegally are just two examples of fronts designed to mislead observers.

In other words, the world and its inhabitants are not always what they appear to be, just as a given research study may not be exactly what its investigators claim.

Some kinds of respondent bias are *un*intentional, as in the general tendency of people to give socially acceptable answers. Researchers have also found that there are persons who are yea-sayers (who tend to agree) and those who are nay-sayers (who tend to disagree) no matter what the issue.

Despite such limitations, sociologists continue to study both the macrolevel and microlevel structures and processes that compose social life in all its variety.

SUMMARY

1. Sociologists test their theories through research. The chapter examines the importance of research, the scientific and nonscientific factors involved in the research process, the methods used, the type of information collected, and the description and analysis of data.

2. Knowledge is gained partly through subjective understanding based on one's own understanding of the world or on intuition. It is also gained in objective ways.
3. The scientific method involves objective observation, precise measurement, and full disclosure

of research methods and results. Findings should be capable of replication.

4. The research process involves five major steps:
    a. Selecting the research question.
    b. Choosing the most appropriate method for collecting the necessary information.
    c. Gathering the data.
    d. Analyzing the data.
    e. Drawing conclusions and reporting the findings to colleagues.

5. Nonscientific factors, such as the researchers' values and attitudes or consideration of funding and time available, affect the choice of what is studied.

6. Framing the research question involves selecting variables and formulating hypotheses about the relationships among the variables.

7. Operationalizing the variables involves translating the variables and hypotheses into observable and measurable items.

8. The most appropriate research methods depend on the nature of the information needed, the type of data, and the kinds of respondents sought.

9. Research methods that may be used include cross-sectional studies; panel or longitudinal studies; large-scale social surveys; interviews; observations; secondary analysis of available official, historical, and comparative data; and/or experimental designs.

10. Groups of respondents and variables are compared by using statistics such as percentages, rates, ratios, and measures of central tendency (mean, median, and mode).

11. Research findings are often reported or published for colleagues. This allows others to evaluate the research and to replicate a study.

12. The choice of research topics and the decision to report findings are influenced by nonscientific factors such as the value judgments of researchers, the use of data and results, and the extent to which funding agencies shape and control the findings.

13. Deception by researchers and/or subjects is an additional non-scientific factor.

SUGGESTED READINGS

Babbie, Earl. *The Practice of Social Research.* 6th ed. Belmont, CA: Wadsworth, 1992. A good introduction to social research methods.

Ball, Michael S., and Gregory W. H. Smith. *Analyzing Visual Data.* Newbury Park, CA: Sage, 1992. This book explores strategies for understanding visual aspects of culture utilizing content analysis, symbolic interaction, structuralism, cognitive anthropology, and ethnomethodology.

Bradburn, Norman, and Seymour Sudman. *Polls and Surveys: Understanding What They Tell Us.* San Francisco: Jossey-Bass, 1988. A comprehensive overview of public opinion research and its uses including its history, policymakers, the workings of federal and academic survey organizations, how interviewing is organized, the selection of respondents, guidelines for question construction, the interpretation of survey responses, and the many functions of polls in our daily lives.

Burawoy, Michael, Alice Burton, Ann Arnett Ferguson, Kathryn J. Fox, Joshua Gamson, Nadine Gartrell, Leslie Hurst, Charles Kurzman, Leslie Salzinger, Josepha Schiffman, and Shiori Ui. *Ethnography Unbound: Power and Resistance in the Modern Metropolis.* Berkeley: University of California Press, 1991. Based on a field seminar, this interesting book combines a collection of ethnographic studies with discussions on methods and pedagogy linking biography and history, the personal and the political.

Denzin, Norman K., and Yvonne S. Lincoln, eds. *Handbook of Qualitative Research.* Thousand Oaks, CA: Sage Publications, Inc., 1994. Moving from the theoretical to the specific, this handbook examines the various paradigms for doing qualitative work, the strategies developed for studying people in their setting, and a variety of techniques for collecting, analyzing, interpreting, and reporting findings.

Feagin, Joe R., Anthony M. Orum, and Gideon Sjoberg, eds. *A Case for the Case Study.* Chapel Hill: University of North Carolina Press, 1991. The authors make a strong case for interpretive sociology, fieldwork and naturalistic research.

Josselson, Ruthellen, and Amia Lieblich, eds. *The Narrative Study of Lives.* Vol. 1. Thousand Oaks, CA: Sage Publications, Inc., 1993. This cross-cultural and interdisciplinary collection provides rich stories and analyses of life history narratives.

Park, Peter, Mary Brydon-Miller, Budd Hall, and Ted Jackson, eds. *Voices of Change: Participatory Research in the United States and Canada.* Westport, CT: Greenwood Publishing Group, Inc., 1993. Using participatory research case studies, the authors use a methodology, developed in Third World settings, to promote social change in communities using self-generated knowledge.

Stanfield, John H. II and Rutledge M. Dennis, Eds. *Race and Ethnicity in Research Methods.* Newbury Park, CA: Sage, 1993. A compendium of thirteen multidisciplinary articles that illustrate the variations in methodology used for conducting research about ethnic groups and ethnic relations.

3

The Cultural Context

- Among the Maring peoples of New Guinea, the most admired men are those who have as little contact with women as necessary, fearful that sexual intercourse will cause them to lose their health (Buchbinder and Rappaport, 1976), but in the United States, male high school students have constructed an elaborate system of prestige points for the sexual conquest of young girls.
- Nursery school children in Italy have long and serious disagreements about opinions and ideas, whereas American children fight mostly over toys and other possessions (Corsaro and Rizzo, 1988).
- Similar to recipes in today's gourmet cookbooks, a very detailed set of rules were devised by the ancient Aztecs for the killing, cooking, and eating of their enemies (Visser, 1991).
- Because their view of health is based on the idea of energy and spirit ("chi") in the body, Chinese pay special attention to herbs and exercise to preserve their physical well-being, and appear to be as successful as Americans who depend on the exclusively physical model of health and medicine practiced in the United States (Moyers, 1993).

These are only a few of the countless examples we could use to illustrate the influence of *culture* on ideas and actions, which is the subject of this chapter.

Culture consists of the ways of thinking, believing, and behaving that are shared by members of a given society. Culture is learned, primarily through language and experience, and the various elements of culture combine to produce the unique nature of that society at that particular historical moment. Because culture is a human construction and transmitted through interpersonal contacts, it is never fixed. It is always in flux.

THE EVOLUTIONARY BASIS OF CULTURE

Culture is possible because of gradual and cumulative changes over a period of four million years that transformed one line of tree-dwelling apes into human beings (see Figure 3-1). The story began with the first *prehumans* who ventured out of trees onto high grassland, where the ability to stand upright was a great advantage in finding food and spotting enemies (Coppens, 1994).

Standing on two feet, in turn, allowed the front paws to develop into hands that could ultimately make tools. A shift to a more varied diet led to changes in the structure of the jaw, leaving more room for brain growth. The placement of the human head at the top of the spinal cord freed space for the development of a voice box in the throat. Major changes in the female reproductive system transformed human sexuality into a predominantly social relationship. Throughout this entire chain of bodily

Figure 3-1 The evolution of humans.

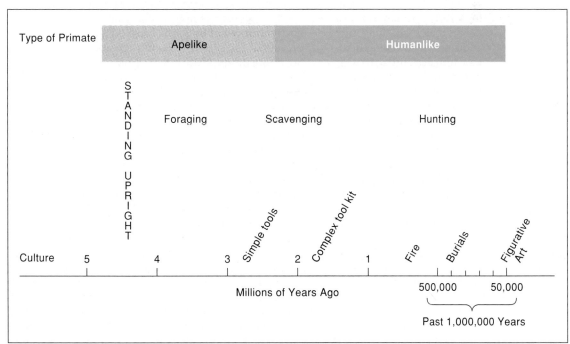

changes, the brain itself became increasingly complex in order to process new types of information.

At the same time, a narrowing of the birth canal meant that the human infant had to be born when its head and shoulders could easily slip down, before the nervous system matured—which meant long before fixed responses could be coded into the human brain. The helplessness of the human infant also meant that its survival depended on the ability of other humans to care for it over a period of many years.

Human behavior, as noted in Chapter 1, is characterized by *flexibility* and *adaptability* rather than by instinct. Born without any preprogrammed behaviors, human beings must *learn* how to interpret and respond to the world about them. The same evolutionary process that made learning necessary also provided the necessary equipment: a uniquely complex brain coupled with the ability to utter a large number of very different sounds. The result is the human capacity to create languages of great variety and sophistication through which people share knowledge and communicate feelings. Each generation does not need to reinvent the wheel but can instead build on the accumulated wisdom of the collectivity—its culture.

The Emergence of Culture

Culture began to replace physical evolution as a means of adapting to the environment, in East Central Africa, with the first apelike individuals who walked on two feet and had to use their brains to outwit other animals. Members of these small groups survived by **foraging,** which involves picking readily-available foodstuff such as fruits, nuts, berries, and edible roots. Contrary to the image you may have of fierce males clubbing one another and dragging helpless females into caves, it now appears that the basic group of prehumans consisted of a female and her children, joined periodically by one or more of the adult males who followed them around and who were chosen as mates because of their willingness to share food and help with the young (Strum, 1988; de Waal, 1989). Similar to the chimpanzees, who are our close primate cousins, these groups roamed across broad spaces, rarely having to compete for food; relationships among adults were essentially peaceful and marked by equality; and because each day brought different challenges, leadership changed with the circumstances (Power, 1991). Thus, from the very beginning of the path to "humanness," our ancestors realized that cooperation is superior to aggression as a survival strategy (Lepowski, 1994).

Foraging involves picking readily available foods for immediate consumption.

Gathering involves transporting, storing, and preserving readily available foods.

As a mental exercise, imagine that you and a dozen of your classmates, evenly divided between men and women, are the earliest prehumans faced with the challenge of staying alive as a group in a new environment, without any of the knowledge that you now have in your mind, and without language. How would you communicate to one another? Find enough to eat? Decide how to divide necessary tasks? Pair off to meet sexual needs in a way that minimizes jealousy and conflict? Raise children? And develop a sense of shared responsibility and identity?

You would most likely hit upon the same solutions as your earliest ancestors: foraging and sharing, group decision making, inventing rules that reward cooperation, developing a set of sounds and gestures through which you could understand one another, and then creating stories that explain the world around you. In short, you will have constructed a unique way of life—your culture—which can be transmitted directly to the children, so that they do not have to start from scratch.

Around 2.5 million years ago, apelike individuals were replaced by those with more humanlike characteristics: larger brain, smaller jaw, longer legs, heavier muscles, narrower birth canal. As shown in Figure 3-1, these earliest humans added meat to their diet, not as hunters but as *scavengers,* outwitting other animals for a share of already dead meat. For this, superior brains, as well as tools to cut skin and sinews, were necessary, and it was a mere one million years before the tool kit of early humans grew in range and sophistication to include scrapers and hand axes.

About 700,000 years ago, some of these groups discovered fire, and a whole new set of adaptations were possible: cooked meat as a major part of the diet, and living in colder climates. Foraging was replaced by **gathering** whereby foods were collected, stored, and preserved for later use. Soon thereafter, we find signs of populations that could truly be labeled "fully human," and that spread rapidly from Africa to southern Europe and across Asia. Called *Homo sapiens*—thinking people—because of their relatively large, complex brains, they engaged in small-scale *hunting,* developed a tool kit including needles for sewing skins, and buried their dead with ceremony. The best known of these early *Homo sapiens* are the Neanderthals, whose remains have been found throughout Europe, Asia, the Middle East, and Africa.

Then, between 100,000 and 75,000 years ago, a more "modern-looking" *Homo sapiens* appeared, gradually replacing Neanderthal as the dominant population. Called *Homo sapiens sapiens* to reflect the ultimate importance of mind over body, these are the people from whom *all* living humans are descended. There are no significant differences in evolved potential or abilities among contemporary racial or ethnic populations; we are products of the same evolutionary history—more alike than different. Body, mind, and culture have all developed together to produce the modern human, a creature specialized only for flexibility.

WHAT IS CULTURE?

Culture is often described as the blueprint for living of a group (or society) whose members share a given language and territory, and who recognize their shared identity. Culture consists of: (1) solutions to the problems of survival, (2) ideals and values that shape rules of conduct, and (3) tools, weapons and other human-made objects (**artifacts,** or material culture). We become functioning members of a society as we learn the content of its culture.

Another way of looking at culture is to emphasize the way in which it shapes how we perceive the world and interpret our experience (Swidler, 1986). Because the human central nervous system develops within a social setting, there can be no "human nature" independent of culture. In this view, there are as many human natures as there are cultures (Geertz, 1973). To be human, therefore, is to be capable of both great kindness and gross cruelty, of both sacrifice and selfishness. Other theorists, particularly those in the biosocial tradition, suggest a number of traits that could be considered basic to human nature, either because they are found in all societies to some degree, such as male dominance, or because they are shared with our closest primate cousins, such as individualism, or because evolution has favored sociability and helping behaviors (J. Q. Wilson, 1993; Maryansky and Turner, 1992).

Symbols and Language

The key to culture is the evolution of the capacity for using **symbols.** A symbol is a sound or object or event that signifies nothing in and of itself but which is *given meaning by members of the group.* For example, a vertical line –|– stands for the number "one" to people who use the Arabic numeral system; in other cultures, it could mean anything on which people have agreed. When joined at right angles by an intersecting line, Christians will recognize the sign of the cross with all the emotions aroused by that symbol; other people will be quite untouched.

The most important symbol system is language—a set of sounds and gestures whose significance depends on the common understanding of all who use them. *All human communication is symbolic,* through words and actions whose meanings are socially defined. Our prehuman ancestors must have devised such a set of shared symbols; it was more complex than those used by chimpanzees, but was limited by their relatively small brain through which symbols are coded, and by an undeveloped voice box.

With *Homo sapiens,* both brain and voice box reach a level of development that permits processing complex pieces of information and producing a wide range of sounds. Over time, each human group or society creates a unique language shaped by their particular history, so that none is precisely similar to another. Languages spoken in other cultures will sound strange to our ears—for example, the variety of clicking sounds spoken by the !Kung San of the Kalahari Desert in Africa—just as we must sound very unusual to them. But no language should be considered superior to any other; all are of equivalent value and validity, and all represent the crowning achievement of human evolution: the capacity for reflexive thought (Diamond, 1992).

> **Culture** is the map for living of a collectivity whose members share a given territory and language, feel responsible for one another, and recognize their common identity.
>
> **Artifacts,** or material culture, consist of tools and other human-made objects.
>
> A **symbol** is a sound, object, or event that is given meaning by members of a group.

True, animals can be taught the meaning of certain gestures, to recognize their name, and to answer to simple commands. A few chimpanzees, after many years of training, have mastered some elements of Standard American Sign Language, and one or two have even produced untaught gestures. But such abilities are extremely limited when compared to the average 2 1/2-year-old human's seemingly endless flow of words, sentences, and untaught concepts.

Indeed, long before they actually speak their native language, human infants are aware of its basic sounds. As newborns, infants are capable of learning any language, but as they grow increasingly familiar with the one spoken by their parents, they come to pay atten-

> The lenses through which any nation looks at life are not the ones another nation uses. It is hard to be conscious of the eyes through which one looks. Any country takes them for granted, and the tricks of focusing and of perspective which give to any people its national view of life seems to that people the god-given arrangement of the landscape.
>
> —Ruth Benedict, 1946: 14.

tion to only some sounds and not others. It appears, then, that language shapes perception even before the child speaks (Kuhl et al., 1992). Recent research on deaf babies shows that they, too, are early learners, using their hands in the same way hearing infants use their voice, a language of gestures rather than sounds, but following very similar patterns of development (Pettito and Marenette, 1991). Furthermore, whereas apes and other animals may communicate effectively among themselves, they have not created cultures that extend across entire groups or that grow more complex over time (Bickerton, 1991). Only humans have produced religion, poetry, and painting.

It is through language that we have been able to bring order out of chaos, to give shape to the world around us. The primary mechanism for doing this is by making *distinctions,* separating one thing from its opposite: day and night, self and other, good and bad, male and female, animal and human (Zerubavel, 1991). These distinctions do not exist in nature itself, but are imposed by humans through language. The boundaries created by distinctions are essential to maintaining social order, and much of our thinking involves sorting what we see into culturally-created categories.

Kinesics is the study of nonverbal communication.

NONVERBAL COMMUNICATION.   Not all language is spoken or written. Gestures, facial expressions, and body movements are all ways of sending a message. The study of nonverbal (unspoken) communication is called **kinesics** (Birdwhistle, 1970). As with spoken language, the meaning of the gesture depends on the culture. The significance of some gestures can vary

Kinesics is the study of nonverbal communication such as gestures, facial expressions, and body movements. What messages are being expressed by these American soccer players celebrating their victory in the FIFA Women's World Championship Soccer tournament?

widely from one society to another, whereas other gestures, such as a smile or a frown, have much the same meaning everywhere. Within a society, the same gesture will have different meanings depending on

Percent Speaking a Language Other Than English at Home by County, 1990

Source: U.S. Bureau of the Census, 1994, p.53; *American Demographics*, April 1993, p.40.

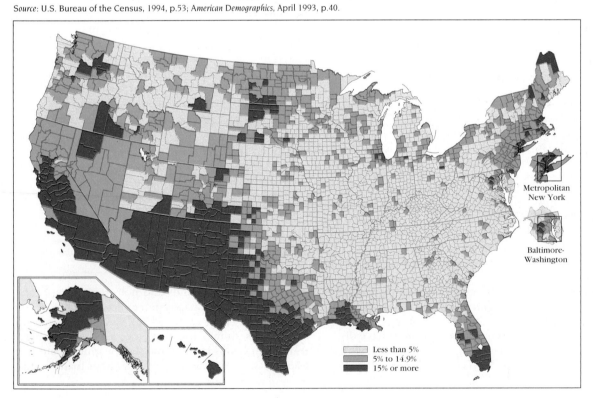

Metropolitan New York

Baltimore-Washington

Less than 5%
5% to 14.9%
15% or more

The Symbolic Significance of Words

The conflict over reproductive rights in the United States over the past 20 years illustrates the profound symbolic power of words. Those who seek to limit a woman's reproductive options call themselves "pro-life," which automatically makes their opponents "anti-life" (or its equivalent, "pro-death"). They refer to "unborn children," so that abortion is equated with homicide. These words immediately produce strong negative images. The red rose they wear symbolizes both beauty and blood.

Supporters of reproductive rights, seeking equally powerful positive symbols, speak of "choices" and the "right to privacy," calling on the traditions of individualism and freedom from government control that are also highly valued in our society. Their symbol of the coat hanger, signifying the lengths that women would go to in the absence of legal and safe medical options, is designed to focus attention on potential physical harm to the woman.

Thus, each side has sought to manipulate public opinion through linguistic constructions, in a battle being fought for the minds and hearts of the American public, as well as in the political arena.

---

the context: saluting an officer on a military base is a sign of respect; saluting one's parents in the home may symbolize quite the opposite.

Each culture also has ideas about privacy and the "bubble of personal space" to which a person is entitled, as seen in the distance between people speaking to one another (Hall, 1959). In the United States, we stand about two feet apart; in many Arab societies, speakers stand head-to-head. The bubble of personal space will also vary by a person's power in the society. Bosses have more privacy than employees; men are more likely than women to impose themselves on someone's personal space; and adults have no hesitation in violating the private bubble of a child (Thorne, 1993).

LANGUAGE AND PERCEPTION. Language and gestures both reflect and create reality. Members of a society develop a vocabulary and grammar that allows them to understand and communicate their experiences. At the same time, one's language serves to channel and shape perception, so that those who share it tend to see and evaluate the world in the same way, which will be different from the reality of people speaking another language. We do not confront the world directly, but only through the screen or lens of culture as embodied in our language.

Thus, what you consider as basic, unquestionable realities, such as color, time, and space are actually perceived quite differently from one language group to another. Many societies have only a few words to describe color, while other languages have dozens; the Inuit of Northern Canada have a dozen different words to cover the fine distinctions among various forms of snow and ice, whereas Fijians of the South Pacific only invented their one word for snow after Europeans settled on their island (Howard, 1986). Just as an American teenage male can identify dozens of automobiles by model and year, a young Nuer herder has over 400 words to describe the cattle on which his society depends. To learn another language is to enter another world of experience.

Words also have an evaluative dimension. Some carry a positive meaning, and others have negative overtones as shown in the box on the symbolic significance of words (above). Throughout history, words have been used to define some people as so different or inferior that they could be enslaved or murdered without guilt; even today, in our society, we can speak of a "fallen" woman or "wild animal" gang member (Brown, 1993).

THE INDIVIDUAL AND CULTURE. As descendants of the original *Homo sapiens sapiens,* all 5.5 billion inhabitants of our planet today share a common physical and mental structure, alike in certain needs and capacities. Yet because each culture is a unique blend of socially constructed beliefs and rules of behavior, members of one society will share certain characteristics different from those of other societies. It is also the case that each individual is a peculiar bundle of inherited traits and predispositions (tendencies to respond in a particular way), but when these tendencies are filtered through the common culture, people become more alike than different in values, beliefs, and predictable patterns of behavior. Thus, to paraphrase a classic observation (Kluckhohn and Murray, 1948): As human beings there are some respects in which we are like *all* others; and as members of a particular culture, there are ways in which we are similar only to *some* others; but as an individual, there are ways in which we are like *no* other person.

CULTURAL DEVELOPMENT: FROM SIMPLE TO COMPLEX

All known cultures—from the past as well as today—can be arranged along a line (continuum) representing degrees of difference between the *most simple* and *most complex* as measured by technology, knowledge base, social structure, and material artifacts. As shown in Figure 3-2, a society's adaptation to its environment,

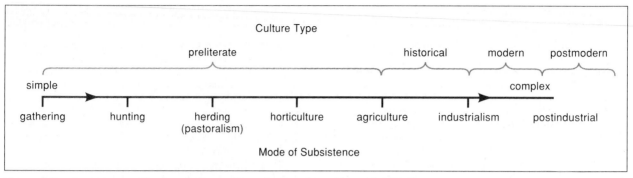

Culture Type

preliterate   historical   modern   postmodern

simple   complex

gathering   hunting   herding   horticulture   agriculture   industrialism   postindustrial
                                (pastoralism)

Mode of Subsistence

Figure 3-2   A continuum of cultural change. (See also Lenski and Lenski, 1991.)

or **mode of subsistence** provides the economic base for supporting a certain size population.

As the food supply becomes more varied and certain, the the larger the population that can be supported. As the population expands, a division of labor results, with some people performing different tasks than others, adding to problems of order and coordination of efforts. These problems lead to increasingly elaborate arrangements for making and enforcing the rules, pairing off the unmarried, and training the young. In all these ways—economic, political, familial, and educational—the culture base expands and the society becomes more complex.

Mode of subsistence refers to the way in which a group adapts to its environment through the production of goods and services.

Preliterate societies do not have a written language.

Historical societies have left written records.

Types of Cultures and Societies

In the discussion of culture types we will use the terms *simple* and *preliterate* in place of such value-laden words as *primitive* or *uncivilized*. There are no "uncivilized" people, only those whose cultures are relatively simple. **Preliterate** means without written language and correctly describes most preagricultural societies, although the spoken language can be very elaborate, containing a range of sounds not found in our language. Agricultural societies are referred to as **historical** because some written records usually exist. *Modern* societies are those that have entered the industrial era.

For most of our evolutionary past, humans lived in small bands of between 20 to 60 persons who subsisted by foraging, gathering, and scavenging and where both women and men tended their young, shared the fruits of their labors, and remained united by bonds of blood and marriage. With the introduction of *hunting* perhaps as early as a half million years ago, a division of labor took place in which young men specialized in the hunt while the women continued to forage and gather, limited by childbearing from being away from the campsite for long periods or distances. Hunting added knowledge, tools, and skills to the group's culture base, including how to cook and store meat and how to use other parts of the animals for clothing, weapons, and new tools. Hunting societies were often organized into tribes of several

Both traditional and modern modes of subsistence are found around the globe today. How efficient is the traditional agriculture of Ethiopia compared to the modern agriculture of Idaho? What are the consequences of these technologies for the populations involved?

Drawing by S. Harris; © 1988 The New Yorker Magazine, Inc.

families, in which women gathered for their own kinfolk, whereas meat from the hunt was usually distributed among all who shared the campsite. Sharing the hunt linked individuals and families in relationships of giving and receiving. By at least 30,000 years ago, some hunting–gathering societies had grown large, with semipermanent base camps and relatively elaborate tools. They were involved in trading surplus goods with other tribes and in producing objects of art such as beads and ceramics (Headland and Reid, 1989).

Herding added such specialties as the care and breeding of animals, and *horticulture* (simple farming) involved learning about plants, how to prepare land, and when to harvest crops. Each of these modes of subsistence was technologically more complex than the preceding one. Settlements became larger; the number and variety of activities increased; and new skills such as basketry, pottery, and weaving were invented or borrowed from other cultures.

The introduction of *agriculture,* some 10 to 12 thousand years ago, marked a major shift in social and cultural development. More systematic than horticulture, agriculture involves plowing furrows and irrigating crops, thus ensuring a more dependable food supply. A surplus in good seasons leads to new adaptations such as trading with other societies and building storage facilities. In turn, the need for record keeping led to the invention of number systems and writing, primarily to keep track of who owns what.

The very size and permanence of agricultural communities tend to produce relatively elaborate political systems in which power becomes centralized in the hands of a chief or small group (elite), whose authority overrides that of family heads, and who can pass on their positions to their children. The informal exchanges of goods and services found in less complex economies are replaced by market systems dominated by the impersonal laws of supply and demand. As division of labor increases, so also does inequality in power and wealth among the citizens.

These key characteristics are shown in Table 3-1, which greatly simplifies the enormous variety of cultural types found among preliterate and historical societies. These cultures are also referred to as *preindustrial* to distinguish them from the profoundly different ways of thinking and behaving and of organizing social life that emerged with the Industrial Revolution of the past two centuries. The industrial way of life is associated with an increasingly complex knowledge base, technology, and material culture. The United States is located at the most complex end of the continuum illustrated in Figure 3-2, along with the nations of Western Europe, Japan, Australia, and Canada. These societies are also moving into a new phase of adaptation called *post-industrial,* as discussed in Chapters 13 and 19.

TABLE 3-1   Types of Preindustrial Societies

Type	Size	Mode of Subsistence	Specialization of Labor	Political Structure	Economic Distribution	Degree of Inequality	Integrating Mechanism
Band	20–60 people in one place	Gathering	Minimal	Informal, based on skill	Communal sharing	Minimal	Kinship (blood and marriage)
Tribe	Hundreds in several residential groups	Hunting Herding Horticulture	On basis of age and sex	Informal, family- and residence-based	Redistribution of group's goods	Relatively low	Residential groups and cross-cutting task groups
Chiefdom	500 to several thousand in large communities	Agriculture and other specializations	Moderate	Chiefs and other recognized leaders	Gift exchange (reciprocity)	Relatively high	Centralized leadership
Early state	Many thousands in cities and towns	Intensive agriculture and professional crafts	Extreme	Formal, legally structured, usually hereditary	Market exchange	Clear political and economic divisions	Monopoly of force by political religious leaders

Gone with the Rain Forests

The world's small population of gathering/hunting bands has diminished rapidly over the past three decades. Across the globe—the Philippines, the Amazon River basin, East Africa, and throughout Southeast Asia—the rain forests that have nurtured and protected these small groups for thousands of years are being destroyed by large-scale logging operations. The growing demand for building material by the more "modern" nations has led the rulers of poorer countries, often for their own personal gain, to sell logging rights to foreign companies.

On the Island of Borneo, in the territory called Sarawak, some of the world's oldest and most unusual forest land has been so thoroughly denuded that what took ten million years to create will now be logged out by the end of this century. As in other countries where logging has been allowed to proceed unregulated, the bulldozers have destroyed the native environment of simple people such as the Penan (Sesser, 1991).

Penan culture is similar to that of other hunting and gathering bands: perfectly adapted to its environment, based on the ideal of sharing. The Penan hunters and gatherers are careful to take only what is needed, preserving the forest and its food for future generations. The people are gentle and nonaggressive; children are never physically punished; power differences between men and women are minimal. Before contact with Christian missionaries, the Penan had no written language, but delighted in long, detailed, oral narratives. The Penan worshipped the spirits that lived in the trees which they were forbidden to cut down.

But since the 1960s, logging has destroyed the wild plants and driven away the animals, leaving the Penan without a place in the world, without food or hope. Their special skills in knowing every inch and aspect of the vast rain forest, its rivers and trees and plants, are of no value to the new lords of the land. Having always been nomads, the Penan have a very different sense of time and space than that required for farming; nor do they have a claim to any usable farmland. They are unequipped for logging jobs, so far removed is their culture from that of the outsiders. In the past few years, under pressure from the government and missionaries,

most Penan have left the deepest forest to live in settlements, but these communities remain without adequate schools, sanitation, or suitable work for the adults.

In any event, the Penan way of life has forever vanished, along with the rain forests that were once the glory of Sarawak. So, also, have the other gentle people of the Philippines, Africa, and the Amazon—the last remnants of a culture that sustained *Homo sapiens* for tens of thousands of years (Shenon, 1994).

From Stan Sesser, "Reporter at Large: Logging in the Rain Forest," *The New Yorker*, May 27, 1991: pp. 42–67. Reprinted by permission of Stan Sesser.

Across the globe, rain forests that had been the home to many cultures and millions of species of animals, insects and plants are being destroyed by large-scale logging. On the Island of Borneo, in the territory of Sarawak, forests that took ten million years to create will be destroyed by the end of the century. Why is this happening?

No one society has passed along the entire length of this continuum. Some have changed greatly; others very little; but when we add up all that we know about human cultures, past and present, we can say that the general direction of change has been toward increasingly more complex modes of subsistence and, consequently, of social structure. Every now and then, a leader will seek to stem the tide of change by calling for a return to a simpler way of life from the past, as in contemporary Iran, but eventually these attempts fail.

Today, more than 3,000 distinct cultures are located at all points along the continuum, each with a unique history of contact with other societies, of environmental pressures, and of changes from within that produce a way of life like that of no other society. Thus, there is probably no "pure" simple society today that could be said to represent fully the way of life of the earliest human groups. Nonetheless, contemporary hunters and gatherers offer fascinating clues regarding the culture of our ancestors.

Cultural Development in a Conflict Perspective

In taking the mode of subsistence as the prime determinant of cultural complexity, we are following an essentially conflict model. As our description of hunting-and-gathering societies suggests, equality within the group is possible when most adults perform similar tasks and when there is very little in the way of material culture. Because hunting, gathering, and herding require constant movement (nomadism), people do not accumulate many things, and because the foods must be eaten fresh, sharing is essential.

Once the group becomes more geographically settled (sedentary), people can hold on to certain possessions—land, animals, and artifacts—and communal sharing is often replaced by private exchanges among individuals or families. As a result, cultural complexity is typically associated with increased inequality, reaching its most systematic form in agricultural societies, especially those based on slavery and/or hereditary ownership of land and other resources.

Conflict over the distribution of goods and services is also common in societies with private ownership where there is no overall authority that can resolve disputes between families or among individuals. Changes in the direction of greater complexity will be resisted by those who enjoy power under the existing system (unless they also control the new resources). The sheiks who rule Near Eastern societies today, for example, have accepted Western oil-producing techniques and even military protection as in the case of Kuwait in 1991, while fiercely resisting other aspects of Western culture that threaten their total control over their subjects, such as free elections and voting rights for women.

ANALYZING CULTURE

Culture is an *abstraction;* most of its elements cannot be seen or touched; we can only describe what people do and the explanations they give for their conduct. This chapter is entitled "The Cultural Context" to convey the idea that culture provides a blueprint or framework for social arrangements that regulate daily life and that meet personal and collective needs.

Cultural Universals and Cultural Variability

Because every culture must deal with human limitations and possibilities, and because every group must solve the same problems of survival, certain types of arrangements are found in every culture. These are the **cultural universals** or basic social *institutional spheres* shown in Table 3-2. As illustrated in the mental exercise on page 52, the earliest prehumans had to find solutions to immediate problems of both personal and collective survival: securing food, maintaining order, producing and training new members, and developing group unity. When organized into patterned regularities of behavior these necessary elements of individual and group survival are called institutional spheres: the society's economic system, its political structure, its family system, its educational processes, and its belief system. Practices responding to these needs will be found in all cultures.

But the *content,* the specific details of the institutional spheres, and the ways in which these traits are linked together will be different from one society to another, shaped by geography and history. These processes account for **cultural variability,** the astonishing variety of customs, beliefs, and artifacts that humans have devised to meet universal needs. For example, although the need for orderly reproduction has led to rules regulating courtship and marriage in all societies, these can range from a communal ceremony among individuals who may never live together to arranged marriages and child brides to the seemingly hit-or-miss choices of contemporary Americans.

Customs that seem odd to us are the natural way to do things in other societies. Because every group must transform sexual impulses into patterned and therefore predictable behavior, we find great variability in sexual beliefs and activities among the world's cultures (see Chapter 8). Some permit open displays of sexuality among children; we find it upsetting. Some allow, even encourage, homosexuality among males; we scorn and try to forbid it. Tibetan monks and Catholic priests are required to remain celibate; in other societies, men are expected to spend their entire lives trying to seduce women. In still other cultures, women are thought to have the stronger sex

Cultural universals are basic elements found in all cultures.

Cultural variability reflects the variety of customs, beliefs, and artifacts devised by humans to meet universal needs.

TABLE 3-2   Cultural Universals

Universal Needs	Group Response (Institutional Spheres)
Adaptation to the environment; food, shelter	Economic activity: production and distribution of goods and services
Maintenance of order; rule enforcement; dispute settlement; protection and defense	Political behavior; lawgiving, policing; defending; judging
Orderly reproduction and recruitment of new members	Marriage and family rules
Transmitting the culture to new members	Training and education
Constructing beliefs that relieve anxiety and give members a sense of shared identity	Belief systems

Cultural variability (the variety of customs, beliefs, and artifacts developed by humans) is illustrated in these photos from societies around the globe. Outward appearances are most obvious—note the contrast shown here among the Masai mother from Kenya, the Aini woman from China, the Inuit Eskimo man from Labrador, Canada, and the Holy Man from India. Despite these differences, all humans are concerned with similar basic needs such as securing food, maintaining order, producing and training new members, and developing group unity.

drive and they behave accordingly. Thus, the same human impulse becomes subject to widely varying rules governing its expression, and in all societies, people are taught that their behavior is normal and natural.

Ethnocentrism is the belief that one's own culture is the best and therefore the standard by which other cultures are consequently judged.

Ethnocentrism and Cultural Relativism

When looking at other cultures, we tend to evaluate their customs in the light of our own beliefs and values. Members of all societies assume that their way of life is the best and only correct way. Often, the very name of the group translates into "the people," implying that those who do not share the culture are not people, but "them," outsiders who are often identified by words that consciously dehumanize (for example, calling police "pigs" or many of the words commonly used to describe women or minorities).

The belief that one's own culture is the only true and good way, and the tendency to judge other cultures by those standards is called **ethnocentrism** (*ethno* = race, people; *centric* = centered upon). Ethnocentrism serves important functions for individuals and collectivities. Certainty about the rightness of one's culture reinforces the tendency to conform and to defend it. In this sense, ethnocentrism is the glue that holds the society together. When we refuse to budge, we are a "proud people;" when they refuse to budge, they are "stubborn" and deserve a kick on the behind.

Ethnocentrism becomes *dysfunctional* (reduces the ability to adapt to change) when belief in one's superiority leads to open conflict with other societies. If other people can be seen as less than human, they

Bodies and Beauty: A Cross-Cultural Perspective

In a now-classic study of cultural relativism, Horace Miner (1956) described the way of life of the Nacirema, a North American group whose chief lives on the banks of the Camotop River. The tribe is obsessed with rituals centered on deforming the human body: changing its color, its smell, and its shape. Under the guidance of "holy mouth men," for example, the Nacirema engage in a daily ritual of inserting bundles of bristles and magical powders into the mouth and "then moving the bundle in a highly formalized series of gestures." Nacirema ceremonies can be quite painful, as when the men scrape their faces with sharp instruments and the women bake their heads in small ovens.

Described in this way, such customs appear very strange. Perhaps you'd be tempted to call them "primitive." Surely a person from the modern industrial world would not behave in this fashion. Yet Miner was simply looking at the American (Nacirema spelled backward) from a different perspective. Can you see it? Look at some of our other behaviors, such as breast implants and liposuction for women or tattooing for men, or the relatively painful procedures for hair transplants and other processes designed to counter baldness.

The lessons of cultural relativism teach us that no behavior should be considered out of the context of the culture in which it originates and that what is "natural" to us will not necessarily be so to members of other societies.

---

can be treated differently from those we consider "like us." Thus, Jews, Gypsies, and gays have frequently been perceived as undeserving of humane treatment.

The social scientist must rise above ethnocentrism and try to observe all cultures objectively. Aspects of any culture can be understood only in terms of the meanings attached to them in that society. This attempt to see the world through the lens of another culture is called **cultural relativism.** Value judgments are replaced by an appreciation of the content of other cultures. The social scientist does not ask if a culture trait is good or bad according to some absolute yardstick, but rather, why does this trait exist, how is it maintained, and what purposes does it serve for members of that society? The standard of evaluation is whether or not the culture pattern enhances the well-being of individuals and the survival of the collectivity.

The basic assumption of the cultural relativity model is that each society's solutions to the tasks of survival are as valid as any other's, however unappealing such customs may seem to someone from another society. Above all, we must avoid the tendency to think of people in simple societies as less evolved or less intelligent than members of modern societies. We may appear to be wiser but this is only because we "stand on the shoulders of giants" (Merton, 1965). That is, we may see further than other peoples because we can draw upon the accumulated culture of Western civilization. In actuality, we are members of one and the same human species, alike in more ways than not. (Let us not forget that there was a very sophisticated society in Mexico at a time when most of Europe was mired in the Dark Ages.) Nor, perhaps, for all our possessions should we claim moral superiority over the gentle, peaceful sharers and protectors of the environment who still live in gathering and hunting bands.

SOCIAL POLICY

Modernization and Its Discontents

Is modernization good for you? Will people in the less economically developed societies called the Third World be better off when they become part of a world economic system dominated by the industrialized nations? What can we learn from the lessons of the past three decades of intervention into Third World economies? Assuming that there is a single path to modernization, in the image of the Western experience, policymakers in the 1960s and 1970s thought that they could best help the developing countries by encouraging them to (1) increase food production through modern farming techniques and machinery, (2) build up cash reserves by growing a few crops for trade in the international market rather than engage in small-scale diversified farming for one's family or village; and (3) provide a source of low-paid labor for light manufacturing,

Although such policies were clearly designed to help the economics of the industrialized nations, it was also thought that modernization would bring benefits to the less-developed societies: political and economic stability, higher income for individuals, a demand for improved education, democratic political institutions, and eventually, greater equality between men and women. The policymakers were not only ethnocentric in their faith in the superiority of modern institutions, but they also looked at the world through a male perspective. Men would be trained for the new roles and taught the new farming techniques, with the expectation that benefits would filter down to wives and children (Blumberg, 1989).

Cultural relativism involves an effort to understand the world as seen by members of other societies.

In some countries, economic growth has had a positive effect on health and infant survival (Firebaugh and Beck, 1994). But in many other cases, reliance on cash crops reduced economic stability in the society because they are linked to a world market in which crop prices can plummet overnight, as in the case of sugar and coffee in the 1980s. At the individual level, starvation is common where the cash crop replaced the varieties of food previously grown. The introduction of farm machines has driven small farmers off the land, and because few other jobs are available, large numbers of unemployed men drift into the major cities. And because governments are weak, civil wars are common, as seen so recently in Somalia and Rwanda in Africa.

In addition, the position of women within the developing nations has often deteriorated (Flora, 1992). When plow agriculture replaces horticulture, women lose their role in food production and local markets. The shift of economic power from women to men is often accompanied by loss of control over reproductive decisions, leading to higher birthrates and the confinement of women to household labor and childcare (Ahlberg, 1991). The transition from agriculture to light industry, however does open up educational and labor force opportunities for women. Employers actually prefer women workers because they can be paid less and can be given longer hours. But women's labor force participation does not necessarily translate into personal power, as they remain under the control of their husbands and fathers to whom they turn over their wages (Tiano, 1994).

Clearly, economic changes in the Third World have done little to improve the living conditions of many members of developing societies (Acosta-Belen and Bose, 1990). In addition, economic development interacts with culture to produce different outcomes in different parts of the world. Thus, in Muslim societies and throughout Catholic Latin America, cultural expectations of female dependency and male dominance have outweighed the liberating aspects of modernization for women (Clark et al., 1991).

To reduce world hunger and political instability, and to improve the quality of life for Third World people, the industrial nations must become less ethnocentric and consider the well-being of women as well as men. As an advisor to the President of the United States, what policies would you advocate to achieve these goals? How would Congress and the general public react to your suggestions?

Ideal culture reflects the highest virtues and standards of a society.

Real culture refers to the actual beliefs and behavior.

Social norms are rules of behavior.

Ideal and Real Culture

When we look at another society, we must distinguish between **ideal culture** (standards of perfection) and **real culture** (the actual beliefs and behaviors of everyday life). When people are asked about their culture, they typically describe it in ideal terms, even though these standards are rarely met. For example, most Americans would mention such ideals as equality, freedom of speech, and tolerance, even though racial inequality is widespread, books are removed from school libraries, and homosexuals are routinely harassed.

The gap between ideal and real adds a dynamic tension to the study of culture. The ideals serve as targets toward which people should strive, while the real culture often consists of explanations for failing to achieve such goals. Think, for example, of the many explanations you have recently heard for why equality between the sexes or among the races is impossible at this time.

Norms and Values

Rules of behavior are a major component of any culture. New members of the society learn what is expected of them from their caregivers, teachers, and friends. These rules are called **social norms,** and can be either *prescriptive* ("thou shalt") or *proscriptive* ("thou shalt not"). Prescriptive norms define acceptable behavior in given circumstances; proscriptive norms spell out forbidden behavior (taboos).

The norms emerge from the history of human groups, and represent the collective wisdom regarding right and wrong; that is, they are socially constructed rather than given in human nature or by some divine power. The fact that similar norms can be found in a variety of cultures is due to the need of any collectivity to maintain social order, hence most cultures have rules against trespassing, lying under oath, committing adultery, and taking the law into your own hands. It is also in the interest of those who make the rules that the norms reinforce obedience to authority, whether from parents, priests, or pharaohs. Not all norms are of equivalent weight. For example, those norms that involve behavior essential to social order ("thou shalt not steal") will have more serious consequences than those that govern personal hygiene ("brush your teeth"). Yet behaviors that are thought of as essential in some societies will be a matter of taste in another. Coloring one's face is optional in America but of great importance in Hindu societies where such markings indicate a person's position in the society.

CLASSIFYING NORMS. Following the classification of William Graham Sumner (1906), we distinguish several types of norms (see Table 3.3).

TABLE 3-3	Classifying Norms		
	Behavior	Sanction	Example
Folkways	Nonessential customs	Informal face-to-face	Brush teeth
Mores	Morals, ethics	Informal public scorn	Respect parents
Law	Essential to survival	Formal	Do not steal

Folkways. **Folkways** are customs and habitual standards of behavior passed from one generation to the next simply as "the way we do things here." Typically, folkways involve activities not absolutely essential to group survival. Eating with a knife or fork, for example, is an American folkway. Our society would not collapse if children threw away their spoons, although the kitchen would get dirty and parental authority would be challenged. Yet, even the most seemingly trivial folkway can tell us something about major cultural themes such as the American obsession with personal cleanliness in the case of deodorants and mouthwash, or male dominance in the case of opening doors for women.

Folkways, however, are not considered important enough to be strictly enforced. No court will punish the child who eats with her fingers or the man who refuses to hold open a door. Such violations of the folkways are usually handled on a face-to-face, informal basis through words and gestures of disapproval.

Halpoular girls from Mauritania in West Africa share a midday meal communally. How do their folkways differ from those of your classmates?

These reactions of other people are called **sanctions.** The norms are enforced through positive sanctions that reward conformity and negative sanctions that withhold approval. The more important the norm, the stronger the sanctions.

Mores. **Mores** (always in the plural and pronounced "more-ays") are norms that govern ethical and moral behaviors more crucial to social order than those covered by folkways, and therefore are more severely enforced. Examples include the obligation to help a relative, to show respect to teachers, and to maintain community standards of decency in conduct and appearance. Violations of these expectations bring scorn and public condemnation, possibly a visit from a minister or an appointment with a psychologist, but rarely an appearance in court. The sanctions are largely informal, but strongly expressed and forcefully applied.

But the mores of one historical period may not be the same at another date. For example, it was the duty of a Puritan parent to beat the evil out of a child—behavior that could be considered abusive today. In the case of sex before marriage, many of today's college students would have been expelled from school only a few decades ago and most certainly placed in the stocks of a New England village in the eighteenth century.

Laws. Norms that are formally adopted, that apply to all members of the society, and that govern behavior most essential to collective survival are called **laws.** Laws are enforced by *formal sanctions* by officials specifically charged with maintaining public order: police, judges, and those who staff prisons and asylums. Laws reflect the accumulated wisdom of the society, making clear just what is acceptable behavior and what is the cost of disobedience—*customary law.* Other rules, those *enacted* by lawgivers, are responses to changes in the society and typically reflect the ideal culture.

The Ten Commandments of the *Old Testament,* for example, are a minimal set of rules necessary for social order: obey authority, minimize jealousy and violence, give honest testimony, and respect other people's property and marriage. Something similar can be found in most societies. But to be law, the rules do not have to be "carved in stone," only considered essential to social order and backed by formal sanctions.

Folkways are approved standards of behavior passed on from one generation to the next.

Sanctions refer to reactions that convey approval or disapproval of behavior.

Mores are norms that cover moral and ethical behavior.

Laws are norms that govern behavior considered essential to group survival.

You Are What You Eat and Wear

Because culture is the water in our fishbowl, we are usually unaware of the extent to which culture has shaped seemingly "natural" activities such as eating and dressing. Hunger and thirst are powerful human drives, yet we rarely eat or drink the first thing at hand. Except under extreme conditions, for example, Americans would not drink urine or eat human flesh, although both have been done in other societies.

Eating, a simple and universal activity, is surrounded everywhere by norms and rituals, symbols, and taboos. Think of the Thanksgiving turkey in the United States and you can see that we are not talking about unusual customs among preliterate peoples. In this feast, the nation's settlers are honored, the ideal family is sentimentalized, and faith in God is reaffirmed in this version of the worldwide custom of celebrating the harvest. In other societies, the end of growing season is an occasion for excesses—overeating and drinking and sexual freedoms not otherwise approved; a release of energy in preparation for the quiet winter ahead.

Within a society some people are distinguished from others by what and how much they can eat. Most common are different food taboos for men and women, adults and children, strangers and natives. In the United States, food preparation for the family is defined as an act of love and expression of femininity, which makes it difficult for many women to share the task with others (DeVault, 1991). You can gain some insight into the relative power of members of your own family by observing what happens at the dinner table. Who is served first and last? Whose preferences determine what everyone has for dinner?

People are also distinguished by what they wear. Clothing, accessories, and make-up—what anthropologists call dress and adornment—have great symbolic content. A person's social value is often indicated by what they are permitted to wear or how their body is decorated (Rubinstein, 1994; Davis, 1992). Uniforms are clear-cut examples of clothing that signify social rank, as in the case of those worn by military personnel, but so also are the uniforms worn by business people, from executives to custodians. The nature of the uniform may convey added symbolic information, as when a nun's habit or Muslim woman's veil obscures the individual and her sexuality. For men, brass and leather speak volumes for "tough guys." Nonuniforms, especially leisure clothing, allow us to relax, and wearing no clothes is often viewed as an absolute freedom from the restraints of conformity to the norms. Think of the many ways you use dress and adornment to say something about yourself, or to judge other people.

In general, the norms of any society are derived from basic ideas about good and bad, right and wrong. These central concepts are called **values.**

> **Values** are the central beliefs of a culture that provide a standard by which norms are judged.
>
> **Rituals** are culturally patterned ways of expressing central values and recurring concerns.

Values.   **Values** are basic beliefs about the ultimate good that form a standard against which norms can be judged. Specific rules such as "Thou shalt not kill" reflect both a respect for human life and the collective need to avoid internal feuding. There are, however, exceptions even to the highest values. Killing innocent people in defense of one's country is not only approved but superior killers are rewarded with medals; and public executions can become sacred spectacles.

Although norms are thought to embody a culture's values, the link between the two is not always direct or consistent. We need only to compare the folkways, mores, and laws that governed race relations in the United States until the late 1960s with the American values of equality and justice.

Rituals.   **Rituals** are culturally patterned ways of expressing some central value or recurring concern of the collectivity. Among the most universal rituals are ceremonies that reinforce the unity of the society and that help individuals over some major transition in their lives (Kertzer and Hogan, 1988). For example, most societies have highly ritualized courtship and mating patterns that are taught to each generation of young people. Birth, death, and the transition from childhood to adulthood are typically marked by elaborate rituals such as baptisms, funerals, and confirmation ceremonies.

Public ceremonies that mark some change in a person's position in the society are known as *rites of passage* (Van Gennep, 1909/1960). Initiation ceremonies in adolescence (puberty) are among the most common. The precise ceremony varies from culture to culture: Plains Indian boys are left on a mountainside to have a vision; at age 13, Jews recite the Holy Scriptures during a Bar/Bat Mitzvah; and in the Andaman Islands, a dance is held in honor of the boy who is soon to become a man, as his back and chest are ritually scarred.

In every society, certain life changes are recognized as potentially dangerous or challenging for the individual and the group—a cultural universal. In each society, the ritual and its symbolism are different—a cultural variable. The function of ritual, everywhere, is to reinforce collective values, to relieve anxiety about the unknown, and to bring human drives and emotions under the control of the group through time-honored ceremonies. Take, for example, the ritual surrounding passage from college student to full-fledged adult, with costumed celebrants, songs and chants, solemn processions, prayers, and tension-relieving cheers. An Andaman Islander might not feel out of place at your graduation ceremony.

These, then, are the essential elements of culture: symbols, language, norms, values, and rituals. Beliefs, behaviors, attitudes, and artifacts make up the unique adaptations of any human group to its environment.

Subcultures

We have defined *culture* as a group's response to the conditions of existence, that is, the adaptive coping solutions to the problems of survival and the effects of history. If subgroups within a society have unique experiences, and if needs and opportunities vary from group to group, then we would expect great diversity in life-style among these subgroups. Such differences in values, beliefs, norms, and behaviors are called *subcultural adaptations,* or **subcultures.**

Subcultures appear whenever access to the general culture is different for some members of a society. As

In many cultures, children are the focus of a special ceremony as a rite of passage to adulthood. Here a young Jewish boy reads the Torah at his bar mitzvah, a ceremony which occurs at the age of thirteen when a boy is considered to be a man.

all but the most simple societies have division of labor, specialization, and differences in power and prestige, subgroups can be identified in almost every society. The more complex the culture and the more diverse the population, the more numerous its subcultures.

The subculture consists of variations on general cultural themes that make sense of the society as it is experienced by members of the subgroup, under conditions different from those faced by members of the dominant group. In many traditional societies, for example, the male and female worlds are so separated and dissimilar that women have developed a special vocabulary and way of speaking (Shibamoto, 1987).

Because of its large number of racial, ethnic, and religious minorities, the United States is a mosaic of subcultures. Some, such as the Amish and Orthodox Jews, survive by minimizing contact with the dominant group and its institutions; others, such as Jehovah's Witnesses and Mormons, have slowly blended into the mainstream while still preserving many unique beliefs and customs (Kephart and Zellner, 1993). Our many waves of immigrants adapted to being uprooted by settling near one another in urban neighborhoods where they were able to maintain the old ways and language until they and their children learned how to survive in the New World. Because their racial and cultural distinctiveness has excluded them from full participation in the dominant cultural institutions, Asian Americans, African Americans, and Latinos have developed complex subcultural responses to exclusion (see Chapter 11).

BOUNDARY   MAINTENANCE. Members of subgroups can protect themselves from outsiders by creating and reinforcing group boundaries. This is the function of special languages, or **jargons.** Just as doctors, lawyers, and sociologists talk to one another in a specialized vocabulary that identifies group members while confusing patients, clients, and other "outsiders," so also do members of gangs or racial and religious minorities have secret handshakes, special clothes, and other signs of recognition, as well as a jargon that cannot be understood by others.

American teenagers have a way of talking and dressing that sets them apart from both children and adults. Such barriers generate solidarity within the in-group and protect against invasion by out-groups. In some respects, people who regularly perform specialized tasks tend to construct barriers, as seen among athletes, musicians, military personnel, firefighters, and police officers.

Subcultures consist of variations in values, beliefs, norms, and behavior among societal subgroups.

Boundary maintenance refers to the ways subcultures/subgroups protect themselves from outsiders.

Jargons are special languages of subgroups/subcultures.

DEENA WEINSTEIN

Rock Music in the Trenches of the Culture Wars

Deena Weinstein is Professor of Sociology at DePaul University in Chicago. Her research and teaching interests are centered in sociological theory and cultural sociology. She teaches courses in mass media, social theory, popular culture and sociology of rock.
Her recent publications include Postmodern(ized) Simmel *(Routledge, 1993) and* Heavy Metal: A Cultural Sociology *(Macmillan, 1991). Under a nom de rock she also writes rock criticism for a variety of popular press publications.*

*I*n the mid-1980s, the United States was undergoing one of its periodic moral panics. This time, it wasn't comics or communists, but the old favorite, rock music. In 1985, Tipper Gore (wife of then-Senator Albert Gore) and the Parents' Music Resource Center (PMRC) convinced the United States Senate to conduct hearings on rock music.

Rock's history has been paved with opposition from a variety of authorities, including a Congressional investigation in 1958 into payoffs to disc jockeys. The PMRC claimed that rock music, especially the genre known as "heavy metal," encouraged suicide, sexual perversion, and satanism. At the time of the 1985 hearings, I had been teaching a course in the sociology of rock music for several years, a field that mainstream academicians considered to be commercial entertainment and therefore unworthy of serious attention. Yet the music was taken seriously by its appreciators, including my students, as well as by its detractors.

As a teenager in the 1950s, I'd been a fan of rock 'n' roll, but had not

been engaged by the music in the two following decades. Beginning in the late 1970s, my students became enthusiastic guides into the elaborate worlds of rock. I learned that the cultural power of rock resided far more in the music, the fans, and the concert, than in the lyrics that most bothered the critics.

Students made tapes for me, showed me their rock magazines, attended concerts with me, and shared their knowledge and judgments. At some point I turned from an eager and apt pupil into an investigator. The warnings that pleasure would disappear as understanding increased turned out to be baseless. The two roles, fan and investigator, easily coexist and reinforce one another.

As I got further into my investigation for studying rock as a complex cultural form, rather than treating a single aspect with a narrow method, I took the totalizing approach of the anthropologist who uses all sources of information. I am a participant and non-participant observer of fans, artists, and the music industry; a rock critic; an empirical researcher; and a sociological theorist. Each approach provides knowledge that the others do not, and serves as a check on the insights of other methods. The use of multiple techniques allows us to interpret rock in all of its dimensions.

My investigation of rock as a complex cultural form sustained by social relations moved back and forth between teaching and research. The Senate hearings were producing an extremely distorted picture of rock and particularly of heavy metal, based on incompetent reading of lyrics and no understanding at all of life within music-based youth subcultures.

At first, I saw the PMRC's denunciations of heavy metal as simply amusing. Much comedy is based on people "not getting it," and the PMRC really didn't get it at all. They saw, for

example, AC/DC's songs, such as "Highway to Hell" and "Hell Ain't A Bad Place to Be," as recruitment propaganda for Satanism. They blamed the increase in adolescent suicide rates on the music, focusing especially on Ozzy Osbourne's song "Suicide Solution." Had they listened to, or read, the lyrics, instead of focusing on the song's title, they would have seen that the song was a strong plea *against* suicide. Ozzy mourns the death by alcohol of a friend, and damns his own massive boozing. His message is that alcohol is not a solution for one's troubles, rather it is death in a bottle.

I was particularly disturbed that the mass media, the American Medical Association, parent-teacher organizations, and law enforcement agencies were endorsing the views of religious right-wing critics. Thus, when I was asked to do a book on heavy metal that would include a focus on its standing as a "social problem," I applied my totalizing method. My conclusion was that the claims that heavy metal encouraged suicide, sexual perversion, and Satanism amounted to a campaign of *discursive terror* (the use of false accusations to intimidate heavy metal performers and their audiences).

How could such false claims succeed in shaping mainstream opinion? The heavy-metal audience, composed predominantly of white lower-middle and working-class male youth, has little credibility and, in addition, wears its outsider status as a badge of honor. Why attack them? Although the music does not encourage the three sordid sins, it is, socially and lyrically, a symbolic rebellion against societal authorities, including parents. The attack on heavy metal is one of the numerous "culture wars" that rage in contemporary society. In this case, the symbolic rebellion of young people was met by an effort at state repression.

COUNTERCULTURES. Some subcultures contain elements of clear opposition to dominant values and beliefs. A **counterculture** provides an alternative life style to those who cannot or will not conform to the dominant culture. Whereas the subculture is a means of adapting to the larger society, the counterculture is based on rejection of such compromises.

Several types of counterculture have been described by Yinger (1982): (1) the *utopian/commune* in which members withdraw from society and perfect their own set of countervalues, as in the case of the flower children of the 1960s; (2) the *mystical/religious* in which members also separate themselves from the dominant society, the better to pursue their unique vision of eternal truth, as in the case of the Branch Davidians who died during a stand-off with authorities in Waco, Texas, in 1993, or others who leave their home community and move to some remote spot to await the end of the world; and (3) *radical/activist* in which the goal is to change the dominant culture, as exemplified by some of the student organizations of the 1960s, and by various skinhead and white supremacy groups today.

Countercultures emerge and flourish in periods of rapid and often confusing social change, and, through their opposition to dominant institutions and values, will have a variable effect on the direction of future change (Adler and Adler, 1992). The most visible impact of countercultural phenomena today is on fashion and musical taste, as displayed by participants in the heavy metal, rock, and rap scenes whose performances and life-styles mock and defy conventional standards (see Chapter 22). Indeed, artists throughout the twentieth century have been a powerful countercultural influence, with the goal of shocking ordinary citizens by rejecting established ideas of worth and beauty.

The Value System of the United (Untied?) States

Given the many subcultural and countercultural influences on American values and institutions, it should be no surprise that rock star Madonna and the humble nun Mother Teresa both appear on lists of most admired women. Possibly, no society containing so many different racial, religious, and nationality groups could have "a" standard culture, one clear set of values and approved behaviors.

Yet social unity requires some overarching value agreement that binds the various subgroups to the whole. This is the function of *patriotism,* an ethnocentric belief in the unique goodness of one's own society, reinforced by such rituals as national holidays and saluting the flag. Do Americans agree on more than Americanism; or, more precisely, what does America mean?

CORE VALUES. Robin Williams, Jr. (1970), presents a list of 15 dominant value orientations representing a conception of the good life and the goals of social action, of what might be called the **American ethos:**

1. *Achievement and success* as the major personal goals.
2. *Activity and work* favored above leisure and laziness.
3. *Moral orientation,* that is, absolute judgments of good/bad, right/wrong.
4. *Humanitarian motives* as shown in charity and crisis aid.
5. *Efficiency and practicality,* a preference for the quickest and shortest way to achieve a goal at the least cost.
6. *Process and progress,* a belief that technology can solve all problems and that the future will be better than the past.
7. *Material comfort* as the American Dream.
8. *Equality* as an abstract ideal.
9. *Freedom* as a person's right against the state.
10. *External conformity,* the ideal of going along, joining, and not rocking the boat.
11. *Science and rationality* as the means of mastering the environment and securing more material comforts.
12. *Nationalism,* a belief that American values and institutions represent the best on earth.
13. *Democracy* based on personal equality and freedom.
14. *Individualism,* emphasizing personal rights and responsibilities.
15. *Racism and group-superiority themes* that periodically lead to prejudice and discrimination against those who are racially, religiously, and culturally different from the northern Europeans who first settled the continent.

This is a bewildering list, combining political, economic, and personal traits, some of which actually conflict with others. As seen in U.S. history, equality is an uneasy partner of beliefs in racial superiority and patriotism often limits the exercise of freedom of speech. The coexistence of such contradictory values accounts for a certain vitality as well as divisions within American society. Furthermore, the content and the importance of any set of value orientations change over time.

> **Countercultures** represent alternative life-styles for those not conforming to the dominant culture.
>
> The **American ethos** is a set of core values guiding the beliefs and behaviors of Americans.

For example, the dominant values proposed by the founders of America in the 1780s included such virtues as moderation in eating and drinking, cleanliness, chastity, silence, and thriftiness (Benjamin Franklin, 1784/1970)—ideal behaviors not always found at the top of a contemporary list. But there are some values that have endured: the centrality of work, performance as a measure of personal worth

There has been a resurgence of national pride and patriotic values in recent years. What does being American mean to you?

and individual responsibility. These continuities reflect the underlying strength of a particular value system that emerged in western Europe in the sixteenth century, originally described by Max Weber as "the Protestant Ethic" but now simply called the **work ethic.**

The behaviors supported by the work ethic allowed the emerging merchant class to accumulate wealth, to hold onto profits, to claim a wide area of personal freedom, and generally to lay the foundation of modern capitalism. (See Chapter 13 for a full discussion of capitalism).

Central to this ethic are the following concepts:

Work as a "calling."   A *calling* is a sacred task. In most societies throughout history, work has been something people did to survive. To regard physical labor of whatever type as a divine duty is a powerful motive for producing more than what is required just to survive. So strong is the work ethic in our society that even enjoyment of leisure must be presented as an extension of work-related meanings; it must be earned and must present challenges to be overcome (Lewis, 1982). "This Bud's for you" only after the cattle are back, the sun has set, or the 5 o'clock whistle has blown.

> The **work ethic** refers to a set of beliefs that emerged in western Europe in the sixteenth century and was associated with the rise of modern capitalism.

Success as a sign of grace.   If work is a sacred task, there must be some way of distinguishing those who perform well from the lazy and the careless. Success in one's chosen occupation seems a clear and simple sign of divine favor and inner virtue.

Individuals as monitors of their own state of grace. The Protestant revolt against the Catholic church was primarily an attempt to do away with the layers of religious authority that interfered with a person's direct communion with God. In this view, the individual alone was responsible for his or her own fate. The Protestant symbol was the lonely pilgrim, overcoming the terrors and temptations of earthly life, always anxious and never certain that God's will was being done. The inner fears of eternal damnation served to regulate social behavior.

These were the concepts that provided a motivational basis for working hard, striving for success, and accumulating private profits in the early stages of industrialization. How else could one persuade people to labor 12 to 14 hours a day in filthy factories for barely survival wages except by convincing them that they are doing God's will? And how else could one reassure the owners that they are not exploiting workers except to suggest that their success is a sign of grace? Furthermore, if success is due to one's own efforts, then failure must reflect a personal flaw, some lack of moral virtue *within the individual.* If those who fail have brought it upon themselves, the rest of us need feel no responsibility for their situation, although we might choose to offer assistance in the form of charity.

Originally, also, the early Protestants stressed *simplicity in life-style.* Displays of wealth were considered vulgar and scorned. Rather, people should practice "worldly asceticism," to live in this world as if one had taken a vow of poverty. Clearly, this concept would be extremely important in the early stages of modern economic development. If one works hard, does well, and cannot spend the profit on material possessions, then the money is available for investment. In other words, the practice of worldly asceticism is a precondition for the accumulation of capital required to begin new businesses.

Just as surely, however, the continued success of profit-making businesses depends on increasingly higher levels of demand for products. Although worldly asceticism may be important for generating start-up money, a lot of other people must be willing to part with their earnings in order to buy what is being produced. Thus, a "culture of materialism" is essential to the later stages of industrial capitalism (Mukerji, 1983). **Materialism** refers to a desire for owning and consuming goods and services. Because materialism is so much a part of our culture, we tend to think of it as a universal aspect of human nature. But the urge to own is no more basic than a willingness to share; both behaviors reflect cultural values.

The culture of materialism is based on the accumulation of worldly goods as symbols of the "good life" and of the owner's prestige. Gradually, then, worldly asceticism has given way to its precise opposite. The American economist Thorstein Veblen (1899) used the term **conspicuous consumption** to refer to lavish displays of wastefulness designed to impress others with one's ability to throw away money, a thought that would surely shock our Puritan forebears and that also produces some ambivalence today. The "most admired women" mentioned at the beginning of this section, for example, include one who has rejected all the symbols of worldly comfort (Mother Teresa), and one who has made a fortune spoofing materialism (Madonna, the "material girl").

The values enshrined in the original work ethic and the changes that have been made over the past three centuries form the basis of the American emphasis on individualism, achievement, progress, personal morality, and public charity only for the "worthy poor."

CULTURAL HEGEMONY. In the perspective of conflict theory, values and norms are not neutral; they do not affect all members of a group in the same manner. On the contrary, what is considered good and true and fair benefits some people and not others. Ideas, no less than things, are cultural artifacts—creations of the group and of its most powerful members. The concept of **cultural,** or **ideological, hegemony** refers to the control over the production of values and norms that is exercised by those who are in a position to create and enforce rules of conduct. It is achieved by defining a reality in which the ruling elite seems to have some natural or inevitable right to be in charge (Gramsci, 1959, 1971). We have just seen

how the ideology of the work ethic promotes the interests of the successful at the expense of the less fortunate.

CHANGING VALUES? But surely, some of you may have been saying, there are other ideals and goals that motivate our behavior. What about caring, openness, cooperation, and community? Didn't the 1960s produce another set of values, at least for young adults?

Yes, there is some evidence that the strength of the work ethic has diminished in recent years. Much has been written about young, well-educated upwardly-mobile, urban professionals—"yuppies"—whose devotion to work is modified by considerations of personal fulfillment, family involvement, and enjoying the good life. Older people, too, appear to be less tied to the work ethic than previously thought, as the data on retirement suggest. Leisure, once thought to be the breeding ground for sin, is now valued by most adults to the same degree as work.

There is no question, either, that the 1960s left a legacy of openness to new experience; a concern for the environment and its preservation; support for the civil rights of women, racial minorities, and homosexuals; and a strengthened desire for peace, at least among college stu-

Materialism refers to the desire for owning and consuming goods and services.

Conspicuous consumption is the open display of wastefulness designed to impress others.

Cultural, or **ideological, hegemony** refers to control over the production of values and norms by those in power.

The diversity of the American value system is illustrated by the popularity of both of these women, Mother Teresa on the left and Madonna on the right, who each represent very different ideas. Why is the emphasis on individualism and materialism more prevalent than a focus on communalism and social responsibility?

Meet the Class of 1997

From its annual survey of entering college students, the American Council on Education reports that the Class of 1997 is similar to other 1990s collegians in seeing their education as primarily a means to a well-paying job, in contrast to students in earlier decades who tended more to value education for personal growth (American Council on Education, 1994). In addition, 26 percent of the men and 17.5 percent of the women, among the highest since the survey began in 1965, describe themselves as politically conservative, and unusually high proportions supported the death penalty (78 percent) and mandatory drug testing by employers (80 percent). On other social issues, however—environmental protection, abortion rights, and disarmament—students overwhelmingly supported traditionally liberal positions.

A 1993 survey of Ivy League students, usually more liberal than the majority of collegians, also found high levels of support for social causes such as reproductive freedom and racial justice combined with conservative views on economic matters (U.S. *News and World Report*, April 12, 1993). Politically, 38 percent identified themselves as Democratic, 15 percent Republican, and 42 percent Independent. The trend toward conservatism can be partly explained by Reagan–Bush administration cutbacks in student-loan programs, reducing the campus presence of lower-income youth. The continued support for liberal social programs is due largely to the dramatic increase in women students—from 40 percent in 1970 to 53 percent of all undergraduates today. How would you measure the attitudes of students on your campus? And how would you characterize their values?

dents. At the same time, "traditional" values centered on individualism and materialism remain very much alive, if not dominant among Americans of all ages (Thomson, 1992). One of the most sociologically fascinating characteristics of the 1980s and early 1990s has been the fierce backlash against many ideals of the 1960s and the movements for change that marked that decade: civil rights, feminism, gay liberation.

The 1980s will go down in history as the "me decade," personified by Donald Trump and the bank managers who bilked the public out of hundreds of *billions* of dollars while announcing the new American ethic "greed is good" and that concern for the common welfare is "wimpish." This is a focus in sharp contrast to the emphasis on collective responsibility—to family and community—found in most preindustrial societies.

Is it possible to revive a sense of community in a society where individualism and materialism appear to reign supreme? Where all messages encourage us to fulfill our own desires at whatever cost to others or to the common good? This is a question that many sociologists are asking today, out of a deep concern that the bonds that link us together are fast unraveling. But it is easier to describe the problem than to propose solutions.

At the personal level, members of your generation will have to discover some way of avoiding the pitfalls of either extreme: of losing your individuality and creativity as part of a larger group, or of becoming so self-absorbed that you find yourself incapable of intimacy. And at the societal level, the task is to create institutions that bring us together in projects that benefit the collectivity. It is the hope of the authors of this textbook that an understanding of sociology will be of great value in both these efforts.

SUMMARY

1. Culture consists of ways of thinking, believing, and behaving shared by members of a society, as well as all the material objects produced within a society.

2. With the emergence of the first pre-humans several million years ago, culture began to replace physical evolution as a means of adapting to the environment. Culture became dominant around 100,000 years ago with the appearance of *Homo sapiens sapiens,* the common ancestor of all living persons.

3. The key to culture is the ability to use symbols through language, both verbal and nonverbal, which serves as a screen through which people perceive their world.

4. All known cultures can be arranged along a continuum from the most simple to the most complex in terms of subsistence technology and division of labor. Cultures range from small gathering bands to modern industrialized societies.

5. Cultural universals such as political, economic, family, and belief systems are basic elements

found in all societies. Cultural variability refers to the specific patterns developed within each society to meet these universal needs.

6. Ethnocentrism refers to the belief that one's own culture is superior to all others and to the tendency to judge others by those standards. In contrast, the perspective of cultural relativity involves the ability to appreciate the content of other cultures without value judgments.

7. Norms are rules of conduct—prescriptions and proscriptions—derived from central values of the culture. Folkways, mores, and laws are three types of norms, distinguished by their importance to group survival and the strength of the reaction to their violation.

8. The more complex the society, the more likely it is to be characterized by subgroups with varying

experiences that produce subcultural adaptations to the general norms. At the extreme, countercultures provide alternative lifestyles and values for their members.

9. The American value system is rooted in the work ethic of the Protestant founders of the nation, emphasizing the sacredness of work and individual responsibility for success or failure.

10. From a conflict perspective, values and norms are not neutral but reflect the interests of the people who have the power to define and enforce the rules.

11. The essential tension in the American value system is between individual fulfillment and collective responsibility, with the former most dominant today.

SUGGESTED READINGS

Bellah, Robert, Richard Madsen, William M. Sullivan, Ann Swidler, and Steven M. Tipton. *Habits of the Heart: Individualism and Commitment in American Life.* Berkeley: University of California Press, 1985. A widely read study of American culture argues that while Americans pursue their individual dreams, they have difficulty making connections with others and forming meaningful communities.

Benedict, Ruth. *Patterns of Culture.* Boston: Houghton Mifflin, 1934. A still unsurpassed statement of the need to view culture as an integrated whole, reflected in all aspects of social structure and personality. Splendid portraits of Zuni, Dobuan, and Kwakiutl cultures.

Bodnar, John. *Remaking America: Public Memory, Commemoration, and Patriotism in the Twentieth Century.* Princeton, NJ: Princeton University Press, 1992. The author traces changing patterns of commemorative activity in the United States, integrating a wide array of materials, including ethnic festivals and public celebrations in ethnically-diverse cities and the people and organizations behind the activities. There is a distinction and tension between "official memory" (state-sponsored recollection of national events) and "vernacular memory" (ethnic, local, and regional communities' memories) of the past.

Dyson, Michael Eric. *Reflecting Black: African-American Cultural Criticism.* Minneapolis: University of Minnesota Press, 1993. Dyson combines race, class, and gender in his theoretical analysis of current black culture and its reflection of postmodern culture in the United States.

Gibson, James William. *Warrior Dreams: Paramilitary Culture in Post-Vietnam America.* New York: Hill and Wang,

1994. An analysis of a new conservative culture that blames the loss in Vietnam on the media, liberals, and the government, and encourages individuals to redeem this loss by acting above the law and fighting for one's own definition of justice.

Hall, Edward T. *Understanding Cultural Differences.* Yarmouth, ME: Intercultural Press, 1990. In examining business and management practices, this book focuses on national cultural contrasts between France, Germany, and the United States.

Kephart, William M., and William W. Zellner. *Extraordinary Groups: An Examination of Unconventional Life-Styles.* 5th ed. New York: St. Martin's Press, 1993. A very readable sociological description of various contemporary American subcultures and modern communities, including the Amish, the Hasidim, the Mormons, Jehovah's Witnesses, and the Oneida Community.

Lamont, Michele. *The Culture of the French and the American Upper-Middle Class.* Chicago: The University of Chicago Press, 1993. Comparative study of the cultural aspects of social structure.

Ritzer, George. *The McDonaldization of Society.* Newbury Park, CA.: Pine Forge Press, 1993. The sociological imagination applied to modern times, rationalization, bureaucratization, assembly lines, "The Magic Kingdom," "The Wheel of Fortune," and, of course, the ever present McDonald's.

Zerubavel, Eviatar. *The Seven Day Circle: The History and Meaning of the Week.* Chicago: University of Chicago Press, 1989. A fascinating sociological account of how the week originated and how it shapes daily life.

Social Structure: Systems, Groups, and Organizations

The more I talked to people, the more I realized that there was a grieving for the past. People miss their jobs and lifestyle, of course, but they also miss the bonds of community that have been broken with so many people moving away (Feder, 1993).

These words could have been spoken by a survivor of a typhoon in the Indian Ocean or a hurricane in the Caribbean. It is the voice of an unemployed American steelworker after the plant that sustained the community for decades was closed down. He recognized that the end of steel milling also destroyed the web of relationships that hold a community together—its social structure. Under normal circumstances, we take these patterns of interaction for granted, but in times of crisis, both the fragility and strength of such ties are revealed as people cope with the disruption of daily life (K. Erikson, 1976).

Social structure refers to a collective reality that exists apart from individuals but forms the context in which they interact. Culture is realized in everyday life through the patterned ways in which people relate to one another to accomplish the necessary tasks of individual and collective survival. These structures preexist each new generation and endure over time—just as the web of relationships that constitute your college predated your arrival and will survive after your graduation, although each set of classmates may challenge and modify some aspects.

In the first part of this chapter, we discuss key concepts in the analysis of social structure: system, status, role, norms, and interaction patterns. The second part examines how these elements are combined into various types of groups and organizations.

THE IMPORTANCE OF SOCIAL STRUCTURE

Culture and society are possible only when behavior is orderly and predictable. This is the function of the norms that regulate behavior and minimize uncertainty. Imagine what life would be like if you could not predict the actions of other people; if, for example, at each class period, the room and instructor were changed, no one knew what had happened to your term paper, and the grading system was revised daily. So, also, must there be predictable patterning in the other areas of your life. As you learned in Chapter 3, a society is composed of five institutional spheres, and each of these is characterized by patterned relationships and norms—all of which compose the collective reality called **social structure,** as shown in Table 4-1.

The idea of structure as an external, limiting reality is difficult for young Americans to grasp because our cultural emphasis on individuality and personal effort obscure the extent to which structural factors determine a person's life chances and choices (Hewitt, 1990). However, the central subject matter of sociology is the interplay between social structure and **personal** action (or **agency**). For example, your choice of college major may have been guided by its potential value on the labor market (an act of personal agency), but you cannot control the number of such jobs that will be available when you graduate (a structural variable).

> **Social structure** refers to a collective reality that exists apart from individuals, constructing the context in which people interact.
>
> **Personal agency** is the ability to have an effect on one's own environment.

TABLE 4-1 Components of Social Structure

Society				
Composed of five institutional spheres				
I. Politics	II. Economics	III. Religion	IV. Family	V. Education

Components of Each Institutional Sphere		
Macro	A.	Institutional structure
		1. Organizations (larger, more formal groups)
↓		2. Groups (two or more interacting people, sharing an identity)
		3. Statuses (positions within an organization or group)
		4. Roles (behavior attached to status)
Micro	B.	Institutionalized moral beliefs and behavioral rules that support structure
		5. Values (moral beliefs)
		6. Norms (rules of behavior based on moral beliefs)

Source: Janice M. Saunders, "Relating Social Structure Abstractions to Sociological Research," *Teaching Sociology* 19 (1991): 270–271. Reproduced by permission of the American Sociological Association and Janice M. Saunders.

In times of economic crisis both the fragility and the strength of community ties become evident as people cope with the disruption of everyday life. As factories, plants and other businesses close and move out of communities, social structures are destroyed. The citizens of Bridgeport, Connecticut have had to face such hardships.

The importance of the context can be seen in the simple example of eating out and how very differently you act when dining at a Roy Rogers in contrast to a place called Ristorante Rodolfo (Finkelstein, 1989). Or in the case of helping behaviors, researchers found that personality traits had little value in predicting whether or not a college student would try to keep a drunken driver off the road. Far more important were such aspects of the situation, or social structure, as how many other people were watching and whether they were known to the student (Rabow et al., 1990).

COMPONENTS OF SOCIAL STRUCTURE

System

A key concept in the analyses of social structure is that of a **social system** as an arrangement of relationships that exists apart from the individuals who compose it (Linton, 1936). From a *functionalist* perspective, a social system consists of mutually dependent parts (people, groups, institutions) joined in more or less stable patterns over time (Parsons, 1951). Change in one part affects the connections among all the other parts. Consider your own family. We could not describe it by listing the unique traits of each member. The family as a whole is an entity in its

A **social system** is an arrangement of relationships existing apart from the specific people involved.

own right, with characteristics that do not exist in each individual but in how they combine to form a separate reality. The family has its rules, its division of labor, its history, and its special language—patterns that have developed out of interaction over time. (For an example of a family system, see the box entitled "Systems Theory at Work: The Genogram".)

The classroom, whether in elementary school or in college, is a social system consisting of statuses and roles. How do these statuses and roles and the nature of the social system change as you advance in the educational system?

Systems Theory at Work: The Genogram

A genogram, as shown in Figure 4-1, is a graphic picture of the biological and emotional relationships among family members, in this case the family of Ben Abbott, a first-year student who is having difficulty adjusting to college. In a genogram, deaths are marked by an X; divorce by //; close relationships by double lines; and conflicted relationships by a wavy line. The

Abbott family genogram shows that, following his parents divorce, Ben was close to his father, who died in 1993, but not to his mother or stepfather (Brad). He also feels close to an older brother, Joe, who remained close to their mother. Note that their mother was a college graduate and the daughter of professionals, in contrast to their father and his parents. The family is also divided in terms of religious and ethnic loyalties, although they are all linked by blood or marriage.

Figure 4-1 Abbott family genogram. (Adapted from McGoldrick and Gerson, 1985.)

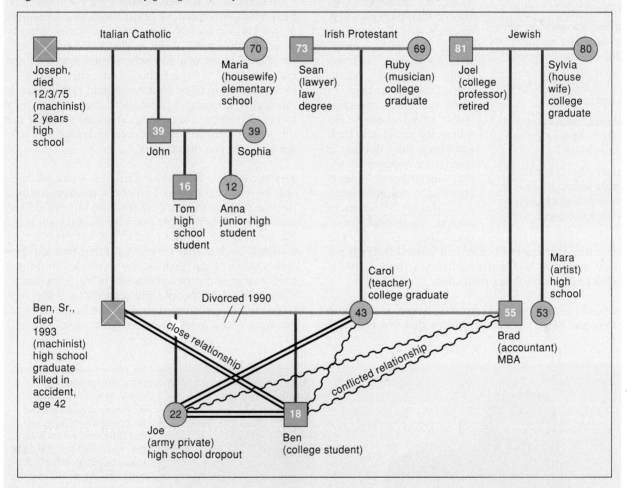

Status

A social system is an arrangement of positions, or **statuses,** characterized by certain rights and obligations that exist apart from the specific person who occupies the position. The statuses in a family are parent and child, each of which has a normative pattern of duties and responsibilities attached to it. The norms about how a Sudanese parent and child should relate to one another differ from those that guide Japanese parents and children.

A person occupies as many statuses as the number of systems in which one interacts. In addition, you can have several statuses within the same system: son/daughter, sister/brother, and grandchild in the family. In your school you occupy the statuses of student, classmate, roommate, and club member in a variety of subsystems within the larger structure of the college. The bundle of statuses that you occupy

> A **status** is a position in a social system and is characterized by certain rights and obligations.

at any moment is your **status set** (Merton, 1968). As you move along the life course, you will leave some systems and enter others, subtracting from and adding to your status set as you go. Status sets tend to expand from childhood to midlife and begin to contract with retirement, widowhood, and the other losses of aging.

Because a system involves more than one person, statuses are always linked. One cannot be a teacher without students, or a parent without a child. The social system of the classroom, for example, consists of such patterned regularities as the instructor at the head of the room, with a big desk, and students clustered below, with little chair flaps to write on. There are clear rules about who talks when and to whom. Each classroom may develop a special atmosphere as status incumbents (occupants of a position) interact; despite differences among classrooms, however, there is a general structure that existed before you walked through the door and that will remain after you leave—this is what makes schooling predictable.

ASCRIBED AND ACHIEVED STATUSES. Some social positions are based on characteristics that are relatively unchangeable or over which a person has no control. Sex, race, and age, for example, are not easily changed (although some people may attempt to disguise them). They are **ascribed statuses**, given at birth, and often associated with positions assigned without effort or choice. To be a certain age or sex is to be permitted to do some things and not others, although what is allowed will vary from culture to culture and change over time. In most preindustrial societies, ascription is all-powerful, so that the social position of one's parents determines the course of a person's life, whether born a prince or a pauper.

In contrast, **achieved statuses** are positions occupied by choice, merit, or effort. Becoming a husband or wife in our society is an achieved status, whereas in many other parts of the world, young people have no choice about when or whom they marry. In general, the more complex the society, the more likely that statuses are filled by achievement rather than ascription. For example, in modern societies, political leaders are elected because it cannot be assumed that the son or daughter of the current leader will have the ability to run the country.

MASTER STATUS. Within the status set, some positions will be more central than others. A **master status** is the one that has the greatest effect on our self-identity and on how other people perceive us. A master status has *generalized* symbolic value, so that people automatically assume that anyone with that trait also possesses other characteristics. For example, a nun may have a large and varied status set, but it is the master status of nun that people will respond to; if she were to take part in an antiwar protest, the headline would not read, "Aunt Arrested in Demonstration." Similarly,

> A **status set** consists of all statuses occupied by a person.
>
> **Ascribed statuses** are positions based on relatively unchangeable characteristics over which a person has little control, such as sex, age, and race.
>
> **Achieved statuses** are positions occupied by choice, merit, or effort.
>
> A **master status** has the greatest impact on a person's self-identity and appearance to others.

Ascribed statuses are social positions based on characteristics that are relatively unchangeable and over which a person has little control such as sex, race, and age. Despite movements to achieved statuses, the position of many women has remained unchanged as symbolized by these Muslim women in Morocco wearing the traditional veil in public.

In traditional Indian society, caste marks are worn on the forehead representing the person's master status. Such identification directs that person's behavior and the responses of others. What observable characteristics illustrate master status in American society?

people with physical disabilities often find that other aspects of their identity are assumed to be similarly "spoiled" (Charmaz, 1991).

In the United States, one's master status is typically based on achievement: occupational for men, family-linked for women. Notice how, when meeting someone for the first time, you are likely to ask, "What do you do?" as a quick source of information on education, income, and other characteristics. Yet even in America, the ascribed characteristics of race and sex often become master status traits, regardless of individual achievements. Notice, also, how often a well-spoken person of color is referred to as "articulate," as if this were unexpected. In the case of women, being female is generalized to a host of other attributes such as an inability to balance a checkbook or an obsession with weight.

Role

Each status carries with it a set of expected behaviors, or **role.** There are no roles apart from social positions, or statuses without prescribed behaviors (Linton, 1936). To use the analogy of the theater, each social situation is a stage on which each actor has a part to play (status); the content of that part (role) is specified in the script (culture); and together, they compose the social system of that performance. In each of our interactions, we occupy a particular status and enact the role, so that individual behaviors become organized into predictable patterns.

Because the status of *student* involves many different relationships, the student role is similarly varied, as when you are expected be respectful of instructors but an equal among classmates—two very different behaviors. It is expected that you will attend class, do the required work, pay your bills, and graduate. In this way, the structure of the school is maintained despite a changing student body.

At the microlevel, behavior, or role *performance* varies greatly from person to person and within the same individual from one setting to another. You are undoubtedly a better student in some courses than in others, either because the material interests you or because the atmosphere of the classroom makes learning easier. But such role variations must be kept within limits, or you find yourself expelled from the system.

Roles, as with the statuses to which they are attached, are relational; that is, they organize behavior toward others in the system—*role partners*. Each sta-

A **role** consists of the expected behaviors associated with a particular status.

A **role set** is a collection of roles associated with a given status.

> A status, as distinct from the individual who may occupy it, is simply a collection of rights and duties....A role represents the dynamic aspect of a status. The individual is socially assigned to a status and occupies it in relation to other statuses. When [we put] the rights and duties which constitute the status in effect, [we are] performing a role.
>
> — RALPH LINTON, 1936, pp. 113–114.

tus links the person to different sets of role partners. The bundle of roles associated with a given social position is called the **role set** (Merton, 1968). Figure 4-2 on page 78 illustrates the role set of a college student.

ROLE COMPLEXITY AND FLEXIBILITY. In general, the more complex the role set, the more people and information with which we must deal, and the greater the opportunity for learning as well as the need for flexibility (Coser, 1991). People with limited role sets tend to have relatively simple and unsophisticated views of the world; whereas varied role sets enhance the ability to handle many different and often conflicting pieces of information, or *cognitive* (that is, thinking) *growth*.

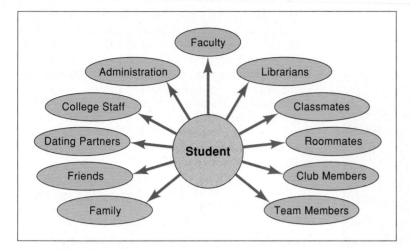

Figure 4-2   The role set of a college student.
In the status of student, you enact a variety of roles with different role partners. What behavioral expectations do each of these have for you? How compatible are they? And which are easier to fulfill?

The flexibility permitted in a given status or role set is always constrained by the other statuses occupied at the same time, especially the master statuses of age and sex. To be middle-aged, for example, is to have a larger and more complex role set than that of either younger or older persons, who are less likely to be in the labor force, to be married, or to be raising children. To be male is to have access to more and more complex role systems than typically allowed to females. For example, in most families, sons are permitted to wander further from home and at earlier ages, and to meet more different kinds of people than are daughters. These adventures allow for learning less available to girls who are kept closer to home and tied to a more narrow set of relationships (Thorne, 1993; Entwisle et al.,1994).

MULTIPLE STATUSES AND ROLES.   Multiple statuses and roles have many advantages. The skills and contacts acquired in one role can be useful in another context, as when former college friends provide introductions to potential employers. Multiple statuses can also soften the impact of personal loss, as when the pain of ending a dating relationship is lessened by plunging into the class play. Indeed, multiple roles can be psychologically beneficial, so that success in one area can make up for shortcomings in another (Barnett, 1994).

SOCIOLOGY AROUND THE WORLD

Widowhood: A Variable Status

Widowhood is instructive. Each society has a very different set of role expectations for widows, because the status of widow rearranges existing family structures in different ways. In modern industrial societies, based on achieved statuses, the widow has little social value or power in the family or workplace and has few role obligations other than a suitable period of mourning (Lopata, 1987). In the United States, she is basically left on her own, with limited resources, whereas most other Western industrial societies provide public supports and services.

Among the Tiwi of Northern Australia, in contrast, older women have built up considerable economic and social power through a series of marriages and a complex set of relationships with sons-in-law. In addition, the Tiwi have no status for a single woman, so that a new husband must be immediately found for a Tiwi widow, with the remarriage taking place at the late husband's funeral (Martin and Voorhies, 1975).

Throughout the Caribbean, the widow and other female relatives are expected to preserve the memory of the dead man and to do the work of mourning for the entire family. Unrestrained displays of grief earn compliments for "crying well." And whereas male relatives may quickly return to their daily work and social life, the women must remain in mourning for an extended period (Kerns, 1992). The Japanese widow in a traditional household also has no status of her own, losing family-based power over sons- and daughters-in-law when her husband dies. This leaves her totally dependent on the good will of the son with whom she takes up residence (Kamo, 1991).

In many parts of India, not only does a widow have no power or value, but she is a definite burden on those who must now support her. Thus, although now illegal, the traditional custom of *suttee* is still practiced: The widow, often a young woman, throws herself on the funeral pyre and is consumed by the fire that cremates the husband's body, which neatly solves the problem of what to do with her.

We can see in these examples how the enormous cross-cultural variations in the status and role expectations of widowhood are related to the widow's value in the family and economic systems and to the resources she can or cannot command from others.

Role Conflict, Strain, and Overload

ROLE CONFLICT.   **Role conflict** refers to the competing and conflicting demands that can arise in a role set under the following conditions (Lang, 1992):

1. When incompatible or conflicting demands come from two or more partners in the same role set: The family, for example, is a major source of role conflict because each member occupies dual statuses in the same role system: father/husband, wife/mother, child/sibling. As a child, one is expected to obey parents; as a sibling, to protect a brother or sister. What, then, do you do when you discover that a younger brother is smoking pot? Tell your parents, or keep his secret? Can the father role be adequately performed by earning money, even when this conflicts with his being able to attend to his daughter's championship basketball game?

2. When the same person conveys conflicting demands: How often have you been told to enjoy yourself and stay out of trouble? Indeed, interpersonal relationships often present us with seemingly incompatible expectations: to be strong yet sensitive, succeed but be your own person, and so forth.

3. When conflicting demands come from members of different role sets: The most notable examples today are the problems often faced by mothers in demanding careers (Galinsky and Stein, 1990b). Do you work late at the office on an important case, or go to your son's first piano recital? Notice that you might have given a different answer to this question than you gave in the first example about a father's role conflict under similar circumstances.

4. A fourth type of conflict lies *within* the individual rather than among role partners, when we are expected to do something that conflicts with our deepest feelings about the kind of person we are. Although few of us think of ourselves as capable of consciously inflicting pain on another person, a researcher had little difficulty constructing an experiment in which a majority of college students administered what they believed to be severely dangerous electric shocks. (See the box entitled "To Obey or Not to Obey.")

> **Role conflict** results from the competing and conflicting demands stemming from a role set.

How can role conflict be avoided or minimized? Some role requirements are designed to prevent conflict, such as when surgeons are generally not per-

---

RESEARCH IN ACTION

To Obey or Not to Obey

The following research was conducted by the psychologist Stanley Milgram (1965, 1974), whose findings provide one of the clearest tests of the basic sociological point that *behavior is largely determined by the definition of the situation.*

How can we explain why thousands of Germans took part in the cold-blooded murder of millions of Jews in death camps in the early 1940s. Was there some kind of character flaw in the German personality, or were extremely sadistic people recruited for the camps? What of the American soldiers who mutilated and raped villagers during the war in Vietnam? Were they also unusual in their psychological make-up? Is obedience a personality trait or a situational response?

In a series of experiments over a decade and involving many different populations, Milgram told unknowing (naive) volunteers that they were participating in a study of learning that would require them to administer electric shocks to people who gave incorrect answers. Sitting before an elaborate machine featuring a voltage dial numbered from 15 ("Slight Shock") to 450 ("Danger: Severe Shock"), the naive subjects placed in the role of "teacher," received orders from experimenters in laboratory coats and clipboards about when and what voltage to apply to the

"learner" (a paid assistant). What proportion of college students like yourself do you think would administer a full 450 volts? A panel of psychiatrists had guessed about 1 percent and that these would be emotionally abnormal. As it turned out, about two-thirds of all subjects—women as well as men, old and young, college educated and not—could and did obey the teacher right up to the "danger" point.

The factor that distinguished levels of obedience was not any personality variable but the experimental situation itself, which Milgram manipulated in many ways, for example, by whether or not the subject saw the learner, by the loudness of moans and screams from the "learning room," and by the distance between the "teacher" and the authority figure. Although most subjects showed signs of great role conflict and emotional distress, vocally protesting, they nonetheless obeyed orders to continue. Obedience was highest when the "teacher" neither saw nor heard the learner, when the experimenter stood directly overhead, and when it was known that peers had also followed the same orders.

These were not unusually cruel people, only ordinary men and women who believed that the situation required their obedience to "legitimate authority." Unfortunately, under certain conditions, almost any of us could become a concentration camp guard.

mitted to operate on members of their own family. In other cases, the role partners are partially segregated, such as when military officers and enlisted personnel are forbidden to "fraternize," that is, to interact on a purely social basis. At the level of the individual, one can construct a priority chain in which some statuses have greater weight than others: being a parent, for example, over the demands of being an employee, or, as a student, giving priority to raising your grades rather than conducting a nonstop social life. Note that some statuses can be more easily downgraded than others, and that priorities are likely to differ by age and sex.

Roles can also be *compartmentalized,* separated from one another by time or space: weekdays for work, weekends for play, library for study, laundry room for homemaking tasks. Wealthy people avoid conflicts by *hiring role replacements,* such as a nanny or bookkeeper. Those with fewer resources must *negotiate* among themselves over who does the wash or takes the children to the dentist. Redefining roles and reallocating tasks is an example of personal agency modifying the accepted pattern; when enough role systems have changed in the same way, new norms emerge, as in the role of father today.

ROLE STRAIN.   Similar to role conflict, the concept of **role strain** has been applied to situations in which a single status calls for incompatible behaviors. The coach of a college team, for example, must walk a delicate line between preserving discipline and being a counselor to the players. The former requires keeping one's distance, the latter, coming close. Parenting is a stressful role for the same reason and lasts much longer.

ROLE OVERLOAD.   **Role overload** occurs when the total number of statuses becomes so overwhelming that all role performances suffer. Overload can be eased by giving up the less important roles, for example, resigning from a club, cutting the time spent on any one activity, or by any of the mechanisms for reducing role conflict discussed previously. Some statuses are easier than others to leave. Dropping out of school and quitting a job are relatively easy compared to leaving a marriage or abandoning one's children. Ascribed statuses, by definition, cannot be easily changed or ignored.

Conflict and strain are the cost we pay for the freedom and flexibility that contemporary Americans enjoy in choosing and arranging role obligations,

Role strain results from situations in which a single status calls for incompatible behaviors.

Role overload occurs when the total number of statuses and role sets overwhelm all activity.

Definition of the situation is the process by which people interpret and evaluate the social context to select appropriate attitudes and behavior.

This mother has tried to balance the competing demands of family and work by working at home. What other role conflicts might be introduced as a result of this decision?

rather than being bound by the force of tradition and ascription, as in most preindustrial societies.

THE CONTEXT OF SOCIAL INTERACTION

Definition of the Situation

To a large extent, social behavior is determined by the **definition of the situation** (Thomas and Thomas, 1928), a stage of deliberation when we interpret the context in which we find ourselves and decide how to respond. Is the situation one of danger or safety? Must I be on good behavior or can I relax? Notice how, with the same role partners, you act very differently when seated together in class or in the stands for a football game.

As noted in Chapter 2, *what people believe to be real is real in its consequences;* that is, when people agree on a definition of the situation, they create a shared reality and will act in a predictable way. because a situation does not define itself but has its meaning conferred by the participants, we continually check our perceptions with other people. Reality is a collective product.

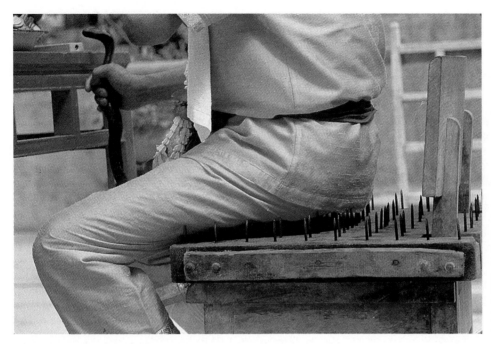

Social behavior is determined by how people come to define social situations. The magic ritual for this Siamese shaman would be defined as a painful experience by most Americans.

ANOMIE.   Although no society leaves potentially troublesome encounters to chance, sometimes a person is faced with a new situation in which the rules are unclear. **Anomie** is a French word that means "without norms." Emile Durkheim (1897/1966) used the concept to refer to situations in which norms were absent, unclear, or conflicting. In these circumstances, confusion reigns. Humans are rule-making and rule-following creatures; we cannot tolerate anomie. Without norms, social structure dissolves. Therefore, creating norms and imposing meaning on anomic situations is a personal and collective necessity.

In unusual or new situations, people tend to define who they are and what they are doing in a way that maintains the system and supports a positive self-identity. How, for example, do members of a nudist colony define their situation in a socially acceptable way when the norms of the broader society equate naked bodies with uncontrolled sexuality? One classic research (Weinberg, 1968) pointed to both the ideology of nudism and the social structure of the nudist camp. The ideology of nudism holds that not wearing clothes is more natural and healthy than wearing them and that shame and sexuality are in the mind and not necessarily related to clothing. The social structure of the camp is designed precisely to minimize problems; young single people, especially men, are not welcome; no cameras or alcohol are allowed; and rules of interpersonal conduct are strictly enforced: no staring, no sex talk, and no body contact. Under these conditions, a new definition of the situation is created and sexuality is controlled, often more successfully than outside the camp.

In this part of the chapter, we have examined the nature and components of social structure, the web of patterned relationships that makes social life predictable. When these patterns are disrupted or cannot be modified to meet changing circumstances, the system breaks down. Thus, marriages dissolve, economies are ruined, governments cease to function, and entire communities are destroyed.

GROUPS AND GROUP INTERACTION

A **group,** in the sociological sense, has the following characteristics: (1) its members are linked by a distinctive set of relationships; (2) they are interdependent; (3) they feel that the behavior of each is relevant to the others; and (4) they share a sense of togetherness, a "we" feeling. Groups vary in size, in the intensity of their bonds, and in stability over time, but all share two elements: *mutual awareness* of and *responsiveness* to other members.

> **Anomie** refers to situations in which norms are absent, unclear, or confusing.
>
> A **group** is characterized by a distinctive set of relationships, interdependence, a feeling that the behavior of others is relevant, and a sense of membership.

Group Characteristics

PRIMARY GROUPS.   A basic distinction is made between small and close-knit groups, on the one hand, and larger, impersonal groups on the other. As de-

During World War II, the London underground (subway) was used as a bomb shelter during night-long raids on the city by Germany. British citizens developed new norms and behaved in an orderly manner despite an otherwise anomic situation.

A **primary group** is a group in which members have intimate personal ties with one another.

An **expressive relationship** is valued in its own right, as an end in itself.

Secondary groups are characterized by few emotional ties and limited interaction.

scribed by Charles Horton Cooley (1864–1929), **primary groups** are characterized by warm personal ties among members—"the nursery of human nature" and the source of our earliest and most complete sense of social unity (Cooley, 1909). The family is the first and ideal example of a primary group; it gives its members a sense of being special, and its

survival depends on their shared identity and concern for one another (Stone, 1988).

Primary group relationships are called **expressive relationships** because they are valued in their own right; belonging is an end in itself. We remain in primary groups for the sheer pleasure and satisfaction of being there. Face-to-face contacts, spontaneous interaction, involvement with the whole of one's being, intensity, and relative permanence are all characteristics of the primary group, as shown in Table 4-2.

SECONDARY GROUPS.   In contrast to primary groups, **secondary groups** are characterized by few emotional ties among members and limited interactions

TABLE 4-2   Comparison of Primary and Secondary Groups

Structural Characteristics	Processes	Sample Relations	Sample Groups
Primary Groups			
Physical proximity	Whole person relationships	Husband–wife	Family
Small number of members	Spontaneity	Parents–children	Neighborhood, gangs
Long duration	Informal social control	Close friends	Work team
Shared norms and values	Expressive behavior	Close work group	
Shared goals			
Secondary Groups			
Large number of members	Segmented role relationships	Student–teacher	College freshmen
Limited sharing of norms and values	Formality	Officer–subordinate	Army
Limited shared goals	More formal social control	Boss–worker	Corporation
No physical proximity necessary	Instrumental behavior		Alumni association
Contacts of limited duration			

involving only a part of the self. Formal relationships replace the spontaneity of the primary group. Members share a common interest in reaching a particular goal, but their contacts are temporary and their roles highly structured. Because interaction is viewed as a means toward a goal, rather than an end in itself, we call these relationships **instrumental.**

Often, primary groups are formed within instrumental settings, such as workmates on the assembly line or office cliques (friendship circles) (Marks, 1994). Moreover, primary groups can influence the larger impersonal system. For example, studies of the behavior of men in combat showed that the average soldier was driven neither by patriotism nor hatred of the enemy but rather by loyalty to one's buddies (Shils, 1950; Stouffer et al., 1949).

COMMUNITY AND SOCIETY. The difference between primary and secondary groups is similar to the distinction made by the German sociologist Ferdinand Tönnies (1853–1936) between *Gemeinschaft* (community) and *Gesellschaft* (society). The *Gemeinschaft* exists where primary groups are dominant, where people have known one another for generations, and where they associate informally, united by a common history and geographic closeness. In the *Gesellschaft,* relationships are limited and businesslike. Major social bonds are voluntary, based on self-interest in achieving limited goals, and characterized by instrumental behavior.

Community/*Gemeinschaft* and society/*Gesellschaft* are **ideal types;** that is, they are models that tend to exaggerate distinctive features to understand them better. Most relationships will have elements of both expressiveness and instrumentality. For example, the authors of this book teach sociology to make a living (an instrumental relationship) but also for the sheer expressive pleasure of interacting with students and passing on sociology to a new generation.

Many sociologists have observed an ongoing dynamic tension between the ideals of *Gemeinshaft* and *Gesellschaft* in American culture. Communities are portrayed as warm and supportive but also as closed and stifling of individualism, whereas society is impersonal and risky but also open and accepting of individual differences and desires.

Most of you are in the process of moving away from the primary group closeness of family and college friends toward the task-oriented secondary groups of the wider society and the workplace. In general, modern societies are characterized by a progressive expansion of the *Gesellschaft,* as impersonal institutions replace primary groups as the source of education, protection, and employment. The *Gesellschaft* provides opportunities for individual achievement and personal choice that the *Gemeinschaft* tends to thwart. But the cost is often a loss of community, of warmth and acceptance. One of your major

life tasks will be to create and nurture circles of intimacy and caring, a haven of *Gemeinschaft* within the *Gesellschaft* settings of modern society.

Primary group ties have important positive effects on physical and mental health (Messeri et al., 1993). For example, researchers found that death rates from heart attacks were strikingly different in two neighboring Pennsylvania communities served by the same health care facilities. The town with the lower rate had been settled by Italian immigrants who maintained the communal solidarity of their native village, a supportive *Gemeinschaft* that protected members from stress. In the 1960s, as younger generations adopted a more modern life-style, the strength of primary group ties declined, and the heart attack rate increased sharply, approaching that of the neighboring community (Egolf et al., 1992).

In-Groups and Out-Groups

Group **boundaries** are essential to distinguishing members from nonmembers. Boundaries can be formal or informal. Formal boundaries are based on some clear criterion such as ancestry (Daughters of the American Revolution), wealth (country clubs), college graduation (alumni associations), or "turf" (neighborhood gang). Specific symbols such as a badge or uniform are also used to signify membership, as in the cases of athletic teams, the police, or the clergy. In other instances, boundaries are not as clear-cut, such as in peer groups where the line between members and hangers-on becomes blurred.

Boundaries are reinforced by a distinction between "us" — the **in-group** — and "them" — the **out-group.** As analyzed by the American sociologist William Graham Sumner (1840–1910), the distinction between "us" and "them" generates solidarity among members of the in-group but at the same time creates hatred and contempt for members of out-groups (Sumner, 1906). Such hostility is an outgrowth of *ethnocentrism,* the belief in the superiority of one's own

---

Instrumental behavior is a means to some other goal.

Gemeinschaft refers to small, traditional communities, characterized by primary-group relationships and intergenerational stability.

Gesellschaft refers to contractual relationships, wherein social bonds are voluntary, based on rational self-interest, and characterized by instrumental behavior.

Ideal types are theoretical models that exaggerate distinctive features.

Boundaries, which may be formal or informal, differentiate group members from non-members.

In-groups are primary or secondary groups to which a person belongs.

Out-groups are primary or secondary groups to which others belong.

SOCIOLOGY AROUND THE WORLD

Nigerian Novels and the Imaginary Community

The concept of community is often romanticized and colored by a longing for security and satisfaction associated with a traditional way of life. Seemingly natural communities—those linked by blood or emotion, such as the "Spanish-speaking community," the "Jewish community," the "African community"—are now understood to be artificial constructions (Anderson, 1991). For example, a study of novels about rural life in the African country of Nigeria by British-educated Nigerian authors indicated that the traditional village has been "imagined" in misleading ways.

Although precolonial African villages had many of the characteristics associated with community, they also had aspects of society. People were bound by real or fictitious kinship ties, in which the individual was subordinate to the good of the community. At the same time, rural African villages "had extensive contacts with the outside world and were highly competitive, riddled with rivalries that belie any image of a peaceable kingdom under a shared normative rule" (Griswold, 1992, p. 710).

The idealized picture of the village as close-knit community before "things fell apart" as a result of the influence of colonialism presents a distorted view, both to outsiders and to most Nigerians. Emphasizing external causes such as colonialism or world capitalism for Nigeria's problems, these novelists divert attention from internal tensions and social inequality. In the "imaginary village" of Nigerian community, the oppression of women and children is obscured, rivalries between tribes are reinforced, and exploitation by traditional rulers is ignored.

Why did the "imaginary" Nigerian village of community emerge in novels? Griswold suggests that the answer lies in part in history. The novel, whose basic form developed in Western Europe during the eighteenth century, "was imported into Nigeria during the colonial period. Nigerians, who had their own social and aesthetic agendas, soon began to write their own novels. To reach publication, their literary productions had to satisfy the aesthetic sensibilities and market considerations of British publishers" (Griswold, 1992, p. 723). The view of Nigerian-village-as-community fits not only Western romanticism of a past that never was but supports local Nigerian elite interests and increases tensions in a nation filled with tribal conflict and ethnic rivalries. As with most areas once ruled by European colonists, various tribes had been played against one another, so that when independence came and new nations were created with artificial boundaries, the old hostilities remained unresolved. Civil wars have plagued these regions ever since, as can be seen most vividly today in Somalia and Rwanda.

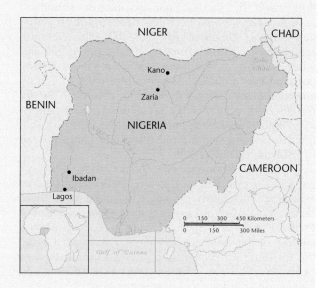

group. You must have noticed how members of your campus club are so very much nicer than members of other clubs.

Because the need for in-group solidarity is especially strong under condition of competition, when each member depends on the others for achieving a goal, out-group hostility becomes increasingly intense, as demonstrated in the Robber's Cave experiment (see the box entitled "Boys at Play"). If you were the ruler of a country marked by widespread internal unrest, wouldn't you be tempted to find an enemy "out there" to unite your own people and direct their hostility out of the in-group and toward "them"? Throughout Western history, witches, Gypsies, Jews, and gays have served as convenient out-

groups when the in-group is under stress. In recent history, such "politics of exclusion" have produced several instances of mass slaughter, most notably the extermination of European Jews by Nazi Germany in the early 1940s, the atomic bombing of the Japanese city of Hiroshima in 1945, and today's "ethnic cleansing" in Bosnia (Gamson, 1995).

When people change membership groups, they also change behavior, because one's sense of self-worth is linked to the approval and acceptance of other members. For example, in one study, people who changed their church memberships also underwent changes in their drinking habits to bring their behavior into line with their new-found beliefs (Beeghley et al., 1990).

BARRIE THORNE

Learning from Children

Barrie Thorne is Streisand Professor in the Program for the Study of Women and Men in Society in the Sociology Department at the University of Southern California, Los Angeles. Her recent book, Gender Play: Girls and Boys in School *(Rutgers University Press, 1993) is part of an ongoing effort to bring the experiences of children more fully into sociological and feminist thought. She co-edited* Rethinking the Family: Some Feminist Questions, Revised Edition *(Northeastern University Press, 1992), with Marilyn Yalom, and* Language, Gender, and Society *(Newbury House, 1983), with Cheris Kramarae and Nancy Henley. She has served as Vice President of the American Sociological Association and is former Chair of the American Sociological Association Section on Sex and Gender.*

*R*esearch topics sometimes seem to choose us as much as we choose them, in a rich and complicated interplay between living one's life and doing sociology. My first large research project—a participant-observation study of the draft resistance movement of the late 1960s—grew out of my opposition to the Vietnam War and my interest in learning about, and making, political change.

Participating in the radical movements of the late 1960s placed me at the origins of the contemporary women's movement. I joined an early consciousness-raising group and became a feminist, a transformation of self and social context that, in turn, shaped the questions I asked as a sociologist. I was especially interested in studies that found differences in the ways men talk with men, and women with women and the dynamics of gender separation and possible differences in the ways women bond with other women, and men with men.

By that time, however, my attention had begun to shift from women and men to boys and girls. My four-year-old son took me into the worlds of children in parks, in our neighborhood, and in day care centers. I noticed a striking fact: even pre-school-age children tend to divide by gender; boys play more often with boys, and girls with girls. As a sociologist, I knew such patterns are not "natural" but are socially organized. And as a feminist and a mother I wondered about the effects of gender separation on children's daily experiences and on their present and future gender relations.

Analyzing my field notes as a participant observer, I found that girls and boys who shared the same formal curriculum, sometimes mixed and interacted in relaxed ways. But they also spent a great deal of time apart from one another, occasionally dramatizing group gender boundaries with games such as "chase and kiss" and "cooties." I also found complex interactions between gender and ethnic minority status, as when two mostly Spanish-speaking boys were repeatedly maneuvered by other boys into sitting next to the girls, a position seen as contaminating.

Erik Erikson once wrote, "Children bring up their parents as much as parents bring up their children." That adage describes my experience not only as a parent but also as a researcher. I am often surprised by the perceptiveness and social competence of children; they create their own complex cultural worlds. We tend to ignore children, assuming their daily actions are trivial and worthy of notice only when they seem cute or irritating. And we may assume that we already know what children are "like," both because they are a familiar part of our environment and because we were once children ourselves.

Adults find it difficult to take children seriously because of the ways our society organizes age divisions. We locate children in families and age-graded schools, excluding them from public life. Children are relatively powerless, although their subordination is extremely complex. My relatively modest empirical study led me to the realization that children were a neglected topic of sociological research, yet there is much to be learned by seeing children not as the next generation's adults, but as social actors who participate in a range of institutions. Children don't just acquire adult culture; acting both alone and collectively, they resist, rework, and help create the worlds in which they live. They influence adults as well as being influenced by them. To bind children more fully into our understanding of social life, we will have to examine the complex group relationships of childhood.

RESEARCH IN ACTION

Boys at Play

In-group/out-group dynamics were strikingly illustrated in one classic experiment from the late 1950s (Sherif et al., 1961). The researchers brought eleven- and twelve-year-old boys to a summer camp at Robber's Cave Park in Oklahoma. The boys were similar in social background, mentally and physically healthy, and unknown to one another before coming to camp. The boys were split into two units—Eagles and Rattlers—located in separate parts of the campsite.

Each unit was given a set of problems to solve that required collective effort. As Eagles and Rattlers worked with their own teammates on a problem, they developed strong in-group feelings. When asked to list their best friends at camp, choices were almost entirely from teammates, despite any friendships spontaneously formed during the first few days of unstructured activity. The need to cooperate to accomplish a task led to a high degree of interaction and the more the boys worked together, the better they liked one another.

Then the researchers began a series of competitions between Rattlers and Eagles, in which the prizes would go to the winning team. The success of one team came at the expense of the other, a condition that almost immediately generated out-group hostility. The boys engaged in fierce name-calling, fistfights, and cabin raids. Indeed, the level of hostility rose much faster and further than the researchers had anticipated.

As out-group hostilities became more intense, feelings of in-group solidarity were also strengthened. An effort to bring the boys together for a fancy meal broke up when the campers turned the dinner into a food fight. How, then, would you reduce intergroup (*inter* means "between") conflict and restore peace to the camp? One obvious answer would be to have the whole camp compete against a new out-group such as a different camp. The other possibility, and the one chosen by the researchers, was to invent tasks that required all the boys to cooperate, such as pooling resources to pay for a trip to the movies, or working together to fix a truck that had broken down.

Slowly, the boys began to make friends with their former enemies, so that by the end of camp, many friendship choices crossed team boundaries. The moral? Working together can reduce conflict and promote harmony within the group.

REFERENCE GROUPS.   One does not always have to be a member to be influenced by group norms. **Reference groups** provide checkpoints or standards against which to judge one's own role performance, whether or not one is a member (Hyman, 1942). Reference groups are often those to which we aspire to gain admittance, such as, for example, a campus club or fraternity or sorority that we would like to join and whose attitudes and behaviors we adopt as our own. For many Americans, the relatively wealthy families portrayed on television are a reference point for judging their own lifestyles.

> A **reference group** exerts a strong influence on one's identity, norms, and values.

Reference groups provide checkpoints against which we judge our own role performance, whether we live in the United States or among these Mayan Indians in Guatemala.

GROUP STRUCTURE AND PROCESSES

Although social groups differ widely in size, purpose, and stability, they share several common structural elements and processes.

Group Structure

GROUP FORMATION AND MEMBERSHIP.   Group membership is a circular process. The more people associate, the more they come to share common norms and values; and the more they think alike, the more they tend to like one another (Newcomb, 1943). Surely, you have also noticed that people who agree with you are smarter than those who do not. People gravitate toward groups that reinforce their own beliefs and reduce the likelihood of value conflict.

When caught between groups with competing values and demands—family and friends, for example—we tend to select the one that offers the most immediate rewards of affection, approval, and companionship. In some cases, this will be one's family; in others, the peer group.

GROUP SIZE.   The size of a group is a structural variable that influences interaction among members. The German sociologist Georg Simmel was particularly interested in the effects of group size. He noted

that the smallest unit of sociological analysis is the **dyad** or two-person group. The dyad is characterized by both the closest intimacy and the greatest fragility because either person can destroy it by leaving. This may explain why your most emotionally intense relationships are also tinged with utmost anxiety.

The **triad** or three-person group, is typically more stable and less intimate than a dyad, with a more complex division of labor. Triads can be maintained as long as the same two people do not consistently unite against the third. The number of possible combinations of role partners increases dramatically with group size. A six-person group will produce 15 dyads, many more triads, and a total of 720 possible relationships!

Social Networks

The **social network** is the sum total of a person's group memberships and represents the support available to a person as a result of social ties, whether primary or secondary. Networks have both structural and interactive dimensions.

The **structural dimensions** of social networks include its range (how many different groups); density (how many overlapping relationships); diversity, and size. **Interactive dimensions** include frequency of contact, strength of the bonds, duration of relationships, and willingness to seek assistance.

Primary group networks provide both general support and specific services, generating ties of giving and receiving (Uehara, 1990; Wellman and Wortley, 1990; Messeri et al., 1993). Some network ties will remain close and strong across the life course, but most will be relatively "weak," infrequently activated but nonetheless helpful as sources of information and assistance (Granovetter, 1973). For example, from whom do you expect to find out about jobs when you leave college and throughout your career? As noted earlier, networks provide emotional and material support. The more deeply embedded the person, the better able to cope with crisis—a finding that would not have surprised Emile Durkheim (Dean et al., 1990; Lin and Ensel, 1989). Conversely, absence of a social network as a buffer to stress is associated with relatively poor physical and mental health across the life course (Thoits, 1989; Kraus et al., 1993).

The **dyad,** a two-person group, is typified by intimacy, joint responsibility, and great opportunity for total involvement or conflict.

The **triad,** a three-person group, is more stable than a dyad and has a more complex division of labor.

A **social network** offers support to individuals through social ties to others.

Structural dimensions of social networks include density, diversity, and size.

Interactive dimensions of social networks include frequency of contact, strength of bonds, and duration.

The dating couple, one example of a dyad, can provide a setting for intimacy, exchange of information, good times, and involvement. Dyads are also fragile, with either partner being able to break up the couple.

Group Interaction Processes

The term **interaction processes** refers to the ways in which role partners agree on the goals of the interaction, negotiate behaviors, and distribute resources. Although each encounter has an element of uniqueness, role partners have a limited repertory of choices. These processes fall along a continuum from willing and positive exchanges of goods, services, and feelings to forced (coerced) responses. As long as two or more people are involved, their potentially conflicting needs and resources must be taken into account.

In any small group, a pattern emerges in which some members assume the **instrumental roles** required to achieve the group goals—from completing a project to selecting a place for dinner. In contrast, **expressive roles** are designed to help release tensions within the group The student who cracks a joke at a particularly tense moment, or whose remarks are greeted with groans, is playing an expressive role in the task-oriented classroom. Each role helps the group to stick together and achieve its goals.

Interaction processes refer to ways in which partners agree on their goals, negotiate behavior, and distribute resources.

Instrumental roles are oriented toward specific goals.

Expressive roles are oriented toward the expression of group tension and emotion.

The **dramaturgical model** views role partners as actors who perform roles as series of minidramas.

Frontstage interaction occurs in full view of the public.

Backstage interaction is free of the constraints of public performance.

THE DRAMATURGICAL MODEL.   The analogy of the theater, as developed in Ervin Goffman's **dramaturgical model,** is especially helpful in analyzing interactions (see Chapter 1). If we think of the context as a stage, the actors as status incumbents, and their performance as role enactment, each encounter is a minidrama in which our identity is at stake. Interactions continue as long as role partners (the audience) accept each other's claims and break off when the performance is no longer accepted.

As in the theater, interaction has a **frontstage,** where public roles are performed, and a **backstage** where actors are free to relax. The example of a restaurant is illustrative. Before the customers arrive, the staff set the stage by arranging tables and preparing food, playing frontstage roles with one another. When customers arrive, the dining room is frontstage and the kitchen backstage, two clearly separated worlds linked by the waiting staff, who act very differently when serving a table than when interacting with the cooks. Restaurant work is also highly gendered: the higher the prestige of the establishment, the more likely to have an all-male staff. Female and male servers are also expected to interact with customers differently—the women to be warm and friendly, the men cold and aloof (Hall, 1993).

THE EXCHANGE MODEL.   All interaction involves an exchange in which each partner gives up something (goods, energy, time, affection, approval) to receive a desired object (love, money, attention, approval). What is considered a fair exchange depends on each person's needs, resources, and alternative sources for getting what one wants.

For example, when a group of !Kung San hunters makes a big kill, the food they bring home is divided

Competition is a mode of social interaction in which the players accept the "rules of the game," whereby only one competitor wins. What are the rewards and costs of such intense competition?

among members of the tribe, with the expectation that when someone else makes a kill, the debt will be repaid. Whether an exact balance is reached is not as important as maintaining the norm of reciprocal exchange. In all societies, gift giving is a basic process for establishing and strengthening social ties. To receive a gift is to be bound by an obligation to repay something of equivalent value in the future. The value of the gift symbolizes the strength of the relationship. For example, think of the fine distinctions you make when selecting Christmas gifts, and how carefully each is chosen to express a certain degree of closeness (Waits, 1993). How do you feel when someone has given you something of greater value than the gift you sent?

Short of **coercion,** interaction processes are characterized by some degree of willingness to follow the norms. Competition, cooperation, and compromise are *modes of exchange* involving different rules of the game.

Competition occurs when the situation is defined as one in which scarce resources will be unequally distributed. Members of the group agree that only people who possess some quality such as intelligence, beauty, or strength will win the prize. On many campuses, for example, a "rating-dating" system

Cooperation involves considering others; forms the basis of social order. Ismale Wala puts his arm around Rabbi Levi Shapiro in the Crown Heights section of Brooklyn, New York, following clashes between African Americans and Orthodox Jews.

still determines who are the most desirable dates, typically those who belong to elite clubs and Greek societies, who have money and good looks (Waller, 1937). As long as all participants agree that the competition is fair, the losers can accept their failure.

Cooperation is a social relationship in which people agree to pool their resources to achieve a collective goal. The welfare of the group comes first, although individuals must also perceive that their needs are being met. From an exchange perspective, cooperation is the most social mode of interaction, and the one that has the most positive effect on group well-being (Orbell and Dawes, 1993).

Compromise represents a cooperative effort to minimize the all-or-nothing aspects of competition. Here, too, participants must agree on their definition of fairness, to give up extreme demands and settle for a limited goal. Compromise succeeds to the degree that all parties appear to receive some of what they want.

Conflict occurs when participants cannot agree on how to distribute resources, so that goal achievement requires the destruction of opponents. Conflict represents the breakdown of social order and shared definitions of the situation. The reaction of authorities is typically to suppress conflict. Conflict can be reduced through force, such as when the military crushes a demonstration, or through cooptation, mediation, and ritualized releases of hostility (Marullo, 1992).

Cooptation occurs when members of the dissenting group are brought into the established political system so that they now have a stake in public order, such as when women and eighteen year-olds were given the vote. Cooptation can also occur when the ideas of the opposition filter into the mainstream, such as with the concept of equal pay.

Mediation, or the use of third parties to resolve issues, is frequently used in our society to settle labor–management disputes and to work out divorce settlements. Most recently, sociologists concerned with reducing the threat of nuclear war and promoting world peace have carried out extensive studies on conflict reduction through mediation (e.g., Lofland and Marullo, 1990).

> **Coercion** is the use of force to induce compliance.
>
> **Competition** is the result of situations defined as ones in which scarce resources are unequally distributed.
>
> **Cooperation** is the sharing of resources to gain a common goal.
>
> **Compromise** involves cooperation to reduce the all-or-nothing results of competition.
>
> **Conflict** occurs when groups try to destroy or disable their opponents.
>
> **Cooptation** occurs when members of a dissenting group are absorbed by a dominant group.
>
> **Mediation** refers to the use of a third party to resolve issues.

A **ritualized release of hostility** is a social pattern devised to limit actual hostilities. In many simple societies, warriors engage in mock combat and carefully patterned displays of courage. The hostility is real, but its expression is carefully controlled to save both lives and reputations. In the United States, men in camouflage suits run through the woods shooting ink at one another and safely ridding themselves of hostility toward employers, politicians, wives, and others.

THE SOCIOLOGY OF EMOTIONS

Although the classic theorists were aware of the importance of personal feelings in social interaction, only recently have sociologists examined how emotions are socially constructed, exchanged, and maintained (Kemper, 1990). Because we tend to think of emotions as internal psychological traits, it is difficult for Americans to grasp the idea that love, hate, jealousy, anger, shame, guilt, sympathy, and other feelings are shaped by cultural and situational forces, as structured as any other aspect of behavior.

As we grow up in a given society, we learn a set of **feeling rules** about how, when, where, and with whom an emotion should be expressed (Hochschild, 1983). Children are taught how to recognize feelings, select the appropriate expression, suppress inappropriate emotions, and change behavior to match the feeling rules (Pollak and Thoits, 1989). As adults, we have mastered the manipulation of emotion. Indeed, a number of occupations require "emotion work," that is, hiding one's own feelings and putting on a display of friendliness to please the customer (Hochschild, 1983). These are primarily female occupations—flight attendant, waitress, beautician, and sales clerk—because women in our society are expected to smile and make other people feel good.

Sports contests offer a natural laboratory for the study of emotion management. Because victory is uncertain, the participants are likely to experience a range of feelings as events unfold, including anxiety, fear, shame, frustration, anger, and joy—some of which are associated with changes in body chemistry in a circular process whereby the emotion arouses the physical reaction and the physiological change heightens the emotion. Athletes must constantly seek to maintain a balance between too much and too little tension and excitement (Snyder and Ammons, 1993). The difficulty in doing so can be seen in the frequent

Ritualized release of hostility occurs when hostility is expressed under controlled situations.

The **sociology of emotions** demonstrates that emotions are socially constructed, exchanged, and maintained.

Feeling rules shape how, when, with whom, and where emotions are expressed.

As we grow up we learn a set of feeling rules about how, when, where, and with whom an emotion should be expressed. Love, anger, jealousy, and shame are some of the emotions people feel in intimate relationships. Have you ever been in this situation? How did you feel?

outbreaks of fighting during a game, and the lavish displays of personal pride after scoring a touchdown or hitting a home run.

Emotions that you largely take for granted, such as love or jealousy, are also constructed within a historical context. For example, as you will see in Chapter 8, definitions of love and sexuality have changed many times over the centuries. Cupid's arrow rarely strikes at random, and the expression of sexual feelings varies greatly over time and among subgroups.

Feelings can be manipulated and managed. We can give, withhold, reject, fake, or "work on" our emotions (Hochschild, 1983). In general, people who have been brought up with similar values will share a "grammar" (emotional language) that makes them more accurate perceivers of the other's emotion than are people whose backgrounds are very different. Sharing a grammar also allows role partners to "play the game" rather than express genuine feelings. Stringing someone along requires knowledge of the rules and cues that bring particular responses. The role partner may feel obligated to play along simply to maintain the interaction.

Love is not the only emotion to be put under the sociological microscope. Pride (positive self-feelings) and shame (negative self-feelings) reflect the state of our social bonds. We feel good when ties with others are strong and rewarding, and we feel bad when our overtures are rejected. When faced with the possible end of an important relationship, a person is likely to feel shame, humiliation, or embarrassment, emotions that can lead to destructive behavior toward the self or others (Scheff and Retzinger, 1991). Shame not only reflects broken ties but can impede further efforts to form social networks. Think of how "breaking up" reduces one's sense of self-worth and makes it difficult to become attached to someone else. Because expressions of rage and shame are not socially acceptable, people tend to push these feelings below conscious awareness.

Shame can be experienced by entire categories of people as a result of their treatment in society. At various times in our history, Catholics, Jews, immigrants from every part of the world, persons of color, women, gays, and the poor in general have endured the types of prejudice and discrimination that produce feelings of shame and inferiority, shared negative emotions that can also become the basis for expressions of pride and solidarity.

FORMAL ORGANIZATIONS

Formal organizations are the defining feature of the *Gesellschaft* and are a major aspect of modern industrial society. Formal, or *complex,* organizations are more structured than small groups and are characterized by the following:

- Clearly defined impersonal rules
- Statuses ranked by authority
- Large size
- Relatively complex division of labor
- Duration longer than that of current members

You will spend much of your life as a member of, or being processed by, formal organizations such as school systems, businesses, hospitals, and government agencies. The structure of the formal organization is an arrangement of statuses in which everyone has a set of responsibilities and duties toward other members of the group, as illustrated in Figure 4-3 on page 92. Role behavior is determined by the requirements of one's position in the system and is therefore less flexible than in informal groups.

The formal organization is an effective mechanism for achieving tasks that require coordinating the work of a large number of people. In any society, as the complexity of work increases, and more and more specialization is necessary, the level of organization and size of the group also increase. For example, the one-room schoolhouse of the past was much like an informal group, with the teacher able to move at will from one task to another. In contrast, the modern school is a formal organization in which teachers have a specific and limited set of duties and area of knowledge, where students and faculty and administrators are responsible to layers of higher authority.

Bureaucracy

These characteristics are most perfectly realized in the complex organization known as a **bureaucracy,** from *bureau* the French word for "chest of drawers." Instead of a piece of furniture, think of a set of offices, arranged one on top of the other in the form of a pyramid, as shown in Figure 4-4 on page 93. These offices—or statuses—are occupied by people who do only the task assigned to that office. As described by Max Weber (1922/1968), the bureaucracy has the following characteristics:

1. A clear-cut division of labor, with people at the same level doing the same type of task.
2. Each level is under the supervision of the next higher level. Authority flows down, responsibility moves up, level by level. This arrangement of statuses ranked by power is called a *hierarchy,* the rule of those in a higher position.
3. A consistent set of rules that govern each office, ensuring uniform performance and minimizing individualism.
4. Impartial treatment. Officeholders must perform their tasks without bias or favoritism and without fear of arbitrary discipline for doing their job.
5. Employment is based on tested skills, and promotions are awarded on the basis of merit.
6. Records are kept of all transactions.

> **Formal,** or complex, **organizations** are social structures characterized by impersonality, ranked positions, large size, relative complexity, and long duration.
>
> The **bureaucracy** is a formal organization characterized by rationality and efficiency, so that large-scale administrative tasks can be accomplished.

Weber's description is an *ideal type,* conveying the essence of the bureaucratic form. In real life, few bureaucracies function with ideal efficiency and rationality, but all have some of the characteristic listed.

SOCIAL POLICY

Bureaucracy: Boon or Boondoggle?

Are bureaucracies good for you? Do they stifle originality and turn employees into cookie cutters? Are clients routinely ill-treated? And will we all drown in paperwork? These are some of the most common complaints about either working in or dealing with bureaucracies. How valid are these criticisms?

Advantages of the Bureaucratic Ideal. The clear-cut division of labor and chains of command make work life predictable and theoretically ensure that promotions are based on merit. In complex modern societies, the simplicity of a *Gemeinschaft* organiza-

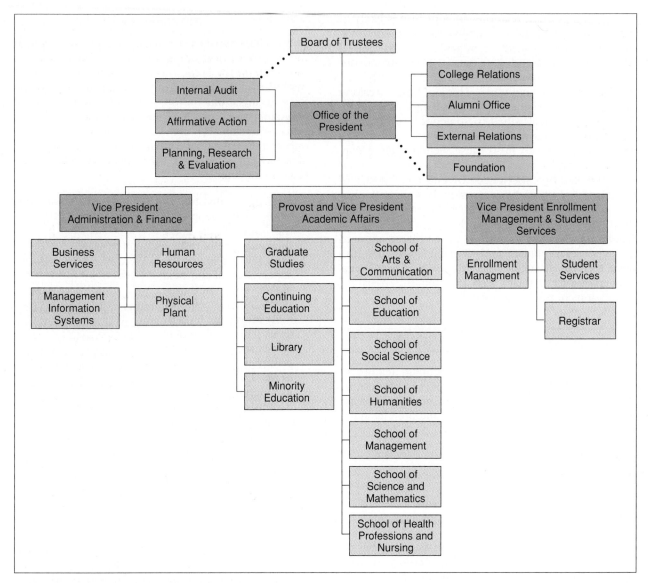

Figure 4-3   Organizational chart.
This formal organization chart illustrates the hierarchical chain of command in a typical college setting. How does your institution's organization compare to this one? P.S.: Where are the faculty and students on this chart?

tion (for example, a mom-and-pop store) is incapable of producing automobiles or treating a heart attack victim. The knowledge required for these tasks is more than one person can master, requiring the coordinated efforts of many specialists. In addition, the job security provided by many bureaucracies is protection against arbitrary demotions or dismissals. Research data suggest that job security frees the bureaucrat to be more innovative than other workers (Kohn, 1971; Foster, 1990).

Negative Features. Most Americans have had experience with the worst in bureaucratic behavior: buck-passing, red tape, faulty communication, and endlessly complex regulations and instructions. Any-

one who has received an official notice from the Internal Revenue Service is aware of these problems, but the organization must have rules to cover every possibility.

Rewarding incompetence cannot always be avoided. As noted only half in jest in *The Peter Principle* (Peter and Hull, 1969), bureaucrats tend to rise to the level of their incompetence. That is, if people are promoted on the basis of their ability to do the job at one level of competence, they will eventually be promoted to a level one step higher than they can handle.

Another criticism is expressed in *Parkinson's Law:* Work expands to fill the time allotted to it (Parkinson,

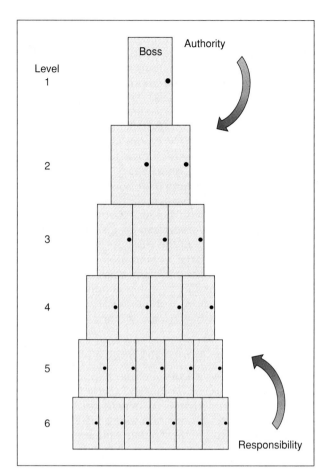

Figure 4-4   A model of bureaucratic structure.

1957/1980). Employees will find something to do to fill up the work hours; otherwise, their superiors might add to the work load. Parkinson also noted that "officials beget officials." For example, in many colleges the number of full, associate, and assistant deans has grown at a faster rate than either the faculty or student body.

The ideal of impersonality annoys many who must deal with "faceless" bureaucrats, but we doubt that you would prefer to be judged on the basis of personal traits such as skin color or religion. Impersonality is designed to guarantee equal treatment; each client is dealt with similarly, however nasty or nice this may be.

Perhaps the greatest problem of any formal organization is that of **goal displacement,** whereby the original goal of the organization is replaced by that of maintaining the structure itself. For example, charitable organizations tend to spend increasing proportions of their income on administrative costs rather than on the stated goal of the charity. In one case, the Girl Scouts of America cookie drive grew from local bake sales in the 1920s to a $400 million business today, but many local troops receive only 14 percent of the profits from their sales, barely enough to sustain the scouting program (E. Graham, 1993).

Do these negatives outweigh the advantages of this form of structure? Can you think of a more efficient way to build a pyramid?

> **Goal displacement** occurs when maintaining the structure replaces the stated goals of the organization.

Among the negative features of bureaucracy are buck passing, red tape, faulty communications, and the endlessly complex regulations and forms that we all have to fill out. President Bill Clinton and Vice-President Al Gore set out to correct many of these problems, but by the time the Washington bureaucrats finished revising the Vice-President's recommendations, most of the innovations for streamlining bureaucracy were scrapped. How can bureaucracies be made more responsive to their citizens?

Corporate Bureaucracies

In addition to public agencies, many private institutions are organized along bureaucratic lines. This has not always been the case. In the early part of this century, many American factories and businesses were still small enough to be operated more informally. But growth leads to organizational complexity as layers of managers and supervisors are added. The day-to-day operation of a large business or university or hospital, for example, is now in the hands of an administrative staff. The growth of the management component in corporations is a central feature of modern business, separating ownership from day-to-day decision making. In theory, managers pursue organizational goals rather than their own personal ends, as in any well-administered bureaucracy.

CORPORATE CULTURES. Traditionally, corporate structures have been studied in terms of the formal organizational chart of power relations or in terms of performance efficiency. More recently, sociologists have also examined the "corporate culture" as an independent variable (Trice and Beyer, 1993; see also Chapter 13). That is, each corporation, similar to a small society, has its own beliefs, rituals, norms, rules about dress and adornment, boundary-maintaining mechanisms, and often a particular language—all of which create an "atmosphere" that characterizes the organization and its employees. Some corporations operate like a military establishment; others claim to be one big family; and still others attempt to recreate a campus environment.

Research on corporate culture generally takes one of three approaches, in which the culture is viewed as integrative, differentiating, or fragmenting (Martin, 1992). In the *integration* perspective, corporate beliefs and behaviors bring employees together in the pursuit of common goals. From a *differentiation* perspective, the corporation is characterized by diverse and overlapping subcultures that add to the complexity of the organization. For example, the culture of the production team will differ from that of the public relations staff or the legal department. And management as a whole has little in common with the hourly employees. Carrying this observation one step further, the subcultures can be viewed as *fragmenting*, reflecting conflicting interests that impede goal achievement.

DEALING WITH CONFLICT AND IMPERSONALITY. Max Weber also described bureaucracy as an "iron cage" in which people feel trapped by impersonal structures over which they have no control. One way to reassert human agency is through the **informal primary group** that emerges within the bureaucratic setting. These informal systems may either reinforce the purpose of the organization or work against its goals. For example, as noted earlier in this chapter, primary groups within the military typically provide the motivation needed for battlefield success. In other cases, workplace primary groups develop tactics to manipulate situations to their own advantage.

Conflict within the bureaucracy is often handled through the informal networks, such as when office gossip and passive resistance are used in place of direct confrontation with bosses (Bartunek and Reid, 1992). Production workers can tie up the line simply by sticking closely to all the rules. As any of you who have worked in a large organization, including the university, know, there are many ways in which low-level groups can modify working conditions to their advantage. This is how workers resist the iron cage and express solidarity with one another.

The Nonprofit Sector

Nonprofit organizations such as charities and foundations form a third or "voluntary" sector of the economy, engaged in activities of benefit to the general public that entitle the organization to tax-exempt status. Organizations in the "public sphere" include a wide variety of nongovernmental and nonprofit groups, from the Neighborhood Watch committee to the International Red Cross. These organizations are called "nonprofit" because any surplus funds cannot be distributed among private individuals. But many administrators do receive sizable salaries, and many organizations are money-makers (with the surplus plowed back into reserves). Indeed, few voluntary associations can survive for very long if they are not run efficiently (Kushner, 1993). The United States has always had a vital third sector and a reputation as a nation of joiners. The French visitor de Tocqueville (1830/1956) was struck with this aspect of American life 150 years ago, and it is estimated that at least 200,000 such associations are active today (Krysan and D'Antonio, 1992).

Voluntary and nonprofit associations emerge to meet a number of needs: for pure sociability, the Elks or Kiwanis; to further a particular cause, the National Association for the Advancement of Colored People; to collect money for charitable work, the March of Dimes; to conduct research, the Russell Sage Foundation; to promote the arts, a local ballet company; or to provide a direct service, a local hospital. In large part, the recent surge of interest in the nonprofit sector reflects a loss of trust in either government or business to provide needed services at an affordable cost (Wuthnow, 1991).

However, it is not altogether clear who benefits from the nonprofit sector (Clotfelter, 1992). Because

Informal primary groups develop within bureaucracies as a buffer against impersonal relationships.

Nonprofit organizations form a voluntary sector of the economy, typically involved in charitable work.

most nonprofits depend on widespread public support for fundraising, they are affected by the state of the economy. Unfortunately, when the economy is not growing, the nonprofits have difficulty raising money precisely when their services are most needed. In any event, nonprofit assistance falls far short of what the most needy can expect from government-sponsored programs. Yet so disillusioned are many Americans with the public sector that many states and cities are contracting with nonprofits and private companies for the services previously provided by state and local governments. It remains to be seen whether the current fad for "privatization" can both save money and meet public needs (Smith and Lipsky, 1993).

THE WORK OF VOLUNTARY ASSOCIATIONS. In addition to providing services and meeting personal needs, the nonprofits are also a natural laboratory for experimental forms of organization. For example, one of the goals of the Feminist Movement has been to develop service delivery organizations that are democratic rather than hierarchical, in which all participants make decisions jointly (Ferree and Hess, 1994). This has worked best for small-scale organizations and relatively simple goals, but the larger the group and the more complex the task, the greater the need for some more formal line of authority and responsibility.

Nonetheless, there are important lessons to be learned from the nonprofits, several of which may be more useful to the business sector than trying to copy a Japanese management style. One lesson has to do with motivation. Successful nonprofits persuade donors, employees, and volunteers that their contributions serve goals that are in the best interest of society as a whole. It may be impossible for a profit-oriented corporation to generate a similar sense of shared mission, but more involvement in the local community and greater support of local voluntary associations might enhance employee commitment.

Structurally, many nonprofits have successfully experimented with more decentralized approaches to decision-making than found in the typical bureaucracy. Problem-solving work teams that bring together experts at the same level of authority are by definition sets of equals who will interact very differently from members of a hierarchy. Delegating authority and spreading decision making among employees not only empowers and motivates workers but enhances the solidarity of the group as a whole.

On the down side, nonprofits are no more immune than other complex organizations to goal displacement and inefficient management. Indeed, freedom from having to make a profit can lead to overlooking basic business practices. Moreover, many nonprofits today are not fully independent of other bureaucracies, such as the government agencies that are a major source of funding and that, therefore, have regulating and oversight functions as in the case of local arts centers (Blau and Rabrenovic, 1991).

The voluntary sector also includes tens of thousands of locally organized support groups, from Bible study circles to meetings of children of alcoholics. These **self-help groups** bring together people with similar interests or problems to talk to one another and, in the process, to feel less alone. Members give helpful advice and provide encouragement and comfort to each other. Although support groups are thought to replace the lost *Gemeinschaft* of village and neighborhood, most people are introduced to the group through existing social networks. In addition, members do not join in order to create and nurture an authentic community, but to gain some personal benefit (Wuthnow, 1994). The goal is individual betterment; the group is only the vehicle.

> **Self-help groups** offer support to people who share a common problem or condition.

From informal primary groups to formal organizations, we live out our days in patterned relationships with other people, attempting to reconcile our need for personal comfort with the achievement of collective goals. Perhaps this introduction to social structure will be of some help in balancing *Gemeinschaft* and *Gesellschaft* in your own future.

SUMMARY

1. *Social structure* describes the patterns of social interaction through which behavior is carried out. The key concepts in the examination of social structure include systems, status, roles, interaction, and groups.

2. A status is a position in a social system, linked to other statuses by norms that provide rules and guidelines for behavior.

3. *Role* refers to a set of behaviors expected of a person in a given status.

4. Social systems represent specific arrangements of statuses and roles composed of interdependent parts.

5. From a functional perspective, social systems consist of elements with mutually dependent parts that remain stable over time.

6. From a conflict perspective, the most important aspect of social structure is the organization of a society's economic production, which determines relationships of domination.

7. Microsystems refer to face-to-face interaction, such as a specific family, while macrosystems refer to social systems at a higher level of abstraction, such as the American family system.

8. Statuses may be acquired at birth (ascribed) or gained through one's own efforts (achieved). Modern societies increase the importance of achievement compared to ascription in determining social positions.

9. Most of our daily activities are structured by the demands and possibilities of the roles we perform. The number of roles we perform may cause strain, whereas the diverse expectations of role partners may lead to conflict between role partners and within individuals.

10. Guidelines for role expectations reduce the anxiety of normlessness, or anomie, as people define their situations and develop appropriate rules of behavior.

11. Groups are collections of people linked by a distinctive set of shared relationships. Groups may be primary or secondary, depending on the degree of closeness, formality, intimacy, and totality of the relationship.

12. Groups have characteristics of their own including size, division of labor, and interaction involving elements of exchange, cooperation, competition, and conflict. In-group solidarity is often enhanced by directing hostility toward out-groups.

13. Emotions are interactive processes, governed by a set of rules and characterized by exchange processes.

14. Groups are also the building blocks of larger systems, termed *organizations*. The sum of the organizations in any one sector of society forms institutions that are the interdependent parts of the larger society.

15. In modern societies, small groups are often overshadowed by formal organizations.

16. Bureaucracy is a type of formal organization characterized by rational specialization of tasks, hierarchical structure, and a merit system of promotions.

17. Positive aspects of bureaucracy include a division of labor that promotes efficiency and discourages favoritism. Negative features include buck passing, red tape, and complex regulations.

18. The informal structure within bureaucracies may reinforce or hinder the purposes of the organization.

19. Nonprofit organizations such as tax-exempt charities and foundations form a third, or voluntary, sector of the economy.

SUGGESTED READINGS

Blieszner, Rosemary, and Rebecca G. Adams. *Adult Friendship*. Newbury Park, CA: Sage, 1992. Using a structural, cultural, and historical approach to the development of friendships, this book examines friendships among young adults, primarily college age, the middle aged, and the elderly.

Demchak, Chris C. *Military Organizations, Complex Machines: Modernization in the U. S. Armed Services*. Ithaca, NY: Cornell University Press, 1991. This interesting study of the U. S. Army's efforts to control the uncertainties of war through the deployment of the M1 battle tank shows how the increasing reliance on complex machines leads to changes in organizations, introducing uncertainty and unintended outcomes.

Erikson, Kai. *A New Species of Trouble: Explorations in Disaster, Trauma, and Community*. New York: W. W. Norton, 1994. A well-written documentation of communities that have experienced major disasters and traumas leading to long-term psychological stress and social breakdown.

Hochschild, Arlie. *The Managed Heart*. Berkeley: University of California Press, 1983. An insightful study of the management of emotions by flight attendants and of emotional labor in the workplace.

Jackall, Robert. *Moral Mazes: The World of Corporate Managers*. New York: Oxford University Press, 1988. Basing his work on hundreds of interviews with managers, the author reveals how the world of corporate managers works and why managers behave as they do.

Kolb, Deborah M., and Jean M. Bartunek, eds. *Hidden Conflict in Organizations: Uncovering Behind-the-Scenes Disputes*. Newbury Park, CA: Sage 1993. An impressive collection of essays on conflict in organizations. Two main themes are prominent: People in organizations tend to refrain from dealing with their conflicts in public forums, and the social context—especially disputants' relationships—is a major influence on conflict management.

Martin, Joanne. *Cultures in Organizations: Three Perspectives*. New York: Oxford University Press, 1992. This useful book seeks to clarify and organize the conflicting perspectives in this research area.

McLaughlin, Margaret L., Michael J. Cody, and Stephen J. Read, eds. *Explaining One's Self to Others: Reason Giving in a Social Context*. Hillsdale, NJ: Lawrence Erlbaum, 1992. A collection of articles reflecting the latest thinking on the microsociology of accounts by focusing on how observers reconstruct and react to negative events and when, how, why, and under what conditions actors do or do not offer accounts for their actions.

Merton, Robert K. *Social Theory and Social Structure*. 2d ed. New York: Free Press, 1968. A revised and enlarged classic sociological analysis of social structure.

Mills, Albert J., and Peta Tancred, eds. *Gendering Organizational Analysis.* Newbury Park, CA: Sage, 1992. The articles collected here bring gender to the center of organizational analysis, revealing the masculine substructure of the workplace. The authors emphasize women's experience and analyze how the modern organization contributes to women's persistent disadvantage.

Scott, John. *Social Network Analysis: A Handbook.* Newbury Park, CA: Sage, 1991. A good introduction to network analysis, this book covers intercorporate relations, as well as community and national elites and personal support systems as topics for network analysis.

Simonds, Wendy, and Barbara Katz Rothman. *Centuries of Solace: Expressions of Maternal Grief in Popular Literature.* Philadelphia, PA: Temple University Press, 1992. The authors trace the changing meaning of motherhood in America through a historical comparison of women's writings on the loss of an child. How the grief was expressed in books and magazines aimed at helping other women cope with their emotions reflects changes in the broader society and the role of women.

5

The Social Self

A Robinson Crusoe is impossible!

—Wolfe, 1993

So, too, are Tarzan and the various "wolf children" regularly featured in the tabloids sold at supermarket checkout counters. Stated most simply: We become fully human and maintain contact with reality only through our interaction with other people. Neither apes nor wolves, however gentle and well-meaning, can do the job. The human infant, remember, is born without preprogrammed responses to the social world, without a particular language or culture. What we do have is that wonderfully sophisticated reflexive mind and capacity to learn any language and culture. The human newborn (neonate) becomes a functioning Aztec, Kwakiutl, or American through interaction with those who speak the language and carry the culture, who teach the norms and prepare the child for various life experiences. This learning process, from infancy to old age, is called **socialization** and involves the transmission of role expectations, values, and beliefs from one generation to another. At the same time, through the same set of interactions, we learn about our "self"—who and what kind of person we are.

Socialization, then, is a twofold process: As we internalize the culture, we also develop a sense of self. Both behavior and self are learned, and both are shaped by culture and expressed in social structures. That is, socialization provides a bridge between culture and social structure. Socialization is also *lifelong*. As long as there are new roles and situations requiring adaptation, humans must depend on learning the appropriate responses.

In this chapter, we first examine socialization as it involves transmission of the culture and then turn to the process of developing a self-image.

SOCIALIZATION

The Effects of Extreme Isolation

Most sociology textbooks begin the discussion of socialization by asking what would happen to an infant who was deprived of all contact with humans. That is, under conditions of extreme isolation, what kind of speech or social behavior would develop? The short answer is none. The longer answer takes the next few pages.

Assessing the effects of extreme isolation is difficult, first because such events are extremely rare. A second problem is that a lack of normal physical and mental development could be due not to extreme isolation but to a birth defect that led the parents to reject the infant in the first place. Because the classic study, involving only two cases of extreme isolation,

was published more than 50 years ago (Davis, 1940), we scoured the literature for more recent examples and could find only two.

In the most thoroughly documented case, 13-year-old Genie had been systematically deprived of supportive human contact. She was kept in a small shuttered bedroom, restrained by straps, barely spoken to, given only baby food to eat, and often severely beaten by her father. Yet in 1970 Genie and her almost totally incompetent mother managed to escape and find the Los Angeles county welfare office (Rymer, 1993). What made Genie an instant object of fascination to social scientists was her inability to say more than a few words and her complete lack of grammar. Although an apparently normal infant at birth, Genie was without language, that essential key to culture and to imaginative thought. She was also physically undeveloped, with a bunny-hop walk, little coordination, and minimal control over her bowels. Clearly, human physical and mental capacities do not unfold automatically but require a supportive social environment.

> **Socialization** is the lifelong process whereby one internalizes culture and develops a sense of self.

Unfortunately, Genie's new caregivers—the academics and welfare officials—were unable adequately to improve her skills at language or self-care, eventually admitting her to a mental institution, although she now lives in a board-and-care home. In addition, the various experts fought among themselves over theory, practice, and ethics, so that the lessons of this sad case remain partly ambiguous, with each authority pushing a special viewpoint. Yet two conclusions are inescapable: that without sustained nurturing interaction, humans cannot become fully social, and that language is *the* key to humanness.

In adulthood, too, extreme isolation has severe consequences. Solitary confinement is a cruel and unusual punishment precisely because we need contact with others to maintain a sense of reality, including our own identity. People who are placed in solitary confinement lose their sense of time—that's why they are often portrayed as trying to keep track of days by scratches on the wall—and ultimately come to doubt every aspect of their lives. Among prisoners in Nazi concentration camps in the 1940s, for example, the most isolated men and women experienced the most extreme losses of self-awareness and mental stability (Rose et al., 1979).

The essential point is that reality is socially constructed, and that without others to help us define reality, we risk "losing our senses." That is why social isolates are so vulnerable to mental problems. The human capacity for social life and our great need to be with other people are the basis of socialization and have roots in the evolutionary development of *Homo sapiens*.

The Evolutionary Bases

As we have discussed in Chapters 1 and 3, humans differ from other animals in our reliance on learning rather than on instinct. Not only *must* we learn, but, thanks to our reflexive mind and capacity for language, we *can* learn. The human infant is born at a less developed stage than any other animal young; it cannot take care of itself, and it remains helpless for several years. Hence, one crucial biological basis for socialization is the extraordinary vulnerability of the human neonate.

PHYSICAL HELPLESSNESS.   You may have observed newborn kittens or puppies that, within weeks, can get around on their own and even be parted from their mother. In contrast, those animals closest to us on the evolutionary scale, the great apes, have newborns in a manner similar to that of humans: typically one at a time, several years apart, and relatively helpless—clinging to the mother. And, for a year or two, there are many parallels between the infant ape and human child.

Validation of self requires assurance that one is who one claims to be.

In the first two years of life, ape and human infants move through basic stages of growth in the same sequence. A crucial difference, however, is that apes do not follow the human course of language development. The human being is, at birth, a bundle of potentials, unguided by instinct, but capable of learning any language and culture, and totally dependent on the social environment. In contrast to this physical dependency, the newborn's brain is actively recording sensations, processing information, and organizing experience.

DEPENDENCY.   This physical dependence on others is an essential precondition to learning. Because the brain and the nervous system are developed at the same time that an infant is being fed and cared for, a basic sensitivity to the expectations of others is built into our earliest experience. This dependence never leaves us, although the objects may shift—from parents to friends to lovers and even to one's own children. But throughout life, humans need other people to provide them with social support.

The mind that reflects on itself, it seems, is never altogether certain: Who am I? What am I? Am I loved? Am I good? These are the questions that we ask over and over again. Because we are not born with such knowledge, we seek the answers from others—beginning with the caregivers of infancy.

Each society has evolved some relatively stable unit to care for helpless young, typically a group centered on the mother. Having carried the infant and given it birth, the mother is the obvious person to care for it. She is also restricted in moving around, somewhat weakened by childbirth, and often limited by the

Physical dependence on others is an essential precondition to learning. This dependence never leaves us even though the objects shift from parents to friends to lovers and even our own children. A Tibetan mother introduces her child to life in this Asian country.

need to breast-feed. There is no maternal (mothering) instinct, but there are many reasons that women behave maternally: for example, the sheer helplessness of the newborn, and the mother's own emotional and physical investment in the product of her body. But given the very high maternal death rates in most societies throughout history, there is an evolutionary advantage to the human infant's being able to relate to any adult nurturer, and to the willingness of nonparents to care for other people's offspring.

The newborn becomes especially sensitive to cues from its caregivers. Over time, the infant discovers that it, too, contributes to the interaction: a wail brings attention, a gurgle thrills an audience, and whining can bring harsh words. An *interdependence* develops between infants and caregivers, although overwhelming power resides in the adults.

EMOTIONAL NEEDS.   Nurturance for physical survival is only one need of the infant. We propose that three other responses from others are essential for well-being across the life course: affection, approval, and some assurance that one is who one claims to be (**validation of self**). A similar set of needs was suggested by W. I. Thomas (1923) in terms of "four wishes"—for new experience, mastery, recognition, and security. The people whose approval and affection we most care about are those whose rejection would hurt most. Throughout our lives we are especially sensitive to the reactions of a few very important people.

INDIVIDUAL DIFFERENCES.   Newborns are not, of course, identical. Some will learn faster than others, be slim or heavy, calm or fidgety, more or less musical, and so on through a long list of traits—largely matters of taste and temperament—that have some *genetic component.* That is, there are inherited tendencies toward some types of behavior and appearance.

But—and this is the crucial point—genetic tendencies do not automatically produce behavior. A tendency is a predisposition, the likelihood that one response will occur rather than another. Such predispositions emerge within social structures that can stifle or encourage their expression.

Biology and culture interact to produce our particular characteristics; neither can be understood without knowing the influence of the other. Indeed, as we saw in Chapter 1, the newer versions of sociobiology/biosociology are based on the assumption that individual personality and behavior emerge from the interaction between genetic potentials and social environments. Sociologists are most interested in the context in which human development takes place (Lerner, 1992).

For example, research on the genetic basis for criminal behavior generally concludes that any inherited traits have a limited and indirect effect, given all the other influences on people who become career criminals, including poor mental and physical health, school failure, abusive home life, and crime-prone neighborhoods (Goleman, 1992.)

Even people born with a great talent—for music, or mathematics, or a sport—do not realize their potential without the support and encouragement of parents and teachers. The environment of the home and the availability of trained instructors are the keys to becoming exceptionally skilled. Because almost everyone has a special talent, we have to look to these social factors to explain why some young people develop the desire to excel and why others do not.

Bearing in mind that each person is a unique combination of innate and learned traits, we turn now to the process by which people learn the rules of the culture and the particular roles that they are expected to play throughout life.

THE SOCIALIZATION PROCESS

Each newborn could learn any culture, speak any language, and organize experience in different ways as it matures. A function of primary (early) socialization is to present a single world of meaning as the only possible way to organize perceptions (Berger and Luck-

mann, 1966). At the microlevel, this information is given through direct training for social roles.

Learning One's Place

When people occupy a particular status, they must learn the appropriate role behavior. Role learning involves several elements: information, opportunities to rehearse, feedback from role partners, and social supports.

INFORMATION.   At some point the learner must be given guidance for adequate role performance. The military recruit receives detailed descriptions from a drill instructor, parents-to-be can attend child-care classes, and children are prepared in advance for kindergarten. There are how-to books for people interested in everything from being a successful golfer to finding a compatible marriage partner.

REHEARSAL.   Knowing *what* to do is one thing; doing it is something else. Most performances benefit from practice. Opportunities for trial-and-error learning under relatively safe conditions are usually given to people just entering a role—the "honeymoon" period for newlyweds, political newcomers, and first-year college students. Notice also that the honeymoon must always end—at some point, the role incumbents are expected to fulfill the obligations of the new status in maintaining the social system as a whole (Slater, 1963).

Another form of rehearsal is called **anticipatory socialization,** involving practice in advance of assuming the role. Thus, children play sex-typed roles, high school seniors begin to act like college students, employees expecting a promotion dress more carefully, and older adults take up the hobbies they intend to follow in retirement. Somewhat related to anticipatory socialization is the behavior called **modeling,** or copying the characteristics of admired people. Parents, movie stars, and sports figures are common role models for children.

FEEDBACK.   Role performances take place before an audience of role partners who transmit messages regarding the performance. **Positive sanctions** are those reactions indicating that the role is well played. **Negative sanctions** involve open criticism or at least the withholding of approval. Depending on the importance of the sanctioner, people will modify their behavior to receive positive feedback. The opinions of most people may have little effect, but the judgments of some are crucial.

> **Anticipatory socialization** involves rehearsing before assuming a role.
>
> **Modeling** is the copying of characteristics of admired people.
>
> **Positive sanctions** indicate approval of role performance.
>
> **Negative sanctions** convey disapproval of role performance.

Success in mastering a role depends on the social support of people who are willing to train the learner. In the case of a father teaching his young child to read, patience helps a lot.

SOCIAL SUPPORTS.   Success in a role often depends on the help of people willing to train the learner and to tolerate role rehearsals. For children, parents and friends are the most important sources of information and support. For adults as well, social networks are crucial to good health and a sense of well-being.

Friends and relatives serve to buffer many life stresses, providing a protective environment in which to cope with major role changes throughout the life course (M. A. Davis, et al., 1991; Ensel and Lin, 1991).

Subcultural Differences

In the United States, many important subcultural differences are apparent in both the content and style of childhood socialization. To the extent that ascribed statuses such as race, religion, and ethnicity are associated with certain marriage or employment patterns, parents will raise their children to meet these expectations. Achieved characteristics such as parental income and education are also powerful indicators of socialization goals and techniques. But of all subcultural differences, the most crucial appears to be *parental occupation.*

PARENTAL OCCUPATION.   Although it is linked to income, education, race, religion, and ethnicity, parental occupation exerts a strong and independent effect on the socialization experience. The work of Melvin Kohn and his associates over three decades, in the United States and elsewhere, has shown the strength and cross-cultural validity of the relationship between parents' work experiences and what and how they teach their children (Kohn et al., 1990).

The major occupational distinction is between those jobs that involve dealing with (1) people and/or ideas, or with (2) machines and other inanimate objects. The first type of work is associated with "white-collar" occupations, where solving problems and

Number of Children under 15 in Paid Employment (per 1,000 households). Some children are socialized to work at a very young age.
Source: Peters Atlas of The World, New York, Harper and Row, 1990, p. 176.

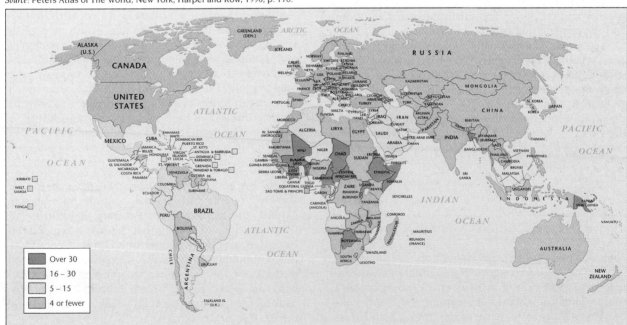

manipulating symbols are the key to success. These jobs tend to be nonrepetitive and loosely supervised, allowing room for *autonomy* (self-direction). In contrast, most "blue-collar" jobs require being on time, following instructions, heavy supervision, and little if any leeway for creativity. As a consequence, white-collar parents encourage their children to be intellectually curious, flexible, and self-controlled, even when this challenges parental authority. Blue-collar parents, however, place a high value on respect for authority and on obedience, punctuality, conformity, and technical skills. Both worldviews are derived from occupational experience, but the former encourages questions whereas the latter emphasizes routine.

In this way, social structural variables (the nature of one's work) affect parental values that, in turn, influence socialization practices and, ultimately, personality traits of the child. For example, in both Poland and the United States, fathers whose occupation calls for self-direction place a high value on personal responsibility in their offspring, whereas men whose work is heavily supervised tend to value conformity (Kohn and Slomczynski, 1990). Similar findings are reported for working mothers in the United States (Spade, 1983; Parcel and Menaghan, 1994a) and in Japan (Naoi and Schooler, 1990).

The experiences of socialization vary dramatically around the world. Orphaned or abandoned children such as those pictured here live in the streets of many large cities in Asia, Africa, and Latin America.

"We found her wandering at the edge of the forest. She was raised by scientists."

Drawing by W. Miller; © 1993 *The New Yorker Magazine*, Inc.

These differences are also reflected in disciplining techniques. Parents in highly supervised work tend toward physical punishment of children, whereas those in self-directed work favor a more psychological approach, especially the threat of the withdrawal of affection. As described in Table 5-1, the two patterns have been labeled *traditional* and *modern*.

The distinction between traditional and modern can be illustrated by the parents' reactions to a child who has broken a neighbor's window. "Traditional" parents are likely to spank the child for destroying property and to worry about the expense of replacing the window. The "modern" parent tends to focus on the child's state of mind—"Why did you do it?" Guilt feelings are reinforced by parental threat of withholding approval. The goal is to teach the child self-control rather than fear of being caught and punished.

SOCIAL POLICY

Spare the Rod and Save the Child

The issue of *corporal* (bodily) *punishment* in our homes and schools reflects conflicting strands in American culture. On the one hand, is the tradition of concern for the welfare of children; but, on the other hand, is the stronger tradition of family privacy and the right of parents to discipline their children free of government intervention. One person's "abuse" may be another's "necessary punishment" or even "God's will." As a result, the United States is one of the few modern societies without a national child welfare program and that permits school authorities in many states to hit students.

American attitudes toward child punishment have hardened dramatically in the 1990s. Apparently believing that adolescents are out of control, a majority of respondents support treating teenage offenders as

TABLE 5-1 Two Patterns of Child Rearing

"Traditional" or Status-Centered	"Modern" or Person-Centered
1. Each member's place in the family is a function of age and sex status.	Emphasis is on selfhood and individuality of each member.
2. Father is defined as boss and more important as agent of discipline: he receives "respect" and deference from mother and children.	Father more affectionate, less authoritative: mother becomes more important as agent of discipline.
3. Emphasis on overt acts—*what* child does rather than *why*.	Emphasis on motives and feelings—*why* child does what he or she does.
4. Valued qualities in child: obedience, cleanliness.	Valued qualities in child are happiness, achievement, consideration, curiosity, self-control.
5. Emphasis on "direct" discipline: physical punishment, scolding, threats.	Discipline based on reasoning, isolation, guilt, threat of loss of love.
6. Social consensus and solidarity in communication: emphasis on "we."	Communication used to express individual experience and perspectives; emphasis on "I."
7. Emphasis in communication from parent to child.	Emphasis on two-way communication between parent and child; parent open to persuasion.
8. Parent feels little need to justify demands to child; commands are to be followed "because I say so."	Parent gives reasons for demands—e.g., not "Shut up" but "Please keep quiet or go into the other room; I'm trying to talk on the telephone."
9. Emphasis on conforming to rules, respecting authority, maintaining conventional social order.	Emphasis on reasons for rules; particular rules can be criticized in the name of higher rational or ethical principles.
10. Child may attain a strong sense of social identity at the cost of individuality, poor academic performance.	Child may attain strong sense of selfhood but may have identity problems, guilt, alienation.

Source: Skolnick, 1992a, p. 413. From *The Intimate Environment: Exploring Marriage and the Family,* 5th Ed., by Arlene S. Skolnick. Copyright © 1992 by Arlene S. Skolnick. Reprinted by permission of HarperCollins Publishers.

if they were adults, including being subject to the death penalty. In 1994, when the government of Singapore announced that an American teenager who was found guilty of vandalism would receive the traditional punishment of six powerful lashes with a rattan cane on the bare buttocks, most Americans thought that the penalty was deserved. In the same year, the Florida legislature overwhelmingly passed a measure called the "spankers' Bill of Rights" permitting parents to spank their children provided only that they did not leave "significant" bruise marks. And in California, there is popular support for legislation that would punish graffiti vandals with 10 whacks of a wooden paddle to be administered in open court by the child's parents.

How effective is physical punishment in reducing undesirable behavior? Not very. The data suggest that hitting a child has a short-term effect and only when administered immediately, predictably, and in proportion to the offense. For long-lasting behavior change, the most powerful techniques are not punishments, but the selective giving or withholding of rewards, including affection and approval (Kohn, 1993).

Furthermore, physical discipline has several negative consequences. Hitting a child is not harmless.

Physical punishment produces feelings of powerlessness and lowered achievement motivation (Straus and Gimpel, 1992). Low grades and low self-esteem combine to limit the child's occupational goals; the more frequent the punishment, the lower one's economic level as an adult and the more likely to be depressed, even when the parents were perceived as loving. Sons tend to feel powerless, and daughters to be depressed. In addition, violence toward one's wife was significantly associated with having been physically punished as a child.

The lessons that a child learns from being hit are not the ones most parents intend: namely, that big people can violate the body of smaller ones; that those who claim to love you can also hurt you; and that violence is an acceptable way to deal with problems (Molm, 1989; Greven, 1991). It is very difficult to teach a child self-control while losing one's own temper. The children grow up perceiving the world as dangerous place, to which boys respond with aggressive behavior, and girls with depression and self-blame. Disobedience is as much a *result* as a cause of physical punishment (Hyman, 1990).

When you become a parent, there will be many occasions when it will be easier to strike out at a child than to take the time to find a nonviolent socializing technique. It may also be tempting to turn the job over to the schools. Yet, if you wish to raise children who are guided by internalized norms rather than fear of external authorities, you might want to question school policy as well as your own responses. How would you respond to a child who runs out into the street or who talks back to you? What is it you really want to teach your child?

GENDER DIFFERENCES.   Although we will have more to say about gender socialization in Chapter 10, there is no doubt that parents, teachers, and friends behave differently toward girls and boys (Thorne, 1993). Such differential treatment has important consequences not only for personality but also for how a child thinks. For example, because of her expected family roles, a girl is encouraged to stay close to home, a confinement in space and relationships that enhances her verbal skills but limits her opportunities to explore the outside world and to develop the abstract thinking skills necessary for mastering science and mathematics (Entwisle et al., 1994).

Role expectations of boys and girls have become somewhat less rigid, which is largely due to the influence of the New Feminist Movement, but children's television programs and books continue to feature many more male figures than female ones (Grauerholz and Pescosolido, 1989). Advertisers and publishers have learned that girls will follow stories about boys, but boys will not watch programs or read stories about female characters. Similarly, the division of household labor among children still follows a fairly traditional pattern: Boys do outside work only, girls do all the rest of it (Blair, 1991).

Nonetheless, early childhood socialization is relatively asexual compared to the experiences of pre- and early adolescence, when schoolmates define and reinforce conformity to gendered norms. Among elementary school children, for example, boys become popular on the basis of active and achieved statuses, especially athletic skills and toughness, while a girl's popularity hinges on passive and ascribed statuses such as her physical appearance and parents' economic position, although recent trends in the broader society have made it easier for the children, especially the girls, to absorb cross-sex elements into their gendered subcultures (Adler et al., 1992).

In early adolescence, when the biological changes associated with puberty become visible, peer-reinforced highly sexualized gendered systems dominate the socialization process (Thorne, 1993). This period appears to be more problematic for girls than for boys. The boys typically gain in size and strength, finding it increasingly easier to meet the standards of masculinity; the girls, however, are beset by self-doubts as the ideal of femininity seems ever more elusive.

Agents of Socialization

The individuals and organizations charged with transmitting the culture to newborns and newcomers are called **agents of socialization,** primarily, parents, peers, teachers, and in modern society, the media.

PARENTS.   The first and most important agents of socialization are the people who care for helpless infants, typically, the biological parent(s). The child learns the culture into which it has been born, as interpreted by these socializers, through words and gestures. Much of this information is nonverbal, matters of mood and feeling, expressed in how the child is touched or spoken to, played with, and held. These impressions are crucial for establishing trust between the child and its socializers. The *quality* of early interaction is as important as its quantity and content. Of special importance is the ability to *empathize,* to put yourself in the place of the other. Empathetic care givers teach a child to try to imagine the feelings of others.

The culture is *internalized* when caregiver expectations become part of the child's own thought, so

> **Agents of socialization** are individuals and organizations responsible for transmitting the culture.

The child learns the culture into which it has been born through words and gestures. Much of this information is nonverbal, matters of mood and feeling, expressed in how the child is touched and spoken to.

that guilt over failing to live up to these expectations becomes an important motivator of role performance throughout the life course. Most parents, if not all, attempt to prepare their offspring for success in that particular society.

In a simple society, parents can probably teach the growing child everything necessary to function as an adult. In a rapidly changing industrial society, however, one generation's knowledge can quickly become obsolete, so that other agents of socialization are needed. Although parental controls tend to weaken in modern societies, many attitudes are transmitted across the generations, especially when parents and children occupy similar occupational statuses (Glass et al., 1986).

Reciprocal socialization takes place when parents and children have a mutual influence on one another. For example, one recent study found that a mother's attitude toward living together without marriage (cohabitation) influenced her children's behavior, but also that the adult child's experience of cohabitation changed the mother's attitude (Axinn and Thornton, 1993). Thus, reciprocal socialization operates at several levels to reduce conflict between generations.

> Through **reciprocal socialization,** children modify their patents' view of the world.
>
> **Peers** are equals and an important source of information and socialization.
>
> **Mentors** are teachers who act as guides and sponsors.

PEERS.   Another powerful source of information and socialization is the friendship group of *age peers.* **Peers** are equals, whereas parents are the child's superiors. The inequality of the parent–child relationship makes some kinds of learning difficult. In contrast to the respect that should be shown to parents, peer interaction is more relaxed. Friends will tease and insult, tolerate mistakes and role rehearsals, without the heavy emotional overtones of family interaction.

More sociologically, the peer group is a social system in which young people negotiate reality with one another. Rather than looking at individual children as they are influenced by friends, we should view the peer group as reality in its own right, creatively adapting to the adult world by reworking selected elements of the broader culture (Corsaro, 1992).

Children need friends in order to learn many things about being a child, such as how to take turns, share, fight fairly, deal with adults, and prepare for the next stage of growth. At school, the peer group provides important knowledge about how to handle authority, manipulate the system, and approach members of the opposite sex. Even in adulthood, peer groups are important agents of socialization—to marriage, parenthood, retirement, and widowhood. But the adolescent peer group has received the most popular and scientific attention.

Adolescent Peer Group.   For several decades, American parents and other adults have looked with amazement and anxiety at the friendship groups of young people between ages 13 and 18. Parents fear the power of the group as a challenge to family values and as a rival for the teenager's loyalty.

Yet, the adolescent peer group is necessary for young people in their journey from dependence to independence, from childhood to adulthood. In a society where adult statuses are achieved rather than ascribed, a young person needs the peer group in order to learn how to meet the objective (*universalistic*) standards of performance of the school and workplace, in contrast to the ascribed and individualized (*particularistic*) standards of the family (Figure 5-1).

In adolescence, peers often replace or compete with parents as a source of affection, approval, and validation. As in childhood socialization, the power of the peer group is based on members' fear of rejection. Typically, however, parents and peers divide the labor of socialization, with parents remaining important socializers to values and long-term goals (finances, education, career), whereas peers have the most influence on immediate life-style choices such as appearance, sexual behavior, and dating activities (Sebold, 1986).

Because the major task of adolescence in modern society is precisely to outgrow dependence on one's parents, the strength of the adolescent peer group reflects the difficulty of achieving independence. In the extended period when one is too old to be a child but too young to be an adult, a subculture of adolescent roles and attitudes allows the person to rehearse and prepare for adulthood. Perhaps the most a parent can do is to try to guide the choice of peers and hope for the best.

Parents can influence their childrens' choice of friends by joining a particular church, or enrolling the children in after-school programs (for music, art, sports, dance, and so forth), and encouraging membership in organizations such as the Boy or Girl Scouts and Little League (Magrass, 1986; Fine, 1987).

TEACHERS.   Much formal socialization today is in the hands of professionals (see Chapter 15). Teachers, from nursery school on, receive pay for being agents of socialization. Ideally, a teacher has both special knowledge and the skills needed to transmit it. Teachers are also role models for responsible adulthood and for the importance of education. Some may even convey the excitement of learning itself. These are usually the teachers we remember.

In high school and college, many students form especially close relationships with particular instructors, who become their **mentors** (guides and

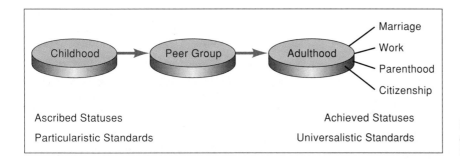

Figure 5-1 The adolescent peer group as a medium for the transition from childhood to adult statuses.

sponsors). At the college level, mentors can influence one's career decisions and open doors to advanced training. In graduate school, the mentor is essential for research and publication opportunities.

THE MEDIA. As discussed in Chapter 22, the mass media—printed and electronic—produce information as well as entertainment. Newspapers, magazines, books, radio, and television tell us what is important, desirable, and beautiful or ugly. Although it has been very difficult to demonstrate a direct cause-and-effect link between media presentations and subsequent audience behavior, there can be little doubt about the power of mass media to capture and channel public attention, to set political and social agendas, and to manipulate emotions.

FORMATION OF THE SELF

Transmission of the culture is only one aspect of socialization. While people process information about the culture and role expectations, they also learn about their *self.* **Self-identity** is an organization of perceptions about who and what kind of person one is. Humans are not born with such knowledge. It is learned and developed gradually through precisely the same socialization experiences by which the culture is internalized.

> **Self-identity** is an organization of perceptions about who and what kind of person one is.

Self-concept as a central component of personality has, for the most part, been studied from the symbolic-interaction perspective. For it is through language, the symbol system of culture, and in the intimacy of face-to-face interaction that messages about the self are conveyed. How the individual interprets and evaluates this information is central to the social construction of identity.

James, Cooley, and the Social Self

Only gradually does the infant come to distinguish itself from its nurturer. It is, of course, impossible to question a newborn (or even a young child) about its

In adolescence, peers often replace parents as significant agents of socialization. The power of the peer group in the United States or in Singapore, pictured here, is based on members' fear of rejection, and has most immediate influence on lifestyle choices such as one's appearance.

feelings and perceptions. Social scientists can only imagine how it must feel to be an infant. Without more certain knowledge, they have devised this scenario:

> The newborn is totally absorbed in the nurturer-in-fant system. But the human mind is reflexive, and at some point, the infant begins to perceive itself in contrast to the overwhelming other. As the care giver coos and murmurs, addressing a "you," the infant dimly begins to differentiate (separate) itself, to see it-self as being that "you."

As people talk to you, handle you, and discuss you with others, you learn who you are and become an active agent in creating your self.

THE SOCIAL SELF.   The concept of a *social self* was introduced by the psychologist William James (1842–1910), who stated that a person has as many social selves as there are others who recognize that person and carry an image of him or her in their minds. The self, therefore, is rooted in social interaction.

The **looking-glass self** suggests that we see ourselves reflected back in the reaction of others.

THE LOOKING-GLASS SELF. Building on James's concept of the social self, Charles Horton Cooley (1864–1929) proposed that the self is composed of a basic self-feeling that is then shaped and given specific content through interactions with important others, especially within primary groups.

Cooley is best known today for his image of the **looking-glass self.** Just as a mirror reflects a reverse image, one's perception of oneself is never direct.

> The self has a character that is different from that of the physiological organism proper. The self is something which has a development; it is not initially there, at birth, but arises in the process of social experience and activity.
>
> —GEORGE HERBERT MEAD, 1934, p. 135

Rather, we see ourselves reflected back in the reactions of others. According to Cooley, our ideas of our self come from (1) our imagining how we appear to other people, (2) how we think they judge our appearance, and (3) how we feel about all this. In other words, our sense of self is more like a process than a fixed object; it is always developing as we interact with others, whose opinions of us are ever-shifting. For example, a child who hears only positive feedback from parents may be confused later when a teacher's reactions indicate a less than satisfactory performance.

Cooley's looking-glass imagery, however, does not imply that the child—or the adult—is a passive receiver of impressions. On the contrary, a person actively manipulates the reactions of others, selects which cues to follow, and judges the relative importance of role partners. Not all reflected images influence the self-process. In general, we tend to accept impressions that reinforce a basic identity and to resist those that do not. Cooley's suggestion that some

Cooley's image of the looking-glass self suggests that we see ourselves reflected back in the reactions of others. We begin to develop our image of ourselves at an early age as we evaluate the responses and reflections of others in the social world around us.

role partners have more effect than others was elaborated by George Herbert Mead (1863–1931).

Mead and the Self-Process

As noted in Chapter 1, George Herbert Mead's view of social action was based on the human ability to use symbols to communicate, to create rules, and to adjust behavior to the expectations of others. A person can do all these things by developing a "self" that reflects on its own behavior while interacting with others. Society is the sum of all these ongoing activities, constantly changing, always becoming something else. Society is also in our minds, through internalized rules, roles, and relationships. Mead's masterwork is titled *Mind, Self, and Society* (1934), in recognition of the complex links among the three levels of reality.

TAKING THE ROLE OF THE OTHER.   If, as Cooley proposed, we learn about ourselves from imagining how we appear to other people, then the reflexive mind not only sees itself as an object but can see into the minds of others. For Mead, this imaginative leap into the mind of others and the taking of that person's attitude toward oneself is central to the development of self-concept.

Following Cooley, Mead noted that our first socialization experiences take place within a primary group where we learn the shared meanings of our culture. We are able to guess what others are thinking precisely because we have a common language and shared experiences.

The child learns by precept (being told how to behave) and practice (trial and error and then feedback). This learning takes place through language, both verbal and nonverbal. Mead used the word **gesture** for a symbol that is shared by group members and that is made part of a role performance. Simply put, we internalize the culture and social structure by taking on the role of others. Thus society becomes part of our self, and the self becomes social.

SIGNIFICANT OTHER.   Particularly important to the formation of self are those specific persons whose approval and affection are especially desired. Parents at first, then peers, role models, and lovers, can all become **significant others,** with special power to shape one's perceptions. Even children can become significant others, as only they can validate an adult's identity as a "good parent."

GENERALIZED OTHER.   Another type of expectation is embedded in role systems, in which a person's status is both different from that of role partners and dependent on them. Mead uses the image of a baseball team to describe what he calls the **generalized other,** an organization of roles and responses. These expectations reflect societal standards of acceptable behavior for anyone in the role. Thus, we learn both *particular*

Because of the human need for approval and affection, our significant others have a very strong influence on our attitudes, perceptions, and behavior.

standards from significant others and the *universal norms* applying to the role from the generalized other.

PLAY AND GAMES.   According to Mead, it is through play and games that the child develops the ability to internalize these expectations. Self-consciousness emerges from situated experiences, as one learns the content of the culture and develops the ability to take the attitude of the other.

The first stage in the development of self involves playacting, in which the very young child takes on the role of parent, fire fighter, doctor, and so forth. Children playing with toys respond to their own behavior in the voice and attitudes of adult care givers; that is, the child engages in an internal conversation between self and other. Child's play is a very serious business, the learning ground for language and relationships. Recent research suggests that play is important for adult development in animals as well as for humans, stimulating the brain and reinforcing group controls (Angier, 1992).

Although animals may roughhouse, they cannot play games! Games have structure and rules that are

> A **gesture** is a symbol whose meaning is shared by group members
>
> **Significant others** are persons whose affection and approval are particularly desired.
>
> The **generalized other** reflects societal standards of acceptable behavior in roles.

JOHN P. HEWITT

The Sociology of the Self

John Hewitt is Professor of Sociology at the University of Massachusetts, Amherst. He is the author of Dilemmas of the American Self (1990), *in which his lifelong fascination with "the self" takes literary shape.*

From the start of my career as a sociologist, I have been asking what the self is, where it comes from, what sustains or undermines it, and what difference it makes for individuals and society. What explains this interest? Although chance plays some role, life-long intellectual pursuits are strongly influenced by one's personal experiences and statuses.

My life experience has involved a considerable amount of social mobility that has affected how I see the world. When I was 12 we moved from a coal-mining town of fewer than 700 people to a large city, which took me from a world I knew to one where I was a stranger, but also liberated from the limited opportunities of the town where I was born.

Gradually, I found a place for myself, and a few friends, yet I never felt entirely at home; I remained marginal, as sociologists would say. I couldn't totally reject the rural culture in which I was raised, and I couldn't assimilate completely the urban middle-class culture to which I was exposed in the

city. When I went to Princeton University to get my doctorate in sociology, I had similar experiences. I was eager to move to the strange new world of the Ivy League but also fearful. Again I felt marginal—not fully a member of the elite social world I was joining and not fully divorced from the less exalted one I had left behind.

These experiences made me acutely self-conscious, concerned with how I appeared to others and how well my efforts to join their social world were succeeding. I cultivated the skills of self-presentation, striving to meet what I thought were the expectations of others. At the same time my heightened self-consciousness itself became something of which I was aware.

Thus, I realized how socially dependent a person is. What we call the "self"—our feelings about ourselves, our images of what we are, our sense of where we fit in society—emerges from our encounters in the social world, our group memberships, and from those that reject us or to which we feel only marginally attached. It develops as we participate in an organized and regular round of activities with others and seek a place in their/our social world.

In *Dilemma of the American Self*, I suggest that a distinctive set of cultural tensions shapes the self. Americans have a strong desire to put down roots, to find a patch of social territory they can call their own, and to encourage their children to accept that way of life. At the same time, Americans want the freedom to define themselves as they see fit, to strike out for

new places. They want to stay where they are but also to leave; to conform to social demands but also rebel against them; and to live with others in the warmth of an accepting community but also to stand alone and independent on their own feet. Americans adapt to these tensions in a variety of ways. Some reject the constraints of their communities and seek to be as free as possible. Others find security in conforming to their narrow religious, neighborhood, or life-style communities. Still others juggle the demands of an autonomous life in the wider society and the obligations of communal life.

Should one define oneself by one's membership in and conformity to the demands of an enveloping community on which one can always depend? Or should one define oneself by striking out one one's own, rejecting whatever one must reject to be free and independent? Can one reconcile these conflicting ways of building a self?

My biography has led me to emphasize the tendency of American culture to make people ambivalent about where they should anchor their sense of self. Because individual experiences limited and limiting, the truth of such ideas ultimately lies in their capacity to aid others in understanding their own life. Social scientists do not study society from some lofty perch where they can disregard the lessons and the difficulties of their own lives. Rather, their experiences sharpen their interest and direct their attention to the social world.

socially constructed and transmitted, involving a more complex level of mental functioning than that of play. Typically, when children enter school and the society of age peers, they are exposed to situations that require internalizing entire role systems. As Mead notes, one must not only take the role of the other, as in play, but must assume the various roles of all participants in the game. This is the skill that we carry into adulthood and even to old age (Chappell and Orbach, 1986).

THE EMERGENCE OF SELF.   Learning to take the role of the other is only one part of the *process of self.* If internalization were all that was necessary for the formation of the self-concept, individual behavior would exhibit little novelty or spontaneity. But Mead's "self" is not a mere passive reflection of social norms.

Rather, the self is dynamic, ever capable of change. Mead distinguished between two aspects of self: the "I" and the "me." The "I" is the more spontaneous and creative element, reflecting on and responding to the "me," which is the socialized self composed of the internalized attitudes of others. This dialogue produces an *organization of perceptions* that forms the self-concept and guides behavior at any one time.

For example, you are constantly engaged in conversations with yourself, in which part of your self is longing to be free of reading assignments and homework, whereas the other part is reminding you of the expectations of your teacher and the college. Sometimes the "I" will win out, and you will put the books aside in favor of a night out with your friends, and at other times the "me" will triumph because you do have long-range goals that require passing exams and earning a diploma.

Mead saw no necessary conflict between "I" and "me," as both are needed to form the social self, although there is always the possibility of tension between meanings derived from experience and those taken from culture at a particular historical moment. In this view, the relationship between self and society is reciprocal rather than in opposition (Burkitt, 1991). Society and the self are both possible because humans can make the imaginative leap into the mind of others and share their world of meaning—the ultimate triumph of our unique capacity for reflexive thought.

Goffman and the Presentation of Self

Many sociologists view the self as a reflection of the cluster of roles being performed by an individual at any point in the life course. For Erving Goffman (1922–83), the key process is *self-presentation,* that is, an impression that we present to others. The self, then, always risks being rejected, and every encounter becomes a drama in which we "manage" the impression we give so that others will accept who we claim to be. In *The Presentation of Self in Everyday Life,* Goffman (1959) showed how carefully we construct a presenting self as the "real me" in order to influence the reactions of role partners and to control the situation.

In this view, a self exists for every situation. Goffman wrote of a **virtual self** (or possible self) that awaits us in every role—what society expects of a person in that role. Whatever our innate tendencies and abilities, each role offers an opportunity to become a particular type of person.

But some possible selves are not very appealing to our self-image. For example, students who have part-time jobs at fast-food counters will resist being thought of as "hamburger helpers." Therefore, there may be a gap between self-image and the virtual self-in-the-role.

ROLE DISTANCE.   Goffman used the term **role distance** to describe the space that a person can place between the self and the self-in-the-role. People use several distancing techniques to warn others not to take them as the virtual self implied in the role. Those of you who have had temporary jobs—busboy, waitress, cashier, stock clerk—that you consider inferior to your true status have probably let others know that you are really a college student or on your way to better things. Perhaps you brought a textbook to the job or did slapdash work so that no one could possibly take you seriously in such a role. Role distance protects the self and offers some freedom for the expression of personal style.

In many situations, however, we have little choice but to become the self-in-the-role, as seen in the experiment described next.

> The "**I**" is the creative spontaneous part of the self, whereas the "**me**" consists of the internalized attitudes of others.
>
> A **virtual self** awaits us in each role we perform.
>
> **Role distance** is the space placed between the self and the self-in-the-role.
>
> **Deindividualization** is the process of removing a person's civilian identities.

THE MIND AS A JAILOR.   In a classic experiment that has received much publicity, Philip Zimbardo and his colleagues (1973) found that the line between the self and the self-in-the-role can be erased in a short time under extreme circumstances. After answering an ad in local and campus newspapers to participate in "a study of prison life," at $15 per day for 2 weeks, 21 average, middle-class, college-aged men, carefully screened for physical health, emotional maturity, and respect for the law, were accepted. The experimenters randomly assigned the subjects to the status of either prisoner or guard in a "mock prison."

Every step was taken to make the prison as realistic as possible. Both prisoners and guards were **deindividualized,** or "depersonalized," through the

The Marine Corps uses deindividualization, the process by which a person's civilian identity is removed, to build a new identity. The process creates loyalty and cohesion among recruits and makes them members of the fighting team.

typical prison processes of removing their civilian identities. The prisoners wore uniforms and had to ask the guards for permission for most normal activities. The guards also had their uniforms: khaki, with nightsticks, handcuffs, whistles, and reflector sunglasses.

Neither group was given much formal instruction in how to play their role yet within days each person had *disappeared into the appropriate role*. The guards quickly learned to enjoy unchecked power, and the prisoners began to act in ways that encouraged the guards' dehumanizing treatment. The researchers were amazed at the speed and ease with which the assigned roles and the definition of the situation controlled the behavior of emotionally sound people.

One prisoner was released after a day and a half due to extreme depression. On each of the next three days, another prisoner developed similar symptoms and was released. A fifth man broke out in a psychosomatic rash. By the end of six days, the entire experiment was called off, so transformed had these "normal, healthy, educated young men" become. What caused the transformation? Obviously, nothing in the subjects' personality, for all had been carefully screened and randomly assigned. As the experimenters concluded, in a ringing endorsement of the sociological perspective:

Rather, the subjects' abnormal social and personal reactions are best seen as a product of their transaction with an environment that supported the behavior that would be pathological in other settings, but was "appropriate" in this prison. Had we observed comparable reactions in a real prison, the psychiatrist undoubtedly would have been able to attribute any prisoner's behavior to character defects or personality maladjustment, while critics of the prison system would have been quick to label the guards as "psychopathic." This tendency to locate the source of behavior disorders inside a particular person or group underestimates the power of situational forces. (Zimbardo et al., 1973, p. 41)

OTHER VIEWS OF SELF-DEVELOPMENT

Guided by Mead's model of the social self, more recent scholars have expanded our understanding of how social environments affect people's self-image. It is also possible that people at different ages organize self-concept differently, suggesting a more complex and lifelong process than that proposed by Mead. Not only is the self-concept an intricate system of abilities, tendencies, and identities formed and reformed over the life course, but it is also an active agent in selecting, interpreting, and shaping its own environment (Rosenberg and Kaplan, 1982).

Yet precisely because the concept of the social self is so basically sociological, it has been criticized for being too narrowly focused on role and interaction. In a classic essay, Dennis Wrong (1961) criticized what he called the "oversocialized" view of self, or personality, that neglects the biological and emotional components of behavior. The purely sociological model cannot easily account for impulsive acts or the range of individual differences within groups of people who have been socialized similarly.

Other critics object to the extreme emphasis on flexibility and change, arguing that some aspects of self are relatively stable throughout the life course. Indeed, recent research indicates that some personality traits do not change greatly with age: friendliness, anxiety level, and openness to new experience (Costa et al., 1987). In contrast, feelings of satisfaction and well-being and of connectedness to others showed little stability across time and were strongly influenced by experiences. In general, predicting adult personality on the basis of childhood behavior would be very risky. One relatively stable trait, however, appears to be what Clausen (1993) calls "planful competence," involving self-confidence, dependability, and intellectual commitment. Emerging in late adolescence, under parental guidance, planful competence prepares the young person to make choices about career, marriage, and life-style that maximize success and will, therefore, lead to high levels of personality continuity.

Until recently, sociological models of the self-process had paid little attention to either **affective** (relating to feelings) or **cognitive** (how people think and process information) factors. The study of emotions and thought processes had been left largely to psychologists, whose work has greatly influenced emerging models in the fields of social psychology and the sociology of emotions. A few of these theories will be briefly reviewed in the following section.

Sigmund Freud and the Control of Impulse

The Austrian physician Sigmund Freud (1856–1939) is best known as the founder of psychoanalysis, which involves both the study of the unconscious motivations and the treatment of symptoms of emotional distress. Although many of his concepts reflect the experience of educated Europeans of the late nineteenth century, several of Freud's insights remain enduring contributions to sociology. We will mention only the most important here: the conflict between the individual and society, the construction of self as a social/psychological process, the role of ego defenses, and the general concept of the unconscious (Kurzweil, 1990).

THE CONFLICT BETWEEN SELF AND SOCIETY.   In the essay *Civilization and Its Discontents* (1930/1962), Freud explores, from a psychological perspective, much the same assumption that underlies sociology in general: that social life is possible only when people can control their behavior. Culture, remember, consists of norms that govern conduct, but humans are also biological organisms with drives and desires. Therefore, a dynamic tension exists between the individual and the collectivity: The individual strives to satisfy basic urges, but cannot survive without the support of others. Social order depends on members of a collectivity being able to forego instant gratification. In other words, as human beings, we are born a bundle of wishes, but if each of us sought to satisfy every need immediately, we could not form the kind of stable groups required for security and well-being. Society—or, as Freud called it, civilization—is based on the control of impulse. Socialization is the process of renouncing (giving up) instant pleasure.

STAGES OF DEVELOPMENT.   According to the Freudian model, these renunciations of instant pleasure take place in a series of emotionally stressful episodes in infancy and childhood. First we must give up the all-embracing comfort of being fed and cuddled, as we are weaned from the breast or bottle. As infants, we can do little except cry a lot, repress anger in the unconscious part of the mind, and learn two of life's most important lessons: Rules are made by others, and life will be full of hard knocks.

Then we must learn to control our bladder and bowels, to become toilet trained, with all the anger brought on by this loss of freedom. As children, we now confront a powerful social system "out there," eventually give up the struggle for control of our body, and deposit another residue of anger into the unconscious. Finally, still in childhood, we must deal with strong and disturbing sexual feelings of either attraction or dislike, originally directed toward our parents. The resolution of this crisis involves renunciation of sexual gratification within the family, the **repression** of unacceptable impulses (placing them below the level of consciousness), and a redirection of sexual feelings toward members of the opposite sex who are not relatives.

Notice that while Freud emphasizes processes within the child's mind (*psyche*), these events take place in a social context, in interactions with adults who represent the wider society. Social/psychological development does not unfold automatically; becoming an adult is an achievement, and not an easy one. The powerful bonds that link the child to its nurturers are used to manipulate guilt feelings, so that fear of losing affection and approval motivate the child, and then the adult, to conform to the expectations of significant others.

But unlike the individual in Cooley and Mead's theories of the social self, Freud's child does not necessarily achieve harmony within the group. Those repressed feelings can bubble up from the unconscious at any time, causing the mental distress that requires the services of a psychoanalyst. The fear of losing control leads us to develop protective mechanisms called **ego defenses.**

> **Affective** factors refer to feelings and emotions
>
> **Cognitive** factors refer to how people think and process information.
>
> **Repression** involves placing unacceptable impulses below the level of consciousness
>
> **Ego defenses** protect the self-image.

THE ROLE OF EGO DEFENSES.   The Freudian psyche has three aspects: (1) the *id,* consisting of impulsive desires; (2) the *superego,* consisting of internalized norms, often called the conscience; and (3) the *ego* that links the self to the real world, mediating the drives of the id and the control of the superego.

Ego defenses are techniques for dealing with impulses that are unacceptable to the self and that could endanger social solidarity. Defenses include denial, repression, blame, displacement of anger onto socially acceptable objects, and rationalization (finding acceptable reasons for thinking or doing the unacceptable). Because we must depend on one another, loss of self-control would have collective as well as personal consequences. And because the Freudian self is always

Defending the Ego: Idealism and Reality at Harvard Law School

What happens to all those idealistic young men and women who enter graduate schools of medicine or law with the expressed goal of serving the most needy? Typically, they become socialized to the very beliefs and behaviors they claim to despise. Such is the "fate of idealism" under the intense pressure of graduate training, especially at elite institutions such as Harvard Law School, whose graduates fill the top ranks of the legal profession.

For students who are politically conservative, there is no conflict between self-image and practicing corporate law. But what about the students who still see themselves as liberals concerned with the well-being of the less fortunate; how can they accept employment in major firms that serve corporate clients (hardly a needy population)? Researchers Robert Granfield and Thomas Koenig (1992) found that such students employed a variety of psychological strate-

gies to defend their ego identity against the charge of selling-out.

The many rationalizations offered included the following: the need to repay a college loan, or to meet family expectations; the belief that they could use the firm's resources to sponsor liberal causes or at least avoid unethical work within the firm; the claim that their new associates were really very moral people, and that the firm was not as unprincipled as most others; and, finally, an attempt to redefine "public interest" to include serving corporate clients.

As the researchers note, professionals are very sophisticated people, so that they can construct extremely imaginative defenses. But even ordinary people must often invent complex reasons or excuses for doing things that conflict with their personal values. How well do your career goals fit your self-image, and how have you reconciled any potential conflict between idealism and reality?

Source: © 1992 by the Society for the Study of Social Problems, *Social Problems*, Vol. 39, pp. 315–331, by permisssion.

somewhat discontent, unable completely to satisfy the body's desires, the ego must constantly be protected from our worst impulses and from challenges to one's image of being a good person (Swanson, 1988).

Erikson and Ego Development

The idea of *psychosocial development* has been taken up by other psychologists who depart from Freud in two directions. First, the newer theories are primarily concerned with the *ego* as an organized set of self-perceptions. The most influential of these post-Freudian theories of life stages and **ego development** is that of Erik Erikson. Erikson extended the stages of personality growth and change to cover the entire life course. By proposing that the life course is composed of a series of challenges that require reorganization of the ego, Erikson opened up the possibility of continual personal change and growth (see Chapter 7 for an extended analysis).

Ego development involves the possibility of change and growth across the life course.

Erikson (1959) described eight stages, each of which involves a person's ability to adapt to life changes.

Stage 1. From experiences with nurturers, the infant develops a sense either of *basic trust* or of *mistrust.*

Stage 2. In the first three years of life, the child learns and practices all kinds of new skills, emerging with a feeling either of *autonomy* (self-regulation) or of *doubt* and *shame* over one's ability to cope with events.

Stage 3. The four- to five-year-old's success in exploring the environment and in dealing with peers can lead to a sense of *initiative* and self-confidence; failure can produce feelings of *guilt.*

Stage 4. Between the ages of 6 and 13, the focus shifts from family to school, where the child can develop the self-concept either of *industriousness* or of *inferiority.*

Stage 5. In adolescence, the developmental task is *identity formation,* and failure to create a firm sense of self leads to *confusion* about one's identity.

Stage 6. The great challenge of young adulthood is to establish stable love relationships, and the outcome is *intimacy* or *isolation* and loneliness.

Stage 7. Citizenship, work, and family formation are the primary tasks of mature adulthood, and they lead to *generativity,* in contrast to the *self-absorption* and *stagnation* of those who do not contribute to the well-being of others.

Stage 8. Even the end of life poses a developmental challenge: finding continuity and meaning in one's life—*integrity*—or being unable to break out of isolation and self-absorption, giving way to *despair.*

Erikson's eight stages are best understood as ideal types, that is, as descriptions of the characteristics of the very best or the very worst outcomes. Few people go through these precise experiences at just the right ages. Most of us meet life's expected and unexpected challenges with only partial success or failure—some self-confidence, a little guilt, general satisfaction, and continued anxiety.

Although Erikson's model is presented as basically psychological, note that his transition points coincide with major changes in the person's *social* environment and the sequence of status changes. Each

For Erikson, the years near the end of one's life pose the developmental challenge of finding continuity and meaning in one's life—that is integrity. Members of four generations of this family come together to celebrate a birthday and to affirm family ties.

change provides the opportunity for reorganization of the self because the person now interacts with different role partners who have new expectations in a new situation.

Central to Erikson's model is the concept of **ego identity,** a sense of continuity and sameness in the self across time and in different situations. Symbolic interactionists have long been fascinated by the question of how, if identities are socially constructed, people can maintain an image of continuity of the self when roles are constantly changing. Working in the area of overlap between sociology (collective realities) and psychology (internal meanings), a growing number of social psychologists are mapping out the ways in which the self is both product and producer of group processes (Howard and Callero, 1991).

Ego identity refers to a sense of continuity and sameness in the self-concept across time and situations.

Older adults do not typically lead lives of isolation or despair. A strong sense of self is based in part on life-long friendships. In this picture, graduates of Vassar College enjoy their fortieth reunion.

Piaget and Cognitive Development

The concept of **cognitive development** refers to changes over time in how people understand and organize their experience (*cogito* is Latin for "I think"). The key figure in this field is Jean Piaget (1896–1980), a Swiss psychologist who spent a lifetime observing children at play and listening to their answers to his questions. From his effort to see the world through their eyes, Piaget concluded that children of different ages had very different ways of processing information and solving problems. These new mental skills emerge in part through the maturing of the child's mind and in part as a result of interaction with other people and the surrounding culture.

Cognitive development refers to change over time in how people understand and organize their experiences.

Moral reasoning involves the application of standards of fairness and justice.

In this view, cognitive development does not unfold automatically with increasing age, and it is not a simple reflection of the child's social environment. Rather, as children experience situations or receive information that does not fit comfortably into existing structures of thought, they have the opportunity to rearrange their view of the world and produce a new way of thinking. Cognitive growth is a product of the child's active efforts to cope with new information.

For example, in the games of marbles that Piaget observed, very young children accepted the rules as absolute and unchangeable; slightly older youngsters were more flexible, able to modify the rules to fit changed circumstances; and at a more advanced age, they realized that the rules were based on common agreement and that whole new games could be invented. Notice how this formulation echoes the basic sociological insight that *rules and roles are socially constructed.* Piaget's most cognitively developed subjects were actually amateur sociologists.

Not all children will have the same growth-producing experiences, and some may reach adulthood with limited cognitive sophistication. You probably know adults whose rigid thinking resembles that of a Piagetian three-year-old. And as the example of Genie and other isolated children reminds us, environmental stimulation and supportive feedback are all essential to physical as well as mental growth. One recent large-scale study of teenage mothers and their first-born children found that the most important predictors of the child's cognitive ability were the mother's own intellectual skills and amount of mental stimulation provided in the home (Moore and Snyder, 1991).

Although Piaget places the growing child within a web of relationships, he still retains the psychologist's focus on the individual. A more sociological view is suggested by observations of children's peer groups. It is through their shared activities that children collectively create their peer culture and socialize one another (Corsaro, 1992). That is, socialization does not take place privately, within an isolated mind, but as part of a creative group process in which the children together confront and cope with the adult world (see also Thorne, 1993).

Not only did Piaget find shifts in the complexity of thinking, but he also noted changes in **moral reasoning,** that is, the way in which children evaluated

The devleopment of self involves taking on the role of others. Through play and games, children internalize the expectations of parents, peers, and other agents of socialization. What are these 3 and 4 year olds learning, and how useful will these lessons be in the 21st century?

situations and made judgments about right and wrong. As the mind is able to deal with increasingly complex information, so also do we learn about such abstractions as fairness and justice.

Kohlberg, Gilligan, and Moral Development

Inspired by Piaget's work, Lawrence Kohlberg has spent several decades conducting longitudinal and cross-cultural studies of "the child as moral philosopher." In essence, Kohlberg (1981) proposed that, given the necessary experience and stimulation, children go through a sequence of six stages in their ability to handle moral problems.

Between the ages of 4 and 10, the child's sense of good or bad is linked to obedience to those in positions of power, based on fear of punishment. In adolescence, conformity to the rules is accompanied by the belief that the existing social order is right and true and deserves to be defended. But with the appropriate moral education, older children and young adults can reach the two highest stages of reasoning, in which considerations of community welfare, general rights, and universal ethical principles—such as justice, equality, and the dignity of individuals—become the guides of action and self-judgment.

Although cross-cultural studies show striking similarities for the early stages of reasoning among children in other complex societies, Kohlberg has been criticized for an ethnocentric bias in defining the highest good as essentially the values enshrined in the work ethic, individual rights, and absolute values (Cortese, 1990; Snarey, 1987).

The major criticism of Kohlberg's work, however, is that he based his theory on data from boys and men. When Kohlberg discovered early in his work that girls did not make judgments in the same way as boys, he, like Freud and Piaget before him, simply assumed that females were somewhat deficient in moral reasoning, and he proceeded to construct a model of "human development" from the male experience. While teaching with Kohlberg, the psychologist Carol Gilligan noticed that many women students were dropping his course, and she decided to find out why.

IN A DIFFERENT VOICE.   Gilligan's research showed that girls and women brought a different set of values to their moral judgments than did men (Gilligan, 1982; Gilligan et al., 1989). For example, in one of Kohlberg's dilemmas, respondents are asked whether or not a man named Heinz should steal a medicine he cannot afford to buy, to save the life of his dying wife. Males approached the problem in terms of abstract standards of right or wrong, saying, for example, that laws must be followed without exception because they ultimately protect all members of the society. In other words, boys and men distanced themselves

from the particular people and from the emotional aspects of the dilemma. In contrast, girls and women wondered about the interpersonal consequences to Heinz, his wife, their children, with minimal emphasis on universal norms.

According to Kohlberg's scoring system, the females' answer would rank at about Stage 3, whereas the males' would be at Stage 6. But, asks Gilligan, by what standard is an "ethic of care" a lower level of moral development than an "ethic of rights"? Or separation a higher value than connectedness? Are these not just two different ways to approach a moral dilemma, with the male pattern rated higher by male researchers? If such gender differences are not innate, but the product of socialization and of life experiences, then they are changeable. If men were to raise children, they would think in terms of attachments, and if women had to spend their lives competing for occupational status, they would think in terms of individual rights. And, indeed, subsequent studies have found minimal sex differences in cognitive development in modern societies (Greeno and Maccoby, 1986; Snarey, 1987).

The theories discussed in this section of ego development, psychosocial stages, cognition, and moral reasoning—are all concerned with processes going on within the individual, even though prompted by events in the social environment. However, there is also an area of psychological research on learning that is not primarily concerned with egos, emotions, feeling, or the inner workings of the psyche.

B. F. Skinner and Behaviorism

Behaviorists, as the name makes clear, concentrate on behavior: observable and measurable actions. The behaviorist who most influenced sociologists is B. F. Skinner (1904-1990). Applying to humans the findings from his years of experiments on pigeons and other laboratory animals, Skinner viewed behavior as shaped by the manipulation of rewards: When an action is rewarded, it is likely to be repeated; when it is not rewarded, it is less likely to be repeated. If a change in behavior is desired, the easiest way to achieve it is to manipulate the conditions under which a reward is available. The sociological implications of Skinner's experiments are one source of contemporary exchange theory and rational choice theory (Homans, 1961; see Chapter 1). These implications are best understood by the concept of the *Skinner box.*

> **Behaviorism** concentrates on the study of observable activity as opposed to reported or inferred mental and emotional processes.

SKINNER BOXES.   Skinner achieved some notoriety in the 1940s by tending his infant daughter for part of the day in a completely controlled environment that became known as the **Skinner box.** (The child, incidentally, not only survived but thrived, contrary to the expectations of many.) The concept of the environment as a box has important sociological applications. Although humans, unlike pigeons, construct and modify their own environments, they, like pigeons, base later actions on a knowledge of what happened before. Social structures can be thought of as Skinner boxes, in which people act within a system of rewards received and withheld. It is important to note again that punishments are never as effective as the manipulation of rewards in producing behavioral change.

The **Skinner box** is a completely controlled environment.

The traditional behaviorist approach is disturbing to many sociologists, who claim that the model is too mechanical, overlooking the fact that people are not passive reactors to an impersonal environment but are active participants in creating and interpreting their situations. Nonetheless, almost all agree that choices take place within a context (matrix) of benefits and costs. Because not all social actors perceive costs and benefits in the same way, or have similar resources to draw on, the task of the sociologist is to reconstruct the cost–benefit matrix for people with different degrees of social power (Pescosolido, 1992). People are not pigeons, but we do have memories and expectations.

SOCIALIZATION ACROSS CULTURES AND THE LIFE COURSE

The Cultural Factor

As described in Chapter 3, each culture is a selection of traits from the range of human possibilities. Some cultures, such as ours, place high value on individualism; others, such as the People's Republic of China, emphasize obligations to the group. Typically, also, one type of personality is desired for females, another for males; one set of traits for children, another for adults, and even a third for the elderly.

SOCIOLOGY AROUND THE WORLD

Culture, Social Structure, and Personality

The idea that cultural ideals are reflected in social structures that then produce certain kinds of personality traits is one of the most interesting and problematic in the social sciences. In the 1940s and 1950s, the concept of "national character" was an intellectual fad, spurred by a need to understand the behavior of our enemies in World War II. Landmark publications from this period include analyses of the "authoritarian personality" characteristic of Germans (Adorno et al., 1950) and of the combination of delicacy and brutality of the Japanese—the "chrysanthemum and the sword" (Gorer, 1945; Benedict, 1946).

Even earlier, the anthropologist Margaret Mead (1928) sought to link child-rearing practices and national character in her comparative study of adolescence in the Samoan Islands and the United States. Although much of this early work was impressionistic and overgeneralized, it left one important legacy: an appreciation of the influence of cultural values on the way in which children are raised and taught, which, in turn, affects adult personality.

Earlier in this chapter, you read about how the features of a parent's job affect personality traits such as creativity and self-direction and lead to child-rearing practices that reproduce these characteristics in their children. In another study of child-rearing practices in 93 nonindustrial societies, the relationship between father and child was the most important variable in explaining cultural-level differences in displays of male power: In societies where father–child relations were most distant and impersonal, men are likely to engage in acts of aggression and sexual superiority (Coltrane, 1992). In contrast, where fathers are expected to have close and warm relationships with their sons, open displays of male power are rare.

The content and organization of schools is another structural variable that reflects cultural values and encourages the development of certain personality traits. In China, for example, where the culture supports loyalty to the group over the individual, preschool children play, learn, and even go to the bathroom in small groups. The American preschooler, in contrast, is both encouraged to be an individual yet sharply disciplined for breaking the rules, producing the particular tension between self and society so characteristic of our culture (Tobin et al., 1989). The Japanese preschooler has an entirely different experience; there is a sharp break between the undisciplined freedom a child enjoys at home and the demands of obedience first encountered in school (Peak, 1991). Japanese teachers depend heavily on the manipulation of rewards rather than on physical punishment for the internalization of the norms. In adulthood, Japanese tend to be more self-disciplined and Chinese to be more group-oriented than their American peers.

Whereas earlier investigations of national character were influenced by a Freudian emphasis on the effects of breast-feeding and toilet training, the newer research examines broader patterns of socialization in the home and school to trace specific links between cultural values, structural practices, and personality traits (White, 1993).

This variety of personality styles is possible because each culture, through its symbol system, creates a particular way of thinking, reinforces certain emotions, and shapes the self-image of its members. The cultural blueprint also determines socialization practices that produce the desired personality types (Mandell et al., 1990).

Adult Socialization

Socialization in childhood cannot prepare a person for the many different roles of adulthood in a modern industrial society. Just think of the major role changes of early adulthood: graduation from school, entry into an occupation, marriage, parenthood, community and civic involvements. These changes require **desocialization** (learning to give up a role) and **resocialization** (learning important new norms and values). Each major role change carries with it the potential for a reorganization of the self.

How many times have you said of someone, "How he's changed since he has married" or "That job certainly made a new person of her" or "My mother's impossible now that she's retired"? These are not new people, of course, but the same people undergoing important role transitions. Their way of life has been altered and so, accordingly, has their view of themselves and their way of dealing with others. Under conditions of stress that threaten one's reflected self-esteem, people will make a conscious effort to rework their "self"—and with sufficient need and support, many will succeed (Kiecolt, 1994).

The transitions of middle and late life have often been thought of as "crises." It was long assumed, for example, that women in midlife are especially vulnerable because they have lost their mother role and that men in retirement are particularly unhappy at the loss of the worker role. Research, however, does not bear out these predictions, which are based on assumptions about the necessity of parenting to women and of work to men. In fact, most women actually enjoy their freedom from child rearing, particularly if they are employed. Many men look forward eagerly to retirement, and those who can afford it are leaving the labor force at increasingly earlier ages (see Chapter 7).

Most role transitions in adulthood are fairly predictable and can be eased by anticipatory socialization. It also helps if one's friends are going through similar status changes. Just as the peer group of adolescence provides support for role learning at an earlier age, the friends of adulthood help us adjust to later changes. It is the unexpected "off-time" transitions, such as early widowhood, that are difficult to handle (Neugarten and Hagestad, 1983).

Reflections on the Nature of the Self

Each culture and historical era has its view of the essential nature of the child and, consequently, of the adult. The Puritans assumed that children were little savages who needed to have evil impulses beaten out of them. In the 1940s and 1950s, under the influence of Freudian psychology, Americans believed that childhood experiences left an indelible mark on the adult psyche. Since the 1960s, in contrast, it has become fashionable for adults to attempt to overcome these childhood limitations through self-improvement therapies, self-help groups, or weekends in the wilderness (Simonds, 1992).

Desocialization is learning to give up a role.

Resocialization is learning important new norms and values.

Professional opinion has also changed over time, from an emphasis on traits fixed at birth to the idea of biologically determined stages of development, and finally, today, to a recognition of the essential changeability and flexibility of personality traits throughout life. Childhood may be the most intense period of socialization—there is so much to learn about society and self—but it is only the beginning of a lifelong process.

Neither can behavior be understood apart from its context. The earlier "either/or" debates over the relative effects of nature (biology) and nurture (socialization) have been replaced by a more sophisticated understanding of the interplay between individual tendencies and the social environment, whereby each affects the other in a complex feedback loop. As sociologists we are most concerned with examining the situational determinants of behavior yet must be careful not to minimize the self as an active interpreter and shaper of one's own experiences (Kagan, 1994).

SUMMARY

1. Socialization is the two-fold process through which a person internalizes the culture and develops a sense of self. Both are learned in interaction with other people, through words and gestures.

2. The evolutionary base of socialization is the physical helplessness of the human infant and our later emotional dependency on others for approval, affection, and validation.

3. Agents of socialization provide information, feedback, and social supports for role learning. The most important socializers are parents and peers and, in modern society, teachers and the

mass media. Peer socialization is necessary for the transition to adulthood.

4. One of the most important subcultural differences in socialization patterns is based on parental occupation, producing either a traditional or modern approach to childrearing that leads to different cognitive styles. Parents also tend to allow sons greater freedom to explore the world than is permitted to daughters.

5. In general, manipulation of rewards is a more powerful and long-lasting shaper of behavior than is punishment.

6. The self is also a social product, shaped through the same socialization experiences by which the culture is internalized. Charles Horton Cooley's "looking glass self" captures the idea of seeing one's self through the reflected reactions of role partners.

7. For George Herbert Mead, the social self is based on the unique human capacity for taking the role of the other toward oneself, through play and games. This perspective is elaborated in Erving Goffman's work on self-presentation and impression management.

8. The affective dimension of self-image has been analyzed by psychologists, including Sigmund Freud, who focused on the tension between inner desires for immediate personal gratification and the self-control required for a stable social environment.

9. Erik Erikson expanded the concept of identity development to encompass the entire life course, with emphasis on the set of self-perceptions called the ego. Major role transitions offer an opportunity to reorganize the self.

10. Cognitive development refers to changes in the way people process information over time. Jean Piaget proposed a developmental theory of cognitive growth from his observations of childrens' changing cognitive styles.

11. Lawrence Kohlberg extended Piaget's analysis to the study of moral development, that is, stages in the capacity for making judgments of right and wrong—an "ethic of rights" based on data from boys and men.

12. To correct Kohlberg's male bias, Carol Gilligan proposed an alternative model of moral judgment based on the experiences of girls and women—an "ethic of care."

13. The behaviorist approach to human learning, associated with B.F. Skinner, stresses the context of costs and benefits within which decisions are made and remembered.

14. Socialization practices vary by culture, as each society tends to develop childrearing techniques that produce the appropriate adult personality.

15. Socialization is a life-long process, as long as there are new roles to learn and old ones to relinquish. Some traits show relative stability across the life course, but most are flexible and responsive to experience.

SUGGESTED READINGS

Adler, Patricia A., and Peter Adler, eds. *Sociological Studies of Child Development: A Research Annual.* Vol. 5. Greenwich, CT: JAI Press, 1993. An annual publication of the latest and most useful articles dealing with the study of children and child development from a sociological perspective.

Burkitt, Ian. *Social Selves: Theories of the Social Formation of Personality.* London: Sage, 1991. Fine coverage of the relevant theories of the self and its relationship to society.

Charmaz, Kathy. *Good Days, Bad Days: The Self in Chronic Illness and Time.* New Brunswick, NJ: Rutgers University Press, 1991. A sensitive account of the issues involved in chronic illness and its impact on self-identity.

Duetscher, Irwin, Fred P. Pestello, and H. Frances G. Pestello. *Sentiments and Acts.* Aldine De Gruyter, 1993. This book updates and expands the classic sociological analysis of the relationship between what we say and what we do.

Hewitt, John P. *Dilemmas of the American Self.* Philadelphia: Temple University Press, 1990. This insightful book explores stability and change in the American social character and identity.

Morris, Brian. *Western Conceptions of the Individual.* Providence, RI: Berg, 1991. A clearly written introduction to the philosophical and social theories of the individual.

Parcel, Toby L. and Elizabeth G. Menaghan. *Parents' Jobs and Chldren's Lives.* Hawthorne, NY. Aldine De Gruyter, 1994. The authors discuss the effects of parental working conditions on children's cognitive and social development.

Taylor, Ronald L. *African-American Youth: Their Social and Economic Status in the United States.* Westport, CT: Praeger Publishers, 1994. The book shows the increasing polarization of Black youth into haves and have nots.

Zelizer, Viviana. *Pricing the Priceless Child: The Changing Values of Children.* Revised Edition. Princeton, N.J.: Princeton University Press, 1994. An important historical and sociological contribution to our understanding of the place of children in American society.

Conformity, Deviance, and Social Control

hat do these very different people have in common?

Rigoberta Menchú, winner of the Nobel Peace Prize
Robbie Beale, a British skinhead
Saki, a 500-pound Japanese Sumo wrestler
The class nerd in high school
Donald Trump, a very wealthy businessman
Hedi Fleiss, the "Hollywood Madam"

Each of these individuals in some way violates the definition of "normal"—Donald Trump by great wealth; Saki by exceptional size; Rigoberta Menchú, an uneducated Guatemalan Indian, by reaching the highest level of international respect; Robbie Beale, a working-class lad who has become a violent racist; the high school student who is ridiculed for placing a higher value on getting good grades than on having a good time; and the high-class madam.

Behavior or characteristics (both ascribed and achieved) that depart from the approved, expected, or statistical norm are what sociologists call **deviant**. If we think of the norms as defining a band of acceptable conduct or appearance, that which falls outside the band is, by definition, nonnormative, or deviant. The Latin *via* means *"road,"* and deviance is literally "off the beaten path" (Figure 6-1).

Although this definition covers exceptionally meritorious conduct, the general tendency is to use the term *deviant* to describe socially *disapproved* or extremely unusual behavior. Deviance that falls within the definition of criminal behavior will be discussed in Chapter 17. In this chapter we examine how conformity and deviance are socially constructed; the functions and dysfunctions of deviance; the kinds of people most likely to be considered deviant; and how authorities respond to nonconformity.

Figure 6.1 Deviant 〉〉 Normative 〉〉 Deviant

STRUCTURING CONFORMITY

Which line, A, B, or C, matches the standard in Figure 6-2? If you were alone when you looked at these lines, you would correctly guess "B," but if you were in a group that unanimously selected "C," it is likely that you would change your original perception and say "C." How can a person deny the clear evidence of one's eyes? All too easily, because to be human is to depend on others for a sense of reality.

In this classic experiment, after having answered correctly while alone, a naive subject was placed in a group of other students, all of whom had been coached to agree on an incorrect answer, after which a majority of subjects changed their original opinion (Asch, 1956). As you might expect, manipulating the

Standard Line ——————
Line A ——————
Line B ——————
Line C ——————

Which line (A,B, or C) is the same length as the Standard Line?

Figure 6.2 In an experiment, naive subjects were asked whether line A, B, or C matched the standard line on top.
Source: Adapted from Asch, 1956.

experimental conditions will modify the outcome; for example, having one other nonconforming person in the group dramatically reduces the probability of changing one's mind. Changers were primarily motivated by a fear of appearing weird or difficult, as well as a desire to win the approval of peers (Scheff, 1988).

If this is so for something as seemingly obvious as the length of a line, how much more difficult it must be to resist group definitions of less clear-cut events, such as values, beliefs, and norms. Because social life is possible only when the behavior of most people most of the time is predictable, there are powerful pressures toward conformity to expectations. But life is not lived in a laboratory, and despite all the societal and personal benefits of conformity, none of us is so perfectly socialized as to follow all the rules all of the time. Deviance is a fact of social life, as are efforts to control it.

> **Deviant behavior** refers to behavior that departs from approved, expected, and generally held norms.
>
> **Prescriptive norms** dictate what is expected.
>
> **Proscriptive norms** govern forbidden conduct.

Constructing the Norms

As noted in Chapters 3 (culture), 4 (social structure), and 5 (socialization), norms are collective constructions, reflecting the specific experience of social groups. By defining appropriate role relationships, the norms account for predictability and stability in social systems.

As we saw in Chapter 3, some norms are more important than others: *laws* are rules essential to collective survival; *mores* set standards of ethical conduct; and the *folkways* are traditional customs. The strength of the norm is measured by the severity of sanctions; that is, the collective response. Norms are also either **prescriptive** ("thou shalt") or **proscriptive** ("thou shalt not"), with violations of proscriptions typically more severely punished than failure to observe prescriptive norms.

Yet you have also learned that norms are essentially arbitrary, a selection from the full array of human pos-

Behavior or characteristics that depart from expected norms are called deviant. Each of these persons violates the definition of normal in some way—Donald Trump, the wealthy businessman; Rigoberta Menchú, a poor Guatemalan peasant who won the Nobel Peace Prize; and Heidi Fleiss, who ran a high-class prostitution business.

sibilities, neither engraved in our genes nor sent from on-high, although we are brought up to believe that our way of life is both "natural" and "sacred." Furthermore, every time a norm is established, another set of activities—the nonnormative—is automatically created: unacceptable behavior, or deviance. Deviance is behavior that violates generally accepted standards and can be defined only with reference to conformity. In one sense, the two are bound together in that one cannot exist without the other, like two sides of a coin.

Constructing Deviance

When the circus was invented, so was the sideshow (Doob, 1971). The major function of the sideshow is to reassure viewers of their own normality while holding up to ridicule people who are extremely different—taller, shorter, fatter, uglier. It is norms of beauty that define what is called ugly, as can be seen in societies where men and women whose bodies have been ritually scarred are considered extremely attractive, and the typical *Vogue* model would be a wallflower.

But the line between normative and deviant is continually shifting. At one time or another in the United States, all of the following activities, currently considered within the range of normal, were sufficiently deviant to warrant imprisonment: printing a book, claiming that the earth was round, not attending church, selling food on Sunday, and prizefighting.

Conversely, although people who are thought to consort with Satan are still considered dangerous, they are no longer burned at the stake. Many behav-

iors that are harshly condemned in America today were once considered relatively normal. Opium-based narcotics, for example, were widely available in syrups advertised in family magazines earlier in this century, and the original Coca-Cola contained a small amount of cocaine for medicinal purposes. Possibly, more Americans were addicted to narcotics in the nineteenth century than at the present, typically a middle-class middle-aged white married woman hooked on over-the-counter medications. Another high-use population was children, for whom soothing syrups laced with tranquilizing drugs were frequently prescribed (Douglas and Waksler, 1982).

In contrast, the image of the typical American addict today is much less respectable—poorer, dark-skinned, and living in a high-crime neighborhood—and drug use has been redefined as a grave social menace and criminal act. The same law enforcement energy has not been directed at another high-risk category—doctors, nurses, and pharmacists with ready access to "legal" (prescription) drugs. Thus, while the effects of drug use may not differ, the ways in which addiction is defined, tolerated, and controlled will vary from one population to another.

In other words, *both conformity and deviance are socially constructed.* It is important to remember that ideas and actions do not exist as good or bad in themselves: What is acceptable or unacceptable—a social problem or nothing to worry about—is the outcome of a struggle among competing groups over the power to define right and wrong. Just think of the conflict today in the United States over the definition

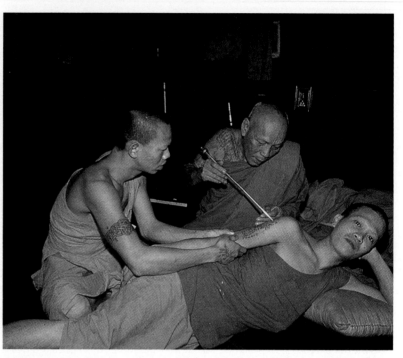

Cross cultural beauty: Every culture develops norms regarding the altering of physical appearance. As seen here, a Thai monk is undergoing ritual scarring, while a woman from Burma wears a collar to elongate her neck. How do Americans alter their appearance to adhere to cultural norms of beauty?

of abortion: Is it an acceptable exercise of personal choice or a form of murder?

Although it is always tempting to locate deviance within the individual—a moral flaw or a sickness of mind or body—sociologists view deviance not as a quality of the person but as a result of how the behavior is evaluated by others. Consider the case of marijuana, the meaning of which varies from one society to another and from one historical moment to another. In India, where the Hindu religion forbids the use of alcohol, a liquid form of marijuana mixed with fruit (*bhang*) is freely served at wedding feasts. In contrast, an American wedding will feature vast amounts of alcohol, with pot smoking considered deviant enough to be done in secret.

Defining marijuana use as a *social problem* requiring public sanctions is relatively recent. Up to the 1930s, marijuana was a common component of non-prescription medications for everything from epilepsy to tooth decay and was not considered addictive. But once the Federal Bureau of Narcotics (FBN) was established in 1930, it needed a mission, and marijuana was a logical target because there were no powerful business interests to oppose (unlike liquor, which had just won the prohibition war). The FBN began a media campaign to convince the American public of the evils of dope (including that great film classic *Reefer Madness*), thus transforming a relatively harmless drug into a symbol of evil and threat to social order (Becker,

The ingestion of some drugs condemned harshly today was quite acceptable 80 to 100 years ago. When Coca Cola first came on the market, the "real thing" ingredient was cocaine, and when aspirin was first marketed in the U.S., one of its ingredients was heroin.

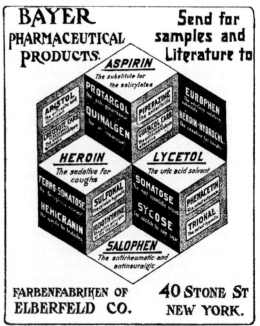

From Normative to Deviant in One Puff

The history of smoking in America illustrates the shifting boundary between normative and deviant. In the 1920s, a period of cultural liberation similar to the 1960s, smoking cigarettes was a symbol of modern sophistication for women, signifying freedom from the sexually restrictive mores of the early twentieth century. If you watch movies from the 1930s and 1940s, you can barely see the actors for the smoke. For the next two decades, a nonsmoker was considered rather odd, even a bit "square."

But as information about the health risks of smoking became widely known, the normative was slowly transformed into the deviant, redefined as harmful behavior. Today, it is smokers who violate the norms, forced to huddle outside the office building to indulge in their vice and perceived as persons unable to control self-destructive impulses. The people who smoke on television and the movies are clearly the villains. And smoking has now been added to the list of addictive diseases requiring psychiatric treatment, the ultimate step in the social construction of deviance.

In Japan, smoking continues to be widely acceptable and taxes from the sale of cigarettes provide an important source of revenue for the government. Many Japanese youth learn to smoke at an early age and flaunt their habits.

1963). But by the late 1980s, when courts and jails became clogged with minor offenders, the laws regarding marijuana possession were once more changed to decriminalize limited use. In this way, time and place and political considerations influence definitions of normal and abnormal, determining which behaviors are viewed as social problems and which are tolerated.

DURKHEIM'S CONCEPT OF SOCIETAL REACTION.   As Emile Durkheim pointed out a century ago, deviance is not internal to an act but can be recognized only by the external reactions to it (Durkheim, 1893/1964). When a rule of conduct is violated, sanctions are set in motion to oppose the wrong-doer. But what constitutes a violation is a cultural variable. For example, the act of killing a person is called murder only in specific circumstances. It is considered "justifiable homicide" under some conditions and "extreme heroism" when committed by a soldier in wartime: same act, different circumstances. Similarly, throughout most of the world today (and in parts of the United States until recently), a man who found his wife in bed with her lover was justified in killing them both to defend his honor. A wife who shot her husband and his lover would be a cold-blooded killer, because women do not have personal honor and ought not to be allowed to shame their husband: same act, different cultural norms.

As another example, if a wealthy woman and her maid were each caught shoplifting, would their behavior be similarly defined? One suspects that Mrs. Van Arsdale's attorney would claim his client suffered from kleptomania; whereas Masie, the maid, would be a thief, without the luxury of a psychological impulse: same act, different people.

These examples neatly illustrate one of the key insights of the sociological perspective: *All social behavior must be interpreted in context: Who does it, to whom, and under what circumstances.*

SOCIAL FUNCTIONS OF DEVIANCE

Because deviance consists of socially disapproved behavior, it is typically perceived as a threat to social order. But Durkheim also noted the positive functions of nonconformity. To hope to wipe out all sin and waywardness is not only an exercise in futility but actually could be harmful to the health of the society as a whole. Behavior that offends and disturbs us personally can nonetheless have great social value.

Deviance as Unifying Force

In the process of organizing against those who violate the norms, we reaffirm and strengthen our commitment to the rules and to one another. Uniting in righteous anger is a powerful source of cohesion within the society, creating what Durkheim called the *public temper,* a set of shared feelings. Through such a consensus, a common identity is reinforced, as when Americans of all types united in righteous anger against Iraq, and enveloped the country in a sea of yellow ribbons symbolizing our support of military sanctions against a violator of international law.

Deviance as Boundary Setting

Public identification and punishment of deviants strengthens the existing belief system by demonstrating where the line is drawn between "us," the virtuous, and "them," the offenders. **Boundary setting** occurs when the limits of acceptable behavior are made very clear, reducing confusion and stabilizing normative consensus. But because this boundary is continually shifting, some individuals and groups will always be testing its limits through **confrontation** (K. Erikson, 1966). Such confrontations, acts that press the extremes of the boundaries, are essential to reminding the public just where the lines are drawn at any particular moment. For example, television programs have steadily tested the limits of acceptable presentations of sexuality —a line that has shifted greatly in just the last few years.

> **Boundary setting** occurs when shared norms set the limits of acceptable behavior.
>
> **Confrontations** test the limits of acceptable behavior.
>
> Some deviance serves as a **safety valve,** allowing controlled expression.
>
> **Moral entrepreneurs** define what is virtuous and combat the forces of evil.

WITCH HUNTS AS BOUNDARY-SETTING MECHANISMS. In some cases, members of a society undergoing internal crisis will attempt to shore up moral boundaries and unify the collectivity by identifying neglected forms of deviance and pursuing the wrongdoers. This appears to have been the case in the witch hunts in Europe and some New England colonies in the fourteenth through the seventeenth centuries. The search for witches became most intense when church authorities thought they were losing control over their flock and ceased only when even more powerful political figures came under attack (Riforgiato, 1993). Today's witchhunts—for terrorists, subversives, and sinners—also tend to come at times of great threat to the ruling elite (Oplinger, 1990).

Deviance as Safety Valve

All societies must deal with human impulses that threaten to disrupt its essential institutions. Anger, frustration, and inappropriate sexual desires must somehow be siphoned off in relatively harmless ways so that they do not disturb such important systems as the family, the workplace, or school. Thus, some deviant behavior is acceptable because it serves as a **safety valve,** permitting controlled expression of potentially destructive activity. This is the function of "red light" districts in the major cities of the world, in which prostitution and adult sex shops are allowed to flourish even as the mass of citizens unite in righteous condemnation.

Notice that brawling is acceptable as long as it is confined to the parking lot outside the bar. Stock car races and professional wrestling in the United States and soccer games in Europe and South America allow spectators vicariously to play out their more violent impulses: to crash a car or smash an opponent's face. While authorities deplore the overdrinking and fighting in the stands, they permit it rather than have such anger and antisocial behavior displayed at work, school, home, or anti-government marches.

PROSTITUTION AS SAFETY VALVE. The example of prostitution illustrates many of these points: condemned yet tolerated throughout human history in all types of society, possibly the oldest profession (the priesthood being second). What functions are served by prostitution? In many cultures, it preserves the distinction between "good women," whom one marries, and "bad women," those a man sleeps with but doesn't marry— a double standard of morality that permits sexual freedom to men while preserving the integrity of marriage.

Prostitution also allows men the opportunity to explore unconventional sexual practices without emotional involvement and in circumstances where, as the one paying for the service, they can maintain control. For the women who enter the profession, this is a way to make a living in a trade that requires little training or skill. Highly paid prostitutes (call girls) who earn thousands of dollars a week are frequently employed by legitimate business firms as entertainment for important clients. Others are streetwalkers, working for whatever the traffic will bear and increasingly vulnerable to acquired immune deficiency syndrome (AIDS) and other sexually transmitted diseases and violent attacks (E. Miller, 1986). And then there are bored and unhappy teenagers such as Amy Fisher who "turn tricks" to impress schoolmates and dismay their parents.

There are also others who profit from the business: the "pimps" who protect their women, the madams who run "houses of ill repute," the lawyers who defend them, the police who accept bribes, and the people who make a living by condemning sinners and leading crusades against prostitution and pornography. These latter are what sociologists call **moral entrepreneurs,** people who make it their business to define what is virtuous and to defend it by destroying the forces of evil. Some moral entrepreneurs are legiti-

The line between conformity and deviance is ever-shifting. When vast crowds of Germans attended rallies of the Nazi Party in the 1930s (shown at left), persecution of Jews, Gypsies, and homosexuals was a patriotic duty. Today, a revival of Nazi beliefs in the inferiority of nonChristians and nonEuropeans is considered a threat to social order. The rally on the right took place in 1994, a year in which the homes of foreign workers were firebombed by young men shouting Nazi slogans. Same beliefs; different eras.

mate members of the clergy; others are laypersons who have assumed the role of gatekeeper of morality, such as Senator Jesse Helms today. In recent American history, in addition to prostitution and pornography, moral entrepreneurs have fought the demons of drink, dope, communism, and obscenity in art.

Another recent addition to the status set of prostitutes is an organization called COYOTE (Call Off Your Old Tired Ethics). COYOTE advocates repealing laws that criminalize prostitution, redefining sex work as a respectable occupation, and protecting sex workers' rights and health (Jenness, 1990).

Expressing Discontent

A society without deviance would be one in which nothing new ever happened—a clearly dysfunctional situation in which existing patterns remained rigidly in place regardless of other changes in the environment. Deviance is thus the cutting edge of social change, a source of flexibility and vitality as well as strain within the social system.

In most societies, young adults are the vehicle through which discontent with the existing order is expressed. Because they are not yet fully integrated into the larger systems of family and work, young people have greater freedom to challenge norms than do older adults. In most of the world today, movements for social change are largely fueled, if not led, by students who have the time, energy, and intellectual commitment to engage in protest. The only time that American students showed similar tendencies was in the 1960s, leading a youth revolt against the repressive morality and materialistic values of the 1950s. Long hair, casual dress, experimentation with drugs and sex, and campus antiwar demonstrations not only were boundary-testing activities but were attempts to discover a "higher set of values" than money-making and conformity.

> An act is socially bad because society disproves of it [and] the true function of [punishment] is to maintain social cohesion.
>
> —EMILE DURKHEIM (1893/1964), pp. 82, 108.

Predictably, other segments of American society closed ranks in defense of the existing moral boundaries: flag-waving hard hats broke up student demonstrations; college authorities called in the local police; parents and politicians created a public temper of shared moral indignation over the ingratitude of youth; and the National Guard fired real bullets. Order was restored and traditional values reaffirmed, although with some relatively harmless modifications.

The long hair and sloppy clothing could be tolerated, but not the challenge to authority.

Principled Challenges to the Norms

Some expressions of discontent are deliberate attempts to confront the norm setters. For example, the young black college students who defied custom and law in the 1960s by sitting down at a department store lunch counter were making a strong challenge to the boundaries that segregated the races throughout the American South. Their deviance and that of other protesters ultimately brought profound changes to every institutional sphere.

Principled challenges today may be found among antinuclear activists, animal rights crusaders, and both sides of the great debate over abortion in the United States (see Chapter 23). Defying the law carries great risks—not only the scorn typically heaped on deviants but the full weight of the forces of social control.

SOCIAL CONTROL

The term **social control** refers to the planned and unplanned processes by which people are taught, persuaded, or forced to conform to norms. Because the survival of any human group depends on most members behaving in a predictable manner most of the time, rewards for conformity and negative sanctions for deviance are a crucial element of all social systems. Social controls can be either informal or formal. **Informal controls** include those expressions of approval and affection by significant others that are crucial to the internalization of norms in the process of socialization. *Socialization* is every group's first and most powerful defense against deviance, as we saw in Chapter 5. A person's conscience is the most effective and least expensive form of social control. But few of us are ever so thoroughly socialized that we do not deviate from the norms at some time or another. These are the times when informal sanctions from significant others—a raised eyebrow, a slap on the wrist, the silent treatment—can bring us into line. The fear of losing their affection and approval is sufficient to make us think twice about repeated deviance.

Formal Agents

When informal sanctions fail, formal agents of social control may be called on. **Formal agents** are status incumbents specifically charged with enforcing the norms. In our society, such formal agents include mental health professionals, social workers, law enforcement and criminal justice personnel, and religious leaders.

In their role as formal agent of social control, these people manipulate the rewards for conformity and the punishments for deviance. Mental wellness and personal adequacy are measured by the individual's ability to meet the expectations of role partners. The "sick" or "evil" person is the one whose behavior is unpredictable and who thus threatens the stability of the system.

If the unacceptable behavior continues despite warnings and punishments and the loss of significant others, and if that behavior becomes recognized as a clear threat to social order, the final step in the process of social control is to remove that person from the community. This is the function of prisons and mental hospitals—to contain people who cannot otherwise be brought under control. When such menaces are behind bars, conformists are reaffirmed in their virtue, the boundaries of acceptable behavior are clarified, and the norms are reinforced.

Although all societies have networks of informal and formal controls, societies differ in the leeway allowed for various role performances and in the severity of sanctions applied to wrongdoers. Formal control systems can be either repressive or restrained (Currie, 1968). In **repressive** control systems, agents have extraordinary powers to detect and restrain a wide range of behaviors. For example, in Teheran, the capital of Iran, where very conservative religious leaders also control the government, groups of unofficial agents regularly patrol the streets of the city to make certain that women are appropriately veiled and confiscate such immoral objects as alcohol, cigarettes, and tapes of Western pop music (Hedges, 1993).

In contrast, modern Western nations such as Sweden, the Netherlands, and the United States have **restrained** systems of formal controls, characterized by legal protections for personal privacy and by increased tolerance of nonconformity, despite the efforts of moral entrepreneurs. In general, contrary to popular belief, the severity of formal sanctions do not necessarily reduce deviance but only push it underground, which encourages further rule breaking (Aday, 1989). For example, two generations of "thought police" and control over schooling and the

---

Principled challenges are deliberate attempts to confront the norm setters.

Social control refers to planned and unplanned processes to enforce conformity.

Informal controls include expressions of approval and affection by significant others.

Formal agents of social control occupy statuses specifically charged with norm enforcement.

Agents in **repressive** control systems have extensive powers to detect and control many behaviors.

Restrained control systems use less intense control over fewer behaviors.

media in the former Soviet Union not only failed to curb deviance but positively encouraged opposition to the norms. The United States has thus far failed to control drunk driving, largely because of a reliance on criminal law solutions, which have a limited deterrence effect on any form of deviant behavior (Ross, 1992).

Thus, the degree and direction of social change is a product of the interplay between boundary-testing deviance and boundary-maintaining controls. Typically, agents of social control have greater power than the challengers, but the struggle between the two forces is a dynamic aspect of all social systems, coexisting in an uneasy balance at any given moment (Ben-Yehuda, 1990). On the one hand, too much deviance disrupts the ongoing web of social relationships; on the other hand, a society without deviance would be a very dull and ultimately dysfunctional place.

EXPLAINING DEVIANCE

"Why do they do it?" is the first question most Americans ask in the vain belief that finding a single "cause" will both explain why some people are deviant and how to reduce the level of deviance in society. The social science literature is filled with theories of deviance, none of which is completely satisfying. Least satisfactory are those models that attempt to locate deviance within the individual—in that person's genetic makeup or childhood experiences.

Biological and Psychological Models

BIOLOGICAL THEORIES.   Even if scientists were able to isolate a "deviance" gene, or more likely, a number of interacting genetic influences, this cannot explain why certain types of norm violations are common in one time and place and not another or even why the definition of deviant behavior varies. Furthermore, as with any biological factor, the most that can be claimed is a tendency or predisposition to act in a given way; whether a person actually does act that way depends on an array of social variables.

Nonetheless, with regard to criminality, the lure of a single-factor, easily identified marker has produced one discredited theory after another: head shape, bumps on the skull, body size, and abnormal chromosomes. For example, in the 1970s, the discovery of a greater than expected number of men with an extra Y chromosome (i.e., an XYY pattern rather than the normal XY for males) who were in mental hospitals and prisons set off a flurry of speculation that the extra Y was associated with hypermasculinity in the form of antisocial and aggressive behavior. In fact, the chromosome pattern is linked to low intelligence and high height—precisely the type of person most likely to be identified by witnesses and caught by authorities.

Because deviant behavior is so complex, single-factor explanations are of limited use. At the moment, there is little empirical evidence to support the idea that violence is genetically inherited, although biol-

The agents in repressive control systems have wide powers to restrain a wide range of behavior. Defying a repressive law can bring down the full weight of the forces of social control, as demonstrated by the police in the People's Republic of China.

SOCIOLOGY AROUND THE WORLD

Kamikazi Bikers and Teenage Wastelands

In Japan today, the "Yankees" are not Americans but teenagers dressed in elaborate youth culture fashions, members of motorcycle gangs engaged in *bosozoko* riding (Sato, 1991). A *boso* ride is a noisy mass drag race through a populated area, a test of skill and courage, but also of relatively short duration compared with the amount of time spent just cruising around, posturing to the public, showing off to one another, and generally annoying adults. The entire performance is a spectacle, a collective drama in which the youngsters find an identity in an otherwise drab and conforming society. Although they are from stable working- and middle-class homes, and are receiving the standard Japanese education, these young people are not headed for the top of the economic ladder, and they know it. *Boso* is an alternative means to achieving respect and gaining attention—the attention of ordinary citizens. The public has responded by defining *bosozoko* as a grave social problem, which only enhances the *Yankees'* image.

Similarly bored teenagers in lower-income neighborhoods of Australian cities, without the money for elaborate costumes or customized bikes, and unwelcomed in most public spaces, search for a place to hang out, dabble in drugs, and steal automobiles for joy rides, rather like their American counterparts (White, 1990). The sight of gangs of aimless youth has aroused the general public who blame the young people for their lack of marketable job skills. But as long as modern economies fail to produce well-paying or meaningful employment to noncollege youth, teenage deviance will remain a gesture of defiance against their limited horizons.

Thus, it is no surprise that the United States, also, is currently experiencing a "juvenile crime wave." Large sectors of our inner cities offer little hope of decent jobs, even less in the way of stable family life (Hagedorn, 1991; Pinderhughes and Moore, 1993). Politicians and the general public frame the issue in terms of "wild animals" running loose in the streets, irresponsible fathers, and welfare mothers who continue to have children. Rarely mentioned are the structural causes of teenage deviance: the deterioration of housing and schools, the flight of entry-level jobs to other areas, and the overall shift in the economy toward low-paying service employment for noncollege youth (Wilson, 1991; see also Chapter 13). To correct these conditions would take time and tax money.

Under such circumstances, "respect" is won through displays of superior toughness, so that acts of disrespect (being "dissed") can lead to interpersonal violence. But inner-city youth are not the only ones growing up in what they see as a "wasteland," without respect or hope. Many white suburban teenagers flirt with delinquency and drugs for the same reason. Teenage girls, especially, are similar to inner city youth in being relatively powerless with few avenues for success (Gaines, 1992b). For many young women, sex is the only commodity they have to offer in return for attention.

Until young people, male and female alike, have valued roles in modern, consumer-driven societies, we can expect continued high levels of deviance among teenagers, societal responses that attempt to personalize the problem, and a field day for moral entrepreneurs.

Even in New York City's poorest neighborhoods, some youngsters, with the encouragement of parents and teachers, have successfully competed for academic prizes and scholarships. In this case, conformity to societal norms may be deviant behavior in terms of the neighborhhood adolescent subculture.

ogy is linked to conditions such as learning disabilities, nervous system disorders, and physical handicaps that make some people more vulnerable to social problems. These conditions are *not* behavior traits, but features that set a person apart from otherwise "normal" people who respond to the difference in ways that reinforce deviance (Goleman, 1992).

PSYCHOLOGICAL THEORIES.   The belief that deviant behavior is the result of a moral flaw or particular personality disorder is as popular today as in biblical times. In the nineteenth century, physicians confidently identified people who violated the norms as "moral imbeciles," even though their intelligence was not impaired. In this century, a new, presumably more "scientific" vocabulary was introduced: psychopath, sociopath, and antisocial personality (American Psychiatric Association, 1987). The problem here is circular reasoning: the diagnosis is applied to people who have already committed an antisocial act; that is, they are antisocial because they have a certain set of traits, and the proof of the traits is that they committed the acts. The test of any psychological theory is to predict in advance what kind of person will do what, and this has not been accomplished by the use of these concepts.

Other psychological theories focus on childhood experiences that lead to imperfect impulse control. Here, too, predictive power has been limited. Because almost everyone had some unpleasant episodes in childhood, apparently no patterns predict which experiences lead to what specific forms of deviance. Childhood conditions such as those associated with poverty—overcrowding, malnutrition, family violence—are far more important than personality variables. But it can also be argued that people with differing psychological traits will be more or less able to change their environments.

THE EXAMPLE OF LEAD POISONING.   The most productive research today examines the intricate and mutually influencing links among social, biological, and psychological variables. For example, one fairly consistent finding is the link between lead poisoning in childhood and later trouble with the police (Denno, 1990). Obviously, the physical condition of high lead levels in the blood does not "cause" delinquency. Exposure to the lead is a social variable, having to do with the construction and maintenance of low-income housing, while curiosity and hunger will cause some children to put lead flakes in their mouths. Lead poisoning has biological and psychological effects on a child's nervous system, lowering IQ and reducing the ability to control oneself (hyperactivity), which in turn makes school success problematic. School failure translates into a lack of job skills, leading to low wages and spells of unemployment that, in turn, reduce the chances of success in marriage, and so on. About the only sure avenue to survival is illegal activity, in which case some will be able to move into lead-free homes. For those who remain in poverty, the next generation of children will also be exposed to dangerous lead levels, the cycle is repeated, and some researcher will claim to have discovered that deviance is inherited.

Sociological Models

As you are well aware by now our focus as sociologists is primarily the *context of the act and its meaning.*

As shown in Table 6-1, sociological theories vary along two major dimensions: the *level of explanation* (macro or micro) and the *causal focus* (on social origins or social reactions) (Bridges, 1992). This gives us a four-cell table in which the theories to be discussed in this section can be placed .

FOCUS ON ORIGINS.   This approach examines the environmental conditions that make nonconformity likely and rewarding.

Macrolevel.   This is the "big picture" at the level of the entire society or its subsystems, presented in very abstract terms, with an emphasis on structural variables. One early twentieth-century macrolevel explanation of deviance centered on the belief that the poorer neighborhoods of large American cities were characterized by *social disorganization,* as *Gemeinschaft* ties were replaced by impersonal *Gesellschaft* relationships (Park, 1924). Later research showed that such neighborhoods were disorganized only in the eyes of middle-class observers. However, the extreme destruction of inner-city communities brought about by current economic and political trends has revived

TABLE 6-1   A Typology of Theories of Deviance

Level	Focus	
	Social Origins	Social Reaction
Macro (societal level)	Disorganization Anomie Opportunity structure Poverty Deviant subcultures	Conflict models Social control models
Micro (individual's environment)	Social learning Differential association Group controls	Labeling Primary and secondary deviation Stigma Deviant career

From George S. Bridges, Deviance Theories. Adapted with permission of Simon & Schuster/Macmillan Reference from ENCYCLOPEDIA OF SOCIOLOGY, Edgar F. Borgatta, Editor in Chief. Volume 1, pp. 476–487. Copyright © 1992 by Edgar F. Borgatta and Marie K. Borgatta.

concern over the breakdown of institutional supports for the poor who cannot move out (Hagedorn, 1991).

Merton's Anomie Model.   Another early systematic attempt to explain the origins of deviance in macrolevel terms was Robert K. Merton's elaboration of the concept of *anomie* to refer to the "fit" between valued goals (culture) and legitimate means for achieving these (structure).

As shown in Table 6-2, people who accept the approved goals and have access to institutionalized means of achievement tend to conforming behaviors. In contrast, deviant adaptations are likely to occur when support for culturally approved goals is withdrawn or when people are denied access to legitimate avenues of achievement. In the United States, wealth and occupational success are the valued goals, and education, hard work, and honest business practices are the approved means of reaching these goals. *Innovators,* therefore, are those who devise new and typically illegitimate means of achieving success. *Ritualists,* recognizing that fame and fortune are out of reach, measure success by rigid conformity to the rules (as in the example of the bureaucrat who becomes obsessed with the details of the job). The *retreatist* rejects both the socially sanctioned goals and means and drops out—into an alternative life-style, drugs, or mental illness. In contrast, the *rebellious* adaptation links rejection of the current structure with efforts to bring about social change—as in the example of political and religious radicals.

Clearly, the major structural factor in predicting deviant adaptations is poverty. Yet, while most poor people may have to adopt innovative means of survival, only a small proportion actually become official deviants. What are the steps whereby the strains of being unable to achieve valued goals are transformed into visible acts of deviance? Here is where the subcultural environment becomes an intervening mechanism.

As elaborated by Cohen (1955) and others, **delinquent and criminal subcultures** originate in the lack of fit between high hopes for legitimate success and limited means of achievement. The subculture offers friendships and provides alternative and attainable definitions of success (e.g., being cool). As a result of *blocked opportunity structures* (Cloward and Ohlin, 1960), different types of subcultures develop innovative sources of gratification: in criminal activity, acts of violence, or withdrawal into drugs and alcohol.

Microlevel.   Microlevel theories of the social origins of deviance look more closely at the individual's immediate social environment. Assuming that all behavior is learned, but that rejection of the norms requires special conditions, the question becomes, How and under what circumstances does this learning take place? Edwin Sutherland's (1939) influential model of **differential association** can be summarized as follows:

1. Criminal behavior is learned in interaction with others and has no unique biological or genetic basis.
2. It is within primary groups, rather than from the larger society, that one learns motives and techniques for committing crimes, reasons for conforming to or violating particular rules, and what behavior is permissible in which situation.
3. A person becomes a criminal when definitions favorable to the violation of law outweigh the unfavorable ones; that is, one becomes a criminal because more factors support such activity than oppose it.
4. The differential associations most likely to result in criminal behavior are frequent, long-lasting, and intense, and they occur relatively early in life.

Delinquent and criminal subcultures originate in the differences between hopes for legitimate success and limited opportunity for achievement.

The **differential association** model states that deviant behavior is learned in primary groups and involves the same learning processes as nondeviant behavior.

TABLE 6-2   Merton's Typology of Individual Modes of Adaptation to Cultural Means and Goals

Individual Mode of Adaptation		Accepts Cultural Goals	Access to Institutionalized Means of Attainment
Other Adaptations	Conformity	Yes	Yes
	Innovation	Yes	No
	Ritualism	No	Yes
	Retreatism	No	No
	Rebellion	No/but seeks to replace with other goals	No/but seeks to restructure means of attainment

Adapted from permission of The Free Press, a Division of Simon & Schuster from SOCIAL THEORY AND SOCIAL STRUCTURE by Robert K. Merton. Copyright © 1957 by The Free Press; copyright renewed 1985 by Robert K. Merton.

DONNA GAINES

Understanding the Teen Scene

Donna Gaines is a journalist with a doctorate in sociology and a New York state certified social worker. She writes for such publications as the Village Voice, SPIN, *and is the author of* Teenage Wasteland: Suburbia's Dead End Kids *(1992,* HarperCollins Perennial*). She is the organizer and founding Chair of the American Sociological Association Section on Culture and serves on the editorial boards of two interdisciplinary journals. She is currently a research professor at The Institute for Social Analysis at the State University of New York, Stony Brook.*

Vernon Reid, guitarist for *Living Colour,* once said, "People say just to be yourself. But if you really do that, it's the most threatening, subversive thing you can do." That is a sociological statement, a fact. Finding the courage to be yourself is a critical social act. At home, in the family, the neighborhood, at work, and at school, you may feel pitted against the whole of culture and social structure. Sometimes the social order seems designed to kill you, to make you feel worthless. Being who you are and doing what you want with pride and dignity is a political act. People who can't or won't go with the program can be punished, labeled, beaten, jailed, or thrown into a psychiatric hospital. Any cultural outlaw or social outcast

understands this through lived experience. Sociologists understand this through the study of deviance.

I grew up on the south shore of Queens, New York. Bored by high school, I cultivated the fine art of hanging out on the boardwalks, street corners, train stations, and candy stores of Rockaway Beach. Like most of my friends, I tolerated the order of things. I was known in the neighborhood as a problem child, a wild kid. My friends too, were tagged as troublemakers.

Around 1970, I ended up at a local community college, looking for something to do. I started taking sociology courses. I was pleased to learn that activities such as "hanging around" and "making the scene," done purposefully, were useful methods of sociological analysis. The weird feelings that I had taken for granted could be explained as alienation and anomie. Subsequent readings showed me that there have always been marginal people, individuals and small groups who couldn't or wouldn't fit in. Through sociology, I located the tools and the courage to articulate my particular truth. I understood myself historically, as a social being, a member of a race, a sex, a class, as a participant in culture. I saw that my personal experiences were both political and sociological.

Today I work as a "free" or "public" sociologist. I write and speak about popular culture. In recent years, my primary focus has been youth advocacy. During the 1980s, young people were a low national priority, ignored or devalued by adults. Families weren't functioning, schools weren't educating. After high school, only dead-end "shit-jobs" could be found. The media misrepresented American

kids as losers and thugs, dropouts, and dummies.

Youth suicide rates had adults concerned and alarmed. But instead of examining the harsh social realities American kids were facing, the suicides were blamed on youth subculture—mainly heavy metal, Satan, drugs, and alcohol. Nobody was listening to the kids themselves.

In 1987, after a teenage suicide pact in Bergenfield, New Jersey, involving four kids labeled as "burnouts," I wanted to get the story on youth suicide from the point of view of young people. I wasn't satisfied with the view that they committed suicide because they came from messed up families, used drugs, listened to heavy metal or were involved in Satanism.

I needed to understand the social meaning of the label "burnout" in the high school and the town where the kids lived, and to understand the social context of the music they liked—thrash and heavy metal. How did their scene and subcultural activities protect them from the negative effects of being outcasts in their community? What possibilities did they see for meaningful lives, interesting jobs, or true love. I observed how young people carved out meaning and dignity, and how crucial music, friends, and cars were to their survival.

Sociological knowledge helps us to expose the doctrine behind the veil, to question the "taken for granted" world. We come to view ourselves as historical actors operating within a context much greater than ourselves. We can see who we are in the world we live in, where we came from, and where we can go. This is our gift in passing sociology on to you.

Formal enforcement of the law can provide a powerful social control. Why might people pursue criminal activity, as did this drug dealer, knowing they might get caught? What other factors are at work?

5. Learning criminal behavior is the same as learning any other behavior. For example, people who value money could become robbers, stockbrokers, or physicians. There is thus *no* value or need pattern unique to criminals as opposed to noncriminals. A person becomes criminal when the reinforcement for lawbreaking is stronger than the reinforcement for remaining law abiding.

Differential association is one variety of *social learning theory* based in part on the behaviorist model described in Chapter 5. Most simply, behavior is conditioned by the environment in which it occurs and the responses from others that either encourage or discourage repeat performances (Akers, 1985). People learn deviant definitions and acts in specific situations just as they learn conforming beliefs and behaviors. The deviant subculture rewards its members with respect and honor that the rest of society would withhold. The power of significant others to grant or withhold affection, approval, and validation is just as strong in nonconforming as in conforming subcultures. Remember also that punishment is not a very effective mechanism of social control; to change behavior, the manipulation of rewards is far more powerful.

From a different, and basically *functional* perspective, *social control theories* (Gottfredson and Hirschi, 1990) emphasize the investments that most people have in conformity. This is, after all, what brings the greatest rewards in self-respect and in the eyes of others. To the degree that people remain attached to mainstream institutions and are embedded in conforming subcultures, they have a powerful stake in the stability of these systems. But when bonds to conventional norms and social structures are weakened, individuals will be "structurally available" for recruitment into a deviant subculture.

The three crucial links in control theory are (1) ties to parents, (2) involvement in conforming activities, and (3) a commitment to the norms. Parents also set an example by their own behavior. For example, adults who are smokers will have great difficulty convincing their adolescent children to conform to the norm of nonsmoking, regardless of the closeness of the parent–child bond (Foshee and Bauman, 1992).

In addition, control theory incorporates an element of the rational choice model in proposing that people weigh the benefits and risks of conforming (Matsueda and Heimer, 1987). It is not the severity but the certainty of sanctions that have the greatest effect. If the probability of being caught is low, it matters little that the penalty is life imprisonment.

FOCUS ON SOCIETAL REACTION. This is the area in which sociologists have made their most impressive contributions to the study of deviance.

Macrolevel. The macrolevel study of reactions to deviance focuses on the power structure of the society as a whole: Who has the power to define the norms and, therefore, activity that falls outside the acceptable?

From a *conflict* perspective, definitions of deviance and agents of social control are directed primarily at threats to the existing power structure (Liska, 1992). For example, a case could be made that the U.S. "war on drugs" has been waged largely against poor and black Americans as a means of containing the problems of urban slums (Zimring and Hawkins, 1992). The really big profiteers in the international drug trade are the foreign leaders supported by the American government over the past two decades as allies against communism, while our prisons are overcrowded with "mules," South American peasants hired to bring in small amounts (Marshall, 1992; Weinstein, 1993). Throughout American history, "illegal" drugs are those used primarily by socially threatening subgroups, while the recreational pastimes of the white and wealthy are rarely so described (Kinder, 1992). In 1994, for example, the penalties for dealing and smoking crack cocaine were many times harsher than the penalties for selling and sniffing powder cocaine. The two substances are chemically identical; the major difference is that crack is smoked by poor minority males and the powder is sniffed by relatively affluent whites. Our prisons are full of crack addicts, while the sniffers—if caught—are more likely to be on probation in the suburbs.

In any event, the United States is not alone among modern industrial societies in finding that rounding up street addicts is a lot easier, cheaper, and more pleasing to ordinary citizens than facing the costs of creating jobs and rebuilding community in disintegrating urban centers (Dorn et al., 1992). Social controls are most strongly imposed on people perceived as most threatening, who are typically of a different race or culture from the people in power. In the United States, because minority races are more visible and seen as more threatening than similarly violent white people, they are more likely to be killed by the police (Liska and Yu, 1992).

Despite periodic drug busts (Such as this one in Miami) and pronouncements about wars on drugs, more than 25 million Americans use cocaine and crack. Why is the war on drugs not being won?

SOCIAL POLICY

Saying "No" to the War on Drugs

Is it time to wave the white flag in the "war on drugs" and decriminalize the use of currently illegal substances? Two decades after President Richard M. Nixon opened the hostilities, the annual anti-drug budget has risen from $3 billion to almost $13 billion; arrest rates have doubled, adding hundreds of billions more to the cost of drug enforcement; the total volume of illegal drugs for sale has not diminished; drug-related crime has engulfed urban America; and organized crime is flourishing on the proceeds (Currie, 1993). Although overall use rates appear to have fallen, the number of hard core users has not diminished (Treaster, 1994).

Why, then, do we continue to put more and more money into the effort? In part because once having made the commitment, as in any war, political leaders cannot admit defeat without appearing unmanly. In part because the organizations enlisted to fight the war have a vested interest in its continuance: billions of dollars for offices and staff. Also, for the military, the war on drugs may be the only game in town since the breakup of the Soviet Union. And in part because of the traditional American pattern of framing deviant behavior in moral terms: The use of illegal substances is evil, and sinners must be punished.

Just as in the case of "demon drink" in the 1920s, however, the attempt to prohibit drug use has had the latent dysfunction of causing even more addic-

tion and crime. But calling off the war on drugs will not be as easy as repealing the Prohibition Amendment. The best that current critics might hope for is a shift in focus from the impossible goal of reducing the supply to programs designed to reduce the demand. The problem here is that efforts to reduce supply have greater public appeal than do educational and job-training programs. What is more glamorous to watch on television: a helicopter raid on a poppy field or a grammar class for high school dropouts?

Nonetheless, many Western industrial nations have contained drug addiction and avoided the high cost of drug-related crime by emphasizing rehabilitation of addicts, extensive public health campaigns, and minimal use of criminal sanctions. But in those countries, addicts are not much different from everyone else in terms of race and income, and moral entrepreneurs have had limited success in defining the issue.

At the moment, the United States is clearly not ready to decriminalize the use of many drugs that are less addictive than tobacco or alcohol (Nadelman, 1993). The arguments against decriminalization are that it would give official approval to immorality, increase the number of users and eventual addicts, overwhelm the health care system at no cost savings to the public, and lead to the total destruction of inner-city neighborhoods.

This is another social issue that you will be asked to evaluate in the years ahead. The pressure to decriminalize—if not fully legalize—heroin and cocaine will increase as the costs of enforcement and imprisonment continue to rise. The public temper, however, may not change as rapidly. In addition, reducing demand is not an easy task. Much will have to change in the lives of the populations most at risk, those for whom drug use brings relief from daily problems, and for whom drug dealing is the most available source of money and respect.

Microlevel. Societal reaction at the microlevel refers to the messages a person receives through encounters with other people. How do friends and family, school authorities, and other agents of social control interpret your actions? What self-image emerges? And how does this influence your subsequent behavior (Heimer and Matsueda, 1994)?

Labeling. The key concept here is labeling, the process through which a given act becomes defined as deviant. Most simply put by leading labeling theorist, Howard S. Becker:

> The deviant is one to whom the label has been successfully applied; deviant behavior is behavior that people so label. . . . Whether an act is deviant, then, depends on how other people react to it. (Becker, 1963, p. 9)

Not all violations of the norms become visible; there are "secret deviants" whose behavior has not yet been discovered or labeled. Technically, they, too, are norm breakers but able to avoid the consequences. It often does not matter whether or not the accusation of deviance is accurate. Once in motion, the process develops its own logic. This is the source of the power of moral entrepreneurs—they need only cast the first stone.

That first stone leads to the crucial distinction in labeling theory between *primary* and *secondary deviation* (Lemert, 1972). **Primary deviation** consists of violations of the norms that a person can "normalize" by making excuses and explaining it to oneself. After all, you drove over the speed limit today because you couldn't be late to class; you certainly are not a "dangerous driver." **Secondary deviation** refers to how a person deals with the problems created by being identified and labeled as a deviant. If you had been caught speeding often enough to be publicly labeled in court and to have your license revoked, think how this would change the way other people see you and how you see yourself, as well as your subsequent behavior—such as violating the law by driving without a license. And as long as you've been labeled, why bother to stay within the speed limits? No one would believe you anyway. And you will, indeed, become a danger-

Labeling refers to the process by which action becomes defined as deviant.

Primary deviation refers to violations of norms that can be normalized by making excuses and explanations for oneself.

Secondary deviation refers to how one deals with the problems of being identified as a deviant.

The **deviant career** refers to a journey of stages from one deviant status to another.

A **deviant subculture** is a group or network providing acceptance of deviant behavior.

Contingencies refer to possibilities that open or close opportunities for change.

Stigma refers to a moral blemish that is attached to the characteristic defined as deviant.

ous driver—another example of the self-fulfilling prophecy.

This process illustrates the concept of the **deviant career,** a set of stages in a continuous journey from one status to another (Becker, 1963). In the case of deviance, the career begins with that first stone, is deepened by the effects of secondary deviation, until the deviant label is internalized and becomes central to one's identity. The final step in the career involves seeking out others who share the label. Because interaction with conformists is so painful, the deviant avoids them, finding acceptance and approval only within the **deviant subculture.** Heavy drinkers hang out in the neighborhood *Cheers;* drug users find a supportive network; couples without children socialize with other nonparents; and people of above-average weight are most comfortable with others of similar size.

One recent analysis of data from a large random sample of American youth, followed over many years, supports many features of the labeling model (Matsueda, 1992). Boys who had committed a juvenile offense and whose parents labeled them as rule breakers developed a self-image that encouraged further delinquency.

Not all violators of the norms embark on a deviant career or, once labeled, follow the typical career path. Life is full of **contingencies,** possibilities that open up or close off opportunities for change. But these options are more possible for people with a wide range of resources. For the poor and already powerless, alternative outcomes will be more difficult to achieve.

Central to the labeling process is the concept of **stigma,** a "sign of moral blemish" that attaches to the deviant characteristic, becoming a "master status" trait through which all other perceptions are filtered. Notice how much else you assume about people who are much larger or much smaller than average—how the trait of body size overwhelms all other perceptions. Indeed, simply calling a particular physical condition a "disability" is a clear case of social construction when what actually limits the person is a disabling environment—stairs that cannot be mounted; bathroom fixtures that cannot be reached; chairs that are narrow or too high, and so forth (Higgens, 1992).

Sometimes the effect of the stigma is indirect, as when an overweight person's dieting reduces their overall health status, leading to feelings of depression (C. Ross, 1994).

Once applied, stigma can have a powerful effect on the individual, as seen in the case of mental patients who were unable to overcome the negative attitudes of other people despite efforts to cope with their disability (Link et al., 1991). Indeed, the harder they tried to educate others and to avoid severe rejection, the more distressed they became over their inability to shake the label. Especially difficult to counteract are the labels applied by bureaucratic

Although dieting continues to be multi-million-dollar business, not all women subscribe to the cultural ideal of the slim, trim, female body. In a society stressing slimness, organizations such as Women at Large can provide a source of validation and social support for large women, encouraging them to participate in activities from which they ordinarily feel excluded.

authorities: drug control agencies have a vested interest in finding junkies; the Bureau of Alcohol, Tobacco, and Firearms needs their Branch Davidians (the religious sect whose defiance ended in death); and social workers in a child-abuse unit would be out of a job if they could not identify and label assaulters (Margolin, 1992).

TOLERATED EVASIONS OF THE NORMS. Not all violations of the norms evoke negative labels. Many people avoid stigma because their deviance is secret; some are given relatively harmless labels—"oddball" or "character"—and others are just considered "eccentric." **Eccentrics** are rule breakers whose violations are not perceived as either disruptive or threatening to the social order. Some eccentrics are tolerated because they are generally perceived as harmless (the town drunk); or are expected to be different from everyone else (artists); or are protected by powerful colleagues (womanizing politicians); or are so rich and famous that they are above ordinary standards of behavior (Madonna, Ross Perot).

THE MEDICALIZATION OF DEVIANCE

A major issue in the sociology of deviance today is the tendency in United States and other industrial societies to treat many types of deviant behavior according to the medical model, as diseases, rather than as social constructions. The debate has raged most fiercely around sexual practices and drinking behaviors but has recently extended to smoking, gambling and even poor writing (Kirk and Kutchins, 1994). Since 1980, the number of mental disorders recognized by the American Psychiatric Association has increased from 106 to over 300. Although this may seem to be an intellectual debate regarding the origins of deviance, it is also, perhaps primarily, a turf war over who has the power to define the issues, access to the funding for research, and control over treatment.

The Case of Gambling

One example of this trend is the question of "compulsive gambling." Just defining compulsive is not easy and the label is typically applied to someone who loses. Winners are thought of in the same way as any professional deeply involved in their work; one rarely speaks of a "compulsive physician." As more and more gambling casinos are opened and state lotteries established, largely as a source of income in lieu of raising taxes, the issue has come into prominence—a perfect instance of official actions creating a new category of deviants. But is excessive gambling a disease or behavior carried beyond the range of "normal"? As you may have guessed, the medical model has been embraced by the psychiatric establishment and organizations such as Gamblers Anonymous, using the grammar of addiction ("highs" and "lows"). The issue is not simply a matter of treatment, but one of funding. Americans are more willing to spend public money to research a disease than a disreputable behavior. More important, health insurance does not cover bad habits.

> Violations by **eccentrics** are not regarded as disruptive or threatening to the social order.

Arguments against the medical model follow: (1) Gambling is rather ordinary behavior, enjoyed by a majority of citizens, only a few of whom cannot tear themselves away from the gaming tables. It is very similar to overeating, overworking, and a range of actions that suggest low impulse control rather than disease. (2) The results of biomedical research will, at best, be only suggestive and very limited in predictive ability. Nonetheless, based on a small sample of clients in therapy, a psychiatrist has already declared that compulsive gamblers suffer from "early deprivation . . . emotional losses that go way back" (Marriott, 1992).

Is Alcoholism a Disease?

The medicalization of deviance has been most successful in the area of alcohol use and abuse, where the physical *effects* of overindulgence are much more obvious than in other forms of deviance. Some evidence suggests a genetic influence—again, *not* "a drinking gene" but possibly several genetic tendencies in combination and limited to men whose problems began before age 20 (Pihl et al., 1990; Svikis et al., 1992). Environmental influences were more important than an inherited predisposition for the great majority of problem drinkers—men whose drinking problems emerge later in adulthood and women.

Although studies of children of alcoholics (COAs) find them at risk of a variety of emotional and behavioral problems (Sher, 1991), the evidence is difficult to evaluate, because the family situation is so greatly influenced by the effects of the drinking parent. In most respects, COAs are similar to children from any troubled family. That is, their problems are not related to alcoholism but to the difficulties of growing up in a family where parents do not function well, for whatever reason.

The medical model personalizes the issue. That is, overdrinking is perceived as a problem of the individual. From the sociological perspective, however, drinking is social behavior. People take a drink or refuse it depending on the situation, on the meaning of alcohol in their subculture, and on the role of significant others.

A second issue is the difficulty of defining "heavy" drinking, which is basically not a medical judgment but a socially and culturally determined description. What is accepted as ordinary alcohol consumption in Finland would be considered excessive in the United States (Alasuutari, 1992). The distinction between socially approved drinking and "overdrinking," therefore, is an arbitrary and flexible line drawn by the norms for that situation and enforced by agents of social control (Orcutt, 1991). Think of the times you may have had "just one more" at the urging of friends rather than from an inner craving. Thus, although drinking presents clear health risks, it becomes a "problem" only when family or work roles are affected; that is, when others become disturbed.

Sociologists also point out that the most common treatment for alcohol problems is not medical but profoundly social, based on the interpretive/symbolic interaction model described in Chapter 1. In an Alcoholics Anonymous meeting (or any other 12-Step Program) people use the group setting as a *Gemeinschaft* within which appropriate behavior is redefined and a new identity forged (Pittman and White, 1991). Fear of losing the approval and validation of the new significant others is a powerful motivator.

> Much mental illness is defined as **residual deviance** because normative expectations are more ambiguous.

The medical jargon is designed to help the "addict" overcome guilt. It is easier to live with a disease ("it happened to me") than with a moral flaw ("I did it"). In addition, much of the language in these therapies is so vague it could fit anyone or any situation—a variety of "fortune cookie wisdom." For example, does a strong need to be loved become "codependency" only when exhibited by a COA?

Historically, these social dimensions to drinking were well recognized up to the 1970s, when most money for alcohol research went to social-science-based centers. The medical/psychiatric model came into prominence when the number of practitioners and academic departments were expanding. In addition, the media have a great fondness for the biological and "scientific." Thus, over the last two decades, the medical model has become widely accepted, enjoying support from government funders, the press, the people labeled "alcoholic," and the powerful industries that have developed to treat the afflicted.

Yet even if a drinking gene were discovered, researchers would still need to explain why it should vary systematically by such non-biological variables as education, occupation, ethnicity, region of the country, and strength of religious belief. There is also evidence that drinking behaviors and the reactions of role partners vary systematically by sex (Robbins and Martin, 1993).

These same observations hold for other forms of drug use and abuse. Yes, people become addicted, and this has clear medical consequences, but the weight of the evidence strongly suggests that "what goes on outside of a person's body is more significant in understanding drug use, including alcoholism, than what goes on inside the body" (Schaler, 1991, p. 46).

MENTAL ILLNESS AS VIOLATION OF RESIDUAL NORMS

Various forms of deviance have been classified as "mental illness," diseases of the mind that impair a person's ability to function. Psychologists and psychiatrists (medical doctors) have listed the symptoms of various mental diseases in great detail. The problem for sociologists is that the list and the details are subject to change. What is acceptable behavior in one time and place and for certain persons may not be appropriate at other times and places or for other kinds of people. In the early part of this century, both masturbation and homosexuality were considered evidence of severe mental disorder; yet when they were taken off the list, many newly discovered illnesses were added (e.g., tobacco addiction), which may have more to do with health insurance reimbursement than science (Mirowsky and Ross, 1989). Value judgments of labelers have also shaped the list. Until recently, for example, girls who liked to climb trees were routinely diagnosed by mental health professionals as having "gender-identity disorder."

Clearly, much mental illness is norm violation in the same sense as other forms of deviance, determined largely by societal standards of correct behavior. But because these normative expectations are so ambiguous and difficult to use predictably, they are often referred to as **residual,** left over in the sense of not being covered by other categories of behavior (Scheff, 1966). At what point does hearing the voice of God become madness rather than a religious experience? Considerations such as these have led some social scientists to propose that most of what is called

SOCIOLOGY IN EVERYDAY LIFE

Roll Out the Barrel

How does your school rate on the college drinking scale? Figure 6-3 is based on a survey of 58,000 students on 78 campuses in 1989–90 and 1991. As you can see, both average and "binge" drinking (5 or more drinks at a single sitting) is most common among students in the Northeast and least among those in the West. Male students drank more than their female peers; younger students more than older ones; and four-year college students more than 2-year college students (which is probably due to the presence of a

higher proportion of women and older students at two-year colleges).

Why the regional difference? The research organization suggested that the key factor was the size of the campus, with students at the smaller institutions dominant in the Northeast being subject to greater peer pressure to conform to group norms. Another factor might be the composition of the student body, with the western and southern schools having relatively high proportions of students from traditional and deeply religious backgrounds. From your knowledge of your own campus, how would you explain these patterns?

FIGURE 6-3   Average number of drinks per week and proportion of students who binged in the previous two weeks.

Source: Chronicle of Higher Education, May 26, 1993, p. A-28.

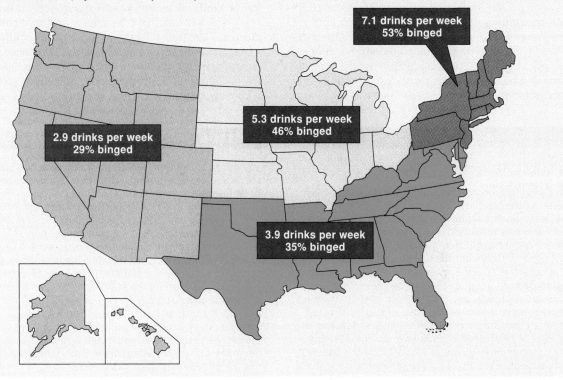

mental illness refers to problems in everyday living that role partners can no longer tolerate (Szasz, 1993; Holstein, 1993). For example, in an earlier era, mentally retarded people were teased but tolerated and cared for at home, in the community. But in the middle of the nineteenth century, "feeble-mindedness" became medicalized and those so labeled were placed in institutions or sterilized, under medical orders, "for their own good" (Trent, 1994).

Critics of the concept focus on the distinction between **organic disorders**—due to some disease or malfunction in the brain or nervous system—and **functional disorders,** an inability to meet normative expectations. The former can be considered truly mentally ill, while the latter suffer primarily

from the effects of societal reaction to nonconforming behavior—the labeling and stigmatization discussed earlier in this chapter. Both types of illness, however, are included in the U.S. Public Health Service's definition of *serious* mental illness (SMI) as "any psychiatric disorder during the past year that seriously interfered with one or more aspects of a persons daily life." According to this standard, between 4 and 5 million, or about two percent of American adults, only some of whom are

Organic disorders result from disease or malfunction of the brain or nervous system.

Functional disorders refer to the inability to meet normative expectations.

in institutions, suffered from SMI at the time of the survey (U.S. Department of Health and Human Services, 1992). Over the course of one's lifetime, however, the figure will be much higher. For example, a recent large-scale mental health survey, using an expanded list of ailments, reported that almost half of Americans experienced a mental disorder at some time in their life, typically an extended period of depression or severe anxiety attack (Kessler et al., 1994).

Rates of SMI are higher for women than men, for African Americans than for other races, for the less educated, and for the poor—in general, people who are most likely to experience problems in daily living with the least coping resources and who are least likely to be able to meet societal standards of adequacy (Markson et al., 1992). In addition, African-American adolescents are overrepresented at community mental health facilities largely because they come to the attention of social and legal referral agencies while equally disturbed white youth are protected by family and agency personnel (Takeuchi et al., 1993).

Gatekeepers regulate the entry of patients into different kinds of treatments.

The Career of the Mental Patient

As with any persistent deviant, the person officially labeled and processed by mental health authorities embarks on a career, with its contingencies and agents of social control (Goffman, 1961). Being labeled mentally ill carries the additional burden of having a disorder that role partners perceive as being more within the control of the individual than are other types of sickness—"just pull yourself together!" One recent study of auto workers using mental health services found that the self-blame experienced by the clients *increased* rather than reduced their level of distress (Broman et al., 1994).

Especially important in the career of the mental patient are the formal agents known as **gatekeepers,** the people who regulate the entry of patients into different kinds of treatments (Holstein, 1993). Personal resources will also have an effect: privately paid psychiatrists are most likely to be treating individuals who can afford several months at the Betty Ford Clinic rather than the alcoholic ward of the city hospital. People without health insurance will have difficulty receiving treatment even at the city hospital, so that

---

RESEARCH IN ACTION

Iatrogenic Madness

The word *iatrogenic* refers to an illness caused or made worse by the treatment taken to cure it. One of the major arguments against mental hospitals for anyone not extremely disturbed is that the asylum itself is an environment that produces and reinforces symptoms of madness (Goffman, 1961). In one classic study (Rosenhan, 1973), researchers got themselves admitted to different mental hospitals by presenting symptoms of "existential psychosis," a completely made-up disease. Once admitted, the "pseudopatients" acted normally. But the hospital staff, having made a firm diagnosis of illness, had a strong investment in having their professional judgment validated by the patient's subsequent behavior. Thus, everything the patient did was perceived as a sign of that illness. For example, although the pseudopatients continued to take field notes even as they interacted with staff, no one paid any attention except to report that the patients "indulged in writing behavior." Eventually, the pseudopatients were discharged as improved by their treatment. The staff congratulated one another on their therapeutic skills; but the other, legitimate, patients had not been fooled—they know madness.

More recently, Bruce Luske (1990) spent 18 months as a participant observer in a halfway house for mental patients. His findings illustrate many of the points in this chapter, especially the way in which a psychiatric diagnosis is jointly constructed by the patient and the professional staff during the intake interview. Both the structure and content of patient–staff interaction create and reinforce emotional disorders. What is especially interesting in this study, however, is the analysis of staff behavior as a form of boundary maintenance.

The people who supervise institutionalized mental patients are typically drawn from marginal populations—immigrant doctors, minority custodians. Many have picked up enough psychiatric jargon to worry about their own mental stability ("closet insanity," in Luske's term). Much of the staff's energies are devoted to drawing and clarifying the line between their own insecurities and the patient's "real" illness. Unfortunately for the patient, this process only magnifies their symptoms, and the psychiatric staff is torn between the professional goal of curing the ill and the need to see the patient as seriously disturbed.

Life outside the institution, however, may be no more helpful to the mental patient. In Belgium and France, people released from mental hospitals are often placed as lodgers in the homes of villagers who are paid for their efforts. The idea is to integrate the ex-patients into ordinary life by erasing the barriers between sane and insane. In one such village, however, the researcher found that, because the local people believed that mental illness was contagious, they did everything possible to exaggerate and maintain the boundary between themselves and the "crazies," separating eating utensils and laundry, and minimizing any contacts (Jodelet, 1992). Needless to say, the mental health of the boarders was not greatly improved.

their condition deteriorates to the point at which they can no longer survive in their communities. The ultimate stage in the career of the mental patient is **institutionalization** in an asylum, or mental hospital.

Because an asylum is a total institution (see Chapter 5), the labeling process is intensified. There is nowhere to hide; nowhere else to go for information about the self. As described by Goffman (1961), the patient is stripped of outside roles and possessions, losing every shred of privacy. Information is shared among the staff who resist the patient's slightest effort to maintain a positive self-concept. For a new self to be constructed, the old one must be thoroughly discredited. Only then can the patient be reconstituted into an acceptable human being, but this new self, unlike the old one, is no longer a "fortress" but a small open city (Goffman, 1961).

Once released, the former inmate will bear forever the label of "mental patient," a master status that colors every interaction. The public image of someone on the verge of doing something outrageous is difficult to dislodge. It is true that some people being treated for mental illness will engage in violent illegal behavior, but this is a very small percentage with severe symptoms; the great majority are as law-abiding as the ordinary citizen (Link et al., 1992).

Restoring community and family ties and finding a job will be difficult. Many will not succeed, joining the number of other people made homeless for a variety of reasons. It is estimated that at least one in four homeless persons suffers from a serious mental disorder, and many others display various deviant behaviors (Rossi et al., 1987). But homelessness in America has more to do with a lack of affordable housing for poor families than with the failure at all levels of government to fund community mental health centers to treat former patients—although both have contributed to the current visibility of "street people" (see Chapter 21).

From the Streets to the Asylum and Back

As an example of how economic and political trends in the broader society affect the creation of deviance and its treatment, several recent studies follow the rise and fall of the mental asylum in America. For example, historical data demonstrate that the huge influx of asylum patients between 1880 and 1920 had nothing to do with a sudden increase in the supply of mentally ill people (Sutton, 1991). Rather, as social reformers succeeded in closing down the system of local poorhouses, large numbers of impoverished elderly were left without housing. The burden of caring for them became the responsibility of state governments, which were able at that time to raise money to build asylums, thus providing jobs for local workers as well as shelter for the elderly. And so the mental hospital system expanded to fill several different kinds of social needs, few of which were related to mental health.

Three decades after this expansion, in the late 1950s, another set of reformers set out to empty the

> **Institutionalization** refers to the commitment of mental patients to asylums or mental hospitals.

People who suffer from mental illness have been institutionalized in asylums or mental hospitals for centuries. Since asylums are total institutions, the labeling process becomes intensified. With no place for patients to hide they are stripped of outside roles and possessions, thereby losing every bit of privacy, as in this "madhouse" in England during the eighteenth century. Why do many of the problems of institutionalizing mental patients persist two centuries later?

mental hospitals. By this time, the development of effective drug therapies and a shift in psychiatric thought in favor of the healing power of social involvement offered the hope of allowing mental patients to live in "the least restrictive environment." These trends combined with a shift toward a more activist federal government role in social welfare, to produce the Mental Health Centers Act of 1963 (Grob, 1991).

Deinstitutionalization refers to the release of mental patients into the community.

The **deinstitutionalization** of people who could function on the outside was to be accompanied by a network of community-based services to monitor medication and to assist afflicted individuals and their families. This plan, too, fell victim to circumstances—in this case, the costs of the Vietnam War and the inability of state and local governments to raise the money needed to operate the local centers. And so the fate of mental patients was decided not by their medical needs but by the "politics of madness."

SUMMARY

1. Conformity is structured by collective agreement on the norms, both prescriptive and proscriptive.

2. Because the norms define what is acceptable, they also define the unacceptable, what comes to be called deviant behavior.

3. The sociological perspective on deviance emphasizes the context of behavior: who does what to whom under what circumstances.

4. Deviance serves a number of social functions: unifying the collectivity, setting boundaries, providing a safety valve for antisocial impulses, and serving as the cutting edge of social change through principled challenges.

5. Conformity to the norms is encouraged and enforced by informal and formal agents of social control.

6. Biological and psychological models of deviance locate nonconformity within the individual and have been of limited explanatory power.

7. Sociological models focus on the social origins and societal reactions at both the macro- and microlevel.

8. Sociological theories of the origins of deviance at the macrolevel include Merton's typology of anomie, blocked opportunity structures, and deviant subcultures. Social learning, differential association, and group controls operate at the individual level.

9. Concepts in societal reaction models include social control, labeling, secondary deviation, stigma, and the deviant career.

10. A major issue in the study of deviance is the trend toward medicalization, treating nonconformity as a disease rather than as a social construction.

11. From the sociological perspective, mental illness is viewed as a violation of residual norms, and the patient embarks on a career of labeling and treatment.

12. Institutionalization is the ultimate stage in the deviant career, whereby the offender is removed from the community and the deviant label firmly attached.

SUGGESTED READINGS

Patricia A. Adler and Peter Adler. *Constructions of Deviance: Social Power, Context, and Interaction.* Belmont, CA: Wadsworth, 1993. A lively presentation of how deviance is socially constructed.

Barrows, Susanna, and Robin Room (Eds). *Drinking Behavior and Belief In Modern History.* Berkeley: University of California Press, 1991. A fascinating collection of essays on historical and cross-cultural drinking patterns, from Puritans to modern Irishmen, and from regulating alcohol in the British colonies to the American temperance movement.

Becker, Howard S. *The Outsiders: Studies in the Sociology of Deviance.* New York: Free Press, 1963. A classic study in which the labeling perspective is applied to the study of jazz musicians and marijuana smokers.

Currie, Elliot. *Reckoning: Drugs, Cities, and the American Future.* New York: Hill & Wang, 1993. Three decades of research explains why drugs have become an epidemic in America's inner cities and why the federal war on drugs has failed.

Ettore, Elizabeth. *Women and Substance Abuse.* New Brunswick, NJ: Rutgers University Press, 1992. Insightful analysis of women's use and abuse of alcohol, prescribed drugs, heroin, tobacco, and food.

Goffman, Erving. *Stigma: Notes on the Management of a Spoiled Identity.* Englewood Cliffs, NJ: Prentice-Hall, 1963. Goffman's essay deals with reactions to labeling, the ways in which stigmatized individuals protect their self-image and learn to negotiate social interaction.

Gupta, Giri Raj. *Sociology of Mental Health*. Boston: Allyn & Bacon, 1993. Comprehensive overview of the sociological perspective on definitions and treatment of mental illness.

Pfuhl, Erdwin H., and Stuart Henry. *The Deviance Process.* 3d ed. New York: Aldine de Gruyter, 1993. A social constructionist perspective for the study of deviance.

7

Aging and the Life Course

ere is the Riddle of the Sphinx:

What creature walks in the morning on four feet, at noon upon two, and at evening upon three?

Here is the answer, given by Oedipus:

A human being who crawls as an infant, stands as an adult, and uses a cane in old age.

From the earliest recorded legends of Western civilization to this very day, and in all societies, the possibilities and limitations of chronological age have shaped the passage of individuals across the life course. Although aging is a biological process, it is also socially constructed. Different societies recognize different sets of age categories, and the roles attached to these age strata vary greatly across cultures and time. The norms that govern entry and exit from valued roles will change from one society to another and from one historical period to another. For example, the age at which a young person becomes an adult varies greatly, from age 13 among the Mundurucu of the Amazon forest to anywhere between 18 and 21 for modern Americans, depending on the particular role.

In this chapter we will focus on two dimensions of the social construction of aging and age groups. First is the creation of systems of *age stratification*: the extent to which structured inequality is created on the basis of age. If important roles such as spouse or worker are open to people of a particular age and not to others, inequality among age strata is the result. In this sense, age operates in the same way as gender, race, or ethnicity to divide the society. The general processes of stratification are discussed in Chapter 9.

The second focus of this chapter is the *life course perspective* in which aging is viewed as a life-long process shaped by the particular history and culture in which the individual is embedded (Elder, 1994).

THE SOCIAL CONSTRUCTION OF AGE AND LIFE STAGES

As a status—a determinant of social location—age has several important characteristics. First, age, like sex and race, is an **ascribed characteristic.** Although people may try to look older or younger than their chronological years, at any particular moment, age is a given trait and therefore provides a clear basis for division of labor. There are also age-linked requirements for holding other statuses. In the United States, for example, laws define the ages for attending school, drinking beer, joining or leaving the labor force, voting, and getting married.

Second, unlike sex and race, age is a **transitional status.** We are always moving from one age category to another. At various points along the way, most societies have ceremonies that mark important transitions—**rites of passage** from one age-linked identity

> Age is an **ascribed characteristic** that determines people's social location.
>
> Age is a **transitional status** as people move from one age category to another.
>
> **Rites of passage** are ceremonies marking important transitions from one age status to another.

Age is an important dimension of social structure, affecting opportunities, experiences, and relationships throughout life. A group of Sun City residents enjoy the relaxation of retirement from work roles.

to another, such as confirmation rituals, graduation ceremonies, and retirement parties (Van Gennup (1909/1960). In both simple and modern societies, these ceremonies regulate the flow of people into and out of valued statuses.

Third, *age categories or strata* form a hierarchy of power and prestige. During one's lifetime, a person can expect to move through this system, occupying positions of varying dominance based on age, from powerless childhood to relatively powerful adult, and finally to the frailty of old age. In other words, age is a kind of "career," in which one moves along a pre-planned path (Marshall and Rosenthal, 1994).

Fourth, age statuses generate **age norms,** socially constructed expectations of persons of a given age. The expression "act your age" means exactly that: Conform to age-based norms or be negatively sanctioned by role partners. Nine-year-olds who cling to their mothers or 75-year-olds who wear skimpy swimwear are violating generally accepted age norms in our society. In other societies, these behaviors might be approved. "Young" and "old" are relative concepts. Notice how very important even a one-year age difference was when you were a child, and how your definition of "around my age" is much broader today.

The number of recognized age-status groups in a society is also culturally variable. The Nandi of Kenya, for example, recognize 28 different age categories, while the Nupe of Nigeria have only three, and modern Americans use six: infancy, childhood, adolescence, young adulthood, middle age, and old age.

Age norms are social expectations of persons of a given age.

An **age structure** of a population is based on the number of persons in each age category.

The **role structure** of a population consists of the number of roles available to persons of a given age.

Age stratification refers to inequality of both people and roles in terms of control over valued resources on the basis of chronological age.

Rites of passage are ceremonies that mark important transitions in societies. These young Masai boys in Kenya have just been circumcised in a ritual that marks their passage into adulthood. What rites of passage characterize entry into adulthood in our society?

Age as an Element of Social Structure

Age is more than a personal quality. It is an element of social structure in two ways: (1) The entire population has an **age structure** based on the number of persons in each age category, as shown in Figure 7-1. (2) There is a **role structure** that consists of the roles available to persons of a given age. The role structure is composed of arbitrary age norms that regulate the flow of people in and out of valued positions. For example, age norms control entry into marriage roles; governments that want to limit population will raise the legal age for marriage, whereas those seeking population growth will lower the legal age (see Chapter 20).

These two aspects of social structure and the processes that channel people of different ages into productive roles produce an **age stratification** system (Riley et al., 1972) That is, both people and roles can be analyzed as unequal or stratified in terms of access to or command over valued resources. In a modern society, children and the very old are generally excluded from the most valued positions, whereas in simple societies, the elderly may be honored for their accumulated wisdom. In the following sections we take a closer look at the both age and role structures.

> There is a dynamic interplay between people growing older and society undergoing change. People age in different ways because society changes, and in turn the ways in which people age are continually shaping the society.
>
> —MATILDA WHITE RILEY, 1982, p. 11

AGE STRUCTURE

The age structure of any society can be graphically illustrated in the form of a **population pyramid,** as in Figure 7-1, where each bar represents the number of males and females in each age category. The shape of the pyramid will vary from society to society, depending on birth and death rates and, as you can see in Figure 7-1, can also change over time. A full discussion of population processes can be found in Chapter 20. In this chapter, we are interested in how the entire age structure and the size of a given age stratum affect the life chances of its members.

Birth Cohorts

A **birth cohort** consists of the people born during a given set of years. Many of you are members of the birth cohort of 1975-77. Cohort members age together through a particular slice of history. Thus, while members of a cohort share certain experiences, such as being a particular age during a war, each cohort is historically unique, different from every other. In modern societies, patterns of schooling, marriage, and work may vary widely from one birth cohort to another, in large part as a consequence of the very size of the birth cohort. For example, in Figure 7-1, you can follow the aging of two very different birth cohorts: the small numbers born in the depression era of the 1930s in contrast to the "baby boom" cohorts of 1947-67. The former are shown in the shorter bars of girls and boys ages 10-19 in 1950 compared to the longer bars of boomers ages 0-9 in that year. The baby boom cohort creates a bulge in the pyramid as it ages: the large numbers of young adults in 1980, and the very large number of elderly in 2030. Most of you are located in the very small birth cohort ages 0-9 in the 1980 pyramid.

In general, chances of economic success are highest for members of small cohorts because of less competition for good jobs (Easterlin, 1987). Members of large cohorts face greater competition for jobs, educational opportunities, and marriage partners. The baby boomers were able to compensate for their large size through later marriage, remaining single, having fewer children, and increased labor force participation of wives. Your cohort, however, as noted in Chapter 9, may have difficulty because of the extra large number of people who preceded you into the labor force and who will clog channels of promotion for some years to come.

In addition, the effects of birth cohort size and historical contexts interact with social class, ethnicity, race, and sex to influence life course experiences.

Life Expectancy

The age structure of any society is affected not only by the original size of its birth cohorts but also by subsequent death rates (mortality). **Life expectancy** refers to the average number of years a person can expect to

> A **population pyramid** is a graphic representation of the age and sex distribution of a society's population.
>
> A **birth cohort** consists of people born during a specified time period.
>
> **Life expectancy** refers to the average number of years a person is expected to live.

A birth cohort consists of people born around the same set of years. Experiences at schooling, work, and family vary from one birth cohort to another. What are the similarities and differences in the experiences of the men and women of this cohort?

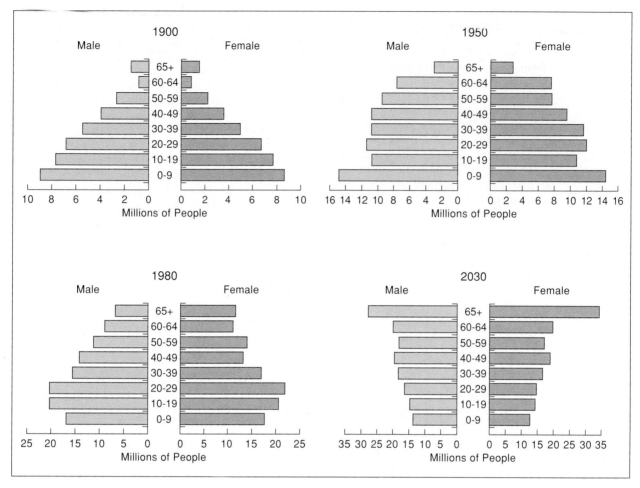

FIGURE 7-1   U.S. population pyramids: 1900, 1950, 1980, and projected for 2030.

Sources: U.S. Bureau of the Census, *Current Population Reports*, P25–1092, 1992.

live. For example, as seen in Table 7-1, average life expectancy for an American born in 1900 varied by sex and race, approximately 48 years for whites and 34 for African Americans. This does not means that there were no old people in the society, but that infant mortality was so high that the average was lowered dramatically; anyone surviving childhood could expect to live to a ripe old age. For example, if in a group of 100 people, 50 died in infancy and the rest lived to be 100, the average life expectancy of the group would be 50 years.

SOCIAL CHANGE

Generational Memories:
The Importance of Cohort

The concept of cohort increases our understanding of the meaning that history may have for people born within the same time period. Schuman and Scott (1989) found that specific memories and interpretations of historical events distinguished one age cohort from another. People of all ages remembered social and political events occurring during their adolescence and young adulthood most clearly; for example, almost half of respondents ages 16–24 during World War II re-

called it as a key event; for those ages 15–27 during the Vietnam War, the majority mentioned it as key. Moreover, birth cohorts perceive an event experienced in common differently. For example, a 60-year-old may view the recent reunification of Germany as a restoration of one nation; a 20-year-old, born during the Cold War, may experience it as a change from the way things have been. The experiences of young men and women who served in Vietnam in 1965 differed from those who served in 1971. The intersection of personal memory and social and political history shapes the perspective of each birth cohort's interpretation of the world.

Life Expectancy throughout the World

Source: Population Reference Bureau, 1994 World Population Data Sheet, PRB, 1875 Connecticut Ave. N.W., Suite 520, Washington, D.C.

As Table 7-1 indicates, average life expectancy at birth has risen greatly over the course of this century, doubling for African Americans, and increasing by over 60 percent for whites. In addition, the gap between women and men has widened as women face lowered risks of death during childbirth. The sex gap also reflects the poorer health habits of men and their heightened risks of heart diseases (see Chapter 18). These differential life expectancies affect the numbers of males and females within each cohort. The resulting age structure has direct effects on people. For example, returning to Figure 7-1, if you were a baby boom male in the ages 20–29 cohort in 1980 looking for a bride five years younger than yourself, would you have a larger or smaller number to choose from than does your brother who is ten years older than you? How easy will it be for a woman born in 1963 to find a husband five years older than herself?

TABLE 7-1   Life Expectancy at Birth, United States, 1900 and 1993, by Sex and Race (in Years)

| Year of Birth | White | | African-American | |
	Male	Female	Male	Female
1900	46.6	48.7	32.5	35.0
1993	73.0	79.5	64.7	73.7

Source: U. S. Bureau of the Census, *Historical Statistics of the United States*, 1975; U.S. Department of Health and Human Services, *Monthly Vital Statistics Report* Vol. 42, No. 13, October 1994.

THE AGE STRUCTURE OF ROLES

The **age structure of roles,** as illustrated in the example of finding a marriage partner, refers to the statuses open to people of a given age. For example, as the number of jobs available either expands during a period of economic growth or contracts during a recession, the flow of workers can be controlled by changing the age norms for entry or exit from the work force. Child labor and mandatory schooling laws can be manipulated to regulate entry of younger workers, and older ones can be encouraged to stay or leave by changing the age of pension eligibility.

> The **age structure of roles** refers to the statuses open to persons of a given age.

Where there is a greater supply of role players than the institutional sphere can absorb, social unrest can result. Large numbers of unemployed and/or unmarried young people are a threat to social order, as can be seen throughout Eastern Europe today and in many American cities. Maintaining a balance between the supply of role players (age structure) and available statuses (role structure) is a major problem for governments. Social institutions must adapt to population shifts, and these institutional changes, in turn, affect the age structure by encouraging or discouraging births or by reducing age-related mortality.

Age-Related Capacities

Entry and exit from some roles is often dictated by biological factors. Few females younger than age 12 or

Elderly Men in Short Supply

The *sex ratio* refers to the number of men for every one hundred women. Because women live longer than men, the sex ratio will become increasingly unbalanced in old age. In the United States today, for example, there are 80 men for every hundred women aged 65 to 69, but only 32 men for every hundred women aged 90 to 94. For all Americans age 65+, the sex ratio is 67/100.

Throughout Eastern Europe and in the territories that once made up the Soviet Union, however, sex ratios are much lower than in the United States. In Russia today, there are only 36 men for every 100 women aged 65+, and the ratios range from 42 to 55 in the former republics. The ratios for Hungary, Poland, and the Czech Republic are about 60/100. Indeed, male life expectancy actually declined in the 1980s, due largely to poor health habits (U.S. Bureau of the Census, P95/93-1, 1993). Compared to their American counterparts, men in these countries drink more and smoke more (unfiltered cigarettes); work in unsafe and unsanitary workplaces; take less exercise; and are less likely to seek health care. Although generally poor nutrition and widespread air and water pollution also affect women, men's health is more negatively affected. At the same time, because of poor economic conditions, the fertility rate for younger couples has fallen drastically, which means that there will be very few young adults to support a growing population of elderly widowed or never-married women.

older than age 55 can become mothers. Football players are typically "over the hill" by age 40. But most age limits are culturally or socially defined. When flight attendants were originally defined as air-borne cocktail hostesses, no airline would hire a woman older than age 30; the age range has been expanded since (because of an age-discrimination lawsuit), but few attendants are older than age 40. Few norms are as variable as the legal age of consent for marriage—from country to country, from year to year, and they are often different for men and women. The variations have nothing to do with biology, but everything to do with cultural beliefs about sexuality and the society's need to control fertility.

DEVELOPMENT AND STRUCTURE OF ROLES ACROSS THE LIFE COURSE

As noted in Chapter 5, various theories of personality development have emphasized the importance of experiences in infancy and childhood. The notable exception is Erik Erikson (1959) who defined the entire life course as a series of developmental challenges. Each of Erikson's eight stages involves a crisis or turning point that must be successfully resolved before the next developmental stage can be reached. Table 7-2 summarizes each stage, its crisis, setting, and favorable outcome. In this model, failure to take advan-

TABLE 7-2   Erikson's Eight Stages of Development

Development Stage/Age	Psychosocial Crisis	Social Setting	Favorable Outcome
Infancy (birth to 18 months)	Basic trust vs. mistrust	Family	Trust in self, parents, and the world
Toddler (18 months to 3 years)	Autonomy vs. shame and doubt	Family	Self-control and self-esteem
Preschooler (3–6 years)	Initiative vs. guilt	Family	Purpose and direction in activities
Preadolescence (6–12 years)	Industry vs. inferiority	Family, school, peer group	Mastery and competence
Adolescence	Identity vs. role confusion	Peer group, reference group, family	Ego identity, coherent sense of self
Young adulthood	Intimacy vs. isolation	Same/opposite-sex friends	Ability to share and care with others
Mid-life	Generativity vs. stagnation	Marriage, parenthood, work, friendships	Selflessness, concern about others' welfare
Old age	Integrity vs. despair	Retirement	Acceptance of one's own life patterns and accomplishments

JON HENDRICKS

The Context of Aging

Jon Hendricks, (Ph.D., Pennsylvania State University) is Professor and Chair, Department of Sociology, Oregon State University. He has been chair of the Behavioral and Social Sciences Section of the Gerontological Society of America and the American Sociological Association Section on the Sociology of Aging and currently serves on the editorial board of several journals. Hendricks is co-author of Aging in Mass Society: Myths and Realities and co-editor of Gender and Aging and The Remainder of Their Days: Domestic Policy and Older Families in the United States and Canada.

N one of us lives a life entirely of our own choosing. The choices we make, the successes we enjoy, even the nature of our failures reflect our membership in larger social groupings. It is no different for old people than for young people.

Think for a moment about when you have been a guest in someone's home or bring a guest into your home. What kinds of questions are asked? Information is exchanged about where you live, what your parents do, who you know, in order to establish common ground. All very innocuous question asked to get to know one another. At the same time they "peg" you in whatever pecking order is relevant.

As you move through adulthood, the nature of the questions changes but the spirit and intent remain the same—a search for common ground, social background and personal preferences. The answers provided will help those who study aging to predict what your old age may be like.

When I was an undergraduate, I had to work to go to school. As I neared graduation, a nice older faculty member suggested that I consider graduate school. After I had him explain what it was, I figured "Why not?" and off I went to earn a master's degree. When offered an opportunity to pursue a Ph.D. on a National Institute of Child Health and Human Development fellowship to study developmental change over time, I jumped at the chance.

What I hadn't anticipated was that I would develop an abiding interest in how the process of individual aging is shaped by broader social currents. Only gradually did it dawn on me that no one gets to the doorstep of old age without accumulating a lifetime's experience and that whatever they encounter in old age could be nothing but an extension of earlier experiences. If people felt powerless their whole lives, it is unlikely they will feel differently in their later years. If they had struggled to obtain health care, there isn't much chance things will change. If they worked jobs without pensions, or held jobs not covered by Social Security, it is not likely there will be much in the way of financial security after retirement—if they retire at all. Eventually I realized, too, that what most of the textbooks talked about as typical patterns may not be typical of any but mainstream, middle-class men. But what of women, minorities, the poor, people like my father, my mother? How do they age? How are their lives affected by their experiences? I had read, or had read to me, the same nursery stories as other children; I know about putting nuts away for the winter, that deferred gratification brings dividends, that hard work pays off. But what if there were never enough nuts to put any away, that gratification deferred might be gratification foregone? What if hard work was merely hard work, and the myths we live by are often merely myths?

I don't really care for questions such as how many angels can dance on the head of a pin. I want to know who decides who gets to be an angel and be invited to the dance. What I, and others, found out is that old age is very much what we—collectively—make it by virtue of the societal arrangements under which we live. Having the right job, the right benefit package, the right experiences means old age is probably going to be pretty good too. The hard part is being able to get such resources in the first place, which depends more on group memberships than individual skills. Moving into the later years without the "good things" in life leads to a far different experience. That is, those who are advantaged at an earlier age receive comparable advantages when they are old. Our so-called safety nets are designed to provide minimal coverage but not to upset any "applecarts" or to redistribute whatever rights and privileges have been doled out previously. Never mind a lifetime's hard work or contributions, how will the pie be divided in light of today's priorities?

When I think about what I am going to do with the rest of my academic career, one of the things that occurs to me is that relatively few of us appreciate how much our lives are shaped by forces beyond our understanding and beyond appreciation. Maybe if I redouble my efforts, a few of you coming along behind me will have a better understanding of the things that make a difference and maybe, just maybe, a few of you will want to make a difference yourselves.

tage of the opportunity for emotional and cognitive growth will limit the person's ability to cope with subsequent challenges. The infant whose needs remain unfulfilled is likely to view the world with fear and suspicion; the toddler who has been shamed will have difficulty establishing a sense of self-worth; and the preschooler with a low level of self-esteem will have difficulty with school work, and so forth.

There is, however, little empirical evidence that people move through these stages in as systematic a way as the theory suggests, or that the infant who fails to develop a sense of trust at 18 months is doomed to personality problems. Many things that have a long-term effect do not have an obvious immediate impact, and the effect of seemingly unbearable events can be overcome by later experiences. The life course is a long chain of happenings, and it is usually an accumulation of incidents that eventually produce a full-fledged personality problem (Wadsworth, 1991).

Nonetheless, Erikson's model is very useful as a broad outline of life course development. It is also more sociological than most such theories in recognizing the importance of the social setting, the interactions between the individual and others, and how role performances at one stage shape future performances and expectations. Let us now examine each stage in greater detail.

Infancy and Childhood

Because the proportion of people available to play socially defined roles is constantly changing, age-based requirements for entering or exiting the statuses must also shift in order to maintain a rough balance between people and roles. This is one factor in explaining historical changes in the meaning of childhood. For most of European history, and still in many societies, infant and childhood mortality rates were so high that many young people who died did not even have their names recorded. As one mother in the seventeenth century observed, "Before they are old enough to bother you, you will have lost half of them, or perhaps all of them" (Ariés, 1962, p. 38). Nor for most of human history were children regarded as innocent lovable creatures to be especially treasured. Quite the opposite: The sixteenth century Protestant leader John Calvin expressed the common view that because children are born in sin they are hateful in God's eyes and must therefore be treated harshly. Such feelings were highly functional in keeping parents from making an emotional investment in an infant who might not survive childhood. Smallpox, a major cause of early death, was known as the "poor man's friend" (van de Walle and Knodel, 1980). As late as 100 years ago in Europe, infanticide, abandonment, and starvation of children were common solutions to poverty (Skolnick, 1992).

In less complex, nonindustrial societies, children are socialized early to help gather food and tend animals. In more complex economies, children are expected to assume adult roles at an early age, with their continued economic contribution to the family essential to the support of their parents in old age. In most preindustrial societies, in the past and today, living quarters were small and privacy limited, so that even young children witnessed all adult talk and activity, even sexual intercourse. The idea of childhood as a special, protected phase of the life course is a uniquely modern conception.

In the early days of industrialization, children continued to be valued for their economic contribution to the family, working on farms, apprenticed to craft

In subsistence economies children are socialized very early to work roles which require many hours of labor. These girls of the Lisu Hill Tribe work at the rice harvest in northern Thailand.

The experiences of children can vary dramatically from one society to another. Victims of glue sniffing, these abandoned children live in the streets and parks of Bangkok, Thailand. Some of the several hundred "glue children" are less than 10 years old. To make matters worse, organized gangs control them and pay them with a jar of glue at the end of the day.

workers, placed in factories, or, in the case of nobility, being married off at an early age for political reasons. At the same time, the industrial revolution separated the workplace from the home, so that family life became more private, cut off from other areas of social activity (Chapter 12). Although middle-class people came to sentimentalize the family, motherhood, and children, poor parents with an unwanted child had few options: to place the infant in an orphanage, abandon it, or pay a "baby farm" for its care, in the hope that wealthier people might adopt it. As late as 1870 in the United States, the primary value of a child was his or her ability to occupy a work role; if the courts decided that the death of a child was due to the negligence of a non-family member, the parents could receive financial compensation for the loss of the child's labor (Zelizer, 1994b). And since the labor value of boys was higher than that of girls, the preference for male offspring was extremely strong.

By the early 1900s, improvements in public health and nutrition increased the likelihood that infants would survive to adulthood and at the same time reduced the need for child labor. Legislation was passed to prohibit employment of minors and to make education compulsory. Out of the factory and into the schools, children ceased to be an economic asset to parents. This shift is reflected in legal decisions. By 1930, the death of a child due to negligence by a non-family member entitled the parents to receive compensation for "emotional pain" (Zelizer, 1994b). Thus the financially useful child became economically worthless but emotionally priceless. Nonetheless, sex differences persisted; the greater freedom enjoyed by boys in childhood made masculinity far more desirable than femininity to the average child of both sexes

(Brown, 1992). Modern parents, however, came to value girls for their cuteness.

This shift in the meaning of the child and the nature of childhood in the twentieth century also produced a new field of "scientific" theory and research: the study of child development, typically based on observations of white middle-class American families, and featuring a multi-stage model. These theories proved popular among American parents even though the underlying assumption of developmental stages remains empirically unsupported (Kagan, 1994). As our brief review of the history of childhood suggests, what is appropriate behavior for children (or adults) is highly variable across time and place. And as discussed in Chapter 5, even in modern societies, conceptions of childhood vary by family income and parent education, the sex of the child, and region of the country (West and Petrik, 1992).

In general, young children in America today are idealized as clean, playful, and innocent. Carefully excluded from adult roles and often pampered, they are considered an important emotional asset; so much so that childless couples will pay thousands of dollars for fertility treatments or adoption. This public image, however, contrasts sharply with the reality of childhood for large numbers of America's youngest citizens. In 1994, the poverty rate for children was over 22 percent, the highest for any age group of Americans, and triple the rate for most other modern societies. One in five American children is without adequate nutrition, health care, or shelter, and the gap between poor and nonpoor children continues to widen (Hernandez, 1993; Children's Defense Fund, 1994). The United States also has the highest infant mortality rate among industrialized nations.

The Double Life of America's Children: The "G" Factor versus "Psy" Controls

As the emotional value of children has increased, so has their spending power. According to a 1993 survey, the 34 million American children aged 4–12 had a combined income of $14.4 billion dollars or an average of $8.13 per child per week, of which $4.90 was spent immediately. Parents spent an additional $146 billion on items from audios to vacations for their offspring. Clearly, the youth market is big business and a sizable proportion of America's children enjoy a very pampered existence. Analysts suggest that some of this spending reflects a "G factor" or high guilt level among parents, perhaps to compensate for the time spent at work (Antilla, 1993). A more important factor is probably the need to maintain the appearance of success in the eyes of others, a competition for prestige that their children learn quite quickly.

However, there is a dark side to the image of children in the United States today, a growing fear of what many adults perceive as uncontrollable youth (other people's offspring). The range of tolerance given to young people has narrowed greatly in recent years. Children who are rebellious, physically aggressive, school failures, drug users, or otherwise deviant are no longer given the slack to "grow out of it." They are increasingly likely to be referred to social institutions for punishment rather than support. The "psy" sector—a coalition of despairing parents, school personnel, social workers, psychiatrists, psychologists, and medical staff—regularly dispense questionable diagnoses and medications to children whose behavior troubles adults (Armstrong, 1993).

Giving the child a few pills a day is simpler and less expensive than dealing with the conditions that produce "problem children," such as poor nutrition, family violence, poverty, overcrowding, and the like. By defining the child's condition as an individual pathology, these wider issues can be ignored. Under the guise of medical treatment for mental illness, the children who most need help are isolated and sedated. Those who continue to make trouble and commit crimes are now treated as adults and institutionalized.

Adolescence

Adolescence, generally defined as the teenage years and a major transition between childhood and adulthood, is a more recent "discovery" than childhood as a distinct life course stage. The concept of adolescence as a special period of great psychological turmoil emerged in the early 1900s (Hall, 1904). As a socially constructed stage of development, adolescence is a unique product of the industrial revolution.

For all the preceding centuries, the transition from childhood to adulthood took place in one's early teens, often celebrated by a rite of passage. The teenager was expected to fulfill adult roles as soon as capable. And because no extended period of training for complex tasks was required, the young person could move easily into the adult world. Under these circumstances adolescence is rarely recognized as a problem or period of crisis.

Modern industrial societies, in contrast, have little use for untrained teenagers. Too old to be children but too young to be fully integrated into mainstream institutions, contemporary teens exist in a self-contained world of the adolescent subculture. As with any subculture, there are rituals, a special language, folkways and mores that allow members to recognize one another while keeping the adult world at a distance. The American youth culture received a major impetus from the large number of baby boom children who reached their teens between the late 1950s and late 1970s, a period of relative prosperity for the nation

Role slack occurs when capabilities are underdemanded, as in adolescence.

and individual families. Here was an enormous consumer market for youth-oriented goods and services: clothing, cosmetics, books and magazines, electronic equipment, films and TV programs, rock concerts and records.

The baby-boom adolescents were also remarkable in their involvement in politics; many participated in the civil rights and antiwar movements; others served in the military in Vietnam. Contemporary teens appear to have largely withdrawn from confrontation with the wider society, absorbed primarily in consumer-oriented activities, with the shopping mall as their native territory.

But not all teens are affluent. As noted in the case of younger children, the gap between poor and nonpoor has widened over the past two decades. And for both rich and poor, adolescence can be a period of extreme turmoil. Constructing a positive self-image out of the experiences of these years is not a simple task. Even the biological changes of puberty come with mixed messages—yes, you are sexually developed, but no, there are things you should not do (at least "good girls" shouldn't). In addition to their own difficulties, adolescents are sensitive to stressful events in the life of their parents (Ge et al., 1994). Nor is the legal system much help in clarifying the status of adolescents: An 18 year old may serve in the military, become a parent, or face the death penalty for certain crimes but be unable to buy an alcoholic drink.

In our society, adolescence is a period of **role slack** in which the young person's capabilities are underdemanded; there is a lot of energy and little constructive to do with it. Defined by Erikson as the stage of identity formation as opposed to role confusion, adolescence is often characterized by experimentation as the teenager searches for entry into adult roles. Role slack leads many teenagers to overidentify with their peer group or figures from popular culture; others engage in deviant behavior. For example, rates of mental illness are relatively high during adolescence, especially for schizophrenia, a disorder characterized by false perceptions and withdrawal from the agreed-upon reality. Criminal behavior, rare among 12 year olds, rises rapidly. In the United States in 1993, teenagers accounted for almost half of all arrests for property crimes; unwed teens gave birth to 650,000 infants; and a teenager committed suicide every 90 minutes.

Much juvenile deviance—drinking, drug use, sexual experimentation, running away from home, dropping out of school—can be seen as a premature attempt to exit the ambiguous and unsatisfying roles of adolescence. The status and role of student is often defined as "childish" and unrewarding. But lack of success in school is linked to deviant behaviors that will make success in work difficult (Schulenberg et al., 1994). In any event, there are not many well-paying jobs for high-school dropouts or even for most high school graduates. Teenage unemployment rates are three times higher than for adults, with African-American youth twice as likely to be unemployed as their white age peers, illustrating the effect of both age and race on life chances.

Young people who feel unwanted or distant from their parents are especially likely to seek premature exit from adolescence. Girls from such homes may see early parenthood as a way out of the bleak possibilities of unrewarding jobs punctuated by unemployment that characterized their mother's life (Hagen and Wheaton, 1993). Ironically, early marriage and parenthood will only reproduce the type of unstable family from which these young women are trying to escape (see Chapter 12).

In contrast to the role slack model, some critics believe that today's youth are being "hurried" into adulthood by parents and schools, unable to enjoy the slow process of maturation. This argument makes for best-selling books of popular psychology but overlooks the historical data on the social construction of the life course. If some children of affluent families are stressed by pressures to achieve, many more find themselves without opportunities to reach adult goals (Lynott and Logue, 1993).

Young Adulthood

In our society, the beginning of adulthood is typically marked by completing one's education, taking a full-time job, or getting married, and it continues until midlife, roughly ages 40–45. In contrast to the role slack of adolescence, young adulthood is a period of great **role strain,** when the demands of work, marriage, parenthood, and civic responsibility all converge in a short time span (Chapter 4). Indeed, rates of stress-related emotional problems rise sharply at this stage before falling in midlife (Mirowsky and Ross, 1992). Violent crime rates also peak in young adulthood. And for African Americans, the stresses of establishing stable work and family careers are reflected in sharply elevated suicide rates for men in their early 20s.

> **Role strain** occurs when demands on time and energy exceed one's capacity to meet them.

In many societies, adolescence is often a period of role slack when teenagers' capabilities are underdemanded. Searching for adult roles and identities, teens may find themselves at odds with themselves and others, like these French teenagers. What were your experiences?

In Erikson's terms, the challenge is between establishing relationships of intimacy in contrast to becoming isolated from others. Work and family and community roles bring us into a web of social supports and bind us to a wider community. Although there is considerable variation by income and education, the age structure of roles is a type of "social clock," delineating the "best age" for a man or woman to marry, become a parent, settle into a lifetime occupation, and so forth. These **age norms** are internalized and used by people to measure their conformity to age-appropriate role behavior and their success or failure in achieving age-appropriate goals.

Age norms for young adults have undergone important changes in just the past two decades. As you will see in Chapter 12, the "best age" for marriage and parenthood has shifted upwards. One consequence is greater tolerance for people living together before marriage. Age norms regarding education have also been greatly modified, with four in ten college students today over age 25 (Chapter 15). Where the age norms once separated childrearing years from periods of employment for women, a majority of contemporary American mothers have combined the two. If one can generalize about this life course stage today, it would be to note the enormous diversity of patterns. Indeed, people appear to have become increasingly detached from age norms.

The life course is profoundly affected by the specific historical context in which members of a birth cohort reach adulthood. The challenges and opportunities facing young adults aged 18–24 today are shaped by such economic trends as higher housing costs and declining incomes, affecting the age and family stage of home-owning. As we detail in Chapter 13, the likelihood of finding an occupation with a clear career ladder is much lower than in the past, so that job changes will be more frequent at any life course stage. For the 56 percent of 20–24 year olds without a college education, the economic prospects are dimmer than just a decade ago and are not expected to improve in the immediate future (Kalish, 1992).

The interplay of birth cohort and economic conditions may also be seen in differences in projected earnings for high school-educated fathers and sons. If the economy does not dramatically improve in the 1990s, it will be harder for a man with a high school education to earn his way into the middle class than it was for his father (Levy and Michel, 1991). Not only will mobility hopes be crushed, but failure to find rewarding work in young adulthood can undermine one's sense of self-worth and lead to rejection of societal norms, as can be seen in America's inner cities today, especially among young men. Lack of career advancement is also associated with lowered life expectency for men (Pavalko et al., 1993).

Because of changes in both the age structure and the historical context, the idealized view of the 1950s young couple, seen in television reruns of such programs as "Father Knows Best," no longer portray the realities faced by most young couples today.

Middle Age

The most recent life stage to be discovered as a unique period is middle age, variously defined as "older than young adulthood and younger than old age." In societies with low life expectancy, there was no need to distinguish different stages of adulthood; thus, the "discovery" of middle age is a product of being able to live longer.

THE APPEARANCE OF AGING. The visible effects of aging are typically greeted with fear and resistance in America and probably most other modern societies. People will go to elaborate lengths to hide hair loss and graying, remove wrinkles, or maintain their waistline. Because of the sexual double standard of aging, these cosmetic changes have a greater impact on women than on men. Despite the many recent changes in gender relationships, femininity remains largely associated with sexual attractiveness and fertility, so that a woman's social value tends to diminish with age. Conversely, masculinity is associated with control and power, qualities that are enhanced with maturity, if not old age. These gendered images are reflected and reinforced in the media. When was the last time you saw an "older" male actor paired with a woman close to his age? In fact, when was the last time you saw an older woman portrayed as sexually active or desirable—outside of a situation comedy?

ECONOMIC DIFFERENCES. Middle-aged men and women also differ in labor force participation, the type of jobs they occupy, and their earnings. Many of these differences, however, are narrowing as (1) younger cohorts of women expect to remain in the full-time labor force throughout adulthood and (2) older men are retiring at an increasingly earlier age. According to recent projection, much of the increase in the labor force over the next decade will be from middle-aged women, while men aged 25–54 "are expected to lose some of their inclination to work" (Exter, 1992, p. 59).

Wage differentials may also narrow, but the current cohort of middle-aged women is very disadvantaged in the labor market. Men continue to retain and find employment in industries that provide both better pay and retirement benefits than do the occupations in which women are concentrated (Korczyk, 1993).

MID-LIFE CRISIS. Defined by Erikson as a period of *generativity versus stagnation*, mid-life is commonly thought to be a period of intense "crisis." The concept of mid-life crisis may sell a lot of popular psychology books, but it, too, has minimal empirical

Changes in appearance are probably the most dramatic evidence of aging, and both men and women spend considerable sums of money to keep their youthful looks. Do you think it's worth the effort?

For both men and women, middle age is typically a period of maximum social power. People age 45–64 enjoy the highest levels of income and occupational prestige. Marriage partners who have stuck together for three decades or longer consider themselves as happy as when they were newlyweds. The tribulations of child rearing are over, and marital happiness increases sharply once the children have left home (White and Edwards, 1990). Yet this is also a period of preparation for the status changes that are now a part of modern life, heralded by concern, care, and perhaps the death of one's parents and grandparents.

Old Age

Despite lip service to the concept of "productive aging," few respected roles are currently available to older people in modern societies. The cultural construction of old age encourages elders to internalize their limitation and settle for less than their actual capacities (Philipson, 1982). Age bias in both developing and industrialized nations tends to exclude the elderly from roles that could be occupied by younger people (David, 1993; *Aging International,* 1993). Yet it is at the oldest age levels that age-related capacities become a major social and personal issue. There are few role prescriptions for old people other than to avoid being "odd" or "troublesome." This situation

support. Mid-life may bring its particular strains but not extreme mental disorder (Mirowsky and Ross, 1992; Clausen, 1993).

But the myth persists. Women are assumed to suffer from various "losses"—of sexual attractiveness, of the mothering role, and possibly of one's husband (through divorce or death). Yet the great majority of middle-aged women find mid-life a highly satisfying period. There will, of course, be some women whose world has been so centered on home and family that they have no other source of self-worth; for them mid-life can bring on a crisis of identity that leads to physical or emotional illnesses. But these outcomes are uncommon among American women today.

For middle-aged men, the problem is one of adjusting earlier expectations of success to their current situations. Some will use the concept of mid-life crisis to justify or explain a major change in life-style: divorcing the wife of 25 years and marrying a younger woman, taking up flying, or, perhaps, buying a red sports car. Note that these descriptions of mid-life crisis are based on the white middle-class experience. Indeed, Erikson's "universal" scheme of developmental stages is derived almost exclusively from observations of upper middle-class white men in mid-twentieth-century industrial society. The great majority of American men negotiate mid-life without engaging in extreme behavior of any variety.

What are age-appropriate activities and practices in old age? What are the benefits of an active life, whether in the People's Republic of China or in the United States?

should produce high rates of deviance, but precisely the opposite is the case.

DEVIANCE. The rates for almost all forms of deviance decline across adulthood—especially for crime and drug and alcohol abuse. To a large extent, these data simply reflect the fact that people with bad habits do not live as long as those without. They may also reflect differing age cohort patterns, because today's elderly were socialized in an era with more restrictive views about the recreational use of drugs or alcohol. Therefore, the cohort that grew up in the 1960s may be very different in this regard than today's old people. Another explanation for the relative lack of deviance among the elderly is based on a biosocial model (Gove, 1985). In this view, the kinds of deviance that involve risky and physically demanding behavior will decline with age, especially among men, as their hormone levels drop and their physical strength declines.

The one deviant behavior that does increase, but only among white males, is *suicide,* as shown in Figure 7-1 on page 148. Contrary to popular belief that retirement drives men to suicide, there is no sharp increase at age 65. Rather, it is men who have become widowed or who have lost other social contacts, with friends or their adult children, who are most at risk—as Emile Durkheim had predicted.

AGE AND POWER. When is a person "too old" for a given role? In the past, this was not too difficult to answer because few lived long enough to outgrow some form of usefulness—as a source of knowledge or household helper. In agricultural societies, the older the male, the greater his power over younger members of the family. In many societies, the social power of women is enhanced once child rearing is completed.

These powers, however, are based on the elders' ability to control things of value either to the whole society or to their children: information, land, other forms of wealth, the choice of marriage partner. It is precisely these forms of control that are lost to the elderly in the course of industrialization. Children become less dependent on parental resources; they can make their own way in educational and occupational systems that reward achievement; and they can select a marriage partner without consideration of kinship obligations. In other words, the elderly lose power in modern societies because of social structural changes and not because adult children have become suddenly hard-hearted.

The status honor shown to the elderly in the past or in nonindustrial societies today flows less from deeply felt affection than from fear of offending the elders who could cut off access to resources. There was no "golden age" in history and there are no "golden isles" of simple natives today in which elders have been automatically loved or respected (Nydegger, 1991). And there is no reason to believe that younger members of the family enjoyed their powerlessness more in the past than they do today. The Bible and Greek drama are filled with stories of dysfunctional families, rebellious children who murder their parents, and tyrannical parents who cause the death of their children. More recently, the commonly assumed culture of respect for the elderly in Asian nations such as China or Japan has not withstood the pressures of industrialization. In the majority of developing nations, not only have elders lost their control over scarce resources, but national governments

The respect and care of the elderly has not withstood the pressures of industrialization in many nations. A number of older women and men in Moscow, Russia, have had to sell their belongings at a "beggars" market in order to buy food for themselves.

are too poor to finance programs for their older population.

One of the hallmarks of a modern society, in contrast, is the ability to provide income and health care to the elderly, thus reducing dependency on one's own family. But this security is the other side of the coin of losing control over valued resources at both the family and societal level. The occupational skills of older workers are rendered obsolete in a rapidly changing economy. Increased life expectancy adds to the numbers who require old age health and income supports. These trends all combine to change the meaning of old age itself, as the elderly come to be viewed as a social burden.

THE ELDERLY IN MODERN SOCIETY

Theoretical Perspectives

In functional terms, older people in modern society are relatively disadvantaged in terms of power and prestige, although not necessarily in terms of income. But the shift in responsibility for the well-being of older people from families to the society as a whole is also functional in that most old people will be better off than if totally dependent on the resources of kin (Haber and Gratton, 1994).

In *exchange* terms, status losses leave older people with little bargaining power. Their major claim to societal resources is based on the expectation of reciprocity for the contributions they once made to society and for the care they once gave their own offspring, as well as their voting power in a democracy. In exchange, their own children and current wage earners have an obligation to return the favors.

Some elderly are more favored than others. Many come to old age with all the advantages they enjoyed earlier in life. In the United States, unlike other modern societies, retirement income is based on previous earnings while social programs in housing, transportation, and health care are underfunded (Pampel and Hardy, 1994).

From the *conflict* perspective, therefore, many older Americans endure the same struggle for resources that they waged when younger. The same subgroups that were disadvantaged earlier in the life course are even less well off in old age: women, the unmarried, African Americans, Hispanics, and low earners in general. Particularly disadvantaged are very old women (80+), most of whom have outlived their husband and even their own children, whose only income is Social Security, and who are likely to have one or more long-term illness (Hess and Markson, 1991).

DEVELOPMENTAL PERSPECTIVES. In Erikson's formulation, old age is a period of integrity versus despair. Integrity refers here to looking back on one's life and seeing it as a meaningful whole in which one can take satisfaction (*integrity* means both oneness and virtue). Despair, in contrast, suggests dissatisfaction and a lack of continuity. As with much of Erikson's theory, empirical tests of this assumption are lacking, and until recently, few researchers have paid attention to sex differences in old age. Both men and women were lumped together as "elderly"—implying that gender is irrelevant—while models based on the experience of men were defined as "normal aging."

More recently, however, researchers have probed the differences between men and women's experience of aging. In many respects, despite their lower income and lesser social worth, women cope with the changes and losses of old age more successfully than do men (Hurwich, 1993).

Whatever power and prestige are to be gained from the role of wife and mother must come through one's children (a situation that often leads to overprotecting, especially of sons). But in many nonindustrial societies, once a woman has completed her major tasks of bearing and rearing children, her status in the society improves. Middle age often brings personal freedoms and enhanced social power. When her children are grown, a woman has fewer restrictions on her physical movements; she can exert influence on her children's marriage choices and give orders to her daughters-in-law; and she can even be eligible for roles in the larger community (Brown and Kerns, 1985).

We have already noted that widowhood is particularly difficult for men, many of whom have been totally dependent on their wife for social support. In contrast, women are likely to be embedded in friendship networks that provide continuing support and companionship (Akiyama and Antonucci, 1993).

Growing evidence also suggests that men and women undergo personality changes in mid-life and old age that reduce the extremes of masculinity and femininity that characterize earlier stages of the life course. Women become more independent and aggressive, while men become more nurturant and dependent—a transformation that appears to hold cross-culturally (Gutmann, 1987).

Myths of Aging

The well-being of older Americans today has been profoundly affected by a number of untested or untrue assumptions: myths of aging.

THE CHANGING DEPENDENCY RATIO AND THE "GREEDY" ELDERLY. Because Americans live longer and have fewer children than in the past, there has been a marked change in the composition of the "dependency ratio": the number of people younger than age 18 or older than age 64 compared with the number of people between the working ages of 18 to 64. In 1900, for example, an average couple had four children, compared to two today. In 1900, there were 7 elders for every 100 people of working age; today there 12. For the first time in history, the average American couple has more living parents than children (Preston, 1984).

Because Social Security benefits are based on a worker's previous earnings and are funded by a payroll tax on current workers, the shift in the old-age dependency ratio means that fewer workers are supporting more retired elderly than in the past. Conservative critics of Social Security claim that this is an unfair burden on current and future workers whose wages are lowered by Social Security deductions. The counter argument is that the *total* dependency ratio remains unchanged because the increase in elderly is offset by the decrease in younger dependents. In addition, the United States is the only industrial nation that funds old-age pensions with a payroll tax rather than from generally collected revenues. If the United States adopted the policy of other nations, current and future workers would have less cause for intergenerational resentment.

The same critics of Social Security also claim that the nation has been overly generous to its elderly and that the portion of the federal budget dedicated to programs for older Americans is responsible for the national deficit. The "greedy" elderly are portrayed as taking money that could be spent on children and other more worthy targets. The counterarguments are that no new programs for the elderly have been enacted since 1972 and that existing benefits have been steadily cut back. For example, the taxable share of Social Security payments has been increased and the cost of living adjustment reduced. Since its introduction in 1965, Medicare (a federal program that reimburses health care providers to the elderly) has been pared down so that older Americans today pay the same proportion of their medical bills out-of-pocket as they did before 1965 (see Chapter 18).

Nonetheless, health care of the elderly remains a major cost to the nation, which has led some politicians and scientists to suggest rationing medical treatment to older people. Denying health care to any individual to contain costs raises a number of ethical as well as practical issues. In Great Britain, where kidney dialysis and heart transplants are rationed on the basis of age, decision makers have found the guidelines helpful in reducing stress over choosing who will live or die. The age cutoff is simple and objective, and it also has been a great money saver (Halper, 1993). Are the elderly less worthy of care than younger people? Is age alone a suitable criterion considering the enormous variation within the category of persons 80 and older? If age today, what characteristic will it be tomorrow?

PARADISE LOST AND FAMILY ABANDONMENT.   The myth of a lost paradise of happy families gives rise to the myth of family abandonment of its elders. Although par-

No new programs for the elderly have been enacted in the United States since 1972. Despite that, volunteers continue to help the elderly such as in this senior center in Hackensack, New Jersey.

ent–child relationships may have always been somewhat conflicted, it is also the case that family members remain the primary source of assistance across the life course (Stoller, 1985). Resources flow from the more to the less able, so that parents typically provide more support over a longer period of time to their children than do the children provide to their parents in later life (Hogan et al., 1993).

Refuting the myth of abandonment, study after study has shown high rates of concern, contact, and caring (Bengtson and Achenbaum, 1993; Harootyan et al., 1993). Today, over 80 percent of middle-aged Americans have at least one living parent, in contrast to less than one-half in 1900. Despite increasing residential mobility, the great majority of older people live within one hour's driving distance from at least one of their children. Family members remain the core of an older person's social support system, with friends and neighbors in secondary roles (Stoller and Pugliesi, 1988; Akiyama and Antonucci, 1993).

INSTITUTIONS AS DUMPING GROUNDS FOR THE UNWANTED. The extreme form of the myth of family abandonment has large numbers of frail elderly being "dumped" into nursing homes by uncaring kin. The very opposite is the case. Only 5 percent of Americans age 65+ are housed in long-term care units. The increase in *numbers* (but not proportion) of nursing home patients is due both to the actual increase in numbers of frail elderly and to the growth of the nursing home industry. Nursing home patients are overwhelmingly women, age 85 and older, white, widowed, with multiple disabilities, and likely to have lived alone before admission. Older men typically are cared for at home by a wife. African Americans and Latinas are very unlikely to enter a long-term care facility; consequently, their families bear a great burden for their care when they become severely impaired (Worobey and Angel, 1990a).

Because Medicare covers only a few special cases, and because few beds are reserved for poor people in the Medicaid program, the vast bulk of nursing home costs are born by patients and their family. At an average of over $100 per day, or $40,000–60,000 per year, not many families could afford to "dump" granny, even if they wished to. To the contrary, families try every possible alternative to institutionalization. Nursing home placement is the last resort and typically follows a serious medical setback or major change in the family's ability to care for a frail relative (Aneshensel et al., 1993). It is people *without* children or friends nearby who are most likely to be institutionalized and to remain for a longer period (V. Freedman, 1993).

Disabled elderly are most often taken care of in the community by family members with assistance from neighbors and paid helpers. Most prefer to remain in their own home rather than move in with an adult child, but many frail elderly have no choice but to join the household of one of their children, usually a daughter. In general, women—wives, daughters, and daughters-in-law—perform the bulk of care-giving tasks, at great emotional and physical cost (Pearlin et al., 1990).

Yet as long as the myths persist, social policy toward the elderly will be affected, even when the myths conflict—for example, that old people are living it up in Florida at the expense of hard-working young adults but are also being dumped by heartless children. In the final section, we look at the life situations of America's elderly today.

Life Situations of Older Americans

MARITAL STATUS AND LIVING ARRANGEMENTS.   As you can see in Table 7-3, marital status and living arrangements among persons 65+ differ greatly by sex. Older men are twice as likely as their female age peers to be married and living with a spouse. These data reflect the facts that women live longer than men and that wives are typically younger than their husband.

The great majority of elderly, couples or single persons, live in their own household, but 10 percent of men and 18 percent of women are in the household of someone else, usually an adult child. African-American and Latino elderly are more likely than whites to be in the household of a relative, as are recent immigrants from Asia and the Pacific Islands (Woroby and Angel, 1990b; Yee, 1990). In part, this pattern reflects ethnic cultural norms but is largely dictated by economic circumstances that make separate households impossible. Of the 8.5 million older Americans who live alone, 80 percent are women, primarily white

TABLE 7-3   Marital Status and Living Arrangements of Noninstitutionalized Elderly (65+), by Sex, Race and Hispanic Origin: 1993 (in Percents)

	White		African American		Hispanic	
Marital Status	Men	Women	Men	Women	Men	Women
Married, spouse present	77	42	56	26	69	37
Widowed	13	47	23	56	17	44
Divorced, separated	5	6	15	13	9	10
Never married	4	4	6	4	4	8
Living Arrangements						
Alone	15	43	29	40	11	25
With spouse	76	41	54	25	73	36
With relatives	6	14	12	33	14	36
With nonrelatives	3	2	5	2	2	3

Source: U.S. Bureau of the Census, P20-478, 1994.

Although the media have focused on women in nontraditional jobs, most people over the age of 55 are employed in traditionally low-paying job categories, including the service sector's fast-food chains.

and widowed, but many will have never married. Contrary to popular belief, never-married elderly are not socially isolated, enjoying a high level of interaction with friends and siblings.

LABOR FORCE PARTICIPATION AND INCOME. As more Americans live longer, one might expect that they would remain in the labor force until later ages. But such is not the case. Since 1950, the median age at retirement for both men and women has declined; from age 66.9 in 1950 to 62.3 today for men; and from age 67.7 to 62 for women (Gendell and Siegel, 1992). The typical American 25-year-old today can expect to spend 1.2 years out of the labor force for every year at work (Kotlikoff, 1992).

Many older workers have been encouraged with financial incentives to retire before age 65 to make room for the large baby boom cohort; others have been let go by employers in the process of "downsizing" their work force to increase profits (see Chapter 13). Large numbers have also elected to retire as early as health and income permit. Although most analysts expect retirement ages to continue to decline, much depends on whether or not Social Security benefits, private pensions, and personal savings provide sufficient income.

Social Security is the single largest source of income for Americans age 65 and over, roughly 36 percent. An additional 18 percent comes from private pensions; 24 percent from income from assets, 18 percent from earnings, and 3 percent from "other." Despite the claim that America's elderly are being spoiled by an array of government benefits, older people in the United States derive a *smaller* proportion of income from government programs than do their counterparts in other in other modern industrial societies (Quinn and Smeeding, 1993; Williamson and Pampel, 1993). For example, Sweden and the Netherlands provide about 70 percent of retirement incomes, twice the proportion for the United States, in addition to broader health care programs. And benefits do not reach all Americans entitled to receive them: only 30 percent of poor people are enrolled in Medicaid, and only 60 percent receive Supplementary Security Income (SSI) or food stamps (*Update,* 1993).

The aggregate data on sources of income obscure wide differences on the basis of sex, race, and class. Few women or African Americans or low-skill manual workers have access to private pension plans or income from investments. As a result, as shown in Table 7-4, poverty rates among the elderly vary by sex and race. Although overall poverty rates for older Americans declined by half in the 1960s, thanks to the introduction of Medicare and changes in the Social Security system, there are pockets of extreme poverty among women in general and women of color in particular.

People who live alone ("unrelated individuals") are more likely to be poor than are those who live with a spouse or other relative; and because women predominate among unrelated individuals, the poverty rate for older women is twice that of older men. Elderly American women who live alone are much more likely to be poor than their counterparts in other Western societies (Quinn and Smeeding, 1993). The poverty rate for elderly Latinas is 51 percent; among African-American women age 65+ living alone, 58 percent have incomes below the poverty level! Fortunately, not many minority women are in this category, because most will be in the household of a daughter or other relative. In contrast, 24 percent of white unrelated elderly women live in poverty.

The poverty threshold for persons 65+ in 1993 was $6,930 for an unrelated individual and $8,740 for a two-person household. These numbers, calculated with such precision, are based on the assumption that

TABLE 7-4   Poverty Rates for Americans Age 65+, by Sex and Race: 1992 (Percentages)

	White	African American
Men	6.4	23.2
Women	13.7	31.0

Source: U.S. Bureau of the Census, *Current Population Reports,* P60-188, 1994.

Early Retirement in Europe: The New Age Grading?

In the United States, the age at which workers must leave the labor force (*mandatory retirement*) was raised, largely to reduce the cost of the Social Security program through delaying retirement. Throughout Europe, however, the opposite strategy has been adopted: The retirement age has been lowered to open up jobs for younger workers. Widespread unemployment and other effects of the worldwide recession were causing much social unrest. In addition, from the employer's viewpoint, it is cheaper to hire a younger worker at entry-level pay than to retain an older one. Thus, employees over age 55, or even age 50, have been targeted for layoffs and early retirement incentives (Drury, 1993).

Removing older people from the labor force is changing the terms of social exchange, the unspoken bargain between generations, by increasing competition among age strata for societal resources. New conflicts regarding employment, promotion, and retirement have developed in the workplace. Especially hard hit are workers in Greece and Spain. Spanish workers are forced to retire at age 60, resulting in a 40 percent permanent reduction in basic pensions. In Greece, working mothers gain the right to a government pension at age 55 and are typically then dismissed by employers, even if they need the work to maintain their family.

These policies affect age stratification patterns. Unemployed European workers over age 50 have little hope of finding other employment. Use of age limits in job advertisements is widespread everywhere, except France, where it is illegal. Displaced workers find that their expected movement through the life course has been suddenly rearranged; normative definitions of appropriate mid-life roles are no longer applicable. As one British man put it: "I feel as though I should be working at my age. When I wake up I feel I should be going to work" (Taylor and Walker, 199, p. 37).

The large number of unemployed workers in their 50s is producing a new social age category: the "prematurely retired." Are they still "middle-aged" or have they become "young–old"? In this way, the trend toward early job loss not only changes the interaction context of everyday behavior but also calls for a revision of the models that until recently ordered both individual lives and theories of life course development.

---

people age 65 and over need less money than younger persons. For example, the poverty line for a single person age 65+ is exactly $588 lower than the threshold for someone age 64.

To summarize, the life situation of America's elderly has improved greatly since the mid-1960s, when one-third lived in poverty. Nonetheless, the economic situation of older widows remains fragile, as does their health status (health issues will be covered in Chapter 18, along with a more detailed discussion of the Medicare and Medicaid programs). Because women greatly outnumber men in the older population, their inability to maintain an independent household is likely to become a major social problem in the decades ahead. Being forced to share the home of an adult child is not a satisfying solution for members of either generation. Yet any attempt to balance the federal or state budgets by cutting into programs for the elderly will have a powerful negative effect on the most vulnerable: persons of color, working-class families, and widows who live alone.

For many elderly, then, the last stage of the life course brings elements of despair. Perhaps the most amazing aspect of the research data is the relatively high degree of integrity displayed by so many older women and men.

Because incoming cohorts of older Americans will be different from those who are aged 65+ today, the experience of aging will also undergo change. Most important, the elderly of the future will be better educated than in the past and education is associated with better mental and physical health. This means lower disability rates, as well as less decline in cognitive skills (Schaie, 1994). In other words, tomorrow's old people will enjoy many years of active well-being. But they will also live long enough to spend time in a nursing home (especially those without adult children) and higher proportions of women will have never married and/or had children. There is also evidence of a lessened sense of responsibility for elder care among adult children of divorced parents (Riche, 1993).

SOCIAL POLICY

What if We All Live Longer?

Will the maximum number of years people can live (the **life span**) change dramatically within the next century? What would be required to extend life expectancy, that is, the average amount of time any of us could expect to live? The United States now has more people 85 years of age and older than any other nation. Some scientists argue that there is no biological limit to life itself but

> The **life span** refers to the oldest age to which it is possible to live.

only age-related physical decline for which intervention is possible in the future. To date, however, there is no definitive proof that the human life span itself can be increased. If mortality conditions were to improve as much as they did during the past few decades, the number of people aged 85 and over could quadruple by 2030, accounting for 4 percent of the total population (Olshanskey, 1992).

For most developed nations, this would mean eradicating the major causes of death in old age including heart disease, cancer, and stroke. Thus, if heart disease—the major cause of death—were eliminated in the United States, people at age 65 could expect to gain another five years of life, another two years if cancer were obliterated. The effect on the length of human life would be to condense mortality into a few short years: people would live out their lives relatively free from heart disease or cancer but would know that normal biological deficits that are due to aging would result in death at about age 100.

An opposing view has been offered by scientists who suggest that such gains are unrealistic, because science and medicine have pushed human life expectancy to its natural limit of about 85 years—close to the current life expectancy in Japan. Dramatic breakthroughs in modern health care and medicine such as the development of antibiotics and organ transplants have increased average life expectancy but have not pushed the maximum length of life (the life span) much beyond what it had been in ancient times.

If life expectancies do increase, issues arise about the quality of life for older people: the number of years of active life expectancy versus the number of years of chronic illness or incapacity. An increase in life expectancy without good health would expand the proportion of people who may live long enough to suffer from dementia, arthritis, diabetes, and so forth. A growing area of inquiry thus is that of biotechnology to detect and modify disease processes. Studies in human genetics now enable discovery of many genetic disorders before their onset: not only unusual diseases but also genetic susceptibility. As techniques become available to repair genetic defects or replace the genes, many diseases can be treated at their source. Searches for specific drugs, supplanting the loss of genetic function that directly or indirectly regulate the rate of age-related diseases and perhaps aging itself, are underway.

Genetic engineering and gene therapy seem to hold the promise that we shall be able to bring about radical changes in the physical and psychological attributes of human beings. Because gene therapy alters the genetic structure of the person and his or her offspring, it presents a new twist on eugenics, or selective breeding. But this new twist also presents profound social policy issues: Who should define "normal" human functioning for selective breeding? If, indeed, the human life span can be extended so that there are no natural limits, how many years should people live? How would social construction of the life course and the age structure of roles be affected? And what changes in our social institutions would be required if life expectancy increases dramatically or if there is no limit to the life span?

SUMMARY

1. Age stratification means the differential distribution of social resources on the basis of age. The life course perspective of aging is directly related to age stratification. This perspective focuses on continuity and change across the life course.

2. Age is an ascribed characteristic that has several important features: It is transitional; it has a hierarchy of power and prestige through a lifetime; and socially constructed norms exist for each age stratum.

3. The age structure of a society varies with each society and can vary over time. Birth cohorts represent groups of people who were born at the same time. Life expectancy refers to the average number of years members of a cohort can expect to live.

4. Although biological factors often set limits on behavior, most age limits are socially and culturally defined.

5. The psychologist Erik Erikson identified the life course as a series of dynamic developmental periods through which each person much pass successfully to avoid later problems. An important function of this approach is that it includes the interaction of the individual and society at each stage.

6. The notion of childhood has changed over time as infant mortality declined and because children are no longer required to be income earners.

7. The newly identified life stage of adolescence is a socially constructed bridge between childhood and adulthood. It is a time of role slack, where the capabilities of adolescents are underused. Role slack is also evident during old age.

8. Young adulthood is a period of role strain, when many varied demands are made on people.

9. The newest stage of adulthood is middle age, the stage of maximum social power. The term "mid-

life crisis" is another social construct that has little empirical support.

10. Deviant behavior tends to decrease across the stages of adulthood, partly as a result of early death of those with bad habits, and partly as a result of a decline in physically risky behavior.

11. In modern society, the loss of power and control for the elderly is a result of changes in social structure. Even in some Asian cultures, traditionally known for respecting elders, industrialization has brought with it a loss of power for elders.

12. From a functional viewpoint, the loss of power and prestige by the elderly is a logical outcome of the limited contribution they make to society. Responsibility for the elderly has shifted from the family to society.

13. According to exchange theory, loss of status leaves the elderly with little bargaining power.

14. From a conflict perspective, older people struggle for resources as they did when they were younger.

15. Researchers who study aging from a developmental perspective report that women cope with the changes of aging more easily than men do. In some ways, women become more aggressive and independent, while men become more dependent and nurturant as they age.

16. The untrue myths of aging are numerous: That aging "dependency ratio" has created an excessive burden on those now paying social security, that family elders have been abandoned by family members, and that institutions have become a dumping ground for the elderly.

17. The living arrangements of older people show great variability, although older men are twice as likely as older women to be married and living with a spouse. People who live alone are more likely to be poor than are those living with a spouse or other relative.

18. The median retirement age for both men and women has declined, to about 62 for each. Social security is the largest single source of income for those over age 65.

SUGGESTED READINGS

Abel, Emily K. *Who Cares for the Elderly? Public Policy and the Experiences of Adult Daughters.* Philadelphia: Temple University Press, 1991. The author examines care givers and public policies by focusing on the relationships between the person being cared for and the people who assist in care giving–doctors, nurses, and nursing home administrators. Interviews with adult daughters caring for older mothers and fathers show that in addition to physical care, care givers are really care managers with many different types of responsibilities.

Bengtson, Vern L., and W. Andrew Achenbaum, eds. *The Changing Contract across Generations.* New York: Aldine de Gruyter, 1993. An assessment of generational ties by gender, race, and class, and a look at how societal changes create conflict in family members relationships and social ties.

Blieszner, Rosemary, and Rebecca G. Adams. *Adult Friendship.* Newbury Park, CA: Sage, 1992. Using a structural, cultural, and historical approach to the development of friendships, this interesting book examines friendships among young adults—primarily college aged, the middle aged, and the elderly.

Cahill, Spencer E. ed. *Sociological Studies of Child Development: A Research Annual. Vol. 5: Perspectives on and of Children.* Greenwich, CT: JAI Press, 1993. Includes current thought, advances, and techniques in theoretical, global, institutional, interactional, and retrospective childhood studies.

Clair, Jeffrey, David Karp, and William Yoels. *Experiencing the Life Cycle: A Social Psychology of Aging.* An organized framework for thinking about aging through the use of subjective, personal responses to aging made by people in their daily lives.

Elder, Glen H. *Children of the Great Depression.* Chicago: University of Chicago Press, 1974. A classic study of the depression-years cohorts and the impact of social-historical events on their lives.

Gubrium, Jaber F. *Speaking of Life: Horizons of Meaning for Nursing Home Residents.* Hawthorn, NY: Aldine De Gruyter, 1993. An ethnographic compilation of narratives from people living in nursing homes. The focus of the research is to assess the quality of long-term care by interviewing the people receiving the care.

Hess, Beth B., and Elizabeth W. Markson, eds. *Growing Old in America. 4th ed.* New Brunswick, NJ: Transaction Books 1991. A collection of original essays and recent reprints at the cutting edge of social gerontology, with special emphasis on the political economy of aging.

Keith, Pat H., and Robert B. Schafer. *Relationships and Well-Being over the Life Stages.* New York: Praeger, 1991. A comparison of marital and gender relationships and their effect on the psychological well-being of men and women in different family configurations; single-parent households and married couples divided on the basis of parent status, employment status, and life-course stage.

Kohli, Martin, Martin Rein, Anne-Marie Guillemard, and Herman van Gunstern, eds. *Time for Retirement: Comparative Studies of Early Exit from the Labor Force.* Cambridge, England: Cambridge University Press, 1991. Most high-income countries have experienced a decline in the participation of men ages 55–64 in the workforce. This volume examines the trends of early retirement in seven countries, including the Netherlands, France, Germany, Great Britain, the United States, Sweden, and Hungary.

Marshall, Victor W., ed. *Aging in Canada: Social Perspectives.* 2d ed. Toronto: Fitzhenry and Whiteside, 1987. An interesting anthology of articles examining the diverse experiences of aging in Canada.

Minkler, Meredith, and Carroll L. Estes, eds. *Critical perspectives on Aging: The Political and Moral Economy of Growing Old.* Amityville, NY: Baywood, 1991. The political economy of aging is connected to the concept of the moral economy with special attention on the effects of gender, race, and class in regard to access to resources throughout the life course.

Schulz, James H., Allan Borowski, and William H. Crown. *Economics of Population Aging: The "Graying" of Australia, Japan, and the United States.* New York: Auburn House, 1991. A probing macroeconomic comparison of the implication of economic aging in Australia, Japan, and the United States that examines retirement policies, the relative income adequacy and net worth of older persons, government and private pension provisions, the labor market for older workers, and the ability of the countries to deal with the future economic "burdens" that may result from a growing older population.

Szinovacz, Maximillian, David J. Ekerdt, and Barbara H. Vinick, eds. *Families and Retirement.* Newbury Park, CA: Sage, 1992. Retirement is usually viewed as taking place solely in the workplace, but retirement also occurs in relationship to events and situations in the family. This volume looks at the timing of retirement, the family lives of retired persons, and gender differences in the social activities of retired persons.

Waksler, Frances Chaput, ed. *Studying the Social Worlds of Children: Sociological Readings.* New York: Falmer Press, 1991. Includes previously published and often-cited articles with a helpful commentary by Waksler, which make it useful for the classroom.

8

Sexualities: Identities and Behaviors

SOCIOLOGICAL PERSPECTIVES ON SEXUALITY
Functional Perspective
Conflict Perspective • Interpretive Models
SEXUALITY IN THE UNITED STATES
Historical Perspectives
Sexual Norms and Behaviors Today
Adolescent Sexuality
Adolescent Pregnancy and Parenthood
SOCIAL POLICY Abortion—Whose Body? Whose Baby?
Reproduction, Sexuality, and the Law
HOMOSEXUALITIES: THE LESBIAN AND GAY MALE EXPERIENCE
Cross-Cultural and Historical Perspective
Roots of Homosexuality
Prevalence of Homosexuality
SOCIOLOGISTS AT WORK "Researching the Social Contexts of Sexuality" by Beth E. Schneider
Organizing for Gay Rights • Life-Styles and Pair Relationships
SEXUAL VIOLENCE
Child Molesting • Violence against Women
Pornography • Sexual Harassment
THE FLIP SIDE OF THE SEXUAL REVOLUTION
SUMMARY ■ SUGGESTED READINGS

*S*exual notes across time and space:

- The most successful military forces of ancient Sparta and Thebes were composed of pairs of older and younger male lovers (Cohen, 1993).
- Among the weightier matters decided by the United States Supreme Court in 1993 was the custody of seven frozen embryos, fertilized in a laboratory but not yet implanted.
- The Hijra cult of modern India is composed of men who choose to live as women, undergoing castration as teenagers, and spending their life in close-knit communes whose members share income earned from blessing babies and begging on the street (Nanda, 1984).
- Several recent studies suggest that close to half of American women have been subjected to an unwanted sexual encounter (M. Smith, 1994).

Clearly, sexuality is not always what we think it is or should be. In the United States, sexual taboos have lessened; one need only compare television programs from a decade ago to what can be seen nightly on the "family" networks today (not to mention MTV). At the same time, the Puritan streak in American culture remains strong, as seen in the resistance to sex education and in the fierce condemnation of homosexuality. Thus, although most Americans accept the liberating potential of varied sexual expression, fears and anxieties persist, as do sexual violence and exploitation.

This dual image of sexuality, as both pleasurable and frightening, is found throughout human history. Although human sexuality is a powerful basic drive, the reflexive mind that sets us apart from other animals also means that our sexual feelings and actions are not automatic responses to biological urges. Sexual reproduction is essential to group survival, but unregulated sexuality can threaten social order and divert attention from other survival tasks. Therefore, no society leaves sexual feelings and actions to chance; such potentially disruptive impulses must be brought under normative control. Each society has defined certain expressions of sexuality as acceptable or forbidden, so that the range of "normal" sexual conduct is as varied as the human imagination itself (Davis and Whitten, 1987).

In recognition of the flexibility and variability of sexuality, this chapter is entitled "Sexualities." We begin with an overview of sociological perspectives and the history of sexuality in America. The next section examines contemporary norms and behaviors, including adolescent sexuality and childbearing, and the current debate over abortion. This is followed by an extended examination of homosexualities and the politics of the gay male and lesbian experience in America. The chapter closes with a discussion of sexual violence and a consideration of both the confining and liberating potential of today's broadened range of sexual possibilities.

SOCIOLOGICAL PERSPECTIVES ON SEXUALITY

Sexuality is private and public, personal and political, praised or punished—depending on who does what to whom and under what conditions. In other words, it is the definition of the situation that constitutes "normal" sexual conduct in any society. The norms that govern sexual expression are social products, the result of conflicting pressures, and subject to change over time (Callero and Howard, 1989). Sexual attraction and expression are complex experiences, shaped by culture, learned through socialization, and sanctioned within social networks (Simon and Gagnon, 1986).

In addition to the regulation of behavior, culture and social structure also interact with biology to influence the development of a person's *sexual identities*. These identities are of three types: (1) **sex identity,** a basic definition of the self as female or male; (2) **gender identity,** a sense of being appropriately feminine or masculine; and (3) **erotic identity,** based on the object of sexual attraction, persons of the opposite or same sex. Of these, gender identity is most thoroughly socially constructed, and sex identity most linked to biological forces. Erotic identity, as we see later in this chapter, has been contested terrain.

> **Sex identity** is a definition of the self as female or male.
>
> **Gender identity** is a sense of being feminine or masculine.
>
> **Erotic identity** is based on the object of sexual attraction—persons of the opposite or same sex.

Functional Perspective

The functional approach emphasizes how sexuality is channeled in socially productive directions. For example, restricting legitimate sexual activities to marriage partners will encourage family formation and high levels of marital childbearing. This norm is reinforced by defining homosexuality and sex outside of marriage as "sick" or "evil," a view that dominated American society and sociology up to the 1960s. Even today, American law and the courts continue to reflect traditional mores (Green, 1993). In 1986 the Supreme Court upheld the right of states to define "correct" positions for sexual intercourse, with all other acts being "sodomy" and therefore illegal.

Sexual attraction and expression are complex experiences, shaped by culture and learned through socialization.

Conflict Perspective

The conflict model focuses on who has the power to define "normal" sexuality (Foucault, 1978; Connell, 1987). In the U.S., regulation of sexuality is a state matter, so that there are actually 50 different standards of legal conduct in our nation. Religious authorities have also had great influence in defining proper behavior, not only from the pulpit but also by influencing legislation.

Customs and laws that limit sexual expression are instruments of social control, typically exercised by dominant groups over relatively powerless populations such as women or racial/ethnic minorities. In most societies, men are allowed greater sexual freedom than women, and the native-born are considered sexually superior to "promiscuous" immigrants. For many Americans, a man with many love affairs is an admired "stud;" a woman with lovers is a "slut" (Stombler, 1994). Think, also, of how the media portray sexuality among minorities, feeding fears that once justified lynching and that are still used to condemn black men for acts that are rarely punished when committed by whites (Collins, 1990).

The laws imposed by the powerful can be challenged by the less powerful as behaviors and attitudes change, though slowly. Only in 1965 did the Supreme Court recognize the right of unmarried persons to receive birth control information and purchase contraceptives, and only in 1974 did the American Psychiatric Association remove homosexuality from its list of mental illnesses. The struggle today is over who has the power to define pornography and obscenity in art and popular music, or which reproductive choices will be legally available to American women.

Interpretive Models

From the perspective of interpretive sociology, the focus shifts from the macrolevel to the microlevel, away from a drive-based model to one that views sexuality as a social construction, and to an emphasis on sexual identities rather than roles (A. Stein, 1989). In this perspective, sexuality is a set of meanings pieced together from the values, expectations, and images of the culture (Kimmel, 1989). Heterosexuality, therefore, is no more "normal" than homosexuality but in most societies it has been defined as normative because of the collective need to maintain high levels of reproduction.

SEXUAL SCRIPTS.   A key concept in the interpretive approach and an attempt to link the macrolevel and microlevel, is the idea of sexual scripts (Simon and Gagnon, 1986; Gagnon et al., 1995). Scripts emerge out of interactions in situations that provide broad guidelines (scenarios) for behavior. The script allows us to organize our perceptions and feelings so that we respond appropriately. For example, the classroom is typically defined as nonsexual, but if the same people go from the classroom to a singles' bar, their behavior will also change because a different scenario and interpersonal script apply to the situation.

> **Sexual scripts** allow individuals to organize their perceptions and experiences to behave appropriately in particular situations.

Sexuality, in this view, is a flexible set of responses that change from one situation to another and over the life course. In childhood, we develop a sex identity (male or female) without necessarily linking these to explicitly sexual motives or meanings. In adolescence, these various elements—meanings, motives, identities, and behaviors—coalesce into a sexual script more problematic for girls than for boys (Tolman, 1994). However, most will enter adulthood with a fairly conventional set of expectations. Sexual activity peaks during ages 18 to 29 and gradually declines with the responsibilities of marriage, parenthood, work, and community involvement (Bachrach and Horn, 1988; T. Smith, 1993). In addition to differences across cultures and over the life course, scripts often vary from one subculture to another within a society, on the basis of race, religion, ethnicity, education, and occupation. In most societies, males and females have separate scripts. Scripts also change over

Sexual Scripts in Five Contemporary Societies

On the island of Mangaia in the Pacific South Seas, sexuality is both more common and more casual than in the United States. Sexual learning and experience come early in adolescence, and the culture emphasizes the virtue and value of sexual pleasure. Although, as in most societies, what is sexually appropriate and permitted to males and females is defined from a male point of view, both boys and girls, women and men appear to derive great enjoyment, and little guilt, from their open and accepted sexuality. Homosexuality and female frigidity are rare (Marshall and Suggs, 1971).

In contrast, extremely rigid sexual norms continue to characterize modern Ireland, especially in the countryside. Dominated by a traditional Roman Catholic clergy, the schools teach the norm of heterosexuality, "artificial" contraception is forbidden, divorce difficult to obtain, and sexuality outside of marriage discouraged. As a consequence, average family size is the highest of all Western societies—despite the fact that people marry at relatively late ages, when a man can support a family. Late marriage and general sexual repressiveness are often said to contribute to Irishmen's drinking habits (Kennedy, 1989).

At the other end of the spectrum of modern industrial societies, Sweden is more similar to Mangaia than to Ireland. In Sweden, equality between women and men is a stated societal goal and built into the legal structure. Sex education is an integral part of schooling from early grades, contraception is freely available, and all forms of sexual violence are officially condemned. Sexual activity among consenting adults, regardless of marital status or sexual orientation, is widely tolerated. Single parents and children born outside of marriage are entitled to all citizen benefits. Adolescent childbearing is very low, but so, too, is the overall birthrate.

Another variation on sexual themes is found among the Sambia of New Guinea, where adolescent males are expected to have sexual relations only with other males until marriage, after which they remain exclusively heterosexual. In several other societies, ritualized homosexuality between boys and older men continues even after the men are married. These are typically cultures in which it is believed that males are in danger of losing their masculinity through contact with women, so that young boys are taken from their mother's home to live in a longhouse with other boys and men (Herdt, 1987).

Clearly, human sexuality is as varied as the cultures that define and shape other attitudes and behaviors. Had you been born a Cheyenne, you would practice extreme sexual control, never touching or being touched by a person of the opposite sex until marriage and even rarely as a married person. Highest respect among the Cheyenne is given to those adults most able to control their impulses, a very different scenario from other American subcultures (Nanda, 1984).

Sexual scripts vary from one culture to another. In this initiation ceremony in Gabon, Africa, adult women teach younger women about appropriate sexual scripts in their society.

Out of the learning experiences of adolescence, most young people enter adulthood with a socially conventional set of heterosexual expectations and behaviors.

time, as seen in the dramatic changes in the script for female sexuality in America since the 1960s, from one organized around being a passive object of male desire to one in which women can become active seekers of pleasure.

SEXUALITY IN THE UNITED STATES

Historical Perspectives

A review of sexual norms and behaviors in America reveals three distinct periods up to the 1970s (D'Emilio and Freedman, 1988):

1. From the 1600s to the mid-1800s, sexuality was closely linked to reproduction, and the norms of faithfulness were enforced by the community. The same couple that now tells all to Oprah or Phil would be an object of public ridicule and shame. Punishing wrongdoers united the virtuous and reinforced their commitment to the norms.

2. As the nation became industrialized and a white middle-class emerged in the cities, a more "romantic" and privatized conception of sexuality in marriage emerged, and the birthrate dropped dramatically. At the same time, single young people left the constraints of village life and flocked to the cities to make their own way in the world, which eventually led to a loosening of norms re-

garding sex before marriage (premarital) and same-sex intimacy. All this brought a sharp counterattack from religious conservatives, so that by the end of the century, sexuality was once more defined as potentially dangerous to personal health and public order.

3. The 1920s to the 1960s saw additional changes. In the 1920s, the modern view of sexuality once more dominated city life. The sexually liberated "flapper" was the female ideal for the new century; women won the right to vote; and family planning became a public issue. Sexuality was also becoming highly commercialized, used to sell all types of products in the emerging consumer marketplace. At the same time, sexual intimacy, preferably within marriage, was becoming defined as a private matter, especially within the educated middle class. Love as a powerful attraction based on sexual desire replaced the nineteenth century notion of love as a desexualized spiritual union. In part, this shift reflected the impact of Freud's focus on the dangers of sexual repression and in part the increasing availability of effective contraception.

4. Finally, the 1970s brought strong challenges to the last vestiges of sexual traditionalism: gender inequality and the taboo on homosexuality. In this context, the New Feminist Movement and the Gay/Lesbian Liberation Movement are logical extensions of the century-long trend toward moving sexuality from the public to the private sphere and defining it as a source of personal fulfillment. In the process, however, love and sex may also have become uncoupled; that is, although a lasting, loving relationship remains the ideal, much sexual activity today appears to take place without deep attachment. (Giddens, 1992; Seidman, 1992). And as long as power and perceptual differences between men and women persist, the ideal of mutual and uncoerced sexual encounters is also unfulfilled. For example, in one study in which 22 percent of women said that they had been forced to commit sex acts they did not wish to commit (even within an intimate relationship), only 3 percent of men thought that they had forced themselves on an unwilling partner (Laumann et al., 1994).

> Sexual love is undoubtedly one of the chief things in life, and the union of mental and bodily satisfaction in the enjoyment of love is one of its culminating peaks...all the world knows this and conducts its life accordingly; science alone is too delicate to admit it.
>
> —SIGMUND FREUD, 1915/1958, pp. 169–70

Sexual Norms and Behaviors Today

PROBLEMS OF DATA COLLECTION.   Obtaining accurate information on sexual behavior is extremely difficult. This is not information willingly given to an interviewer, and, when people respond to a survey, they may not report accurately: Men tend to exaggerate and women to minimize their sexual histories. Until 1994, most studies involved either limited representative samples (e.g., college students) or large, nonrandom and scientifically useless samples such as the readers of *Redbook* or *Playboy* magazines.

One early attempt to collect systematic data on American sexual practices was conducted in the 1940s by Dr. Alfred Kinsey and his colleagues who questioned anyone willing to talk to them—hardly a representative sample! Kinsey's findings were shocking, with many men and women reporting behaviors considered deviant at that time, but it may be that only the less inhibited were willing to be interviewed (Kinsey et al., 1948, 1953). A more scientific survey by the Department of Health and Human Services in the early 1990s was cancelled under pressure from conservatives in Congress, but the researchers were able to secure funding from private foundations. Their findings are the most reliable source of information on contemporary sexual mores and behaviors in the United States (Laumann et al., 1994) In combination with other, more limited research, the data suggest many changes over the past few decades, but also a much less dramatic "sexual revolution" than commonly assumed.

CONTEMPORARY ATTITUDES AND BEHAVIORS.   The emerging picture is one in which American men and women are becoming sexually active at ever earlier ages, over half by the time they complete high school. Because Americans are marrying at later ages than in the 1950s, only a small proportion of adults today enter marriage without sexual experience. In addition, a woman's first partner is no longer a fiancee or her eventual husband. Increasingly, also, women report having been sexually assaulted in childhood by a male family member or friend (Wyatt et al., 1988). Compared with earlier data for both men and women, the number of life-time partners and the range of sexual expression have become increasingly varied, although there is evidence that fear of AIDS has made many unmarried adult women more cautious in their choice of partners (Mosher and Pratt, 1993).

The 1970s and 1980s also saw dramatic changes in attitudes toward contraception and sex before marriage, even among American Catholics (Yankelovich et al., 1992; T. Smith, 1993). It was during these decades that (1) inexpensive, effective contraception became both legal and widely available; and (2) age at first marriage rose dramatically. The two trends re-

inforced each other: The contraceptive revolution made premarital sex less risky, which made it possible to delay marriage, which made contraception more acceptable, and so forth.

In most other respects, however, Americans are relatively conservative in both attitudes and behaviors. The percentage disapproving of extramarital sex remains as high today as in the early 1970s. At the same time, while most respondents believed that such affairs were commonplace, the overwhelming majority of married people are actually very faithful. Indeed, a number of recent studies have found that over 90 percent had had sex only with a husband or wife in the past year (Billy et al., 1993; Kost and Forrest, 1992; T. Smith, 1993; Laumann et al., 1994). In addition, nearly 75 percent of men and 85 percent of women claim never to have been unfaithful to their spouses. Furthermore, despite the belief that single people are enjoying a glorious, nonstop sex life, married couples are almost twice as likely as unmarried adults to have intercourse several times a week and to find the experience satisfying.

In general, the 1994 study also found many expected gender differences, with men over twice as likely as women to think about sex daily (54% versus 19%); to have had more lifetime partners (typically 6 for men versus 2 for women); and to have experienced a more varied set of sexual behaviors. Even so, a great

AIDS information and education can have an important effect on the sexual behavior of young men and women. Where have you received most of your information about AIDS?

majority of men, and a higher percentage of women, had very conservative sexual tastes. Fewer than one in four couples bought X-rated videos or engaged in oral sex—and even fewer enjoyed the experience.

It appears, then, that the "sexual revolution" of the past three decades has been largely limited to relationships before marriage. In addition, the contraceptive revolution has had a major impact on American women, permitting them to be sexually active and to delay marriage, as well as to control the number and spacing of their children. Of greatest concern to the American public today, however, is the effect of these changes on adolescents.

Adolescent Sexuality

All available data indicate that American adolescents are becoming sexually active at increasingly younger ages. For example, the proportion of women who had premarital intercourse by age 19 has doubled since 1972, from about 30 percent to close to 60 percent in the early 1990s (Judkins et al.,1991; Kost and Forrest, 1992). For women aged 15, the proportion has also doubled: from 15 percent in 1972 to about 30 percent today.

Some teenagers are more likely to be sexually active than others. For many adolescent males, hormone levels at puberty may be associated with early sexual experience (Udry and Billy, 1987), but the strongest effects are exerted by the teenager's sociocultural context. Young women who live in communities that offer little hope of success in either school or work are more likely to become sexually active compared with those who live in communities with opportunities to succeed (Brewster et al., 1993; Luster and Small, 1994; Lauriston, 1994). Family and community characteristics affect attitudes toward school and self-expectations; where young women feel in control of their future, they are likely to delay sexual activity (Plotnick, 1992). Racial differences in early sexual activity are largely due to neighborhood differences in income and adult role models (Brewster, 1994).

Neighborhood quality and parents' educational level also affect young men's attitudes toward sexuality, contraception, and paternity. Neighborhood poverty, poorly educated parents, and traditional attitudes toward women are all associated with an adolescent male's feeling that impregnating his girlfriend has enhanced his masculinity (Marsiglio, 1993). Having little else to boast about, visible signs of one's sexual power become crucial to self-image.

In addition to school failure and low expectations of occupational success, early sexual activity for adolescents is linked to other high-risk behaviors such as delinquency and drug use (Ketterlinus et al., 1992; Mensch and Kandel, 1992). Another risk factor, especially in light of the current epidemic of sexually transmitted diseases, is having multiple sex partners.

Among sexually active adolescent women, the proportion having two or more partners has increased dramatically since the 1970s, even among college undergraduates. One study at a midwestern university reported an average of 5.6 partners among sexually active women and 11.2 among men (Reinisch et al., 1992).

With regard to contraceptive use, the data show a general increase, among adult women (Mosher and Pratt, 1993). But as adolescent males age, their sexual activity increases while condom use declines because they now expect their female partners to take responsibility (Ku et al., 1993). The risks of pregnancy, then, are especially high for teenaged women, who are least likely to use contraception or to be protected by their partners. Because contraception use requires some foresight and planning, many young women think that to take a pill in the morning would make them seem promiscuous, violating the script that excuses sexual activity only if one is swept away by the passion of the moment later that night. "Good girls" do not plan in advance to do something "bad."

Adolescent Pregnancy and Parenthood

Contrary to popular belief, the pregnancy rate for sexually active teenagers has not risen dramatically and is lower today than it was in 1975 (Alan Guttmacher Institute, 1994). As a proportion of all U.S. births, the rate for women aged 15–19 has remained steady since the late 1980s (Ventura et al., 1992). One in ten adolescent pregnancies will be terminated by natural causes, and another 40 percent are ended by abortion, as shown in Figure 8-1.

The "teenage childbearing epidemic" is an excellent example of the social construction of a social problem, largely through the success of moral entrepreneurs in blaming sexually active adolescents for a range of social ills (Nathanson, 1992; Trent, 1993). In fact, over 90 percent of the fathers of children born to teenage mothers are not themselves underaged (Males, 1992). Teenage births would not be considered a social problem if, as in the past, the mothers were married. But most pregnant adolescents today are not married and either cannot or choose not to marry the father of their children (Farber, 1990). Indeed, teenagers are not alone in this respect; 30 percent of all births in the United States in the mid-1990s were to unmarried women (U.S. Department of Health and Human Services, 1996; Parnell et al., 1994).

Adolescent birth rates are highest in the South and West, where sex education programs are minimal and abortion services severely restricted. In general, African-American and Latina teenagers are least likely to have family planning services in their communities and most likely to live in urban areas with high rates

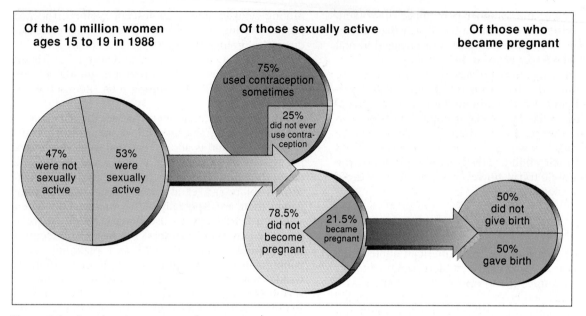

Figure 8-1 American teenagers and pregnancy.

Reproduced with the permission of the Alan Guttmacher Institute from Jacqueline Darroch Forrest and Susheela Singh, "The Sexual Reproductive Behavior of American Women, 1982–1988," Family Planning Perspectives, Vol. 22, No. 5, September/October 1990

of early and nonmarital childbearing (Crane, 1991; St. John and Rowe, 1990). Nonetheless, nonmarital birth rates rose more rapidly for white than minority teenagers in the early 1990s.

Nonmarital pregnancy and early parenthood are associated with various measures of family and community disorganization, namely, poverty, lack of employment opportunities for women, divorce and separation in one's own family, and being the child of a teenage mother (Billy and Moore, 1992; Kahn and Anderson, 1992; Plotnick, 1992; Wu and Martinson, 1993). For many young women, parenthood represents an island of certainty in a sea of unpredictable, largely negative events. Conversely, the more predictable one's environment, and the higher the income and educational level of one's parents, the less likely will a young woman become a teenage mother.

Despite generally high income and education levels in the United States compared to other modern industrial societies, our teenagers have the *highest* rates of unintended pregnancies, abortions, and births, as shown in Table 8-1. Because rates of teenage sexual activity are similar in all these countries, the difference in pregnancies, abortions, and births is almost entirely due to limited access to sex education and low-cost family planning services and failure to use effective contraception consistently. Adolescent pregnancy rates are lowest in societies that make contraception widely available and where there are few pressures on young people to prove themselves sexually, where attitudes toward sex are open and accepting, and where

men are also expected to take responsibility for birth control (Jones et al., 1987; Kondo, 1991).

RISKS OF TEENAGE PARENTHOOD. Teenage childbearing involves risks to both mother and child. Among the common physical outcomes for infants born to teenagers are low birth weight, breathing difficulty, birth defects, delayed growth, and behavior problems by the time they reach school age (McCormack et al., 1992). Although the mother's immature reproductive system may account for some health problems, background variables such as low income, limited educa-

TABLE 8-1 Birth Rates to Teens Aged 15–19 for Selected Countries, 1970–1989

Country	1970	1980	1985	1989
United States	68.3	53.0	51.3	58.1
Denmark	32.4	16.8	9.1	9.2
France	27.0	17.8	11.6	9.2
Germany (western)	35.8	15.2	8.6	11.1
Japan	5.0	7.6	9.0	9.8
Netherlands	17.0	6.8	5.0	5.9
United Kingdom	49.1	30.5	29.6	31.7

From Dennis A. Ahlberg and Carol J. DeVita, "New Realities of the American Family," *Population Bulletin*, 47 (2) August, 1992.

tion, and overcrowding are far more important (Geronimus and Korenman, 1993).

In addition, a pregnant teenager in a poverty area has limited access to prenatal care, usually a few visits to a crowded and understaffed hospital clinic late in the pregnancy. Poor nutrition and health habits, combined with emotional stress, contribute to high rates of maternal death, miscarriage, and stillbirth among impoverished American teenage women. Infant mortality rates in the United States, though declining, are among the highest of all industrial societies.

The social consequences of early childbearing are also largely negative, including failure to complete high school, low life-time earnings, unstable marriages, and welfare dependency (Center for Population Options, 1992; Grogger and Bronars, 1993; Ahn, 1994). Some of these negative outcomes can be avoided through special outreach and educational programs for pregnant and parenting teenagers (Warrick et al., 1993). These programs are expensive, but in the long run are more cost-effective than long-term welfare dependency.

Given all the problems associated with early parenthood, it is not surprising that four out of ten young women will elect to terminate their pregnancy. Because most states have denied Medicaid coverage for abortions, only women with sufficient funds can make this choice. In general, abortion is chosen by young women who face no strong opposition from parents and friends and who have relatively high educational and occupational goals (Brazell and Acock, 1988). They must also have access to a facility that performs abortions—a major problem today for American women of any age.

SOCIAL POLICY

Abortion—Whose Body? Whose Baby?

Throughout most of this century, state laws made it illegal for women to terminate a pregnancy voluntarily. Although wealthy women could always find a helpful physician, an unknown number of American women risked their lives and health at the hands of "back alley" abortionists. But in 1973, in the case of *Roe* v. *Wade,* the Supreme Court interpreted the Constitution as providing an implied "right to privacy" that covered a woman's decision, in consultation with her physician, to end a pregnancy. This right, however, was not absolute and must be weighted against the "compelling interest" of government in preserving the health and life of mother and child.

Accordingly, the Court ruled that: 1. During the first three months (trimester) of pregnancy, the states could not interfere in a woman's choice; 2. during the second trimester, states could enact rules designed to protect health; and 3. during the final trimester, when a fetus could survive outside the womb, the interests of the state could supersede the wishes of the mother. In other words, abortion was defined as a medical issue rather than as an absolute right.

The number of abortions rose steadily from 1973 to 1980 before leveling off at about 1.6 million a year through the 1980s, primarily to white, young, unmarried women. Ninety percent take place within the first 12 weeks, and all but a very few by the sixth

Abortion is an important political issue in the United States. This group of women and men is demonstrating in support of the 1973 Supreme Court decision that it is a woman's right, in consultation with her physician, to end a pregnancy.

month. Despite the opposition of their church, the abortion rate for Catholic women is close to the national average (Henshaw and Van Vort, 1994).

Roe v. *Wade* unleashed a powerful backlash among religious and political conservatives that led state legislatures to impose severe limits on a woman's access to abortion services. These limiting conditions include refusal to allow Medicaid coverage for poor women, requiring teenagers to receive parental permission, and enforcing waiting periods of several days. In addition, abortion opponents have successfully pressured hospitals and physicians, so that a majority no longer perform the procedure (Henshaw and Van Vort, 1994). Today, 94 percent of nonurban counties have no abortion providers, even though the health risks of abortion are lower than those of giving birth, particularly for teenagers.

The six Justices of the Supreme court appointed by Presidents Reagan and Bush were selected in large part for their willingness to review *Roe v. Wade.* As a consequence, the Court has given priority to state interests over the woman's right to privacy but have stopped short of overturning *Roe.* The new standard announced by the Court in 1992 was whether or not the state requirements constitute an "undue burden" on a woman exercising her rights, with the definition of "undue" left to lower courts. In 1993, the Court decided that requiring a minor to get the written permission of both parents was not an "undue burden" for a 14- or 15-year-old.

Thus, the battleground has shifted from challenging the constitutionality of abortion to restricting

> **In vitro** fertilization is a procedure in which an egg is fertilized outside the mother's body and then replanted in the womb.

access, with greatest impact on the very young and very poor and women living in the South and Mountain states. The antiabortion movement has been enormously successful in reducing the availability of services despite continued high levels of public support for the legality of abortion, as seen in Table 8-2.

Over the next decade or more, your vote will determine who has reproductive choice and who does not, in your community and state. You will decide whether or not the unborn has rights independent of the woman in whose womb it lives (Daniels, 1993). Is the fetus entitled to medical treatment regardless of the wishes or health of the mother? Can courts order a pregnant woman to have a cesarian birth? Can two legal persons exist in one body? And what rights may the father fairly exercise?

Reproduction, Sexuality, and the Law

Still deeper legal and sociological issues arise from the introduction of reproductive technologies that effectively separate sexuality and reproduction: artificial insemination, *in vitro* (test tube) **fertilization,** surrogate childbearing, and embryo transfers (Rothman, 1989; Addelson, 1990). Lawmakers and the courts are struggling to deal with the practical and ethical implications of these developments.

Several of the most interesting cases have involved frozen embryos, fertilized *in vitro,* but not yet transferred to the woman's uterus because the couple have decided to divorce. Are the fertilized eggs "preborn children" with the legal status of persons, as one judge decided? Or are they community property, and, if so, to whom do they belong? Can an ex-husband, or any man,

---

RESEARCH IN ACTION

When Adolescents Choose Abortion or Adoption

What are the social and psychological effects of voluntary termination of a pregnancy? One longitudinal study of African-American teenage women from similar backgrounds found that those who chose abortion were more likely than women who elected to complete the pregnancy to finish high school, to be economically secure, and to practice effective contraception, thus avoiding a second pregnancy within the following year (Zabin et al., 1992).

In addition, the women who terminated their pregnancy did not experience heightened levels of emotional distress. There are no significant differences in self-esteem or psychological well-being among women who have had no abortions, one abortion, or more than one (Russo and Zierk, 1992). Apparently, no scientific data support the idea of postabortion trauma. Indeed,

quite the contrary: The women with lowest self-esteem scores were those who had had an unwanted birth.

Other adolescent mothers will choose to place their infants for adoption. Studies indicate that whereas some expressed regret, the great majority would make the same decision again (Kalmus et al., 1992). Compared with women of similar background who decided to mother, those who gave up their babies had higher educational goals, were more likely to remain in school, and were less likely to be on public assistance. Other data from a national survey found that unmarried white women who chose to place their children for adoption, compared with women who chose to keep their infants, are more likely to have a well-educated mother, to have been in school at the time of conception, to have no labor force experience, and to be somewhat older (Bachrach et al., 1992). It is interesting that sons are less likely than daughters to be given for adoption.

TABLE 8-2   Attitudes toward Legality of Abortion by Demographic Characteristics, United States, 1994

Question: "Do you think abortions should be legal under any circumstances, legal only under certain circumstances, or illegal in all circumstances?"

	Always legal	Legal under certain circumstances	Never legal	No opinion
All Respondents	33	52	13	2
Sex				
Male	30	53	14	3
Female	32	49	17	2
Age				
18–29 years	37	45	16	2
30–49 years	34	53	12	1
50–65 years	20	54	23	3
65 years and older	28	51	14	7
Race				
White	32	51	14	3
Nonwhite	26	46	24	2
Education				
College post graduate	39	52	7	1
College graduate	34	56	8	2
College incomplete	27	53	18	2
No college	12	56	25	7
Politics				
Republican	28	56	16	*
Democrat	39	49	10	2
Independent	33	50	14	3
Income				
$75,000 and over	46	50	4	*
$50,000–$74,999	36	56	7	1
$30–$49,999	32	54	12	2
$20–$29,999	30	50	19	1
Under $20,000	28	48	21	3
Religion				
Protestant	28	52	16	4
Catholic	26	54	18	2
Not church member	47	42	7	4

*Less than 1 percent.

From George Gallup, Jr., The Gallup Poll Monthly, No. 316 (Princeton, NJ: The Gallup Poll, January, 1992), pp. 8,9. Reprinted by permission.

be forced to become a father against his will? These are only some of the questions raised in recent court cases, with no clear answers in sight.

In addition, what is permitted to men is often considered inappropriate for women. In the mid-1990s, for example, the artificial insemination of post-menopausal women produced a storm of outrage from those who contended that the women were "too old" to be effective mothers. No one questioned the ability of their even older husbands to enact the father role.

The case of **surrogacy,** in which one woman agrees to carry the child of another woman, also raises a number of sensitive sociological issues. Many feminists object to the practice because, if no money changes hands, it appears to exploit one woman for the benefit of another (Anleu, 1992; Shanley, 1993). But if the surrogate is paid for her

Surrogacy is the stiuation in which one woman agrees to bear a child for another woman.

177

In surrogacy, one woman agrees to carry the child of another woman. In a rather unusual case in Aberdeen, South Dakota, a mother (on the left) agreed to help her daughter bear children. Twins were born to the grandmother.

services, the whole arrangement comes close to baby selling (Rothman, 1989). But why should surrogacy be more acceptable when the newborn is donated rather than paid for? Why do Americans think that children should be born for love alone and never for money? The process of childbearing is the same, and others are just as likely to take advantage of the birth mother and never pay a cent for it.

If the ultimate effect of the new technologies is to separate sexuality from reproduction, does the state's compelling interest in encouraging reproduction still extend to sexual behavior? That is, can the states continue to regulate sexual conduct if this behavior is no longer linked to the societal need for reproducing new members? The trend in all modern societies is toward extending the area of privacy in intimate relations based on affection, choice, and relative equality. The same liberating currents that have transformed heterosexual behavior have also had a profound impact on the lives of American homosexuals.

HOMOSEXUALITIES: THE LESBIAN AND GAY MALE EXPERIENCE

Cross-Cultural and Historical Perspective

Throughout human history, in most societies, some proportion of the population has been attracted to partners of the same sex. Whether **homosexual relations** are encouraged, ignored, or punished is a cultural and social variable.

Homosexual relations involve persons of the same sex.

In some societies, for example, same-sex relationships among men are considered superior to those with women, especially where warfare and male bonding are highly valued, and women are treated with great contempt (Herdt, 1984). In ancient Greece and Rome, it was expected that an older warrior would have a younger male as his student and sexual servant until

Cultures and societies vary as to whether homosexual relations are encouraged, ignored, or punished. In many of the nation's largest cities homosexual subcultures offer protection and support. After a lengthy opposition by some residents of New York City's Greenwich Village, these statues commemorating the 1969 Stonewall uprising were unveiled.

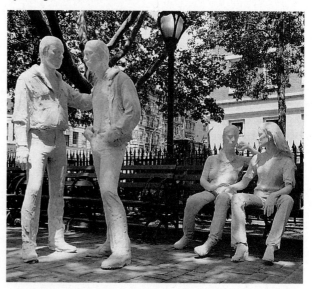

the boy reached the age when he, in turn, could exercise power over an inferior male (Canterella, 1992).

Many scholars believe that "homosexuality" is a concept that has meaning only in societies where only two sexes are recognized, and where maleness and femaleness are assumed to be inborn (Laqueur, 1990). Where the lines of sexual identity are less rigidly drawn, other possibilities exist, as with the **berdaches** of certain native American tribes. *Berdaches* are men, relatively passive by nature but not altogether womanly, who enjoy same-sex lovers yet are also highly honored. The *berdaches* were in essence a third sex, thought to have supernatural powers combining the wisdom of male and female (W. Williams, 1986). Some Native American cultures were also receptive to the "manly hearted" woman who shared in the activities of men and often lived with another woman (Blackwood, 1984).

In modern America, we are not yet able to recognize more than two sexes, although nature actually provides a number of gradations from female to male (Fausto-Sterling, 1993). Possibly four of every hundred births involves an infant with some characteristics of both sexes (intersexed), but so strong is our need to maintain a clear distinction between male and female that we have no word or place for such a person (Raymond, 1994). The intersexed child is immediately subjected to hormonal and surgical "correction." Similarly, people who cross-dress disturb our sense of sexual identity because they challenge the either/or two-sex classification scheme (Bullough and Bullough, 1993). Men who cross-dress are treated as mental cases, whereas women who wear male clothing are tolerated as long as they do not try to pass as a man.

Homosexuals challenge the group's gender norms as well as people's sexual identity and can therefore be condemned on both grounds (Martin, 1993). In the United States, the range of tolerance or condemnation has varied over time. In the early part of this century, the concentration of unmarried young people in cities, and the privatization of sexuality, combined to encourage sexual experimentation, including same-sex relationships. Freed from the constraints of family and community, gay men and lesbians created a social space hidden from the broader society. In the largest cities, emergent **homosexual subcultures,** centered in bars and other places of entertainment, offered protection and support (Kennedy and Davis, 1993).

But most gay men and lesbians, then as now, led a double life, fearful that acknowledging their homosexuality would cost them their jobs, housing, and standing in the community (Adam, 1987; Duberman et al., 1989). American culture, shaped by Puritan sexual mores, is characterized by a strong streak of **homophobia,** an intense fear of homosexuals and of doing or saying anything that might cast doubt on one's own sexual and erotic identity.

Roots of Homosexuality

Americans tend to look for direct, single-cause answers to questions about nonnormative behaviors: genes, hormones, weak fathers, and domineering mothers are the most common. Decades of research have proved only that they are negligible factors in predicting homosexuality. That leaves genetic markers and brain structure as the currently favored research directions.

With regard to genetic influences, recently published studies of twins have found a statistical correlation between sexual orientation and degree of genetic closeness for both men and women (Bailey and Pilliard, 1991, 1993). Other research has isolated a particular marker on the sex chromosome that appears to increase the likelihood of homosexuality among family members (LeVay and Hamer, 1994). But these researchers have been very careful to note that their findings apply only to some homosexuals and that the precise mechanisms whereby genes affect behavior remain unknown. Genes guide the production of protein, not bodies or minds. In addition, the scientific track record on genetic markers for behavioral traits is not reassuring, because previous claims have not stood up to later investigation (Hubbard, 1993).

Similarly, research on the brain and the nervous system (reviewed in Burr, 1993) indicate some structural differences by sexual orientation, but no one has yet discovered how or why a particular brain formation should affect sexual behavior (Byne, 1994). Something as complex as sexuality has multiple roots; biological tendencies interact with social environments in mutually influencing patterns; and some individuals

> The **berdaches** of certain Native American tribes were treated as a third sex, neither fully male nor female.
>
> **Homosexual subcultures** offer protection and support for gay males and lesbians.
>
> **Homophobia** refers to intense fear of homosexuals.

State Anti-Sodomy Laws

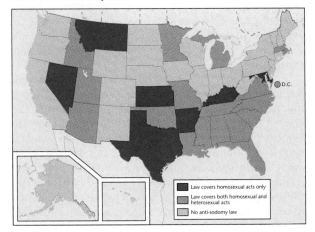

Law covers homosexual acts only
Law covers both homosexual and heterosexual acts
No anti-sodomy law

may be more predisposed than others to being attracted to same-sex partners. As sociologists, our focus is on the social processes that influence how a person comes to define herself or himself sexually.

In the sociological perspective, sexual and gender identities are constructed along the same lines as other aspects of the self: through experiences, the reactions of role partners, and our interpretation of these responses. Labeling and the internalization of self-definitions create a frame in which one type of sexual expression becomes more comfortable than others, reducing the attractiveness of alternative behaviors (Risman and Schwartz, 1988).

Even if homosexual tendencies are biologically based, the processes of self-definition and of learning how to behave as a gay male or lesbian are social. Each society and historical period has its own expectations of heterosexual and homosexual conduct, so that erotic identities are constructed through a chain of events and multiple experiences. The power of the heterosexual script and rewards for conformity ensure that the great majority of girls and boys emerge from adolescence with a socially appropriate sexual preference, however uncomfortable this may be for some. Indeed, a large proportion of lesbians and gay men have at one time been in a heterosexual relationship (Kitzenger, 1988; Fay et al., 1989).

THE POLITICS OF SEX.   The issue of the roots of homosexuality is no longer primarily an academic matter but has become an important political issue. If homosexuality is rooted in biology, then it is an ascribed characteristic, given and fixed, and clear from the very beginning, as many gay men and lesbians believe to be true in their own case. Politically, this is an attractive position, because it allows homosexuals to claim that they cannot be otherwise and that no amount of therapy, religion, or will-power can change their orientation. In addition, as an ascribed trait similar to race and religion, sexual orientation ought to fall within the protection of antidiscrimination rules. The biological argument should also reassure heterosexuals who are fearful of being seduced. If it's not in their genes, they cannot be swayed.

In contrast, the social constructionist approach suggests that homosexuality is primarily a chosen identity, a life-style preference. This is precisely the claim of anti-gay forces: Lesbians and gay males are sinners because they refuse to change their wicked ways, and therefore do not deserve "special treatment" under antidiscrimination laws. From a political standpoint, then, the sociological view is harmful to the cause of gay rights. Yet to deny personal agency in the construction of one's erotic identity is to give

Bisexuality involves the ability to enjoy sexual relations with both males and females.

up responsibility for one's conscious decisions and life-style choices (Plaskow, 1994). One solution for many lesbians and gay men is to feel that their sexuality is both given and constructed.

This dilemma is played out in vocabulary. In an attempt to accommodate both views, we have spoken of both sexual "preference" and "orientation." But they do not mean the same thing: a *preference* implies choice, an achieved status; an *orientation* is an ascribed characteristic. Antigay forces use the word "preference;" most gay rights activists now use "orientation." As seen in Table 8-3, whether one sees homosexuality as chosen or given makes a big difference. People who see homosexuality as a life-style choice are much less likely than other Americans to sympathize with the goals of the Gay Rights Movement.

Prevalence of Homosexuality

Gay rights and antigay forces have also argued over the prevalence of homosexuality. One of the goals of the massive demonstration in Washington in March 1993 was to impress Americans with the sheer number of gay men and lesbians, the vast majority of whom look just like your next-door neighbor and may actually live there. Once gays are perceived both as numerous and nonthreatening, it is easier to convince voters that they deserve protection from discrimination.

How widespread is homosexuality? The generally accepted estimate for modern societies is that at least 5 percent of men, and a smaller percentage of women, are almost exclusively involved in same-sex relationships. The major problem is in defining homosexuality. Who, indeed, is gay? What about all those who might be attracted to persons of the same sex yet never act on that impulse? Or what of those who have a few homosexual episodes in an otherwise heterosexual life? Or the homosexual who had a few heterosexual experiences and who technically is not therefore "exclusively" gay? Depending on how the question is worded, researchers will come up with very different numbers (Stokes and McKirnan, 1993). For example, one 1988 national survey found that 20 percent of American men had had at least one homosexual "experience" but that less than 3 percent could be classified as "exclusively homosexual" (Fay et al., 1989). Other studies range from a low of 2.3 percent of men aged 30–39 with any homosexual contacts in the past ten years (Billy et al., 1993) to a high of 5.7 percent checking the category "gay/homosexual/lesbian" in a representative sample (Yankelovich Partners, 1994). Over a person's lifetime, the proprtion with some homosexual experience rises to 16–20 percent for men, and from 6–10 percent for women (Laumann et al., 1994; Selk et al., 1994).

A considerably higher percentage of Americans are **bisexual,** that is, able to enjoy sexual relationships with both women and men, than are exclusively ho-

TABLE 8-3 Attitudes Toward Gay Issues

How the Public Views Gay Issues

Do you think being homosexual is something people choose to be, or do you think it is something they cannot change?

Choose to be gay	44%
Can't change	43%
Don't know	13%

Total Adults		Those who say homosexuality	
		Is a choice	Cannot be changed
Jobs and Rights			
78%	Say homosexuals should have equal rights in terms of job opportunities	69%	90%
42	Say it is necessary to pass laws to make sure homosexuals have equal rights	30	58
11	Object to having an airline pilot who is homosexual	18	4
49	Object to having a doctor who is homosexual	64	34
55	Object to having a homosexual as a child's elementary school teacher	71	39
Personal Judgments			
46	Say homosexual relations between consenting adults should be legal	32	62
36	Say homosexuality should be considered an acceptable alternative life style	18	57
55	Say homosexual relations between adults are morally wrong	78	30
43	Favor permitting homosexuals to serve in the military	32	54
34	Would permit their child to play at the home of a friend who lives with a homosexual parent	21	50
36	Would permit their child to watch a prime-time television situation comedy with homosexual characters in it	27	46
Familiarity			
22	Have a close friend or family member who is gay or lesbian	16	29

Based on telephone interviews with 1,154 adults nationwide conducted Feb. 9–11, 1993.

From: "The New York Times/CBS News Poll; How the Public Views Gay Issues," March 5, 1993. Copyright © 1993 by The New York Times Company. Reprinted by permission.

mosexual (Weinberg et al., 1994). Bisexuality illustrates the conceptual and practical distinction between gender and erotic identities. In this category, women outnumber men. For most, situational factors outweigh any deeper impulses; that is, people take comfort and sexual gratification where it is available, with different opportunity structures for women and men.

BETH E. SCHNEIDER

Researching the Social Contexts of Sexuality

Beth E. Schneider is associate professor of sociology at the University of California, Santa Barbara. Publications include "The Office Affair: Myth and Reality for Hetero-sexual and Lesbian Women" (Sociological Perspectives, 1984), "Coming Out at Work" (Work and Occupations, 1986), "Female Sexuality" (with Meredith Gould in B. Hess and M. M. Ferree, eds., Analyzing Gender, 1987), and "AIDS and Class, Gender and Race Relations" (in J. Huber and B. Schneider, The Social Context of AIDS, 1992). A member of the Sociologists' AIDS Network, the sex/gender section of the American Sociological Association (ASA), she chaired the ASA Committee on the Status of Homosexuals in the Profession, the Sociologists' Lesbian and Gay Caucus, and the Sexual Behavior Section of the Society for the Study of Social Problems.

S o much of the sociology I learned in college and graduate school was concerned with the public world, with those activities and institutions such as the church, the university, the state. The domestic, private, or intimate world was, for many sociologists, off limits, set aside for psychologists. Thus, despite talk about sexuality and its cultural importance, the topic still carries a heavy burden of moralism and myth that stigmatizes its researchers. The sociology of sexuality remains a marginal subfield.

In the 1970s, the feminist critique of sociology, coupled with the development of the women's and the lesbian/gay political movements, argued for a reconsideration of the ways scholars understood sex, sexuality, and gender. I began work on my dissertation dur-

ing this period, being interested primarily in the experiences of lesbians in the workplace. Because many lesbians I knew had met their partners at work, I was particularly curious about how they handled the complexities of interpersonal relations in the workplace and how questions about their sexuality were managed. Research on gay men involved processes suggesting that those with higher income and more prestigious jobs were relatively unlikely to reveal their sexual identity to co-workers; that is, they stayed "in the closet". But there was virtually no research on lesbians.

Studying the interplay of sexuality and work calls for complex thinking because it challenges long-standing sociological assumptions about the workplace. Weber claimed that bureaucracies should be impersonal, and Freud warned of the havoc sexuality might bring to normative relationships. Yet sexuality as a set of social relations occurs in all types of social settings.

I found myself altering my original research to parallel the feminist dialogue about violence against women, and to test the assumption that the sexual scripts of lesbians were similar to those of heterosexual women. To explore the various dimensions of sexual relationships, sexual harassment, and social relationships at work, I chose to study both heterosexual and lesbian women in many types of employment.

I found that sexuality was a far more pervasive aspect of everyday life at work than has been recognized. Both heterosexual women and lesbians "in the closet" (and, hence, thought to be heterosexual) experience much more sexual harassment than do women who are openly lesbian. Because most women work in settings where there are more women than men, lesbians can become friends with status equals,

whereas the heterosexual women find themselves involved in more problematic relationships because the men with whom they interact are likely to be in positions of authority.

My more recent study of the social world of lesbians has led me to an interest in AIDS and the question of how lesbians had been socially and politically affected by an epidemic among gay men. I discovered that the vast majority of women with AIDS or HIV infection are not lesbians, but heterosexual women about whom little research existed. Most of my professional energy over the past several years has been devoted to constructing a social science on women with AIDS.

In addition, a disease that can be sexually transmitted poses challenges to current sexual scripts; the meanings applied to sexual relations and sexual practices become important features in any effort to change interpersonal behavior. Social scientists are studying if, when, and how AIDS prevention education can alter individual behavior. I have undertaken a parallel study of institutions in which this education occurs. Colleagues and I are examining the political and bureaucratic means through which AIDS prevention education was introduced and managed in a public school district in California. We have already observed that school administrators and teachers fearing that AIDS education would arouse parental and community opposition because of its association with male homosexuality, adopted mechanisms such as extra permission slips and programs whose content often avoided any mention of homosexuality. It remains to be seen whether the school's concern with deflecting controversy will undermine the stated goal of AIDS education.

Organizing for Gay Rights

Because of the stigma and real harm that can result from an open declaration of one's erotic identity, the earliest organizations of and for homosexuals were primarily concerned with helping members adapt to the prevailing mores. The highly conservative 1950s, however, saw a revival of intense homophobia, spurred by the increase in white collar jobs that led some experts to fear for the masculinity of men trapped all day in their offices (Adam,1987). Nonetheless, gay rights activists continued to organize in several cities, where companionship and comfort could be found in a flourishing bar scene (Marcus, 1992).

The societal mood shifted once again in the liberating currents of the 1960s, as one social movement after another surfaced, demanding full rights of citizenship for students, racial/ethnic minorities, and women. In such a climate, a **Gay Rights Movement** was no longer an impossibility. The event that symbolized the shift from passive adaptive goals to active militancy occurred in New York City in 1969, when police routinely raided a gay bar, the Stonewall Inn, and the customers fought back rather than retreating (Duberman, 1993). This incident and the spirit of the times encouraged gay men and lesbians to **"come out"** (publicly acknowledge their erotic identity) and join organizations such as the National Gay and Lesbian Task Force, as well as a variety of local and professional groups, including gay caucuses on most large college campuses.

The 1970s and 1980s saw major gains in public tolerance; several cities added "sexual orientation" to their antidiscrimination laws; and most states changed their statutes to protect the sexual privacy of consenting adults. But the recognition of an AIDS epidemic in the 1980s, associated with the sexual practices of gay men, stalled many of these initiatives. Since then, AIDS has killed hundreds of young men and women, bringing enormous grief to the gay and lesbian communities, and it has brought a new level of organization and cooperation among homosexuals to reduce health risks and to deal with its devastating effects on the ill and their companions. At the same time, AIDS has fueled public fears and energized the antigay backlash movement. (Gagnon et al., 1995).

Having temporarily lost the battle to outlaw abortion, many religious conservatives have turned their attention to homosexuality. In the early 1990s, these forces succeeded in passing local ordinances condemning homosexuality and in blocking statewide efforts to include sexual orientation in antidiscrimination statutes (Holmes, 1994). Hate literature is being widely disseminated, and cases of arson, assault, and even murder of people suspected of homosexuality appear to have increased dramatically (Jenness, 1995; Herek and Berrill, 1992).

Yet even where protected by law, gay men and lesbians are confronted daily with open and subtle discrimination in employment and housing. Many find it wisest to remain "closeted," even though this delays their ultimate acceptance by others. This is an instance of individual self-preservation working against the well-being of the population as a whole, which is why "coming out" is a central issue today. People who have a gay or lesbian family member, friend, or co-worker tend to be more supportive of gay rights than are people without such personal knowledge (Schmalz, 1993). Thus, it is in the best interests of the Gay Rights Movement that homosexuals be open about their identity, so that more and more Americans will know that they do indeed have a gay friend, relative, or colleague.

The dilemma of remaining closeted or being "out" was a central theme of the debate over gays in the American military (Scott and Stanley, 1994). Officially, gay men and lesbians are barred from joining in the armed forces, but in reality many have served, often with great distinction, and always voluntarily. Most often, superior officers have ignored the situation, especially in wartime, when discharges for homosexuality decline dramatically (Shilts, 1993). President Clinton's 1993 attempt to reverse the official ban, however, brought a firestorm of protest from the military and its supporters among religious conservatives and Southerners.

> Along with other civil rights movements, the **Gay Rights Movement** emerged in the 1960s; it attempted to extend full rights of citizenship to all homosexuals.
>
> **"Coming out"** refers to the public acknowledgment of one's homosexual identity.

One major objection to openly gay military personnel was the widespread fear that heterosexuals would be subjected to sexual harassment and loss of privacy; indeed, the list of fears—being stared at, propositioned, rubbed against—are precisely what some women experience from heterosexual men. Apparently, what heterosexual servicemen fear most is becoming feminized. The compromise ultimately agreed on permits lesbians and gay men to serve in the military without being subject to surveillance and discharge on that basis alone, provided that they do not make their erotic preferences public: "Don't ask, don't tell, and don't pursue."

Life-Styles and Pair Relationships

Contrary to common perception, lesbians and gay men do *not* typically re-create the stereotypical heterosexual pattern of dominant male and submissive female. To the contrary, homosexual relationships tend to be characterized by greater equality and mu-

After an extensive debate the U.S. military agreed to permit lesbians and gay men to serve in the military, provided they do not disclose their sexual orientation. Prior to this policy, homosexuals were discharged solely on the basis of their sexual preference, despite their often distinguished contributions to the military. These two soldiers, Heidi DeJesus and Laura Little, accompanied by their lawyer, have appealed their dishonorable discharge. Will the "don't ask, don't tell and don't pursue policy" allow homosexuals to serve in the military?

tuality than found among heterosexual couples (Connell, 1992; Nardi, 1992). Survey data indicate that the educational and income levels of gay men and lesbians are well above the national average, with a majority currently in a relationship of at least three years' duration (*New York Times*/CBS News Poll, 1993; Yankelovich Partners, 1994).

If couples are valued on the basis of the quality of their commitment, the depth of caring, rather than the sex of the partners, many homosexual relationships would be judged healthier (or at least less destructive) than many heterosexual unions. Nor is the homosexual scene any more violent or sexually exploitive than the "straight" world. Above all, it is important to recognize that there is no *one* gay life-style; the homosexual population is as varied as the heterosexual, and the experience of being gay will vary from one subpopulation to another (Herdt, 1992).

Domestic partners include homosexual and nonmarried heterosexual couples who in some U.S. cities enjoy some of the same legal rights as married couples.

The great majority of lesbians and gay males seek intimacy in a stable relationship, but given the relatively small pool from which to select a partner, success is more problematic than for heterosexuals. Increasingly, however, gay couples have established households, adapting the kinship terms of the broader society to their own situation (Weston, 1991). The idea of homosexual marriage is no longer dismissed automatically, and the reality is that a grow-

ing number of couples are exchanging solemn vows, often with the support of clergy (S. Sherman, 1992). In addition, these families are as successful as heterosexual parents in raising children. One analysis of three-dozen current scientific studies found *no statistically significant differences* between children from homosexual and heterosexual households on a range of measures of social or emotional development (Patterson, 1992).

In recognition of the fact that gay and lesbian couples are likely to be living together under the same circumstances as legally married couples—sharing and caring through illness and health—courts and local governments are extending some marital rights to **domestic partners.** Today, in several American cities, an unmarried couple, whether homosexual or heterosexual, can formally register their partnerships with the city clerk and receive a certificate and some of the rights of married couples such as parental leave, hospital visitation, and limited inheritance.

Most difficult for the courts are cases of child custody. A few states have laws that specifically forbid adoption by same-sex couples. In other jurisdictions, judges have been reluctant to extend parental rights to lesbian and gay couples seeking to adopt biological offspring from a previous marriage or to recognize parenthood in the case of children conceived artificially. Nonetheless, many adoption claims have succeeded, and more are being brought to court.

By 1992, several universities, including Stanford and the University of Chicago, extended to gay couples the benefits offered to married couples, including health insurance. In 1993, the Supreme Court of

Several American cities have passed ordinances that extend some legal rights and benefits to domestic partners. Among New Yorkers to register as domestic partners were these two women who also decided to combine their family names.

the State of Hawaii overturned a ban on same-sex marriages on grounds of sex discrimination without a showing of compelling state interest. As a sure sign of the times, several newspapers now include announcements of domestic partnerships on the wedding and engagement page.

Although the overall trend is toward expanding the concept of "family" to include same-sex partnerships, the antigay backlash has also recorded many local victories. This is another issue on which you will have an impact every time you enter the voting booth. Some states have passed legislation banning discrimination on grounds of sexual orientation, while others retain antisodomy laws. The ultimate outcome remains very much up in the air. Stay tuned.

SEXUAL VIOLENCE

The same long-term trends that have loosened traditional social controls and opened up previously forbidden areas of sexual pleasure have also increased the opportunities for acting out harmful sexual impulses. But because so few solid data exist for earlier years, we cannot say whether or not acts such as child molestation or rape have increased or only appear that way because people are now willing to report them. In addition, some behaviors have only recently been given a name and defined as unacceptable, for example, sexual harassment.

As sociologists, we are less concerned with the personal characteristics of molesters, rapists, and harassers than with questions such as: What are the common features of various forms of sexual violence? What does this tell us about our society and culture? The most obvious generalization is that this type of violence is directed against relatively powerless persons, namely, children and women, as much for purposes of social control as for sexual pleasure (Grauerholz and Korelewski, 1991; Chancer, 1992; Bart and Moran, 1993).

Such acts remained unnoticed and unstudied until recently, especially when they took place within the privacy of the family. But private matters become public issues when large numbers of people are involved and when the definition of the situation changes so that the public temper shifts from indifference to anger.

Child Molesting

Child molestation outside the family became a public issue following claims of sexual abuse in child care facilities, or stories of runaway children involved in prostitution. The runaway children data turned out to be greatly inflated (Best, 1990), while most of the day care prosecutions have resulted in acquittal or dismissal. More recently, claims of sexual abuse by Catholic priests have surfaced, the majority of which have been settled out of court by the church.

More difficult to identify and respond to legally are incidents of sexual abuse within the family. Although some child welfare experts advocate a "Child's Bill of Rights," including freedom from coercion and mistreatment, other people fiercely resist state interference with family relationships. The testimony of children is difficult to produce in court, and adult memories of childhood experiences are often unreliable, so estimates vary widely; it seems clear today, however, that many families are dangerous places for young girls. Over half of all rapes reported to the police in 1992 involved girls under age 18. Sixteen percent of the girls were under age 12, one in five of whom was raped by her father. Other relatives accounted for most of the remaining incidents (U.S. Department of Justice, 1994).

Some sexual encounters take place among classmates or neighborhood age peers (Erikson and Rapkin, 1991). Indeed, several studies indicate that rituals of sexual abuse of girls occur at ever earlier ages, as a form of male bonding among boys from relatively wealthy neighborhoods as well as in the public swimming pools of large cities (Hood, 1992; Henneberger, 1993).

Violence against Women

Redefining violence against women has been a central goal of the New Feminist Movement (Ferree and Hess, 1994). Sexual violence has often been equated with masculinity in a society in which only a wimp would let a woman boss him around (Kimmel, 1994; DeKeseredy and Schwartz, 1993). From the feminist standpoint, sexual violence is not so much about sex as about power, with the effect of limiting the freedom of women in their home, workplace, or streets. The few studies of male rapists found that their primary motive was anger against women rather than any sexual pleasure from the episode (Scully, 1990; Goleman, 1991).

In the United States today, estimates of the likelihood of being a victim of sexual assault range from one out of four to almost half over a woman's lifetime (Harlow, 1991; National Victim Center, 1992; M. Smith, 1994). The American rape rate leads the industrial world: 20 times higher than Japan and 13 times higher than England (U.S. Department of Justice, 1991). In the great majority of rapes, the attacker was known to the victim—a family member, friend of the family, or date. Very few rapes were reported to the police, although more victims might have done so if assured that their names would not be published (Bachman, 1994).

The incidence of **date rape** (nonconsenting intercourse in the dating context) on college campuses is a matter of increasing concern to women (Sanday, 1990; Martin and Hummer, 1989), but these are difficult situations to report. Men and women come to the dating situation with very different attitudes and expectations and may not be accurate interpreters of the cues that each is sending (Fonow et al., 1992). The resulting ambiguity is reflected in studies of acquaintance rape that find considerably less sympathy for the victim than when an assault is committed by a stranger (Bourque, 1989; Scritchfield and Maskar, 1989).

Date rape in nonconsenting sexual intercourse in the dating context.

Statutory rape occurs when sexual intercourse takes place with people under age 15 or 16, whether willingly or not.

And this being America, we must always be sensitive to the racial dimension in judgments of which victims are more worthy of sympathy than others. Rapes of women of color go largely unreported by the media, and minority victims are less likely than white women to be thought of as "innocent," thus perpetuating the myth of African-American and other minority women as sexually promiscuous. Rapes of minority women by white men are rarely publicized or prosecuted, in comparison to the overwhelming media attention paid to the much rarer cases in which white women have been attacked by minority men (Collins, 1991; Benedict, 1992).

In most cases of rape, especially those committed by an acquaintance, the victim may feel that she is to blame for not resisting more forcefully or for sending an ambiguous message by simply being on the date (Pitts and Schwartz, 1993). Having entered a relationship willingly, one cannot easily claim that subsequent events were completely out of one's control, unless the victim is underage. **Statutory rape** refers to state laws (statutes) that define as rape any act of sexual intercourse with a female under age 15 or 16, regardless of the circumstances.

If it has been so difficult to define physical assaults as impermissible sexual violence, attempts to make a similar claim for pornography and sexual harassment have met even greater resistance among advocates of the First Amendment's guarantee of freedom of speech and of the press.

Research has shown that fraternities create a sociocultural context in which the use of coercion in sexual relations with women is common and in which there is little effort to keep such behavior in check. Some national fraternities have decided to educate their brothers, seeking to change their behavior.

TODAY'S GREEKS CALL IT DATE RAPE.

Just a reminder from Pi Kappa Phi. Against her will is against the law

Pornography

Pornography (from the Greek, *porne,* for "sexual slave") refers to sexually detailed pictures that may or may not be judged obscene. The line between art, which is protected under the First Amendment, and obscenity, which can be censored, is difficult to define. At the moment in the United States, it is left to local officials to decide which material offends community standards and is without any serious artistic or political value. Thus, statutes and enforcement will vary from place to place. What many men perceive as a harmless world of fantasy and impossible freedom (Kimmel, 1990) is experienced by many women as a world in which they are degraded and abused (Berger et al., 1991).

Despite the establishment of a special division in the Justice Department in 1987, pornography in the United States has grown into a multibillion business, including adult book stores, mail order merchandise, videotape rentals, and "dial-a-porn" telephone services (*New York Times,* June 4, 1993c). Although it is difficult to prove that pornography directly incites attacks on women, experimental evidence suggests that exposure to violent pornography tends to increase men's tolerance of physical aggression (Russell, 1993).

Although many people are more concerned with the sexual component of pornography rather than its link to violence, the feminist argument against pornography is precisely that it violates a woman's constitutional right to feel secure in her person. In this view, the association of sexual pleasure with acts of extreme cruelty socializes people to believe that women should be willing victims of pain and humiliation, further reinforcing their general subordination in the society (MacKinnon, 1993).

The major arguments against censorship of sexually explicit material follow: (1) Once one exception is made to the First Amendment, others will follow, until the guarantee of free speech is meaningless. (2) Repressive norms will once more be used to deny women the right to define and control their own sexuality (Segal and McIntosh, 1993). This, too, is an issue upon which you will be asked to vote.

If defining pornography and proving its harmful effects has been difficult, identifying even more subtle forms of potential violence is filled with problems of meaning and enforcement.

Pornography refers to sexually detailed pictures and stories.

Sexual Harassment

Wherever men and women are in daily contact, in school or at work, shopping or merely walking down the street, it is not uncommon to hear sexually suggestive comments, antigay remarks, and jokes that put down men as well as women. Nonverbal behaviors such as staring and uninvited touching are also common. To what extent can these acts be considered a form of discrimination or social control?

Most people would agree that when a student or co-worker is pressured for sexual favors by someone with the power to award grades or promotions, saying "no" could have a negative effect on one's career. But what about a wolf call, a professor's suggestive comment in class, a supervisor's invitation to have a drink after work, or a pat on the behind? Many, perhaps most, Americans consider these relatively harmless gestures part of the natural byplay between the sexes. Yet, increasingly, these acts have been given a new name and meaning: sexual harassment.

Increasingly, citizens in a number of communities are protesting against pornography in their neighborhoods. What are the ordinances in your community?

Sexual harassment is legally defined as unwelcome sexual advances that affect a person's chance of employment or promotion, or that negatively influence one's working environment (including the school atmosphere). Although the statutes are gender neutral, and some men have successfully sued, the great majority of sexual harassment cases have been filed by women because they usually have inferior status in the workplace.

Although the data indicate that four out of ten women experience unwanted sexual advances at their workplace, only a few incidents are ever reported (Kolbert, 1991). If rape is hard to prove, harassment is doubly difficult. Many men are surprised to learn that their sexual advances are not taken as a compliment, whereas some women will misinterpret an otherwise friendly gesture (Mazer and Percival, 1989; Giuffre and Williams, 1994).

Nonetheless, harassment complaints from a variety of workplaces increased by 50 percent in early 1992 (Gross, 1992). This sudden surge followed a number of highly publicized events, including the televised testimony of Professor Anita Hill at the confirmation hearings on Clarence Thomas as a justice of the Supreme Court and the senators' responses that ridiculed her charges and accused her of all sorts of character flaws. Another major story of the early 1990s was the annual convention of the Tailhook Association, composed of present and former naval airmen. As in past years, the conventioneers routinely attacked female passersby, ripping their clothing, pawing their bodies, and generally living it up. The only difference this time was that some of the victims were themselves naval officers, and one of them reported the incident to her superior. Even so, it took another year of bureaucratic infighting before any high-ranking officers were sanctioned. In the end, however, all the cases were dropped because of the cover-ups, one admiral took early retirement, and the officer who brought the original complaint resigned as a result of continued negative treatment from her colleagues.

Regarding sexual harassment in the workplace, the Supreme Court in 1993 ruled that a complainant need not prove that the offending behavior caused severe psychological harm or impaired the ability to do one's job, but only that it created an environment that could reasonably be perceived as hostile or abusive for one sex but not the other.

Sexual harassment in elementary and high schools is almost never reported because the victims are doubly powerless, as girls and as children in a world governed by elders. These difficulties are compounded again at the college level, where a commitment to

Sexual harassment is unwelcome sexual advances that affect a person's chance of employment or promotion or that negatively influence one's working or school environment.

free expression is central to the mission of the school. Attempts by university authorities to create a comfortable learning atmosphere for all students by regulating "hate speech" are in direct conflict with the First Amendment and the institutional goal of open discussion. At what point does trash talk and sexual innuendo produce a hostile environment for students?

How far can a university go in setting guidelines on potentially exploitive relationships between instructors and students? In theory, teachers should be bound by the code of ethics of their professional association, which in most cases clearly prohibits the use of one's power over grades and scholarships to secure sexual favors. In actuality, such behavior is not uncommon (Rubin and Borgers, 1990). But do not students and instructors have a right to free association? This debate may be taking place on your campus at this moment. You might find it interesting to examine your school's policies regarding all forms of harassment, or to conduct a survey of your classmates' experiences. How well are individual rights protected? How secure do students feel? How do those who have been harassed handle the situation?

To the extent that all forms of sexual violence reflect the lesser status and power of women and children, as well as a fear of the feminine (Reilly et al., 1992), the key to reducing such incidents is the trend toward sexual equality. Eventually, it is thought that rates of sexual assault in the United States will decline to the levels of other industrial societies when girls and women respect themselves and are treated as persons rather than sexual objects and when sexual conquest ceases to be a means of gaining honor among men. The solution to harassment is to define the workplace as a setting for work-related activities, the schoolroom as a place for learning, and stores and streets as area where everyone can feel safe. These are distant goals, to be sure, but ones that will enhance the quality of life for all.

THE FLIP SIDE OF THE SEXUAL REVOLUTION

Despite the problems and ambiguities of the many recent changes in sexual attitudes and behaviors, we doubt that most Americans would want to return to the 1950s. The past is always idealized, and there really was no golden age of family love and sexual fulfillment. Sexuality has always been contested ground, in the society at large and in personal relationships. Insofar as sexual relationships involve wide differences in social power, they will tend to be exploitive and hardly helpful to the personal growth of either partner. The sexual revolution and other liberating currents of this century have shifted the focus from one of maintaining social order to individual pleasure and from duty to love. Although the self-centered pursuit of happiness has led many critics to condemn the selfishness of contemporary women and men, there is another possibility.

When Sigmund Freud, the founder of psychoanalysis, was asked the recipe for personal fulfillment, he answered: *love and work*. In our society, we have considered love to be the responsibility of women and work the obligation of men, leaving each only partially fulfilled (Cancian, 1987). The current trend toward sex equality means that relationships between men and women can be characterized by mutual dependence, so that both can realize their full potential for love and work. This is not an easy goal, which may be why so many fall short, but it is increasingly appealing to modern Americans of any age, and especially to college students.

SUMMARY

1. Sexual attraction and expression are complex experiences, shaped by culture, learned through socialization, and sanctioned within social networks. There is great cross-cultural variation, as well as change over time.

2. From a functional perspective, sexuality is a powerful drive that must be channeled into socially productive directions.

3. The conflict perspective focuses on the question of who defines appropriate sexual norms and enforces public morality.

4. Interpretive models emphasize the social construction of sexuality and how sexual scripts organize perceptions and experiences.

5. In the United States, sexual scripts have changed over time, from being linked strictly to reproduction in the sixteenth through the nineteenth centuries to the relative decoupling of sex and marriage or love today.

6. Studies of sexual habits and attitudes in the United States indicate the persistence of many traditional norms in the face of widespread changes in behavior, especially among women.

7. Adolescents in all industrial societies are becoming sexually active at earlier ages, but American teenagers have the highest rates of unintended pregnancy, abortion, and teenage motherhood. This is a result of limited sex education in the schools, lack of access to family planning services, and exploitive attitudes toward women.

8. Teenage childbearing has largely negative outcomes for both mother and child, including poor health, low lifetime earnings, unstable marriage, and welfare dependency.

9. Current attempts to restrict abortion rights raise issues of the control of women and the power of the state to control reproduction.

10. New developments in reproductive technology have changed the definition of motherhood and parental rights, separating sexuality from reproduction entirely.

11. In most societies, some proportion of the population has preferred same-sex sexual partners. The prevalence and meaning of homosexuality varies greatly across cultures and over time.

12. The United States is characterized by widespread and intense homophobia, although attitudes appear to have become more tolerant in the past two decades.

13. Since the 1970s, gay and lesbian rights organizations have been successful in reducing many forms of discrimination and in encouraging homosexuals to "come out." Most recently, however, a powerful backlash has stalled these efforts.

14. Homosexuality has multiple roots, involving complex interactions among biological tendencies, life course experiences, and the sociocultural environment.

15. The prevalence of homosexuality in American is difficult to determine, but most data suggest a range of 5–10 percent, higher for men than for women.

16. Several states and cities now recognize the legitimacy of "domestic partners," unmarried couples who are committed to caring relationships.

17. Sexual violence is most often directed at the powerless, primarily women and children. Sociologists view these acts as expressions of power rather than of uncontrollable sexuality.

18. Child molestation is extremely difficult to confirm but appears to be more widespread than previously thought. Most assaults take place within the family.

19. Most rapes are committed by someone known to the victim, but go largely unreported because of the publicity and tendency to blame the victim.

20. The issue of pornography has divided scholars between those who feel that the First Amendment must be protected and those who claim that pornography is a form of violence toward women.

21. Increased attention has been focused on various forms of sexual harassment, generally defined as deliberate, repeated, and unwelcomed comments and gestures that create a hostile environment for one sex and not the other.

SUGGESTED READINGS

Bart, Pauline B. and Eileen Geil Morgan. Eds. *Violence against Women: The Bloody Footprints*. Newbury Park, CA: Sage, 1993. A compilation of articles about the types of violence perpetrated against women, the structural supports in society that condone this violence, institutional repsonses to the violence after it occurs, and overviews of the current information about women and violence.

Chancer, Lynn S. *Sadomasochism in Everyday Life: The Dynamics of Power and Powerlessness*. New Brunswick, NJ: Rutgers University Press, 1992. Using a model based on critical theory and object-relations theory from psychoanalysis, the author analyzes a wide range of social phenomena involving power and powerlessness, dominance and subordination.

Chodorow, Nancy. *Feminites, Masculinites, Sexualities: Freud and Beyond*. Lexington, KY: University Press of Kentucky, 1994. A sociologist reworks Freudian and more contemporary psychoanalytic theories to illuminate the construction of sexual identities. Richly textured but very readable, and essential to understanding psychosocial processes of gender formation.

D'Emilio, John, and Estelle B. Freedman. *Intimate Matters: A History of Sexuality in America*. New York: Harper & Row, 1988. A lively history of sexuality in America with particular focus on the complex issues of race, gender, and social class and the movement of sexuality from the privacy of the bedroom to its commercial exploitation and inclusion in the general culture.

Faderman, Lillian. *Odd Girls and Twilight Lovers: A History of Lesbian Life in Twentieth Century American*. New York: Columbia University Press, 1991. An informative history of lesbian life in the United States.

Fairstein, Linda A. *Sexual Violence: Our War against Rape*. New York: William Morrow & Company, 1993. Fairstein, director of the Sex Crimes Prosecution Unit within the Manhattan District Attorney's office, details the positive change in prosecution of sexual violence.

Gagnon, John, Cathy Greenblat, and Michael Kimmel. *Human Sexualities*. 2d ed. New York: Allyn and Bacon, 1995. An excellent overview of the meanings of sexualities, sexual development, and sexual expression from a sociological perspective. Includes latest U.S. and global material on current issues such as AIDS, child sexual abuse, rape, and sexual identity.

Gullota, Thomas P., Gerald R. Adams, and Raymond Montemayor, eds. *Adolescent Sexuality*. Newbury Park, CA: Sage, 1993. An interesting collection covering topics such as anatomy, gender, roles, heterosexuality and homosexuality, pregnancy and parenting, sexually transmitted diseases, and sexual responsibility.

Hemphill, Essex, ed. *Brother to Brother*. Boston: Alyson Publishers, 1991. A compelling collection of essays, poems, and nonfiction by black gay men about their homes, sexuality, AIDS and social movements.

Huber, Joan, and Beth E. Schneider, eds. *The Social Context of AIDS*. Newbury Park, CA: Sage, 1992. An anthology of studies of gay men, sexual partners of IV drug users, people with AIDS, care givers of persons with AIDS, prostitutes, in the United States.

Michael, Robert T. , John H. Gagnon, Edward O. Laumann, and Gina Kolata. *Sex in America: A Definitive Survey*. Boston: Little, Brown & Company, 1994. The short and more popularly written version of the most thorough recent national survey of sexual practices in the United States. All you wanted to know, and more, about who's doing what.

Rubin, Lillian B. *Erotic Wars: What Happened to the Sexual Revolution?* New York: Farrar, Straus & Giroux, 1990. A lively and empathetic portrait of men's and women's participation in and reaction to the sexual revolution.

Sprecher, Susan, and Kathleen McKinney. *Sexuality*. Newbury Park, CA: Sage, 1993. A useful source of information about sexuality including the influence of culture and family on close relationships, physical attraction, sexual decision-making, and the variety of sexual expressions.

Weinberg, Martin S, Colin J. Williams, and Douglas W. Pryor. *Dual Attraction: Understanding Bisexuality*. New York: Oxford University Press, 1994. A team of well-known sociologists of sexuality use the topic of bisexuality to explore all forms of sexual identity and to propose a broad new theory of human sexuality. Provocative and fascinating.

9

Social Stratification

W ho shall live and who shall die? Although Americans do not like the idea of "playing God," we make decisions daily that affect the likelihood of other people living or dying—decisions about welfare policy, crime control, speed limits, and health care. For example, although many people might need to have a heart transplant, the supply of healthy hearts for this purpose are extremely limited. If you were a hospital administrator with the final say, which of the following eight patients would you select to receive one of the four available hearts?

- An African-American 50-year-old woman doctor
- A white gay male 30-year-old physicist
- An unmarried Hispanic-American pregnant teenager
- An Asian-American 25-year-old woman artist
- A white male 55-year-old priest
- A white 45-year-old female homemaker
- The 20-year-old mentally impaired son of wealthy parents
- The 65-year-old white male governor of the state

Each of these descriptions contains a mix of ascribed and achieved characteristics, some of which are valued more highly than others in our society. In addition, as a hospital administrator, you have the financial health of your organization to think of, in which case, the state governor or the son of wealthy parents might go to the top of the list. In fact, high-income patients are more likely than those with low income to jump to the head of the line waiting for a transplant (Friedman et al., 1992), and in 1993 it took less than one day to find a suitable *heart and liver* donor for the Governor of Pennsylvania (Belkin, 1993).

When we rank some kinds of people as more deserving than others, we are making judgments of moral worth. Although each society has different criteria of worthiness, the result is similar everywhere: **systems of stratification** in which the more worthy receive more of the society's resources than do those of lesser quality. In this chapter, we examine the general processes of stratification and the consequences of inequality. In the two following chapters, we will pay attention to stratification on the basis of the specific ascribed traits of sex, race, religion, and national origin (ethnicity).

PRINCIPLES OF STRATIFICATION

In all societies, three kinds of resources are valued: (1) **power**—the ability to impose one's will on others; (2) **prestige**—respect from others; and (3) **property**—wealth owned, whether measured in yams, land, wives, or green rectangles. And in all societies more complex than a simple gathering band, these resources are unequally distributed among individuals and groups.

When people who differ in their ascribed and achieved characteristics are evaluated differently, a **social hierarchy** is formed. A hierarchy is a set of ranked statuses from highest to lowest. Because both the most- and least-valued traits are likely to be relatively rare, status hierarchies tend to be diamond-shaped, narrow at the very top and bottom, as can be seen later in Figure 9-2 on page 200.

Within the hierarchy, people at different levels, or *strata* (the plural of *stratum*, the singular), can claim different amounts of power, prestige, and property. In this way, a set of ranked statuses based on evaluations of social worth is transformed into a hierarchy of control over societal resources. Stratification systems, thus, are both a cause and consequences of inequality.

Although we can imagine a society in which all members are equally valued and rewarded, this is a rare phenomenon. Once the division of labor expands beyond gathering, some tasks will be considered more important than others, and the people who perform such tasks are rewarded with power, respect, and material goods. At the very least, labor is divided on the basis of sex and age, so that all societies have gender and age stratification systems. The more complex the division of labor, or the more heterogeneous the society in terms of race, religion, and national origin, the more ways there are to judge people differently—by what they do (achieved statuses) or by what they are (ascribed statuses).

Systems of stratification rank some individuals and groups as more deserving than others.

Power is the ability to impose one's will on others.

Prestige refers to the respect given by others.

Property refers to forms of wealth.

A **social hierarchy** is a set of ranked statuses.

THEORETICAL PERSPECTIVES

Why are stratification systems nearly universal? The idea that it is in human nature to create "pecking orders" is not sufficient because it cannot explain variations across cultures and history. For a sociological understanding, we must look at characteristics of the society, at the level of the collectivity, to understand stratification patterns.

The Functional Theory of Stratification

The *functional perspective* explains social structures in terms of the consequences of a given arrangement: What does it do for the collectivity and for individuals? The classic expression of this view, by Davis and

Moore (1945), goes like this: Not all persons have the same abilities. Some will have qualities that are most needed and valued at a particular historical moment, such as physical strength, wisdom, or artistry. The other side of the equation is that desired rewards are always limited in quantity, either naturally or artificially (if everyone can have it, "it" loses its value as a symbol of superiority). Therefore, it is in the interests of the society that those with the most ability use their skills for the well-being of all. In return, they deserve greater rewards—in respect, power, and material goods—than do people of lesser talent.

In this view, inequality is functional for collective survival. As elaborated by Talcott Parsons, the functional perspective fit the mood of prosperity, social order, and celebration of individual achievement of the 1950s (Grimes, 1991). It was assumed that the resulting hierarchy of talent, called a **meritocracy,** was best equipped to lead the nation, and it was taken for granted that these leaders would be white, middle- and upper-middle class, Protestant men.

The functional position has been challenged by several generations of sociologists, beginning with Melvin Tumin (1953), who point out that inequality is due more to a scarcity of top slots than to a shortage of talent. In addition, many advantages are inherited rather than earned.

Conflict Perspectives on Stratification

As described in Chapter 1, the conflict perspective explains social structure as the outcome of struggles over scarce rewards, in which some individuals and groups may already have an advantage, being in the positions of power that set the rules of the competition, as well as defining what constitutes merit and virtue. As Karl Marx observed, the dominant ideas of an era are those of its dominant strata. Conflict theorists have expanded on this insight—that ideas are social products—with the concept of **ideological hegemony** (Gramsci, 1959). *Hegemony* means influence and control, and *ideological hegemony* refers to control over the production of cultural symbols—beliefs, values, ideas of justice, and so forth (Bourdieu, 1984). If you think about the people who own the media, dominate the educational system, and govern the nation, it is clear that they come from the more privileged strata, and it should not surprise you that they promote definitions of reality that justify their own positions. Thus, from the conflict perspective, the functional theory of stratification is itself a prime example of ideological hegemony.

> A **meritocracy** is a hierarchy of talent, in which rewards are based on one's abilities.
>
> **Ideological hegemony** refers to control over the production of cultural symbols.

The conflict perspective focuses on such structural variables as the distribution of occupations (how many openings for particular jobs), past and present hiring practices, the degree of unionization of the labor force, and the number of different kinds of employers in a community. These are characteristics of the economy, not of individuals, and they play a major role in creating and maintaining inequality among various types of workers (Althauser and Wallace, 1991).

The functionalist and conflict perspectives differ in their explanations of how people come to hold certain jobs. How would each perspective explain why so many data entry operators are women and most business executives are men?

A Unified View

The functional and conflict perspectives are not necessarily mutually exclusive (Lenski, 1966; Milner, 1987). The functional model may well account for the origins of inequality, which is then maintained by the mechanisms studied by conflict theorists. Thus, individuals with unusual luck or ability can amass great power and wealth at a particular historical moment. But once established, they will seek to pass their status to their children, regardless of the talents of the offspring—even in societies ideologically committed to equality, as in China today (Lin and Bian, 1991).

The transmission of social advantages occurs because members of the next generation are unequal from the very beginning. As in a foot race, some runners may be naturally faster than others, but others will receive better training and equipment. In the stratification system, contestants do not begin at the same starting line; children from high-status families have a big head start.

> **Social stratification** refers to the unequal distribution of societal resources.

DIMENSIONS OF SOCIAL STRATIFICATION

Social stratification refers to the unequal distribution of power, prestige, and property. In many ways,

there is a basic unity to these three hierarchies: wealth is often power, and both can be used to command respect. Max Weber, however, emphasized the need to consider three different ways of ranking, even though they cannot always be separated in real life (Weber, 1922/1968):

1. *Class* refers to people at the same economic level, who may or may not be aware of their common interests.
2. *Status groups* are based on prestige, whose members share a common life-style. Just what qualities earn respect will vary from one society to another.
3. *Parties* are political groupings that may or may not be organized around class interests.

In sum, political parties, prestige groupings, and social classes are different (although often overlapping) dimensions of stratification. Let us examine the distribution of power, prestige, and property in the United States today.

Power

Power, as defined by Max Weber, is the ability to impose one's will on other social actors, regardless of their own wishes. Power is a social resource that is unequally distributed in most societies, groups, and relationships. Power is also *relational,* that is, it can be realized only when other people obey.

Per Capita Gross National Product (GNP). Gross national product is computed by dividing the total monetary value of all domestic and foreign goods and services by the number of people in the population. It is an indication of a society's overall wealth and well-being.

Source: Population Reference Bureau. World Population Data, 1994.

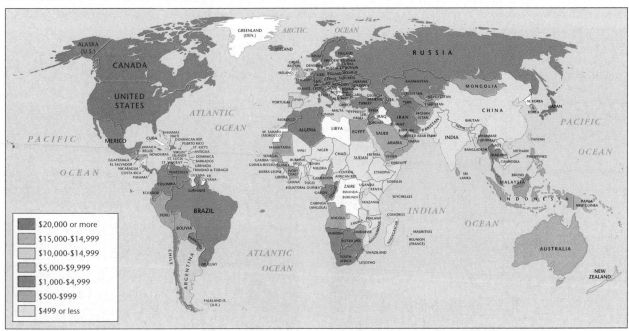

Authority refers to the power residing in a socially recognized status. Pope John Paul II, the leader of the Roman Catholic church, toured the United States to reach his flock. After a Papal Mass attended by over 500,000 people in Cherry Creek Park in Colorado, the Pope met with leaders of a tribe of Native Americans.

Authority refers to power that belongs to a socially recognized status, such as president, police officer, or employer, and therefore considered to be legitimate by other members of the society. Although a full discussion of political power appears in Chapter 14, it is worth noting here that most positions of authority in government and business in the United States are held by people who come from the upper levels of the wealth and education hierarchies. Other forms of authority are more widely distributed, such as the power of parents over children, of husbands over wives, and of teachers over students. But not all power is socially legitimated, as in the case of leaders of organized crime families.

Influence, in contrast to authority, is the ability to persuade others to bow to your will and is based more on interpersonal skills than on occupying a particular position. Influential people are often close to those in authority, or possess unique skills and knowledge.

Prestige

Prestige, or *status honor,* is uniquely social in that it depends on the respect that others are willing to give. Some societies honor the wise and humble, others the boastful and warlike, but everywhere respect from others is a valued resource. In modern industrial societies, prestige is based largely on occupational status, although income is also important. As shown in Table 9-1, when people are asked to rank various occupations, the highest scores are given to *professionals,*

such as physicians, lawyers, scientists, and college professors. A **profession** is an occupation that requires a long period of training and for which those already in the field control the number and type of people allowed to practice, monitor peer performance, and protect their members from public review.

Lowest rankings, in contrast, are given to people whose jobs require little training, who do "dirty" work, or who must take orders without question; for example, nursing home aides, janitors, and gas station attendants.

In general, the higher the social value of the occupation, the more justified do high incomes appear to respondents (Kelley and Evans, 1993). Prestige judgments are also affected by whether women or men dominate the occupation, with "women's work" rated lower. In the United States, for example, a circular process is at work whereby low-ranked low-pay jobs, generally shunned by white men, are relatively open to persons of color and white women, further reducing the prestige of the occupation (Xu and Leffler, 1992; Carlson, 1992).

Authority refers to socially legitimated power.

Influence is the ability to persuade others to follow one's will.

A **profession** is an occupation requiring lengthy training and in which practitioners control entry and monitor performance.

The link between income and occupational prestige has a number of interesting exceptions. College teachers, for example, enjoy high prestige but moder-

TABLE 9-1   The Prestige Ratings of Occupations in the United States

(Scale runs from 100 (highest) to 1 (lowest); Score = average score for the sample)

Occupation	Score	Occupation	Score	Occupation	Score	Occupation	Score
Physician	82	High school teacher	63	Secretary	46	Baker	34
College professor	78	Registered nurse	62	Real estate agent	44	Shoe repairer	33
Judge	76	Pharmacist	61	Fire fighter	44	Bulldozer operator	33
Lawyer	76	Veterinarian	60	Postal clerk	43	Bus driver	32
Physicist	74	Elementary school		Advertising agent	42	Truck driver	32
Dentist	74	teacher	60	Mail carrier	42	Cashier	31
Banker	72	Accountant	· 57	Railroad conductor	41	Sales clerk	29
Aeronautical		Librarian	55	Typist	41	Housekeeper	25
engineer	71	Social worker	52	Plumber	41	Dockworker	24
Architect	71	Funeral director	52	Farmer	41	Gas station	
Psychologist	71	Computer specialist	51	Carpenter	40	attendant	22
Airline pilot	70	Stockbroker	51	Welder	40	Cab driver	22
Chemist	69	Reporter	51	Dancer	38	Bartender	20
Minister	69	Office manager	50	Jeweler	37	Waiter	20
Civil engineer	68	Bank teller	50	Watchmaker	37	Farm laborer	18
Biologist	68	Electrician	49	Bricklayer	36	Maid/servant	18
Geologist	67	Machinist	48	Flight attendant	36	Garbage collector	17
Sociologist	66	Police officer	48	Meter reader	36	Janitor	17
Political scientist	66	Insurance agent	47	Mechanic	35	Shoeshiner	9
Mathematician	65	Musician	46				

Source: Davis and Smith, 1984

ate income. Conversely, some low-ranked workers benefit from relatively high, union-negotiated wage scales, for example, sanitation workers in New York City. Many people in low-prestige jobs maintain their sense of self-worth by deemphasizing work and focusing on family and friends (Gecas and Seff, 1990), or by mastering whatever skills are required for the occupation, such as the bartender with the best memory (Walsh and Taylor, 1982). In addition, criminal activities are often well rewarded with high income and prestige, as seen in both inner-city neighborhoods and Wall Street offices.

Net worth consists of the value of all assets less all debts.

Property

Every society has certain objects that signify material success: yams, wives, cattle, and coral necklaces, to mention only a few. In the United States, we measure wealth by counting the money value of everything owned by a person, family, or household, including houses, cars, bank accounts, stocks and bonds, life insurance, retirement funds, artwork, and jewelry.

WEALTH.   The distribution of wealth is very difficult to determine because many assets go unreported—in foreign banks and complex business arrangements.

Table 9-2 shows the most recent data on the **net worth** (the value of all assets minus outstanding debts) of all American households. As you can see, one-third of U.S. households have assets of $10,000 or less. Most others have some money in the bank, own a car, and are partial owners of their home, but only 4 percent have a net worth of $500,000 or more. In

TABLE 9-2   Household Net Worth, 1991

Net Worth in Dollars	Percent of U.S. Households
Negative or zero	12
1–4,999	14
5,000–9,999	6
10,000–24,999	11
25,000–49,999	12
50,000–99,999	16
100,000–249,999	18
250,000–499,999	7
500,000 and over	4
	100 %

Source: U.S. Bureau of the Census, *Current Population Reports,* P70-34, (1994): 6.

other words, a very few households account for most of the wealth of the nation. The *median* net worth (the point at which half of all households are above and half below) was about $31,000 in the mid-1990s, mostly represented by the value of a house minus the outstanding mortgage.

Using a different sampling frame and a longer list of assets, the Federal Reserve Board found a much higher degree of the concentration of wealth, with the top wealth holders accounting for 37 percent of the nation's privately owned assets (Kennickel and Woodburn, 1992). Figure 9-1, which compares 1989 data with similar information from 1963 and 1983, shows that most of the increase in the concentration of wealth is accounted for by the top *one-half of 1 percent* of households.

Wealth and asset ownership vary by many background characteristics. The largest difference is by race, with white households accumulating assets worth *ten* times those of African-American households. Married couples own more assets than the nonmarried, and households headed by persons age 55 and older are wealthier than those headed by younger people.

INCOME.   Because accurate information on assets is so difficult to gather, social scientists typically rely on the Bureau of the Census's yearly data on *earned in-*

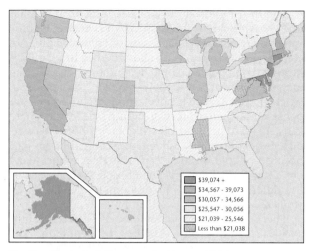

Median Household Income, by States, 1994.
Source: U.S. Bureau of the Census P60–184, 1994.

come. This refers to annual earnings from wages, dividends, and money gained from sale of stocks and bonds, as reported by individuals, families, or households. These data will underestimate the income of people whose earnings can go unreported, typically at both the highest and lowest income levels.

FIGURE 9-1   Distribution of wealth (% share of total net worth) in 1983 dollars.

(*Sources:* Economic Policy Institute, 1992; Reprinted by permission of the Wall Street Journal, August 15, 1986. Copyright © 1986 Dow Jones & Company, Inc. All Rights Reserved Worldwide.)

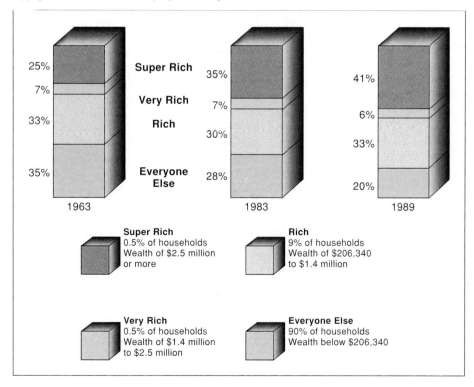

The distribution of incomes for American families in 1992 is shown in Table 9-3. As you can see, income varies by race and ethnicity, sex of earner, number of earners, educational level, and whether the family is headed by a couple or only by a mother. The median income for married couple families is more than twice that of female-headed families, and whites are considerably better off than Latinos or African Americans, in part because of a higher proportion of female-headed families among the latter, but in part because people of color earn less than white workers, even at the same level of job skill. Note especially the difference it makes if you complete your college studies!

There is also a major difference between family and household income. Families, by definition, consist of more than one person related by blood, marriage, or adoption. Households can consist of a single individual, usually a young person early in his or her work life or an older widow living on Social Security benefits and therefore with relatively low incomes. Clearly, in terms of the income hierarchy, it is best to be married, to be white, and to have more than one earner. Yearly income of $1 million or more a year is quite rare, with only 65,000 individuals reporting such earnings in 1991.

THE DISAPPEARING MIDDLE. During the 1960s and 1970s, the income gap between the richest and poorest Americans narrowed. Federal programs reduced poverty among the elderly and Appalachian whites, while a progressive tax system (where higher incomes are taxed at higher rates) limited income gains among the wealthy. High-skill factory workers and public employees benefited from union-negotiated contracts, and white-collar employment increased. Most Americans could consider themselves part of the comfortable middle.

TABLE 9-3   Median Income of American Families and Individuals, March 1994

Family Characteristics	Median Income (Dollars)		
All races			
All families			
Married couples	43,005		
Female householder, no husband present	17,443		
White			
Married couples	43,675		
Female householder, no husband present	20,000		
African American			
Married couples	35,218		
Female householder, no husband present	11,909		
Hispanic[a]			
Married couples	28,454		
Female householder, no husband present	12,047		
Number of earners			
No earner	15,536		
One earner	26,292		
Two earners	45,779		
Earnings of year-round, full-time workers			
Male	30,407		
Female	21,747		
Education (year-round, full-time workers, age 25+) (1993)		Male	Female
Less than ninth grade		12,206	7,942
High school graduate		22,756	13,226
Some college		26,878	16,611
Bachelor's degree		36,691	24,126
Professional degree		70,728	37,249
Per person income	15,574		

[a]Persons of Hispanic origin can be of any race.

Source: Adapted from U.S. Bureau of Census, *Current Population Reports*, P60–188, 1994

The economic differences between wealthy Americans and those with limited incomes is reflected in many ways, including where they shop and what they can afford to buy. Where can you afford to shop?

The 1980s, however, were another story. Between 1977 and 1989, the rich got very much richer, the poor got poorer, and the middle began to shrink (Morris et al., 1994; U.S. Bureau of the Census, P60–184, 1993). The top 1 percent of wealth holders received 70 percent of all income gains during that period, the bottom fifth lost 9 percent of their income, and the middle gained slightly (Krugman, 1992; Congressional Budget Office, 1992).

What has kept most families from falling even further is having a second wage earner. That is, when wives enter the labor force, the family is able to maintain its standard of living; families with only one wage earner have lost ground.

Workers in low-income families have actually increased the number of hours worked, compared to higher-income earners, yet their wages have grown only slightly, and their pretax income, even including welfare payments, has declined. In other words, the poor are not poor because they are working less; quite the contrary, they are working more but at jobs with stagnant or declining wages (Burtless, 1990). The failure of men's earnings to keep pace with inflation and life-style expectations is the single most important factor in the shrinking of the American middle strata over the past 15 years (Duncan et al., 1992; Wolff, 1992).

In the 1980s the Reagan and Bush administrations reduced taxes on the wealthy and cut programs that assisted the poor, reversing the trends of the previous decades. Other factors contributing to increasing income inequality in the United States include the following (to be discussed in Chapter 13):

- Changes in the composition of the labor force, as women and entry-level baby boomers earn relatively low wages
- Breakdown of union power to negotiate favorable wages and benefits
- Relocation of manufacturing jobs overseas or to low-wage, anti-union states
- Decline of employment in high-pay "smokestack" jobs
- Increased use of part-time employees, who do not receive benefits such as health insurance and retirement pensions
- Growth of jobs at the lowest end of the skill and wage scale

Socioeconomic Status

Social scientists have attempted to construct one simplified measure of social rank that accounts for all three dimensions: power, prestige, and property. The common usage today is to refer to **socioeconomic status (SES),** a construct based on income, occupational rank, and education. SES is then used as a measure of another abstraction, *social class.* Figure 9-2 shows the distribution of American adults on the basis of education, occupation, and income in 1993, from which a rough SES hierarchy can be derived.

> **Socioeconomic status (SES)** is a measure based on a combination of income, occupational prestige, and education.

Social class is a powerful variable in the social sciences because it influences almost every other variable of interest to us from how long one lives to age at first marriage to the likelihood of mental illness. Thus, the measurement of social class and the tracing of its effects have been a major field of sociological inquiry.

SOCIAL CLASS IN AMERICA

Measuring Social Class

Social class can be measured by a person's reputation in the community, by life-style, and by a self-identification, as well as various SES indexes. But because these

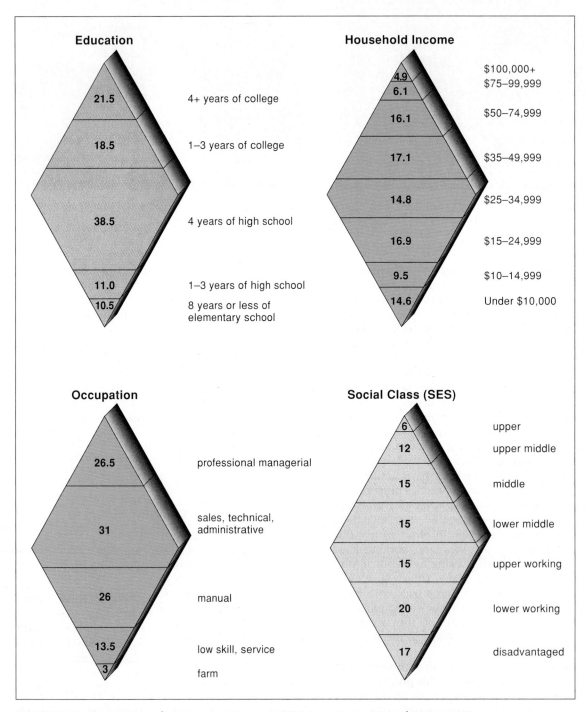

FIGURE 9-2   Dimensions of socioeconomic status (SES), in percents, United States, 1993.

(*Sources*: U.S. Bureau of the Census, *Statistical Abstract of the United States*, 1994; U.S. Bureau of the Census, *Current Population Reports*, P60–188, 1994)

Social class reflects dramatic differences in the income, occupation, and education of individuals and families. What are the obvious and less apparent differences between the wealthy and poor in the United States? How do you think the social class differences will affect the children of these families?

methods are based on characteristics of individuals, they are not fully sociological. An alternative approach examines features of the job and the *social relations of production* (Wright, 1985).

> It is . . . this division into working class and business class that constitutes the outstanding cleavage in Middletown. . . . tending to influence what one does all day long throughout one's life; whom one marries; when one gets up in the morning; whether one belongs to the Holy Roller or Presbyterian church; or drives a Ford or Buick.
>
> —ROBERT S. LYND and HELEN MERRILL LYND, 1929, pp. 23–24

This approach focuses on where a person is located in the process of production and in a web of relationships. How much control does the worker have over his or her own tasks or those of others? This definition contrasts with the simple division of workers into *blue-* and *white-*collar, or *manual* (using ones hands) and *nonmanual* (using one's brain). Many white-collar nonmanual jobs (e.g., bookkeeping, bank telling) allow less job autonomy and are more heavily supervised than some blue-collar/manual jobs (e.g., carpentry, equipment repair). To illustrate the social relations of production model, Figure 9-3 cross-tabulates the two variables of (1) ownership of the workplace and (2) control over one's labor, to create four cells. *Capitalists* enjoy ownership and control over the work of employees. *Managers* control the work

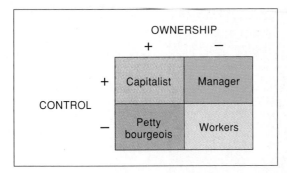

FIGURE 9-3 A property space for relational social class.

(*Sources:* Robinson, 1984; Wright, 1985.)

of others but are employees of owners. The term *petit* (or *petty*) *bourgeois* is the French phrase for the self-employed or small-scale owners such as shopkeepers. The authentic *working class* that forms the bulk of the labor force neither owns nor controls the conditions of their work. But it is not a very unified class, disproportionately composed of women and minority employees, along with blue-collar white men.

Class Awareness and Self-perception

How do Americans perceive the stratification system and their position in it? **Class awareness** refers to recognizing differences in wealth, occupational prestige, and social power and accurately locating oneself in these hierarchies. Most research suggests that Americans are aware of class distinctions, have strong feelings about their own location, and tend to associate with others in the same stratum (Simpson et al., 1988; Vanneman and Cannon, 1987).

In addition, when assigning a class position to oneself and others, respondents not only use the standard objective variables of education, occupation, and income, but they also take into account the social relations of production: job autonomy, supervisory authority, and self-employment (Vallas, 1987). Although many respondents misclassify themselves, with people in both the higher and lower strata claiming membership in the middle class, they also showed a rather sophisticated sociological understanding of the complexities of class location.

Class placement is particularly problematic for employed women whose jobs may place them in different categories from those of their husbands. What, then, is the class status of the couple? For most respondents in the United States and other modern societies, the husband's occupation remained the

> **Class awareness** refers to recognizing differences in income, occupational prestige, and life-style and accurately locating oneself.
>
> **Class consciousness** occurs when class awareness becomes the central organizing point of self-definition and political action.

primary determinant of the couple's subjective class location, regardless of the wife's employment status or educational level (Baxter, 1994).

The placement of full-time homemakers has also presented problems to researchers. Because unpaid labor is typically not counted as "work," homemakers have been excluded from the population used to compute occupational distributions, with the effect of making the stratification system look less polarized, especially by sex, because homemakers would be clustered at the lower end of the hierarchy (Szelenyi, 1992).

Class Consciousness

Being aware of the class system is one thing, **class consciousness**—making this awareness central to self-image and political action—is quite another. Most of you have been brought up with the idea that although there are differences in wealth, job prestige, and control over others, social class really doesn't matter in America; anyone can make it to the top if they have the right stuff.

The American "myth of classlessness" could be considered a form of ideological hegemony that obscures the degree to which class-based interests have prevailed at the top of the hierarchy. A number of other conditions have made class consciousness less obvious in the United States than in other industrial societies: the ideals of individualism and equality; the lack of a hereditary aristocracy; the image of a nation of immigrants; failure of organized labor to create a self-conscious political party in opposition to employers; ties of racial, religious, and ethnic loyalty that cut across class lines; and the reality of upward movement in the class structure as a result of two centuries of economic growth.

Social Class and Social Order

Societal resources in the United States are more unevenly distributed than in many other modern industrial societies (United Nations, 1994). Because inequality tends to produce discontent and reduce social cohesion, we must ask why this society has remained so stable.

> Wealth and opinion were practically worshipped before Washington opened his eyes on the sun . . . and the worship of Opinion is, at this day, the established religion of the United States.
>
> —HARRIET MARTINEAU, 1837, Vol. 2, p. 153

Inequality alone does not necessarily produce disorder; it is when inequality is defined as unfair (*inequitable*) that the legitimacy of the stratification

Most of the unrest in Central and South America is due to extreme inequality in the distribution of wealth. The dramatic differences in living conditions are illustrated in this photo of extreme poverty on the outskirts of Mexico City and in the modern skyline in the background.

system is threatened. As long as most people perceive that the rules are fair, inequality will be tolerated. Only when inequality reaches extremes, and/or the have-nots withdraw their support for the system, is class warfare likely, as seen in Latin America today. In Guatemala, for example, where 65 percent of farmland is owned by 2.5 percent of landowners, a civil

war between landless peasants and the ruling elite has been in progress for over 20 years (Cabrera, 1993).

IDEOLOGICAL SUPPORTS FOR THE AMERICAN CLASS SYSTEM. Beliefs that justify inequality are deeply embedded in our value system. Most Americans adopt a functional perspective on stratification, in which effort and self-reliance will be rewarded (Bobo, 1991; Ritzman and Tomaskovic-Devey, 1992; Feagin and Feagin, 1994). Among the most enduring ideological justifications of inequality are the following:

- *The promise of equal opportunity,* the belief that with hard work and a bit of luck, anyone can rise from "rags to riches."
- *Survival of the fittest,* or "social Darwinism," based on an image of society as a jungle in which the naturally superior will win out.
- *Psychological determinism* reflects the individualistic emphasis of American culture, whereby such traits as motivation and innate intelligence determine success or failure (Hernnstein and Murray, 1994).
- *The work ethic,* as described in Chapter 3, gives a touch of the sacred to many of these beliefs. If work is a "calling" and success a sign of grace, then failure can only signify some moral flaw in the individual.
- The "*culture of poverty*" concept claims that poverty is the outcome of dysfunctional values and behaviors that are transmitted from one generation to the next, creating a distinct subculture that reinforces a cycle of failure (Lewis, 1959; Mead 1992).

As Table 9-4, from 1969 and 1980, indicates, the general public believes that people are poor because they lack thrift, effort, ability, and morals. Although

TABLE 9-4 Percentages of Americans Who Felt the Following Reasons for Poverty Were Very Important or Somewhat Important, 1969 and 1980

	1969		1980	
	Very	Somewhat	Very	Somewhat
1. Lack of thrift and proper money management	59%	31	64	30
2. Lack of effort by the poor themselves	57	34	53	39
3. Lack of ability and talent	54	34	53	35
4. Loose morals and drunkenness	50	32	44	30
5. Sickness and physical handicaps	46	39	43	41
6. Low wages in some businesses and industries	43	36	40	47
7. Failure of society to provide good schools for many Americans	38	26	46	29
8. Failure of private industry to provide enough jobs	29	38	35	39
9. Prejudice and discrimination against African Americans	34	39	31	44
10. Being taken advantage of by rich people	19	32	20	35
11. Just bad luck	8	28	12	32

Source: © 1987 by the Society for the Study of Social Problems. Reprinted from Social Problems, Vol. 34, No. 1, pp. 82–99, by permission.

Class, Self, and Society

A large body of research has examined class awareness and class consciousness. An additional question is whether or not citizens of a country ideologically committed to eliminating class distinctions, such as an Eastern European communist nation before 1989, would have different perceptions of social class and their own location than do citizens of a Western democracy.

To explore these issues, researchers conducted large-scale national surveys in Hungary and Australia

in the late 1980s (Evans et al., 1992). Their basic theoretical assumption was that a person tends to view the world in the same terms as the people with whom one interacts. In other words, because members of the same occupational or income group live with people similar to themselves, as family, friends, and co-workers, they believe that most others in the society see things the same way. Respondents were shown diagrams of a five-class system, as in Figure 9-4 and were asked which one best described their society, where they would place themselves, and which diagram

(continued)

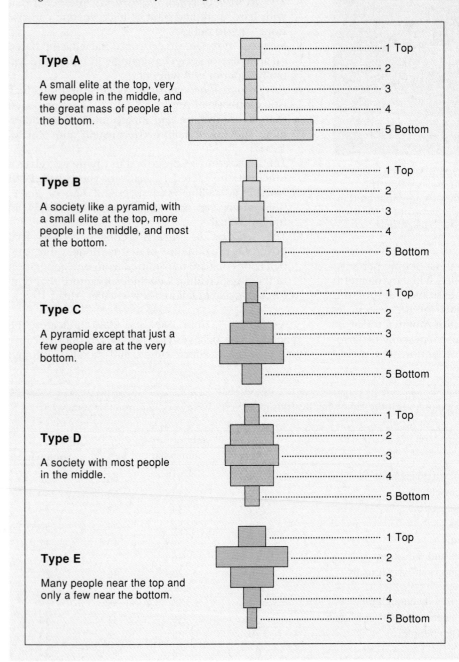

Type A

A small elite at the top, very few people in the middle, and the great mass of people at the bottom.

Type B

A society like a pyramid, with a small elite at the top, more people in the middle, and most at the bottom.

Type C

A pyramid except that just a few people are at the very bottom.

Type D

A society with most people in the middle.

Type E

Many people near the top and only a few near the bottom.

FIGURE 9-4 Perceptions of Social Class. Respondents were asked to decide which pattern characterized their society. Which type do you think best represents the U.S. today?

Source: M. D. R. Evans, Jonathan Kelly, and Tamas Kolosi. "Images of Class: Public Perceptions in Hungary and Australia." *American Sociological Review* 57 (1992), p. 461-482. Reproduced with permission.

would be their preferred social system. Types A and B were the most elitist, with few on top and most on the bottom; Types D and E were the more egalitarian, with most people clustered at the higher end.

Despite the great differences between then-Communist Hungary and democratic Australia, and despite their perception of the existing system, a majority of respondents placed themselves exactly in the middle. This was so regardless of the person's actual occupa-

tional location, education, income, and degree of job autonomy. In other words, when we assume that the people around us represent "the" society, we rearrange the social class system to minimize the size of the strata above and below us.

The authors concluded that social-psychological processes of status placement are more powerful than the effect of actual position in the class system.

Source: Evans et al., 1992.

---

this exact study has not been replicated recently, comparable data from the early 1990s indicates no significant shift in these attitudes (Kluegel and Bobo, 1994).

Not all Americans hold these opinions. Many place norms of equality and social responsibility above the norm of economic individualism, but these are subgroups with little political power—the poor themselves, minority populations, traditional liberals—so that the dominant values are only weakly challenged (Bobo, 1991; Ritzman and Tomaskovic-Devey, 1992; Jackman, 1994).

sponses to the reality of "living poorly in America" (Beeghley, 1983). These attitudes and behaviors are not consciously transmitted from one generation to another. Most poor parents—white and minority alike—like the nonpoor, want their children to stay in school, study hard, and succeed in marriage and work. But when the children are faced with the same obstacles and limited options as were their parents, they adapt with the same set of limited responses (Harvey, 1993).

POVERTY IN AMERICA

Explaining Poverty

Although the public tends to perceive income inequality as the outcome of personal qualities, sociologists focus on *structural* variables such as items 6 through 9 in Table 9-4. This distinction has important political implications. On the one hand, conservatives claim that persistent poverty is a result of the behaviors of poor people, such as a lack of attachment to the labor force, poor work habits, family breakdown, single parenthood, and dependency on welfare (e.g., Mead, 1992).

On the other hand, liberals and most sociologists point to a lack of jobs in the inner city, the low wages of those who do find work, a shortage of marriageable men in high-poverty areas, cutbacks in assistance programs, residential segregation, and continued employment discrimination by race, sex, and ethnicity (Wilson, 1991; Thomas, 1993; Bernstein and Adler, 1994). That is, the poor are poor because they compete for a declining number of jobs in low-wage, low-security sectors of the economy (Burton, 1992). In this view, poverty is the involuntary outcome of powerlessness, as employers shift jobs from the cities to the suburbs and beyond.

Thus, the personality traits so often thought of as *causes* of poverty (lowered ambition, lack of thrift, enjoying what one can at the moment) are logical *re-*

In a successful innovative effort the city of Los Angeles has brought together public and private support to provide shelters for homeless families. A village of inexpensively constructed dome structures accommodates 24 families. How can such housing be made available on a large-scale basis to homeless people throughout the U.S.?

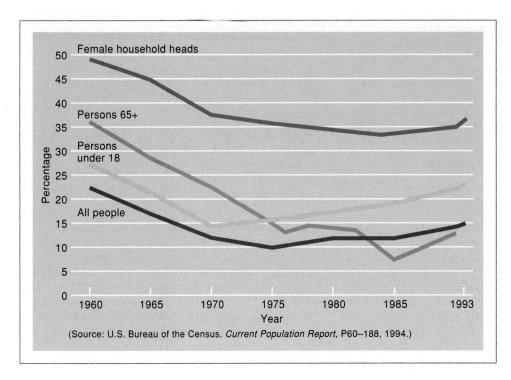

FIGURE 9-5 Poverty in the United States: 1960–1993.

(Source: U.S. Bureau of the Census. *Current Population Report*, P60–188, 1994.)

Who Are the Poor?

As seen in Figure 9-5, the composition of America's poverty population has changed over the past three decades. The "War on Poverty" of the mid-1960s dramatically reduced the overall rate, mostly through programs targeted to the elderly and other "deserving poor" (Appalachian whites and unemployed fathers). But the 1980s saw an equally dramatic rise in poverty, concentrated now among women and children in single-parent households. In early 1994, slightly over 39 million Americans, or 15 percent of the population, including 22.7 percent of the nation's children, lived in households with incomes below the official **poverty level** (U.S. Bureau of the Census, P60–188, 1994).

> The **poverty level** represents the minimum income needed to feed, house, and clothe household members.

THE POVERTY THRESHOLD.   The official poverty level is a dollar amount considered to be the minimum income needed to feed, house, and clothe household members. The formula for establishing the poverty level is based on a 1955 government survey that found that poor households spent about one-third of their income on food. The researchers determined the yearly cost of a minimally nourishing diet, multiplied by three, and came up with a number that has been adjusted annually for changes in the cost of food.

Unfortunately, for most poor people, the cost of housing has risen far faster than that for food and now absorbs over half their income (Scott and Wehler, 1992). Rather than the one-third budget share built into the poverty index, food expenses are only about 20 percent today. Thus, for most poor households, the choice is between rent and food, especially toward the end of the month.

The magic numbers for 1993, calculated with great precision, follow:

One person, under age 65	$7,518
One person, age 65+	$6,930
Two people, under age 65	$9,728
Two people, age 65+	$8,740
Three people (1 adult, 2 children)	$11,522
Four people (1 adult, 3 children)	$14,763

How well could you and two children live on $11,000 a year?

Although 75 percent of poor Americans are non-Hispanic whites, this represents under 10 percent of that population. The poverty rate for African Americans in 1993 was 33 percent, and for Hispanic Americans, 30.6 percent. And although we tend to associate poverty with the inner cities of the Northeast, the rate has always been highest in the South, for persons of any color. The poverty rate for families is 6 percent for married couple families, and 35 percent for female-headed families. The statistic that has caused most concern, however, is the proportion of children in the United States being raised in households with inadequate resources: one-fourth of all children under the age of 6, and two-thirds of those living in a single-parent household, clearly, a "generation at risk" (Carnegie Corporation, 1994).

Children now comprise 40 percent of the American poverty population, and the income gap between rich and poor children increased greatly in the 1980s (Lichter and Eggebeen, 1993).

THE WORKING POOR. Most nonelderly poor adults spend some time in the labor force each year, but very few have been able to find full-time, year-round employment. Among those with full-time jobs, at minimal wages, about 20 percent will earn less than the poverty threshold for a family of four, even before taxes are withheld. Although many of these low earners are aged 18–24 and unlikely to be supporting a family, such low wages are a strong barrier to marriage and stable family life.

It is important to note that the number of adults who remain poor despite working full-time is *twice* as high as the number of nonworking adults receiving welfare. Clearly, poverty in America is not due to lack of commitment to the labor force but to a shortage of jobs with decent wages and family-related benefits.

THE NEAR POOR. Another 10–12 million Americans live in households with incomes that are 25 percent or less above the poverty line, and as a consequence they do not qualify for "means (income) tested" programs such as Food Stamps, school lunches, and Medicaid, available only to the officially poor.

An estimated additional 15–20 million people live in a household with at least one full-time, year-round worker whose net income is under 150 percent of the poverty level, or under $22,000 a year for a family of four. These "forgotten Americans" (Schwarz and Volgy, 1992) are committed to the work ethic, often working two jobs, but never really able to scrape by, much less eat out or subscribe to cable TV. Some are entry-level employees, but, today, many are people who have lost higher-paying jobs and have had to settle for much less. In other words, one in every four Americans lives in poverty or so close to the threshold as to make little difference in their quality of life.

THE FEMINIZATION OF POVERTY. The great majority of poor people in the United States today are female: teenaged mothers, single parents and their daughters, divorced women of any age, and elderly widows (Pearce, 1985). Many of them are employed but in low-wage jobs without benefits; others are unemployed because there are few jobs where they live; and others are caring for small children at home. For white women, poverty is typically the result of divorce or desertion by a husband (Arendell, 1987). For African-American women, the problem is a shortage of men earning stable wages.

> The **feminization of poverty** refers to the fact that a majority of the adult poor are women.

The poverty gap between women and men in other industrialized nations is narrower than in the United States because of policies that encourage employment (Sweden), or support marriage (Italy), or provide gen-

Close to 40 million Americans live in poverty. The number of employed adults who remain poor is twice as great as the number of nonworking adults receiving welfare. The poverty of those who work full time is due to the lack of jobs with decent wages and family-related benefits. Seasonal workers, such as these cauliflower pickers in California, are particularly affected because they have to move from place to place to find work, the hours are long, and the work is physically strenuous.

A single mother works through some family issues with her social worker. A large proportion of the poor are women and children. Why is this so in the wealthiest nation in the world?

erous welfare benefits (Netherlands) to all needy citizens (Casper et al., 1994).

Welfare Programs

Despite growing numbers of poor and near poor, most assistance programs were reduced or eliminated in the 1980s as the economy worsened and politicians rode an anti-tax rebellion. By the mid-1990s, state and federal funding had been slashed by one-third, primarily in the four major social welfare programs affecting poor women and their children:

- *Medicaid* repays doctors and hospitals for services to the poor, but the reimbursement rate is so low that patients are often turned away by health care providers.
- *Food Stamps* are available to impoverished households and the temporarily unemployed. By 1994, a surge in applications brought the percentage of recipients up to 10.5 percent, or about 27.5 million Americans. In most states, the average monthly value of the stamps, under $150 per household per month, has not been adjusted to increases in the cost of food since the 1970s.
- *Supplemental Security Income (SSI)* provides cash assistance to the blind, disabled, and elderly whose income (even after Social Security) remains well below the poverty threshold. Monthly payments average about $420, which many states supplement with an average of $32; but by 1994, each state had either frozen or reduced even that small amount.

- *Aid to Families with Dependent Children (AFDC)* is an income support program for unemployed single parents, almost all of whom are women. Costs are shared by the federal government and the states, which set eligibility rules and benefit limits. *Average* monthly AFDC benefits thus vary greatly from one state to another: from a low of $125 per family in Mississippi to a high of $725 in Alaska, with the national average about $375 a month for a mother and two children. The actual purchasing power of the cash benefits has declined over 40 percent since 1972.

As minimal as the programs are, *over half* of all poor Americans are *not* enrolled, due to lack of efforts to inform people of their rights, as well as increasingly tight eligibility rules. For example, a recipient cannot own items worth more than $1,000 in total, excluding furniture and cooking utensils and an automobile that is valued at no more than $1,500. Therefore, only half of all poor children receive cash benefits, and less than half of eligible households receive Medicaid or Food Stamps.

WELFARE FACTS. Despite such low participation rates and the minimal benefit levels, many Americans believe that vast numbers of ineligible recipients are "ripping off" the system. The data indicate otherwise:

- Very few (less than 2 percent) of federal welfare recipients are able-bodied men, most of whom are single fathers. Two-thirds are mothers and their children (AFDC); another 26 percent are SSI beneficiaries; and the remainder are in small, special programs.

■ Only 7 percent of AFDC mothers remain in the program for 8 or more continuous years; the great majority—85 percent—receive benefits for four continuous years or less.

■ Most poor families drift in and out of poverty because of changes in health, marital status, or employment (Bane and Ellwood, 1994). Thus, over their lifetimes, one in four AFDC families will be on welfare a total of 8 years or more, but close to two-thirds will receive benefits for 5 years or less. Most likely to remain in persistent poverty are women who enter the program as unwed teenaged mothers, with low educational and work skills (Devine et al., 1992).

■ Poor women do *not* have additional children in order to increase their AFDC benefits. Exactly the opposite: Women receiving welfare are less likely to have another child than are other poor women (Rank, 1989; Congressional Budget Office, 1994). Seventy-one percent have only one or two children, and less than 10 percent have four or more. Average family size of welfare recipients has declined steadily since the early 1970s and is only slightly higher than the U.S. average today.

■ Living on welfare is not a happy-go-lucky existence. Because benefits are still below the poverty threshold, recipients must scramble to make ends meet, while also coping with poor health, violent neighborhoods, failure in intimate relationships, and children suffering from crippling diseases (Edin, 1991; Jarrett, 1994). Being poor is very hard work.

■ Although a tempting target for budget-cutters, AFDC is *not* a major expense item: under 2 percent of the 1994 federal budget and under 5 percent of state budgets.

■ In comparison with other industrial societies, the United States spends proportionately *less* on social welfare programs. All but a few modern societies provide family allowances, extended disability and unemployment payments, and old-age pensions as a right of citizenship, unrelated to work history or current assets. As a consequence, even though poverty rates in these countries are comparable to ours, the transfer payments allow most families to enjoy an adequate income and sense of financial security (Casey, 1991).

In the United States, people remain poor because the transfer payments are so minimal and reach so few. We do not have a policy for reducing poverty but only for minimizing some of the worst effects of being without money for food and housing, and only for some. But the politics of poverty—the strong public temper against welfare—has moved the nation from a "war on poverty" in the 1960s to a "war against the poor" in the 1990s. Many states have recently passed laws that limit benefits to one or two years, reduce payments to unwed mothers, and deny assistance to immigrants or mothers whose children skipped school (DeParle, 1994).

SOCIAL POLICY

How Fair Is *Workfare*?

Given the American belief in the redeeming virtue of work, it is not surprising that the most popular new idea for reducing both the cost and extent of welfare is to put able-bodied recipients to work. Those in favor of **workfare** programs cite the following potential benefits: (1) breaking the cycle of "welfare dependency" by providing job training for single parents; (2) restoring a sense of self-worth through gainful employment; and (3) lowering welfare costs as people move into the work force and as those who refuse to participate are dropped from the welfare rolls.

The arguments against the concept follow: (1) It subverts the intent of the original 1935 legislation, which was to give poor women some of the privileges enjoyed by the nonpoor—the right to privacy and to choose whether or not to stay home with their children. (2) Unless well-designed and well-financed, the programs come close to being the kind of "forced labor" Americans would heartily condemn in a Communist country. (3) Money savings will be minimal because the women who succeed in the programs would probably have been able to escape poverty anyway, leaving the mentally and physically disabled and mothers of preschool children still needing support. (4) Countries with the *most generous* welfare benefits have the highest rates of people who eventually escape poverty (Duncan, 1994).

> **Workfare** programs are designed to prepare welfare recipients for permanent positions in the labor force.

Practical problems are involved in implementing an effective workfare program. First, it will be more expensive than welfare initially, requiring extensive educational and social work resources, plus child care and other family support services. Second, clients must be trained for jobs that will lift them over the poverty line, but few such jobs are currently available to poor people. A woman with two children working full-time year-round in a nursing home would earn slightly more than a woman on welfare, but she would end up with much less because of having to pay for child care, health insurance, and transportation. In other words, a woman entering a workfare program today will probably lose out both financially and emotionally, having experienced another failure in her life (Cloward and Piven, 1993).

The evidence from several evaluation studies published in the early 1990s presents a mixed picture:

Some programs in some states have shown limited success, but the overall impact has been minimal (Hagan and Lurie, 1992; Friedlander and Burtless, 1995). In general, the programs that work best are those that depend on positive incentives such as allowing participants to retain most of their welfare grants while working. Conversely, programs with the lowest success rate are those with a strong punishment component such as reducing welfare grants for an additional child or if a child fails to attend school (Sack, 1992). The punishment-oriented policies simply push recipients into illegal activities to make up for lost revenue, as well as adding to the number of homeless families.

Nonetheless, the "Contract with America" endorsed by victorious Republican party candidates in national and state elections in 1994 embraced the punishment-oriented philosophy on the grounds that, if receiving welfare were made more difficult, single poor women would enter the labor force and stop having additional children. Among the various proposals in the "Contract" are the following: (1) an absolute two-year limit on receiving benefits, with no further assistance in training, schooling, or income supports, regardless of the state of the local job market; (2) immediate loss of all benefits to any mothers for whom the paternity of her children cannot be established; and (3) encouraging states to use the funds thus saved to build and operate group homes for children whose mothers can no longer provide economic support. At the same time, the new majorities in Congress and many state legislatures oppose any effort to raise the minimum wage to a level that might make single-parent families self-sustaining.

In fact, a majority of welfare mothers do find some kind of employment, typically part-time or "off the books," and most prefer to remain in the labor force, but their wages cannot compensate for loss of AFDC or Medicaid (K. Harris, 1993; Spalter-Roth and Hartmann, 1994). The problem is not commitment to work but a lack of steady, well-paying jobs in the private sector near where they live.

Additional problems include the tendency for welfare officials to treat clients in a demeaning fashion, emphasizing their shortcomings and blaming them for their continued failures, which only undermines whatever self-confidence the clients have managed to salvage (G. Miller, 1991). A well-planned and well-staffed educational and job training and placement program, plus tracking and follow-up, is actually more expensive than maintaining single families on welfare. Restructuring this system and providing pathways out of poverty remain crucial and unrealized goals that you will have to deal with in the immediate future. What type of program would you design, and how would you gain public support for it?

HOW THE OTHER ONE-TENTH OF ONE PERCENT LIVE

At the other end of the stratification system are the slightly more than 1 million Americans whose *net assets* are valued at $1 million or more. All but a very few are white men or their widows, and most are in their early 60s. Their way of life is a source of endless fascination to the tens of millions who buy books by Donald Trump and watch television programs devoted to displays of conspicuous consumption.

Although a few sports and entertainment figures are millionaires at least for a few years, most people with *new* wealth (the "nouveau riche") fit the classic mold of the American Dream, having accumulated their wealth through hard work and risk-taking in business. *Old* wealth, in contrast, is inherited. The great founding fortunes of this country have been preserved across generations through asset management, careful investment, and favorable inheritance laws. The intergenerational transmission of wealth allows inheritors to maintain the family's economic status across time (Maurer and Ratcliff, 1989; Rosenfeld, 1992).

The secret marriage of Lisa Marie Presley and Michael Jackson was covered extensively by tabloid and non-tabloid magazines and television shows. Why are we so fascinated with the life-styles of the rich and famous?

In general, millionaires enjoy a luxurious life-style, but it is typically the newly wealthy who engage in the public displays shown in tabloids; old wealth tends to be less obvious or visible. Then, too, a million dollars does not go very far these days, because the cost of living on a grand scale has risen at a rate twice that for ordinary consumers. But the very wealthy are protected from extreme hardship by the tax system, especially by the changes made in the 1980s. Yet such advantages have not made high-income earners any more willing to pay taxes than in the past. For example, a sample audit of tax returns of millionaires working in New York State but claiming to live elsewhere found that every claim was false (Gutis, 1989). And the Internal Revenue Service regularly finds large numbers of wealthy citizens paying taxes at much lower rates than an average income earner (Bartlett and Steele, 1994).)

Wealth and Class

Although wealth can buy you such luxuries as a Rolex wristwatch for $130,000, it is not an automatic entry card into the upper class. The American upper class is a very exclusive group, consisting of about 60,000 families and individuals, based primarily on "blood" (family background) rather than money (Baltzell, 1964; Ostrander, 1984). Until quite recently,

our uppermost stratum was composed almost exclusively of white Anglo-Saxon Protestant families whose roots in America go back to the 1700s. The upper class is still all white, but a few highly successful people from other religious and class origins have managed to win acceptance (e.g., the late Jacqueline Kennedy Onassis, Lee Iacocca, and Henry Kissinger).

The upper class maintains its continuity over time through intermarriage and the socialization of its children in private schools (Chapter 15). From infancy to old age, private clubs, schools, and other activities isolate and insulate members of the upper class and provide them with a distinct set of values and behaviors that set them apart and account for their high level of solidarity (Domhoff, 1983).

Despite the glaring differences between the lifestyles of this fraction of 1 percent of the population, on the one hand, and the conditions of poverty or near-poverty that affect 20 percent of Americans, on the other, few people express a sense of outrage or even unfairness. Public opinion data find that a majority of Americans feel that the wealthy are entitled to their success if they played according to the rules. Most also believe that with more hard work and a bit of luck, they or their children can join the ranks of the rich, if not the upper class itself (Kluegel and Smith, 1986).

But just what are their chances for upward movement in the American stratification system?

RESEARCH IN ACTION

Welfare for the Wealthy

Among the antipoverty programs suffering the largest cuts in the 1980s were those that offered housing assistance—rent subsidies, low-cost loans, or direct housing. In 1994, fewer than 20 percent of low-income Americans were enrolled in any of these programs, but 100 percent of the wealthy benefit from a variety of federal housing policies (Dreier and Atlas, 1992).

The big gainers from government housing programs in the 1980s were (1) high officials of the Department of Housing and Urban Development (HUD), many of whom successfully engaged in illegal activities for personal gain, (2) banks that made risky HUD-guaranteed loans to builders whose losses must be covered by all taxpayers; (3) homeowners in general and the wealthy in particular.

Homeowners can deduct property taxes and mortgage interest payments from their taxable income. This amounts to a massive subsidy—over $60 billion in 1994, or four times the federal budget for AFDC that year.

But there are more welfare programs for the rich:

- Corporations and executives enjoy a $5 billion-a-year Food Stamp program in the form of tax deductions for business-related meals and entertainment.
- Farm-aid programs originally designed to maintain family farms now distribute over $10 billion annually to very wealthy landowners and corporations.
- Medicaid for the rich consists of $47 billion of tax-exempt health insurance plans that typically cover management but not all other employees.

The wealthy are also the primary beneficiaries of their own charitable giving. More than two-thirds of their tax-deductible gifts are directed to institutions that serve their interests almost exclusively: private schools and elite universities, museums, ballet companies, symphony orchestras, private hospitals, and conservative think tanks. Very little is given to nonprofit agencies that serve the less affluent (Odendahl, 1990; Goodgame, 1993).

Even the national debt works to the advantage of the affluent. The deficit is financed by treasury bonds purchased by the wealthy, with the interest paid out of general taxes.

SOCIAL MOBILITY

The term **social mobility** refers to the movement of individuals and groups within a stratification system. The distinction between a caste and class system is the degree to which status lines can be crossed.

Caste and Class

In a **caste system,** one's place in the stratification hierarchy is determined at birth. This ascribed status affects the kind of education received, the occupations that one can enter, and whom one may marry. In this way, the hierarchy is preserved over time, with a few exceptions for unusually talented or lucky individuals. Although caste systems are associated with preindustrial societies, caste remains an important feature of modern India and, until just a few years ago, the Union of South Africa. In South Africa, the system of rigid segregation between whites and people of color, called **apartheid,** ensured white control over the best land, the government, and the economy.

Similar laws existed in many American states right up to the 1960s, forbidding cross-race marriage, segregating school-children, denying voting rights, and failing to provide public services to nonwhite neighborhoods. Our society still has elements of a caste system at the very top and very bottom, and apartheid-like patterns continue to characterize many occupations, housing markets, and school systems in which few, if any, Hispanic Americans or African Americans are welcome. Thus, elements of both a closed and open class system can exist within the same society.

Open class systems, based largely on achieved statuses, permit individuals and groups to cross class boundaries. *Upward mobility* refers to improvement in social status; *downward mobility* to a loss of rank; and *horizontal mobility* to the slight gains or losses that accompany job changes or geographic mobility. When the comparison is between parents' social rank and that of their adult children, we speak of **inter-**

Social mobility is the movement of persons and groups within the stratification system.

Caste systems are based on ascription, with minimal movement across stratum boundaries.

Apartheid refers specifically to the South African policy of segregation and political and economic discrimination against people of color within that country.

Open class systems allow individuals and groups to cross class boundaries.

Intergenerational mobility involves status change between parents and their children.

Intragenerational, or **career, mobility** refers to status changes over an individual's lifetime

In a caste system, one's place is determined at birth. Although the caste system no longer exists legally in India, this woman is still considered an untouchable and is allowed to do only the lowliest work, such as sweeping the streets.

generational (*inter* means "between") **mobility.** Change in social status over the course of an individual's lifetime is **intragenerational** (*intra* means "within") or **career mobility.** The American Dream is based on a belief in both forms of upward mobility through hard work and clean living.

SOCIAL MOBILITY IN THE UNITED STATES

There is some truth to the dream of continued upward mobility, but it is not a uniquely American reality. All industrial societies with a democratic political system, low birthrates, and an ideology of equal opportunity experienced similar patterns of upward mobility between 1945 and 1965 (Lenski, 1966; Erikson and Goldthorpe, 1992). During this period, in all modern Western societies, there was a massive shift of jobs from manual to nonmanual—a shift that by definition creates upward mobility because white-collar employment is considered of higher prestige than blue-collar manual labor. Most of this movement was intergenerational, with sons' exceeding their fathers' status, rather than being accomplished within the sons' work lives. We speak of fathers and sons because mobility data were typically gathered only for men. Mobility for women was assumed to be a function of marriage and

PATRICIA HILL COLLINS

Silenced Voices, Invisible Lives

Patricia Hill Collins is associate professor of African-American studies and sociology at the University of Cincinnati. She is the author of Black Feminist Thought: Knowledge, Consciousness, and the Politics of Empowerment *(Routledge, Chapman, & Hall, 1990) and winner of the American Sociological Association (ASA) 1993 Jessie Bernard Award. She is a newly elected Councilmember of the ASA.*

While I was growing up, my working-class parents stressed the importance of education. I listened, got good grades, followed the rules, and did well. But my success came at a price. My public school education stressed conformity to a set of values that I found troublesome. I kept silent on the rare occasions when the classroom discussions turned to race and excelled in mathematics by minimizing the fact that I was a girl. By speaking so-called proper English to my teachers and assuming other trappings of middle-class culture, I succeeded. Over the years, the little silences added up. The "me" in me was virtually educated out of existence.

My education was problematic because it told me that my experiences as a working-class African-American girl were unimportant. I knew that to be successful I had to master the distortions of the established curriculum. But to ensure my own intellectual and emotional survival, I had to learn never to accept those distortions or to trust any so-called truths that rendered any group inferior or invisible.

As an undergraduate, I was fortunate enough to major in sociology and to discover C. Wright Mills's description of the sociological imagination. To Mills, sociology enables us to grasp history and biography and the relations between the two within society. Up to that time, my entire education had been designed to teach me that talking from my own experiences made me less rational and "educated," but sociology encouraged me to see my own experiences as part of a much larger story.

Here was a way that I could begin to reconcile my two "educations"—my formal studies, which silenced me and rendered me invisible, and the critical posture that grew from that treatment. As I learned to trust my own inner voice, I became increasingly able to use the skills gained from my formal studies to articulate my own criticisms.

I came to see that what I had defined as an individual issue affecting only me was instead a collective struggle influencing African-American women as a group. Moreover, African-American women were not the only group that had been silenced and rendered virtually invisible. In America, the "white, thin, male, young, heterosexual, Christian, and financially secure" individual is defined as possessing the normal and universal experience. But, far from being the majority, those fitting the profile of the mythical norm are remarkably few.

For the past few years, I have actively challenged this mythical norm by researching the experiences and ideas of African-American women. My book on black feminist thought revived the rich wisdom of African-American women's communities and ended their invisibility in academic scholarship.

My own experience led me to seek ideas in places that had previously been neglected. For example, I realized that many African-American women who had been denied access to literacy had turned to music as a forum for their ideas. The great black women blues singers, such as Ma Rainey, Bessie Smith, Billie Holiday, and Nina Simone, all spoke to the larger community of African-American women. By examining black women's music, literature, poetry, speeches, and everyday conversations with new angles of vision, I found that they have produced a rich intellectual tradition infused with a critical posture toward race, class, and gender inequality.

My work shows that black women's ideas and experiences produce new definitions of work, family, community, power, and oppression that affect a range of silenced groups.

Transforming the curriculum to reflect diversities of race, class, gender, sexual orientation, age, and ethnicity is not only necessary today but desirable. Knowledge that embraces only the mythical norm is harmful to both the privileged and the silenced. Thus, I see my work as one small part of de-centering knowledge based on a mythical norm. I hope that other silenced and invisible groups will now be seen and heard and, in the process, transform knowledge and our society.

could be measured simply by comparing the social status of a woman's father with that of her husband. Only recently has women's mobility been studied as a complex process in its own right.

Although there are variations depending on the unique history of each modern industrial society, the striking similarity in mobility patterns supports the sociological assumption that the *structure of the economy* is the prime determinant of mobility rates (Ischida et al., 1991; DiPrete, 1993). In other words, most occupational mobility can be explained in terms of societal-level variables rather than by differences among individuals.

Structural Mobility

The term **structural,** or **demand, mobility** refers to the societal-level variables that affect mobility rates. Two factors are of prime importance: (1) the number of jobs in different occupations that are open at any particular historical moment and (2) the number and types of people prepared to fill those jobs. The distribution of jobs depends on economic system changes, such as the sharp reduction in the need for farm labor since 1900 or the growth of manufacturing through 1960 and the current increase in low-level service jobs. The number of competitors for these jobs depends on variations in birthrates and in education/skills training.

As shown in Figure 9-6, for example, the proportion of American workers in different occupational strata has changed dramatically over the century. Farm employment dropped from 37 percent of the labor force in 1900 to 3 percent today, while professional/managerial employment doubled, and other white-collar positions quadrupled. These shifts are typical of modern societies: from farm to factory to office. Such structural changes mean that most occupational mobility is forced by circumstances with local job markets linked to the forming or folding of particular firms (Haveman and Cohen, 1994).

Occupational shifts were not the only structural factor accounting for the spurt in upward mobility between 1945 and 1965. Equally important were the extremely low birthrates, especially for middle-class couples, during the Great Depression of the 1930s and World War II in the early 1940s. This meant that the pool of job applicants was relatively small at the very time when white-collar employment was ex-

> **Structural,** or **demand, mobility** refers to societal-level factors affecting mobility rates.

FIGURE 9-6 Changing structure of occupations, United States, 1990–1992 (in percents).

Sources: U.S. Bureau of the Census, *Historical Statistics of the United States*, Vol. 1, 1975, p. 139; Bureau of Labor Statistics, *Employment and Earnings*, January 1993.

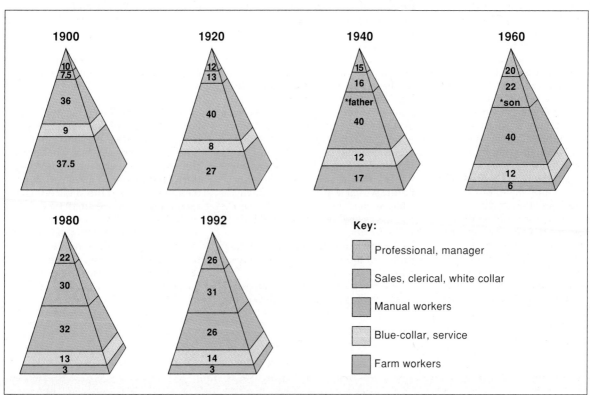

panding in the 1950s. Managerial jobs were opening up at a faster rate than children of the middle class could fill them, creating a job vacuum into which young people from the working class could move.

In addition, if they were veterans of World War II, men (and a few women) from working-class backgrounds could take advantage of a program that provided a full college education financed by a grateful nation. This was an option open primarily to whites, as few African-American veterans could afford to remain out of the labor force for an additional four years. Thus, a combination of a free college education, a shortage of middle-class youth, and the expansion of white-collar occupations accounted for the upward mobility surge of the 1950s.

Absolute and Relative Mobility

As they surpassed their fathers in education, occupational prestige, and income, sons enjoyed *absolute social mobility*. But because the entire occupational structure was upgraded, the son's position relative to other workers might not be so different from that of the father. If, for example, the father had been a skilled carpenter (high-level manual) and the son is an insurance underwriter (white collar), the son occupies a higher occupational status than the father. Yet if many others in the son's generation also moved into white-collar jobs, the location of father and son compared to all workers has not greatly changed, as shown by the asterisks in Figure 9-6.

What, then, are the mobility prospects for young people today? Looking at the structure of occupations and the number of people born in the two decades before 1970, upward mobility rates are expected to be lower than in the past (Krymkowski and Krauze, 1992). This is so because job growth at the top of the occupational hierarchy is limited, with most expansion today occurring at the lower end of the white collar stratum, in service-related employment (Chapter 13). In addition, today's college students follow two decades of baby boomers who will clog avenues of job advancement for many years to come. The best bet for college students is to stay in school as long as possible; the more one knows, the fewer competitors one will have and the better able one is to adapt and take advantage of new opportunities.

STATUS ATTAINMENT

The assumption of continual upward mobility obscures the high level of **class immobility,** the general tendency for class status to be reproduced from one generation to another (Corcoran, 1992; Western, 1994). Most mobility—between generations or within a person's lifetime—is a matter of small steps rather than dramatic changes. Success in the United States, as in other industrial societies, remains profoundly influenced by the ascribed status of one's family at birth. Although the effect of family background can be modified by a person's educational achievements, the length and quality of schooling often depend on

> **Class immobility** occurs when class status is reproduced from one generation to another.

SOCIOLOGY IN EVERYDAY LIFE

Falling From Grace: Downward Mobility

If success in life is a sign of God's grace, then downward mobility represents a "fall from grace." Because of our fascination with upward mobility, downward movement has been a neglected topic in sociology. Yet over their lifetime, close to one-third of Americans will experience status loss.

Among examples of downward mobility studied by Katherine S. Newman (1993), three involved intragenerational loss of middle-class security: (1) high-level executives who were laid off and unable to find comparable employment; (2) members of the air traffic controllers union (PATCO) who were fired as a group by President Reagan in 1981; and (3) divorced wives of middle-class men. How did members of these three groups deal with the self-perception of personal failure and the public image of being morally flawed?

The former executives had the most difficult time reconciling what had happened to them with their deep belief in individual responsibility; they blamed themselves and suffered from low self-esteem. The PATCO members maintained a high level of group solidarity and morale, blaming their fate on Reagan's betrayal of workers' rights. The divorced women had a double burden: adapting to downward mobility for themselves and their children while also dealing with the stigma of failure in marriage.

Newman's fourth case consisted of blue-collar workers who lost their jobs because of a plant closing in a city with few other opportunities for skilled labor. The workers avoided self-blame by directing their anger toward the company, but nonetheless suffered a loss in self-esteem when they had to take lower-paying jobs in less prestigious occupations.

Similar findings are reported from a study of displaced steel workers by Allison Zippay (1991). Hardworking believers in the American Dream, their hopes of attaining some of the symbols of middle-class status (home ownership, college education for their children) were dashed by the economic recession and loss of real income in the 1980s.

family resources (Chapter 15). Even in Japan, thought to be relatively open to the influence of education on mobility chances, the pattern is similar to that of other industrial societies—strongly influenced by family background with a limited education effect (Ishida, 1993).

In the United States, it also helps to be white, male, and an only or first-born child and to be raised in a home that emphasizes **deferred gratification** (putting off immediate pleasure in order to achieve a distant goal) and high achievement expectations (Kerckhoff, 1989). In Chapter 5, we described how the parent's occupation was reflected in childrearing techniques that encouraged or inhibited intellectual flexibility in their offspring. Upward mobility is also associated with coming from a small family, having relatively older parents, and spending one's childhood in a two-parent family (Amato and Keith, 1991; Biblarz and Raftery, 1993). In dual-earner families, the mother's labor force participation has a strong effect on her children's schooling, a distinct advantage that may widen the gap between poor and nonpoor youth in the future (Kalmijn, 1994a).

> **Deferred gratification** is the postponing of current pleasure to achieve future goals.

The strength of class boundaries is a variable, stronger in some societies than in others, even among industrial societies. In addition, some dimensions of class are easier to cross than others—for example, friendships and marriages between adjacent strata. In general, property ownership remains a powerful determinant of mobility chances (Western and Wright, 1994).

The Basic Model of Status Attainment

The dominant model of status attainment is shown in Figure 9-7. Family SES at birth is represented by father's occupation, which influences both the length

and quality of the son's education, as well as assistance in finding a job for the son (Marsden and Hurlbert, 1988; Wegener, 1991). Once launched, the son's education and his ability to handle the first job determine his later occupational status.

Although family background is the single most powerful predictor of social mobility, it is not all-determining. Men from similar backgrounds, even the same family, can vary widely in eventual class status. There is always an element of luck that cannot be measured—pure chance, being in the right place at the right time, getting a tip from a friend, following a hunch.

The process of status attainment for women today is not as well understood as that for men. As increasing numbers of women establish an identity separate from that of their father or husband, and carve out their own educational and occupational careers, new mobility models may be required. In addition, future mobility studies will have to take into account the extent to which a wife's income maintains or raises the family SES and makes a college education possible for her children. Chapter 10 examines stratification as a deeply gendered process, both in the very meaning of power and prestige and in the ways that women and men are assigned class positions (Andes, 1992; England, 1992a), while Chapter 11 traces the effects of race and ethnicity on mobility opportunities.

Criticism of the Status Attainment Model

The belief that underlies the basic American model is one of optimistic faith in a meritocratic process based on equality of educational opportunity (Knottnerus, 1987). Yet working class youth continue to be channeled into jobs with limited chances for advancement, and their distribution in the stratification system has not greatly changed in three decades. Location in the

FIGURE 9-7 The status attainment model.

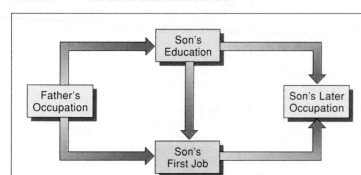

labor force is far more important than motivation or attitudes in explaining mobility patterns (Dewart, 1991). Indeed, U.S. Department of Labor data indicate that a combination of low-paying jobs and lack of educational credentials have produced a growing underclass of white and minority youth and women workers in general (Manegold, 1994).

Inequality is structured when the wealthy transmit assets and advantages to their offspring, regardless of talent—an aspect of stratification referred to by Robert K. Merton (1973) as the "Matthew effect" from the New Testament: "For unto everyone that hath shall be given . . . in abundance, but from him who hath not shall be taken away even that which he hath."

Nonetheless, the American Dream of individual achievement remains a powerful vision. Young people from all social classes have high expectations of personal success. Yet at some point, reality must intrude; not everyone rises to the top. How do people deal with the gap between their early high hopes and their actual achievements? Typically, by reducing aspirations and expectations to bring them into balance with reality (Chinoy, 1955; Jacobs et al., 1991). Surrendering the dream is difficult but very common among working class men and women from every racial/ethnic group.

Thus do race, sex, and social class at birth affect mobility opportunities and outcomes. If the system is not altogether open and fair, however, neither can personal characteristics be totally overlooked in the process.

SOCIAL STATUS IN EVERYDAY LIFE

From the interpretive perspective, at the level of face-to-face interaction, social status is an aspect of identity that affects how people relate to one another. In Chapter 5 we spoke of Goffman's concept of *impression management,* the ways in which we manipulate the image we present to others. The goal is to protect the "self" while trying to assume control of the interaction. Because people behave very differently to those perceived as social superiors, or equals, or inferiors, it is important to be able to locate one's role partners in the prestige hierarchy (Berger et al., 1992).

Status Symbols

We are all rather skilled at picking up status cues—speech patterns, dress, hair styles, and the like. In one recent study, subjects identified higher- and lower-status brides in wedding pictures primarily on the basis of their education and physical beauty, but even when facial features were blanked out, hair and hat styles served as effective status cues (Mazur, 1993). This kind of information tells us how to deal with the other person. Think, for example, of how you decide whom to call "sir" or "hey, you." Status considerations influence who speaks first or who ends the conversation, who can impinge on another person's private space, and countless other details of daily encounters.

Status symbols are outward signs of social rank by which people manage the impression they give to others. A sure way to impress others is through displays of conspicuous consumption. What status symbols are being displayed here?

The Waiting Game As A Power Ploy

A friend of ours who is the personal secretary of a high-level corporate executive has a whole repertory of tricks for ensuring that the person her boss is calling is on the line *before* her boss picks up the phone. The other secretary is trying to do the same thing, and the result is an often hilarious, but deadly serious, game of one-upmanship. Why? Because the last one on the line has done the least waiting, and in a society where time is money, time is also a status symbol. Keeping others waiting is a sign of power as well as prestige.

The waiting game is played in almost every social setting. For example, who in your family waits longest for the bathroom or to eat? Do faculty members wait in the same lines as students? Are there ever checkout lines in fashionable shops or only at stores such as K-mart? Who goes to the head of a line? And who *never* waits? The answers to these questions should provide a rough outline of the stratification system of the family, the college, the workplace, and society as a whole (Levine, 1987).

Status symbols are the outward signs of social rank. "Keeping up with the Jones's" describes people who try to equal the status displays of neighbors. Appearing to have less brings instant loss of social standing, just as appearing to have more than your neighbors confers esteem. Displays of conspicuous consumption are the ultimate in impression management in the United States. The advertising industry is devoted to stimulating ever-higher levels of consumption, signifying success and earning the esteem of others. In France, in contrast, "cultural resources such as elegant taste and a knowledge of the arts and literature are generally accepted symbols of high status" (Lamont, 1992).

> **Status symbols** are outward signs of social rank.
>
> **Status consistency** occurs when a person occupies a similar position across different hierarchies.
>
> **Status inconsistency** refers to occupying different positions in different hierarchies.

Consumption patterns are often used to identify social class placement. How would the consumption patterns of working-class families differ from those of the middle class, even assuming similar levels of income? What would you select, today, as the clearest symbols of social status?

Status Consistency and Inconsistency

As individuals send and receive status information, they adjust their responses. This is a relatively easy task when role partners present clear and unambiguous cues. In modern society, however, people occupy a variety of social statuses.

The term **status consistency** refers to occupying similar positions in different hierarchies: the ascribed hierarchies of sex, race, age, ethnic background, and social class at birth, as well as the achieved hierarchies of education, occupation, and income.

A white male executive is status consistent, ranking high across ascribed and achieved categories. Similarly, a dark Latino cleaning women has a consistent position at the lower levels of these hierarchies. Indeed, the status consistency at both the top and bottom of the stratification constitutes a caste system.

The high degree of social mobility in modern societies, especially at the middle levels, creates the possibility of **status inconsistency**—of occupying positions at differing levels across status hierarchies. For example, a minority athlete or entertainer may have great wealth and esteem but little social power.

Status inconsistency affects interpersonal encounters. The female doctor or African-American lawyer present inconsistent cues: low ascribed and high achieved statuses. Some role partners will resolve the ambiguity by assuming that the woman or person of color is less qualified, thus creating consistency in their own mind. For the status-inconsistent person, the problem is being accepted at one's higher status (lawyer, doctor) while others respond to the lower status characteristics (female, nonwhite).

At the other extreme of status inconsistency are people with high-ascribed and low-achieved traits such as a white, European-American man who is a high school dropout and works at the local gas station. Believing that their ascribed characteristics entitle them to more than they have achieved, such men are likely to resent the achievements of people they perceive as their inferiors—women, blacks, Jews, Catholics, immigrants, and homosexuals (Roebuck and Hickson, 1982). It is precisely among men of this type that organizations such as the Ku Klux Klan or American Nazi Party (ANP), with their emphasis on the superiority of maleness and racial purity, find most of their recruits. This is a purely *structural* explanation of recruitment to the Klan or ANP; it is not prejudice that fuels resentment but social locations that feed attitudes (See Chapter 23).

SUMMARY

1. Valued social resources—power, prestige, and property—are unequally divided among people and groups in all but the most simple societies.

2. From a functional perspective, stratification is an inevitable and necessary outcome of individual differences. In this view, stratification processes develop a hierarchy of talent, the rule of the most worthy and deserving.

3. From the conflict perspective, inequality is socially structured and transmitted from one generation to another. Stratification hierarchies result from struggles over scarce rewards, with those in power setting the rules of competition.

4. Weber's distinction among class, status groups, and parties is used to frame our discussion of power, prestige, and property as distinct, though interrelated, dimensions of stratification. Power can be exercised legitimately (authority) or through interpersonal influence. Prestige refers to respect received from others, typically on the basis of occupation. Property is measured by wealth and income.

5. Socioeconomic status (SES), based on a combination of occupation, income, and education, is used by social scientists to place people and groups within a hierarchy of social classes. Other sociologists prefer to use variables that measure the social relations of production—control over one's work and that of others.

6. Contrary to the myth of "classlessness," researchers have found that most Americans are aware of class distinctions, hold strong beliefs about their place in the stratification system, and associate with others of equal rank.

7. However, when it comes to class consciousness, which occurs when awareness becomes central to a person's self-definition and when members of a class act together politically, the only strata to have succeeded in advancing their class-based interests are the upper classes.

8. Social inequality is not a threat to social order unless it is also perceived as unfair. In our society, there are strong ideological and institutional supports for inequality and, hence, little pressure for change.

9. Poverty remains a major social problem, primarily affecting women, children, and members of racial and ethnic minority groups.

10. Social scientists locate the sources of poverty in structural rather than personality factors, interpreting the latter as responses to, rather than causes of, poverty.

11. Although the numbers of poor Americans increased steadily, most federal assistance programs were reduced or eliminated in the 1980s.

12. To reduce the cost of welfare, workfare programs, which require welfare recipients to seek employment, have been introduced in many states.

13. Despite the long-term negative effects of poverty on people and the society as a whole, there is little public pressure for redistribution of resources.

14. The wealthy enjoy an affluent life-style that combines conspicuous consumption with institutional arrangements that preserve their status.

15. In contrast to caste societies, most modern industrial societies are characterized by relatively high levels of upward mobility both between generations and within a person's own work life. Most of this mobility can be accounted for by changes in the occupational structure and fluctuations in birthrates.

16. Although absolute social mobility has occurred in the United States, the relative position of people and groups in the SES hierarchy is unchanged. Current college students face relatively limited prospects for upward mobility.

17. Studies of status attainment—the paths that lead from social placement at birth to adult occupational level—focus on individual-level variables, with family background and education the primary determinants of one's social status.

18. But there are also powerful structural barriers to mobility, such as hiring practices and differential wage scales between and within job categories.

19. Social rank influences everyday interaction. From a symbolic interaction perspective, status symbols are essential to impression management and serve to guide behavior.

20. In modern societies, people are likely to display status inconsistencies that create problems in self-presentation and social interaction.

SUGGESTED READINGS

Baltzell, E. Digby. *The Protestant Establishment Revisited.* Edited by Howard G. Schneiderman. New Brunswick, NJ: Transaction, 1991. Another look at the provocative thesis proposed by Baltzell in his 1964 classic, *The*

Protestant Establishment, namely, that the American upper class provides a pool of dedicated political leaders who function to protect the society from mindless bureaucrats and greedy rabble-rousers.

Bian, Yanjie. *Work and Inequality in Urban China.* Albany, NY: State University of New York Press, 1994. The author shows how membership in work organizations has produced a system of stratification based on wages and access to consumer goods, thus creating a powerful hierarchy of inequality within a socialist society.

Devine, Joel A., and James D. Wright. *The Greatest of Evils: Urban Poverty and the American Underclass.* New York: Aldine de Gruyter, 1993. In this incisive book, Devine and Wright argue convincingly that the social and economic costs of poverty-related problems exceed what it will cost to find remedies that address its underlying causes.

Goldsmith, William W., and Edward J. Blakely. *Separate Societies: Poverty and Inequality in U.S. Cities.* Philadelphia: Temple University Press, 1992. An innovative look at the global economy and urban poverty. The authors examine how industrial change has locked the poor in place.

Hacker, Andrew. *Two Nations: Black and White, Separate, Hostile, Unequal.* New York: Charles Scribner's Sons, 1992. An insightful look at the persistence of inequality and racial tensions in a country that is supposed to be dedicated to freedom and equality for all.

Jencks, Christopher. *Rethinking Social Policy: Race, Poverty, and the Underclass.* Cambridge, MA: Harvard University Press, 1992. The author critically reviews contemporary social science and social policy controversies surrounding affirmative action, the War on Poverty, crime, the urban underclass, and welfare reform.

Jones, Jacqueline. *The Dispossessed: America's Underclasses from the Civil War to the Present.* New York: Basic Books, 1992. Jones asserts that underclass or "stranded" communities have a long history in America and come in all colors and time periods, thus transcending race, culture, and region.

Lamont, Michele. *Money, Morals, and Manners: The Culture of the French and the American Upper-Middle Class.* Chicago: University of Chicago Press, 1993. A revealing portrait of the upper-middle-class managers, professionals, entrepreneurs, and experts at the center of power in France and the United States.

McNall, Scott G., Rhonda F. Levine, and Rick Fantasia, eds. *Bringing Class Back in: Contemporary and Historical Perspectives.* Boulder, CO: Westview Press, 1991. A collection of articles discussing Marxism and its place in the analysis of inequality.

Mandle, Jay R. *Not Slave, Not Free: The African American Economic Experience since the Civil War.* Durham, NC: Duke University Press, 1992. A good basic text that presents the argument that current racial differences in poverty rates are closely linked to the historic economic roles of African Americans.

Marmor, Theodore R., Jerry L. Marshaw, and Philip L. Harvey. *America's Misunderstood Welfare State: Persistent Myths, Enduring Realities.* New York: Basic Books, 1990. The authors clarify facts and misperceptions of the origins and workings of American welfare policies.

Massey, Douglas S., and Nancy A. Denton. *American Apartheid: Segregation and the Making of the Underclass.* Cambridge: Harvard University Press, 1993. Essential reading for anyone interested in the causes, and possible solutions, of urban poverty. Redirects our attention to racial segregation as part of the debate on the causes and consequences of urban poverty.

Perrson, Inga, ed. *Generating Equality in the Welfare State: The Swedish Experience.* Oslo: Norwegian University Press, 1990. Focusing on the period from 1960 to the late 1980s, ten economists and three sociologists discuss distribution and redistribution in the Swedish welfare state. A rich source of data on policy initiatives, documenting both successes and failures of the Swedish model.

Phillips, Kevin. *Boiling Point: Republicans, Democrats, and the Decline of Middle-Class Prosperity.* New York: Random House, 1993. An exploration of the phenomenon of middle-class decline from a wide perspective, including Victorian Britain, the seventeenth-century Netherlands, the Spain of Philip II, as well as different decades in American history.

Sennett, Richard, and Jonathan Cobb. *The Hidden Injuries of Class.* New York: Random House (Vintage Books), 1973. A sensitive discussion of the subjective experience of social class of working-class Americans.

10
Gendered Inequality

100,000,000 of the World's Women Are Missing!

Population experts, applying standard formulas for sex ratios at birth and across the life course, have discovered that there are at least 100 million fewer females than there would be if boys and girls received similar nutrition and health care (Sen, 1990; United Nations, 1993).

The People's Republic of China and India account for almost two-thirds of the missing children and adults. These are both societies with a long tradition of valuing males more highly than females; the birth of a son is greeted with great joy; that of a daughter with sadness. But it has always been thus, so what can account for the sudden recent shortage of females? Quite simply, the ultrasound scanner, which can identify the sex of a fetus.

In China, the government's effort to control population growth has emphasized the ideal of one child per couple (see Chapter 20). Because the family's preferred child is a boy, girl babies often contract a fatal illness or simply vanish, allowing the couple to try again for a son. And many girls are never born. Whereas the typical sex ratio at birth is 104–5 boys for every 100 girls, the ratio was close to 120/100 as ultrasound technology spread throughout China until sex screening was banned in 1995.

In parts of India, the low cultural value placed on females is reinforced by their even-lower economic worth. A daughter is a financial disaster, producing little and needing a dowry to marry. Thanks to the low-cost ultrasound machine, Indian physicians do a brisk business in sex determination tests, followed by the termination of almost all pregnancies involving a female fetus (Gargan, 1991). For families without access to ultrasound, daughters typically receive much less food and health care than sons do, with consequently higher death rates throughout childhood. The only variable that increases the survival chances of a daughter is living in an area dependent on rice cultivation, where women play an important economic role (Kishor, 1993).

Throughout the world, systems of social stratification are *gendered*, that is, they are based on a differential evaluation of males and females. The result of this **gendered inequality** is that, in all but a very few societies, power, prestige, and property are unequally distributed on the basis of sex. It is a cultural universal that where men and women know and do different things, men's work and wisdom is more highly valued than that of women. Sex is also a prime determinant of a person's location in other hierarchies, such as those based on religion, race, ethnicity, and age as well as education, occupation, and income.

In this chapter, we examine the origins and history of gendered inequality, cross-cultural variations in sex stratification, and the possibilities for future change. Our emphasis is on the statuses of women, because these have only recently become the object of intensive study, but the changing roles of men are also discussed here and in Chapter 12.

SEX AND GENDER

The terms **male** and **female** describe a person's biological sex, even though, as noted in Chapter 8, this is not always a clear-cut distinction. **Feminine** and **masculine** are socially constructed identities—gendered realities that vary highly from one culture to another and within a society, by class, race, and ethnicity (Lorber and Farrell, 1991).

> The principle which regulates the existing social relations between the sexes—the legal subordination of one sex to the other—is wrong in itself, and now one of the chief hindrances to human improvement. . . .
>
> —JOHN STUART MILL, 1869/1984, p. 259

But gender is more than behavior. We act and think as men and women because our language and social structures divide us, on the basis of biological sex, into distinct categories. Observing gendered differences, we then assume that they reflect biological differences (Lorber, 1993). However, because gender *is* socially constructed, it cannot be taken for granted, which is why we experience such powerful pressures to conform to gender norms. We become gendered persons living in gendered worlds and doing gendered work (Leidner, 1991). But, as with other power relationships, gender boundaries are continually being redefined and renegotiated; both men and women can and do resist the gendered expectations of their culture (Gerson and Peiss, 1985; Leahy, 1994).

Before describing the gender-stratification system of the contemporary United States, let us examine the nature of sex differences, various models of gender stratification, historical trends, and cross-cultural patterns.

Gendered inequality refers to the differences between men and women in the distribution of power, prestige, and property.

Male and **female** refer to biological sex. **Feminine** and **masculine** are social constructions.

THE NATURE OF SEX DIFFERENCES

Biological Perspectives

"Few areas of science are as littered with intellectual rubbish as the study of innate . . . differences

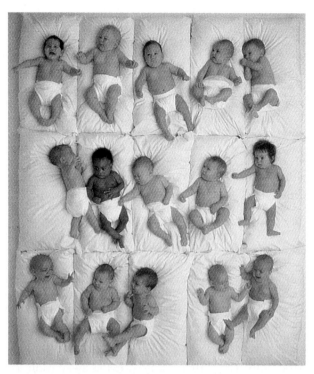

We are born male or female, but without socialization, our gender might only be as evident as it is for the infants in this photograph.

between the sexes" (Ehrenreich, 1992). The list is endless and never-ending: from brain size to brain side, from evolutionary pressures to the production of hormones. And in each case, the findings have been highly questionable, if not simply the product

of wishful thinking (Reinharz, 1986). In each case, also, the reported differences are far smaller than the similarities between women and men (Bem, 1993; Lorber, 1994). But the search goes on, and interest in the topic never fades. The most current research, however, actually reinforces many insights of the sociological perspective: (1) our species is enormously adaptable; (2) any effects of brain structure are subject to modification by experience; and (3) behavior is the outcome of complex interactions between the organism and the social and physical environment.

Arguments that explain male superiority by reference to men's greater body size and aggressiveness are the least persuasive. Size is not necessarily associated with intelligence, and highly aggressive individuals are usually labeled dangerous and are locked up. Regarding *hormones,* most research finds only a weak link between hormone levels and specific behavior, and the cause-and-effect is unclear; in many cases, hormone levels rise *after* a contest is won.

As for the *evolutionary* argument that human behavior is an extension of earlier primate adaptations, the evidence suggests wide variability among species in patterns of cooperation and competition between the sexes (deWaal, 1989). In fact, among chimpanzees, our close primate ancestors, aggression in males and submissiveness in females appears less frequently than among most other species.

From a sociological perspective, it is most useful to see sex differences as rooted in social experience rather than being fixed in our genes, hormones, or evolutionary past. For example, social psychologists suggest that because women nurture infants and

The stereotype of women as physically weak is contradicted by many activities pursued by women, including service in the armed forces.

raise children, they tend to develop a strong sense of connectedness to others (Chodorow, 1994; Gilligan et al., 1989). Males, in contrast, who must separate from the mother to become fully masculine, tend to be detached from other people; the closer the original attachment, the more violent the rejection (Gilmore, 1990). In this view, such early experiences produce girls and women fearful of abandonment, and boys and men fearful of commitment—not the best recipe for fulfilling adult relationships.

The Distribution of Sex Differences

When evidence of sex-linked traits is found, the data describe group differences or averages. For example, if a researcher is studying acts of helpfulness among school children, the total score for all the girls in the sample likely will be higher than for the sample of boys. Let us say that 100 girls produced 600 helpful acts compared to 400 for an equal number of boys. This finding does not mean that every girl was more helpful than every boy. Rather, when each child's score is plotted along a line, the pattern in Figure 10-1 emerges.

Patriarchy refers to male dominance.

Note that some boys outscore the average girls, and some girls score below the average boy. Most scores are extremely close, clustering around 5. In addition, the difference between the highest and lowest scoring girls and boys (0–10) is five times greater than the difference between group averages (2). Thus, more variation exists *within* each group than between the two sexes. An observer guessing on the basis of sex alone which child would be more helpful would be correct 6 out of 10 times. By chance alone, the observer would be correct 5 times out of 10. The advantage of the sex-linked guess is only slightly greater than drawing names from a hat.

A SOCIOLOGICAL MODEL OF GENDERED INEQUALITY

Although all gender stratification systems favor men, degrees of male dominance, or **patriarchy** (the rule of fathers) vary. At one extreme are societies in which a woman's power is minimal and in which she may be physically confined to the household. At the other end of the continuum of male dominance are relatively egalitarian societies in which power differences are narrowed and women have important roles outside the family. Only scattered evidence exists of societies in which women may have had power equal to or greater than that of men (Gimbutas, 1991).

If no "natural" or innate abilities produce male dominance, how can we explain its universality? Most scholars today point to the earliest division of labor, based on the one crucial biological distinction between the sexes—only women bear and nurse infants. Weakened by pregnancy and limited by the need to breast feed, it was logical that women assumed tasks centered on the campsite and child care. In contrast, men took on the more physically risky jobs, those that required being away from the campsite for long periods, that brought them into contact with other tribes, and that led to control over space, tools, weapons, and certain kinds of knowledge. Throughout most of human history, extremely high infant death rates have meant that an adult woman spent most of her short life either pregnant or nursing. Only recently, in industrial societies, have women been freed from the demands of high fertility.

Gendered inequality is most minimal in small gathering bands where the food supply is plentiful and any neighboring tribes are peaceful (Hope and Stover, 1987). In these societies, both men and women gather food and care for children, trap small animals, make decisions, and share resources. Human groups probably existed this way for tens of thousands of

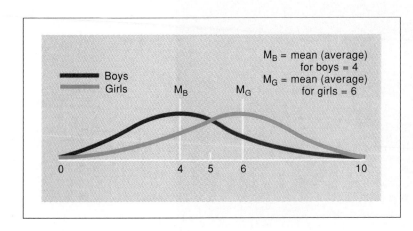

Figure 10.1 Comparison of girls' and boys' scores on acts of nurturance.

M_B = mean (average) for boys = 4
M_G = mean (average) for girls = 6

Boys
Girls

M_B M_G

0   4   5   6   10

Paradise Island

Because the few thousand inhabitants of Vanatinai Island in the South Pacific have had minimal contact with other societies, they have been able to maintain their traditional ways even as the rest of the world enters the twenty-first century (Lepowsky, 1994). Similar to other simple cultures known to anthropologists, the Vanatinai are essentially egalitarian. The economic base is a combination of fishing, horticulture, and pig farming in which both men and women participate equally. Decision-making is shared by all adults; no

chief is needed. Even the language is gender-neutral, and both sexes have ritual powers and access to the supernatural.

Where egalitarianism stops is precisely where we might expect it to—with a division of labor in which young women spend more time on child care and the household garden, while the men gain prestige through their skill at spearing wild pigs. Nonetheless, the example of the Vantanai supports the theory that inequality is not the original condition of human societies, but, rather, an accompaniment of cultural complexity.

years before their economic base expanded to the hunting of large animals. With the introduction of hunting, men and women developed different skills, and stratification systems emerged. Some men became more important than other men, but all men became more important than women.

Male dominance, as with other forms of stratification, tends to increase with the amount of private property held by the family—cattle, land, wives, children. Where possessions can be directly passed from father to son, patriarchy and control over women reach a high point, as in herding and plow-agricultural societies (Clark et al., 1991). The link between mode of subsistence and male dominance is illustrated in Figure 10-2.

Conversely, male dominance is reduced in societies in which women have effective control over eco-

nomic resources (Blumberg, 1991; Coltrane, 1992). It is not enough that a woman produces goods and services crucial to the family's survival—this is the case in all societies—or even that some property is owned in her name; what is necessary is that she has the power to decide how to use such resources and that she keep the income earned from her efforts.

Although the general pattern in industrial societies is toward egalitarianism, that is, a lessening of male dominance, the trend is uneven. It is important to distinguish between formal (official) equality and the actual distribution of power, prestige, and property. In the formerly Communist countries of Eastern Europe, for example, official ideology proclaimed equality between the sexes, but actual practice left women in complete charge of the household while also being employed full-time (Rueschemeyer, 1989). But they

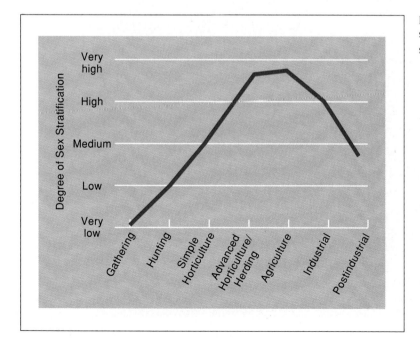

Figure 10.2 Degree of gender stratification by mode of subsistence.

Sources: Adapted from Chafetz, 1990; Huber, 1990.

The Seclusion of Women and the Honor of Men

The most effective way to control women is to restrict their movement—from the locked towers of medieval Europe to the foot binding of Chinese women. Today, throughout much of the Islamic world and parts of Hindu India and South Asia, women of relatively well-to-do families are secluded in special residences and required to veil their faces in public. These practices, called *purdah*, are designed to protect a woman's husband's family from the potentially disruptive force of female sexuality (Ahmed, 1992; Mule and Barthel, 1992). In these societies, the bonds between blood relatives are more important than those of marriage, so that a husband feels more closely attached to his male relatives than to his wife.

Outside the household, a woman must be fully veiled and covered and must never be alone or make eye contact with a man who is not a relative.

Today, in many Muslim countries, wearing the veil has become a major political and religious issue. In reaction to the modernizing trends of the recent past, a new emphasis on traditional Islamic values has resulted in a return to the practice of purdah. In Iran and

(continued)

In many Muslim countries today in reaction to modernizing trends there has been an emphasis on traditional Islamic values such as the wearing of the veil by women. This practice symbolizes loyalty to one's religion and nation even as it signifies loss of personal power. For these Muslim university students the veil allows participation in public events without offending those in power.

Saudi Arabia, patrols of religious police roam the streets to ensure that no violations occur; women are forbidden to drive automobiles and must sit in the back of a bus; those in Western dress are attacked. Against the combined forces of church, state, and family, few have dared to resist. Many hope that, when the current wave of religious fundamentalism has run its course, the more egalitarian aspects of Islam will once again emerge (Afary, 1994).

Returning to the veil symbolizes loyalty to one's religion and nation, an important source of esteem and acceptance in the Muslim world today, even as it signifies a loss of personal power (Mule and Barthel, 1992). Only under conditions of open revolt against a common enemy, as experienced by Palestinians in land controlled by Israel, have Muslim women realized a degree of independent empowerment (Haj, 1992). For many, taking the veil is a transitional attempt to reconcile the traditional and modern, allowing them to take part in public events without offending those in power (Moghadam, 1994).

are no better off under capitalism; indeed, the situation of women has deteriorated greatly in Eastern Europe and the former Soviet Union under "free-market" conditions (Moghadam, 1993a; Broschart, 1993). Where there had at least been price stability, subsidized child care and health care, rent control, and job opportunities, these are all now gone. The benefits of economic change have been enjoyed by a very small stratum of businessmen, leaving these societies even more stratified than before, especially in terms of gendered inequality. What the media hail as a great victory for freedom and democracy has thus far benefitted only a few. The condition of women and children (and most working-class men) has worsened greatly, but they do not write the headlines.

Functional and Conflict Perspectives

From a *functional perspective,* gendered inequality reflects the sex-linked requirements of survival: toughness for men, nurturance for women; the public arena for men, the private household for women. In this view, the division of labor is functional for individuals and the society as a whole. Male and female traits are seen as complementary—independent/dependent, instrumental/expressive—and based on innate natural differences.

From the *conflict perspective,* the division of labor and its resulting inequality are primarily socially constructed. Sex stratification is both cause and consequence of differential access to the means of production (tools, land, knowledge) and the products themselves (goods and services). Patriarchy rests on control over both the production and distribution of resources, within the family, the workplace, and the nation (Acker 1991; Coltrane, 1992).

Whatever its original basis, gender inequality is enforced by powerful agents of social control, especially legal and religious authorities. Ultimately, there is physical force or the threat of sexual violence. Of all mechanisms of social control, none is stronger than women's responsibility for bearing and raising chil-

dren (Calasanti and Bailey, 1991). Where women cannot control the number and spacing of their children, and where they are solely responsible for child care, they cannot participate fully in other activities. This is why reproductive choice is a central goal of feminist movements throughout the world.

To understand how gender hierarchies at the macrolevel are maintained, we must examine how gender identities are established and reinforced at the microlevel of face-to-face interaction (Huber, 1990; Risman and Schwartz, 1989; Coltrane, 1992).

Increasingly, women are challenging gender stereotypes in a number of ways. Lynne Hill, a pioneer in rockclimbing and a member of the U.S. rockclimbing team, is one example of a woman who has pursued an activity regardless of gender limits.

SOCIALIZATION TO GENDERED IDENTITIES

Learning about the gendered self and gendered world is similar to any other socialization experience and is taught by the same agents: parents, peers, teachers, and the mass media. No society leaves this process to chance or to the unfolding of inborn tendencies. Socialization pressures will be more or less severe depending on how much the sexes are thought to differ.

Gender stereotyping begins *before* birth, as parents create mental images of their daughter or son, and continues to death, as seen in the Research in Action box on page 229. Throughout life, a person is constantly reminded of how a "real" boy/man, girl/woman looks and acts. From an early age, people become active agents in their own socialization, developing a strong motivation to display sex-appropriate behavior. Thus, men and women tend to give stereotypical answers to researchers' questions, reinforcing the image of extreme gender differences, although detailed observations reveal less variation and more overlap (Walker, 1994).

As we saw in Chapter 5, gendered socialization affects **cognitive structures,** that is, how the mind processes information. In many societies, including the United States, girls continue to be encouraged to remain close to home, to limit their exploration of physical space, and to have a few but intense friendships. As a consequence, compared to boys, they have fewer experiences of expanding control over their environment, of dealing with abstract ideas, and of weaving complex role systems (Entwistle et al., 1994; Coser, 1991). Overprotective fathers, especially, tend to inhibit daughters from developing a sense of mastery (Avison and McAlpine, 1992).

Cognitive structures shape how the mind processes information.

Differential socialization by parents is reinforced by everyday activities in school and at play, where boys and girls interact in sex-segregated friendship groups, within which they socialize one another to traditional gendered values and behaviors (Thorne, 1993). Then, too, there are the toys, books, and television programs that reflect the same highly gendered world of experience, both imaginary and real. Although evidence indicates that prize-winning children's books have become more egalitarian over the past two decades, male characters still outnumber females and continue to be more adventurous (Weitzman et al., 1972; Grauerholz and Pescosolido, 1989; Clark et al., 1993). A major problem for toy makers and television producers is that while girls will watch boy's programs and play with male-oriented games and toys, most boys will not participate in female-oriented games or play with their toys.

As you learned in Chapter 5, socialization includes the formation of a self-image as well as internalization of the norms. One of the most consistent findings in social psychology is the lower self-esteem and greater self-hatred of females compared with males (Avison and McAlpine, 1992). Women and men both think less of a woman's accomplishments, attributing them to luck or manipulation rather than to talent or skill.

But as powerful as socialization pressures may be, it is also important *not* to reduce gender inequality to individual learning experiences, thus personalizing success or failure. Inequality is a structural characteristic and low self-esteem is a logical outcome of occupying statuses of little power or social worth. For American girls, the crucial period appears to be preadolescence. Self-assured and confident through childhood, a majority have a lower sense of self-worth by the time they enter high school, with white teenagers generally losing self-assurance at an earlier age than their African-American and Latina counterparts who appear to derive strength from social supports in their families and communities (Brown and Gilligan, 1992). Some of this loss can be traced to the schools and the subtle ways in which girls are discouraged from achieving and are vulnerable to harassment (Sadker and Sadker, 1994; Orenstein, 1994).

In adulthood, as in adolescence, uncertainty over the worth of one's work makes women more sensitive than men to the evaluations of others (Schwalbe and Staples, 1991). Even motherhood, while lavishly praised, offers few societal rewards and increases dependency (Sorensen and McLanahan, 1987). Several scholars have suggested that women's eating problems, including bulimia and anorexia, are not simply responses to a cultural ideal of thinness but are a means of coping with daily problems of powerlessness (Thompson, 1992; Bordo, 1993).

Drawing by Cheney; © 1992 The New Yorker Magazine, Inc.

Gendered Perceptions from Birth to Death

So deeply are gendered images embedded in our minds that we often see sex differences in appearance and behavior that are not really there. For example, researchers interviewing parents immediately after the birth of a first child found that both mothers and fathers described their son as alert, strong, and hardy; daughters were small, cute, and cuddly. In fact, there were no significant differences by sex in the infants' weight, length, muscle tone, or alertness. Knowing the sex of the infant, parents immediately perceived the culturally approved gendered traits (Rubin et al., 1979).

Similarly, at the other end of the life course, gendered images prevail. In cases in which a judge must decide whether to withdraw life supports from a terminally ill patient who has left no written instructions, researchers found that the court reconstructed a woman's preference and competence differently from those of an equally helpless man (Miles and August, 1990). Judges consistently referred to women patients by their first name, described them as emotional, immature, and incapable of expressing a thoughtful preference to guide the court. Men patients, in contrast, were referred to as "Mister," assumed to be rational and decisive, and as once having expressed a firm opinion for the court to honor. Nothing in the evidence before the courts supported any such distinctions.

Microlevel Processes

From the interpretive perspective, gendered inequality is reflected and re-created in everyday interactions. How people talk to one another, how they use space, who opens doors, and who sits where in the bus—these are all acts with deep symbolic meaning. The analysis of conversations, for example, explores such questions as who controls the subject matter, interrupts others, changes topics, and brings it to an end? You can see this power clearly in conversations between employer and employee or teacher and student. But at the same rank, if one participant is female and the other a male, it will be the man who opens and closes a conversation, changes topics, and interrupts (Lakoff, 1990; West and Garcia, 1988; Smith-Lovin and Brody, 1989).

Space is also gendered, because its use and organization typically reflect power differences between women and men (Spain, 1992). Especially important are the patterns that segregate people by sex and therefore physically remove women from places of

In a positive effort to encourage girls to broaden their perspectives of the varied careers women pursue, Ms. Foundation has sponsored an annual "Take Your Daughters To Work" Day. The idea has caught on as more and more women each year show their daughters where they work.

For most women around the globe, work continues to be physically difficult, monotonous, sex segregated, and low paying. These workers in Brazil are removing defective cashew nuts from an assembly line so people in developed countries can eat perfect nuts.

power. Although this process is most clearly illustrated in preindustrial societies (see the Sociology Around the World box "The Seclusion of Women," on page 226), the contemporary American scene offers many examples including the skewed sex ratios within many professions and occupations, the isolation of the suburban household, single-sex private clubs, and the privacy of a boss's office compared to the "steno pool."

It is in the details of everyday life that sex differences are socially produced and reproduced and gender is continually being constructed. The following section explores current systems of gendered stratification in the United States.

SYSTEMS OF GENDERED INEQUALITY

The umbrella term *status of women* obscures many variations depending on the dimension of stratification (power, prestige, property) and the institutional sphere (family, economy, politics, education, religion). Great differences also exist *within* the population of women—by age, race, ethnic origin, and social class (Wilkinson et al., 1992). Even though all women may be subordinate to men, women of higher social strata enjoy advantages denied to other women, and, in the United States, women of color must deal with multiple systems of inequality. Thus, the status of women is highly variable across cultures and within any society (Mason, 1986; Bradley and Khor, 1993).

The Power Dimension

All but a very few positions of great power in America—in politics, business, education, and religion—are occupied by white men. This outcome is typically explained by the belief that women do not project an image of leadership, are not comfortable with power, and lack the driving ambition to reach the top. This set of beliefs takes white male achievement norms as the standard against which others are seen to fall short.

In contrast to explanations based on personal qualities, most sociological research focuses on structural factors that encourage or inhibit moving to the top: on informal networks, workplace characteristics, support from senior personnel, and the availability of child care, to name only a few that tend to disadvantage women (Acker, 1991; McIllwee and Robinson, 1992). From this viewpoint, the barriers are in the situation rather than in the individual. Most obviously, as long as women assume major responsibility for child care, they cannot compete on equal grounds with men for positions that are thought to require extraordinary investments of time and energy.

Despite such structural obstacles, the number of women seeking high positions in politics and business have risen dramatically over the past decade throughout the industrial world.

Politics.   Even after their remarkable victories in the early 1990s, women still compose a small percentage of members of Congress (Table 10-1). Greater gains have been realized at higher ranks of the federal gov-

TABLE 10-1 Percentages of Women in Selected Elective Offices: United States, 1995

U.S. Senate	8
U.S. House	10.8
State legislature	20.8
Statewide elective executive office	26
Country governing boards	9
Mayors of cities with populations over thirty thousand	18

Source: The National Information Bank on Women in Public Office (NIB), a service of the Center for the American Woman and Politics, Eagleton Institute of Politics, Rutgers University, 1995.

ernment with President Clinton's appointment of women to positions of power and visibility, where it is expected that they will mentor junior staff.

The female candidate is no longer an oddity or without support, as both male and female voters at all social class levels have become more accepting (Clark, 1991). Nonetheless, women candidates do have more difficulty than men in raising money and in being perceived as a forceful leader. People still tend to remember what a male candidate said and what a female candidate wore. Opportunities are even more limited for women of color, who are greatly underrepresented in elective office compared with their male counterparts.

Throughout the industrialized world and in some developing nations women are slowly moving into national politics. But women still cannot vote in some countries and actually only won the right to vote in national elections in France in 1944 and Switzerland in 1971. Where women have been elected or appointed

to office, they typically occupy positions associated with women's interests such as health, education, and welfare rather than such "masculine" areas as defense and finances. Nonetheless, in mid-1994 a woman was prime minister or president in over a dozen nations. The countries with the highest percentage—between 33 and 40 percent—of women in high office are Finland, Sweden, Iceland, Norway, Denmark, and Cuba, compared to about 10 percent for the United States (Inter-Parliamentary Union, 1994).

BUSINESS.   In the world of big business, women now fill 44 percent of all management posts (compared to 19 percent in 1972), but very few reach the top. Less than one-half of 1 percent of the 4,000 highest paid officers or directors of major American firms are women (*Newsweek,* 1993). At the same time, women are flocking to graduate schools of business administration, where they now compose over 40 percent of the student body.

Because the world of big business is stratified by race as well as sex, the number of women of color in business schools and executive positions is extremely small and lower than that for nonwhite men. African Americans account for only six-tenths of 1 percent of senior corporate officials, almost all of whom are men (*Newsweek,* 1993). Against these odds, few Latinas or African-American women are willing to invest time and money in executive training. Successful women of color are primarily located in self-owned, neighborhood-oriented businesses primarily in the fields of cosmetics and fashion.

The career paths of women executives differ from those of men. Within corporations, women tend to be located in human resources, public relations, and other "people-oriented" departments rather than in

Gendered inequality refers to the differences in power, prestige, and property between men and women. Despite some advances by women, most positions of power are still held by white males. Twenty six of the 28 Major League Baseball teams are owned and managed by men. (The two women owners inherited their teams from their husbands.) The owners (right side) and players (left side) meet for talks with federal mediators during the long 1994–95 baseball strike.

Norwegian Prime Minister Gro Harlem Brundtland and almost 40 percent of the cabinet are women. The experiences of Norway suggests that as more women are elected to political office, greater attention will be paid to "women's issues" such as child-care subsidies, paid parental leave, and other benefits for working parents and children.

production and financial management—the royal roads to corporate power. Across economic sectors, women executives are concentrated in the fields of book publishing, retail sales, fashion, cosmetics, and advertising. The big-money, high-power fields of real estate, investment banking, communications, transportation, and oil and chemicals remain almost totally male and white.

Tokenism. In terms of directorships on corporate boards, women occupy about six percent of directors' chairs in the 1,000 leading American companies, usually one per board. This is a form of **tokenism,** the placement of one or two "outsiders" (not like those already there) in a high position, largely for display and without great power in the organization (Kanter, 1977). One study of token women lawyers found that, compared with their male colleagues, the women were more likely to be called by their first names, and to be complimented on their looks rather than on their work (MacCorquedale and Jensen, 1993). Tokenism is particularly difficult for minority women in male occupations such as law enforcement (Martin, 1994).

In contrast, the problem for token men in professions such as nursing, social work, or elementary school teaching, is having to explain their career choices to other men (Yoder, 1991). Although they earn less than they would in a male-dominated profession, token men are on a "glass escalator"—rising to the top more rapidly than their female colleagues (Williams, 1992). These findings suggest that it is not being merely a token but being male or female that determines how one is treated (Zimmer, 1988).

Tokenism refers to the appointment or promotion of one or two "outsiders" to high positions.

The **glass ceiling** blocks the way to the very top for women and nonwhutes.

Although women in the upper ranks of business are earning more than they did a decade ago, they still feel somewhat lonely at the top, are likely to experience stress due to family obligations, have experienced sexual harassment, and expect to retire before age 65 (Korn/Ferry, 1993).

The "Glass Ceiling." The way to the very top for the vast majority of women executives is blocked by a **glass ceiling**—you can see above but cannot pass through. A mixture of corporate tradition and gender stereotyping makes it difficult for most men to deal with women as occupational equals (Acker, 1991). Success in the corporate world depends on access to information and the informal relationships that men establish in the dining areas, locker rooms, and golf courses of private clubs that do not admit women (or Jewish or nonwhite men).

"Fast tracks" and "mommy tracks." The corporate "fast track" is very demanding—60+-hour work weeks, weekend meetings, constant travel, unexpected crises—all of which conflict with the requirements of stable child care. Because most companies have not yet made the changes necessary to retain women managers, such as on-site day care, parental leave benefits, and flexible work schedules, American women are faced with difficult choices (Galinsky and Stein, 1990).

Some will decide to stay on the fast track and delay childbearing or forego motherhood altogether. Most will opt for the "mommy track," reducing occupational goals to balance work and family obligations. And others will leave to establish their own businesses, with greater control over working conditions. But few self-owned businesses are successful. Women are less likely than men to be able to secure funding and tend to be pushed into the most risky and least prosperous areas of small business (Loscocco and Robinson, 1991; Devine, 1994). Thus, although over 30 percent of small businesses in the United States are women-owned, most are retail shops, beauty parlors, or launderettes with few, if any, employees.

Overall, although the presence of women in positions of political and economic power is only slightly greater than it was a decade ago, the idea of their being there has become taken for granted. A determined and talented few who are also wives and mothers will make it to the highest levels with the assistance of a supportive husband, affordable child care, and household help. Most, however, will face the choice between fulfilling career dreams and the demands of parenthood.

Prestige

If prestige is measured by occupational rank, very few American women enjoy high prestige as a function of their employment. Prestige ratings for women tend to be more ambiguous than those for men; respondents do not penalize women for their low-status jobs, including work as a housewife, but neither are they honored for high status employment. Being female is a master status that obscures other bases of social worth (Tyree and Hicks, 1988).

Despite lower rewards for high occupational achievement, women are entering professional fields in increasingly higher proportions ever since the emergence of the New Feminist Movement in the mid-1960s. As shown in Table 10-2, the percentage of women graduating from professional schools has risen dramatically since 1960.

In two previously all-male fields, women now earn 62 percent of new degrees in pharmacy and 57 percent of doctorates in veterinary medicine (now that it is largely concerned with household pets rather than large farm animals).

The example of medicine illustrates several key processes that limit the number of women in high-status occupations. Although similar proportions of women and men enter undergraduate premedical programs today, men far outnumber women in applications to medical school, even though the women's grades and chances of acceptance are quite high. What happens to discourage women from entering medical school (or any other professional graduate school)? The key factor is that only the very brightest women will apply, whereas many men with relatively poor academic records seek entry (Fiorentine, 1987). Not only do women receive less encouragement, but there are also fewer obstacles to their lowering career goals when confronted with difficulties (Fiorentine and Cole, 1992). Men are expected to persevere in a career path, but women are given cultural permission to reduce investments in nonfamily roles. The women who ultimately enter and complete graduate school, therefore, are highly self-selected for excellence.

Nonetheless, they tend to be clustered in the low-prestige sectors of their profession: pediatrics

TABLE 10-2 Professional Degrees Earned by Women, United States, 1960 and 1993 (in Percents)

	1960	1993
Medicine	5.5	36
Law	2.5	43
Dentistry	0.8	32
Theology	—	23

Sources: Statistical Abstracts, 1993, p. 174; *Chronicle of Higher Education,* September 1, 1994, p. 13.

rather than surgery; family law rather than corporate mergers; ecology rather than aerospace engineering (Hagan, 1990; National Research Council, 1992; Roach, 1991). Women are also more likely than similarly trained men to work in the public rather than private sector—as district attorneys and public defenders in the law, or in clinics and health departments in medicine—where pay and prestige are lower but so are discrimination and harassment (Wharton, 1989; Rosenberg et al., 1993). These processes are especially marked in the careers of women of color (Sokoloff, 1992).

In higher education, women faculty are clustered in the less prestigious departments and institutions, in the lower academic ranks, and, at any rank, earning less than their male peers (DePalma, 1993). The higher the academic rank and the more elite the school, the fewer women in high places, even in sociology departments (Beeghley and Van Ausdale, 1990). Nonetheless, increasing numbers of women have recently become deans, provosts, and presidents of universities and professional societies.

Science and engineering, however, present enormous barriers to girls and women. Traditional attitudes and career choices discourage girls from doing well in science and math in adolescence (T. E. Smith, 1992; Catsambis, 1994). In college, the overwhelming masculine context of science and technology majors serves as yet another inhibitor for women (Wilson and Boldizar, 1990). However, in countries where women have access to training and technical jobs, the sex gap in mathematical performance has narrowed (Baker and Jones, 1993). In the United States, the few women who receive graduate training typically lack access to mentors and the informal networks that lead to promotions and publications (Long, 1992; Fox, 1993).

Conversely, when women enter a field, it becomes less attractive to men. Men begin to leave an occupation when better prospects open up, creating vacancies that can then be filled by women. Once the women arrive, the occupation is redefined downward, pay scales are lowered, and very few men are left (Reskin and Roos, 1990). Bank telling,

Despite lower rewards for occupational achievement, higher proportions of women are entering professional fields. In the field of law women are more likely than similarly trained men to work in the public rather than private sector where pay and prestige are lower. This is particularly true of women of color, such as this Hispanic-American legal defense attorney.

for example, was once the first step in a banking career for men, but after 1945, when more attractive white-collar occupations opened up, the men left, the banks were forced to hire women, and bank telling became a dead-end job (Cohn, 1985). One exception is computer work, where the entry of women has not yet brought "male flight," most likely because men continue to monopolize the higher levels of what is still perceived as a masculine field (Wright and Jacobs, 1994).

It is also often the case that just when women and persons of color achieve a toehold in well-paying blue-collar occupations, these types of jobs disappear, as in automobile and steel production in the United States in the 1980s. Seniority rules protect the holders of the remaining jobs, so that the last hired are the first fired; and the very last to be hired was probably a minority woman (Woody, 1992). In general, race appears to have a more powerful negative effect than sex on the prestige level of one's job (Xu and Leffler, 1992; McGuire and Reskin, 1993). These are the workers for whom the glass ceiling has been replaced by the "sticky floor" that locks them into the lowest levels of the occupational hierarchy (Berheide, 1992).

Labor Force Participation

Most women, like most men in the labor force, do not have "careers," they have "jobs," fairly repetitive, closely supervised, and with limited potential for promotion. But a job of her own, however routine, provides income, a chance to leave the home, and friendships—all of which reduce a woman's dependency on a male wage-earner (Voydanoff, 1987).

Women's labor force participation is nothing new. Women of the working class, immigrants, and especially African-American women have always worked

for a living—if not in the paid labor force, then by taking in boarders, tending shop, and producing goods and services within the home (e.g., as a dressmaker, baker, or laundress). Their numbers have always been undercounted because the Bureau of the Census classifies them as "housewife" (Bose, 1987). And many continue to do home-based work for pay, even though it does not reduce the hours spent on housework (Silver and Goldscheider, 1994).

Full-time motherhood has always been a luxury reserved for the well-off. Only after 1945, when many families were able to move from cities to the suburbs, were large numbers of American women cut off from the stream of community life, becoming totally absorbed in homemaking and child care. But not all women left the labor force following World War II, although they were often shifted to lower-paying jobs when the veterans returned. In 1940, before the war, 27 percent of American women worked outside the home, a figure that rose to 35 percent at the height of the war effort. Yet in 1955, at the peak of the baby boom, 33 percent were still employed outside the home, a percentage that has risen steadily every year since.

Today, close to 60 percent of all American women aged 16 to 65 are in the labor force, compared with about 75 percent of men, 80 percent of whom are full-time year-round workers. In the age range 35–64, labor force participation rates for women are almost the same as for men. And among married women with children younger than one year of age, 57 percent were in the labor force in 1993 (Statistical Abstract of the United States, 1994; p. 402). Indeed, women now compose over 45 percent of the total labor force, so that if you had to describe "an American worker," you would be almost as accurate depicting a woman as a man (see Figure 10–3 on page 235).

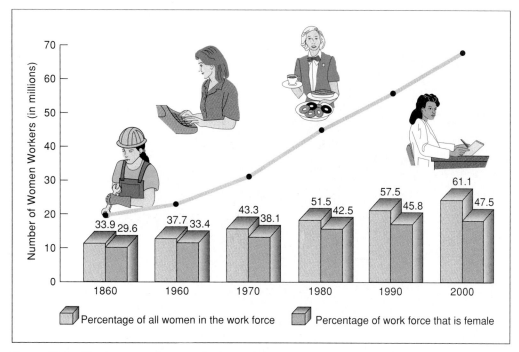

Figure 10.3 The increase of women in the work force.

Source: U.S. Bureau of the Census, *Statistical Abstract of the United States*, 1993.

Clearly, American women are out to work, especially those who are not currently married and those who are the sole breadwinners for their families. While some may withdraw from the labor force for a few years to care for infants, the trend is toward continued employment, as seen in Figure 10-4 (page 237) for married women, husband present (Hayghe, 1994). The higher the cost of leaving the job in terms of lost wages and job training, and her contribution to the family income, the more likely is the new mother to continue working (Desai and Waite, 1991; Wenk and Garrett, 1992.) For some mothers, however, child care costs, especially for preschoolers, outweigh the benefits of employment (Maume, 1991).

Most women not in the labor force are also working, though not for pay. They provide a range of services for other household members—shopping, food

As the labor force participation of women with young children increases, there is an increasing need for child care facilities. But there is a dramatic shortage of licensed child care centers—those available often have waiting lists and are too expensive for most working mothers.

While some progressive corporations provide on-site child care, many others believe that it is up to employees to make their own arrangements. What options are available for today's working mothers?

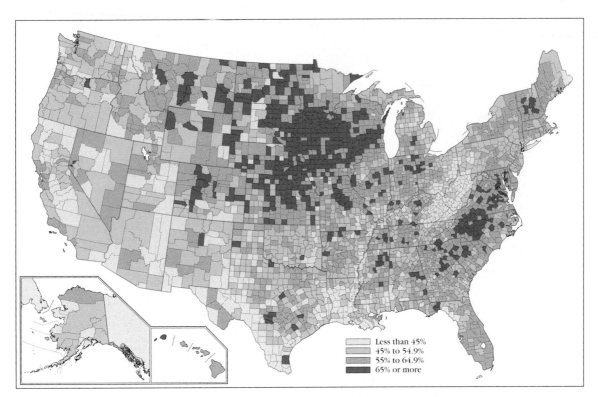

Labor Force Participation Rates of Women Age 16 and Over with Children under 6, by County, 1990.
Source: Statistical Abstracts of the U.S., 1993; American Demographics, October, 1993.

preparation, laundering—that need not be purchased from outsiders. In a society where people are judged by their labor value, housewives are greatly disadvantaged, which may be one source of their higher rates of emotional distress in comparison with employed women (Rosenfield, 1992). Also, many tasks previously done by paid workers have been shifted to homemakers, especially in the area of home-based health care to frail elderly (Glazer, 1993; Gerstel and Gallagher, 1994).

Gendered Work

Women workers enter a labor force that is thoroughly gendered (Baron, 1991). For every one who finds a nontraditional or high-paying position, several others enter at low-skill, low-pay levels. Most employed women today and in the future will work at dead-end jobs in the service sector (see Chapter 13). The overall effect of these employment patterns has been to maintain the **gender wage gap** in earnings that has changed only slightly since 1950. On average, full-time women workers earn between 65 and 72 cents for every dollar earned by a man, even in the same job (Rigdon, 1993; U.S. Department of Labor, 1994b).

> The **gender wage gap** refers to the discrepancy between average earnings of women and men.
>
> **Sex segregation** occurs when women or men are concentrated in a given occupation or in particular jobs within an occupation.

Some of the earnings gap can be traced to working women's family obligations and household responsibilities that reduce labor time and limit their ability to change employment or to relocate for a better job (Shelton and Firestone, 1989; Bielby and Bielby, 1992). But these obligations alone cannot account for the pay differential between people with similar qualifications and commitment in the same jobs. Only one-third of the wage difference by sex, or by race, can be explained by "human capital" variables such as education, job experience, skill level, work continuity, motivation, or working conditions (Jacobs and Steinberg, 1990; Seccombe and Beeghley, 1992).

The crucial factor in explaining the gender wage gap is **sex segregation** in the workplace, both by occupation and specific types of job within the occupation, as well as within the particular workplace. Although the degree of sex segregation has declined somewhat since the early 1970s in the United States, the great majority of men and women work in occupations dominated by members of their own sex. This permits employers to apply different pay scales and fringe benefits, even when workers have similar levels of skill and responsibility (Bridges and Nelson, 1989; Perman and Stevens, 1989). In the 1980s, however, wage inequality by

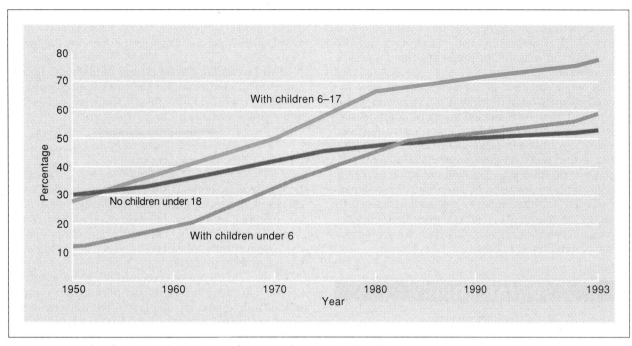

Figure 10.4   Labor force participation rates for married women, 1950–1993.

Source: U.S. Bureau of the Census, Statistical Abstract of the United States, 1994. p. 402.

sex, race, and ethnicity increased slightly (Carlson, 1992), especially for women of color (Tienda et al., 1992). In general, occupations that employ many women and/or have nurturing aspects about them have low pay scales (England et al., 1994; Kilbourne et al., 1994)

A third factor in the wage gap is, quite simply, **employer discrimination,** a tendency to treat employees differently on the basis of sex or race or whatever. Usually, the pay differential begins with starting salaries, which is then reinforced by decisions on promotions and raises that tend to favor male employees (Acker, 1991). These practices are

> **Employer discrimination** is the tendency to treat employees differently on the basis of sex, race or other characteristics.

Laundry day on the Ivory Coast finds both men and women working side by side. Why is laundering defined as women's work in most other societies?

technically in violation of the law, but the burden of proof is on the employee, and the legal process is extremely slow and often costly. Employers can cite any number of reasons for preferring one employee over another.

The work situation of women is even more restricted in Japan, often thought of as a society in which education rather than ascription opens doors to success. Not when it comes to a person's sex, however. Japanese firms both in Japan and in the United States prefer to hire and train men, who will be totally loyal, dependent on their jobs, and will not leave for family reasons. Without antidiscrimination laws, young Japanese women find the attractive occupations closed to them. As a consequence, mothers invest their energies in preparing sons rather than daughters for work roles (Brinton, 1992; Sanger, 1994).

SOCIAL POLICY

Comparable Worth

What is a fair wage? Most Americans would agree that people in the same job should be paid the same. But the wage gap that is due to sex segregation is not a matter of equal pay for equal work, because the jobs held by women and men are different. To remedy this situation, women's right groups have introduced the concept of **comparable worth,** or **pay equity,** (Steinberg, 1990; England, 1992b). This means that people who occupy jobs that require similar levels of training and supervisory responsibility and that are carried out in similar conditions of safety and comfort should receive similar wages. Thus, different jobs can be compared and given ratings on a strictly technical basis.

Comparable worth, or **pay equity,** means that people who occupy jobs that require similar skills and supervisory responsibility and are carried out under similar conditions should receive similar wages.

One of the earliest pay equity cases, for example involved nurses at a state hospital, almost all of whom were women, who received lower wages than the groundskeepers, almost all of whom were men. The principle of pay equity (fairness) would strongly suggest that nurses should be paid more than people who mow lawns. The counterargument is that wages are established by a person's market value, and if women are willing to work for less, or select themselves for low-paying jobs, the employer is not at fault.

Despite resistance from business leaders a number of pay equity settlements have been won in the private sector, and a majority of state governments are in the process of revising pay scales to reflect comparable worth standards. As with so many of the issues that become public policy debates, the solutions are largely political, depending on pressure from voters or federal agencies, and most often involve compromises among competing interests (DiPrete and Grusky, 1990; Baron et al., 1991; Fudge and McDermott, 1991).

If you were hired by a political candidate to measure public opinion on this issue, what questions would you ask? And how do you think pay equity will affect you personally in the years ahead?

Education

Educational attainment is a central component of location in the social class system, through its link to occupational status and life-style choices. The educational system is highly gendered in the classroom, in the expectations of teachers, and in a student's choice of what to study.

Cross-culturally, gender inequality can be measured by the rate at which girls are permitted to attend school and women are allowed in the universities. In many traditional societies, limiting female education to the minimum needed to run a household is a powerful form of social control. Thus, the great majority of the world's women remain illiterate and powerless and more likely than men to live in abject poverty (Jacobson, 1992).

In the United States, the elementary school is a "feminine" setting. Most teachers are women, and students are expected to sit still, wait to be called on, and show other female virtues. The more "feminine" the students, boy or girl, the better their school performance (Burke, 1989). Characteristics of schools and teacher expectations will be considered in Chapter 15, but your own experience should suggest the many ways in which boys and girls are encouraged to behave differently or are differentially sanctioned for the same behaviors.

Although girls outperform boys in elementary school and in high school subjects requiring verbal skills, the situation is reversed in applying to college. Men do better than women on SATs, win more academic as well as athletic scholarships, and are more likely to apply to college, regardless of school grades. The key variable in attending college is family resources, and sons are more likely than daughters to be encouraged to apply and to be helped financially (Stage and Hossler, 1988). The more brothers in the family, the less likely that all the children can get financial help from parents, a situation having the greatest impact on the college plans of sisters (Powell and Steadman, 1990).

Nonetheless, the rate at which women high school graduates entered college rose dramatically over the past three decades: from 25 percent in 1965 to 42 percent in 1993. At the same time, the rate for men *declined* from 45 to 41 percent. This means that the probability of going to college in the 1990s is the same for women and men, but because there are more women than men at all adult ages, the number of women attending college is now greater than that of men. Today, 55 percent of America's college students are women—a historically unprecedented situation. As you might expect, however, women are more likely than men to attend a public rather than private school, to be enrolled in a two-year rather than four-year college, to worry about finances, and to have selected the school for financial reasons (American Council on Education, 1994). In addition, women and persons of color do not receive the same income return on years of education as do white males. A woman with a college degree still earns less than a male high school graduate.

Unlike elementary and secondary schools, colleges and universities are essentially masculine, founded to provide employment to men of learning and to prepare younger men for citizenship. Men designed the curriculum and established standards of excellence. Just as boys feel out of place in the feminized grammar school, higher education is often experienced as a hostile environment for women students and scholars. For example, academic fields with a high proportion of female faculty have lower payscales than male-dominated disciplines (Bellas, 1994).

Gradually, the content of courses and textbooks is expanding to include women's experience, and many schools now offer a major or a concentration in women's studies. Although many scholars welcome these additions to the curriculum, there is always the danger that such courses will be of interest only to women and that the material will be "ghettoized," that is, segregated and set apart from "standard knowledge," rather than incorporated into every field of study.

WINDS OF CHANGE

As a result of all these trends—increased labor force participation, lower fertility, expanded educational and occupational opportunities—many American women today have a greater sense of independence and self-respect than in the past. But this would not have been possible had not their experience with gendered stratification systems in the 1960s led some women to organize actively for change. The goal of the New Feminist Movement, now three decades old, is to challenge gendered inequality in every major institutional sphere: the family, economy, politics, health care system, religion, education, and law (Lopata, 1993; Ferree and Hess, 1994).

Since the early 1970s, the women's movement has spread across the globe, to developing nations as well as the industrial world (Moghadam, 1993; Margolis, 1993). The strength and structure of women's organizations will vary from one society to another, as will their immediate goals and tactics. The basic goals essential to gender equality everywhere are the right to vote, to control fertility, to receive an education, and to keep one's own earnings or inherited property. In these terms, the countries of Northern Europe come closest to an egalitarian ideal, followed by Canada, Israel, and the United States, with much of Africa and the Muslim world least egalitarian. But even in many traditional societies, the ideas and ideals of the women's movement have led some women to protest openly, at great personal risk (Afary, 1994). At the very least, once-tolerated practices of female subordination have been challenged and exposed to international view. It is probably safe to say that gendered stratification systems will never again be quite the same.

Not surprisingly, the far-ranging agenda of contemporary feminism has unleashed a powerful backlash. Opposition comes from the many women and men who have a vested interest in existing gender relations, from employers who would have to change their ways of organizing work and doing business, and from people with firm ideas about the essential differences between women and men. From their perspective, there are many losses and few gains from any change in systems of gendered inequality.

At this writing, although the media refer to a "postfeminist" generation in the United States, presumably disillusioned with the feminist movement, or at least unwilling to be identified with it, recent survey data indicate otherwise (Ferree and Hess, 1994). Vast and probably irreversible changes have taken place and are likely to continue to shape the lives of men and women in the twenty-first century. In this section we examine two of these: changes in men's lives and changes in public opinion.

Changes in Men's Lives

In comparison to the sweeping changes that have reshaped the life of American women, it is much more difficult to chart similarly deep and widespread changes in the cultural images and actual practices that define the life space of men (Segal, 1990). Although we often speak of "masculinity" as if it were a universal set of deeply ingrained impulses, the sociological perspective treats masculinity (and femininity) as a socially constructed reality, highly variable across cultures, historical time, and an individual's life course (Kimmel, 1994). Furthermore, in our society today, the components of masculinity differ by race, religion, ethnicity, social class, and sexual preference (Craig, 1992).

For example, the construction of manhood for African Americans will differ from that of whites because their life circumstances and chances are so very different. The more disadvantaged African-American man may adopt a *cool pose,* "a ritualized form of masculinity that entails behaviors, scripts, physical posturing, expression management, and carefully crafted performances that deliver a single message: pride, strength, and control" (Majors and Billson, 1992, p.4). For other African-American men, coping with the often contradictory demands of the dominant and minority cultures produces a more complex conceptualization of masculinity, in which family and friendship and spiritual values are also incorporated (Hunter and Davis, 1992). And as with white males, social class locations affect definitions of masculinity and the quality of friendships (Franklin, 1992).

Yet among this diversity of masculinities a few core elements partially explain resistance to change in men's behaviors and their concepts of manliness. First, *maleness* is invariably defined in opposition to femaleness, a generally devalued quality. Second, maleness is associated with power, which few have ever given up willingly. Although scholars have pointed out that the aggressive individualism of "masculinity—American style" is no longer functional for success in either work or intimate relationships, this ideal remains the dominant image. The socialization of boys at home, in school, and within the peer group all reinforce the very qualities that make American men extremely vulnerable—the extreme fear of being considered either gay or a wimp/wuss (Gaylin, 1992; Kupers, 1993). Although parents may no longer fret over a tomboy daughter, they remain extremely anxious about encouraging "feminine" traits in their sons (Lawson, 1989; Nardi, 1992).

To the extent that women have become less dependent on men and in some cases are in direct competition for jobs, many men will feel threatened by their loss of economic and social power. It is no coincidence that so many recent television programs and hit films revolve around men unattached to women. Especially popular is a traditional American theme: the "buddy" relationship of men, preferably alone together in the wilderness, but often modernized to include women as either victims of sexual attacks or background "bimbos." When men were portrayed as warm and caring, however, it was not as a husband but as a single father—a statistical rarity, but the subject of half a dozen television series in the 1980s.

Another popular image today is of a wild-man primal self that can be rediscovered on an all-male retreat in which the traditional buddy theme is played out by thumping drums and shouting together in a display of male bonding. The basic idea is that a man can discover his true essence only when removed from the world of women, reinforcing distinctions of both sex and gender.

Despite these backlash maneuvers, many men will have experienced major change in their relationships with women and with one another, in self-concept, and in expectations of family life. The area of greatest impact is child care. There is wide consensus in the scholarly literature that men should become more involved in family life, for a man's own emotional well-being as well as that of his wife and children. In fact, the actual *amount of time* spent by a married man on home and child care activities has not changed greatly since the 1960s. What has risen is the proportion of total household work performed by husbands of working wives. As she reduces her homemaking hours, his input becomes a higher percentage of the total without any increase the time spent (Pleck, 1989). Because housework is a form of "doing gender," husbands may be reluctant to do very much of it (South and Spitze, 1994).

With regard to child care, research suggests that a father's involvement has a positive effect on the marriage and on the parent–child relationship. But it is not easy for men to invest time and emotional energy in fathering. Few employers look kindly on men taking time from work to attend to family matters. It is perceived as less than manly and as a sign of less than full devotion to business (Stein, 1989P.). Even in Sweden, where fathers are entitled to several months of paid leave, very few take more than 10 days, although the great majority do take at least one week (Haas, 1992).

A father's involvement in child care has positive benefits in the marriage and in the parent-child relationship. What sort of social policies are needed to get fathers more involved in the care of their children?

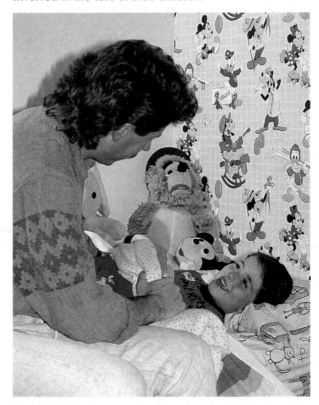

MICHAEL S. KIMMEL

The Sociology of Masculinity

Michael S. Kimmel is associate professor of sociology at the State University of New York at Stony Brook. Among his books are Against the Tide: Profeminist Men in America, 1776–1990 (*Beacon*, 1992), Men's Lives (*2d ed., edited with Michael Messner, Macmillan*, 1992), Men Confront Pornography (*Crown*, 1990), Changing Men (*Sage*, 1987), *and* Manhood: The American Quest (*HarperCollins*, 1994).

W hen I first mentioned that I was preparing a course on "the sociology of the male experience," my colleagues and friends wondered why a separate course was needed; after all, wasn't anything that didn't have "women" in the title really about men? Perhaps, but only by default. We study men as historical actors—soldiers and politicians—or as artists, workers and consumers. Rarely, if ever, are men discussed *as men*, and rarely is the male experience analyzed objectively. But the core insight of the women's movement was that gender, like race or social class, was a "master status," one of the central organizing principles of social life and self-identity.

I decided to look at men's lives as *gendered*, in which masculinity is no longer taken for granted, but becomes the lens through which a man's life is viewed. It was like putting on a new pair of glasses. I was seeing the world—one that I thought I knew quite well—in a completely different way (which is, after all, the essence of the sociological imagination). I remembered how architect Louis Sullivan admired "masculine"

forms—strong, solid, commanding respect—and how composer Charles Ives referred to a rival's work as "feminine," lacking in vigor and power. I thought of how a founder of the Boy Scouts of America in 1910 explained its mission as protecting boys from a culture that was turning them into sissies. I realized how the idea of masculinity, as the polar opposite of femininity, had become the metaphor around which men could understand their experience.

With this realization, themes of masculinity appeared everywhere I looked, especially over the past decade when scores of books and magazine articles claimed to define the "real" man, and my students were unclear about whether they should be more like Alan Alda or Sylvester Stallone. As a historical sociologist, I realized that ours was not the first era to experience confusion over the meaning of masculinity. As the example of the founder of the Boy Scouts illustrates, during the period around the turn of the last century, 1880–1920, many people thought that masculinity was threatened by rapid industrialization, taking men from the outdoors and placing them in factories and offices, and that our culture was being "feminized" as women began to dominate the socialization process in schools as well as at home.

What were the parallels between this earlier period and today? The American economy is once again being reshaped, this time by a massive shift from manufacturing to service jobs and by the emergence of a global system of production and trade. American economic and political control over other nations has been greatly reduced. And, again, renewed fears are expressed about the "feminization" of America—a nation "gone soft," in which the successes of the women's movement and the

emergence of a visible gay culture are taken as evidence of the decline of "real masculinity." Both eras saw the rise of an active women's movement.

Not all men in the earlier period or today reacted with fear to these events. My continuing research project has been to chronicle the history of "pro-feminist" men in American history, men who actively supported women's claims to equal opportunity, equal education, family reforms, political participation, sexual autonomy, and an end to male violence.

My interest in this topic began in my college years, as one of the first male students at Vassar College in 1968–72. I had heard about earlier "men of Vassar," such as the founder of the college, Matthew Vassar, who wanted to give woman an education every bit as demanding as that received by men at Harvard or Yale. My female classmates lost no time in introducing me to the ideas of the new Feminist Movement. After graduation, I became a leader of the National Organization for Men Against Sexism (NOMAS), a group that supports the goals of the women's movement and of gay and lesbian right organizations. Its members counsel men who batter women and seek ways to expand men's options as friends, lovers, husbands, and fathers.

My course on the sociology of the male experience explores what it means to be a man in the United States today, what we mean by masculinity—not as a fixed role, but as a socially and historically constructed set of attitudes and behaviors that change over time and across the life course. The variety of experience of my students—by age, social class, race, and sexual orientation—has been a significant subtext, leading us to the realization that we are speaking of *masculinities* and not a singular, "one size fits all" identity.

In the infrequent cases in which men are raising children as single fathers, they tend to develop attitudes and behaviors similar to those of mothers, further evidence that it is the *role* and not any in-born tendencies that determine behavior (Risman, 1986). Cross-culturally, fathers' participation in child rearing is associated with a lessening of male dominance and a reduction in violence against women (Coltrane, 1988). In the United States, married men who chose to invest themselves in child rearing tend to be very secure in their masculinity and to have a wife who is equally secure in her femininity (Snarey, 1993).

When asked about their expectations, young college-bound American men consider family life as important as their work life, plan to spend more time with their children than did their fathers, and support egalitarian marriage relationships (American Council on Education, 1994). Whether they will realize their hopes remains unclear. Much will have to change in the workplace, in employer attitudes, in a realistic family leave policy, and in cultural supports for doing "women's work."

Paradoxically, although men are seeking warmer, closer family relationships than in the past, they are increasingly reluctant to establish long-term commitments to marriage or parenthood (Gerson, 1993; Griswold, 1993). Attempts by individuals to institute change are often overwhelmed by the rigidity of institutional structures. Yet amid all this ambivalence are signs of more egalitarian relationships at work and at home, especially among younger, more educated men (Crispell, 1992; Potuchek, 1993).

For many midlife men, the past three decades have been a period of identity confusion, as can be seen in the recent flood of books about the "true meaning" of maleness and masculinity, no two of

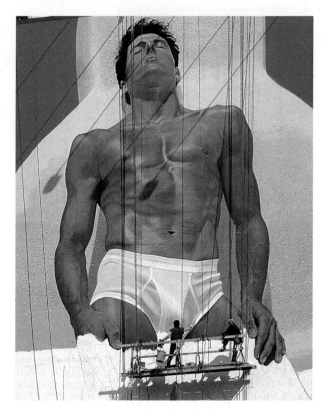

As a result of changing attitudes and a further emphasis on equality in the treatment of men and women, men are now baring it all in the media. Now that men are also objectified, have we reached equality?

which say the same thing (Shweder, 1994). Some of these books emphasize the dysfunctional elements of traditional masculinity, while others claim that the

---

RESEARCH IN ACTION

Restroom Parity, or, When Is Equality Unequal?

To illustrate how the goal of equal opportunity may actually require providing unequal facilities, Harvey Molotch (1988) directs our attention to public restrooms. On the basis of strict equality, the area allocated in public buildings for toilet space for women and men should be precisely the same. But it is a fact of physiology that women will take more time than men to use the facilities. In addition, urinals take up less space than full-sized toilets, so that more men than women can use the restrooms at any given time. The result is that women spend more time than men do waiting in restroom lines—clearly an unequal outcome that you must have noticed!

In this example, distributing a resource (toilet space) equally produces gendered inequality. What can be done? The "liberal policy" would involve en-

larging the size of the women's restroom until fairness (equity) is reached, but this would require men's giving up some of their space. The "conservative" approach, in contrast, would require women to change their toilet habits; after all, nothing in nature requires that women have private cubicles.

Although the tone of the article is tongue-in-cheek, there is a serious point: Sometimes it is impossible to provide equal opportunity without taking differences into account. Not long after this study appeared, the New York State legislature passed a bill amending the state building code that had required equal numbers of toilets for men and women (Verhovek, 1989). One correspondent (Nelson, 1993) wrote us about a theater in California that starts each performance with the announcement that half-way through the intermission, the men's room will become a second women's restroom. It works, everyone is good natured, and all are in their seats for the second half of the show.

TABLE 10-3 Changing Attitudes toward the Roles of Women and Men, United States, 1977-1994

	Percent Agreeing		
	1977	1991	1994
It is better for everyone involved if the man is the achiever outside the home and the woman takes care of the home and family.	65	41	35
It is more important for a wife to help her husband's career than to have one herself.	55	36	21
A working mother can establish just as warm and secure a relationship with her children as a mother who does not work.	50	66	70

Source: National Opinion Research Center, General Social Survey, 1977, 1991, 1994.

women's movement is destroying the authentic core of maleness.

Changing Attitudes

A large majority of American men and women today support the major goals of the New Feminist Movement: reproductive choice, improving the status of women, and sharing both breadwinning and household tasks. It is interesting that the politically conservative 1980s saw major increases in public approval of feminist positions, gains that have carried into the early 1990s, as seen in Table 10-3 (Mason and Lu, 1988; Losh, 1988; Piirto, 1991; Grigsby, 1992).

In general, these opinion shifts have taken place across all age and race categories and for men as well as women. In particular, attitude change has been most marked for women, for younger adults, for the more educated, and for African Americans in contrast to whites. Indeed, both African-American men and women are more positive toward gender equality than are their white age and education peers (Wilkie, 1993).

As might be expected, men's attitudes are more conflicted than those of women, especially with respect to the role of breadwinner, a major source of male identity and self-esteem. For example, men's attitudes toward the provider role grew steadily more egalitarian between 1972 and 1989, in terms of wife's contributing to a family's income. But most of the difference was due to younger respondents' being far more egalitarian than the oldest men rather than to any change in attitude among older men (Wilkie, 1993). Men with employed wives were more egalitar-

ian than those whose wives were not in the labor force, suggesting that the actual experience of sharing the provider role leads to change in gender expectations. Because this sharing is most likely among younger people who are already more egalitarian than their elders, we can expect continued support for reducing gendered inequalities.

Among American teenagers, however, traditional attitudes remain stronger for boys than for girls. In one recent national survey, only 58 percent of the boys expected their wives to work while 86 percent of the girls expected to work when they got married (*New York Times*/CBS News Poll, July 1994d). Interestingly, the girls were much more likely than the boys to say they could be happy without marriage.

Although only a minority of female respondents today self-identify as "feminist," an overwhelming majority say that they have personally gained from the women's movement, and an equally large percentage support the major goals of the movement (Ferree and Hess, 1994). This support has grown over time in all age groups, but primarily among younger respondents, despite expressions of stress over the double burden of work and child care. The more dependent the woman, the less likely she is to complain about inequality in the household division of labor (Kane and Sanchez, 1994). Yet there are compensations: a variety of role commitments is associated with good physical and emotional health, for both women and men (Menaghan, 1989; Barnett, 1994). Despite the difficulties of "having it all" and the possibility of a husband's resentment, wives employed outside the home enjoy higher levels of psychological well-being than do wives not in the labor force.

SUMMARY

1. Gendered inequality is produced by the differential evaluation of people's social worth on the basis of biological sex, resulting in hierarchies of power, prestige, and property in which men have higher status than women.

2. *Female* and *male* refer to biological sex; *femininity* and *masculinity* are socially constructed gender identities subject to continual redefinition and negotiation.

3. Biological differences are frequently used to explain gendered inequality but have failed to withstand empirical examination.

4. The sociological perspective examines how sex and gender differences are rooted in social experience.

5. Although all gender-stratification systems favor men, the degrees of male dominance (patriarchy) and its opposite, egalitariansim, vary.

6. From a functional perspective, gendered inequality reflects sex-linked requirements for individual and collective survival.

7. The conflict perspective focuses on the social patterns that produce and maintain male dominance over production and reproduction, including the forces of social control.

8. Socialization to gendered identities begins before birth and continues to the end of life. Socialization produces gendered cognitive structures and self-images that are reinforced in everyday experience.

9. From an interpretive perspective, power relationships are reflected and recreated in face-to-face interaction.

10. All but a few positions of great power and prestige—in politics and the economy—in the great majority of societies are occupied by men.

11. Women who enter high-ranking occupations are often treated as tokens and soon hit a "glass ceiling" that bars entry to the very top positions.

12. The primary barrier to high occupational achievement for women is their continued responsibility for household and child care tasks.

13. Women workers compose 45 percent of the U.S. labor force, largely concentrated in sex-typed occupations. Women enter and remain in the labor force for many reasons: to support oneself and children, to increase the family income, for the challenge of the job, and for workplace friendships.

14. Sex segregation of jobs and employer discrimination have produced a gender wage gap in which women workers earn about two-thirds the wages of similarly skilled men workers.

15. Education is a gendered process, in the schoolroom, teacher expectations, and students' choices of field of study. Higher education is gradually adapting to the influx of women students and scholars.

16. Increased labor force participation, lower fertility, and expanded educational and occupational opportunities have contributed to increased independence of women in the United States and other industrial societies.

17. The women's movement has also had an effect on men's lives, as they must adapt to changes in the wider society.

18. The construction of manhood varies by race, ethnicity, social class, and sexual orientation. In general, *masculinity* is defined in opposition to femininity and is associated with power.

19. Despite many signs of backlash, younger college-educated men are generally supportive of egalitarian relationships in which they expect to share some of the obligations of homemaking and child care.

20. Public opinion today is highly supportive of gender equality, reproductive choice, and shared roles in the family and the workplace.

SUGGESTED READINGS

Andersen, Margaret L. *Thinking about Women: Sociological Perspectives on Sex and Gender.* 3d ed. New York: Macmillan 1993. This excellent undergraduate text provides a comprehensive and up-to-date analysis of women's lives. Included are issues of sexism, culture and biology, socialization, work, family life, health, religion, crime and deviance, and social change.

Baca Zinn, Maxine, and Bonnie Thorton Dill, eds. *Women of Color in American Society.* Philadelphia, PA: Temple University Press, 1991. A collection of articles that represent the new scholarship on the interaction of race and gender in various systems of stratification. The impact of these social arrangements on the lives of Hispanic, African-American, Native American, and Asian-American women are detailed as examples of resistance and organizing for change.

Cordova, Teresea, Norma Cantu, Gilberto Cardenas, Juan Garcia, and Christine M. Sierra. *Chicana Voices: Intersection of Class, Race and Gender.* Austin, TX: National Association for Chicano Studies, 1990. A collection of papers exploring the complexity of women's roles within the Chicano and Mexican societies.

Dunk, Thomas W. *It's a Working Man's Town: Male Working Class Culture in Northwestern Ontario.* Montreal: McGill-Queen's University Press, 1991. An insightful narrative about a group of young men in Thunder Bay, Ontario. It explores social relationships among themselves and with the native peoples and women.

Gaskell, Jane. *Gender Matters from School to Work.* Philadelphia: Open University Press, 1992. A solidly researched book that raises issues about the education of women.

Kimmel, Michael S., and Michael A. Messner, eds. *Men's Lives*. 2d ed. New York: Macmillan, 1993. A splendid collection of essays dealing with men's socialization experiences, sports and war, work, sexuality, health, family life, and relations with women and other men.

Lorber, Judith. *Paradoxes of Gender*. New Haven, CT: Yale University Press, 1994. A brilliant and detailed argument for the social construction of gender and for considering gender as a major dimension of social structure, a set of institutional arrangements that generate and maintain inequality.

Nardi, Peter M., ed. *Men's Friendships*. Newbury Park, CA: Sage, 1992. A collection of essays describing and analyzing the dynamics and variety of friendships among men—gay and straight, black and white, middle and working class.

Reskin, Barbara F., and Irene Padavic. *Women and Men at Work*. Thousand Oaks, CA: Pine Forge Press, 1994. A brief but comprehensive and clear analysis of the intersection of gender and work, the gendered workplace, sex segregation, wage differentials, and the work-family dilemma as these affect both men and women.

Vogel, Lise. *Mothers on the Job: Maternity Policy in the U.S. Workplace*. New Brunswick, NJ: Rutgers University Press, 1993. A detailed historical analysis of how public policies regarding maternity and employment have shaped the debate over whether women should be treated the same as men or differently because of their uniqueness as bearers of children.

11

Minority Groups: Race, Religion, Ethnicity, and the Emerging American Mosaic

As we sat down to write the first page of this chapter, the following headlines grabbed our attention:

- Youths in France and Germany attacked the homes of workers of Turkish and Algerian descent.
- In Rwanda, Africa, Tutsi and Hutu tribesmen continued their centuries-old warfare, now with modern weapons.
- Eastern Orthodox Serbs, Catholic Croatians, and Muslim Bosnians renew historic hostilities, turning the former Yugoslavia into a vast killing field.
- Brazilian tin miners ambushed and massacred dozens of native Yanomami Indians.
- As Palestinian and Israeli Jews ended three decades of violence, extremists on both sides continued to attack one another.
- The Governor of California's popularity soared when he vowed to end emergency medical care and schooling for the children of undocumented immigrants.

In fact, similar headlines could have been found on any day since records have been kept. But we also know that humans are not preprogrammed for intergroup conflict, and that sharing and coopera-

Ethnic, racial, and religious conflicts occur around the world. Here Hindus storm and destroy a Sikh temple at a holy site near Calcutta, India. How can we understand such conflicts around the world?

tion are essential to collective survival. How are differences in appearance and customs transformed into grounds for violence?

In this chapter we examine the concept of *minority group*, with special emphasis on the social construction of race, ethnicity, and religious differences. These are ascribed characteristics that affect both (1) the placement of individuals and groups in the stratification system, and (2) the stability of the society as a whole. Social order is in large part based on the public's sense of fairness about the distribution of scarce resources; conflict occurs when people believe that their treatment is unfair in relation to their ascribed statuses.

WHAT IS A MINORITY GROUP?

A *minority group* is defined in contrast to the society's **dominant group:** those who control the central institutional spheres, including the power to define standards of beauty and social worth. The dominant group need not be a numerical majority, as in the case of light-skinned ruling elites in many South American countries. In the United States, although White, Anglo-Saxon, Protestant (WASP) males comprise only a small fraction of the population, their influence on our culture, language, laws, and beliefs have shaped the nation, and their control over major institutions remains largely intact. It is their standards against which all are judged. Thus, those who are not white, male, northern European, or Protestant have traits that not only set them apart but that become cues for special, typically unequal, treatment.

> A **dominant group** exercises control over societal resources.
>
> **Minority group status** involves visible traits, differential treatment, shared identity, and self-image.

Minority group status involves four necessary elements:

1. A *visible* ascribed trait by which a person can be clearly recognized.
2. *Differential* (unequal) *treatment* on the basis of this trait.
3. *Organization of one's self-image* around this identity.
4. *Awareness of a shared identity* with similar others.

For example, people with red hair are not a minority group in this sense, but if red hair came to be seen as a sign of the devil, redheads would probably be barred from certain jobs. That would constitute differential treatment, which could lead to a self-perception organized around the trait that was setting you apart. If, finally, one felt a sense of unity with other redheads and joined them in protest, we could speak of redheads as a minority group.

Are left-handers a minority group? They are physically different; they suffer from negative stereotyping and from accidents caused by the fact that the material world is structured for right-handedness; and many are developing a sense of shared fate and joining clubs and organizations where their concerns are central (Gaydosh, 1993). More obviously discriminated against are people whose physical disability makes it difficult even to move around. Only in 1990 did Congress pass legislation ordering places where people are invited to enter (shops, offices, restaurants, and transportation systems) to provide reasonable access to the disabled. This outcome was largely due to the organized efforts of disabled persons as a self-conscious minority group.

The concept of minority group status has most often been applied to people whose skin color, nationality background, and religious beliefs set them apart from the dominant group. Members of such a group often form a *subculture* that nurtures and protects, provides a supportive primary group network as well as an alternative interpretation of reality in which the ascribed trait is given a positive value. Belonging to a minority group, however, often makes it

Cultural homogeneity refers to populations whose members share a similarity in language, race, religion, national origin, and a common culture.

Cultural heterogeneity refers to populations having many subgroups, who differ in language, race, religion, national origin, and culture.

difficult to avoid stigmatization when subcultural norms are not understood or accepted within dominant institutions (Lempert and Monsma, 1994)

ETHNICITY, RELIGION, AND RACE

Societies vary greatly in the number of different populations they contain. Most simple societies and some modern ones (e.g., Sweden or Norway) are **culturally homogeneous** in that the great majority of citizens share a language and religion and are of similar racial and nationality origin. In contrast, the United States, Israel, China, Canada, and others, are **culturally heterogeneous**, composed of many distinct subgroups.

Within basically homogeneous countries such as Sweden and West Germany, a number of "guestworkers" were recruited from poorer sections of Europe in the 1960s to provide low-wage labor during economic boom years. The expectation was that the guestworkers would return to Turkey or Albania once they had accumulated enough money. When the immigrants did not leave but established their families in the guest country, these nations, too, began to have minority group problems similar to those in the United States.

Thus, although the United States is now the most diverse country in the world in its variety of subgroups, the American experience is both unique and universal. An underlying theme in this chapter and the book as a whole is that no nation today is an island; all are joined in a global system of economic and political ties, in which the movement of people

The cultural heterogeneity of American society is illustrated in this naturalization ceremony in Miami's Orange Bowl, during which 10,000 people, from a number of other countries, were sworn in as U.S. citizens.

across national borders is a worldwide phenomenon, causing outbursts of hostility and terror in all types of society. The three major bases of such hostility are ethnicity, religion, and race.

Ethnicity refers to cultural variables derived from a common ancestry and place of origin. The customs, language, and family names that people bring from one country to another and retain over time are aspects of ethnicity, as are categories such as Irish American or Polish American.

Religion refers to a set of beliefs and rituals through which people make sense of this world and the next and that unite a community of believers in shared worship (see Chapter 16).

Race is almost impossible to define in scientific terms, because human populations have become so intermixed that no "pure" racial types exist today and perhaps never did. In addition, aside from a few physical traits such as skin color, eye shape, or hair texture, people classified as Caucusoid (white), Negroid (black), or Mongoloid (yellow) have no major biologically based differences. That is, *all innate human abilities, including intelligence, are distributed in much the same way within any racial population.*

The problem of the twentieth century is the problem of the color line—the relation of the darker to the lighter races of men in Asia and Africa, in America and the islands of the sea.

—W. E. B. DuBois, 1903/1953, p. 13

Race is, however, a powerful social construction, because of the meanings assigned to it (Omi and Winant, 1987). It is the *definition of the situation* (what people believe to be real is real in its consequences) that defines race and the outcomes for different minority groups. In the United States, throughout most of our history, "nonwhite" has been equated with lack of ability, justification enough for not providing adequate education or job training. Drawing the line between black and white was especially crucial for maintaining white privilege once slavery was ended in the 1860s; by that time, decades of racial mixing had made whiteness and blackness matters of very fine shading. The solution was the "one drop" rule, whereby one drop of black blood was sufficient to make a person nonwhite, and subject to differential treatment (Davis, 1991).

In general, minority groups face higher or lower barriers to success depending on such factors as (1) how closely they resemble the dominant group in appearance and customs (which didn't keep Irish immigrants from being called "uncivilized barbarians"); (2) the job skills they bring with them; and (3) the state of the economy. For example, both blacks and Jews have been the targets of great hostility in this country, but the Jews came to the United States with certain educational and job skills at just the right time to find an economic foothold in urban trades such as the garment industry (Steinberg, 1981).

In contrast, blacks were brought to the United States as slaves when white Southern landowners needed farm workers but could not find enough white laborers for the low pay they offered (Williams, 1990). The solution was unpaid labor justified by an ideology of black childishness and white paternalism (acting as father), a belief later adopted by working-class whites to distinguish themselves from people with even fewer rights (Roediger, 1991). Ultimately, racial violence, including lynching, was used to discourage blacks from seeking employment that might displace white Southern factory workers (Soule, 1992).

The history of other religious and ethnic minorities has also been determined by the interplay between their skills, the job market, and competing sources of labor. The first waves of Irish, Italian, and Polish and other Eastern European immigrants consisted largely of poorly educated rural folk pushed out of their country of origin by famine and loss of farm jobs. They found employment in American cities as unskilled factory workers, gradually working their way out of the slums over several generations, but always one step ahead of blacks migrating from the South.

> **Ethnicity** refers to cultural identity derived from a common ancestry and place of origin.
>
> **Religion** is a shared set of beliefs, rituals, and worship.
>
> **Race** is a social construction influenced by the meanings assigned by a given society.

At one time or another in American history, race, religion, and ethnicity have served as *caste* boundaries, severely limiting entry into mainstream positions of power, prestige, and property. Over time, fear of Catholics and Jews has lessened. Today, a visit from the Pope is a national celebration, and Jews are found at the highest levels of business and government. Ethnicity has also ceased to be a caste-like barrier to upward mobility, and one's identity as a hyphenated American today is optional rather than imposed (Alba, 1990; Waters, 1990).

Constructing Ethnicity

Although ethnic identity is largely a matter of ancestry, the reality is that generations of assimilation and intermarriage have made it difficult for most Americans to claim a single ethnic origin (Lieberson and Waters, 1993). Increasingly, ethnicity is a constructed

Race, Ethnicity, Skin Color, and Early Death in Brazil

The American South was not the only port-of-call for African slave traders; Brazil also had large landholdings and few white workers. A small white elite controlled the labor of both native Indian and African slaves, and because the white men had few opportunities to marry within their race and class, a great deal of racial intermixing occurred, resulting in a population of varied racial backgrounds and skin colors.

Unlike the United States' "one drop" definition of race, Brazilians recognized many gradations within the three major categories of white, brown (mulatto), and black (Harris et al., 1993). Because of the difficulty in assigning a racial identity, Brazil never erected a vast system of legal barriers to integration as in the American South. Nonetheless, despite an official policy of racial democracy, race does matter in Brazil— today as well as in the past.

For example, two important measures of racial inequality are residential segregation and child death rates. In terms of residential segregation, although this has never been legally enforced in Brazil (e.g., through zoning codes as in the United States), the same goal has been achieved by virtue of income and occupational inequality (Telles, 1992; Brooke, 1994). Skin color is strongly associated with economic inequality in both Brazil and the United States, where lighter skinned blacks enjoy greater occupational success than their darker peers, regardless of parental SES (Keith and Herring, 1991).

With regard to infant mortality, in both Brazil and the United States, the likelihood of a child's surviving birth and early childhood are considerably reduced for black compared with white children (Wood and Lovell, 1992). In both countries, lack of access to the health care system is an important cause of high death rates among children of color. Brazil also has a large number of orphaned, abandoned, or runaway mixed-race children who roam its major cities, begging and stealing and sleeping in the streets. Several dozen such street children were shot and killed by fun-seeking adults in 1993; no one claimed the bodies.

reality, as individuals seek to define themselves and create a collective reality (Nagel, 1994; Hurtado et al., 1994). For many ethnic groups, the shift has been from "being" a hyphenated American in the first generation—an identity as much imposed by the dominant elites as adopted by new immigrants—to "feeling" culturally attached to a particular heritage (Bakalian, 1993).

> The **melting pot** model of integration assumes that immigrants will lose their ethnic uniqueness through exposure to the dominant American culture.

Race, however, remains a major barrier to social acceptance and upward mobility, more powerfully for African Americans than for Asian Americans, but strong enough to suggest that *racism* is a fundamental aspect of the American character rather than a temporary condition (Bell, 1992). In the remainder of this chapter, we look at patterns of dominant-minority group relations and the specific stratification outcomes of selected minority groups in the United States.

MODELS FOR THE INTEGRATION OF MINORITY GROUPS

How can a heterogeneous population be welded into a unified whole? From a functionalist perspective, social stability depends on establishing a common set of values and norms and on bringing minority groups into mainstream social structures such as the workplace, schools, and the political process. Because the United States is a society of immigrants, the integration of minority populations has been a long-standing problem to which solutions have ranged from early attempts to eliminate cultural differences to today's mix of celebrating diversity while fearing further immigration.

The Melting Pot Model

For much of American history, the basic model for the integration of immigrants was that of a **melting pot,** in which ethnic differences would melt away through exposure to the dominant culture and mass education. This model was based on the assumption that WASP values and standards of beauty and conduct were the ideals required for success. It was assumed that immigrants wished to become fully Americanized and would willingly abandon all traces of their former identities. People of color were considered an exception; not only was race an unmeltable trait, but law and custom created strong barriers to integration. It was even hoped that Jews and Catholics would gradually renounce their strange practices.

Despite the successes of public education in socializing the children of immigrants to a common language and culture, ethnic and religious differences were never completely erased. Supporters of the melting pot ideal had overlooked the crucial importance of religion and ethnicity as sources of identity and community (Nagel, 1994).

Nonetheless, over time, the children and grandchildren of immigrants have become well Americanized, strongly attached to its values and institutions and, today, are among our most vocal patriots and at the forefront of the movement to restrict further immigration (see "Social Policy: Lock the Door and Throw Away the Key!" p. 259). To ease their entry into the mainstream earlier in this century, many changed their names to disguise their ethnic or religious background. This was necessary because elite universities were known to have quotas for "Jews and people whose names ended in a vowel." Up until the 1950s, few minority group members could aspire to national political office, and fewer still were accepted into the higher ranks of corporate power. Most people would have laughed at the idea of a Catholic president, or a man named Lee Iacocca running a major corporation, or a Jewish Secretary of State, much less a black man on the Supreme Court!

By the late 1950s, however, there were few new immigrants, and the ethnic populations once concentrated in large cities were now scattered to the suburbs, the Americanized children had intermarried, and ethnicity ceased to be a major barrier to upward mobility (Alba, 1990). Nonetheless, many aspects of ethnicity remain quite strong, especially such optional elements as food preferences, cultural and religious customs, and self-identification (Waters, 1990). Ethnic differences within the three major religions—Protestantism, Catholicism, and Judaism—had also diminished greatly, although marriages *across* religious categories remained relatively rare, leading to the concept of a **triple melting pot**. Yet the persistence of race and religion (and ethnicity to a lesser extent) as sources of personal identity and continued barriers to achievement suggested that the pots were melting away only surface differences.

Cultural Pluralism

Recognizing that many differences are unmeltable and that intergroup tensions are inevitable, critics of the melting pot model have proposed an alternative ideal: *cultural pluralism.* The **cultural pluralism** model emphasizes the special contributions of each minority group to the diversity and vitality of American life. If the melting pot can be likened to a plate of hash, where the ingredients are blended together, the pluralist meal is a stew, where each ingredient remains separate yet contributes to the dish as a whole.

Cultural pluralism requires acceptance of differences in personal matters such as family relationships, religious customs, and community associations. It does not extend to tolerance for separatism, that is, a demand for complete isolation from mainstream institutions.

The ideals of pluralism have been tested over recent decades as many minority groups, previously barred from full participation in the mainstream, began to claim their rightful place: Native Americans, African Americans, Hispanics, and Asian Americans. For these minority groups, the road to self-respect and political power began with a renewal of ethnic and racial pride. The theme was that group members would no longer be judged by traditional American standards of beauty and worth but on the basis of their own talents and skills. Furthermore, the pluralist model implies that members of the dominant culture should attempt to understand and appreciate the values and life-styles of minority subcultures. As we shall see throughout this chapter, such acceptance has never been easy or complete.

The **triple melting pot** model of integration suggests that ethnic differences were melting within but not across religious categories.

The **cultural pluralism** model emphasizes the special contributions of each minority group to the diversity of American society.

Segregation refers to isolating a minority from contact with other members of the society.

PROCESSES OF MINORITY GROUP INTEGRATION

Minority groups are linked to the larger society in several ways that can be placed along a *continuum* from near isolation (segregation) to complete blending into the dominant culture (amalgamation), as shown in Figure 11-1.

Segregation

Segregation refers to isolating a minority from contact with other members of the society and can be ei-

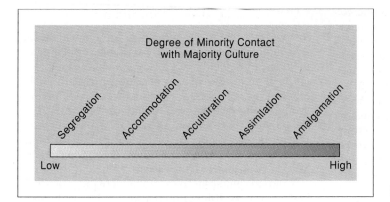

Figure 11-1   Processes of integration.

ther *de jure* or *de facto*. **De jure** means supported by laws, such as those that restricted Jews to living only in certain parts of Eastern European towns (ghettos), or that once marked relationships between a white minority and black majority in South Africa (apartheid). In American history, after slavery was abolished in 1862, an elaborate legal structure (Jim Crow laws) ensured that blacks and whites did not live together or share schools, workplaces, restaurants, movie theaters, buses, trains, or voting booths.

De facto means "in fact" but not necessarily supported by law. Although *de jure* segregation in the United States was finally declared unconstitutional in the 1950s, *de facto* separation persists because whites typically choose not to live near blacks and are able to maintain residential segregation through a variety of real estate practices (Farley et al., 1994; see Chapter 21).

Accommodation

Accommodation occurs when members of a minority become aware of the norms and values of the dominant culture but adapt just enough to deal with mainstream institutions while remaining culturally and linguistically distinct. Contemporary examples include many Hispanic and Asian populations in the United States, where the language and customs of the "old country" remain strong in the ethnic community, but individuals can negotiate the job market and the school system. This has been a typical pattern for almost every immigrant group in American history, as well as other modern societies with a visible but low-status minority: Pakistanis in England; guestworkers in Sweden; Roma (Gypsies) in Hungary; and native-born Arabs in Israel. In some cases, the accommodation is voluntary, but more often it is forced on the minority group.

Acculturation

Acculturation, or *cultural assimilation,* occurs when minority group members adopt the dominant culture as their own, replacing ancestral patterns, and participate fully in the economy, political system, schools, and community groups, but are still refused entry into more intimate social groupings. For example, even Jews who are directors of corporations are rarely invited to join the elite clubs to which many of their WASP colleagues belong.

Acculturation without full social acceptance creates the condition of **marginality,** in which a person is caught between two cultures, without being completely at home in either (Park, 1928; Weisberger, 1992). For example, the middle-class African American, suspended between the dominant and minority cultures, is accepted and rejected to some degree by each (Feagin and Sikes, 1994). Marginality has the advantage of providing a viewpoint from outside as well as inside, and it is no accident that many leading social critics occupy marginal statuses (e.g., Jews, homosexuals, women).

Assimilation

Authentic **assimilation,** or *structural assimilation,* takes place when minority group status is no longer recognized as a barrier to full integration into the social world of the dominant group. The rate of assimi-

De jure segregation is created by laws.

De facto segregation is not necessarily supported by law but does in fact occur.

Accommodation occurs when members of a minority are aware of the norms and values of the dominant culture but do not replace traditional ways of life with a new ones.

Acculturation, or cultural assimilation, occurs when minority members adopt the dominant culture and participate in the economy, schools, and so on, but are refused entry into intimate social groupings.

Marginality is the experience of being caught between two different cultures.

Assimilation, or structural assimilation, occurs when minority group status is no longer a barrier to full integration into the dominant group.

Guess Who's Coming To Dinner?

As a class exercise, each student should distribute the following questionnaire to a dozen people, together with an unmarked envelope in which to return it anonymously (adapted from Morrissey, 1992).

"Below is a list of seven activities and ten American minorities. Please answer "Y" for yes or "N" for no if you feel comfortable engaging in this activity with a member of this group."

This type of questionnaire is called a "social distance scale" and is intended to measure the degree to which people of different backgrounds are accepted by others, literally how close one is willing to get to someone unlike oneself in terms of race, religion, or ethnicity, or someone who departs greatly from the white Anglo-Saxon Protestant standards of beauty and

social worth. This relates to the distinction between "us" and "them" described in Chapter 4, and to the concept of ethnocentrism discussed in Chapter 3.

But some minority groups are less negatively evaluated than others, as this social distance exercise will demonstrate. When the class has pooled its data, certain patterns should emerge: for example, which status barriers are strongest? Do female classmates answer differently from males? Does region have an effect? What do the findings tell you about the future of minority group relations in the United States? And who let the Wisians in, anyway?[a]

[a]The Wisians are a fictional category added to a list of over 30 other ethnic groups in surveys conducted by the National Opinion Research Center. In the 1989 survey, they were ranked ahead of Mexicans, Puerto Ricans, and Gypsies (Lewin, 1992).

	Turkish	Italian	Jewish	Japanese	African American	Russian	Wisian	Mexican	German	Iranian
1. Work together on homework										
2. Join the same club										
3. Invite to your home										
4. Have as a roommate										
5. Date										
6. Have a sexual relationship										
7. Live with and/or marry										

What is your ethnic/racial background?_____

Sex:_____ Home city: _____

lation of a minority group varies by the degree to which members' physical and cultural traits depart from the dominant ideal. In the United States, having a light skin and speaking English are associated with high levels of assimilation, even though ethnic and religious identities may remain strong, as for Irish-Americans.

The *social distance scale* in the box "Guess Who's Coming to Dinner?" is designed to tap into this dimension of integration. What kinds of people are you more or less likely to date, or bring home to meet your parents, or consider seriously as someone with whom you could share your life? In general, low ethnic or racial status tends to be associated with low socioeconomic status and, therefore, the highest barriers to structural assimilation. In Israel today, for example, social distance research shows that Jews who came to Israel from North Africa and the Near East (Egypt, Algeria, Tunisia, Iran, Iraq, Lebanon, and Syria) are lower

on the ethnic status hierarchy than are those who migrated from Europe (Schwartz et al., 1991). But being Jewish does put the North African migrants ahead of native-born Arabs and Muslims on the Israeli social desirability scale.

Amalgamation

The opposite of complete segregation is **amalgamation,** a process involving the gradual loss of minority group traits through social acceptance and intermarriage—the melting pot ideal. The degree to which a minority group has been fully accepted by the dominant group can be measured by *intermarriage rates* (Spickard, 1991; see also Chapter 12). Since the early 1970s in the United States, mar-

> **Amalgamation** is the gradual process of loss of minority group traits through social acceptance and intermarriage.

Intermarriage rates reflect the degree to which a minority group has been accepted by the dominant group. Over time, intermarriage reduces the differences among ethnic, racial, and religious groups. In the United States today, marriages across racial lines involve about 2 percent of all marriages.

riages across ethnic categories have become widespread, although typically within the same religion (the "triple melting pot").

Marriages between Protestants and Catholics have also become more common, as has intermarriage between Jews and Christians. But marriage across racial lines remains quite rare: In 1993, for example, only 2 percent of all American marriages involved persons of different races, and the majority of these were between Asian and European Americans. Among Asian Americans born in the United States, one-half will marry outside their race, a trend especially marked among Japanese Americans.

> **Prejudice** occurs when members of a racial, ethnic, or religious group are assumed to have a single set of favorable or unfavorable characteristics.
>
> **Stereotyping** is the tendency to generalize favorable or unfavorable traits from one person to an entire population.

Black/white intermarriage remains very rare, evidence of the persistence of powerful barriers to integration in neighborhoods, schools, and the workplace (Alba and Logan, 1993; Massey and Denton, 1993). Such marriages typically involve an African-American husband of higher socioeconomic status than his white wife (Kalmijn, 1993).

Over time, intermarriage reduces the sharp differences among ethnic, racial, or religious groups. By the same token, where intermarriage is resisted, traditional inter-group hostilities are maintained and reinforced over time. For example, the intensity of fighting among Serbs, Croats, and Bosnian Muslims in the former Yugoslavia reflects a long history of refusing to have any cross-ethnic contracts and consequently low rates of intermarriage (Botev, 1994).

BARRIERS TO INTEGRATION

The assimilation of minority groups is typically resisted by dominant groups, both consciously and unconsciously. Three major mechanisms of resistance to integration are *prejudice, discrimination,* and *institutionalized racism.* Prejudice and discrimination are primarily individual-level responses; institutional racism is a structural characteristic.

Prejudice

Prejudice literally means "prejudging," making up one's mind in advance. Members of a racial, ethnic, religious, or any other social category are all assumed to have a single set of characteristics, favorable or unfavorable. The tendency to generalize these traits from one person to an entire population is called **stereotyping.** Thus, at various times in American popular opinion, Swedes were dumb; Irish, drunken storytellers; Italians, highly emotional; Jews, overly clannish; blacks, lazy; Hispanics, murderously jealous; and WASPs, rigidly unemotional. Even today, negative stereotypes are widespread. A major survey in 1991 found that three in four white respondents felt that African Americans and Hispanic Americans were more likely than whites to prefer welfare to work, and a majority thought that nonwhites were less patriotic and less intelligent than whites (*New York Times,* January 10, 1991). Although these figures actually represent a *decline* in traditional prejudice since the 1940s, whites remain strongly opposed to social policies designed to reduce the effects of past discrimination (Bobo and Kluegel, 1993). There is also evidence that whites are moving out of states with the largest influx of recent immigrants (U.S. Bureau of the Census P25-1111, 1994).

These attitudes are learned in one's home and school, through primary relationships with parents and peers, and often reinforced by self-interest as an adult. If you believe that the value of your home is diminished by nonwhite neighbors, you will resist their moving in, and invent other, more socially acceptable, reasons for doing so ("they really wouldn't be happy here"). And if you think that your job is in jeopardy because your employer is under pressure to hire a minority worker, you will obviously feel that that person is much less qualified than you are. Conversely, members of minority groups will feel resentful toward members of the dominant group who they believe are unfairly monopolizing societal resources, regardless of ability. It also appears that minority respondents hold extremely negative stereotypes about one another. A recent national survey found that Hispanic Americans, Asian Americans, and African Americans were almost as resentful of other minority groups as they were of whites, or at least they were more willing than whites to express their beliefs (Louis Harris Research, 1994).

As we saw in Chapter 8 regarding attitudes toward homosexuals, people who actually socialize with members of a minority group have less stereotypical views than do people without contact. Can social contact also reduce racial prejudice? Early research on this hy-

pothesis found mixed results, but a recent study of national data suggests that in several cases, interracial contacts have led to positive changes in racial attitudes (Sigelman and Welch, 1993). In general, those who are already relatively unprejudiced are more likely to be in situations where they meet people from other races, but these contacts can also lead to a lessening of negative stereotypes among formerly prejudiced persons (Lamphere, 1992). Yet the very conditions of modern city life that bring people into contact and promote tolerance also bring them into competition over housing and jobs (Hodson et al., 1994; Olzak et al., 1994).

One of the purest examples of prejudice comes from Japan, where a minority group, the *Burakumin,* have been considered the lowest of the low for over a thousand years (Rhim, 1993). In reality, the Burakumin look exactly like any other Japanese, but such is the force of prejudice that anyone known to have a trace of their blood is denied employment and refused as a marriage partner (Sayle, 1993).

SCAPEGOATING.   Prejudice is also reinforced by **scapegoating,** or finding someone to blame for one's own misfortune. The term refers to the Biblical practice of sacrificing a goat to appease God for human sins. In Nazi Germany, for example, Jews were blamed for the country's massive economic problems in the 1930s, reinforcing existing anti-Jewish prejudice *(antisemitism)* and leading to the mass murder of Europe's Jewish population. Jews, Roms/Gypsies, and homosexuals have long served as universal scapegoats.

> **Scapegoating** occurs when someone else is blamed for one's own misfortune.

Jewish concentration camp prisoners at Buchenwald peer out at American soldiers who liberated them at the end of World War II. In Nazi Germany, the Jews were blamed for economic problems, which reinforced existing anti-Jewish prejudice. Millions of Jews were killed in death camps such as Buchenwald. How can we understand the systematic slaughter of women, men, and children?

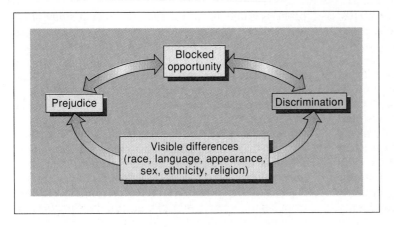

Figure 11-2 The vicious circle of prejudice and discrimination.

Prejudice is an attitude, and attitudes do not necessarily lead to behavior. Indeed, from the sociological perspective it is just as valid to assume that behavior shapes attitudes; that is, we act and then justify that action to ourselves and others. This is why sociologists typically focus on behavior rather than feelings.

Discrimination

Discrimination is behavior, the actual practice of treating people unequally. Usually, discrimination and prejudice are linked in a mutually reinforcing circle, as shown in Figure 11-2. A visible difference triggers either prejudgment or discriminatory behavior, or both, which leads to blocked opportunities and lack of training, which then reinforce the original judgment ("I knew that an Irishman was too dumb to do that job").

> **Discrimination** is the practice of treating people unequally.

Yet prejudice and discrimination are two separate variables, as seen in Table 11-1. A person can be very prejudiced without behaving in a discriminatory way, as when a classmate who fears Jews will nonetheless vote to admit them to his fraternity if the other members are strongly in favor. Conversely, the least prejudiced among us could easily find herself denying equal treatment to a minority person. For example, a real estate broker in a community where a certain area is "off limits" to racial minorities would probably not show those homes to an African-American buyer for fear of losing any future business ("You really wouldn't be happy in that neighborhood.")

What these examples illustrate is the basic tendency to act in ways that bring approval from significant others. If behavior and attitudes are not necessarily linked, then discrimination can be reduced *without* attitude change by encouraging group norms that define such behavior as unacceptable and by rigorous enforcement of antidiscrimination laws. If the costs of a behavior outweigh its benefits, people are likely to stop doing it.

Institutionalized Racism

Reducing unequal treatment is not simply a matter of getting individuals to change their ideas or their ac-

TABLE 11-1 The Relationship between Attitudes and Behavior

		Attitude	
		Prejudiced	Accepting
Behavior	Discriminatory	Not only hates having strangers next door but actively attempts to prevent having them (e.g., by cross burning and retaining exclusionary zoning laws).	Does not care who lives where but will not fight institutional racism/inequality.
	Nondiscriminatory	Does not want strangers next door but will not do anything to prevent their moving in or their continued residence.	Does not object to and may even welcome strangers' moving into neighborhood.

Institutionalized racism was practiced in many communities throughout much of American history and was enforced by formal agents of social control. This 1963 photo shows the reaction of Birmingham, Alabama, police officers to attempts by African Americans to register voters. To what extent is institutionalized racism prevalent in the U.S. today?

tions. Many discriminatory practices are built into the very structure and conduct of everyday activities. Such **institutionalized racism** is evident in the example of the real estate broker or the loan officer of a bank who fears taking an unnecessary risk with the bank's money. What is it worth to jeopardize your own job when you have a mortgage to pay and children who might be teased at school? Clearly, you do not need to have a racist mind-set to engage in essentially racist activities. It is these practices that are the most difficult to change and that continue to determine the life chances of millions of Americans. Racism has also been built into most federal legislation, especially the laws regarding poverty (Valocchi, 1994; Quadagno, 1994).

COSTS OF DISCRIMINATION.   Victims of prejudice and discrimination lose the opportunity to participate fully in society. They also risk their health, property, and even their life. Discrimination and prejudice affect a person's sense of self, as negative images are internalized and self-esteem lowered.

But there are also costs to the dominant groups. An enormous amount of energy and resources must be devoted to shoring up their position of superiority, and much talent from both groups is lost to the society as a whole. People who feel themselves superior are often unable to adapt to change, and dominance easily shades into the abuse of power.

Throughout American history, intergroup conflict has strained the social fabric, as when two or more minority groups, unable to coexist peacefully, engage in violent struggle for political and eco-

nomic power in multi-cultural cities such as Miami, Los Angeles and New York (Olzak, 1992). Confrontations, demonstrations, and riots destroy property and divert scarce public resources from schools and health care to law enforcement. Today, the lines of conflict are increasingly directed at the newest immigrants. The United States is not unique in this process. Throughout Europe, as well, a combination of economic recession, technological change, and reawakened feelings of national identity have heightened tensions among dominant and minority groups.

> **Institutionalized racism** is systematic discrimination of a racial or ethnic group that is built into social structures.

IMMIGRATION TO THE UNITED STATES

The original settlers reached the American continent tens of thousands years ago across a land bridge between Siberia in Northern Asia and the ice fields of Alaska. They moved gradually down the Pacific coast to the very tip of South America and westward to the Atlantic coast. By 1492, several million Native Americans, comprising dozens of tribes, were scattered across North America, and many millions more had created vast and culturally sophisticated civilizations in Central and South America.

In the fifteenth and sixteenth centuries, settlers arrived from Northern Europe, a few from Spain, France, and Holland, but the overwhelming majority

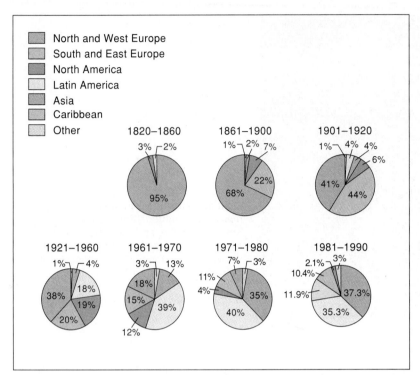

Figure 11-3   Place of origin of legal immigrants to the United States, 1820–1990.

From: "The Making of Americans," THE NEW YORK TIMES, 4/10/88; and "New Americans," THE NEW YORK TIMES, 5/31/92. Copyright © 1988/92 by The New York Times Company. Reprinted by permission.

from England, Scotland, and Ireland (80 percent of the U.S. population in 1790). As you can see from Figure 11-3, this pattern persisted up to 1900, when migrants from Southern and Eastern Europe were allowed to enter, largely in response to the need for low-skilled factory labor.

The flow of immigrants can be best understood as the outcome of pressures that "push" people out of one country (poverty, famine, persecutions) and the "pull" of another country (jobs, reunion with relatives, and favorable immigration rules) (Jasso and Rosenzweig, 1990; Parrillo, 1994a). As a consequence of all these forces, between 1900 and 1918, the United States absorbed millions of Catholics from Italy, Poland, Hungary, and Slovakia; Jews from Russia and Poland; and a host of others whose language, religion, customs, values, and norms differed greatly from those of the dominant culture. Each of these ethnic and religious minorities was greeted with fear, resentment, and discrimination. As soon as the demand for workers declined in the 1920s, new immigration restrictions effectively cut off the flow of "strangers," as shown in Figure 11-4.

In 1965, American immigration policies were revised to be less restrictive and more welcoming to people from the rest of the world. The results can be seen in the increased migration rates of Figure 11-4 and the dramatic shift from European to non-European populations shown in Figure 11-3. In addition, the Immigration Reform and Control Act of 1986 le-

galized the status of many Asian and Hispanic aliens already in this country while it also tightened the eligibility rules for new migrants. It is this influx of non-European and minority populations that has sparked the current debate over the changed appearance of America (Portes and Rumbaut, 1990).

Drawing by Handelsman; © 1992 The New Yorker Magazine, Inc.

"Well, it all depends. Where are these huddled masses coming from?"

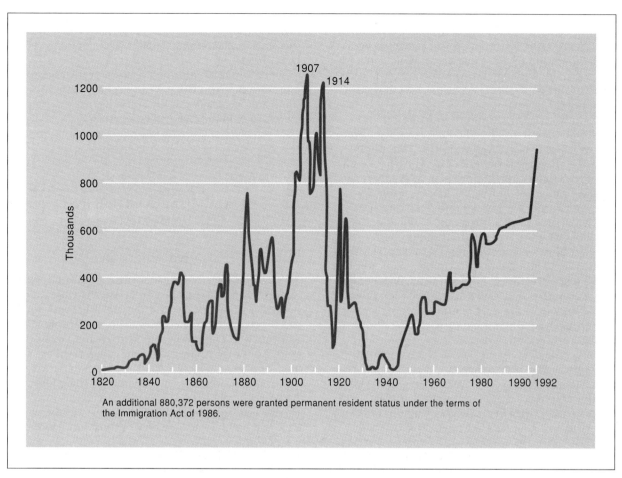

Figure 11-4   Legal immigration (new arrivals) into the United States, 1820-1992.

Sources: Statistical Abstract of the United States, 1994.

Foreign-born Population, United States, 1990, by Region/Country of Birth

Country/Region	%
Asia	25
Mexico	22
Europe	20
Latin America	11
Caribbean	10
Canada	4
Africa	2
USSR	2
Other	4
	100

Source: U.S. Bureau of the Census, *Statistical Abstract,* 1994, p. 52.

SOCIAL POLICY

Lock the Door and Throw Away the Key!

Is the United States being overwhelmed by a high tide of immigrants bringing poverty, disease, and crime? Will they take away jobs from American citizens, dilute our European heritage, and bankrupt the social welfare system? These questions incorporate words used by a respected television newscaster, a governor of a major state, and several congressional candidates in 1994. Actually, something like this was also said in the nineteenth century about Irish and Chinese immigrants and earlier in this century about Jews and other Eastern Europeans. Each generation of Americans seems to feel that it is now time to lock the door and throw away the key.

Should immigration be restricted to persons with a socially valued skill or those who promise not to use public welfare and health services? What about people fleeing from certain death, as in the case of the European Jews in the 1930s whom we did not assist? There is obviously an ethical as well as economic dimension to these questions, which should make for an interesting classroom debate. The complexity of this issue also ensures that is will remain on the public agenda.

As you have learned from this chapter, the world's most poor and huddled masses have never been welcomed in the United States. Xenophobia ("fear of strangers," pronounced zen-uh-foh-bee-uh) often overwhelms other, more generous American impulses, especially in times of high unemployment. And at this writing, xenophobia appears to be widespread, with three out of four Americans today believing that immigration should be restricted. These fears are reinforced by data showing that most new immigrants are young Asians and Hispanics, whose relatively high fertility will account for most of the population growth between now and the middle of the next century, feeding fears that European Americans could soon be a minority (see Figure 11-5).

Another element in this debate is the argument from conservative research groups that immigrants not only take jobs away from American citizens but that they and their families use up more public money than they pay in taxes (e.g., Huddle, 1993). Other data, from liberal think tanks, suggest that both job loss and public costs have been overestimated and that, on balance, immigrants add more to the American economy than they take out (e.g., Clark et al., 1994).

Once you have informed yourself of the arguments on both sides, you will have to decide where you stand and what will this say about the nature of American society in the twenty-first century.

RACIAL MINORITIES IN THE UNITED STATES

Native Americans

The Native American tribes that populated North America before the arrival of Europeans were quickly defined as biologically and morally "inferior" to the more "civilized" newcomers who were only doing God's will in conquering the natives and taking their land. All Native Americans were categorized as "Indians," and their widely varying cultures were treated with equal contempt. In addition to their losses in battle with the settlers, the tribes were also ravaged by diseases brought by the Europeans, against which they had no biological defenses (Thornton, 1987).

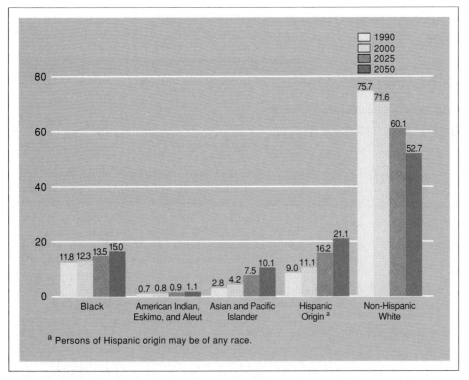

Figure 11-5 Percent distribution of the population, by race and Hispanic origin: 1990, 2000, 2025, and 2050.

Source: U.S. Bureau of the Census, "Population Projections of the United States, by Age, Sex, Race, and Hispanic Origin," *Current Population Reports,* P25-1092, 1992, p. xix.

Ethnocentric assumptions followed the westward flow of white settlers, who displaced the native tribes and absorbed their lands on the basis of treaties that were not intended to be taken seriously. During the late 1800s, entire tribes were forcibly relocated to reservations in sparsely populated areas with few natural resources, far from the farming and grazing lands that had been the basis of their traditional way of life.

By this time, also, an unknown number of Native Americans had joined the industrial labor force, intermarried, and disappeared into the multicultural urban population. In the 1950s and 1960s, many more left the reservations to live and work in cities, but rather than melt into the urban masses, these newcomers often formed cohesive communities in which Native American traditions were maintained (Weibel-Orlando, 1991).

Today, there are about 2.2 million Native Americans, including Eskimo and Aluet populations in Alaska. Slightly over one-third live on reservations or other areas held in trust by the federal government and administered by the Bureau of Indian Affairs (BIA) as part of the treaties whereby land was exchanged for protection of Indian rights. Although the treaties promised adequate housing, education, and health care, the history of the BIA has been one of almost total neglect and goal displacement, in which the billions allocated to the tribes have gone mostly to maintaining the bureaucracy that administers the funds. Not one of the 300 treaties between the tribes and the United States government has been fully honored (Richardson, 1993).

As a consequence of this pattern of **internal colonialism,** whereby native populations are treated as if they were foreign colonies, life on the reservation remains marked by high rates of poverty and its consequences: homicide, suicide, family violence, school failure, infant mortality, alcohol-related diseases, diabetes, and tuberculosis (Snipp, 1989; Bachman, 1992). Yet the past decade has also brought benefits. Court cases asking for compliance with the treaties have resulted in favorable judgments, including 300,000 acres of prime land in Maine returned to the Penobscot and Passamaquoddy, and fishing rights restored to Great Lakes tribes. College graduation rates are inching upward, although they remain very low (Cage, 1993).

> **Internal colonialism** is the practice of treating native populations as if they were colonies.

The major factor in the improving economic status of American Indians, however, has been the introduction of gambling casinos on the reservations. The original treaties guaranteed the tribes rights to local resources as well as freedom from control by the state governments. These conditions brought great wealth to the Oklahoma reservations where oil deposits had been discovered earlier. More recently, the tribes have invoked the treaty rights to exempt the reservations from prohibitions against gambling establishments. As a result, casinos have been opened on several Indian reservations, bringing jobs and millions of dollars in profits to formerly poverty-stricken tribes. For example, the Pequot Indian casino in Connecticut is one of the state's leading employers and has been so successful that tribal leaders hope to expand it into one of the largest in the world, prompting Donald Trump to file a lawsuit arguing that the Indians are taking advantage of honest businesspersons such as himself (Johnson, 1993a).

Native Americans remain the poorest and most disadvantaged of all racial and ethnic groups in the United States. Nevertheless, they are reclaiming rights and traditions that were violated by their resettlement onto reservations in the 1800s. There has also been a revival of cultural pride and an increasing interest in preserving the diversity of tribal history, customs, and crafts.

African Americans

The history of slavery in America illustrates many of the processes discussed in this chapter and this book. How can one group of people treat another as if they are not human? Only by defining "the other" as so very different as to be "nonhuman." Obviously, this process is easiest when the "other" has little resemblance to "us," as in the case of black Africans compared to the white Christians who bought and sold them. Within the overall system of dehumanization and degradation, the actual conditions of slave life varied greatly from colony to colony, by the type of agriculture involved, and over time as the black popu-

Kwanzaa is a recently created holiday that blends African traditions and American culture. More and more people are adopting this tradition which emphasizes the family and community life. Here an African-American family celebrates the holiday.

lation grew and the proportion born in America increased (Kolchin, 1993).

Of all enslaved Africans brought to this hemisphere, the great majority went to South America, with about 10 percent, or 650,000, sold to owners in the North American colonies. This relatively small population grew rapidly, making further trade with Africa unnecessary, so that by 1860 most of the 3 million blacks in the United States were American born. Racial stereotypes changed to reflect a more paternalistic (fatherly) view of slaves as children rather than as untamed savages.

Over time, African-American slaves developed a unique culture, blended from native elements and those imposed by their owners, within which some degree of self-direction could be exercised. The subculture of slavery, as with any other, provided a supportive environment, alternative definitions of reality, a basis for positive self-image, and the strength necessary for survival. Originally, the owners were of two minds about introducing Christianity to the slaves, but eventually the idea of converting "heathen" won out over the definitions of blacks as unredeemable. Not only did Christianity spread rapidly among the slaves, but it was reworked by blacks and many whites in such a way as to become a force for ultimately challenging the system of slavery itself.

Not all African Americans lived as slaves in the South; many had made their way to the North and West, where they also met with prejudice and discrimination but were at least free from everyday controls. Similarly, the formal end of slavery in 1862 brought one kind of freedom but left former slaves under the control of "Jim Crow" laws and a system of *de jure* segregation that was dismantled only in the 1960s.

Today, African Americans comprise about 12 percent of the population of the United States but remain disadvantaged along many dimensions of social stratification. As we saw in Chapter 9, blacks are overrepresented at the lower end of the income and occupation hierarchies and underrepresented in positions of political and economic power (see also Chapters 13 and

Among the advances made by African Americans in recent years was the selection of General Colin Powell to head the Joint Chiefs of Staff. One of his major achievements was the swift defeat of Saddam Hussein's army in Kuwait in 1991.

14). In addition, the employment and income gaps that had been narrowing between 1965 and 1980 began to widen once again during the 1980s.

The result has been labeled *American apartheid* to refer to the systematic residential segregation of African Americans in areas where employment opportunities are almost nonexistent today (Massey et al., 1994). Unlike the experience of other urban minorities, the isolation of blacks has been more intense over a longer period of time while the kinds of jobs available to earlier waves of immigrants have been moved to where the labor force is whiter (Neckerman and Kirschenman, 1991). Even Atlanta, Georgia, once thought to be a symbol of black political and economic progress, is experiencing the effects of the new apartheid (Orfield and Ashkinaze, 1991).

Institutionalized racism remains a powerful determinant of the life chances of African Americans. A short list of recent research findings should suffice:

■ Rejection rates for mortgage and home improvement loans were twice as high for blacks as for whites *at the same income level* (Quint, 1992).

■ Employers prefer to hire immigrant workers who do not speak English rather than American-born blacks willing to work for lower wages (Massey and Denton, 1993).

■ Social Security disability benefits are refused more often to African Americans than to whites at similar levels of physical impairment (Labaton, 1992).

■ Blacks are twice as likely as whites to be fired from the U.S. Postal Service, despite identical education and work records (Zwerling and Silver, 1992).

■ Even middle-class African Americans continue to face hostile treatment in restaurants and stores (Feagin and Sikes, 1994), and in trying to establish their own businesses (Feagin and Imani, 1994).

The employment and income gulf between white and black will grow even larger as American taxpayers demand cuts in the government workforce, because minorities have always found the government a more willing employer than private businesses. Thus, any reduction in public employment will have its strongest impact on African Americans, reducing mobility opportunities and reversing one of the more favorable statistical trends of the past three decades (Zipp, 1994).

What happens when immigrants are also black? Their fate depends on the skills they bring, their family structure, and whether or not they speak English. Thus, French-speaking unskilled, black Haitians are intercepted at sea and turned back. In contrast, English-speaking, relatively well-educated blacks from the Caribbean region have enjoyed unusual economic and political success in New York City, but only within the limits to upward mobility set by race as a master status (Kasinitz, 1992). Overall, however, systematic discrimination in employment and earnings accumulate over the life course, producing an ever-widening income gap between white and black Americans (Thomas et al., 1994).

Asian Americans

Asian Americans represent at least a dozen distinct cultures and language groups, yet a tendency to classify all Asians together has dominated immigration policy and popular attitudes. In fact, the Pan-Asian (*pan* meaning "all") community not only is increasingly varied, but its composition has changed dramatically between 1970 and 1990, as shown in Figure 11-6. Whereas Americans of Japanese origin were the largest Asian subgroup in 1970, today, they rank below Americans of Chinese and Philippine ancestry.

Figure 11-6 Distribution of Asian-American population, 1970–90.

From: The US Bureau of the Census, "We, the Asian Americans" (Washington, D.C.: GPO , 1973)p 2; and The US Bureau of the Census, "We, the Asian and Pacific Islander Americans" (Washington, D.C.: GPO , 1988)p 2; Statistical Abstract of the United States, 1992, p. 21; and Population Today, Vol. 19. No. 2, April, 1991, p. 6. Reproduced by permission of the Population Reference Bureau, Inc.

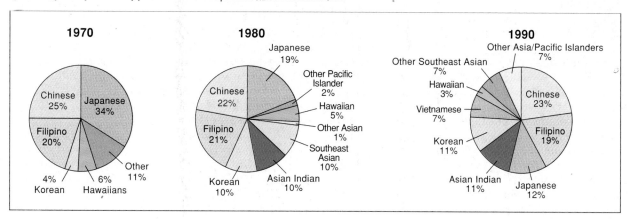

The recent wave of immigrants from Southeast Asia has added diversity and numbers to the Pan-Asian population.

In general, Asian Americans are considered to be examples of a *model minority* for having fulfilled the American Dream of upward mobility as a result of hard work. And indeed, poverty rates for most Asian subgroups are lower than for the nation as a whole. Average family income is even slightly above that of non-Hispanic whites, and educational achievement highest of any racial or ethnic subgroup (Lott and Felt, 1991). Asian Americans are also more highly mobile geographically than other minority groups, translating their economic success into residential assimilation (White et al., 1993). These overall patterns, however, hide great variation between and within various Asian populations.

CHINESE AMERICANS.   In both the United States and Canada, in the mid-nineteenth century, young Chinese men were imported (often forcibly put on ships in the port of Shanghai, hence, "shanghaied") to work on the transcontinental railroad. Not allowed to become citizens and forbidden to send for a wife or marry an American, those who remained on this continent formed almost exclusively male communities in West Coast cities in the United States and Canada. The gambling, opium smoking, and prostitution that characterized these all-male communities only reinforced the socially constructed image of Chinese as antifamily and immoral (Anderson, 1991). These neighborhoods were targets of white mob violence fanned by periodic fears of the "yellow menace," right up until the outbreak of World War II in 1941, when the Chinese suddenly became the "good" Asians in contrast to the "evil Japs." Over the past three decades, the Chinese-American community has grown in size and wealth. The educational success of Chinese-American youth has been exceptional, which is due in part to the traditional high value placed on learning in Chinese culture. The more important influence, however, appears to be the achievement motivation derived from the parents' involvement in family-owned small businesses such as restaurants, laundries, garment manufacturing, and Chinatown tourist stores (Sanchirico, 1991). Such success is not without cost. Because women in racial/ethnic minority groups must try harder than other women to achieve occupational success, they are also likely to have fewer children (Espenshade and Ye, 1994).

Studies of the assimilation patterns of minority groups often focus on the degree to which the group has carved out a special place in the urban economy—an *ethnic/racial enclave*—in which they control local businesses and establish a protective subculture, often reinforced by discrimination and other segregating forces (Logan et al., 1994). The en-clave nurtures economic stability and serves as a springboard to upward mobility. In the case of Chinese Americans, various Chinatowns have served this purpose well, thanks in large part to an influx of money from Hong Kong, Taiwan, and other "offshore" territories. As a result, banks and mortgage companies can provide loans for new businesses and homes, ultimately encouraging assimilation among the children and grandchildren of immigrants who move up and out to the suburbs (Zhou and Logan, 1991; Zhou, 1992; Nee et al., 1994).

Despite the general prosperity of the community, many Chinese Americans who remain in the enclave and most new immigrants live in poverty and are exploited at work. In addition, with so much offshore money entering the enclave, the line between legitimate and illegitimate business is often blurred, and local merchants have become targets for gangs of young Asians involved in the protection racket, as well as prostitution, drugs, and gambling, in the grand tradition of organized crime in America.

JAPANESE AMERICANS.   The path to structural assimilation for Japanese Americans has also been marked by discrimination, prejudice, segregation, and official violence. Lacking the numbers and resources to form an enclave of the size and influence of a Chinatown, Japanese communities on the West Coast were located in areas where members could succeed as farmers and gardeners. Like all Asians, Japanese immigrants were forbidden to own land or become citizens; they had, however, been able to emigrate as husband and wife, and because their children were born in the United States, the second generation, which soon outnumbered the first, had American citizenship.

Nonetheless, following the Japanese attack on Pearl Harbor and the outbreak of war in 1941, all Japanese Americans living on the West Coast were forcibly rounded up and sent to detention camps for the duration of the war. Although the reason given for this forced evacuation was "national security," the more powerful motives were economic and emotional, as their white neighbors eagerly took over the property that had been confiscated without compensation. Emotionally, the social construction of the Japanese as untrustworthy Asians could go unchallenged because of their relative isolation. In contrast, in Hawaii, where national security was really at stake, the Japanese had become so integrated into mainstream institutions that they were able to avoid such fear and mistrust (Parrillo, 1994a).

The experience of the detention camps had several long-term effects on the Japanese-American community, primarily through the erosion of power of men over women and of elders over juniors (Fugita and O'Brien, 1991). Many of the younger detainees were able to leave the camps to attend school elsewhere in

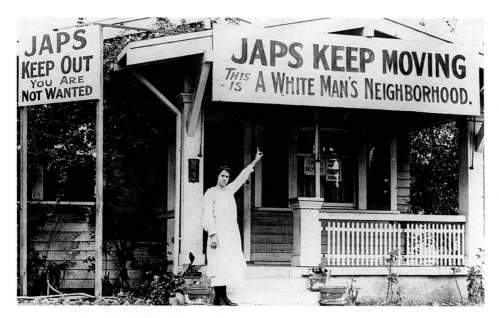

Following the Japanese attack on Pearl Harbor and the start of World War II in 1941, many Japanese Americans were forcibly rounded up and sent to detention camps for the rest of the war. Their property and belongings were confiscated without compensation until much later. The Hollywood Association started a campaign to force Japanese from the community with signs like these posted throughout the neighborhood. Do you think this type of situation could occur again in the United States?

the United States or to serve in the armed forces. This weakening of traditional authority speeded up the process of assimilation once the war ended and the camps were emptied.

No longer tied to agricultural occupations or to an ethnic enclave, native-born Japanese were both geographically and socially mobile, attending college in large numbers, moving into white-collar jobs in electronics and engineering, and marrying outside the Asian community. Few are left who remember the camps, and only in 1988 did Congress approve legislation that officially apologized for the detention and offered a tax-free payment of $20,000 to surviving victims—very little and extremely late.

OTHER ASIANS.   Policy changes in the 1980s led to lifting restrictions on immigration from various parts of Asia. The outcome, as shown in Figure 11-6, has been a large influx of people from Korea, Cambodia, Thailand, Laos, and Vietnam, representing dozens of ethnic groups, each with its unique language and culture. Many of these new immigrants are from rural areas, with minimal education and job skills, and little knowledge of English—traits likely to arouse fear and hostility as well as inhibit economic integration. The most recent arrivals have evoked greater than usual resentment because of growing competition for jobs among workers at the lower end of the occupational system. It does not take a crystal ball to predict that

The decade following the Vietnam War brought some 840,000 refugees from Vietnam, Cambodia, Laos and Thailand to the United States. Despite major social and political barriers, many of these people have achieved considerable educational and economic success in this country.

their assimilation will be slower and more problematic than that of earlier Asian immigrants.

Other Asian immigrant groups have found a variety of occupational specialities. Those from the Indian subcontinent entered the United States with high educational and technical skills and have found a niche in the pharmaceutical and health care industries. Recent arrivals from the Philippines also tend to be well educated, many with professional degrees, although most have had to settle for less prestigious employment. Immigrants from Korea lack educational background but compensate with a powerful commitment to self-employment for the entire family, especially in owning and operating small grocery stores in large cities, although this often brings them into conflict with other urban minorities. Nonetheless, the failure rate for small, family-supported businesses is much higher than for immigrant enterprises that have more solid financial and management bases (Bates, 1944).

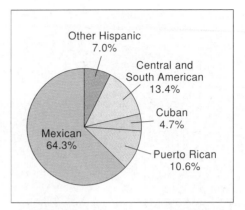

Figure 11-7 Subgroups within the Hispanic population of the United States, 1993.

Source: U.S. Bureau of the Census, "The Hispanic Population of the United States: March 1993," in *Current Population Reports,* Series P20-475, 1994.

THE NEW ETHNICS

The *old ethnics* refers to the waves of immigrants from Europe. The *new ethnics,* and fastest growing subgroups, come from South and Central America and from the Middle East.

Latinos

The census categories of *Hispanic* and *Spanish Origin* and the more recently preferred *Latino/Latina* are umbrella terms that cover a diverse, largely Catholic, population. The four major subgroups, shown in Figure 11-7, are very different from one another in racial and ethnic ancestry, immigrant history, and current status. Together, however, they currently comprise 10 percent of the population of the United States and are expected to outnumber African Americans as the nation's largest minority group by 2010. Their political influence, however, is diluted by the diversity of the subgroups, which are also stratified by socioeconomic status (SES) and skin color (Knouse et al., 1992).

MEXICAN AMERICANS (CHICANOS/CHICANAS).   The single largest subgroup (64 percent) is of Mexican origin. Some are descendants of people who settled in the Southwest before that area was annexed by the United States in 1848; others have lived in the United States for several generations; and many have entered more recently in response to employment opportunities in American factories close to the border.

Most Chicanos continue to live in the Southwest and in distinctly Mexican neighborhoods, or *barrios.* While language and culture set the Chicano community apart from the world of European Americans, appearance also has an impact on employment and earnings. Mexican-American men with dark skin

and/or Native American features receive significantly lower earnings than their more "Anglo-looking" peers, all other characteristics being equal (Telles and Murguia, 1990). Although the stereotype of the Mexican farmhand persists, about 90 percent live in urban areas, where the men typically work as laborers and machine operators and the women as domestic servants or office cleaners (Pinderhughes and Moore, 1993).

Despite the fact that the great majority are legal residents, the social construction of "illegal alien" is often applied to all Chicanos (and even to all Hispanic Americans). Upward mobility has been limited by job discrimination and social isolation (Morales and Bonilla, 1993). Family income and educational attainment remain below the U.S. average, while family size is higher. Although the traditional extended family remains a major source of economic and emotional support, many aspects of family life have undergone change, particularly with respect to the power of men and of elders. As Mexican-American women become acculturated, educated, and part of the labor force, their power in the family and marriage is enhanced (Segura, 1993). Similarly, the children, who are educated in American schools, often have an advantage over their parents.

PUERTO RICANS.   American citizens since 1917, Puerto Ricans arrived on the North American mainland in large numbers in the 1950s because of the collapse of the sugar industry on their island. The majority have settled in the Northeast, especially the New York/New Jersey/Connecticut area, where they have found employment in low-skill, low-pay service jobs. The ethnic community has not yet generated the kind of resources or opportunities for self-employment that many Asian communities have (Logan et al., 1994). Nor has the overall economy produced the type of jobs that could serve as a springboard to upward mobility (Melendez et al., 1991).

Puerto Ricans are characterized by a mixture of Spanish, Indian, and African ancestry, which subjects them to racial as well as ethnic barriers to upward mobility. Although the poverty rate for Puerto Rican Americans is over one-third, and labor force participation rates for both men and women are below those for the population as a whole, their expectations of success are higher than are those of Puerto Ricans remaining on the island.

Some signs of positive upward movement are seen in high school and college graduation rates, political influence, representation in the arts, and community control. On the negative side, dropout and unemployment rates remain high, and four in ten families are headed by a single parent (U.S. Bureau of the Census, P20-475, 1994).

CUBAN AMERICANS.   The first wave of Cuban immigrants consisted of relatively well-educated and affluent people fleeing the Castro revolution in the mid-1950s. This cultural and social elite, many of whom were descended from European Spaniards, settled in Miami, Florida, where a very successful ethnic enclave was established, which has gradually accumulated great political influence. Cuban Americans continue to be wealthier, better educated, and more assimilated than other subgroups. In contrast to other Hispanic Americans, this is an extremely conservative population, allied to the Republican party.

Nonetheless, Miami's citizens remain mistrustful of their Spanish-speaking neighbors, especially after Fidel Castro expelled another wave of immigrants in 1980, who were much poorer and less educated. Opposition to Cuban American power today also comes from local African Americans who feel that authorities have favored Latino immigrants over native-born African Americans.

Middle Easterners

In recent years, a new group of immigrants have emerged as a visible urban minority: newcomers from the Middle Eastern countries of Egypt, Syria, Jordan, Lebanon, Iran, and Iraq. Relatively light-skinned, they bring many diverse cultures, languages, and religions to the United States. Some are ethnic Arabs, others not; most are Muslim, but not all; many are from affluent families, but others are working-class youth; some are political refugees, but the majority seek economic opportunities (Parrillo, 1994a). Their common denominator is their geographic area of origin. The best estimates are that between 3 and 4 million Middle Easterners, primarily Muslims, currently reside in the United States. But because this is primarily a young adult population from countries with traditionally high fertility rates, the number could soon exceed 6

million, surpassing the size of the American Jewish population (Bernstein, 1993).

Assimilation has been made difficult by the demands of the Muslim religion, particularly, the need to stop other activities and pray at particular hours during the day and to observe many dietary (eating) rules (see Chapter 16 for a detailed discussion of Islam). Family relationships and the role of women are also very different from those of the surrounding culture. But these typical problems of any new minority in the United States were compounded in the 1990s by the war against Iraq and the emergence of terrorist groups on American soil. All "Arabs" have become objects of fear, although few are a danger to public safety (Esposito, 1992). This reaction is similar to the "yellow menace" scares that led to anti-Asian riots in California in the 1920s and to detention camps for Japanese Americans in the 1940s.

In reality, the Middle Eastern populations have in many ways fit the pattern of a model minority, establishing ethnic and religious enclaves that provide employment and funding for businesses within the community. Middle Eastern communities depart from the model, however, in that their goal may not be assimilation but, rather, maintaining a unique heritage in the face of modernizing influences. The key institu-

The discovery and celebration of one's cultural roots can serve to strengthen the identity of an ethnic group. What is your cultural heritage and how do you celebrate it?

tion here is the religious center, called a mosque, which serves as a unifying element and source of shared identity, reinforcing traditional customs and power relationships. It remains to be seen whether exposure to the modernizing influences of American culture, especially on the part of youth and women, will produce a major challenge to these traditions as it has with other newcomers (Ansari, 1992).

RELIGIOUS MINORITIES

We have dealt at some length with race and ethnicity as ascribed traits that affect access to power, prestige, and property. In heterogeneous societies, religion also serves to set some people apart from others. Because the specific nature and practices of various religions are analyzed in detail in Chapter 16, this section will consider only the stratification dimensions of religious minorities in the United States. In general, religion has ceased to be a major barrier to upward mobility. The absence of an "official" American religion, Constitutional protection for freedom of belief, increasing tolerance, and widespread intermarriage have eroded the sharp lines that once isolated Catholic and Jewish minorities in the United States, and that linked religion and ethnicity (Hammond and Warner, 1993). In addition to social class distinctions *among* the major religious groups in the United States, there are stratification hierarchies *within* the religious communities on the basis of ethnicity, education, income, and political power.

Protestants

Numerically and ideologically, the United States is predominantly a Protestant nation. Although the framers of the Constitution refused to establish a state religion, being Protestant was an expected requirement for political and economic leadership until very recently. The various types of Protestant congregations today account for between 65 and 70 percent of Americans; Catholics are about 25 percent of the population; Jews, 2.5 percent; and Muslims, 1.5 percent. Because Protestantism is composed of a number of subgroups, called *denominations* (see Chapter 16), the faith embraces Episcopalian Wall Street brokers at the highest level of socioeconomic status as well as Southern Baptist tenant farmers, at the other extreme. In general, the various denominations can be ranked in terms of their members' wealth, educational attainment, and occupational status. In this hierarchy, white Episcopalians rank highest, followed by Presbyterians, Methodists, and Lutherans, with Southern Baptist and African-American denominations at the bottom.

Intermarriage rates are highest among the subgroups closest to one another in the hierarchy and lower still across religious lines (although intermarriage to a Catholic is more likely than to a Jew).

In terms of acculturation and assimilation, Protestant norms of conduct and standards of beauty remain dominant. If there is a fault line within American Protestantism today, it is less related to ethnicity than to the split between "liberal" wealthy (Northeastern) and "conservative" (Southern, Midwest) denominations (Hammond, 1992; Wuthnow, 1988). Only in the past decade has the conservative wing challenged the political and economic power of the liberals (see Chapter 16).

Catholics

Although individual Catholics have enjoyed high prestige throughout American history, Catholics as a group have long been regarded with deep suspicion by the Protestant majority. Protestantism was originally founded in opposition to the practices of the Catholic Church, and much of this hostility was brought to North America by the colonists. This mistrust was also based on a fear that loyalty to the Pope would outweigh allegiance to the United States, a fear that was dispelled only in 1960 with the election of President John F. Kennedy.

Although a single church, Catholicism embraces social class extremes—from the wealthy, such as the Kennedy family, to the most recently arrived Chicano family. The stratification hierarchy within American Catholicism is based on the time of arrival of the immigrant group, its closeness to Northern European ancestry, and its whiteness. For most of its history in the United States, the Catholic community was dominated by the Irish, who monopolized the top positions in the religious hierarchy, Catholic educational institutions and charities, and American politics. Only in the last three decades have the Irish been replaced by leaders with Italian, Polish, and Latino names.

At one time, because of the extreme social class divisions within the American Catholic community, it was a matter of great anguish for both families if an Irish Catholic chose to marry someone of Southern or Eastern European ancestry. Over time, as non-Irish Catholics have caught up in educational attainment and occupational status, class differences based on ethnicity have become blurred, as seen in the relatively high level of intermarriage among Catholics of varying ancestry.

Although they still may not be asked to join an elite private club, American Catholics today face few barriers to integration and upward mobility. As for self-imposed restrictions, it had long been thought that the emphasis on community fostered by the parish church and the close family ties of Southern and Eastern European immigrants would reduce the motivation for individual achievement among second-generation American Catholics. And for many decades, the pull of the ethnic and religious enclave, combined with anti-Catholic discrimination, limited their integration into mainstream institutions. Since the 1950s, however, barriers within and without the community have fallen so that, today, Catholics are found at the highest levels of politics, business, and education.

At the same time, the church remains a powerful source of self-identity and primary group ties. A large majority of Catholics marry within the faith, and many continue to send their children to church-run schools. But it is a more "optional" Catholicism than in the past, less bound to the schedule of observances or to official church positions on matters of everyday conduct (Sweeney, 1992).

Jews

Prejudice and discrimination are nothing new or unusual for Jews, the eternal minority (with the exception of the State of Israel since the mid-1960s). Most American minorities, whatever else divides them, at least share the Christian faith. Jews thus stand apart, *in* but never quite *of* the dominant social systems. In the United States, Jews have avoided the extreme hostility faced throughout Europe, thanks in part to the Constitutional guarantee of freedom of religion. For many decades, also, the bulk of the American Jewish community was numerically small and self-contained geographically. Nonetheless, anti-Semitism has been a continuing theme in American history, especially among conservative Christians, Southerners, and Midwest farmers, but also deeply embedded in the culture of the Protestant elite.

The internal stratification of American Jewry is based largely on the time of immigration, which is associated with both ethnicity and occupational achievements (Sachar, 1992). At the top of the hierarchy are the descendants of several Jewish families who fled the Spanish Inquisition in the sixteenth century and settled in the Carolinas and Virginia before the Revolutionary War. By the 1860s, the Jewish population was 150,000, and they were soon joined by several thousand highly urbanized, educated, and affluent immigrants from Germany. The German Jewish enclave prospered in areas of merchant banking that the established elite believed was beneath their dignity. Not especially religious in background and largely concerned with assimilating as readily as possible, this second wave blended in by deemphasizing any and all differences with the Christian majority.

The major wave of Jewish immigration came between 1890 and 1920, when one-third of European Jews migrated to the United States, mostly from villages in Poland and Russia. Compared to the German Jews already established in the United States, this new population was very strange indeed—Yiddish-speaking, deeply superstitious, relatively uneducated, and very poor. For many decades, the German Jewish elite

had little direct contact with the newcomers, who slowly worked their way out of poverty and residential isolation. Intermarriage between German and Russian or Polish Jews was almost as agonizing to the families as if the children had married out of the faith altogether.

Over time, as both the internal and external barriers to integration gradually weakened, American Jews have enjoyed great success in education and business, so that today, in comparison with their absolute numbers, they are overrepresented among college graduates and high-income earners. Excluded from the elite eating and country clubs, they formed a parallel system of upper-status Jewish clubs. Until very recently also excluded from the top levels of corporate power, Jews took other avenues to economic success—medicine, law, publishing, investment banking, entertainment, and self-employment, especially in the manufacture and selling of clothing and household goods (Korman, 1989).

As the second generation was encouraged to enter college and to move to regions where economic opportunity beckoned, the ethnic and religious enclaves began to break up, although pockets of Jews can still be found in inner cities in neighborhoods that have now become home to newer immigrant groups. Moving up and out of the enclave was accompanied by an increase in intermarriage, further eroding the sense of community that protected and nurtured earlier gener-

Religious diversity can be found even within one denomination. Here, Orthodox Hasidic Jews, a very traditional branch of Judaism, celebrate a marriage. How do other Jews or Catholics or Protestants celebrate marriages?

ations (Waxman, 1990). Not only has intermarriage reached historically high levels, involving perhaps one-half of marriages of Jewish men today, but birth rates are at a historic low (Keysar et al., 1991; Mott and Abma, 1992). Both the low fertility and high intermarriage are characteristic of any population with high educational and occupational statuses. Thus, the great irony for American Jews is that their very success in integration and upward mobility may ultimately undermine the survival of the American Jewish community, as more men and women drift away and lose the sense of unique identity.

The exception to these trends is the small subgroup of extremely traditional and deeply religious *Orthodox Jews,* who have retained their way of life by isolating themselves from both mainstream Judaism and the dominant culture. Living in closely knit neighborhoods, educating their children within the community, and choosing employment that does not conflict with religious obligations, the Orthodox are a people who pride themselves on their separateness (Heilman, 1991). Orthodox fertility is very high, but given the small size of this population to begin with, this will not be enough to keep the number of American Jews from declining further (Mott and Abma, 1992).

Muslims

The newest arrivals and fastest growing religious minority in America comprises followers of the Islamic faith, called Muslims. This is an enormously varied population in terms of race, ethnicity, culture, and language, united only by their religion (Ansari, 1992).

The earliest Muslim immigrants came to the United States from Syria and Lebanon in the 1920s and moved to the Midwest, where the first American mosques were founded in North Dakota and Iowa. Similar to the Jews who worked their way westward in the early decades of this century, these light-skinned migrants were primarily engaged in peddling household goods and clothing to local farmers and villagers. Despite their adherence to a strange faith, they settled in small towns and cities throughout the Midwest, where they gradually became integrated into the mainstream community (Parrillo, 1994a).

The largest wave of Muslim immigrants arrived only in the past decade, primarily from Pakistan and Iran, and is concentrated in large cities such as New York, Chicago, and Los Angeles, where there is a supportive ethnic enclave. As noted earlier, depending on the skills with which they came, some will find professional employment and others entry-level jobs. In New Jersey, for example, well-educated Pakistanis are employed in the pharmaceutical industry, but their working-class counterparts have found an economic niche in gas station franchises, where it is not uncommon for a man pumping gas to be wearing a turban.

In addition to increased immigration and relatively high fertility, the American Muslim community has grown through the conversion of several hundred thousand African Americans, including the political leader Malcolm X, the prizefighter Muhammad Ali, and the basketball star Kareem Abdul-Jabbar. The appeal of Islam lies in part in its very difference from the existing structures of dominance, offering a fresh

The newest, fastest growing religious minority in the United States are Muslims, followers of the Islamic faith. The great majority are non-Arabs from Pakistan, Iran, Egypt and more than two dozen other Asian, Middle-Eastern and African nations.

VINCENT N. PARRILLO

Global Ethnoviolence

Vincent N. Parrillo is professor and chair of the Department of Sociology at Wm. Paterson College of New Jersey. He is the author of Strangers to These Shores, *Fourth Edition, Allyn and Bacon, 1994, and of* Diversity in America, *Pine Forge Press, 1995, and co-author, with John Stimpson and Ardyth Stimpson, of* Contemporary Social Problems, *Third Edition, Allyn and Bacon, 1995.*

I was exposed to the richness of ethnic diversity early, growing up as third-generation, Italian/Irish-American and living near a Dutch-American neighborhood. My boyhood friends in Paterson, N.J., were a mix of Dutch, German, Italian, Irish, or Polish backgrounds. I also developed school friendships with African-American, English, Jewish, Lebanese, and Syrian classmates.

When I think of those boyhood experiences, I realize now that they enabled me to learn an important lesson: ethnicity is simply other people's humanity. Those differences in others, which some find a cause for concern or open hostility, enriched my life. It was more than the special foods, words, games, places, and sights, all of which were wonderful.

When I became a sociologist, race and ethnic relations became my specialty, probably as a natural extension of my life experiences. Whenever I teach, do research, write, or give public presentations, I use the sociological perspective to promote understanding and appreciation of cultural diversity. These insights were reinforced in 1993–4, when I lectured throughout Europe under the sponsorship of the United States Information Agency (USIA).

Knowing the positive side of intergroup relations makes me even more opposed to the negative side, particularly when it results in ethnoviolence, action taken against others as a result of racial or ethnic hatred. In my recent travels, questions about ethnoviolence were frequent, sparked by the senseless killing in Bosnia and vicious neo-Nazi attacks in Austria and Germany.

Ethnoviolence has been a global phenomenon for thousands of years. Throughout world history, we can find widespread examples of brutality against people because of their race, religion, or ethnic background. Today's violent episodes may be similar to those of the past, but that is hardly comfort for the victims or for a generation that considers itself more sophisticated and tolerant than earlier cohorts.

Religious and political issues are at the core of the conflicts between Catholics and Protestants in Northern Ireland, Jews and Muslims in the Middle East, and Hindus and Sikhs in India. Racism is a key element in the "genocide by ecocide" currently waged by several South American states against indigenous tribes as well as in violent episodes in western Canada and in the 1992 Los Angeles riot. Economic fears and xenophobia in 1992 in Germany triggered over 1,800 attacks on foreigners and 17 deaths. Elsewhere, the Hutu in Rwanda, the Tamils in Sri Lanka, and the Ixil in Guatemala have all recently suffered brutality at the hands of ethnically different dominant groups.

Whether perpetrator or victim of the ethnoviolence, each group believes its situation is unique, but when we gather data about all these so-called isolated incidents, we have a basis for determining their prevalence and trends over a period of time. Next, sociological analysis enables us to identify cross-cultural similarities and patterns.

In many ways, ethnoviolence is like an active volcano. Neither type of eruption is inevitable, but occurs as a result of a set of preexisting conditions. Sociologists can measure past patterns of human activity not readily observable by most people and predict the probability of certain outcomes, although not with the time-line accuracy of a geologist predicting a volcanic eruption.

In the case of the volcano, we can do little against the powers of nature. In the case of ethnoviolence, however, knowledge is power. If we know the pre-existing conditions that trigger attacks, we may be able to prevent it or, if it happens, we may be able to prevent or contain them.

At the very heart of the issue is the perception of other people as "different." Well, we are different. We are not all the same. We don't really "melt" into one people. We can never eliminate the differences. The task is not to make us all the same but to understand our commonalities and at the same time to appreciate the diversity that enriches us as a society. Ethnicity is, as I said earlier, other people's humanity. Until "we" replaces "us vs them," hate and ethnoviolence will persist.

line of departure for rebuilding African-American communities. Islam also demands a high level of personal and sexual discipline, akin to the Protestant work ethic that underlies our cultural emphasis on achievement through self-control.

THE EMERGING AMERICAN MOSAIC

All American minorities have experienced some degree of prejudice, discrimination, and segregation, with varying levels of success in overcoming barriers to upward mobility. Periodically, the public has been aroused by fears that these "strangers" would soon outnumber white, native-born Americans and destroy our unique culture. Today is another such period in American history, when xenophobia has erupted in a wave of anti-immigrant sentiments and actions, although the nation is in many ways *less* culturally diverse than in several earlier periods (Parrillo, 1994b).

Multiculturalism brings together people representing many traditions, religions, and racial types.

These fears are grounded in the prospect of major population changes in the United States, in transition from a society dominated by whites and shaped by Western culture to a society in which a majority may not be white or European in origin (O'Hare, 1992). This is what is meant by **multiculturalism,** the bringing together of peoples representing many traditions, religions, and racial types. Your school has a more diverse student body today than ever before, and your neighborhood and workplace will also be less homogeneous in the future. Your children will play with friends from a number of cultures. Indeed, because fertility rates among white native-born Americans have fallen so low for so long, the new immigrants will be the major source of new Americans for our schools and workplaces.

Although many Americans lament the declining dominance of Western culture in our schools and our lives, others celebrate the diversity of the "new mosaic" as the realization of the American ideal of tolerance and personal freedom. In a mosaic, each piece retains its unique color and shape as it contributes to a larger picture. Is this the death of Western civilization or the revitalization of the nation? Will the United States become a model for the rest of the world in the twenty-first century when all countries will be linked by the continual movement of populations and trade and ideas? Can the United States avoid major intergroup conflict? In large part, the answers are up to your generation; you will decide whether to welcome diversity or resist it by demanding rapid acculturation. Welcome to the twenty-first century!

SUMMARY

1. Race, religion, and ethnicity are ascribed characteristics that influence the placement of individuals and groups in stratification hierarchies.

2. Minority groups are defined in contrast to the dominant elites in terms of control over societal resources and ability to establish standards of beauty and worth.

3. Minority group status is characterized by visible, ascribed traits, differential treatment, organization of self-image around this identity and awareness of shared fate with similar others.

4. Race, religion, and ethnicity are social constructions that affect how people are perceived and treated. Major differences among minority groups or between dominant and minority groups are cultural rather than biological in origin.

5. Barriers to entering mainstream institutions vary with how closely minority group members resemble the dominant group in appearance and customs, the job skills they bring with them, and the state of the economy.

6. Models of minority group intregration in the United states range from the melting-pot ideal of erasing differences to the cultural pluralist vision of emphasizing diversity.

7. Minority groups are integrated into the mainstream along a continuum from segregation to amalgamation through intermarriage.

8. Obstacles to integration include individual responses such as prejudice and discrimination, as well as the institutionalized patterns of racism built into the structure of economic and political life.

9. Discrimination and institutionalized racism have negative outcomes for both minority and dominant groups and for social solidarity in general.

10. The United States is a society of immigrants. Whereas the majority have come from Europe, the most recent waves are from Central America, Asia, and the Middle East.

11. Racial minorities have met the greatest resistance to integration, from the slaughter of Native Americans, through slavery, to residential isolation today.

12. The history of each racial and ethnic minority in the United States is unique, due largely to its

time of arrival and the type of community developed in this country.

13. Religion is another ascribed status with stratification outcomes, not only between religions but within each depending on time of arrival and economic success.

14. The United States is in transition from a society in which whites of European descent are a majority to one that will be less white and more ethnically diverse.

15. The prospect of change has aroused xenophobic reaction among many Americans, while others perceive diversity as a dynamic and creative force.

SUGGESTED READINGS

Barakat, Halim. *The Arab World: Society, Culture, and State.* Berkeley: University of California Press, 1993. This wide-ranging examination of Arab society and culture offers a unique opportunity to learn about the Arab world from an Arab point of view.

Fraser, Angus. *The Gypsies.* Oxford: Blackwell, 1992. A valuable interpretation of current thought and research on a population that has fragmented into a number of different ethnic groups. Included is an analysis of current racial prejudice against Gypsies in postcommunist Europe.

Gold, Stephen J. *Refugee Communities: A Comparative Field Study.* Newbury Park, CA: Sage, 1992. This book provides insight into the largest refugee populations currently entering the United States.

Halbwachs, Maurice. *On Collective Memory.* (Edited and translated by Lewis A. Coser.) Chicago: University of Chicago Press, 1992. This book deals with the representation of the past, specifically with the concept of "collective memory," a term that Halbwachs developed and that has generated a considerable recent interest.

Helmreich, William B. *Against All Odds: Holocaust Survivors and the Successful Lives They Made in America.* New York: Simon and Shuster, 1992. A moving ethnographic exploration of the way Holocaust survivors have dealt with their experience and proceeded to construct new successful lives in the aftermath of this horrible tragedy.

Hill, Herbert, and James E. Jones, Jr. (eds.) *Race in America: The Struggle for Equality.* Madison, WI: University of Wisconsin Press, 1993. Original essays on the current status of race relations in the United States from a number of contemporary sociologists.

Jhally, Sut, and Justin Lewis. *Enlightened Racism: The Cosby Show, Audiences, and the Myth of the American Dream.* Boulder, CO: Westview Press, 1992. An examination of television's influence on racial stereotyping, media images, and their effect on patterns of thinking.

Knouse, Stephen B., Paul Rosenfeld, and Amy L. Culbertson. *Hispanics in the Workplace.* Newbury Park, CA: Sage, 1992. A compilation of articles focusing on Latinos and employment, including discrimination, job stress, and career mobility.

Leonard, Karen I. *Making Ethnic Choices: California's Punjabi-Mexican Americans.* Philadelphia: Temple University Press, 1992. A case study of the Punjabi-Mexican families of California and the ethnic choices these multi-ethnic people confront in all phases of life.

Levine, Hillel, and Lawrence Harmon. *The Death of an American Jewish Community.* New York: Free Press, 1992. A compelling book documenting the "changing" of a neighborhood and the relationship between Jews and blacks in the Northeastern United States.

Massey, Douglas S., and Nancy A. Denton. *American Apartheid: Segregation and the Making of the Underclass.* Cambridge, MA: Harvard University Press, 1993. Essential reading for those interested in the causes, and possible cures, of urban poverty.

Parrillo, Vincent N. *Strangers to These Shores: Race and Ethnic Relations in the United States.* 4th ed. New York: Macmillan, 1994. An excellent account of the experiences of the major racial and ethnic groups in the United States, including the older and newer European groups, Native Americans, African Americans, Hispanics, Asian immigrants, and Near Easterners.

Spickard, Paul R. *Mixed Blood: Intermarriage and Ethnic Identity in Twentieth-Century America.* Madison: University of Wisconsin Press, 1991. A comparative study of the intermarriage patterns of Jewish, Japanese, and African Americans, including variations in the strength of pluralism and integration.

12

Courtship, Marriage, and Family

he condition of American families became an issue in the presidential election of 1992. Conservative politicians, led by Vice President Dan Quayle and his wife, Marilyn, claimed that much of what was wrong with America was a product of "liberal permissiveness" that destroyed the "traditional family," by which they meant the 1950s version as depicted in the TV show "Father Knows Best." The former Vice President cited the TV series *Murphy Brown*, as an example of media glorification of single parenthood and male irresponsibility. The basic assumption in this view is that there is a natural, moral form of family that has been destroyed by welfare and feminism.

In this chapter, we place the American family in a cross-cultural and historical context and examine its interface with other institutional spheres, then and now. From a sociological perspective, the family system of any society must be viewed as *a set of socially constructed norms and behaviors essential to the survival of individuals and groups.* These rules and roles regulate the conduct of courtship, the selection of marriage partners, relationships among family members, inheritance of property, and the circumstances under which a marriage can be ended.

We open the chapter with an examination of the origins of family systems and their variations across cultures and time. The second part of the chapter focuses on the contemporary American scene and the strengths and weaknesses of various family structures. Then, perhaps, you can answer some of the questions raised by Dan Quayle: Has the system broken down? What is the proper role of public policy? How do trends in the broader society affect family life? Have all of the changes had negative consequences for collective and personal well-being?

BASES OF THE FAMILY

Every human group must solve these problems: controlling sexuality, pairing people off for reproduction, and meeting needs for intimacy and care. The norms designed to solve these problems constitute that society's **family system.** The precise details of such rules are as varied as human culture itself, reflecting the group's particular history, but all serve the same function of adapting sexual impulse to collective goals. Family life, therefore, is not a biological given but a social construction.

> The **family system** reflects society's solutions to certain basic issues such as controlling sexuality and pairing people off for reproduction.

Despite considerable family diversity, many politicians continue to glorify the one-breadwinner family such as the one depicted in "Father Knows Best." In contrast, programs featuring single parents such as Murphy Brown are criticized for exemplifying much of what is wrong with the United States today and representing media glorification of single parenthood and male irresponsibility. As you read this chapter think about the various forms of American families and evaluate the advantages and limitations of each.

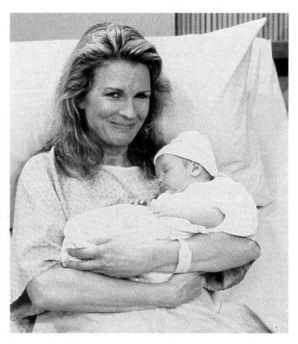

The human family differs from that of primates because of the unique qualities of culture: language, foresight, self-control, and the ability to plan collectively. Relatively permanent relationships between adult females and males are possible only when attraction is based on more than immediate sexual gratification. It is likely, therefore, that the first and most powerful set of norms were those that directed sexual attraction into socially productive patterns.

Functional Explanations

INCEST TABOOS.   The social control of sexual impulses is accomplished through rules that specify (1) who can legitimately have sexual intercourse with whom and (2) who can marry whom. The **incest taboo** prohibits sexual contact among people defined as relatives, typically between parents and children, and between brothers and sisters, although there are rare exceptions. The taboo is found in all societies, although who is included as "family" varies widely, from only a few close blood relatives to everyone remotely related. As cultural constructions, the taboos are often elaborate and arbitrary, but the goal is always the same: to regulate sexuality and reduce conflict within and between families.

> The **incest taboo** forbids sexual relations between people defined as relatives.
>
> The **rule of reciprocity** obligates the receiver of a gift to return something of equivalent value.
>
> The **principle of legitimacy,** or social fatherhood, identifies one man as responsible for the protection of a woman and her children and for placement in the social system.

The taboo is also the foundation of group survival. By forbidding sexual relations within the family, the taboo forces sons and daughters to marry *outside* the set of blood relations. This produces alliances between one family and another, so that ties of kinship and duty replace potential hostility, and the society as a whole is strengthened. Although it was not known scientifically until the mid-nineteenth century, marrying outside the blood line also reduces the likelihood of mental and physical defects among newborns.

There is a sense, then, in which the 1960s bumper sticker "Make Love, Not War" represents one of the earliest and most important human insights: It is better to establish ties of mutual obligation than to create enemies.

EXCHANGE FACTORS.   Anthropologists have suggested that the exchange of brides and grooms is the original *social bond,* linking individuals and families into enduring systems (Mauss, 1925/1967; Levi-Strauss 1969). Underlying all relationships is the **rule of reciprocity:** To receive a gift is to be obligated to return something of equivalent value—from the gift of a bride or groom to all the other presents and exchanges that accompany a marriage and bind individuals and families to one another and to the larger community.

THE PRINCIPLE OF LEGITIMACY.   Another basis for marriage and family systems is the **principle of legitimacy,** whereby one man is socially designated as responsible for the protection of a given woman and her children (Malinowski, 1929/1964). This is necessary in societies where social status is ascribed and where the father's position determines the social placement of his children. Note that the "father" does not have to be the biological parent. What is important is that there be a *social father* who assumes responsibility for the family unit.

Conflict Explanations

From a functional perspective, the incest taboo, exchanges of brides and grooms, and the concept of social fatherhood all serve to strengthen the collectivity while meeting individual needs. The conflict model goes one step further and asks: Who benefits from these arrangements? The clear answer is family heads, kinship groups, and men in general.

Incest taboos are often manipulated to enhance family power and to protect property rights. For example, exceptions to the taboo—as in brother-sister marriage in ancient Egypt or cross-cousin marriages through much of the Muslim world today—are designed to keep family property intact.

The exchange of marriage partners among kinship groups is a power game played by family elders who "give away" sisters and daughters for their own benefit, reinforcing men's control over female members of the family.

Similarly, the concept of social fatherhood reflects the greater power of men over women. Legitimacy ceases to be important precisely in those societies or strata where fathers cannot transmit resources to offspring. Thus, high rates of illegitimacy will occur among the poor in any society and in entire societies whose culture has been destroyed by outside forces—not because the people are less moral, but because legitimacy confers no advantages.

KINSHIP IN CROSS-CULTURAL PERSPECTIVE

Kinship, or family-based relationships, is the central organizing principle in most nonindustrial societies. The particular kinship system of any society varies along five dimensions: how many marriage partners (spouses) are permitted at one time; who can marry whom; how descent and inheritance are determined;

Family systems and marriage ceremonies represent socially constructed norms and behaviors necessary for the continuity of groups. This neotraditional wedding ceremony combines elements of Christianity and traditional Algonquin culture. As the bride and groom exchange vows, can you identify the traditional elements in the ceremony?

where the couple lives; and the power relationships within the family. The major differences between traditional (preindustrial) and modern societies are shown in Table 12-1.

These variables, along with rules governing courtship, child rearing, divorce, and widowhood constitute the family system of a society, and no two are exactly alike. The only common thread in prein-

dustrial societies is the protection of the interests of the kinship group.

In all societies, marriage involves a public ritual because the collectivity as a whole has a stake in marital stability and orderly reproduction. For most people throughout human history, marriage has been a family affair rather than a personal commitment. Many of you have grandparents whose marriage was arranged

TABLE 12-1   Kinship in Cross-Cultural Perspective

	Traditional Societies	Modern Societies
Number of spouses at one time	One (**monogamy**) or plural (**polygamy**) **Polygyny**—two or more wives **Polyandry**—two or more husbands	One (**monogamy**)
Choice of spouse	Choices made by parents to enhance family power	Relatively free choice
Line of descent (inheritance)	From males (**patrilineal**) From females (**matrilineal**)	Both equally (**bilateral kinship**)
Couple's home	With groom's family (**patrilocal**) With bride's family (**matrilocal**)	Place of one's own (**neolocal**)
Power relationships	Various degrees of male dominance (**patriarchy**)	Greater equality (**egalitarian**)
Functions of family	All-embracing, to protect the kinship group as a whole	Specialized to provide a stable environment for child rearing and emotional support
Structure	Extended	Nuclear
Focus of obligation	Blood relationships	Marriage tie and children

by family elders, and this remains the pattern in most societies today. Only with industrialization does mate selection become solely a matter of personal choice, as we will discuss later in this chapter.

THE FAMILY IN HISTORICAL CONTEXT

Extended Family Systems

The kinship, or descent, group that so dominates the needs or interests of its members is referred to as an **extended family**—a large unit composed of several related households. Most often, the extended family consists of a father, his sons, and their families. In some societies, the unit consists of a mother, her brother, and her daughters, and their families. Other relatives are added as circumstances dictate. Another type of extended family is created by **polygamy,** where a man or woman has more than one spouse, all of whom share a household with their children.

The extended family provides many benefits:

The **extended family** is a relatively large unit composed of several related households, most often involving three or more generations.

Polygamy creates extended households composed of a woman or man with more than one marriage partner at the same time.

The **nuclear family** is a unit composed of a married couple and their dependant children.

shared wealth and power; a supply of brides and grooms to exchange with other families; and protection and care for its members. Most importantly, the extended family is an economic unit, producing and distributing its own resources. Before the rise of the modern state with its public provisions for educating the young, protecting property, and caring for the elderly, the extended family was the only source of support for its members, which explains its great power over the individual.

Nuclear Families

A **nuclear family** is a unit composed of a married couple and their dependent children. Nuclear units are more or less closely linked to one another in the kinship group. The major distinction is not extended *versus* nuclear family systems, but the degree to which nuclear units in the same kinship line share residence, resources, work, and a sense of responsibility for one another.

Because extended families are typical of nonindustrial societies and rural regions of industrial nations, they are considered *traditional,* in contrast to the independent nuclear units of *modern* societies. Yet, not all families in the past or in preindustrial societies were extended; in fact, nuclear families were quite common throughout Europe by the seventeenth century (Lee, 1987). At the same time, extended kinship groups supported family members in the transition to industrial labor (Lavely, 1990).

Similarly, today, in countries undergoing the transition from agriculture to industry, urban households

Although found mostly in Third World countries, polygamous families have existed in the United States, especially among Mormons. While the Mormon church officially abandoned polygyny a century ago, fundamentalist Mormons have pursued the practice in small towns like Big Water, Utah where the town's mayor lives with his nine wives and twenty children. As state law enforcement officers have adopted a policy of "live and let live," more polygamous families have gone public.

SOCIOLOGY AROUND THE WORLD

What is a Family?

Almost every characteristic that we think of as essential to defining family has at least one cross-cultural exception. Here are just two examples from the anthropological literature (Nanda, 1984):

■ The Nayar of South India represent the most fascinating challenge to the ideal of marriage as the essential basis of the family. Among the Nayar the basic family unit consists of a woman's sons and daughters and their children, who live together in the household of her brother, their uncle. At some point before puberty, a Nayar girl will take part in a ceremony whereby she is "married" to a man, but they never live together and need not have sexual relations. She is then free to take additional "visiting husbands," preferably of higher social rank, one of whom will officially become the father of her children. Responsibility for raising the children and caring for the mother belong to her blood family.

What possible function can these patterns serve? The kin-based family of daughters is well suited to the type of agriculture practiced by the Nayar, and the men are free to pursue their traditional careers in the military, which takes them away from the village for long periods. Rather than be home alone, the wife has the company of her kin.

■ The Nyakyusa of Southeastern Africa deal with the temptations of incest and intergenerational hostility by creating age villages. At age ten, a group of boys will build their own set of huts at the edge of the settlement where they will grow up together and bring their wives to live. Why is this isolation of father and son so necessary? Because the Nyakyusa also practice polygyny, a young man is a potential lover of one of his father's younger wives. Under these circumstances, fathers are fearful and jealous of their sons, so that the age villages are a means of reducing tensions within the kinship group and the society as a whole.

Thus, what might seem to us to be "unnatural" customs are actually quite functional. Had you been born a Nayar or a Nyakyusa, you would accept these patterns as the only correct and natural way to behave, and wonder at the strange ways of Americans, with only one husband or wife and forced to live alone together!

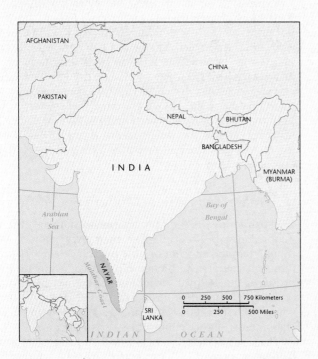

expand or contract in response to economic necessity. In Mexico, for example, several extended families will share a single household or adjoining homes so that earnings can be pooled and child care provided while some find work and others are unemployed (Selby et al., 1990).

The Family in American History

As helpful as the extended family is in the early phases of industrialization, it has never been the dominant form in the United States. There was no golden age in American history when most people spent most of their life in a three-generation household. The typical pattern was the nuclear unit joined for a few years by a widowed grandparent but rarely containing other relatives (Coontz, 1992).

Furthermore, no evidence exists to indicate that past generations of parents and children wished to live together any more than they do today. As noted in Chapter 7, relationships between parents and children have always been marked by fear, jealousy, and hostility. In American history, for over two centuries, young people could "go west," and so they did, leaving kin far behind.

And although we tend to picture immigrants as arriving in extended families, with white-haired grandfathers and grandmothers in babushkas, the vast majority were single young adults who established families only after settling in the United States. Many of these families became extended when adult children remained in the parental household because they could not yet afford their own home. As soon as they could, the children of immigrants established nuclear households. In other words, most extended-family households in America have been temporary adjustments to economic realities and not a matter of cultural preference.

> The **romantic love syndrome** involves the selection of a mate on the basis of love rather than on kin-based needs.

This is still the case among the very poor, and especially among African Americans who have coped with economic disadvantage with extended households for the past 125 years (Morgan et al., 1993).

From Traditional to Modern

People who live in industrial societies come to share certain "modern" attitudes about individual rights and family obligations and the balance between the two. The crucial distinction between traditional and modern concerns the primary focus of duty: Is it to the blood line of kin or to one's marriage partner? What makes a family modern is not its structural isolation but its shift of sentiment inward to the nuclear unit. For example, if you were to receive two messages at the same time, one reporting the serious illness of your father and the other an accident to your spouse, to which hospital would you go? In most traditional societies, you would be at the bedside of your father.

Industrialization erodes the power of elders. Young people move from villages to the city, they become educated, choose their jobs, live on their own, select their partners, and have smaller families. When young men and women can make their own way in society and no longer depend on parents and kin, they come to value personal freedom over obligation to the extended family.

THE MODERN FAMILY

The transition from traditional to modern involves a shift in dependency from the kinship group to the broader society. Tasks once performed by the extended family are now handled outside the family. In the *economic* sphere, families are no longer self-sufficient, but depend on the wages of the one or two adults who work outside the home. The Industrial Revolution dramatically changed the relationship between home and workplace (the two become physically and emotionally separate) and changed the relationships among family members. The modern family became a consuming rather than producing unit, and in many households, women and children lost their economic value and became totally dependent on the earnings of the male worker.

The challenges of modern life created a need for intimacy and affection that cannot be easily met by relatives with whom one has relationships of unequal power. Thus, the modern family became specialized for emotional support and the early socialization of children, that is, for the gratification of expressive rather than instrumental needs.

Expressive needs are best met through intimacy with a few chosen friends and lovers—hence, the importance of mate selection, no longer for kin-based goals but for personal well-being. The **romantic love syndrome** became the modern basis for choosing a marriage partner (Goode, 1959). Although romance and strong sexual attraction were always possible in a traditional marriage, they were rarely the sole or even primary basis for mate selection. In a modern society, however, love is the only socially approved grounds for choosing a marriage partner, however risky the outcome.

Mate Selection in Modern Society

If romantic love is the only legitimate standard, then people must be free to make their own choice. Although parents may not be able to arrange a marriage, they can exert an influence directly (by signs of approval or disapproval) or indirectly (by moving to another area). But the burden of choice rests on the young people themselves, and each generation has elaborated a set of dating rituals to assist them.

These rituals usually begin with a form of group dating, a convoy of protective friends, gradually changing into smaller groups as the young people mature and become more comfortable with the dating situation. As in simple societies, the relationship is marked by gift exchanges that draw the couple closer together. Up to the formal engagement, there is still time to be released from the relationship, but once the public announcement is made, family, friends, and the world at large are witnesses to the intention to marry. Larger and more expensive gifts are exchanged, no longer between the couple, but from outside, progressively bringing the weight of the community to bear. Notice how difficult it now becomes to withdraw from the commitment, to face other people, return all the gifts!

> All courtship systems are market or exchange systems. They differ from one another with respect to who does the buying and selling, which characteristics are more or less valuable in that market, and how open or explicit the bargaining is.
>
> —WILLIAM J. GOODE, 1963, P. 8

Although you are theoretically free to marry anyone, your actual selection is limited to the people you are likely to meet and whom you can confidently bring home to dinner or introduce to your friends. These factors automatically exclude all but a small "pool of eligibles"—people likely to be very similar to you in terms of social background and physical attractiveness (Stevens et al., 1990). The tendency to select

An example of a homogamous marriage market exists in India. This young man and woman, both members of the Brahmin caste, celebrate their marriage. What American institutions function to reinforce homogamy in mate selection?

a mate of the same race, religion, social class, ethnicity, educational level, and age as yourself is called **homogamy** (*homo,* meaning "similar"; *gamy,* meaning "marriage"). People similar to oneself are easy to be with. You begin with a set of shared values and attitudes as a result of similar socialization experiences, reducing the likelihood of disagreement and misunderstanding (Kalmijn, 1994b). In addition, people who agree with us are very rewarding to be with because they reinforce our own sense of rightness. Haven't you noticed that people who agree with you are so much nicer and smarter than those who do not?

But modern societies provide expanded opportunities to meet people from different social backgrounds and geographic areas—at school, in the armed forces, the workplace, singles bars, personal advertisements, and video dating services. As a result, an increasing proportion of American marriages are **heterogamous** (*hetero,* meaning "different") in terms of race, religion, ethnicity, and social class. At the same time, age and educational level are becoming more alike. The great benefit of heterogamy is that it exposes partners to other ways of doing and thinking, adding an element of variety and challenge to the relationship.

Regarding the various dimensions of homogamy, the trend over recent decades indicates that achieved characteristics such as education and employment status are more important than ascribed traits such as religion and social class (Kalmijn, 1991a, 1991b; Stevens, 1991). That is, brides and grooms today are more likely to have the same educational characteristics than to share religious and/or family background (Quian and Preston, 1993).

> **Homogamy** is the practice of selecting a mate with similar social background characteristics.
>
> **Heterogamy** is the practice of selecting a mate with different social background characteristics.

One ascribed barrier remains almost insurmountable: race. It is true that the percentage of interracial marriages in the United States has almost doubled since the late 1970s. However, when you start with a very small number—1.2 percent of all American marriages in 1980—any addition will be an enormous percentage increase. Thus, the 2.2 percent of all marriages in 1992 is an increase of 83 percent but still represents a very small number of couples, most of which involve an Asian-American partner. Marriages between white and African-American couples remain a statistical rarity: one-half of 1 percent of all marriages in 1992 (U.S. Bureau of the Census, P20-468, 1993).

How stable are heterogamous unions? The data are not altogether clear because so many dimensions are involved. Apperently, however, interracial couples, especially when one spouse is African American and the other is white, experience extra stress from a vari-

SOCIAL CHANGE

Loving Versus American Apartheid

Fittingly, an interracial couple named Loving were the focus of the Supreme Court case ending laws against *miscegenation* (racial mixing). In 1958, Virginia police broke into the Loving's home and arrested them for unlawfully living together, even though the couple had a valid marriage certificate from the District of Columbia. The local judge sentenced the Lovings to a year in prison but offered to suspend it if they agreed never to live as man and wife in Virginia for the next 25 years.

The Lovings left for a few years, before returning to challenge the Virginia law in court. Finally, in 1967, not long before many of you were born, the Supreme Court of the United States unanimously struck down anti-miscegenation statutes in Virginia and 15 other states. Thus, 104 years after the Emancipation Proclamation, African Americans and other racial minorities received equal protection of the laws in marriage choice, and one more vestige of slavery was erased (Margolick, 1992).

ety of sources: unaccepting parents and friends, the public in general, and the effects of other background differences. Religious intermarriage is also relatively unstable, with about one in three such unions ending in divorce within five years (Lehrer and Chiswick, 1992). Divorce rates are also high for marriages between liberal and very conservative Protestants. Clearly, lack of agreement on fundamental values and beliefs can be very destructive of an intimate relationship.

THE MARRIAGE MARKET. When marriages are not arranged, people must make the best bargains they can. The word *bargain* is intentional, because the modern process of mate selection has many features of a marketplace in which sellers advertise their valuable qualities and buyers seek the best trade. A person's value on the market is determined by possessing qualities desired by others. A woman's youth and beauty are traits most desired by men, while women look for occupational potential in men. This means that, over time, her market value will decline, while his is likely to increase.

Social class is also an important determinant of market value. Although most Americans marry within the same stratum, men can "marry down" because their achieved statuses determine the couple's location in the stratification system. A woman is urged to marry at the same level as her father or at a higher one (Schoen et al., 1989); marrying down is form of "social death." Those of you with a sibling of the opposite sex may remember your parents' reaction to your telling them you just met a very nice guy/girl. Our guess is that the daughter was asked "Where does he live, dear?," a subtle probe for social class location, whereas the son was asked, "What does she look like?"

From a functional perspective, the market represents a mutually beneficial exchange whereby a woman receives economic support and social rank in return for emotional services, home maintenance, and child production. But from the conflict perspective, as long as women and men have different levels

of social power, the exchange is not entirely fair. Men have a wider range of choice, do not lose market value with age, and retain independence outside the home. Conversely, women have fewer options, lose their market value over time, and will often remain in an unsatisfying relationship rather than risk reentry into an unfavorable mate market (England and Kilbourne, 1989).

The marriage market is also affected by the number of eligibles in a particular geographic area. For example, in American history, a shortage of nonmarried women in the Western states meant not only that many men never married but that those who did often chose women older than themselves or married into Native American families. Today, the shortage of eligibles is most acute for women of color (Fosset and Kiecolt, 1991; South and Lloyd, 1992). In many local African-American marriage markets, young women far outnumber young men as a result of many factors: military enlistment, long-distance job searches, and relatively high rates of suicide, homicide, and imprisonment. For every three unmarried African-American women in their 20s, there is only one unmarried man with earnings above the poverty level (Lichter et al., 1992). As a result, African-American women are less likely to be married than their nonblack age peers.

Age at First Marriage. As a consequence of several trends over the past few decades, American women of all races and social strata are delaying marriage. Many choose to complete their educations, others are preparing for demanding careers, and a majority simply enjoy independent living. American men also show a disinclination to marry at an early age, for many of the same reasons (Gerson, 1993). Evidence also indicates that young women have become more egalitarian in their views of family life than have young men, which means that it will take longer for women and men to find a compatible partner (Goldscheider and Goldscheider, 1992).

As a result, median age at first marriage in the United States has risen steadily from a low in the

1950s of 20 years for women and 22 for men to an all-time high in 1993 of 26.5 years for men and 24.5 for women. As shown in Figure 12-1, age at first marriage today is higher than it was 100 years ago, when men could not marry until they could support a family. This is a major change in individual lives and in societal patterns of family formation.

Because the search for an appropriate mate takes longer and as the pool of eligibles becomes smaller, more women than in the recent past may never marry: possibly 25 percent of African-American women and more than 10 percent of their white age peers, double the proportions of never-married women in earlier cohorts (U.S. Bureau of the Census P23-180, 1992; Lichter, 1990). Remember, however, that the period between 1947 and 1967 was most unusual for its low age at first marriage, high fertility, and very high marriage rate—almost 96 percent of all Americans! Before then, one or more adult children remained unmarried to take care of an elderly parent or because they could not afford to support a household.

EGALITARIANISM.   The modern family is also characterized by **egalitarianism,** the reduction of power differences between husband and wife and between parents and children.

HUSBANDS AND WIVES.   Equality within the marriage, however, is possible only when partners have similar resources, and as you saw in Chapter 10, male dominance is the rule, especially in agricultural societies. Women's power in marriage is highest in gathering bands, where all resources are shared, and also in matrilineal, matrilocal societies where she can remain among her kinfolk (Warner et al., 1986). In modern industrial society, egalitarian relationships are again possible, as men and women seek affection and emotional support in marriage—feelings that are more likely to flow from mutual respect among equals than from fear or duty.

PARENTS AND CHILDREN.   Relationships between parents and children are more egalitarian than in the past for both material and ideological reasons. Material conditions include the dramatic decline in infant mortality, sharply lower fertility rates, and reduced need for child labor. As a result, children come to be valued for their expressive contributions rather than as economic assets or potential pawns in the marriage game. Parents have fewer children but invest more emotional resources in each child.

As the ascriptive bases of stratification are weakened, the power of parents to command respect and obedience is diminished. Intergenerational affection can no longer be demanded; it must be earned, and this requires a more egalitarian relationship than was possible or necessary in the past.

> **Egalitarianism** refers to reduced power differences between husbands and wives and between parents and children.

THE FAMILY CYCLE.   As detailed in Chapter 7, the timing of family events has changed greatly during this century. In 1900, for example, marriage followed a rather long courtship until the husband-to-be could support a family. Despite the long wait, both man and woman entered marriage with limited sexual experience. The typical couple had four children, and

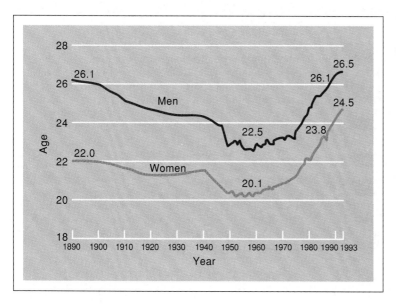

Figure 12-1   Median age at first marriage, 1890–1993 by sex.

Source: U.S. Bureau of the Census, P20-478, 1994.

The childbearing part of the family cycle for most American couples today consists of two children fairly close in age. Why is this so?

TABLE 12-2 Household Composition, United States, 1970–2000 (percentage)

	1970	1990	2000
Family households	**81.2**	**70.9**	**68.2**
Married couple with children	40.3	26.3	23.5
Married couple no children	30.3	29.8	29.2
Other, with children	5.0	8.3	8.5
Other, without children	5.6	6.5	7.0
Nonfamily households	**18.8**	**29.2**	**31.8**
Men living alone	5.6	9.7	10.4
Women living alone	11.5	14.9	16.4
Other	1.7	4.6	5.0

Sources: U.S. Bureau of the Census, P23–181, 1992, p. 15; Dennis Ahlburg and Carol De Vita, "New Realities of the American Family," Population Bulletin 47, no. 2, 1992, p. 7.

by the time the youngest was ready to leave home, one parent had died.

Today, in contrast, people enter marriage after a short courtship and long history of sexual experience. A typical couple has two children, closely spaced, and the children are out on their own while the parents are in their early 50s. The dramatic increase in life expectancy since 1900 has added two decades to the parental life course,

> The **empty nest** stage of the family cycle occurs when all children are out of the house and the parents are alone together again.

creating an entirely new phase of the family cycle—the **empty nest** in which the parents are alone together again, except when the nest is temporarily refilled.

The effects of delayed marriage, low fertility, extended life expectancy, and current divorce rates are shown in Table 12-2. Compared to 1970, fewer households contain a *family*—technically, two or more per-

SOCIOLOGY IN EVERYDAY LIFE

Baby Boomerangs

As a young adult living away from home before marriage, many of you are part of a relatively new phenomenon in American life. Before 1945, few men and even fewer women in their early 20s left home to attend college, and only a small proportion had the economic resources for independent living. In the 1950s, however, postwar economic growth, the expansion of higher education, and the cultural emphasis on personal development all led to the expectation that young people would and *should* leave home as soon as possible, even if not yet economically independent. Between 1954 and 1974, the proportion of unmarried adult children living with their parents declined dramatically, especially in the middle class, and most particularly for sons.

The resulting "empty nest" has been hailed as a triumph of modern childrearing, the successful launching

of an independent young person, and the freeing of the parental couple for new forms of personal fulfillment. But many nests do not stay empty for long these days (Schnaiberg and Goldenberg, 1989). Since 1980, the proportion of American households with at least one adult unmarried offspring has increased steadily, so that by 1993, almost 60 percent of unmarried persons age 20–24 lived in the parental home—the same level as in 1954!

The most important factor appears to be money, or, more precisely, lack of it, and the return typically for a brief interlude between marriages or jobs. Interestingly, it is a *son* rather than a daughter who is most likely to remain at home or to return, largely because a mother will continue to provide food and laundry services to a son without expecting assistance in housework. Daughters are reluctant to return because they fear losing their recently won independence (Goldscheider and Goldscheider, 1994; South and Spitze, 1994).

sons related by blood, marriage, or adoption—and a higher proportion contain persons living alone or in nonfamily relationships. Among married couple families, a declining percentage contain a child. These trends are expected to continue into the next century but at a much slower pace than in the 1990s.

MODERN MARRIAGE: REWARDS AND RISKS

If one chooses one's own mate, marries for love and love alone, and is expected to provide emotional support in a relationship that could last five decades in the privacy of a nuclear household, can it be any wonder that many will fail? The relatively high divorce rates of modern society are the other side of the coin of free mate choice and the expressive functions of marriage today. At the same time, social surveys report high levels of satisfaction in marriage, largely because unhappy couples will have dissolved their union. Also, many people will find any marriage preferable to being unmarried.

Functional and Conflict Perspectives

Under the influence of the functional model, it was long assumed that "the family" was a unit of shared interests, in which husbands and wives performed complementary roles: *she* as keeper of the household, *he* as representative to the larger society. From a conflict perspective, however, value consensus and harmony of interests cannot be taken for granted (Curtis, 1986). Not only do wives and husbands have individual, often conflicting interests, but the nuclear household may not be well suited to a modern economy where both adults are in the labor force. Relatively isolated from kin, shielded from others by a veil of privacy, the modern nuclear household is an emotional hothouse, in which a variety of intense needs and feelings are concentrated on its very few members.

Under these circumstances, family roles are subject to *negotiation,* never fixed but continually being redefined. Our culture's idealized emphasis on romantic love has obscured the very real contests for control and self-definition within a marriage. Today, especially, given the major changes in women's lives, traditional expectations have lost much of their validity. But marriage partners still bring very different levels of power into their struggle to define the relationship (Ferree, 1990).

BENEFITS AND RISK FACTORS. In general, because of their higher income and alternative sources of esteem, men are thought to be *less* dependent than women on marriage for their physical and emotional well-being. One result is the common belief that men can do quite well without a family but that a woman's life would be empty and meaningless without a husband and children. In reality, however, as Durkheim noted over a century ago, marriage has benefits for both men and women.

In contrast to the nonmarried, married persons live longer, report higher levels of personal happiness, and are in better physical and mental health (Doherty and Campbell, 1988). Most research also suggests that these benefits are somewhat stronger for husbands than for wives, in the sense that nonmarried men are especially at risk of accidents, suicide, homicide victimization, poor health, and mental disorders. For women, such risks are more closely associated with low income than with marital status. These effects are also magnified by race, with nonmarried African-American men particularly vulnerable to mental disorders and early death (Williams et al., 1992).

Contrary to popular myth, then, marriage is most beneficial to men—at least in terms of life expectancy and mental health. Its major benefit for women is in the higher income enjoyed by married women. But marriage and parenthood can be especially stressful for mothers compared with fathers,

In many developing countries, poor families will sell their daughters to those who will pay. In this case, a ten-year-old Indian girl was sold by her father and forced to marry a sixty-year-old Saudi sheik. Here, she steps down from a police bus after being rescued by an Indian Airlines' hostess.

and even more so for women in low-wage jobs (Simon, 1992; Lennon and Rosenfield, 1992). Clearly, contemporary American marriage is the site of both conflict and reconciliation, personal fulfillment and role overload, stress and satisfaction. The same emotional closeness that promises the greatest rewards can also produce tension and hostility, as seen in the data on domestic (within-family) violence and on divorce and separation.

Violence in the Family

The very virtues of the modern family—its emphasis on personal fulfillment, privacy, and emotional bonding—have a darker side: people who are intensely dependent on one another are also very vulnerable. It is very difficult to measure the extent of family violence: participants do not easily admit it to themselves or willingly give this kind of information to an interviewer; and neighbors and friends are reluctant to inform authorities. Furthermore we cannot tell whether such violence has increased or decreased over time, because no comparable pre-1970 data exist.

One study comparing survey data from 1975 and the late 1980s found that in both time periods about 16 percent of American couples experienced at least one violent episode during the year, and two-thirds reported some act of physical punishment of children (usually slapping or spanking). Reports of severe punishment (beating, kicking, threatening with a weapon), however, declined from 14 to 11 percent (Straus and Gelles, 1989).

What has greatly increased is the research literature, spurred in part by the women's movement and

child rights advocates (Straus, 1992). This is another example of the process whereby private problems are transformed into a public issue (Loseke, 1992). Only when the experience is recognized as a matter of social concern can public resources be directed at finding causes and seeking solutions.

Although husbands and elderly parents are often targets of household violence, the most common and severely injured victims are wives and children (Brush, 1990). Family violence has more to do with *threats to authority* than with the personality of either abuser or victim, and is the outcome of factors at the levels of culture and social structure as well the interpersonal: the cultural equation of masculinity and physical aggression, the structural privacy of the nuclear household, and the effects of alienating labor and persistent poverty (Kurz, 1989; Kruttschnitt et al., 1994). Under these circumstances, it is not difficult to imagine how frustration and failure outside the home can be vented within its relative privacy. Despite claims that family violence crosses all class lines, it remains strongly associated with low educational and occupational status, early marriage, and unplanned pregnancy. Children in households with unplanned births are two to four times more likely to be abused than are children from homes with no unplanned offspring (Zuravin, 1991). Violence against a wife and children is also characteristic of families involved with organizations that demand absolute obedience, such as the military and extremely religious groups (Schmitt, 1994).

Does childhood abuse lead to violent behavior in adolescence and adulthood? Research suggests that the answer is "yes"—in violence toward parents as a teenager, in one's own marriage, and in various forms

Violence in families, particularly toward women, is a growing national concern.

of juvenile and adult criminality (Seltzer and Kalmus, 1988; Straus and Gimpel, 1992; Widom, 1992). The experience of childhood family violence is also associated with depression among people who experience stress as adults (Kessler and Magee, 1994).

Although comparable data are lacking, it is probably safe to assume that the United States outranks most other modern industrial societies in the rate of domestic abuse, as it does in other forms of interpersonal violence (see Chapter 17). One also assumes that family violence is lower in industrial than in nonindustrial societies, where women and children are especially powerless. In contemporary India, for example, where daughters are an economic drain on a family's resources, prospective grooms can demand as much dowery money, goods, and livestock as the bride's family can afford. A very high rate of "accidental" deaths of young wives then leaves the widowed husband free to contract a new marriage and receive many more gifts. Conversely, in Egypt today, the growing concern is the number of husbands "accidentally" killed by a wife. Under Islamic law, a man can divorce his wife by simply stating his intention; the wife cannot object because her testimony has no weight in religious courts. As a result, a woman who fears that her husband is about to leave her may choose to strike first.

DEALING WITH WIFE ABUSE.   Battering takes place in an emotional and financial context that often makes it difficult for victims to define their situations as intolerable (Fernandez et al., 1994). It is far easier to blame oneself for having caused the problem than to admit that the most important decision of your life was a horrible mistake. Think of the women you know who are in abusive relationships and the reasons they offer for remaining: "I really should stop nagging." "He's O.K. when he's not drunk." "He's really sorry afterward." "What are my choices?" However, women need not always remain as helpless victims; they can take charge of their lives and leave their abusers, as difficult as it is for most (Schwartz, 1986).

Increasingly, law enforcement personnel are being trained in the complexities of family violence, in contrast to the previous "hands-off" practice (Ferraro, 1989). Intervention, including arresting the abuser, appears to reduce future incidents of wife battering for men who already have a stake in conformity to community norms, namely those who are employed and married (Berk et al., 1992; Pate and Hamilton, 1992; Sherman et al.,1992). For the unemployed and unmarried, arrest only increased the likelihood of further attacks.

Divorce and Remarriage

Contrary to popular belief, although the divorce rate in the United States is at an historical high, it is *not* rising, and has not risen since the mid-1970s and even declined in 1993 as shown in Figure 12-2. An un-

Figure 12-2   Marriage and divorce rates per 1,000 population in the United States: 1930–1993.

Source: U.S. Department of Health and Human Services, *Monthly Vital Statistics Report*, Vol. 43, No. 1, 1994.

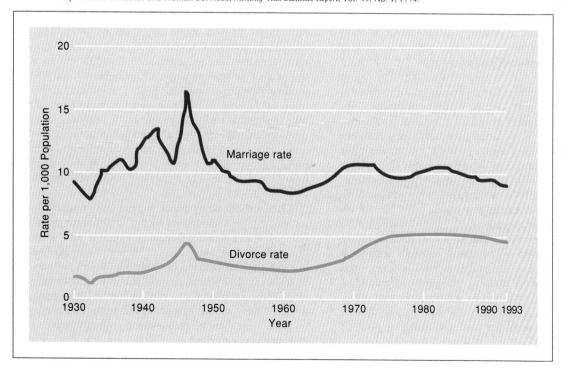

known number of marriages are also dissolved through separation and desertion, but these rates were probably higher in the past, when divorce was more difficult to obtain. The best current estimate is that less than half of all marriages and four of every ten first marriages today will eventually end in divorce (U.S. Bureau of the Census, P23-180, 1992). Although these numbers are higher than for other modern industrial societies, so also are American marriage rates.

Remember that a large proportion of marriages in the past were ended by the early death of one spouse (most often the wife), so that the average duration of a marriage has remained relatively stable throughout the twentieth century. However, the effects of divorce on the emotional well-being of offspring are stronger than the effects of parental death (Acock and Kiecolt, 1989; McLeod, 1991).

EXPLAINING DIVORCE RATES.   Since 1950, divorce rates have risen in all industrial societies. Divorce is an essential component of the romantic love syndrome and modern marriage market; the one is necessary to the other (Goode, 1993). If people choose a mate on the basis of sexual attraction, marry for emotional well-being, and expect personal fulfillment, what reason is there to remain in a relationship that provides none of the above and that may even be dangerous to mind and body? Any marriage system based on expressive needs rather than instrumental goals must provide a way out of unsatisfying unions.

Among the many characteristics of modernity that increase the likelihood of divorce are the high value attached to companionship in marriage, the uprooting that results from geographic and social mobility, and the ability of women to become self-supporting (Kitson and Holmes, 1992). In addition, as divorce becomes more common, it also becomes more acceptable, although not necessarily less stigmatizing as a sign of personal failure (Hopper, 1993).

RISK FACTORS.   In general, the probability of divorce is associated with young age at first marriage, unplanned and premarital pregnancy, limited education, low income, husband's unemployment, and residential moves (South and Spitze, 1986). Controlling for other variables, employed wives are more likely than nonemployed wives to leave an unsatisfying marriage. Whereas it was usually a husband who initiated divorce in the past, today it is women who file for divorce in six of ten cases (DeWitt, 1992).

Conversely, factors tending to preserve a marriage include participation in religious services and relatively late age at first marriage, which is associated with shared decision making, planned pregnancies, adequate income, completed education, and emotional maturity. It is precisely the rise in age at first marriage that accounts for the stabilizing of divorce rates since 1975.

Once a couple is married, the most powerful predictor of continued stability is, quite simply, the length of the marriage itself: The longer it lasts, the less likely it is to dissolve. The bulk of divorces occur in the first five years and, contrary to popular belief, there is no "second peak" once a couple reaches mid-life.

The presence of children, particularly older ones, does not appear to keep a troubled marriage together (Waite and Lillard, 1991). To the limited extent that young children reduce the likelihood of divorce, the effect is stronger for sons than daughters, because the father is more likely to be involved in shared activities with a son and therefore more closely linked to the nuclear family (Morgan et al., 1988; Schwartz, 1944).

In many cases, high levels of psychological stress appear to be more of a *consequence* than a cause of problems in the marriage and tend to diminish following the divorce especially for people in very troubled relationships (Booth and Amato, 1991; Aseltine and Kessler, 1993). And conflicts over appropriate gender-linked behavior are not a major cause of marital problems today (Kitson and Holmes, 1992). The single most commonly cited reason for divorce today is incompatibility—a clear signal that the goal of personal fulfillment remains paramount.

CONSEQUENCES OF MARITAL DISRUPTION.   Although it is a solution to many problems, the end of a marriage can have severe negative consequences, especially for women and children (Morgan, 1991; Furstenburg and Cherlin, 1991). For children, although it is often difficult to disentangle the effects of the divorce from those of the turmoil preceding the breakup and the financial problems that follow, lack of economic resources appear to be the most powerful (Booth and Amato, 1991; Wells and Rankin, 1991; Thompson et al., 1994). Evidence indicates that, compared with children living with both parents, those who live with one parent show more behavior problems, are less likely to complete high school, and are more likely to engage in juvenile delinquency (Free, 1991; McLanahan and Sandefur, 1994). In addition, women who spent part of their childhood in a single-parent family are themselves more likely than other women their age to marry early, have a premarital pregnancy, and ultimately experience divorce (Sandefur et al., 1992).

Children in one-parent homes are negatively affected by the parents' example, a sense of personal failure, lack of supervision, role overload of the custodial parent, and most of all, a lowered standard of living in a mother-headed household. However, living in an intact family where parents are continually fighting does little to enhance a child's mental and physical health. Many of the symptoms thought to be caused by the divorce are already present in response to family tension (Cherlin et al., 1991).

After Divorce: Who's Supporting the Kids

Following divorce, only 15 percent of former wives are warded *alimony* (personal support payments), and fewer than half receive the full amount, typically less than $5,000 a year. Divorced and separated women with children may also be eligible for *child support* payments from the absent father, but only half of eligible women are awarded anything, and only half of these receive the full amount. While the likelihood of support has increased slightly, its dollar value continues to decline.

Clearly, divorce and separation are an economic disaster for women and children; instant poverty for the youngest and least educated mothers. Some former husbands are themselves poor and unemployed, but the great majority have incomes at least twice the poverty level (Larson, 1992). Most fathers give no material assistance to their children other than support payments, but it is those already providing child support who also make other contributions (Teachman, 1991).

For children, the costs of divorce also include loss of contact with a father. In 1990, joint custody was awarded to only 7 percent of absent fathers, and visitation rights to 55 percent, not all of whom took advantage of the opportunity. The remaining 38 percent had no official role in the life of their children. Sixty percent of children of divorce see the nonresidential father less than once a month; only 23 percent see him at least once a week (Stephen et al., 1992).

At the interpretive level, absent fathers tend to view their failure to visit as a means of regaining control of the situation and striking back at the former wife, a regrettable outcome for future parent–child relations, but one that the fathers saw as essential to maintaining their self-respect (Arendell, 1993). Other fathers are engaged in an organized effort to win custody and visitation privileges against what they see as the vindictive acts of a bitter ex-wife and the bias of the courts. Both the fathers' rights movement and women's organizations working for enforcement of support decrees are attempting to sway public opinion with claims of acting in the best interests of the child, thus translating their private troubles into public issues (Coltrane and Hickman, 1992).

REMARRIAGE.   The great majority of divorced persons (and a small proportion of the widowed) will remarry. In 1994, four of every ten marriages in the United States were at least the second time around for one or both the participants. The younger the age at divorce, the more likely is remarriage. Remarriage rates for women are highest for the young and less educated and lowest for the older and more educated. At all ages, non-Hispanic whites are more likely to remarry than African Americans or Hispanics, and men are far more likely to remarry than are women. Not only do men have a larger pool of eligibles from which to select (e.g., younger, less-educated, or never-married women), but as mentioned, their value on the marriage market tends to increase throughout middle-age.

As in the case of first marriages, remarriage is more beneficial for men than for women in terms of mental and physical health and life expectancy. For women, remarriage typically brings immediate financial benefits; it is the major factor in raising a family above the poverty line. In comparison with first marriages, the probability of divorce after remarriage is somewhat higher, but this is largely due to the smaller pool from which a second or third mate can be chosen. More compromises must be made between one's ideal and what is available, with a higher risk of incompatibility. Although most Americans are willing to take such risks, preferring marriage to singleness, increasing proportions are choosing not to remarry, especially women with a satisfying career and adequate income (Gross, 1992). Predictions for the rest of this century are that the remarriage rate for divorced women will be lower than the 75 percent of earlier decades (U.S. Bureau of the Census, P23-180, 1992).

BLENDED FAMILIES.   Remarriage among parents creates a **blended family** that combines offspring from the previous marriage(s) and any from the new union. Although a mother's remarriage often lifts her children out of poverty, stepchildren are more likely than those living with both parents to be in a low-income household. This is so because both divorce and remarriage rates are highest among the relatively poor. Despite its potential for stress, the blended family does provide the advantages of a two-adult household.

> **Blended families** consist of a husband and wife, children of previous marriages, and any children from the new marital union.

Compared with two decades ago, American children today live in increasingly varied households, and over the course of childhood, they may experience several types of family life: from living with one's biological parents to being with one parent to joining a stepfamily. Although some critics see these trends in a purely negative light, little evidence suggests a return to the "traditional" family structure.

FAMILY DIVERSITY IN CONTEMPORARY AMERICA

When Americans think about "the family," they have an image based on the cultural ideal of a nuclear unit composed of a married couple and their minor children, with the father as breadwinner and mother as homemaker, against which all other forms are judged deviant (Baca Zinn, 1990).

In actuality, as seen in Table 12-3, there is no "American family" but rather a range of household structures that meet peoples' needs at various points in their lives or that are forced on them by circumstances, in addition to variations by race and ethnicity.

Minority Families

In contrast to the ideal derived from the white, middle-class experience, ethnic and racial minority families are more likely to be extended. Although often interpreted as a reflection of cultural differences, these families are primarily a response to economic circumstances. Poor families of all ethnic and racial types depend on kinship ties and shared resources for survival (McAdoo, 1993). For most immigrant groups, the nuclear household was the norm by the third generation, as young people acculturated and assimilated into mainstream institutions.

LATINO FAMILIES IN THE UNITED STATES. Because of racial and ethnic discrimination, and their recency of migration, many Latino families remain relatively unassimilated. Under conditions of structural isolation, many traditional patterns are retained at least for one generation. For example, fertility rates are higher than for other American women; male dominance is more marked; and women's labor force participation is lower. This pattern is often referred to as **familism.**

Familism is a pattern of family closeness, traditionalism, and male dominance.

The earlier literature on Latino-American families assumed that familism and patriarchal relationships in marriage limit mobility opportunities, but that acculturation would erode such traditional patterns. More recent analysis, however, has shifted the emphasis from cultural factors to the continued economic segregation of Latino workers. As long as minority workers are channeled into low-paying employment, often in the nonindustrialized sector (agriculture, food service, janitorial), upward mobility is highly problematic, regardless of family structure. From this viewpoint, Latino family patterns are a means of coping with economic and social isolation. Given the many differences among Hispanic Americans, family patterns will also vary greatly (Vidal de Haymes and Kilty, 1994).

In addition, familism and "machismo" (excessive masculinity) have increasingly been challenged by Hispanic women and modified by migration and resettlement (Segura and Pierce, 1993). For example, a Mexican man can migrate to the United States, while expecting his wife to remain chaste until he calls for her. Usually, however, the wife is empowered by making decisions on her own and is reinforced by egalitarian norms once she joins him in the United States (Hondagneu-Sotelo, 1992.) Conversely, the husband's power is diminished by his low status in the U.S. economic system, so the outcome actually undermines patriarchy. Because the wife now enjoys greater control over her life and the husband less than was the case in Mexico, it is the women who wish to remain in the United States and the men who yearn to return.

AFRICAN-AMERICAN FAMILIES. The effects of discrimination and segregation are most clearly seen in data on the African-American family. Compared to other racial and ethnic groups, American blacks are more likely to postpone marriage or never marry; to experience divorce, desertion, and separation; and to forego remarriage. As a result, less than half of African-American family households contain a married couple (compared with 82 percent for whites) and 46 percent are headed by a woman (compared with 13 percent for whites) (U.S. Bureau of the Census, P20-478, 1994).

The low marriage rates have more to do with the sex ratio than culture (Lichter et al., 1992). The family ideology of African Americans is the same as for whites, but conditions for realizing the goal of a stable marriage differ. Large numbers of young men are unemployed because the jobs have moved elsewhere. It is not the expectation of receiving welfare that depresses marriage rates in the inner city, but lack of employed men (Testa and Krogh, 1989). For well-educated African Americans, the problem is also that women outnumber men, and the men are more likely than the women to marry across racial lines. Thus, both high and low income African-American women will have low marriage rates.

TABLE 12-3 United States Households: 1970–1993

Type	Percent of All Households	
	1970	1993
Married couple, children, one-earner	24	8
Married couple, children, dual-earner	16	17
Married couple, no children under 18	30	28
One adult with children	11	17
One person household	17	25
Two or more nonmarried persons	2	5

Source: U.S. Bureau of the Census, P20-478, 1994; P23-181, 1992.

A major reason for egalitarian relationships among many middle-class African-American couples is the likelihood that partners have similar educational and occupational backgrounds.

The Stable Middle-Class African-American Family. Despite all the problems, almost two-thirds of high-income African-American men are in a stable marriage. An increasing percentage of black families have an income over the national median—from 10 percent in 1950 to one-third today. These middle-class families differ from their white counterparts in being composed of two adult wage earners, often both professionals but whose combined income still falls short of that earned by one white professional. Because husband and wife are similar in educational and occupational status, the marriage relationship is typically more egalitarian than that for middle-class whites (Wilkinson, 1987; McAdoo, 1993).

Most public attention, however, has focused on the growing number of African-American families at the lower end of the income spectrum and particularly the inner-city, female-headed household.

Inner City Matrifocal Households. Although the term *matriarchy* has often been used to describe the female-headed black family, a more accurate description is **matrifocal,** meaning ' "women-centered." Where wage-earning husbands are in short supply, the extended line of female kin shares a household and pools resources. If the women have power within the family, it is typically by default.

Research on the matrifocal family has taken two directions. One type of study points to the strengths of this pattern in maintaining generational continuity and providing services to kin while resisting the negative impact of outside conditions (Hogan et al., 1990). Another type details these outside forces: unemployment, low pay, residential segregation, and other outcomes of institutionalized racism. In both views, the matrifocal family is seen as a *response* to the conditions of poverty rather than its cause.

The matrifocal family is "deviant" only in terms of the white, middle-class ideal that defines "normal." When viewed in the context of historical experiences, the kinship patterns of minority groups have been extremely functional. These are families that have endured. For African Americans, the struggle to preserve kinship ties has survived more than two centuries of slavery, economic discrimination, social segregation, and cultural insults (Billingsley, 1993). But the strengths of inner-city Latino and African-American families today may not survive the effects of long-term unemployment, diminishing social welfare services, deteriorating housing and schools, and uncontrolled levels of crime and drug use (Hogan et al., 1993)

> **Matrifocal** refers to families centered on the woman.

ALTERNATIVE LIFE STYLES

Other variations on the ideal American family reflect the array of options that has become increasingly common over the past several decades: living alone, living as an unmarried couple, single-parenting, voluntary childlessness, and dual-earner couples.

Living Alone

One in every four American households today consists of one person, twice the proportion in 1960. This category includes three subpopulations that differ by age, marriage expectations, and financial resources.

NOT YET MARRIED.　Today, close to two-thirds of American women and about four-fifths of American men aged 20–24 are still single, compared with only 28 percent of women and 53 percent of men in 1960. Most of these single young people are economically independent and able to maintain their own households. For both men and women, the widespread availability of effective contraception permits an active sex life without the fear of pregnancy. In addition, public attitudes have become more supportive of singlehood and of sex before marriage (Chapter 8). However, the glamorous singles' scene portrayed in the media is far from the norm for most young nonmarrieds, who lead lives not very different from their married friends (P. Stein, 1989b).

DIVORCED.　Divorced people account for one-fifth of live-alone households and tend to be somewhat older than the never-marrieds. Although most will remarry, a larger percentage of women than men will maintain their single-person households for several decades.

WIDOWED. The third category of live-alones, and the fastest growing subgroup, comprises elderly widows (and a few widowers), almost all of whom prefer independent living as long as health and income permit.

Cohabitation

Not all single adults live alone. Many share a household with another unmarried person, a pattern called **cohabitation** (from *co-*, meaning "together"; *habitation,* meaning "dwelling place"). In 1993, about 5 percent of American households consisted of two or more unmarried persons, but the Bureau of the Census does not ask if or how they are related sexually. Some of these households will consist of siblings, others of same-sex couples, and a majority will fit the Census category of POSSLQs: persons of the opposite sex sharing living quarters.

For every 100 married couples today, there are 6 unmarried couples (up from 1 per 100 in 1970). And although we tend to think of cohabitors as college-aged, most are somewhat older, between ages 25 and 44, with only a high school education or less (U.S. Bureau of the Census, P20-478, 1994). Aside from age and education, the most significant variable in distinguishing cohabitors from noncohabitors is *religiosity.*

Cohabitation occurs when unmarried people share living quarters.

Involuntary childlessness refers to the inability to conceive.

Voluntary childlessness refers to the decision to remain child free.

The effects of religious commitment are reciprocal (working both ways). People who are more religious are less likely to cohabit, and the experience of cohabitation reduces religiosity (Thornton et al., 1992). Similarly, parental attitudes toward cohabitation influence the behavior of their offspring, and the children's behavior affects the parents' view of cohabitation (Axinn and Thornton, 1993).

Does cohabitation affect the stability of a subsequent marriage? Some evidence from Sweden and the United States indicates that divorce rates are higher for cohabitors than noncohabitors, but this may only reflect the fact that the kind of people who cohabit are also less likely to remain in an unsatisfying marriage (Bennet et al., 1988). Although cohabitors account for less than 5 percent of all households at any given time today, four in ten Americans will probably spend some years as part of an unmarried couple before or between marriages.

Childlessness

When marriage is delayed, so also is childbearing, accounting for most of the fertility decline since the early 1970s. Delayed childbearing, in turn, increases the risk that a couple might wait until conception is unlikely. Thus it is probable that a higher percentage of couples than in the past will remain childless—possibly 20 percent compared to the 10–12 percent of earlier decades (U.S. Bureau of the Census, P20-470, 1993).

In the past, **childlessness** was typically **involuntary,** a matter of inability to conceive rather than preference. For poor people, inadequate diet and lack of access to health care continue to account for high levels of infertility. Wealthier couples may choose to experiment with the new reproductive technologies discussed in Chapter 8; others will adopt; and still others gradually adapt to remaining childless.

Because not bearing children is a form of deviance from the norms of marriage and womanhood, the couple must learn to manage a stigmatized identity. This is especially difficult for the wife, whose femininity is called into question, and who generally seeks to protect her husband. In contrast, husbands tend to treat the problem as an unfortunate event rather than as a personal tragedy (Greil, 1991).

VOLUNTARILY CHILD-FREE COUPLES. Increasingly, couples choose not to become parents. Women in professional careers may postpone both marriage and childbearing until the odds of a safe pregnancy turn against them. Upwardly mobile couples could decide that parenthood would be inappropriate to their lifestyles. And still others will be inhibited by the emotional and financial costs of raising offspring.

Single-Parent Households

As a result of divorce and nonmarital childbearing, approximately 27 percent of American children under age 18 live with one parent, compared with 12 percent in 1970. Large numbers of white children and a majority of African-American children will spend some years in a single-parent household—86 percent of which are headed by the mother.

As noted, compared with two-parent families, those headed by one adult have many problems, the most severe being low income (Weitzman and McLean, 1992; Smock, 1994). More than half of all children living with a mother only are poor compared with 10 percent of those living with two parents. The single-parent must handle the role obligations of both mother and father; and those in the labor force are doubly pressed for parenting time. In terms of psychological well-being, long-term single-parenting is a long-term source of distress for single mothers (Thompson and Ensminger, 1989).

In the case of divorce, the children must adjust to a changed household structure as well as to reduced economic circumstances. Although most will eventually find success in marriage and work, the path is

Increasing numbers of American children live in single-parent households headed by women. What are the major problems such families face?

rockier than for other children, and the failure rate somewhat higher. Children of divorce do very well, however, when family income is adequate and assured, when the custodial parent has satisfying employment, when the noncustodial parent maintains contact, and when social networks—relatives, friends, and child care services—are available. But as we have seen, these are not typical conditions in the United States. Divorce does not impoverish women and children in societies with welfare policies designed to protect all types of family. It is not the end of the marriage, but the lack of supportive policies and services that makes divorce a social problem in the United States (Goode, 1993).

NEVER-MARRIED MOTHERS.   In 1992, TV's Murphy Brown was joined by over 4 million other mothers, twice the number of only a decade earlier. Seventy percent of these births were to women aged 20 and older, with the largest increase for women aged 35 to 44 (U.S. Bureau of the Census, P20-470, 1993). The number who were white, middle-class, and with some college education more than doubled over the decade. Presumably, these women chose to become single parents rather than marry their children's father. In other words, for many women, the link between marriage and maternity has become optional. These are also the women who can provide the financial and child care services that reduce the negative consequences of single parenting.

SINGLE FATHERS.   In 1993, 13 percent of single parent families were headed by fathers, up from 10 percent in 1980. Limited research suggests that single-parent fathers feel quite comfortable and perform competently in the role (Risman, 1987). Compared to single-parent mothers, however, fathers typically enjoy a higher income; they can more easily hire household help; and they will remarry much sooner. If they have fought for custody, they are also very likely to form warm and close ties to their children. Similar to single-parent mothers, balancing workplace commitments with child care duties and responsibilities is easier when employers and co-workers are supportive (Greif et al., 1993).

DUAL-EARNER FAMILIES

Although a deviation from the 1950s ideal, the **dual-earner family** is the new statistical norm. Three-fourths of married mothers are in the full or part-time labor force, including almost 70 percent of those with children under age 6 and two-thirds of those with children under age 3 (Hayghe and Bianchi, 1994). Dual-earner families enjoy an income almost double that of single-earner families, except for men at the highest occupational ranks, whose nonemployed wife contributes to his career by providing emotional support and extensive homemaking services (Bellas, 1992).

> In **dual-earner** families or couples, both partners are in the labor force.

Compared with nonemployed wives, married women in the labor force enjoy better physical and psychological health (Barnett, 1994), and her children benefit from her personal well-being and added income (Parcel and Meneghan, 1994b). These positive effects, however, are moderated by (1) whether her job brings more than material rewards and (2) how much assistance she receives with household tasks (Lennon and Rosenfield, 1992; Ross and Mirowsky, 1992; Spade, 1994). For many women, low pay, low job autonomy, and little help at home negate the positive effects of employment. The meaning of her employment—as a plus or minus factor—will also vary by the income and occupational status of the husband (Pyke, 1994).

The effects of a wife's employment on her husband's emotional well-being are similarly complex. Some men feel relief at sharing economic responsibility and they enjoy the higher standard of living provided by a second income; others have difficulty giving up the traditional role of sole provider (Bielby and Bielby, 1989; Vannoy-Hiller and Philliber, 1989). Her employment is most likely to have a negative effect when it decreases his share of family income and increases his homemaking responsibilities (Rosenfield, 1992). And some husbands will respond to economic dependence on their wives by lowering their share of housework (Brines, 1994). But as dual-earner families become the norm, some of these issues will diminish (Trovato and Vos, 1992).

Nonetheless, divorce rates for dual-earner families are higher than for single-earner families, but this could reflect an employed wife's greater ability to leave an unsatisfying marriage, as well as the possibility that women in unrewarding relationships are more likely than other women to seek employment. In any event, marriages that are already troubled will be most vulnerable. Those that remain intact typically undergo many adjustments—in the balance of power and the meshing of work and leisure schedules. Just finding time together is a problem, and the more time spent together, the more satisfying the dual-earner marriage is (Kingston and Nock, 1987).

> In **dual-career** families or couples, both partners have careers.
>
> The **wife as senior partner (WASP)** model involves a family organized around the wife's career.
>
> **Commuter marriages** occur when husband and wife work in different cities and typically maintain separate households.

Dual-Career Families

One variation on the dual-earner family is the **dual-career** model (Hertz, 1986). A career differs from a job by its greater demands. People with careers are typically in high-status occupations that require enormous commitments of time and energy. But it is pre-cisely their high incomes that permits such couples to purchase the services necessary to run a household and care for children.

Variations on the dual-career family that although rare now could become more common in the future include the **wife as senior partner (WASP)** model, organized around her career (Atkinson and Boles, 1984). This is most possible when the husband's working conditions are highly flexible and when there are no small children. In the **commuter marriage,** both partners are equally committed to careers located in different cities (Gerstel and Gross, 1984). This usually involves two separate households, with partners alternating weekend visits.

Although both the WASP model and commuter marriage are extreme departures from normative expectations and have a number of built-in stresses, there are also compensations, including great flexibility in negotiating marital roles and tailoring these to achieve success in both work and love.

Men in Families: The New Division of Labor

The family role of men in modern society has typically been viewed as secondary to that of worker, but there are signs of change today, at least in attitudes if not always in actual behavior (Hood, 1993; Kimmel and Messner, 1993; Gerson, 1993). Despite late marriage, early divorce, small families, and father absence, more than 90 percent of American men will marry at least once, most will become fathers, and a higher proportion of men than women, at all ages, will be living with a spouse.

Successful dual career couples may take turns supporting each other's careers. For example, Ruth Bader Ginsburg, shown here at her swearing-in as Associate Justice of the Supreme Court with her husband, Martin, (third from the left) mutually supported each other as they advanced in their separate careers. He is looking on as President Clinton and Chief Justice Rehnquist congratulate Justice Ginsburg.

PHYLLIS MOEN

Child Care as a Public Policy in the United States and Sweden

Phyllis Moen is The Ferris Family Professor of Life Course Studies and Director of the Bronfenbrenner Center for Life Course Studies at Cornell University. She is the author of Working Parents: Transformations in Gender Roles and Public Policies in Sweden (*University of Wisconsin Press, 1989*) *and* Women's Two Roles: A Contemporary Dilemma (*Greenwood, 1992*).

W hat attracted me to the field of sociology was C. Wright Mills' view of the relationship between private troubles and public issues. Individuals and their families confront many problems and challenges. But these seemingly personal difficulties must be placed against the backdrop of social and economic conditions within the larger society. This proposition also provides a useful perspective on women's lives generally and my own in particular.

A continual challenge for me has been to reconcile my educational and career aspirations with my family responsibilities. Like most women who grew up in the 1950s and early 1960s I thought that to be a good wife and mother was to be a full time homemaker, at least while my children were young. But I also aspired to be a college professor. As a consequence, the path to my educational and career goals was inevitably marked by interruptions and delays.

As many other American women began to combine mothering with employment, dilemmas that we thought of as personal troubles emerged as public issues.

I had been taught that only by comparing and contrasting different societies or social groups can we hope to understand stability and change in the human condition. Following this advice, I looked for a society where public policies and attitudes kept pace with changes in gender relationships, where supports were provided to help parents combine employment with the raising of children. What I found was Sweden.

What makes the Swedish case especially instructive is the concerted effort made by government, organized labor, and other institutions to distribute the burden of parenting between men and women, and to facilitate the employment of all adults, including those caring for infants and children. These policies included paid parental leaves for both mothers and fathers and the option of a reduced work week without the loss of benefits, for parents of young children.

There are two competing views in sociology regarding the psychological consequences of maternal employment. One holds that women who perform both work and family roles will experience increased role strain. The other emphasizes the positive consequences of employment for mothers' well-being, resulting from their reduced social isolation. I suggest the need for a third approach, the life course perspective, which highlights the context of lives. Whether maternal employment has positive or negative effects depends

on the social and historical context in which it occurs. The policies adopted in the 1970s to support working parents by reducing the costs and promoting the benefits of employment for mothers of young children have allowed mothers in Sweden to spend more time with their children than can mothers in the United States, where to be employed often means working full-time with little or no leave available following the birth of a child. The options available to working parents in Sweden are used primarily by working mothers, although they are available to fathers also. The generous paid parental leave and part-time work options (with benefits and the option to moving back to full-time hours) allow mothers to maintain an attachment to the labor force while devoting time to their children, thus reducing the strains of combining mothering with employment.

Sweden's experience illustrates potential limits in achieving gender equality; women continue to be the principal caretakers of children. Yet the Swedish example shows that legislation can facilitate the balancing of work and family responsibilities. For example, a significant percentage of Swedish fathers take at least a few week's parental leave, an option that is rarely available to American fathers. We in the United States can no longer cling to an outdated vision of the American family and of American society. By framing issues of employment policy with specific reference to the needs of working parents, the United States can begin to address today's (and tomorrow's) realities, public issues of growing urgency.

Although few comparable data are available from the past, it is thought that men's involvement in housework and parenting has increased, largely as a response to a wife's labor-force participation and the ideology of egalitarianism. Some of the increase is more relative than absolute. That is, as the time spent on household work by an employed wife declines, the husband's share of the total will automatically increase even though he invests no more time at it than before (Pleck, 1989). In addition, his participation in homemaking remains highly gender-linked, largely confined to yard work and paperwork (Goldscheider and Waite, 1991; Galinsky et al., 1993).

The effect of social class on men's participation in household labor is not altogether clear. To the degree that middle-class couples tend to share an egalitarian ideology his participation should be enhanced (Coltrane, 1994). Conversely, workplace demands will limit participation regardless of ideological commitment (Presser, 1994). Thus, although Swedish men assume a greater share of household work than do American husbands (25 percent compared to 20 percent), there was no difference by social class.

Nonetheless, the trends associated with sharing family labor show no sign of abating: women's continued employment and higher education; men's involvement in infant care; later age at marriage; small families; and endorsement of gender equality (Coltrane, 1994). It seems likely, therefore, that men in modern industrial societies will increase their involvement in domestic tasks. In developing nations in contrast, men's generally low participation in childcare and household work appears unrelated to any changes in the wife's resources or power (Sanchez, 1993).

Furthermore, the gendered division of household work does not change when either the wife or the husband uses the home as a workplace (Silver, 1993). The wives experience less conflict between domestic and work responsibilities but end up doing the major share of both. Despite saving commuting time, the husband's share of housework is no greater than that of men working outside the home.

THE NEW FATHER. It is in the area of child care that most change appears to have taken place, although perhaps not as great as commonly assumed, in either the United States (Hochschild and Machung, 1989) or Europe (Bjornberg, 1992). The clearest change has been in participation in childbirth. As part of the "natural childbirth" movement, most young husbands have joined their wives in birthing courses and taken part in assisting the delivery. This experience alone does not create a mystical bond between parent and child, although there may be many positive benefits from being included in what was once a purely mother/child event. In addition, men who choose to

participate in birthing probably differ from those who do not along a number of dimensions likely to enhance the parent/child relationship.

A small proportion of new fathers assume primary care of the newborn, typically those with flexible schedules and a commitment to gender equality (Kimmel, 1994). An increasing proportion of American men are involved in daily care of a preschool child. In the early 1990s, 20 percent of children younger than age 5 were cared for by their father while their mother worked outside the home; this was due in part to the high cost of commercial child care and to an increase in part-time and split-shift work (O'Connell, 1993). This arrangement can create strains in the marriage: the couple has little time together, the father may feel feminized, and the mother may feel guilty. Women who depend on a husband for child care, especially those in low-wage jobs, are more likely to leave the labor force than are other working mothers (Maume and Mullin, 1993).

Despite men's desires to spend more time with their children, throughout the industrial world the nature of employment and the demands of the modern

Although fathers may take part in the birth of their children, they are discouraged from parental involvement if it involves time away from their jobs. A dramatic example of this lack of employer support occurred when David Williams, a starting tackle for the Houston Oilers pictured here, was fined $111,111 for missing a football game in order to be present at his son's birth. Do you think Williams should have been fined?

workplace make it difficult to realize this goal (Pleck, 1993). This conflict could be lessened by flexible work schedules and family leave policies for men as well as women. However, most American employers continue to resist such changes, even though "family-friendly" benefits increase loyalty and reduce employee turnover (B. Noble, 1993). But because an employed mother usually earns less than a father, the "opportunity costs" of her leaving the labor force are lower. This is especially true for the United States, where very few wives earn more than their husbands or work in jobs with characteristics that reduce the conflict between family and work (Glass and Camarigg, 1992).

In both Europe and the United States, new cohorts of young adults express a more egalitarian view of marriage roles than do older people, especially among those already in dual earner households (Bjornberg, 1992; Snarey, 1993). As a consequence, young people in modern societies enter marriage with flexible role expectations, and many who begin with traditional views will change in response to their actual situations.

While the day of the "househusband" remains distant, the division of household labor, particularly child care, is becoming more varied if not fully shared. The long-term benefits of nurturent fathering for both daughters and sons have only recently been studied and appreciated, even though the stereotype of father as the stern disciplinarian continues to dominate American culture (Snarey, 1993; Schwartz, 1994).

SOCIAL POLICY

Who's Minding the Children?

Who's minding the children? Are family settings naturally superior to group care? With a majority of mothers of preschoolers in the labor force, most of whom return to work within a year of giving birth, child care has become a major problem for dual-earner parents in the United States. Unlike other modern societies, our society has defined children's welfare as a private family matter rather than as a public responsibility, so that each family is left to find its own solution. The resulting variety of child care arrangements is shown in Figure 12-3.

About one-fourth are in an organized day care facility, some provided by employers, but most are in private, profit-making facilities, for those who can afford them. For low-income families, the child's father and other relatives provide the bulk of care, with 18 percent cared for in the home of a paid but unlicensed provider.

Does it matter who cares for a child? Most research has found few, if any, significant differences in the cognitive or emotional development of children cared for by others and those cared for at home by the mother, especially after the child's first year (Lamb et al., 1992). Daughters often do better in day care than at home with an overprotective mother (Mott, 1991). The important factor is the quality of

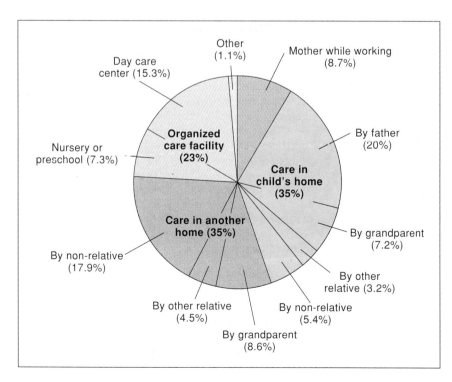

Figure 12-3 Primary child care arrangements of working mothers with children under age 5.

Source: U.S. Bureau of the Census, P70-36, 1994.

Many "new fathers" share child care and housework with their wives. Recent studies indicate long-term benefits for both sons and daughters when their fathers take on a more nurturing role. How can we increase fathers' child care participation? What is the importance of a relationship between a father and his children?

care, regardless of who provides it. Providing a stimulating environment for her child in any setting will be most difficult for women with limited resources and the greatest need for employment.

Only in 1993 was a Family Leave Act passed by Congress and not vetoed by the President. But this legislation was extremely limited: A worker may take up to 12 weeks of *unpaid* leave to care for a newborn or a seriously ill family member. Part-time employees and employers with fewer than 50 workers are excluded, and the leave-taker cannot collect unemployment insurance. In other words, family leave is available only to those who can do without a weekly paycheck. In contrast, Sweden provides 12 months of leave, to either parent, at close to full pay, plus additional days and weeks to care for ill family members (Haas, 1992; Moen, 1992).

Despite its limited scope, the Family Leave Act was opposed by organized business on grounds of the expense of hiring new workers and continuing health benefits and by conservatives who fear government intrusion into the privacy of the family. Do we really want state officials to set standards for households and for care-giving relatives?

Supporters of family leave legislation note that worker morale is raised and turnover reduced and also that families are strengthened, as in Sweden, where one in four fathers now take some time off to care for a newborn. The more time taken, the closer the parent/child bond, and the more likely the father is to assume child care duties beyond infancy.

Because most of you will want to combine work and child rearing, child care will become a major concern in the years ahead (Galinsky and Stein, 1990). What would be your ideal child care arrangement? Can all working parents take advantage of such arrangements? You might also want to familiarize yourself with the research on the effects of day care on infants and young children.

We now return to the questions raised at the beginning of this chapter. Is the American family in a state of collapse? Are children and adults worse off today than in the past? Is there a role for public policy? From a sociological perspective, we argue that the variety of family structures in the United States today is an adaptive response to the conditions of postindustrial society: extended life expectancy, the decline of patriarchy and the power of kinship groups, the emancipation of women and children, and the modern emphasis on self-fulfillment (Skolnick, 1991). Not only is it impossible to return to what is often called the "traditional" pattern, we suspect that few of you would find much satisfaction there. No law forbids extended family relationships, therefore, we assume that most Americans choose to live independent of blood relatives.

True, for many, the choice will be between the "new family," characterized by greater egalitarianism, flexible roles, and joint involvement in child care and breadwinning, or "no family," by foregoing marriage or parenthood (Goldscheider and Waite, 1991). But short of forcing couples to stay together, there seems to be no alternative to allowing people to dissolve unsuccessful marriages. Yet much can be done to strengthen families through the types of public policy initiatives found in all other modern societies: family allowances, day care facilities for children and the frail elderly, housing assistance, and social welfare services. Opposition to government programs focused on the family, however, remains very strong, unless, like Social Security, the benefits are enjoyed primarily by the nonpoor. Yet it is largely families already at or below the poverty line who experience the most negative effects of failure in both love and work.

For many critics of the current scene, including academics as well as politicians, the American obsession with material success and personal happiness represents a serious threat to the sense of responsibility for others that underlies a strong family (Glenn, 1992). The traditional family functioned by denying members' personal needs. Today, we exalt the individual above the needs of the family as a unit. In this view, the most difficult task of your adulthood will be finding a balance between self-fulfillment and caring for others. The good news is that you will be able to choose among a range of family forms—from new to none and all stops in between—that were not readily available in the past.

SUMMARY

1. As with any other institution, the family can be understood as a set of socially constructed norms and behaviors vital to the survival of individuals and societies.

2. In the family system, these norms are clustered around the essential activities of reproduction, socialization, protection, care, and intimacy.

3. The functionalist explanation of the bases of the family focuses on the incest taboo, reciprocity between families, and the principle of legitimacy.

4. The conflict explanation of the bases of the family focuses on who and what groups benefit from given family arrangements.

5. Though kinship systems vary from one society to another, they can be described in terms of how many spouses are permitted at one time, who can marry whom, how lines of descent and the flow of resources are determined, where the new couple lives, and what power relations exist within the marriage and the family.

6. The major historical change has been from extended family systems to the nuclear family; an increasing number of tasks once assumed by the kinship group are now performed outside the home.

7. The stresses and demands of modern life create needs for emotional support, which people seek from their marriage partners and their children. Thus, the modern family has become a unit specializing in emotional support and the early socialization of children.

8. From a functional perspective, the marriage market has traditionally represented a mutually beneficial exchange. From a conflict perspective, mate selection takes place under conditions that generally favor men.

9. The modern family is characterized by reduced power differences between husbands and wives and between parents and children. This move toward egalitarianism has been influenced by ideological trends, legal changes, the influence of psychological theories of child development, and the decline in parent's abilities to control the social mobility of their children.

10. Modernization has also changed the timing of family events, including age at first marriage, premarital sexual experiences, the spacing and number of children, mothers reentering the labor force, the empty nest stage, and widowhood.

11. Marriage and parenthood continue to be almost universal among Americans, and social surveys consistently indicate high levels of satisfaction among marrieds.

12. However, evidence that conflict is also a feature of family life comes from reports of domestic violence and divorce. Most violence is directed at wives and children, and the economic impact of divorce is especially hard for them.

13. No one "American family" exists today. Instead there is a variety of American families. These include minority families (both Latino and African-American), singles living alone, cohabitors, childless couples, single-parent households, and dual-earner and dual-career families.

14. There is conflicting evidence as to how much change is occurring in men's participation in child care and housework.

15. Evidence suggests support for flexible family roles, sharing of child care and homework tasks, and greater support for each other's work and careers, especially among younger Americans.

SUGGESTED READINGS

Cherlin, Andrew J. *Marriage, Divorce, Remarriage.* 2nd ed. Cambridge: Harvard University Press, 1992. In the original work, Cherlin examined the social upheaval of the 1970s and 1980s—doubling of the divorce rates, decline in marriage, and the rise of cohabitation. In the updated edition, he expands his treatment of racial issues, out of wedlock childbearing, and poverty.

Coontz, Stephanie. *The Way We Never Were: American Families and the Nostalgia Trap*. New York: Basic Books, 1992. This enlightening book brings together statistics and facts that show that diversity in the American family is the norm. Coontz shows that concerns over declines in family values and the crisis of the family are contrived to alleviate anxiety over social change.

Gelles, Richard J. and Donileen Loseke, eds. *Current Controversies on Family Violence*. Newbury Park, CA: Sage, 1993. This volume highlights the most current research and controversies on the subject of family violence.

Gonzales, Juan L. *Racial and Ethnic Families in America*. Dubuque: Kendall/Hunt, 1992. The author traces the assimilation processes of numerous racial and ethnic groups in the United States by looking at the changes in their family systems.

Gubrium, Jaber F. *Out of Control: Family Therapy and Domestic Disorder*. Newbury Park, CA: Sage, 1992. Clearly written, of interest to those concerned with dysfunctional families, therapy, and social welfare.

Hochschild, Arlie, with Anne Machung. *The Second Shift: Working Parents and the Revolution at Home*. New York: Viking, 1989. This often-cited study of working couples indicates that women do most of the second-shift work—the job they do before they go to the office and after they return home—and looks at why many men are still unwilling to share housework and child care.

Hood, Jane C., ed. *Men, Work and Family: Research on Men and Masculinity*, Vol. 4. Newbury Park, CA: Sage, 1993. A collection of the most current social science research on how men are balancing work and family commitments, comparative analyses of men in other countries, and the impact of public policy on men's experience of family and work.

Kibria, Nazli. *Family Tightrope: The Changing Lives of Vietnamese Americans*. Princeton: Princeton University Press, 1993. An analysis of the change in Vietnamese immigrant families in Philadelphia utilyzing in-depth interviews and participant observations to show how they respond to the social and economic challenges posed by migration and resettlement.

Kissman, Kris and JoAnn Allen. *Single Parent Families*. Newbury Park, CA: Sage, 1992. The authors discuss the many challenges facing single female caregivers, which represent nearly 90 percent of single parent families.

McLanahan, Sara, and Gary Sandefur. *Growing Up with a Single Parent: What Hurts, What Helps*. Cambridge, MA: Harvard University Press, 1994. A thorough examination of several national data sets that carefully explain the links between family structure and the child's chances of success in school, marriage, and work. The authors present practical policy prescriptions for strengthening single parent families.

Rubin, Lillian. *Families on the Faultline: America's Working Class Speaks about the Family, the Economy, Race and Ethnicity*. New York: Harper Collins, 1994. Nearly 400 interviews with working-class men, women and children of different races and ethnic groups explore feelings about the pressures on family life.

Sherman, Suzanne. *Lesbian and Gay Marriage: Private Commitments, Public Ceremonies*. Philadelphia: Temple University Press, 1992. The debate regarding gay and lesbian marriages is documented in a thoughtful book that asks us to consider the meaning of commitment, marriage and family life.

South, Scott J. and Stewart E. Tolnay. *The Changing American Family: Sociological and Demographic Perspectives*. Boulder: Westview Press, 1992. This collection of papers probe current topics in family demography from cohabitation, absentee fathers, to division of household chores.

Taylor, Ronald L. (ed.) *Minority Families in the United States: A Multicultural Perspective*. Englewood Cliffs, NJ: Prentice-Hall, 1994. A comprehensive overview of cultural and historical trends in family formation and functioning of the United States' many racial/ethnic minority groups.

13
Economic Systems and the Organization of Work

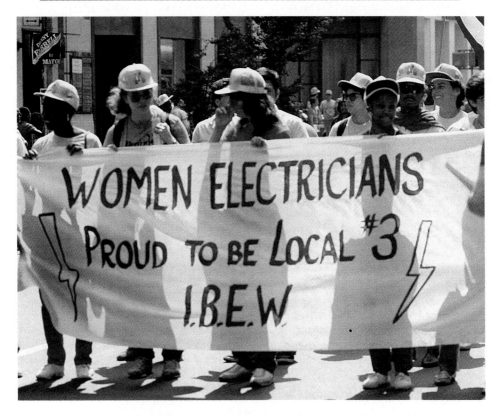

- For most of human history, the world's people lived in small gathering bands, and, by 10,000 years ago, most had added hunting or fishing to their economic base. Anthropological studies of contemporary hunter-gatherers such as the Mbuti of Africa, the Tiwi of Australia, and the Copper Eskimo of North America indicate that food sharing is central, personal possessions few, and social relations egalitarian (Haviland, 1993).
- The Trobriand Islanders of the Western Pacific engage in an extensive trading system called the *kula ring*, through which the "big men" of the Islands exchange shell necklaces and armbands of little intrinsic worth but high symbolic value. The elaborate rituals that surround the canoes as they transport the shell jewelry from island to island provide a ceremonial context for a lively trade in yams, mats, vines, and other goods. The *kula ring* creates a network of trading partners, who redistribute the products of the various islands through direct exchanges with one another (Malinowski, 1922/1955).
- The Kwakiutl Indians of the Pacific Northwest and British Columbia are famous for their spectacular feasts in which the host showers gifts on the guests, engages in boasting contests, and even destroys some of his family's property. This is the *potlatch*, a ceremony that establishes a stratification system based on the accumulation and distribution of wealth, similar to displays of conspicuous consumption in our society today. Guests remain status inferiors until they can return more than they have received. As wasteful as the *potlatch* may appear, it does redistribute goods from the wealthy to the less favored and encourages high productivity among all families (Rohner and Rohner, 1970).

These are only three of the thousands of different patterns whereby members of a society produce, distribute, and consume goods and services. In each society, the economic system is linked to other institutional spheres—especially to family and political systems. Economic behavior also has a symbolic dimension, embedded in the belief system and reinforced in ongoing social relationships.

ORIGINS AND HISTORY OF ECONOMIC SYSTEMS

Economic systems originate in the trial-and-error attempts of human groups to survive in a specific geographic location. The term **mode of subsistence** refers to how the group adapts to its environment to produce and distribute the goods and services necessary for individual and collective survival. As you

saw in Chapter 3, Figure 3-1, we have arranged these adaptations along a continuum from the most simple, foraging and gathering, to the most complex, modern industrial and postindustrial economies. Once a mode of subsistence is established, its customary patterns of behavior (folkways) become defined as natural and even sacred (mores) and are ultimately supported by rules and sanctions (laws). This is the process of **institutionalization,** whereby an adaptation becomes a way of life.

Over time, however, most societies change in response to contact with other cultures, wars or invasion, and natural disasters, although some will remain relatively untouched. The long-term trend, however, has been toward increased division of labor, specialization of tasks, more efficient uses of energy, and linkages to the economic system of other societies. Such changes are not always beneficial to members of simpler societies, such as when the Tanzanian government converted Masai pasture lands into a game park to attract foreign visitors on safari, or when the South African government used !Kung San villages as staging areas for a war against black guerrillas (Keller, 1993). In the industrialized world and throughout most of Eastern Europe today, drastic economic change is causing great turmoil in the life of ordinary citizens, adding to the flood of refugees across the continent (see Chapters 19 and 20).

> **Mode of subsistence** refers to the how a group adapts to its environment through the production and distribution of goods and services.
>
> **Institutionalization** is the process whereby a given adaptation becomes an established pattern.
>
> An **economic system** consists of the norms and activities regulating the production, distribution, and consumption of goods and services.

COMPONENTS OF ECONOMIC SYSTEMS

The **economic system** of any society consists of norms and patterned activities regulating (1) the *production* of goods and services; (2) their *distribution* throughout the society; and (3) patterns of use or *consumption.*

Production

Primary production consists of taking from the earth and using directly, as in gathering, hunting, fishing, farming, and mining. Secondary production involves making something new out of raw materials, such as pottery, cloth, bows and arrows, automobiles, or nuclear weapons. Modern societies are characterized by a third, or *tertiary,* level of production: **service work,** providing assistance and information, ranging from baby-sitting to international banking. Sales, health care, education, entertainment, government, sports, transportation, information processing, and hair dressing are all service occupations.

Service work refers to providing assistance and/or information.

As seen in Figure 13-1, the United States is fast becoming a service society, as the proportion of workers in primary and secondary production declines relative to those in the service sector. The occupations projected to gain the greatest number of new workers between now and 2005 are seen in Table 13-1.

Notice that Table 13-1 consists primarily of support personnel, often part-time, and not necessarily the best paid. Job loss will continue to be greatest among high-wage, high-skill unionized factory workers and middle-management white-collar employees. Most job gains in the late 1980s and early 1990s have come in the low-paying service sector, so that people entering

TABLE 13-1   Change in Employment, 1992–2005

Occupation	Percent	Numerical
Registered nurses	42%	765,000
Computer scientists and system analysts	111%	737,000
Homemaker and home health aides	136%	645,000
Nursing aides and psychiatric aides	44%	616,000
Preschool workers	65%	611,000
Guards	51%	408,000
Teacher aides	43%	381,000
Human services workers	136%	256,000
Restaurant and food service managers	46%	227,000
Correction officers	70%	197,000

Source: U.S. Department of Labor, 1994a.

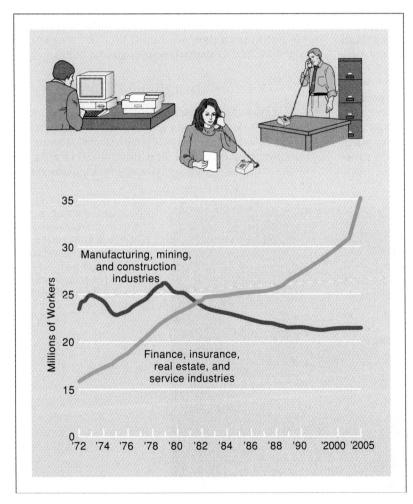

Figure 13-1   Number of workers in selected occupations, 1972–2005.

Source: Statistical Abstract, 1994, p. 413; Silvestri, 1993.

There are many ways in which members of a society produce, distribute, and consume goods and services. Both traditional and modern societies use markets to make goods available to buyers. How many different items are available in this Myanmar floating market?

the labor force today will earn much less than other workers in general, and many will be *underemployed* in jobs for which they are overqualified as the earnings gap between more and less educated workers contiunes to grow (Ryscavage, 1994).

What are your prospects in the labor market of the late 1990s? Job growth at the upper skill and prestige levels will increase, although at a much lower rate than jobs at the lower levels. The very high-prestige and high-income occupations require the ability to think abstractly, to express oneself articulately, to view problems in context, and to be creative and flexible—precisely the capacities developed through higher education. The lesson here is that you should stay in college, not just to get a diploma, but to broaden your knowledge base and to sharpen your cognitive skills.

Distribution

Once goods and services are produced, each collectivity must develop rules for their distribution. When group resources cannot be equally shared, a stratification hierarchy is created. In gathering and hunting societies, the day's yield is typically divided among all

Primary production in the United States takes place on a grand scale today. The mechanization of agriculture has replaced tenant farmers, sharecroppers, and most family farms.

In a market economy system, the value of any item depends on how much others are willing to pay for it.

members of the group. In more complex economies, some goods can be preserved over time, and often a surplus is produced. The simplest way of distributing the surplus within the group or between societies is by barter, the exchange of goods and services judged to be of equivalent value by the traders. The process can be direct, as in the case of the kula ring, or indirect, as in the potlatch. Underlying these exchanges is the **rule of reciprocity,** whereby giving a gift obligates the recipient to return something of equal value at a later time. Gift exchanges not only redistribute surplus goods but also create social ties and a sense of community—in modern as well as simpler societies (Carrier, 1991).

Once a society has reached the degree of complexity that requires a centralized government, the rulers can collect taxes from citizens and weaker neighbors. Rulers then decide how to *redistribute* this wealth to maintain their own power and keep most citizens content. In modern societies, some redistribution takes place through social welfare programs such as Food Stamps or subsidies to farmers. But the major mechanism of distribution in complex societies is the **market system,** in which the worth of any item depends on what other people are willing to pay for it. Ideally, supply and demand should tend toward balance in the long run, but such ideal conditions rarely apply.

Consumption

Literally, to *consume* means to "eat up." Every society has rules about consumption—how, who, when, and where. In most societies, throughout history, the household has been both a unit of production and consumption; that is, members work together and share the fruits of their labor among themselves. The unique feature of an industrial society, however, is the separation of work and home. Productive activities take place outside the household, in a factory, shop, or office, and are done by one or two adult members of the family. The household becomes primarily a consuming unit, and its nonemployed members become dependent on the wage earner(s). Figure 13-2 illustrates the typical consumption pattern of American households in 1992.

As discussed in Chapter 9, consumption patterns reflect and reinforce social class locations. The ability to shower gifts is a form of power, for wealthy party givers in Hollywood as for the Kwakiutl. The symbolic significance of consumer goods as status symbols is reinforced through advertising. An advanced capitalist economy depends on ever-higher levels of demand for newer, bigger, better, and just plain more of anything. Specific consumer choices are further influenced by subcultural standards of beauty or quality, as can be seen in automobile purchases. For example, what kind of person buys a Volvo or a pickup truck?

Despite many parallels in economic behavior between preindustrial and modern societies, industrial-

> The **rule of reciprocity** obligates the receiver of a gift to return something of equivalent value.
>
> In a **market system,** the value of goods and services is determined by supply and demand factors.

Figure 13-2 How Americans spent their money in 1992.
Source: Bureau of Labor Statistics, 1993.

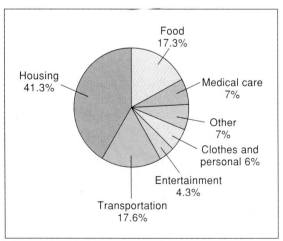

Food 17.3%
Medical care 7%
Other 7%
Clothes and personal 6%
Entertainment 4.3%
Transportation 17.6%
Housing 41.3%

ization brings major changes to traditional patterns of production, distribution, and consumption.

CONTEMPORARY ECONOMIC SYSTEMS

Modern economic systems can be arranged along a continuum representing the degree to which economic activity is regulated by **public agencies** representing society as a whole (e.g., government bureaus) or is left to the **private interests** of individuals, families, or corporations. This continuum is shown in Figure 13-3. At one extreme is **free-enterprise capitalism,** with minimal public supervision or ownership. At the other extreme, characterized by central planning of production and distribution, is a fully **socialist economic system.**

These terms describe economic systems and are not necessarily linked to any particular form of government (discussed in Chapter 14). Capitalist economies have been found in democracies (the United States), dictatorships (Latin America), and caste societies (South Africa before 1993). Conversely, elements of socialism are found in democracies (Sweden) as well as dictatorships (Cuba). Nonetheless, there are strong pressures toward democratic rule in modern industrial societies, provided that workers are allowed to organize and that the government remains somewhat independent of the economic elite (Rueschemeyer et al., 1992). Note that Figure 13-3 is a *continuum* and not an either/or situation; the extremes are "ideal forms" rarely found in any society over an extended period.

Public agencies are institutions, such as governments, that represent the society as a whole.

Private interests refer to property held by individuals, families, or corporations.

Free-enterprise capitalism is an economic system with minimal public ownership or controls.

A **socialist economic system** is marked by central planning of production and distribution by the government.

Welfare, or **state, capitalism** refers to free markets existing within limits designed to ensure social stability.

Capitalism

In a capitalist economy, the means of production (land, factories, capital, knowledge, businesses) are privately owned and operated for profit. In theory, open competition will drive out inefficient producers, leading to lower prices, plentiful goods, and personal and societal well-being. Both owners and workers are motivated by the promise of keeping what they earn. In practice, capitalism has been remarkably successful in unleashing productive power and raising standards of living over the long run, and where accompanied by democratic government it has also enhanced personal liberty (Bell, 1991).

Unregulated capitalism, however, can also produce widespread inequality and social injustice. These were the conditions that so distressed Karl Marx in the early years of the Industrial Revolution. They are also the conditions that exist today in Russia, where "shock treatment" capitalism led to an inflation rate of 240 percent in 1993 and left more than 35 percent of the population in poverty, and millions unemployed (Specter, 1994a).

When ability to pay determines who gets what, some people will gain control of more resources than others, regardless of need, and the most needy will be unable to claim even the most basic goods and services. To reduce the potentially destabilizing effects of extreme inequality, most capitalist countries, especially the democracies, have hedged market forces with a variety of social welfare programs such as old-age pensions, unemployment benefits, health insurance, and family allowances.

Because of these modifications, it is more accurate to speak of **welfare** (or **state**) **capitalism** when de-

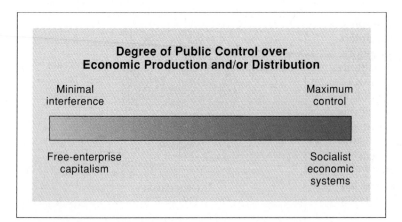

Figure 13-3 A continuum of economic systems.

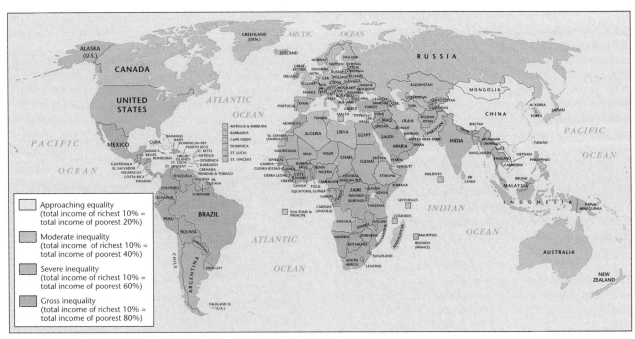

Inequality among Countries of the World. Nations vary in the degree of inequality between the richest and poorest citizens.
Source: Peters Atlas of the World, New York, Harper and Row, 1990, p. 179.

scribing the economic system of most modern industrial societies. Welfare capitalism is a far cry from the unfettered free-enterprise system of classic theory, and, while conservatives still call for less government, most economists view the system's ability to adapt and change as the key to its survival and success (Block, 1990). As noted in Chapter 9, most government spending has actually benefited the wealthy rather than the poor: landowners, shipping companies, construction firms, and the managers of savings and loan institutions.

Despite its overwhelming successes, capitalist economic behavior has a number of built-in aspects that could have a negative effect on the American economy in the future. For example, an emphasis on short-term gain and private profit encourages speculation, mergers, buyouts, and takeovers of other businesses rather than investment in improving productive capacity—a trend that marked the 1980s and led to increased concentration of wealth and less competition (Useem, 1993). Profit can also be maximized by moving manufacturing jobs to countries where the pay scales are very low and environmental regulations nonexistent. In the United States, short-term profit making has ruined the environment and left communities jobless, as in the case of Montana's forests, now treeless, as distant corporations cut and ran (Egan, 1993).

Another trend that distorts the free play of the market is the tendency toward concentration of economic power in fewer and fewer hands. **Monopolization** occurs when smaller firms are bought out by larger ones, so that only a few competitors dominate a given market. For example, where once dozens of daily newspapers flourished in American cities, today these cities have only one or two (and the two are often owned by the same local publisher or national chain). **Conglomerates** are formed when one company holds commanding shares in other businesses, so that one board of directors makes decisions affecting firms in a variety of different fields. BAT Industries, for example, is a conglomerate that itself employs only a few hundred people in its London and New York offices but which owns retail store chains, paper mills, tobacco companies, and financial institutions located in five continents. The 1980s surge toward conglomerate growth appears to have diminished in the recessionary 1990s (Davis et al., 1994).

Economic power is literally concentrated when the same individuals serve on a number of corporate boards of directors (Mintz and Schwartz, 1985). Such **interlocking corporate directorates** in the financial field, for example, mean that a small group of leaders in banking and insurance companies control the flow of money throughout the economy and large parts of the world.

Monopolization refers to the tendency for a company to acquire exclusive control of a commodity or service in a particular market.

Conglomerates exist when one company owns controlling shares in a variety of commercial areas.

Interlocking corporate directorates involve the same individuals sitting on several boards of directors.

The international expansion of trade, communication, and flow of capital has also produced **multinational corporations** whose ownership spans several nations and is therefore responsible to the laws of no one country. Decisions are based primarily on corporate needs, and although some economists hail the potential of multinationals to improve the economy of developing countries, others see *economic imperialism* replacing the political and military imperialism of the past (Barnet and Cavanagh, 1994).

In these many ways, then, contemporary capitalism differs greatly from the ideal of competing small firms in a perfect market. But the system has shown enormous staying power, and, with the collapse of socialist economies throughout Eastern Europe and Asia in the early 1990s, capitalism has emerged as the dominant economic system throughout most of the world. But it will be a capitalism with many variations, adapted to the unique history and characteristics of each nation. Some forms will succeed in raising the standard of living of the masses (Nee, 1991), and other forms may only add to continued underdevelopment (Burawoy and Krotov, 1992).

Socialism

Socialism, in its ideal form, is an economic system in which the means of production are collectively owned and in which the distribution of goods and services is guided by public needs. Socialist goals include (1) the reduction of inequality based on inherited wealth and status and (2) the widest distribution of basic resources such as education, housing, and health care. Just as the promise of prosperity for all under capitalism remains unfulfilled, so also do the egalitarian ideals of socialism.

The real world is considerably more complicated than its theoretical representations. And as Marx and Weber were well aware, economic systems cannot be understood in isolation from other institutional spheres. We have seen, for example, how the work ethic (Chapter 3) was essential to the rise of capitalism and how the family's dependence on a male wage earner produced a disciplined labor force. In turn, major changes in the mode of subsistence cause change in other institutions, such as when industrialization reduces the power of the extended family over young people.

In socialist theory, which owes much to Marx's critique of capitalism, the ultimate goal is the transformation of private property into a public good. When the forces of production are claimed in the name of all citizens, the distinction between owners and workers, the cause of social conflict throughout history, no longer exists. Reflecting the new economic order, family and gender relationships will become more egalitarian, education and belief systems less authoritarian, and politics more representative. How close has any modern society come to this ideal?

CONTEMPORARY SOCIALISM.   Socialism has many contemporary forms. At one extreme, in the former Soviet Union and East Germany, centralized controls of production brought the economy close to total collapse in the late 1980s, leading to the downfall of their Communist governments. Contrary to the socialist ideal, shortages of goods and rising prices led to increased inequality in the standard of living between the political elite and the rest of society, causing spiraling rates of alcoholism, crime, and other social problems (Jones et al., 1991). In addition to an elite of government officials, the workers themselves were stratified by benefits from their employing organization (Nee et al., 1994; Walder, 1992).

More limited and flexible forms of economic planning are found in almost all Western democracies, especially in Sweden and Denmark, where production remains largely in private hands but the distribution of essential services is a public responsibility. This

Multinational corporations are firms with branches and factories in many countries and whose ownership is not linked to one nation.

Socialism is an economic system is which the means of production are collectively owned and the distribution of goods and services is guided by public needs.

Many consumer goods have been in short supply in the Eastern European countries and in the new countries of the former Soviet Union for some time now. The supply of goods has not yet improved, as is evident by these very long lines inside GUM, a major department store in Moscow, Russia.

system is often called **democratic, or welfare, socialism.** In Sweden, for example, inequality in income and access to education, housing, and social services was greatly reduced throughout the 1970s and 1980s (Olsson, 1990). Since 1990, however, the world economic recession has caused cutbacks in socialist programs throughout Europe.

Welfare socialism involves very high rates of taxation: over half the value of total goods and services produced in Sweden, about 44 percent in France, and 38 percent in Germany and Italy, compared with only 30 percent for the United States. In return, citizens of most European countries receive family allowances, health insurance, and other benefits for which Americans must pay out of pocket. Indeed, when we total an American family's payments for medical expenses, college costs, and care of elderly relatives, the financial burden is at least as high as that paid in taxes by Swedes. The major difference is that the costs and benefits are spread more evenly among Swedes than among Americans, where ability to pay determines the quantity and quality of services received.

Another major problem for socialism is the deadening effect of the layers of bureaucracy required for central planning. An expanding number of jobs in government is functional in providing white-collar employment for college graduates but can be equally dysfunctional when speedy and risky decision making is required. The process of *goal displacement* leads to an emphasis on protecting one's job over making any decisions and was a major problem in Eastern Europe and the former Soviet Union, where college graduates were produced at a faster rate than the economy could absorb them (Zaslavskaya, 1990).

THE FUTURE OF SOCIALISM.   The socialist ideal of an economy fully responsive to the needs of all citizens was one of the most powerful intellectual currents of the modern era, with an impact on the political and economic development of both industrial and developing nations. Today, however, the failure of the most self-consciously socialist systems in Europe, Asia, and Africa has brought the entire project into question. Does socialism have a future? Is free-enterprise capitalism the key to universal well-being?

Many scholars claim that any system of planned production is fatally flawed by constant shortages and bureaucratic and political controls that no reform can overcome (Kornai, 1992; Poznanski, 1992). Other observers claim that socialism should be distinguished from the communist version and that when combined with a democratic political system it is an essential corrective to the excesses of capitalism (Lemke and Marks, 1992; Roemer, 1991).

In reality, contemporary capitalism has already been transformed by the expansion of social welfare programs, more thoroughly in Europe than in the United States, and by state regulation of the money supply and business practices. Indeed, as the capitalist promise of prosperity is realized in developing nations the demand for public services such as education, health care, and old-age pensions will increase also.

Postindustrial Society

Many of the trends discussed earlier in this book combine to characterize the **postindustrial society,** different enough from the industrial society to deserve its own name (Fiala, 1992). The postindustrial economy is based on continued expansion of the service sector, the importance of theoretical knowledge over mechanical skills, a decline in patriarchy and other forms of inequality, a concern with quality of life, heightened awareness of the self, and an emphasis on interpersonal relationships and consumption values in contrast to the self-restraints of the work ethic (Bell, 1973; Block, 1990).

The term *postmodern* is often used to describe the social and cultural aspects of postindustrial society, such as the breakdown of traditional hierarchies, a blurring of reality, and an emphasis on high-tech self-gratification at the expense of traditional values (Baker, 1990). If modern society is based on *differentiation* (reinforcing hierarchical distinctions), the postmodern world is characterized by *dedifferentiation,* a blurring of class differences in patterns of consumption and a dissolving of centralized structures such as the assembly line and bureaucratic organizations. The outcome could be increased equality and democratic workplaces, such as in Sweden, *or* wider differences between the privileged few and the vast majority of the population, such as in Japan or the United States (Clegg, 1990; Burris, 1994).

Under **democratic, or welfare, socialism,** goods and services may be privately produced, but the distribution of essential services is centrally controlled.

Postindustrial society is characterized by an expanding service sector and the importance of knowledge.

Division of labor is the separation of work into distinct parts, each of which is performed by an individual or a group of people.

THE ORGANIZATION OF WORK

While awaiting the postindustrial transformation of society, the structure of most work organizations continues to be characterized by extreme specialization, or **division of labor** in which tasks are divided into distinct parts, each of which is performed by an individual or group. The very complexity of modern economies and the expansion of technical knowledge ensures that most workers will be trained in a limited range of skills. The U.S. Department of Labor publishes a *Dictionary of Occupational Titles* with over 20,000 entries!

The film *Modern Times*, with Charlie Chaplin, satirizes the effect of machinery and assembly lines on workers. Have you ever felt like a cog in a wheel at your job or at your college?

Such specialization has led social theorists from Durkheim, Weber, and Marx to Talcott Parsons and Kai Erickson to view the organization of industrial work as potentially harmful to social unity. When each person participates in the society and culture in a limited way, it is difficult to generate a sense of shared values and common fate.

Durkheim's concern was the lack of intermediate groups between the worker and the impersonal forces of government and employers, such as family, worker associations or religious groups. Weber spoke of the "disenchantment of the world" as science and technology expand their hegemony over daily life. And Marx saw it all leading to **alienation,** a sense of powerlessness, of being cut off from one's own labor, from other people, and eventually from oneself (Blauner, 1964; Seeman, 1972). The concept of alienated labor has most recently been applied to a variety of contemporary workplaces, from an automated factory to a sweatshop (Erikson and Vallas, 1990; Geyer and Heinz, 1992).

Alienation is the feeling of powerlessness, normlessness, and being cut off from the product of one's labor, from other people, and from oneself.

The dominant structure of industrialization is the factory, which brings workers out of their home to a central location where machines and labor power can be used most efficiently under direct control of management. The perfect embodiment of this system is the assembly line, with each worker repeatedly performing a single function. The link between an assembly-line worker and the finished product is all but invisible. For example, an old-fashioned shoemaker makes an entire shoe, from selecting the material to fitting the customer and has a feeling of creative pride. The assembly-line worker who attaches a heel to each shoe as it passes down the line will have little sense of personal pride in the finished product.

Robots have replaced humans on the assembly lines of all major auto manufacturers. Their virtue? Neither American nor Japanese robots complain, take coffee breaks, join unions, gossip, come to work late, or have personal problems.

This process has been described as "de-skilling," in contrast to the accumulation of skills often required of workers in the past (Braverman, 1974; Feldberg and Glenn, 1982). But many changes in occupational technology require *skill upgrading,* such as when typists learn the intricacies of word processing (DiPrete, 1988; Vallas, 1993).

Automation

The ultimate in impersonal production is **automation,** whereby workers are replaced by a machine. Although initial costs are high, machines are cheaper in the long run, and easier for management to control. Machines do not join unions, take coffee breaks, or expect a pension at the end of their worklife. For many tasks, however, they may be no more efficient than humans, and they require highly skilled operators who tend to keep their knowledge to themselves to maintain control of the work process (Zuboff, 1988). But many more workers are displaced than find upgraded jobs.

Worker Satisfaction

Despite the routine dullness of most work and the fact that only 40 percent hold the job they planned, a majority of American workers express satisfaction with their employment (Gallup, 1990). Many will have lowered aspirations to fit reality and to avoid a sense of failure; others take pleasure in workplace friendships or the goods they can purchase with earnings.

Worker satisfaction is highest in jobs where the employee can make decisions regarding the pacing and sequencing of the work and where supervision is light. Such **job autonomy** reduces alienation and job stress by giving the employee control over the work process and boosting self-esteem (Kohn et al., 1990; Mortimer and Lorence, 1989; Galinsky et al., 1993; Link et al., 1993). In general, high autonomy is most often found in high-pay and high-prestige occupations.

> **Automation** is the replacing of workers with machines.
>
> **Job autonomy** involves making decisions about the timing and sequence of tasks, exercising judgment, and having an impact on the outcome.

In contrast, work satisfaction is lowest among employees who are kept to a tight schedule, closely monitored, expected to use complex skills on repetitive tasks, and who feel pressured—typical features of low-pay, low-prestige occupations. These conditions have a similar effect on women and men, but women are more likely to be found in low-satisfaction jobs (Loscocco and Spitze, 1990).

As shown in Figure 13-4, income and promotion come last in a list of desirable job characteristics; they are also the aspects with which respondents felt least satisfied in their own job (Galinsky et al., 1993). Other goals, however, were highly valued: interesting work, recognition from co-workers, and ability to help others.

Figure 13-4 Reasons considered "very important" when taking current job (in percents).
Source: Galinsky et al., 1993

#	Reason	%	#	Reason	%
1	Open communication	65%	11	Job location	50%
2	Effect on personal/family life	60	12	Family-supportive policies	46
3	Nature of work	59	13	Fringe benefits	43
4	Management quality	59	14	Control of work schedule	38
5	Supervisor	58	15	Advancement opportunity	37
6	Gain new skills	55	16	Salary/wage	35
7	Control over work content	55	17	Access to decision makers	33
8	Job security	54	18	No other offers	32
9	Co-worker quality	53	19	Management opportunity	26
10	Stimulating work	50	20	Size of employer	18

Changes in the Industrial Workplace

Because satisfied workers are likely to be more productive, many American companies in the late 1980s adopted some form of employee involvement system similar to those used in Japan and Europe (Cole, 1989; Florida and Kenney, 1991). One of the most common is the **quality circle** in which teams composed of workers and managers meet weekly to discuss how to raise productivity and improve working conditions. Although ordinary workers may get to call the bosses by their first names, the essential relationship of inequality between employee and employer remains unchallenged.

> **Quality circles** are teams of employees and managers who meet to discuss how to improve their work performance.
>
> **Workplace democracy** occurs when the workers become the managers and often the owners.

In many cases, management has used employee involvement techniques to increase its control over work processes or to ward off unionization (Grenier, 1988). Evidence on the effectiveness of employee participation plans suggests that such programs do little to improve productivity or worker morale compared to the effects of a strong labor union (Kelley and Harrison, 1992; Vallas, 1993).

WORKPLACE DEMOCRACY.   The ultimate in employee participation is **workplace democracy,** whereby the workers become the managers and, often, the owners (Rothschild and Whitt, 1987). Worker-owned firms in the United States are usually ones that a capitalist owner has abandoned as unprof-

itable, with good cause. Despite its limited success, the democratic workplace remains a valued goal of labor activists, even though little evidence indicates that worker-owners embrace egalitarian and cooperative values (Greenberg, 1986; Krimerman and Lindenfield, 1992).

Experiments in workplace democracy are more common and more successful outside the United States—most notably in the Mondragon cooperative complex in Spain (Whyte and Whyte, 1988)—and also in some developing nations (Bayat, 1991). In Canada, one of the largest experiments in worker ownership, the Algoma steel plant, recently showed a profit as well as a dramatic increase in worker morale (Farnsworth, 1993a).

In the 1970s, new forms of worker–management cooperation were established in Britain, France, West Germany, and Sweden. Since the early 1980s, however, economic recession, managerial resistance, and a more conservative political climate have halted or reversed many of the workers' gains (Hancock et al., 1991; Ferner and Hyman, 1992). Whatever the lessons of the European experience, they will have to be applied selectively to the United States, which lacks a tradition of economic cooperation and egalitarianism in the workplace (MacShane, 1993).

ESOPS.   Short of any meaningful role in management decisions, the closest that most American workers will come to ownership is through *employee stock ownership programs (ESOPs)*. Under these plans, shares in company stock are part of the worker's benefit package. Because receipt of the stock is usually deferred until the employee leaves or retires, management continues to have voting power and certain tax

Although current quality circles in American firms are adapted from a Japanese model, the United States and England introduced employee participation during World Wars I and II. Following World War II, the Japanese perfected the concept, incorporating it into their management systems. These American workers, participating in a quality circle, are employees of a Japanese automaker in the United States.

Do They Really Do It Better in Japan?

Throughout the 1980s, Americans were bombarded with pictures of throngs of happy Japanese workers, dressed in the company uniform, doing gymnastics before starting another productive workday, assured of lifetime employment, and deeply committed to the employer (Lincoln and Kalleberg, 1990).

In reality, only about 20 percent of Japanese workers have lifetime tenure, and these are primarily men employed in government and large corporations, some of whom lost their jobs in the recession of the 1990s. Class and sex inequality are more characteristic of the Japanese economy than of our own and Japanese

unions weaker than the American model. The emphasis on group goals and dependency on the the employer for social services (*paternalism*) co-opted the workers, with the willing assistance of politicians who received vast sums from major corporations (Gerlach, 1992). The Japanese worker does show a high level of commitment to work, as demonstrated by the low rates of absenteeism and turnover, but this is primarily a result of pressures from family and co-workers rather than of positive feelings toward the employer (Besser, 1993). The cost of living in Japan is very high, wages are low, and households are crowded because few can afford homes of their own, unless it's a three-room residence with a two hour commute to work (Sterngold, 1994). Nor are the elderly treated with any more respect than in the United States. In short, few American workers would want to change places with their Japanese counterpart.

The economic boom of the 1980s did not last into the 1990s. Banks have collapsed along with the real estate market, factories have closed, jobs have moved to other parts of Asia, and social welfare programs have been reduced (Sassen, 1992; Sanger, 1993.) A few businessmen have amassed great wealth while a growing underclass fills the major cities.

All these problems have not kept American employers from adopting Japanese manufacturing techniques, most recently a system called *lean production*, whereby parts are delivered only at the very last moment, thus cutting inventory and overhead (Holusha, 1994). Because the process requires great discipline from workers, critics have called it the "lean and mean" system, a far cry from the humanized workplace envisaged in the 1980s. But in tough economic times, worker morale is not a high priority in either country.

advantages (Adams and Ellerman, 1989). As with other forms of employee involvement, ESOPs appear to have minimal effect on worker productivity or company profitability (Russell, 1990).

In summary, the new industrial workplace looks very much like the old one, despite cosmetic changes. The workers who benefit most are those who already enjoy many advantages in the labor force: older, better educated, nonmanual, supervisors, and members of the dominant racial and ethnic groups (Taylor et al., 1987). The best hope for workplace democracy remains with organized labor.

Throughout Europe, the economic interests of the working class have been represented by a political organization called the "Labor" or "Social Democratic" party in a system of other class-based political parties. In contrast, in the United States, although capitalists tend to vote Republican and manual workers tend to vote Democratic, the two parties embrace issues and voters across class and status lines. The interests of

American workers have been largely represented by self-governing labor associations (trade and craft unions) rather than by a centralized, nationwide political organization.

THE AMERICAN LABOR MOVEMENT

How capable of protecting worker interests are American unions? Among modern industrial societies, Japan and the United States are unique in the weakness of their labor organizations. From its beginning in the period following the Civil War, the American labor movement was fiercely resisted by employers and all levels of government, to the point where, in 1886, Chicago police opened fire on workers supporting the radical idea of an eight-hour workday. Just over 100 years ago, at the Carnegie Steel plant in Homestead, Pennsylvania, a pitched battle

The strong resistance by employers and the government in the United States to a broad-based union movement was often harsh and violent, as seen in this wood engraving of Chicago police firing at a workers' rally in Haymarket Square in 1886. Today, the proportion of the U.S. work force private industry organized for collective bargaining is smaller than in 1936, when labor law reforms were enacted. Greater antagonism against unions by big business and the government reflects the decline of Big Labor's political clout.

between unionized workers and Pinkerton guards hired by Carnegie led to the state militia occupying the town and protecting the mill while it hired nonunion workers (Krause, 1992). These are only two examples of attempts to organize factory workers meeting with crushing defeat at the hands of state and local government.

These tactics delayed legal recognition of unions and their right to bargain on behalf of members until 1935, during the presidency of Franklin D. Roosevelt, in return for their cooperation in reducing labor violence and in ridding themselves of their more radical members (McCammon, 1993, 1994). The result was a labor movement more often opposed to immigrants, women workers, and racial minorities than to management, even though the few remaining radical unions won the most favorable contracts (Schutt, 1987; Olzak, 1989; Asher and Stephenson, 1990; Stepan-Norris and Zeitlin, 1991).

Within American labor, a fierce struggle for power pitted unions representing skilled craft workers such as carpenters or machinists (American Federation of Labor) against those representing all workers in a given industry such as steel or garment manufacturing (Congress of Industrial Organizations). Only in 1955 did the two join ranks to form the AFL-CIO. But by then, organized labor in the United States was already in decline, slipping from a high of 35 percent of the work force in 1945 to a little less than 16 percent today—only 12 percent of private sector workers but an increasing proportion of employees in the public sector (government, education, health care). This decline in membership can be traced to a number of broader trends in the economy and the society (Cornfield, 1989; Jaffee, 1986; Bluestone and Bluestone, 1992):

■ Deindustrialization: The loss of jobs in highly unionized "smokestack" industries such as automobile and steel production, which was due to plant closings and foreign competition

■ Reagan–Bush administration policies that made imports cheaper and that were openly hostile to most unions

■ Failure of union leadership, until recently, to organize service industries with large numbers of women and minority employees

■ Employers' threats to relocate and actually to move to states and countries with weak labor organizations

■ State and local policies that make union organizing difficult and that protect business interests

■ Negative public perception of unions, as a result of successful "demonizing" by employers and highly visible cases of criminal involvement (e.g., the Teamsters)

Not all attacks come from conservatives. The unions have also been criticized by liberals for their failure to become a class-based force in opposition to the overwhelming economic power of owners. Critics claim that union leaders have become co-opted; that they suffer goal displacement; and that the workers who have benefited most from the movement (highly skilled white men in blue-collar occupations) have turned their back on the original goals of the labor movement: to improve the status of all workers, reduce inequality in the society, and bring democracy to the workplace. These were the "Reagan democrats" of the 1980s who thus contributed to the decline of organized labor.

In reality, unionized workers enjoy higher pay, greater job security, and better protected benefits than do their counterparts in nonunionized work-places (Wiatrowski, 1994). All American workers have benefited from such union-initiated achievements as the eight-hour day and five-day workweek, health and pension benefits, sick leave and unemployment insurance, the minimum wage, and a safer and more sanitary workplace (Nyden, 1984; Shostak, 1990). But with the current decline in union power and the threat of employer relocation and firings, workers are losing ground in wage settlements and fringe benefits, and in many cases have agreed to "givebacks" of previously won gains (Hathaway, 1993).

To the argument that unions have made the American economy less productive than foreign competitors, the evidence suggests otherwise: Unions tend to increase productivity, although employer profits may be lowered (Mishel and Voos, 1992). With the exception of Japan, unions are much stronger and more representative of the entire labor force in other industrial societies, where membership has grown while remaining competitive in the world markets (Brody, 1992; Western, 1993). The key difference appears to be that American employers and governments have never overcome their deeply ingrained opposition to unions. In contrast, in Canada and most of Europe, management and labor have been able to work together to increase production while protecting worker's jobs and health.

The Future of American Unions

If American unions are to survive, they must attract previously nonunionized types of workers: high-tech white-collar employees as well as low-wage service personnel, part-timers, and women workers in general. Organizing white-collar employees is difficult, because they do not perceive themselves as being similar to factory workers; but increasingly they are forming "professional associations." Public employee and teachers' unions are the fastest growing segment of the labor movement today. But the future of organized labor may rest in the hands of women workers.

WOMEN AND THE LABOR MOVEMENT.   Historically, organized labor in the United States has been a white-male fellowship, even though the early factories were filled with women and children. From the early 1800s to the 1930s, women workers were among the most militant supporters of the rights of labor, producing remarkable leaders such as Lavinia Wright, Sarah Bagley, "Mother Jones," and Mary Mc-Cloud Bethune. They were supported by middle-class reformers such as Lillian Wald and Jane Addams, concerned about the poverty of working-class mothers and children.

Nonetheless, the unions remained dominated by the white male leaders of skilled trade unions, who grew increasingly conservative, anti-Communist, and not very supportive of civil rights or women's rights. Even today, only a few women are in leadership positions, yet it is precisely the fields in which women workers predominate that offer the best chance of reversing the unions' decline: government offices, health care facilities, schools, and the communications industry (Cook, 1992; Cobble, 1993). Two out of three new union members in both Canada and the United States today are women, and in both countries women will be a majority of the workforce by the end of the century (International Labor Organization, 1993). Even now, women account for 40 percent of union membership.

LABOR SEGMENTATION

Although organized labor has raised the status of some workers, it has failed to reduce inequality within the working class. A major source of inequality among workers is the stratification of the economy itself, especially between the "core" and "periphery" sectors (Weakliem, 1990). The **core sector** consists of major industries (steel, auto, chemical) with heavy investment in plants and equipment, a unionized labor force, monopoly status, and relatively high profitability. The **peripheral sector,** in contrast, is composed of smaller, highly competitive, low-profit, labor-intensive businesses (clothing manufacture, fast food).

This **dual economy** is complemented by a **split, or segmented, labor market,** with core workers drawn from a largely white male pool and peripheral workers from a pool composed largely of women and minority employees. Depending on one's location in this labor market, a worker receives very different wages despite similar years of education and training. Within either the core or the periphery, firms vary in opportunities for job mobility and skill upgrading (Kelley, 1990; Sakamoto and Chen, 1991). But these variations should not obscure the larger insight of the dual economy: Wage inequality by sex and race is primarily determined by the organization in which one is employed rather

The **core sector** of the economy consists of major industries, large investments in plants and equipment, unionized labor, monopolies, and high profits.

The **peripheral sector** of the economy consists of smaller, competitive, low-profit firms employing low-pay, nonunion manual workers.

Dual economy refers to the existence of two separate types of employing firms: core and peripheral.

The **split,** or **segmented, labor market** is differentiated by race and gender, core workers being white men, and peripheral workers being primarily women and minorities.

Organizing on Campus: From Haymarket Square to Harvard Yard.

One key location for organizing today is the college campus, where women compose the vast majority of support staff, at wages well below the private sector, and without the benefits enjoyed by teachers and administrators. Up until the late 1980s, attempts to organize staff workers were fiercely resisted by university administrations that openly threatened and fired the "ringleaders" (Sacks, 1988). It became increasingly difficult, however, for major universities such as Harvard and Yale to claim that they were somehow exempt from the laws of the workplace.

After a bitter battle and a finding of misconduct on the part of the university, Harvard finally recognized a union of technical and clerical workers. The union pro-

ceeded to negotiate a contract that raised pay and benefits and brought the staff into the governance structure (Hoerr, 1993). The contract is most unusual in that the typical list of work rules has been replaced with a commitment by the parties to remain in a participatory relationship for joint problem solving.

Many observers believe that this "new type" of union, rooted in the daily experience of workers and drawing them into partnership in decision making, both within the union and between workers and management, will be the best hope for revitalizing the American labor movement (Bruyn, 1991). The old adversarial model has lost its effectiveness, and the co-opted leadership of the 1970s and 1980s has lost much of its legitimacy. It remains to be seen whether the participatory model can bring people back to the unions by bringing the unions back to the people.

than on the basis of personal qualifications (Coverdill, 1988). But even core workers may be losing their wage advantage as union power declines (Kilbourne et al., 1994).

> If we compare one country of the civilized world with another . . . we find that the degradation of the working classes varies almost uniformly with the amount of rough work done by women.
>
> —ALFRED MARSHALL (1890/1961)

Workplaces vary not only in terms of wages and promotion opportunities, but also with respect to

benefits such as health insurance, parental leave, paid vacation time, and most importantly, pension plans (Pearce, 1987; Perman and Stevens, 1989). Because such benefits are most common in the core sector and among white-collar employees, inequalities within the labor force accumulate over a person's work life and continue into retirement (O'Rand and MacLean, 1986).

Most negatively affected by the growth of the peripheral sector are women of color who often work in nonunionized, unsafe, and unsanitary jobs. The three "Ds" of the 1980s—deregulation, discrimination, and deindustrialization—have combined to worsen the labor market situation of women and minorities, and minority women in particular (Woody, 1992; Tienda et al., 1992).

The Global Assembly Line

The situation in the United States is mirrored in the international economy. As the industrial West and Japan drift into the postindustrial era of high-tech services, much of their manufacturing, core and peripheral, has been exported to the Third World. Most of your clothing and electronic equipment is now made in Asia and Latin America. Even the items marked "Made in the USA" are likely to have been manufactured in the Western Pacific islands of Saipan and the Marianas, technically American territory, by imported Chinese and Philippine labor (Shenon, 1993).

Wages are cheap, benefits low, and environmental regulation minimal. Along the Mexican–U.S. border, for

example, employment in assembly plants (*maquiladoras*) rose from 130,000 in 1981 to over 500,000 today. Although worker productivity increased greatly during this period, wages did not. In many such industries, across the globe, the work force is composed of young women, who work for lower wages than men and who are easier for employers to control. The women also remain dominated by family relations and obligations (Lee, 1993). Training programs for the more skilled and better paying jobs are reserved for men, so that traditional power relationships by gender, age, and social class are reinforced (Scoville, 1991). The Third World and its most powerless citizens have become the "periphery" to the developed nations' "core" (Ward, 1990).

MARY ROMERO

Coping with Exploitation of Domestic Workers

Mary Romero is an associate professor of sociology at the University of Oregon. She is the author of Maid in the U.S.A. *(Routledge, 1992).*

My mother, sister, sister-in-law, and cousins were employed as private household workers. As a schoolchild, I worked with my mother during holidays and summers, and as a college student, I returned to domestic service as a second job when necessary. But it was not until after graduate school that an event occurred that led me to see issues of paid and unpaid housework as serious subjects for research.

Before beginning a college teaching post in Texas, I stayed at the home of a colleague who employed a live-in domestic worker. Until then, I had been unaware of the practice of hiring teenage undocumented Mexican women as household help. Nor had I had access to the social or "private" space of an employer. I was shocked at the way my colleague and his family treated the 16-year-old domestic whom I will call Juanita. Only recently hired, Juanita was still adjusting to her new environment; her shyness was reinforced by my colleague's constant flirting. I observed many encounters that served to remind Juanita of her subservient role. For example, one evening I walked into the kitchen as the employer's young

sons were pointing to dirty dishes on the table and in the sink and yelling "Wash! Clean!" Juanita stood frozen, angry and humiliated. Aware of the risks of my reprimanding the boys, I chose instead to suggest that Juanita and I would wash and dry the dishes, while the boys cleared the table. When my host returned from his meeting and found us cleaning the last pan, his expression told me how shocked he was to find his houseguest and future colleague washing dishes with the maid. His obvious embarrassment confirmed my suspicion that I had violated the normative expectations of class-based behavior within the home.

That experience focused my attention on the situation of young undocumented Mexican women living in the country club environment of border cities. They worked long hours in the intimacy of middle-class American homes but were starved for respect and positive social interaction. Curiously, although employers rarely treated a domestic as "one of the family," they did not see themselves as "employers" in an impersonal economic sense; rather, they defined hiring a domestic as a way of "helping those poor Mexican women." I began to wonder professionally about the Chicanas employed as domestics that I had known throughout my own life and about their vulnerability to exploitation, racism, and sexism.

I also began to question the feminist analyses of household labor that ignored or obscured the experience of domestic workers, most of whom are women of color. Although the burden of housework unites women, the question of who does it clearly divides them on the basis of class, race, and ethnicity. Resources for

purchasing household assistance differ greatly among women. Working-class women who cannot afford paid help typically reallocate tasks among other family members, most often to other females. Women with financial resources can hire people to do "their" work: low-wage women to do general cleaning and men to handle the household tasks defined as requiring specific skills. Both the first and second wave of feminism encouraged women's involvement outside the home yet failed to achieve the goal of making men assume some responsibility for the household and children. Consequently, the need for domestic service has increased along with women's labor force participation.

Not long after my encounter with Juanita, I began systematic research on Chicana household workers. The women I interviewed were aware of the stigma attached to doing degraded work but continued in the occupation because it paid more than other alternatives available to them. In addition, the job offered autonomy, room for negotiating the employee–employer relationship. Chicana domestics struggled to maintain instrumental (i.e., task-related rather than personal) relationships, defining the employer's home as a workplace, and establishing a business-like environment. Strategies used included (1) increasing job flexibility; (2) bargaining for higher pay and benefits; (3) establishing a contractual basis for the relationship; (4) minimizing contact with the employer; and (5) defining themselves as a professional housekeeper. Thus were these women able to upgrade their occupational status and eliminate vestiges of servitude.

TRENDS IN EMPLOYMENT AND UNEMPLOYMENT

Employment and unemployment rates reflect the dual economy as well as the overall state of the economy. These rates are based on a large probability sample of U.S. households contacted each month and asked whether or not any family member was working for wages the previous week. Until January 1994, the survey defined any paid work as "employment," regardless of the time involved. If a person was not employed but actively seeking a job, he or she was officially classified as "unemployed." This definition understated the amount of joblessness on the part of discouraged job seekers who have given up looking as well as underemployment of those forced to settle for part-time work or employment below their skill level. Most crucially, the survey underestimated unemployment rates for working women who were also homemakers. In response to these distortions, the questionnaire was revised in January 1994 and came up with higher rates than found with the older method. This also means that we cannot accurately compare rates from before 1994 with those after that date.

It does appear that overall unemployment, which hit a postdepression high of over 10 percent in 1982–1983 has now declined to about 6 percent, higher for minority workers, and especially so for Hispanics during the 1990-92 recession (Boisjoly and Duncan, 1994).

Relocation

Unemployment is also high in the industrial Midwest, where plant closings have left the predominately white labor force without jobs or hope of employment in their home towns. In addition to income loss, unemployment has a negative effect on family ties, friendships, and a person's mental and physical health (Hamilton et al., 1990; Catalano et al., 1993). When laid-off workers find new jobs, it is usually at reduced wages, thus limiting upward mobility for their children as well (Rosen, 1987; Perrucci et al., 1988; Moore, 1990; Kilborn, 1993).

Especially hard hit are the Appalachian region and the South, where the flight of capital and jobs has brought massive unemployment among miners, farmers, home workers, and factory employees of both sexes, all races, and age groups (Gaventa et al., 1990). Having lured businesses to these areas with promises of low taxes and no unions, the states of the region have few defenses when employers find even more attractive locations in Asia, Mexico, and Central America.

Downsizing

Another way to lower the corporate payroll is through *downsizing,* a polite way of referring to lay-offs of white-collar employees. One of the ways in which the recession of the early 1990s differs from those of the past is that employers are now trimming administrative and managerial staff. These are primarily white middle-aged men whose value on the job market is problematic and who, for the most part, will be forced to settle for a job with lower pay, prestige, and pension benefits. Some will become consultants or will establish small businesses with a high risk of failure (Harrison, 1994).

Another way in which the current economic scene differs from earlier patterns is that the good factory and office jobs will not return even when the economy recovers from the recession. To the contrary, almost all of the new jobs created today are relatively unstable and unattractive, and more often than not, part-time.

The Temping of the Labor Force

America's offices and factories are increasingly filed with part-time—contingent (conditional)—workers. Over the past decade, as the total labor force has grown by less than 20 percent, contingent employment has increased *250 percent,* and by the year 2000, one-half of all American workers will be tempo-

A number of American manufacturers have established plants in Third World countries with few safety standards, where workers receive very low wages and cannot form unions. In many developing countries governments have no laws against child labor and products are made by children and teenagers. What is the impact of such practices on Americans?

rary or part-time workers (Morrow, 1993; Uchitelle, 1993). Contingent labor has many advantages for employers: Workers can be hired and laid off as the firm's requirements fluctuate; they do not require health, pension, and other fringe benefits; and they are powerless. Because most of the increase in part-time employment since 1970 has been among those who would prefer full-time jobs, many Americans now work two part-time jobs, still without benefits (U.S. Department of Labor, 1994d).

Outsourcing is another type of contingent employment and refers to shifting tasks from within to outside the the corporate setting: temporary employment agencies, independent contractors, service suppliers, consultants, freelancers, and home-based workers—an "invisible work force" (Lozano, 1989). Advantages for the employer are, once again, relief from fringe benefits or even tax withholding; and terms of employment are negotiated in a situation favoring the employer. Advantages for workers are less clear. Parents may prefer a flexible work schedule; and others enjoy the independence of freelancing. But most will be working for less pay as well as fewer benefits than comparable full-time, in-house employees.

Many of these workers will join the **underground economy,** or informal labor force, in which the independent contractor is paid in cash with a minimal paper trail to avoid reporting taxable income. The underground economy also includes workers engaged in illegal activities (e.g., drug dealing) that pay far more than regular employment and often bring greater status rewards. For obvious reasons, it is impossible to measure the extent of the underground economy, but it undoubtedly expands when opportunities for legitimate, stable employment contract. To this extent, official unemployment data may underestimate the number of full-time workers.

Nonworkers

In addition to the millions of students and retired persons who are out of the labor force voluntarily and homemakers whose labor is not counted as "work," another 15–20 million are involuntary nonworkers. This category includes discouraged job seekers, single mothers for whom employment would lower their standard of living because of the cost of child care and the loss of medical insurance, and people who have worked only a few months of the year (officially "employed" but actually not working).

> The **underground economy** is an informal labor force in which the independent contractor is paid in cash to avoid reporting taxable income.

Despite the large number of adults among the unemployed, underemployed, and nonworkers, a potentially more serious social problem is the lack of stable job opportunities for young people.

Youth Unemployment

For the 50 percent of American youth who do not continue their education after high school, steady em-

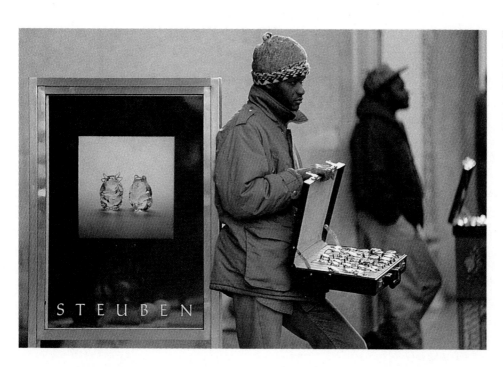

Some of the workers of the underground economy include street vendors selling many items such as watches, jewelry, clothing and books. They can be found in all the major cities of the United States.

ployment is the normatively legitimated means of achieving adult status. Unfortunately, unemployment rates for young people are two to three times higher than for people age 25 and older. As seen in Figure 13-5, unemployment among teenagers has risen sharply in the 1990s, with a continuing gap between white and African-American and Hispanic youth.

Among men in their early 20s, nonwhite unemployment rates remain over twice as high as those of white youth. Remembering that official data greatly understate the lack of full-time year-round employment, we can appreciate the seriousness of the problem for young Latinos and African Americans, for whom the likelihood of establishing a stable marriage and a long-term commitment to the labor force become particularly problematic. The major problem is that the kinds of jobs required for a successful adulthood are very few and far between in the urban areas in which so many minority youth are concentrated (Massey and Denton, 1993).

For a majority of inner-city teenagers, low-skill jobs at below the minimum wage will not go very far in solving their problems. Much more is needed: family stability; decent housing; adequate schooling; strong community organizations; and control of street crime, the drug culture, and random violence (Ogbu, 1989). Although many white ethnic and Latino teenagers are unemployed and unemployable, the situation of young African-American men appears to be the most

Studies of inner-city African-American youth show that most are as serious about getting good jobs as are white youths, but many fewer jobs exist, and those that do pay lower wages. Here inner-city teens are being trained for summer jobs.

potentially costly to society—a "lost generation" of men without labor force experience or legitimate means of supporting a family.

Why is this young woman happy? She just learned that she was accepted for admission to the highly selective Tokyo University, and, like other college students, she won't have to find full-time employment for the next four years.

Figure 13-5 Unemployment among men and women age 16–19, by race and Hispanic origin, 1980–1994.

Sources: U.S. Bureau of the Census, *Statistical Abstract of the United States*, 1993:413; U.S. Department of Labor, *Employment and Earnings*, 1994.

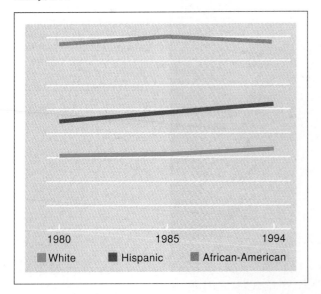

THE ORGANIZATION OF BUSINESS

The Sociological Study of Business Organizations

The sociology of economic systems also embraces the study of business organizations as social actors and carriers of a special culture. Research in this area spans a wide spectrum of topics. Some studies deal with the effects of characteristics of the organization on the people in it. For example, one study addressed how mobility opportunities for white-collar employees may depend less on individual traits than on the size, complexity, and share of market power of the organization (e.g., Villemez and Bridges, 1988).

Other research is more purely macrolevel, examining the population of corporations. Here, the vocabulary of social ecology is often used to describe how firms relate to one another and to their external environment, adapting more or less successfully to changes in consumer demand, labor markets, and competition (Hannan and Freeman, 1987; Singh, 1990). Looking at the spatial restructuring of the American automobile industry, for example, we can trace major shifts in the geography of plant locations, in response to labor market conditions, declining sales, and rising transportation costs (Rubenstein, 1992). The most recent move, from plants located in Michigan and coastal areas to the Midwest can be explained in terms of the need to consolidate production where freight costs are lowest and workers least likely to be militant. The effect of big business on the economic well-being of communities can be positive or negative, depending on the structure of the community. The more urbanized and open to a variety of subgroups, the more positive the impact of a branch plant on the local area (Young and Lyson, 1993).

Another type of ecological analysis centers on the question of why some new firms succeed and others fail. As one recent large-scale study of newly formed business organizations in Germany shows, the answer involves a complex set of both internal and external factors: individual traits of the founders, structural characteristics and strategies pursued by the organization itself, and the firm's location in labor and consumer markets (Bruderl et al., 1992). In a study of American manufacturing plants, the researchers found that the most crucial factor was investment in research and knowledge (Hage et al., 1993).

Another tradition in organizational studies examines internal processes, for example, how information is used or decisions made (e.g., Stinchcombe, 1990). Once the organization has been successfully launched and expanded its share of a particular market, it typically becomes more internally complex, splitting into divisions with a hierarchical, bureaucratic administrative structure—all of which make organizational change difficult. Changing an organization requires coordination among the top strategists, middle-level implementers, and the mass of employees who must adapt to the new demands (Kanter et al., 1992).

American corporations have shown a remarkable ability to adapt to broad changes in the economy. Although specific firms rise and fall, the power of the business sector has not diminished and may even be strengthened by bad times because workers are rendered even more powerless. Indeed, what at first might have appeared to be a major threat to company executives, the "hostile takeover" by outside investors, has typically been turned into an opportunity to walk away with an enormous personal profit—the "golden parachute" that cushions the fall of high-ranking corporate executives.

Corporate Power and Pay

Out of a total labor force of over 132 million workers in 1995, almost 100 million were employed in the private sector's 6.3 million businesses. Eighty-six percent of these firms have fewer than 20 employees, and the great majority are single-owner—America's small business sector. But economic power is concentrated in the 8,000 companies with 500 or more employees—big business. The 200 largest industrial corporations account for 90 percent of the nation's industrial assets (U.S. Bureau of the Census *Statistical Abstract*, 1994).

A **corporation** is a formal organization that is a legal actor in its own right (Marrett, 1992). Corporations can enter into contracts, accumulate assets or debts, and declare bankruptcy without individual owners, managers, or employees being held responsible. Ownership in American corporations is widely held: 45 million people own shares in one or more companies, usually through a pension plan. Although this might suggest that corporate profits are spread across the stratification system, the vast majority of stockholders are in the upper socioeconomic status strata, and over 90 percent of shares are held by other corporations, banks, and company executives, as well as by pension funds. Corporate power is further concentrated through the interlocking directorates described earlier in this chapter.

Corporations are formal organizations that are legal actors in their own right.

One of the defining features of the corporation in a capitalist economy is the separation of ownership (stockholders) from management (the executives who run the business). This distinction, however, has become blurred as executives are rewarded with corporate stock as part of their benefit package (Zeitlin, 1989). In 1993, the average yearly compensation package (salary, bonus, stock options) for a chief executive office (CEO) was over $2.5 million, compared to the average worker's total compensation of $18,000 (*Business Week,* 1993). The bottom line for the boards of directors who award these packages is the profit margin of the firm, which today does not necessarily depend on producing and selling a product but on buying and selling other companies (Useem, 1993).

This shift in how profit is made—from production and marketing to mergers, buyouts, takeovers, and acquisitions—is reflected in a change in how top management is selected (Fligstein, 1990). Before 1940, most corporate leaders were either the person who founded the company or who came from the manufacturing division. Between 1940 and 1970, top slots were occupied by people from sales and marketing. Most recently, it is financial experts who have risen to the highest positions. All but a handful of top executives are white men. Middle management, however, is more diverse; it is more female than in the past, with a sprinkling of darker faces, and a growing number of part-timers and outside consultants (Waldrop, 1993).

> **Corporate culture** refers to the beliefs, values, and norms that define the organization.

Corporate Cultures

Just as corporations have social structure, so also is there a **corporate culture:** beliefs, values, and norms that define the organization, establish boundary relationships with other entities, and confer meaning on daily activities. Corporate symbols (the logo, company colors, semi-uniforms) and rituals (the company picnic or the executive fishing trip) serve the same functions as a totem pole or rain dance. Fine distinctions of power are marked not by facial paint or a feathered headdress but by the size and location of an office, whether or not it has a window, and the quality of its carpeting (Reynolds, 1987). There are taboos and ceremonies, beliefs and sacred texts, folkways, mores, and laws, ideal culture, and the reality of the executive suite and shop floor (Trice and Beyer, 1993; Kunda, 1992). Thus, organizations attempt to foster loyalty and cohesion while minimizing conflicts and retaining control (Vallas, 1993).

Although often conceptualized as gender-free environments, business organizations are highly sexualized. The basic culture is a celebration of masculine activity and values, an extension of the peer culture of adolescence or the college fraternity, which is why the presence of women in executive roles is so disruptive (Hearn et al., 1989). The language of organizational life is filled with images of aggression and sexual competition. Its norms reward displays of gendered power in which women and homosexuals symbolize weakness (Mills and Tancred, 1992).

In this respect, the executive suite does not differ much from the shop floor where working-class men engage in displays of expressive masculinity, less in competition with one another than as an expression of social worth in what is often a dehumanizing envi-

Although more than 45 million people own shares in American corporations, most shares are held by other corporations, banks, and domestic and foreign conglomerates. Annual meetings, such as the one shown here, where management reports and shareholders vote, do not usually provide a true picture of who really controls corporations.

ronment (Collinson, 1992). Women, and in many cases men from racial minorities, intrude on this culture at great risk of physical harassment on the shop floor and equally intense hostility in the executive suites (Reskin and Padoric, 1994).

CORPORATIONS AND THE COMMUNITY.   Business organizations are located in particular geographic environments. With the growth of conglomerates and multinationals, and the quest for short-term profits through mergers and takeovers, the links between a large national organization and the communities in which its plants and offices are located have weakened. Gone are the days when the founder-owner of the corporation lived in the area. Today's top executives may never have seen the local plant or office building, which is primarily a piece of property to be kept or sold to enhance the book value of the corporate stock. Thus, plants are closed, sold, or moved without much concern for the community in which it was often the major employer.

Public goodwill, however, is also a corporate asset for those who produce consumer goods. Thus, many corporations seek to legitimate their economic power by making well-publicized contributions to national and local charities (Mitchell, 1989). McDonald's efforts on behalf of the developmentally disabled is a striking example. Most **philanthropy** (gift giving), however, is local: to the United Fund, the community orchestra, or regional hospital. Although corporate giving reached $2 billion in the early 1990s, this amounted to only 1 percent of pretax income of the reporting firms (U.S. Bureau of the Census, *Statistical Abstract,* 1993; Sweeney, 1994). In some cases, charitable giving has become a status symbol, with corporations competing with one another to donate the most to local charities and reach the top of the prestige hierarchy in that community— a form of "corporate potlatch" (Galeskiewicz, 1985; Padgett, 1986).

> **Philanthropy** refers to charitable giving.

Another form of philanthropy is practiced by the foundations established by the most successful capitalists of the past, such as the one established by Andrew Carnegie, the man who hired the Pinkertons to break up the Homestead strike. In general, these foundations support causes that maintain the economic status quo and reward institutions that serve the interests of the upper and upper middle classes such as private universities and symphony orchestras (Odendahl, 1990). The Carnegie Foundation, for example, until quite recently was a prime funder of cultural projects that reinforced the elitist control of knowledge (Lagemann, 1989). Little of this knowledge would have empowered Carnegie's steelworkers, but the factory closed down anyway.

SOCIAL POLICY

How much is Too Much—or Too Little?

Is a CEO really worth $2 million a year? If the executive increases the value of the corporation by hundreds of millions of dollars, the compensation package appears well worth it. And surely, it is argued, his value to the society is higher than that of a multimillion dollar sports figure. But what of the 8 million Americans at the opposite end of the spectrum who work at or below the minimum wage?

During the Great Depression of the 1930s, Congress mandated a minimum wage of 25 cents an hour. Before this, high unemployment and the absence of income support programs left workers at the mercy of employers who paid less than $10 for a 50-hour workweek. For the next 50 years, all attempts to raise the minimum were fiercely resisted by employer groups and conservatives who felt that government had no right to dictate private business practices. Each nickel and dime became a battleground.

Nonetheless, by 1981, the minimum was up to $3.35 per hour, where it remained until 1989, when Congress proposed a raise to $4.55, which was immediately vetoed by President Bush. Ultimately, Congress and the administration reached a compromise: an increase to $3.80 in 1990 and $4.25 in 1991, plus a *sub*minimum wage of $3.35 for teenagers in their first job. Although the Clinton administration has promised another look at the issue, it is unlikely that a conservative Congress will approve any increase.

Yet even at $5.00 an hour, a person working full-time, year-round would earn only $10,400 before taxes and work-related expenses such as transportation and child care. These expenses would drive the worker's income well below the poverty level for a parent with two children. Furthermore, when adjusted for inflation, today's amount is 30 percent *lower* than the minimum wage in 1970.

Who are the 7 percent of hourly rate workers currently receiving $4.25 or less? Roughly one-third are teenagers; 80 percent are non-Latino whites; 62 percent are women; and 92 percent are in the private service sector (U.S. Bureau of the Census, *Statistical Abstract* 1994). These numbers, however, apply only to people counted by the Department of Labor; many more are working "off the books," including large numbers of recent immigrants, both documented and undocumented, for whom even the minimum here is higher than they could earn in their country of origin. Most mimimum wage workers work in fast-food outlets, dry-cleaning establishments, garment factories, and migrant farm camps. The major argument against raising the minimum is quite simply that, because such workers are in the low-profit peripheral sector, any additional expense for the employer would lead to cutbacks in hiring.

But empirical tests of the 1991 raise to $4.25 indicate that any job loss is minimal, and that the higher wage might increase employment (Uchitelle, 1994). There is general agreement that the amounts in question will do little to lower the poverty rate, but also that a wage that could help struggling families is politically impossible unless the economy shows great improvement.

The fierceness of the struggle over a few pennies for low-income workers suggests the degree to which conservative and liberal positions diverge on the issue of the proper role of government in the economic sector, reflecting two very different

philosophies. Should the state be neutral in its effects on individuals to avoid distorting the play of market forces? Should it assist only the most needy, and then only minimally, to avoid reducing the motivation to work? Should it favor the wealthy in the expectation that they will use their money to create more jobs? Or does the state have an obligation to ensure that most citizens have access to such public goods as education, health care, housing, and income security? Even though these questions are raised in an economic context, they will be answered in the political arena. Every time you step into the voting booth, you will be making a statement about the meaning of "America."

SUMMARY

1. Economic systems consist of the norms and behaviors regulating the production, distribution, and consumption of goods and services. Such modes of subsistence originate in the group's adaptation to its physical environment to ensure individual and collective survival.

2. Over human history, economic systems, or modes of subsistence, have become increasingly complex in terms of knowledge and technology.

3. Modern societies are in the process of shifting from economic activity centered on the production of goods to one based on service industries, a postindustrial mode.

4. Modern economic systems vary in the degree to which private economic interests are regulated by public agencies. At one end of the continuum is free-enterprise capitalism, and at the other, a fully planned socialist economy.

5. In a capitalist economy, the means of production are privately owned and operated for profit. Positive effects include high levels of productivity and an enhanced standard of living for most. The negative features are extremes of wealth and poverty and increasing concentration of economic power.

6. Socialism, in its pure form, is an economic system in which the means of production are collectively owned and the distribution of goods and services are guided by public needs. Positive outcomes include a reduction of inequality; negative features are inefficiency and goal displacement.

7. In reality, most economies today contain features of both free enterprise and state regulation, called *welfare capitalism* or *democratic socialism.*

8. The organization of work is based on a division of labor, with extreme specialization in the industrial economy and the replacement of human labor by automated equipment.

9. Worker satisfaction is highest where employees enjoy autonomy in the pacing and sequencing of their labor and is lowest in repetitive heavily supervised jobs.

10. Changes in the modern workplace include various forms of worker participation, some borrowed from the Japanese model, with minimal impact thus far on productivity or lessening of management control.

11. The American labor movement has suffered membership losses among manufacturing workers but is currently organizing in sectors that employ women and white-collar workers.

12. Inequality within the working class is partly a result of the dual economy (core and periphery) and the segmented labor market that divides pools of workers.

13. In the United States, relocation of manufacturing has led to widespread job loss among relatively high-skilled blue-collar workers, many of whom are forced into lower-paying jobs.

14. American corporations are boosting profit margins by reducing their white-collar managerial staff through downsizing, use of contingent labor, and outsourcing.

15. Increasing numbers of American workers are in jobs with lower pay and fewer benefits than a decade ago.

16. Youth unemployment, especially among African Americans and Latinos, is a major social problem.

17. Organizations are social actors and can be studied with the same sociological tools as any other structures and systems.

18. Corporations have a unique culture composed of symbols, rituals, norms, and values designed to enhance solidarity.

19. The struggle over the minimum wage reflects a basic ideological difference between a conservative and liberal approach to defining the role of public agencies in the workings of the economy.

SUGGESTED READINGS

Blum, Linda M. *Between Feminism and Labor: The Significance of the Comparable Worth Movement.* Berkeley: University of California Press, 1991. A passionate analysis of the plight of low paid working women and the search for a comparable worth strategy to politicize and mobilize women.

Colcough, Glenna, and Charles M. Tolbert, III. *Work in the Fast Lane: Flexibility, Divisions of Labor, and Inequality in High-Tech Industries.* Albany: State University of New York Press, 1992. The authors investigate the relationships of high tech work to the U.S. economy and growing trends in social and economic inequality.

Costello, Cynthia B. *We're Worth It! Women and Collective Activism in the Insurance Workplace.* Urbana: University of Illinois Press, 1991. A case study of four different work environments and the conditions that will promote or hinder activism among women, including the place of unions in the empowerment of working women.

Ferber, Marianne A., and Julie A. Nelson, eds. *Beyond Economic Man: Feminist Theory and Economics.* Chicago, IL: University of Chicago Press, 1993. A collection of important essays on the social construction of modern economics, which has been based on a view of the world that reflects the experience of educated man. What we assume to be objective rational economic analysis is actually theoretically and empirically flawed.

Jackall, Robert. *Moral Mazes: The World of Corporate Managers.* New York: Oxford University Press, 1988. An important contribution to the sociology of business, based on hundreds of interviews with managers and an in-depth look at three organizations. Jackall concludes that managers only survive by supporting their bosses with complete loyalty and by constructing events so that it is very difficult to pin blame on anyone.

Kaufman, Bruce E., and Morris M. Kleiner (eds). *Employee Representation: Alternatives and Future Directions.* Ithaca, NY: ILR Press, 1993. A timely collection of essays on various forms of worker representation within American businesses, especially the relative strengths and weaknesses of unions and employer-dominated systems. Another excellent volume from the Industrial Relations Research Association.

Morales, Rebecca, and Frank Bonilla, eds. *Latinos in a Changing U.S. Economy: Comparative Perspectives on Growing Inequality.* Newbury Park, CA: Sage, 1993. A search for theoretical and empirical reasons for the increasing economic inequality experienced by Latinos as compared with other Americans.

Zuboff, Shoshona. *In the Age of the Machine: The Future of Work and Power.* New York: Basic Books, 1988. This very important study of the computerized workplace is based on observations and interviews with workers and managers in eight different workplaces, including pulp and paper mills at different levels of computerization, an international bank, and a pharmaceutical firm.

14

The Political System: Power, Politics, and Militarism

*N*otes from the world political scene in the mid-1990s:

- Fifty years after the Allied invasion of Europe that ended the dictatorships of Adolph Hitler in Germany and Benito Mussolini in Italy, neo-fascist candidates won victories in democratic elections in both nations.
- Less than a decade after being removed from political power in Hungary and Poland, former communists were elected to high office with overwhelming majorities.
- The political elite that governed Japan since the 1950s was turned out of office after thousands of politicians and businessmen were indicted for bribery and kickbacks in the awarding of government contracts.
- Only one in three Americans can correctly identify the Bill of Rights, and over half thought the government should ban "hate speech."
- The 1995 U.S. defense budget contains $100 million for a type of spy plane that was retired in 1990.

These news items help to illustrate the range of phenomena covered in the sociological study of politics and power: for example, the fragility of democracy, the corruption of power, the tension between freedom of speech and the limits of tolerance, and the military as a unique institution. In this chapter, we examine the concept of power, the origins and types of political systems, political socialization and participation in the United States, and the structure and role of the military.

POWER

In its broadest sense, politics is the exercise of **power,** defined by Max Weber as the probability of achieving one's goals regardless of the wishes of others. Power therefore involves having the resources required to bend others to your will and is itself a resource that is distributed unequally among members of a collectivity or among subgroups within a society. Thus, control over resources is a crucial aspect of power, and dependence on the resources of others is a form of powerlessness. This dimension of power is clearly seen in one-earner families as well as in the structure of most workplaces.

Power is also *relational*, embedded in relationships that link followers and leaders who mutually influence one another (Lawlor and Bacharach, 1987). Power is an aspect of all interactions, from the dating dyad to a summit meeting of world leaders. People who are without power are usually expected to make a public display of their subordination—to bow or beg, and to appear weak and dependent—which then reinforces the superiority of the powerful.

But such displays often mask a subculture of resistance, a secret language and behaviors that mock the dominators and restore a sense of dignity to the oppressed (Scott, 1990). During the Communist control of Eastern Europe, for example, "underground" nightclubs featured comics and singers who ridiculed the government. And among women of the Bedouin tribes of North Africa, a literature of stories and poems permits them to assert a limited autonomy in their strongly patriarchal society (Abu-Lughod, 1992).

Authority

Weber distinguished **authority**—the exercise of control over others through normatively recognized channels—from *influence*—informal persuasion. This chapter is primarily concerned with authority, power that is considered legitimate by members of the collectivity. Authority flows from the status occupied by an individual: Parents have power over children; typically, husbands control the behavior of wives; religious leaders guide their flock; and teachers enjoy legitimated power in the classroom. The institutional sphere in which the dynamics of power are most central is the political system itself.

In the arena of politics, Weber (1922/1968) described three very different bases of legitimated power: traditional, charismatic, and legal-rational.

Traditional authority is based on custom and the force of habit. Patriarchy (the rule of men as fathers, husbands, kings, and religious leaders) is an example of traditional authority. Weber regarded this type of authority as essentially irrational, because there are few restraints on traditional leaders and because it is not related to a person's having the special skills required for the task.

Charismatic authority is based on some extraordinary quality of the person or ideology that makes followers obey without question (*charisma* means "a gift"). Among historical figures with charismatic qualities are religious leaders such as Jesus, Muhammad, and the Biblical prophets. In modern times, charisma is more often associated with political figures such as Franklin Roosevelt, Adolf Hitler, Winston Churchill, and Fidel Castro. The American civil rights leader Martin Luther King, Jr., was the essence of a charismatic figure—a forceful speaker with a powerful message

> **Power** is the probability of achieving one's goals regardless of the wishes of others.
>
> **Authority** refers to socially legitimated power.
>
> **Traditional authority** is based on custom and the force of habit.
>
> **Charismatic authority** is based on some extraordinary quality of the leader or the leader's ideas.

Traditional and legal-rational authority are two bases of political power. Queen Elizabeth of England holds authority that is based on heredity and custom. Legal-rational power is based on impersonal contract between ruler and the ruled. At the time of the peace accord between Israel and Palestine, President Bill Clinton and Prime Minister Yitsak Rabin held elected offices while Yassar Arafat held power as the head of the Palestinian Liberation Organization.

and commanding physical appearance. With few exceptions (e.g., the faith healer Aimée Semple McPherson and Argentina's Evita Peron), women are rarely perceived as charismatic leaders.

Because charismatic authority is based on a unique gift and because followers obey out of blind faith, it too is irrational in Weber's terms. In addition, because of the very power of their appeal, charismatic leaders also attract powerful enemies, so that their life is often cut short. To achieve the leader's goals, followers must create a formal organization that survives over time. Weber referred to this process as the *routinization of charisma,* whereby the divine gift is translated into everyday structures of power: a political party, church, or social movement (see Chapter 23).

Legal-rational, or **bureaucratic, authority,** according to Weber, is the most rational form of power because is is based on an impersonal contract between ruler and the ruled. Power is limited by laws that apply to all office holders, regardless of their personal qualities or other statuses. It is legal-rational authority that offers greatest protection against arbitrary force and that is, therefore, most suited to a modern society.

Legal-rational, or **bureaucratic, authority** is based on laws that limit the power of officeholders.

The three forms of authority can be found in varying mixtures in most political systems. For example, while modern societies are primarily legal-rational, some traditional features remain (e.g., the monarchy in Great Britain), and some traditional leaders automatically assume charisma (e.g., the Pope).

THE ORIGINS AND HISTORICAL DEVELOPMENT OF POLITICAL SYSTEMS

From a functional perspective, political systems serve the basic survival need of maintaining order within the society and defending it against outside enemies. The political system consists of the patterned interactions through which the norms, rules of conduct, are defined and enforced. In a simple gathering band, all adults can take part in making the rules and seeing that they are obeyed. Much control is also exercised informally, as among the Kwanga of Papua New Guinea, relatively egalitarian horticulturalists who live in densely populated villages (Brison, 1992). Kwanga men are fiercely competitive but outright hostilities are forbidden lest they disrupt village life. Instead of physical attacks, Kwangans use gossip as a weapon, spreading rumors designed to lessen the prestige of competitors. But even rumors have their limits and the targets are allowed to present a defense so that hostilities rarely get out of control.

In societies of greater size and complexity, different degrees of power become linked to specific statuses; at the very least, elders give orders to juniors,

Put Out More Flags

Just in case you thought that national anthems and flags are produced by random historical forces, you haven't yet learned that nothing escapes sociological analysis. Because the flag and anthem represent the nation, they carry enormous symbolic weight, sending a message not only to members of that society but to other nations. Therefore, they are typically very carefully constructed. Is there a global patterning to the structure of these central symbols?

Sociologist Karen A. Cerulo (1993) studied the musical components of national anthems and the content of national flags adopted in the same year as the anthem (which excluded the United States). Cerulo found a significant relationship between the elaborateness of the song and flag and that country's political and economic centrality in the world system. The nations with the earliest adoption dates, which were also likely to

be at the center or "core" of the world system, had the most basic structure, while nations on the "periphery" of the world system tended toward busy and embellished symbols.

Cerulo suggests that the less central nations had to cram more symbolic information into their flag, especially, to impress their identity on other states and also to accommodate a greater variety of ethnic, religious, and language groups within their borders. For example, the new flag of democratic South Africa has seven colors, and there are now two national anthems: "Nkosi Sikele' iAfrika" with verses in the Xhosa and Sotha languages and a chorus in Zulu; and "The Call of South Africa" based on the English translation of a Dutch Afrikaaner poem.

Cerulo's study is also an example of the range of work being done in the relatively new but rapidly growing field of the sociology of culture, linking symbols and social structure.

and men to women. The more complex the society, the greater the need to coordinate the efforts of many specialists and to settle disputes among kinship groups or other social units (Glassman, 1986). At some point, loyalty to the society as a whole must replace family and local allegiances. Rules are then made by a small group that represents the entire society—a council of tribal elders or the U.S. Congress. Leaders can be witch doctors, queens, emperors, generals, or presidents. Loyalty to this larger collectivity and its leaders is created and reinforced through *rituals* and other unifying symbols (Kertzer, 1988; Cerulo, 1989; Berezin, 1994). When ceremonies and sacred objects fail to maintain solidarity, the collectivity disintegrates into hostile factions, as seen in the civil wars that followed the end of Communist rule in the Soviet Union and Yugoslavia in the late 1980s.

The manipulation of collective symbols is an important part of legitimating the power of ruling elites, from the circuses of ancient Rome to the massive demonstrations staged by the Nazis in Germany in the 1930s to the coronation ceremonies for a British monarch (Edelman, 1988). Unifying symbols are especially important in wartime, as witness the speed and thoroughness with which the United States was wrapped in yellow ribbons signifying support for the troops engaged in the Persian Gulf War of 1991.

Historically, as a society becomes larger and its members more specialized in skills and resources, the political system itself grows more elaborate. As shown in Table 3-1, p. 57, the integrating force of kinship relationships is replaced by centralized leadership, ultimately involving a web of lawmaking bodies, courts to settle disputes, officials to enforce the law, and a military to defend the society.

Political Institutions in Complex Societies

The political organization of a complex society is called the **nation-state,** a set of institutions that governs and defends a given territory (see also Chapter 19). Up to the 1970s, political sociology was dominated by two oversimplified visions: (1) The "convergence" view that the logic of industrialization produces similar social policies in all modern societies, and (2) the Marxist view that the state is simply the political arm of capitalism. Recent studies suggest a more complex reality in which the state operates as a relatively autonomous sphere, with its own momentum and logic, while also linked to other institutions (Gilbert and Howe, 1991; Skocpol, 1993).

THE POLITICAL ECONOMY OF THE WELFARE STATE.   As discussed in Chapter 13, modern industrial societies are characterized by varying degrees of government intervention in the workings of the economic system. Over the past century, the range of the *welfare state* has expanded, beginning with public education and old-age pensions, and gradually extending citizens' entitlements to include unemployment insurance, health care, housing, and family supports. The role of state agencies and political leaders in initiating and expanding these programs is a major focus of research in political sociology (Orloff, 1993; Quadagno, 1990; Meyer, 1994).

> The **nation-state** is an overarching political unit that emerged as a consequence of modernization in complex societies.

Government policy is also influenced by national values and by the power of business and labor and

The United States lags behind other Western industrial societies in providing universal health care, income security, and other social services to its citizens. Why are these defined as individual rather than collective rights in the U.S.?

other special interest groups. In Sweden and Norway, for example, a cultural "passion for equality" and a popular labor movement produced a rapid expansion of citizen rights in the 1960s and 1970s (Piven, 1992). In contrast, the United States, with its weak unions, powerful business elites, and cultural emphasis on individual rather than collective rights, lags behind other Western societies in providing a range of social services.

American politics are profoundly influenced by the power of special interest groups. Thus, the National Rifle Association has been largely successful in defeating gun control legislation; the American medical and pharmaceutical establishment gutted much of President Clinton's health care reform; and organizations representing the elderly resisted changes in Medicare (Street, 1993).

A Continuum of Political Systems

Political systems can be arranged along a continuum from totalitarian to democratic, based on the degree to which the right to oppose the state is institutionalized and protected, as seen in Figure 14-1.

TOTALITARIAN GOVERNMENT.   As the name implies, **totalitarian regimes** attempt to regulate all aspects of social life and personal behavior. Leaders, or dictators, can be civilians, military figures, or religious authorities. What they have in common is absolute power, maintained by repressing dissent.

In terms of its structure and effects, it makes little

In **totalitarian regimes,** the government attempts to exercise total control over society and its members.

difference whether the dictatorship is of the "right"—fascist—or "left"—Communist. Fascist dictators rule in the name of racial or religious elites; Communist dictators do so in the name of the masses. Either way, power is in the hands of a few who rule by force and who demand total obedience.

Totalitarian governments tend to flourish in societies without the preconditions for democracy, which are widespread literacy, economic stability, and an egalitarian ideology. But even modern industrial states are vulnerable when economic conditions deteriorate, as in the late 1930s in Germany and Italy, where the dictators Adolf Hitler and Benito Mussolini came to power through democratic processes. So, also, as Western European economies faltered in the early 1990s, political groups modeled on Hitler's Nazis and Mussolini's fascists have reappeared and enjoyed electoral success.

An important aspect of totalitarian rule is control over cultural products. The contents of the media, schools, and theater are regulated; only certain kinds of music and art are allowed. Books are burned, and

FIGURE 14-1   A continuum of political systems.

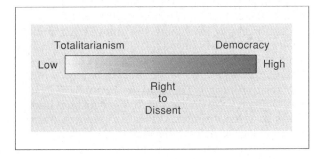

the people who wrote them are sent to prison or exile. Public meetings are forbidden. Up to 1990, this was as true of capitalist South Africa as of socialist Cuba.

DEMOCRATIC GOVERNMENT.   What distinguishes a democratic system, then, is not how many people vote (dictatorships tend to have a very high turnout) but whether or not the right to oppose the government is protected. In the United States, the basic guarantees of democracy are contained in the second clause of the First Amendment to the Constitution (italics added):

> Congress shall make no law respecting an establishment of religion, or prohibiting the free exercise thereof; or *abridging the freedom of speech, or of the press; or the right of the people peaceably to assemble, and to petition the government for a redress of grievances.*

These rights—to speak, to publish, and to meet—that we have as citizens and that cannot be taken away by government are called **civil liberties.** Most Americans, however, have an extremely low level of awareness and support for these rights. A 1991 survey found that only one in three respondents could correctly identify the Bill of Rights, and fewer than one in ten knew that it was designed to protect ordinary citizens from the misuse of power by their government (American Bar Association, 1991). Such lack of political sophistication leaves the public open to manipulation even by its freely elected leaders.

Liberty is not a means to a higher political end. It is itself the highest political end.

—J. E. E. D. ACTON, 1878/1985, p. 22

Manipulating Public Opinion

Democratic and totalitarian governments alike depend on influencing public opinion for legitimacy. The flow of information from leaders to the masses can be manipulated through propaganda, censorship, chilling dissent, and repression.

PROPAGANDA.   **Propaganda** refers to the selective release of information favorable to those in power. In wartime, especially, civilians are continually told how well their side is doing, in order to maintain high levels of morale and support for the war effort. In peacetime, as well, leaders try to present themselves in the best light, or at least to control the "spin" on potentially harmful information.

CENSORSHIP.   In contrast to propaganda, **censorship** involves the selective *withholding* of information (Jansen, 1988). In totalitarian societies, newspapers often appear with entire columns blacked out by gov-

ernment censors, theaters are closed down, and radio and TV are operated by agents of the state. In democracies, it is far more difficult to censor news and art, but governments never stop trying, as when material is classified "top secret" and kept from public view on grounds of "national security."

The United States, however, is unique in the First Amendment's protection of freedom of speech and the press. The state cannot forbid publication in advance, which is called *prior restraint.* Only after it can be shown to have an unlawful outcome can speech or print be suppressed. For a few months in 1979, the government was able to stop publication of an article on how to build a nuclear weapon, in a small left-wing magazine, the *Progressive,* before being overruled by a higher court— the only case of extended prior restraint in our history. Because the article was compiled from material available in any public library, this was hardly a major breach of national security.

Ironically, during the ceremonies marking the bicentennial (200th) anniversary of the very Constitution that contains the First Amendment, National Park rangers prevented a group of protesters from carrying placards objecting to U.S. policies in Central America! This action was immediately overturned by a local judge.

Censorship is most obvious, and considered most necessary, during wartime. Reporters depend on military and civilian authorities for information and are, therefore, very vulnerable to manipulation. This was very evident during the Persian Gulf War, when the press acted more like cheerleaders than critical reporters (MacArthur, 1993; see Chapter 22).

Chilling Dissent.   A government can use numerous tactics to make people think twice about what they say and with whom they associate. Such "chilling" tactics include wiretaps, opening mail, questioning neighbors and employers, and direct surveillance— part of everyday life in totalitarian states but also used effectively by democratic regimes (McCormack, 1990). In the United States, the whole array of chilling tactics, in violation of Constitutionally protected rights, was employed against suspected Socialists in the 1920s and 1930s, anyone who got in the way of Senator Joseph McCarthy in the 1950s, and antiwar protesters in the 1960s.

As late as 1988, the FBI was engaged in a "Library Awareness Program," whereby librarians were requested to report on the "reading habits of people with foreign accents and funny-sounding names"

Civil liberties are the rights to speak, publish, and assemble.

Propaganda involves the selective release of information favorable to those in power.

Censorship involves the selective withholding of information.

Political dissidents are found all over the globe and even in countries that are formally democratic. Leonard Peltier is an American Indian Movement (AIM) leader falsely convicted of murdering two FBI agents on the Pine Ridge Indian Reservation in 1975. His case illustrates the FBI's ability to "neutralize" dissenters by using slander and arrest. Peltier is currently serving two life sentences in a federal penitentiary although the government has admitted they have no idea who did the killing. Ms. Aung San Suu Kyi (right), the daughter of Burma's national hero General Aung San, has been under house arrest since 1989. She was a founder and general secretary of the Burmese National League for Democracy (NLD), which won a landslide victory. In 1991 Ms. Kyi was awarded the Nobel Peace Prize for her efforts to free her country from the military dictatorship that continues to keep her under house arrest.

(Gentry, 1991). And until the election of Bill Clinton, the Department of Energy routinely photographed antinuclear protesters and wiretapped its own employees who complained of safety conditions at government nuclear facilities (Pear, 1992). This is the same Department that conducted tests on unsuspecting and powerless civilians (prisoners, retarded children, poor blacks) in the 1960s, to learn about the effects of radiation on humans and managed to keep it all secret for 30 years. The amount of information being stored runs into the billions of documents and the cost of securing information runs into tens of billions of dollars. A recent Congressional study found that seven million items are classified each year and that some files date to World War I, still stamped "secret" on grounds of national security (Weiner, 1994).

Because the FBI and other national security units operate in secrecy, it is difficult for higher authorities to check their excesses and to ensure that the veil of secrecy is not being used to hide the agency's own misdeeds (Jeffreys-Jones, 1989). These considerations present us with an essential paradox, where one goal cancels out another: Can unconstitutional means be used to preserve social order in a democracy without compromising the very meaning of democratic rule? What is it worth in lost liberties to be protected against potential terrorists? What is the price of privacy (Nock, 1993)?

Repression involves the forceful denial of civil liberties.

Genocide is the systematic, intentional killing of an entire population.

COERCION: REPRESSION AND GENOCIDE.   The ultimate in social control is the use of force, or *coercion,* to eliminate dissent and dissenters. **Repression** includes house arrest and imprisonment, a public trial, and even execution. In Iran, in the late 1980s, religious leaders declared the writer Salman Rushdie to be a heretic and placed a price on his head, driving Rushdie into hiding, where he remains today.

Curfews (ordering people off the streets at certain hours) and requiring people to carry identifying papers are coercive techniques for controlling movement, common in dictatorships, less so in a democracy. Nonetheless, fear of being swamped by refugees from Eastern Europe and of violent antiforeigner demonstrations by their own citizens has led many Western democracies to take just such steps today. In the United States, fear of teenage youth has prompted many local governments to enact curfews.

The final step in eliminating opposition is **genocide,** the systematic, intentional killing of an entire population (Chalk and Jonassohn, 1990; Fein, 1992).

Big Brother Never Sleeps

In 1948, the British author George Orwell wrote a novel called *1984*, depicting England under the totalitarian rule of Big Brother. Civilians were kept under constant electronic surveillance, and their ideas were subject to "thought control." *Big Brother* has come to refer to all the ways a government can regulate the daily life of its people.

In 1984, sociologist Gary Marx (1986) compared the current American scene with Orwell's vision and found it essentially free of the physical, more violent techniques of control used by totalitarians. But he noted the many subtle nonviolent threats to privacy in our society—a "velvet glove" rather than an "iron fist." The list includes many items that you might have met in the course of an ordinary day: video cameras in the workplace and shops; lie detector tests by employers; arbitrary drug testing; data banks that contain everything from health records to credit card purchases; sophisticated wiretapping and taping devices; magnetic-tape ID cards that monitor movement in a building; hotlines for anonymous tips; and neighborhood watch groups on the lookout for "suspicious" behavior.

To this list, we may now add such up-to-date developments in the workplace as clip-on microcomputerized badges that transmit signals as an employee moves around, a monitor that counts each keystroke at a word processor, or an undetectable tap on a voice mail station (Sloane, 1992; Kilborn, 1994). Typically, the technology is introduced for its productivity value and only later becomes a means for controlling employees (Rule and Brantley, 1992). In addition, an entire industry has emerged to buy and sell information on individuals—for example, buying medical records from doctors and hospitals and selling them to insurance companies or employers, who can then weed out high-risk applicants (Rothfeder, 1992).

According to Gary Marx and others, if totalitarianism ever comes to America, it will do so by the slow acceptance of the new surveillance and loss of privacy. No invasion, no violent revolution is necessary. We become willing participants in our own loss of liberty in our eagerness to catch a thief, arrest a junkie, plug an information leak, and uncover a terrorist.

Many examples can be found in this century but none more devastating than the systematic slaughter of millions of European Jews by the German government before and during World War II. The 1990s "ethnic cleansing" that has destroyed and displaced Muslim communities in Bosnia and Herzegovina is only the most recent example of government-sponsored mass murder. Genocide is most likely to occur where state power is unchecked by democratic institutions, although there are examples from our own history: the massacres of Native Americans; the atom bombs dropped on Hiroshima and Nagasaki, Japan, in 1945; and the systematic destruction of Vietnamese villages and civilians in the 1970s. But it is totalitarian governments that have accounted for the overwhelming majority of "megamurders" in this century, precisely because absolute power is, by definition, unchecked and unaccountable (Rummel, 1992).

The most recent example of government-sponsored mass murder (genocide) has been the practice of "ethnic cleansing" that has destroyed and displaced Muslim communities in Bosnia and Herzegovina in the former Yugoslavia. Overall about 200,000 men, women, and children have been killed in this civil war.

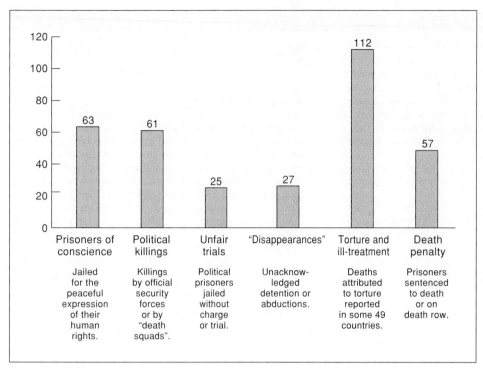

FIGURE 14-2   Number of countries committing various human rights abuses, 1994.

From: Amnesty International Annual Report, 1994. Copyright © Amnesty International USA.

The Iron Law of Oligarchy

When all power is in the hands of a small group of people, a ruling elite, abuses of power are inevitable. As the British historian Lord Acton put it: "Power tends to corrupt; absolute power corrupts absolutely." No matter how "good" their original intentions, power holders find that exercising authority becomes an end in itself. Given control over others, any one of us could become contemptuous and cruel in our dealings with the less powerful, as shown in the study of the "mock prison" in Chapter 5.

Yet even in organizations formed to represent "the masses," leaders, whether elected or appointed, tend to become cut off from their followers. **Oligarchy** means "rule of a few," and the *iron law* proposed by Robert Michels (1911/1962) states that because decision makers have a crucial interest in being considered correct, they tend to manipulate information and individuals to gain support. The few who rule have a full-time commitment to their task; the masses are only periodically concerned or involved. A gap is opened between rulers and the ruled, and the corrupting influences of power appear: censorship and propaganda; opponents are removed from office; and the leaders are shielded from dissent by the people who surround them and screen out bad news.

> **Oligarchy** is the rule of the many by the few.

Regardless of the leaders' personality, the exercise of power feeds arrogance (a feeling of superiority coupled with contempt for the less powerful). Eventually, the corrupting influences of power and the growing distance between the elite and the masses could lead to a revolution in which the oligarchy is overthrown. But the iron law suggests that the new ruling elite will, in turn, tend to control information and limit dissent. In other words, the new rulers will be pushed by the logic of exercising power to behave very much the same as the old ones. For example, the revolutionary leaders who deposed the absolute monarch of Iran in 1979 have become every bit as totalitarian as the Shah they replaced.

The beauty of democracy is that every two, four, or six years, our rulers must appear before us and justify their actions, in competition with other candidates. We can replace one set with another, so that even if the Iron Law cannot be repealed, we can ensure that no one stays in office long enough to become fully corrupted by power. An elite may always govern, but its power is limited by democratic politics. But in nations without longstanding democratic traditions, hierarchical power relations cannot be easily dismantled and replaced.

Examples of the Iron Law at work can be seen in recent American history. President Lyndon Johnson pursued an increasingly unpopular war, fed false information to the people and the press, was shielded

Public executions are used by totalitarian governments to destroy dissent. These prodemocracy demonstrators are about to be executed by a firing squad in Shanghai, a scene shown on prime-time television in the People's Republic of China. What effect do you think such public executions have on the population?

from negative information by his staff, and until the last moment, had little idea of his situation. President Richard Nixon engaged in a criminal cover-up, lied, and resigned the presidency only as he was about to be impeached. And advisors to President Ronald Reagan thought that they could conduct a secret foreign policy in direct opposition to the will of Congress.

If the modern state is a semiautonomous institution capable of representing the interests of "the people" against the interest of political and economic elites, and if the best guarantee of protection against corrupt rulers is open elections, then democracy does matter. But democratic institutions are of limited effect unless citizens participate in the political process and diligently protect their right to dissent, as guaranteed in the First Amendment.

SOCIAL POLICY

Protecting the Protectors

How secure are your First Amendment rights of speech and assembly? From the moment it was adopted, more than 200 years ago, the Amendment has been under attack from those claiming to act in the interests of democracy. They ask, Why should our enemies be allowed access to the American press? Or students permitted to demonstrate against the government? Or pornographers to send obscene material through the mails? Or American Nazis to march down Main Street? The list is endless, but the basic issue is the same: How secure is the right to dissent if it is not

extended to those whose ideas we most fear and despise? Three current examples suggest the difficulties in taking the First Amendment seriously.

1. Many campuses are trying to draw the line between the free exchange of ideas for which higher education exists and speech that creates a climate of fear and intimidation for students who are members of a minority group, lesbians and gay men, and women in general. What some observers call thought control ("political correctness") is what others feel to be a necessary protection against harassment.

2. "Symbolic speech," such as burning an American flag in protest of government actions, is another relevant issue. In 1989, the Supreme Court ruled that flag burning fell within the protection of the First Amendment, a decision that sparked a movement to amend the Constitution specifically to forbid "desecration of the flag." The counterargument is that the flag symbolizes precisely the freedom to burn it. In addition, once one exception has been made, what about others with broad popular appeal: barring anti-Christian speech, for example, or obscene pictures in art galleries?

3. Is burning a cross on a person's lawn an act of vandalism, or is it a hate crime involving symbolic speech outside the protection of the First Amendment? What about "fighting words" that encourage someone to commit a crime out of racial or antigay hatred? These cases were resolved in such an ambiguous manner by the Supreme Court in the early 1990s that they are bound to come before the Court again.

Throughout your years as an active citizen, your vote will make a difference not only in how well the First Amendment protects you but in how well the Amendment itself is protected. Who shall guard the guardians? Citizens such as yourself.

Another problem for democracy is that the very dependence on public opinion that is its glory can also be its undoing. Lawmakers must act slowly and seek widespread support for policies. They cannot demand obedience or silence dissenters, and they cannot easily violate the legal-rational limits of their authority. Often, as in the case of responding to the civil wars that destroyed Bosnia and Rwanda in the early 1990s, democratic leaders do nothing because they cannot command enough support in their own countries to take decisive action. Always, democratic rule is a slow and inefficient process of compromise and consensus building (Marks and Diamond, 1992). Thus, there is always a possibility, even in the United States, that the public will become impatient and look for "a man on horseback," a decisive leader who will rescue the nation from its economic or political stalemate, if we just relax those "bothersome" restraints on power. This may have been the appeal of General Douglas MacArthur, Colonel Oliver North, and businessman Ross Perot. Today in Russia and South America, where fragile democratic structures have been unable to cope with vast economic problems, many people yearn for the return of the very same military dictators that were overthrown only a few years earlier (Brooke, 1993b; French, 1993).

POLITICS

In this section, we examine several aspects of political practice in the United States today: participation in the democratic process, political socialization and attitudes, and the structure of politics at the national and local levels.

Political Participation

Citizens of a democracy may participate in politics in a number of ways: running for office, contributing money to parties or candidates, working on a campaign, voting, or doing none of the above.

OFFICE HOLDING.   As we saw in Chapters 10 and 11, despite recent gains, few women, African-Americans, or Latinos hold high public office, whether elected or appointed. The higher the office and the more important its duties, the less likely to be occupied by someone other than a white man. President Clinton's cabinet is the first to have more than a token woman or African

Political action committees (PACs) are special organizations that use funds to support causes and candidates.

American and to have them in positions of great power (e.g., as attorney general rather than secretary of transportation).

The low representation of women and minorities in high office is due in part to the self-fulfilling prophecy that people without economic or interpersonal power are not perceived as strong candidates, and that without legitimated authority, they remain powerless. For the same reason, they have difficulty raising money. There are also structural barriers: The major path to becoming a candidate is by working one's way up the political party organization. At this time, few African-Americans or Latinos have this background experience, and women are only now emerging from the political pipeline. The other route is to buy one's way into candidacy, which immediately screens out almost everyone but a few white men, such as a Ross Perot or Michael Huffington.

CAMPAIGN ACTIVITY.   Only a small number of Americans become active as volunteers in a political campaign, although many millions will contribute money to candidates or organizations that support a particular viewpoint. Although the amount an individual can spend on a particular candidate is limited by law, there are no restrictions on the number of organizations supporting that candidate to which one can contribute.

PACs.   The restrictions on campaign contributions led to the creation of large numbers of **political action committees (PACs),** which solicit funds for causes and candidates. Most of the money goes to members of Congress who sit on committees over-

Although the U.S. Senate and House of Representatives remain centers of male power, women have made important advances in being elected to the Senate and House of Representatives. What factors have accounted for the increase in representation of women in political leadership? And what factors account for their relatively low numbers?

seeing an area of activity of special importance to PAC contributors, which is why people already in office (incumbents) have an advantage over challengers (Theilmann and Wilhite, 1991; Clawson et al., 1992).

Although most research has centered on the political power of PACs representing employers and business interests, labor unions are among the biggest givers. As you might expect, labor and entertainment PACS contributed primarily to Democratic candidates, whereas business, insurance, oil and gas, tobacco, and liquor PACs supported Republicans (Makinson, 1993). Overall, Republican PACs can raise more money than those supporting Democrats, especially when contributions to local and state political party organizations are taken into account (Goldstein, 1993).

When their candidate wins office, PAC representatives expect at the very least to have access if not a strong influence on the congressperson's vote, which is why most business groups support the candidates from both parties who are most likely to win (Clawson et al., 1992). Influence is more important than ideology. The way to reduce PAC power is to adopt the European model of publicly financed campaigns, in which each candidate receives a similar amount of money collected for that purpose through a tax form write-off.

VOLUNTEER WORKERS. Although some volunteer workers are motivated by powerful personal or ideological motives, most are drawn into political activity by friends. Thus, participation is socially structured and recruitment is linked to interpersonal networks (Knoke, 1990; Abowitz, 1990).

Voting

The minimal act of political participation is voting. As you can see in Tables 14-1 and 14-2 and Figure 14-3, not all eligible Americans exercise this right. Indeed only 68 percent of those eligible—persons age 18 plus and citizens of the United States not in prison or a mental institution—are even registered. Voting rates are higher in presidential election years than in years when only members of Congress are on the ballot. In 1994, for example, a nonpresidential year, fewer than four in ten potential voters chose the persons representing them in Congress, and even fewer elected their governor and state legislators.

American voting rates are roughly half those of other Western democracies. In part, this difference is structured by the timing of the vote. European elections are held on the weekend rather than on a workday, making it easier for hourly wage earners to take the time to vote (Beeghley, 1986). Voting in the United States is further complicated by eligibility rules and registration processes that vary from one state to another (Bauer, 1990).

TABLE 14-1 Voting in Presidential Elections, United States, Selected Years, 1968–1992 (Percentage of Voting-Age Population)

	Percentage voting		
	1968	1988	1992
Total	67.8	57.4	61.3
White	69.1	59.1	63.6
Black	57.6	51.5	54.0
Spanish Origin	—	28.8	28.9
Men	69.8	56.4	60.2
Women	66.0	58.3	62.3
18–20	33.3	33.2	38.5
21–24	51.1	38.3	45.7
25–44	66.6	54.0	58.3
45–64	74.9	67.9	70.0
65–74	} 65.8	} 68.8	73.8
75+			64.8

Source: U.S. Bureau of the Census, P20–466, 1993.

TABLE 14-2 Percentage of Voting-Age Population Voting in the Election of 1992 by Education, Employment, and Income

	Voting
Years of School Completed	
Elementary	35.1
High school: 1–3 years	41.2
High school: 4 years	57.5
College: 1–3 years	68.7
College: 4 years or more	81.0
Labor Force Status	
Unemployed	46.2
Agriculture	56.5
Private wage and salary	60.2
Self-employed	69.2
Government worker	78.7
Not in labor force	58.7
Family Income	
Under $5,000	32.4
5,000–9,999	39.5
10,000–14,999	46.8
19,999–15,000	55.7
20,000–24,999	62.5
25,000–34,999	69.5
35,000–49,999	75.7
50,000 and over	79.9

From: The US Bureau of the Census, P-23, No. 102, 1980; P-20, No. 405, 1986; and "Nonvoting Americans," THE NEW YORK TIMES, December 17, 1992. Copyright © 1992 by The New York Times Company. Reprinted by permission.

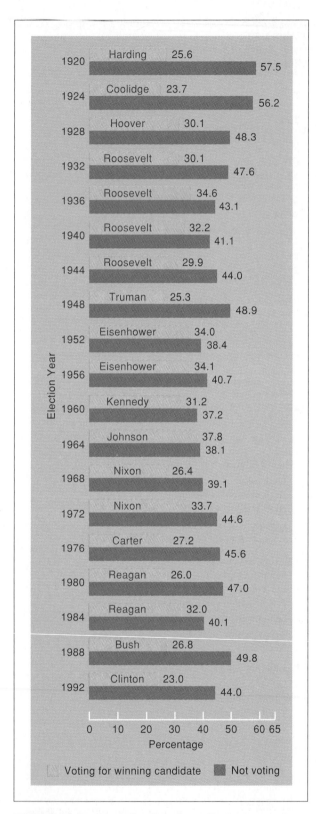

Election Year		Voting for winning candidate	Not voting
1920	Harding	25.6	57.5
1924	Coolidge	23.7	56.2
1928	Hoover	30.1	48.3
1932	Roosevelt	30.1	47.6
1936	Roosevelt	34.6	43.1
1940	Roosevelt	32.2	41.1
1944	Roosevelt	29.9	44.0
1948	Truman	25.3	48.9
1952	Eisenhower	34.0	38.4
1956	Eisenhower	34.1	40.7
1960	Kennedy	31.2	37.2
1964	Johnson	37.8	38.1
1968	Nixon	26.4	39.1
1972	Nixon	33.7	44.6
1976	Carter	27.2	45.6
1980	Reagan	26.0	47.0
1984	Reagan	32.0	40.1
1988	Bush	26.8	49.8
1992	Clinton	23.0	44.0

Percentage (0 10 20 30 40 50 60 65)

■ Voting for winning candidate ■ Not voting

FIGURE 14-3 Nonvoting Americans. Percentage voting for the winning candidate and percentage not voting: 1920–1992 (after universal suffrage).

Sources: U.S. Bureau of the Census, P–23, No. 102, 1980; P–20, No. 405, 1986; *New York Times*, December 17, 1992. Copyright © 1992 by The New York Times Company. Reprinted by permission.

Between 1968 and 1988, American voting rates declined steadily, before picking up slightly in 1992, as seen in Table 14-1. This might be due to the particular election and the presence of a third-party candidate, because voting rates returned to their historic lows in the 1994 Congressional races.

WHO VOTES. As Table 14-1 also shows, voting rates vary by sex, race, ethnicity, and age. In addition, as seen in Table 14-2, the probability of voting is associated with such indicators of social class as education, occupation, and income. Because these data are no secret, it should be no surprise that political party platforms are not typically constructed around the interests of the poor, racial minorities, or the young.

To a large extent, the lower voting rates of African-American and Latino populations reflect racial and ethnic differences in education and occupational status. When social class is statistically controlled, some African-American subgroups have higher voting rates than comparable whites, especially among those with a high sense of personal control and who are integrated into community networks (Guterbock and London, 1983; Ellison and Gay, 1989; Tate, 1993).

THE GENDER GAP. Of all the changes in voting patterns since the 1960s, the one with the most long-term political significance is the increase in voting rates for women. In 1980, for the first time since they gained the suffrage (right to vote) in 1920, the voting rate for women was higher than that for men, a gender gap that has grown wider with each succeeding election. This trend is doubly significant because women also outnumber men at all adult ages, so that the electorate today is predominantly female and will become more so as the population ages.

Among white voters women are more likely to support the Democratic Party and women candidates and to be concerned with a different set of issues than are men (Center for the American Woman and Politics, 1994; Sprague, 1991). Among African-American voters, both men and women tend to concentrate on issues of race rather than gender and both are more likely than whites to vote for Democratic candidates (Howe, 1992; Welch and Sigelman, 1989).

The power of the women's vote was shown in the Presidential election of 1992, when only 3 points separated the male vote for Bush and Clinton, but Clinton ran 9 percentage points ahead of Bush among women, who won the election for him. In the 1994 Congressional elections, women were more likely than men to favor Democrats, but men overwhelmingly preferred conservative candidates, thus giving the Republican Party its great victory in both the Senate and the House of Representatives. In many ways, the 1994 election could be considered an anti-feminist backlash vote, in which a white male majority asserted itself decisively at the polls. The topics thought of as "women's issues"—health care, child welfare, sexual violence, and world peace—took second place to is-

Despite the liberation of Kuwait by American forces in 1991, the country has not adopted political reforms promised by the ruling Al-Sabah family. To date only 14 percent of the adult population are allowed to vote, while women are completely excluded from the political process. Recently, for the first time in Kuwaiti history, groups of women took to the streets to demand their political rights. Defiantly bare-headed and dressed in Western clothing, the march was led by professional women who demanded women's inclusion in the political process. Why aren't women allowed to vote in a country that was "liberated" by American armed forces?

sues of greater importance to men—national defense, taxes, the right to firearms, and criminal punishment.

In a very real sense, then, American politics has become gender politics, with future elections hinging on which sex turns out to vote and how strongly men and women feel about gender-related issues. While some predict that the women's vote will determine most elections, other data suggest that as the baby boomers age and move to the suburbs, especially in the South and West, the electorate will become increasingly conservative (Lyons, 1994; U.S. Bureau of the Census P25–1117, 1994).

WHO DOESN'T VOTE. As Tables 14-1 and 14-2 indicate, many subgroups with much to gain from government assistance have the lowest voting rates: African-Americans, the poor, the young, and the less educated. This list would not surprise Emile Durkheim, because these populations are least likely to be fully integrated into mainstream institutions. The greater a person's investment in ongoing social networks, the higher the probability of voting (Teixeira, 1992).

In the case of young people age 18–24, many will not have lived in one community long enough to

qualify. Young adults are also likely to be in the midst of many status changes—from student to full-time worker, from single to married, and from nonparent to parent—so that politics might be a low priority at this time in their life.

But because so many Americans do not vote (more than 72 million in 1992), those who do get to the polls can exert an influence far beyond their numbers. For example, as shown in Figure 14-3, all but a few presidents elected since 1920 have been placed in office by *fewer* than one-third of the voting-age population! Before 1920, because women could not vote and men who were members of racial minorities were discouraged from doing so, our presidents were elected by no more than 15 percent of American adults!

Only in 1993 did Congress pass and a president sign the "motor voter" bill allowing states to send voter registration forms in the mail along with motor vehicle renewal forms. Permitting people to register on election day would bring out even more voters. The problem for politicians is that the added voters come from groups that could demand support for programs aiding the poor and other marginal populations, thus alienating the majority of taxpayers, which is no way to win an election.

POLITICAL SOCIALIZATION AND VALUE ORIENTATIONS

The term **political socialization** refers to the influences and experiences that lead people to define their political orientation as either conservative or liberal. Because 18-year-olds do not confront the political system as blank slates, the basic question is one of the relative impact of early learning in the home and community compared to adult experiences that lead to a reexamination of attitudes formed in adolescence.

As Figure 14-4 illustrates, the process of political socialization combines elements of both early and later influences. There is a direct link between political attitudes formed by the time one enters college and those held in later adulthood, but intervening experiences also have an effect. In general, it appears that political orientations formed during the "impressionable years" of young adulthood tend to become increasingly stable with age (Alwin and Krosnick, 1991).

> **Political socialization** includes the influences and experiences that determine one's political orientation.

With regard to social class, it is important to distinguish (1) attitudes toward "economic" issues such as private ownership, taxation, and budget priorities from (2) attitudes on "social" issues such as women's rights, school prayer, and racial integration. In general, the upper middle class is most liberal on social issues and the working class the least. On economic matters, the class positions are reversed, with the

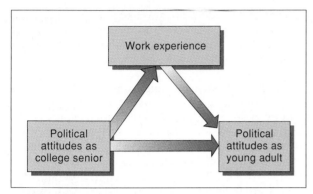

FIGURE 14-4   A model of political socialization.

Source: Adapted from Lorence and Mortimer, 1979.

working class most liberal. These differences, however, appear to be more related to *educational level* than to income or occupation (Zipp, 1986). The middle-class is not a homogeneous voting bloc; lower-level white-collar employees are likely to identify with working-class interests while managers and petty bourgeoisie share political goals with the capitalist class. But voters will change party identification in response to macrolevel economic trends such as unemployment or inflation (Haynes and Jacobs, 1994). Academics and other "knowledge workers" tend to be the most liberal of all occupation/education groups in terms of support for personal freedoms, gender equality, homosexual rights, and racial tolerance.

Thus, both the Democratic and Republican parties are split today between what should be the role of government (a public responsibility) and what should be left to the individual (private interests). For example, many conservatives who deplore government intervention in the economic sphere also support censorship of obscenity and limits on reproductive choice. Conversely, liberals would use public powers to promote economic equity while insisting that government stay out of art galleries and people's bedrooms (Wolfe, 1993). Thus, the same person can hold political opinions that are of the "left" (liberal) or "right" (conservative), depending on whether the issue is one of economics or culture.

The difference between social and economic attitudes is illustrated by data on yuppies, the name given to young, upwardly mobile professionals in the 1970s. Although only about 15 percent of their baby-boom birth cohorts, yuppies captured media attention and, because of their high voting rates, they have had a major impact on public policy. Influenced by the liberating currents of the 1960s during their youth, they remained liberal on social issues, but, also very career conscious, they have become very conservative on economic matters (Jennings and Markus, 1986).

These data illustrate how political attitudes are shaped by historical experience at a particular point in the life course, with a common impact on members of a birth cohort (Braungart and Braungart,

RESEARCH IN ACTION

Bennington Women: Fifty Years Later

In the late 1930s, social psychologist Theodore Newcomb began a study of the political attitudes of students at Bennington College, an exclusive college for women. Then, as now, Bennington's goal was to foster personal autonomy and intellectual growth through close contact between students and faculty. Newcomb (1943) found that their college experience had made these women considerably more liberal than when they entered or than their affluent parents. This shift was due to several factors: contact with a young and progressive faculty; the whole spirit of that historical era, centered on President Franklin Roosevelt's use of government policy to solve social problems; and the reinforcing effect of sharing attitudes with classmates—the reference group effect (see Chapter 4).

But would these attitudes have staying power over the life course? When reinterviewed 25 years later, in their mid-40s, the women displayed a remarkable persistence in the political and social orientations formed during their college days (Newcomb et al., 1967). They continued to view the world through the lens of values shaped by that era.

Researchers located almost two-thirds of the original sample for a third interview in the mid-1980s. Fifty years later, entering old age, the Bennington women were as liberal as ever if not more so (Alwin et al., 1991). In addition, when compared to other women of similar social background, age, and educational attainment, the Bennington graduates were both more liberal and politically active.

This remarkable longitudinal research tells us a great deal about political socialization. First of all, people do not necessarily grow more politically conservative with age. Much depends on one's social environment; if that does not change, neither will a person's attitudes. In this respect, the Bennington women maintained an environment of progressive liberalism through their choice of husband and friends. Second, the surrounding historical context at the time when political attitudes are formed has long-term effects.

Overall, by creating continuity in reference group values, these women maintained the political orientation shaped by their generational history and the unique experience of Bennington College in the 1930s.

1986; see the box entitled "Bennington Women"). Your political generation, for example, came of age during the Reagan and Bush years, and follows a cohort of unusually conservative college students. Typically, young people are more liberal than older persons, but in the 1980s, they were more supportive of Ronald Reagan than any other age group, and more willing than past cohorts of college-age youth to call themselves "conservative" without actually adopting conservative positions on social issues such as sex equality and reproductive choice.

It appears that in the 1980s it was socially desirable for young people to be called conservative, so that there were reference group rewards in applying the label to oneself (Miller, 1992). In the election of 1992, however, young voters were second only to people older than age 50 in their support of Bill Clinton. You might want to examine both the reference group and cohort experiences that could account for this shift in political identity.

WHO RULES? THE STRUCTURE OF POLITICAL POWER IN AMERICA

A recurring theme in political sociology is the debate over who rules America. How is power distributed in *mass society* where traditional authority has been replaced by distant and formal bureaucracies? The specific issue is whether there are many and competing bases of power (the *pluralist* model) or whether decision making is concentrated in the hands of a small homogeneous class (the *power-elite* model).

The Power-Elite Model

In 1956, sociologist C. Wright Mills published a book entitled *The Power Elite* in which he traced the social class backgrounds of leaders in business, government, and other major spheres of influence and authority. It is not necessary to prove a conspiracy among these people or even to show that they are in contact with one another, in order to suggest that the decisions made in one power sector reinforce those made in others. As products of similar class locations and socialization experiences, these leaders will think alike, share a vision of what is fair and good, and act in ways that maintain the existing stratification system. These relationships are shown in Figure 14-5.

The empirical tests of Mills's thesis have centered on identifying a "national upper class" whose members own most of the nation's wealth, manage its corporations and banks, run the universities and foundations, control the mass media, and staff the highest levels of government and the courts (Schwartz, 1987; Domhoff, 1990). It is worth noting in this regard that contrary to the "log cabin" myth, all but five of our presidents were from the upper or upper-middle classes, including Abraham Lincoln (Pessen, 1984; Baltzell and Schneiderman, 1988).

Yuppie stands for young upwardly mobile professional.

The **power-elite model** assumes that decision making is concentrated in the hands of a few similarly socialized people.

The emphasis in recent research has been less on the content of socialization than on the structural links among the members of this elite: from schools and clubs to marriages and jobs. These are interlocks that extend beyond the world of business to involve politics, education, and control over information. This phenomenon is most obvious in presidential appointments and in the actual movement of people from one sphere to another, as when corporate officers become cabinet members, or when heads of regulatory agencies leave government for jobs in the industries they previously regulated.

Other studies trace the flow of campaign contributions from major business groups and individuals. Throughout the 1980s, corporate interests showed a high degree of unity in support of the Republican party and conservative causes in general, as the

FIGURE 14-5 The power elite is composed of members of the upper classes who have achieved the highest possible positions in each of these centers of power.

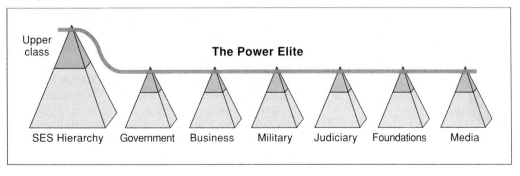

power-elite model would suggest (Clawson and Neustadtl, 1989; Mizruchi, 1992). Labor and public-interest PACs were also relatively united in support of Democratic candidates, lending further support to a class-based theory of political interests (Goldstein, 1993).

The Pluralist Model

Critics of the power-elite model suggest that it over-simplifies reality, assumes a greater uniformity among leaders than actually exists (not everyone can graduate from Harvard, Yale, and Princeton—and even their graduates do not always agree on values), and underestimates the sources of conflict within the ruling class.

> The **pluralist model** assumes there are many different and competing bases of power, with no one group dominating the other.
>
> **Self-help** groups allow people to derive strength from one another in face-to-face interaction.

Pluralists contend that business interests are very diverse; policies that benefit core industries may be disastrous for peripheral firms. Furthermore, the various power sectors are usually in competition for scarce resources, as when the military competes with consumer industries for electronics experts, or when the government competes with private enterprise in providing health care. In the political sphere itself, pluralists point out that power is widely diffused across the three layers of government: local, state, and federal.

The basic assumption of pluralism is that the diversity of interests in mass society ensures that no one group can control decision making throughout the system (Riesman, 1950). As shown in Figure 14-6,

FIGURE 14-6 Model of countervailing forces. Competing power sectors may form coalitions to prevent the uncontrolled expansion of another sector.

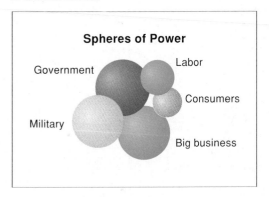

Spheres of Power

Government
Labor
Consumers
Military
Big business

each power sector serves as a potential buffer against uncontrolled expansion of other sectors.

Although the two models are often presented as mutually exclusive, they are best seen as alternative explanations depending on the system under analysis. The power structure of your home town probably resembles the elite model, with local leaders in frequent contact and making decisions that are mutually beneficial. The power structure of a college or university, however, might come close to the pluralist ideal, with administration, faculty, staff, and students competing for scarce resources and serving to limit the concentration of power in any one group. Faculties continually test their power against those of administrations; staff members go out on strike; and teachers and students may refuse to cross picket lines in defiance of the administration.

Pluralist and elitist theorists agree on one point: The great mass of people remains relatively uninvolved in politics, so that power holders are rarely challenged. In recent decades, however, there has been a revival of interest in neighborhood and community organizing to empower "ordinary" people to resist corporate or political decisions that might have a negative effect on their area.

Community Action

In the 1960s, the best-known efforts at community action were directed by Saul Alinsky and his associates, who taught inner-city residents how to organize, demonstrate, and put pressure on local merchants and politicians. The goal was to give a relatively powerless population a sense of control over their destiny (Horwitt, 1989). Another, more limited effort to empower poor people was the Highlander Folk School, founded by Myles Horton in the 1930s, to help poverty-stricken Appalachian whites and blacks resist racism and economic oppression (*Social Policy*, 1991).

Although Alinsky's work was soon overshadowed by the urban riots of the late 1960s, he left a legacy of ideas and techniques for organizing at the grass roots (or, in this case, asphalt). In the 1970s and 1980s, many activists from the civil rights and antiwar movements turned their attention from trying to influence policy at the highest level to trying to make a difference at the lowest level, the backyard.

As is true of **self-help** groups in general, neighborhood organizations are a means of bridging the enormous gap between isolated individuals or families and the impersonal bureaucratic powers "out there." This search for community is an enduring theme in sociology, a major concern of Durkheim, Weber, and Marx, and one that takes on special significance in modern, mass society (Milofsky, 1988). Organizations that bridge this gap allow members to develop a collective identity and shared strength, to learn cooperation and techniques for generating change from the bottom up (Krauss, 1989; Rubin, 1994).

NEIGHBORHOOD ORGANIZING. Local organizations emerge in response to immediate and specific problems such as housing quality, utility rates, access to health care, safety in the streets, and environmental threats. Although followers of Horton and Alinsky are committed to empowering the poor, it is actually communities with greater resources that are best able to unite to resist unwanted changes, such as waste disposal facilities or halfway houses for mental patients that then end up in the poorer neighborhoods (Krauss, 1989).

Organizing residents of poor neighborhoods to act on their own behalf is extremely difficult. Many are overwhelmed with the problems of daily survival, and the cost of participation appears to outweigh any perceived benefits (Oliver, 1984; Wandersman et al., 1987). But where successful, for however short a period, the experience of taking control of one's life has had greatest impact on those most powerless at the start: women and people of color (Bookman and Morgan, 1988). Although only a few-dozen Alinsky-style groups are active today, interest in community organizing has revived among African-American leaders who see this as a necessary step toward stemming further deterioration of America's inner cities.

THE MILITARY

A primary characteristic of the state is its monopoly over the legitimate use of force. Governments—whether tribal councils, absolute monarchies, or modern democracies—are expected to settle disputes within the society and protect it from outside enemies. To serve these functions, two sets of specialists emerge: (1) makers, interpreters, and enforcers of the law to secure internal order (see Chapter 17) and (2) the military for national security. In this section, we examine the military as an institution, the increasing militarization of our society and culture, and the consequences for world peace and human survival.

The American Military

Until recently, the United States was unique among modern nations in *not* having a large professional military. The ideal, rather, was the "citizen soldier," a civilian who could be called on to join the military only when the need arose and who would return to civilian life once the emergency was over (Moskos, 1988; D. Segal, 1989). Examples include the militias of the Revolutionary War and the state National Guard units, which still exemplify this ideal. But when volunteers were lacking, citizens could be forced (conscripted) into the military for temporary duty, such as during the Civil War, both World Wars, and the Vietnam War. From 1945 to 1973, conscription (the draft) continued in peacetime as well.

THE ALL-VOLUNTEER FORCE. In 1973 the citizen-soldier ideal was replaced with a new concept: the "economic man" model of military service. In this model, serving in the armed forces is viewed as a job, like any other, to which recruits would be attracted by relatively high pay, a chance to travel, educational op-

Governments can direct the use of military force against their own citizens. In Thailand, the military was used to crush a popular revolt against an undemocratic government resulting in many arrests, injuries and some deaths as soldiers battled crowds. Thousands of demonstrators were arrested on the streets of central Bangkok.

DAVID R. SEGAL AND MADY WESCHLER SEGAL

Studying the Military as a Social Institution

David R. Segal and Mady Weschler Segal are Professors of Sociology at the University of Maryland at College Park. Both have received awards for teaching excellence, as well as the Department of the Army's Medal for Outstanding Civilian Service. Both have published extensively, individually and jointly. Their most recent joint publication is Peacekeepers and their Wives; *(Westport: Greenwood Press, 1993), a report on the American soldiers who served as peacekeepers in the Sinai Peninsula in the 1980s.*

For the past two decades, our teaching, research, and public service have focused on personnel and organizational issues associated with the all-volunteer armed services. We view the military as a unique institution and profession, as well as an arena in which to study many basic social processes. Having done our graduate work at the University of Chicago in the activist 1960s, with its emphasis on the practical uses of sociological knowledge, we view the application of our training to issues outside the academy as a professional responsibility.

We came to sociology from different paths (neither of us was originally interested in studying the military) and we do not think of ourselves as exclusively military sociologists.

David: I started college as a geology major, but found social stratification more lively than geological stratification. It was my interest in stratification and political sociology that brought me to graduate school at Chicago.

Mady: I wanted to be a teacher for as long as I can remember, and started college as a mathematics major, but by senior year had discov-

ered that sociology interested me more, so I changed my major and applied to graduate programs. Since discrimination against women in admissions was common—and legal—I was thrilled to be accepted at the University of Chicago, where I met David. From Chicago, we went to Michigan, where David joined the faculty at the University of Michigan, and I, at Eastern Michigan University.

David: In 1973, we both took a leave of absence from our academic positions to join the staff of the U.S. Army Research Institute for the Behavioral and Social Sciences (ARI). ARI had been established to apply social science knowledge to the needs of the Army and its personnel. A fascinating social experiment was underway: the transition from conscription to the all-volunteer force.

Mady: I was reluctant both to leave Ann Arbor and to stop teaching in order to work for the army. This was the kind of compromise decision that dual career couples often face. We were fortunate to obtain jobs in the same location, and I knew there were many opportunities in the Washington, D.C., area if I wanted to return to college teaching before David was ready to leave ARI.

Because we had both been active opponents of the Vietnam War, we were surprised and pleased that our anti-war activity had not disqualified us from government employment, but we also had students who were veterans of that war and believed that neither the soldiers nor the army were responsible for the prolongation of the conflict. Our system of civilian control means that it is elected officials who bear ultimate responsibility for the wars that our soldiers fight.

David: I was responsible for a research program that reflected the social problems of the 1970s: race and ethnic relations; drug and alcohol abuse; and issues of morale, motivation, and discipline. Mady worked in

a unit engaged in manpower research, with the goal of understanding what motivates young people to join the military. She quickly became aware of the army's increasing dependence on women as a source of qualified recruits and of the implications of a married volunteer force in contrast to the previous predominantly male and unmarried conscripted force.

Although our time at ARI was stimulating, our first love was teaching, and in 1974 Mady joined the faculty at the University of Maryland, where I joined her the following year. We have always enjoyed working together, and in recent years our collaborative research has returned to military issues, a topic almost completely ignored by American sociologists. We believe that it is much too large and powerful an institution to be left unstudied. Today, although we teach a range of courses on military topics, from the Sociology of War to Military Families, we also continue to teach such sociological basics as statistics, social psychology, and theory.

Mady: And we have continued to carry our sociological perspective beyond the university. In recent years, David has conducted fact-finding missions for the military and has appeared before several Congressional Committees during hearings on sexual orientation and military service. He has also directed a major study of how contemporary trends will affect the structure of the army in the next century. I have served as a consultant to the Secretary of the Army on racial and gender issues and have directed a project to translate the findings of the army's large-scale family research program into concrete policies and practices that would make the armed forces more family friendly.

In these many ways we believe that we have been able to make sociology useful in the real world while constructing a fulfilling life for ourselves.

portunities, and health and retirement benefits. It was thought that an **all-volunteer force (AVF)** would be smaller and more professional than the citizen force, and because volunteers would be making a career out of military service, the higher pay scales would be offset by lower turnover rates and training costs (White, 1989). This is a profound ideological and organizational change in the nature of the American military, and the contemporary AVF is a very different establishment from its predecessor.

RACE AND ETHNICITY.   The AVF has a higher proportion of African-American and Latino men and women than did the conscripted forces: 27 percent of enlisted (nonofficer) personnel today, somewhat higher than their representation in the general population. Indeed, the U.S. Army is the most integrated institution in our society, if only at the lower ranks. Among officers, only 5 percent are African American. Nonetheless, the American armed forces offer greater equality of opportunity for education and training for minority youth than does the civilian labor force (Daula et al., 1990) or the military in other societies (Dietz et al., 1991). Although military service removes large numbers of minority men from local marriage pools, it also provides many with the means to marry and to support a family.

Interracial relations in the military reflect those in the wider society. When on duty together, segregation is minimal, but once off duty, service people tend to associate exclusively with members of their own race. This is not surprising, when we consider that the military tends to attract whites from the South and Midwest rather than from the North.

EDUCATION.   Contrary to public perception, today's recruits, because they can be more carefully selected, are not low achievers from marginal subgroups. To the contrary, most are drawn from upwardly mobile lower-middle class families (Berryman, 1988), and all but a few are high school graduates. This is a more committed and professionalized military than before, as reflected in relatively high reenlistment rates.

WOMEN IN THE MILITARY.   Although women have served in the American armed forces since the early 1940s, the AVF has actively recruited women to its ranks. In 1993, women were 11.5 percent of all troops on active duty and 13 percent of reserve forces: 12.2 percent of Army personnel, 10.4 of the Navy, 4.5 percent of the Marine Corps, and 14.7 of the Air Force (M. Segal, 1995). These percentages are the highest of any modern military, as seen in Figure 14-7. In addition, many women have moved up in rank so that they now compose about 15 percent of

> The **all-volunteer force (AVF)** is composed of people who enter the military as a full-time career.

FIGURE 14-7   Women in combat: how other nations rank. The walls restricting women to nonfighting roles in the United States military cracked when the Defense Department in 1993 lifted bans against women in aerial combat and asked for the repeal of a law forbidding women on warships. The United States is not blazing the trail; other countries have women in combat jobs. Examples of military policies are shown.

From: "Women in Combat: How Other Nations Rank," *The New York Times*, May 2, 1993, (Week In Review, p. 4) Copyright ©1993 by The New York Times Company. Reprinted by permission.

Country	Women in active-duty forces, 1992

Canada   10.9%
Women are in combat jobs in every area except submarine duty. Future submarine designs will have separate quarters for women.

Israel   11.0%
Drafts women, but they are barred from combat jobs. In the early fight for nationhood in the 1930s and 1940s, women had served in combat positions, reaching levels as high as 20 percent of all soldiers. But the use of women in combat was never formally recognized and was discontinued in 1948.

Norway   2.4%
Women are allowed in every job in the armed forces.

Russia   0.7%
Women are allowed in combat-support and non-combat positions. In World War II, women served as machine gunners and snipers and on artillery and tank crews. The Air Force had three all-woman fighter and bomber units.

United States   11.5%*
Until 1993, women were allowed only in combat-support jobs. In 1991, 35,000 women served in the Persian Gulf war. Five were killed and two were taken prisoner by the Iraqis.
*1993 figure

Today, increasing numbers of white women and minority men and women are in the armed forces of the United States and have gradually worked their way into the officer corps. How do women's experiences in the military differ from those of men?

all officers below the rank of colonel or lieutenant commander.

Originally, the job categories open to women were limited to the clerical and medical areas, on the grounds that they were emotionally and physically unsuited to other tasks, especially combat duty. The line between combat and noncombat positions has blurred greatly under conditions of modern warfare, as seen in the Persian Gulf War when women served close enough to combat to be killed and wounded. Over time, most of the other limitations were gradually eroded, and with the election of Bill Clinton, the Department of Defense moved to open most of the remaining positions, with the exception of some types of armored units and combat ships. All positions in the Coast Guard and Air Force are now open to women, although not without resistance from male colleagues and their wives (Hertz, 1991).

One persistent problem for military women is sexual harassment, reported by close to two-thirds of those surveyed by the Department of Defense in 1990, with one-third having experienced a direct unsolicited assault. Nonetheless, the American AVF has been less openly sexist than other modern military establishments, including the Israeli army (Yuval-Davis, 1985).

> **Militarism** refers to a social emphasis on military ideals and a glorification of war.
>
> **Militarization** occurs when an entire society is mobilized around militaristic goals.

MILITARY FAMILIES. In the past, only officers' families were permitted to live on base in a highly stratified society in which the husband's military rank determined the interactions among wives and children (e.g., the Colonel's wife could open a conversation with the Major's wife but not the other way around). With the AVF, to attract and retain personnel, enlisted men and women can also live on base with their spouses and children, so the base commander must now deal with a community of military families (Bowen and Orthner, 1989). Like the mayor of any town, the commander must worry about schools, health care, and social services, and must provide support for single-parent families and those in which the mother is away on active duty.

But because both the family and the military are "greedy institutions," demanding full commitment from members, there is a strong potential for conflict between the demands of service to one's country and obligations to spouse and children.

Militarism and Militarization

Militarism refers to a societal emphasis on military ideals and virtues and a glorification of war and warriors. Militarism is associated with heavy expenditures on weapons as well as an aggressive foreign policy. **Militarization** refers to the mobilization of an entire society around war-related goals. Until the 1960s, the United States had been relatively nonmilitaristic, with a small permanent army, and bound by the constitutional principle of civilian control over the military. The government could periodically whip up a fever pitch of support for particular wars, but the ideal of the citizen soldier predominated; men went reluctantly into battle and came home as soon as possible.

Until recently, the United States avoided the militarism of other nation states by physical and ideological isolation from the rest of the world—protected by two oceans and inclined to look inward. Limited wars were conducted against native tribes, and the British, French, and Spanish for territory on this continent. The United States has not hesitated to invade or create revolutions in the Latin American countries in which American corporations have important investments. But involvement in European wars came slowly and reluctantly.

Today, however, the United States ranks among the most militarized nations, due largely to our assuming the role of "leader of the free world" following the end of World War II. The 1950s saw the beginning of a cold war between the United States and the Soviet Union that ended only in 1990 with the breakup of the Soviet empire. But during those four decades, each superpower was caught up in a spiral of fear, devoting an increasing amount of national resources to the weapons and preparations for war.

"Put simply, the mission is to discover a potential enemy who could justify our three-hundred-billion-dollar defense budget."

Drawing by Stevenson; © 1992 The New Yorker Magazine, Inc.

Militarism is a major problem for a democratic society because, by its nature, the military is a totalitarian, antidemocratic institution. It is a rigid hierarchy where blind obedience is the goal, and no opposition is permitted. Thus, the military mind is ill equipped for democratic tolerance of dissent. The authors of the Constitution therefore were very clear about ultimate civilian control: The President is Commander in Chief, and if a military person runs for any political office, it is without the uniform or the commission (Kohn, 1994).

Militarism also invades the culture. Movies, television programs, children's toys, video games, and cartoon programs all glorify combat as a solution to political and social problems (Gibson, 1994). There are also war games and toys for adults: camouflage suits, paintball weapons, soft-air guns, and training camps for would-be Rambos. Dozens of magazines such as *Soldier of Fortune* carry advertisements for mercenaries and mail-order catalogues that show the latest in advanced weaponry. And because militarism is so closely associated with masculinity, it unites men from across all social statuses and sets them as a class apart from women, thus reinforcing gender stratification in the society as a whole (Jeffords, 1989; Enloe, 1993).

The strength of the link between masculinity and militarism is illustrated by the reaction of the U.S. Joint Chiefs to a proposal to lift the ban on openly gay personnel and their fear that the military would then be perceived as less of a "man's world." The equating of homosexuality with femininity, and femininity with fear, is very strong among military men. Being referred to as a "lady" is an insult that brings instant obedience. Some critics claim that American officers are not isssued an umbrella because it would make them appear to be afraid of the rain (Enloe, 1993).

Another area in which the impact of militarism will be felt throughout the society is its effect on domestic policy and the federal budget.

THE MILITARY-INDUSTRIAL STATE. In his Farewell Address to the nation in 1961, President Dwight D. Eisenhower, a former general, warned of a new threat to democratic government and the pursuit of world peace: the combination of a large permanent military establishment and an immense defense industry. This

Globally, war and military life remain a male experience. Most boys are exposed to war toys, both make-believe and real ones, whether in the United States or in war-torn countries such as Somalia where more than 30,000 people died as a result of a domestic war.

military-industrial complex could become an independent power in setting priorities in domestic and foreign relations. Funds would have to be diverted from social programs to support the arms buildup. Once entrenched, with billions of dollars and thousands of jobs at stake, the complex would have a vested interest in world conflict rather than peace. Thirty-four years later, out of a total U.S. budget of 1.5 *trillion* dollars, over 17 percent, or 261 billion dollars, was earmarked for military spending. In comparison, roughly 1.5 percent is alloted for Aid to Families with Dependent Children, and another 14 percent is for interest on the national debt (U.S. Bureau of the Census, *Statistical Abstract* 1994). Contrary to campaign promises, not a single major weapon system has been eliminated by the Clinton administration, despite a government report that military officials and defense contractors consistently lied about the costs and effectiveness of these projects (Burton, 1993).

> The **military-industrial complex** consists of a large permanent military establishment combined with an immense armament industry.

Warfare Welfare

As Eisenhower foretold, the vast numbers of dollars and people involved in the production and procurement of weapons have become a force of their own. Members of Congress compete to secure defense contracts for their own districts; retired military officials take jobs with defense industries; military contractors contribute to political campaigns; communities depend on defense plants for jobs and other income. As a consequence, a vast system of "warfare welfarism" has evolved in which billions of taxpayer dollars subsidize war industries, with minimal supervision by civilian authorities (Feagin and Feagin, 1994.)

The purchase of weapons has less to do with rational calculations about need and effectiveness than with political considerations and the sheer force of institutionalized patterns of behavior throughout the military-industrial complex (Suchman and Eyre, 1992). From the 96 B-1B bombers that have been grounded by mechanical problems from the day they were built to the thousand dollar toilet seats, hundreds of millions of taxpayer dollars have been transferred to the defense industry with little increase in military readiness. For four decades, bureaucrats in the Department of Defense have commanded a budget greater than the combined profits of all U.S. corporations, thus determining a large share of American industrial policy (Hooks, 1991). This kind of power has also reshaped the industrial map of the nation, creating a "gunbelt" of states where defense spending has been concentrated and where regional economies now depend on maintaining these industries (Markusen et al., 1991; Hooks, 1994). Not coincidentally, these states are often represented in Congress by members of the Armed Services Committee.

In addition, once a complex weapons system is in place, the temptation to use it grows, and when the world today is filled with a variety of powerful offensive armaments, the possibility of an accidental war also rises (Tetlock et al., 1991; Burrows and Windrem, 1994). Although the Soviet Union no longer supplies weapons to its allies, the international arms traffic has barely slowed down. The United States today is the largest single supplier of weapons to the rest of the

As a result of "warfare welfarism" trillions of dollars have been spent on various defense systems and machines of destruction. These expensive B-52 bombers, now obsolete, rest at an Air Force Base in Arizona. How many schools, hospitals, and families could have been helped with the money spent on these bombers?

world, especially to the less developed nations where, despite widespread poverty and starvation, the military absorbs the bulk of government spending. In part, our share, 73 percent, has risen as Russia's share has declined, for a total of almost 15 billion dollars.

The cost of weapons also strains the economy of developed nations by diverting money that could otherwise be spent producing civilian goods. In general, the lower the percentage of income spent on the military, the stronger the nation's economy.

NUCLEAR WAR. The arms race that has overtaken countries at all stages of economic development has also spread to the atmosphere. Today's nuclear weapons are faster, more accurate, and far more powerful than envisaged only a decade ago. Although only a few nations admit to having a nuclear arsenal, another two dozen could be well on their way. The combined firepower of just the *known* stock of nuclear weapons in the world today is *3,000* times greater than the total firepower of all weapons used in World War II.

Social scientists, along with most Americans, were slow to recognize the destructive implications of the atomic age, but the threat of nuclear extinction has focused attention on the high cost of war and the potential for accidents (Sagan, 1993). As a result, the Sociology of War and Peace is now a recognized subfield. Research topics include many of the issues examined in this chapter: the power of the military-industrial complex, the manipulation of public opinion, the military as an institution, militarism and masculinity, the militarization of societies, the dynamics of international cooperation and conflict, and the consequences of nuclear war (Tetlock et al., 1991; Grimshaw, 1992). Clearly, nuclear war is too important to be left to generals and physicists.

The U.S. capacity for nuclear warfare was built up in response to a perceived threat from the Soviet Union but is also the result of the sheer momentum of having the technical capacity, another example of a complex system taking on a life of its own (MacKenzie, 1990). Yet the greater the buildup, the greater the chance of unintended consequences (Schwartz et al., 1990; Burrows and Windrem, 1994). And with such weapons in the hands of many relatively unstable governments, the probability of an accidental nuclear holocaust is a reality that will haunt the international scene throughout your life.

SUMMARY

1. The study of political systems begins with an analysis of power, a resource unevenly available to members of a society and an important dimension of social stratification.

2. The type of power called *authority* refers to the exercise of control through legitimated and institutionalized structures.

3. Weber distinguished three bases of authority: traditional, charismatic, and legal-rational.

4. As social systems become more complex, the political organization becomes elaborated.

5. Political systems, although relatively autonomous, are linked to other institutional spheres, particularly the economy. Political and economic forces led to the establishment of the welfare state in most modern societies.

6. Political systems can be ranged on a continuum from totalitarian to democratic.

7. All governments attempt to manipulate public opinion through selective control over information—propaganda and censorship—and to chill dissent through surveillance. The iron law of oligarchy suggests that all power holders are tempted to manipulate their citizens.

8. The ultimate form of social control involves coercion, repression, and genocide.

9. In a democracy, citizens participate in the political process by running for office, working on campaigns, and voting. Participation is socially structured so that certain groups are overrepresented. The major change in U.S. voting patterns involves women's high voter turnout.

10. Political socialization refers the influences and experiences that lead people to define themselves as either politically conservative or liberal.

11. Sociologists developed two models for analyzing power in the United States—the power-elite and the pluralist. Each is useful for explaining certain types of power systems, and both note that the majority of American citizens are politically inactive. This may be changing through the spread of community-action groups.

12. A defining characteristic of the state is its monopoly over the use of legitimate force—the police for internal order and the military for external defense.

13. Historically, the American military has been guided by the ideal of the civilian-soldier, but

since 1973 it has been composed of volunteers. The AVF has a greater proportion of African-American, Latino, and women ranks than did the conscripted military.

14. The military-industrial complex is a dominant feature of our economy and of our foreign trade. Military spending has increased dramatically in the past few decades.

15. Although the threat of nuclear war has receded somewhat recently, the absolute number of weapons available to the United States and the other nations continues to feed fears of an accidental outbreak of war.

SUGGESTED READINGS

Block, Fred. *Revising State Theory: Essays in Politics and Postindustrialism.* Philadelphia: Temple University Press, 1987. A series of important essays spanning a decade of state theory, that examines the political economy of postindustrialism, its new productive forces, and the existing relations of control.

Dunn, John. *Democracy: The Unfinished Journey, 508 B.C. to A.D. 1993.* Oxford: Oxford University Press, 1992. A collection of thought-provoking essays discussing both historic and contemporary democracy.

Dye, Thomas R. *Who's Running America? The Clinton Years.* Englewood Cliffs, NJ: Prentice-Hall, 1994. An overview of America's power elite.

Enloe, Cynthia. *The Morning After: Sexual Politics at the End of the Cold War.* Berkeley, CA: University of California Press, 1993. A collection of essays by a leading feminist academic analyst of all things military. Enloe's sharp wit pierces one illusion after another, revealing the deeply gendered nature of militarism.

Gibson, James William. *Warrior Dreams: Paramilitary Culture in Post-Vietnam America.* NY: Hill and Wang, 1994. An analysis of the "New War" culture that has presented the warrior role as the ideal identity for American men, in movies, magazines, politics, and paramilitary organizations.

Hooks, Gregory. *Forging the Military Industrial Complex: World War II's Battle of the Potomac.* Urbana: University of Illinois Press, 1991. An analysis of the development of America's military industrial complex with a timely discussion of issues crucial to the conversion from a military economy to a civilian one.

Lewis, Anthony. *Make No Law: The Sullivan Case and the First Amendment.* New York: Random House, 1991. Free Speech and the Constitution are discussed in this lively historical analysis of the New York Times vs. Sullivan case over a "libelous" article that appeared in the Times. The watershed case went all the way to the Supreme Court.

Rueschemyer, Marilyn. *Women in the Politics of Post-Communist Eastern Europe.* Providence, RI: Brown University, 1993. An examination of the social upheaval of the post-Communist era and transition to a market economy and how this changed social structure and the political power of men and women.

Washburn, Philo, C. (ed.) *Research in Political Sociology: A Research Annual, Volume 6.* Greenwich, CT: JAI Press, 1993. This edited edition addresses four important themes in political sociology: political involvement, American politics, the welfare state, and the development of collective political orientation.

15

Education and Schooling

*E*ducational notes from late twentieth century America:

- As Congress passed legislation designed to improve the intellectual performance of American school children, a librarian in Montana was fired for allowing a student to read a book on witchcraft; a school district in Florida required teachers to inform students that American culture was inherently superior to all others; and the New York City Board of Education scuttled a curriculum intended to teach tolerance for diversity.
- Even as college tuition costs rise yearly, more than half of all new college and university faculty will be part-time employees.
- Twenty-three of the 50 states faced court challenges to public school funding that allows wealthy (and white) districts to spend more than six times the amount per student than is raised in districts with many poor and minority residents.
- The Department of Education reports that one-half of American adults do not have the skills to read a bus schedule or write a letter about a billing error.
- And 40 years after the Supreme Court struck down racially segregated school systems, 70 percent of African-American students attend schools in which they are the majority.

Clearly, education in the United States is not now, and never was, a smoothly operating institutional sphere, above politics, and dedicated to nurturing the intellect. To the contrary, the schools have always been a battleground of competing interests, reflecting the tensions generated in other parts of the society (Willie and Miller, 1988; Fass, 1989).

This chapter examines the history of education in the United States, its functions and dysfunctions, and its links to other institutional spheres. We also explore the social system of the classroom, the structure of higher education (colleges and universities), and current controversies about quality, equality, and funding of public schools.

FUNCTIONS OF EDUCATION

Formal education extends the socialization process begun in the family. Because family members often cannot teach all that a child needs to know, other agents assume the task of presenting specialized knowledge. The more complex the society, the less family bound and more lengthy the educational process.

In simple societies, girls and boys learn similar skills by watching their elders. In societies with specialized occupations, families will try to keep skills within the kinship line through apprenticeship but not all knowledge or jobs can be handed down from parent to child. Some tasks require long periods of special training for which the earliest schools were established: for example, those for scribes in China and Egypt and for priests in Judea.

Today, in addition to the transmission of occupational skills, a major function of education is to pro-

Schools function to prepare children for adult roles in the community, family, and workplace, whether in India, (left), Nigeria (right), or the United States. What similarities and differences exist between these two classrooms and those you have experienced?

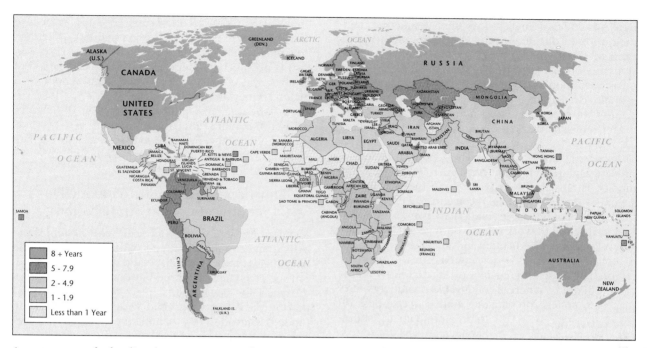

Average years of schooling, by country, 1990. This map illustrates the wide variation in the level of education of the world's population.

Source: Human Development Report, 1993 © United Nations Development Programme, I UN Plaza, New York, N.Y. 10017, 1993, pp. 135–137.

mote social unity, in both complex and developing nations. The assumption is that when school children learn a common culture—language, values, beliefs—there will be agreement on fundamental societal goals (Benavot et al., 1991; Fuller, 1991). In most developing nations, however, this education is primarily directed at boys and men because there are not enough resources to educate all children (Clarke, 1992). But because one unintended consequence of not educating girls is continued high birthrates, economic growth for the entire nation is impeded (London, 1992). These countries would, therefore, benefit more from educating girls as well as boys.

Manifest Functions

TRANSMITTING THE CULTURE.   Because of its great diversity of subgroups, "an" American culture is not easily defined. Finding common ground is made more difficult by the fact that our educational system is based on local control by elected school boards in over 16,000 separate districts representing extremely diverse populations. As a consequence, the task of presenting a standard version of the culture and society has fallen to the writers and publishers of textbooks.

This is why parents and political/religious groups have fought so fiercely over textbook content. Just as feminists and civil rights organizations sought to correct the sexist and racist biases in school material in the 1960s and 1970s, so today, extremely conservative religious groups seek to mold the curriculum and text-

books to reflect their world view (Wong, 1991). For example, since 1992, candidates of the very conservative Christian Coalition won a large number of seats on local school boards, precisely to influence textbook selection and the curriculum, to eliminate sex education and any positive mention of homosexuality, and to promote the Biblical account of creation.

The economics of textbook publishing are that a publisher must produce books that will be adopted by school boards throughout the country. One way to avoid offending board members is to omit mention of controversial topics such as world hunger, the women's movement, sexuality, and, of course, evolution. Books that might awaken interest among young people could also arouse the fears of adults.

Thus, the culture that is transmitted is typically dull and colorless (literally as well as figuratively), downplaying conflict, extolling the status quo (things as they are), and locating success and failure within the individual. The books reflect the world of those who have succeeded, a world from which many students are excluded and to which they feel inferior (Freire, 1985; Apple, 1993). No educational system intentionally trains students to reject existing values, and few encourage critical thinking, at least until the college level.

ACCULTURATION OF IMMIGRANTS.   During the great waves of immigration from Europe between 1880 and 1920, it was thought that urban public schools would be the "melting pot" in which diverse ethnic populations would learn English, lose their uniqueness, and pick up the skills needed for industrial employment. Because these were years of great economic expansion, the schools were relatively successful as avenues of upward mobility. But not all children entered the schools or stayed for long. Today, however, city schools must accept almost all students, keep them longer, and send them into a deteriorating job market.

TRAINING FOR ADULT STATUSES.   The schools function to prepare children for their eventual roles in the community, family, and workplace. From the first day in school to the last, students receive instruction in conformity, good work habits, and obedience to authority.

Socialization to work roles is both general (punctuality, discipline, obedience) and specific (vocational or college preparation). In general, *vocational education,* largely sex segregated, is targeted to working-class children, whereas middle-class students are placed in college preparatory courses, regardless of their intellectual skills. Similar patterns are found in other modern societies with ethnic minorities, such as Malaysia's (Pont, 1993) or Israel's division into Arab and European or Eastern Jewish populations (Shavit, 1990).

> The **hidden curriculum** refers to what is learned, such as ethnocentrism and respect for authority, but is not part of the official curriculum.
>
> A **meritocracy** is a hierarchy of talent, in which rewards are based on one's abilities.

Although it is often assumed that industrialization leads to an expansion of education, the demand for cheap, unskilled workers often makes child labor attractive to employers and families (Walters and James, 1992). Only when child labor is forbidden does schooling become a legitimate alternative for children whose work is no longer needed on the farm or within the household.

In the United States, in addition, African-American children in the South were denied even the basics of public education, not only during slavery but for decades following emancipation. The lesser resources available to predominantly black school districts has ensured that Southern states rank last on any measure of educational input or outcome, even today.

Latent Functions

Manifest functions have unacknowledged, if not necessarily intended, consequences. The term **hidden curriculum** refers to the unannounced lessons learned by school children, such as ethnocentrism, respect for authority, homophobia, and a belief in the superiority of nonmanual labor (even though most will have jobs with little autonomy).

Critics charge that the hidden curriculum is actually the heart of American schooling. Learning to know one's place, to obey superiors, and to believe that the system is fair are lessons that last a lifetime, long after one has forgotten the dates of the Civil War. In this perspective, kindergarten has been likened to "boot camp" (Gracey, 1977) and high school to a prison (Haney and Zimbardo, 1975).

Perhaps the most important function of schools, with both manifest and latent functions, is to serve as gatekeeper to the occupational system, sorting students into "winners" and "losers" at an early age.

Functional and Conflict Perspectives on Education and Stratification

A central element of the American value system is the belief that schools offer an equal opportunity for individual talent to be recognized and developed. In modern society, where achievement replaces ascription as the basis for occupational placement, it is claimed that by providing each child with a "free" (publicly funded) education, the schools become the link between ability and mobility.

From the functional perspective, schools encourage competition to distinguish the better students from the less able, thus creating a hierarchy of talent, or a **meritocracy** based on the innate qualities of individuals. The underlying assumptions are that (1) teachers can accurately identify bright and dull students; (2) standardized tests are objective measures of intelligence; and (3) differences in test scores reflect differences in innate abilities. Thus, if students are given an equal opportunity to learn, unequal outcomes are due to personal qualities. In this way, functionalists claim that society as a whole benefits from the talents of its brightest members, while all individuals are helped to find their "natural" level.

Each of these assumptions has been challenged from the conflict perspective and its focus on the hidden curriculum. Research in this tradition suggests the following:

- Ascribed statuses such as race, sex, and social class play at least as important a role as academic performance in sorting students into winners and losers (McClelland, 1990).
- The entire system is designed to reproduce economic inequality by turning out a mass of obedient workers and an elite of owners/managers.
- The belief in meritocracy leads people to blame themselves for failure.
- The approved culture reflected in the curriculum serves to delegitimate other ways of seeing and living (Bourdieu, 1984; Bernstein, 1990).
- Middle-class parents can influence school authorities and secure advantages for their children in contrast to the relative powerlessness of working-class parents at the same school (Lareau, 1989; Useem, 1992).

■ Standardized tests do not measure innate intelligence so much as socialization to the approved culture and therefore the ability to perform well in the schools.

At the macrolevel, critics suggest that the very structure of the school is a lesson in conformity to bureaucracy. At the microlevel, interpretive studies of the classroom show how students and teachers actively construct a definition of the situation appropriate to the students' expectations of failure or success (Wexler et al., 1992; Mehan, 1992; Kelly, 1993).

One of the least noted effects of compulsory schooling is that it succeeds in obtaining from the dominated classes a recognition of legitimate knowledge . . . entailing the devaluation of knowledge and know-how that they effectively command.

—PIERRE BOURDIEU AND JEAN-CLAUDE PASSERON, 1977, p.42

Both the functional and conflict approaches see schooling as a "filtering process," channeling students into different programs and thus into different academic and adult careers. The models differ in (1) the relative importance of talent or social background in determining educational outcomes and (2) their claims regarding the goal of the system, developing needed skills for the benefit of the society as a whole, or in reproducing the socioeconomic status (SES) hierarchy.

Schooling and Social Class

In general, children from the middle and upper strata score higher on standardized tests and complete more years of schooling, regardless of test scores, than do children from other strata. In part, this is the result of simply having more money: Services such as tutoring can be purchased; the children's earnings are not essential to family well-being; the local schools are well funded and filled with students from other affluent homes; and college costs can be covered for all offspring. In addition, growing up in such households brings nonfinancial benefits that have a strong bearing on school achievement.

CULTURAL CAPITAL.   College-educated parents in white-collar occupations transmit **cultural capital**—a style of thinking and speaking, and a knowledge of music, art, and literature, that allows a person to feel comfortable in educational settings and to understand the world as defined by dominant elites (Bourdieu, 1984; DiMaggio, 1982a).

> **Cultural capital** refers to a style of talking and thinking, as well as to knowledge of music, art, and literature, that prepares individuals for membership in the dominant strata.

RESEARCH IN ACTION

Fast Tracks, Slow Tracks, No Tracks

Many of the issues raised in this chapter are illustrated by the widespread practice of placing children who are at the same grade level into separate learning groups called *tracks* or "ability groups." The assumption is that children who differ in intellectual abilities will do best when grouped with students similar to themselves, rather than being held back by slower learners or embarrassed by faster ones.

Most research shows that ability grouping tends to have negative effects on the intellectual development of lower-track children while adding to the cumulative advantages of high-track students (Kerckhoff, 1993; Oakes, 1994). Conversely, heterogeneous groups appear to benefit *all* the children, as the fast learners serve as peer tutors to their slower learning classmates (Lee and Smith, 1993). Because the amount and quality of instruction vary greatly between tracks, their primary effect is to perpetuate inequality in the schools and society. (Hoffer and Gamoran, 1993; Natriello et al., 1989). In addition, overwhelming evidence shows that race and social class are closely related to track placement, regardless of the child's test scores (U. S. Department of Education, 1994).

Sociologists are also interested in how the structural and organizational characteristics of the school (teacher work loads, class size, instructional resources, and activity schedules) affect the number and size of tracks regardless of changes in the student population (Hallinan, 1994). For example, where students and their parents have most influence on track placement, typically in higher-income districts, the high tracks tend to be more exclusive than in schools where teachers' preferences are crucial (Kilgore, 1991; Useem, 1992). Another significant structural variable is the amount of movement from one track to another permitted in the school; the greater the mobility, the greater the improvement in students' achievement (Gamoran, 1992).

In recognition of these findings, many school districts today are rethinking the tracking system and, if not eliminating it entirely in favor of cooperative learning and peer tutoring, are at least trying to make tracking more flexible and responsive to the individual student (Strum, 1993).

Family background influences both a student's ability and level of effort, the major mechanisms for educational success, so that as the schools reward achievement they also reproduce class inequalities (Katsillis and Armer, 1992).

Children with cultural capital are so attractive to educational authorities that some among them are singled out as particularly "gifted." The discovery of gifted children in the early decades of this century is a fascinating example of the social construction of a category of persons, a product of scholars seeking to reinforce the superiority of the white upper classes over people of darker skins and lower social status (Margolin, 1993). Even today, special classes for presumably gifted children tend to be found only in wealthy, largely white school districts.

Another type of family resource is *social capital,* defined as supportive relationships, especially those between parent and child (Schneider and Coleman, 1993). The greater the parental involvement, the higher the child's achievement, often overcoming the lack of other resources, but most often found in middle-class families.

ACHIEVEMENT EXPECTATIONS. As noted in Chapter 5, the use of psychological rather than physical discipline in middle-class homes leads to internalized guilt and high achievement motivation in their children. The work habits encouraged by these parents not only enhance school performance but also affect the teacher's perception of the child and subsequent grades (Farkas et al., 1990).

Because affluent parents have control over their environment, they can make *deferred gratification* pay off, and their children know that by putting off immediate pleasure they will reap benefits later. In contrast, children from low-income families accurately perceive their parents' lack of social power and have no guarantees that working hard in school now will have any future payoff.

FAMILY SIZE. Children from middle-class households also benefit from having fewer siblings than their working-class peers. In general, the smaller the family or more widely spaced the children, the greater the parental investment in each child, and the higher the child's academic achievement, regardless of other background variables (Blake, 1989; Poston and Falbo, 1990; Grissmer et al., 1994). Indeed, family size often outweighs the effect of social class, as seen in the achievements of working class youth from small families, or from families in which an older child serves as a peer tutor to younger siblings (Shavit and Pierce, 1991; T. E. Smith, 1990).

HOUSEHOLD COMPOSITION. In general, children from a two-parent household have higher school grades and test scores and stay in the school system longer than do children from a one-parent household. Much of this difference disappears when family income is taken into account; that is, poor school performance is related more to low income and its problems than to living with one parent *per se* (Alstone and McLanahan, 1991). Also, limited parental education has an effect on the child's school grades regardless of household composition. Nonetheless, compared with SES peers who live with two parents, children from one-parent households receive less adult supervision and less help with homework, and display behaviors that limit school performance, such as tardiness, truancy, and frequent dating (Mulkey et al., 1992). In general, two adults in a household provide the supervision, homework assistance, and achievement expectations that translate into enhanced academic performance (McLanahan and Sandefur, 1994). In addition, teachers' perceptions of a child's ability are influenced by the composition of a student's family, lowered for those in a one-parent household, and higher for those in an intact family (Thompson et al., 1988).

NEIGHBORHOOD EFFECTS. Middle class children appear to benefit from the characteristics of the neighborhood in which they live. The more affluent one's neighbors, the more positive the effects on childrens' IQ and the likelihood of staying in school—outcomes that benefit white children to a greater extent than their African-American counterparts (Brooks-Gunn et al., 1993).

For all these reasons, regardless of individual ability, youth from the higher social strata, compared to other students, do better in school, stay longer, enjoy cumulative advantages, and are ultimately poised for success in the adult world (McClelland, 1990). Educational attainment has long-term positive effects on cognitive capacity and on earnings. The longer one stays in school, the greater the benefits in average income, as shown in Table 15-1. As you can also see, at each education level the benefits are greater for men than for women, and for whites than for persons of color.

THE STRUCTURE OF THE AMERICAN EDUCATIONAL SYSTEM

In all modern societies, education has become increasingly *differentiated* and *specialized*. Where a one-room schoolhouse once sufficed, age-graded classes are now divided among elementary, junior high, and high schools. Knowledge is similarly separated into categories and taught by specialists. Eventually, students are expected to choose one distinct package of knowledge (their "major"), which will prepare them for the world of work.

TABLE 15-1   Mean 1992 Earnings by Education Attainment, Sex, Race and Hispanic Origin, for Persons Ages 18 and Over

Characteristic	Total	Not a high school graduate	High school graduate	Some college or Associate degree	Bachelor's degree	Advanced degree
Total	$23,227	$12,809	$18,737	$20,866	$32,629	$48,653
Male	$28,448	$14,934	$22,978	$25,660	$40,039	$58,324
Female	$17,145	$9,311	$14,128	$16,023	$23,991	$33,814
White	$23,932	$13,193	$19,265	$21,357	$33,092	$49,346
African American	$17,416	$11,077	$15,260	$17,768	$27,457	$39,088
Hispanic Origin*	$16,824	$11,836	$16,714	$19,215	$28,260	$41,296

*May be of any race.

Source: U.S. Bureau of the Census. "Educational Attainment in the United States: March 1993." *Current Population Reports* P20-476, May 1994, p. ix.

Inclusiveness

The American educational system is also **inclusive,** that is, open to large numbers of students, in contrast to being selective, or exclusive. The ages at which children may enter and leave the schools have been gradually extended so that today almost all children age 5 to 16 are enrolled in a mandatory system of elementary and high school. In addition, educational opportunities are open to almost everyone both before and after the mandated years.

PREKINDERGARTEN.   Although early childhood education is increasingly common, the United States lags behind other modern societies in providing an extensive network of publicly funded, early learning programs. Private nursery schools, stressing cognitive development and social skills, are widely available to children of the well-to-do, where competition for a place in a high-quality nursery school is often more fierce than it is for college entrance (Antilla, 1994). The quality nursery school is the first stepping-stone on the path to educational achievement.

HEAD START.   For disadvantaged children, the federally funded **Head Start** program has had a positive but limited impact on the children served. As originally designed 30 years ago, the program also included health examinations and hot meals for the children and referrals to needed social services for other family members (Zigler and Muenchow, 1993). But all this is very expensive, and the program is a tempting target for budget cutters because it serves a politically powerless population.

The American education system is **inclusive,** or open, to almost all children of given ages.

Head Start is a federally funded preschool program for disadvantaged children that provides learning experiences and social services to the family.

Ideologically, Head Start has been consistently opposed by religious and political conservatives who see it as a plan to supplant family-based child rearing with communal care. Critics also claim that the real problem is the personal behavior of parents, so that helping the children is a waste of both time and money. As a result, the program remains greatly underfunded, reaching only a small fraction of needy students for only part of one year, so that gains to many participants are soon overwhelmed by all the other effects of poverty (Entwistle and Alexander, 1994).

Research indicates, however, that adults born in poverty who attended a well-designed preschool pro-

This one room school house was home to children from grades one through six who shared one teacher. How did their experiences compare to today's schools where each grade meets separately, and there is considerable division of labor among teachers?

SOCIOLOGY AROUND THE WORLD

A Tale of Two Chinas

The People's Republic of China (PRC), a nation ideo-logically committed to egalitarianism, practices an ex-treme form of educational inequality. A few highly selected boys and girls attend subsidized elite high schools that prepare them for study abroad and eventual leadership positions in the PRC (Kristof, 1993). Primarily motivated by a sense of obliga-tion to parents and of duty to country they share a dormitory with a dozen classmates, spend up to 12 hours a day on formal studies, and use their spare time for homework or other learning experiences.

Because of the PRC's attempt to limit family size (Chapter 20), many of these students are only-children, the center of family pride and future dreams, pampered by parents and grandparents. The result is a child with high motivation to suc-ceed, to avoid shaming the family name.

Another outcome is a widening gap between the few with the subsidized elite education and the great mass of Chinese children whose parents cannot pay even the small sum required for admis-sion to elementary school. Village schools are overcrowded, short on pencils, paper, books, and teachers. Only 13 percent of the children will enter high school, and a much lower proportion will graduate. To the degree that universal public edu-cation is the key to reducing inequality in a mod-ernizing society, the PRC has betrayed its ideological roots. Yet with hundreds of millions of young people to educate and so few resources, the government has made what it considers the best choice for the moment.

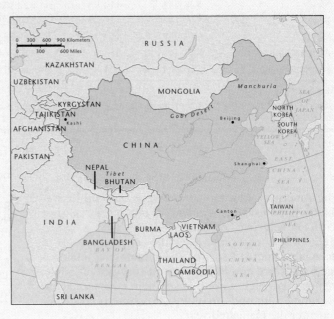

gram have a higher commitment to marriage, they earn more, and they are less likely to have a criminal record than a control group of age peers from the same neighborhood who did not attend preschool (Schweinhart et al., 1993).

POST-HIGH SCHOOL. Today, about half of all high school graduates enter an institution of higher educa-tion, although not all com-plete the four-year degree program. Those who do not enter college directly have a choice of options including apprenticeship programs or vocational school. In addition, millions of Americans are enrolled in adult education classes, both academic and vocational. In all, one in four Americans age 3 and older is a student.

Parochial schools are pri-vate schools operated by religious organizations.

EDUCATIONAL ATTAINMENT. As a result of such inclu-siveness, in terms of school years completed, Ameri-cans are among the most schooled people in the world. The proportion of young adults (age 24–29) who have completed high school is now about 87 percent compared with 38 percent in 1940. The per-cent of all American adults aged 25 and over with a college degree is now 22 percent, and the proportion of women enrolled in colleges and universities is the highest among industrialized nations. Differences in educational attainment by race, age, and region have also narrowed over time.

Public and Private Systems

Another structural feature of American education is the existence of two separate school systems: one supported by public taxes and open to all; the other funded by private fees and selective in admissions. Today, about one in ten elementary and high school students attends a private school.

PAROCHIAL SCHOOLS. By far the largest number of pri-vate schools are church related, or **parochial** (the word means "confined to the parish" or "narrow"). The most extensive parochial system in the United States is operated by the Roman Catholic Church, en-compassing close to 2.6 million students in about 8,700 elementary and high schools. These figures are one-third smaller than in the 1960s, largely as a result of the movement of Catholics out of central cities, where the schools were located, into the suburbs, where there may not be enough families in a given

Millions of adult Americans continue their formal education in degree and non-degree academic and vocational courses, making adult education the fastest-growing segment of the educational market. Why do so many adults enroll in classes?

suming positions of power and thus to reproducing the social class system (Cookson and Persell, 1985; Kingston and Lewis, 1990). The SES hierarchy is also literally reproduced when the friendship networks among prep school students define the pool of eligibles for dating and marriage.

There are also private day schools that cover elementary as well as high school grades. Although many now prefer to call themselves *independent* schools, and are somewhat less exclusive than in the past, admitting a higher proportion of scholarship students, working-class, and young people from racial minorities, the link between family income and attending a private school remains quite high. For example, only 2.7 percent of children from low-income households are enrolled in a private high school, primarily parochial, located in the community, in contrast to 12 percent of children from higher-income families.

> **Preparatory schools** are private schools developed primarily to prepare children of well-off parents for entry into elite colleges.

A small number of children are being taught at home by their parents. These are typically extremely religious families that do not want to expose their

area to support a parish school. In addition, the cost of operating these schools has escalated with the hiring of lay teachers to fill in for the declining numbers of nuns and brothers in teaching orders. In 1960, three of four Catholic school teachers were members of a religious order, compared with about one in ten today (U. S. Bureau of the Census *Statistical Abstract,* 1994).

The fastest growing sector in parochial education today, however, is the American Christian school system operated by conservative Protestant churches, reflecting the revival of fundamentalist beliefs (see Chapter 16).

Parents—whether Protestant, Catholic, Jewish, or Muslim—send their children to religious schools not only to preserve tradition but to insulate their offspring from exposure to other views and values and to channel friendships and ultimately, mate selection.

PREPARATORY SCHOOLS.   The latent functions of private schooling are especially important for most of the 20 percent of nonpublic schools that are not church related. These are places where the sons and daughters of the upper strata are groomed for success and prepared for entry into elite colleges and occupations, hence the term **preparatory** (Persell et al., 1992). At the top of the hierarchy are the elite WASP boarding schools, covering grades 9–12 and typically single-sex, where children of affluence develop the high level of self-esteem and confidence so essential to as-

The most extensive parochial school system in the United States is operated by the Roman Catholic church. What are the advantages and limitations of parochial schools?

Achievement expectations, including computer literacy, will differ in content and complexity depending on the occupational goals expected of the particular student population. What resources are needed by a school system to provide career training for its students?

children to competing values. Home-based instruction has been largely successful in terms of how much the children have learned. At this writing, the courts have been reluctant to order the children into the public system, in many cases on grounds of religious freedom.

PUBLIC SCHOOLS. In contrast to both parochial and private education, the public school system was designed precisely to fulfill the egalitarian promise of America, to reflect the pluralism of the society at large, to bring together children of varying backgrounds, to nurture tolerance of differences, and to reward merit regardless of family status. Ninety percent of American children attend one of the 86,000 elementary and secondary schools funded by local taxes and operated by a locally elected board of education.

The American public school was not always the inclusive institution we know today. Indeed, many were highly selective in admissions, and large numbers of children were never enrolled because their labor was necessary for family survival (Walters and O'Connell, 1988).

Today, the public school system is characterized by compulsory attendance, acceptance of all but a few severely disabled children, a professional teaching staff, and school boards responsible to the local electorate.

EDUCATIONAL QUALITY. Are there major differences in the quality of education provided by private and public schools? Some evidence indicates that private high schools produce higher test scores and are less racially segregated than public schools (Coleman, 1990). This outcome, however, may say less about quality than about the many advantages enjoyed by private schools.

Most important is the fact that private schools can select their students, screening out low achievers and troublemakers, whereas public schools must accept all but the most "uneducable." Furthermore, most private schools place all their students on an academic track, which produces higher test scores. In addition, the parents of private school students have already shown an interest in their children's education and are likely both to have high achievement expectations and to provide supportive encouragement.

Schooling occurs through interaction among students and teachers that reflect the larger societal values, whether in South Africa (left) or Mauritania in West Africa, as seen in the photograph on the chapter opening page. How do these classrooms reflect the relative poverty of Mauritania (per capita income of $530 per year) and the relative affluence of South Africa (per capita income of $2700 per year)?

Parents, teachers, and students in private schools also share a set of values about the importance of education and the duty of students as citizens. In the Catholic schools this ideology takes on a sacred, inspirational dimension that lends an air of moral authority to the school and its activities (Bryk et al., 1993). Students also benefit from the smaller size of most private schools (American Legislative Exchange Council, 1994).

Because of these many differences, comparisons of public and private school test scores are of limited value (Kreft, 1993). In fact, the differences between public and private school students are not always very large, as seen in 12th grade mathematics tests where similar percentages of public and private school students reached the highest level (U.S. Department of Education, 1994).

Nonetheless, the general perception today is that the public school system has somehow "failed." This charge comes primarily from the political right, where mistrust of all public services and teachers' unions has always been high (Chew, 1992). In addition, a lot of money could go to private sector educational ventures if parents could be persuaded that the public system no longer works. The facts are that overall test scores for elementary and high school students have *improved significantly,* especially among minority youth, due largely to increased spending on city schools, smaller families, and higher parental education levels (Grissmer et al., 1994).

If the public schools, despite a number of drawbacks, are not necessarily inferior to American private schools, are they, as critics charge, grossly inferior to their European and Japanese counterparts? (See box below.) Despite its successes, our school system has many problems. Too many young people are lost along the way, either as dropouts or turn-offs. Complaints come from all directions of the political spec-

SOCIOLOGY AROUND THE WORLD

A *Comparative Report Card*

When compared to age peers in other industrial societies, test scores of American youth are indeed lower. But it is important to point out that the formal educational system of the United States differs in many important ways from that of other modern nations. Five of these differences are of special importance (Dougherty and Hammack, 1992):

1. *Size.* The American system is far larger than any other, in both sheer numbers and inclusiveness, especially the proportion in postsecondary education—more than three times as high as for Japan and twice that of West Germany.
2. *Local control, decentralization.* Control over primary and secondary schools is in the hands of elected local school boards and funded by local school taxes, which gives American parents greater control over their children's schooling compared with the centralized systems of other countries.
3. *Testing.* Although testing has become widespread, our system is actually *less* driven by examinations than most others. In Japan and most of Europe, for example, all students take a standard test at tenth grade that determines whether they will go to an academic or vocational high school. They are tested again after high school to determine the type of higher education, if any, they are entitled to receive. The anxiety caused by the preparation for these tests has led to a system of "shadow education," in Japan where children of the wealthy are tutored after school hours (Stevenson and Baker, 1992). In contrast, American high school graduates can go on to college despite low test scores and school grades.
4. *Comprehensiveness.* Most American teenagers are enrolled in a "comprehensive" school, that is, one that provides both academic and vocational programs. This allows a student who may not go to college to receive a general academic training and to build up some cultural capital. In the other nations, the line between academic and vocational is more sharply drawn and also more closely linked to social class.

One attempt to reduce class differences in educational attainment without taking away from the privileged is through expanding the education system itself (Shavit and Blossfeld, 1993). But, when Ireland eliminated fees for attending high school and children from poorer families entered and graduated from high school, the overall class structure was only minimally affected (Raftery and Hout, 1993). Similarly, in both the Netherlands and Hong Kong an expansion of higher education had a limited effect on the link between family SES and educational attainment (Dronkers, 1993; Post, 1994).

5. *Range of tasks.* American schools also address a broader range of needs than do their counterparts abroad, such as special education, driver training, health and nutrition services, and sex education. In fact, most of the new money put into school systems since 1965 has gone to these areas and not, as critics claim, to teacher salaries or general programs. Indeed, in constant dollars, teacher salaries have risen less than 3 percent since 1988.

For all these reasons, international comparisons have limited validity. In fact, it could be argued that, given its unique nature, the American system is the most successful in keeping a higher proportion of young people in schools for a longer period of time, with more flexibility and a greater range of services.

trum: business leaders complain that graduates lack essential skills; other critics point to the lack of satisfying or secure employment, and the deadening effects of poverty. Almost everyone believes that something is wrong inside the schools.

INSIDE THE SCHOOLS

The functions and structure of education are macrolevel topics. But schooling takes place at the microlevel—in face-to-face interactions among students and teachers. These interactions compose the social system of the classroom, a system that cannot be understood without reference to the enduring values of our society: success, competition, and individualism. Children learn that their success depends on the failure of others, competition is encouraged, and a recognition of hierarchy and inequality is built into the school experience. In addition, there are special lessons to be learned by students in working-class, middle-class, and inner-city schools, which differ greatly from one another in what is offered and how it is taught (Wexler et al., 1992).

Suburban Schools

Schools in middle-class suburbs have been very successful in encouraging self-discipline and a taste for competition, with high rates of college entry and completion. Yet, for many, the suburban high school is a place where boredom rules and the student body is fragmented into subcultures of nerds, headbangers, trendies, jocks, and skins (Kinney, 1993). This fragmentation helps administrators to maintain order. In working-class suburbs, the inability of students to break out of their peer subculture prepares them for a lifetime of political apathy and concentration on per-

sonal relationships, thus reproducing the stratification system (Eckert, 1989; Wexler et al., 1992).

Nonetheless, suburban schools typically operate with a core of motivated students and concerned parents, under favorable funding conditions, within a supportive community—advantages that are less likely to be present in today's inner city schools.

Urban Schools

Unlike in the past, city schools today must absorb more children of the very poor, keep them longer, and send them into a disappearing labor market. The buildings continue to deteriorate, experienced teachers leave, neighborhoods are terrorized by gangs of unemployed youth, and powerless parents have difficulty imparting high expectations to their children.

The learning problems of most inner-city poor children are not due to lack of ability or even to their relatively deprived cultural context. Much depends on the atmosphere of the school and commitment of its staff (Lee and Bryk, 1989). Urban schools can work where there is a climate of expectation in which no child will be allowed to fail, when classes are small, and when disciplining is fair but effective—precisely the characteristics that account for the scholastic success of suburban and private schools. Although such practices can overcome many of the disadvantages associated with the inner-city environment (Grant, 1988), the major barriers to learning are the correlates of poverty: hunger, uncertainty, interpersonal violence, and a sense that things will never get better no matter how hard one tries.

Renewing the schools means reawakening hope that the effort of staying in school will have a payoff in the form of decent jobs at wages above the poverty level (Ray and Mickelson, 1993). Where city youth have been guaranteed that staying in school will have

---

RESEARCH IN ACTION

From Nerd to Normal

Those who believe that the educational shortcomings of American youth can be traced to the low evaluation of intellectual pursuits in our society need only point to the student culture of middle schools. In these settings, the bright student is a "nerd" whose spoiled identity leads to social isolation. The most popular in middle school are male athletes and female cheerleaders, whose later life successes tend to be extremely limited. The nerds, who will eventually reap the rewards of their education success, undergo a social death as teenagers.

To investigate the processes by which the nerds overcame their unpopularity and established a posi-

tive identity, David A. Kinney (1993) conducted an extensive microlevel study of peer groups and peer culture in a Midwest high school. By now, you should be a good enough amateur sociologist to have guessed at the answer: through participation in peer groups that "normalized" their stigmatized identity. Compared to middle schools, high schools offer a far more varied and less rigidly hierarchical social system in which young people can find others who share their interests and who provide that protective environment in which one can establish a positive self-image. Without losing their academic edge, these young people found ways to achieve in other areas that won them the respect of classmates and allowed them to practice social skills denied them in the middle school.

College Dreams

In 1981, the principal of P.S. 121, in one of the poorest sections of New York City, asked an old graduate to speak to the 62 sixth graders about to enter junior high. Eugene Lang, a millionaire businessman, had attended the school 50 years earlier when the neighborhood was primarily white ethnic. The Class of 1981, however, was African-American and Latino, survivors of extreme poverty and family breakdown. Lang threw away his prepared address on the virtues of hard work and spoke from his heart: He would personally finance the college education of any child who stayed and graduated from high school. He called this the "I Have a Dream" program in honor of Rev. Martin Luther King, Jr. (Rohter, 1986).

Ten years later, in a school with a 75 percent dropout rate, almost three-fourth's of Lang's students had finished high school and more than half were in college. Similar programs have been underwritten by other philanthropists and a few businesses, with high success rates. The sociological point is that once assured of a payoff, students will stay in school and do well: *Behavior is largely determined by the structure of opportunity* (Ogbu, 1989). The major problem with these programs is that they favor some children over others on the basis of whim. Should the chance to go to college depend on what side of the bed a wealthy person got out of that morning?

a payoff, they have been able to defer gratification, graduate from high school, and succeed in college (see the box entitled, "College Dreams" above). But until such opportunities are generally available, many youngsters will take the easier route to survival and peer prestige: drop out and live on the streets, where success is less problematic and more immediate than in the schools.

DROPPING OUT.   Among Americans aged 18 to 24, the high school dropout rate has fallen from almost 20 percent in 1967 to about 10 percent in 1993 (U.S. Bureau of the Census, P20-476, 1994). In the inner city, however, between one-third and one-half of students either leave or are pushed out by authorities. On the one hand, this process clears the schools of troublemakers and "difficult cases," thus improving the educational environment for those who remain. On the other hand, it leaves the youngsters most in need with no help at all.

The traits that are used to identify dropout risks are the same as for "troublemakers"—problems of attention and attendance that disproportionately afflict poor minority children (Bowditch, 1993). The most common reasons for leaving high school are being disciplined for bad behavior, boredom, poor health, learning difficulties, family needs, pregnancy and parenthood, and limited job prospects. Given the immensity of such problems, city school systems are underfunded and overwhelmed; teachers burn out readily; and students become increasingly alienated (LeCompte and Dworkin, 1991; Kelly, 1993).

For young people of all races and ethnicity, but especially Hispanic youth, the most powerful predictor of graduating or dropping out is family income (Ortiz, 1989). But at any income level, least likely to drop out are those from two-parent families, where adults are involved in the children's educational plans, and

where the mother has herself completed high school (Rumberger et al., 1990; Ensminger and Slusarcick, 1992; Fitzpatrick and Yoels, 1992).

Although some dropouts may experience instant success on the streets, most will find that their disadvantages multiply. Because high school graduation is now the norm, employers can screen out "high-risk" cases by requiring the diploma, regardless of its appropriateness for the job (Burstein and Pitchford, 1990). Without an education or job prospects, young people are trapped in a cycle of economic disadvantage (Olneck and Kim, 1989; Ray and Mickelson, 1993).

In the Classroom

It is often assumed that the way a teacher reacts to a student will influence the pupil's self-image and subsequent achievement, encouraging the children perceived as bright and subtly discouraging those thought to be slow learners (Rosenthal and Jacobson, 1968). The research data, however, do not support the idea that a *self-fulfilling prophecy* can account for the high rates of academic failure among the poor (Kingston, 1992). Lower-income or minority youth do not necessarily feel out of place in the middle-class culture of the school; the crucial variable appears to be the fit between social class status of teachers and students. High-status teachers, regardless of race, tend to perceive lower-income and minority pupils as immature; they expect minimal performance of these students and grade accordingly (Alexander et al., 1987).

RACE.   In general, African-American boys, especially those who are disruptive, are most likely to be caught up in a spiral of failure, as the gap between expectations and achievement widens. They are also singled out for discipline much more frequently than are their white classmates (McCarthy and Hoge, 1987). This has led some minority educators to call for establishing special schools designed to enhance the self-image and academic skills of African-American boys. The arguments against such schools are that they reinforce racial segregation, use resources that ought to be shared with African-American girls and other minority youth, and subvert the pluralistic ideal of public schooling.

SEX.   Few classroom differences are more fully documented than those on the basis of sex (Sadker and Sadker, 1994). Teachers still make very traditional assumptions about the abilities of girls and boys, and many textbooks continue to reflect such a worldview. In general, boys receive more attention in the classroom, and their contributions are taken more seriously by the teacher even though the girls will typically receive better grades, at least through middle school. Conversely, from sixth grade on, girls are subjected to higher levels of sexual harassment and are penalized for putting grades ahead of popularity (Orenstein, 1994). The high achievement level of girls in single-sex private schools is partly due to their insulation from overt sexism and the highly sexualized adolescent subculture (Riordan, 1990; Lee et al., 1994).

Can Schools and Classrooms Learn?

The focus on classroom interactions and school environments is uniquely sociological, in contrast to an emphasis on learning as something that goes on within a child's head. But a classroom is more than a teacher and pupils. It is a collectivity in its own right, with characteristics that cannot be reduced to the individuals involved—a division of labor, level of technology, and way of arranging work. Different types of classrooms and schools have differential effects on student achievement (Cohen et al., 1989).

For example, many behavioral problems of junior high students can be traced to a mismatch between the autonomy needs of the children and the rigid structures of most of the schools (Eccles, 1994). As noted earlier in this chapter, classrooms based on **cooperative learning,** or "peer tutoring," are far more effective than those divided into tracks in raising the performance level of all students.

Cooperative learning occurs when students pool talents and help one another.

Sociologists have also questioned another sacred element of American educational ideology—the meaning of standardized tests.

The Politics of Testing

It is now generally agreed that standardized IQ tests cannot measure a fixed ability or "intelligence quo-

tient," because intelligence is not a single trait but a bundle of capacities that are combined in different ways and strengths at various ages in each person (Gardner, 1989). To the extent that some components of intelligence are inherited, they may account for variations *within* a given racial or ethnic group but not the variations *between* populations at different economic levels (Taylor, 1992). Inherited abilities emerge and develop within social environments, and most research has concluded that cognitive differences by race are largely due to these background variables (Berry and Asamen, 1989). Thus, statements about the intellectual abilities of any racial or ethnic population are more political than scientific, closing off educational opportunities for the less favored, including thousands of minority children erroneously classified as "learning disabled" (Hanson, 1993; Richardson, 1994).

Since 1976, scores on the Scholastic Assessment Test (SAT) for minority youth have increased dramatically whereas those for white students have declined (College Board, 1994b). The general decline in SAT scores during the 1980s is due primarily to the larger pool of test takers, although some critics suggest that television watching has a negative impact on verbal abilities (Glenn, 1994). On other standardized tests, today's students are doing as well as in the 1970s. While SATs are useful in predicting college performance, high school grades are just as accurate.

A study by the National Science Foundation (1992) found that standardized tests had more negative than positive effects because teachers spent their time drilling the students on test items rather than on developing broader cognitive skills. But these data are unlikely to lessen the politically popular demand for more such tests in the United States.

HIGHER EDUCATION

Functions and Structure

The manifest functions of higher education are (1) the transmission of existing knowledge, (2) production of new information through free inquiry, and (3) preparation of the next generation of scholars. Universities reflect the general tendency of modern societies toward specialization and are organized into discrete units: departments, programs, schools, and divisions. Each unit enjoys some degree of professional autonomy because only peers can judge one's work. Yet the entire institution must run as a unified whole, which is the job of the administration.

The administration does not operate in a vacuum. Although *private* colleges and universities are relatively independent (financed by student fees, alumni contributions, and endowment fund investments) they are under the nominal control of a board of

Drawing by M. Stevens; © 1992 The New Yorker Magazine, Inc.

trustees and are bound by some government guidelines if they receive federal assistance.

Public institutions (state universities and colleges, and the county colleges), in contrast, are largely funded by tax dollars allocated by state and county legislators and are much more vulnerable to political pressures than are the private schools. Because their survival depends on the goodwill of the public, these schools are very sensitive to their social environment.

Faced with declining numbers of teenagers to fill their ivied halls and with the need to find sources of revenue other than government subsidies or ever-higher tuitions, both private and public institutions of higher education have been forced to seek funds elsewhere—through intensified money raising among alumni/ae, appeals to foundations, the business community in general, and research firms in particular.

THE UNIVERSITY GOES INTO BUSINESS. Beginning with World War II and continuing to this day, leading research universities (e.g., M.I.T. and Stanford) have reaped enormous profits from contracts with the Department of Defense. Indeed, the military-industrial complex described in Chapter 14 might more accurately be labeled the military-industrial-academic complex (Leslie, 1993). With cuts in the military budget, however, these universities and other major research institutions have replaced their military links with profit-making arrangements with private industry (Etzkowitz, 1989; Cordes, 1993). This trend raises two ethical issues: (1) Should profits from research subsidized by American taxpayers go to private businesses rather than back to the nation? (2) Because research for private profit requires secrecy and exclusive ownership of data, it violates the commitment to open inquiry that is the essence of the scientific method and higher education.

Furthermore, with profits distributed between a private company and a university (often including the university officers) other nonprofit-making parts of the university tend to receive less attention and support, especially undergraduate teaching compared with graduate-level research activity.

STRATIFICATION WITHIN HIGHER EDUCATION. Institutions of higher education in the United States (and elsewhere) form a ranked hierarchy. At the top are a handful of private universities (e.g., Harvard, Yale, Princeton) followed by the elite private colleges (e.g., Dartmouth, Vassar, Amherst). Then come the major research-oriented state universities, second-tier state universities, state colleges, and at the base, the community colleges. The more highly ranked the institution, the higher its admission standards and, typically, its fees. Also, the more highly ranked the institution, the lower the proportion of students and faculty who are female, minority, or of working-class origins. Conversely, the lower ranked the institution, the more diverse its student body and faculty.

The Faculty

The faculty are also stratified by academic rank within the institution: distinguished professor, full professor, associate professor, assistant professor, instructor and adjuct faculty. Promotions and tenure (job security) are based on years of service, and quantity and quality of publications. Except in the community college, teaching skills are rarely a major factor; indeed, the higher one's academic rank, the *fewer* hours spent on classroom teaching.

Faculties reflect the race and gender stratification systems of the broader society. There are very few African-Americans and Hispanics—perhaps 1 percent of the faculty at predominantly white institutions and only a handful at the highest ranks. These figures are lower than in the late 1970s and will not rise soon, because the number of African Americans in graduate schools has also declined. Talented men and women of color today can enter a variety of better-paying occupations that do not require a graduate degree, or they could pursue a career in medicine or law. As long as the average salary for an assistant professor is $35,000, college teaching will not be a very attractive career choice.

The gender hierarchy of higher education is slowly changing, although the top ranks remain almost exclusively male, especially at schools that emphasize research rather than undergraduate teaching. Male faculty also predominate in fields such as business and physics, which command higher salaries and greater prestige than, for example, English or sociology, where women are well represented.

THE NEW ACADEMIC NOMADS. One way for colleges to lower costs is to use part-time and temporary "ad-

The number of new full-time professors has declined dramatically as the ranks of the tenured are getting older and grayer. What are the ramifications of this trend for the faculty, the students, and the colleges themselves?

junct" faculty in place of full-time teachers (Gappa and Leslie, 1993). Adjuncts are hired by the semester, paid by the course, and are excluded from fringe benefits such as medical or pension coverage. To earn a living, an adjunct must teach at four or five different schools and spend a lot of time in transit—hence the label "academic nomad"—and all for a total income less than half that of full-time faculty (Rosenblum and Rosenblum, 1990; Kean, 1994). The proportion of part-time faculty has doubled in the past two decades, from 20 to 40 percent of the teaching staff!

THE GRAYING OF THE FACULTY.   Because so few new full-timers have been hired, the average age of the faculty is rising, and most schools are top-heavy with older, tenured teachers hired in the 1960s. This means that many will be retiring over the rest of this decade, so that opportunities for academic employment may open up and college teaching become an attractive option for young intellectuals (Hill, 1989). By the time you finish graduate school, many colleges may be competing to hire a sociologist of your brilliance.

The Student Body

In 1995, about 15 million women and men were enrolled in the 3,500 institutions of higher education in America. Despite a drop in the proportion of the population of traditional college age, college enrollments have remained high because of the entry of "nontraditional" students—older and part-time students, and working class youth who could not have afforded a college education before the community colleges.

INCREASED DIVERSITY.   In comparison to the past, today's student body is far more diverse in terms of age, race, ethnicity, sex, and foreign birth. Forty-one percent of college students today are older than age 25, raising the median age above 21, the age at which most students once graduated.

RACE.   Since the early 1980s, the proportion of persons of color in the student body increased from 10 to 18 percent. After rising through the early 1970s, the number of African-American students dropped somewhat and has remained relatively stable at about 10 percent since 1985. This figure masks a shift in the sex distribution of African-American students, increasing for women, but declining for men. The largest percentage increase among racial minorities is for

---

SOCIOLOGY IN EVERYDAY LIFE

College Choices

Remember how you sweated the SATs or ACEs? Spent hours looking over college catalogues, spoke with friends and family, checked out finances, and then waited for word from the school of your choice, hoping for a fat rather than a thin envelope? These agonies are a yearly *rite of passage* for more than half of high school graduates today.

How do colleges select their incoming class? With the exception of a few hundred elite schools, most are not all that selective (Altbach and Lewis, 1994). The SATs really don't matter that much; your high school transcript would do as well. But grades are only one criterion. Admissions officers take many factors into ac-

count: extracurricular activities such as volunteer work, special talents such as athletics or music, race, ethnicity, letters of recommendation, and the interview impression. The goal is a diversified student body.

At elite institutions, it helps to be a "legacy," that is, to have parents who attended, to come from a preparatory school, and to have cultural capital as measured by family background. But even here, a heterogeneous student body is an important institutional goal. A minority applicant from Nevada who volunteers at a soup kitchen and who plays an antique musical instrument would go to the front of the line. Admissions staff are also concerned with the long-term interests of the school that employs them and to whom they owe primary loyalty (Karen, 1991).

Segregation's Last Stand

If a college education was beyond the means of most white families until the mid-1940s, a much smaller proportion of African-American families could afford higher education for their children. Nonetheless, a number of highly motivated and talented students of color graduated from Northern campuses in the early and mid-1900s. But most blacks at that time lived in the South, where custom and law maintained segregated schools at all levels.

An attempt to integrate the University of Alabama in 1956 by a young woman, Autherine Lucy, led to burning crosses, death threats, and her expulsion after less than a month on campus. The media spotlight, however, focused on Governor George Wallace, who had sworn to "stand at the schoolhouse door" to resist racial integration. In 1963, Governor Wallace stood at the door of the university's admissions office while federal marshals escorted two black students. After a brief symbolic gesture, Wallace turned aside and the University of Alabama was integrated, 100 years after the Emancipation Proclamation, and only a decade before many of you were born.

In 1992, Autherine Lucy received her master's degree in education, and the university accepted an endowed scholarship in her name (Clark, 1993).

In 1956, Autherine Lucy was the first black woman in 136 years to enroll at the University of Alabama. She was denied the right to use the dining rooms and dormitories used by the white students. She was expelled a month later, but persevered with her education, eventually earning a graduate degree.

Asian Americans, from less than 4 percent in 1985 to close to 7 percent today.

The decline in African-American enrollments in the early 1980s was not due to any change in college plans or aspirations but to a shift in college tuition assistance during the Reagan administration from direct grants to a bank-loan program (Hauser and Anderson, 1991). Because even at the same income level, the economic security of black families is more fragile than that of whites, the likelihood of receiving a bank loan is considerably reduced. When coupled with today's increasing tuition costs, a four-year college education is a financial impossibility for many minority families even though they have made a greater effort to save for this purpose than have their white SES counter-parts (Steelman and Powell, 1993; Carter and Wilson, 1990). One outcome is that African-American students are more likely than their white age peers to be in a two-year college and to terminate their education at that point despite recruitment efforts by four-year colleges (Kane and Spizman, 1994).

Another outcome has been to reduce the overall supply of black students, so that the most qualified are heavily recruited by elite institutions, although some schools will have difficulty recruiting and retaining

minority students because of an increase in racial tensions on predominantly white campuses (Allen et al., 1991). Many white students, born after the civil rights struggles of the 1960s, resent what they consider to be preferential treatment for students of color, while the latter are angered over what they perceive as insensitivity on the part of nonminority students, faculty, and administrators. As a sociology student, if you are not a member of a minority, you might try an exercise in *Verstehen* by imagining that you are a minority student at your school. How would you interpret campus life from that perspective?

GENDER.   The 1980s saw a major shift in the sex composition of the American campus, where women now outnumber men. Women's academic performance today equals and often surpasses that of their male colleagues, even though their education, as with minority graduates, brings lower occupational and income rewards (Mickelson, 1989; Hyllegard and Lavin, 1992). Once welcome on only a few campuses, women today are everywhere, including such traditionally elite campuses as M.I.T., where they account for one-third of entering students, and Harvard, where women are one-half the student body.

Students today are far more diverse in terms of sex, race, ethnicity, age, and foreign birth than in the past. What is the ratio of women to men on your campus? What ethnic and racial groups are represented on your campus? What proportion of students are "nontraditional?"

As noted in Chapter 10, higher education is an essentially masculine world in which women may feel uncomfortable despite their numbers. As a result, enrollment in predominantly women's colleges has risen in the 1990s (Newman, 1994), where graduates have traditionally enjoyed higher career accomplishments than have women from coeducational colleges (Riorden, 1990). What are the pros and cons of single-sex vs. coed colleges?

SOCIAL CLASS. As campuses have become more diverse in terms of sex and race, four-year colleges have become increasingly *exclusive* by social class, as federal aid dropped and costs soared. As seen in Table 15-2, tuition, room, and board at an elite institution in 1994 was more than two-thirds higher than the median income of all American households. Costs are much lower at state universities—around $7,000 on average—and lower still at state colleges. Because community college students are commuters, they pay only tuition and fees—probably the best academic bargain in the world at $1,230 a year. These numbers mean that regardless of ability, children from large and/or lower-income families will attend the less prestigious institutions, although they will not necessarily receive an inferior education. Only at the level of graduate school does family SES lose its power, as students are self-selected primarily on the basis of perceived rewards (Stolzenberg, 1994).

Is a college education worth the time and money? You bet. The diploma signifies that you are a person of ambition and self-discipline, and as shown in Table 15-1, the longer you stay in school, the higher your income. But earnings should be only one consideration for remaining in school. Educational attainment is associated with feelings of control and competence, with cognitive flexibility, with good health and long life, and with high overall satisfaction.

At the societal level, higher education is a major factor in maintaining the stratification system. At elite schools, up to the 1960s, there were quotas for Jews and Catholics on the faculty and in the student body (Oren, 1985). Since that time, and up to the late 1980s, the links between family SES and the length and quality of education were gradually loosened. In the 1990s, however, lowered family incomes and cuts in student loan programs have reversed this process, leading to "middle income melt" whereby students who might once have attended a private college are enrolled in a public institution, and others are taking their first two years at a community college (Honan, 1994).

Community Colleges

Two year public colleges emerged in the 1960s to: (1) relieve the pressure on state universities from anticipated baby-boom enrollments, and (2) provide local industries with a reliable pool of trained workers. The community college system expanded over the next two decades, along with certificate-granting technical schools and a few private junior colleges. In 1994, over 6 million students were enrolled in the nations 1,200 community colleges, representing almost half of all entering undergraduates.

TABLE 15-2 Fees for Tuition, Room, and Board, in Selected "Ivy League" Colleges and Universities, 1993–1994

Brown	24,618
Columbia	23,358
Cornell	22,896
Dartmouth	24,249
Harvard	24,880
Pennsylvania	24,442
Princeton	24,650
Yale	25,110

Fees for Tuition, Room and Board in other institutions, 1993–1994

Four-year private	$15,818	
Four-year public	6,207	
Two-year public	1,229	(Tuition, fees only)

Source: College Board, 1994a.

Community colleges offer convenient locations, low tuition, part-time programs and evening and weekend courses. The student body is usually more varied by race, ethnicity, age, and social class than many four-year colleges. Here students in a writing class at a community college in Austin, Texas, share their work with one another.

The mix between academic and skill-oriented courses varies with the location of the college. Those in urban industrial areas are primarily "institutions of the higher voc-ed" (Pincus, 1986), in which low-income students are prepared at taxpayer expense for entry-level jobs in local firms (Dougherty, 1988). At the same time, these schools offer "the best hope for a generation of Americans that have virtually no other opportunity for education, training, and in some cases, economic and social survival" (Brint and Karabel, 1991, p.12).

Community colleges in suburbs and wealthier communities have maintained their college-transfer program but primarily for white, middle-class students. Even here, a majority of students today are enrolled in "career" courses such as secretarial, business, accounting, and mechanical technology. These programs receive most of the college's budget and generate high levels of community support, especially from local employers. Overall, only one in four community college students today is in the college-transfer curriculum.

Thus, critics claim that the community college actually serves to *limit* rather than expand educational opportunity, "cooling out" the losers by giving the impression that they had a chance to improve their prospects (Pincus, 1986; Lee and Frank, 1990). Most research indicates that enrolling in a two-year school significantly reduces the likelihood of earning a bachelor's degree or reaching high occupational status (Pascarella and Terenzini, 1991; Monk-Turner, 1990).

On the plus side, community colleges offer low tuition, convenient location, part-time programs, and evening and weekend courses. At least two years of college can therefore become a reality for many who could not otherwise have had the opportunity. As a result, the student body is more varied by race, ethnicity, age, and social class than the typical four-year school. In addition, there are extensive remedial services, small classes, and close contact with professors as instructors (in contrast to teaching assistants). Maintaining high academic standards while retaining an open admissions policy is a difficult task that many community colleges have accomplished, with honors (Kirp, 1992).

CONTEMPORARY CONTROVERSIES

A Question of Equality

The most important issue in American education today brings us back to the functions of public schooling as a means of individual achievement and collective well-being. The issue has two dimensions: (1) continued segregation of minority students and (2) inequality in school financing.

Segregation, Desegregation, and Resegregation. Before 1954, school systems throughout the country systematically drew school district lines that kept white and black students apart, while also investing three to four times more money in the white districts. In 1954, the Supreme Court, in the case of *Brown v. the Board of Education of Topeka, Kansas,* declared that segregated districts created by local authorities violated the Fourteenth Amendment's guarantee of "equal protection of the laws" and that such systems must be dismantled "with all deliberate speed." Thirty-nine years later, in 1993, Linda Brown, the original plaintiff, went back to court on behalf of *her* children because the Topeka schools were still largely segregated as are schools in most urban areas (Kluger, 1994).

In many places, the schools have been successfully integrated, with stable enrollments and improved test scores, especially where community leaders support the policy (Fuerst and Petty, 1992; Celis 1994). Elsewhere, resistance to integration has led to unrest, especially in working class, white ethnic neighborhoods. These local conflicts tend to siphon off working-class discontent while leaving the real power structure intact (Monti, 1985). Yet when working-class students from different racial and ethnic groups make common cause against their middle-class critics, they forge strong friendship ties (Peshkin, 1991).

Magnet schools are designed to attract students by offering specialized educational programs.

In most urban communities, however, school systems have become resegregated, no longer through the drawing of district lines *(de jure)* but in part through families moving from one district to another *(de facto)*, as a continuation of the decades-long migration from city to suburb rather than a sudden response to fears of school integration (Smock and Wilson, 1991). The primary factors in resegregation, however, were not "white flight" or an increase in private school enrollments, but major changes in birth rates and immigration patterns (Orfield et al, 1993). Birth rates for urban whites dropped sharply while those for Hispanic newcomers remained high, creating a massive shift in race and ethnic balance in the schools. Another type of resegregation takes place *within* integrated schools when students of different races and ethnicity are separated by tracking or similar devices (Pressman and Gartner, 1986).

Solutions to Resegregation.   Under court orders, districts have been forced to take various approaches to reducing racial segregation and its effects.

Magnet Schools.   **Magnet schools** are designed to attract students by offering an unusual educational experience, with special emphasis on a specific talent such as music, art, or science, or by featuring a particular teaching philosophy (Metz, 1986). Many magnets have been very successful in recruiting students from wealthier neighborhoods to predominantly minority schools. Potential drawbacks include (1) resegregation within the school as outsiders monopolize the special programs and (2) skimming off the most aware parents and students, leaving the other schools with a less knowledgable base (Henig, 1990).

Grade Differentiation.   Districts can be desegregated by assigning specific grades to each school. Thus, all students in the district attend school *X* for kindergarten through second grade, school *Y* for third to fifth grade, and so on. All children spend some time in their neighborhood school and the burden of busing is equally shared.

Merging School Districts.   If whites are in the suburbs and minority children are in the city, one mechanism for integration is merging the districts so all children are in the same one, with busing to ensure racial balance among the schools in the new district. Politically, this is not a popular solution but may be mandated by the courts.

In many places, schools have been successfully integrated, with stable enrollments and improved test scores, especially where community leaders support the policy. What are your experiences with school integration?

Enrichment of Minority Schools. If integration cannot be achieved, then an enrichment of inner-city schools could at least provide equal, if separate, education, which is exactly what the Court found unconstitutional back in 1954. This solution requires the nonpoor to support higher taxes for the benefit of other people's children, another politically unpopular course in an era of antitax fervor.

One or more of these solutions, however, is precisely what state courts will order for segregated school districts throughout the country in the years to come.

SCHOOL FINANCING. Because our public schools are financed by local property taxes, widespread differences have developed among districts in the amount of money that can be raised per student. For example, in 1992, one poor district near Chicago was able to raise only $1,600 for each student, while a nearby wealthy community with an extremely low tax rate could put $14,000 behind each pupil (*Time,* April 5, 1993, p.35). If the state constitution guarantees each pupil a "thorough and efficient" education, and if it can be shown that $14,000 buys more education than $1,600, the property tax is an unconstitutional financing mechanism. Although some critics claim that money spent on schools has a minimal effect on student outcomes, the most recent national data show that money does matter significantly (Hedges et al, 1994). At this writing, a majority of states have been ordered by the courts to come up with a more equitable formula to reduce wide spending differences between rich and poor districts. This is yet another social issue that will be decided every time you step into the voting booth.

DISABLED STUDENTS. Questions of equal treatment and fairness also come into play in the matter of educating the disabled. That guarantee of a free public education for all cannot be arbitrarily applied, yet until only a few years ago, most districts regularly refused to educate large numbers of children judged unable to fit into the "normal" classroom. Although Congress passed legislation in 1975 mandating "an appropriate" education for all those "needing" or "requiring" it, school boards continued to claim that, because disabled children could not benefit from the education, they therefore neither needed nor required it. Finally, court rulings in 1989 and 1991 made it clear that "all" meant "all" and ordered the districts to provide a suitable education for each child.

Despite the mandate, the high cost of special education and shortage of trained personnel have effectively limited the number of children served and range of services offered. Of the 8 million disabled youngsters in the United States today, only half receive educational assistance from the public school system, most for only a few hours a week.

The largest category (49 percent) are classified as "learning disabled," a nonscientific grab-bag term for a host of behaviors thought to render a child unfit for the regular classroom (Carrier, 1986). If the concept has such little scientific validity, sociologists must ask how, why, and for whom has the term been socially constructed? Some suggest that the label serves primarily to validate the middle-class performance standards that we call "normal" (Coles, 1987). But blaming children for their failure and consigning them to a lifetime of underachievement obscures the role of the schools in producing failure and diverts attention from institutional arrangements that could benefit such students. In addition, for many children so labeled, the major problem was unfamiliarity with the language and approved behaviors of the schools.

Mainstreaming. The negative effects of labeling and isolation can be partially minimized by integrating disabled pupils into regular classrooms for part if not the whole school day. **Mainstreaming** normalizes the child's experience and encourages classmates to interact with someone who differs from them. But mainstreaming is difficult to implement; it requires a supportive parent body,

> **Mainstreaming** integrates disabled pupils into regular classes.

Mainstreaming makes the school experience different for both the disabled and the non-disabled by breaking the pattern of isolation that often exists between these groups. Mainstreaming is particularly helpful in providing less restrictive educational experiences for those who are physically or mentally challenged.

trained teachers, and funding from the district board. Where these are lacking, teachers are overwhelmed, and parents of other children feel that too much is being spent on a few children (Mouseley et al., 1993). Thus, in most districts, only a few disabled children spend full time in a regular classroom. Most remain segregated in special classes, especially in the overcrowded and underfunded inner-city schools with large numbers of special education students (Richardson, 1994).

SOCIAL POLICY

Vouchers and Vendors

Should parents be able to use their school tax money to send their children to any school they select? Most Americans might answer "yes" to this question. Do you think that parents should be given public funds to send their children to private school? Most Americans would probably answer "no" to this question. Yet both are asking about the same program: school choice through the use of vouchers.

Originally the brainchild of liberals concerned with empowering parents of inner-city children, voucher plans have become the centerpiece of conservative efforts to replace the public school system.

> The **voucher system** allows families to spend a given sum of tax money for any type of schooling available.

Under a **voucher** system, school funds raised in a given district are redistributed to families in the form of certificates ("vouchers") worth a sum of money that can be applied to tuition at a school of the parents' choice. The assumption is that vouchers will create a demand for a variety of educational settings, so that each child can be placed most appropriately. The supply of schools will increase, competing to attract students. Advocates argue that a lack of competition has allowed the public schools to resist change (Chubb and Moe, 1989).

A few school districts have experimented with versions of school choice, with mixed success. The two major problems with these plans are (1) that they subsidize private schools at public expense, and (2) that the program will increase inequality in the society as a whole.

The use of public money for private education is a touchy issue. In the case of preparatory schools, poorer taxpayers would be subsidizing the wealthy, because the voucher would not cover the entire cost for most families. As for parochial schools, the First Amendment appears to prohibit using state funds for religious education. The Bush administration argued that the public money actually went to the student who might then choose to spend it on a parochial ed-

ucation, rather than directly to the school, thus avoiding the constitutional issue. These cases are still in the courts at this writing.

As to who benefits, the research evidence overwhelmingly indicates that better-informed parents use the choice programs and move their children to the most desirable schools. This leaves children of poorer and less-educated parents in schools that now have fewer resources than before, thus increasing class and racial/ethnic segregation—not only in the United States but in other modern societies that permit school choice (Walford, 1992). Thus, middle-class French children avoid going to school with peasants and North Africans; Israelis insulate their children from North African and Russian immigrants; Dutch children are shielded from contact with the offspring of Turkish guest-workers; and middle-class Scots are separated from blue-collar age peers (Rothstein, 1993).

School choice is only one part of the conservative attack on the public schools. If Americans believe that the public schools are failing, they will be receptive to interventions from the business sector (Ray and Mickelson, 1990). It is very tempting for a school board to accept a corporate gift or offer of technical assistance rather than raise property taxes. The outcome, however, may be that the business community's interests in preparing students for the local labor force will replace the goal of a general education.

The final conservative challenge to public education is the movement toward commercialization/privatization, turning the schools or particular programs over to profit-making firms. For example, in 1990, a company called Whittle Communications offered to provide public schools with thousands of dollars of video equipment in return for a daily showing of a 12-minute "newscast" complete with commercials. Eventually, the service reached millions of students in thousands of schools, before the Whittle company went bankrupt in 1994.

Another Whittle project, now scaled down for want of start-up funds, is a chain of for-profit grade schools, but there are a number of other companies with similar plans already operating in several urban districts. The concept will undoubtedly remain a cherished goal of politicians seeking to reduce the power of teachers' unions and local governments through privatization of public services. If the public can be convinced that there are tax savings at no loss of school quality, many other districts may explore this option. In other words, control over the content of schooling will pass to commercial interests whose view of reality will become "official knowledge" (Apple, 1993). This is clearly a development for which you should stay tuned.

MARTIN D. SCHWARTZ

A Curmudgeon's Guide to College Survival

Martin D. Schwartz is the author or co-author of over 50 journal articles, book chapters and books, mainly on the victimization of women but also on teaching and learning, criminological theory, and corrections. He has been chair of the Department of Sociology and Anthropology at Ohio University, and suffers badly from the feeling that something important has been left undone, probably by one of his co-authors. He has no felony convictions worth mentioning.

Sometimes, as I get older and more grouchy, I get tired of hearing about how hard the current generation has it in college. Students of your grandparents' era also struggled with problems of good grades versus good times, the opposite sex, alcohol abuse, sexual violence, loneliness, no jobs on graduation, paying for tuition, and incredibly boring teachers who tried so hard to be friends with them all. Many of them got through. You will too.

Although my generation wore beanies, drank legally but couldn't vote, I have been asked to pass on my pearls of wisdom on college survival. So, what *did* I learn that I can pass on?

First and most important, lighten up. Let's face it, most of you are going to get your jobs by luck or hard work or both. Your mother may hate me for saying this, but someone with a good appearance, good interpersonal skills and reasonable grades will be at a serious advantage over uninteresting grinds with a 3.8 GPA. Of course, if you want to get into Harvard Law or

get a fellowship to work on your doctorate in Sociology, I recommend the 3.8. For the rest of you, join clubs, organize field trips, and make the club work despite the jerks your classmates are.

So, what else did I learn in college? Most important is a lifelong lesson that has always stood me in good stead: learn to hold your liquor well. After a few freshman stunts, I can't say that avoiding serious drunkenness has harmed me much. I learned that many of the worst experiences women have in college come when they are blind drunk, and alcohol use certainly is associated with the worst behavior my sex has to offer. At my university, we have banned alcohol from the campus itself, and some people have discovered an extraordinary thing: you can have a great time without throwing up afterwards.

What else? You may never again have the time and resources to engage in learning. Take the time to become educated, whether or not your school encourages it. The real reason for college is that all high school seniors think they know everything. College is where you learn that there are dozens of areas in which you are ignorant. Graduate school is where you learn that it is hundreds! Percy Bysshe Shelley said: "The more we study the more we discover our ignorance." Find out who Shelley was.

Read some books. Read some classics. My students' lack of factual knowledge is astounding. I teach at a selective admission school, and the number of students who don't know when the Civil War was fought scares me. But don't read to show off. Read for yourself. Many of you are now enjoying the music of the 60s, even though your parents like it. Find out why your grandparents thought Virginia Woolf and Ernest Hemingway

were so wonderful. You may be surprised.

This will probably also be your best shot at learning to work with other people. The nature of college is that if you want to meet and learn about people different from yourself, you probably can. Seek out people of other races, the opposite sex, opposing politics, a different sexual orientation, varied interests. Try to *hear* them. Maybe they will hear you. You may never again have the opportunity to learn to hear, work with, and get along with such a diverse group of peers.

It is also a great chance to become computer literate if you are not already. This computer stuff is not taking over because it makes your life worse. Look, if God wanted you to be using an old typewriter she wouldn't have allowed the invention of spell-checking and grammar-checking programs.

Finally, don't believe those Sunday newspaper stories about how life is so different today. Well, the tuition is a lot higher, the music is a lot louder, and the cafeteria food is a heck of a lot better—a really scary thought!

I hope that reading this book will convince many of you to become Sociology majors. Whatever else we are, we have interesting ideas. Sociologists study people, culture, heavy metal music, crime, politics, deviant behavior, race, poverty, sex, gender, the environment and almost everything else worth thinking about. I became a Sociology major because I couldn't imagine taking 13 courses in anything else without becoming so bored I would have to drop out of school. The more interesting the subject, the more you read, the higher your grades. See, I did give you a grades tip: become a Sociology major. Good luck, people!

PROSPECTS FOR THE FUTURE

Can the American education system build on its successes and overcome its failures? In the process of idealizing the past, we forget that there never was a Golden Age when schools operated without conflict or provided an impartial education. But today's criticism from all directions suggests a higher level of discontent than before. If so, the trend for the remainder of this century is likely to be toward *pluralism—* greater diversity among schools. Some will feature innovative classrooms, others a more traditional approach. Some will appeal to artistic students, others to budding scientists. Although most will be public schools, many will be private, profit-making businesses, and others nonprofit religious institutions. The major issue will be whether or not nonpublic schools receive taxpayer assistance. As one sociologist put it, this is the "struggle for the soul of American education" (Cookson, 1993; also Walters, 1993).

SUMMARY

1. Educational institutions are formal extensions of the socialization process designed to transmit the culture, to train people for adult statuses, to develop talent, and to generate new knowledge.

2. Functionalists see the education system as a meritocracy based on objective measures of innate talent, while conflict theorists view schools as mechanisms for reproducing the stratification system, especially the elite.

3. In modern society, the education subsystem is increasingly differentiated and specialized.

4. The American educational system is inclusive, providing a general education to all but a few children, although pupils are often separated into college preparatory and vocational tracks.

5. The American educational system includes a private sector dominated by church-related parochial institutions, with a smaller number of preparatory schools for the children of high-status families.

6. Ninety percent of American students are enrolled in public schools operated by a locally elected board of education and funded by property taxes.

7. There are many differences between and within urban and suburban school districts in terms of funding levels, student characteristics, and the quality of instruction.

8. Dropout rates are especially high in inner-city school districts, largely because there is no payoff for staying.

9. Sociologists also study the school and classroom as social structures, as well as the interactions between teachers and students.

10. Recent research strongly supports the effectiveness of cooperative learning rather than competition or tracking in raising student achievement.

11. The major functions of higher education are the transmission of existing knowledge, the production of new information, and training the next generation of scholars.

12. Higher education is stratified by private versus public universities and colleges and two-year institutions. Within the schools, faculty are stratified by academic rank, race, and sex.

13. Over the past 20 years, faculties and student bodies have become more diverse in terms of age, race, ethnicity, sex, and social class, more so at the less prestigious than at the elite institutions.

14. Current controversies in American education concern racial resegregation and inequality in funding among districts.

15. Another issue is the education of disabled students, only half of whom currently receive instruction in the local schools. Stigmatization and isolation can be reduced by mainstreaming.

16. Prospects for the future include increased pluralism among types of schools and increased diversity of the student body.

SUGGESTED READINGS

Cookson, Peter W. *School Choice: The Struggle for the Soul of American Education.* New Haven, CT: Yale University Press, 1994. Cookson analyses the many school choice plans currently being proposed or in place and explores their potential effects on students, teachers, school systems and communities.

DelFattore, Joan. *What Johnny Shouldn't Read: Textbook Censorship in America.* New Haven: Yale University Press, 1992. A review of federal textbook lawsuits and an analysis of the statewide textbook adoptions process indicate that conservative and liberal groups are equally represented in trying to change textbooks and are more effective at protesting textbook contents if they are in large states or register their complaints with the elected state board members.

Kozol, Jonathan. *Savage Inequalities: Children in America's Schools.* New Haven: Yale University Press, 1991. A stark indictment of the public school system and its funding practices. Deplorable and unsafe conditions are repeatedly documented in low-income, minority neighborhood schools in this moving and often shocking description of inequalities and their impact on the lives of children.

Peshkin, Alan. *The Color of Strangers, the Color of Friends: The Play of Ethnicity in School and Community.* Chicago: University of Chicago Press, 1991. A thoughtful book that asks the question, what are the elements that allow adolescents to overcome their ethnic differences and come together as friends? Peshkin draws on interviews, observation, historical and demographic data to discover how a high school, characterized by ethnic diversity, established racial respect and harmony.

Rury, John L. *Education and Women's Work: Female Schooling and the Division of Labor in Urban America.* Albany: State University of New York Press, 1991. This fine book examines the link between women's secondary education and the labor market from 1870 to 1930. Interesting questions are raised regarding gender equality in education and the emergence of a sex-specific curriculum as women wage earners increased.

Solomon, R. Patrick. *Black Resistance in High School: Forging a Separatist Culture.* Albany: State University of New York Press, 1992. How do schools fail minority children? This book presents a case study of why minority students fail to reach their academic potential despite high aspirations. Their failures are due to curriculum content, tracking and placement policies, authority structure, and intergroup relations.

Thorne, Barrie. *Gender Play: Girls and Boys in School.* New Brunswick, NJ: Rutgers University Press, 1993. An ethnographic study of boys and girls in the classroom that challenges the previous theory that boys and girls inhabit different worlds. Thorne's research points to exceptions, qualifications, and ambiguities in the previous theory.

Zweigenhaft, Richard L. and William G. Domhoff. *Blacks in the White Establishment: A Study of Race and Class in America.* New Haven: Yale University Press, 1991. An examination of the experiences of blacks who attended elite preparatory schools as part of the "A Better Chance" program, aimed at academically promising but low-income minority junior high school students. The authors found that not only race but class and schooling play major roles in the success of minority students.

16

Belief Systems: Religions and Secular Ideologies

THE SOCIOLOGICAL STUDY OF BELIEF SYSTEMS
Durkheim • Weber • Marx

A SOCIOLOGICAL MODEL

FUNCTIONS AND STRUCTURE OF BELIEF SYSTEMS
Manifest and Latent Functions • Dysfunctions of Belief Systems
SOCIOLOGISTS AT WORK "The Sociology of the Holocaust" by William B. Helmreich
Structure of Belief Systems

VARIETIES OF THE RELIGIOUS EXPERIENCE ACROSS TIME AND PLACE
Sacred and Profane • Magic

BELIEF SYSTEMS AND SOCIAL CHANGE
Priests and Prophets • Nativistic Revivals

MODERNIZATION
Secularization • Fundamentalism Revived

**ORGANIZED RELIGION AND RELIGIOUS BEHAVIOR
IN THE UNITED STATES**
Belonging and Believing • Participation
Civil Religion • African-American Churches

CONTEMPORARY TRENDS
The Decline of Mainstream Religious Institutions
Women and the Church • Church and State
The Fundamentalist Revival in America
Cults and the New Religious Movements • The Unification Church
SOCIAL POLICY Brainwashing or Normal Conversion?
Cults and the Courts • Cults Demystified • The New Age Movement

LAST WORDS ON BELIEVING AND BELONGING
SUMMARY ■ SUGGESTED READINGS

*V*arieties of the religious life as the twentieth century draws to a close:

- The uncertainties of modern life have revived witchcraft beliefs among the Ibos of Nigeria.
- Insomniacs in both the United States and Russia find their late night television screens awash in psychics.
- The last ceremonial eunuch of the Middle East still tends the sacred gardens of the Lalish Valley in Northern Iraq.
- Some delegates to the Parliament of the World's Religions refused to sit down with goddess worshipers, but the group finally produced a Declaration of a Global Ethic based on nonviolence. During the same week, Christians killed Muslims in Bosnia, Hindus killed Muslims in India, Muslims killed Christians in Egypt, and Jews and Muslims killed one another in Israel.
- In the Kalahari Desert of Africa, !Kung San hunters still apologize to the spirits of the animals they must kill to feed their own children.

Throughout the world there are thousands of different stories about how the world was formed, tens of thousands of ceremonies designed to purify individuals and help them cope with life events, and millions of people thought to have mystical powers. Each human group has constructed a set of beliefs and activities that give meaning to existence and unify the believers, and no two are exactly alike. Although many of these beliefs may strike us as quite strange, even bizarre, imagine trying to explain the story of Adam and Eve to a Jivaro headhunter.

THE SOCIOLOGICAL STUDY OF BELIEF SYSTEMS

At the beginning of Chapter 3, you were asked to create a culture and social structure on the deserted island to which your sociology class had been miraculously transported. At some point members of the group will retell the story of their amazing good fortune, marvel at their norms, and decide that they must have some grand mission in the world. In essence, you will have constructed a **belief system**—shared ideas about the meaning of life.

If these beliefs included the idea of a divine power guiding human destiny, we would speak of a **religion.** But not all belief systems are based on faith in supernatural forces, so we will use the broader term in this chapter, although most of the material does concern religions.

Because belief systems are based on faith and emotion, they may appear to be unsuited to empirical analysis. Yet the topic has fascinated sociologists from the very start. August Comte wished to substitute the scientific study of society, a **secular ideology** (*secular* means "of this world") for what he saw as the irrational superstitions of the past. Weber and Marx explored the links between beliefs, behaviors, and the economic system. And Durkheim saw belief systems as the celebration of society itself.

Durkheim

In *The Elementary Forms of the Religious Life* (1912/1961), Durkheim proposed that beliefs and the ceremonies expressing them—like any other aspect of culture—arise out of the collective history of the group (Chang, 1989). At the same time, the abstraction *society* is experienced through the beliefs and rituals that bind people to one another and reinforce their collective commitment.

In Durkheim's view, *all* systems of belief, regardless of specific content

> have the same objective significance and fulfill the same function everywhere. . . .There are no religions that are false. All are true in their own fashion; all answer, though in different ways, to the given conditions of human existence. . . .
>
> A religion is a unified system of beliefs and practices that unite into one moral community all those who adhere to them (1912/1961, pp. 15, 17, 62)

Weber

Weber's concern was less on the emergence of beliefs than on the relationship between ideas and actions. In *The Social Psychology of the World Religions* (1922–1923), Weber described how the central ideas of Islam, Buddhism, Hinduism, Judaism, and Christianity each provided a particular psychological and practical context for economic activity. For example, as seen in Chapter 3, Weber showed how the ideas of early Protestantism were essential to the development of capitalism and the value system that still characterizes American culture. The Protestant emphasis on personal responsibility generated anxieties about salvation compatible with the demands for hard work and clean living that were necessary for accumulating capital in the early stages of industrialization.

In contrast, Hinduism and Buddhism tend to deemphasize this world and its daily struggles in favor of reaching a mystical oneness with the universe through contemplation. The most revered figure is not the money maker but the propertyless wise man. Confucianism, the traditional religion of China,

> A **belief system** is a set of shared ideas about the meaning of life.
>
> **Religion** is a belief system based on the concept of a divine power guiding human destiny and directed toward the supernatural.
>
> A **secular ideology** is a belief system based on worldly rather than supernatural forces.

Religion is a belief system based on the idea of a divine force guiding destiny. This supernatural force is called on in matters of war as well as peace. Here, Christian Bosnian soldiers celebrate Easter Mass while the Civil War rages.

although firmly focused on this world, nonetheless inhibits individual achievement by its emphasis on ascribed statuses and obedience to elders. All these are different beliefs with different psychological motivations and different economic outcomes.

Marx

For Karl Marx, belief systems reflect existing power relationships and justify inequality by giving it divine sanction. If oppressed people can be convinced that it is the will of God or Allah or some other higher power that they accept their fate in this world in return for rewards after death (when "the last shall be first"), they will not challenge the status quo. This is the context of Marx's statement that religion is the "opium" [painkiller] of the masses, the "sigh of the oppressed," lulling them into the belief that their condition is part of a divine plan and cannot be changed by organized effort (Marx, 1844/1975).

If one must believe in a larger force at work in the world, at least let it be based on the facts of history and material conditions of everyday life. This is the essence of Marxism or any other *secular ideology:* it must be rooted in this world rather than the next one and explanations must be based on human experience rather than on blind faith.

A SOCIOLOGICAL MODEL

Regardless of one's own beliefs, a sociologist must examine all religions and ideologies objectively. We do not question the truth of any belief system; each is true to those who believe. We do not ask, "Is there a God?" but, rather, "What happens because people be-

lieve in this God or that one?" or "How did such ideas arise?" or "Whose interests are served?" These are questions that can be answered empirically.

Although the contents of a belief system are unique to each society, there are certain universal aspects that answer the same human need for meaning and the collective need for solidarity.

A belief system exists when the following conditions are met at the three levels of social analysis (Yinger, 1969):

- People become aware of continuing problems of daily life (individual level).
- Explanations and rituals have developed to reduce the anxiety of this awareness (cultural level).
- Specific roles have been assigned for the maintenance of the rituals and meanings (social structural level).

In the sociological perspective, cannibalism, Calvinism, Confucianism, and communism are of equal validity if they reduce individual anxiety and bring unity to the community of believers. Only when the belief system fails to satisfy either need can we make a value judgment: not that it was "false," but only that it "didn't work."

FUNCTIONS AND STRUCTURE OF BELIEF SYSTEMS

Systems of belief and ritual thus fill individual and group functions. As you have probably noticed, people turn to worship at times of great personal misery or happiness and at moments when group unity is under strain.

Of Sacred Cows and Black Magic

Anthropologists and sociologists are keenly aware that seemingly irrational beliefs and behaviors can serve positive functions for the collectivity. For example, the Hindu taboo against killing cattle is very important in their economic system because a live cow is more valuable than a dead one, regardless of widespread hunger. The cattle provide milk, energy for plowing, and dung for flooring, mortar, fertilizer, and cooking fuel. During bad times, the taboo keeps peasants from killing their cattle for short-term gain at the cost of long-term well-being (Harris, 1985a).

Likewise, the Voodoo rituals among Haitians serve important manifest functions for the community: pleasing the gods, honoring dead parents and grandparents, and warding off vampires. Honoring one's dead ancestors requires the construction of an elaborate tomb, which typically costs more than the mud huts of

the living. How wasteful, you might say. Perhaps, but if the money for the Voodoo ceremony must be raised by selling land to other members of the village, the process actually keeps land in circulation and prevents its accumulation in a few hands (Murray, 1980).

Some religious rituals and rules may outlive their original purposes but remain unchanged. The dietary law of Orthodox Jews that forbids eating pork, for example, was not created to reduce the risk of disease, but to discourage people from raising pigs, which required more shade and water than was economically profitable at that time (M. Harris, 1985a). But why, then, do such taboos remain in effect long after their original purpose is served? Because they accomplish even more important goals: to reaffirm the power of the collectivity over the individual, and to set believers off from all others. That they are arbitrary is precisely their value, because they celebrate the triumph of the social over the biological.

The Hindu taboo against killing cattle is important in the Indian economic system because live cows are more valuable than dead ones, despite widespread hunger in India. What are the positive and negative consequences of making cows "sacred"?

Manifest and Latent Functions

Beliefs and rituals have both manifest (open, intended) and latent (unintended, unanticipated) functions. Ceremonies such as Holy Communion, Bar/Bat Mitzvah, rain dances, witch hunts, and even human sacrifice are openly intended to help groups and individuals deal with unknown or threatening aspects of life—the fu-

ture of a young person, the fate of one's soul, natural disasters, and enemies within and without.

These rituals also have the latent function of reinforcing tradition and providing an immediate experience of social cohesion. Thus, although the rain dance may not produce a thunderstorm, it will bring people together to relieve the personal and social stresses caused by prolonged drought.

WILLIAM B. HELMREICH

The Sociology of the Holocaust

William B. Helmreich is Professor of Sociology at CUNY Graduate Center & City College of New York. He is the author of eight books, including Against All Odds: Holocaust Survivors and the Successful Lives They Made in America *(1992), winner of the National Jewish Book Award, and* The Things They Say Behind Your Back: Stereotypes and the Myths Behind Them *(1984). Professor Helmreich is currently working on a book about the influence of large metropolitan areas upon nearby smaller cities.*

My most recent book *Against All Odds: Holocaust Survivors and the Successful Lives They Made in America* is about how those who survived the Nazi era in Europe were able to learn to live again, hope again, trust again and even love again. The reasons why I wrote it go back all the way to my childhood.

I grew up in New York City, five blocks away from the Harlem border. It was a tough neighborhood whose inhabitants were a mosaic of America's immigrant groups—Irish, Puerto Rican, African American, Jewish, Italian, and Polish. Most of the Jews had already left by the time my parents arrived in 1946. I eventually became accustomed to epithets directed toward me as a Jew and this aroused my curiosity as to why people hated Jews and what it was that caused them to cling to a belief system that seemed capable of evoking such great hostil-

ity in others, such as my own family had experienced at the hands of the Nazis. Once, after yet another fight with a local tough, I asked my father: "Why do we have to stay here?" His response: "I came to America, a free country, after the holocaust and nobody is going to chase me out."

Under such circumstances it was only natural that I became a "street sociologist" at about the age of seven. In order to survive I had to develop an understanding of my social environment. I became an untrained yet highly intuitive participant observer. And because it was a poor neighborhood I was imbued with a sympathy toward the oppressed that has never left me and that has shaped my work and my views of life.

Every Sunday my father and I traveled on a different subway line to the last station, walked around the neighborhood, and stopped for a simple treat. Is it surprising, then, that today, at City College, I teach a graduate course, called The Peoples of the City of New York, that involves taking walking tours through the various neighborhoods?

My first project in college days was to interview skid row derelicts in New York's notorious Bowery area and try to learn how and why they became addicted to alcoholism. Part of the project included a five-week stay in a Bowery flophouse, my first formal attempt at doing ethnographic fieldwork.

At Washington University, in the late 1960s, I learned how to apply what I learned in the classroom. My doctoral dissertation was based upon a participant observation of the Black Panthers. I lived, worked, and traveled with them, trying to see how their belief system developed and how the

larger political power structure responded to them.

It was not surprising that, as a child of Holocaust survivors, I should eventually write a book about them, especially since sociologists have written so little about the topic. For me the most interesting question was how these people, who suffered so much, were able to pick up the pieces and go on. The answers to that, I reasoned, could provide valuable lessons on how people in general can overcome tragedy, crisis, and adversity.

I spent six years interviewing survivors from Massachusetts to Georgia, and from New York to California. Some were businessmen, others farmers, still others, lawyers and doctors. Respondents included atheists and God-fearing Hasidic Jews, rich and poor, men and women. One of the more important conclusions was that success in coping often depended on the belief-systems— secular or religious—that survivors created for themselves as they struggled to understand the meaning behind the terrible things that happened to them.

Finally, there was the question of Holocaust denial. Survivors are both outraged and mystified as to how something so obviously true can be challenged. After all, they lived through it. The fear that large numbers of people will come to believe what deniers say has prompted more and more survivors to testify by speaking out. My project became an unintended beneficiary of that apprehension. Many respondents expressed satisfaction, even relief, that yet another vehicle could be found for telling others what had transpired during those years in World War II.

Religions of the Middle and Far East

As the United States enters the world economy and becomes home to immigrants from Asia and the Middle East, Americans are increasingly exposed to belief systems very different from the Judeo-Christian tradition. Of the 5.5 billion people in the world today, 33 percent are Christian, 18 percent are Muslim, 16 percent are nonreligious, and most of the rest practice an Eastern religion or Chinese Folk Religion (*World Almanac*, 1994).

Islam. Islam, the religion of Muslims, was founded by the Prophet Muhammed in 622 CE (Common Era). Its holy book, the *Koran*, embraces both the Jewish and Christian *Bibles*, with the addition of Allah's (God's) words to His Prophet. Similar to Christianity and Judaism, Islam is *monotheistic*, centered on one god who created the world, all-powerful but just and merciful. Humans are created in Allah's image but are an imperfect reflection, open to Satan's temptation, yet capable of repentance. Islam imposes a strict code of behavior on secular rulers. Although theoretically egalitarian and nonhierarchical among men, this blending of political and religious authority can slide into **theocracy** (religious dictatorship) and the subordination of women. Male believers have five duties: to accept Allah, pray five times a day, give to charity, fast during the month of Ramadan, and make at least one pilgrimage to Mecca.

Eastern religions: In contrast to Islam, Christianity, and Judaism, the major belief systems of the Far East are more oriented to nature and the afterlife, less insistent on conformity to a single version of truth, and typically *polytheistic* (accepting many gods). Each of these religions has its own particular history, rituals, and doctrines, as well as variety of local sects.

The grand theme of H*induism*, the religion of India, is of an everlasting cycle of life in which all things are reincarnated (born over and over again). The goal of existence is to transcend this cycle through meditation, bringing peace from earthly desires.

Buddhism is also based on a cycle of birth and rebirth in a world filled with evil. One's misery can be ended through contemplation, with the goal of *nirvana*, a complete emptying of the self so that Buddha's insights can enter.

In contrast, *Confucianism* is founded on a reverence for the past and obedience to authority. A key concept is *piety* (respect), established in the family and extended to secular rulers. Only friendship is egalitarian.

Shintoism, the native religion of Japan, combines worship of nature and ancestors. The Emperor is a descendant of the sun goddess and rules by divine right. Shinto as the state religion was abolished during the American occupation following World War II, but millions of Japanese continue to practice the religion at thousands of shrines.

Ceremonies such as Holy Communion, Bar/Bat Mitzvah, and baptism are intended to help individuals and groups deal with the unknown aspects of life—the future of the young person, the fate of one's soul, etc. These children are taking their first communion. This religious practice takes months of preparation by the children and functions to reinforce Catholic religion and tradition for their kin and community.

Dysfunctions of Belief Systems

Because most religions assume that one and only one set of beliefs—their own—reflects "the" truth, all others must be false. Thus, there is always the potential for conflict among those who hold different beliefs, especially if possessing the one and only True Word involves an obligation to spread it. With so little room for compromise, religious wars have been among the longest and bloodiest. History is filled with religious persecutions, forced conversions, and wholesale slaughter, even though most faiths proclaim an ideal of mercy and brotherhood, at least among believers. Beliefs unify the faithful but divide them from nonbelievers.

Within a given society, the presence of more than one faith is often associated with **sectarian conflict**—open violence between religious groups. The United States has largely avoided such hostilities by making religious freedom a legal principle, although historically there have been periodic attacks on Catholics, Jews, followers of Asian religions, and open season on atheists. Sectarian violence is widespread today: between Catholics and Protestants in Northern Ireland, Muslims and Hindus in India, Christians and Muslims in Lebanon and Bosnia, and Jews and Muslims in Israel. In many cases, however, the conflict is less about religion than about

> **Sectarian conflict** refers to interreligious strife.
>
> A **theocracy** is a religious dictatorship.

381

For India's Hindus (left), the Ganges River is sacred and its waters are spiritually purifying. The women and men worship separately. Buddhist monks (right) regard materialism as a barrier to spiritual development. Prayer and study allow these monks to look beyond the constaints of this world.

inequalities in economic and political power that are exploited by religious leaders.

These examples illustrate a major sociological principle: *The same pattern can be functional or dysfunctional depending on the context.* The beliefs that unite one group can lead to conflict with others. Internal cohesion, remember, is often gained by increasing outgroup hostility.

Structure of Belief Systems

To fulfill these functions, every belief system contains three essential elements:

1. An origin story telling how the group came into being, as in the biblical story of Creation, the Tiwi belief that they originated in the waters, or the humanist reliance on the forces of evolution.
2. *Rules of behavior* that must be obeyed, such as in the Ten Commandments and similar codes of conduct, giving the norms a sacred dimension.
3. Most belief systems also contain a *vision of the future,* of belonging to some broad sweep of history. The idea of an afterlife or the return of the Cave God or the triumph of Communism serve to unite believers and give meaning to individual existence.

These three elements are found in the religions of the most simple and the most complex societies, in the beliefs of astronomers as well as astrologists, and even among those who follow secular ideologies.

> If there were only one religion in England, there would be danger of tyranny; if there were two, they would be at each other's throat; but there are thirty and they live happily together in peace.
>
> —VOLTAIRE, 1732/1961, P. 26

MARXISM AS A SECULAR IDEOLOGY.   Ironically, the antireligious ideas of Karl Marx formed the basis of a belief system that gave its followers the same certainty that Christianity or Judaism brings to others. As the official ideology of a Communist country such as Cuba or the People's Republic of China, Marxism contains the essential elements of any belief system: an explanation of human history, a code of conduct in the present, and a vision of ultimate good, and all without mention of a divine being.

Rituals are also important, but in place of religious holy days, Marxist holidays celebrate key events in the history of the nation's class struggle and are designed to reinforce commitment to the secular government. At the individual level, important moments in the life course are also marked by secular ceremonies.

Marxism, like many political ideologies, celebrates its heroes and past achievements, reinforces the authority of current leaders, and motivates citizens to sacrifice for the nation and the group. The annual May Day Parade in Havana, Cuba, features posters of Che Guevara, a legendary revolutionary leader who helped establish Communism in Cuba.

SECULAR HUMANISM.   As a nonpolitical belief system, **secular humanism** is based on the assumption that human beings can solve their problems through their own efforts. This belief reflects the Enlightenment's emphasis on rationality and science as a corrective to blind faith. In 1933, a small group of intellectuals founded the American Humanist Association and published a *Humanist Manifesto* based on the following tenets (American Humanist Association, 1988):

- A faith in human intelligence and abilities
- A commitment to democracy and civil liberties
- A belief in the importance, if not the divine origin, of the Ten Commandments and the ideals of equality, the human community, and world peace
- A compassionate concern for all human beings

Although the Association membership is only a few thousand, these ideas are profoundly upsetting to deeply religious American Protestants who believe only a firm faith in God can solve personal problems. As a result, secular humanism is a prime target of the religious right in the United States.

VARIETIES OF THE RELIGIOUS EXPERIENCE ACROSS TIME AND PLACE

Although belief systems must have emerged with the earliest human bands, the earliest traces of religious rituals date from Neanderthal grave sites of 100,000

to 60,000 years ago where the dead were arranged in a ceremonial position, amid offerings of seeds and flowers. But it was not until about 10,000 years ago, when some groups of modern *Homo sapiens* developed agriculture and herding to the point of producing a surplus, that we find relatively elaborate funerals (Grandjean and Fuller, 1993). Burial gifts of tools, weapons, and food strongly suggest a belief in an afterlife when these necessities would be needed. In addition, differences in the amount and value of grave gifts indicate a stratification system. Economic developments apparently preceded the elaboration of religious ritual, which supports the view that beliefs reflect material conditions.

But this emphasis on belief systems as rooted in social structure and relationships does not always satisfy those who seek a more spiritual and individual (rather than social) foundation for this universal phenomenon. Through the years, philosophers and social scientists have suggested that religion is based on such factors as awe at the power of nature, fear of death, guilt over the wish to kill one's parents, and the need to wash away original sin. Some sociologists speak of a need for **transcendence,** to escape the limits of everyday life through union with a divine power (Berger, 1992).

Secular humanism is a belief system that assumes that people can solve their problems without divine intervention.

Transcendence is the escape from everyday life through union with a divine power.

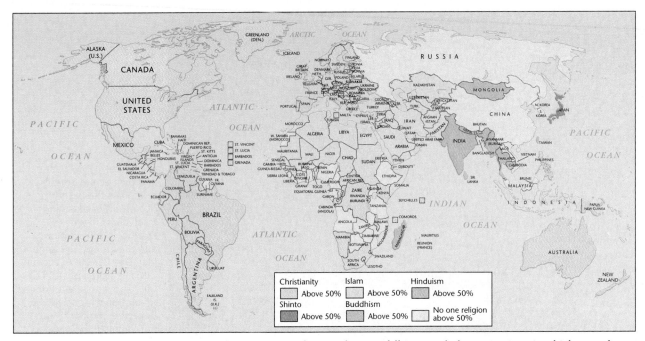

The major religions of the world include Christianity, Hinduism, Islam, Buddhism, and Shinto. Nations in which one of these religions is practiced by more than half the population are noted in the legend.

Source: The World Almanac and Book of Facts, 1994.

Such universal longings can explain only why people need to believe in the supernatural but not the endless variety of belief systems or changes over time. For this type of understanding, we must follow Durkheim, Weber, and Marx and ask how a particular type of society tends to produce a particular type of belief system. For example, we know that fertility goddesses were worshiped in early horticultural societies where it was important to guard against crop failure and that warrior gods are prominent in societies engaged in struggles for land and power.

The gods that people worship also reflect the quality of social relationships within the society (Harris, 1985b). In simple gathering and hunting bands, for example, the gods, like the people, are an egalitarian bunch, with little distinction between male and female. In contrast, highly centralized agricultural societies with well-defined social classes worship gods that are also stratified under a male leader who demands strict obedience.

Despite such general similarities, it is the diversity and richness of beliefs and rituals that fascinate the social scientist. Ritual life tends to be more elaborate in simple than in complex societies, probably because of the wider range of events that appear to be outside of human control. Some beliefs, however, such as the idea of an invisible "soul" existing inside the visible body (*animism*), are as common in modern as in preindustrial societies.

Sacred and Profane

In all societies, there are two very different sets of objects and behaviors. One set is **sacred** and invested with holy, divine, mystical, or supernatural force. The other is the realm of the **profane**, earthly and understandable in its own terms. Just what goes into which category is a cultural variable. Sacredness is not built into an object; it is imposed by the group. Thus, what to one society would be two pieces of wood joined together becomes "the cross," with all its mystical significance, to another group. The sacred burial places of Plains Indians are just so much good pastureland for Midwest farmers.

In all societies, certain individuals are put in charge of the sacred objects and places. **Religious roles** are among the very first to emerge in human history ("the second oldest profession"). Shamans, witch doctors, priestesses, ministers, rabbis, and Islamic mullahs are all religious specialists whose duties are primarily the protection of sacred things, places, and ceremonies.

Magic

People throughout the world attempt to control the forces of the unseen. **Magic** refers to behaviors de-

Sacred behaviors and objects are invested with holy, divine, mystical, or supernatural force.

Profane behaviors and objects are not holy but rather earthly and understandable.

Religious roles involve supervision of sacred objects, places, and ceremonies.

Magic refers to behavior designed to manipulate unseen forces.

"When Jesus Came, the Corn Mothers Went Away"

All divine beings probably were once thought of in feminine terms, as givers of life and therefore close to nature (Gimbutas, 1991). Evidence also indicates that important religious roles were given to women as priestesses and protectors of holy places in ancient Britain and Rome (Pace, 1985). Wall paintings and statues of a mother goddess suggest widespread mother worship throughout the prehistoric world and even in many societies today (Preston, 1983).

But the introduction of agriculture brought an entirely new religious imagery, based now on the powerful father who rules through chosen sons, reflecting the social patterns of male ownership of lands and herds as well as inheritance through the male line. The leaders of the biblical Hebrews were called *patriarchs*; Christianity is built on a masculine triad; and Islam is almost exclusively male oriented, forbidding women entry into the main body of the mosque. Although the major Eastern religions (Buddhism, Hinduism, and Shintoism) are less openly masculine, women's role in traditional ritual is extremely limited.

The exclusion of women and the triumph of male religious authority is maintained through the widespread practice of sacrifice, a ritual that is everywhere associated with patriarchy and hierarchy (Jay, 1992). From the ancient Hebrews to the contemporary Ashanti of West Africa, from offering a lamb to the sacrament of Eucharist, sacrificial ceremonies are led only by men, establishing a clear boundary between men and women and between religious leaders and their followers.

Long before Europeans settled in North America, certain of the Pueblo Indians of the American Southwest had developed a belief system centered around the Corn Mothers, givers of food and life, and a celebration of all forms of human sexuality (Gutierrez, 1991). This quite naturally upset the seventeenth-century Spanish missionaries with their strict sexual mores and views of cor-

rect gender relationships. Ultimately, the missionaries won the ideological battle, a masculinized religion and social system replaced the egalitarian culture of the Pueblos, and the Corn Mothers went away.

This figure, thought to have originated about 30,000 years ago in the Upper Paleolithic Era, was found in a cave in Austria. Called the "Venus of Willendorf" and representing the life force itself, it is one of the earliest religious objects linking the fertility of women and nature.

signed to manipulate the supernatural, whereas religion involves coming to terms with a superior power. Magical formulas and gestures are used to reduce uncertainty. For example, among the Trobriand Islanders of the South Pacific, fishing in the calm waters of a lagoon requires little in the way of ceremony because success depends only on skill; but when the same men and boats venture into the ocean outside the lagoons, where the winds are unpredictable, the departure of the vessels is marked by solemn rituals (Malinowski, 1922/1955).

Magic and superstition are applied when an outcome cannot be predicted or controlled with scientific knowledge, which is why they are most often found in preindustrial societies and among the powerless. Yet, even we "moderns," when faced with the

unpredictable, cross ourselves, stroke a rabbit's foot, or make bargains with the gods. Professional athletes, whose performances are always problematic, respond with all types of superstitious tics and twitches.

BELIEF SYSTEMS AND SOCIAL CHANGE

Because belief systems deal with the eternal—either truth is everlasting or it is not truth—most religions tend to be very conservative and supportive of the existing economic and political structures. Yet secular ideologies and religions have often been agents of social change (Billings, 1990). New movements are continually being generated within established religions, typically by a charismatic leader who calls for reforms that ultimately become the basis of a new religion, as with Jesus, Muhammad, and Martin Luther.

Priests and Prophets

The dual nature of belief systems—as support of the status quo and as agent of change—is captured in Max Weber's distinction between the *priestly* and the *prophetic.* In general, **priestly** functions involve the protection and maintenance of existing religious structures and traditions. The priest is a manager of the sacred. **The prophet,** in contrast, is a disturber of the peace, often charismatic, who challenges the existing system. Just as prophets will attract an enthusiastic following, they also rouse fierce opposition, so that their life is often short and violently ended.

This is why, in Weber's terms, the prophet's message must be institutionalized and the spiritual mission transformed into a worldly organization—**the routinization of charisma.** The resulting structure, dominated now by priests, often becomes the conservative oppressive system described by Marx, and the ground is prepared for a new prophet.

A basic tension exists between religion and its emphasis on the pure and otherworldly, on the one hand, and the impurity and imperfections of real life, on the other hand. Some religious communities will survive by withdrawing from the rest of society, as in the example of the Amish in the United States or the Buddhist monks in Tibet. Or believers can divide their activities into two separate realms with different rules for each. Thus, Orthodox Jews can be devoted to secular business during part of the day and, for the rest, follow a purely religious way of life.

Nativistic Revivals

Charismatic figures are most likely to emerge during periods of rapid social change. Although some will welcome the weakening of traditional authorities, others will lead an effort to return to a glorified past. **Nativistic revivals** are attempts to cope with cultural disintegration by resisting the impact of new ideas and recalling better days.

Examples include the Native American chief Wovoka who briefly revived the Ghost Dance religion among the Plains Indians, 100 years ago, as the native culture was being destroyed by U.S. troops. More recently, the Ayatollah Khomeini of Iran was the charismatic focus of a revival of traditional Islam and anti-Western emotions throughout the Near East. Similar revivals are also found in industrial societies in response to the strains of modernization.

MODERNIZATION

The most powerful source of social change today is **modernization**—the spread of industrialism and urbanization and the development of a world economy (Chapter 19). In the Third World, kin-based production has been replaced by cash crops and the assembly line. Family members drift to the towns looking for work. Tribal leaders are displaced by weak and corrupt national governments. Few societies can absorb all these changes without personal stress and social strain. The old ways no longer work, and new norms are unclear. The destabilizing effects of rapid change have led to many nativistic revivals—in the United States as well as the developing world and within all traditional religions—as a response to the conditions of modernity and the threat of secularization.

Secularization

One of the crucial dimensions of modernization is the process of **secularization** with its focus on this world and on the ability of human reason and technology to solve problems. The secular way of thinking is a profound challenge to traditional faith and its emphasis on unquestioned obedience to religious authority. The secular spirit celebrates the individual and consumption values, the enjoyment of life rather than the contemplation of an afterlife.

Ever since Comte, it was assumed that the march of science would eventually diminish the importance of religion in daily activities. At the least, religion would be a matter of private personal devotion with minimal impact on secular affairs. Although science need not be viewed as an enemy of faith, the current controversy between creationists and evolutionists suggests that many still view science that way. In any event, science as a secular ideology cannot answer ultimate questions such as "What is the meaning of life?" or even "Is there a God?" As long as these questions are asked, people will look for answers in the realm of the

---

Priestly functions deal with specific traditions of the faith, supporting the existing structure of power.

The **prophet** is a charismatic figure, witnessing a revelation calling for a new order.

The **routinization of charisma** occurs when the prophet's beliefs are institutionalized and transformed into a worldly organization.

Nativistic revivals arise when a culture is disintegrating under the impact of profound change.

Modernization involves a global process of change whereby industrialization and urbanization are spread to nonindustrial societies leading to the development of a world economy.

Secularization is the shift in focus from the next world and unquestioned faith to this world and reason, science, and technology.

Islamic Fundamentalism: The New Satan?

Although resistance to modernity is worldwide, including many Christian churches in the United States, the American public appears to be uniquely aroused by the revival of religious traditionalism in the Muslim world. This fear is grounded in part on the reality of Islamic–American relationships in the Middle East, beginning with the taking of American hostages in the Iranian Revolution of the late 1970s, and continuing through the bombing of New York City's World Trade Center in 1993 by members of a fundamentalist mosque. For many years, American television viewers have become used to seeing the angry faces and gestures of what seems an endless sea of young Muslim men.

Islam can also arouse anxiety by its very reach—covering countries from the Mediterranean Sea to the Pacific Ocean and south through much of Africa—and its potential wealth in oil and other resources. One billion people, or close to one-fifth of the world's population, are Muslim. And to a greater degree than other major world religions, Islam is militant, motivated by a command to conquer and convert nonbelievers (Juergensmeyer, 1993). In addition, the American media have "demonized" the Islamic fundamentalist movement by consistently using such descriptive words as "militant terrorist," and "radical extremist," as if there were no rational reasons for their anger. In many ways, Islamic fundamentalism has replaced the Soviet Union as the new global threat against which the West must mobilize.

These fears have obscured the real failures of Middle East rulers to provide either democracy or economic security and have diverted attention from American support for the most repressive regimes. To equate all Islamic political activity with terrorism is to overlook the legitimate hopes for peace of the vast majority of Muslims, as well as the diversity of cultural traditions within the faith (Esposito, 1992). But because Muslims remain foreign and exotic, we tend to use a different standard of judgment for Islam than for Christianity or Judaism. Each of these has its extremists, but we do not judge the entire religion by their acts.

Ultimately, the West will have to accommodate these new currents in the world. The major question appears to be whether, like previous revolutionary religious movements, Islamic fundamentalism will lose its crusading enthusiasm as it confronts the realities of the material world. Or are the current waves of fundamentalist activism within all major world religions a type of nativistic revival, the last gasp of a disappearing way of life, or the beginning of a new world order in which faith once more becomes the basis of civil society?

One billion people, about one fifth of the world's population, are Muslim and their worldwide numbers are increasing dramatically. Here a group of Muslims are worshipping at a mosque in Old Delhi, India.

nonscientific (Appleyard, 1993). It has also been claimed that the secularization thesis—that religious faith would gradually wither away—reflects an ideological bias on the part of social scientists in favor of positivism and the ultimate triumph of the intellect (Hadden, 1987; Esposito, 1992).

If, as sociologists, we look at religious structures rather than beliefs, it is clear that the power of religious authorities over much of everyday life has diminished greatly in modern industrial societies (Chaves, 1994). In this sense, the secularization thesis is supported, with one major contemporary exception—the revival of fundamentalism among a growing segment of the world's population.

Fundamentalism Revived

Not only has religious faith survived the impact of modernization, it has recently emerged in a particularly militant form throughout the world. The old gods have not gone away; some have been transformed by their encounter with modernity, but others have been revived by a newly energized body of true believers (Crippen, 1988). The most significant contemporary development in religion is the global emergence of **fundamentalism,** a rigidly traditional set of beliefs, based on an unchanging sacred book, which sees the world as divided into clear-cut forces for good or for evil, with no middle ground (Marty and Appleby, 1993; Kaplan, 1992; Misztal and Shupe, 1992). In general, the stricter the belief system, the more committed the members because the less devoted are screened out, leaving a core of "true believers" (Iannaccone, 1994).

Fundamentalism is a rigidly traditional set of beliefs that sees the world as divided into clear-cut forces for good or for evil.

As a response to secular society and its imperfections, fundamentalists define their task as one of purification, of cleansing all evil in preparation for a grand transformation of the world—an expectation that may have something to do with the fast approaching end of the twentieth century. Unlike earlier fundamentalist revivals, however, contemporary movements have a political agenda that often involves replacing secular governments with a religiously guided regime if not a full theocracy.

In the Third World, the failure of civilian governments to cope with the effects of industrialization and the world economic system has brought widespread corruption and poverty, providing a fertile base for religious organizing. As a consequence, revivalist Hindus are a major political force in India; fundamentalist Muslims threaten the secular regimes of Egypt, Algeria, and Tunisia; and smaller movements are waging sectarian wars in Southeast Asia. In the United States, Christian fundamentalists have become important players in the political system.

At this writing, it is unclear how successful these groups will be in transforming politics, or if they do triumph, whether they will be able to meet their followers' expectations for spiritual and material well-being. Yet the depth of this yearning for a personal, emotional, religious experience can be seen in South and Central America and in Eastern Europe, where American and native fundamentalist organizations have won millions of converts at the expense of traditional Catholic and Orthodox churches (Martin, 1990; Brooke, 1993; Schmemann, 1993). If history is any guide, however, the current revivalist forces will ultimately have to make compromises with modernity, perhaps preparing the ground for another wave of nativistic activism. If secularization was not quite the overwhelming force once predicted, it nonetheless remains a major contemporary trend. Neither the strength of faith nor the depth of yearning for spiritual fulfillment can turn back the clock; modern ideas cannot simply be erased from human memory; and the lure of material goods has been known to overwhelm religious purity from the beginning. Secularization is an uneven process, and the extent to which the old gods have been banished varies greatly. In general, among industrial societies, Western Europe is most secularized, Japan the least, and the United States, only partially (Sasaki and Suzuki, 1987). Let us now turn to a closer examination of the American scene.

ORGANIZED RELIGION AND RELIGIOUS BEHAVIOR IN THE UNITED STATES

Belonging and Believing

Today, almost two-thirds of Americans are formally linked to (affiliated with) a religious congregation, but some churches include children and others count only adults or people officially baptized. Because the Census Bureau no longer asks about religious affiliation, the data come from information provided by church groups or sample surveys. The best guess is that 60 percent of Americans are Protestant; 24 percent, Roman Catholic; with Jews, Mormons, Muslims, and followers of Eastern religions each accounting for between 2 and 2.5 percent (*Yearbook of American and Canadian Churches,* 1994). Although not all of these people are officially affiliated, the numbers who profess a faith make the United States appear to be more religious and far more religiously diverse than other Western societies. In addition, the level of faith in the United States is the highest among modern nations, with over 90 percent saying that they believe in God, and over half also believing in heaven and an afterlife (Kosmin and Lachman, 1993).

Participation

Despite such strong expressions of faith, attendance at religious services is quite low, although many may listen to religious programs on television or radio. For many years, a consistent finding was that about 40 percent of respondents said that they had recently attended services. But when researchers compared actual attendance figures with answers to a telephone survey, they found that only 20 percent of Protestants and 28 percent of Catholics had actually been in the pews that week (Hadaway et al., 1993).

Historically, the most likely to participate in organized prayer are women, the elderly, city dwellers, and the religiously conservative (Finke and Stark, 1992). Today, young teenagers are also more likely to attend than most adults (Gallup, 1993). Participation rates fall among young adults, especially those in college, but pick up as people experience the life course events that turn one toward the church—marriage, parenthood, divorce, or death in the family.

Types of Religious Organization

Religious identity and practice are shaped by the organizational settings in which people worship. Several distinctions are crucial:

- *Denomination* or *church* refers to the formally organized body of believers as a general category, that is, the Catholic church in contrast to a specific congregation such as St. Jude's parish in Chicago. Although there is only one Roman Catholic church, there are dozens of Protestant denominations (e.g., Methodist, Episcopal, or Lutheran). The Jewish faith embraces three traditions, or denominations: Orthodox, Conservative, and Reform, based on their degree of adaptation to the secular world. Among Muslims, history has produced many denominations that remain a source of continual conflict within the faith.
  New denominations typically develop through *schism* (division), when members of a large church split off to form a religious body that differs somewhat in belief or practice but is not entirely different from the original church.
- *Mainstream* or *mainline churches* refers to recognized religious organizations that support the central cultural values of the society. For example, within Protestantism, Presbyterian churches are mainline in contrast to those that practice snake-handling or that reflect the beliefs of the person who founded the congregation (e.g., Pat Robertson).

- *Ecclesia* refers to the "official" church, embracing all members of a society, and where religious and political leadership are mutually supportive if not one and the same. The Anglican denomination is the established Church of England; Judaism, the state religion of Israel; and Roman Catholicism, the official religion of The Republic of Ireland. In modern societies, the political structure is typically separate from that of the ecclesia, although religious leaders may also exercise great political authority, as in Islamic Iran.
- *Sect*: Often the result of a denominational schism over doctrine or ritual, sects tend to be more exclusive in membership and less tolerant of differences in beliefs than the denomination from which they split. The mode of worship is relatively personal and emotional. Over time, however, as a sect gains members, its charisma may become routinized to the point at which the sect loses its extreme features and assumes the respectability of a recognized denomination, as with Seventh Day Adventist, Jehovah's Witness, and Christian Science churches in the United States.
- *Cult*: This term covers a wide variety of belief communities, some of which are religious, others secular, and still others that combine features of both but which are essentially unattached to any other religious group. Later in this chapter, we examine contemporary cults and the current controversies surrounding them.

Another factor that might depress attendance rates is the steady increase in religious intermarriage (see Chapter 12). Couples can resolve religious differences by reducing the importance of religion in their life. This is a special problem for the already small number of American Jews, with intermarriage rates among men currently as high as 50 percent, although some non-Jewish spouses will convert to Judaism (Kosmin and Lachman, 1993). Not only marriage but other primary group relationships today involve contact with people of very different backgrounds. Because religious commitment takes place in a social context in which personal ties are often more important than ideology, the heterogeneous family and friendship networks of young people tend to weaken the influence of inherited religious identities (Cornwall, 1989; Wilson and Sandomirsky, 1991).

Finally, geographic and social mobility loosen ties to ascribed religious identity. For example, church attendance is relatively low in communities characterized by high mobility and religious diversity (Bainbridge, 1990; Land et al., 1991; Kosmin and Lachman, 1993).

Does participation matter? One extensive study of African Americans found that involvement in religious activities was associated with high self-esteem and feelings of personal well-being (Ellison, 1993). In addition, the interviewers reported that religious respondents were friendlier and more open than their less religious counterparts (Ellison, 1992). Yet there is also evidence that extremely religious people can be very intolerant and suspicious (Wilcox, 1992). Some of these negative traits, however, could be due less to religious factors than to the regional cultural context, such as the relative intolerance of Southerners in general (Ellison and Musick, 1993).

> **American civil religion** is a common faith that the nation is divinely blessed, has a mission in the world, and is guided by ethical standards of good citizenship.

Civil Religion

The United States is unusual in its religious variety and unique in the range of religious expression protected by law. How, then, under conditions of such denominational pluralism, can there be a unifying belief system? Sociologist Robert Bellah (1975) found the functional equivalent of a common faith in the **American civil religion,** by which the nation and its institu-

American civil religion sees our nation and its institutions as divinely blessed. The members of the University of Texas football team pray before a game. Does blurring of the line between the sacred and the secular dilute or revitalize religious experiences in everyday life?

tions are seen as divinely blessed, with a mission in the world, and guided by ethical standards.

In other words, the civil religion is a secularized version of Protestant morality. As the "universal religion of the nation" it serves the essential functions of any belief system: to legitimate the social order and integrate its diverse members, despite other differences. The mixing of secular and religious in the United States is visible both when we make secular holidays sacred, as on the Fourth of July, and when we transform sacred holy days into commercial orgies, as at Christmas. In sum, the civil religion provides an ideological umbrella under which a variety of religious communities can congregate (Demerath and Williams, 1992).

Other analysts are less optimistic. One early critic (Herberg, 1960) foresaw a loss of authentic spirituality in a vague sea of secularized worship, where having a religious affiliation is more important than deep involvement in a particular faith. For example, is school prayer a religious or secular practice? Do students derive any moral benefits from a moment of silence or from reciting a nondenominational blessing (Althauser, 1990)?

Another criticism of the civil religion is that religious symbolism can be easily co-opted, for example, by politicians who wrap themselves in religion and the flag; by business leaders who join a prayer breakfast before closing down a factory; and by athletes who conduct locker-room services to ask God's help in scoring touchdowns. It is difficult to tell whether this blurring of the line between the sacred and secular signifies a diluting of the religious impulse or its revitalization in everyday life.

African-American Churches

Religion has always been a major spiritual resource for oppressed people, but the African-American churches were of special importance as the only basic institutions not under white control. The church is the center of community life, serving as a political, social, and educational resource (Gilkes, 1985; Freedman, 1993). The great majority of African Americans are Protestant and denominationally Baptist but are also extremely diverse in blending elements of African and Southern American culture. Services involve a high level of personal participation, with an emphasis on music as an integral part of the religious experience.

A small percentage of African Americans are Roman Catholic, often as a result of sending a child to a parochial school (Rath, 1993). A growing number have become converts to Islam, which represents a clean break with what many perceive to be a failed past. Islam is a more disciplined and demanding faith than contemporary mainstream Protestantism: no music or choirs; strict dietary laws; prayers five times a day; no alcohol, gambling, or nightclubs. The majority of recent converts have joined established mosques rather than the Black Muslim movement founded by Malcolm X in the 1960s and now led by Louis Farrakhan.

African-American religious life, even today, can be understood only in the context of the pervasive racism of the larger society and the tension between adapting to the dominant culture while also preserving a separate heritage (Lincoln and Mamiya, 1990; Baer and Singer, 1992). The churches are especially important as agents of integration *within* the black community and as a source of contact with mainstream institutions.

Because the African-American church was the only avenue of upward mobility for talented and ambitious young blacks who were excluded from high-status occupations in the larger society, it should be no surprise to learn that all but a few leaders of the 1960s civil rights movement come from the clergy. Today, however, when men and women of color can pursue careers in high-paying professions, proportionately fewer have entered religious studies.

The role of women in the black church has historically been more visible than in the white churches, as participants and leaders if not as ordained ministers. To the extent that the church has been the heart of the black community, the preserver of a distinct tradition, and catalyst for collective action, women have been its lifeblood (Higgenbotham, 1993). These varied functions have allowed women to forge an area of autonomy in the face of both racism and sexism.

As long as African Americans continue to experience barriers to achievement in mainstream institutions, the church has a vital mission. Indeed, as sources of outside support have dwindled in a period of backlash and economic recession, the church *must* function as an all-purpose social center and welfare agency. It is notable that African-American churches have been able to retain their membership through the very decades that saw a sharp decline in white mainstream denominations (Sherkat and Ellison, 1991).

CONTEMPORARY TRENDS

The Decline of Mainstream Religious Institutions

The great paradox of contemporary American religion is this: Amid widespread religiosity, the *mainline* Protestant churches have lost membership and influence. Between 1965 and 1989, membership declined by 29 percent among Episcopalians, 32 percent among Presbyterians, and 45 percent among Disciples of Christ. Conversely, large membership gains were realized by denominations that until recently had been marginal to the Protestant mainstream such as Seventh Day Adventists (up 92 percent), Assemblies of God (up 121 percent), and the Church of Latter Day Saints (Mormon), up by 133 percent (*Time,* April 5, 1993; pp. 46–47). To a large extent, these changes reflect the major line of division today among American churches—between liberal and conservative denominations *within* each faith (Wuthnow, 1993; Hart, 1992; Olson and Carroll, 1992).

This division also reflects social class differences, with conservatives more likely than liberals to be from small towns in the South and Midwest, to be working- and lower-middle class, and to have experienced economic dislocation. At the moment, the conservatives appear to outnumber the liberals, or at least to be voting with their feet by shifting their affiliation.

SPECIAL CONCERNS OF THE CATHOLIC CHURCH IN THE UNITED STATES.   Although the Catholic church has not lost members, it shares many of the problems of mainstream Protestantism and has other problems unique to its hierarchical and patriarchal organization. Membership will continue to grow as a result of higher-than-average fertility among recent Hispanic immigrants. But as the new migrants become acculturated, they will most likely follow the pattern of earlier Catholic ethnics whose fertility rates have declined to the same level as the Protestant majority. In the process of acculturation and upward mobility, many Catholic couples engage in contraceptive practices still forbidden by the church. The normative conflict between church teaching and private behavior has caused large numbers of young couples to stop at-

Catholic priests who follow liberation theology are actively involved in changing the lives of the poor and oppressed. An activist priest in Brazil is leading his parishioners seeking agrarian reform in their opposition to wealthy Brazilian landowners who control most of the land.

tending mass, although they remain "communal Catholics" and rejoin the church at a later date (Hout and Greeley, 1987; D'Antonio et al., 1989).

In addition to rejecting church doctrine on birth control, a majority of American Catholics disagree with their leaders on premarital sexuality, women as priests, allowing priests to marry, permitting divorce and remarriage, and abortion (*New York Times*/CBS News Poll, 1994c). Indeed, after decades of fierce opposition by the clergy, support for legal abortion under most conditions has *increased* among American Catholics.

A more serious problem is the steep drop in men and women in holy orders, from 60,000 priests in 1967 to 45,000 in 1992, and from 173,000 to 93,000 nuns. In terms of the ratio between the Catholic population and its clergy, the decline began in the 1940s and was due to structural changes rather than any loss of faith (Castillo, 1992; Schoenherr and Young, 1993). As Catholic families became smaller, the pool of potential priests and nuns also diminished. After 1945, other educational and occupational opportunities were opened to working-class Catholic men, and in the 1960s, the women's movement increased the range of choices for women seeking a calling in social service.

The tension between church doctrine and personal feelings is particularly intense for the large minority (possibly 20 percent) of Catholic clergy who are homosexual (Wolf, 1989; Berry, 1993). Sexuality has been a problem for the church in other ways, as seen in the inability of American Bishops to agree on the wording of a pastoral letter on the role of women after ten years of trying. The rule of celibacy has caused many nuns and priests to leave holy orders to marry and fulfill their calling in secular roles (Waite, 1989). And, most recently, the issue of sexual abuse of children and the church's response has surfaced, involving several thousand priests and tens of thousands of underage victims over the past 40 years (Berry, 1993; Greeley, 1993a). The slowness of the hierarchy to take adequate steps to remove the priests and to acknowledge the harm done to victims has further eroded its authority.

Women and the Church

Another recent trend that has brought some turmoil to American churches is the participation of women in all aspects of religious life, including admission to the clergy. Despite long and strong resistance, over half of American Protestant denominations now accept women in the ministry, as do the Reform and Conservative branches of American Judaism. Today, almost one-third of theological school students are women.

Greatest resistance has come from the more patriarchal denominations: the Catholic churches, the Orthodox branch of Judaism, and the Mormon church. The subject has never been raised within the ranks of Islam. In Orthodox Jewish synagogues, women must remain in a special section, screened off from the main sanctuary lest they distract men from their sacred tasks. Some changes, however, have occurred in Roman Catholic ritual, in part to compensate for the shortage of ordained priests and in part to meet the demands of women for a more visible role. Many parishes have permitted girls to serve at the altar even though the practice was forbidden by the Vatican until 1994, and women have taken part in all priestly functions except hearing confessions and celebrating the Eucharist (Wallace, 1992). The door to the priesthood was firmly closed by Pope John Paul II in 1994.

For many Americans, the role of women within the church is related to broader issues of gender and sexuality (Jelen, 1989; Neitze, 1993). Here, we can clearly see the split between liberals and conservatives within the various denominations, with liberals supporting equality for women in all areas of social life, as well as acceptance of homosexuals and recognition of loving unions outside of marriage. In contrast, conservatives approve of sexual relations only in marriage, resist the ordination of homosexuals, and support norms of male dominance (Grasmick et al., 1990; Lehman, 1990; Hawley, 1994).

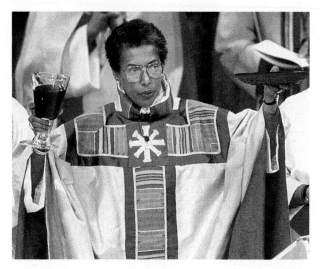

Despite a lengthy resistance, the mainstream Protestant churches, as well as reform and conservative branches of Judaism, have decided to ordain women. Barbara Harris is the first woman to be ordained as Bishop in the Episcopal Church.

Despite such obstacles, Catholic feminists continue to organize for the ordination of woman, with the support of Catholic nuns, who although fewer in number than in the past, are far more assertive and worldly and approving of feminist goals (Neal, 1991; Quinones and Turner, 1992; Ebaugh, 1993). Among Protestant and Jewish women with religious training, many are rethinking their traditions, reinterpreting sacred documents, and reconstructing rituals to include women's experience (Erikson, 1992). Other religious women, giving up hope of changing the established churches, have rediscovered centuries-old beliefs and rituals and woven them into a *women's spirituality movement* (Eller, 1993). Female centered and female controlled, the movement blends a variety of images of female power, from the ancient fertility goddesses to the beneficial witches of medieval Europe whose knowledge of herbs and healing comprised the sum of medical information for many centuries.

The issue of women and the churches illustrates a built-in problem for any religion: If the faith is "the" truth, it cannot be influenced by new ideas; however, if religious organizations cannot adapt to changing social currents, they lose their relevance. In the case of the Mormon church, for example, initial strong resistance gradually gave way to greater accommodation to women's changing roles. This shift pleased younger members but reduced the participation of older ones (Iannaccone and Miles, 1990). Outright feminists, however, are still expelled (Johnson, 1993). The difficult task for religious leadership is to adapt to social change without appearing to make a radical break with tradition.

Church and State

Another area of current debate concerns the line between church and state, which is continuously being tested. One problem lies in the First Amendment itself, which contains two rules that can come into conflict: "Congress shall make no law respecting an establishment of religion, or prohibiting the free exercise thereof." The first part, the *establishment clause,* says that the state can in no way impose religious practices or favor one faith over another. The second part, the *free exercise clause,* says that the state can in no way interfere with religious practices. The wall between church and state is tested by both religious leaders who feel called on to influence public morality and by politicians who manipulate religious symbols in support of secular goals (Johnson and Tamney, 1986).

Political activism by religious leaders takes many forms. In the 1960s, the challenge of the civil rights movement brought many clergy out of their pulpits and into the streets, where they were conspicuous in the front ranks of antisegregation marchers. Younger and more liberal clergy were thrilled at the opportunity to practice what they preached: to work for social justice. Their flocks, however, were less than thrilled and preferred to have their minister at home visiting the bereaved rather than in jail in Alabama. As a result, contributions to mainstream Protestant churches fell sharply in the 1970s. Forced to choose between the general goal of social justice and their specific duties to congregants, most clergy redefined their mission as one of serving local needs. Thus, the prophetic impulses of the 1960s gave way to an emphasis on priestly functions in the 1980s.

For church leaders still dedicated to social activism and liberal goals, the 1980s and 1990s brought new and less controversial causes: protecting the environment, preventing nuclear war, reducing world starvation, ending apartheid in South Africa, and encouraging corporations to be more ethical. In the same decades, conservative denominations also embarked on their crusades: banning abortion and pornography, restricting homosexual rights, combatting feminism and secular humanism, and returning prayer to the schools.

Given the various trends and problems confronting mainline religious organizations, it should come as no surprise that the recent religious revival in the United States is taking place outside the mainstream: (1) among the more charismatic Protestant sects, and (2) in the emergence of a wide variety of cults.

The Fundamentalist Revival in the United States

The worldwide revival of fundamentalism has affected American religious life as well. Within the Catholic church, a more emotional and participatory *charismatic movement* has special appeal to Spanish-speaking congregations (Neitz, 1987; Newman, 1992). Some scholars detect a religious revival among Orthodox Jews, although the actual numbers are quite small (Davidman, 1991; Waxman, 1992). But the major fun-

Another form of the fundamentalist revival in the United States is the annual "Success" road show, which in 1994 featured guest speakers including famous athletes, preachers, military heros, and three former presidents, Ronald Reagan, George Bush, and Gerald Ford. These practicing Christians visited 41 cities to deliver their message of how to put God to work for you. More than 16,000 people paid $49 to $225 for an eight-hour seminar in self-improvement. Here the organizer of the seminar in San Francisco's Cow Palace pumps up the crowd of eager success seekers.

damentalist movement in the United States today is rooted in a variety of Protestant sects, although extemely conservative factions have also taken over the top positions in mainline denominations with strong Southern roots.

Fundamentalism refers to a "back-to-basics" approach to religion. Fundamentalist Protestants believe that every word of the Bible must be taken literally, that Satan is a living force in this world, that a fearful destruction will precede the return of the Messiah, that humans are inherently sinful, and that there is a clear line of authority from God to His chosen ministers and then to the husband and father as head of the family (Barnhart, 1987; Ellison and Sherkat, 1993). By drawing a firm line between themselves as "true believers" and all others, fundamentalists create close-knit communities in which intensive interaction reinforces faith (Ammerman, (1993).

Because such beliefs did not fit the image of "modern" Protestantism projected by the mainline churches, the more extreme fundamentalist sects were pushed to the margins of the Protestant establishment, where they organized independently. During the first four decades of this century, periodic fundamentalist revivals, in the form of traveling tent shows featuring such charismatic figures as Aimée Semple McPherson and Billy Sunday, drew hundreds of thousands of followers eager to witness healing miracles (Epstein, 1993).

Since the early 1970s, a new set of fundamentalist sects and leaders has emerged, moving from the margins to the very center of American religious and political life (Marsden, 1991). As mainstream churches lose members, fundamentalist congregations grow and grow. Services are marked by an immediacy and

emotionality that empowers the participants. Throughout Latin America today, fundamentalist Protestantism is winning converts from Catholicism in large numbers, precisely because its rituals embrace local folk practices and give believers the feeling of taking power over their own life rather than having to work through a priestly hierarchy (Martin, 1990; Stoll, 1990; Tamney, 1992).

Another explanation for the fundamentalist revival focuses on its functions for people who believe that they are losing control over their way of life and that their traditions are mocked by a cultural elite. This interpretation is supported by data on the social characteristics of fundamentalists— Southerners and Midwesterners who grew up in small towns, the elderly, and people with limited educational and occupational statuses (Hunter, 1987). These are subgroups whose sense of mastery has been eroded by the forces of secularization and by the shift from local to national economic and political decision making. In their eyes, the failures of modernity were plain to see as the 1960s and 1970s offered one example after another of the breakdown of social order: student protest, antiwar demonstrations, assassinations, riots, civil rights activism, the women's movement, homosexual marches, the ambiguous ending of the Vietnam war, the Watergate scandal, and Supreme Court decisions on school prayer and abortion (Paloma, 1989).

The enemy was clear: the spirit of the modern age that places people rather than God at the center of life. The solution was renewed faith in the old-time religion, based on an unchanging, eternal truth. But this "new" old-time religion differed from earlier versions in two important ways: its involvement in electoral politics, and the use of such mod-

Aimée Semple McPherson was a charismatic evangelist who toured the country healing and saving souls. In 1933 she delivered a sermon in New York City's Bowery section where a group of homeless men knelt and prayed with her.

ern devices as the electronic media by "prime-time preachers."

THE NEW CHRISTIAN RIGHT.   Because of their vulnerable position as unaffiliated sects, fundamentalist congregations had historically been strong supporters of the separation of church and state, desiring only to be left alone to worship as they saw fit. It was a major shift, therefore, when, in the late 1970s, fundamentalist leaders joined forces with extremely conservative political action groups to form the **New Christian Right (NCR)** (Liebman and Wuthnow, 1983). By combining their mailing lists, media know-how, and funding sources, organizations that had once been considered "too extremist" entered the political mainstream.

The alliance gained legitimacy in the presidential election of 1980, when its candidates won the White House and a dozen Senate seats. Although studies now suggest that the NCR was not as powerful a voting bloc as the media originally claimed, the publicity gave its leaders an opportunity to define a "Christian agenda" on a range of issues reflecting deeply held beliefs and values: *against* abortion, homosexual rights, the women's movement, gun control, and sex education; and *for* school prayer, defense spending, "family values," and removal of offensive library materials (Wilcox, 1992).

The alliance held together for the 1982 and 1984 elections, thanks to the great popularity of its friend in the White House, Ronald Reagan, and generous funding from wealthy families such as the DuPonts and major corporations such as Pepsico and Mobil Oil (Magrass, 1986). But with so many different organizations and interests, conflict among its leaders was inevitable. Nor are followers always obedient or even of one mind on the issues (Ammerman, 1993; Berke, 1994b). By the end of the decade, the NCR appeared to have lost much of its unity and clout. At the 1992 Republican Convention, the uncompromising positions of its representatives actually diminished rather than enhanced its political influence. But reports of the death of the Christian Right were premature. From the ashes of the NCR, a new religious-political organization has risen, called the Christian Coalition.

THE CHRISTIAN COALITION.   A grassroots movement with the same agenda and following as the NCR, the **Christian Coalition** is much more politically sophisticated. For example, instead of focusing on such divisive issues as abortion and school prayer, its candidates talk about topics with wide appeal, such as lower taxes, more crime control, and family-centered concerns (Reed, 1993). In 1992, the Coalition won hundreds of races for state legislatures, town councils, and local school boards, as well as control of the Republican Party organization in several states. In 1994, the Coalition was the big winner

in the Republican sweep of Congressional seats. The ability of the Christian Coalition to activate its core of highly motivated members gives it an advantage in off-year elections, when voter turnout is typically very low.

PRIME-TIME PREACHERS.   The decline of the NCR is partly linked to the spectacular rise and fall of television ministries in the 1980s. Some aspects of modernity were eagerly adopted by fundamentalist leaders: radio, television, and mass mailings. Mainstream ministers considered themselves above such commercial techniques for spreading the word. Fundamentalist preachers, however, immediately grasped the opportunity to reach large numbers of people with a clear and simple message. Noting the success of Billy Graham in the 1970s, whose positions were close to mainstream Protestantism, the "prime-time preachers" of the 1980s used similar techniques to send out a much more conservative and more politicized message (Hadden, 1993).

During the heyday of televised religious broadcasting, fundamentalist Protestant preachers such as Jerry Falwell, Jimmy Swaggart, Pat Robertson, Oral Roberts, and Jim and Tammy Faye Bakker reached tens of millions of viewers each week and collected hundreds of millions of dollars each year from responses to the televised toll-free phone numbers displayed throughout the telecasts. Viewers were hungry for plain talk and emotionally moving experiences; they did not want intellectual discussions of moral ambiguities by graduates of mainstream theological seminaries. In contrast, the fundamentalist preachers were products of Bible schools, and they spoke in the earthy accents of the American South and Midwest rather than the upper-class tone of the Eastern private schools attended by the mainline clergy. Because they were not part of the network of mainline churches, they founded their own congregations. Clearly, prime-time preachers are close to their audience, not only in terms of social class but also ideologically and emotionally. During the 1980s, the preachers used their electronic pulpits to support the political agenda of the Republican Party and both Ronald Reagan and George Bush addressed their annual conventions as the line between church and state blurred and eroded.

Then, in the late 1980s, came "the fall," in biblical fashion, of Jimmy Swaggart and Jim Bakker for sexual misconduct. Bakker was also convicted on charges of fraudulently selling partnerships in his theme village, Heritage USA. By 1993, Jerry Falwell's religious organi-

> **The New Christian Right (NCR)** was formed by a combination of fundamentalist leaders and extremely conservative political action groups.
>
> **The Christian Coalition** is a politically sophisticated grassroots movement with the same agenda and following as the NCR.

Billy Graham is one of the pioneers of the electronic ministry who has remained popular in the United Sates and in Europe. A few years ago he attracted 250,000 people to the Billy Graham Crusade in New York's Central Park; later he visited Russia and again drew huge crowds, including this one in Moscow

zation was close to bankruptcy, which was due to a sharp drop in viewer contributions as well as losing its tax-exempt status for engaging in illegal political activity. Only Pat Robertson survived relatively untouched, to become the inspirational leader of the Christian Coalition and the scourge of Bill and Hillary Clinton.

Yet, despite the falloff in television ratings and contributions in the late 1980s, religious broadcasting has not disappeared from the airwaves. Can you identify the rising stars of "Pray TV"? Or of the 1,200 Christian radio stations around the nation?

EVANGELICALISM. Although the term **evangelical** is often used interchangeably with *fundamentalist,* the two forms of Protestantism are not the same. Not all evangelicals share the fundamentalists' extremely conservative social and political positions (Warner, 1988). Evangelicals stress personal witnessing of God's presence and an oblig-

> **Evangelical** refers to an emphasis on the personal witnessing of God's presence coupled with an obligation to spread the Word.
>
> **Born again** means having an experience that changes one's life through the acceptance of the Lord.
>
> **Cults** and **New Religious Movements (NRMs)** have developed outside the mainstream religions, compete with them for members, and have attracted attention as a result of members' unusual behavior and fear generated among joiners' families.

ation to spread the Good Word. A central concept is being **born again,** having a personal revelation that changes one's life through complete acceptance of the Lord. A public announcement of this rebirth brings` the weight of the community to bear on future conduct.

Although the enthusiasm of their witnessing and relatively lower social status originally set the evangelicals apart from mainstream Protestantism, they were never as distant as the fundamentalists. In addition, the evangelicals' encounter with modernity has moderated much of their traditional conservatism. They have become less strict regarding drinking and sex and less rigidly patriarchal (Hunter, 1987).

Cults and the New Religious Movements

Another source of competition with mainstream religions is the variety of cults attracting both young and older adults. Although politically and numerically less important than the fundamentalist revival, the cults have attracted much media attention because of the sometime unusual beliefs and behaviors of joiners. Some of the modern cults are offshoots of fundamentalism, others derive from Eastern religions; some are focused on the supernatural, others on the self.

The New Religious Movements (NRMs) based on non-Western belief systems include Zen Buddhism, very popular among young students in the 1960s; Yoga as a form of self-discipline; Hare Krishna followers; and dozens of smaller groups centered on obedience to a guru, or "wise one." One such guru, the late Bhagwan Shree Rajneesh, brought his educated middle-class following to the backwoods of Oregon, where he also collected dozens of Rolls Royces before being deported as an illegal alien (Carter, 1990). Other frequently studied NRMs are the Church of Scientology (a self-improvement cult with a spiritual overlay) and the Unification Church (nominally Christian) created by a charismatic leader, the Rev. Sun Myung Moon, whose followers are popularly known as Moonies.

The Unification Church

Although the Unification Church claims a membership of 50,000 in the United States, most scholars place the actual number at a few thousand (Berger, 1992). Despite such small numbers, the Unification Church has drawn an enormous amount of publicity, in part because of what some observers perceive as illegitimate recruitment activities, and in part because of its links to the New Religious Right and its apparent wealth and political influence. The Unification Church departs from mainline Christianity in its belief that the Rev. Moon is the new Messiah and in the practice of recruiting mostly young people who then live in group quarters and work full time for the church, selling flowers and flags on the streets, or in one of the church's commercial enterprises.

Parents of recruits have difficulty understanding how their children can cut themselves completely off from previous ties to follow the word of a Korean businessman who claims to have spoken with Jesus, Moses, and Buddha. The only explanation that parents can accept is that innocent youngsters have been brainwashed, weakened by poor diets, and held against their will. Under such circumstances, it is perfectly legitimate to rekidnap their children and to "deprogram" them. In addition, critics claim that such groups are not real "religions" deserving of First Amendment protections.

SOCIAL POLICY

Brainwashing or Normal Conversion?

Do cults kidnap innocent victims and hold them by force? If so, should the government decide which are true religions and which are not? Parental concerns over NRM recruitment led to formation of a Cult Awareness Network, supported by many psychologists and religious leaders who claim that recruits are forcibly detained and subjected to mind control and coercive persuasion (Ofshe and Singer, 1986).

A different viewpoint is held by most sociologists of religion, who consider the attacks on the NRMs empirically unfounded and a dangerous threat to religious freedom (e.g., Richardson, 1989). Although there may be a few cases of extreme force, the career of a typical joiner follows a fairly standard scenario. Recruitment takes place among young people who are *structurally available,* that is, temporarily without other close ties—a first-year or transfer student or someone between jobs or relationships (Miller, 1992b). They are befriended and introduced to the group by another young person. Seeking community and acceptance, they find it.

Without any major ideological conversion to the beliefs of the NRM, the recruit will nonetheless become committed through a series of small tasks (selling flowers at an airport, chanting on a street corner). Once these actions are taken, the mind invents reasons for having done so; otherwise, one would have to admit having made a dreadful mistake. This process is not "brainwashing" in any technical sense, but it operates with great speed to produce conversion to the new belief system. Nor is it very different from the process of joining a "respectable" church through interpersonal ties and a desire to become part of a community of believers.

The longer one stays, the deeper the investment of self in the role, and the harder it is to leave. Yet recruits do leave, in large numbers, voluntarily, and almost immediately (Wright, 1991). The NRM is not interested in forcibly restraining unwilling members. Under what circumstances might you become a likely recruit to a New Religious Movement? How would you deal with being kidnapped and deprogrammed by people hired by your parents?

Cults and Public Fears

There are many dangers in attempting to define what is a "true" religion or "real" conversion experience. All the major world religions began as cults that aroused great suspicion, and most were led by charismatic figures as unusual in their day as the Rev. Moon is today. Yet, under pressure from parents and the media, legislators often try to define some cults as outside the protection of the First Amendment, attempts which the courts have generally held unconstitutional. Where cult leaders have been successfully prosecuted, it has been for secular crimes such as tax evasion or consumer fraud. Church rituals, beliefs, and finances are largely protected from government oversight. Several recent events, however, have reopened this debate, including fears of satanic cults and the fiery deaths of the Branch Davidians in Waco, Texas, in 1993.

SATANIC SACRIFICES OR SCARES?   The fundamentalist revival of the past two decades produced a heightened awareness of evil in the modern world, leading to a sharp increase in reports of satanic rituals, of music recordings with hidden messages, of movies and games with evil themes, and of devil worship among the wealthy and powerful. How else to explain the temptations of modern life that cause children to turn away from traditional values (Richardson et al., 1991)?

There is also money to be made from the satanism scare—from books and lectures and workshops to alert local police and parents about the dangers that lurk in the popular culture (Shupe, 1990). All this has occurred despite a continued lack of empirical evidence of widespread satanic sacrifices, or of any large-scale organized cult activity other than the usual incidents of unstable people claiming to be possessed, or teenagers trying to shock their elders (G. Goodman, 1994). Most of the evil in this world, it appears, has perfectly human roots.

RELIGIOUS WARFARE IN WACO: DAVID KORESH AND THE BRANCH DAVIDIANS.   In 1993, as television screens played on, members of the U.S. Bureau of Alcohol, Tobacco, and Firearms (ATF) launched a full-scale attack on a compound occupied by a breakaway sect of Seventh Day Adventists called Branch Davidians. Official grounds for the 51-day siege were that weapons had been illegally stockpiled (not uncommon in that part of Texas), but the more immediate reason appeared to be that after four agents had been killed during a botched raid, the ATF could not appear to back down.

The Branch Davidians had lived in the Waco compound for several years, relatively isolated from the rest of the community, following an earlier shootout with a rival sect. Their charismatic leader was David Koresh, who had worked for the Seventh Day Adventist church until he broke away to form his own "branch" of the faith. But the Waco group shaded from sect into cult as the intensity of their dependence on Koresh increased. They believed that the end of the world was near, that it would take the violent form prophesied in the Bible, that Koresh was the Messiah, and that they needed to stockpile food and weapons for the coming cataclysm. The ATF obliged by conducting precisely the bloody attack that the Davidians awaited.

But the answer to the question of how seemingly ordinary people could follow such a leader to their death lies less in ideology than in the social structure of any cult.

Cults Demystified

The Waco incident was reminiscent of the mass suicide of several hundred followers of the charismatic leader, Jim Jones, over a decade earlier. In both cases, the key to power was the leader's total control over information and over sexual relationships. The cult must be isolated from regular contact with surrounding communities and the outside world in general. Both Jones and Koresh were the only ones to have access to a radio or television set, so that followers had no way to check the accuracy of the information received from their leader. Both men also disturbed existing primary relationships, between husbands and wives and between parents and children. They alone were entitled to have many partners, so that competing ties of intimacy were destroyed in favor of sexual links to the leader. Under such extreme conditions, followers become pawns in the hands of someone whom they have endowed with superhuman qualities.

Most cults, however, stop short of such total control. Of the approximately 2,000 cult-like groups in the United States, only a few hundred live in self-confined isolation, and the vast majority are peaceable in doctrine and behavior (Raschke, 1990). Indeed, there is much in American society that ensures the persistence of cults, in addition to the legal protections offered all

The New Age Movement (NAM) includes an array of beliefs seeking to understand the universe through contact with the supernatural, psychic healing, reincarnation, and similar mystical experiences.

believers: a long history of unusual religious fads and periodic revivals of fundamentalism, the dislocations of modern industrialism, and the coming of the millennium (the end of one century and beginning of another). Thus it is likely that the next few years will see both an increase in exotic end-of-the-world cultism and renewed efforts to outlaw them.

The most common pattern for cults and sects, however, is that over time, the strangeness wears off, compromises are made with the secular world, and public hostility declines (Wilson, 1990). This process may also come to characterize another type of popular cult-like activity, less openly religious and more attuned to nature and self-awareness.

The New Age Movement

The fastest growing spiritual trend in the United States today embraces a variety of beliefs generally referred to as the **New Age Movement (NAM).** The NAM attracts a more educated and occupationally secure set of searchers for meaning than do other NRMs. New Agers seek to understand the universe through a mix of mysticism, contact with a spirit world, and other paranormal (outside the everyday) events. The 1994 Whole Life Exposition in New York City, for example, featured psychic readers, lectures on the thousands of Americans kidnapped by aliens from Unidentified Flying Objects, consultations with an angel and other departed spirits, discussions of near-death experiences, hundreds of astrologers, books on reincarnation, displays of rock crystals with healing properties, and products for the nonmedical health care of pets as well as humans.

Interestingly, although most Americans consider such beliefs harmful to traditional religious faith, they, themselves, believe in psychic healing, astrology, and extrasensory perception (Gallup, 1991; Hess, 1993). As modern life appears increasingly out of personal control, some people seek new ways to understand complex mysteries.

In their emphasis on the nonmedical dimensions of health and healing, the New Age philosophies also fit into a larger movement toward a *holistic* view of the relationship between body and mind and of self and the natural world (McGuire, 1993). The NAM appeal to many relatively sophisticated people may lie in its attention to environmental themes and to an individualistic spirituality that bypasses established modes of worship through yoga and meditation (Harris, 1994).

LAST WORDS ON BELIEVING AND BELONGING

What, then, can we conclude about the current state of sacred and secular ideologies in the United States? It seems clear that many children of the Baby Boom, and their children, are abandoning the religious mainstream, although some will eventually return to their traditional affiliations (Roof, 1993; Johnson et al., 1992). Most continue to believe in God but prefer to remain unaffiliated. Some will find their faith renewed and redoubled in a fundamentalist/charismatic congregation, and still others will be attracted to the New Age Movement.

In terms of both believing and belonging, Americans are more religious today than ever before, in part because of the wide range of choices available to believers (Finke and Stark, 1992). The tendency for denominations to divide into sects, the emergence of cults, and the variety of faiths brought by recent immigrants have all produced a *religious pluralism* to match all the other pluralistic aspects of American society as well as the multicultural world system in which we participate.

Indeed, many sociologists now speak of a "religious marketplace," where various belief systems compete for the allegiance of an increasingly individualized public (Hammond, 1992; Finke and Stark, 1992; Nauta, 1993; Warner, 1993). In this competition, the more expressive and personally empowering faiths appear to be the winners, at least for the moment. There is something here for everyone who seeks meaning and community. There are so many choices and so few certainties. Is it any wonder, then, that many Americans have become "spiritual junkies," moving from one to another of the experiences available in our pluralistic religious universe? In the long run, however, we have more to fear from those who would narrow the definition of "true religion," than we do from those who seek to expand the boundaries of belief.

SUMMARY

1. Shared ideas about the meaning of life constitute a belief system.

2. Religion is a belief system based on the concept of a divine being guiding people's destiny and directed toward the supernatural.

3. All belief systems have certain elements in common: ideas about the meaning of life, the use of rituals, and a community of believers. The beliefs relieve personal anxiety and bring members of the group together.

4. Every belief system has an origin myth, rules of conduct, and a vision of the future. This is true both of religions, based on faith in supernatural powers, and of secular ideologies, based on human efforts in this world.

5. According to sociologists, the specific beliefs of any group emerge from its history and social structure.

6. Every religion distinguishes between the sacred and the profane and constructs rituals that help people deal with major transitions and times of danger.

7. Belief systems have a dual nature: They are conservative and support the status quo, but they also serve as agents of social change. Weber's distinction between the priestly and the prophetic function focuses on this duality.

8. Modernization and secularization have had profound effects on contemporary religious practices and organizations. The secular way of thinking emphasizes scientific explanations and rationality, thus challenging beliefs in divine forces and values based on faith.

9. Religious beliefs and affiliation remain important to the majority of Americans. Our tradition of religious tolerance has led to the institutionalization of an American civil religion in which patriotism and faith are blended.

10. While religion has always served as a spiritual source for the oppressed around the world, African-American churches represent the only major institution in the members' world that is not under white control.

11. Religious divisions within our society are no longer between churches but between religious liberals and conservatives within each church. Such differences are linked to social background and to different reactions to political and economic changes.

12. The Roman Catholic church shares the problems of mainstream religion, but its hierarchical and patriarchal organization generates some specific issues for Catholics.

13. The participation of women has increased in all aspects of religious life. Today, women account for one-third of all students at theological seminaries.

14. Over the past four decades, dramatic changes have occurred in involvement in secular matters by church leaders.

15. Much spiritual renewal is taking place outside mainstream churches through the rise of Protestant fundamentalism and the emergence of various cults.

16. Fundamentalism represents a back-to-basics approach to religion, resisting modernity and the

many changes taking place in our society. The growth in memberships of fundamentalist sects has become a powerful force in conservative politics.

17. Cults appeal to younger, more highly educated believers, who are attracted by the companionship and acceptance of others, by the seeming certainty of the beliefs, and by the authority of the leader.

18. For older, educated believers, a number of New Age and self-improvement cults enjoy widespread popularity.

19. In America today, belief systems seem to be available for any person who seeks identity and meaning in a spiritual context.

SUGGESTED READINGS

Beckford, James A. *Religion and Advanced Industrial Society.* London and Boston: Unwin Hyman, 1989. The author challenges traditional theorists of religion and builds a convincing argument for parallels between the New Social Movements and contemporary forms of religious behavior.

Boyer, Paul. *When Time Shall Be No More: Prophecy Belief in Modern America.* Cambridge, MA: Belknap Press, 1992. Fascinating and witty, American premillennialist prophecy pamphlets since the 1940s are the subject of study in this engaging book. Premillennialism (the belief that the end of the world is imminent and foretold) is tracked through its historical roots and societal attitudes and opinions.

McNamara, Patrick H. *Conscience First, Tradition Second: A Study of Young American Catholics.* Albany: State University of New York Press, 1992. A unique contribution to the study of religious identity that sheds light on the relationship between cultural and institutional changes and subsequent changes in believers' religious identities.

Reader, Ian. *Religion in Contemporary Japan.* Honolulu: University of Hawaii Press, 1991. An overview of contemporary religious behavior in Japan.

Richardson, James T., Joel Best, and David G. Bromley. *The Satanism Scare.* New York: Aldine de Gruyter, 1991. A critical look at our fascination with "satanic cults," our fears of cults and how those fears develop, and the industries spawned by anti-Satanists.

Roof, Wade Clark. *A Generation of Seekers.* New York: Harper Collins, 1993. The religious lives of baby boomers are probed and a diversity of patterns discovered.

Stein, Stephen J. *The Shaker Experience in America: A History of the United Society of Believers.* New Haven: Yale University Press, 1992. A fascinating look at Shaker history that strips away the myths that surround this group and indicates a dynamic culture deep in conflict.

Wallace, Ruth A. *They Call Her Pastor: A New Role for Catholic Women.* Albany: State University of New York Press, 1992. A discussion of the issues, interactions and responses to female pastors in twenty Roman Catholic parishes across the United States.

Wuthnow, Robert. *Rediscovering the Sacred: Perspectives on Religion in Contemporary Society.* Grand Rapids, MI: Eerdmans, 1992. An examination of religion's steady presence not always evident in a traditional sense but transformed into new patterns and expressions.

17

Law, Crime, and the Criminal Justice System

THE ROLE OF LAW
Theoretical Perspectives on Law
Theoretical Perspectives on Crime

CRIME IN THE UNITED STATES
Crime in the Streets
Female Criminals
Organized Crime
Crime in the Suites: White-Collar and Organizational Crime
Crimes without Victims

THE POLICE AND LAW ENFORCEMENT
Private Policing

JUVENILE DELINQUENCY AND THE JUVENILE JUSTICE SYSTEM
Juvenile Justice

ADULT COURT SYSTEMS
Processing the Criminal
SOCIOLOGISTS AT WORK "Studying the Death Penalty" by Michael J. Radelet
Prisons and Jails
SOCIAL POLICY Alternatives to Prison
SUMMARY ■ SUGGESTED READINGS

*I*n mid-1994, the following news items made the front pages:

- Defense contractor admits falsifying test data on a missile system used in the war in the Persian Gulf.
- Drive-by shooting claims the life of another bystander.
- Vice squad officers testify about their off-duty careers as thieves, extortionists, and drug dealers.
- A well-known entertainer dies from inhaling heroin, the latest drug of choice of the jet set.
- Fans cheer a former football star accused of the brutal slaying of his ex-wife and her friend.
- Major hospital chain is fined for Medicare fraud and pattern of bribes and kickbacks for physician referrals.
- Convictions of low-level drug dealers climb, as state prisons overflow.
- Another prisoner is executed in Texas.

The different events in the preceding list suggest the wide variety of illegal activity and societal reactions to be discussed in this chapter. In Chapter 6, we described the tension between conformity and deviance, and the mechanisms of social control that maintain social order. In this chapter, we examine violations of the rules that are defined as *criminal*, actions specifically forbidden by law and that therefore require the intervention of formal agents of law enforcement.

As Emile Durkheim noted, deviance is a necessary part of social life for its latent functions of (1) continually reminding citizens of the limits of acceptable behavior and of (2) generating solidarity around support for the rules and condemnation of violators. What varies across societies and historical periods are the range of activities covered by law and the effectiveness of social controls.

The idea that crime is more than a wrong against another person but is also a wrong against society is very old. For much of human history, however, punishment was left to the injured persons and their family. Gradually, as a society becomes more complex, enforcement of important norms is defined as a function of the community as a whole, whose powers are also limited by the law. The ancient principle of an "eye for an eye," for example, ensured that the punishment would be no greater than the original harm.

Over time, criminal codes and systems of social control become increasingly elaborate, and variations across societies become so great that cross-cultural comparisons are difficult. In this chapter, then, we are primarily concerned with the extent and variety of criminal activity in the United States, and the ways in which crime and criminals are controlled through police, courts, jails, and prisons.

THE ROLE OF LAW

Laws are norms that cover behaviors essential to collective well-being: they define what actions are legitimate and what will be treated as criminal, and they also specify how the legal system itself must operate (Sanders, 1992). In simple societies, social order is maintained through informal sanctions, and individuals conform out of custom and the fear of losing the support of the primary group. In a complex society, enforcement of the folkways and mores also tend to be localized and limited, with most disputes resolved without going to court (Ellickson, 1991). But an increasing number of laws become *institutionalized*—embedded in a universal code enforced by formal authorities.

A distinction is usually made between acts that violate the interests of private citizens (the *civil law*) and acts that are considered a threat to the best interests of the community (the *criminal law*). Just what is covered by the criminal law varies over time. Many of the acts etched in the Ten Commandments are still considered criminal in the United States today: murder, stealing, perjury (giving false testimony), and adultery. Other behaviors, such as worshiping many gods or being envious, are matters of individual choice. And many new crimes have been added: selling drugs, sexual harassment, and blowing up a public building. For a short period in the 1920s, it was illegal to make or sell hard liquor, a law that was so widely violated it was soon repealed.

> **Laws** are norms that govern behavior considered essential to group survival.
>
> A **conflict approach** to criminal justice assumes that laws serve the interests of the dominant social strata.

Theoretical Perspectives on Law

It is commonly assumed that the law protects citizens from harm and promotes societal well-being. This *social injury* approach evades the issue of who has the power to define the social interest and to decide what is harmful to whom.

From a functional perspective, norms become laws when they reflect general agreement, or *consensus*, about appropriate behavior. Debate over values ultimately strengthens social cohesion. Although recognizing the importance of economic inequality in encouraging crime, functionalists tend to see such problems as temporary and capable of being corrected through social policy (Gibbons, 1987).

In contrast, a **conflict approach** assumes that economic inequality and power differences are cen-

The United States Supreme Court is the final court of appeals, and through their decisions the justices interpret American law. Capital punishment, privacy issues, racial and sexual discrimination, abortion, and who gets custody of frozen embryos have been some of the legal issues considered in recent decisions.

tral to constructing laws and to guiding the agents of social control (Quinney, 1977; Mosher and Hagan, 1994). Thus, the law tends to reflect the interests of the social strata that dominate the government and the courts, at the expense of the powerless, while also claiming to represent an objective, rational, universal truth (Fitzpatrick, 1992; Turk, 1993). For example, current efforts to control the movement of street people or that set curfews for teenagers clearly protect the property of shopkeepers and homeowners by limiting the rights of the poor and young, just as laws against public drunkenness in the early 1900s were aimed at immigrants whose life-style offended middle-class Americans (Brown and Warner, 1992). At the same time, many actions extremely dangerous to the general public are not as clearly defined as criminal: faulty bridge construction, inadequate asbestos protection, performing unnecessary surgery.

> The law in its majestic equality forbids both rich and poor alike to sleep under bridges, to beg in the streets, and to steal bread.
>
> —ANATOLE FRANCE, 1894/1917

In addition, critics claim that the law is used not only to control potentially disruptive populations but also to remove surplus workers from the labor pool by imprisonment (Chiricos and DeLone, 1992). Finally, from the conflict perspective, the field of *crime control* itself is seen as a profitable activity, employing a cast of tens of thousands of lawyers, judges, prison guards, police officers, court personnel, and social workers—all of whom would be out of a job if the crime rate decreased.

Theoretical Perspectives on Crime

The major sociological perspectives on crime build on models of deviant behavior presented in Chapter 6: blocked opportunity, differential association, inequality, and anomie. The gap between aspiration and reality is a breeding ground for illegal behaviors that are learned and reinforced in primary groups and supported by norms and values generated within criminal subcultures. Not surprisingly, unemployment rates are directly and indirectly linked to crime rates, especially property offenses (Britt, 1994). Much crime can be viewed as attempts to "do" masculinity when legitimate sources of power are not available (Messerchmidt, 1993).

In contrast to an emphasis on inequality and poverty, the **social control model** highlights the bonds that reinforce law-abiding activity: marriage, steady employment, religious affiliation, and community ties (Kempf, 1993; Jensen, 1993). Can such ties overcome the effects of early exposure to a crime-promoting environment? Some sociologists argue that children who fail to develop *self-control* at an early age are destined for a life of deviance, especially in the absence of "good" role models (Gottfredson and Hirschi, 1990; DiIulio, 1993). Yet evidence also indicates that troubled youths can become conforming adults, with the help of a stable job and strong marriage

The **social control model** highlights the bonds that reinforce law-abiding activity.

(Sampson and Laub, 1993). Peer influence can also be reduced by other aspects of the school culture and by time spent with parents (Warr, 1993; Felson et al., 1994).

Other researchers utilize the **routine activity,** or **lifestyle opportunity, approach** (Hindelang et al., 1978). This model assumes that criminals make rational choices about which targets offer maximum rewards at the least risk. As ordinary citizens engage in the routine activities of daily life (going to work, shopping, taking a bus, dining out, or staying at home), they offer more or less attractive targets to thieves. If these activities take place where there is a low probability of being caught, the criminal will be highly motivated; where police are visible, the criminal is less likely to strike. Therefore, a major shift in routine activities will produce a change in crime rates. For example, when women enter the labor force or when there is an increase in dining out, more homes are left unguarded during the day, and more people with money are out at night; theft and robbery rates will rise because of *increased opportunities* (Cook, 1986; Messner and Blau, 1987). But increased opportunity may not produce higher crime rates if it also leads to increased use of protective devices such as burglar alarms, guard dogs, and private police (Miethe et al., 1991).

This model has great appeal to sociologists for its focus on aspects of the social environment that encourage or discourage criminality rather than on the psychological makeup of the criminal (Blau and Blau, 1982). For example, in explaining rates of interracial crime, the most powerful variable is the extent to which members of different races are likely to come into contact with one another. It is the structure of urban life that predicts rates of black–white homicides and rapes in different cities (South and Felson, 1990; Messner and South, 1992).

The assumption that criminals make **rational choices,** weighing costs and benefits, is also open to question, at least for crimes of violence. An increase in arrest rates in New York City, for example, did not reduce rates for murder, rape, and assault, although robberies declined (Corman and Joyce, 1990). The decision to commit a property crime, however, is based less on fear of punishment than on the likelihood of being caught (Tunnell, 1992).

> The **routine-activity,** or **life-style/opportunity, approach** assumes that criminals will target situations that offer the maximum rewards at the least risk.
>
> **Rational-choice theory** assumes that criminals weigh costs and benefits of committing crimes.
>
> **Street crimes** are actions that directly threaten people or property.

CRIME IN THE UNITED STATES

Crime in the Streets

Although fear of crime is widespread and crime stories fill our newspapers and television screens, overall rates for most crimes have actually *declined* since 1981, as seen in Figure 17-1. The rate for **street crimes,** acts that directly threaten a person's life or property, rose during the 1970s and then declined to a fairly stable plateau in the 1980s before rising slightly in the mid-1990s. In part, this pattern reflects major changes in the age distribution of the population, as the baby boomers outgrew their crime-prone years. That is, because most crime is committed by men age 18–24, crime rates will fluctuate as members of this age group form a smaller or larger part of the entire population. Although rates for assault, rape, and robbery remained steady in the 1990s, the number of murders increased, especially those committed by younger teenagers (U.S. Department of Justice, 1994h). Because these juveniles have not yet reached their peak crime-prone years, it is possible that the American homicide rate will mushroom in the late 1990s. In addition, the proportion of serious violent crime involving handgun use also rose in the early 1990s (U.S. Department of Justice, 1994d).

Figure 17-1 Households reporting victimization by selected crimes, 1975–1992.

Source: U.S. Department of Justice, 1994a.

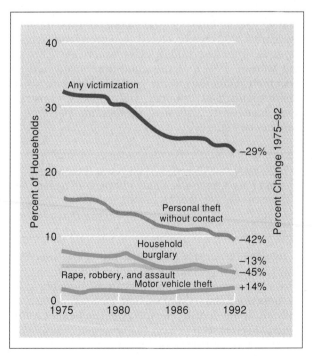

TABLE 17-1 Victimization Rates for Personal Crimes of Violence and Assaults: United States, 1992

	Number per 1,000 persons age 12+
Race	
African American	111
White	89
Other	88
Sex	
Male	101
Female	82
Age	
12–15	171
16–19	173
20–24	177
25–34	111
35–49	75
50–64	43
65+	21
Family income	
Under $7,500	65
7,500–14,999	35
15,500–24,999	33
25,000–29,999	36
30,000–49,999	27
50,000+	22
Place of residence	
Central city	116
Suburbs	85
Other	72

Source: Department of Justice, 1994a.

MEASURING CRIME. In the United States, two major data sources are used to measure the extent of crime. The ***Uniform Crime Reports*** (**UCR**) are compiled by the Federal Bureau of Investigation (FBI) from monthly and yearly reports submitted by state and local law enforcement agencies. The eight most serious offenses that form the base of the FBI crime index are: (1) violent crimes such as murder and nonnegligent manslaughter, forcible rape, robbery, and aggravated assault and (2) property crimes such as burglary, larceny, motor vehicle theft, and arson. Rates for most of these **index crimes** in 1992 are shown in Table 17-2. Note that these are acts most likely to be committed by poor people; the crimes of the wealthy and powerful do not appear in the Index, and will be discussed later in this chapter.

> *Uniform Crime Reports* (**UCR**) are compiled by the FBI from city, state, and county police information.
>
> **Index crimes** include the violent crimes of murder, forcible rape, robbery, and aggravated assault.
>
> The *National Crime Victimization Survey* (**NCVS**) collects self-reported experiences of victimization from U.S. households.

Although the UCR are widely cited by the mass media, they have two major shortcomings: (1) The data reported by various agencies are not always comparable; states and localities differ in crime definition, reporting techniques, willingness to do paper work, and deliberate falsifications. (2) Fewer than 40 percent of all crimes are reported to the police, because many victims are unwilling to make the effort or to run the risk of retaliation. Thus, the UCR greatly underestimates the actual volume of criminal activity.

To supplement the UCR, the Department of Justice conducts a ***National Crime Victimization Survey*** (**NCVS**) of close to 50,000 randomly selected households. Twice a year, household members are asked about any experience of victimization,

Table 17-1 shows the rates of criminal victimization for various subgroups. The most likely to be victims of a street crime are men, young adults, African Americans, city dwellers, and people with low income. Curiously, the people most fearful of crime—women and the elderly—are the least likely to be victimized. Most violent crime in the United States involves victims and offenders of the same race; indeed, the great majority are acquainted with one another (U.S. Department of Justice, 1994b). Nonetheless, fear of strangers is very common (Riedel, 1993), and an influx of minority youth into a neighborhood will generate high levels of fear among current residents (Taylor and Covington, 1993).

TABLE 17-2 Offenses Known to Police (Index Crimes), 1992. (Rate per 100,000 population age 12 and over.)

Murder	9.3
Rape	42.8
Robbery	263.6
Aggravated assault	441.8
Burglarly	1168.2
Larceny/theft	3103.0
Motor vehicle theft	631.5

Source: U.S. Department of Justice, 1994h, p. 352.

Chris OBrion, *The Freelance Star*, Fredericksburg, Va.

whether reported or not. By comparing these data with the UCR, we can see that only four in ten victimizations are reported to local authorities. The data in Figure 17-1 and Table 17-1 are from the NVCS. Interestingly, while the NCVS shows a sharp drop in household victimizations, the UCR records only a slight decrease. Apparently, the volume of crime has declined, but victims are more likely to report an incident, perhaps because of insurance requirements.

Property crimes such as burglary, larceny, and theft are much more prevalent than crimes against people.

HOMICIDE. The United States has the dubious distinction of having the highest rate of homicide (intentional murder) in the industrial world. For example, in 1992, the U.S. homicide rate per 100,000 people was 10.0, ten times higher than for France or Germany and 17 times that of Japan (Yanagishita and MacKellar, 1995).

Although it is widely believed that access to handguns is a major factor in the American homicide rate, the empirical evidence is mixed. Gun ownership in the United States is so widespread that it is difficult to prove a direct link with violent crime (Kleck, 1991). Nonetheless, firearms are a leading cause of death among young Americans, accounting for almost half of all deaths among African-American men aged 15–24 (Fingerhut et al., 1994). In addition, having a gun in one's home almost triples the chances that someone will be killed in that home, and the victim won't be a stranger: In one large-scale study, 77 percent of home-based handgun homicides were committed by a family member or friend (Kellerman et al., 1993).

Even if every homicide victim had been shot, we would still have to explain variations in homicide rates among subgroups. The variables shown to have the greatest impact on homicide rates in modern democratic societies are social and economic inequality and racial segregation (Balkwell, 1990; Rosenfeld and Messner, 1991; Peterson and Krivo, 1993). And the United States has more of both than do other industrial nations.

In the United States, men accounted for two of every three victims and 96 percent of the offenders. Men are killed by other men, and women by men whom they know (U.S. Department of Justice, 1993a). Cross-cultural data indicate that a woman's risk of being a homicide victim is highest when she is not embedded in traditional roles, that is, in societies with high divorce rates, single-parent households, delayed marriage, and high levels of women's labor force participation (Gartner et al., 1990). In the United States, female homicide rates are highest in those states where gender inequality and exposure to pornography are highest (Messner, 1991). Conversely, female victimization rates are lowest where women's social power and educational level are more equal to that of men. When U.S. states are ranked by handgun murder rates, all twelve Southern states appear among the top 20 (Morgan Quinto, 1994).

PROPERTY CRIMES. As you saw in Table 17-2, the number of crimes against people is relatively small compared to the number of property crimes such as burglary, larceny, and theft. The UCR data, remember, are only of crimes reported to the police, and **property crimes** (except for motor vehicle theft) are less likely than personal assaults to be reported. As might be expected, larceny and burglary rates are highest in communities with marked differences in economic power. In Russia, for example, rates for robbery, theft, and burglary soared after the introduction of Western economic practices that produced widespread income inequality (Voigt, 1993). The opportunities provided by an unregulated market coupled with a breakdown in law enforcement have turned sections of Moscow into a battleground of criminal gangs (Specter, 1994b).

With the exception of burglary, a "professionalized skill," the great bulk of property crime is committed by young men with limited education and job skills, drawn from the most recent urban minority group. Or, more precisely, these are the ones who get arrested; middle-age or middle-class offenders have many ways of avoiding criminal labeling. The high level of street crime in America can thus be largely accounted for by poverty, poor job prospects, the destruction of the economic base of inner cities, decreased funding for social services, and failure to contain the spread of drugs—all of which have produced a large pool of potential criminals, isolated from mainstream institutions (Currie, 1993). In addition, because the United States is a heterogeneous society, with many racial, ethnic, and religious minorities, it is difficult for citizens to develop a sense of shared identity with people who do not look like themselves. In countries such as Norway, where the population is racially and ethnically homogeneous, it is easier to feel akin to others and to support programs that minimize the effects of social isolation.

The level of street crime in the United States is also related to our strong reliance on punishments that have had minimal deterrent effect and that often encourage further criminality (Chambliss, 1994; Pepinsky and Quinney, 1993). Diverting scarce resources to imprisonment rather than to family support programs, job training, and drug treatment will only ensure continued high rates of street crime. This emphasis on punishment over prevention runs counter to the policies of other modern societies, all of which have lower crime rates than the United States (Savelsberg, 1994). But moral entrepreneurs have pushed "street crime" to the top of the American political agenda (Beckett, 1994).

Female Criminals

Although the gender gap in arrests and imprisonment has narrowed in recent years, women are much less likely than men to commit any type of crime, especially one of violence. In part, this difference reflects men's greater freedom of movement, their socialization to using physical force, and permission to express anger openly. In contrast, women have fewer opportunities to commit crime, are less concerned about "respect," and are more likely to have acted under the influence of drugs or alcohol.

The types of crimes committed by women are gendered, as are those of men. Women are arrested for prostitution, larceny (primarily shoplifting), drug pos-

session or dealing, vagrancy, and domestic violence, and only rarely for major acts of violence toward strangers. These are not the crimes of liberated women. To the contrary, their crimes are those of women trapped in sex-typed roles—as mothers, wives, and girlfriends. Typically, they steal to feed their children; run drugs for their boyfriend; and turn violent after years of abuse from a husband or lover (Pollack-Byrne, 1990).

Random violence, however, has increased among female members of street gangs who act like their male counterparts and for similar reasons: to gain respect from peers and a sense of mastery over some part of a world that appears to ignore their existence (Taylor, 1993; Chesney-Lind, 1993).

In 1993, women accounted for 18 percent of arrests and almost 6 percent of state prison inmates, an increase of one-third in arrests and of 75 percent in imprisonment since 1986 (U.S. Department of Justice, 1994c). Because there are so few women inmates, the cost of their imprisonment is twice as high as it is for males. Small prisons are more expensive to run than are large ones. Other difficulties include protecting inmates from sexual assaults by guards and finding homes for their children. Eighty percent of female inmates are mothers, and the great majority are single parents who have been the family's primary wage earner (U.S. Department of Justice, 1994c). Thus, a woman's imprisonment creates an enormous burden for the state's social welfare system, adding to the cost of sending her to prison. Although judges are more willing than in the past to imprison a woman, public officials are torn between meeting the popular demand for harsher punishments and the practical reality of paying for it.

Although women are much less likely than men to commit violent crimes, there has been an incrcase in violence among female members of street gangs who in many ways act like their male counterparts. The young women in this East Los Angeles gang seek to get respect from peers and a sense of control over a piece of the urban turf.

SOCIOLOGY IN EVERYDAY LIFE

Living in Fear and Anger

There is enough seemingly senseless violence in the United States to have hardened the public attitude toward crime and criminals. Thus, despite a statistical decrease in victimization rates, the great majority of citizens believe that crime rates have risen dramatically, particularly in their own communities. National surveys in the mid-1990s report that crime and violence had replaced the economy and health care as the nation's #1 problem. One study found that 73 percent of respondents thought that the amount of crime in the country had increased in the past five years, compared with only 3 percent who thought it had decreased. Forty percent expressed fear of walking in their neighborhoods at night (*New York Times*/CBS News Poll, January 1994a). In another survey, 61 percent thought that local crime had increased, and over half worried about being victims, even though very few would ever have that experience (*Time*, 1993). Also contrary to the evidence, 80 percent thought that increasing the number of police would reduce crime. Three in four favored the death penalty, and 60 percent favored paying more taxes to build more prisons. Clearly, Americans are fearful, and they are also angry.

To what extent are these attitudes shaped by the coverage of crime stories in newspapers and television? Research on the effects of newspaper coverage suggests that a reader's level of fear is raised only by initial front-page reports of local murders, while reports of crime in other cities can make a reader feel safe by comparison (Liska and Baccaglini, 1990). When the front pages feature violent crime stories, the city gains a reputation as dangerous, affecting the area's chances of attracting homeowners, businesses, and cultural activities—all of which tend to reduce crime—another example of the principle that what is believed to be real is real in its consequences.

Spurred by these fears and by the need to appear effective in combatting crime, Congress passed an Omnibus Crime Bill in 1994 that expanded the federal death penalty to cover an additional 52 offenses, most of which are extremely rare as federal cases. Other acts, such as "conspiring to join a criminal street gang," were made federal offenses, even though this type of charge could apply to almost anyone in a poor neighborhood. Because most crimes still fall under state statutes, the bulk of the $30 billion in the Omnibus Bill is to go toward hiring and training more local police officers and building and staffing prisons, leaving very little for crime prevention. And much of these funds were shifted to law enforcement by the conservative Congress of 1995.

At the state level, politicians have been equally active, with proposals for mandatory life imprisonment for a third felony ("three strikes and you're in") and various other tough-sounding policies, none of which is likely to be any more effective in controlling crime than past efforts because lack of "toughness" is not the problem (Clear, 1994).

Organized Crime

The *Godfather* movies sum up what most Americans know about organized crime: an import from Sicily, run by close-knit families, and led by a patriarch who demands total loyalty from lieutenants who kill rivals in restaurants and barbershops. The term *Mafia* has become synonymous with organized crime in the United States, but not all organized efforts to accumulate wealth in defiance of the law have been new or alien or particularly Italian in origin. Criminal organizations succeed because (1) its members supply goods and services not available legally, such as pornography, drugs, and risky loans; (2) public officials are easily corrupted; and (3) the organization is willing to use force.

When those at the bottom of the status hierarchy find access to legitimate success blocked, they have always used illegal activities as a ready, if crooked, ladder of social mobility (O'Kane, 1992). In the late nineteenth century, criminal gangs in the United States were dominated by Irish and German immigrants. By the turn of the century, many leaders where Jewish, and by the late 1920s, Italians came to dominate crime "families." Most recently, African-American, Latino, and Asian-American criminal organizations have taken control of most low-level activity, as the third generation of traditional crime families has moved off the street and into semirespectable ventures. Thus, today, inner-city residents live in fear of turf wars among gangs competing for control of the local narcotics trade, and the country's "Chinatowns" are terrorized by gangs offering "protection" to shopkeepers (Chin, 1990). For the organized criminals working out of business offices, the money involved is so staggeringly high that they have a major impact on the U.S. economy through stock market manipulations, control over union pension funds, and the corruption of public officials.

Crime in the Suites: White-Collar and Organizational Crime

When Americans talk about fear of crime and criminals, they are usually referring to street crime and young minority men. But in terms of the sums of money involved and eventual harm to public health and safety, and possibly the sheer number of criminal acts, most crime in America is not committed on the streets but in the office suites of white, middle-aged, middle-class executives.

The term **white-collar crime** was coined in 1949 by Edwin Sutherland to describe illegal acts intentionally committed by respectable, high-status people in the course of their employment. More recently, criminologists have limited the concept to those crimes committed for personal gain, such as embezzlement and theft from an employer or selling or buying insider information (Geis and Jesilow, 1993). In contrast **organizational crime** refers to illegal actions undertaken by a corporation and its officers for corporate rather than personal advantage, such as bribing government officials, conspiring to set prices, falsifying test data, or intentionally disregarding safety rules. In both cases, the essential sociological point is that the extent of such crimes has little to do with the personal characteristics of the people involved and everything to do with the positions they occupy and the opportunities provided for undetected illegitimate acts in a capitalist economic system (Snider, 1993).

WHITE-COLLAR CRIME. In the case of white-collar criminals, the necessary conditions for any type of crime—motivation, opportunity, and neutralization of social controls—are not as visible as in the case of street criminals, which makes white-collar crime very difficult to recognize and prosecute. The *motivation* is usually greed, but white-collar criminals are less ob-

The United States has the highest murder rate in the industrial world. This Gunfighters Deathclock, an electronic billboard in New York City's Times Square sponsored by a man who lost a relative to gun violence, counts the number of guns, the number of people killed by guns in the United States, and names some of the victims. Why has gun control become such a politically explosive issue?

viously desperate than are their streetwise counterparts, although both are driven by the pursuit of personal gain in a society that values material success above all else (Currie, 1991). There are abundant *opportunities* for illegal acts, and because physical violence is not necessary, the white-collar criminal is rarely perceived as a public danger. *Social controls are neutralized* when the likelihood of being found out is very low, and when law enforcement agencies lack the technical skills needed to unravel complex financial deals.

How can we tell when a physician performs unnecessary surgery, or when a banker makes a fraudulent loan? Both have abused the trust of their occupational status, but proving illegality rather than incompetence is almost impossible (Shapiro, 1990). In the 1980s, for example, a change in banking regulations made it possible for executives of savings and loan associations to make unsecured loans to friends and relatives, to siphon off company funds for personal use, and to falsify bank records. The total bill for this bankers' orgy will be $500 *billion* out of the pockets of American taxpayers, to the tune of over $4,000 each. Only a few of the people involved have been prosecuted, and hardly any of the ill-spent funds have been recovered.

> **White-collar crimes** are illegal activities committed by individuals of high status, usually by nonviolent means, in the course of their employment, for their own benefit.
>
> **Organizational crimes** are illegal activities taken by a corporation or its officers for the corporation's benefit.

An economy increasingly centered on money management rather than on production of goods and services expands the opportunities for white-collar crimes and widespread abuse of trust (Calavita and Pontell, 1991; Zey, 1993).

But the overwhelming bulk of white-collar crime is much less dramatic than these well-publicized multibillion dollar scams. Most cases involve low-level offenders and relatively small sums of money: a false insurance claim, petty theft, minor tax evasions, and credit fraud. The typical offender is an otherwise ordinary individual who is temporarily under financial pressure perhaps because of gambling losses, overdue credit card bills, loss of child support payments, and who sees an easy way out because the employer's money is just sitting there and "no one will ever know" (Weisburd et al., 1991).

ORGANIZATIONAL CRIME. In contrast to white-collar crimes committed for personal gain, organizational crimes are committed for the benefit of one's employer. A small sample of recent newspaper headlines will give you an idea of both the extent and variety of organizational crimes: "Maker of Sleeping Pill Hid Data on Side Effects," "Company Admits It

SOCIOLOGY IN EVERYDAY LIFE

Heigh-o Silverado

When many U.S. banks were deregulated in the 1980s, their officers managed to spend and lose hundreds of billions of dollars, ultimately paid for by ordinary tax payers. The Silverado Banking Savings and Loan Association of Denver, Colorado, was typical of hundreds of similar institutions that took advantage of this relaxation of banking rules to engage in questionable activities (Wilmsen, 1993). Silverado became well known because one of its directors was Neil Bush, son of then-President George Bush. The bank's ultimate failure cost the American taxpayers $1 billion. Among its many high-risk ventures were largely unsecured loans to real estate developers who had loaned money to Mr. Bush and invested in his oil company. When the real estate market collapsed, Silverado's managers began to falsify their records to cover up losses from many other poorly financed loans to friends and relatives.

For almost a decade, Silverado's directors and officers felt secure in the knowledge that federal regulators and the company accountants would "look the other way." Only when the situation became impossible to ignore did the government step in, asking for only $200,000 in fines and restitution, and settling for far less. Some officials were accused of "gross negligence," but none has gone to jail, and Neil Bush acknowledged that some dealings were "a bit fishy."

Neil Bush

Faked Tests on Missile-System Part," "U.S. Says Empire Blue Cross Billed Improperly on Medicare Claims," "Cigarette Makers Debated Risks They Denied Existed," "City Workers Doctor Records To Allow Illegal Dumping of Waste." Defense contractors and pharmaceutical companies appear to have engaged in almost universal and systematic fraud. When the corporate bottom line is profits to enhance the value of the company's stock, there is enormous pressure to take shortcuts. And when the costs of getting caught are minimal, there is little to restrain the eager executive (Clinard and Yeager, 1980). In cases of price-fixing, several different corporations will cooperate, acting in much the same way as any illegal conspiracy, although ultimately driven more by the need to conceal their activities than by the goal of increasing efficiency (Baker and Faulkner, 1993).

Because a corporation cannot be sued in the same way as an individual, it has been almost impossible to hold particular people responsible for illegal acts committed in their role as corporate employees. Most cases are settled out of court for fines much smaller than originally asked. A major corporation cannot be threatened with being shut down; too many workers and communities would be negatively affected. Corporations can afford a legal staff that will keep a case in court for a decade or more.

Strategic Bankruptcy. When push comes to shove, and the company has been successfully sued, it can declare bankruptcy and avoid court-ordered payments to victims of their faulty products and fraudulent testing (Sobol, 1991; Delaney, 1992). The reorganized corporation, with the same officers, is then clear of all personal and company liabilities incurred by the former corporation. This tactic was used with great success by the Johns-Manville Company to avoid paying victims of its asbestos products, and by A. H. Robins Pharmaceuticals to evade a court-ordered settlement to women injured by a falsely tested and marketed contraceptive device that the manufacturer refused to withdraw. When finally ordered to remove the product from the U. S. market, Robins simply exported its remaining stock overseas to be sold to Third World women who were not likely to initiate lawsuits (Grant, 1992).

In pursuit of corporate goals, ordinary citizens are placed at risk. Pollution and price-fixing eventually take their toll on peoples' health and pocketbooks. Although no one is openly mugged, corporate crimes ultimately lower the quality of life for all; corruption spreads to the highest levels of responsibility; and the

Pollution takes its toll on peoples' health whether it occurs under capitalism or Communism. Under Communism the government was a major polluter and citizens had no recourse. This town in the former East Germany is typical of that government's disregard of citizens' health.

financial costs are at least ten times greater than that of all the street crimes committed during the same year (Spence, 1989). In both Italy and Japan in 1993 and 1994, reports of decades-long wholesale corruption of public officials by corporations led to the downfall of governments and political parties. So many politicians were involved in the scandals that it was difficult to find enough "clean" leaders to put together a government.

For obvious reasons, detecting and prosecuting such crimes is extremely difficult. The American legal system tends to protect organizations and private property against the acts of individuals rather than protecting individuals and the nation from organizations (Hagan, 1989). Although fraud and bribery are widespread, few companies have suffered from negative public opinion, and even fewer executives have lost their jobs on this account. The general public's fear remains concentrated on street crimes and petty offenders.

Because organizational deviance has not been dented by regulation from the outside or by policing from within, we must conclude that, similar to organized crime, it provides goods and services to its clients (corporate executives and stockholders) that are worth the cost of increasing the level of criminality in the society.

Patriotic Crime. Events of the past few decades suggest a new category of corporate crime: crimes committed in the name of achieving important national goals. **Patriotic crimes** involve actions taken outside legitimate channels as well as the perjury needed to maintain secrecy and to cover up the original offense (Hausknecht, 1992). The Iran-*Contra* affair, in which secret deals for money and weapons were made by White House officials in defiance of the will of Congress, is the classic case of patriotic crime. The officials believed that their cause was pure and that any means to achieve it were proper. National security overrides all other goals, so that telling lies to Congress and the American people is fully justified. Many of the same individuals were involved in covering up arms sales to Iraq, even as U.S. soldiers were invading that country (Friedman, 1994).

Other types of crime that can be committed by governments include violations of international law, undeclared warfare, false imprisonment, failure to regulate pollution, tax codes that favor campaign contributors, and using the military to terrorize dissenters (Barak, 1991). Such acts are common in dictatorships but also are present in democratic societies, such as when U.S. officials falsified documents and lied to Congress about our role in the massacre of civilians in El Salvador in the 1980s (Krauss, 1993). In 1994, the Department of Energy released information about hundreds of government-sponsored tests carried out in the 1950s on the effects of low-level radiation. Experiments were conducted on hospital patients, prison inmates, nursing home residents, children, and the mentally ill—all populations unlikely to understand or to question "informed consent" clauses (Wasserman, 1994).

> **Patriotic crimes** involve actions taken outside legitimate channels in the name of achieving important national goals.
>
> **Victimless crimes** violate moral standards, but those involved are willing participants.

Crimes without Victims

Victimless crimes are acts believed to threaten the moral integrity of a community but in which people participate willingly. Few individuals are forced to sit at a poker table, solicit a prostitute, purchase pornography, take out a loan at 100 percent interest, or buy illegal drugs. People who do these things may get hurt, but they cannot claim to be victimized by anything other than their own desires. But because such acts are defined as a public harm, the police are charged with protecting morals and eliminating sin.

SOCIOLOGY IN EVERYDAY LIFE

Pyramids in the Sky and Other Con Games

The circus founder, P. T. Barnum, is supposed to have remarked that there is "a sucker born every minute." He posted signs at the entrance to the sideshow pointing to "Egress," which many customers thought was another type of freak on exhibit. Because *egress* means "exit," the people who followed the sign soon found themselves outside the circus tent from where they had to pay a second admission fee.

Modern-day Barnums have a host of highly successful scams for separating innocent (naive) citizens from their money. Most confidence games depend on the greed of those who participate and who would, therefore, have difficulty admitting that they had been cheated. "Cooling out" the mark (target) refers to techniques for minimizing awareness of the con and the likelihood of reporting it to the police. One of the most common scams today is a variation on the classic "pyramid scheme," where people at the base of the pyramid give money to those at the top and then recruit new members; the new members pass their money upward and draw more people into the scheme, so that those on the bottom gradually work their way to the top. It might seem that everyone stands to gain eventually, but in practice only those who enter early realize big profits before authorities step in.

Confidence games that depend on earning the trust of the mark are often targeted toward elderly women. Among the most popular of these con games is the *pigeon drop*, in which an appealing stranger (typically a young woman) offers to share a stake in some "found" money in return for a small amount of the mark's money "as a show of good faith." Then there's the lottery ticket that that person can't cash because they're an illegal immigrant, so it is offered to you for a small sum. Oh, yes, and all the free gifts you've won if you'll pay a fee for shipping and handling. Not to mention the 900-number products and phony phone services. And, of course, the wonderful once-in-a-lifetime chance to purchase land in what will soon be Arizona's most attractive retirement community.

Alas, the list is endless, and P. T. Barnum may even have underestimated the number of Americans eager to believe that you can get something for nothing— well, almost nothing.

Clearly, law enforcement would be simplified if victimless offenses were *decriminalized,* that is, no longer defined as violations of the law although not exactly legalized either. Such a step would reduce opportunities for the corruption of police officers, especially those in the vice or morals squads who are particularly vulnerable to bribery because of the wide range of discretionary power given to them. ("Why not raid someone else's gambling parlor?") The sheer volume of drugs and untraceable money is very tempting. ("Who'd miss a few ounces or C-notes?") Officers who can pick and choose whom to arrest are tempted to substitute personal feelings for objective criteria; that is, to be especially harsh on people whose appearance they do not like. These incidents violate the ideal of equal treatment and further erode respect for the law and its agents. Police corruption can encourage further lawlessness by giving citizens an excuse for breaking the law ("The cops do it, too"). Despite such drawbacks, victimless crimes remain on the books as a relic of our Puritan past that few politicians dare to renounce.

DRUG USE. The victimless crime with the greatest impact on crime rates, law enforcement, and the social temper today is drug use. Although alcohol-related acts of criminal violence far outnumber those involving other drugs, the sale and consumption of alcohol is not illegal in most parts of the United States and in most circumstances. Thus, the "drug problem" has been defined in terms of substances such as marijuana, cocaine, heroin, various hallucinogens, and pills that either pep you up or bring you down. With an estimated 6 million hard-core addicts, and millions more only periodic users, there is a lot of money to be made in providing illegal substances to eager buyers.

Since 1980, drug use declined among high school and college students and among the relatively affluent but increased explosively among the urban poor and teenagers, who are least likely to be able to afford their habits without becoming low-level pushers or committing some other crime (Inciardi et al., 1993; Currie, 1993). The drug problem in America, therefore, has many dimensions: the crimes committed under the influence of drugs; the much larger volume of crime committed by people who need money to support their habit; the violence stemming from warfare among suppliers; the devastation of inner cities; the corruption of law enforcement agents, international banks, and entire governments that is due to drug trafficking and money laundering; and the strains on the criminal justice system caused by the public reaction. This is all very costly, indeed.

The latest data from the Department of Justice indicate that between 30 and 40 percent of violent crimes today are committed by a person under the influence of an illegal drug and that about 80 percent of prison inmates had been drug users at some time. Arrests of adults for the sale and/or possession of drugs have more than doubled in the past decade, even as federal funding for drug control programs has increased by 800 percent (U. S. Department of Justice,

The tragic deaths of six American astronauts and a civilian teacher in the 1986 Challenger explosion revealed that profit motive and political pressure appear to be more important than the protection of human life. Which model of society helps us understand this outcome?

1994h). The federal "war on drugs," however, involved largely futile efforts to stop the production of drugs overseas and to bar their entry into the United States. This is essentially a "supply-side" approach to drug control. The alternative "demand-side" approach would try to reduce the number of users and/or their level of use. A recent large-scale study of these strategies concluded that treatment programs would be seven times more cost effective than the best efforts to control the supply of cocaine entering the United States (Rydell and Everingham, 1994).

However, the emphasis today is on law enforcement rather than on treatment of users or on reducing poverty and joblessness among inner-city youth (Currie, 1993). Any attempt to change these priorities has thus far met with resistance in Congress and among the public, even though the cost of treating addiction among inmates is lower than that of maintaining them in a cell. Indeed, the public temper continues to support **mandatory sentencing,** in which judges must impose a specific prison term rather than use their discretion in disposing of a case. As a result, the proportion of drug offenders in local jails has increased by 150 percent since 1983. Drug law violators now compose 60 percent of all Federal prisoners, almost 30 percent of first-time state prison inmates, and an increasing proportion of juvenile offenders. The current overcrowding of prisons and the soaring cost of new facilities are direct consequences of drug-related crime and sentencing.

Under these circumstances, the debate over legalization or decriminalization of drugs has been renewed—at least by academics (Inciardi, 1991). When the Surgeon General of the United States in 1993 merely suggested that it might be worth examining the issue, a firestorm of outrage led President Clinton to repudiate the idea immediately. An interesting exercise for you would be to draw up a list of costs and benefits of making some drugs available to addicts under medical supervision. Would it work? How could the public be persuaded to support such a program?

Another approach, pioneered by Miami's Dade County, offers detoxification treatment and job training services to first-time nonviolent offenders arrested for drug possession. Most would either have been released on probation or given short jail terms, but they would probably have reappeared in the courts. Thus, while rehabilitation is more expensive in the short run, it saves money by reducing the likelihood of a return to crime (Finn and Newlyn, 1993).

> **Mandatory sentencing** requires judges to impose specific prison terms rather than use their discretion.

THE POLICE AND LAW ENFORCEMENT

Police are formal agents of social control, with the right to use force to enforce the laws. The unique aspect of police work is its on-the-spot, situational nature. The officer must react to intense, immediate threats to social order (Bittner, 1990). Thus, police are allowed wide discretion in choosing how to respond. This same discretionary authority, however, can open the door for excessive use of force. To maintain public peace, officers will concentrate their power on populations perceived to be especially threatening, so that the poor and powerless inevitably become the primary targets of policing (Jackson, 1989; Mann, 1993).

Dirty Linen and Laundered Money

Between the crop planted by a Third World farmer and the illegal substance taken by an addict, a lot of money changes hands many times over; from producers to sellers to "mules" who carry the material from country to country, to packagers and repackagers who dilute the product, to distributors to street dealers and their "associates." It is estimated that over $500 billion are spent worldwide each year on buying illegal drugs, with $200 billion spent in the United States alone.

In addition to drug money, hundreds of billions of dollars involved in illegal arms sales, tax evasion, fraud, and bribes to public officials must be circulated in such a way that they cannot be traced to people committing illegal acts. **Money laundering** refers to techniques for transforming "dirty" money into "clean" income, and it is today a leading component of international trade. How can a drug producer in Columbia, South America, hide hundreds of millions of dollars from the tax collectors? The money is hidden in "offshore deposits" into a bank whose officials will not report the transaction.

Just such an obliging financial institution was the Bank of Credit and Commerce International (BCCI), involving thousands of people from Middle Eastern oil countries, South American drug-producing nations, and a number of respected American bankers, all engaged in extremely complex and sophisticated transfers of money among several countries.

Money launderers are especially attracted to Switzerland, with its strict guarantee of the secrecy of bank accounts, and to several smaller Caribbean nations (the Cayman Islands and Netherlands Antilles) with similar protections for depositors. Getting the money out of one country to another has been greatly facilitated by electronic fund transfers. Within a country, money-changing stores and gambling casinos permit instant exchanges. In one famous case in the 1980s, the money from sales of Southeast-Asian heroin was channeled through New York pizza parlors, brought in gym bags to leading stock brokerages, and then wired to Europe, where it was used to purchase more heroin. This is truly international trade in an unregulated free market.

U. S. authorities are trying to establish an international approach to enforcement of currency laws, but each country has its own banking regulations, and some small nations depend on international banking for economic stability. Cultural and procedural differences make cooperation difficult, and even with it, the sheer complexity of unraveling the paper trail requires a team of experts who must be able to spend years on a single case .

Source: Barbara Webster and Michael S. Campbell, "International Money Laundering: Research and Investigation Join Forces," *Research in Brief*, National Institute of Justice, 1992, 17.

Police work has a number of built-in contradictions and strains. While officers have discretionary power on the street, the organization of police work is a bureaucratic hierarchy with its own rigid structures. Individual officers are both kings of the streets and dependent on the citizenry to assist them in reporting crime, identifying suspects, and showing respect for the law. When not on duty, the officer is also a civilian, a family member, and a community participant. An added stress on family intimacy comes from the fact that police share the dangers and triumphs of their workday with their partners, to the exclusion of their spouses, who might justifiably become jealous. Split shifts and irregular hours strain marriages, producing relatively high rates of family violence and marital problems.

Most frustrating of all, however, may be the realization that not much works; the more policing, the more crime. The current war on crime has only given the public the illusion that something is being done, while actually it has diverted funds from dealing with the basic causes of violence, namely, the economic trends that have turned large areas of American cities into the domestic equivalent of a Third World nation

Money laundering refers to techniques for transforming "dirty" money into "clean" income.

(Gordon, 1992; Currie, 1993). Although police work today is far less risky than two decades ago, their world remains a dangerous place to which they respond by becoming increasingly hardened and doubtful about everyone's motives (Egan, 1991a). And the everyday violence in the lives of police officers often results in high rates of suicide among officers in large cities. It is truly a jungle out there.

Given all these built-in strains—family stress, work-related frustrations, and physical dangers—combined with relatively low pay and prestige, while criminals are dealing in oceans of drugs and dollars, how long could you remain squeaky clean? In addition, everyday police work is full of opportunities to vent one's anger on those who threaten the public safety. Only rarely does the use of excessive force come to public attention, and very few such cases result in criminal charges, much less a jury conviction. For example, only because the scene had been videotaped and released to the media was it possible to bring misconduct charges against officers in the beating of Los Angeles motorist Rodney King in 1993, and even then the state jury refused to convict. One key element in police culture is the "blue code of silence" about misconduct of other officers, thus seeming to place the police above the law they are charged with enforcing (Skolnick and Fyfe, 1993).

In terms of lawlessness, however, your local police department is probably a model of honesty compared with the Federal Bureau of Investigation under J. Edgar Hoover from the 1920s to 1970. During these decades, the FBI operated without oversight from other branches of government largely because Hoover blackmailed presidents and politicians with material from files he had secretly and illegally gathered (Theoharis, 1991).

Private Policing

The United States has a long history of private policing. The Pinkerton Agency provided the Carnegie Corporation with strikebreakers; citizen posses imposed their idea of justice on the Wild West; and vigilante groups lynched Southern blacks in the name of Christian values. The concept of private policing is being revived today, which is due in part to the perceived failure of local police to control street crime, and in part to the belief that "privatizing" public services will save taxpayer money. But police work differs from other government services in that one foundation of democracy is that only the state has a legitimate right to use force, and the state is run by elected officials (Johnston, 1992). Law enforcement must always be answerable to the public, however inefficient or expensive this might be. Nonetheless, some tasks could be turned over to private companies: collecting fines, controlling illegal parking, and providing security at public events. Privatizing is a "hot" issue that will appear on local election ballots for many years to come.

In reality, a great deal of white-collar crime is already being dealt with privately, through employer sanctions such as job transfers, demotions, and firings. Low-level crimes such as shoplifting are handled by store security personnel usually without resort to the criminal justice system. The problem here is that private justice does not have to meet standards of fairness or be concerned with civil liberties. Thus, one study found that shoplifters were treated differently on the basis of social class: The relatively affluent paid damages in a civil proceeding; the poor were referred to the local police (M. G. Davis et al., 1991).

Gigantic profits are made by those who mastermind the illegal shipments of drugs from South American countries into the United States and Europe. This U.S. government map shows the major routes of cocaine shipments. The topography and climate of Bolivia, Peru, and Columbia are ideal for cultivating coca, while the inaccessible mountain slopes make these areas very difficult to police. Poor economic conditions generate incentives to traffic drugs. Given the complexity of this process what can the U.S. government do to halt the flow of drugs into the U.S.? Can the supply of drugs really be reduced without also reducing the huge demand among Americans?

PRIVATE GUARDS. The use of private guards is widespread and is one of the fastest growing occupations in America. Your college or university probably employs a private police force larger than that of the local community. Many businesses hire private guards around the clock; and wealthy residents of crime-prone neighborhoods are increasingly willing to pay for additional protection. As a result, private security is the nation's primary source of protection, employing three times as many workers as the public police force, and costing twice as much (Cunningham et al., 1991). In other words, the security of most Americans today, under most circumstances, is in the hands of workers hired for that purpose, whose primary obligation is to their private employer.

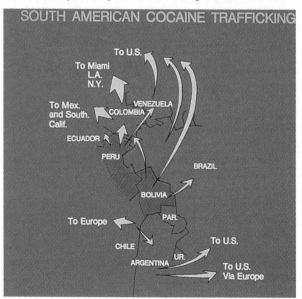

JUVENILE DELINQUENCY AND THE JUVENILE JUSTICE SYSTEM

Young people come to the attention of the legal system for three reasons: (1) They have committed a crime; (2) they are neglected or abused; or (3) they have committed a **status offense,** which is an act that would not be a crime if done by an adult, such as running away from home, skipping school, drinking alcohol, or being ungovernable (incorrigible).

> A **status offense** is an act that would not be a crime if committed by an adult.

In every society the police have the right to use coercive force to control others' behavior. Whose interests do the police serve?

The upper age for juvenile status varies by state, and ranges from 16 to 19 for different offenses. Because of such variation, plus changes in both law and reporting, and fluctuations in the proportion of teenagers in a population, it is difficult to compare yearly rates. What has changed is the proportion of offenses that involve violence against persons, even though the vast majority of juvenile crimes are property offenses. Thus, although arrest rates for crimes of violence have doubled since 1970, this accounts for only 5 percent of juvenile arrests (J. Miller, 1991).

From a sociological viewpoint the key variables are structural: poverty, unemployment, school failure, lack of adequate housing, and breakdown of community networks (Bunsik and Grasmick, 1993). In the absence of jobs and stable communities, the gang offers a place to hang out, a set of supportive peers, and opportunities to prove one's manhood, often in turf wars against other ethnic/racial youth (Pinderhughes, 1993). Given the current drug scene and the careers to be made in dealing, many street gangs have turned from the minor hustles of the past to serious criminal activities (Huff, 1990). The mean streets of our central cities have become much meaner over the past 15 years. Millions of young people are growing up with minimal attachment to mainstream institutions and little expectation that things will get any better, and thousands have already taken to life in the streets (McCarthy and Hagan, 1992; Inciardi et al., 1993; Cummings and Monti, 1993).

Although youth from single-parent households are at greater risk than those from two-parent families, this correlation is strongest for minor status offenses and relatively weak for violent crime. In addition, the larger and more representative the sample, the smaller the effect of household type on delinquency (Wells and Rankin, 1991). Boys are four times more likely than girls to be brought into juvenile court, and whites are twice as likely as blacks to appear in court, but when it comes to disposing of the case, minority youth are more likely than their white age peers to be placed in a correctional facility.

Juvenile Justice

What to do with the youthful offender? American law and public opinion have cycled between extreme harshness and leniency (Bernard, 1992). On the one hand, there are strong arguments for keeping a young person out of the formal justice system. Most juveniles outgrow their illegal activities, whereas being processed as a criminal tends to reinforce antisocial impulses. On the other hand, fear of crime, especially when committed by young minority men, often labeled "animals" in the media, has fueled public demand for harsh punishment (Champion and Mays, 1991; Schwartz et al., 1992). The 1994 Crime bill permits treating 13 year-olds as adult criminals under some circumstances.

The *juvenile court system* was designed to be more flexible than the adult system, allowing judges wide discretion to deal with young offenders in an individualized way. But it is now more of a criminal processing system than one aimed at diverting youth from a life of crime (Krisberg and Austin, 1993). Over time, juvenile offenders have gained some of the protections of the adult system, such as the right to counsel, to question witnesses, and to appeal the court's judgment, but much of the work of the juvenile court is done outside the formal channels by officials who are acting out their occupational roles (Cavender and Knepper, 1992).

The last resort—placement in a secure juvenile facility—is very costly (about $80,000 a year). These are largely populated by minority youth, while white offenders are more often sent to private treatment facilities or half-way houses. In 1994, an all-time high of slightly over 100,000 juveniles were behind bars (U.S. Department of Justice, 1995).

Are there alternatives to reform schools? For all but a handful of extremely dangerous young persons, there are a variety of effective programs that maintain the juvenile in the community. In 1970, Massachusetts closed down its reform schools, found alternatives for the majority of inmates, and greatly reduced the rate at which juveniles returned to a life of crime (J. Miller, 1991).

ADULT COURT SYSTEMS

The judicial process has three principal participants: the **prosecutor** (district attorney), the **defense attorney,** and the **judge.** Many others, including the defendant, appear in supporting roles. The prosecutor represents the interests of society ("the people") and any injured parties. The defense attorney represents the accused, and the judge personifies the law and impartial justice. The image of Justice, found in most courthouses, is blindfolded—she does not see distinctions of sex, race, or social class—with a sword in one hand symbolizing swift justice and a scales in the other hand referring to the protection of rights of the accused individual against the overwhelming resources of the state.

Although the cornerstone of the American legal system is the right to a jury of one's peers (status equals), most cases are settled by a guilty plea or the release of the accused because of lack of evidence, as shown in Figure 17-2. Of the few cases that go to trial,

the majority of defendants choose to appear before a judge without a jury.

The American court system is very complex, with separate courts for adults and juveniles, for civil and criminal cases, and for federal or state offenses. Each system has higher courts to handle appeals from the trial courts, and at the top is the Supreme Court, which can hear appeals from all lower courts that involve a constitutional issue or federal/state conflict. This complexity is a source of frustration to some, but it also protects citizens from arbitrary acts by government officials.

Processing the Criminal

Once arrested, the suspect embarks on a mini-career in the judicial system. As shown in Figure 17-2, the case can be terminated or continued at a number of steps. A *felony* is a crime that carries the possibility of a prison term of more than one year. Assuming that about 40 percent of felony victimizations are reported to police and that half of these are cleared by an arrest, the 100 accused felons in Figure 17-2 are responsible for only a small proportion of criminal acts.

> The **prosecutor, defense attorney**, and the **judge** are the three major parties in the criminal justice system, each representing different interests.

Once booked, 6 suspects will be diverted to programs that bypass the courts, and 18 cases will be rejected by the prosecutor's office as too flimsy for trial. Once in court, 21 cases will be dismissed by the judge for lack of evidence or improper police procedure. Of the 55 cases carried forward, 52 will be concluded by a guilty plea, and 3 will actually go to trial, typically without a jury. One defendant will be acquitted and two found guilty. Of the 54 guilty persons, 18 will serve a jail term (less than one year), 14 will be

Figure 17-2 Tracking felons through the criminal justice system.
Source: U.S. Department of Justice, 1993b.

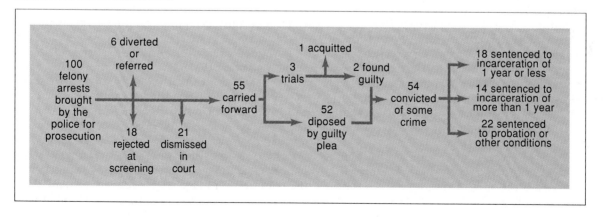

sent to prison (more than one year), and 22 will be placed on probation or given a punishment such as community service. In murder cases, the proportion carried forward and convicted is much higher: 73 percent, of whom 90 percent will be sentenced to prison. But whatever the crime, at each step, the lower a person's income and the darker their skin the more likely the individual will be processed to the next stage and be incarcerated (placed behind bars), in part because of the defendant's low status itself and in part because he or she cannot afford adequate legal assistance (Smith, 1991). It is difficult to believe that many other black men accused of a particularly bloody double murder in Los Angeles County would have been as successful as O. J. Simpson was in avoiding a prosecutor's asking for the death penalty.

PLEA BARGAINING. One way in which a competent lawyer can help a client is in negotiating with the prosecutor's office for a compromise solution. Of the 52 who pleaded guilty before trial, few will actually have confessed to the crime for which they were arrested. **Plea bargaining** involves an offender admitting to something in return for a reduced sentence. Critics claim that plea bargaining makes a mockery of the system. But without it, many cases would have to be dropped for lack of evidence, while the remainder would clog the courts. The bargain saves the public the cost of a trial and adds to the district attorney's record for clearing cases. Both the accused and the state avoid the risk of losing in court.

Plea bargaining is a negotiation between the prosecution and the accused to reduce the charges if the defendant pleads guilty.

Capital punishment is another term for the death penalty.

PUNISHMENT. Traditionally, American judges have been allowed great leeway in determining an appropriate punishment for a convicted offender. This practice has been criticized by both liberals and conservatives. Liberal critics point to the arbitrariness that sends the poor and racial minorities to prison, while wealthy white offenders are sentenced to community service. When the affluent serve time, it is likely to be in a minimum-security facility; and because they are also more likely than the poor to have committed a federal offense, they are incarcerated in a federal facility that resembles a "country-club with bars." Although Justice may often be blind to sex and race, she has a keen sense of class.

In contrast, conservative critics argue that sentences for street criminals are too short and that parole boards release prisoners too early. As a result, federal district courts and some states have now established guidelines for uniform sentencing. It is still too soon to determine whether or not the new guidelines result in greater fairness or simply more plea bargaining. One clear outcome of longer sentences has been prison overcrowding. It is less clear whether stricter sentences have reduced the volume of criminal activity.

Does Punishment Deter Crime? The rational choice model suggests that criminals calculate the benefits of illegal behavior against the costs in terms of the likelihood of being caught and the harshness of the penalty. Research shows that neither certainty nor severity of punishment (including imprisonment) has much effect on crime motivation. As you saw in Figure 17-2, only 2 or 3 percent of criminal acts end in imprisonment, so that even if the probability of being caught and convicted was *doubled,* we are still talking about a very small proportion of all criminals. Nonetheless, most of the public and lawmakers favor longer sentences and building more prisons, with an overwhelming 75 percent favoring the death penalty for convicted murderers.

CAPITAL PUNISHMENT. The history of **capital punishment** (another term for the death penalty, from the Latin *capo* meaning "head") in America provides a fascinating study of how the public temper shifts. Up to 1967, death by hanging, firing squad, or electric chair was an accepted part of the criminal justice system. By this time, the United States was the only modern industrial democracy that had not abolished the death penalty. The late 1960s were also a period when many repressive aspects of the society were being questioned. Thus, in 1972, the Supreme Court heard a case that challenged the death penalty on grounds (1) that it violated the Eighth Amendment's prohibition of "cruel and unusual punishment," and (2) that because the penalty was used overwhelmingly against poor minority men, it violated the Fourteenth Amendment's guarantee of "equal protection under the laws." The Court failed to find the death penalty unconstitutional but did issue a temporary ban on executions until the states could devise procedures to ensure uniform treatment of people accused of capital crimes.

In the following years, one state after another enacted legislation designed to meet the Court's standards, finally succeeding in 1976. All but 15 states now permit capital punishment, and between 1976 and 1994, more than 250 executions took place. As of mid-1994, more than 2,700 prisoners were under sentence of death, as shown in Figure 17-3. Death row inmates are almost evenly divided between whites and minorities (although whites compose 80 percent of the population) and are largely concentrated in Texas, Florida, and California (U.S. Department of Justice, 1994h).

MICHAEL L. RADELET

Studying the Death Penalty

Michael L. Radelet is a Professor of Sociology at the University of Florida. He is the author of three dozen articles and four books on the death penalty, including one which documents over 400 cases in which people convicted of homicide were later found to be innocent (Radelet et al., 1992).

*I*n 1979, I arrived in Florida after seven years of studying medical sociology. I had no interest in, knowledge about, or opinions concerning the death penalty. But when a friend told me that the NAACP Legal Defense Fund was collecting records to see whether the death penalty in Florida was being applied with a racial bias, I volunteered to analyze their data. It sounded quick and easy, exactly what new professors need if they hope to earn tenure. I naively thought the results might show no racial disparities, and made sure that everyone knew that I would publish the results no matter what they were.

One of the strongest attractions of sociology is that it offers the opportunity to learn about some very interesting groups. People on death row are one such group. Not wanting to be accused of being an ivory-tower intellectual, I began to write to one of the men on death row. Later I visited him and did so twenty more times until he killed himself a year later. For the next four years, I paid monthly visits to another condemned inmate, who was executed in 1985. Since then I've worked with attorneys as a paralegal on a hundred more cases, testified in death penalty trials all over the country, and have gotten to know

dozens of condemned inmates and their families.

More than anything else, it was these families that made me take a stand opposing capital punishment. Their agony, coupled with the data showing strong racial bias in the administration of the death penalty and the occasional execution of the insane or innocent far outweighs in my mind any justifications for the death penalty voiced by the executioner's friends. Prisoners suffer, and given that in most states the alternative to the death penalty is life imprisonment without parole, eliminating the death penalty will not mean that murderers will go free. I have seen case after case in which the death penalty punishes the prisoner's (innocent) family as much as the prisoner himself. The death penalty doesn't help families of homicide victims—it simply doubles the number of innocent families who mourn the loss of a loved one. Holding the hands of mothers while their sons are being executed has only strengthened my commitment.

Given this perspective, my involvement in capital punishment quickly grew beyond the purely academic. In the last few years I have sprinkled the ashes of one dead inmate in Africa, stored the inherited possessions of a half dozen more in my closets, and visited with numerous inmates in the hours before their executions. In 1993, I spent the night before an execution with the inmate in his cell, sharing his last meal. Seeing this side of capital punishment and realizing that each execution today costs millions of dollars more than life imprisonment, makes me wonder why we aren't spending our resources on more effective approaches to the crime problem in the United States.

Does publicly being opposed to the death penalty violate ethical principles about "objectivity?" I think not.

As I see it, objectivity is not the same as neutrality and *not* to shout out at what one sees as a moral outrage is in itself a moral outrage. After all, when I lecture about racism in my sociology courses, I do not feel obliged to give equal time to the Ku Klux Klan. Sociologists and their students need to have informed perspectives, but these perspectives need not be "neutral" (even though neutrality is often easier).

Others, of course, see the death penalty differently. That too, is part of the excitement that sociology has to offer, as part of what it teaches is an ability to argue issues from several different perspectives. It seems to me that on an issue such as capital punishment, one's position is less important than simply taking a stand, learning how to defend it, and respecting informed opinions of those who differ. What turns me off are those who are apathetic or who take a position without bothering to learn anything about it.

Sociology is a discipline that teaches concern for the powerless. There are lots of relatively powerless people who need help—the homeless, the poor, the elderly, victims of racism or sexism, migrant farm workers, battered women and kids, prisoners, and yes, even death row inmates. Sociology can teach compassion for those less fortunate, the value of making a commitment to make things better, and the competence to make one's voice heard—no matter what stand on what issue one chooses to take.

Sources: Miller, Kent and Michael L. Radelet, *Executing the Mentally Ill* (Sage, 1993); Radelet, Michael L. (ed.), *Facing the Death Penalty: Essays on a Cruel and Usual Punishment* (Temple University Press, 1989); Radelet and Pierce, "Choosing Those Who Will Die: Race and the Death Penalty in Florida," *Florida Law Review* 43 (1991):1–34; Radelet, Michael L., Hugo Adam Bedau, and Constance Putnam, *In Spite of Innocence* (Northeastern University Press, 1992).

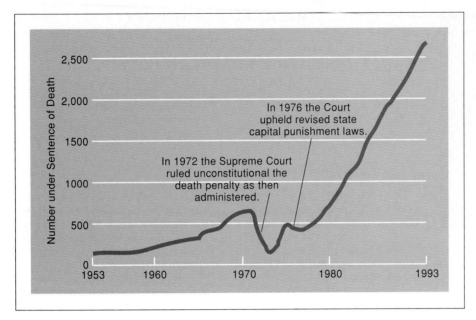

Figure 17-3 Persons under sentence of death, 1953–1993.

Source: U.S. Department of Justice, 1994h.

The last major challenge to the death penalty was turned back by the Supreme Court in 1987 in a case in which social science data were used to demonstrate that the death penalty was still being applied arbitrarily according to the race of the *victim*. Taking all other variables into account, the researchers found that a person who killed a white was 4.3 times more likely to be sentenced to death than was a person who killed an African American. The Court acknowledged the validity of the statistics, but a majority held that the data did not prove intent to discriminate. Yet of all American executions, only two involved a white offender and black victim, and of the more than 250 from 1976 to 1994, all but a few were poor and/or black, or of limited mental ability.

Capital punishment reaffirms the norms of society and unites the community in condemning criminals. What are the differences in the effects of a public execution, such as this one of a terrorist in Lebanon, and the more "sanitized" and hidden execution using an electric chair in a State of Louisiana prison? Why is the demand for capital punishment on the rise in the United States?

In 1989, the Supreme Court also ruled that juveniles and mentally retarded persons can be executed, and they were. Finally, the Court has let it be known that it does not wish to be bothered with further death sentence delays, turning down an appeal on the technicality that the lawyer had been one day late in filing the proper papers.

Those who support the death penalty claim that it serves both to deter further crime and to balance out a social wrong (retribution). The evidence for *deterrence,* as noted in the case of other crimes, is not very convincing, although it is true that the executed person will not commit another crime. There is no evidence of a significant or long-term deterrent effect on other criminals (Stack, 1987a; Baily, 1990).

PUNISHMENT AS RETRIBUTION.   Here we return to one of the grand insights of Emile Durkheim: Punishment reaffirms the norms of the society and unites the community in shared condemnation of the criminal. A public execution focuses attention on the wrongdoer and allows law-abiding citizens to congratulate themselves on their virtue. When punishment was removed from the town square to behind prison walls, some of its social impact was lost, but the revival of capital punishment allows the public to unite in righteous indignation (Garland, 1990).

The theme of retribution and the death penalty also taps into Max Weber's analysis of the work ethic and individual responsibility for one's acts. Support for the death penalty among white Americans is linked to their belief that criminal behavior is due to some moral flaw within the person rather than to aspects of the environment (Young, 1991). Thus, the death penalty and other punishments that cannot be justified on the basis of their deterrent effect nonetheless meet deep societal needs by reaffirming that justice has been done and that the law-abiding are distinctly different from the criminals. In this perspective, visible punishments are highly functional for social solidarity, however unfair they may appear to be to individuals.

Prisons and Jails

The most obvious effect of the demand for stronger and longer punishments has been to overload the criminal justice system, clogging the courts and filling America's prisons to overflowing. By early 1994, 5 million people, or 2.5 percent of American adults, were under some type of criminal supervision. The majority, 3.5 million, were being supervised by probation or parole agencies, 1,013,000 were being held in federal or state prisons, and 445,000 in local jails, where people serve terms of less than one year (U.S. Department of Justice, 1994f).

Between 1983 and 1993, as shown in Figure 17-4, even as overall crime rates were declining, the number of inmates doubled. But because the number of beds increased only marginally, American prisons are now filled to 125 percent of capacity. Close to 70 percent of state prisoners share cells that provide an average of 56 square feet of living space per inmate, to which they are confined for all but a few hours a day. In those states where overcrowding is most intense, the prison system is under court order either to reduce the inmate population or expand correctional facilities. Because politicians do not want to raise taxes

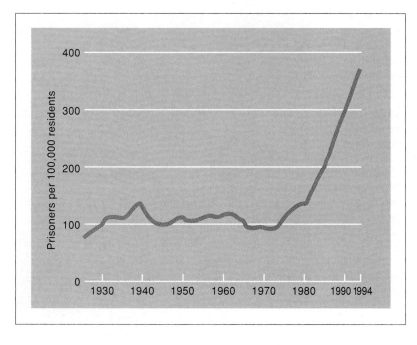

Figure 17-4 Inmates in state and federal prison, 1980–1994. An additional 170 per 100,000 Americans were in local jails in 1994.

Source: U.S. Department of Justice, 1994f.

The increase in the number of prisoner in American jails exceeds the available space, resulting in dramatic overcrowding. Two prisoners share this 9-foot by 6-foot cell. How do you think you would cope with imprisonment?

to pay for the new cells, but are equally reluctant to appear to be "soft on crime," the solution to over-crowding has been a backdoor arrangement whereby less dangerous convicts are released early to make room for the newly sentenced (typically on drug charges), most of whom are not violent offenders.

COST. In 1994, the cost of maintaining a prison in-mate averaged $17,000 per year. By early 1994 the total bill for building and operating prisons, as well as supervising people on probation and parole, came to more than $34 billion for 5 million offenders. The bulk of the prison budget is spent on custodial ser-vices, with only a small fraction available for social, educational, and job training programs. Under these conditions, little can be done to improve employment chances following release. And, under a "3 strikes and you're in for life" policy, the cost per prisoner (for in-stance, a 22-year-old with a life expectancy of 72 years) would be at least $1,250,000 in 1994 dollars.

RECIDIVISM. Most prisoners are released after serv-ing five to six years for a violent crime, two to four for property or drug offenses, and about one year for lesser charges. In other words, all but a few are even-tually returned to the community, where, within a few years, over 70 percent will be arrested again, and almost half will be back in prison (U.S. Department of Justice, 1992). The term

A **recidivist** is a repeat offender.

used for a repeat offender is **recidivist,** literally "one who has fallen again"—a concept that beauti-fully evokes the Puritan emphasis on punishment of sinners.

PUNISHMENT VERSUS REHABILITATION. The history of American corrections has been one of fluctuation be-tween two basically incompatible goals, each of which derives from the Protestant value system. On the one hand, sinners must be punished and the com-munity avenged. On the other hand, repentance and

Boys from low-income homes have higher rates of arrest than do boys from higher-income homes. Why do they get involved with criminal activities?

Today about 1.5 million Americans are incarcerated in prisons and jails at an annual cost of $17,000 per prisoner. By comparison, we spend about $9,500 per year on each child in the educational system. Do you think that if our society did a better job of educating young people, fewer would wind up in prisons?

redemption can be realized through **rehabilitation,** restoring the sinner to a previous state of virtue. The two goals cannot easily be reconciled in a correctional setting because of the very nature of a prison as a total institution.

THE PRISON AS A TOTAL INSTITUTION.   Prisons and jails are **total institutions,** in which people live together in an enclosed world, where all aspects of living are regulated by bureaucratic authorities (Goffman, 1961). Similar to other total institutions such as military bases, mental hospitals, monasteries, and nursing homes, life in prison is closely scheduled and carried out in full view of others. The inmate is stripped of civilian identities, given a number in place of a name, and subjected to ceremonies of degradation and submission. Activities are organized on the basis of the needs of the institution and its staff. The primary goal of any total institution is to resocialize its inmates into the routines of the institution, not to prepare them to reenter civilian life. Prison norms are incompatible with the requirements of community living, and in

the absence of family ties and job skills, civilian failure is inevitable. Unfortunately for today's largely poor and illiterate inmates, not many opportunities for education or job training are available on the outside, either. In addition, the inmate subculture itself works against rehabilitation.

Prison Subculture.   Until recently, prison conditions produced a traditional subculture among the inmates that emphasized "doing one's time," staying out of trouble, and being tough. But recent changes in both the prison and the characteristics of inmates have created an increasingly unpredictable and violent environment (Hunt et al., 1993). In place of a relatively stable hierarchy of inmate leaders and an unwritten code of inmate behavior, prisons are being taken over by groups of young men linked by their pre-prison gang memberships and shared ethnic or regional identity. In seeking to control the gangs, authorities have often created a power vacuum that encourages more violence.

Lack of privacy, the impersonality of the system, the brutality of guards and other inmates, loss of contact with family, boredom, poor food, inadequate medical care, and overcrowding have turned today's prison into a "jungle"— one that frequently erupts into open warfare. Prison riots are the result of a serious breakdown in administrative control of the facility that adds to the intolerable conditions experienced by inmates, who then use the uprising to attract attention and force the state to remedy the situation (Useem and Kimball, 1989). Assaults on guards are especially likely in prisons that primarily hold young convicts, unsocialized to the traditional inmate culture and its rules (Light, 1990).

> **Rehabilitation** means restoration to a former state.
>
> **Total institutions,** such as prisons and jails, control and monitor all aspects of inmates' lives.
>
> **Probation** allows a felon to remain in the community under close supervision.

SOCIAL POLICY

Alternatives to Prison

Are there cost-effective and crime-reducing alternatives to total imprisonment? One possibility is **probation,** whereby the felon remains in the community under close supervision. The cost of probation is about one-tenth that of incarceration, and the recidivism rate is somewhat lower: Within three years of sentencing, 62 percent had been rearrested or violated their probation requirements, and 46 percent had either disappeared or been sent to prison (U. S. Bureau of Justice Statistics, 1992). Probation works best for nonviolent, first-time offenders with strong roots in the community, who are low risks for recidivism in any event.

Other *intermediate sanctions* include fines, community service requirements, house arrest (out to work during the day; home at night), and electronic monitoring. Because offenders are employed, they can pay part of the cost of their supervision. In addition, remaining in the community reinforces the ties likely to reduce recidivism.

A recent variation on the typical prison sentence is *shock incarceration,* or "boot camp," a short-term, semi-military program involving physical training, manual labor, and strict discipline. This concept has great appeal to many Americans, who believe that strict discipline builds character, even though all the social science evidence suggests more negative than positive effects. Indeed, a Justice Department evaluation of one such program found that while the attitudes and self-image of some inmates improved, the overall recidivism rate was not much lower than for other prisoners (MacKenzie et al., 1993).

Another alternative is based on the fact that a large number of convicted felons have preexisting drug problems, so that any *drug treatment program* would be more rehabilitative than imprisonment. These efforts would also have to be backed with educational, social, and employment services—all of which add to the cost of this option. In the long run, however, the costs of continued drug-related crimes are much higher.

Most recently, conservative critics of public prisons have suggested the use of *privately-operated facilities,* run for profit under contract from the state. Although the state retains its monopoly over disposing of offenders, it can delegate its powers to supervise their sentence. In theory, competition among providers would lower the cost and improve the quality of imprisonment (Logan, 1990). It is difficult to argue that the public system cannot be improved; the question is whether or not the state can do it on its own. Limited experience with private management has thus far shown that inmate conditions and job training can be improved at no added public expense, largely through hiring nonunion personnel (Ramirez, 1994).

We can also look to *other societies.* Japan's incarceration rate is one tenth of the United States'; Norway has the lowest in Europe (60 per 100,000 population in contrast to more than 520 today for the United States.), and Poland has set a ceiling of 100,000 prisoners. In these societies, the prison population is kept under control through a variety of alternatives for nonviolent offenders. When imprisonment is necessary, the facilities tend to be small, with an emphasis on rehabilitation programs and the reinforcement of family and community ties.

The Norwegian prison system stands in greatest contrast to the American. In Norway, all but the most dangerous offenders must make a reservation to get into prison after being sentenced; the most serious offenders go to the head of the waiting line, while lesser criminals can wait for years before a place is available (Pepinsky, 1993). To shorten the wait, placing two inmates in one cell was introduced in 1990 but soon withdrawn because of objections by prison staff. At this writing a new prison is being built, with private showers, writing desks, and other home-like touches. Because the average prison term is four to five months, a prisoner has little time to enjoy the surroundings. Prison guards receive two years of training and are expected to cultivate friendly, helpful relationships with prisoners, and to assist them in the transition to civilian life. A happy prison is the warden's goal; and politicians and the public have little interest in raising the costs of the prison system. The waiting line therefore is periodically shortened by changing sentencing guidelines or by offering amnesty for minor crimes.

Would such a system work in the United States? Why or why not? Could you use your sociological knowledge to design a correction system that protects the public, eliminates overcrowding, reduces recidivism, and improves the quality of city life?

SUMMARY

1. Every society has rules considered so important to social order that their violation is severely sanctioned. In simple societies rules are enforced through customs and informal sanctions; in modern societies rules are formalized into laws.

2. Criminal law punishes conduct violating the interest of society or the state. Civil law punishes conduct violating the interest of private citizens.

3. The social injury, consensus, and conflict models represent three different explanations of how norms become laws.

4. Contrary to popular belief, most violent crimes occur between members of the same race.

5. The two major sources of data used to measure crime are the *Uniform Crime Reports* and the *National Crime Victimization Survey.*

6. Several theories, sometimes contradictory, have been proposed to explain why fewer women than men have been arrested or imprisoned. It has also been proposed that differences in the types of crime women commit result from gender socialization.

7. Organized crime represents attempts to gain wealth illegally. When immigrant groups found access to legitimate economic opportunities blocked, some turned to crime as a way out of the poverty of urban ghettos.

8. Although most attention in the United States has been focused on street crime because it is violent, in terms of money involved and lives affected, white-collar and organizational crime is far more serious than street crime. Business scams, corporate greed, and government/industry corruption are increasingly publicized, although criminal penalties remain lighter for white-collar than for street criminals.

9. Crimes without victims, or vice crimes, are believed to pose a moral threat to society. In fact, they are likely to provide extensive opportunities for corruption of law enforcement personnel and violation of the ideal of equal treatment under the law.

10. Juveniles come to be identified by the law when they commit a crime, are neglected or abused, or commit a status offense. They are usually processed by the juvenile court system.

11. The police in every society are formal agents of social control, charged with maintaining public order.

12. The criminal justice system involves the prosecutor, the defense attorney, and the judge, each representing different interests. In the course of the complex judicial process, most offenders avoid being brought to trial, and very few are ultimately sentenced to prison.

13. Although there is little evidence that harsh punishments have a deterrent effect, the great majority of Americans support them, especially the death penalty.

14. Prison life is extremely dehumanizing and most ex-convicts eventually return to crime. The prison experience reinforces antisocial impulses in the absence of job training or family supports.

SUGGESTED READINGS

Bernard, Thomas J. *The Cycle of Juvenile Justice.* New York: Oxford University Press, 1992. An historical overview that explains policy changes in juvenile justice. Discussion of important legal cases is accessible for undergraduates.

Chambliss, William J., ed. *Making Law: The State, the Law, and Structural Contradictions.* Bloomington, IN: Indiana University Press, 1994. A compilation of articles by legal scholars, sociologists, political scientists, and anthropologists who have formulated a structural theory of law.

Colvin, Mark. *The Penitentiary in Crisis: From Accommodation to Riot in New Mexico.* Albany: State University of New York Press, 1992. Key issues in corrections, namely, safety, order, and productivity are discussed and recommendations are made for some self-governance by inmates, which improves stability.

Daly, Kathleen. *Gender, Crime, and Punishment.* New Haven: Yale University Press, 1994. A strong challenge to the assumption that women are sentenced more leniently than men.

Ellickson, Robert C. *Order Without Law: How Neighbors Settle Disputes.* Cambridge: Harvard University Press, 1991. An important work that explains social control as the result of five subsystems: personal ethics, two-party contracts, informal control, organizational control, and the law. The author focuses on intimacy and group cohesion as foundations of informal social control.

Jacobs, Mark D. *Screwing the System and Making It Work: Juvenile Justice in the No-Fault Society.* Chicago: University of Chicago Press, 1990. Juvenile probation, rather than incarceration, is seen as the most effective way of correcting deviant behavior. Jacobs paints a disheartening picture of a system that too often fails the juvenile offender.

Kelly, Robert J., Ko-lin Chin and Rufus Schatzberg, eds. *Handbook of Organized Crime in the United States.* Westport, CT: Greenwood Press, 1994. Survey of the diverse ethnic and racial groups in today's criminal underworld with an assessment of law enforcement efforts.

Mann, Coramae Richey. *Unequal Justice: A Question of Color.* Bloomington, IN: Indiana University Press, 1994. An illuminating, thoroughly researched, and comprehensive treatment of the experiences of people of color in the criminal justice system.

Miyazawa, Setsuo. *Policing in Japan: A Study on Making Crime.* Albany: State University of New York Press, 1992. In any given year, Tokyo has never had more than 29 murders. Focus is placed on the criminal justice system: is it the effectiveness of the Japanese police or the law-abiding nature of the people that accounts for such relatively low numbers?

Radelet, Michael L., Hugo Adam Bedau, and Constance Putman. *In Spite of Innocence.* Boston, MA: Northeastern University Press, 1992. The authors document over 400 cases in which people convicted of homicide were later found to be innocent.

18
Health, Illness, and the Health Care System

- One-third of American men age 20 to 39 have engaged in types of behavior that place them at risk of infection with human immunodeficiency virus (HIV).
- Americans spend more of their total income on health care than do citizens of other modern societies, but are less likely to be fully insured for a range of services.
- More Americans drive over the border to Canada for free health care than Canadians who come to the United States for health services.
- Female physicians are more likely than their male counterparts to perform gender-related cancer-screening tests on women patients.
- A child born in Chile or Malaysia is more likely to survive the first year of life than an African-American infant born in parts of Mississippi.

The preceding data illustrate the many facets of the sociology of health. Patterns of health, illness, and medical practice are influenced by social variables such as sex, race, social class, and the organization of medical care. Health and illness are only partly biologically determined; they are primarily social constructions:

> Health is shaped fundamentally by culture, society, and environment. . . . Physical and psychological illness, however influenced by inheritance and biology, arise in no small way from conditions in the family, at work, and in the community more generally. (Mechanic, 1986, p. 230)

In addition, conditions viewed as an illness during one historical era may not be considered "real" diseases during another. For example, in nineteenth-century America, when well-bred women were thought to be extremely fragile, an illness called "the vapors" (fainting fits) was quite common among young middle-class women, most likely in response to the many constraints on their behavior. Today, when physical weakness is no longer a sign of good breeding, the vapors have been replaced by such culturally acceptable illnesses as "chronic fatigue syndrome," food allergies, and other disorders unrecognized during the nineteenth century (Shorter, 1991).

Not only were men and women thought to have different illnesses, but they were also expected to respond differently to the same condition. In the case of tuberculosis in the early nineteenth century, men were urged to overcome their disability by traveling to European clinics where exercise and fresh air were stressed. In contrast, women were advised to remain in the home, seek support from family and friends, and continue their domestic duties (Rothman, 1994).

Patterns of health and illness also vary greatly from one society to another and by the level of technological development. Industrialism has introduced both new medical problems and the means of treating them. For example, the widespread use of chemicals in wartime as well as for peacetime agricultural production has been tied to higher than expected rates of cancer and birth defects, both of which are now the target of new treatment technologies.

The meanings of health and illness are culturally determined. What is considered healthy or normal in one society may be viewed as abnormal in another. This is not to say that disease is not real but that members of a society develop norms about what is to be treated as an illness or as a normal condition. In our society, for example, *epilepsy* is defined as a serious illness to be aggressively treated with medication. In other societies, people who have epileptic fits are thought to possess magical powers. And in still others, the condition is viewed as a minor ailment. Moreover, depending on the society, those who treat the ill can be priests, magicians, herbalists, witches, barbers, or graduates of medical school.

Finally, some illnesses are more socially respectable than others. Heart disease among executives is thought of in very different terms from that of AIDS among gay men or African Americans. People who contract HIV from blood transfusions, however, have a semi-respectable status ("they are really not to blame").

In this chapter, we examine in more detail the social construction and distribution of health and illness, as well as the organization of medicine and health care in the United States and other societies.

PATTERNS OF HEALTH AND ILLNESS

One of the most important indicators of quality of life in any society is the health status of its population. Physical and mental diseases are not distributed randomly; they are patterned by age, sex, race, ethnicity, place of residence, social class, occupation, and personal habits such as drinking and smoking.

Social Epidemiology

The study of the patterning of specific disorders within a population is called **epidemiology** (Rockett, 1994). Epidemiologists analyze the links between a specific disease agent (such as a virus or bacterium) and the victim's social and physical environment. Why, for example, is black-lung disease

> **Epidemiology** is the study of the patterns of occurrence of illness in a population.

common among miners, cancer among asbestos workers, and drug addiction among nurses and doctors? In the case of tuberculosis, the Industrial Revolution, which brought people from the countryside to overcrowded, unsanitary city slums, led to an epidemic of the disease, which declined only when living conditions improved. That is, it was life-style change rather than any major medical breakthrough that made tuberculosis a rarity in industrial societies by the mid-twentieth century. The disease, however, has recently reappeared in a particularly strong form among America's urban poor as a consequence of extreme impoverishment.

INCIDENCE AND PREVALENCE OF DISEASES.   Epidemiologists chart both (1) the number of new cases of a disease within a specific time period, the **incidence rate,** and (2) the total number of cases in the population regardless of when they began, the **prevalence rate.** Incidence rates tell us how new cases are distributed, which subgroups are most at risk, and whether the condition is increasing or on the wane. The total prevalence rate tells us how widespread the condition is and how treatment resources should be allocated.

> The **incidence rate** of disease is the number of new cases of a disease within a population during a stated time period.
>
> The **prevalence rate** of disease is the number of all the known cases of a disease in a population, regardless of when they began.
>
> **Life expectancy** refers to the average number of years a person is expected to live.

The frequency of cancer as a result of job-related exposure to radiation illustrates the distinction between incidence and prevalence. If we look only at incidence, the rates today would probably be very low because of recent workplace safeguards. The prevalence rate, however, would include all the people exposed in the past and would therefore be quite high, justifying the expansion of cancer treatment facilities.

The Social Distribution of Illness

The four most important variables in epidemiological research are age, sex, race/ethnicity, and social class. Each is related to differences in health, illness, and access to medical care.

AGE.   As noted in Chapters 7 and 20, one of the most striking features of modern industrial societies is a great increase in **life expectancy**—the average number of years that a person born in a particular year can expect to live. For an American born in 1900, life expectancy was slightly over 47 years, which was due to very high rates of infant mortality. Once a person survived childhood, he or she could expect to live into their 60s. Average life expectancy for an American today is slightly over 76 years, thanks to major improvements in living and working conditions and public health advances such as pasteurization, indoor plumbing, and childhood vaccination programs.

One outcome of extended life expectancy is that people are less likely to die of infectious diseases such as influenza, tuberculosis, gastroenteritis, diphtheria, or typhoid—among leading killers in 1900. The major

Industrialism has introduced a number of work-related medical problems. For example, black lung disease is an occupational hazard among coalminers the world over. These Rumanian workers in a carbon black factory are exposed to dust and pollution every day, at substantial risk of contracting cancer.

PETER CONRAD

Studying Emergency Medicine in Indonesia

Peter Conrad is the Harry Coplan Professor of Social Sciences at Brandeis University. He is the author or co-author of many professional articles and several books, including Deviance and Medicalization: From Badness to Sickness; Sociology of Health and Illness: Critical Perspectives; *and* Health and Health Care in Developing Societies. *He is currently studying the social implications of the new genetics.*

After spending 15 years studying aspects of health and illness in the U.S., I wanted to learn more about health in other countries, especially developing nations. Did medical sociology have any relevance in societies with very different cultures from our own? The only way for me to learn about health in the Third World was to go and live there.

My wife and I decided to spend my sabbatical year in Indonesia, an archipelago of a few large and many tiny islands covering the same distance as from Alaska to Georgia. At the time Indonesia had the fifth largest population in the world and a very rich and diverse culture. In June, 1989, I went with my wife and two children (then aged 9 and 4) to Yogyakarta, Indonesia, to teach medical sociology at a large university and do research on emergency medical services. Although on balance I learned more in Indonesia than I taught, I sometimes thought of myself as bringing the gospel of medical sociology to Indonesian students.

Because my wife is an emergency physician, we felt that we could combine our expertise to research emergency care in Indonesia. We hoped that if we were successful, we would provide information that was useful to Indonesian physicians and policymakers and make a small contribution to the accumulated knowledge about health care in a developing society.

Yogyakarta was a great place to live and do our research. It is a city of 800,000, known as the cultural capital of Java, the largest of the Indonesian islands. In addition to the largest Indonesian university, Yogya (as the locals called it) was also a center for Javanese dance, *wayong* (shadow) puppets, gamelon music, batik fabrics, and other traditional arts and crafts. Related to our research interests, there were four hospitals with active emergency departments (EDs).

In our first few months in Yogya we studied the Indonesian language intensively and gained some facility with everyday conversations. I got to the point where I could teach my class about 15% in Indonesian and have the ability to ask all the questions I needed to (although I didn't always understand the answers!)

In early 1990 we began our research. We wanted to collect data about all patients who came to the four emergency departments for a month. We hired 22 student research assistants (RAs) and spent a week training them how to use our observational survey to collect the data we wanted.

Becuase EDs can't control the flow of patients, our assistants were sometimes overwhelmed and at other times became bored waiting for patients. The overall number of patients meant that the surveys came back to us in huge stacks, quicker than we could process them or provide useful feedback.

After a month we had data on virtually all patients who came to the EDs for care; a total of 4,527. As we began to analyze the data we encountered some provocative findings. For example, we found that although Yogya had virtually no ambulance system and few people owned cars, 42% of the trauma (injury) patients arrived at the ED within 30 minutes of the accident and 64% within 60 minutes. The question became, how did they arrive so quickly? Equally interesting was the finding that more than a quarter of the patients who came to the ED really did not have urgent problems. Why did these patients show up at the ED which cost them more money than did the inexpensive community health centers? It appears that in developing countries EDs are frequently used for primary care.

Living in Indonesia was fascinating and conducting the research was challenging and interesting. It provided me with a firsthand view of health care in a developing country and enriched my understanding of the sociology of health. As we continue to publish articles from our research, my hope is that our findings will be useful to our Indonesian colleagues and encourage other sociologists to further expand the purview of medical sociology into the developing world.

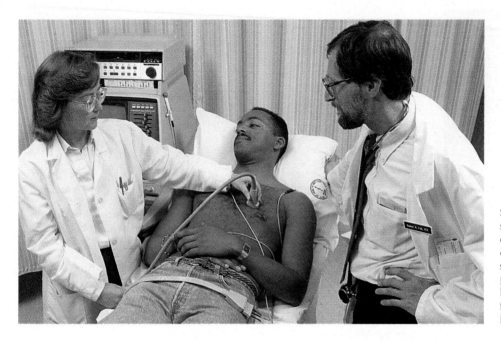

Social epidemiologists study the occurrence of specific diseases and disabilities within a society. Epidemiological patterns are determined by accumulating data from a large number of individual cases.

causes of death today are long-term *(chronic)* conditions such as heart and lung diseases and cancers. The high death rate from cancer today does not necessarily signify a major increase in cancer-causing conditions but simply the fact that people are not dying of other diseases earlier in life. The shift from infectious to chronic causes of death is shown in Table 18-1.

Because Americans live longer than they did in the past, 40 percent of the population experiences some limitation on their daily activities due to chronic conditions such as arthritis, heart disease, and vision and hearing losses, and half of these experiencing severe limitations (U.S. Bureau of the Census, P70-33, 1993). When hospitalized, elderly patients have longer hospital stays and require longer periods of recuperation than do younger patients, who are typically hospitalized for acute (short-term, one-incident) illness or accidents. This shift from a largely acute to a primarily chronic patient load is a major component of increasing health care costs in modern societies.

Old age, however, is not inevitably linked to poor health. The great majority of Americans rate their health as good, regardless of age (Verbrugge, 1989). The health status of older Americans continues to improve, thanks to government-funded health insurance for the elderly and a greater awareness of the benefits of exercise and proper nutrition. Health and disability at any age is strongly related to income. Among Americans aged 65 and older, the proportion with extreme disability was 53 percent among those with lowest incomes compared to 23 percent for those with high income (U.S. Bureau of the Census, P70-33, 1993).

Although the United States currently spends more of its gross national product (GNP) on health care

TABLE 18-1   Leading Causes of Death, United States, 1900 and 1993, by Number per 100,000 Persons

1900	1993
Heart disease (137)	Heart Disease (286.9)
Pneumonia and influenza (202)	Cancers (205.8)
Tuberculosis (194)	Stroke (58.1)
Gastroenteritis (143)	Chronic Lung Disease (39.2)

Sources: U.S. Department of Health and Human Services, National Center for Health Statistics, *Vital Statistics Report,* Vol. 42, No. 13, 1994; *Historical Statistics of the United States, Vol. 1.* Washington, DC: U.S. Government Printing Office, 1975:58.

than any other industrial nation, the health status and life expectancy of its citizens rank among the lowest of modern societies. There is some link between the number of physicians and life expectancy, but this alone does not explain the differences. For example, the people of the Netherlands, Sweden, and Australia have longer life expectancies than Americans have, but the ratio of physicians per population in those countries is the same as in the United States; the Japanese, with a lower ratio, can expect to live 2 years longer than Americans. The explanation lies in the organizational aspects of health care, to be examined later in this chapter.

SEX.   Another powerful epidemiological variable is sex. In modern societies, life expectancy of females is much higher than that of males (about 7 years more on average in the United States today, compared to about 2 years more in 1990) and is not expected to narrow until well into the twenty-first century (U.S. Bureau of the Census, P25–1104, 1993). The percentage of males dying at all ages, from conception on, is higher than that for females for all causes except diabetes, suggesting that women have a greater resistance to both infectious and chronic illness and especially to the heart diseases that are the leading killer of men. It is *not* true that men die because they work harder and are therefore under greater stress than women; rather, they have a more vulnerable heart system and engage in more unhealthy behaviors than do women.

Paradoxically, although they live longer, women have both a higher incidence and prevalence of illnesses than men and are more likely to use the services of physicians and hospitals but less likely to receive major diagnostic tests and preventive intervention, especially if their doctor is a man (Clancy and Franks, 1993; Scully, 1994).

Why, then, if women have more illnesses and receive less aggressive treatment, do they live longer than men? There are a number of reasons, including the following: (1) Women are more likely than men to cut down activities because of ill health, thus conserving their energy. (2) Their willingness to visit a doctor brings them into the health care system at an earlier stage in the development of disease than similarly afflicted men, and they are more likely to follow the doctor's orders. (3) Women are more attuned than men to changes in their body. (4) They have lower rates of drinking, smoking, and reckless driving. In other words, sex differences in health behaviors work to the advantage of women. If the life expectancy gap is to narrow, it will be because men begin to watch their diet, exercise more, visit a doctor regularly, and take their medications.

RACE AND ETHNICITY.   One reflection of social inequality in the United States is the difference in health among various racial and ethnic groups. African Americans, Hispanic Americans, and Native Americans continue to have a lower life expectancy than non-Hispanic white Americans. For example, the infant mortality rate for African Americans is 2.2 times higher than for non-Hispanic whites (Hummer, 1993). The relatively poorer health status of minority infants and adults has many causes: poor nutrition, lack of maternity care, residential overcrowding, and limited access to health services (Aday, 1993).

In addition to lower life expectancy, certain diseases have higher rates of prevalence among minority populations. Native Americans, especially those living on reservations, have relatively high rates of typhoid fever and diphtheria, which is due primarily to substandard living conditions and absence of health care facilities. Latino factory workers, many of whom are recent immigrants, experience high rates of serious work-related injuries (Kilborn, 1992). African Americans are most likely to suffer from heart disease, and to die from these at a younger age than whites but are far less likely to receive bypass surgery (Hilchey, 1993). These data indicate the complex relationship between health, life-style, and ability to afford medical treatment. Although some minorities are genetically predisposed to a few conditions—Tay-Sachs disease among Jews, or sickle cell anemia among African Americans— most race and ethnic differences in disease rates are social in origin (McKenzie, 1994).

The effects of social/cultural factors can be seen in the changing rates of heart disease among Japanese

Certain diseases are more likely to affect minority populations such as Native Americans, Latinos, and African-Americans. Recently, scores of Native Americans in Arizona and New Mexico were exposed to an undetermined viral infection linked to the environment of the reservations.

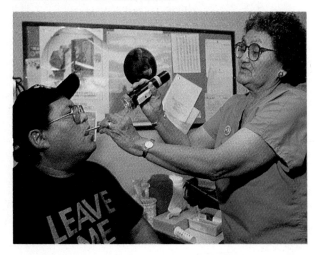

living in the United States and in Japan. In general, Japanese Americans rarely develop heart diseases, but their rates are higher than for their age peers living in Japan, largely as a matter of diet. Now that meat consumption has risen in Japan, however, heart disease rates are also rising in that country.

SOCIAL CLASS. As already noted, life expectancy is shorter and death rates higher among the poor than the nonpoor, as a result of living conditions, limited access to care, and differential treatment of patients. The way in which health care in America is financed also plays an important part. For example, wealthier patients and those with private health insurance are twice as likely to receive a heart transplant despite the likelihood that they will not benefit from the operation than are poorer, noninsured patients who would benefit greatly (Friedman et al., 1992). Furthermore, the health gap between poor and nonpoor Americans in all racial categories has widened since the 1960s, despite the introduction of a government program to pay health care costs of the poor (Pappas et al., 1993). In large part, the racial differences in life expectancy are a reflection of differences in income and education. That is, social class rather than race *per se* is the prime determinant of health status (Guralnik et al., 1993). Social class is directly linked to having health insurance, and people without insurance are less likely to seek medical care or to be welcomed at a doctor's office, placing them at increased risk of premature death (Franks et al., 1993; Schwabe and Rushing, 1994). In addition, having an adequate income gives a person a sense of control over one's life that often leads to taking care of one's health through exercise and proper diet (Grembowski et al., 1993).

The poor are also subject to different risks and stressful events such as fatherlessness, unemployment, divorce, and death of a spouse (Angel and Angel, 1994; Turner et al., 1995). In many cases, neighborhood and family support can cushion the impact of stressful life events, but long-term exposure to a series of such stresses can overwhelm the support system, as illustrated in Figure 18-1.

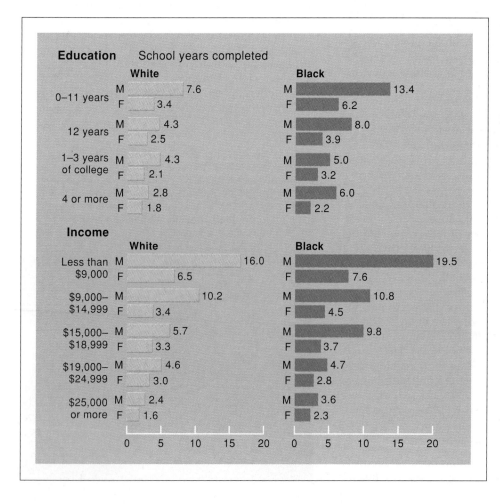

FIGURE 18-1 Class, race, and death: deaths per 1,000 people in 1993 among people 25–64 years old. (M, male; F, female.)

(*Sources*: Pappas et al., 1993; graph from *New York Times*, July 8, 1993. Copyright © 1993 by The New York Times Company. Reprinted by permission.)

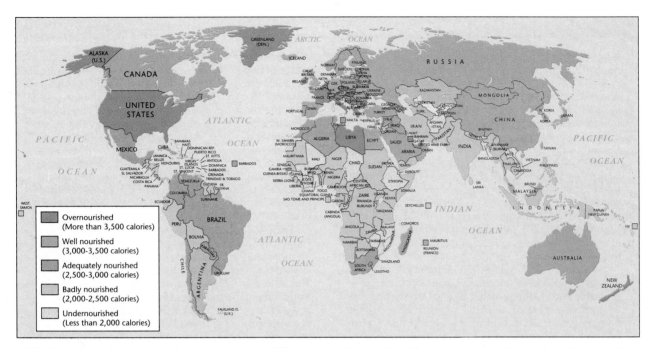

Global Calorie Consumption. There are dramatic diffferences in the nutritional consumption patterns of people around the globe ranging from those who are overnourished and consume more than 3,500 calories per day to those who are undernourished and consume fewer than 2,000 calories a day.   (*Source:* Peters, p. 138)

HEALTH AND ILLNESS AS SOCIAL IDENTITIES

From a sociological perspective, health and illness are relative concepts. Although we can identify serious illness, usually in terms of a person's inability to carry out daily tasks, other conditions may or may not be considered signs of incapacity. Much depends on cultural definitions of desirable appearance or behavior. For example, *overweight* is clearly a relative concept, depending on the definition of *proper weight*. In many societies, large bodies are admired and though to be sexually attractive. In the United States, slimness is highly valued, so that those who depart from its standards are often defined as suffering from obesity, an illness—a medical judgment heavily influenced by aesthetic values. Mental health practitioners, for example, are more likely to assign negative psychological traits to relatively heavy women patients compared to slimmer patients with identical symptoms (Young and Powell, 1985).

> . . . health is, sociologically defined, the state of optimum capacity for the effective performance of valued tasks.
>
> —TALCOTT PARSONS, 1972

The high value placed on slimness in our society has produced a number of industries whose financial health depends on maintaining this definition: fitness centers and spas, psychologists, weight-loss doctors, exercise machine manufacturers, and producers of diet foods and medications. As part of the entire **health promotion** movement, these industries have helped perpetuate the belief that good health is an individual responsibility, a sign of good character and moral worth, very much in the tradition of the work ethic described in Chapter 3. Health is virtue personified and illness a source of guilt for having no will power or for letting oneself go (Becker, 1993). In this view, the cure lies in individual actions and not in government efforts to reduce poverty, provide access to health care, or control environmental pollutants.

> The **health promotion** movement perpetuates the belief that good health is an individual responsibility.

The Sick Role

If health is defined in terms of peoples' ability to enact their usual social roles, illness threatens to reduce the effective functioning of social systems, removing a role player and draining resources in the provision of care. Therefore, social stability (especially in the workplace or nuclear family) requires the control of illness. It is in this context that Talcott Parsons (1951) defined the

SOCIOLOGY AROUND THE WORLD

The Social History of an Epidemic: The Case of HIV/AIDS

The interaction among social, biological, and medical variables is well illustrated in the case of the human immunodeficiency virus (HIV) and its frequent outcome, acquired immune deficiency syndrome (AIDS). Once thought to be a local virus confined to rural areas in the Third World, HIV spread dramatically with urbanization and the flow of people from the countryside to the cities, especially in the poorer nations. Nearly two-thirds of the estimated 17 million HIV carriers in 1994 lived in Africa, while the most rapid increase in reported cases took place in Southeast Asia. In these countries, the virus is spread primarily through heterosexual contact.

As Figure 18-2 shows, the HIV epidemic is now worldwide. However, the actual number of cases is probably several times higher due to underreporting by governments because of the stigma attached to the primary avenues of transmission—prostitution, homosexual sex, and intravenous drug use. For example, China, with a population of 1.2 billion, has reported only 35 AIDS cases to the World Health Organization

(WHO). In contrast, the United States had reported a total of 412,000 AIDS cases by mid-1994. The current best estimate is a worldwide total of 4 million full-blown AIDS cases (WHO, 1994).

In the years since AIDS was recognized and the HIV virus discovered, drugs have been developed to slow down the process, but no cure is in sight. Drug therapies, however, are expensive and therefore not widely available. Race and class affect other aspects of treatment in the United States: people of color are less likely than whites to receive outpatient care and more likely to be admitted to a public hospital (Piette et al., 1993).

The virus and risk of AIDS is transmitted by an exchange of body fluids, through blood transfusions, conventional heterosexual sex, in the womb to a fetus, by shared drug needles, and by some homosexual acts. The fastest growing source of transmission here and worldwide is the the heterosexual sex trade, especially in Asian counties such as Thailand, where "sex travel" is a major source of revenue from the West (Backhaus et al., 1994). This has produced an extremely high incidence of HIV among child and teenage prostitutes and their clients (Brown and Xenos, 1994).

(continued)

FIGURE 18-2   Estimated cumulative distribution of adults infected with HIV, the virus that causes AIDS, 1993.

Sources: *Science Magazine* and *New York Times,* June 6, 1993. Copyright © 1993 by The New York Times Company. Reprinted by permission.

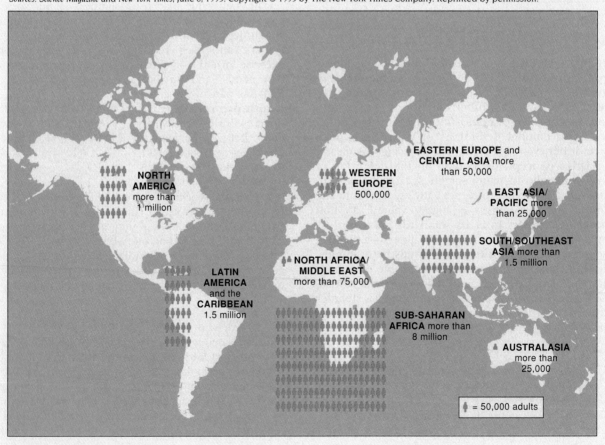

By 1994 about one-and-a-half million Americans were infected with the HIV-AIDS virus and more than 17 million were infected worldwide, more than 200,000 Americans had already died of AIDS-related diseases, and it has been the leading cause of death among men and women aged 25–44. One of the most prominent victims is basketball star Earvin (Magic) Johnson. Johnson's wife Cookie Kelly tested negative, as did their daughter, born after the diagnosis. While Magic wanted to continue his basketball career, the NBA banned his participation with the LA Lakers and forced his early retirement. Do you think athletes that test HIV positive should be allowed to compete in team sports?

As of this writing, no evidence indicates that the HIV virus can be transmitted through casual contact, even with an infected person, or from a cough, sneeze, toilet seat, or restaurant food. Nevertheless, young AIDS victims have been barred from school, adults have lost housing and jobs, and physicians have re-fused to treat them (Yedidia et al., 1993). The fear of infection is compounded by the stigma attached to ho-mosexuality and drug addiction, allowing many Ameri-cans to see the disease as punishment for sinful behavior.

Today, AIDS is a leading cause of death among Americans aged 25–44, especially minority men and women. Because the infection typically takes a decade or more to develop into full-blown AIDS, these victims must have contracted the disease as adolescents or young adults, when people are least likely to protect themselves from the risk of sexually transmitted dis-

eases (Chapter 8). The risk of infection also varies by education and income, with college students a low-risk population despite their young age. In addition, many high-risk populations also have a low level of knowl-edge about the disease and how it can be transmitted (Le Blanc, 1993).

How can the incidence of HIV/AIDS be reduced? Abstinence from sex and drugs is the surest way. A monogamous relationship with an uninfected partner is low risk. Condoms are relatively effective and inex-pensive, but their distribution to high school students in the United States has been opposed by powerful religious groups. Thus, while most Western European nations have undertaken massive media campaigns advocating condom use and "safe sex" in general, the U.S. Department of Health and Human Services has

(*continued*)

Children may contract AIDS at birth or through blood transfusions (blood screening did not begin in the U.S. until 1985). Elizabeth Glaser, wife of actor Paul Michael Glaser, contracted AIDS through a transfusion while pregnant with her first daughter, Ariel, who subsequently died of AIDS at the age of seven. Before her death in December, 1994, Glaser founded the Pediatric AIDS Foundation. She advocated for more government support for, and a change in attitudes toward, people with AIDS. Some communities have ostracized school-aged children by boycotting classes and even using violence. Are children and adults with AIDS the new lepers?

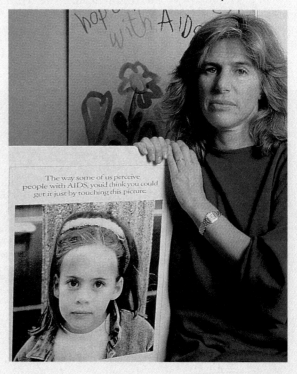

been unable to make a similar effort, unless it is to promote complete abstinence. Along the same lines, programs offering clean needles to drug addicts have been opposed by people who claim that this would give a governmental stamp of approval to illegal and immoral conduct.

As you saw in Chapter 8, however, evidence indicates that fear of AIDS has had some effect on the dating behavior of young Americans, with increasing percentages reporting fewer sexual partners and more consistent use of condoms (Kalish, 1993; Mosher and Pratt, 1993). The impact of HIV/AIDS on sexual prac-

tices is an ongoing illustration of the effect of a disease on other aspects of life. Nonetheless, because large numbers of Americans continue to engage in unprotected and risky sexual acts, the AIDS epidemic will remain with us, claiming an increasing proportion of heterosexuals (Billy et al., 1993).

The costs of the epidemic have already been enormous in terms of research funding, expensive drug therapies, and medical and nursing care, but most of all in terms of premature death and what our responses say about the public temper.

"sick role." The **sick role** has the following characteristics: (1) A person, through no personal fault, cannot meet her or his normal role obligations; (2) that person is then exempted from these responsibilities; (3) this exemption is granted with the proviso that the patient seek appropriate medical help and try to get well as soon as possible.

The sick person is excused only temporarily. Notice how our sympathy tends to turn to annoyance when the patient is not making a serious effort to regain health. The word *malingering* refers precisely to the situation of staying too long in the sick role and testing the patience of role partners.

> The **sick role** is a set of rights and obligations attached to the status of being ill.
>
> The **pathological model** of disease focuses on biological symptoms and abnormal functioning in the organism.

One criticism of this concept is that it once more places full responsibility for getting well on the individual, thus allowing health care providers to escape criticism. In general, definitions of health and illness emerge from the dynamic interaction between physician and patient, in which the doctor has the greater power to impose meaning and determine subsequent behavior.

CLINICAL MODELS OF ILLNESS AND DISEASE

How can we tell whether a given condition is healthy or not? Two models, the *pathological* and the *statistical* are used to identify abnormality within individuals or a population (Mercer, 1973). The **pathological model,** preferred by medical practitioners, looks at specific symptoms and how they cause the organism

While health spas offering "proper diets," therapeutic baths, and massages are relatively new to the United States, they have existed for a long time in West and East European countries. This spa in Budapest has been a favorite for many generations of Hungarians. Mineral water, anyone?

The Medicalization of Childbirth

In 1900, the great majority of births in America took place at home. Since 1966, however, all but a few have been performed in hospitals, attended by a physician. In addition, an increasing percentage of births occur through medical interventions such as drug-induced deliveries or cesarean sections, accounting for approximately one-third of all American births today. How did childbirth become so thoroughly medically managed?

The answer lies in part in the political struggle of the medical profession for control over health issues (Weitz and Sullivan, 1986). In colonial America, births were attended by a midwife, with female relatives and friends gathered in the home for assistance and support. At that time, physicians tended to believe that caring for pregnant women was beneath their dignity. When medicine became more professionalized in the nineteenth century, physicians began actively to seek out patients for their new "scientific" procedures. To extend their influence, they first needed to drive out existing health care providers such as midwives and traveling medicine men. The attack on midwives was particularly fierce, with the women portrayed as drunken, dirty, and un-American. A medical vocabulary was employed—*parturition* rather than *childbirth*—as the all-male establishment emerged victorious. The next task was to relocate birthing from the home to the hospital, where medical power was unquestioned. In addition to financial rewards, this move helped change the image of the hospital from a place of dying to one of hope.

To justify these changes, birth had to be redefined as a basically dangerous event, so that as additional technologies and drugs became available, they could be put to use. In the 1970s, however, these developments came under challenge from feminists concerned with women's total powerlessness in what ought to be a situation in which they should participate. When the "natural childbirth" (without drugs or other invasive conditions) movement appeared to threaten the medical establishment, doctors responded by co-opting the movement—providing instruction classes for parents and creating "birthing rooms" in the hospitals (Scully, 1994). Midwives remain controlled by requirements for licensure and practice, as well as difficulty in obtaining malpractice insurance.

Medicalization represents the triumph of the belief in science as objective and morally neutral, so that decisions based on a host of subjective factors are presented as technical judgments "for your own good" (Zola, 1990).

---

to function abnormally. This model (1) is based on biological explanations for individual pathology; (2) often assumes that each illness has a specific cause; and (3) emphasizes what is wrong with the person. Although the model has been useful in the study of acute physical diseases, it is less successful for understanding long-term, complex disorders, which tend to have multiple causes, including many environmental effects. The pathological model also overlooks the cultural, evaluative factors we have already noted. Why for example, are chubby babies thought to be so healthy and chubby adults not?

In contrast, the **statistical model** defines health and illness in terms of the average for a population. In this model, "normal" is what characterizes the majority, with the few cases at the extremes being considered "abnormal." While it emphasizes what is most common, the statistical approach can be criticized for labeling nonconformists as abnormal. For example, children from minority groups who do not do well in school because of language problems may function perfectly normally within their own communities, yet be defined as "learning impaired" by school authorities (Mercer, 1973).

Which of the two models is applied to any given condition has important effects. Viewing drug use and emotional problems as illnesses is different from seeing them as deviant behavior. The broader the definition of illness and the more behaviors that are la-

beled symptoms of disease, the greater the power of health care professionals to define *normal* and *abnormal.* Physicians and other medical personnel assume the roles of agents of social control once occupied by priests, parents, and police. Forms of behavior once tolerated as unusual or minor deviance become defined as medical problems, requiring active intervention. The process of **medicalization** can be seen when overactive schoolchildren are reclassified as *hyperactive* and treated with drugs. The box entitled "Medicalization of Childbirth" describes how giving birth has been transformed from a natural to a medical event.

> The **statistical model** of disease defines health or illness in terms of the average of a population.
>
> **Medicalization** occurs when forms of behavior once tolerated as unusual become defined as medical problems requiring active intervention.

THE GROWTH OF AMERICAN MEDICINE

The American health care system as we know it evolved in the past 100 years in response to changing technology and social needs. Although hospitals can be traced to ancient Greece, it was only in the late nineteenth century that they provided care to large numbers of patients and eventually became the health care center of a community. Until the end of the nineteenth century, hospitals were as much a source of infection as of cure: Conditions were very unsanitary, without antiseptic procedures, and hospitals were staffed by poorly trained practitioners.

As odd as it may seem to us today, physicians in the nineteenth century were held in low esteem, financially insecure, and engaged in fierce disputes over medical matters (Starr, 1982). But by 1950, American physicians were a united, prosperous, and powerful interest group, expanding both the range and costs of their services.

The Rise of Medical Dominance

The development of modern health care was spurred by work in social epidemiology, the rise of the public health movement, and medical discoveries such as the germ theory of disease, anesthesia, and immunization. The professionalization of medical practice in America dates to 1910 and the publication of the *Flexner Report,* which set standards for the training and licensing of doctors and the content of a medical education. As diploma mills were put out of business by the new medical universities, the general quality of health care improved, standards for training and practice were raised, and the power of medical people over American health care was firmly established (Starr, 1982).

From the Hippocratic Oath, taken by physicians

Sometimes give your services for nothing. . . . And if there be an opportunity of serving one who is a stranger in financial straits, give full assistance to all such.

—HIPPOCRATES (C. 400 BCE)

The medical establishment—in the organizational form of the American Medical Association (AMA)—controlled not only the demand for services but the supply of practitioners. Up to World War II, the field was perceived as a "gentlemen's club" of like-minded experts, from which women, racial minorities, and Jews were largely excluded. Smaller medical schools that had once trained women and African Americans were forced to close, and admissions to accredited institutions were carefully controlled. Where women had once composed 20 percent of all physicians in some American cities in 1900, they were now refused admission to medical schools on the grounds that their frail constitutions could not withstand the rigors of a medical education. For the next five decades, women were channeled into nursing, social work, and public health organizations (Morantz-Sanchez, 1985). It was not until the civil rights legislation of the

1970s forced medical schools to adopt nondiscriminatory admissions that women or persons of color gained entry in large numbers. Yet even today, over 80 percent of practicing physicians are white males. The proportion of women will, however, increase, because they now compose close to 40 percent of medical students. The outlook for persons of color is less optimistic; the costs of a medical education and the number of years required for training preclude many qualified people from entering the field.

THE NEW MEDICAL-INDUSTRIAL COMPLEX. The absolute power of the American doctor is being challenged today by several developments. In some areas, solo and small group practices are gradually being absorbed by profit-making companies that own chains of hospitals, nursing homes, medical office centers, and walk-in clinics (Estes et al., 1992). In such facilities, the doctor ceases to be self-employed and becomes a salaried employee of corporate owners, with nonmedical administrative decisions made at regional or national corporate headquarters. In return for selling their practices to the company, doctors are provided with cash, stock in the corporation, office space, nurses, technicians, secretaries, and the security of a steady income. The combined annual business of medical groups acquired by profit-making chains exceeded $1 billion in 1993 and is growing at a rate of 30 percent a year (Freudenheim, 1993).

In other cases, medical people compete among themselves for control of technology and health care profits. Increasingly, a group of doctors will invest in medical support facilities such as laboratories or diagnostic centers to which they refer their own patients and at higher rates than do doctors without these additional sources of income. For example, physicians who own diagnostic imaging centers were *298 times* more likely than other doctors to refer patients for CAT scans (*Productive Aging News,* 1993). Although government regulations forbid doctors from owning a stake in clinical laboratories serving patients covered by the Medicare and Medicaid programs, these rules do not extend to privately insured or self-paying patients, nor do they cover physician investments in health care companies that provide services to homebound patients. None of these practices has been condemned by the AMA, despite obvious conflict-of-interest problems (Meier, 1993).

The scramble for profits and income security is partly fueled by an increase in the number of physicians. In 1960 there were about 150 doctors per 100,000 Americans; today there are approximately 250. Competition for patients, especially those covered by insurance or who can pay in full, has become intense in some parts of the country, leaving other areas underserved. Despite the relative glut, it has been difficult to find doctors to practice in the inner

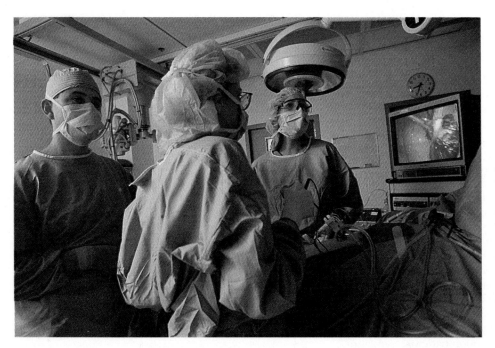

Technological advances have dramatically changed medical procedures. For example, the gall bladder that is being removed during this laproscopic surgery can be observed by the surgeons on the adjacent television monitor. Such expensive technology is generally available only in well-funded hospitals.

city, places with concentrations of elderly people, and regions where the patients are few and far between. (Just think of the complaints of Dr. Joel Fleischman on the TV program *Northern Exposure,* repaying his medical school bills by treating the residents of Cicily, Alaska, while dreaming of eventually having a prosperous practice in New York City.)

In large part, this problem reflects the higher prestige and income given to a specialist rather than to a family doctor. Specialists must practice where there is a concentration of potential patients, such as in the wealthier sections of major cities or large suburbs. As a result, New York's Park Avenue is home to hundreds of psychiatrists, heart specialists, and surgeons, while entire counties in the midwest are without a single physician.

Other Health Care Providers

NURSING: A PROFESSION IN FLUX.   Although we tend to think of physicians as the major providers of health care, nurses compose the single largest category of health professionals in the United States. The history of modern nursing dates from 1854 and the well-to-do women organized by Florence Nightingale to care for the British wounded in the Crimean War. Nightingale was the first to define nursing as paid work rather than as an act of mercy or a woman's natural duty. By the 1920s, nursing was a popular career choice of upwardly mobile American women seeking a respectable and responsible occupation. But as physicians and hospitals came to dominate health care delivery, demanding cheap and controllable

labor, nursing became less attractive and less easily professionalized.

The history of nursing is closely linked to that of gender politics. Throughout most of human history

Nurses represent the single largest category of health professionals in the United States. Recent attempts to professionalize nursing have included upgraded training, four-year college degree programs, higher pay, and greater job autonomy.

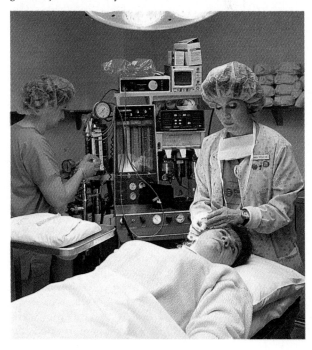

healers were women, people with knowledge of herbs and home remedies, until they were labeled as witches. With the rise of modern medicine as a male profession, the role of nurse was defined as that of doctor's helper, with an emphasis on such female virtues as obedience and nurturance. She could dispense tender, loving care, while he diagnosed and prescribed.

Recent attempts to professionalize nursing, therefore, must first deal with gendered stereotypes. Gradually, training has been upgraded, with a four-year college degree program replacing two- or three-year hospital-based nursing schools. Graduate nurses are no longer willing to perform many of the unskilled and semi-skilled tasks that were once expected. The American Nursing Association has become a more aggressive professional association, fighting for such un-lady-like things as higher pay and greater job autonomy, but the vast majority of nurses are not members of any bargaining organization. Notice how, on the few occasions when nurses have gone on strike, the first question by a reporter is invariably, "How can you leave those poor patients?" and not, "Why are you striking?"

Nonetheless, rising health care costs plus increased specialization within medicine have encouraged the development of new career paths for nurses. The relatively new positions of *nurse administrator* and *nurse practitioner* require additional training and bring added autonomy and prestige. A nurse administrator supervises the nursing staff of a hospital or long-term care facility, with decision-making powers independent of the attending physicians. The nurse practitioner is trained in a particular specialty, such as obstetrics or geriatrics, where she can handle many of the procedures usually done by a doctor, short of prescribing medication. Not surprisingly, these efforts to upgrade the profession and to enhance autonomy have drawn opposition from physicians' organizations. Yet, where doctors are loath to go—into slums and nursing homes—the nurse practitioner will probably find little competition.

But several trends are limiting the pool of registered nurses. Given the long hours and low pay, the life-and-death responsibilities with little recognition, the field is not as inviting as it was when women had few other choices. The young woman who wants to become a health care professional today can as easily apply to a medical school as to a nursing program. The other trend is that hospitals are reducing overhead costs by turning more bedside

Chiropractic is the treatment of disease through manipulation of the body, especially the spine.

Osteopathy, a treatment of disease that originally emphasized bones and muscles, has become very similar to mainstream medicine.

Nurse practitioners are trained in specialties, such as adolescent development, and handle many of the procedures usually done by doctors. What factors have led to this increased specialization within medicine?

tasks over to lower-paid, lower-skilled support staff, which has the effect of creating an underclass of health care workers, typically minority men and women.

UNCONVENTIONAL HEALTH CARE PROVIDERS. A variety of health care providers are not yet fully accepted into the mainstream of the medical establishment. In addition to midwives, there are chiropractors, osteopaths, acupuncture specialists, and Christian Science healers. All share a distaste for the use of drug therapies and surgical interventions, although they differ on other aspects of care.

Chiropractic, for example, treats illness through the manipulation of the body, especially the spinal column. The field was founded in 1895 and has been subjected to ridicule from medical doctors ever since, even though chiropractors take much the same course work as physicians and must pass rigorous licensing tests. Local medical societies have been successful in denying the use of hospital facilities to chiropractors. The range of services that a chiropractor can provide is also limited by law. Nonetheless, chiropractic has enjoyed a new popularity among people interested in holistic health, that is, the treatment of the body through natural techniques rather than through surgery or drugs.

Osteopathy also began as an alternative to nineteenth-century medical practice. From an original emphasis on bones and muscles, osteopathic training has become very similar to that of mainstream medicine. Osteopaths are not limited in the services they can provide and typically enjoy hospital privileges and re-

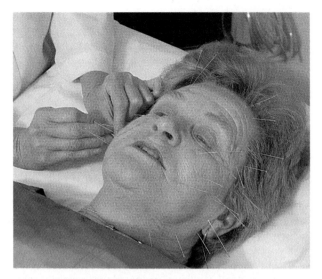

Among the less conventional medical technologies gaining popularity in the United States is acupuncture. Acupuncture has a long history of use in Asia, especially in China, and consists of the insertion of needles into various areas of the body. Practitioners claim that the procedure balances the body by unblocking the flow of energy. Acupuncturists have mapped the connections between various areas of the body and know which points to puncture in order to help the patient feel better.

ferrals from conventional physicians and their practices are becoming indistinguishable from mainstream medicine.

Acupuncture is an ancient Chinese technique for relieving pain and reducing addiction through the manipulation of fine needles inserted into designated parts of the body thought to affect specific functions.

Christian Science healers depend on the powers of mind and spirit to combat poor health and other problems such as psychological tension and family conflict. The emphasis is on health rather than illness and on individual control over one's body.

Although long ridiculed and opposed by mainstream medical practitioners, nonconventional and holistic medicine and various folk remedies were given new respectability in 1994 with the creation of an Office of Alternative Medicine in the National Institutes of Health, the U.S. government's medical research complex in Bethesda, Maryland.

THE GROWTH OF THE AMERICAN HOSPITAL

Paralleling the physician's dominance of medical practice has been the emergence of the hospital as the major center for health care. In 1873, there were only 100 general hospitals in the United States, most of which were owned by state or local governments or by religious organizations. Today, there are about 5,300 general hospitals (somewhat fewer than in 1972) under a variety of ownerships. **Hospital ownership** falls into three broad categories: (1) for-profit (*proprietary*) private, (2) nonprofit private, and (3) public.

The growth of hospitals in the early twentieth century was encouraged by physicians who needed teaching and research facilities. As the practice of medicine became more respectable, people who could afford it began to demand professional care. To meet these needs, nonprofit community hospitals were founded, providing acute and surgical care financed by patient fees. As a result, physician control was reinforced, because only they could order the admissions that filled the beds. The monopoly over health care was further strengthened when the AMA succeeded in limiting the number of free clinics and in preventing public health offices from offering direct care (Starr, 1982).

Acupuncture is an ancient Chinese technique for relieving pain and reducing addiction by manipulating fine needles into designated parts of the body.

Christian Science healers combat poor health and other problems by using the powers of the mind and spirit.

Hospital ownership is either for-profit (proprietary) private, non-profit private, or public.

Proprietary Hospitals

Today, the rapid growth of for-profit (proprietary) hospital chains has posed a profound challenge to the traditional community-based nonprofit hospital. By 1994, close to one in three acute-care hospitals in the United States was part of an investor-owned chain—a kind of medical Kmart—involving almost 2,000 facilities. In addition to acute-care hospitals, the proprietary chains have also purchased or constructed psychiatric hospitals and treatment centers for addictions and have contracted to manage nonprofit institutions.

The early momentum for proprietary companies came from the purchase of smaller community hospitals that were in financial trouble as a result of rising costs and declining ability to raise money from patients and the public. By centralizing purchasing and other administrative tasks, the chains claimed to be able to lower overhead costs while bringing businesslike efficiency to the health care system, but the evidence has not been very convincing (Lindorff, 1992). The major criticism of proprietary hospitals is that quality of care may be sacrificed to the goal of making a profit for shareholders. Indeed, the average length of stay is lower in the proprietary than in nonprofit hospitals, occupancy rates are lower, and fewer staff per person are employed (American Hospital Association, 1992).

Most of these effects, however, are related to the ability of proprietary facilities to select their patients, avoiding the very sick and the very poor, who tend to require the most care. Almost all patients are privately insured or eligible for Medicare reimbursement. Although the proprietary chains have not yet produced competition in the price of health care, they have stimulated a market for recruiting staff physicians. The typical for-profit facility can offer steady work, high salaries, rent-free offices, paid nurses and clerical assistants, centralized billing, and even country club memberships (Dallek, 1986). Few nonprofits or public facilities can compete in this league.

Nonprofit Facilities

The majority of American hospitals are owned and operated as nonprofit institutions by a Board of Trustees composed of civic leaders. Their nonprofit status allows certain tax advantages, and governance of the hospital is divided between medical and administrative staffs. In general, the local medical society determines who can admit patients to the hospital. Financing comes from patient fees, insurance reimbursements, charitable fund-raising in the community, and government grants. Without community support, nonprofits may find themselves unable to remain financially healthy and become targets for a takeover by a proprietary chain. Unlike a proprietary facility, nonprofits that receive government funds are obligated to treat all members of the community. Whether they can do so and how well is problematic.

Because the community nonprofit hospital serves some patients who are not insured and who cannot pay for their care out-of-pocket, a surcharge must often be added to the bill of insured patients. Otherwise, some services would have to be eliminated or the hospital staff reduced. There are therefore strong financial pressures to provide uninsured and underinsured patients with the minimum care required to stabilize their condition before releasing them or arranging a transfer to a public hospital.

Another major expense item is the purchase and use of increasingly complex and expensive diagnostic and treatment technologies, which tend to be used regardless of their immediate benefit. For all these reasons, including adequate pay for nurses and other staff, the cost of an average stay in a nonprofit hospital has risen dramatically over the past 25 years, from $600 in 1970 to about $5,500 today.

Because of the high overhead costs, it is in the interest of the hospital to fill its beds, and to do so with paying patients. In reality, hospital use rates (days of care per population, length of the average stay, and number of beds filled) have *declined* since the 1970s. Ironically, the hospital's contribution to enhancing the health status of community residents has undermined an important source of income. In many places, the hospital has responded by expanding its outpatient services, offering clinics on a variety of health-related problems such as pregnancy counseling and drug rehabilitation.

The Public Hospital

Public hospitals are owned and operated by the federal, state, or local government. In this section we are concerned primarily with city-owned hospitals, whose financial well-being is directly related to the local tax base. For reasons detailed in Chapter 21, America's cities have lost most of their income sources at the same time that their population has grown poorer and sicker. Unemployed people and part-time workers are not covered by workplace health insurance policies, and only some of the very poor are eligible for the state and federal Medicaid program that partially reimburses health care providers. Where do the uninsured and underinsured go for health care? Certainly not to the for-profit chains, perhaps to a nonprofit if there is one in the vicinity, but most often to a city-owned public hospital.

The public hospital, in contrast to the proprietary and nonprofits, is overcrowded with acute care patients, people who require immediate, intense service. The public hospital also tends to be understaffed, given the stressful working conditions and low pay. Although health care professionals take an oath to serve the needful, it is much more pleasant and profitable to do so in a proprietary or suburban facility. At the same time that the patient load has become poorer and sicker, federal and state subsidies to public hospitals have been drastically cut in order to reduce deficits without raising taxes. And just as the the cost of treatment has risen, the rate at which government programs reimburse providers has been lowered. In addition, several states have cut their health care costs by changing the rules for eligibility for subsidized care, leaving many poor and near-poor without any assistance at all (Pear, 1994).

As a consequence, although Americans claim to abhor the idea of rationing health care, that is exactly what is being done informally by private physicians and nonpublic hospitals every day. In our system, health care has been effectively rationed by the ability to pay (Estes et al., 1992).

Why is the American system so different from those of other industrial societies? Why do we spend more on health care that covers a smaller proportion of citizens? The answers lie in the dominance of physicians over all aspects of medicine, already described, and in the unique models of health care delivery and payment that they have devised and maintained, as examined in the remainder of this chapter.

MODELS OF HEALTH CARE DELIVERY

The norms and values of a society determine the extent to which the health needs of a population are met, the level of funding, the delivery system, and the way in which scarce resources are allocated. Such seemingly neutral acts as performing an organ transplant, eliminating pollutants, or advising a pregnant woman are all influenced by nonmedical factors such as social class, political power, and religious beliefs. Among the most enduring American values are those associated with individualism and capitalism, and these have done most to shape our health care system (Birenbaum, 1993).

The United States is the only modern industrial society without a program of government-funded health insurance, providing coverage for medical care to all citizens across the life course. In 1945, when President Harry Truman presented a proposal for a modest national health insurance program, the AMA brought its weight to bear on Congress and the public. Advertisements claiming that the plan was the entering wedge for socialism filled newspapers and airwaves. Major business organizations were also totally opposed, and Truman's proposal died quickly.

Two decades later, in 1965, when rising health care costs associated with the growing elderly population threatened to bankrupt their children, pressure developed for a health insurance system for older Americans. The result was **Medicare,** an insurance program funded by contributions from workers and employers, administered by a federal agency, that re-

Drawing by Cotham; © 1994 The New Yorker Magazine, Inc.

"This patient has a rare form of medical insurance."

imburses health care providers for certain services given to older patients. The plan does not cover many health care needs of the elderly, including routine physical examinations, eyeglasses, hearing aids, most dental care, or prescriptions. In the following decades, premiums for supplemental insurance have risen, the range of covered services has narrowed, and the reimbursement rate has fallen further below costs, so that older Americans pay as much out of pocket for their health care as they did in 1960. Hardest hit are the very poor and ill who have difficulty negotiating the health care system in the first place. Once in a hospital, poor and black Medicare patients tend to receive less and lower-quality care than that given to their equally ill, white age peers (Kahn et al., 1994).

Also in 1965, Congress initiated a federally funded state-administered program, **Medicaid,** for reimbursing providers of health care to the very poor. Because their health needs are enormous and costly, the program has been troubled from the beginning. Fewer than 40 percent of those eligible are enrolled, most states have reduced the reimbursement rate, and few physicians or hospitals accept Medicaid patients. Women and nonwhites are disproportionately represented among Medicaid patients and are subjected to discriminatory treatment and stigmatization (Meyer, 1994). Yet even this limited program is currently under attack in Congress and in state legislatures. All other Americans are on their own in a system dominated by the professional model of health care.

Medicare is a federally administered insurance program, funded by workers' and employers' contributions, to reimburse providers for certain services given to older patients.

Medicaid is a federally funded, state-administered program for reimbursing providers of health care to the very poor.

The **professional model** of health care delivery is based on physicians' control of health care.

The Professional Model

The **professional model** is based on the power of physicians to control the health care system. Payment is on the basis of *fee-for-service,* with the doctor setting the appropriate fee and the patient paying only for specific services rendered. As with any profession, monitoring quality of service and establishing a "fair fee" structure are the responsibility of one's peers; that is, other physicians sit in judgment on their colleagues. The distribution of doctors is determined by the individual practitioner's specialty and other personal preferences rather than by considerations of the health needs of the population.

As noted, the autonomy of individual physicians has already been eroded by the growth of medical chains. In addition, rising health care costs have led employers to seek alternatives to the professional model. Thus, from a 73 percent share of the health care market in 1988, fee-for-service now accounts for only 38 percent of privately insured patients. The new leaders in health care delivery are health care maintenance organizations and other forms of "managed care."

The **health maintenance organization (HMO)** is uniquely American in its combining of features of both private enterprise and group insurance. The HMO consists of a group of health care providers who contract with employers to offer a full range of medical services to covered employees for a fixed yearly fee (paid by the employer but often in lieu of a wage increase). Subscribers must use doctors, pharmacies, and hospitals in the HMO network or pay on a fee-for-service basis elsewhere. Typically, also, the worker makes a token co-payment—$2 or $5 or $10—for each visit or prescription. Unlike the fee-for-service system, the HMO makes money when people do *not* use its services; the emphasis is on preventive medicine, such as promoting beneficial health habits; and when the fee is prepaid, people are more likely to visit a doctor during the early stages of an illness, thus reducing the eventual cost of treatment. If you thought that the visit would cost $100 or more out-of-pocket, you would probably delay as long as possible.

Since 1980, the number of HMOs has more than doubled, from 236 to over 600 and the number of subscribers has quintupled, from 9 to 50 million. Most dramatic has been the number of HMOs owned by national for-profit corporations. Although it was originally assumed that competition among HMOs would produce high-quality and cost-effective health care, the trend toward monopolization has reduced the competitive element. Nonetheless, from the subscriber's viewpoint, the HMO provides full care at relatively low cost, with less paperwork than conventional insurance plans. The trade-off is limitations on choice of provider and treatments.

One common variation on the HMO model is the **individual practice association (IPA)**, which al-

> The **health maintenance organization (HMO)** is based on prepayment for health care by patients who agree to use member physicians and hospitals.
>
> In **individual practice associations (IPAs)**, physicians accept patients under a prepayment arrangement but can also accept fee-for-service reimbursement.
>
> The **preferred provider organization (PPO)** is based on an agreement between health care providers and third-party payers to provide health care at a discount.

Health maintenance organizations (HMOs) combine features of private enterprise and group insurance. HMOs emphasize preventive medicine, such as promoting beneficial health habits. This worker, whose employer belongs to an HMO, makes a $10 co-payment while receiving prenatal care.

lows physicians to have fee-for-service patients as well as prepaid subscribers. The doctors practice in their own offices rather than in a centralized clinic-like facility of many HMOs.

Another variant is the **preferred provider organization (PPO),** involving an agreement between providers, employers, and health insurance companies to provide fee-for-service health care at a discount. The providers are ensured of a steady supply of patients, at lower cost to the employer. Some companies with thousands of workers and retirees have built their own clinics to provide low-cost basic care.

The functioning and quality of HMOs vary greatly from region to region, as does that of fee-for-service providers. Both systems are essentially physician-dominated, with costs covered primarily by employer contributions and secondarily by patient co-payments. Because the employer's share is a fringe benefit, workers often forget that they also pay this share in terms of wages foregone. But linking health insurance to employment status, while in perfect keeping with the work ethic, is a major problem for people not currently employed, those who work part-time, and those not covered by employers (a majority of low-income hourly employees). The retired and the very poor are covered to a limited extent by Medicare and Medicaid, but about 40 million other Americans, or one in six, are not insured at all.

National Health Insurance Models

The United States, as noted, is the only modern industrial society without some form of government-sponsored health insurance system that enrolls all citizens from birth to death. There are a number of variations on these cradle-to-grave systems, but none relies on private insurance companies as in the United States (Hurst and Poullier, 1993). Indeed, the fact that there is a "single-payer"—the government insurance fund—reduces costs by eliminating the need for profit-oriented private insurance companies.

In some societies, the national health system is financed by a general income tax and patients are reimbursed for their out-of-pocket, fee-for-service payments to a provider of their choice. In other societies, notably Japan and Germany, the cost of coverage is shared by employers and employees, with employers doing the bookkeeping. And in still other systems, health care providers are salaried employees of the state, and patients are served free of charge. Wealthier patients can always go outside the system to purchase additional care at their own expense, but each citizen is guaranteed a basic level of care regardless of the person's health status, income, or employment.

CRITICISMS OF THE NATIONAL INSURANCE MODELS. National health insurance, often referred to as "socialized medicine" by its opponents, has been criticized on several grounds. One claim is that free services will lead to "overuse" as people seek care for minor ailments. The evidence from Europe, however, is that the number of yearly visits to a doctor is not significantly higher than in the United States (Sandier, 1989).

A second criticism is that the doctors will be overworked and underpaid, lowering morale and the attractiveness of medical training. In terms of hours worked, however, the American fee-for-service general practitioners put in more hours (53.3 hours per week) than their salaried British counterparts (38.2 hours). Nor has there been a dramatic drop in applications to European medical schools.

A third criticism is that government controls invariably produce a bureaucratic maze in which providers and consumers lose control over health care. In most nations, however, the rules and regulations are formulated in negotiations among representatives of medical professions, consumer advocates, and the agency administering the health care funds. Also, the trend is away from direct government intervention, as illustrated by Canada's single-payer system where the role of the state is to balance the interests of providers and consumers and to contain costs by removing the profit-motive from health insurance (Rosenthal and Frankel, 1992). Yet, despite a health care bill that is the highest in the world (Figure 18-3), and a service delivery system that has effectively excluded at least 16 percent of the population, Americans have refused to consider any of the single-payer models. By 1992, however, soaring costs and increasing numbers of uninsured placed the issue high on the public agenda. At this writing, the outcome is still in doubt.

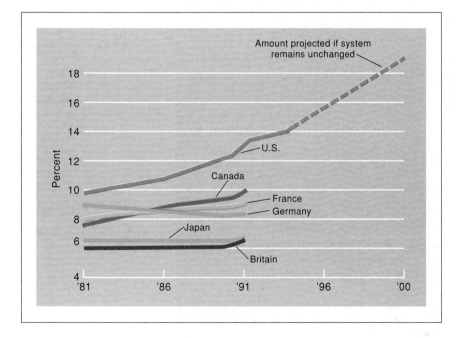

Amount projected if system remains unchanged

U.S.

Canada

France

Germany

Japan

Britain

Percent

'81 '86 '91 '96 '00

FIGURE 18-3 National health spending as percentage of gross domestic product for selected countries.

Sources: Data from Organization for Economic Cooperation and Development; graph data from *New York Times*, September 20, 1993. Copyright © 1993 by The New York Times Company. Reprinted by permission.

THE AMERICAN DILEMMA: RISING COSTS, DECLINING COVERAGE

Rising Costs

As shown in Figure 18-3, health care spending in the United States rose sharply in the 1980s and accounts for 15 percent of all expenditures on goods and services in the nation today. If health care spending continues to grow at the present rate, it could exceed 18 percent of total expenditures by the year 2000 (Dworkin, 1994). Where do the health dollars (more than $1 trillion today) go?

As already noted, hospital care is extremely expensive, and accounted for 44 percent of personal health care costs in the early 1990s. Twenty-two percent was spent on physician care, most of which was paid by private health insurance (47 percent) or Medicare/Medicaid (35 percent). About 9 percent was spent on drugs, and another 9 percent on nursing home care. Dentists, home health care, vision and hearing aids, and "other" expenses accounted for the remaining 15 percent (Employee Benefit Research Institute, 1993).

In part, these expenditures reflect the aging of the population, as most health care dollars are spent on the treatment of chronic conditions and terminal illnesses. As the baby boom generation ages, the proportion of Americans age 65 and over will increase from 13 percent to 21 percent by 2050, so that this type of expense will not decline soon. However, population aging accounted for only about 10 percent of the increase in health care costs in the late 1980s. Far more important were economy-wide and medical price inflation and a large increase in the number of tests performed during each patient visit, which was due in part to the rapid development and use of sophisticated technology. The cost of health care has also been affected by an increase in the number and incomes of health care personnel, high administrative costs of a system financed largely by private insurers, and outright fraud.

Although opponents of national health insurance point to the potential misuse of the system by patients, most illegal and unethical conduct to date has involved providers and insurers. Overcharging, unnecessary testing, billing for treatments not given, and kickbacks for patient referrals account for 10 percent of the total health bill (Jesilow et al., 1994). In addition, much of the overhead for the health insurance companies that serve as a third-party—collecting contributions from employers and individuals, handling claims, and paying providers—is spent on executive salaries in the high six figures, luxury offices, and expensive travel (Fritsch and Baquet, 1993). Despite several well-publicized cases of corruption and excessive overhead in 1993, most current proposals for health care reform would leave the third-party insurance system basically intact, and even modest changes were subject to an extensive negative advertising campaign by insurer and physician organizations.

Can quality care be delivered more cheaply? The case of Canada is instructive, because it resembles

The aging of the population, whether in the U.S. or China, has resulted in greater expenditures of national resources for the treatment of chronic conditions and terminal illness. The government of The People's Republic of China provides free health care for all of its citizens, including the elderly.

Do They Really Do It Better in Canada?

As seen in Figure 18-3, Canadian health care expenditures are a much smaller part of its gross domestic product than those of the United States. Yet Canadian life expectancy is longer and infant mortality lower than in the United States. Administrative costs in Canada account for 3 percent of the health budget in contrast to 12 percent of the U.S. health budget. In addition, the incidence of fraud and mismanagement is lower.

Up to 1969, the Canadian health care system was organized on the professional model and financed through third-party insurers, with costs proportionately similar to those in the United States. In 1969, the Canadians switched to a system of federal funding, administered by the various provinces (comparable to our states). To receive the federal funds, the provinces must provide (1) comprehensive and universal coverage (in other words, every health care item and every person must be included) and (2) a public nonprofit administrative agency.

Despite claims of waiting lists and rationing of health care by American opponents of the Canadian model, a 1991 survey found that 95 percent of all Canadians reported receiving the care that they needed within 24 hours (Coupland, 1993). Indeed, Canadian rates of satisfaction with their health care system are far higher than those of American respondents. Another claim of opponents is that many Canadians prefer to use American medical services, but it appears that many more Americans cross the border into Canada to take advantage of the free care (Farnsworth, 1993b).

Above all, the single-payer model is an enormous money saver, by lowering overhead and controlling price increases, largely through bypassing insurance companies.

---

the United States in many cultural and population characteristics (see box above).

Another factor in the rising American health bill is the fear of malpractice suits that leads to the practice of defensive medicine, that is, prescribing tests and treatments to cover every eventuality, regardless of its immediate necessity. This fear appears to be exaggerated, because few physicians are ever sued, most cases are settled out of court for a few thousand dollars, and the cost of malpractice insurance is relatively low—an average of $15,000–20,000 a year—for people earning ten times that amount (Hay, 1992; Fielding, 1995). The number of malpractice claims might be further reduced if local medical boards were more diligent in pursuing complaints against colleagues. In 1992, for example, peer panels took disciplinary action against only one-half of one percent of all practicing doctors (Verhovek, 1994).

Health care costs in the United States vary widely from region to region, depending on the number and types of physicians and hospitals. For example, where there are a large number of cardiologists and high-tech surgical centers, heart surgery rates will be high. Similarly, the more hospital beds in the area, the higher the rate of medical admissions. This is Parkinson's Law of medicine: Cases will expand to fill all available facilities.

CONTROLLING COSTS.   Because hospital charges are the largest single contributor to health care costs, and because most of this money is spent on elderly patients, the federal government has tried to "cap" (set a ceiling on) hospital use and charges for Medicare patients.   Originally, hospitals were reimbursed for all "reasonable costs" of patient care. In 1985, a new system was introduced involving **prospective payments,** rates set in advance of service delivery, based on diagnostic-related groups (DRGs).

Under this system, the hospital is paid a fixed sum by Medicare for each case; the amount is determined by which of 465 diagnostic categories the patient fits. The advantages are that payment rates are simplified, the hospital is paid in advance, and if the actual cost of care is lower than the DRG payment, the hospital can pocket the difference. If costs exceed the DRG fee, however, the hospital must absorb the difference. Opponents of DRGs claim that there are strong incentives to release patients before they are fully cured. Advocates claim that DRGs force hospitals to review procedures with an eye to reducing unnecessary costs.   At the moment, the evidence is mixed, in part because the average length of a hospital stay was already declining as a result of the expansion of outpatient facilities and the introduction of treatments that no longer require surgery.

Among the European nations, despite the variety of national health insurance models, costs have been controlled by capping physician and hospital fees and by budgeting for entire geographical areas, with local officials deciding how to allocate the funds. But all these countries are currently feeling the crunch of lowered tax revenues during the global economic recession, which may lead to some curtailment of services while preserving universal coverage.

> The **prospective payment system** is based on fixed payment diagnosis-related groups (DRGs) rather than "reasonable costs."

Declining Coverage

As health care costs have risen, so also has the cost of health insurance, followed by a decline in the number of employer health plans, and consequently an increase in the number of Americans who are uninsured. Uninsured people are less likely than the insured to seek medical care, typically waiting until their illness is well advanced (Franks et al., 1993). In 1994, approximately 40 million Americans, or 16 percent of the population, were uninsured. Figure 18-4 shows the distribution of uninsured younger than age 65 in 1992, a majority of whom are in the labor force and over one-third of whom are the primary family earner.

Another large but difficult to calculate number are the *under*insured, whose policies cover only certain illnesses or payments. In addition, the 34 million Americans on Medicaid must also be included here because the reimbursement rate is so low that few providers are willing to accept them as patients. All in all, between one-third and two-fifths (40 percent) of the population are inadequately covered. Most are simply unable to afford the premiums for individual or family coverage; others have been dropped from employer plans through layoffs or plant closings; and still others are turned away by insurers because they are assumed to be at high risk of expensive health problems (U.S. Bureau of the Census, *Statistical Brief 94-6*, 1994).

Private insurance companies can increase their profits by minimizing their risks. American insurers routinely refuse to cover people with potentially

The staggering costs of medical care in the United States and the fact that some 40 million Americans do not have health care coverage have led the Clinton Administration to seek national health insurance for all Americans—coverage available to citizens of all other industrial countries. The American Medical Association, the insurance companies, and a number of other lobby groups have opposed such reform. Hillary Rodham Clinton, addressing a meeting of the AMA, has been a major advocate of health care reform. As of early 1995 no universal health care has been enacted by the Congress of the United States. Stay tuned.

FIGURE 18-4   Nonelderly population without health insurance, by own work status, 1992.

Source: Employee Benefit Research Institute, 1994.

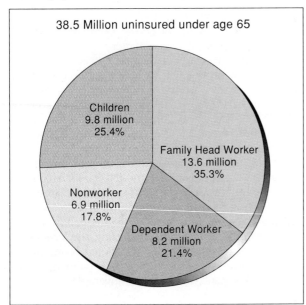

costly existing health problems or whose life style might lead to serious illness. In addition, the companies can impose a surcharge on riskier applicants. For example, as a potential AIDS risk, an unmarried man older than age 30 would have difficulty finding an affordable policy. Another cost-reducing mechanism is limiting the services covered in the policy, so that it is often the insurance company rather than the physician who determines the degree and level of care a patient can receive (Light, 1994). The average premium for a basic family plan from a private insurer today is about $6,000 and rising.

Another factor that limits coverage is the tendency for employers to shift more of the benefit cost to employees, claiming that health insurance expenditures have cut into profitability, even though this represents less than 7 percent of total labor costs (Harris, 1993). Increasingly, employers are also shifting from major insurance carriers to "self-insured" programs, in which the employer can pick and choose what services to cover and at what level, as with any private insurer.

In the light of these trends in costs and coverage, a majority of Americans now consider that there is either a "crisis" or "serious problem" with our health care system. But the power of private enterprise in the American mind and economy are such that most of the proposals now before Congress, including the one presented by President Clinton, not only maintain the dominance of profit-making insurance giants such as Blue Cross and Prudential, but would expand their control of the market. Only one proposal calls for a single-payer system, eliminating private insurers, and offering universal coverage. The most likely to succeed are those that phase in coverage gradually, that refuse to cap provider fees, and that do not force employers to pay for their workers. The coalition of employers, insurers, and physicians that defeated President Truman's attempt at national health insurance 50 years ago won again in 1994.

SOCIAL POLICY

Health Care: A Right or a Privilege?

Is universal and comprehensive coverage incompatible with cost containment? Must some people be sacrificed so that most can receive adequate care? Above all, what services are to be defined as rights of citizenship or as privileges to be enjoyed by those who have earned or can afford them? These are questions that go to the core of the American value system, and the answers will define our nation at the close of the twentieth century.

Up to this point, with the exception of the elderly, health care in America has been defined as a privilege. Costs are largely borne by individuals directly or indirectly, and both the delivery and administrative systems are dominated by private profit-driven entities. Although private market forces should increase competition and ultimately drive down costs, this has not happened. Rather, a three-tiered system of health care has evolved, in which the well-to-do can purchase all the services they require, including luxury accommodations at proprietary facilities. Most other Americans are limited by an employer-determined benefit package that may or may not include most services or cover other family members. And at least one in four Americans is effectively locked out of the system, either because there are no health care providers in the vicinity or because they cannot afford the fees, or both.

Advocates of health care as a right of citizenship argue that when proprietary hospitals screen out the very ill and the uninsured, when insurance companies refuse to cover the sick and the poor, and when physicians turn away those who cannot pay, the quality of life of the nation is lowered. In this view, whatever the potential drawbacks of a single-payer national health insurance system, the savings in administrative costs will allow a more equitable distribution of health services.

Opponents of major change claim that the private market will eventually bring down costs, that public bureaucracies breed inefficiency and corruption, that physicians are in the best position to make medical decisions, that consumers are better equipped than a government agency to decide how much and what type of care they are willing to pay for, and that the tax burden would inhibit economic growth that eventually raises all incomes.

What do you think? Would you be willing to pay more in taxes for health care reform? Would you accept limited choice of physicians in return for guaranteed coverage? Should health care fees be capped? If your class were to debate this issue, what arguments would you consider most powerful in favor or against any of the proposals before Congress, a single-payer system, or minor changes in the current systems?

SUMMARY

1. Health and illness are socially defined, and what may be considered normal or healthy in one society or a particular historical era may be viewed quite differently in another society or a different time.

2. Health and illness are linked to the level of economic development and technology of a country, its norms and values, and its population characteristics.

3. Epidemiology is the study of the patterns of occurrence of illness in a particular population.

4. Rates of incidence and prevalence provide a measure of the increase or decrease of specific diseases in a given time period.

5. Age, sex, race, and ethnicity, and social class are important factors in epidemiological studies. Each is related to differences among subgroups in health, illness, and death rates.

6. The relative social regard given to people with certain kinds of illnesses affects not only their medical treatment but the funding to find causes and cures for such an illness. AIDS illustrates the interplay between medical and social factors.

7. Two different models of physical and mental health, the pathological and the statistical, are used in today's medicine. Each leads to a different diagnosis and treatment. The pathological model focuses on abnormal functioning in an organism, whereas the statistical focuses on the average of a group as forming the norm.

8. A person in a sick role cannot function appropriately, is exempt from normal responsibilities, and is expected to get medical help. The concept of the sick role has been criticized for ignoring the ways in which health and illness are defined and controlled.

9. The current American health care system is relatively new. It is dominated by physicians and third-party payers, who are able to control the market for health care.

10. There are indications that small practices are being replaced by large profit-making companies that own a number of hospitals, nursing homes, medical office centers, and clinics with salaried physicians, nurses, and staffs.

11. Many public and non-profit community hospitals are unable to stay solvent, as proprietary chains increase their share of the market.

12. Nurses, the largest group of health workers, are members of a profession striving for greater recognition and higher pay. But other trends have reduced both the supply and demand for registered nurses.

13. Although various models of health care have been proposed, the most common in the United States is the professional model, based on the physician's control of health care. In contrast, the central planning model is based on public control over health care. The national insurance model places the financing of health care under government control, sets rules and policies, and arbitrates disputes.

14. The United States spends more on health care than several other countries, with poor results, as demonstrated by life expectancy data. Administrative costs, medical waste, unnecessary procedures, and physicians' increasing concern with malpractice suits drive up the cost of American heath care.

15. Controversy about the organizing and financing of health care in the United States continues as health care costs increase.

SUGGESTED READINGS

Aday, Lu Ann. *At Risk in America: The Health and Health Care Needs of Vulnerable Populations in the United States.* San Francisco: Jossey-Bass, 1993. An in-depth study of vulnerable populations such as mothers and infants who are at high-risk, the chronically ill and disabled, people with AIDS, the mentally ill and disabled, alcohol and substance abusers, abusive families, immigrants and refugees.

Albrecht, Gary L. *The Disability Business: Rehabilitation in America.* Newbury Park, CA: Sage, 1992. A highly readable book with the author providing key insights into the power structure of the rehabilitation industry, the fight over control of the industry and, ultimately, control of the lives of the disabled.

Birenbaum, Arnold. *Putting Health Care on the National Agenda.* Westport, CT: Praeger, 1993. A fine overview of the American health care system and its problems—even handed evaluation of complex issues, analysis of dramatic increases in costs of health care, and consideration of health care reform proposals.

Braithwaite, Ronald L. and Sandra E. Taylor. *Health Issues in the Black Community.* San Francisco: Jossey-Bass, 1992. A comprehensive examination of health concerns that affect the black community in disproportionate numbers. Chapters cover topics from heart disease and AIDS to substance abuse, homelessness, and violence.

Charmaz, Kathy. *Good Days, Bad Days: The Self in Chronic Illness and Time.* New Brunswick, NJ: Rutgers University Press, 1991. Charmaz probes beyond basic issues of chronic illness to discover how coping with illness reshapes one's life and one's idea of time.

Fox, Renee C. and Judith P. Swazey. *Spare Parts: Organ Replacement in American Society.* New York: Oxford University Press, 1992. Broad coverage of a topic that raises various moral and ethical dilemmas.

Philipson, Thomas J. and Richard A. Posner. *Private Choices and Public Health: The AIDS Epidemic in an Economic Perspective.* Cambridge, MA: Harvard University Press, 1993. The authors examine the economic effects of AIDS, including the subsidization of AIDS education and medical research, the social and fiscal costs of AIDS, and the political economy of the government response.

Ory, Marcia G., Ronald P. Abeles, and Paula Darby Lipman. (eds.) *Aging, Health and Behavior.* Newbury Park, CA: Sage, 1992. This authoritative, current reference with contributions from major researchers in the field illustrates the recent trend in aging research that integrates the social and psychological with the biological and studies individuals over the life course as well as groups that are the same age.

Rhodes, Lorna A. *Emptying Beds: The Work of an Emergency Psychiatric Unit.* Berkeley: University of California Press, 1991. Deinstitutionalization has imposed the need to "empty beds" in psychiatric health care units. Rhodes' ethnographic study is a fascinating account of psychiatric emergency patients who "travel through the new system."

Rodwin, Marc A. *Medicine, Money, and Morals: Physicians' Conflicts of Interest.* New York: Oxford University Press, 1993. Rodwin documents practices used by physicians which are not necessarily helpful to patients but increase physicians' incomes.

19

Modernization, Technology, and Social Change

*F*or many generations, a tribe of hunter-gatherers, the Teuso, lived in the mountains of east-central Africa. Nomadic bands of Teuso tracked big game in a yearly cycle that led them past food-gathering and watering sites back to their home base. The Teuso were well adapted to their physical environment, careful never to take more from the land than necessary, so that there would be enough animals and plants for the next year. When first visited by anthropologist Colin Turnbull, the Teuso were an open and friendly people, with few distinctions on the basis of power, possessions, or sex.

This peaceful, cooperative society was drastically changed after World War II, when new nations were created in central Africa. Leaders of these emerging nations sought to unify the vastly different tribes within their boundaries by creating a national economy. As part of this process, the traditional hunting ground of the Teuso, now called the Ik, was turned into a national park to attract foreign visitors. The Ik were forbidden to hunt the game that had been their source of food and the center of their culture. Instead, the government tried to turn them into farmers who would stay in one place, but the land assigned to the Ik was a rocky area with little rainfall. Because the tribe had no traditions or technology for farming, disaster was certain.

Indeed, when Turnbull returned to the tribe in the 1960s, he found an unfriendly, inhospitable, and cruel people. All ties of affection had disappeared. Faced with starvation, each Ik acted in terms of immediate self-interest, even grabbing food from the hands of a child or ill person. What had happened?

Major changes in the mode of subsistence had affected every aspect of culture and social structure, even personality (Turnbull, 1972).

Not all social change is necessarily disruptive of order or negative in its effects on people. For example, the recent integration of Greece into the broader European economic system has not only raised living standards but stabilized a democratic government and encouraged personal freedoms. In this case, reducing the power of traditional authorities and adopting modern institutions had positive outcomes for the younger generation.

Yet even if all members of a society resisted new ideas and social patterns and insisted that everything be done as it always had been, forces beyond their control would produce change. Climate shifts, disease, wars, and invasions can wipe out a population and destroy the economic base. Contact with other societies inevitably introduces different culture traits. No society, not even the most simple, is exactly the same today as it was 500 or even 5 years ago.

Social change is the process through which values, norms, institutions, stratification systems, social relationships, and self-identities are altered over time. This chapter describes the processes of change and their consequences at both the macrolevel of culture and social structure and the microlevel of interaction and personality. We also examine the master trend of modernization—becoming an industrial nation—and the role of technology in social change.

> **Social change** is the process through which values, norms, institutions, stratification systems, social relationships, and self-identities are altered over time.

When European settlers colonized South Africa, they created a system of apartheid, a policy of segregation and political and economic discrimination against people of color. Recently, social change has come to South Africa, and in 1993 African National Congress leader Nelson Mandela, (center) who had been jailed for 27 years by the old government, and South African President F.W. deKlerk, (right) were jointly awarded the 1993 Nobel Peace Prize. What further changes are necessary to transform South Africa into a democracy?

SOURCES OF CHANGE

Social change originates in events that are either primarily external or internal. External sources include (1) environmental events, (2) invasion and war, and (3) culture contact and diffusion. Internal sources include (1) innovation, (2) population shifts, and (3) cohort flow. Once in motion, the forces of change affect the entire system.

External Sources

Environmental events include both (1) those produced by nature such as earthquakes, floods, and climate shifts and (2) those produced by people such as overgrazing the land or polluting the air. These events destroy the balance between the society and its natural surroundings and ultimately affect the social ties within the group.

Warfare and invasion of one group's territory by another tribe, colonial nation, or economic power is a major source of change, especially in the countries of the Third World, that is, the less industrially developed regions of Africa, Asia, and Latin America. The far-reaching consequences of colonialism can be seen, for example, in southern Africa, where the European settlers not only displaced native populations and altered the economic base but introduced a stratification system based on skin color. Historically and culturally distinct tribes were lumped together as "blacks," defined as inferior to "civilized" whites, and forced to serve the interests of the colonists.

Can invasion and warfare bring positive changes? Some social scientists would argue that imposing a new way of life by coercion is always a misuse of power, but others point to such beneficial change as forcing Japan to adopt democratic political institutions following its defeat in World War II.

Culture contact is the most common and important source of change, as people from different societies meet and learn about one another's beliefs, artifacts, and social structures. Such contact can occur accidentally, or be deliberately sought for purposes of trade and the exchange of marriage partners, or be imposed from outside. Contact leads to the spread of culture traits from one society to another—a process called **diffusion.**

Some items of culture essential to the survival of humans were probably discovered in only one or two places and then diffused by contact throughout the inhabited world: fire, animal traps, ways of keeping track of time, and the wheel (which never made it to some areas for thousands of years.) Diffusion today typically involves consumer goods such as Coca-Cola, blue jeans, and fast foods—even McDonalds and Burger King in person. These items are often the first form of culture contact between the United States and other societies, and their American names enter directly into the language. Similarly, most Americans have their first contact with Japanese culture through the purchase of an automobile or television set, and their first words in Japanese are Sony or Toyota.

Teenagers throughout the world dance to rock-and-roll, and in the process absorb Western attitudes about sex, authority, and politics. In other cases, the industrial world "borrows" items of culture from traditional societies, also primarily foods and clothing styles. Food plants developed by Native Americans in the sixteenth century—corn, potatoes, manioc, beans, and squash—have diffused to the point where they now account for half the world's food supply (Haviland, 1993).

Culture contact is the most common source of change as people from different societies learn about other cultures through their artifacts. This Australian Aborigine is getting his first lesson in the use of a video camera. What are the consequences of such culture contact?

Environmental events include those produced by nature and by people.

Warfare and **invasion** occur when one group's or nation's territory is overrun and controlled by another.

Culture contact occurs as people from different societies meet and learn about one another's beliefs, artifacts, and social structure.

Diffusion refers to the process by which culture traits are spread from one society to another.

MAURICE RICHTER

Science, Technology, and Social Change

Maurice N. Richter, Jr. is Professor of Sociology at the State University of New York at Albany. He is the author of five books on science and society, including Exploring Sociology *(1987). He is currently editor of the ASA Newsletter on Science, Knowledge, and Technology.*

*M*y specialty, the sociology of science and technology, is often misunderstood. Some friends think that because I wrote several books about science and technology I should be able to tell them what computing equipment they should buy. But my books deal with science and technology only in relation to society, how American society has been changed by the automobile but not how to repair a car.

I grew up in a world without television, computers, atomic energy, jet planes, spaceflight, dial telephones, homogenized milk, penicillin, or cars with automatic shifting. I remember shoveling coal into the furnace every morning at home before going to school, seeing horse traffic mingling with cars on the New York City streets, watching ice delivered for the iceboxes that we had before refrigerators, and seeing several of my playmates crippled by polio that no one knew how to prevent. My interest in technological development has been inspired by such memories of a vanished way of life.

My interest was also stimulated by the fact that my father was a scientist who did research on diseases of the blood, and discovered a new form of cancer. My mother was also a physician. She received her medical degree in 1925, at a time when few women went into medical careers. I grew up in a home filled with books about science and nature. And I also had childhood contact with other scientists, including Dr. Enrico Fermi, the Nobel-Prize-winning nuclear physicist, who was a neighbor in the 1940s and was working on the atomic bomb. Thus, my background led me into the sociology of science and technology.

The central task of the sociologist of science is the study of the organization and functioning of the "scientific community," i.e., the community of scientific researchers. We investigate scientists' values and norms, their careers, their ways of communicating among themselves, inequalities among them, and how they relate to sponsors, employers, governments, and people who seek to use their discoveries.

I consider scientific progress to be essential to the long-range survival of human life. And, unlike many of my colleagues, I think that, despite imperfections and lapses, the scientific community has generally set a strong example for the rest of society by exhibiting less gender and race discrimination, less unfairness, less cheating and fraud, and less irrationality than one finds in most other sectors of society.

Scientists cannot work effectively if their work is too tightly controlled by employers, financial sponsors, or governments. However, they often face difficulties in securing the freedom they require. In totalitarian societies especially, rulers have often recognized that they need science but have also distrusted scientists and have been afraid to give them much freedom.

I also studied what happens when American university scientists obtain financial support for their research from industrial corporations. I found that, although such corporations may impose restrictions on scientists who accept money from them, this effect is more than compensated for by the fact that scientists who have access to money from both government and industry gain some freedom because they have a choice between different sources of funding.

Technology is often regarded as an outgrowth or extension of science, but scientific discoveries often depend on previous technological achievements: thus the invention of the microscope, of the telescope, and much more recently of the computer. Each stimulated numerous scientific discoveries.

The sociology of technology is concerned largely with understanding sources and outcomes of technological innovation. Predictions about new technology and its effects often turn out to be wrong and incomplete. I recently re-examined a book published in 1946 predicting the future of aviation: the author said that within a decade people would probably be traveling in flying automobiles (cars with wings!) but said not a word about the possibility of spaceflight. As the sociology of technology advances we hope to improve our predictive capacities so that technological change will not surprise us so much.

Internal Sources

Innovation refers to the introduction of a new item of culture, either through discovery or invention. A *discovery* involves becoming aware of an aspect of nature that had not been recognized before, such as the law of gravity, the infection theory of disease, or the principles of evolution. Discoveries open the door for further elaborations, such as when the realization that baked clay becomes permanently hard led to unique pottery-making industries and a flourishing of artistic styles throughout the prehistoric world.

An *invention* involves the combination of existing items of culture in a new way, such as when the combustion engine, wheels, piston rings, and dozens of other earlier inventions were all put together to create an automobile. Inventions are usually the result of small (incremental) improvements to a technical process rather than the product of one great brainstorm (Collins, 1988). Whether or not an invention ever gets off the drawing board often depends less on its intrinsic worth than on such factors as adequate funding, prestige of the inventor, and strength of opposition from competing interests (Etzkowitz, 1992).

Population shifts include major changes in birth or death rates or migration in and out of the society. These trends affect the size of various age groups and the sex composition of the population, with important social consequences, as discussed in the next chapter. Sometimes these changes are the result of the spread of disease that has been introduced from outside through culture contact, or result from wars and invasions.

Cohort flow refers to the movement of people born in a given time period across their life course (Chapter 7). As members of a birth cohort move from childhood to adulthood to old age they will typically add to or change some element of the existing culture and social structure. The society is never exactly the same from one generation to the next. The structural changes made by one cohort become the social environment of the next age group, and so forth through time (Riley, 1982).

Whatever the original source of change—external or internal—the outcomes will affect social patterns within the society and its relationship to the physical environment. Once in motion, the ultimate effects of social change are often unpredictable.

> As long as it exists and functions, any sociocultural system incessantly generates consequences which are not the results of external factors . . . but the consequences of the existence of the system and its activities.
>
> —Pitirim A. Sorokin, 1941, pp.600–1

ACCEPTING CHANGE

Not all diffused traits are equally likely to be adopted by the receiving society. In general, technology is most easily diffused because it is relatively easy to determine whether the new technique is superior to the existing one, for example, that a bow-and-arrow is more effective than a spear for hunting game. In contrast, nonmaterial items such as values and beliefs are less readily adopted, as the Chinese discovered since their invasion of Tibet several decades ago. Although monasteries have been closed and traditional rituals forbidden, Tibetans persist in their Buddhist beliefs, refusing to accept the ideology of Chinese communism. After all, who can quickly tell whether one person's gods are more effective than another's?

But even immediately beneficial items may not be welcome if the new trait involves radical changes in other aspects of culture. Diffusion has many outcomes, similar to the ripples caused by throwing a stone into a pond. A major change in one institutional sphere affects all relationships in a system and will be fiercely resisted on that account alone. People fear both the immediate and long-range impact of change. During the early days of the factory system in France, for example, new equipment was literally sabotaged by workers who threw their wooden shoes (*sabots* in French) into the machinery. Although new technologies have usually created more jobs than they have destroyed, the short-term effects on individual workers and whole communities are disastrous. Even a relatively simple shift in material culture, such as using a bow and arrow rather than a spear, requires the development of new skills as well as dramatic changes in the rituals surrounding the hunt and in traditional power relationships.

The innovation must be seen as compatible with the existing culture, or as meeting a crucial need, or as conferring a benefit that outweighs the cost of changing behavior. In addition, in all societies, certain individuals and groups profit greatly from the status quo and therefore have a strong investment (vested interest) in maintaining it. No African witch doctor could have resisted medical missionaries any more fiercely than members of the American Medical Association have fought against universal health insurance to this very day. And what vested interests continue to resist the production of fuel-efficient, nonpolluting automobiles in the United States?

Innovation refers to the introduction of a new item of culture through discovery or invention.

Population shifts include major changes in birth or death rates or migration.

Cohort flow refers to the movement of people born in a given time period across their life course.

SOCIOLOGY IN EVERYDAY LIFE

Reaching Out—and Out

A particularly fascinating example of the consequences of innovation for everyday life is Claude S. Fischer's (1992) study of the social history of the telephone from the 1870s to the 1940s. The men who introduced the telephone to the United States saw it primarily as an instrument for the advancement of business, to be used by men for important purposes or by wives to make their husbands' lives easier by ordering meals and other assistance.

Unlike the automobile, the telephone did not produce major changes in American life. Rather, the tech-

nology was used by ordinary people to expand activities in which they were already engaged, most important, the enhancement of *sociability*. It was women and people in small communities who found the telephone invaluable for instant and continual contact. Although some experts had predicted that telephone calls would depersonalize communication, precisely the opposite occurred: more people could reach out more often to more friends than ever before. Women who might otherwise have been isolated in their homes were the special beneficiaries of the new technology, able to stay in touch with the wider social universe (Rakow, 1992).

Not all authority figures resist the adoption of new technologies or ideas. Some will become **agents of change** by accepting and exploiting the new elements. If the tribal chief accepts the innovation, others are likely to follow. Each society has its trendsetters and gatekeepers who influence the pace and direction of social change. Although the mass media play a significant role in introducing new items in industrial societies, informal channels of communication are just as important to the modern American as to an Australian aborigine. Information on new items is conveyed through social networks. For example, one classic study of innovation in medicine found that a new drug was adopted most rapidly by those physicians who were embedded in a professional network in contrast to socially isolated doctors (Coleman et al., 1957).

Not all agents of change are appreciated. Many are labeled as troublemakers or heretics and subjected to ridicule, imprisonment, and even execution. In these ways, broad currents of change can be temporarily slowed, as when the Romans crucified Jesus or when the medieval Catholic Church imprisoned those who dissented from the doctrine that Earth was the center of the universe.

As a modern example, in 1987, the Communist government of Czechoslovakia convicted several musicians on the charge of corrupting Czech youth with American jazz. Only three years later, when a democratic government replaced the totalitarian regime, an American rock musician, Frank Zappa, was appointed to the post of cultural ambassador to the West. As this example illustrates, it is the *context* in which change is introduced that largely determines the outcome; the music was the same, the

Agents of change occupy statuses through which they influence the direction and pace of change.

Culture lag refers to the tendency of parts of the social structure to change at different rates after a new technology is introduced.

political and social environment had been radically altered.

The acceptance of a specific innovation thus depends on several factors: (1) the extent to which it is consistent with existing ideas and social patterns; (2) the balance between the benefits and costs of change, including a generalized fear of the unknown; (3) the strength of resistance by those with a vested interest in the status quo; and (4) the influence of change agents and networks.

THE PACE AND DIRECTION OF CHANGE

Once innovations are diffused and adopted, the society's culture base is enlarged, which increases the likelihood of further discovery and invention. The larger the knowledge base, the greater the probability of recombining elements into something new. This is why the rate of change is faster in complex than in simple societies. It is not that members of modern societies are more intelligent than people in simple societies, but that they can call on the accumulated knowledge of Western civilization; they can see further because they stand on the shoulders of giants (Merton, 1965). Thus, over the course of human history, the pace of social change has accelerated, so that the experience of one generation in modern society today is no longer comparable to that of their offspring.

But the history of social change in the industrial West is no certain guide to understanding the pattern of change in Third World nations today. It appears that no one set of stages characterizes the course or pace of economic development in contemporary preindustrial societies. These nations vary greatly in their resources, population size, and trade links to other countries (Santiago, 1993).

Within a society, not all aspects of culture change at the same rate. The term **culture lag** refers to the tendency for parts of the social structure to change at varying rates following the introduction of a new technology. For example, the effects of introducing the mass-produced automobile in the United States in the 1920s are still being felt (Ling, 1990). The distribution of population between city and suburb, patterns of work and leisure, and even dating behaviors have been transformed by the ability of most people to own an automobile. New industries have been spawned. The physical environment has been dramatically altered, as shopping malls, superhighways, and drive-in food outlets sprawl across the countryside. In addition, the full effects of air pollution from fuel emissions may not be felt for decades.

The technology–diffusion model shown in Figure 19-1 illustrates various aspects of cultural lag between the introduction of the new item and the many adaptations that follow (Coates, 1983). As you can see, the first step is adoption, when the new technology replaces older techniques. The second step is accommodation, when one institutional sphere is modified to make efficient use of the technology. In the third stage, other areas of social life undergo internal reorganization in response to earlier changes. New institutions could also be created at this time. In the fourth phase, an institutional pattern may become obsolete, be re-

placed, or drastically modified. Throughout, changes in one sphere affect all the others in a feedback loop.

Using the model in Figure 19-1, can you plot the many consequences of the introduction of the personal computer (PC) into millions of American homes, schools, and workplaces? Before the PC, only those businesses and institutions that could afford large expensive computer systems could reap the benefits of the new technology. With the small, affordable PC, these capabilities were within the reach of individuals, schools, and small business. Manual typewriters and paper files became obsolete; workers had to learn new skills to retain their jobs; new industries emerged for creating programs, training workers, and servicing the machines. Electronic mail and desktop publishing have transformed the knowledge business, and anyone who can pay for computer time now has access to vast information banks. Your college library is probably fully computerized, with much of its printed material now stored and retrieved electronically. Gone are the wooden file drawers and the traditional librarian. Welcome to the high-tech "learning resource center!"

As with earlier innovations, the PC has been resisted by those who fear technological displacement or who foresee an office run by machines rather than

Figure 19-1   The technology-diffusion model: how an institution responds to a new technology.
Source: Coates, 1983, p. 80.

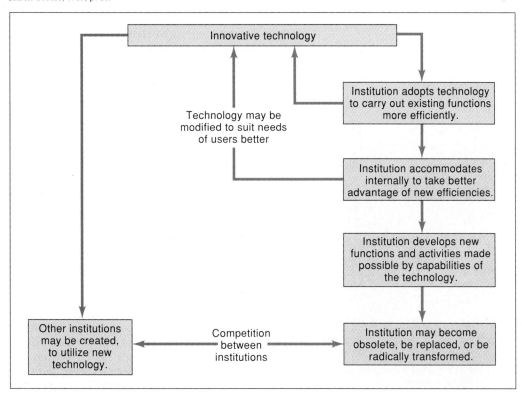

SOCIAL CHANGE

Spin the Bottle

A delightful fictional account of the problems caused by the introduction of a new culture item can be found in the South African film *The Gods Must Be Crazy*. While flying over a remote section of the Kalahari Desert, a bush pilot throws away an empty soda bottle. The bottle falls into the campsite of !Kung San hunter/gatherers, a gentle peaceful people with few possessions and no concept of private property. No one in the band had ever seen such an item, and since it fell from the sky, they assumed it to be a gift of the gods. People invented a wide variety of uses for it: as a musical instrument, a rolling pin for stretching snakeskins, a spinning toy, almost anything except a water container. Each person found a special need for the bottle, but there was only one bottle in a society where goods had always been equally shared by all members.

It was not long, then, before quarrels broke out over who could use "the thing" and for what purposes. Children fought with one another, adults exchanged sharp words. The group's traditional way of life was threatened by these strange and ugly feelings. To restore harmony, one of the hunters offered to take the thing to the corners of the earth and return it to the gods. Thus began a long journey in which the hunter comes into contact with other societies, including modern South Africa. He is naturally confused by their values and behaviors and most of all by their inability to understand how the bottle had almost destroyed the !Kung San way of life. At many points in the film, it also becomes obvious that the !Kung San way of life has many advantages over that of more "advanced" societies whose members typcially appeared on the verge of a nervous breakdown.

people (Garson, 1988). The PC also allows a worker to remain at home rather than travel to an office, a development that has mixed outcomes. Although some parents will be more available to their children, others will become prisoners in their own home, with the employer taking over what was once a private, personal space—a colonization of the household. What do you think might be the long-range effects of the PC on work, family, education, leisure, entertainment, dating, and even social values?

The personal computer (PC) has transformed countless American offices—gone are the office machines of yesterday, replaced with computers, printers, modems, disks, and electronic mail. Remember to save your document!

Incremental Change

Some changes are part of a broad historical trend whose final form emerges over time. Gradual, incremental change occurs through the accumulation of minor alterations in social patterns and may go unnoticed until a major transformation has taken place. The agricultural revolution of prehistory, for example, was not a sudden, dramatic event, but the result of a long process of small changes in planting, irrigating, plowing, and storing. The contemporary women's movement is the product of a century of incremental changes in thinking and behavior that have revolutionized gender relationships. The final outcome of such "silent revolutions" represents a sharp departure from the past.

Gradual, unplanned change occurs in knowledge systems as well as in behavior patterns. Science proceeds by small steps, accumulating data that support or fail to support a particular theory. When enough bits and pieces of evidence emerge that disconfirm a particular model of the world, one belief system will ultimately be replaced by another, until that one, in turn, fails to explain observed realities (Kuhn, 1962). Thus, a belief in the instant creation of the world and an unchanging natural universe was replaced by Darwin's evolutionary model, which is today being modified by recent discoveries of abrupt rather than gradual species' changes. And there are many in modern society who still cling to the Biblical story.

In general, the broad trends in industrial society have been toward increased political participation, civil liberties, civil rights, sexual privacy, and educational attainment. But such trends can be slowed and even temporarily reversed. Modern societies have periodically engaged in political repression and limitations on personal choice and privacy, as seen today in many "backlash" movements in the United States and in the resurgence of antiforeigner sentiments in Western Europe. Thus, despite a long-term trend toward more open and tolerant attitudes, short-term events can stall or reverse the direction of change.

Revolutionary Change

Revolutionary change involves a "sudden, basic transformation of a society's political and socioeconomic (including class) structure" (Skocpol, 1979, p. 5). But revolutions do not just happen; they arise when the ground has been prepared and when a revolutionary situation arises. A **revolutionary situation** exists when (1) two or more political units claim legitimate control over the state; (2) their interests cannot be reconciled; and (3) the opposition party receives substantial support from the population (Tilly, 1993). The revolution ends when only one claimant is left, either the existing power holders or the opposition party. The triumph of the opposition constitutes a **revolutionary outcome.**

Revolutionary events occur along a continuum from a *coup,* in which one segment of the elite displaces another, to the silent revolutions of nonviolent transformation, to the great revolutions that mark a watershed in national and international politics, such as the American and French Revolutions, and the 1917 Russian Revolution (Tilly, 1993). The long-term effects of revolutionary events are more difficult to classify. The high hopes and emotional outpouring of the liberating moment are soon overwhelmed by the practical tasks of everyday life. Many short-term gains are erased in the long-run. For example, the expansion of women's rights in the early days of the Russian Revolution soon gave way to economic necessity and totalitarian controls. Conversely, short-term setbacks, such as the Reign of Terror at the beginning of the French Revolution, can be followed by broad-based liberating reforms. But revolutions do generate revolutionary ideas, some of which take on a life of their own—liberty, equality, the rule of law, civil rights, social justice— inspiring others long after the goals of the original event have been forgotten.

Revolutions can also look backward, to restoring the past rather than embracing the future, as in the case of the Iranian Revolution of the early 1980s (Ansari, 1992; Moaddel, 1993). These revolutionary events are similar to the "nativistic revivals" discussed in Chapter 16, in which modernizing trends are so disruptive of the social system that many people support a return to traditional, predictable patterns.

But whether the revolutionary ideals are initially liberating or resisted, in relatively developed societies or in the Third World, the outcome of most revolutionary events is strikingly similar: increased centralization of power and bureaucratization when the new order is first installed, as well as mobilization of the masses in sup-

A **revolutionary situation** exists when two or more political units claim control over the state, their interest cannot be resolved, and the opposition party receives support from the population.

A **revolutionary outcome** occurs when the opposition party in a revolutionary situation wins.

Revolutionary events occur along a continuum of magnitude of political change.

Citizens may oppose governmental policies for a number of reasons. In 1994 large numbers of French students took to the streets to oppose a government policy to pay students less than the minimum wage. After considerable nation-wide protests and violence, the government reversed their policy. How can citizens voice discontent with official policies? Have you been involved in any protests?

1989: A Year Of Revolutionary Change

From Central Europe to the People's Republic of China, 1989 was a year of revolutionary change, as protesters demanded political and economic reforms in one totalitarian society after another. In China, a short-lived open revolt led by students was forcibly crushed, but throughout Europe communist regimes fell without a shot being fired. With the exception of Romania, these "quiet revolutions" were remarkable for their speed as well as their nonviolence. Demonstrators lighted candles in the path of the police who had terrorized the population only weeks before.

Within a brief two years, the East German government and Communist Party leadership resigned, free elections were held, and the country was reunited with West Germany. In Czechoslovakia, an equally swift "velvet revolution" peaceably removed the communist regime and installed an elected government. The struggle took a bit longer in Poland, but eventually the workers' union, Solidarity, won recognition as a political party and successfully challenged the Communist Party in free elections.

How could 40 years of totalitarian rule be ended so quickly and bloodlessly? Why hadn't the established regimes used force against protesters, as they had in the past? One reason was that the rulers and their Soviet allies were thoroughly discredited by their failed economic policies. Two other factors were the widening gap between the ruling elite and the impoverished masses and the lack of freedom of expression (Burawoy, 1992). The most important reason, however, was that, by 1989, due to its own internal problems, the Soviet Union could no longer support its East European "satellites" with trade, money subsidies, and troops when necessary. Under the leadership of Mikhail Gorbachev, the Soviet Union adopted a hands-off policy toward the satellites—dubbed the "Sinatra Doctrine" (go your own way). Gorbachev also set in motion revolutionary changes in the Soviet economy and political system—*peristroika* (the introduction of open market mechanisms) and *glasnost* (permitting limited freedom of speech and assembly)—that ultimately led to the overthrow of his own government.

The revolutionary changes of 1989 have been compared to an earlier period of political transformation in Europe, the democratic revolutions of 1848 (Ash, 1990). In both cases, the ideology of personal rights and political freedoms fueled social movements that challenged traditional regimes. And in both periods, intellectuals played an important role: poets, playwrights, and philosophers became political activists and public heroes. This is a very different tradition from that of the United States where, with the exception of the 1960s, students and professors have rarely been in the forefront of social movements.

In many cases, the high hopes of 1989 have already turned to disillusion. The transition to a market economy has created widespread unemployment and income inequality, especially among women

(continued)

Nationalism is exhibited not only through flag waving but also through symbols of group unity. In 1989 in Prague, Czechoslovakia, in what has been called the Velvet Revolution, citizens demonstrated and lit candles for freedom, which was gained when the Communist Party relinquished its power without a single bullet being fired. In 1993 the country separated into two independent countries, the Czech Republic and the Slovak Republic.

(Rueschemeyer, 1994). How secure is the budding democracy in nations such as Poland, Romania, or Bulgaria, with a limited tradition of secular democratic institutions? Will the future of Eastern Europe resemble its precommunist past: an area of weak nation-states, characterized by poverty, inequality, and ethnocentrism (Ash, 1990)?

In the former Soviet Union, the process has been one of steady geographic disintegration. A nation of more than 100 different ethnic, religious, and culturally distinct populations—from Westernized areas close to Europe to Asian republics in the east, from Eskimo

herders in the arctic north to Muslim territories in the south—the Soviet Union had been held together by a centralized government in Moscow dominated by ethnic Russians. In a real sense, the Soviet Union was an internal colony, and, when the central government collapsed, the newly freed populations claimed independence. Although the eventual map of the area is still unclear, it is likely that a dozen new nations will emerge from the ashes of what was once seen as a world superpower, and Russia itself will be just another developing country.

port of the regime. As the "iron law of oligarchy" (Chapter 14) suggests, one totalitarian system is likely to be succeeded by another; only the faces will change, and perhaps not even that, as can be seen in Eastern Europe and Russia today.

Once the revolution is stabilized, and when an educated middle class emerges, democratic institutions can take root, especially in societies that have some history and tradition of self-rule (Korzeniewicz and Awbrey, 1992). Such a trend is clearly visible today in the Czech Republic, Hungary, Korea, the Philippines, and even the People's Republic of China. These gains are encouraged and reinforced by foreign economic investment (Firebaugh, 1992).

> It is absolutely false and totally unhistorical to represent work for reforms as a drawn-out revolution, and revolution as a condensed series of reforms. A social transformation and a legislative reform do not differ according to their *duration* but according to their *essence* . . . in the transition from one historical period, one social order, to another.
>
> —ROSA LUXEMBERG, 1899/1971

In the less-developed Third World, however, dependence on foreign economic and military assistance often delays political reforms by reinforcing the power of the ruling elite and increasing economic inequality within the society, thus feeding revolutionary opposition (Boswell and Dixon, 1990) Some sociologists also see Third World dependence on the world market and foreign investment as the source of widespread starvation and social disorganization (Wimberley and Bello, 1992). Other data, however, suggest that economic development reduces starvation, increases life expectancy, and generally benefits the masses (Firebaugh and Beck, 1994).

In many instances in the 1980s, when revolution broke out in Third World countries, intervention

from the industrial nations, especially the United States, helped to crush the revolution and allow the government to become even more repressive, as in Namibia and Angola (Kowalewski, 1991). In some cases, the United States intervened to protect economic interests and in other cases to deny power to revolutionary groups that supported socialism.

Because each revolution is grounded in the particular history of a society, general theories of revolutionary change have been of limited predictive value. There are, however, some basic causal factors that must be included in any such theory: population pressures, infighting among elites, and mass poverty (Goldstone, 1991). Much theorizing about revolution has been done with the goal of refuting or modifying the ideas of Karl Marx.

THE MARXIST MODEL.   In the **Marxist model,** revolutionary situations exist wherever class divisions lead to widespread inequality and increased poverty among the masses. Under some circumstances, a revolutionary movement will take root and grow strong enough to overthrow the dominant elites. This process will cease only when social classes are eliminated. Many of Marx's original predictions have been modified in the light of actual events. For example, modern revolutions have occurred primarily in agricultural societies rather than among the working class of industrialized nations. Conflict between classes has been less important than competition between factions *within* the ruling class. Revolutionary leaders have not been peasants or factory workers but members of the educated intellectual class. And, finally, it is not the class system but the political structure that undergoes immediate change, although this might eventually alter stratification hierarchies, as seen in current revolutionary events in Eastern Europe (Banac, 1992).

> In the **Marxist model,** revolutionary situations occur whenever class divisions lead to widespread inequality and increased poverty among the masses.

THEORIES OF SOCIAL AND CULTURAL CHANGE

Does change take place along a single path (unidirectional), leading to some predestined goal such as the Kingdom of Heaven? Or has there been a gradual decline from some Golden Age? Or does change occur in cycles as civilizations rise and fall? These are common models of social change in the Western world, reflecting the historical locations of their authors.

Evolutionary Theories

In the eighteenth and nineteenth centuries in Europe, unidirectional theories of evolutionary progress were very popular. As Western explorers discovered native tribes and settlers took their lands, it became necessary to establish an ideological basis for colonialism. The idea that humankind had developed in a steady path upward from savagery, as represented by members of simple societies, to the high culture of contemporary Europe, was doubly appealing (Spencer, 1860). The **theory of evolutionary progress** from barbarianism to civilization not only excused colonialism but made "the white man's burden" of bringing the benefits of Western rule to the inferior peoples a sacred task, ordained by God and history. This model was given added intellectual weight with the publication of Charles Darwin's work on the biological evolution of animal and human species.

In contrast to the *upward* model of nineteenth century social philosophers, many Christian authorities claim that the direction of social change has been *downward* from an original state of grace to the final battle in which the world is destroyed to make way for the Second Coming.

The **evolutionary progress theory** assumes that humankind has progressed from the savagery of simple societies to the high culture of the West.

Cyclical theories of social change are based on the view that society resembles a living organism going through phases of growth and decline.

The **neoevolutionary model** traces changes in cultural and societal complexity without making value judgments about the superiority of one society over another.

Cyclical Theories

The notion that society is like an organism, growing from birth to adulthood before losing strength in old age, appears at various historical eras but tapped an especially responsive chord following World War I. In Germany, especially, an intellectual current of profound pessimism fed into the idea that Western civilization, far from being the high point of cultural development, was actually corrupt and in decline. This **cyclical theory of social change** was the basis of a best-selling book of the times, *The Decline of the West* (Spengler, 1928), and similar volumes appeared throughout the 1930s and 1940s.

European civilization has proved far sturdier than its critics assumed, surviving yet another World War, although many today foresee a gradual loss of power in the face of the political and economic growth of the nations of the Pacific rim, especially China and Japan. However, although cultures do flourish and decline over long periods, there is so much variation that the analogy to an organism has little predictive value.

A more sociological theory of cyclical change was proposed by the Russian-born American sociologist Pitirim Sorokin (1941) who saw sociocultural systems as alternating between periods dominated by rationality and those in which sensory knowledge is most valued. That is, some historical periods are characterized by extreme conservatism and are often followed by an era of artistic and personal liberation—just as the restrictive Victorianism of the early 1900s was followed by the Roaring Twenties, and the 1950s gave way to the 1960s in the United States.

Neoevolutionary Models

Many of sociology's classical theories have adopted at least a two-stage evolutionary model to represent the cumulative direction of sociocultural change, from a relatively egalitarian sameness of functions to an increasingly complex division of labor and social differentiation (Sanderson, 1990). Durkheim, for example, contrasted what he called the *mechanical solidarity* of simple societies, a unity based on similarity among group members, to the *organic solidarity* of modern society, a unity based on interdependence among people who occupy different and complementary statuses. Tönnies's contrast between *Gemeinschaft* and *Gesellschaft* reflects the same underlying concept of movement from primary to secondary group relationships (see Chapter 4). Other observers speak of a drift or shift from folk communities to urban society (Redfield, 1947). In all these schemes, structural complexity is associated with changes in the economic base, population density, and specialization of tasks.

The **neoevolutionary model** we have used in this textbook is an extension of these ideas. We assume that the direction of social change is toward increasing complexity in culture, social structure, and social interaction, from the small bands of nomadic gatherers with their limited material tool kit to the technologically sophisticated societies of the modern West (Lenski and Lenski, 1991; Chapter 3). But we make no assumptions about superiority or inferiority, and we do not use words such as *progress* or *advancement*. It would be very difficult to claim that modern Americans are any more content, fulfilled, or

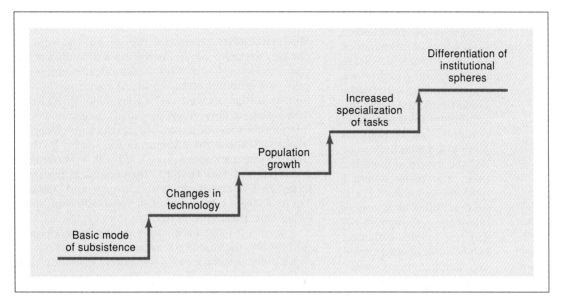

Figure 19-2 Steps in the structural differentiation of society.

intelligent than the hunter-gatherers of the past or contemporary yam growers of the South Sea Islands.

The neoevolutionary model, as shown in Figure 19-2, is based on four propositions: (1) that population size depends on the economic base; (2) that technological changes that make the food supply more varied and secure lead to population growth; (3) that new technologies and increased density lead to division of labor and a need for coordination among specialists; (4) that the tasks of organizing work and controlling larger populations lead to increasingly complex organizations and the emergence of distinct institutional spheres.

To this neoevolutionary view of cumulative and general change, we add the elements of the conflict model to explain the pattern of change *within* a given society.

The Conflict Model

The **conflict view of social change** focuses on recurring and lasting sources of tension and struggle among individuals and groups within a society. At any given moment, social systems consist of competing interest groups. Only by looking at the specific circumstances that give rise to discontent can we understand why some social systems persist and others experience violent revolution (Wuthnow, 1989).

In its Marxist form, the conflict perspective views the process of social change as **dialectical,** the outcome of opposing forces. At any moment, the social system of interconnected parts is the status quo out of which competing elements emerge to challenge the existing order, or *thesis.* As long as there is inequality among subgroups, the forces of opposition, or *antitheses,* will gather strength. Although the conflict between vested interests and protesters is constant, the struggle is not always openly violent. Most change comes slowly, but revolution is always possible and may even be necessary to create a new social order, or *synthesis.*

That is, change within a society can be analyzed in terms of class-based interests, with the outcome uncertain. Ruling elites are typically stronger than protesters, with power to subvert, co-opt, or suppress opponents. We will discuss the roles of social movements, that is, organized efforts at social change, in Chapter 23.

The **conflict view of social change** focuses on recurring and lasting sources of tension and struggle among individuals and groups within a society.

The **dialectical model** views social change as the outcome of a struggle between opposing forces.

SOCIAL CHANGE AND MODERNIZATION

Specific and General Change

Within general models of change, each society is shaped by specific historical events. The rise of nation-states in Africa transformed the Teuso into the Ik; the discovery of oil in Alaska has forever altered the culture of Inuit herders; and 300 years of immigration have literally changed the face of the United States.

Among all the historical uniqueness, however, we have proposed that the direction of **cumulative social change** operating over the tens of thousands of years of human society has been toward increasing complexity of social systems. If we add together the histories of all known human societies, their paths could be plotted along the continuum from simple to complex, as shown on p. 56 in Chapter 3. But not all have moved at the same pace, and many different types of society have coexisted at different historical moments. Although all began as simple gathering bands, some adopted hunting, herding, horticulture, and agriculture earlier or later, depending on their geographical location and specific experience. For example, 1,500 years ago, a high civilization of art and architecture flourished among the Mayans of Mexico while much of Europe was overrun by bands of "barbarians." Today, it is the West that has the more complex culture, but who is to say which societies will dominate the globe tomorrow?

> **Cumulative social change** is the long-range historical trend toward the increasing complexity of social life and interaction.
>
> **Modernization** involves a global process of change whereby industrialization and urbanization are spread to nonindustrial societies, leading to the development of a world economy.

Societies that have undergone rapid change are typically located where they come in contact with other people, such as on the seacoast or where two rivers meet. Others remain isolated and therefore insulated from change. Human history is a graveyard of vanishing cultures, such as the rain-forest people, tribes displaced by nation-states, and the natives of the American continent. Still other societies emerge from prehistory to become sophisticated civilizations—as in ancient Egypt and China—before undergoing a long period of decline and disorganization, and even colonial rule, finally reemerging in the mid-twentieth century as powerful modernizing nations. Each society has its unique pattern of development, its history, and its rate of change. No two are alike in all respects, and the future is not fully predetermined by the past.

Despite such variations, social change tends to be cumulative, because each innovation enlarges the culture base from which other new items can be constructed, and because, once ideas are abroad in the world, it is almost impossible to return to a state of ignorance (once bitten, the apple of knowledge can never be made whole again). Nonetheless, history is filled with attempts to "turn back the clock," as in contemporary Iran where religious authorities seek to stem the tide of Westernization and to reimpose an earlier way of life. Not all institutional spheres become more complex as societies industrialize: governmental, educational, and economic institutions expand, but the scope and power of families and religious organizations tend to be reduced.

Modernization

Modernization refers to the global process of change whereby nonindustrial societies absorb the characteristics of the more economically and politically powerful industrial world. Although modernization is often viewed as a desirable goal for a developing nation, there are many negative consequences for individuals and social structures. People's hopes far exceed the capacity of the society to meet them; local institutions are destroyed; communities are disrupted and families dissolved; and in Africa today half a continent is in poverty and anarchy. There is also a large element of *ethnocentrism* in the belief that "modern is better."

Contrary to the early assumptions of modernization theory, the march to industrialization did not automatically produce a free-market economy and political democracy along the lines of the industrial West. Nonetheless, the broad trends that constitute modernization have by now touched most of the rest of the world: the development of a manufacturing

Modernization refers to the process of change whereby developing societies, such as Mexico, absorb the characteristics of the more economically and politically powerful industrial nations. While modernization is often seen as a desirable goal for developing nations, many negative consequences for individuals and communities follow. The tension between deeply embedded traditional values, embodied in the Guadalupe Virgin, are undermined by modernization symbolized by the Ferrari automobile. How can traditional values and modernization coexist?

base (industrialization), the movement of people from villages to cities (urbanization), and a growing dependence on scientific knowledge (secularization). In the political sphere, modernization is associated with the rise of the nation-state.

THE NATION-STATE. For most societies throughout human history, collective identity and loyalty were based on residential location, kinship, and other ascribed statuses. The **nation-state** as an overriding political unit, embracing many different tribes and subpopulations, emerged only in the past few hundred years, as a necessary consequence of modernization. The nation-state is held together by feelings of shared fate and common history, a **nationalism** that provides an identity stronger than that of other attachments (Greenfield, 1992).

Although the existence of strong, relatively stable monarchies promoted the rise of nationalism in Europe, two other factors favored the development of the nation-state as the basis of political authority and self-identity: (1) the rise of capitalism, and (2) the spread of colonialism. The rise of capitalism in the seventeenth and eighteenth centuries created a constant need for new markets and sources of raw material. The response in Europe was to send bands of

explorers and settlers in search of markets and raw materials and ultimately to create colonies out of the captured areas.

Western traders and colonists easily conquered the geographically isolated and culturally distinct native populations, establishing territories to be ruled from the European mainland. A strong bond of nationalism linked the settlers to their homeland, uniting the colonizers, "the bearers of civilization," against the native peoples, who were defined as inferior and incapable of handling their own affairs.

This was the state of affairs until the end of World War II and the withdrawal of colonial governments in favor of the newly independent nation-states of Africa and Asia. With the end of European rule, a new-found nationalism swept the former colonies, fueled more by anticolonial and anti-Western feelings than by any overriding sense of national identity. Throughout the Third World, nationalism became a liberation movement in which the common element was not language, shared culture, or common institutions but a hatred of the West. Still old tribal loyalties remain strong in many of these countries, especially in Africa, where civil wars continue to destroy the stability of many governments. In response to the civil unrest, these governments, where they exist at all, have become increasingly totalitarian, militaristic, and corrupt, siphoning off resources that could be used to relieve the poverty of their populations.

> The **nation-state** is an overarching political unit that emerged as a consequence of modernization in complex societies.
>
> **Nationalism** is a consciousness of shared identity among the members of a politically distinct territory.

Nationalism has also surfaced today in the developed and developing areas of the former Soviet Union and Yugoslavia, where a centralized communist government had imposed a temporary unity on territories composed of diverse ethnic and religious subpopulations but failed to create an overriding sense of national identity and loyalty to a government of all the people. These attempts to build a universal sense of citizenship led to bloodshed and imprisonment as enemies of the regimes in power were "liquidated." Yet, the surge of nationalism, welcomed by many in the West as a healthy sign of anti-communism, has now turned into the equally bloody "ethnic cleansing" that has killed tens of thousands of people who were relatively peaceful neighbors only a few years ago (Pfaff, 1993).

The nation-state is an overriding political unit that includes many subpopulations. Tensions between traditional and modern values, such as the changing definition of women's roles, are often found within nation-states. These Indian women wearing traditional veils participate in a modern practice—voting in a national election.

From Preindustrial to Postindustrial Society

All modern industrial societies share some traits, regardless of differences in culture and history. Political ideology may have separated the United States and the former Soviet Union, but modernization has pro-

 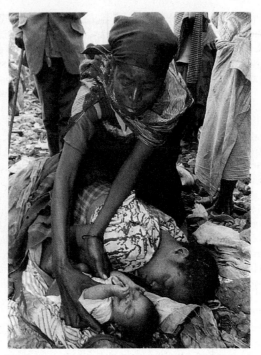

In some countries, such as the former Yugoslavia, nationalism created a bloody civil war and an "ethnic cleansing" that has resulted in over 200,000 deaths and the displacement of hundreds of thousands. Here a family of Croatians flee Serbian shelling of the city of Dubrovnik.

Hundreds of thousands of Rwandans were forced to leave their villages when warfare broke out between the ruling Tutsi and the dominated Hutu tribes. Here an infant is rescued from the side of its dead mother by a caring survivor.

duced many common structural features, such as an emphasis on technology and the bureaucratization of authority.

The sociocultural change associated with modernization has several important aspects: (1) **mobilization,** in which existing economic and social structures and psychological commitments are weakened, as individuals become available for socialization to new beliefs and behaviors; (2) **social differentiation,** a shift from tribal and family loyalties and roles based on ascription to specialized and achieved roles; and (3) an emphasis on *legal-rational* norms and relationships, more instrumental than expressive.

Max Weber (1915/1946) used the term *rationality* to refer to social action based on a logical relationship between means and ends rather than on tradition or emotion. Typical of industrialization, rationality leads to predictable and systematic relationships and practices, to the refinement of technology and science. Modern societies are composed of large numbers of workers and consumers, engaged in the production and distribution of specialized goods and services, whose behavior is largely guided by calculations of cause and effect, costs and benefits.

The emergence of capitalism and democratic ideals in the seventeenth and eighteenth centuries both reflected and reinforced the triumph of rationalism over tradition and faith, at least in the economic and political spheres. And both trends gave the Western nations a great advantage in further economic development. As a result, a few industrialized countries have dominated the rest of the world for four centuries. Now, however, as we enter the **postindustrial era,** the economic base of modern societies has shifted from manufacturing to the production of information and services. A nation's strength will be measured by the proportion of technical and knowledge workers in the labor force and the amount of money spent on research and development rather than how much steel or automobiles it can produce. At the same time, manufacturing jobs have been relocated to the developing nations, which may give their

Mobilization involves the weakening of existing patterns of economic and social structures and psychological commitments, making people receptive to socialization to new patterns.

Social differentiation involves a shift from ascribed tribal and family roles to specialized achieved roles.

A **postindustrial era** is marked by a shift from manufacturing to the rapid development of information technology and services.

In modern society, social action is assumed to be guided by rational consideration of the relationship of means to ends. Thus the development of nuclear power is seen as a rational way to make electricity and those who oppose it are seen as irrational, because of their concern for the safety and well being of people. Who defines rationality?

economies an important boost—if wages are raised and workers allowed to keep most of their earnings, and if pollution controls are instituted.

SOCIAL POLICY

Who's the Boss?

Will workers control the new technologies, or will the machines call the shots? Is it the ultimate fate of *Homo sapiens* to become a glorified button-pusher? We have already noted that the postindustrial society will reward technical skills, knowledge, and managerial abilities. But for how many people? When a microchip can contain circuits that would have taken a worker ten years to put together, and when the 30 volumes of the *Encyclopedia Brittanica* can be transmitted in 30 seconds, a lot of people could be out of work.

In addition, the types of jobs that will be created are likely to consist of a few "expert" slots and a large number of "nonexpert" positions, as seen in Table 13-1, p. 303. In other words, some jobs will require exceptional abilities whereas many will be "deskilled." Notice how the cashier at your local fast food outlet no longer needs to know the price of any item or how to add up a check: just punch the "med coke," "lge fries," and "Big Mac" buttons and the total bill is instantly, magically displayed. Even stockbrokers now rely on computerized trading programs developed by hidden experts. And many predict that computerized catalogs will replace the shopping mall, causing not only a loss of retail jobs but the disappearance of the modern equivalent of the town square.

When almost anyone can learn to punch the correct buttons to sell you a computer or make an airline reservation, the prestige and pay of the job will be re-duced. These developments have led to a renewed interest in Marx's concept of *alienation,* a separation of self from the labor process, in which work is a set of meaningless gestures. But is sitting in front of a word processor really more alienating than standing on an assembly line?

In contrast to the relatively gloomy predictions of many social scientists, the "information revolution" also holds out many promises. More knowledge is readily available to more people than ever before. A shorter work week and work life add up to more

With greater segmentation of tasks, workers neither understand the complexity of the organization nor develop promotable skills. How much do the workers in this supermarket need to know to work in a setting controlled by microprocessors which tell them all they need to know to finish the transaction?

leisure time in which to pursue interests that reduce the boredom of the electronic workplace. Many technologies can expand rather than limit technical skill (just compare the word processor to the typewriter). Because they are new and depend primarily on skill, many high-tech careers are more gender- and race-neutral than are other forms of employment.

All in all, how do you think the new world of information technology and computerized work will affect your future? What will work, family, and leisure look like in the twenty-first century?

THE WORLD SYSTEM

Although nation-states and nationalism are at the center of attention today, the world has actually been moving toward increasing cooperation and trade across national boundaries. Each nation-state is linked to others in a **world social system** (Wallerstein, 1991; Chase-Dunn and Hall, 1993). This global political economy is characterized by the rapid spread of information and technology, by instant culture contact, complex money flows, the exchange of goods and services, and most recently, by large-scale migrations of refugees and workers.

The **world social system** involves increased cooperation and trade across national boundaries and a rapid spread of information and technology, culture contact, flows of money, and large-scale migration of refugees and workers.

One of the most interesting developments in education is the recognition of the importance of the world system in understanding the United States. Recent calls for a more multicultural curriculum reflect not only the changing ethnic composition of our society but also our growing involvement in the world system. It is easy to notice that your VCR was made in Japan, your shoes in Brazil, and your shirt in Sri Lanka. What is less visible is the way in which economic and political power are distributed globally. Will expanding trade make the world a safer place and one in which the benefits of industrial capitalism will spread to all parts of the globe?

Many of the hopes and fears related to international trade were on display during the 1993 debate over the North American Free Trade Agreement (NAFTA). The free flow of money, people, and goods across national borders has also posed problems for Western Europe in its efforts to establish a unified trading area with a common currency. When national interests collide with international goals, few politicians can resist pleasing their own voters. Nevertheless, the nations of the world appear to be stumbling toward the global economy.

The feature of the world system of greatest interest to sociologists is the relationship between the industrialized First World (the "north") and the Third World (the "south"). Even though colonialism in terms of political control of less-developed territories has ended, economic domination continues. The industrial north can be considered the economic "core" of the global system, and the developing south as the "periphery," providing raw materials, labor-intensive manufacturing, and markets for northern products (Smith and White, 1992; Chapter 13).

Dependence on the world system has had variable effects on Third World countries. Oil-producing states such as Kuwait and Saudi Arabia have benefited

The cultural and economic domination of the First World over the Third World occurs in a number of ways. In numerous Latin American countries, even in the smallest mountain villages, the models on billboards and posters are always white and sell various "modern" products. All of the people in the truck are Quechua Indians being enticed to drink the national soda, Inca Cola. Of course, this is Peru, the country of the Incas.

MICHAEL BROWN

Social Change, The World System, and the Former Soviet Union

Michael Brown is Professor of Sociology/Anthropology at Northeastern University. Among his books are The Production of Society *(1986) and* New Studies in the Politics and Culture of U.S. Communism *(1993). He has published numerous articles in professional journals and continues to work as best he can for a better society.*

*I*ronically, of all sociological models, I have found that Marxism is most helpful in illuminating the relationship between the immediate conditions of social change and the enduring long-term conflicts that underlie all historical transitions—even with regard to the events thought to mark the end of Marxism: the disintegration of the Soviet Union and other Eastern European nations in the late 1980s.

Marxism specifies the four factors necessary to analyzing how modern societies are constantly changing: *formation, form, context,* and *problem.* The first, *formation,* refers to the actual institutional arrangements. *Form* refers to how key sectors are mutually oriented, e.g., on the basis of "social values" such as full employment in contrast to one organized around private profit. The *context* refers to the external setting within which the social formation operates. Lastly, the *problem* is either the immediate external or internal challenge to the stability of a society.

How well can this framework be applied to the seemingly sudden end of the Soviet Union after seven decades of Communist government? Some scholars see the break-up of the Soviet Union as the result of popular discontent finally able to express itself. Others blame socialism itself, claiming that it is contrary to human nature and can therefore only be imposed by force.

These views overlook a great deal of contradictory evidence. First of all, socialist institutions—those that are governed by social values in which certain benefits are considered rights of citizenship—exist in some degree in all but a few industrial societies. For example, social security, public health programs, medical insurance, housing subsidies, and family allowances are common in the electoral democracies of Western Europe, designed to minimize the socially destructive effects of unregulated capitalism.

Socialism is not some monolithic, fixed or unchanging system, invariably associated with coercive government. It is, rather, a way of thinking about social order and the interdependence of citizens in any industrial society. The values of cooperation and a sense of public good characteristic of socialism are at odds with those of capitalism and the global market, which is the "context" within which the break-up of the Soviet Union should be placed.

From this perspective, the end of the Soviet Union was hastened by the expansion of the global market in the 1970s and the need to apply market standards to institutions formerly governed by social values made it difficult for political leaders to live up to the promise to provide economic security to all. In addition to existing, long-term problems in the Soviet production and distribution systems, these outside pressures brought the economy to near collapse.

The seeming suddenness of the disintegration of the Soviet Union is also due to the particular formation and form of the society, with all institutions closely connected through government and the political system. The Soviet government retained legitimacy and public support only to the extent that it could provide for citizens' daily well-being, and maintain order in such a geographically vast and heterogeneous nation. An equally complex and sluggish bureaucracy grew ever larger and less able to administer a planned economy. Finally, the need to maintain a strong military to counter threats from both the United States and potential civil strife within the Soviet sphere drained the system of valued resources essential to sustaining a socialist economy.

Thus, the transformation of Eastern and Central Europe in the late 1980s can best be understood as part of a general destabilization of national societies under the impact of the new global economic order dominated by capitalist institutions. In general, these effects are most critical for socialist economies based on the primacy of social values. The legitimacy of the governments disintegrated with their inability to provide economic stability, and citizens lost a sense of personal well-being.

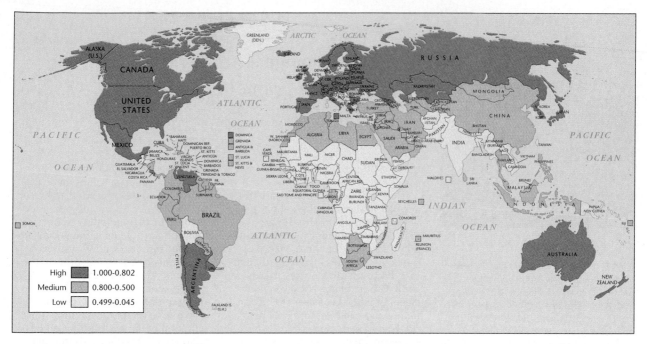

The Human Development Index, devised by the United Nations, combines several variables into one measure of human development refering to conditions that enlarge or expand individual choice.

greatly from their monopoly over a scarce resource, raising prices and draining money from the industrial core. The standard of living has risen dramatically in these countries, but most of the money and all of the political power remain in the hands of a few royal families. In the case of Mexico, however, the expected oil revenues did not materialize, and the country remains relatively poor and dependent on trade with the United States.

Other peripheral countries placed their economic fate in raw materials such as coffee, cocoa, tin, and sugar, whose prices on the world market fluctuate greatly. In these nations, the benefits of foreign trade have largely benefitted a small elite. In other countries, foreign investments have stabilized the economy and reduced starvation (Firebaugh and Beck, 1994). Overall, however, the distribution of the world's wealth has become increasingly uneven. The wealthy nations have gained economic power while the poor nations struggle to survive, and multinational companies draw more profit from the developing world than they invest (Braun, 1990). All these trends have led to widespread political instability in parts of Asia, Africa, and Latin America (Moaddel, 1994).

> The **quality of life** of a population is measured by indices such as life expectancy, health, education, and income.

In terms of the **quality of life** as measured by life expectancy, health, education, and income of its citizens, there are wide variations among the nations of the world. As you might expect, Japan, Canada, Nor-

way, Switzerland, Sweden, and the United States rank highest in quality of life, in that order. At the lowest end are Afghanistan in Asia, Somalia and Angola in Africa, and Haiti in the western hemisphere (United Nations, 1994). In terms of political freedoms such as the right to vote, to dissent, to associate with others, and to travel, the core industrial states rank highest and Third World nations lowest. Clearly, the benefits of international contacts and trade have yet to filter down to most of the world's population.

Despite growing inequality and political instability, and the resurgence of militant nationalism, the long-term direction of change is toward increasing interdependence within the world system. Eventually, most borders will open even wider, with goods and people moving freely around the world. Perhaps, ultimately, the living standards of all people will be improved. But for better or worse, Americans are now deeply embedded in a global network of economic and political relationships.

THE SELF AND SOCIAL CHANGE

What happens to the self when social change occurs? Among the Ik described at the beginning of this chapter, changes in the mode of subsistence were also associated with drastic changes in personality and sense of self. From warm, open people, the Teuso turned into the hostile and cruel Ik. They provide a vivid example of the theory that the self is a product of social structure. Social change consists

Haiti is a dramatic example of a country in which the ruling elite created a repressive dictatorship dominated by the military and supported by a few families who amassed great wealth while the rest of the country lived in poverty. After centuries of oppression by various dictators, Haiti was finally freed in 1994 with the help of U.S. troops. Can Haitians establish a stable democracy or is a return to some form of dictatorship inevitable?

not only of structural, economic, and cultural shifts but also involves psychological changes. Our very selves and our positions in the social structure are mutually reinforcing. For example, from a conflict perspective, the mode of production shapes the self. The alienation that results from a worker's relationship to the modes of production under industrialism is part of his or her very being, so that people in supervised work have different personality profiles than those in more self-directed jobs (Kohn et al., 1990).

As described in Chapter 5, much of the self is molded by the actions and the reactions of others toward us. The variety—and sometimes the unpredictability—of others' reactions to us is far greater in modern, urban societies than in the relative stability of isolated simple societies. Complex societies also provide a greater range of roles than are available in tradition-based or developing nations. This can be a mixed blessing. On the one hand, shifts from traditional primary relationships (*Gemeinshaft*) to relationships based on rational self-interest (*Gesellschaft*) permit us more personal freedom and allow us to live in a variety of social worlds. On the other hand, the range of choices in a complex society requires that each of us must constantly read, process, and select among the cues given us by others to an extent not required in simpler societies.

Modern urban societies, according to Georg Simmel (1902/1950), promote a different kind of consciousness, a "blasé attitude," or indifference to many of the people and the events around us. This indifference is a type of survival mechanism, developed to screen out the constant stimulation of other people, sights, smells, noises, and activities that are part of modern life. The rational-legal mode that dominates modern, urban society also has "side effects." As Weber noted, rationality involves mathematical measurement of the performances of each worker. In the process of rational calculation, each worker becomes a little cog in a big machine, preoccupied with how to become a bigger, more important cog. What then becomes of the individual?

The effect of social structure on personality has been described in a classic study by David Riesman (1950). Contrasting three different ideal types, each associated with a particular level of industrial development, Riesman identified the **tradition-directed** person, whose behavior is governed by custom; the **inner-directed** person, whose behavior is guided by an internal mechanism and who is, therefore, well-suited to industrial society; and the **other-directed** person, who is equipped

The **tradition-directed** person's behavior is governed by custom.

The **inner-directed** person's behavior is guided by an internal mechanism typical of industrial society.

The **other-directed** person, typical of the postindustrial society, constantly reacts and adapts to the expectations of others.

with a psychological radar that scans the environment for appropriate messages to guide behavior. The other-directed person, suggested Riesman, will characterize postindustrial society. Constantly anticipating new roles and aware of the need to adapt swiftly, the other-directed person differs from the other two types in being less certain of how to behave under all, or even most, circumstances. He or she is constantly reacting and adapting to others, reinventing the self with each encounter.

The reactive-adaptive (other-directed) self has advantages and drawbacks. The ability to adapt to a variety of situations allows us to anticipate and prepare for changing roles. Yet, it may also result in anxiety and a crisis of the self. The self is constantly being constructed and reconstructed to fit varying statuses and roles; who and what one is not readily identifiable. Consumer goods become commodities that establish status, part of what Goffman has called one's "identity kit" or "I am what I wear and use." Some theorists even believe that the personality of postmodern individuals will be a "relational" self, searching for social connectedness through interactive television and radio, at home in the virtual world of cyberspace, but actually living in the nonrelational world of the "lonely crowd" of modern malls and suburbia (Inglehart, 1990; Gergen, 1991).

In summary, personality is mobilized as a resource in modern society, and the self is rationalized. Success, achievement, conscious control, and self-improvement are primary goals. The self, as the "me" orientation that dominated the United States in recent years illustrates, becomes treasured above all else as an object to be used to achieve desired ends.

THE FUTURE: WHAT NEXT?

What can we expect in the future? Both social change and the problems of the future will be, in part, results and reactions to the current technology and the institutionalized patterns of social relationships. In the past, the United States and other major industrialized nations have relied on cheap raw materials from preindustrial nations. As a result, the industrialized world has developed social and economic institutions based largely on waste and the depletion of the world's resources. Americans in particular are used to the idea of disposables—the car, radio, dress, cup, or whatever is quickly replaced by another newer model. Repairing items is for many people a lost art.

Yet, there is growing evidence that scarcity can be anticipated in a number of areas—scarcity caused by the demands of technology and by the widespread modification of the environment (see Chapter 20). For example, the supply of water and fossil fuels has limits that may have far-reaching implications for almost every economic system. We could delay these potential shortages by reducing our use of water and fossil fuels, by manufacturing longer-lasting goods and by planned recycling. But this solution, too, has its costs. Longer-lasting goods lead to increased unemployment. After all, fewer workers would be required to turn out fewer but more durable products. Likewise, there is a trade-off between our need for imported sources of energy, such as oil, and balance-of-trade payments. The point here is that latent consequences, by definition, are unknown and often produce effects that are the opposite of intended goals.

Nor can the future be accurately foreseen. Yet, the restructuring of society is proceeding at this very moment and will change social relationships and self-concepts. Various visions of the future have been proposed, all of which emphasize the importance of technological change and the impact of these alterations on human lives. For example, the rise of computer technology has led some futurists to predict a society in which technology will become too complex for the average person to understand. According to this view, a kind of "gods and clods" division of labor will develop, in which a small group of highly educated engineers and scientists control technology, while the remainder of the population is engaged in meaningless make-work. Not all futurists have such depressing predictions. Others foresee a multiple-option society, in which the range of personal choices is expanded by "high-tech/high-touch" developments. That is, technological innovations will stimulate compensating human responses (Naisbitt, 1982). These more optimistic forecasters predict that the United States is moving toward an information society in which short-run interests are giving way to longer time frames in which self-reliance and the importance of informal social relationships will increase and the dependency on bureaucratic organizations will decline (Zuboff, 1988).

Drawing by W. Miller; © 1994 The New Yorker Magazine, Inc.

"Excuse me, I'm lost. Can you direct me to the information superhighway?"

Attempts to describe the future in detail are almost always wrong. The most accurate way to anticipate the direction of social change is through an understanding of past and current events. Within your lifetime, numerous social changes have occurred. New technologies have developed, and the transition from an industrial to a postindustrial economy is under way. Numerous revolutions have been fought and are still going on. Shifts in the political climate of the United States, the former Soviet Union, and Eastern Europe have occurred. Social movements have been born, died, or persisted.

What will the future hold? And what will American society—and the rest of the world—be like in 50 years? The answers depend on crucial choices that you will be involved in making during the half century ahead. A sociological perspective (that is, an awareness of how you are shaped by and shape the world in which you live) is essential to your informed participation in the design of the future. If social systems are human constructions, they can be deconstructed and reconstructed. We've given you tools for such an analysis; you will decide whether you use the knowledge to work for change and in what directions. History, as Marx reminds us, is made by women and men, although the outcome is not always what we intend. Our choices are constrained by both the past and the present.

SUMMARY

1. Social change is the continual process through which values, norms, institutions, stratification systems, social relationships, and self-identity are altered over time.

2. External sources of social change include environmental events, invasion and war, and culture contact and diffusion. Internal sources include innovation, population shifts, and cohort flow.

3. Accepting change depends on the degree to which the new trait is consistent with existing culture, the forces of resistance, and the power of change agents and networks.

4. The rate of social change increases with societal complexity as the culture base expands. *Cultural lag* refers to the tendency for some institutional spheres to change more rapidly than other areas.

5. Incremental changes are gradual, part of a broad historical trend, in contrast to sudden, revolutionary changes.

6. Evolutionary theories of change are based on a model of unidirectional progress from simple to more sophisticated forms of social life.

7. Cyclical theories based on the analogy to an organism see societies or cultures as growing from infancy to maturity and to eventual decay. Other models view culture as alternating between cycles of liberation and repression.

8. Neoevolutionary models, such as the one in this book, see the cumulative direction of change as one of increasing complexity, with each society following a distinctive path, but without any assumptions of superiority or inferiority. This model also incorporates a conflict orientation to the sources of change in struggles for scarce resources.

9. Modernization, the master trend of recent history, involves industrialization, urbanization, and secularization, and has become a worldwide process, with variable outcomes.

10. The nation-state is the political organization of most societies today, involving a central government, and held together by feelings of national identity.

11. Postindustrial society will be increasingly dependent on science and technology and the control of information.

12. A world system approach to the study of social change emphasizes the economic link among nations, especially between the industrialized core and peripheral Third World.

13. As societies undergo change, so also do the components of the self-concept. One major direction of personality change is toward a more flexible, adaptable self in modern and postmodern society.

SUGGESTED READINGS

Brenner, Robert. *Merchants and Revolution: Commercial Change, Political Conflict and London's Overseas Traders, 1550-1653.* Princeton: Princeton University Press, 1993. A forceful analysis of the socioeconomic system that launched political action and the transition from feudalism to capitalism.

Callaghy, Thomas M., John Ravenhill (eds). *Hemmed In: Responses to Africa's Economic Decline.* New York: Columbia University Press, 1993. A collection of case studies of the economic and political transformation of African nations during the 1980s, with many workable proposals for the strengthening of societies "hemmed in" by multiple problems.

Garst, Rachel and Tom Barry. *Feeding the Crisis: U.S. Food Aid and Farm Policy in Central America.* Lincoln: University of Nebraska Press, 1990. By dissecting the intricate web of bilateral, national, and local transactions that make up the food aid chain, the authors indicate that by giving up self-sufficiency in favor of imported food staples, Central American countries have clearly put themselves at risk.

Kahn, Robert L. and Mayer N. Zald. *Organizations and Nation States: New Perspectives on Conflict and Cooperation.* San Francisco: Jossey-Bass, 1990. An updated introduction to the policy and practice of international relations based on the decision to cooperate.

Licklider, Roy. (ed.) *Stopping the Killing: How Civil Wars End.* New York: New York University Press, 1993. A collection of empirical and theoretical essays that examine why civil wars end and why they rarely resume. Includes case studies of seven civil wars.

Pfaff, William. *The Wrath of Nations: Civilization and the Furies of Nationalism.* New York: Simon & Schuster, 1993. The author is a well-known expert on modern politics who writes for ordinary readers as well as for academicians. This volume is easily the most understandable exploration of the origins and current force of nationalism throughout the world, and what it bodes for the future of humankind.

Rueschmeyer, Dietrich, Evelyn Huber Stephens, and John D. Stephens. *Capitalist Development and Democracy.* Chicago: University of Chicago Press, 1992. A comprehensive study of democratic transitions that examines capitalism and democracy in most modern societies.

Sedaitis, Judith B. and John Butterfield, eds. *Perestroika from Below: Social Movements in the Soviet Union.* Boulder, CO: Westview Press, 1991. An analysis of social movements in the Soviet Union from 1987 to 1990 using models of social movement research to show how the foundation of the developing civil society was laid.

Seidman, Steven and David G. Wagner, (eds). *Postmodernism and Social Theory: The Debate over General Theory.* Cambridge, MA: Blackwell, 1992. Leading sociological theorists address the dilemma that postmodernism poses for the study of sociology.

Stokes, Gail. *The Walls Came Tumbling Down: The Collapse of Communism in Eastern Europe.* New York: Oxford University Press, 1993. Very readable, brief volume that details the social, economic, and political processes leading to the end of communist rule in Poland, East Germany, Romania, Hungary, Bulgaria, and Czechoslovakia.

Tilly, Charles. *From Mobilization to Revolution.* Reading, MA: Addison-Wesley, 1978. The classic analysis of revolution. Tilly pulls together historical analyses to develop a model of revolutionary situations and outcomes.

20

Human Ecology:
Population and the
Environment

*T*ake out your crystal ball and ask yourself the following questions:

■ For what kind of occupation should I prepare, and how many job changes will I probably make?
■ What are my chances for a long and happy marriage?
■ How many children and grandchildren do I want, and how many will I actually have?
■ How long will I live, and in what state of health?
■ Where do I want to live when I graduate?

The answers to these personal questions are of great interest not only to you but also to **demographers,** sociologists who study population trends. In Chapter 1, you learned that the sum of individual acts such as being born, getting married, moving to a new residence, retiring from work, and dying constitute social facts, characteristics of a society or subgroup. In this chapter, you will see how these social facts have an impact on individuals. How, for example, the size of your birth cohort affects the social and natural environment in which you make decisions about education, marriage, parenthood, occupation, and where to live (Kennedy, 1989; McFalls, 1991). In other words, although your answers to the opening questions reflect your own desires

and hopes, whether you can realize them or not depends on the choices of all the other people born around the same time as yourself.

The study of populations is called **demography,** from the Greek *demos,* or "people." The size of any population is determined by the three basic demographic acts: birth, death, and migration. **Demographers** study not only the size but also the composition of populations—by sex, race, age, religion, ethnicity, and place of residence—and how these change over time.

But populations cannot be studied apart from their natural environment: available food resources, the climate and its risks, and the effects of various economic systems on the land, air, and water. This chapter is titled "Human Ecology," which is the study of the interplay between populations and their environment, how each affects the other. We begin with a review of basic demographic concepts and data sources, then examine processes of population stability and change, and conclude with an overview of current environmental issues.

Demographers are sociologists who study population trends.

Demography is the study of populations.

Absolute numbers are an actual head count of people, births, deaths, and so forth.

Relative numbers are rates, ratios, and percentages that allow us to compare different societies or the same society at different historical periods.

A **census** is an inventory of an entire population at a given moment.

The People's Republic of China has the largest population of any country in the world. In the late 1980s it took 7 million census takers about two years to count China's more than 1.1 billion citizens.

BASIC DEMOGRAPHIC CONCEPTS

Demographers use either absolute or relative numbers to describe a population. **Absolute numbers** are an actual head count of people, births, deaths, and so forth. But because countries vary in the size of their populations, absolute numbers are of little help in cross-cultural comparisons. It is far more useful, then, to use **relative numbers** such as rates, ratios, and percentages (see Chapter 2) that allow us to compare different societies or the same society at different historical periods. Some of the more common demographic terms are defined in Table 20-1.

SOURCES OF DEMOGRAPHIC DATA

Census Data

A **census** is an inventory of an entire population at a given moment. The practice is as old as ancient

TABLE 20-1   Commonly used demographic terms

Birthrates

The number of children born within a specified time period as a proportion of the entire population. For example, in the United States in 1994, the birth rate was about 15.8.

Fertility rates

The number of children born to 1,000 women age 15–44. Because societies vary in the proportion of women of child-bearing age in their population, the fertility rate is a more useful measure than the crude birthrate. In 1994, the fertility rate of U.S. women was approximately 68.0.

Death (mortality) rates

The number of deaths within a given time period as a proportion of the entire population.

Natural increase of a population

Calculated by subtracting deaths from births within a specified time period.

Life expectancy at birth

The average number of years a newborn can expect to live, given current mortality rates.

Infant mortality rates

The ratio of deaths to live births of infants under one year of age. In 1994, in the United States, of every 1000 live births, 8.3 infants did not survive their first year.

Migration

The movement of people from one geographic area to another. Those who leave are **emigrants;** those who enter are **immigrants**.

Net migration

This is measured by subtracting those who moved out from the number moving into a particular area over a given period.

Population growth

The sum of natural increase (births minus deaths) and net migration.

Greece, Rome, and Egypt, probably begun to collect taxes and locate military recruits. In the United States, a national head count is required by law once every ten years to apportion seats in the House of Representatives on the basis of each state's share of the total population. Although the goal is to reach every household, and citizens are required to answer the questionnaire, some people either cannot or will not provide all the necessary information, and others simply cannot be located. Nonetheless, the *decennial* (ten-year) census provides a remarkably thorough picture of the society at that one moment in time.

The final tally for the 1990 U.S. Census was 248,709,873 persons in 93.3 million households. The population has since risen to over 262 million in about 98 million households. It is also estimated that as many as 5 million people, primarily poor inner-city residents, were not counted in 1990 (Weeks, 1992). Because federal welfare funds are distributed on the basis of how many people need help, this undercount added to many city's financial problems, but the Census Bureau refused to make any adjustment that would embarrass the Bush administration by raising the number of officially poor people. The issue is now being studied in preparation for the 2000 census.

Political considerations have also shaped the kinds of questions asked. The first American census of 1790 asked only five questions: the number of free white men, females, and boys; free blacks or Indians; and slaves. By 1890, the questions mirrored concerns about health and immigrants, with one question asking "Are you a tramp, syphilitic, or habitual drunk?" and another requesting the head size of any mentally retarded member of the household. In 1990, the focus was on data of practical use to the government and a source of endless fascination to social scientists: household size and composition, migration history, sources of income, and socioeconomic characteristics.

The problems encountered by American census takers, however, pale in comparison to the task facing the People's Republic of China in the late 1980s when it attempted the most massive head count in world history. Seven million census takers (more people than the entire population of Switzerland) took almost two years to count 1.1 billion citizens, a number far higher than expected, and most likely an undercount of people in isolated rural villages.

Sample Surveys

The U.S. decennial census is supplemented by **sample surveys** that provide updated information at low cost within a short time.

For example, data on unemployment are gathered monthly from a representative sample of approximately 60,000 randomly

> **Sample surveys** provide updated information at low cost within a short time.

selected households (see Chapter 2 on random sampling). Information on income, poverty, household composition, and living arrangements is updated yearly from the same sample.

"Garbage In, Data Out"

One unusual source of demographic data lies buried in the soil. Archeologists have always studied the past by looking at what people have left behind, the remains of daily life that did not disintegrate over time: tools, weapons, clothing, pottery and baskets, and foodstuffs. From an analysis of the type and quantity of such leftovers, archeologists can tell us about the size of a long-gone community, its divisions by sex and social status, and its overall quality of life.

Can contemporary rubbish serve the same function for the study of modern populations? The Garbage Project at the University of Arizona has devoted two decades of research to the systematic analysis of rubbish heaps and garbage cans (Rathje and Murphy, 1992). Among its more fascinating findings are the fol-

lowing: the use of condoms rose by almost half following publicity given to AIDS; cats are much better fed than are dogs; the most popular baby-food in Hispanic households is squash, which ranks last for other babies, along with spinach; and people who eat the same thing everyday waste the least food.

Currently, the Garbage Project is working with the U. S. Census Bureau on the problem of counting homeless people, undocumented aliens, and male residents of urban slums. The task involves reconstructing a community's age and sex distribution on the basis of what is thrown away. By actually sorting, counting and weighing household garbage over an extended period, the research team was able to estimate the size of populations typically undercounted during the decennial census.

Vital Statistics

Vital statistics are records of births, deaths, divorces, and marriages collected at the state level, and published monthly by the Department of Health and Human Services.

Migration Statistics

Migration statistics are more difficult to maintain. People often leave a country without giving notice, and not all immigrants are counted. The U.S. Immigration and Naturalization Service attempts to keep track of all people entering the country with the intent of working here and/or eventually becoming citizens (see Chapter 11).

Population Projections

Population projections are estimates of future growth or decline based on the assumption that current rates will continue. Because of unforeseen factors, the assumptions often turn out to be inaccurate. For example, few social scientists predicted the length and size of the baby boom of 1947-67; they had assumed only a small and temporary jump in birthrates. Today, demographers typically present several projections, each one based on different assumptions of fertility and mortality. For example, if

Vital statistics are records of births, deaths, divorces, and marriages collected at the state level.

Migration statistics measure the population flow within a society as well as movement across national boundaries.

Population projections are estimates of future growth or decline of a nation, state, or other geographic area.

American birth, death, and migration rates continue as they are today, our population will continue to grow slowly, but if each woman were to have three or more children, and, if large numbers of young people were to enter the country, our population could double by 2050!

POPULATION GROWTH

How many people have ever lived on this planet? Perhaps as many as 50 billion in the 100,000 years since the emergence of Homo sapiens. Up until a few hundred years ago, the total human population numbered 5 million, held in check by high mortality rates. The world's population began to rise gradually around the middle of the seventeenth century and then rose steeply from 1960 on. The world population today is 5.6 billion, or one in ten persons who has ever lived, and is likely to reach 6.2 billion by 2000 (Figure 20-1) (Population Reference Bureau, 1994).

The world's population increased dramatically in the past 50 years, doubling between 1950 and 1991, and currently adding 144,000,000 per year. This growth is due largely to (1) a decline in death rates in societies where sewers, boiling water, and indoor toilets reduced the spread of infectious diseases; (2) continued high fertility in societies where large families are encouraged; and (3) techniques that increase crop yields and support a larger population. The *rate* of growth, however, has recently slowed, even as the numbers climb.

The links between population, the food supply, and technology are much more complex than those first noted by the English demographer Thomas Malthus (1766–1834), who was concerned that unre-

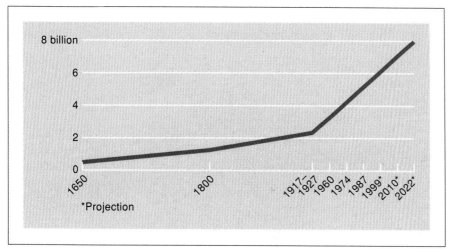

Figure 20-1   Growth of world's population, 1650–2022.

Source: World Almanac, 1993, pp. 817–818.

stricted fertility would outstrip a nation's food supply. When food is scarce, either people must limit fertility or infants will starve to death, thus bringing the population back into balance with resources. Fortunately for English couples, Malthus' prescriptions for controlling the sex life of the masses, especially the poor and less intelligent, never became government policy.

The Demographic Transition

The term **demographic transition** refers to the historical shift from populations kept in balance by both high birth and death rates to one in which the population is stabilized by low fertility and mortality. In Western societies, the shift took place in the eighteenth and nineteenth centuries in a three-stage process at the beginning of the Industrial Revolution.

In the first stage, the decline in death rates with the control of infectious diseases leads to a growth spurt because (1) people are subtracted at a slower rate and (2) more births take place because of the greater number of women who survive through their childbearing years. If, at the same time, food production and living standards are improved, dramatic gains in life expectancy occur.

In the second phase, several decades later, birthrates also begin to fall, as parents realize that most of their children will survive childhood, so that only the desired number need be born. This trend is especially strong among people who live in cities and for whom a large family is a barrier to upward mobility and a higher standard of living. Children, who are an economic asset on the farm, become a major expense in an industrial society.

In the third phase, characterized by both low death and birth rates, the population is stabilized at a very low rate of growth. **Zero population growth (ZPG)** occurs when fertility reaches the replacement

level of the 2.1 offspring required to replace the parental couple (the extra .1 is a demographer's correction for infant mortality and the fact that some couples will have no children). Today, all but a few modern societies have birth rates of 2.1 or lower.

It is somewhat confusing to realize that the United States is almost a ZPG society at the same time that the *number* of births has risen steadily since 1970. This paradox is a result of the fact that women born during the baby boom are now in their childbearing years, adding to the absolute number of babies, even though few mothers will have more than the 2.1 of ZPG. In other words, there is no "baby boomlet" but only an "echo boom" from the large birth cohort of the postwar decades. Nonetheless, the Census Bureau predicts that the rate of natural increase will not decline much further, unless, of course, American couples once more surprise the experts (Pollard, 1994).

> **Demographic transition** refers to the historical shift from populations kept in balance by both high birth and death rates to populations stabilized by low fertility and mortality.
>
> **Zero population growth (ZPG)** occurs when fertility reaches the replacement level of the 2.1 offspring required to replace the parental couple.
>
> **Overpopulation** refers to an imbalance between the number of people and the ability of the society to support them.

Overpopulation

In the second phase of the demographic transition, when fertility remains high while death rates fall, the population could outstrip its resources. **Overpopulation** refers to an imbalance between the number of people and the ability of the society to support them. A large population in itself is not a problem, but be-

■	7.0-7.9 children
■	6.0-6.9
■	5.0-5.9
■	4.0-4.9
■	3.0-3.9
■	2.0-2.9
□	Less than 2.0

The total fertility rate, defined as the average number of children born to a woman in her lifetime, varies dramatically from low rates in developed countries to high rates in developing countries.

comes one when there is not enough food, shelter, or work.

Throughout much of the world today, in the less developed countries (LDCs), or Third World, overpopulation is a major threat to social stability. In many countries, public health programs have reduced infant mortality, but this has not led to reductions in fertility. To the contrary, religious and cultural forces continue to deny access to contraception in most Muslim societies and parts of Asia and Africa, where women typically bear between five and eight children. For example, the countries of eastern Africa have one of the world's highest fertility rates (6.5), highest rate of natural increase (3.1 percent a year), highest infant mortality rate (104 infants per 1,000 live births), lowest life expectancy (51 years), and one of the lowest rates of contraceptive use (less than 15 percent of married women). These are also the nations with the world's lowest per-person income—$210 per person per year in 1994 (Population Reference Bureau, 1994).

Overall, 90 percent of the world's population growth today takes place in the world's poorest regions, breeding illness, starvation, personal misery, and political disorder. At current rates, the population of the LDCs is expected to double within 30 years (Lutz, 1994). Table 20-2 summarizes the demographic differences between the LDCs and the more developed nations. Because of the enormous impact of just one country—the People's Republic of China—the data are presented twice: with and without China.

A major question today is whether or not the LDCs will experience the same demographic transition that characterized Western Europe over the past 150 years. At this moment, it appears that Third World

Ninety percent of the world's population lives in Third World countries where overpopulation (the imbalance between the number of people and the ability of a society to provide food, shelter, and work) is common. Bangladesh is one of the world's most crowded countries with 2,320 people per square mile.

TABLE 20-2   World Population Highlights, 1994

World Population: 5,607,000,000

World Total Fertility Rate: 3.2 children per woman
More Developed Countries: 1.7
Less Developed Countries:
including China: 3.6
excluding China: 4.2

Population of People's Republic of China: 21 percent of world total

World Birth Rate: 25 per 1,000 population
More Developed Countries: 12
Less Developed Countries:
including China: 28
excluding China: 32

World Infant Mortality Rate: 63 per 1,000 live births
More Developed Countries: 10
Less Developed Countries:
including China: 69
excluding China: 77

World Rate of Natural Increase: 1.6 percent per year
More Developed Countries: 0.3
Less Developed Countries:
including China: 1.9
excluding China: 2.2

World Life Expectancy at Birth: 65 years
More Developed Countries: 75
Less Developed Countries:
including China: 63
excluding China: 60

World per capita GNP (in US$): $4,340
More Developed Countries: 16,610
Less Developed Countries:
including China: 950
excluding China: 1,180

World Population Living in Urban Areas: 43 percent
More Developed Countries: 74
Less Developed Countries:
including China: 35
excluding China: 38

Projected World Population
Year 2010: 7,022,000,000
Year 2025: 8,378,000,000

Source: Adapted from 1994 *World Population Data Sheet*, Population Reference Bureau, Inc. Reprinted by permission.

women face greater barriers to fertility control than did their European counterparts in the eighteenth and nineteenth centuries, for whom later age at first marriage offered one contraceptive strategy, as did various "natural" forms of birth control.

However dysfunctional it may be for the collectivity, high fertility is often a rational choice for parents. In societies without public programs for care of the elderly, one's children are the most reliable form of social security in old age. In most agricultural societies, the children produce more than they consume, even though some will starve to death when the crop fails (which is an additional argument for a large family).

High fertility is also characteristic of patriarchal and theocratic societies, where women's health and well-being rarely enter into fertility decisions. To the contrary, pregnancy and child care responsibilities are a means of maintaining male dominance. Although many religious and political leaders claim that women achieve fulfillment through childbearing, fertility rates tend to decline sharply in societies where women have access to contraception or any degree of control over fertility, regardless of the country's level of development (Robey et al., 1993; Sen, 1994).

Second Demographic Transition

As you can also see in Table 20-2, growth rates for the most developed countries are actually well below the 2.1 required for a stable population. In fact, the lowest fertility rates in the world, 1.3 children per woman age 15–44, are found in Italy and Spain, two traditionally Catholic countries. In the rest of Western Europe, the average is 1.6, compared to 2.0 for the United States, and 1.5 for Japan and South Korea. These declines are so steep as to lead some demographers to refer to a "second demographic transition," in which the nation's population actually declines. This situation has led many governments to propose programs to increase fertility, such as providing family allowances, encouraging women to stay out of the labor force, or limiting access to family planning. But because most of these countries are also democratic societies, in which women have the right to vote, such proposals have generally remained on the drawing board.

A useful index for predicting a rise in fertility in modern societies is a combination of measures of women's labor force participation, college enrollment, and age at first marriage. When these rates are rising or remaining stable, fertility will be relatively

SOCIOLOGY AROUND THE WORLD

Demographic Transitions in the Middle East

The geographic area called the Middle East includes countries in all stages of demographic transition. An understanding of their population dynamics is essential to an understanding of the social and political tensions that characterize this part of the world (Omran and Roudi, 1993).

One set of countries such as Jordan, Syria, and the West Bank experienced a sharp drop in infant mortality—from 196 deaths per 1,000 live births in 1950 to only 65 in 1990—that was followed by only a slow decline in fertility. The dramatic decline in mortality has led to an equally dramatic increase in life expectancy, from an average of 40 to 60 years over the four decades. Continued high fertility combined with lowered mortality has produced a high rate of natural increase in this group of countries.

In contrast, Egypt, Lebanon, Turkey, and Iran—that were more influenced by Western culture—experienced faster declines in fertility. Among urban women especially, educational attainment and access to family planning services brought a sharp drop in infant and maternal death rates, with a consequent rise in life expectancy. With both fertility and mortality on the decline, the rate of natural increase remained relatively stable. These countries are also in transition to industrialism despite setbacks due to wars, sectarian conflict, and the influence of fundamentalist critics of modernization.

The demographic picture of a third set of nations, the Gulf states, was determined by the development of oil fields and the foreign money and workers that turned these countries into wealthy societies in a short period of time. Improvements in socioeconomic conditions brought dramatic declines in mortality and a sharp rise in life expectancy among the native population. To reduce dependency on the large number of foreign workers needed to fulfill these nation's ambitious development programs, leaders of these highly traditional Islamic societies have encouraged large families among their own citzens. Thus birth rates have risen, even as mortality has fallen.

Only Israel is at the end of the demographic transition, largely because the country was settled in this century by Westernized Jews who followed the demographic behaviors of their countries of origin. Low fertility and mortality translated into low rates of natural increase, although waves of new migrants have kept population growth relatively high since 1948. The demography of Israel's Arab population, however, is similar to that of Jordan: relatively high fertility and declining mortality. Nonetheless, the balance between Jewish and Muslim Israelis has been maintained by continued Jewish immigration, most recently from Russia. Israel is the most Westernized and industrialized in the region.

Thus, in the same small region of the world, we find a variety of demographic patterns deeply influenced by politics, economics, and religion. These population patterns, in turn, have important implications for the political and economic fate of nations and individuals.

From: Abdel R. Omran and Farzaneh Roudi, "The Middle East Population Puzzle," *Population Bulletin,* Vol. 48, No. 1 (Washington, DC: Population Reference Bureau, Inc., July 1993)

---

low. If, however, age at first marriage declines, and women's college enrollment rates and labor force participation decrease, we can expect an increase in fertility. Keep your eyes peeled.

Migration is the movement of people out of or into a geographic area.

THE DISAPPEARING RUSSIANS. A combination of forces has led to a dramatic decline in the Russian population since 1990 (Haub, 1994). With the end of the communist government's social welfare safety net, the death rate has suddenly climbed while fertility has plunged, leading to a natural *decrease* in population. The introduction of an unregulated market economy has produced even greater shortages of essential goods and services, starvation is widespread, while health care and decent housing are priced beyond the reach of the vast majority of Russians. Under these circumstances, couples stop having children and the aged and ill die off at a rapid rate.

Migration

In addition to birth and death rates, population growth is affected by **migration** patterns, the movement of people out of or into a geographic area. Large-scale population movements can be classified as follows:

- *Environmental migration* occurs in the wake of natural disasters such as famine, drought, typhoons, or volcanic eruptions.
- *Forced migrations* take place when a population is forcibly removed, as when Jews were expelled from Spain in the 16th century, or Kurdish peoples from Iraq, and Muslims from parts of Bosnia today.
- *Free migration* is largely a matter of personal choice, as in the massive immigration to America in this century or the movement westward in the previous century.
- *Mass migration* involves the movement of an entire ethnic or religious group from one region to

another. The migration of Mormons from New York State to Utah is one example, as is the current migration of ethnic Russians from the Baltic states that were once part of the Soviet Union, and of Russian Jews to Israel and the United States.

These types of migrations often overlap. For example, both famine and personal choice led many Irish to leave their island and come to America in the late nineteenth century. And throughout Europe today, mass migrations are bringing people from the economically troubled Eastern areas to the more prosperous West. As we saw in Chapter 11, these migrations have caused many political and social welfare problems for the Western nations. Mass migrations are also characteristic of the Third World, primarily caused by famine and warfare; indeed, 87 percent of the world's 19 million officially designated refugees are in the less developed regions. Overall, at least 100,000,000 people today live outside their country of birth or citizenship (Teitelbaum and Russell, 1994).

The massive influx of relatively poor people strains the resources of the receiving nations, which is why many countries are now refusing to accept them. The United States, for example, has stopped admitting "economic" refugees (especially Asians and Haitian blacks) and will accept only the few "political" refugees who can prove that they would be imprisoned or killed if forced to return. Throughout Western Europe today, political leaders are under great pressure to limit the number and length of stay of immigrants because their economies can no longer support the newcomers. In other times and places, however, immigration has been encouraged, such as in the last century when the United States needed industrial laborers or today in the case of the foreign workers in the oil-producing Gulf states. And Israel desperately seeks Jewish immigrants to maintain its population.

The various pushes and pulls and mediating factors in migration are illustrated in Figure 20-2. In general, it is young, single people who are most able to pick up roots and move to a new country or region. They are also in prime childbearing years and typically boost the fertility rate of their new location, while also causing a fertility decline in the place they left, which is why the migration of Irish to America during the potato famine benefited both countries demographically. Today, however, the mass migrations associated with the global economy have had primarily negative consequences for the poor of the Third World.

COMPOSITION OF THE POPULATION

In addition to the impact of sheer numbers, the age and sex distribution of a population have important effects on the society and its members.

Figure 20-2 Pushes, pulls, and mediating factors in migration.

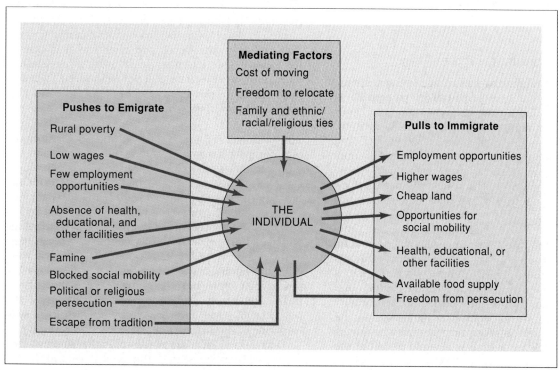

During the economic boom of the early 1980s, large numbers of foreign "guest workers" were encouraged to migrate to Western Europe, including large numbers of Turkish laborers, to work in German factories. When European economies took a downturn in the 1990s, local residents turned upon the guest workers. In this picture, the residence of Turkish migrants was set on fire by German youths.

Population Pyramids

Demographers summarize data on age and sex distributions in the form of a **population pyramid,** as shown in Figure 20-3. Note the very different shapes for Denmark with its negative population growth, the United States at ZPG, and a less developed country such as Kenya in Africa. The pyramids are divided vertically by sex, with males on the left, females on the right. Each bar represents an age group at five-year intervals—a **birth cohort,** or people born during a specified time period. In a high-fertility, high-mortality society such as Kenya, the population will be "bottom heavy," overwhelmingly composed of children, with very few old people at the top. In a low-fertility, low mortality society, such as

A **population pyramid** is used to summarize data on age and sex distributions.

A **birth cohort** consists of the people born during a given time period.

A **dependency ratio** compares the number of children and elderly to the number of working age.

the United States, the pyramid will look more like a rectangle, with minimal natural increase. In the case of negative growth, as in Denmark, the pyramid becomes inverted with the base smaller than the next set of layers. Baby booms will create bulges, as shown among people in their 30s in the United States, while wars cause temporary indentations.

The example of Germany, as seen in Figure 20-4, illustrates the impact of historical events on the age and sex composition of a population. The loss of millions of young men in World War I (1914–18) created a shortage of husbands, as reflected in both low birthrates immediately after the war and the excess of women at the oldest ages. Similarly, you can see the effects of World War II, in which civilians as well as soldiers died, followed by a post-war baby boom as the German economy improved dramatically, which was followed in turn by the current "baby bust" and tiny "echo boom."

Age and sex distributions tell us a great deal about a country. A glance at the pyramid for Kenya in Figure 20-3 should suggest the kinds of problems facing developing nations, such as how to feed and educate the young and provide income for their parents. In contrast, one look at the population distribution of a developed nation is sufficient to understand why health care and social security are major economic and social issues.

DEPENDENCY RATIOS.   The number of people younger than age 15 and older than age 65, relative to the number of people age 16–64, is called a **dependency ratio,** on the assumption that the young and old must be supported by the others. As you can see from the pyramids in Figures 20-3 and 20-4, the dependency burden in developing nations is that of caring for children, while in the developed countries it is care of the elderly. The dependency ratio has a major effect on taxation and welfare policies in modern societies, just as it has a powerful effect on political and economic stability in the Third World.

AGE, SEX, AND LIFE STYLES.   The age and sex distribution of a population also affects marriage patterns and lifestyles. In the frontier West, for example, largely populated by unmarried males, high levels of drinking, brawling, and prostitution created problems for law enforcement. The number of men or women in an age cohort will obviously affect the probability of marriage and age at first marriage. For example, a woman born at the beginning of the baby boom (1947–8) will have difficulty finding a marriage partner because so many fewer men were born in the five years before her birth. Conversely, men born in the last year of the boom (1967) will have heavy competition for a wife from one of the smaller cohorts born after that date.

One influential study of the sex ratios suggests that where women are scarce, the norms will emphasize

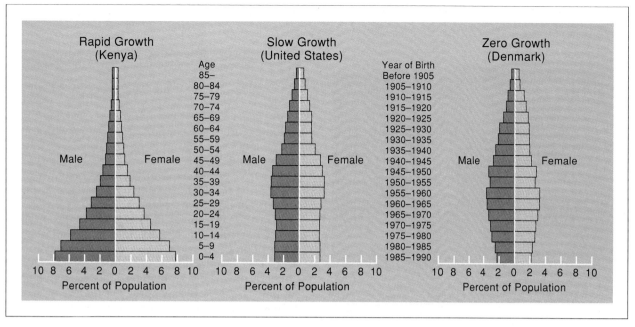

Figure 20-3 Age patterns of population.

From: The US Bureau of the Census and the United Nations; Joseph A. McFalls, "Population: A Lively Introduction," *Population Bulletin* 46, no. 2 (Washington, D.C.: Population Reference Bureau, Inc., 1991).

monogamy and restriction of women to the home, because the men who do have wives do not wish them to come into contact with other men. When men are scarce, other norms are stressed; with all the single women around, a man need not commit to life-long monogamy, and women will find it easier to pursue an education and participate in the labor force (Guttentag and Secord, 1983). Thus do age and sex distributions affect decisions that we tend to think of as highly personal and voluntary.

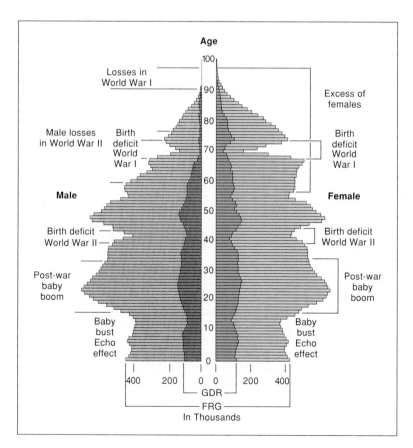

Figure 20-4 The impact of historical events on the age and sex composition of the population of Germany. (FRG, West Germany; GDR, East Germany.)

From: The US Bureau of the Census and the United Nations; Joseph A. McFalls, "Population: A Lively Introduction," *Population Bulletin* 46, no. 2 (Washington, D.C.: Population Reference Bureau, Inc., 1991).

The deaths of soldiers in wars is reflected in the population pyramids of countries. Germany is one country which lost millions of young men in World War II creating a shortage of husbands, a social fact reflected in low birth rates after the war and a surplus of women at the oldest ages. This cemetery contains German soldiers killed in the Second World War.

The population of any society is determined by three factors: births, deaths, and migration. When births exceed deaths, as in Guatemala, the country's population grows.

SOCIAL POLICY

Fertility Control: When the Personal Is Political

As the material in this chapter makes clear, both high and low fertility have important consequences for entire societies and kinship groups as well as for mothers and children, Therefore, only rarely in human history have decisions about the number and spacing of offspring been left to women themselves. In the less-developed nations, high fertility and overpopulation threaten economic and political stability. In the industrial world, low fertility produces a different set of social problems: population aging, high dependency ratios, and rising health care costs.

On the positive side, high fertility ensures a family support system in old age, provides bodies for armies, fills church pews, and creates a pool of inexpensive labor (the more workers there are, the less one needs to pay them). Conversely, low fertility, when linked to parental choice, is associated with enhanced physical and mental health for young and old, close parent–child bonds, and lowered rates of child neglect or abuse.

In practice, however, it is the societal rather than the personal effects of fertility that motivate political leaders, as two opposite contemporary examples illustrate, both occurring under Communist rule. In Eastern Europe, the Marxist governments established in the 1940s were ideologically committed to freeing women from their inferior position in the family and society. Women were given the right to vote, the divorce laws were liberalized, and family planning was encouraged. The immediate consequences were a dramatic rise in divorces and an equally profound drop in the birthrate. By the 1960s, these governments were sufficiently alarmed at the population decline to begin programs of encouraging fertility (pronatalist policy).

No country went further than Romania, whose leader claimed that the fetus was social property and that giving birth was a woman's patriotic duty. In 1966, the legal age of marriage was lowered to 15, contraceptives were forbidden, all employed women were forced to undergo a monthly gynecological examination, pregnant women were carefully monitored, and a special tax was placed on childless adults. The Romanian birthrate rose sharply for a few years but gradually declined to an even lower rate than before 1965, as women found that they were not receiving any support from husbands or the state in raising their children while also holding down jobs. Maternal and infant death rates soared to the highest levels of the West, and when the government was overthrown in 1989, the women joyously trashed the clinics. Among the lasting legacies of this policy, however, are tens of thousands of abandoned children, overwhelming the Romanian orphanage system.

In some countries with low birthrates the government is urging citizens to increase the number of children for the sake of the nation, whereas other countries with high birth rates urge people to have fewer children. This French billboard encourages people to have children. The infant asks, "Do I look like a government regulation to you?", a tongue-in-cheek reference to the French government's policy to increase birth rates. French families receive a monthly government subsidy for each child born after the first. Added, at the bottom right, is "France needs children." Compare the message on this bulletin board in France, promoting larger families with the photo in Chapter 1 promoting one child families in China.

In contrast, the problem for the People's Republic of China was reducing fertility. At 1 billion by 1980 and rising steadily, the population was a threat to economic growth and any rise in the standard of living. The Chinese leadership had tried and failed to enforce a "one-child" policy, except among urban educated elites. Although the one-child goal was somewhat eased, especially for rural, traditional families, the regime's *antinatalist* program is a mirror image of the Romanian: the legal age for marriage was raised to over 21, contraception was made available at no cost, abortions were encouraged, and the tax system favored people with one or no children. The result was a sharply reduced birthrate among the ethnic Chinese but no change for ethnic minorities, raising the possibility of a crackdown on the minorities (Tien et al., 1992). Nonetheless, the very size of its population places pressure on China's environment in an effort to increase supplies of food and water.

The politics of fertility also emerged in 1994 as the United Nations planned an International Conference on Population and Development. Earlier conferences had been dominated by men whose idea of population planning was limited to encouraging contraception. In 1994, however, women's groups from around the world insisted that the delegates deal with broader issues such as educating women, allowing them to vote, providing decent health care, and reducing gendered inequality in general. Advancing women's rights, they argued, is the surest way to lower fertility.

These proposals drew immediate opposition from the Vatican and Muslim countries resistant to changes that would upset traditional gender relationships. The final document was a major victory for supporters of family planning and reproductive health care, recognizing a basic right of people to decide the number and spacing of their children (Cohen and

Richards, 1994). If you were President Clinton, how would you have instructed the American delegates? What role do you think the United States should play in world population planning?

The complex links between population growth and economic development were explored by the world's countries at the International Conference on Population and Development. The conference was better at demonstrating the politics of population control than the countries' willingness to adopt policies that would really deal with these issues. Developed countries supported greater population control, developing countries objected to the imperialism of such policies, and the Catholic Church objected to any strong guidelines on family planning or the use of abortions to limit family size. Women's groups around the world pressed for the discussion of larger issues, such as educating women, advancing their rights, and providing adequate health care.

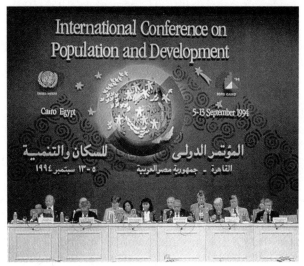

GROWTH AND DISTRIBUTION OF THE U. S. POPULATION

At its founding in the 1790s, there were approximately 4.5 million Americans. By 1820, the population had more than doubled as a result of territorial expansion, natural increase, and immigration. In 1900, the U.S. population was roughly 76 million and stands at over 262,000,000 today. More interesting than its size, however, is the distribution of the population. The history of the United States has been one of massive population shifts: from farm to city to suburb; from the Atlantic coast westward; and most recently, from the Northeast to the Southwest.

Geographic Mobility

Geographic mobility or internal migration is subject to the same push-pull analysis as overseas migration patterns, as shown in Figure 20-2. People move primarily in response to economic opportunities, but also to improve their living standards and/or avoid negative conditions. The United States has even had its forced migrations, in the case of Native Americans in the nineteenth century or Japanese Americans during World War II.

Internal migration patterns also affect the age and sex distribution of various regions. For example, as discussed in Chapter 21, an outflow of young people has dramatically "aged" rural America. Conversely, an influx of young people of child-bearing age will quickly increase a region's population. And because seats in the U.S. House of Representatives are based on the state's population, there are important political consequences to mobility patterns.

Contrary to the popular assumption that the United States is a nation of movers, however, internal migration rates have declined in recent years. In 1992–1993, 16.8 percent of Americans changed residence compared with 20.6 percent in 1960–1961, and the vast majority of these moves were within the same state. Less than 3 percent of Americans moved across state lines in 1992–1993 (U. S. Bureau of the Census P20–481, 1994). Yet compared with other modern societies, ours is considered to experience high mobility (Gober, 1993). As with international migration, movers are primarily young adults in the process of status changes—from school to work, one type of employment to another, single to married, and nonparent to parent.

Migration Streams

Where do they go? Historically, the major population streams have been driven by economic changes. Before the Civil War, large numbers moved West in search of cheap land. In the early phase of industrial-

ization, Americans moved from farms and villages to where the factories were, in the Northeast and around the Great Lakes. Following World War II, young couples moved from city to suburbs in ever-widening circles (Chapter 21). In the 1970s and 1980s, a massive shift took place as millions of workers left the declining manufacturing centers of the Northeast and North Central regions (the Snowbelt states) and moved to where the new jobs were, in the South and Southwest (the Sunbelt states). The Sunbelt thrived on defense-related businesses, low-wage light manufacturing, oil booms, and consequent construction projects. The 1990s have seen a slowing down of the migration rate, but the direction remains southward and westward (Gober and Haub, 1994).

Looking ahead to the next century, official projections are that the South will continue to gain population at the expense of the Northeast (U.S. Bureau of the Census P25-1111, 1994). California, now the largest state, will become even more populous, with 15 percent of the nation's population by 2020, followed by Texas and Florida. California will have the youngest population and Florida the oldest (over 25 percent will be age 65+ in 2020).

Interestingly, African Americans, whose major migration stream was from South to North up to the 1970s, have also joined the flow out of the Northeast (Frey, 1994). Black college graduates tended to move to Texas and the West Coast where job opportunities were expanding. Other African Americans, pushed by unemployment and rising housing costs were more likely to move from the urban North back to the South where their roots were.

POPULATION, NATURAL RESOURCES, AND THE ENVIRONMENT

In the process of securing food and shelter, humans have always brought changes to their natural environment (Bharadwaj, 1992). However careful they tried to be, hunters and gatherers used up the resources in one area before moving to another. Herders and horticulturists replaced an area's natural vegetation with crops, overgrazed the land, and cut down forests. With agriculture and irrigation, the very face of the land is transformed. As cities were built, natural resources were used up at ever increasing rates. Most recently, the industrial economy is based precisely on using natural resources as raw material for the production of other goods, and in the process creates gases and chemicals that pollute the air and water (Schnaiberg and Gould, 1994).

In addition, as detailed earlier in this chapter, the world's population is rapidly increasing, especially in the poor, less developed nations. Are we then doomed to use up the world's resources, or can technological advances and population controls restore the balance between humans and their environment? But even if food production could be increased and natural energy sources harnessed, the world's resources will remain unequally distributed, with nations such as the United States consuming the lion's share while the most populous areas are starved of food and material comforts. Thus, the pressures of both population growth and inequality in the distribution and consumption of resources have led to a sense of crisis among many **ecologists,** scientists who study the adaptation of populations to their environment (Ladd, 1994). Some of the many sources of alarm, particularly in the Third World but also in parts of the United States, are discussed next.

> The environment is not a natural thing; it is a set of interrelated percepts, a product of culture . . . . The relation between a society and its environment can be understood only when we see how the environment is organized in terms of the verbal categories of those who use it.
>
> —EDMUND LEACH, 1965

Negative Effects on the Environment

DECLINES IN FOOD PRODUCTION.   The technological advances in food production known as the "Green Revolution" of the 1970s increased crop yields throughout the Third World and allowed many countries to continue to feed their growing populations. But production can no longer keep pace with unrestrained fertility. In addition, the new strains of crops required enormous amounts of fertilizers and pesticides that are now polluting the ground. Furthermore, water was diverted into irrigation ditches where accumulated salts that result from evaporation spoil nearby land.

LOSS OF FARM LAND.   Overgrazing by cattle, loss of trees and shrubs that kept soil in place, and poor crop rotation have all reduced the amount of topsoil in vast areas of the globe. In Africa, the Sahara desert has grown ever wider, bringing starvation to millions, leading to mass migrations, and creating the type of political turmoil that brought American troops to Somalia in 1993.

DEFORESTATION.   As noted in Chapter 3, many developing nations have allowed foreign companies to exploit the timber resources of ancient rain forests. Once the timber is gone, the money will stop coming in, and the country will be left with even fewer natural resources. When the forests go, so also do thousands of different plants and animals that exist nowhere else. This loss of biological variability, or bio-

Scenes such as this one of young children starving in the Sudan may become all too familiar in the future. The poorest countries in Africa and Asia are expected to experience more famines as civil strife and climate changes create periodic shortages. Even when shipments of food are made to the needy countries, corrupt local governments often hoard and sell the food rather than make it available to those who need it.

diversity, could have a negative impact on the adaptability of the entire ecosystem (world environment).

ENDANGERMENT OF NATIVE (INDIGENOUS) PEOPLE.   The native tribes that occupied the rain forests are also in danger of extinction, as loggers cut down everything in sight, with no obligation to plant new growth. Many other indigenous peoples have been forced out of traditional habitats by farmers and housing developers who seek the best land and push the tribes further and further into less productive areas. This, too, is a major loss of diversity in the world and of an opportunity to expand our knowledge of human capabilities and our understanding of the human condition (Durning, 1993; Wilford, 1994).

> **Ecologists** are scientists who study the adaptation of populations to their environment.

DECLINING SUPPLIES OF CLEAN WATER.   The diversion of streams for irrigation, the drying up of ground water, and the pollution of other sources have created a scarcity of drinkable water. The one answer that appeals to political leaders—building massive new dams—alters the natural environment in a number of ways, none of which enhances the long-term water supply or the diversity of species that live in the lakes and rivers. In addition, local communities upriver are driven out of their natural habitat to places where they can no longer practice their traditional ways of life. The young will drift into the expanding urban slums of the Third World, adding to the masses of unemployed that make these countries so politically unstable.

ACCUMULATION OF UNRECYCLED GARBAGE.   Increased use of plastic, glass, aluminum foil, paper, and metals has created a new environmental hazard in the developed world as well: a growing pile of waste material. Although Americans were vastly entertained in 1987 by the saga of a barge full of garbage that traveled up and down the coast looking for a dumping place, disposal is a real problem for most localities today as landfills reach capacity.

In the United States, recycling efforts have diverted only a small fraction of material from the garbage pit. The most successful programs involve curbside disposal and pickup, anything that makes it easier for a homeowner to comply and to see that neighbors are also participating in a community-wide effort (Derksen and Gartrell, 1993).

AIR POLLUTION.   One by-product of industrial production is the release of toxic (illness-causing) material into the atmosphere: billions of tons each year from American industries. Throughout Eastern Europe and the former Soviet Union, the use of soft coal to fuel factories, combined with a complete lack of concern for environmental protection, has left whole regions blackened by soot, destroyed crops, and fouled the water (Flavin and Lennsen, 1993).

Although there is some controversy over whether these industrial emissions are eating away the layer of ozone that protects the Earth from cancer-producing ultraviolet rays, there can be little question that air pollution creates a health and safety problem of major proportions, such as the effects of smog in Los Angeles.

Another potential problem is called the *greenhouse effect,* a result of gases such as carbon dioxide that act like the glass in a greenhouse, keeping the moisture and heat inside. If enough of these gases accumulate, they can change the world's temperature, altering the climate, and producing drought and storms that shift agricultural belts. This is also a controversial hypothesis, as the evidence for global warming is still unclear. In addition, nature also contributes to changes in the environment, some of which may be beneficial and others less so, such as when volcanic emissions transform the local climate and spread across the globe (Brown et al., 1994).

Energy Sources and the Environment

The interaction between populations and the environment can be seen in the current debate over energy policy. On the one hand, the major sources of energy for industrial development—coal and oil—are limited; it took tens of millions of years for the supply to be created, and only a few hundred to use it up. Coal and oil are *nonrenewable resources;* unlike forests that can be replanted, once the coal and oil are gone, there is no more. In addition, after the easily tapped supply is gone, wells and mines must be dug deeper and in increasingly difficult places, making the product more expensive while spoiling the native environment, such

Garbage has become an important research tool in the gloved hands of demographers at the University of Arizona which started the "Garbage Project." Here a group of students and their professor are examining garbage to determine the consumption patterns of families and individuals. Among the things discovered were differences in the most popular foods among white and Hispanic families, and differences in what people say they prepare as fresh foods compared to pre-packaged food. More recently the Garbage Project has worked with the U.S. Census Bureau on the problem of undercounting homeless people by accurately identifying the age, sex, and social class composition of a community from its garbage. (See Research in Action box, page 478.)

The Tragedy of the Commons

Here is the tragedy of the commons, as described by the American biologist, Garrett Hardin (1968). The commons is an area in each village where all herders can graze their cattle. Herders try to feed as many of their own cattle as possible on the common ground, and as long as the herds remain below the carrying capacity of the land, each herder gains and makes a rational choice whether to keep adding animals. The owner receives all the proceeds from the sale of the animals, whereas the costs of overgrazing are shared with others. But eventually, more animals are added than the commons can support, and disaster is the result. "Freedom in a commons brings ruin to all." What benefits individuals destroys the collectivity.

as when the Alaskan pipeline destroyed the caribou grazing land of the Inuit Eskimo (Egan, 1991).

Coal and oil also carry other environmental risks. For example, coal-using industries emit particles of sulfur that linger in the air and fall back to earth in the form of acid rain. Oil is cleaner to burn but more hazardous to transport, as seen in the many well-publicized oil spills of the past decade.

On the other hand, the *renewable* energy sources most popular today—nuclear power and hydroelectric power—have their environmental risks. The dangers of nuclear energy production were well illustrated by the 1986 meltdown at the Chernobyl nuclear power plant in the Soviet Union. Clouds of radioactive material floated across Europe, contaminating crops and seeping into water supplies, and elevating the risk of several types of cancer (Medvedev, 1991). Problems of plant safety and the disposal of radioactive waste have yet to be solved, which has led to the deactivation of many facilities.

Hydroelectric power, provided by harnessing the energy of falling water, is the cleanest, safest, and most common renewable resource. However, to increase the water flow, large dams must be built that have many unintended and undesirable outcomes: soil erosion, silted rivers, flooded farms and pastures,

and the inevitable displacement of local populations. Proposed hydroelectric projects in India, for example, will involve moving up to 10 million people and providing them with alternative modes of subsistence (Brown et al., 1994).

Other alternative sources of energy (wind power, solar heat, and underground steam) are still in a preliminary stage of research and application. In the United States, research funding on alternatives has been limited by pressure from the powerful oil and mining industries. Several European nations, however, are investing in studies of various nonpolluting and renewable sources of energy.

The problem for people in developing nations is much more immediate and severe: how to stay warm and cook food. People who need wood now for the family hearth do not worry about how or when to renew the forests. In the absence of any help from their government, they will cut down trees and dig up wads of peat, even if in the long run these acts destroy the productivity of the land. It is one of those great ironies of human existence that when each family acts in its own best interests, the total effect may be to reduce the survival chances of the collectivity.

A further hazard is the likelihood that a scarcity of renewable resources will lead to continued violence in the developing world. Shortages of fuel, water, farmland, and forests combined with rapid population growth are a recipe for conflict within each society and for wars between nations. Many researchers believe that if the destruction of the environment continues at its present pace, there will be little peace on Earth (Homer-Dixon et al., 1993). In this view, it is crucial for both rich and poor societies that the world's resources be more fairly distributed within and between nations (Ladd, 1994).

Technological Risks in American Society

Sociologists have long been interested in the effects of harmful events on people and communities, focusing mainly on natural disasters such as floods or earthquakes. More recently, researchers have added

Drawing by Lorenz; © 1992 The New Yorker Magazine, Inc.

"And may we continue to be worthy of consuming a disproportionate share of this planet's resources."

In the United States thousands of cases of cancer are estimated to be caused by the billions of pounds of toxic chemicals released into the air each year. What can we do about this? And why have we not done it?

technological risks to this list, especially those that involve the spread of toxic materials such as radioactive waste, acid rain, and noxious (harmful) gases. Toxic hazards differ from natural disasters in that their effects are not immediately visible and victims are never certain when they are safe from further damage (Clarke, 1992; Hofrichter, 1993).

The sociological study of risk involves both actual and perceived threats, not only how people react to hazardous experiences such as contaminated water in their own communities, but also people's ideas about what is dangerous and why (Freudenberg, 1993; Erikson, 1994). Risk research at the macrolevel has examined the organizational contexts in which risks are generated and managed. For example, in the case of the oil spill from the tanker *Exxon Valdez*, despite all kinds of complex organizational plans on paper, the company had failed to take adequate precautions against such a disaster, and neither the company nor the government had an immediate and effective response. The paper plans gave the illusion of professional knowledge and expertise, a falsehood that had to be believed by employees and the general public because the alternative is too awful to contemplate: that there may be hazards in the modern world that are beyond our ability to control or contain (Clarke, 1992).

Risk research at the microlevel has focused primarily on attitudes and beliefs and how these are shaped and changed over time. In general, the public tends to overestimate the likelihood of relatively rare threats that are dramatic (an airplane crash), violent (being held up at gunpoint), or catastrophic (a nuclear power plant accident). At the same time, the public underestimates the dangers from less sensational but common threats such as car emissions and polluted streams. In large part, this difference reflects the fact that most of us receive information on risk from the mass media. Covering a disaster is cheaper, quicker, and more compelling than doing a well-researched piece of investigative journalism on contamination in ground water. It is these structural factors in the production of news (programming demands, cost, keeping the attention of viewers or readers) that explain why the media cover high-drama risks and ignore other hazards and why the public has such a biased view of the dangers out there.

It is very difficult for any community to resist certain kinds of economic development, despite environmental hazards, if the rewards are jobs and tax revenues (Sheehan, 1993). If the choice is between work or welfare, most people will choose the job now and worry about the health risks later. In economically secure communities, citizens have been more successful in opposing environmentally risky development than have people in poor neighborhoods (Fruedenberg and Gramling, 1994).

Opposition is also found where people have experienced the failure of technology, as in communities near nuclear power plants where "accidental" emissions have been reported (Goldsteen and Schorr, 1991). The word *accidental* is used by authorities to reassure the public, but the very fact that such things could happen unintentionally should be most upsetting (Perrow, 1984). Various interest groups—the energy industry, government agencies, and environment protection organizations—are currently struggling to define "acceptable risk." The difficulty of assigning risk or even responsibility for an accident and its clean-up were illustrated in the case of a fire in a transformer in a Binghamton, New York, office building that spewed toxic coolant through the building and out to the neighborhood (Clarke 1989). Without clear standards of acceptable levels of exposure, none of the eleven federal, state, and local government agencies involved was willing to claim "ownership" of the problem, and the final disposition of the case depended on which interest groups had the greatest political and economic clout. Under such conditions of "organizational anarchy," interest-group power rather than scientific analysis will determine levels of risk and the assessment of responsibility for correcting the problems and coordinating cleanup measures.

The only people not involved in risk assessment are the most vulnerable citizens, those most likely to find a nuclear power facility in their own backyards (Schnaiberg and Gould, 1994; Krauss, 1993).

Environmental Justice

As with most other social phenomena, technological risks are not equally distributed; some communities and people are at greater risk than others. In general, the distribution of ecological hazards is *inversely* related to social status: The higher one's position in stratification hierarchies, the lower the risk. Conversely, the lower the status, the higher the likelihood of being placed in danger. For example, three-fourths of the residents of communities where hazardous-waste landfills are located are poor, African American, and/or Latino. That some citizens are more valuable than others can be seen in the fines imposed for violations of the hazardous-waste laws: 500 times larger when the site was located near a predominantly white community than when located in a minority neighborhood (Hofrichter, 1993).

Each year, hundreds of thousands of Latino farm-workers are exposed to pesticide poisoning under grossly unsanitary working conditions, but the cost of reducing their health risk has been defined as the unacceptable alternative of raising the prices we pay at the supermarket (Perfecto and Valasquez, 1992). Native American communities in the Southwest find their sacred lands taken by the government and turned into radioactive waste dumps, while corporations evade federal regulations by dealing directly with tribal leaders for landfill sites for commercial waste (Churchill, 1992). One such proposed dump on a Sioux reservation, nicknamed "Dances with Garbage," was eventually halted by a grassroots alliance of various native groups. But other Indian nations have been less successful in resisting such offers, and cancer rates have risen dramatically in these areas. Many tribes have also accepted money from multinational companies eager to exploit the natural resources under Indian land (Gedicks, 1993).

These are only a few examples of widespread **environmental racism**—policies that have different impacts on racial/ethnic populations—in exposure to industrial toxins, dirty drinking water, and foul air, as well as the location of dumps and incinerators, and both strip and deep mines (Bryant and Mohai, 1992).

Most of the waste generated in white neighborhoods and communities is eventually disposed of in predominantly black areas. The American South is gradually becoming the dumping ground of the nation. The largest landfill of all—the "Cadillac of Dumps"—is located right in the center of rural Alabama, where African Americans comprise 90 percent of the population. In Houston, Texas, where blacks make up 28 percent of residents, over 80 percent of both public and private landfill sites are located in black neighborhoods, which is an improvement over just a few years ago, when all the landfills and six of eight incinerators were sited there (Bullard, 1993).

> **Environmental racism** occurs when toxins are stored in communities that are inhabited primarily by people of color, who have little political or economic power.

Most hazardous waste landfills are located in communities primarily populated by the poor African Americans, and Hispanics. Toxic waste is found everywhere, including the suburban community of Montclair, New Jersey, where thousands of barrels of soil contaminated with radon were stored in a residential neighborhood. How safe is your neighborhood? and how can you tell?

ROBERT D. BULLARD

The Legacy of Environmental Racism

Robert D. Bullard is Professor of Sociology at the University of California, Riverside. He has published a number of books on the African-American urban experience and environmental issues, most recently Unequal Protection: Environmental Justice and Communities of Color *(1994).*

*A*s a product of the 1960s and the modern Civil Rights Movement, my research focus has always been on questions of fairness, justice, and the rights of powerless groups. At the time I began studying neighborhoods, few people in this field had made the connection between environmental problems and social justice. My first published paper, in 1978, dealt with housing barriers and the built environment in Houston, Texas.

A year later, when I was still an untenured assistant professor at predominantly black Texas Southern University, my attorney-wife, Linda McKeever Bullard, asked me to conduct a study of the locations of municipal solid-waste disposal facilities in the city. Linda had filed a class action suit against the city, the state of Texas, and Browning Ferris Industries—the "Avis of Garbage"—who were planning to locate a garbage landfill in a suburban neighborhood that was 82 percent home-owning African American. The lawsuit was the first of its kind to challenge an environmental decision by using the 1964 Civil Rights Act that forbids discriminatory treatment by government agencies on the basis of race.

My research showed that from the 1920s to the early 1970s, all the city-owned landfills and 75 percent of municipal garbage incinerators were located in predominantly African-American neighborhoods, as were three-fourths of the privately owned sanitary landfills. At this time, blacks composed no more than one-fourth of the city's population.

This is *environmental racism*—a policy or practice that has the effect of treating people differently on the basis of race or skin color, whether intended or not. Environmental racism in the United States has joined public policy with industry practices to shift the burden of waste disposal onto people of color, while exempting white neighborhoods.

Actually, when the new landfill was first proposed in the early 1970s the area was largely white, and officials decided not to build it on grounds that it was too close to neighborhood schools, would lower property values, disrupt the community, and present a public health nuisance. Yet less than 8 years later, after most homes had been sold to black owners, none of these arguments was considered serious enough to delay building a landfill only 1400 feet from the public school.

Houston was not unique. A similar pattern can be found throughout the South where government and industry have responded to white cries of "NIMBY" (Not In My Backyard) with the practice of "PIBBY" (Place in Blacks' Back Yard). But environmental racism is more than a "black and white thing." Many grassroots organizations, environmental groups, scientists, and academics are involved in the movement for environmental justice and livable communities. They have redefined *environmentalism* to include where people live, work, and play.

After more than a decade of studies, public hearings, and neighborhood activism, these efforts are beginning to pay off. Several grassroots groups have successfully resisted further environmental degradation. Yet all too many communities remain prime dumping grounds for a variety of deadly materials, in the North as well as the South and from coast to coast.

The decade of the 1990s is different from the 1970s when I began my work in this area. In the earlier decade, few environmentalists, civil rights organizations, or government agencies were willing to challenge environmental racism. Today, in contrast, a broad-based coalition of civil rights, environmental, and legal-defense organizations are fighting waste disposal decisions that differentially affect poor people and people of color.

Environmental racism and justice are "hot" topics at conferences sponsored by law societies and public health associations. The concept of environmental justice has even "trickled up" to the White House and federal agencies. In 1992, the Environmental Protection Agency (EPA) produced a call to action, *Environmental Equity: Reducing Risk for All Communities*, and created an Office of Environmental Equity. In that year, I was asked to join President Clinton's Transition Team on the Natural Resources, and in 1993 the EPA began drafting an Executive Order on Environmental Justice for the president's signature.

Although the nation is a long way from being a racially just society, academic studies can be used by activists and grassroots organizations to make small steps toward that goal. It is very gratifying to know that one's own work has had real consequences for real people.

The Environmental Justice Movement

The problems outlined in this chapter have led to the creation of an **Environmental Justice Movement (EJM)** in the United States, a culturally diverse grassroots effort to change the way in which decisions that affect the quality of life are made. The EJM differs in composition and goals from the largely middle-class, white environmental movement that placed the whole issue on the public agenda. Protecting nature refuges and shorelines and saving species are all honorable goals but often do not speak to the immediate concerns of the people most affected by environmental degradation.

In contrast, EJM members are more diverse, drawn from the ranks of industrial labor, farm workers, neighborhood associations, women's health groups, civil rights/minority organizations, and antinuclear activists.

This alliance has worked with the mainstream environment movement on limited goals such as consumer product safety, pesticide control, and conservation. The EJM, however, has a broader agenda, no less than "equal access to natural resources and the right to clean air and water, adequate health care, affordable shelter, and a safe workplace" (Hofrichter, 1993, p. 4).

The EJM will have to take on not only City Hall but major American corporations seeking to maximize profits (Cable and Benson, 1993). For example, two logging companies managed to cut most of the timberland in Montana before closing down operations and leaving the state to deal with the destroyed forests and thousands of jobless workers. It will also have to deal with a Congress elected in 1994 on a platform of repealing environmental rules that impede business growth.

Without political clout or representation in the city government, minority populations are typically unable to fight back. Yet some attempts at organized resistance have been successful (Gottlieb, 1994). One such group, Concerned Citizens of South Central Los Angeles, fought off an attempt to locate yet another incinerator in an area already the dirtiest in the state from a combination of freeway car exhaust and emissions from industrial smoke stacks and waste pipes: A one-square-mile area contained a total of 33 million pounds of waste chemicals per year (Bullard, 1993).

When Los Angeles officials then decided to place the new incinerator in a Latino neighborhood, they met their match in the Mothers of East Los Angeles, who conducted a successful campaign against the facility. Much of the membership and leadership in both these organizations was provided by women of color. Local organizing around an issue of immediate concern to their families gives women an opportunity to use their skills effectively and thus to gain a sense of empowerment. Although their involvement begins with a single issue, the experience leads them to broaden their range of concerns (Krauss, 1993).

Corporations, however, driven by market forces and the profit motive, continue to target politically weak communities as sites for toxic chemicals and polluting industries. Few government agencies are powerful enough to resist this pressure: Lawsuits can linger for decades in the courts, and in the meantime, campaign contributions are made to local and state politicians.

Back to our clouded crystal ball. At this writing, there is both good news and bad news. Many of the

most pessimistic ecological predictions may need to be modified. For example, although modernization typically improves the status of women and encourages population controls, this has not been the case for many Islamic nations in the Near East and Africa. Nonetheless, the rate of world population growth is no longer rising as rapidly as earlier in the century, which is due less to the improved status of women than to widespread famine and extensive regional warfare.

> The **Environmental Justice Movement** is a culturally diverse grassroots effort to change the way in which decisions that affect the quality of life are made.

Growing concern over environmental hazards has led to a reduction in the emission of noxious gases and chemicals, suggesting that depletion of the ozone layer could be halted and even reversed in the next century. Attempts to contain and reverse the greenhouse effect are also underway. And many industrial nations, including the United States, have begun the task of cleaning up the radioactive waste and other hazardous material dumped by private corporations and government research facilities (Weber, 1993). Citizens have an important role to play in protecting their environment, by limiting consumption of nonrenewable resources, supporting recycling efforts, and holding government and industry accountable for their treatment of such public goods as air, water, and land. Until these common interests are recognized as more valuable than the pursuit of national security and private profit, however, the quality of our life will hang in the balance.

SUMMARY

1. Demography is the study of population trends. The size of any population is determined by birth rates, death rates, and net migration. Population growth occurs when more people enter a society through birth and migration than leave it.

2. The demographic transition occurs when populations kept in balance by high birth and death rates shift to a balance based on low birth and death rates. Typically, this happens in the transition to industrialization.

3. Overpopulation refers to an imbalance between population size and the resource base, especially agricultural land, of the society, usually in the gap between a decrease in death rates and a much later reduction in fertility.

4. Throughout the industrialized world, a second demographic transition to negative growth is taking place as fertility has fallen well below the 2.1 replacement level.

5. Migrations patterns involve the selective pressures that push people out of one area and pull them toward another region. The world today is characterized by a number of mass migrations spurred by war, starvation, and other dislocations of the global economy.

6. Population pyramids showing the age and sex distribution of a society reflect its history and tell us about current problems such as feeding and schooling of children in a developing country and high dependency ratios and health care costs in the developed nations.

7. Human ecology refers to the adaptation of populations to their environments and to the distribution of resources within the society.

8. Ecologists today see many causes for alarm: declining food production and loss of farm land in the industrial as well as developing world; deforestation; endangerment of native peoples; declining supplies of clean water; accumulation of unrecycled waste; and air pollution.

9. As nonrenewable energy sources are depleted, many nations are turning to renewable sources such as nuclear energy, hydroelectric power, solar energy, and underground steam.

10. Many of the new industrial technologies carry still unknown risks to populations, typically to communities with little social power.

11. Environmental racism involves locating toxic material and facilities in primarily poor and nonwhite communities and has led to the creation of an environmental justice movement in the United States.

12. Environmental racism also affects Third World nations in relation to the industrialized core countries and multinational corporations.

SUGGESTED READINGS

Abu-Lughod, Janet L. et al. *From Urban Village to East Village: The Battle for New York's Lower East Side*. Cambridge, MA: Blackwell, 1994. Based on five years of research and participant observation, this dramatic account describes the battle over the East Village by established and new immigrants, community activists, hippies, squatters, yuppies, developers, artists, drug dealers and users, and the police.

Gillis, John R., Louise A. Tilly, and David Levine. *The European Experience of Declining Fertility: A Quiet Revolution, 1850–1970*. Cambridge, MA: Blackwell, 1992. An important book that shows the significant influence of a decline in fertility on social relations, gender, and family by creating sweeping social change.

Moch, Leslie Page. *Moving Europeans: Migration in Western Europe Since 1650*. Bloomington: Indiana University Press, 1992. A fascinating study of intra-European migrations from the Thirty Years' War to the present. Emphasis is put on the pull of social relations rather than on the means of production including female patterns for migration, economic and emotional needs, and life cycles.

Sagan, Scott D. *The Limits of Safety: Organizations, Accidents, and Nuclear Weapons*. Princeton, NJ: Princeton University Press, 1993. The author documents cases of near-nuclear accident, showing how the system itself enhances the risk of disaster.

Scheper-Hughes, Nancy. *Death Without Weeping: The Violence of Everyday Life in Brazil*. Berkeley: University of California Press, 1992. A gripping narrative, both provocative and insightful, which tells the sad tale of chronic hunger and malnutrition and their effects on the health of a community in Brazil.

Weeks, John R. and Roberto Ham-Chande. *Demographic Dynamics of the U.S.–Mexico Border*. El Paso: University of Texas at El Paso Press, 1992. A valuable source of demographic information and changes in the U.S.–Mexico border area.

21

Rural, Urban, and Suburban Life

*B*y mid-1994 in New York City . . .

- The last bar in the skid-row area called the *Bowery* had closed down—a victim of rising rents and a preference for crack over alcohol.
- 41 percent of residents said crime was the city's major problem; in second place was education at 10 percent.
- Homeless shelters were filled with families, victims of high urban unemployment and a shortage of affordable housing.
- In the surrounding suburbs, lawmakers called for curfews on young people milling around the malls, annoying merchants, and frightening older customers.
- Out in the countryside, the oldest dairy farm in the area auctioned off its remaining herd and buildings—the victim of low milk prices and high property taxes.

Urban, suburban, and rural: three types of residential area, three different life-styles, and all three today driven by fear and taxes. The emergence of cities—sometime between 8,000 and 6,000 years ago in those areas of the world where plow agriculture replaced simpler modes of subsistence—marked a major turning point in human history.

Sociologists have long been fascinated by how social relations are organized differently in the city (urban) than in the countryside (rural). Max Weber (1923/1958) saw the city as the source of art, science, religious institutions, and the concept of citi-

zenship. For Karl Marx (1844/1975), the city was at the very core of the historical process, in contrast to the "idiocy" of rural life. In large part, the distinction between *Gemeinschaft* and *Gesellschaft* reflects the contrast between rural community and urban society (Tönnies, 1887/1957). Georg Simmel (1903/1950) wrote extensively about the intellectually stimulating atmosphere of the large, central city (*metropolis*). And in the Durkheimian tradition, the American sociologists Robert E. Park and Ernest W. Burgess (Park et al., 1924) saw the city as the product of human nature, rooted in the customs of its inhabitants.

In this chapter, we first examine the nature of rural life and its transformation in the modern world. Then we trace the development of cities—the process of urbanization—which, along with industrialization and secularization, is one of the major components of modernization. The third section describes the emergence and unique characteristics of suburban life. The chapter closes with a discussion of the current urban crisis in the United States and the future of the modern city.

RURAL LIFE

Throughout most of human history, people lived in nomadic bands and tribes. With the discovery of agriculture some 10,000 years ago in many parts of the world, people could construct relatively permanent villages and eventually towns, usually near a river or seacoast for ease of transportation. Although there

Sociologists have long been fascinated by how differently social relations are organized in the city compared with the countryside. In Bolivia, the old Indian city of Aymar has been transformed into the booming, modern city of La Paz. Here, two Indian women survey the changes.

were also great cities in the ancient world—in Egypt and Babylonia, for example—most of the population lived outside the city walls, and the basic economy of the society was rooted in agriculture and the small-scale craft occupations of the village.

Today, most of the world's population still lives in rural areas—more than 60 percent in the less developed nations—although the rural population is steadily declining as the spread of the world economy transforms all but the most remote places. Each nation will have its unique pattern of growth, so that the example of industrializing Europe and America may not hold for the Third World. Nonetheless, the American experience illustrates many of the basic processes of change.

Rural America

At the founding of the nation, in the 1790s, more than 90 percent of the American population lived on farmland. Today, 200 years later, under 3 percent of the labor force is engaged in farming, and only 7 percent of rural households are working farms (Chynoweth and Campbell, 1992; U.S. Bureau of the Census H121/93-5, 1993). Most of this change has taken place since 1935, when the number of farms declined from 6.8 million to about 1.9 million today, while the average size tripled. This trend is the result of the *mechanization* of agriculture, whereby machines replace hand labor and push tenant farmers and sharecroppers off the land. And because machines operate most efficiently on large landholdings, owners of small farms are disadvantaged in the marketplace and eventually sell out to owners of large farms.

The final phase in this process occurs when the remaining farmers are bought out by *corporate* owners. As a result, the traditional "family farm" has given way to **agribusiness,** in which a few high-tech corporations produce most of the food consumed in the United States and sold abroad. Furthermore, the many government programs to aid farmers now benefit the corporate owners, so that, in effect, American consumers are subsidizing large profit-making conglomerates. In contrast, the typical remaining family farm goes bankrupt as the cost of equipment and seed rises while prices for farm products are subject to fluctuation due to weather conditions and competition from agribusiness. Many are heavily in debt today, unable to meet mortgage payments because property values have also declined sharply.

The great majority of America's farmers—97 percent—are white, and most live in the Midwest and South. African-American sharecroppers and tenant farmers were the first to be displaced by mechanization. In 1920, for example, nearly half the black population of the United States lived on farms; today only a few are left, often as part-time labor in the South (Smothers, 1992).

Population Changes

One of the major population trends in the United States, especially since the 1950s, has been the exodus of young people from rural areas. Higher levels of education, the lure of upward mobility, and freedom from the constraints of village life, combined with the rigors and uncertainties of farming, have drawn young people off the land and into more populated areas with a wider variety of occupational choices (Summers, 1993). As a result, the median age in rural communities is higher than in the past and higher than for the population as a whole (47 years versus 33 years). Not only are there fewer family farms, but those that are left are increasingly unlikely to be passed down from parents to children.

Village Life

In addition to a farming population, rural places (defined as incorporated areas with fewer than 2,500 inhabitants) include villagers who provide goods and services to the farmers and one another. For most of American history, its villages were the center of economic activity and social life for a majority of the population. The post office, church, and general store—and ultimately, the gas station—were common gathering places. Some residents earned a living by repairing farm equipment or selling farm supplies; and others worked in nearby towns.

> **Agribusiness** is a type of farming in which a few high-tech corporations produce most of the food consumed domestically and abroad.

But as the young people began to leave in large numbers, the villages were rapidly depopulated. In addition, the vast interstate highway system built after World War II bypassed most of small-town America, leaving its villages isolated, without even the occasional income from passing tourists and nightly lodgers.

Poverty

With the loss of its economic bases in farming and village enterprises, rural America is marked by widespread poverty, especially in the South, and particularly among minority populations (Duncan, 1992; Rural Poverty Task Force, 1993). Native Americans are especially hard hit by rural poverty. For example, ten of the nation's poorest counties are in South Dakota, each of which contains a reservation (Falls, 1992). In addition, rural communities are poorly served by government agencies because it is so much more expensive to deal with clients scattered over large areas (Flora and Christenson, 1992). All these factors have contributed to rural homelessness, when couples can

Rural America, especially in the South, has been marked by widespread poverty resulting from the loss of its economic base in farming and village enterprises. What sort of planning would be necessary to alleviate poverty and foster economic growth?

no longer meet their mortgage obligations and rental properties are lost to the commercial market (M. Bell, 1992).

In other rural areas, such as Appalachia, dependency on a mining economy has turned villages into ghost towns. Price declines and rising costs have led many companies to abandon the mines that provided work to generations of residents of the backwoods hollows. The geographic isolation of these areas makes it difficult to establish other kinds of economic activity, leading to even greater poverty and powerlessness (Freudenburg, 1992; Lyson and Falk, 1993).

Rural people are also hindered by the generally low quality of education in such areas. Not much money can be raised from property taxes, and not many teachers willingly choose to work among the rural poor. But education will be of little help if there are no paying jobs at the end of the rainbow. Most of the better jobs have moved to more populated areas where employers can find a larger pool of workers (Teixeira and Swaim, 1992). As a result, any jobs that are available are typically low skill with comparably low wages (Duncan, 1992; Sherman, 1992).

But poverty rates have also increased among educated rural residents: from 29 percent to 43 percent among high school graduates and from 18 percent to 26 percent of college graduates, during the 1980s (Gorham, 1992). This means that better educated

women and men will have to leave to find well-paying jobs, creating a serious "brain drain" in rural communities.

Medical Care

Rural America suffers from a severe shortage of physicians. Few medical specialists choose to practice where the distance between patients is so great and where fees would have to be set very low. Hospitals are rare, and clinics are few and far between. As a result, infant mortality is higher in the countryside than in cities. In the early 1990s, a full 42 percent of rural children had not seen a doctor in the past year, while the growing population of elderly has created a demand for health service, including home care (Gesler and Ricketts, 1992).

Recent Trends

Data from the early 1990s indicate a slight turnaround. Rural unemployment rates have dropped while the population has grown, but most of this has taken place

The number of farms in the United States has declined dramatically as a result of mechanization of agriculture. The traditional farm has been replaced by agribusiness, the high-tech corporations that produce most of the food we consume. Farm equipment is being auctioned in Missouri as the farmers hope to get some money back from their equipment. What has happened to the hundreds of thousands of farmers and their families as they are forced off the land?

on the outskirts of metropolitan areas, as an extension of suburbia rather than as a revival of village life. Nonetheless, many of these areas are far enough from the metropolis to give new residents the feel of being in the country (Satow, 1993).

Rural areas on the urban fringe have also become a "new frontier" in industrial development by companies looking for cheaper land, fewer traffic jams, and a lower cost of living. Industrial relocation is followed by housing developments, perhaps a mobile home park, stores, and restaurants—all of which provide employment for the long-term residents. But the income and life-style gaps between the new and old villagers remain quite wide (Barringer, 1993).

The repopulation of rural America apparently will be a by-product of the trend toward the *decentralization* of businesses and housing in the 1990s. It remains to be seen whether the new rural population will become countrified or whether the countryside will come to resemble a small city.

THE CITY

Urbanization

Urbanization occurs when a population becomes residentially concentrated in the city, originally a walled area set apart from the surrounding farmland. Because of its greater opportunities for division of labor, the city contains a more diversified population than the countryside, with many occupational specialists. Urban areas are characterized by (1) the size of the population; (2) its density, that is, how many people are in a given space; and (3) a variety of statuses. But there are no magic numbers that automatically define

a city; it is more a matter of degree. For example, the average number of people per room (density) is probably greater in most Asian villages than in the United States' largest cities. But those Asian residents are not urbanites; the village is too small and the division of labor, too minimal. Table 21-1 summarizes the major differences between rural and urban settings. (Note that these are ideal types with many gradations.)

In general, however, in comparison to the countryside, the city has more people per square mile; a more diversified population in terms of social background, education, income, and occupation; and greater access to services such as health care, schooling, libraries, and so forth. The city also permits greater privacy and anonymity. Relationships tend to be instrumental, and social controls, formalized. In the urban setting, visible symbols of power, prestige, and wealth—houses, cars, clothing—are more important in defining social status than in the countryside, where a person's family history and economic situation are already well-known to others.

URBANISM. The way of life associated with the city, its impersonality and individualism—called **urbanism**—is often negatively contrasted with the closeness and warmth of the small community. One popular viewpoint in the 1930s was that city life discourages strong primary group ties, forcing people into temporary and segmented roles, loosening informal social controls, and ultimately producing high levels of personal disorganization, alcoholism, mental illness, and criminality (Wirth, 1938). Others suggest that city life exposes

> **Urbanism** refers to the way of life in cities, which emphasizes individualistic norms and styles of behavior.

TABLE 21-1   Rural and Urban Settings*

Characteristic	Rural	Urban
Diversity of population	Low ⟶	High
Availability of formal organizations and services	Low ⟶	High
Division of labor	Low ⟶	High
Potential anonymity of individuals	Low ⟶	High
Major nature of social relationships	*Gemeinschaft* ➤	*Gesellschaft*
Major types of social control	Informal ⟶	Formal
Degree of status ranking on the basis of visible symbols	Low ⟶	High

*An *ideal type* of rural society is described under the heading "Rural," and an *ideal type* of urban society is described under the heading "Urban." As ideal types are rarely seen in real life, the lines between "rural" and "urban" indicate that there is a continuum on each of the dimensions listed.

Source: Edgar R. Butler, *Urban Sociology: A Systematic Approach,* HarperCollins, 1976.

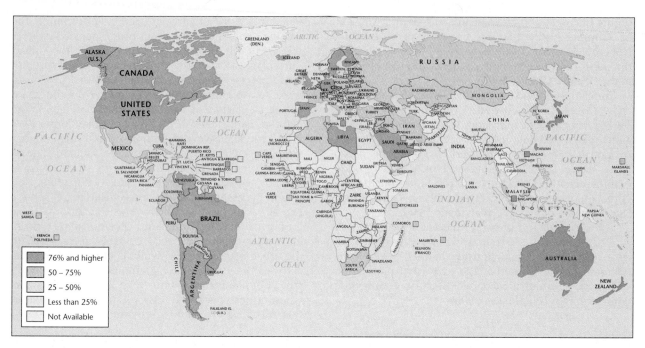

Percent Urbanization. There is considerable variation among nations in the proportion of the population living in urban areas. What factors account for these differences?

people to more stimulation than the mind can comfortably handle—a form of "psychic overload" that leads to an attitude of indifference toward others (Simmel, 1950).

How accurate are these pictures of urban life? Despite their surface plausibility, the evidence is quite mixed. For example, even in the impersonal setting of public places such as a laundromat, people tend to create an "instant community" for the brief period in which they share an activity, but they do so voluntarily rather than being forced by custom. Many prefer anonymity, and others unconsciously cooperate in protecting personal privacy (Karp et al., 1991).

Furthermore, once social class is taken into account, rates of mental illness and alcoholism are no higher in the city than the suburbs or countryside, although criminal activity is greater. Nor are social ties weakened; urban dwellers have extensive and diverse social networks (Fischer, 1984). City residents are no more alienated or isolated than their rural or small-town counterparts, who may know many people but be close to none (Freudenberg, 1992).

Urbanism is not necessarily a way of life confined to the city, but a trait associated with whole societies at a certain stage of economic development. The urban society is literate, dynamic, secular, and worldly (cosmopolitan from *kosmos,* meaning "world"); it allows individual achievement, nurtures artistic creation, stimulates the mind with its contrasts, and encourages tolerance of differences. Many of these influences and attitudes have spread beyond the metropolis to smaller cities and communities via mass

communications. Whether you live in New York City or on Beaver Lake, North Dakota, you are in an urban society, in touch with the world through the same media, reachable by telephone, and able to travel almost at will.

These traits contrast with those of the *ruralized* society, where people value ritual, tradition, kinship loyalty, and stability. But the master trend throughout the world today is toward urbanization if not urbanism.

URBAN GROWTH. Urban growth was gradual for thousands of years before undergoing a rapid expansion in Europe during the late 1700s, on the verge of the Industrial Revolution. Indeed, the introduction of the factory system was hastened by the influx of young laborers from rural areas. The basic conditions for urban growth are (1) an agricultural base capable of supporting both city and countryside; (2) transportation links; and (3) the promise of city jobs to lure young people off the farm. The agricultural base and job opportunities were in place by 1800, but the transportation systems did not reach their peak for another century.

Nonetheless, by 1800, the population of London was almost 1 million, and by 1900, ten cities, including Moscow, Tokyo, and Calcutta, had over a million residents. Since 1900, the world has undergone rapid urbanization, as shown in Figure 21-1. Early in the next century, more people will be living in cities than in the countryside, although this may not translate into a higher standard of living in most of the Third World.

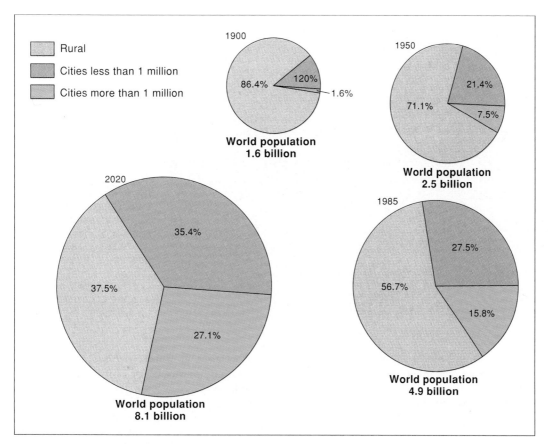

Rural

Cities less than 1 million

Cities more than 1 million

1900

86.4% 120% 1.6%

World population 1.6 billion

1950

71.1% 21.4% 7.5%

World population 2.5 billion

2020

35.4% 37.5% 27.1%

World population 8.1 billion

1985

56.7% 27.5% 15.8%

World population 4.9 billion

Figure 21-1   Patterns of urbanization, 1900-2020.

Source: John J. Palen, T*he Urban World,* 4th Ed., New York: McGraw Hill, 1992.

Urbanization in Developing Nations

For reasons described in Chapters 19 and 20, massive changes in the world economy, population pressures, and widespread famine have forced millions of villagers and peasants off the land and into the nearest city, seeking employment or some means of family survival. In 1994, for example, an estimated 50 million Chinese peasants have left rural villages for cities where they form a vast pool of low-skill, low-pay labor for the nation's newly-built factories (Tyler, 1994). But typically there are not enough jobs for all the migrants, and Third World governments lack both the money and institutional framework necessary to provide housing, work, and social services. The consequence is vast urban slums throughout Asia, Africa, and Latin America, far larger and impoverished than anything most Americans can imagine.

Although patterns of economic development will vary with the specific history of the society and its position in the world capitalist system, the general trend is toward increased concentration in urban areas. The prime target of migration is usually the nation's capital city, for example, Mexico City, Sâo Paulo, Brazil, or Bangkok, Thailand. By the year 2000, 14 of the 19 largest metropolitan areas, with populations over 10 million, will be in the Third World (U.S. Bureau of the Census, *Statistical Abstract of the United States, 1994,* p. 856).

Because urbanization has long been considered a primary index of a country's overall development and power in world politics, leaders have encouraged economic development. But national policies that favored investments in industrialization at the expense of rural projects had the twofold effect of further impoverishing the countryside while failing to provide adequate employment for the urban migrants.

Within most developing nations, the gap between rich and poor widened, with a few families controlling most of the land and its wealth, and its politicians. It was these families rather than peasant farmers who most benefited from international programs of agricultural assistance. In fact, as in the developing countries a century earlier, mechanization and modernization of agriculture displaced most rural small landowners as well as farm laborers.

Unable to find permanent jobs, many people are caught in a circular pattern, living in the city for a

The urban society is cosmopolitan—it allows individual achievement, nurtures artistic creation, stimulates the mind with its contrasts, and encourages tolerance of differences. Prague, in the Czech Republic, has been a center of cosmopolitan life for many centuries.

time, but returning to their rural home community to help with the harvest or to take part in family and religious ceremonies. Without a firm footing in either community, migrants drift between the two worlds, forming a human bridge for other family and friends to make the transition from rural to urban, swelling the ranks of underemployed city dwellers (Kasarda and Parnall, 1993).

Over time, also, the largest cities receive migrants from smaller regional urban centers, the first stepping stone away from the village. When resources of the regional city are exhausted, people move on to the next larger place in hopes of finding a job. In contrast to the pattern in developed nations such as the United States, where poor immigrants locate in the inner core of the city, Third World immigrants set up "squatters settlements" on the ever-expanding outskirts of the major city. These are locations without adequate water, sanitation, or even electricity. Health care, schooling, and other services are either nonexistent or immediately overwhelmed by the next wave of newcomers.

Despite such difficult living conditions, tens of millions of migrants prefer these urban slums to life in the countryside and its deprivations. There is always the hope of finding some way to support oneself and one's children, if not in a proper job, then in the underground economy (Chapter 13).

THE INFORMAL SECTOR.   In any Third World city, as well as in the Western world, a great deal of economic activity takes place on the street. Hawkers and traders of a vast variety of items and services crowd sidewalks and parks, selling to one another but especially to tourists. Other workers in the in-

formal sector labor at home, producing the wares hawked by family members, or doing piecework for commercial buyers.

This sector has long been ignored by formal economic theory on the assumption that it was a precapitalist phase that would disappear when real jobs opened up, as happened in the developed world. But as capitalist development failed to lift most Third-World people out of poverty, the informal sector has spread rapidly, possibly accounting for well over half the economic activity in developing countries (Kasarda and Parnell, 1993). A similar trend may be found today in the developed world, where the loss of well-paying, secure jobs has led to an expansion of the underground economy.

The urban informal sector covers a variety of occupations from street trading to light manufacturing to transportation and repair work "off the books." These businesses are operated without official registration, largely to avoid taxes, but, in developing countries, also, because the procedures are time-consuming and because most workers lack the education needed to fill out the forms and to keep books.

The informal sector also provides low-cost labor to the formal sector, as in the case of Hispanic women and their children who sew garments at home on a piecework basis for licensed manufacturers (Fernandez-Kelly et al., 1990). This arrangement may seem like superexploitation, but it provides earnings necessary for survival in an overcrowded urban labor market. Unless additional formal-sector jobs are created, more workers will enter the underground economy, where they will have to compete with one another for street space or home manufacturing, further depressing already low wages.

The Quality of Urban Life

How can we measure the quality of life, the relative pleasantness of a person's environment? One recent study (Suffian, 1993) of 98 of the world's largest metropolitan areas used ten indicators that could be measured empirically: (1) *public health* (infant death rates); (2) *standard of living* (percentage of income for food); (3) *privacy* (persons per room); (4) *housing* (percentage with water/electricity); (5) *communications* (telephone); (6) *education* (percentage in high school); (7) *public safety* (homicide rate); (8) *quietness* (level of street noise);

(9) *traffic* (rush hour speeds); and (10) *air quality* (pollution level).

On the basis of these data, cities could be ranked high, medium, or low in terms of their quality of life, as shown in Table 21-2. The proportion of income spend on food was a powerful indicator of a city's quality: the higher the percentage of income spent on food, the lower the quality of life. For example, in Lima, Peru, almost 70 percent of a family's income was spent on food, compared to 12 percent for residents of Los Angeles.

TABLE 21-2   Quality of Urban Life, Selected Cities

City	Index Value	City	Index Value	City	Index Value
Group 1 (High)		**Group 2 (Medium)**		**Group 3 (Low)**	
Montreal, Canada	79	London, UK	62	São Paulo, Brazil	43
Seattle, USA	78	Moscow, Russia	61	Ahmedabad, India	40
Houston, USA	77	San Diego, USA	58	Bangkok, Thailand	38
Tokyo, Japan	74	Athens, Greece	56	Mexico City, Mexico	36
Philadelphia, USA	71	Seoul, S. Korea	55	Calcutta, India	33
Chicago, USA	69	Beijing, China	54	Cairo, Egypt	32
Rome, Italy	66	Belo Horizonte, Brazil	53	Lima, Peru	30
Los Angeles, USA	66	Baghdad, Iraq	49	Recife, Brazil	30
New York, USA	65	Santiago, Chile	47	Karachi, Pakistan	27
Paris, France	64	Naples, Italy	45	Kinshasa, Zaire	25
Boston, USA	64	Cape Town, S. Africa	44	Lagos, Nigeria	17

Source: Abu Jafar Hohammad Suffian, "A Multivariate Analysis of the Determinants of Urban Quality of Life in the World's Largest Metropolitan Areas," *Urban Studies,* Vol. 30. No. 8, 1993 Carfax Publishing Company. Reprinted by permission.

Despite some similarities, the quality of urban life in the Third World—where most of the world's population will live in the next century—is very different from that of the developed nations, as seen in the box entitled, "The Quality of Urban Life."

Urban Ecology

Urban ecology refers to the fit between people and land use in the urban setting (Park and Burgess, 1921). Research in this tradition dominated the field of urban sociology until the late 1960s. Early studies indicated that most Western industrial cities developed according to one of three basic models of urban ecology, as shown in Figure 21-2: (1) the concentric zone; (2) the sector; and (3) the multiple nuclei.

Chicago and other older industrial cities in the United States developed along the concentric zone model, with different land uses arranged in circles around the central core (Burgess, 1925). This pattern, however, will be modified if geographic barriers or unusual scenic features divert land uses in particular directions. The three rivers of Pittsburgh, for example, or the unique geography of New Orleans produced an ecology closer to the **sector model,** in which different land use areas radiate from the core along horizontal rather than circular pathways.

> **Urban ecology** refers to the fit between people and land use in the urban setting.
>
> The **sector model** organizes land use areas horizontally from the core of a city rather than circularly.

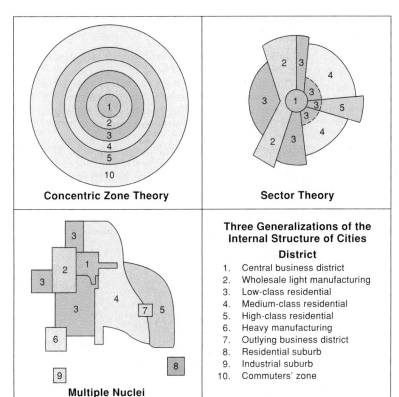

Concentric Zone Theory

Sector Theory

Multiple Nuclei

**Three Generalizations of the
Internal Structure of Cities**

District

1. Central business district
2. Wholesale light manufacturing
3. Low-class residential
4. Medium-class residential
5. High-class residential
6. Heavy manufacturing
7. Outlying business district
8. Residential suburb
9. Industrial suburb
10. Commuters' zone

Figure 21-2   Concentric zone, sector, and multiple nuclei models.

From: C. D. Harris, et al., "The Nature of Cities," Figure 21-3, *The Annals of the Academy of Political and Social Science*, pp. 107 © Copyright 1945. Reprinted by permission.

The **multiple nuclei model** describes cities in which several centers emerge, each specialized in a given activity such as banking, or manufacturing, or government offices. New York City, for example, has its garment district, elite shopping areas, Wall Street financial center, courts and government building clusters, and theater row.

> The **multiple nuclei model** describes cities in which several specialized centers emerge.
>
> **Concentration** occurs when a large number of people settle in a relatively small space.
>
> **Ecological differentiation** occurs with decentralization, when specific activities become associated with a given geographical area, such as the financial or theater district.
>
> **Ecological invasion** occurs when a differentiated area is invaded by new activities and new populations.

URBAN DYNAMICS.   The dynamics of urban growth can be studied as a four-stage process: (1) concentration; (2) segregation; (3) invasion; and (4) succession (MacKensie, 1925). The first phase of urbanization, **concentration,** occurs when a large number of people settle in a relatively small space. When this produces overcrowding, some people and activities will move outward, creating a more diverse and decentralized urban space.

With decentralization comes **ecological differentiation,** in which specific activities become associated with a given geographical area, such as the financial district or theater row. Cities are never static, and any differentiated area is open to **ecological invasion** by new activities and new populations. For example, a warehouse district could be

Drawing by W. Miller; © 1991 The New Yorker Magazine, Inc.

"This area has a long and rich history. First, the Indians lived here, then it was a plantation with slaves, then poor people lived here, and now it's a magnificent condo complex."

CLARA E. RODRIGUEZ

The Puerto Rican Community in the South Bronx: Contradictory Views from Within and Without

Clara E. Rodriguez is an associate professor at Fordham University College, Lincoln Center. She is currently engaged in researching the intersections of race, ethnicity, class, and gender. Her latest books are Puerto Ricans: Born in the USA, *Boulder, CO: Westview Press, 1991 and* Hispanics in the Labor Force: Issues and Policies, *co-edited with Edwin Melendez and Janice Barry-Figueroa, Plenum Press, 1991.*

The South Bronx in New York city has always been home to me. As a young girl growing up there, I was surrounded by a stable family and a sense of community, even though the area was viewed as a place where only "the poorest of the poor" lived.

My earliest recollection of my neighborhood is of an energetic and alive community with a great deal of social interaction. I recall being wheeled with my sister in a huge baby carriage in front of what the *New York Times* would subsequently call those "solid, grimy five-story tenements." My parents would stop to converse with neighbors, part of a network of people who knew each other well and who helped each other.

My South Bronx had a richness of life, a dynamism and stability of relations that few other places have. However, as I matured, I came to understand that the world beyond my community's boundaries had a different view of us. That world saw us as "different" and poor and was often instinctively hostile or afraid of us. Yet, I never felt poor, deprived, or disadvantaged. I also never understood what inspired hostility toward those I held dear.

At an early age I came to puzzle over this contradiction, why the view from within was so different from the view from without; why hostility, fear, or disrespect should exist without cause. This developed in me a basic curiosity about the view of those affected and the factors that affected them.

The world within which I grew up was not all roses and pasteles (a festive Puerto Rican dish). My childhood was as full of traumas, joys, and disappointments as the next person's. There were the usual struggles to survive that all people who have little money or who have strong differences of culture, color, and language experience. Life was hard, but life was manageable. As I was growing up, I witnessed my community and others like it destroyed by forces over which we had little control: drugs, urban renewal, and housing abandonment. Although the South Bronx today is on the rebound, the extent of the housing decline and urban devastation is made dramatic by the following data. Between 1970 and 1980, the Bronx and Brooklyn, the two New York City boroughs with the largest Puerto Rican populations, accounted for more than 80 percent of housing units either abandoned or destroyed in the entire country. During this time, the South Bronx, which has the largest Puerto Rican community in the United States, lost 10.5 percent of all its housing stock. Buildings that had roofs but were abandoned and not inhabited were not included in this count. Moreover, a high proportion of Puerto Ricans still residing there live in units with three or more maintenance deficiencies and live in areas with boarded-up buildings on their blocks.

What were the reasons for this dramatic urban decay? Foremost were the redlining policies of insurance companies and banks, which made very little money available for local residential development, and the policies of the federal government, which emphasized highway construction and suburban residential development. Other reasons included the failure of local government policy, arson for profit, rent control (which did not allow a large enough profit for the maintenance of buildings), drug trafficking and other crimes, poorly planned housing projects, and the gutting of neighborhoods for the construction of the Cross Bronx Expressway. Because the loss of housing was not evenly distributed across the South Bronx, certain neighborhoods were devastated, leaving local landscapes with one or two buildings as lone survivors. The dynamism and stability of the communities of the South Bronx had been destroyed by external forces.

Not all Puerto Ricans fled; some fought to maintain their neighborhoods, fought drug dealers, and organized to get support form the city and federal governments. Currently, the decline has slowed and signs of revitalization have appeared. The South Bronx has bottomed out, but the history lived there will remain a bitter chapter for all concerned.

These experiences were important in my decision to focus my studies on the Puerto Rican community in the United States, to understand how, in the words of C. Wright Mills, my particular community had been affected by the historical period in which it was located. Sociology, as the most interdisciplinary social science, gave me the tools to analyze these events.

Gendered Images of Urban Life

How does the city as viewed by men differ from the city perceived by women. In the nineteenth century (as illustrated by their fiction and painting), men saw urban life as profoundly liberating, a world in which they could wander at will and at all hours, a world to conquer and enjoy. Paris and London were uniquely the domain of the *flaneur*, a French word meaning one who strolls aimlessly, enjoying all about him (the *flaneur* was always pictured as a man of leisure).

For women, too, the city was less constraining than the village, but was also fraught with potential sexual danger. A powerful form of social control of women was the norm that respectable women did not walk the streets alone. Middle-class women, however, could take advantage of the opportunity to go shopping and to do "good works," usually in the company of other women. Working class women had to fend for themselves. The city of "dreadful delight" described by Judith Walkowitz (1992) is one in which both men and women projected their fears onto figures such as Jack the Ripper, but it was women who were the typical victims of urban dangers—then as now.

The contemporary urban scene is no more inviting to women than it was in the past. Fear of the "dark stranger"—strangler or rapist—continues to limit women' freedom to wander the metropolis, but men are also less comfortable with the city streets than before. Indeed the "dreadful" appear to have outweighed the "delights" of urban life in the late twentieth century for men as well as women.

---

converted to artists' lofts, or a Jewish neighborhood could become largely Asian American or Hispanic. Once the newer residents have replaced the former occupants, **succession** has taken place.

Not every neighborhood will undergo the same process of change. Although the pattern of white-to-minority succession was common in the 1950s and 1960s, the pace of change slowed greatly since 1970 and is by no means inevitable (Wood and Lee, 1993). The likelihood and pace of racial invasion and succession depend on the city's housing policies, the supply of affordable units, job availability, and the specific racial mix of the area. In some cases, minority groups will replace whites; in other cases, a neighborhood remains racially stable; and, in still other cases, whites will supplant a minority population. In New York City and other major American urban centers, these factors all reinforce the trend toward racial/ethnic residential segregation (Rosenbaum, 1994).

Succession is the replacement of one activity or population for another in a particular area.

The New Urban Sociology

The basically functionalist and evolutionary approach of the urban ecology school has been challenged recently by a more conflict-oriented perspective sometimes called the "global political economy" model (Palen, 1992; Flanagan, 1993). In this view, urban social and physical changes are the product of conflict among various urban populations (divided by race, ethnicity, and class) for the city's limited resources (jobs, housing, health care, transportation, police protection, educational facilities, and social welfare benefits). Different groups bring different levels of power to the struggle.

The focus is on both the ability of political elites to determine what gets built where and on the reactions of the powerless. For example, case studies from this perspective have shown how racism and economic discrimination account for marked differences in the housing status of blacks and whites in Atlanta (Leigh and Stewart, 1992) and how insurance company practices produced a similar situation in Milwaukee, Wisconsin (Squires et al., 1991). Rather than viewing such outcomes as the result of class- and color-blind evolutionary processes, the new urban sociology looks at concrete social groups pursuing their own perceived best interests.

> Any city, however small, is in fact divided into two, one the city of the poor, the other of the rich; these are at war with one another. . . .
>
> —PLATO (353 BCE), 1982

For example, whereas the ecological school would explain the growth of suburbs as a logical function of the mass-produced automobile, the conflict theorist would also ask why public transportation, which serves the needs of the vast majority of city residents, was allowed to deteriorate. Why was transportation money spent on highways out of the city rather than on urban subways and buses? This is more than a question of consumer preferences, but of the actions of powerful economic interest groups such as automobile makers, oil companies, and the highway construction industry.

URBANIZING THE UNITED STATES

In 1790, there were no places in America with as many as 25,000 residents, and only 5 percent of the population lived in towns of more than 2,500 people. By 1870, the nation was 25 percent urban, and by 1920, half the population lived in urban areas. Today, about 77 percent of Americans live in a place designated by the Bureau of the Census as **urban,** which is any city, town, or village with 2,500 or more inhabitants.

The Bureau of the Census has other designations. An **urbanized area** is defined as consisting of one or more places and surrounding territory with a population of 50,000 and more. A **metropolitan area** consists of a large population center plus any surrounding communities with a high degree of social and economic integration with that center. As of 1994, there were about 250 metropolitan statistical areas (MSAs) in the United States, including Laredo, Texas, and Provo, Utah. Because this definition of an MSA embraces the suburbs and small towns within the range of the central city, not everyone officially designated as a city dweller actually lives under typical urban conditions (for example, overcrowded, noisy, apartment houses).

The two largest MSAs are New York City and its surrounding communities and Los Angeles and its environs—two very different urban areas. The fastest growing MSAs are in the South and West, and most of this growth is in the suburbs rather than central city, reflecting the migration patterns discussed in Chapter 20. In contrast, the MSAs losing population over the past decade are primarily located in the North and East: Gary, Indiana; Newark, New Jersey; and Detroit, Michigan, head the list.

The American population is not evenly distributed across the country. More than 75 percent is concentrated on 16 percent of the land, mostly on or near the two seacoasts. Because so many people live in strings of towns and cities along these coastlines, increased attention is being paid to the *supermetropolitan region,* often called a **megalopolis** (from *mega,* meaning "great" and *polis,"* meaning *"city").* One such stretch is "Bo-Wash," an almost continuous string of urban and suburban communities extending from north of Boston, Massachusetts, to just south of Washington, D.C., and from the Atlantic shoreline to the foothills of the Appalachian Mountains, although many rural pockets have survived throughout the region.

From Commercial to Corporate City

Before 1850, American cities were organized around craft manufacturing, commerce, transportation, and politics. These urban centers, or **commercial cities,** resembled medieval cities in their unplanned character, dominated by informal street life, with shops and residential housing next to one another. Only as land became more expensive was the typical urban pattern of rectangular or square city blocks introduced, and specific land uses identified.

By 1850, this commercial center began to be replaced by the **industrial city,** dominated by factories, the railroad, and tenement housing. The industrial city is especially suited to two functions: (1) economy of scale, whereby many workers are available for factory employment, with room for a surplus supply within the city, and (2) enforcement of labor discipline, as the working class is isolated from the middle and upper strata to a greater extent than in a small town. The industrial city thus becomes increasingly segregated by race, ethnicity, and class.

By the early 1900s, the industrial city was being replaced by **industrial suburban cities,** built up in areas adjacent to the major city. For example, Gary, Indiana, was built by the United States Steel Company for its own factory and workers. The decentralization of manufacturing was encouraged by the development of a vast network of highways in the 1950s. The introduction of the assembly line also encouraged the construction of factories in the suburbs, where the plant could be built on one floor over a large tract of land, so that workers could all be on the same line.

Locating factories outside the major city also served the interests of employers by isolating their employees from contact with other workers and the influence of union organizers. Lower taxes and a shorter commute for executives were also important considerations, then and now. In addition, the process of suburban industrial growth was prompted by a shift in political power. The old commercial and early industrial cities had been run by politicians controlled by the social and economic elite, but the influx of manual workers and immigrants shifted power to political machines able to turn out the vote. With their control over city politics threatened, the owners simply relocated outside the town lines to the suburbs, where they could once again dominate local politics.

A city, town, or village with 2,500 or more inhabitants is considered **urban.**

An **urbanized area** consists of one or more places and surrounding territory with a population of at least 50,000.

A **metropolitan area** houses a large population center plus any surrounding communities strongly connected to that center socially and economically.

A **megalopolis** consists of overlapping metropolitan areas with many social, economic, and transportation links.

American cities before 1850 were **commercial cities,** organized around craft manufacturing, commerce, transportation, or politics.

The large **industrial city** was dominated by factories, railroads, and slums.

Industrial suburban cities developed in vacant areas outside central cities for economic, political, and labor-related reasons.

The typical corporate cities of the United States are the newer cities of the Sunbelt, such as Phoenix, Arizona. Suburban shopping malls have replaced downtown shopping areas, and few factory districts are visible. With the working class scattered, the new corporate city most resembles the fragmented metropolis of the multiple-nuclei model.

The Corporate City

As manufacturing decentralized, the city's economy became increasingly concentrated on financial and other service industries. The office building replaced the factory and even much of the shopping area by the late 1950s. The most typical corporate cities, however, are not transformed industrial centers such as Chicago or New York City but the newer cities of the sunbelt: Dallas, Phoenix, and Houston. With few visible factories, a scattered working class, and suburban malls replacing downtown shopping districts, the corporate city most closely resembles the multiple nuclei model of the fragmented metropolis.

What next? Given the new communications technologies that allow service businesses to be in immediate contact with clients (such as via FAX, computer networks, video phones), these firms can locate anywhere, lured by climate or low taxes. Some cities have fallen into permanent decline; Buffalo, New York, and Detroit, Michigan, are prime examples. Others will find new life in their specialized role in the world economy (Flanagan, 1993).

Global Cities

The most recent stage in the development of the metropolis has been the emergence of the **global city,** one that is oriented to international rather than domestic trade and commerce. The global city is a result of the major shift in economic activity among developed nations from

A **global city** is focused on international trade and commerce.

manufacturing to providing services, primarily banking and investment, and information/communications systems. From their headquarters in the global city, multinational corporations organize the world economy.

New York, Tokyo, London, Paris, Zurich (Switzerland), and Rotterdam (The Netherlands) are examples of urban centers that were once dominated by local businesses and domestic manufacturing but have now become specialized for corporate services (Sassen, 1993). The prosperity created by the newer businesses, however, has not been evenly distributed among the city's population. A three-tiered structure of urban inequality has emerged: a highly-paid elite of primarily male professionals; a low-wage class of (mostly) female clerical workers; and a largely immigrant or minority working class providing low-skill services.

The degree of urban inequality and subsequent social instability varies from country to country. In New York and London, England, for example, inequality and urban unrest have been reinforced by the flight of manufacturing jobs and by the unwillingness of the national governments to pursue policies to help the urban poor (Sassen, 1993). In Tokyo, in contrast, manufacturing jobs and other forms of urban employment were retained, and the government has provided a safety net for the displaced workers, thus reducing the degree of urban inequality and polarization (Fujita and Hill, 1993). Nonetheless, Tokyo also has its urban underclass, Korean immigrants who perform the city's "dirty work" at minimal wages (Rhim, 1994).

The rise and fragmentation of the global city are illustrated by the case of Miami, Florida.

Miami as a Global City: from Beachcombing to International Banking

The city of Miami has undergone several transformations since its founding in the 1890s as a winter resort for wealthy northern whites (Portes and Stepick, 1993). In 1959, the area became the new home of thousands of relatively wealthy, educated Cubans fleeing the Castro revolution. Over the next two decades, the Cubans became a major power in local politics and the economic life of the growing city, challenging both the old Anglo elite and the emerging African-American presence. Because of their cultural ties to the Spanish-speaking countries of Latin America and the Caribbean, the Cubans made Miami into an increasingly cosmopolitan city and a commercial hub for trade and banking throughout the region.

The emergence of Miami as a global city was also aided by its unique geographic location at the tip of Florida, which oriented it outward to Latin America rather than inward to the rest of the United States. The Cuban presence made the city attractive to Latin American investors looking for a safe place to store their wealth. The favorable investment climate, in turn, led American firms looking for markets in South and Central America to establish offices in Miami. It is precisely this concentration of corporate services—banking, accounting, and legal—that are the hallmark of the global city (Sassen, 1993).

As a result of these developments, and as cause of further growth, Miami's international transportation facilities and communications services expanded dramatically. Its airport and seaport are among the busiest in the United States; its television and radio stations beam throughout the region. There has also been a sharp increase in high-income residential and commercial real estate developments, widening the gap between rich and poor, as existing low-income communities deteriorate further.

Thus, while Miami has assumed a privileged position in the global economy, many internal sources of strain have become increasingly severe, and a new "geography of inequality" has emerged. For all their successes in trade and banking, the Cuban business class has encountered a "glass ceiling" that prevents them, and other minority personnel, from rising to the top level of the American corporations in the area. The entire international corporate sector is arrayed against the old local economy and elites. And racial divisions have deepened. African Americans have gained least from Miami's commercial successes, in terms of both occupational mobility and the distribution of public services—circumstances that led to widespread urban rioting in 1992. A tale of two cities, indeed.

THE SUBURBS

A **suburb** is part of the metropolitan area, beyond the political boundary of a city but closely linked to it socially and economically. In earlier times, it was the poor who were forced to lived outside the city walls; today, it is the relatively well-off who can afford a home in the suburbs, and the poor who are left behind. As a result, many metropolitan areas today resemble a doughnut, in which the hole is an impoverished central city, and the doughnut is the prosperous suburban fringe.

A **suburb** is closely linked to a metropolitan area socially and economically, but it is politically independent.

The prosperity found in global cities has not been evenly distributed among the city's population. Well-paid professionals enjoy the urban life-style, including these successful Russian businessmen dining in a fashionable Moscow restaurant. How has this business elite developed in what had theoretically been a classless society?

Although a particular suburb or suburban neighborhood may appear to be a homogeneous expanse of single-family houses, there is enormous variation from one suburb to another. In general, also, the suburbs are characterized by greater residential segregation on the basis of race and social class than found in most cities. As noted in Chapter 11, institutionalized racism in the real estate and mortgage markets establishes and ensures residential segregation. Because few whites choose to move to an integrated suburb, the value of property held by minority homeowners fails to increase as rapidly as that of white homeowners in white neighborhoods. Although the African Americans who live in the suburbs are typically better off financially than those who remain in the city, they are "steered" to the less attractive neighborhoods (Beveridge, 1994). Thus, the suburbs are both heterogeneous, because one differs from the other, and relatively homogeneous, because within each are similarities of race and class and often, also, ethnicity and religion.

Growth of the Suburbs

Suburbanization depends on transportation facilities and the location of jobs. The extension of streetcar lines, often built by land speculators to attract people eager to escape the noise and dirt of city life, made limited suburban development possible by the early 1900s (Baldessare, 1986). But it was the mass production of affordable automobiles in the 1920s that spurred suburban growth. In 1900, only 10 percent of the American population lived in suburbs; by 1929, the suburbs were growing at a rate double that of the cities. The automobile created a demand for highways, constructed with public funds, that al-

> **Suburbanization** resulted from the expansion of the highway system, the spread of housing developments, and the dispersion of industry.

lowed the wealthy to live outside the city and commute to work (Logen, 1992).

When industries also moved outside the city limits, even the less well-to-do employees were eager to relocate in the suburbs. The newer migrants filled the suburbs closest to the city, while the previous residents moved further out, so that gradually, rings of suburban developments circled the central city. The outward-migration of homeowners left the city increasingly unattractive, pushing more people to seek housing in the suburbs.

The complex interplay of all these "pushes" out of the city and "pulls" into the suburbs is illustrated in Figure 21-3. A combination of political, economic, and social factors converged and fed one another to hasten the depopulation of urban America: relocation of industry; racial and ethnic tensions; declining standard of living in the city; taxation policies; highway construction; and mortgage practices.

The outflow, especially of white families, increased sharply in the 1950s, when upwardly mobile veterans of World War II took advantage of the programs offering a subsidized college education and lost-cost mortgages. The availability of mortgage loans created a demand for housing, filled by the developers of such mass housing developments as Levittown, Pennsylvania, as shown in the photograph on p. 513.

Although these units may seem to you today to be rather small and alike as peas in a pod, at that time they were the "American Dream" come true: a single family home, with a yard, a garage, and the latest in home appliances. Sons and daughters of the working class, who might otherwise have had to remain in the city, living with or near one of their parents, were now able to own a home of their own!

Over the next three decades, the suburban population grew as most children of suburbanites also chose to live outside of a city, and the remaining city dwellers who could leave did so, including large numbers of upwardly mobile minority families. The bulk

Figure 21-3 Factors promoting suburban growth.

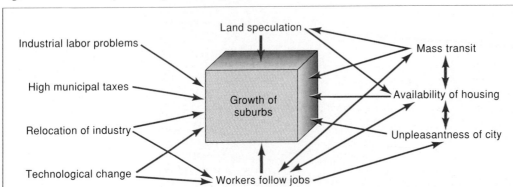

To many people, a house in the suburbs represents part of the American dream, the same freedom that the pioneers sought in the journey across the frontier. Do these houses offer autonomy or represent the conformity critics cite as a drawback of suburban living?

of the American population is now located in suburban areas, and many never leave the suburbs even to go to work. Retail trade centers and office buildings, as well as light industries, followed the population to the suburbs. Today, the amount of office space in suburbia is greater than in central business districts, in part because the fields in which employment is increasing are precisely those service industries that can be located anywhere close to a highway and a computer terminal, such as financial services, health care record keeping, and insurance.

In addition, changes in federal tax and banking policies in the 1980s redirected investment money away from production facilities and into commercial real estate speculation, pouring enormous sums into suburban office parks. Suburban rents are much lower than those in the city, working conditions more pleasant, and labor cheaper. Many suburban businesses draw on a pool of nonunionized, educated, white women willing to work for relatively low wages.

Advantages of Suburban Life

Several generations ago, advocates of suburban life claimed that it offered the best of both possible worlds: close enough to the city to take advantage of its cultural and educational facilities, yet far enough away to provide the wholesomeness and calm of country living (Fischer, 1984). The suburbs reflected and reinforced the dominant ideology of that time of "separate spheres" by literally separating the two worlds of men and women; the isolated single-family home was "hers," the commute and workplace were "his." In the postwar period, from 1945 to 1965, this suburban home was filled with children, the baby-boom cohorts of 1947–67.

There are many advantages to suburban life, especially for families in the child-rearing phase. The suburbs are less anonymous and more homogeneous than many city neighborhoods; outdoor activities are encouraged; the air is cleaner; and the streets are safer. The ideals of domestic privacy and home ownership are within reach of a majority of Americans.

By the 1960s, many of the baby-boom children, particularly those who had left home for college, found the suburbs somewhat confining and returned to the cities to enjoy the "swinging singles" scene of the 1970s. These Yuppies were able to revitalize several urban neighborhoods, but when it came time to settle down and raise a family, they, too, headed for the "'burbs" (Hughes and Zimmerman, 1993). In part, their return was a response to the relocation of white-collar jobs to suburban office parks and in part was due to quality of life reasons: larger homes, better schools, safer streets, and the sense of shared community that comes from living with status equals.

The return migration of Yuppies (young, urban professionals) has altered the character of many suburbs, but these areas were already changing. Dual-earner families were the norm, and many **amenities,** (cultural niceties) had been established far from their urban roots, include symphony orchestras, theaters, elegant shops, and expensive restaurants. Thus, many

Amenities are cultural niceties, such as symphony orchestras, expensive restaurants, and elegant shops.

advantages of being close to a major city were now available in outlying areas, and the "big world" could be brought into the suburban home through cable television, VCRs, and satellite dishes.

Disadvantages of Suburban Life

But all is not wine and roses in suburbia. Residents depend on their cars in the absence of extensive public transportation, making life difficult for those too young or too old to drive and for the family that cannot afford two cars. Shopping malls, health care facilities, and office buildings are rarely accessible by foot, and, when teenagers *can* get to them, merchants and other adults object to their "hanging out."

There are not many services or amusements for different age groups. Teenagers and old people are especially disadvantaged in this regard. The suburbs were originally planned for families with young children, so that playgrounds and barbecue pits abound, but senior centers and youth groups are few and far between. Yet, over time, the suburban population has "aged in place." Many residents are widowed or divorced, some are single parents, others just plain single, and there really isn't a lot for them to enjoy in the typical suburban community. Ideologically and ecologically, suburbia remains dedicated to rearing young children in a two-parent households.

The very sameness of much of suburbia, its internal homogeneity, has been criticized for promoting conformity and reducing opportunities for children to meet people who are different from themselves (Gaines, 1992). It has been suggested that the suburban school prepares students for success in a conformist, bureaucratic society (see Chapter 15). But most parents choose suburban life for this very reason.

The sprawl of suburban communities has brought problems of traffic flow and pollution to many areas.

Among the populations most left out of suburban planning are teenagers. Often their only place to spend leisure time, without spending a lot of money, is the mall.

Haphazard planning and zoning contribute to the destruction of natural beauty, leading residents in many communities to organize to limit further growth or at least slow the pace of development (Cable and Benson, 1993). In other words, many of the urban problems people thought that they had left behind are also moving to the suburbs.

One of the most important of these "urban woes" is that of race relations. In general, problems of race, ethnicity, and social class were minimized by the stratification of the suburbs themselves into homogeneous communities, with higher-status developments the most geographically distant. But in many places, suburban communities have become "contested areas," as minority families seek the advantages of country life for their children. Homes have been vandalized, crosses burned on lawns, and lawsuits filed to keep the newcomers out of white neighborhoods. The white residents fear loss of property values, their homes being their major assets. And, although they do not think of themselves as racists, their actions have the effect of increasing racial segregation (Yarrow, 1992; Wood and Lee, 1993).

Thus, a majority of African-American suburbanites live in primarily black communities (O'Hare and Frey, 1992), just as 86 percent of whites live in predominantly white areas (Judd, 1991). But the move to the suburbs has not brought the same level of social mobility to blacks as it has to whites. The minority-dominated suburbs typically receive less tax support, have lower home ownership rates, and experience more property crime compared with white communities with the same socioeconomic characteristics (Judd, 1991; Beveridge, 1994) African Americans and other minority persons experience similar patterns of discrimination in the suburbs as in the cities; and only the most wealthy or educated gain entry into higher-status white neighborhoods (Alba and Logan, 1993). Nonetheless, the suburban black population is growing at a faster rate than the urban population. Most of this growth, however, is in the areas closest to the city where the better jobs have already left for the further suburbs and where the schools are already deteriorating (Galster, 1991). At the moment, the mobile whites are several jumps ahead of other migrants. And the other migrants are at least one step ahead of those who remain within the city walls.

THE URBAN CRISIS: POOR CITIES, RICH SUBURBS

To understand today's "urban crisis"—the increasing poverty of cities in contrast to the growing wealth of the suburbs—it is necessary to see how all the trends described in this chapter fed on and reinforced one another. The story begins with the first wave of migrants from city to suburb in the late 1940s made possible by two programs subsidized by all taxpayers: (1) the low-interest mortgages to war veterans that stimulated home building on the urban fringes and (2) the massive federal highway program that paved the way out.

Once the people were in the suburbs, shopping facilities and other amenities followed. Huge shopping malls replaced central-city department stores, leaving city residents without jobs or places to shop and leaving city governments without taxable properties (**ratables**). By the 1970s, not only the people and the shops but also the jobs relocated, as office work replaced city-based manufacturing, removing even more jobs and ratables from the city. And by 1980, there was very little to link suburb and city (Goldsmith and Blakely, 1992).

The cities gradually lost home-owning families, taxable businesses, privately owned real estate, and jobs. Factories and stores were abandoned, and absentee landlords allowed rental housing to deteriorate. Because landlords could not raise rents on people with minimal income, they were unable to pay local taxes or maintain the properties, and they simply abandoned the property to the city in lieu of taxes. Because the cities could not raise revenues without ratables, they also lacked the resources to maintain or repair the housing the cities now owned or to provide protection and other services to residents.

Without funds to pay police, teachers, and other employees, the quality of urban life declined sharply and the level of crime and deviance rose, making cities less attractive to the remaining families and businesses. The kinds of entry-level jobs so abundant for previous generations of urban workers are no longer there, while city schools fail to provide graduates with the complex skills for higher-level employment that isn't there either. The result is high unemployment, especially among minority teenagers and young adults precisely when they should be preparing for adult responsibilities; family dissolution; rising crime rates; and abandoned housing. Schools become battlegrounds, and health care facilities close down. Those who can escape, do.

Those most likely to leave the central city are middle-class and white families; wealthy and single people often stay on, isolated and insulated in the remaining high-rent districts. Thus, the depopulation of the cities—often called "white flight"—has sharply raised the level of race inequality in our society, with the cities increasingly darker and the suburbs overwhelmingly white. For example, in 1960, blacks accounted for about 30 percent of the central city residents of Detroit, Michigan; by 1990, that figure exceeded 75 percent. Similar trends are recorded for most major American cities (Garreau, 1994; Farley et al., 1994).

This population shift is reflected in a major change in the balance of political power at the state level. Where state legislatures were once dominated by representatives of urban districts, they are now composed largely of people elected from suburban areas, who are not likely to vote to tax their constituents to help the urban poor. At the national level, in the 1980s, Americans elected administrations pledged to reducing all forms of assistance to the cities and to the poor, and they kept their word. During the Reagan and Bush Administrations, federal aid to cities was cut by two-thirds (Wilson, 1993). Without federal assistance and unable to raise tax revenues locally, most American cities have had to cut services to residents even further, while becoming more and more dependent on increasingly hostile state legislatures and the U.S. Congress.

Racial Segregation

For those left in the cities, racial segregation of schools and other facilities has increased, creating "separate societies" isolated from one another in every respect and reinforced by the employment of private guards (Darden et al., 1992; Goldsmith and Blakely, 1992).

The patterns of *institutional racism* described in Chapter 11 have done much to reduce the stock of livable housing in the inner city. The practice of **redlining,** whereby banks refuse home improvement loans and mortgages in certain areas of the city (those blocks marked in red lines on a city map) ensures that some people cannot upgrade the quality of their housing. Insurance companies also redline, which reduces the value of homes and their resale attractiveness (Squires et al., 1991). In Milwaukee, Wisconsin, for example, homeowners in areas with a large concentration of minority residents were four times as likely as residents of similar-income white neighborhoods to be denied adequate insurance coverage (Kerr, 1993).

As property values decline in redlined areas, landlords leave or hire arsonists in order to collect on existing insurance policies. Local merchants leave, along with other residents, and the neighborhood can be destroyed within a few years. The mortgage and insurance brokers can then claim that they were correct in not making risky investments. In other words, an essentially racist outcome is defined as the result of "good business practices," and the *self-fulfilling prophecy* is realized.

Other business practices intentionally speed the process of producing segregated neighborhoods.

Ratables are properties that can be taxed by a city government.

Redlining occurs when banks refuse to give loans and mortgages to people or businesses in certain areas of a city.

Homeless in Houston (and Every Other American City)

Although homelessness is difficult to measure, most observers agree that the number of Americans living on the streets increased dramatically during the 1980s. Historically, the urban homeless population was primarily composed of male alcoholics living on skid row. Today's homeless, however, are far more varied: young unemployed men and women, the elderly, and entire families, as well as physically and mentally disabled persons. They are found in all types of cities, from the older urban centers of the North and East to the Sunbelt metropolises of the South and West, where many workers had migrated in search of employment before the oil boom went bust in the late 1980s.

Demographic studies of the homeless have found that the population is primarily male, with an average age of 40, largely white, although African Americans are over-represented, extremely poor, with numerous health problems, and a history of long-term social isolation—without family, friends, or previous residence (Rossi et al., 1987; Rosenthal, 1994). They are not on the streets by choice but because of forces beyond their control: because they are jobless and ill, because there is little affordable housing for the very poor, and because social welfare services are inadequate (Blau, 1992; Sosin, 1992; Liebow, 1993).

The career of a homeless person will vary by the supports provided in a particular city. The proximity of soup kitchens and social centers, tolerance by authorities, and welfare policies designed to empower clients will all have a positive effect on a homeless person's self-image and ability to forge a protective network of street friends (Walsh and Rowe, 1992). Unfortunately, in most cities today, policies have become increasingly punitive and nonsupportive.

From an interpretive perspective, homeless people must construct a positive identity in the face of universal stigmatization. One study found that the most com-

mon devices were (1) distancing words that disassociate them from other homeless persons and from the institutions on which their survival depends—shelters, soup kitchens, churches; (2) selective embracement of positive identities such as loyal friend; and (3) fictive storytelling, not altogether accurate stories about one's past and fantasies about the future (Snow and Anderson, 1993). Rather than passively accepting a spoiled identity, these homeless people attempted actively to construct their own sense of self as worthwhile individuals (Wagner, 1993).

From the structural perspective, all the factors involved in the urban crisis are magnified in the production of the homeless population, as illustrated in the case of Houston, Texas (Ringheim, 1990). After growing rapidly in the 1970s, Houston was hit by a sharp recession when the oil boom collapsed in the mid-1980s. Tens of thousands of workers lost their jobs, many were evicted for nonpayment of rent, and in the absence of low-income housing, thousands took to the streets. Hardest hit were minority groups, whose income relative to that of whites was already among the nation's lowest. Job and housing discrimination increased the vulnerability of Houston's black population. In the tradition of Texas and the West in general, the city's spirit of individualism and self-reliance meant that public welfare programs were minimal, so that its poorer residents absorbed most of the cost of the city's development, and then found themselves homeless in Houston.

The solutions are simple: jobs for those who are not physically or emotionally disabled; homes and health care for all. Implementing these has thus far been impossible. Scarce city resources are usually devoted to more socially worthy objects; most Americans can safely ignore the whole issue; and politicians will always find at least one homeless person who embodies all that we most fear and loathe among the urban poor, in general.

Blockbusting occurs when real estate agents generate feelings of panic in otherwise stable white neighborhoods by selling or renting to an African American and then urging neighboring homeowners to sell at once before property values decline. The real estate agent offers to buy on the spot, at well below the market price, fully expecting to sell the property to an upwardly mobile African American at above market value. In these cases, the neighborhood may well be upgraded, but it will not be integrated, and both buyer and seller have been taken advantage of by realtors.

> **Blockbusting** involves generating feelings of panic in stable, white neighborhoods when real estate agents sell or rent to African Americans and then urge neighboring homeowners to sell before property values decline.

Nor can inner-city residents look to local, state, or the federal governments for assistance. As mentioned, the city is without resources to operate, much less repair, the rental units it repossessed for back taxes; the state legislature is dominated by suburban interests; and federal policies have been more destructive than helpful to the urban poor. The "urban renewal" programs of the 1960 and 1970s, for example, resulted in "minority removal" and the construction of subsidized office buildings rather than low-income housing.

It is tempting for observers to look at the state of inner-city neighborhoods and blame the residents ("Why can't they keep the place in decent shape?"), but in most cases, an individual or family can do little to improve an entire neighborhood, especially when so many nonpoor profit from urban decay (R. A. Smith, 1993). As inadequate as it is in terms of safety and sani-

The number of homeless people living on the streets of American cities has increased over the last decade due to the decline in the economy, the loss of jobs, insufficient public housing, and lack of health care. Why are there so many homeless women and men in one of the wealthiest nations in the world?

tation, urban housing is not cheap; poor people of all races pay a larger proportion of their total income for rent than do the nonpoor, often more than 25 percent (U.S. Bureau of the Census, H121/93–95, 1994).

It seems clear that neither the industrial nor commercial city has much to offer today's urban poor. The lack of fit between the job skills of urban residents and the type of work available have led to massive unemployment. When the jobs go, the drug dealers move in; when the housing deteriorates, people sleep in the streets. In this view, the high poverty rate and large proportion of female-headed households in the central city are more the *consequences* than the cause of the urban crisis, and nowhere is this more apparent than in the emergence of homelessness as a social problem.

Can the City Be Revived?

Some cities, such as Boston, New York, Philadelphia, Chicago, and San Francisco, despite their many problems, are major centers of culture and communications, with an ample stock of high-status housing. Others, such as Buffalo, Newark, and Detroit may have reached a point of no return. Yet the urban environment offers that wonderful mix of people and cultures so necessary to creativity and intellectual stimulation, as well as opportunities for mobility unlike those of less densely populated places. For these reasons alone, most cities will remain vital and attractive to young people especially.

In general, cities in the North and East are expected to lose population in the coming decades,

while those in the South and West are expected to gain, as shown in Table 21-3 The metropolitan areas that will grow most rapidly are also those that will offer you the best job opportunities.

But what can be done about the deterioration of the city's core? There are a number of possible solutions, few of which are even remotely politically possible at this time, unless the nation were to experience an era when concern for others becomes a dominant value (Nyden and Wiebel, 1991). Among the most obvious courses of action are the following:

- *Raise federal taxes* to increase funding for the Department of Housing and Urban Development, for a national job training program, and for community health centers.
- *Raise state taxes* to redistribute funds to the most needy areas.
- *Erase the artificial boundaries* that separate a city from its suburbs and create a new political unit, the "metro area," which raises taxes from everyone within it.
- *Regionalize* services among several adjacent urban and suburban areas—for example, water supply, sewage, waste disposal, recycling, parks, highway construction, and transportation. This would save money by reducing duplication.

These are also the most politically impossible choices.

The few approaches that are politically feasible are the least effective in dealing with the roots of the crisis or with its most harmful effects and actually assist the wealthy rather than the poor. For example, *urban*

TABLE 21-3   The Fastest Growing Urban Areas to the Year 2010

Anaheim/Santa Ana, California
Los Angeles/Long Beach, California
Atlanta, Georgia
Dallas, Texas
Tampa/St. Petersburg/Clearwater, Florida
Phoenix, Arizona
Washington, D.C.
San Diego, California
Houston, Texas
Orlando, Florida
Riverside, California
Oakland, California
Nassau/Suffolk counties, New York
Fort Lauderdale/Hollywood/Pampano Beach, Florida
West Palm Beach/Boca Raton/Delray Beach, Florida

Cities can be revived to make them centers of culture, communication, and relaxation. For example, the rundown harbor area of Baltimore, Maryland, was transformed as part of the gentrification process, becoming an attractive and popular spot for local residents and tourists, and for workers taking a lunch-time break.

enterprise zones that provide tax write-offs and other advantages to companies that relocate in the inner city may create a few hundred low-pay, dead-end jobs while subsidizing profits for owners. All too often, when the tax breaks end, the employer closes the plant (W. J. Wilson, 1993).

Similarly, attempts to attract high-income homeowners back into the city have primarily benefited the well-to-do and only indirectly the poor. **Gentrification** (from *gentry,* meaning "propertied") refers to a process whereby high-quality city-owned housing stock is sold cheaply to people who agree to upgrade the property. Entire city areas have been radically changed, as the improved housing eventually lures shops and restaurants to the neighborhood. The streets are safer, and the quality of life substantially elevated. Some of the poorer residents will find employment, and the city as a whole gains new ratables. But if no low-income housing is built, the people displaced by the gentry must double up in the remaining stock or hit the streets. Thus, the upgrading of some neighborhoods is counterbalanced by overcrowding elsewhere.

A classic example of redlining and gentrification is Boston's South End, a stable white ethnic neighborhood of well-built brick two- and three-story houses attached to one another, close to the central business district. In the 1970s, as banks refused to renew mortgages or grant home-improvement loans, the older residents were forced to leave. The units were then purchased by real estate developers and converted into high-price homes for upwardly mobile young professionals.

> **Gentrification** refers to the migration of middle- and upper-income people into urban centers, their displacement of lower-income residents, and renovation of existing housing.

The market for such housing remains strong, leading real estate developers to harass low- and middle-income renters into leaving by doubling or tripling the rents, refusing to make repairs, and even intentionally filling empty apartments with noisy and violent tenants. When the old residents have gone, the housing is transformed into luxury homes, well beyond the reach of all but a few Americans. For example, a two-bedroom luxury apartment on New York City's Upper West Side (not its best) was worth $400,000 in 1994.

The end result is the two cities that Plato wrote about 2,400 years ago: the city of the poor and the city of the rich. Today, however, the gap between

Public housing does not have to be dilapidated. This low-income public housing project is located in a working-class area in the outskirts of Paris, France. It was financed by the French government in cooperation with private businesses. How does this project differ from typical public housing in the United States?

the two has grown ever wider, as the middle class fled outside the city walls. Yet all is not well in suburbia either. After several decades of rapid growth and semi-industrialization, many suburban areas are experiencing their own "crisis" in the form of traffic congestion, lack of affordable housing for low- and moderate-income earners, inefficient delivery of public services, rising taxes, uncontrolled building, racial and class segregation and conflict, and a generation of bored teenagers.

All of this is a far cry from the dream of a more optimistic era, when a leading urban specialist spoke of the city of the future as an **ecumenopolis**— a linking of overlapping urban and suburban areas across nations (Doxiadas, 1968). In this hemisphere, for example, the region from Toronto, Canada, to Havana, Cuba, or, in Europe, from London, England, to Istanbul, Turkey are a cross between the megalopolis and the global city. Yet, if members of smaller geographic divisions within the same society have trouble coordinating services and sharing resources, such a development across national borders may be too much to expect. Nevertheless, the future of the city remains open to a number of potentially revitalizing possibilities.

> An **ecumenopolis** is a linking of overlapping urban and suburban areas across nations.

SUMMARY

1. City, countryside, and suburb are associated with different lifestyles.

2. The proportion of American labor involved in farming has declined to only 3 percent, and most of the country's farmland is owned by corporate interests.

3. Rural villages are increasingly isolated and depopulated, with the exception of areas on the suburban fringe. Rural communities today are plagued by poverty, poor educational systems, and a shortage of health care providers.

4. Although there have been major urban centers for thousands of years, urbanization as the process whereby cities dominate economic and social life is a product of the industrial revolution.

5. Urbanism refers to a particular way of life—fast-paced, worldly and secularized, allowing more personal freedom and anonymity than in the countryside.

6. Urban growth in the Third World is associated with widespread poverty and inequality as displaced rural migrants seek jobs.

7. Urban ecology refers to the fit between population characteristics and land use in the city. Cities are also subject to dynamic changes in the character of neighborhoods as populations compete for jobs and housing.

8. The history of American cities is one of transition from commercial to industrial to corporate as the economic base of the society changes.

9. The most recent stage in the development of the metropolis is the global city, oriented to international rather than domestic commerce.

10. The suburbs emerged after World War II in response to upward mobility pressures and were made possible by the mass-produced automobile, highway construction programs, and availability of mortgage money.

11. Suburban lifestyles are more relaxed than in urban areas, the air is cleaner and crime rates lower, but families are more isolated, and conformity pressures are high. Many urban problems are now spreading to the suburbs, such as overdevelopment, pollution, and racial tensions.

12. The urban crisis involves a number of merging trends that shifted jobs and taxable properties from city to suburbs. As whites and anyone who could afford to move leave the cities, minority poor are locked into a deteriorating urban core, where many have become homeless.

13. In the suburbs, redlining and blockbusting have kept may communities racially segregated.

14. The kinds of policies that might reduce the negative effects of the urban crisis are politically impossible at this time. Gentrification and urban enterprise zones are more help to the middle-class than urban poor.

SUGGESTED READINGS

Budd, Leslie and Sam Whimster. *Global Finance and Urban Living: A Study of Metropolitan Change.* London: Routledge, 1992. An analysis of metropolitan changes over a decade with the focus on London's economic, social, and cultural developments.

Flora, Cornelia B. and James A. Christenson. *Rural Policies for the 1990s.* Boulder: Westview Press, 1991. The authors use social science research to develop a rural policy agenda with respect to economic structure and change, services, and quality control of natural resources.

Jacob, Jane. *The Death and Life of Great American Cities.* New York: Random House, 1961. A classic analysis of the problems of urban planning, urban renewal, and life in North American cities.

Nostrand, Richard, *The Hispano Homeland.* Norman: University of Oklahoma Press, 1992. An historical treatment of the Hispano culture region from formative settlement in New Mexico to the rural communities of the 1980s.

Pederson, Jane Marie. *Between Memory and Reality: Family and Community in Rural Wisconsin, 1870-1970.* Madison: University of Wisconsin Press, 1992. A detailed and lively account of rural life in Wisconsin with excellent treatment of gender issues. The use of diaries, newspapers, and photographs make it most entertaining.

Phillips, E. Barbara. 2nd ed. *City Lights: Urban-Suburban Life in a Global Society.* New York, NY: Oxford University Press, 1995. Focusing on the U.S. city, this book covers new issues facing cities, such as cultural pluralism and the impact of the communications revolution. This edition offers expanded coverage of urban problems, racial and ethnic issues, and suburban and economic life.

Sennett, Richard. *Flesh and Stone: The Body and the City in Western Civilization.* New York, NY: W. W. Norton, 1994. From ancient Rome to contemporary New York City, a noted urban sociologist examines the relationship between the planning of urban spaces and cultural ideas about the body. For example, the ghetto areas of major cities, from 16th century Venice to this day, are designed to segregate contaminated bodies, while the broad boulevards of European cities allow maximum bodily freedoom.

Wagner, David. *Checkerboard Square: Culture and Resistance in a Homeless Community.* Boulder, CO: Westview Press, 1993. Insightful, participant observation of a homeless community, whose residents struggle to maintain their dignity under extremely adverse circumstances.

22

Popular Culture: Mass Media, Popular Music, and Sports

*A*s 1995 begins and the twentieth century draws to a close, the following items have come to our attention as illuminating examples of *popular culture,* the subject of this chapter:

■ The top-rated show on Music Television (MTV) involved the adventures of cartoon teenagers named Beavis and Butthead, who delight in burning objects and blowing up frogs.

■ More people visited Disneyland and Disney World than toured the nation's capital. Only Mecca and the Vatican drew more pilgrims.

■ Two of the most popular radio talk-show hosts were Rush Limbaugh and Howard Stern, who specialize in making fun of gays, feminists, immigrants, and First Lady Hillary Clinton.

■ Some of the highest paid employees in the United States were professional athletes.

■ The second-biggest American export to the rest of the world was "pop cult"—movies, television programs, and fashions (especially baggy pants and baseball caps worn backward).

THE STUDY OF POPULAR CULTURE

Popular culture consists of products designed for mass consumption, typically consumed when a person is not at work or asleep, that is, in *leisure time.* Some scholars use the blanket term *entertainment* to cover the variety of products and processes studied by students of popular culture: everything from comic books to classical music, from baseball cards to ballet (Denisoff and Wahrman, 1983).

Popular culture in the United States is also very big business. It provides employment and wealth to those who produce it, an opportunity for self-expression and pleasure to those who consume it, and endless fascination to those who study it. In other words, popular culture has two aspects: one is based on the human impulse to play and to create (Biesty, 1986), and the other is based on the need of an advanced capitalist economy continually to create new markets (Rojek, 1989).

In this chapter, we can only skim the surface of this fast-growing field of study. We will first examine the role of popular culture in mass society, issues of control and social class, and the processes whereby fun and games are institutionalized. Then we will take an in-depth look at three major subfields: the mass media, especially as a source of news; popular music; and sports.

POPULAR CULTURE IN MASS SOCIETY

Functional Perspectives

THE USES OF LEISURE.   As a species, humans have benefited from the impulse to play and to create things of beauty (artistry). Leisure activities reduce personal anxiety and relieve social tensions. The production of things that give pleasure to the senses brings people together. As Durkheim taught us, commemorative rituals and objects enhance social solidarity, even when the events being celebrated may have been controversial (Wagner-Pacifici and Schwartz, 1991). Thus, popular culture tends to support the social order by providing entertainment for individuals and unifying symbols for the collectivity.

Such personal and group benefits become important in modern societies where leisure time is often defined as the pause that refreshes weary workers and prepares them to resume the rigors of employment. Because play or creativity is an end in itself, it is *expressive* behavior. Work, in contrast, is *instrumental,* a means to other goals. Popular culture thus becomes an expressive outlet that balances the instru-

> **Popular culture** consists of products designed for mass consumption during leisure time.

mental demands of the workplace and is especially functional in societies with an intense commitment to instrumental roles: "The harder we work, the harder we play." Indeed, one survey found that 94 percent of Americans saw their free time as "recuperative," a necessary period for recharging one's energy (Spring, 1992).

The idea that leisure time is "free time," however, obscures the degree to which it is structured by economic and political factors (Wilson, 1994; Butsch, 1990; Hinrichs et al., 1991). Employers and politicians determine the extent of leisure time, as well as when and where people can play. Notice, for example, how much public recreation is devoted to games primarily played by males and also how few public facilities are located in the poorer sections of town.

Contrary to popular belief, the leisure time of employed Americans has *decreased* over the past two decades—by several hours per week on average—as have paid days off (Schor, 1992). This is partly due to the logic of capitalism: It is less expensive for an employer to pay overtime to some workers than to train and extend benefits to additional employees. The decline of leisure also reflects the reduced power of labor unions to hold onto the gains of the past, much less demand a shorter workweek and longer vacations. In addition, because of the declining standard of living provided by a single paycheck, workers must put in extra hours to stay even. Fi-

SOCIOLOGY IN EVERYDAY LIFE

Happy Father's Day! Sort Of

Because they define the occasions and relationships that must be taken seriously and those that permit a degree of humor and even expression of hostility, greeting cards provide a fascinating insight into the popular culture and the management of emotions. A content analysis of Mother's Day and Father's Day cards by sociologist Mario Kravanja (1993) found that sentiments directed toward mothers were universally positive: As a person of little social power, she is not perceived as a legitimate target of a put-down.

Fathers, however, are much more ambiguous figures in the lives of their children—more distant, less nurturant, but representatives of male authority. As a consequence, Father's Day cards tend to be of two types: (1) cards that convey a generalized, but never mushy, "Thanks, Dad," on standard-size paper in "male" colors (browns especially) or (2) cards that have negative undertones of humorously expressed hostility, although channeled into culturally acceptable complaints, such as snoring, being a couch potato, or messing up at a sport or home repairs. Kravanja concludes that, although the fault-finding diminishes the father's power over the sender, it also pushes him even further from the family's emotional center, a form of the self-fulfilling prophecy.

nally, because many women in the labor force are also full-time homemakers, their "free time" has been greatly reduced.

By harnessing people's need for play and games to commercial gain, available leisure time has become another area for profit making and the manipulation of pleasure. The discontented and overworked can be "cooled out" by the illusion of personal freedom in play that deflects anger from employers and other authorities. Every now and then, however, the masses will slip their controls and engage in "rituals of rebellion" such as riots at sports events or doing drugs in the workplace.

PLAY AS WORK.   Popular culture supports the American value system in another way. The work ethic described in Chapter 3 is in part based on the early Puritan distrust of play ("Idle hands are the Devil's workshop"), and many Americans still feel guilty about pure enjoyment. But if leisure activities can be turned into something like work, the discomfort is lessened, such as when play is transformed into a money-making activity or when winning is the only goal (Lewis, 1982). Many how-to books for leisure play sound very much like an operating manual for a machine, using the same goal-directed way of thinking that characterizes the work ethic: If all the right steps are taken in the precise order, success will be yours. Jogging to the point of exhaustion is work, not pleasure. Only after single-minded dedication to a hard day's work or play have you earned that foaming glass of beer.

> A **mass culture** is made up of those elements of popular culture that forge common values in a heterogeneous society and are produced and distributed through the mass media.

Americans participate in a number of nonorganized and noncompetitive athletic activities. What benefits do such expressive activities bring to individuals and the larger society?

MASS CULTURE AND VALUE CONSENSUS.   Those elements of popular culture that are produced and distributed through the mass media (radio, television, newspapers, and magazines) make up a **mass culture** that some scholars believe is essential to forging common values in a heterogeneous society. Because industrialization is based on specialization and the separation of occupational and status groups, the popular culture may be the only culture shared to some degree by most citizens. Whatever else divides us, the World Series and Super Bowl bring us together (Goethals, 1981).

Conflict Analysis

The terms *popular* and *mass culture* suggest something emerging from the creativity of "the people." Yet the production of culture, like any other activity, is socially structured. Who are the artists and entertainers? When, where, and how do they work? Who pays them and distributes their output? Who consumes their products? Who defines standards of excellence? Who benefits?

One major issue from the conflict perspective is that of control over the **production of popular culture**—the issue of cultural hegemony referred to in Chapters 3 and 9. If popular culture is not a spontaneous outpouring of mass creativity, then some people and groups must decide what is made for whom and what vision of the world is portrayed. Popular culture is manufactured in the same way as any other product: There are industries that turn out movies, books, television and radio programs, newspapers and magazines, records, rock concerts, sports events, and art exhibits—primarily for profit, though sometimes for prestige.

> The conflict perspective is concerned with who has control over the **production of popular culture**.
>
> An **elite culture** consists of items consumed and sponsored by the wealthy.

Conflict theorists are also interested in another form of control: Who defines what is authentic or false, good or bad? When does "good" become "what *we* think is good for you?" This is the activity of *tastemakers* or *gatekeepers,* people whose occupation or social position permits them to open or close the gates of success and to impose their standards of value (Greenfield, 1988). Gatekeepers and tastemakers form a cultural elite, typically drawn from the upper middle class.

The belief that "good" music or "fine art" (in contrast to common, or unfine, art) exists in some abstract realm of eternal beauty completely overlooks the cultural, social, political, and economic influences that determine what is produced in any historical era and what is preserved (Lang and Lang, 1988; McClary, 1991). It makes a difference whether a composer is financed by a wealthy patron or must depend on pleasing the general public. Or whether the painter has been hired to decorate a cathedral or a dining room. Artistic products are influenced by nonartistic factors, as when an aria is deleted from an opera score because the tenor cannot reach high C. Even an artist's style may change depending on her or his location in social networks or artistic stratification systems (Finney, 1993). Where profit making is a crucial consideration (when programming classical music concerts, for example, or producing elegant restaurant food), the outcome is determined by the interplay between the artist's creativity (aesthetics), audience taste, and the needs of the management (Fine, 1992a; Gilmore, 1993).

Tastemakers have often created and maintained a distinction between **elite culture**—items consumed and sponsored by the educated and wealthy—and "mass culture" enjoyed by the majority. For example, to set themselves apart from the "lower classes" and Irish immigrants, the commercial elite of Boston founded a symphony orchestra and a museum of fine arts that were then placed off-limits to the masses (DiMaggio, 1982b). Thus, *cultural capital* is reserved for the upper strata, and the class system is preserved over time (Bourdieu, 1984; Chapters 9 and 15).

> Taste classifies, and it classifies the classifier.
> —Pierre Bourdieu, 1984, p.6

Gatekeepers and tastemakers may also have a moral agenda, such as when religious/political leaders attempt to censor art thought to be obscene and corrupting of public virtue. For example, in 1887 in New York City, a leading art dealer was arrested for selling photographic reproductions of nude paintings (Beisel, 1993). One century later, the religious leader of Iran banned a novel and issued a death threat against its author on grounds of blasphemy (Afshari, 1990). And in the United States in the 1990s, Senator Jesse Helms has successfully curtailed federal funding for artistic products of which he might disapprove (Dubin, 1992).

A final concern of conflict theorists is the possibility of using popular culture to resist or oppose the established order (Ross, 1989). Musical styles have been especially important as a channel of protest or of comfort for groups outside the mainstream, most clearly exemplified in the songs of American slaves. Much of the pain of white working-class lives can be heard in the sound and lyrics of country and western. Themes of resistance can be found also in classical music, such as when the servants outwit their master in *The Marriage of Figaro* or, in the past century, in the various schools of "modern" painting that have shocked each generation of viewers.

How effective are these gestures of resistance? Most analyses suggest that the long-term effects are minimal. Although people may feel temporarily empowered, the power of dominant institutions is overwhelming. For example, working-class leisure patterns have long been a center of struggle between workers and employers (Rosenzweig, 1983; Nasaw, 1994). In the early days of the factory system, leisure and work were combined as employees drank and gambled on the job. By the end of the nineteenth century, employers had tightened discipline, and drinking moved to the saloon, the haven of working-class men. By the 1920s, the saloon gave way to vaudeville or the movie house, also controlled by the middle

Watching Weight and Preserving Virtue: Health Nuts and Food Faddists

Among the most interesting aspects of popular culture are the health and fitness fads that periodically sweep the country. Social historians have shown how these trends are shaped by broader currents of change in the society. The history of physical fitness fads is greatly enlivened by the larger-than-life eccentrics who led various health reform movements (Goldstein, 1992).

Particularly fascinating are the three men who founded the food empires that still dominate our breakfast tables: Sylvester Graham, C. W. Post, and J. H. Kellogg. Graham's crackers were a "natural" food answer to widespread fears about the negative health effects of city life and factory work for the urban masses. In addition, members of the newly emerging class of white-collar workers, fearful that they might be "feminized" by the shift from manual to nonmanual labor, were reassured that their masculinity could be preserved by eating natural foods.

C. W. Post, too, was keenly aware of the differences between manual and nonmanual workers; his Grape-Nuts were originally marketed as "brain food" for middle-class employees. Post and others were also worried about declining birthrates in the white middle class, in contrast to the high fertility of recent immigrants and African Americans. All types of health foods were being promoted in the early 1900s to restore virility to WASP middle-class males.

But the most unusual character in the history of health foods was J. H. Kellogg, who had a Puritanical obsession with original sin and the evils of unbridled sexuality. His breakfast products—especially Corn Flakes—were good for you because they reduced the sex drive; eat enough of them and other wholesome grains and you would be freed of sin (Boyle, 1993).

What the three had in common, along with so many other health and fitness leaders throughout our history, was a very American belief in individual responsibility for one's state of physical and moral health. Ill health, therefore, could not be the fault of working conditions or blamed on employers. Such an emphasis on the individual also works against collective efforts to improve the workplace or to narrow life-style differences between middle- and working-class families.

American eating habits have also been shaped by a Puritanical fear of gluttony as sin. Because leanness is thus perceived as the outward sign of inner virtue, American women and men have endured great pain and deprivation to become or remain slim. Perhaps the most unusual approach to weight loss was proposed by Horace Fletcher in the early part of the twentieth century. Fletcher advocated chewing food at the rate of 100 chews per minute and demonstrated its effectiveness through his own weight loss of 50 pounds in a short period of time. Thousands of Americans spent their entire dinner hour chewing a few spoonfuls of food. Eighty years later, Americans spend billions of dollars on diets, visits to spas, and fat-removal surgery.

class. Thus, workers lost the struggle over both leisure and control of the workplace.

Popular culture has also periodically been an arena of gender struggles. Baseball was originally encouraged in the 1870s to amuse the immigrant masses and to allow men an escape from the emerging women's suffrage movement (Lipsyte, 1994). Newly liberated young working women in American cities in the nineteenth century developed styles of leisure activity and dress that challenged the power of parents and employers (Peiss, 1985). Yet at the same time, women were effectively closed off from the liberating currents of the world of modern art, reflecting as it did a basically male world of bars and city streets where men could wander as they please (Wolff, 1990). When museums were organized, they too became male institutions, modeled after business organizations; although women's assistance in raising funds was appreciated, the governing boards remained all male and upper status until recently (McCarthy, 1991).

Mass Culture: Variations and Themes

When we examine what people do in their leisure time, the range of possibilities is enormous. In a soci-

ety as heterogeneous as the United States in terms of race, religion, ethnicity, and social class, great differences will be seen in the experience and expression of popular culture. For example, Irish men spend more time in bars than do Jews; white middle-class men are the major market for pornography; and women of all ages and social classes buy dozens of paperback romances each year. There are also regional cultures, with particularly marked differences between the South and Northeast, and the East and West coasts. Popular music styles differ greatly by race and ethnicity, although there are strong "crossover" effects.

Aspects of popular culture also vary by social class, independently of the relationship between class and religion, race, or ethnicity. The leisure pursuits of the wealthy are very different from those of the less affluent, partly as a consequence of having more money and partly from being socialized to contrasting ideas of fun and play. Upper-status games, for example, tend to be more individualistic—sailing, tennis, golf, skiing, and squash—than such team sports as baseball, basketball, and bowling.

The distinction between elite and mass cultures contains a large element of snobbery, with the elite version assumed to be more pure and worthy in con-

A number of taste cultures exist in the United States, appealing to different portions of the public. For some, an evening at the ballet is wonderful; others enjoy different kinds of dancing. What are your preferred taste cultures?

trast to watered down and vulgar culture forms—the difference, for example, between attending a ballet or a barn dance. The audience for elite culture is extremely small, which gives it its distinction, but which also makes it difficult for non-elites to enjoy because the cost of doing so is very high. Who but a few hundred people can buy "important" art?

CRITICISMS OF MASS CULTURE.   Mass culture has been attacked on many grounds: (1) that it appeals to the lowest levels of taste; (2) that it corrupts the standards of excellence by offering instant fame and fortune to crowd pleasers; (3) that it dulls critical capacities; and (4) that it is not really "art," because it is produced only for profit (Denisoff and Wahrman, 1983; Blau, 1986).

These arguments echo a long-standing fear by elitists that "too much" democracy has had a negative effect on Americans. It is not difficult to find easy targets of ridicule: Mother's Day cards as poetry, movie soundtracks as serious music, television game shows as intellectual contests, and professional wrestling as athletics.

There is a darker vision: mass audiences as passive receivers of entertainment rather than as active agents of their own fate, left vulnerable to the appeal to demagogues (rabble-rousers). The theme of mass culture as a symptom of moral decay has a long tradition in Western thought. How often have you heard the argument that pleasing the masses caused the fall of Rome, or that barbarians are always at the gates, ready to destroy civilized peoples?

IN DEFENSE OF MASS CULTURE.   Contemporary scholars of popular culture tend to view the distinction between elite and mass cultures in less sharp and less value-laden terms. Throughout most of Western history, both ordinary citizens and the wealthy enjoyed many of the same pastimes and entertainments. For most of the nineteenth century in the United States, for example, Shakespeare's plays were regularly performed for working-class audiences, and volumes of his work were second only to the Bible as the most common book in people's homes. It was only at the end of the century, with the influx of non-English-speaking immigrants, that the urban middle class was successful in distinguishing a "legitimate" theater from the "common" music hall, and in defining Shakespeare as too demanding for a mass audience (Levine, 1988).

As a result, certain entertainments came to be the exclusive privilege of the middle and upper classes, who soon turned them into status symbols. This trend reached its most refined point in the late 1980s, when wealthy New Yorkers could rent the Museum of Modern Art for $30,000 a night for a dinner party (Taylor, 1989). Major American corporations also underwrite art gallery exhibits where it is unlikely that material offensive to their corporate sponsors will be displayed (Martorella, 1990).

Nonetheless, there has been much crossover between elite and mass culture. Clothing styles, especially, filter up and down. Elite fashions soon appear in less expensive versions in American malls, while "grunge"-type styles are adopted by wealthy youngsters (Rubinstein, 1994). The ultimate in crossover art probably occurred in the mid-1980s, when elite gallery owners declared that the work of graffiti writers—underclass youth who specialized in spray painting subway cars—was "true art" and wealthy patrons immediately began to bid up the price of their work (Lachman, 1988). Nor are the audiences for elite and mass culture so sharply segregated; individuals typically have both "high" and "low" tastes—both can be found at a professional hockey game, although in different sections of the arena. Conversely, readers of the *National Enquirer* are an entirely different audience from subscribers to the upscale *New Yorker* (Weiss, 1994).

TASTE CULTURES.   The validity of all forms of popular culture has been forcefully argued by Herbert Gans (1974), who uses the term **taste cultures** to suggest the great variety of culture audiences without implying value judgments. Far from being a passive homogenized mass, consumers of popular culture are active participants in interpreting their experience in the light of their own identities (Gottdiener, 1985). Thus, for example, Native Americans' reactions will differ from other Americans' when watching a film about the "Wild West." Members of each group will find something that affirms their own traditional values (Shively, 1992).

THE PRODUCTION OF CULTURE.   In contrast to an earlier emphasis on the people who create and consume culture, many sociologists today are primarily concerned with structural aspects of the **production of culture:** markets, industries, distribution chains, organizations, and other systems that determine what is produced and offered to the public (Ryan, 1985; Crane, 1992). In this view, the final product is the result of an interaction among (1) the object itself; (2) the profit-making producers and distributors of the item; and (3) the social groups that consume it. What is produced and how it is marketed are largely determined by economic factors such as control over markets, dealing with competitors, avoiding regulation, generating consumer demand, and bottom-line profitability.

Yet because sociologists are also interested in the meaning people attach to the products they desire and purchase, the study of popular culture has an interactionist dimension. Popular culture is learned and shared, within families, peer groups, and particular subcultures. But by far the most important element in the spread and homogenization of popular culture— the very condition that makes mass culture possible— is the existence of mass media in modern society.

THE MASS MEDIA

Media is the plural of *medium,* which means a channel through which something is transmitted. The term **mass media** refers to the agents of communication in a mass society: (1) the print media—books,

magazines, and newspapers—and (2) the electronic media—television, radio, and recordings. In the decades ahead, the two will increasingly be combined in the "information highway," whereby print media can be called up on the electronic screen of a home computer.

These are the modern equivalents of the storytellers and singers who were the earliest media of information and entertainment. Such face-to-face communication has been replaced by mass-produced items for use by a wide public. This means that many products must appeal to large numbers, so that the economic requirements of mass production become at least as important as the quality of the product.

This mass-produced cultural product is what critics have condemned for its vulgarity, but sociologists are analysts of culture, not art critics. The topics of interest to us are the manifest and latent functions of the mass media. Manifest functions include selling a product and making a profit. Latent functions, by definition hidden and unintended, are more difficult to pinpoint. How do mass communications support the status quo? What values and behaviors are reinforced? What status groups are co-opted or cooled out? How do the conditions under which information and entertainment are produced affect the product? These are the issues we examine in the following sections.

> The term **taste cultures** is used to give validity to various forms of popular culture without implying value judgments.
>
> The **production of culture** involves markets, industries, distribution chains, organizations, and other systems that determine what is produced and offered to the public.
>
> **Mass media** refers to the print media and electronic media, which are agents of communication in mass society.

IMPORTANCE OF THE MASS MEDIA.   The two most common leisure activities of Americans are watching television and reading newspapers, accounting for at least 40 percent of their leisure time. Ninety-nine percent of American homes have at least one radio, and 98 percent have at least one television set. Sixty-one percent of households receive cable programs, and 77 percent are equipped with a videocassette recorder (VCR). Only slight differences are found in proportions watching television by age, race, education, income, and employment status. In contrast, newspaper reading is strongly and directly related to education and income; the higher the income, the more likely an individual is to read at least one newspaper a day (U.S. Bureau of the Census *Statistical Abstract*, 1994, p. 567).

The mass media also comprise an important sector of the economic system, employing more than a million workers and accounting for tens of billions of dollars in payrolls alone. In addition, over $135 billion will be spent on advertising in the print and electronic media in 1995. Most important, the mass media—in content and advertisements—are crucial for maintaining the demand for goods and services essential to the continued growth of a capitalist economy. The vision of America presented in our media reinforces the values and ideology of materialism (Bogart, 1991). The United States is also unique in the degree to which the media are privately owned, with an extremely limited public sector (McChesney, 1994).

It has been argued that the mass media have homogenized the culture, muting differences among regions and social classes, and have inhibited creativity (Rothman and Lerner, 1988; Crane, 1992). Yet it can also be claimed that the possibilities are greater today than in the past for a wider variety of media products; there is something for everybody on the information highway, from the raunchy to the righteous. Computer networking, cable TV programming, and desktop publishing have greatly expanded the number and type of product that can be tailored to a specific audience.

CENSORSHIP, AMERICAN STYLE.   Although our media are relatively free of direct government censorship (see Chapter 14), they are subject to other pressures, such as the political agendas of their owners, the power of advertisers and special interest groups, and the public temper. Owners, either directly or through the executives they hire, have close to absolute power to determine what is seen or read by the public and how the story is slanted. At the owner's whim, stories can be killed and others played up, usually with a specific political outcome in mind.

Next in power are the advertisers, through their ability to pick and choose the programs that they will sponsor. This is especially important on regular network radio and television, where the sale of commercial time is the sole source of revenue; newspapers and magazines are less dependent on advertising because some of their money comes from subscriptions and newsstand sales; and cable television is partly funded by viewer fees. Because radio and television advertisers want their product to be associated with positive emotions, it is difficult for the networks to sell time on programs with controversial content or

that show the seamier side of the society. For example, many regular sponsors withdrew from an episode of "Seinfeld" in which the topic of masturbation was indirectly mentioned and from an episode of "Roseanne" involving a visit to a lesbian night club. Because these programs were top-ranked, the network was able to replace the advertisers immediately, but any less popular program might well have been cancelled. As one media executive noted: "Sex and violence become love and adventure" when the show is a hit (Carter, 1992). But what is still forbidden on the major commercial networks is now largely "old hat" on cable television.

Special interest groups have long tried to influence program content (Montgomery, 1989). Women, African Americans, Latinos, the elderly, and homosexuals have all protested negative stereotyping. Racial stereotypes have been particularly difficult to dislodge; Clair and Cliff Huxtable of "The Cosby Show" were originally cast as the maid and chauffeur in an upper-class household, yet transforming them into a lawyer and doctor is equally misleading in its obscuring of powerful structural barriers to upward mobility (Jhally and Lewis, 1992). Similarly, from a feminist perspective, it could be argued that moving women out of the home in order to be stalked and raped elsewhere is not much of an improvement. Indeed, the media appear to flourish on unrealistic images of both men and women (Craig, 1992; Press, 1991; Douglas, 1994).

At this writing, the most powerful interest groups are those representing conservative religious constituencies seeking to promote "family values." Letter-writing campaigns have targeted both the networks and advertisers with threats of boycotting their products. Many members of Congress and the general public would like to see limitations placed on the networks. The possibility of government intervention is disturbing to supporters of the First Amendment's guarantee of freedom of the press. They note that attempts to regulate radio and TV content and ownership have not been very successful in the past and that the possibility of thought control is more frightening than the depictions of sex and violence that parents could censor in the home simply by pulling the plug. The most recent attempt at regulation, the Children's Television Act, merely requests stations to document an effort to serve the educational needs of children, which they promptly did by redefining cartoons as educational. G.I. Joe, for example, teaches patriotism; the Jetsons are a model of family life; and Superboy presents the triumph of good over evil according to the networks (Andrews, 1993).

MEDIA GOLIATHS.   The greater threat to press freedom today, however, comes from increasing concentration of media ownership. Throughout most of American history, mass media ownership was widely dispersed and fiercely competitive, so that many competing voices could be heard. The trend over the past two decades is for relatively small, independent, and regional media outlets to be absorbed by nationwide chains. A handful of "media Goliaths" now determine the content and editorial policy of a majority of American newspapers, magazines, and book publishing companies, despite anti-monopoly laws. A similar trend is found in other modern industrial nations, with ownership increasingly concentrated among a few media empires (Tunstall and Palmer, 1991).

Where once several newspapers competed in the same market, there is now typically only one, and that one is probably owned by the same company that controls a local radio or television station (Bagdikian, 1993).

Cross-media ownership refers to the same owner having controlling interest in various media in the same community, giving them total control over the flow of information in that area. At the national level, media Goliaths such as Time-Warner, Paramount Communications, and Rupert Murdoch's American News Corporation have extensive holdings in companies that produce, distribute, and show moving pictures; in companies that produce, distribute, and show television and radio programs; and in all forms of publishing (including the publisher of this book)—and all without a murmur of protest from the antitrust division of the Justice Department. Indeed, in 1992 the Federal Communications Commission (FCC) voted to allow a single corporation to own as many as thirty AM and 35 FM stations, up from a limit of only seven each in 1985.

In the mid-1980s, the independence of the three major national networks was reduced further, as each was sold to a new corporate owner. NBC was purchased by General Electric; ABC merged with Capital Cities, a media chain; and a large share of CBS stock was sold to a family whose fortune was made in New York real estate. The new corporate owners did not disguise their primary interest in bottom-line profit, quickly dropping quality programs that failed to attract a large audience, and scaling back the very expensive but high-prestige news-gathering operations (Auletta, 1991). In most major cities, as a result of arrangements with local affiliates, the televised national news program—once the symbol of network prestige—is now shown at 6:30 so that high-profit game shows can occupy the more popular 7:00 slot. At this writing, two major networks are in the process of being sold once more, this time to two of the largest Goliaths—Time-Warner, Inc., and the Walt Disney Company.

Effects of the Mass Media

Criticism of the mass media is based on the assumption that what people see and hear has a strong and direct effect on attitudes and actions. Conservative critics blame the media for lowering intellectual standards and appealing to the lowest common denominator, while critics on the left see the masses being manipulated by the elites. Both perceive media consumers as a relatively passive audience of individuals. But people absorb information in particular situations; they have past experiences, hopes, and expectations that condition their reactions to what they see and hear, and they are embedded in social networks. Reasons for viewing will also vary by sex, class, and age (Chayko, 1993). Thus, although it is difficult to believe that the media do not have a direct impact on beliefs and behaviors, the research evidence is unclear (Schudson, 1991; Lang and Lang, 1992).

EFFECTS ON CHILDREN. Most research has examined potential negative effects on children from watching televised violence. Although some early studies suggested a link between viewing violent programming and aggressive behavior in some children, most research has found such effects to be weak and temporary (Gunther, 1985). These data, moreover, come from laboratory studies, under artificial conditions removed from the multiple influences of everyday life.

> **Cross-media ownership** occurs when one company controls a variety of media outlets in a single market.

The media have strong influence on the formation of public awareness or ignorance of political and social issues that influence people's everyday lives. In its gatekeeping function, media executives decide what to cover, for how long, and in what context, thereby defining what is "news."

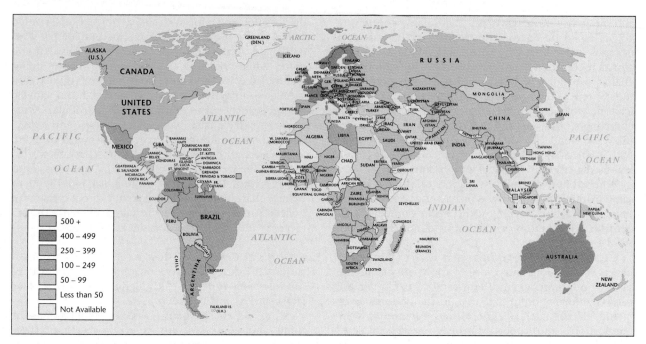

Number of television sets per 1,000 people in each country. Does the spread of television worldwide help or hinder a better understanding of other cultures? Why or why not?

Source: U.S. Bureau of the Census, *Statistical Abstracts*, 1993, p. 856.

One community study of Canadian towns before and after the introduction of TV did find some negative effects on childrens' reading skills and socializing, but such outcomes have less to do with the content of programs than with the fact that watching television took time from other activities (T. Williams, 1986). In addition, other researchers have found that TV viewing can stimulate cognitive development (Hodge and Tripp, 1986) and that high-viewing subgroups have low rates of violent crime (Messner, 1986).

Television viewing may have more subtle long-term effects that have not yet been measured. For example, what messages about race and gender are constantly conveyed in children's media in which the world of action and competence remains largely male and white (Jewell, 1993; Merlo and Smith, 1994)? Because girls will watch programs and read books that have boys as the main character but boys will not watch or read stories that feature girls, the obvious choice for programmers and book writers is to reach the largest audience and omit female characters.

Adults are exposed to similar messages; they see supermasculine men and superfeminine women, all of whom appear to be totally absorbed with their own bodies (Barthel, 1988). A dominant theme of the 1990s in books, movies, and television was the extreme physical violation of women, and often their equally extreme physical retaliation. These "backlash" effects suggest a great deal of ambivalence, hostility, and fear in intimate relationships (Gitlin, 1991).

Although there appears to be an imitative response to media reports of a major accident or celebrity suicide, which tend to be followed by a temporary increase in suicide or accidental death (Phillips, 1982; Stack, 1987b), the impact of most media images is too diffuse to be determinative. There is so much to absorb and our interests tend to be so diverse that it is difficult to argue either that audiences are passive captives or that they have been empowered by the new communications technology (Neuman, 1991).

AGENDA SETTING. Where the media appear to have their strongest effect is in setting the agenda—the list of topics that come to the forefront of public attention. This is a gatekeeping function, so that in their choice of what to cover, for how long, and in what context, the media create reality and define what is "normal" or "problematic." The agenda-setting model appeals to social scientists because it combines an emphasis on media power with an appreciation of the active role of the consumer (Gamson and Mogdiliani, 1989; Iyengar, 1991; Neuman et al., 1992). We must be aware of the context in which consumers process information and entertainment, as well as the institutional context in which such items are created and produced (Saferstein, 1994; Bielby and Bielby, 1994). These considerations are crucial in the analysis of media presentations of current events.

All the News that Fits

It is often assumed that newspapers and newscasts present *the* news, that is, pure factual information. Most media researchers would disagree, as indicated in the titles of their work: *Making News* (Tuchman, 1978); *Manufacturing the News* (Fishman, 1980); *Inventing Reality* (Parenti, 1985); and *Negotiating Control* (1989). The basic theme of these studies is that the gathering and presentation of the news is shaped by the structural conditions under which reporters work and in which editors make decisions about what stories to cover and broadcast. The crucial questions are: Where are the cameras and reporters? Who are the sources? What are the deadlines? and How can the material be made understandable to the public?

Each medium also has space and time limits: 22 ½ minutes on the televised evening news; a fixed number of pages, depending on advertising revenues, for newspapers and magazines; and 3 to 5 minutes per hour of radio time. Stories must then be sifted and shaped to meet these constraints.

For example, of the thousands of events that take place throughout the world every minute, only a dozen or so will become that day's "news." Much depends on where the three or four major news services have their reporters and equipment. In addition, most national and international news comes to reporters in the form of handouts from carefully cultivated sources within governments. These items are passed along without critical commentary. When reporters become too critical, their "sources" dry up. Conversely, total dependence on official sources turns reporters into agents of the establishment, as seen in the Persian Gulf war, when the media acted more as cheerleaders than information gatherers (MacArthur, 1993). Iraqi bombs were called "weapons of terror," while U.S. missiles were "marvels of technology," striking only military targets. Iraq was a "dictatorship," while the equally totalitarian governments of Kuwait and Saudi Arabia were described as "moderate" (Solomon, 1991).

Thus, what finally emerges as the news is a *negotiated reality*, the end product of hundreds of decisions by reporters and editors concerning what is newsworthy, what people might want to know about, where the news crews are located, and what information has been given by sources (Protess et al., 1991). The editors, and especially the anchorperson, then select the items that fill the available slots. Not only do the media set the agenda, but they also serve as the collective memory of the nation, selectively remembering, forgetting, and reconstructing the past (Schudson, 1992).

FRAMING.   Once the story is selected, it must be placed in some frame of reference that makes it understandable to the public. Sports imagery is a common frame, such as when candidates are in a "horse race." The words, tone, and placement of a story are important framing devices. Notice how stories about art and artists are invariably reported with a snicker and placed at the end of a telecast where the audience expects the amusing and trivial (Ryan and Sim, 1990).

Framing is also accomplished through the use of code words, such as when America's enemies abroad are "terrorists" and our equally bloodthirsty allies are "freedom fighters." Racial framing is especially important for its attribution of cause and effect. Heavy metal music, a basically white form, is dangerous on an individual level; black rap music is a serious threat to society as a whole (Binder, 1993). White-collar crime is typically interpreted as a product of our society's materialistic values; black street crime is a matter of personal pathology, committed by antisocial savages (Iyengar, 1991). We leave you to discover the common gender frames for reporting news.

Illustrations are powerful framing devices; even charts and graphs can be drawn to present a particular view of the data, as Ross Perot discovered to great effect (Orcutt and Turner, 1993). An interesting exercise would be to analyze all the illustrations in your favorite newsmagazine and ask yourself what messages the editors are trying convey. What cues are positive or negative?

WHOSE NEWS?   Is the news influenced by the social background and political biases of the largely white, middle-class, college-educated elite who own, manage, and staff the media? Conservatives complain of a liberal bias, and liberals claim that reporters are too respectful of powerful elites. Even if individual reporters and anchorpersons have a liberal bias, the media as a whole must be considered more conservative than not (Lotz, 1991). Often, ideological support for established institutions is very subtle, such as when striking workers in Communist Poland were described in glowing terms at the same time that striking American workers were dismissed as without legitimate grievances (Rachlin, 1986; Puette, 1992).

The great majority of American newspapers, owned by members of the economic upper strata, have consistently supported conservative candidates. Talk radio is dominated by extremely conservative voices, from Rush Limbaugh and Howard Stern to local call-in hosts who hear primarily from people who dislike feminists, immigrants, gays, minorities, and President and Mrs. Clinton (Berke, 1993c).

This debate, however, may be rendered meaningless as network news programs become less oriented toward journalism and more focused on entertainment gimmicks in order to win the "ratings" battle (a head count of consumers) and generate profit for their corporate owners (Greisman, 1987). "Infotain-

The media's coverage of sensational stories involving murder, sexual assaults, and rape is consumed in mass quantities, as witnessed by the dramatic popularity of numerous true life drama programs, such as "Rescue 911" and televised court proceedings. When O.J. Simpson, subsequently accused of murdering his ex-wife and her friend, fled from the L.A. police, 95 million Americans watched the low-speed freeway chase, and hundreds of fans made posters, ran out to the curb, and cheered him on. Why was this event covered by every major network when so many other stories are hardly noticed?

ment" programming has already replaced many of the time slots formerly devoted to in-depth reporting of social issues. For example, "A Current Affair," scheduled in prime time in many regions, is a very different news program from "Nightline," which airs late at night.

Even the national newscasts have increasingly come to resemble "Hard Copy." In 1994, for example, when the future of international peacekeeping was being decided in Bosnia and when our nation's health care system was being debated, the top news items concerned the marital problems of a couple named Lorena and John Wayne Bobbitt, the alleged sexual tendencies of singer Michael Jackson, an attack on an Olympic skater by a rival, the trials of a pair of wealthy teenagers who murdered their parents, and the live coverage by all major networks of pretrial hearings in the O. J. Simpson double-murder case. But this is apparently what the audience wants. When CNN—an all-news television network—cut away from the Bobbitt trial to cover a press conference by the President of the United States, the phone lines were jammed by complaining viewers (W. Goodman, 1994). And when all the networks cancelled their regular afternoon programs to cover the Los Angeles earthquake in 1993, viewers also took to the phone to

protest the preempting of their favorite soap opera. For the O. J. Simpson case, however, they remained glued to their sets during hours of slow questioning.

Nonetheless, the major networks retain some power to affect the public mood over historically significant events. Through their joint coverage of sacred moments, such as the funeral of a President, a royal wedding, or a visit by the Pope, they confer symbolic significance and allow ordinary citizens to participate in the great occasions (Dayan and Katz, 1992). The choice of what stories to cover or not to cover can have an impact on public policy. In 1992, heart-rending pictures of starving Somalis, shown night after night, appear to have changed American attitudes about intervening in that nation and forced the government to act. Yet in another part of Africa, the Sudan, millions of people were also starving to death, and no one at the United Nations suggested a relief mission. The difference was that there were no TV crews in the Sudan, hence there was no nightly reminder and therefore no pressure on political leaders (Goodman, 1992). If the camera does not see you, you are truly invisible.

POPULAR MUSIC

In this brief section we can only indicate the ways in which popular music—perhaps the aspect of the culture with which you are most familiar—illustrates the concepts discussed in this chapter. It is tempting to think of all forms of music and art as spontaneous expressions of one person's creative impulses. But items of culture, even those ultimately considered "classics" and thought to exist in a realm of timeless beauty, are produced in a particular context, at a particular time and place, within a circle of friends, audiences, gatekeepers, and critics (Subotnik, 1991; Sheperd, 1991).

Popular music is possibly the art form most influenced by its context (Ennis, 1993). Rhythm and lyrics emerge from the immediate experience of composers and performers, reflecting subcultural differences, and speaking to both personal and public issues. Yet not every song is recorded, played on the air, or stocked in a music store. Sociologists are interested in the chain of events that transforms one person's inspiration into an object of the popular culture.

The Popular Music Industry

As with any industry, the product—a song, album, group, concert, or video—is packaged for profit making. Today, a few major conglomerates dominate the industry, with the eight top companies producing more than 95 of the top-selling records and albums in 1990 (Lopes, 1992). The conglomerate will own several recording studios, a number of radio and television stations that play the item, the company that distributes recordings and videotapes, a chain of music/video retail stores, as well as the talent agency that represents the artists and arranges concert tours. Many scholars feared that this level of industry concentration and the emphasis on bottom line profit would limit expressive freedom and lead to the same kind of homogenized product found on network television (Firth, 1987). Some evidence indicates that cooperation between record companies and radio stations ensures that a few numbers will be played until listeners "burn out," to be followed by another offering in a similar artistic style, or **genre** (Rothenbuhler, 1987).

More striking, however, is the enormous range of variation, specialized genres, and stylistic mixtures of contemporary popular music. In part this outcome is due to the record companies' openness to innovation and diversity, which in turn reflects the fragmentation of the music audience into specific markets (Lopes, 1992). From country to grunge and "gangsta" rap, with dozens of genres and subgenres in between, and with increasing numbers of minority and women artists, the pop music scene is a kaleidoscope, in which the elements are continually shaken up to produce new combinations. It is perhaps the perfect art form for the postmodern mentality, where nothing remains quite the same for long (Kaplan, 1987).

THE MUSIC TELEVISION REVOLUTION.   This diversity in popular music owes much to the emergence of MTV, where it is on display every moment of every day. Music television stations emerged in the 1980s as part of the expansion of cable broadcasting, which opened up the possibility of specialized markets. Unlike network television, with its limited number of broadcast bands, cable programming can be economically successful by targeting a relatively small segment of the audience and staying with it 24 hours. Today, over 60 percent of American households receive cable programming, with round-the-clock video music channels as part of the basic service.

Originally highly conservative in its presentation and choice of artists, MTV has become increasingly radical in terms of topics, range of performers, and willingness to tolerate controversial views. Certainly, nowhere else on television will suburban audiences be exposed to the realities of working-class and inner-city life, the positive strengths as well as deepest resentments of people rarely shown on mainstream TV except as objects of fear or ridicule (Rapping, 1994). In addition to the expected commercials for the music and other products, MTV now features relatively irreverent news programs, full-length coverage of charity concerts, and documentaries on racism and homophobia, often more probing than those offered on network TV.

At the same time, many of the songs and videos celebrate the supermacho, gay-bashing, women-hat-ing boasting that strikes a responsive chord in its audience, primarily white working-class adolescents and young men painfully aware of their limited chances of upward mobility. MTV is also a world oriented to consumerism and immediate gratification, as befits a profit-making institution. In this sense, music television fully reflects a society in which even emotions of anger and protest can be turned into commodities, and working-class youth can be "cooled out" by the illusion of power.

Music as Protest

The origins of popular music in everyday experience make it a more immediate vehicle for protest than is the case for most other art forms. In American history, from "Yankee Doodle" to "We Shall Overcome," songs have expressed resistance to authority and hopes for change (Dunaway, 1987). The music of African Americans is especially illustrative, creating new sounds and rhythms to capture both the pain of slavery and the possibility of liberation, first in spirituals, then in soul, and now in rap.

A **genre** is a specific type of artistic style.

In the early days of this century, the labor movement provided new words to traditional folk melodies: "Joe Hill," "Union Maid," and "Solidarity Forever" rallied the white working class. In the 1930s, anticapitalist and prounion messages were an integral

Today's popular music is characterized by a wide range of musical styles and tastes that reflect the fragmentation of music audiences along class, race, gender, and age lines. Seattle has been home to a number of trend-setting musicians. Jimi Hendrix grew up there and, more recently, groups such as Smashing Pumpkins, Nine Inch Nails, and Pearl Jam (pictured here) have created the Seattle Grunge scene. Pearl Jam recently got into a battle with Ticketmaster, which they claim was charging their fans too much for tickets.

part of the Broadway musical theater. The songs of the Civil Rights Movement and antiwar movement of the 1960s followed in this tradition, not only in the soulfullness of the sound and emotional longing of lyrics such as "Blowin' In the Wind," but also in the belief that united efforts could change public policy (Garofalo, 1992).

In contrast, contemporary protest music emerges more as a howl of anger rather than an attempt to bring people together in the cause of profound social change. Punk, hard rock, heavy metal, and rap—all words that signify inflicting pain—test the limits of culturally permissible sound and lyrics. The sound is harsh, the words match, and middle-class adults react by "demonizing" the genre and trying to discredit the artists and their audience (Weinstein, 1992).

Heavy metal is the unique genre of white working class youth, lashing out in anger at the world that they know is hemming them in—the "Downward Spiral" of Nine Inch Nails or Pantera's "Far Beyond Driven." The brute strength of the music itself, the names of the bands, and concert behaviors such as thrashing and "moshing" can be viewed as rituals of male bonding that momentarily empower the socially powerless (Weinstein, 1991; Walser, 1993). Attempts to contain the nastiness through a system of voluntary labeling have probably done more to increase sales than to raise consciousness.

The unique protest genre of urban African-American male teenagers is *rap*, or *hip hop*, combining the ghetto game of playing the dozen or "snapping" (increasingly exaggerated and boastful verbal contests) with the beat of punk and rock, and a touch of Caribbean rhythm. In the late 1980s, when groups like Run-D.M.C. were given air time, rap achieved *crossover* success, accepted by the white audiences who compose the vast majority of concert goers, record buyers, and MTV viewers.

Today, 1980s rap appears almost lyrical, as each successive group, in the ghetto tradition of snapping, tries to outdo the other in outrageousness. The blending of rap and heavy metal by Public Enemy, Ice-T, Ice Cube, and N.W.A. has tapped a vein of black anger that also resonates to the rage of white adolescents. But when black artists speak of killing police and politicians, along with the usual sexual abuse of women, the lyrics are taken very seriously by the white establishment, leading to efforts at censorship, boycotts, and criminal charges. All of these reactions feed into the performers' claims of "telling it like it is," to the vast discomfort of the authorities. Their largely white audience revels in a temporary high on power, the vicarious experience of rebellion, shooting police, and raping women (Wurtzel, 1992b). Public Enemy's "Fight the Power" has achieved the status of a classic statement of revolutionary anger and romanticism (Berman, 1993). Even upwardly mobile African-American college students find affirmation of their experience in

rap music, especially when it is condemned by white elites (Kuwahara, 1992).

The most recent version, *"gangsta" rap*, with its roots in the extremely violent world of Los Angeles gangs, openly exalts random murder and raping, not of whites but of other inner-city residents. Record companies sign up performers named Dr. Dre and Snoop Doggy Dog on the grounds of presenting authentic ghetto voices to the enlightenment of the rest of the nation, and the records go right to the top of the charts. It is difficult to believe that anything can top these lyrics in portraying aimless violence and deepest hatred of women, but between now and when you read this book, a new subgenre will undoubtedly appear.

Hardest of all to classify is the genre loosely labeled as *alternative*, built on the punk rock subculture of the 1970s, proudly outside the mainstream and fiercely independent of commercial sponsorship. But the big-time music world has a way of absorbing all types of sound and artists, so that many alternative groups find themselves taken over by professional managers, regulated by concert contracts, and exposed to all the rewards and agonies of fame, as illustrated by the history of Nirvana and the inability of Kurt Cobain to deal with this kind of success (Ross, 1994).

The Lollapalooza festival also walks a fine line between commercial success and distancing itself from the mainstream. One problem is that one summer's "alternative" is next year's big money-maker; the other major problem is that one must still make deals with commercial promoters to find locations, arrange for technical support, and sell tickets. At this writing, Pearl Jam is locked in battle with Ticketmaster over the price of admission to events over which the ticket company has exclusive selling rights. As with so much of contemporary popular culture, business interests and the bottom line intrude on even the most authentic artistic impulses. The 25th anniversary of the Woodstock Music Festival of 1969, which had been attended by a half-million rock fans, most of whom paid nothing for three days of entertainment (they overran the ticket gates), cost the 1994 attendees at least $135 for two days (through Ticketmaster, of course). Although largely attended by footloose college-agers out for a good, non-political time, Woodstock II also ended in rain, mud, confusion, and tons of garbage.

Women in Popular Music

The world of rock music has not been kind to women, either in how they are depicted in the lyrics or in opportunities to perform (Lewis, 1990; Groce and Cooper, 1990). Until very recently, the rock music scene has been the exclusive turf of men—as artists and writers, agents, promoters, disk and video jockeys, arrangers, and company executives. In addition to the routine sexism of any business sector, the particular elements of the music (the beat, loudness, pounding power, and risk-taking) are masculine in sound, a mode of expression thought automatically to exclude women, or at least those who still wished to be perceived as feminine.

In the early 1990s, however, female rock groups began to attract a concert audience, and a few have been picked up by the major recording studios. Some are openly feminist and angry, with a sound as loud and abrasive as the men's groups, and a clear message: "Don't mess with us." Riot Grrrls, L7, Hole, and Liz Phair are not afraid to appear unfeminine even as they explore the female experience. Interestingly, in spite of the openly feminist politics of many of the new groups, women in rock continue to be referred to and to call themselves "girls" (Wurtzel, 1992a). Their challenge to the sexist traditions of the field will depend on audience support. Are enough adolescent men willing to cross over in terms of sex as well as race? Are younger American women willing to appear so angry and independent?

The built-in dilemma of women in rock is that the very nature of the genre—reveling in open sexual-

Since the early 1990s, female rock groups who are openly feminist and angry have begun to attract concert audiences and major recording studios. Among the growing number of female rap singers, Queen Latifah is especially concerned with not turning women into sex objects and in improving the self-image and self-respect of African-American women. She has also crossed over to television with a sitcom called "Living Single," about the trials and tribulations of four twenty-something Black women and the men in their lives.

ity—turns performers into sex objects, which is precisely what the feminist artists are rebelling against (Powers, 1993a).

This dilemma is played out most clearly in music videos featuring girl groups, primarily African American, whose on camera appearance and gestures are extremely provocative, yet who sing about female control over their sexuality and the men they chose to please them (Leland, 1994). The rap singer Queen Latifah is especially concerned about telling young black women that they aren't bitches or whores but are worthy of self-respect and the respect of men—not an easy task in the face of the enormous appeal of the gangsta rappers.

OTHER GENRES.   Other music genres have been much more receptive to women artists than has rock. *Country music* and *blues,* in particular, with their softer sound and romantic themes, are naturals for women singing of unrequited love: No matter how badly he's treated her, she's lonely when he's gone and she would prefer to be mistreated than to be without her man. Because of its origins in the world view of white rural folk in the most conservative parts of the nation, country music has been highly supportive of traditional views of gender, politics, sexual orientation, and religious faith.

But even here, the times are changing. Gender stereotypes are being revised, with the women more assertive and the men less macho than in the past. When superstar Garth Brooks sings about being free to love anyone we choose and to worship from a variety of pews, something new is being added to the usual mix of patriotism and piety (Altman, 1993).

These newer trends may also liberate country music from its obsession with marital problems, alcoholism, and alienation from work—all of which are associated with family violence and self-destructiveness. As reported in one study, the more airtime devoted to country music in the listening area, the higher the suicide rate for whites, regardless of the area's rates of divorce, poverty, gun ownership, or location in the South (Stack and Gundlach, 1992).

The importance of the female audience is also evident in the recent revival of the *New Wave* music of the late 1970s and early 1980s: Duran Duran, Cyndi Lauper, and the B-52s are back. Appealing to girls and women who would prefer not to be beaten and dismembered, as well as others not moved by rock and rap, the old-New Wave sounds are a welcome relief to listeners who have felt somewhat marginal to the pop music scene (Powers, 1993b).

As this brief overview suggests, the sociological analysis of popular music can illuminate the world of creators and consumers and tell us something about the public mood and about race and gender in our contemporary America. Can you apply this model to the form and content of the music that most appeals to you and your friends?

Hate Culture

One of the fascinating aspects of American popular culture in the late 1980s was the degree to which "hate speech" entered everyday life, through the airwaves, in comedy clubs, and most clearly and loudly, in the music (Cruz, 1990). Typical targets for white male performers are minorities, feminists, gays, immigrants, and the disabled. Typical targets for black male performers are whites, the police, feminists, gays, immigrants, and the disabled. If this is the humor and music of people with grievances (young men for the most part) how interesting that it is directed against the even more powerless rather than at the political and economic elites that control the fate of the less fortunate.

But there is a double standard of hate speech. As long as the targets are women, homosexuals, and racial minorities, the speech is considered good fun (Rush Limbaugh and Howard Stern have written best-selling books) and no one suggests that it is not protected by the First Amendment. When the hate comes from African Americans playing at being ghetto cool and is directed at white police ("Cop Killer") or at those perceived as wealthy and powerful (as in the remarks about Jews and the Pope by Nation of Islam speakers), members of Congress immediately vote to condemn it and to suggest ways to limit its expression

At the moment, the audience—white and black—for the talk shows and record albums shows no sign of diminishing, and the speech becomes increasingly outrageous. All of which may say more about the public temper than does anything else in this book.

SPORTS

Sports differ from more playful athletic activities in being organized by rules. In this sense, a marathon differs from jogging, and ice dancing from skating on the neighborhood pond. Sports have the following features (Edwards, 1973): (1) Clear standards of performance, (2) involving physical exertion through competition, (3) governed by norms that define role relationships, (4) typically performed by organized groups, (5) with the goal of achieving a reward by defeating others.

> **Sports** are a form of structured behavior with values, norms, statuses, and roles, linked to other institutional spheres and stratification hierarchies.

As with other aspects of culture, sports are a form of structured behavior with values, norms, statuses, and roles linked to other institutional spheres and stratification hierarchies. As with other modern institutions, sports are characterized by increasing specialization (the designated hitter), bureaucratic organization (NCAA, NBA, etc.), quantification (stats), and a gradual equality of opportunity (Guttmann, 1978).

Sports reflect and reinforce important societal values. In the United States, these include hard work, competition, manliness, and commercialism (Wilson, 1994). In other societies, sports embody varied national problems and goals, such as unifying a new nation (Lever, 1983) or lending prestige to the government (MacIntosh and Whitson, 1990).

It can be argued that organized sport in the United States has become the functional equivalent of a religion, with its gods (the players), high priests (team owners), scribes (writers), shrines (arenas), holy days (Superbowl Sunday), handmaidens (cheerleaders), and rituals such as singing the national anthem (Eitzen and Sage, 1993). When faced with uncertainty, the athletes engage in magic rituals, such as wearing certain items of clothing, crossing themselves, or repeating a set of gestures (Womack, 1992). In many European and South American countries, soccer is the object of fanatical devotion, pilgrimages to championship games, and fierce admiration of star players, whose pictures decorate homes and places of business. In 1994, a disappointed fan murdered the Colombian player whose error had caused the team to lose in World Cup play.

Amateur Sports in the United States

By definition, an *amateur* is one who performs for the sheer pleasure of playing the game; the word comes from the Latin word for love. One's personal best is an end in itself. Playing for pay is instrumental and transforms the amateur into a professional. For most of Western history, only the wealthy could afford to play without compensation, and such sports as tennis and fencing were pastimes of aristocratic men. Badminton was about as strenuous as it got for women. Today, amateur athletics in the United States are associated with college athletic programs or with working-class activities organized at the local level, such as bowling or softball leagues.

COLLEGE SPORTS. Until the 1950s, college athletic programs came close to the amateur ideal, in which the sons of the middle and upper classes combined the rigors of physical competition with academic studies on their way to a comfortable adulthood. As universities grew in size and as a large national audience for sports telecasts was developed, the nature of college athletic programs changed radically.

Sports are activities with a clear standard of performance, involve physical exertion through competition, are governed by norms, are performed by organized groups, and have the goal of defeating others. Rugby is one sport that exemplifies such characteristics. Can you name others?

Universities and colleges today are multimillion-dollar enterprises, with buildings and grounds to maintain, faculty and staff to pay, and thousands of students to house, feed, and educate. Because student fees cover only part of the cost, schools must turn to alumni donors, state legislatures, and television sport fees for the additional revenue. Teams with a winning record enhance all three sources of income. Their games are likely to be televised, which also opens up alumni pocketbooks, influences state legislators to increase funding for the school, and attracts applicants (Alfano, 1989; Fizel and Bennett, 1989). Television fees alone are substantial; millions to the schools with NCAA basketball finalists or football bowl teams.

As a result, college athletic programs have become big business, with a separate budget, and relatively free of academic administrative controls. A head coach with endorsement contracts and television appearances can earn three times the salary of the college president or state governor and be better known. The pressure to field a winning team becomes intense, taking precedence over such concerns as the school's academic rank or the intellectual development of its athletes. Administrators look the other way, faculty advisors are co-opted, and recruitment violations become commonplace (Sperber, 1990).

SOCIAL POLICY

The College Athlete as Professional Amateur

A number of blatant recruitment violations brought the issue of college athletic programs into the national spotlight in the late 1980s, leading the National Collegiate Athletic Association (NCAA) to bar several schools from competition for a short period and to attempt to raise the qualifications for receiving an athletic scholarship.

Many entering athletes, especially in the money-making basketball and football programs, are ill prepared for campus life. They come poorly prepared academically, with naive expectations of breezing through school while spending most of their time preparing for a professional career, only to discover that even the relatively undemanding nature of the course work selected by their coaches is more than they can handle (Adler and Adler, 1991). Scholarship athletes from a middle-class background, white or African-American, will graduate at a rate only slightly lower than that of all students; but those from lower-income homes, especially inner-city black men, will graduate at only half the rate of other athletes (Lederman, 1993a).

Although many college athletes expect to enter the professional ranks, only a very small number will succeed or remain in the pros for more than a few years. The odds of becoming a professional athlete are extremely low, as shown in Table 22-1 for 1990; since then, league expansions have increased the numbers, but odds of reaching the majors have not changed significantly (Coakley, 1994) The average professional career today is between 7.5 years in baseball to under 4 years in football.

Because a majority of nongraduating athletes are minority youth, the schools could be charged with exploiting the athletes' talents. The top players bring up to one million dollars a year to their university but use up only $20,000 in scholarship aid (*Chronicle of Higher Education*, 1994). Yet if academic require-

TABLE 22-1 Major League Career Opportunities, 1990

Approximate number of players in:	Baseball	Football	Basketball
High school	400,000	750,000	550,000
College	21,000	40,000	14,000
Major leagues	625	2,300	280
Rookies per year	100	250	55
Average length of career (years)	7.5	4.0	5

Source: W. Leonard II, *Sociological Perspective on Sports,* 4/e Macmillan Publishing Company, 1993.

ments for admission and eligibility were raised, some minority youth would lose their only chance for higher education. At the moment, African Americans are only 6 percent of all students, but hold 22.3 percent of all athletic scholarships, up to 60 percent for basketball players (Lederman, 1992). If athletic scholarships were withdrawn, would the schools put as much money into academic scholarships for minority students?

What should be done for and about athletes who are academically disadvantaged? Bar them from college? Admit a few and provide extensive and expensive remedial services? Forbid all freshmen from varsity play? Or end the illusion of amateurism altogether by hiring the athletes, just as teachers and other staff are hired, and allowing them to use their earnings for tuition or any other purpose?

HIGH SCHOOL ATHLETES. Many of the problems currently affecting athletes in higher education are already evident in lower grades. As college sports become big business, the interest of fans, recruiters, and TV networks is increasingly drawn to high school contests. When high schools are offered fees for televising championship games, can local school boards resist temptation?

A more immediate problem for the high school athlete is "burnout," complete exhaustion. As with any work-related physical condition in our society, the common explanation is that the individual could not handle the stress—a form of blaming the victim. In contrast, a sociological model would examine the social organization of high school sports, how the athlete gives up control of his or her life to the coach, the structuring of time, the loss of alternative sources of identity, and parental pressures (Coakley, 1992).

Not only is there little evidence of any long-term positive effect of participation in high school sports, but quite the opposite appears to be the case, in terms of school achievement and earnings (Vanfossen et al., 1989). Time spent on sport is time that could be used to improve grades, but the idealization of teenage jocks and the low status accorded to serious students ("nerds") will keep many marginal student-athletes from hitting the books (Stein and Hoffman, 1980). And as Table 22-1 illustrates, the chances of becoming a professional athlete or staying long in the sport remains exceedingly slim.

Sports and American Values

SPORTS AND THE WORK ETHIC. The ideology of sport embraces such basic American virtues as competition, achievement, courage, self-control, discipline, dedication, success, teamwork *and* individual effort. Sound familiar? These are all elements of the work ethic described in Chapter 3. In many ways, socialization to sport is an introduction to industrial capitalism, including an overriding obsession with winning at any cost. As the football coach, Vince Lombardi, put it: "Winning isn't everything, it's the *only* thing." This is a far cry from the amateur ideal of playing your best as an end in itself. The idea that losing represents personal failure is also bound up with traditional conceptions of gender.

SPORTS AND MANLINESS. Sports are a major test of masculinity in our society (and most others). The qualities ascribed to winners, whether male or female, are those typically associated with manliness: strength, courage, coolness under pressure, and self-reliance. Team play is socialization to the uniquely masculine world of the locker room, a haven from the demands of women. Yet the athletes perfect their bodies and skills not to impress women as much as other men, creating a bond among them while also creating a dominance hierarchy within each sport, including body building (Messner and Sabo, 1994; Klein, 1993). Women intrude on this life space (even reporters doing their jobs) at some risk. Traditional masculinity is reinforced through a shared degradation of women (Curry, 1991). The linking of sex, violence, and power often spills over into life outside the locker room as seen in the cases of Mike Tyson and O. J. Simpson (Nelson, 1994; Crosset et al., 1994).

Beginning with Little League, gender identity is a prime motivator of a boy's involvement in sport, with the strong encouragement of parents. In high school and college, the task of constructing a masculine identity continues to attract men to varsity sports and remains crucial to the decision of whether or not to become a professional. The achievement of a masculine identity through sports is more characteristic of men from minority and low-income families than of men whose race and resources permit a wider choice of careers in which to display male competence (Messner, 1992).

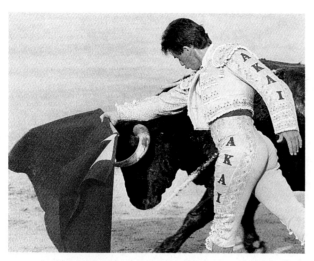

In recent years, athletes all over the world have become living advertisements for various products. The Spanish bullfighter Louis Reina, for example, stunned his audience when he appeared in the ring with advertising on his sequined suit. On his arms and legs he displayed the letters AKAI, the name of a Japanese electronics firm.

Precisely the opposite pressures weigh on female athletes; to become a jock is to place one's femininity in question, as discussed later in this section.

SPORTS AS BIG BUSINESS.   Above all, sports today are big business. Ball players are bought and sold like any other commodity and moved from city to city in the pursuit of profit for the owners. The athletes have also profited from the "industrialization of sport": average salaries in 1993-94 were $1,250,000 in the National Basketball Association (NBA), $1,188,000 in major league baseball, $496,000 in the National Football League (NFL), and $379,000 in the National Hockey League (NHL) (Coakley, 1994; Chass, 1994). These numbers represent major percentage increases from the 1967-68 season, when athletes in all four professional leagues averaged about $20,000.

The big winners, however, are the owners. Money from ticket sales is only part of their income. Millions more come from television revenues and fees from concessions (parking, food and drink, souvenirs, and merchandise). Owning a team is like owning a gold mine; none has sold for less than its previous price. If you don't like the appearance of your arena or stadium, try "sportmail": Threaten to leave town if the city government can't come up with millions of dollars in renovations (Sage, 1993). The owners are, in effect, being subsidized by every local taxpayer, even the poor, while most of the owners' income is sheltered from taxes by a variety of write-offs (Zimbalist, 1992). But as long as the focus is on players' salaries, the owners can claim that high personnel costs have forced them to raise the price of tickets.

The threat of moving the franchise is very real. As the older cities of the Northeast become increasingly poor and populated by minorities, and the regular ticket buyers have moved to the suburbs or to the South and West, the owners would prefer to migrate themselves. Today's owners are different from those in the past, who were superfans with deep roots in the home town. The new breed are primarily business people looking for a profitable investment (Staudohar and Mangan, 1991). Of all the factors that could affect a franchise move—age of the stadium, club record, attendance, other sources of income—the one that most accurately predicted whether or not the team stayed was the racial composition of the neighborhood: the darker the faces, the more likely is the team to move (Lipsyte, 1993).

The commercialization of sports has spread to the Olympic Games, the last bastion of amateurism, but so many nations violated the norms by subsidizing athletes to bring glory to the nation that the pretense has been gradually dropped. In the 1994 Winter Olympics, professional skaters competed with legitimate amateurs, and most of the ice hockey players had played for pay. Rights to telecast the 1996 Summer Games from Atlanta, Georgia, cost NBC $456 million, plus production expenses. The network expects to turn a profit, however, from advertisements.

SPORT VIOLENCE.   A number of factors, cultural and physical, have contributed to an upsurge in sports violence on the field and in the stands. On the field, a sense of male honor and a fear of defeat motivate individual players; owners and coaches are fueled by the

Although athletes on major professional teams have profited from their popularity, it is the team owners who have profited the most. Their money comes from ticket sales, television revenues, concessions, and various tax breaks and tax shelters. By the way, can you find your seat in the bleachers from here?

PATRICIA A. ADLER
PETER ADLER

"Behind the Locker Room Door"

Patricia A. Adler is Associate Professor of Sociology at the University of Colorado. Peter Adler is Professor of Sociology at the University of Denver. In addition to Backboards and Blackboards, the Adlers together have written Membership Roles in Field Research, and edited several books. They are founding editors of Sociological Studies of Child Development and currently edit the Journal of Contemporary Ethnography.

We met as freshmen in college, in the early 1970s, a time of great upheaval and excitement on American college campuses. We, too, were part of the general reaction against the Vietnam War. How could hundreds of thousands of students like ourselves, all over the country and all over the world, get caught up in a movement of action and ideas at the same time? Searching for answers to this question in the classes we took, we found that only the sociological perspective had the power to connect broader cultures and societies with the attitudes and behaviors of groups of people.

Our study of sociology has been fascinating and full of discovery. We have been fortunate in linking our personal biographies to our research endeavors, giving meaning and relevance to our work. Whenever possible, we have studied those things that have been close to us. All along, we have maintained the notion that

the best way to study people was to get close them, to live among them, and to try to share in their lives. Our approach, called ethnography or participant-observation, demands that we, as researchers, become part of the settings we study.

Our work with college basketball players grew out of just such a belief. We both came from strong sports backgrounds. Patti lettered in three varsity sports in high school, at a time when girls could not always legitimately play sports. She often wondered what it would be like to have grown up in a society where women could play sports professionally and why established gender roles did not permit it. Peter has been a rabid sports fan for as long as he can remember, frequently wondering what it was like behind-the-scenes, what went on in the locker room, what the players talked about, and how they prepared for their games.

We began integrating our interest and knowledge of sport with our professional lives in graduate school. Our first published article was about "momentum" in sport, when a team was either streaking or slumping. Peter's ability to apply the sociological imagination to their world made him a regular speaker at the coach's basketball camps and a sociological advisor to the team. He counseled players on academic matters, helped orient them to their new surroundings and the options their futures held (or didn't hold). Peter eventually was made an assistant coach on the team, attending team meetings and practices, travelling with the team on the road, and working in the backstage arena he once glimpsed from afar. Patti took the role of a coach's wife with the coaches, boosters, and other wives,

and, with Peter, as a close friend to many of the players.

Thus, we were able to experience, firsthand, the complex lives of college athletes. Without exception, the recruits had anticipated being big men on campus, handling their coursework with moderate ease, and having fun playing basketball while simultaneously advancing their chances of a professional career. But most were unable to satisfy the competing demands of their academic, social, and athletic roles: their classes were harder than they expected and they often performed poorly; they were separated from other students by housing, practice schedules, and racial and class barriers and their athletic experiences were work infused and demeaning. To the fans and the media, athletes found themselves larger-than-life representatives of the program, expected to live up to idealized images. To the wealthy boosters, they were sources of social status, who could be displayed for friends. To the coaches they were a meal ticket, to be manipulated into maintaining peak emotional intensity for playing basketball. By the time they finally learned to cope, their eligibility was up and they were out, often with no diploma, and few chances at a professional career.

Our investigation showed us that everyday life scenes often look a lot different from the inside than they do to outsiders. Many of the insights of the sociological perspective, in fact, anticipate and predict such an outcome. We urge you to take your sociological learnings and apply them to everyday life all around you, just as we have, to gain a deeper and occasionally surprising understanding of your world.

need to win at all costs. The heightened level of competition and must-win philosophy lead to conditions that have produced an increase in the number and severity of player injuries. Steroid use produces outsized players, so that lighter equipment is required to increase their mobility. Artificial playing surfaces place greater strain on the leg muscles and provide less cushion for falls. But the turf looks green all the time and vacuuming is cheaper than mowing. As a result, the average playing career of a professional football player has dropped from 4.5 years in 1985 to about 3.5 in 1994 (Coakley, 1994). Two-thirds of retiring football players today leave the game with a permanent injury, yet the owners continue to ask for changes in the worker compensation rules to avoid having to make long-term disability payments (Smith, 1992). The athletes learn to accept pain and injury as a normal aspect of their career, despite increasing health risks (Curry, 1993).

Spectator violence also has cultural and physical causes. Seating areas in many arenas and stadiums are uncomfortable and poorly maintained. In many European soccer stadiums, the lowest-cost seat is standing room in a fenced-off pen, often elbow-to-elbow with fans from the other team. Young working-class men with a bit too much to drink, egged on by their buddies, can find a ready target for displays of aggressive masculinity, and the fight is on (Murphy et al., 1990; Buford, 1994). Although this kind of "soccer hooliganism" is relatively rare in the United States, rampaging crowds often engage in vandalism and violence following a major hometown victory.

Sports and Stratification

Sports are both democratic and highly stratified. There is something for everyone, from sandlot ball to polo. Where pure skill is important, the trend is toward democratization, but there is also a prestige hierarchy of sports.

SOCIAL CLASS.   Social class is an important determinant of who plays at what. Activities that require expensive equipment, special facilities, and long periods of expensive training (tennis, golf, swimming, skating, polo) are usually only available to the relatively affluent. In contrast, low-income athletes are likely to take up boxing, basketball, baseball, and track—sports that require minimal outlays of money and that can be practiced almost anywhere. The distribution of athletes by class and race is not a function of talent but of different resources and opportunities. It is as rare to see an upper-class white in professional basketball (such as Bill Bradley) as to find an African American on the professional golfers' tour (such as Calvin Peete). The Winter Olympics is an all-white affair, just as the Summer Games are dominated by black athletes.

RACISM.   The dramatic expansion of professional sports and the impact of the Civil Rights Movement have opened the gates for minority players, but the road to athletic glory was long, lonely, and very ugly (Ashe, 1988). In 1947, the first African American in professional baseball, Jackie Robinson, was openly subjected to abuse from teammates and fans. Because entry into professional basketball and football is typically through college experience, blacks could be effectively excluded from those sports until the 1960s.

Although race is no longer a factor in different salary scales (Sommers, 1990), discrimination remains quite high in the "country club" sports of golf, tennis, and swimming. And even in sports where African Americans and Hispanic Americans now dominate,

Spectator violence has a number of cultural and physical causes and usually involves young working-class men who have a few drinks before and during the game. Here Argentinian and German fans clash outside the soccer stadium where the two teams met in a World Cup soccer championship in Rome, Italy.

racism is not altogether absent. When the players are black and the fans are white, an owner could lose money while winning games. One solution to the problem of hiring minority players without alienating the majority of fans is to practice stacking (Staples, 1989).

Stacking refers to the placement of players on the basis of the importance of the position. In football, the central positions are quarterback, center, and kicker/punters. In 1994, among NFL players, 93 percent of quarterbacks, 79 percent of centers, and 94 percent of kickers/punters were white. In contrast, all but a few running backs and wide receivers were black, as were the great majority of defensive players (Coakley, 1994). Clearly, nothing in nature dictates that whites are destined to be quarterbacks and blacks to be fullbacks.

> **Stacking** involves placing white athletes in positions that involve more responsibility and control than the positions largely occupied by minority students.

In baseball, the central positions are pitcher, catcher, and third base. In 1993, 82 percent of pitchers, 87 percent of catchers, and 75 percent of third basemen were white, in contrast to the largely black and Latino outfield (Coakley, 1994). Even though basketball is now thoroughly dominated by African-American players, stacking can be seen in the likelihood that the few white players (21 percent of the total in the NBA in 1994) are primarily centers. In other words, the further from the center and more removed from decision-making responsibilities, the higher the proportion of minority players.

Breaking into the ranks of coaching and front-office management jobs has been slower and more difficult, but the numbers are slowly changing, especially in basketball (Lapchick and Benedict, 1994). A more subtle form of racism can be found in the comments of sports announcers who tend to explain the success of white players in terms of intelligence and hard work—the "work ethic." Minority athletes, in contrast, are described as having "natural" skills—"raw talent."

UPWARD MOBILITY. In general, sport and entertainment have served as mobility channels for unusually talented Americans from the Irish in the early part of the century, followed by Jews and Italians between 1920 and 1960, and currently by African-American and Latino singers, dancers, and athletes.

The extremely high salaries of today's entertainers and athletes may give the illusion of great upward mobility, but only for a few. The crucial decisions that affect the nation are not made in left field of Yankee Stadium or on a Las Vegas stage, but on Wall Street, the U.S. Senate, and the White House, where one must look very hard for more than the token minority.

Women and Sports

The association of sport with masculinity has served to inhibit many girls and women from becoming skilled athletes, and has also made their presence in sport resented by boys and men. In 1972, however, the Education Act was amended to include a clause, Title IX, forbidding discrimination on the basis of sex to schools receiving federal funds, but few, even today, have programs for girls and women equivalent to those offered to boys and men, and some schools are trying to bypass Title IX by calling cheerleading a sport.

Nonetheless, opportunities for female athletes have improved enormously since 1972, especially in the public schools. While the number of boy participants in school sports declined slightly between 1972 and 1991, the numbers for girls increased more than 600 percent, reaching close to 60 percent of the boys' total by 1990 (National Federation, 1991).

As for higher education, the Supreme Court ruled in 1984 that Title IX applied only to specific programs receiving federal funding rather than the institution as a whole. Colleges and universities therefore are no longer under an obligation to provide equal opportu-

Despite continuing obstacles to sports equity, the performances of women athletes have improved dramatically. For example, at the 1994 Winter Olympics, American women won ten of the eleven individual medals. Bonnie Blair became the first speed skater of either sex to capture a gold medal in the same event, the 500 meters, in three consecutive Winter Olympics. What changes would support greater sports equity?

nity if the athletic program receives no federal funding. As a result, opportunities for female college athletes and coaches remain limited (Theberge, 1993). A 1993 report from the NCAA urged colleges to promote sex equity and to abide by Title IX but proposed no incentives for compliance or suggestions for funding (Lederman, 1993b).

ABSENCE OF ENCOURAGEMENT. Parents and peers are more likely to discourage than to encourage a girl's athletic interests. The evidence, however, indicates that female athletes, like their male counterparts, benefit from testing their strength, endurance, and courage. Nonetheless, they must deal with rumors and innuendos about their sexual orientation (Blum, 1994). For those who persevere, the rewards are typically smaller than for their male counterparts: fewer and smaller trophies for amateurs, less money for professionals. Coverage and description of women athletes in the media continue to reflect this double standard of achievement (Messner et al., 1993).

The sports in which schoolgirls excel are those that require little equipment or other expense: track, gymnastics, and volleyball. They are also encouraged to pursue "ladylike" activities that stress grace and beauty, such as figure skating, swimming, and tennis.

SPORTS EQUITY. Despite lack of support from parents, peers, and authorities, the idea of sports equity has seeped into the public consciousness, and the performance of female athletes has gradually continued to improve. The time gap between men and women racers has steadily narrowed.

The two fields in which women have a long history of professional accomplishment—golf and tennis—have gained in television coverage and prize money for women, although the men's prestige and earnings remain much higher. In the Olympic Games, the inclusion and coverage of women's events have increased dramatically. For example, women comprised fewer than 10 percent of the athletes in the Olympics of 1948, compared with more than one-third of the athletes in 1994. In the Winter Olympics of 1994, American women accounted for the lion's share of medals won by the United States team.

Nonetheless, strong prejudices remain. For many men, sport is the last field of achievement that they can consider their own, embodying all that they value, and setting them apart as unique and superior. Sharing these achievements with women will be difficult but no longer impossible.

SUMMARY

1. Popular culture includes what people do in their free time and the products designed for mass consumption. It serves several functions, including keeping people informed and entertained, reinforcing essential values, and bringing people together in shared rituals.

2. The conflict perspective focuses on who has control over the production of culture and whose values and power are promoted.

3. A distinction is often made between elite culture and mass culture. Mass culture has been criticized for being vulgar and open to political manipulation. However, it has been defended by supporters of cultural pluralism and praised for the variety of taste cultures that typify our society.

4. Popular culture is manufactured the same way as any commodity, involving producers, distributors, and consumers.

5. Popular culture is transmitted through mass media. Most Americans depend on mass media, especially television and newspapers, for their information and entertainment.

6. Whereas, in much of the world, media are owned and operated by the government, in the United States media are privately owned, profit-making enterprises. The current trend is toward increasing concentration of media ownership.

7. Although a debate continues about the direct effects of mass media, there appear to be more subtle long-range effects that cannot yet be measured.

8. Mass media are important in setting agendas, framing and formatting stories, and bringing selected issues to the public's attention.

9. Popular music is an example of the way popular culture is produced. As an industrial product, it is packaged for profit making with a few conglomerates dominating the industry.

10. The expansion of cable programming allows the targeting of small segments of the public. Music television has become increasingly radical in terms of topics, range of performers, and willingness to deal with controversial topics.

11. Even though popular music is controlled by commercial interests, its history lies in songs of political protest. African-American music has a long history of expressing the pain of oppression and the possibility of freedom.

12. The record industry, as with other businesses, is stratified by race and gender. Different music is aimed at divided markets with some "crossover

effect" when African-American music becomes popular with white audiences. The music industry, despite increasing participation by women, continues to be dominated by men.

13. Sports are also an important aspect of popular culture. Both amateur and professional sports express strongly held values regarding work, manliness, and violence.

14. Although amateurs are not supposed to be paid to perform, college recruiting scandals and illegal gifts have focused attention on college athletic programs, raising issues of the academic integrity of the colleges and the exploitation of the athletes themselves.

15. The trend toward commercialization, which is already evident at the high school level, has made sports more democratic but also more prone to inequalities of race, social class, and gender.

16. Although the expansion of professional sports has provided opportunities for minority players, the practice of stacking and limited job opportunities beyond playing days have minimized upward mobility through sports.

17. Women made substantial advances in sports in the 1970s through enforcement of Title IX legislation, but this slowed down in the 1980s, when the law was no longer enforced. The absence of encouragement poses another barrier to fuller participation. Despite these barriers, sports equity has become more acceptable, and the performances of women athletes have improved substantially.

SUGGESTED READINGS

Blumler, Jay G., Jack M. McLeod, and Karl Erik Rosengren, eds. *Comparitively Speaking: Communication and Culture Across Space and Time.* Newbury Park, CA: Sage, 1992. An anthology using a comparative approach to the study of communication in seven different countries.

Epstein, Jonathan S., ed. *Adolescents and Their Music: If It's Too Loud, You're Too Old.* Hamden, CT: Garland Publishing, 1994. A contribution to the sociology of youth culture. A look at the vital issues concerning youth and their relationship to their music, including topics such as rap music's place in urban subculture, social criticism and alienation, and political status of youth and youth culture.

Garofalo, Reebee, (ed.) *Rockin' the Boat: Mass Music and Mass Movements.* Boston: South End Press, 1992. A compilation of timely essays that look at the relationship between mass music and social change in numerous countries and cultures.

Messner, Michael A. and Donald F. Sabo. *Sex, Violence and Power in Sports: Rethinking Masculinity.* The Crossing Press, 1994. After an analysis of such timely topics as homophobia, sports violence, spousal abuse, and gender equity, the authors make suggestions about how sports could be changed in order for men to change.

Neuman, W. Russell, Marion R. Just, and Ann N. Crigler. *Common Knowledge: News and the Construction of Political Meaning.* Chicago: University of Chicago Press, 1992. An exploration of how the media creates public "common knowledge."

Schudson, Michael. *Watergate in American Memory: How We Remember, Forget and Reconstruct the Past.* New York: Basic, 1992. An eloquent work on the fading memory of Watergate and the many "uses" made of this most important Constitutional crisis by politicians, reporters, and political interest groups.

Spigel, Lynn. *Make Room for TV: Television and the Family Ideal in Postwar America.* Chicago: University of Chicago Press, 1992. Fascinating questions are raised about television, family, and gender relations in this study of television and its incorporation into the American family.

23

Collective Behavior and Social Movements

*W*ithin the past few years, the following events have occurred:

- Dozens of schools in Egypt were closed when thousands of teenage girls were affected by spells of fainting and nausea.
- Within days of a report of a hypodermic needle being found in a soft drink can, police received hundreds of other complaints of tampering.
- Every October 30th, murder rumors have made the rounds of American college campuses.
- Millions of Americans made a pilgrimage to a village in Croatia, where several children say that the Virgin Mary has appeared daily.
- Major cities of the world were rocked by street riots. Those most notably affected were in Germany, India, and Russia, and in Los Angeles, California.
- Demonstrators blocked the entrances to family planning clinics.

These very different events are all examples of **collective behavior,** in which a number of people act outside established patterns and social structures, often in response to change and uncertainty in the broader society. Collective behavior is typically less structured than that of a formal group, although personal ties often influence involvement. The category includes everything from a momentary fad to an extended effort to change the society. When the attempt at social change becomes institutionalized in formal organizations, we speak of a *social movement.*

TYPES OF COLLECTIVE BEHAVIOR

One way to impose order on the diversity of collective behaviors is to arrange them along such dimensions as: (1) spontaneous versus structured, (2) short-term versus long-term commitments, (3) expressive versus instrumental goals, and (4) unconscious versus conscious motives for participation. For example, the

continuum for spontaneity might look like that in Figure 23-1.

Relatively Spontaneous Forms of Collective Behavior

In general, events that are relatively spontaneous are also short-lived, expressive, and without clear goals. Fads, panics, and mass hysteria appear to be so unpredictable that they are also assumed to be irrational. But collective behavior, even the most unstructured, is rarely random and usually is linked to social conditions and processes.

Mass hysteria, for example, involves uncontrolled reactions to anxiety, yet most outbreaks can be traced to stresses or strains in the social environment. It is no accident that most contemporary cases involve either school children or women whose job involves simple, repetitive tasks (Golden, 1990). These are relatively powerless people, engaged in extremely boring work, and who have cultural permission to act "irrationally." The episode of mass hysteria breaks up the dullness of their days, produces momentary empowerment, and brings them to the center of attention—in an Egyptian city as well as in your hometown junior high.

Panics are typically grounded in perceived threats and fears, such as among people who leave their home, sell their worldly goods, and flee to survival camps to await the end of the world. The essence of panic behavior is an overwhelming need to escape danger. Panics also occur on Wall Street when brokers who fear a sudden major loss sell off se-

> **Collective behavior** refers to actions outside established patterns and social structures in response to social change and uncertainty.
>
> **Mass hysteria** involves uncontrollable reactions to anxiety, most of which can be traced to stresses or strains in the social environment.
>
> **Panics** are actions caused by the need to escape perceived threats and fears.

Figure 23-1 A continuum of collective behavior.

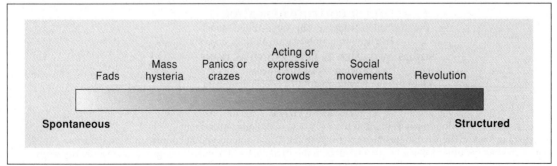

A memorable example of collective behavior occurred in Woodstock, New York, in 1969 when over 400,000 people celebrated their youth, affection for one another, and commitment to peace at a three day rock concert. In the summer of 1994 the two original organizers, now businessmen, organized a "reunion" which drew about 300,000 people including some of those who performed and attended the original Woodstock. Do you think the original "spirit" of Woodstock was recaptured twenty-five years later?

curities, creating a massive drop in values that leads to more selling.

Crazes, in contrast, involve an intense desire to have something that everyone else appears to be enjoying, such as Nintendo games, all-terrain vehicles, or baseball caps. Advertisers play on the American tendency to define success and rank people in terms of material possessions.

Fads are short-lived but widely copied outbursts of unexpected and often playful behavior. Colleges are prime sites for fads, from swallowing goldfish in the 1920s, to running across campus without clothing ("streaking") in the 1970s, to dying one's hair green or red today. These are gestures designed to shock authorities, a last gasp of irresponsibility before settling down, but they tend to be strongly influenced by inter-

personal networks and media attention (Aguirre et al., 1988). To consider fads as the impulsive acts of isolated campus oddballs is to overlook the social pattering that underlies their spread and intensity.

Fashions are more enduring, widespread, and socially significant than either crazes or fads. Trendsetters define what is "in" or "out," and networks of influence carry the message. The direction of influence can be from the top down, such as when

Crazes involve a desire to have something that everyone else appears to be enjoying.

A **fad** is a short-lived but widely copied outburst of unexpected and often playful behavior.

Fashions are more enduring, widespread, and socially important than fads.

designer clothes are copied in inexpensive fabrics, or upward from the masses to the elites, such as with blue jeans and T-shirts.

Dress and body decorations are constructions that convey important information about a person's social status (Rubinstein, 1994; Davis, 1992). For example, in a society without a hereditary aristocracy, members of the upper strata use expensive clothing and jewelry to distinguish themselves from the masses. Conversely, in a caste society, fashion is unnecessary, because status distinctions are very clear without any differences in appearance (Blumer, 1974).

Rumors are unconfirmed stories, usually from anonymous sources, that pass quickly from one person to another. A rumor is a group product; it exists only in the telling. Although some rumors may be intentionally planted, many are unconscious distortions that reinforce existing fears or prejudices, such as when stories of contaminated hamburgers confirm our doubts about fast-food places (Koenig, 1985).

As the rumor circulates, some details are elaborated and others dropped. In one famous experiment, college students were shown a picture of a white man threatening a black man on a subway train; as one student described the picture to the next, the situation was soon reversed, with the black threatening the white, a version that fit the tellers' preexisting view of the world (Allport and Postman, 1947; Goleman, 1991a).

Urban legends are rumors that have become so common and widespread that they can be considered items of modern folklore. You have probably heard at least one version of the story about the baby in the microwave, subliminal messages in movies, sightings of Elvis, and the sexual power of green M&Ms (Brunvand, 1986). There is also the one trotted out by the media every October 30th, warning parents about the "Halloween sadist" who hands out apples with hidden razor blades (Best, 1990). Not one of these stories has ever been verified, and some have been shown to be hoaxes, but they keep cropping up because they help people deal with modern anxieties about events that seem beyond control—the presence of evil in the world, sexual fears, the victimization of children, and corporate arrogance. As the stories pass from one teller to another, details often become linked to local concerns. For example, a legend about corporate evil will be attributed to the area's most important employer—the "Goliath Effect" (Fine, 1992b).

Rumors are unconfirmed stories passed from one person to another.

Urban legends are items of modern folklore involving rumors that resonate to deeply held fears and anxieties regarding aspects of modern life beyond personal control.

Publics are mass audiences of people who share a similar response to an issue.

Other legends are picked up and exaggerated by the media, creating "moral panics" among the general public (Jenkins, 1992). In both Great Britain and the United States, rapid social change has generated fears about the unknown and about personal safety, and, in both societies, stories about the sexual abuse of children and the spread of satanic rituals are immediately given credence by reporters. This process is another example of the social construction of a social problem, in which a limited phenomenon is made to appear widespread, evoking latent fears in the audience.

Rumors tend to originate among the relatively powerless and then spread through the most convenient networks; they are a means of striking back and of generating solidarity by identifying a clear enemy (Wachs, 1988). Rumors become very important in crowd situations where people are milling around with no way to test the truth of what they are told, so that any believable story will be taken at face value.

Publics are mass audiences of people who do not have to be in direct contact with one another but who share a similar response to a given issue. For example, President Richard Nixon's concept of the *silent majority* referred to an assumed public that strongly supported the Vietnam War but that did not take to the streets to demonstrate its approval. The

The fears and fantasies that become the making of urban legends are exploited in the headlines of the more sensationalist press. What are some urban legends you have heard?

Read This Book

Did you know that a message, "read this book," is printed on each page of this volume, but in such faint type that you were not consciously aware of it? One of the more enduring of urban legends concerns *subliminal* (below the threshold of awareness) *messages* enticing people to buy popcorn at the movies or helping them lose weight or to improve their grades (Moore, 1985). Although not a shred of scientific data supports this belief, consumers still buy books and recordings designed to harness the powers of subliminal learning.

But if you have difficulty remembering something spoken aloud, why should something only faintly heard have a stronger impact? In general, the more intense (brighter, clearer, louder) the stimulus, the greater its effect. And even under the best of circumstances, it is extremely difficult to change behavior. Yet if people look or listen closely enough, they could probably hear anything they expected to, including a message from Satan on your hard rock CD. Why do you think people want to believe that they are manipulated by unseen forces?

importance of publics in modern societies cannot be overestimated, when all members of the society can be reached simultaneously by radio and television.

All advertising is designed to create a public for a product, whether a bar of soap or a politician. Other publics consist of people who have a shared interest (protecting the environment, animal rights, or gun ownership, for example) and whose opinions may have been formed individually, but whose commitment can be activated by media reports. Such an unorganized public can become an **interest group** when people feel strongly enough to seek out others with similar views.

Crowds

In contrast to the loosely linked collective behavior involved in panics or expressions of public opinion, crowds are typically characterized by greater mass, consciousness of others, and potential outcomes. Crowds are closer to being authentic groups than are the collections of individuals who pass along rumors or faint in the classroom.

A **crowd** is a temporary gathering of people brought together by some common concern or activity, in which participants are aware of one another. The scope of a crowd is thus limited to the people in it at that time. Yet a crowd is not a group in the sense of having structure, such as a division of labor or specialized roles. Under some circumstances, a person can become "lost in the crowd" and use the opportunity to evade the norms that govern everyday behavior, but this is a rather rare happening. A crowd is typically not a collection of mindless robots who act irrationally or as one body. Rather, as participants pay attention to one another and adjust their behavior accordingly, they can become coordinated enough to achieve a purposive goal (McPhail, 1991).

TYPES OF CROWDS. There are many different kinds of temporary collections, or *aggregates* of people, from shoppers in a store to a lynch mob. Some encounters will be too brief and others too structured

to be examples of crowd behavior. Both the casual and conventional crowd test the limits of the sociological definition.

A **casual crowd** is an accidental gathering of people following individual goals in the same place at the same time (for example, shoppers or travelers) and who then share a common focus (as witnesses to an accident, for example) that makes them temporarily aware of one another. At the other extreme, a **conventional crowd** is composed of people who have intentionally gathered together at events governed by established norms, such as a religious service, hockey game, or opera. Here, behavior is highly patterned and predictable.

Both casual and conventional crowds can be transformed into acting and expressive crowds (Blumer, 1951). This is what is meant by the concept of *emergent qualities*—the possibilities that exist in a crowd situation but are actually shaped as the event plays itself out. An **expressive crowd** emerges when participants are gripped by feelings that overwhelm customary normative controls. Sports fans have been known to tear up a playing field, and worshippers have been trampled at religious rallies. An **acting crowd,** in contrast, has a goal beyond the mere expression of emotion. Fueled by the belief that only immediate action can bring about a desired outcome, the acting crowd can become a mob.

An **interest group** develops when members of a public seek others with similar feelings about an issue.

A **crowd** is a temporary gathering of people brought together by a common concern or activity.

A **casual crowd** is an accidental gathering of people.

A **conventional crowd** is composed of people who are gathered as spectators, audiences, or participants at events governed by established norms.

An **expressive crowd** shows strong feelings with outbursts of emotion.

Acting crowds have some goals beyond expression of emotion: They desire to take action.

RESEARCH IN ACTION

Applauding and Booing as Elementary Forms of Collective Behavior

Using a technique called *conversational analysis*, Steven Clayman (1993) studied the interaction between speakers and their audience. He found patterned sequences of reactions at two levels: between speaker and audience, and among members of the audience, as people adjust their behavior to that of those around them. That is, something as elementary as showing approval or disapproval is an interactive event in which individual responses follow broad social patterns.

Applause and booing, however, involve different processes of collective behavior. Think of the last time you were in an expressive crowd, and how the ap-

plause seemed to begin immediately and independently; remember how you waited to see how loudly others were clapping before committing yourself fully. And remember how embarrassed you were when you found yourself the only one applauding and stopped at once?

Booing tends to be less immediate and is often preceded by whispering, shouting, or jeering. We usually wait to see if others share our disapproval before erupting in sustained booing. Negative responses tend to be more coordinated than are shows of appreciation, because participants monitor one another. The main point is that our behavior in crowds is rarely random. There are customary ways to express feelings and patterned sequences to most interaction.

A **mob** is a relatively cohesive, emotionally aroused acting crowd typically engaged in violent or disruptive behavior. The Boston Tea Party was a mob action, as was the storming of the Bastille Prison in Paris in 1789 or the attack on the American embassy in Iran in 1979—all of which have become sacred events in the history of their nation.

> A **mob** is a cohesive, emotionally aroused crowd, often engaged in violent or disruptive acts.
>
> **Riots** are usually less spontaneous than mob actions and tend to involve more people over longer periods of time.

Riots are another type of violent acting crowd, somewhat less spontaneous than a mob action but involving more people over a longer period. Throughout American history, race and ethnic fears have generated riots, pri-

marily involving white gangs that burned and looted African- and Asian-American neighborhoods. More recently, African-American and Latino rioters have destroyed property in major cities.

Much of this recent unrest is linked to overall feelings of powerlessness and despair. Because the conditions that breed such feelings (economic inequality and the isolation of minority poor in urban ghettos and barrios) have grown more intense, we can expect similar outbursts in the future (Carter, 1992). The rioting that broke out in Los Angeles in 1993, following the acquittal of police officers accused of beating a black motorist, was an event waiting to happen, needing only the spark of justification provided by the jury.

The definition and evaluation of acting crowds depends on who is involved. Students, prisoners, and minorities are usually described by the media as

In an expressive crowd, participants are gripped by overwhelming feelings. When the British rock group, The Beatles, first performed, tens of thousands of young English women reached high levels of hysteria watching them. Was it John, Paul, George, or Ringo?

JERRY M. LEWIS

Kent State: A Personal Memoir

Professor Jerry M. Lewis is Professor of Sociology at Kent State University where he joined the faculty in 1966. He received his Ph.D. from the University of Illinois-Urbana and he was an eyewitness to the shootings at Kent State. He writes regularly on collective behavior topics and his current research involves the study of soccer crowds.

In 1970, I was an assistant professor of sociology at Kent State, having come there in 1966. In the Vietnam era of the 1960s, the controversy over that war was a dominant issue on campus, touching all of us with its strong emotional impact and the protest culture it stimulated. Late in April, 1970, the United States' invasion of Cambodia sparked protests throughout the United States. Two days after the invasion, the Ohio National Guard appeared on campus in response to the burning of a Reserve Officer Training Corps (ROTC) building.

The antiwar protests continued for two more days, culminating in a rally protesting the presence of the Guard on campus. Students had been gathering around the Victory Bell for over an hour when the National Guard troops began to disperse the crowd with a tear gas attack. The students responded with anger, as the Guard continued to push them further away from the rally site.

I was taking care of a student who had been tear gassed when I saw the Guard returning to the commons and watched as almost half of the troops fired their rifles. Some aimed in the

air or at the ground, but a few fired into the crowd of students, killing four and wounding nine.

The Kent State shootings caused the only national college student strike in American history. Ten days later, two students were killed and several wounded during a protest demonstration at Jackson State University in Mississippi.

As a part of my grieving for the dead and wounded students, I began a program of research to understand the crowd dynamics that led to the shootings. This research produced several articles and a book, but documenting the events of May 4 was not enough. As a sociologist, I was looking for principles of crowd management that might help avoid similar tragedies.

Since 1975 I have been doing research on sports crowds in the United States, England, Belgium, and Germany. Most of this research involved participant observation, conducted mainly at the Aston Villa soccer stadium in Birmingham, England. I have been spat on in Aston Villa and had chairs and tables thrown in my direction in Dusseldorf, Germany. My basic technique was to accompany the police and observe how they handled crowds, especially the young men herded into the standing room areas where violence among soccer fans most often breaks out. I discovered that the police develop a system of subtle relationships with potential trouble makers and use a variety of control mechanisms. Because police in England do not use guns in crowd control, they are actually more flexible than their American or European counterparts.

My research has shown me that crowds have a complex structure of roles and norms. The basic structure consists of three sets of role players:

(1) an active core; (2) those who cheer on the core; and (3) the largest group, the observers. The active core represents and embodies the crowd; the cheerleaders act in verbal support; and the observers follow the action from the sidelines. Effective crowd management must focus on the active core.

In the Kent State incident, it was a small group of activist students who did most of the yelling and stone throwing, while the cheerleaders stood on a nearby hill shouting encouragement, and the mass of students stood even further away and watched as events unfolded. I observed a very similar pattern in the soccer stands, where the active core initiates activity, cheerleaders join in the singing and chanting, while observers remain further back and give quiet support to the noisemakers.

In summary, my research shows that crowds are not crazy, nor should they be thought of as a simple aggregate of individuals. A crowd is a complex social system composed of smaller systems of two or more people. I have applied this model to a variety of groups, and as recently as the Gulf War crisis, I trained student and faculty marshals to deal with demonstrations on campus. Much of my time as a scholar of collective behavior has been devoted to teaching off-campus groups and the public, including the media, politicians, and voters. We teach first, that crowd management requires careful planning and execution. Second, that failed management can have tragic effects, as seen at Kent State in 1970. Third, that effective crowd management is an essential feature of democracy—citizens must feel safe as they carry out the rituals of daily life, including the exercise of the right to assemble peaceably.

The opposition to the War in Vietnam increased dramatically on American college campuses in the late 1960s. At Kent State University in Ohio, the protest turned to tragedy on May 4, 1970 when the Ohio National Guard fired on Kent State students who had gathered for a demonstration against the war. Are there any issues today that would lead students on your campus to conduct a schoolwide protest with the potential of bringing out the local police or national guard?

"rioters," whereas police officers, strikers, and desegregation resisters are described as "out of control." For example, when a crush of young people arriving for a concert by The Who in 1979 ended in the death of 11 people, the incident was reported in the press as a "stampede" by "barbarians" high on dope and drink. The image of a rock concert audience stomping over one another in a rush for seats fit the public fear of the effects of the music on young people with long hair and too much money. In actuality, the audience was not rushing to get into the concert but to escape the crush of the crowd and were trying to help others to get out also (Johnson, 1987).

> **Demonstrations** are temporary but highly organized acting crowds with a clearly defined goal.
>
> The **emotional contagion model** focuses on how the intensity of crowds develops.

Demonstrations are acting crowds with a clearly defined goal to support or oppose a particular cause. By definition a demonstration is short-lived but also highly organized. An effective demonstration requires considerable planning: permits, publicity, transportation, portable toilets, speakers, and entertainment. The purpose of a demonstration is twofold: (1) to generate publicity and show widespread support for the cause and (2) to bring "true believers" together and reinforce their shared commitment.

Organizers announce a massive rally at a symbolic location—the steps of the Supreme Court, a nuclear power plant, or a fur salon—and then must ensure an adequate turnout. The size of the crowd becomes crucial. If fewer than expected show up, the cause is described as losing steam; if more than anticipated arrive, the cause is seen as gaining adherents.

COMMON ELEMENTS OF CROWD BEHAVIOR.   Given differences among crowds in size, duration, cohesion, and goals, are there any common elements? One list (Turner and Killian, 1987) of characteristics found to some degree in most crowds includes the following:

- Lack of certainty about what should be done
- A feeling that something should be done
- The spread of this feeling among participants
- Creation of a particular mood based on the uncertainty
- Openness to suggestions about what to do
- Relaxation of customary restraints on behavior

Because crowd behavior is so variable and emergent, outcomes are less predictable than for other social interactions. The models for understanding collective behavior reflect this difficulty.

MODELS OF COLLECTIVE BEHAVIOR

What turns an otherwise ordinary collection of people into a group of panic-stricken survivalists or destructive mob? Early theories of collective behavior were framed primarily from a social-psychological perspective, with an emphasis on individual motives and perceptions. For example, the influential work of Gustave LeBon (1895/1960) explained crowd behavior in terms of people losing their identity and sense of personal responsibility, becoming vulnerable to suggestion and swept up in contagious emotion.

The Contagion Model

A more sophisticated version of LeBon's theory is the **emotional contagion model** (Blumer, 1951). An initial stage of aimless milling around is followed by a focusing of attention on a single theme or leader. This emerging definition of the situation is reinforced as participants interact, creating a circular process that continually raises the intensity level. The crowd is a field for evolving relationships and norms; through their interactions, participants gradually create an "emergent construction of reality" that makes sense of their actions (Wright, 1978).

The Value-Added Model

The **value-added model** (Smelser, 1968) proposes that each of six conditions are necessary and sufficient to produce some form of collective behavior by narrowing the range of alternatives at each step:

1. *Structural conduciveness.* Social institutions are organized to encourage or discourage collective behavior. In the People's Republic of China, for example, an antigovernment rally would have been most unlikely before 1989, and reflects a weakening of the Communist state (Zhou, 1993).
2. *Structural strain* refers to tensions introduced into the situation by inequalities perceived as unfair and structural in origin. Inner-city residents, for example, are structurally situated to experience such conditions.
3. *Growth and spread of a generalized belief* take place when people seek an explanation for their intolerable situation. The source of strain is identified: "whitey," "yos," "them." Through their shared definitions, people are prepared for joint action.
4. *Precipitating factors* are dramatic events that support the generalized belief and crystallize feelings. The event need not have actually occurred; a rumor is often sufficient. A suburban mob can materialize at the slightest hint of a minority family moving into the neighborhood, just as urban violence is precipitated by a report of police brutality.
5. *Mobilization for action* occurs when a leader emerges to give a sense of direction to those ready to follow. The leader is usually a recognized local person, although outsiders can take advantage of an extremely unclear situation (Feinberg and Johnson, 1988).
6. *Social control factors* refers to the response of official agents of social control. Crowds can be encouraged or discouraged from a course of action by how the situation is handled by police, politicians, the media, and the courts. Force can crush or anger a crowd; authorities can recognize legitimate grievances or ignore them; and media reports can calm or inflame the mood. The ultimate fate of a collective action is shaped by the interaction between participants and the forces of social control.

These descriptions of individual motivation and interaction processes cannot, however, answer such questions as, Why does a particular social protest emerge when it does? What accounts for success or failure? Who joins, and how is their commitment maintained?

The Resource Mobilization Model

The dominant model in the sociology of collective behavior today focuses on organizational variables rather than on leaders, followers, or social psychological factors. In this view, protests and organized efforts to produce or resist change (social movements) are *not* abnormal events that attract alienated or marginal or irrational participants. To the contrary, these activities are part of a continuing process whereby social goods are distributed among competing interest groups (Tilly, 1978; Zald and McCarthy, 1987). Protest activity is rarely as spontaneous or disorganized as commonly thought. Even the seemingly unorganized demonstrations against the government by Chinese students in 1989 involved elements of carefully crafted ritual theater to which the world and the authorities responded (Wasserstrom and Perry, 1992; Lin, 1992).

The **resource mobilization model (RM)** of collective behavior emphasizes (1) the financial, political, and personnel resources that can be activated ("mobilized") by protest organizers and (2) the ability of control agents to resist the demands for change. Neither shared grievances nor generalized beliefs are sufficient to explain when and where protest activity takes place; nor are participants typically the most deprived or alienated. To the contrary, isolated individuals are by definition outside the personal networks through which people are recruited to collective action (Opp and Gern, 1993). It was not the most deprived African Americans who led the protests of the 1960s and not the most powerless women who founded the feminist movement.

The RM model assumes that there will always be grounds for protest in a modern society. Issues can emerge from free-floating anxiety without any prior grievance, such as when local residents demonstrate against waste-disposal plants that they fear will contaminate the neighborhood. The success of a protest movement depends on timing and being able to secure a variety of material and symbolic resources: funding, members, communication systems, leaders, and legitimacy in the eyes of the public and politicians (Valocchi, 1993; Amenta et al., 1994).

The RM model also views participants as rational decision makers who have weighed the various costs and benefits of collective action and have decided that the goals of protest are worth the time and effort required to fight for them (Olson, 1965; Opp, 1989; Klandermans, 1993). But this rationality must be understood from the viewpoint of the participant and not that of the "objective" scholarly observer who is most likely to be a white, Western, middle-class male. Indeed, because protest movements usually involve

> The **value-added model** specifies six conditions that are necessary and sufficient to produce collective behavior.
>
> The **resource mobilization model** stresses the supports available to protesters, as well as the tactics used by social control agents.

Resistance movements seek to stop social change, restore traditional values, and resist political compromises. The Palestine Islamic fundamentalist movement, HAMAS, has opposed agreements between Israel and the PLO (Palestinian Liberation Organization), headed by Yasser Arafat. HAMAS terrorists bombed this bus in Tel Aviv, killing 22 Israeli passengers and wounding 40 others.

populations that have been marginalized because they are not white, Western, middle class, or male, we need an expanded view of "rationality" that places participants in a context of experience and commitments (Ferree, 1992).

OTHER MODIFICATIONS OF THE RESOURCE MOBILIZATION MODEL. Over the past decade, the RM model has been expanded to include variables from the social psychological perspective such as goals and grievances, and to link microlevels and macrolevels of analysis (Walker et al., 1988; Cable et al., 1988; Morris and Mueller, 1992). Ideology and beliefs do matter, not only in attracting followers but in gaining public support (Benford, 1993). Most important, however, is the context of recruitment and participation; people are mobilized through networks of friendship and influence, and decisions are not always based on one's own immediate best interest (Rule, 1989; Knoke, 1990; Marwell and Oliver, 1993).

WHY JOIN? What do people receive in return for spending money and time on collective action at some risk to their health or job? If others are willing to do the dirty work, why not stay on the sidelines and get a "free ride" (Olson, 1965)? There are a number of solutions to the "free rider" problem that do not depend on receiving material items such as goods or services. Participants often derive emotional satisfaction and a sense of solidarity from group efforts, whether or not these are successful. If the collective activity has brought victory, participants experience a sense of *efficacy*—being able to make things happen, having an impact on the sys-

tem. And because people want to feel that their contributions are fair as well as effective, they pay attention to what other participants are putting into the joint effort (Gould, 1993).

WHO JOINS? Recruitment to collective activity, as you are well aware by now, is largely through interpersonal contacts. Some participants will seek out the social movement because of their commitment to its goals, but most will learn about it or be urged to join by friends and co-workers (McAdam, 1988). Indeed, the influence of such networks is strongest for people who are not deeply concerned about the issues but who have extensive contact with friends and co-workers, who act as recruiting agents (Dauphanais et al., 1992). Socialization also plays a part. Young people whose parents were socially aware and politically active were more likely to join antiwar protests in the 1960s than were their age peers from deeply conservative Protestant homes where obedience to authority is valued (Sherkat and Blocker, 1994).

It helps if people whom we admire are also committed to the cause, but the most immediate social rewards come from supporting or being supported by a circle of friends (Hirsch, 1990). This is why it is important to organize at the local level, to sustain member's motivation over the long haul by providing a place to meet friends (Barkan et al., 1993).

Peer pressure can operate despite a person's attitudes. One study of doctors' participation in an anti-abortion campaign found that while few agreed with the philosophy or goals of the Right to Life organization, most were willing to support its activities out of fear of being isolated from other physicians and potential patients (Eckberg, 1988). This is another instance in which behavior, in response to the demands of the situation, can be at odds with attitudes and most likely will lead to a change in private beliefs to bring them into line with what one has actually done.

THE MOBILIZATION PROCESS.   Successful mobilization, therefore, depends on a number of factors: (1) creating a potential base of support in the population; (2) forming recruitment networks to tap potential members; (3) arousing motivation among targeted individuals through "framing" the issues; and (4) removing barriers to participation (Klandermans and Oegema, 1987; Gerhards and Rucht, 1992).

Once activated, commitment must be maintained over time, through (1) building a collective identity and (2) continuing to nurture interpersonal relationships (Gamson, 1991). Participants come to define situations collectively and to act together and must be periodically mobilized to reactivate their commitment. In the Iranian revolution of 1978–79, for example, daily street demonstrations kept the protests at a fever pitch until the absolute dictator, the Shah, was deposed, and the Shah's supporter, the United States, was humiliated. What had begun as a limited protest by merchants against state policy picked up support from other aggrieved subgroups such as students and factory workers. The revolution was fueled primarily by economic grievances rather than by ideology. Few began their protest with the goal of installing a religious dictatorship (Parsa, 1988). But the exiled Ayatollah Khomeini, who had come to symbolize resistance to the Shah, was able to unify the opposition, bring down the monarchy, and create an Islamic theocracy.

The Iranian revolution is one example of the most organized form of collective action: the social movement.

SOCIAL MOVEMENTS: BELIEFS AND ACTIONS

Social movements involve mobilizing large numbers of people to either promote or resist social and cultural change. In the RM perspective, it is important to distinguish the goals and grievances that make collective action possible from the organizational structures established to achieve these goals. In this model, a **social movement** is a set of beliefs and opinions in favor of major change in social institutions and the stratification hierarchy. For example, the women's movement exists as a set of ideas and feelings held by people who seek equality between the sexes. A **countermovement** is a set of beliefs and opinions within the population that is opposed to these changes—for example, the profamily movement of re-

ligious and political conservatives. Social movements and countermovements are linked in a dynamic relationship, with each influencing the other to create a new social reality.

> A social movement can rouse people when it can do three things: simplify ideas, establish a claim to truth, and, in the union of the two, demand a commitment to action. Thus, not only does ideology transform ideas, it transforms people as well.
>
> —DANIEL BELL, 1960/1965, P. 401

Social movement organizations are formal associations such as the National Organization for Women or Stop-ERA. These organizations channel the sentiments aroused by the social movement into concrete activities. When several different organizations join forces around the same goal, a **social movement industry** is forged. The coalition of women's groups that coordinated efforts to preserve reproductive choice is an example of such an industry, as is the coalition of antifeminist forces that joined to defeat the Equal Rights Amendment in the 1980s.

Classifying Social Movements

Social movements can be classified along several dimensions, one of which is *duration* (Blumer, 1974). Some movements are agents of *general* long-term gradual change; others are engaged in *specific* goals, limited in time and space. For example, although the long-term (secular) trend in the United States has been toward full inclusion of African Americans, specific movements within this broad trend (the abolition movement of the 1860s and the Civil Rights Movement of the 1960s) have focused on particular goals. In turn, specific countermovements periodically resist and even reverse some of the gains of the movement.

Social movements can be classified along three variables: (1) the degree of change being advocated; (2) whether the goal state is a return to an earlier social order or looks to a new type of society, and (3) whether the tactics involve engagement with ex-

A **social movement** is a set of beliefs and opinions in favor of major change in social institutions and the stratification hierarchy.

A **countermovement** is a set of opinions and beliefs within the population that is opposed to the goals of a social movement.

Social movement organizations are specific formal organizations that channel discontent into concrete actions.

A **social movement industry** is created when several organizations join forces around the same goal.

isting institutions or separation and the development of parallel structures. These three elements can be combined to yield four types of social movement:

- **Reform movements** advocate change within the existing system. For example, extending the Fourteenth Amendment's guarantee of equal treatment to persons of color involves relatively simple legislative and judicial actions. The most effective tactics will be those most likely to influence politicians and the general public: demonstrations, lawsuits, election mobilization, and media attention.
- **Revolutionary movements** call for fundamental changes in values and institutions. Such a radical goal justifies extraordinary tactics, designed to attract attention and to spread uncertainty. Hijacking, kidnapping, fire bombing, and other acts of terrorism are common across the globe—in Iran and India, Northern Ireland, and New York City.
- **Resistance movements** are formed to stop change and restore traditional values and behaviors. Current examples include the New Christian Right in the United States, Islamic fundamentalist movements in the Near East, and neo-Nazis in Western Europe.
- **Utopian movements** seek an ideal society for a select group of true believers, in the hope that their example will spread to the wider society. Ironically, the word *utopia* means "no place," recognizing the impossibility of worldly perfection. Nonetheless, there have been many attempts to create such a community, though few have been successful over time (Berger, 1988).

Reform movements seek changes within the existing social system.

Revolutionary movements call for radical structural and value change in the society.

Resistance movements are designed to stop change and to restore traditional values and norms.

Utopian movements seek an ideal society for true believers.

The **revolution of rising expectations** refers to the gap between expected benefits and actual gains.

Absolute deprivation is a lack of the basic necessities of survival.

Utopian idealism in the United States is most clearly associated with the social organization of the *commune,* in which members pool resources and share common living areas. Major problems include control of sexuality, leadership, and commitment to the group, all of which tend to be strongest in religiously oriented communes and weakest in those created by young people (Kanter, 1972; Zablocki, 1980; Petranek, 1988).

NEW SOCIAL MOVEMENTS. In addition to the major social movements, representing broad currents in the culture and institu-

tions of the United States (the Civil Rights, Feminist, and Gay Rights Movements and countermovements), a number of smaller and more specialized protest movements have emerged in this country and other Western nations. There are organizations to protect the rights of children, the elderly, the disabled, and animals (Jasper and Poulson, 1993), and to pursue world peace, prison reform, nuclear disarmament, physical fitness, and the abolition of the death penalty (Haines, 1992). Among the countermovements are those centered on creationism, white power, family values, and anti-abortionism. Consumers, self-help groups, and neighborhood activists are also represented by movement organizations (Cable and Benson, 1993). Although it is more difficult to organize the poor than the affluent, even the homeless have engaged in successful protest (Wagner and Cohen, 1991).

New social movements have been described as "moral crusades," "the politics of righteousness," and "agents of cultural renovation"—terms suggesting that the goal may be more cultural than political—to change the moral climate of the nation (Aho, 1990; Eyerman and Jamison, 1991; Jasper and Nelkin, 1992). Moral crusades tend to frame issues in absolute terms, leaving little room for compromise, and they often provoke an equally absolutist opposition. This tendency and the sheer number of new social movements could divide citizens and lessen social cohesion, as specialized movement organizations resist incorporation into broader political parties or interest groups (Dalton and Kuechler, 1991; Aronowitz, 1992).

Phases in the Development of a Social Movement

Most models of the life course or "natural history" of a social movement distinguish four phases, characterized by (1) personal discontent and vague unrest in the society; (2) focusing of concern and emergence of information networks; (3) development of formal organizations; and (4) acceptance of the movement's goals or its gradual decline through loss of members (Zald and Ash, 1969; Blumer, 1974).

In phase 1, widespread unrest is usually linked to some condition in the wider society such as an economic crisis, war, mass migration, or major technological change. Some movements will emerge to defend the traditional way of life; others to embrace the changes. In general, also, movements do not arise at the lowest point in a group's fortunes, but when conditions appear to be improving. The gap between expected benefits and actual gains creates a **revolution of rising expectations.** At such times, peoples' feelings of being deprived may be absolute or relative. **Absolute deprivation** refers to a lack of basic necessities, often associated with a sense of powerlessness and withdrawal from collective life.

SOCIAL CHANGE

A Directory of Social Movement Literature

For readers interested in learning more about a particular cause or in participating in collective action to bring about social change, Twayne Publishers (866 Third Avenue, New York City) has produced a series of extremely readable short volumes on past and present social movements. Here is a partial list of the most recent books in this series:

- *The Animals Rights Movement in America* (1994), Susan Finsen and Lawrence Finsen
- *The Anti-Abortion Movement* (1994), Dallas A. Blanchard
- *The American Peace Movement: Ideals and Activism* (1992), Charles Chatfield
- *The Children's Rights Movement: A History of Advocacy and Protection* (1991), Joseph Hawes
- *The Conservative Movement, Revised Edition* (1992), Paul Gottfried
- *Controversy and Coalition, Revised Edition: The New Feminist Movement across Three Decades of Change* (1994), Myra Marx Ferree and Beth B. Hess

- *The Health Movement: Promoting Fitness in America* (1992), Michael S. Goldstein
- *The Hospice Movement: Easing Death's Pains* (1992), Cathy Siebold
- *Self Help in America: A Social Movement Perspective* (1992), Alfred H. Katz
- *The Senior Rights Movement: Framing the Policy Debate in America* (1994), Lawrence A. Powell, John B. Williamson, and Kenneth Branco

Earlier volumes in the series include books on *Abolitionism* (Aptecker), *American Temperance Movements* (Blocker), the *Antinuclear Movement* (Price), the *Charismatic Movement* (Paloma), *Civil Rights* (Blumberg), the *Consumer Movement* (Mayer), the *Creationist Movement* (Eve and Harrold), *Family Planning and Population Control* (Back), *Neighborhood Organizing* (Fisher), *Populism* (Clanton), *Prison Reform* (Sullivan), *The Rise of a Gay and Lesbian Movement* (Adam), and *Social Movements of the 1960s* (Burns).

Somewhere in this list, there should be a social movement that engages your sympathies and provides an opportunity for active participation in the process of social change. Take it!

Relative deprivation occurs when one's condition is compared unfavorably to that of people thought of as similar to oneself. For example, African Americans are not comparing themselves to native Africans but to other Americans with the same level of education and skills, and their sense of unfairness fuels protest.

Such feelings remain vague and unfocused in the early stage of a social movement. One's initial impulse is to blame failure on bad luck or personal shortcomings. The type of leader likely to emerge at this point is the prophet (to believers) or the agitator (to agents of social control).

Phase 2 involves the realization that others share your grievance, but this does not automatically lead to a social movement. To transform personal problems into a social issue requires an ideology, or frame, that locates the structural sources of discontent, provides an alternative reality, and offers a plan of action. At this stage, information networks are crucial to linking individuals. The media have a major role in legitimating the claims of movement leaders, who are often charismatic figures who attract public attention while giving voice to the yearnings of the discontented.

In phase 3, participants mobilize the resources needed to maintain formal organizations: money, mass membership, and public support (or at least the absence of repression). The transformation into formal organizations involves reinforcing charismatic leadership with nuts-and-bolts administrators. Max Weber describes this process as the "routinization of charisma," which partially "demystifies" the movement.

No matter how deep the discontent or righteous the cause, a social movement will succeed only to the extent its leaders can make alliances with other groups, avoid internal conflict, and maintain member commitment over the long term (Staggenborg, 1988). To accomplish these goals, the movement organization tends to become increasingly bureaucratized with power concentrated in a small group of professional leaders, a development that might discourage movement volunteers (Kleidman, 1994). It also helps if the opposition remains disorganized (Walsh, 1986). In summary, the fate of a social movement depends less on the virtue of it goals than on its ability to mobilize resources from within its own ranks and the larger social system (Back, 1989; Minkoff, 1993).

This fate is sealed in phase 4. Complete success, or **institutionalization,** occurs when the movement's ideology becomes part of the taken-for-granted reality, and its goals are embodied in stable organizations. Success can be measured by the degree to which social values and social policy have changed and movement leaders participate in policy making (Rochon and Mazmanian, 1993). Table 23-1 summarizes the phases of social movement development.

> **Relative deprivation** occurs when people feel unfairly treated in comparison to others thought to be their equals.
>
> **Institutionalization of a social movement** occurs when its beliefs are accepted and its goals are embodied in stable organizations.

TABLE 23-1 Model of Social Movement Development

Phase	1 Preliminary	2 Focusing of concern (Crystallization)	3 Organization (Mobilization)	4 Institutionalization
Characteristics	Widespread but isolated feelings of discontent and deprivation	Recognition that others share feelings	Centralization of power Mass membership	Public recognition and acceptance of ideas.
Challenges	Media access Grass-roots organizing	Ideological development Communications network	Organization survival Avoiding internal conflicts Maintain members' commitment	Organizational legitimation Benefiting members Resisting co-optation
Structure	Informal	Local units (cells)	National organizations Alliances with other groups	Bureaucratic formal structures
Leadership	Prophet or agitator	Charismatic leader	Managers (statespersons)	Bureaucrats (priests)

The other extreme outcome is defeat. Early success often provokes powerful opposition, as in the case of the Equal Rights Amendment in the 1980s. Earlier in our history, the Women's Christian Temperance Union enjoyed the victory of the Prohibition Amendment before experiencing total defeat with its repeal only 14 years later, which was due to internal problems as well as to a change in the public temper (Blumberg and Pittman, 1991). In most cases, success is partial, which creates problems in keeping members mobilized. Leaders must stress the unmet goals, while opponents claim that nothing more needs to be done. Today, for example, both the civil rights and women's movements are struggling against the public perception that their major goals have already been accomplished and that policies may have gone too far in correcting past discrimination.

> **Goal displacement** occurs when movement goals are displaced by the goal of maintaining formal structures.

Substantive successes are often hazardous to the health of the movement, such as when the broad-based coalition formed to win the vote for women could not survive the passage of the Nineteenth Amendment in 1920. The struggle for the vote was the only issue on which the various groups could agree, and it was not until four decades later that a new feminist movement emerged to tackle the unfinished agenda of the earlier movement (Ferree and Hess, 1994).

Another danger in becoming institutionalized is **goal displacement,** where maintaining the formal organization replaces the original goal of the movement. As leadership passes from cause-oriented charismatic leaders (prophets) to managers and bureaucrats (priests) whose loyalty is to the organization, the stage is set for goal displacement. Power struggles among successors can also divert attention and energies from the common goal (Ryan, 1989; Valocchi, 1990). In these many ways, then, organizational success and its consequences can corrupt the original goals of the social movement.

SOCIETAL REACTIONS. Success or failure also depends on the actions of outside authorities who may either support or resist the movement's goals. Most often, precisely because they challenge the status quo, social movements are perceived as a threat to social order. Agents of social control resist change through a variety of repressive actions, such as when the National Guard is sent in to beat up labor organizers or fire on protesting students. In totalitarian societies, movement leaders are regularly jailed, deported, and executed—each of which has also happened in American history. Such repressive acts raise the cost of participation but can also be the occasion for further protest (Opp and Roehl, 1990).

Co-optation is another technique for neutralizing social movement activism (see Chapter 4). Cooptation takes place when established leaders claim to embrace the movement's goals or when movement leaders are brought into the leadership structure. A civil rights leader who becomes a presidential advisor or a feminist appointed to a judgeship become part of the power elite against which they had once fought. A few visible acts of co-optation can give the impression that the movement is no longer on the outside, thus reducing public support for further gains, while also thinning the ranks of movement leadership. An-

Agents of social control use jailing, harassment, and executions to repress movements for social justice and democracy. In 1989, members of the Salvadoran army were charged with assassinating six Jesuit priests, their housekeeper, and her daughter. Two of the priests, Dr. Segundo Montes and Dr. Ignacio Martin-Baro, were sociologists at the University of Central America and were active in the struggle for human rights in El Salvador.

other form of co-optation took place when the voting age in the United States was lowered from 21 to 18, in the hope that this would reduce student protests by giving them a stake in the system.

The very structure of American politics, with its checks and balances and various levels, tends to reward compromise and avoid major breaks with traditional policy. Those movement organizations that pursue a moderate course and give the impression of being nonpartisan have the best chance of long-term survival (Minkoff, 1993). By the same token, these organizations often forfeit the opportunity to reach their original goals by becoming fragmented and co-opted (Meyer, 1993). This, then, is the great paradox of social movements: Partial successes can make it impossible to achieve total success. But just as the good (partial victories) can be the enemy of the best (ultimate goals), so, too, can the best be the enemy of the good, when refusing to compromise ruins the chances of making any gains.

Because the power of the state is so overwhelming and is typically used to resist social movements, we

tend to forget that movement activism has an effect on political processes and structures (Quadagno, 1992). New voices are brought to public attention, new interest groups are mobilized, and the political landscape is transformed. Although many goals remain unfulfilled, the civil rights and women's movements have already had a profound impact on the composition and agenda of all branches of government. Cultural redemption may be the ultimate goal, but politics is the battleground between movement and countermovement. Let us examine these issues in the case of contemporary social movements.

CONTEMPORARY SOCIAL MOVEMENTS

Social movements typically appear in clusters. The underlying conditions that make protest necessary and possible usually affect more than one subgroup. Ideas and strategies flow from one group to another. Often, the same people are involved in more than one organizaion. Thus, at some historical moments, a variety of social movements will flourish simultaneously, as in the 1960s and early 1970s in the United States and Western Europe (Koopmans, 1993).

A Decade of Protest

The decade of the 1960s was a period of extraordinary social movement activity in the United States. The period's undercurrent of student activism—a very rare phenomenon in American history—began with the Free Speech Movement on the Berkeley campus of the University of California and the rise of the New Left and ended less than a decade later with National Guard troops firing on student antiwar protesters in Ohio and Mississippi.

At the same time, a massive Civil Rights Movement (CRM), forged within African-American communities, came to national attention with several well-organized protests. By the mid 1960s, a New Feminist Movement entered the spotlight, partly sustained by women who had first been mobilized by the New Left and the CRM (Ferree and Hess, 1994). Members of all these movements were soon joined by other students, religious leaders, politicians, and large numbers of previously inactive citizens protesting the Vietnam War. Also taking root during these years were the Gay Rights Movement (Adam, 1987), the children's rights movement (Hawes, 1993), and the movements against both nuclear power and nuclear war (Price, 1982). In many ways, the movements fed one another rather than competing for members and media attention (Meyer and Whittier, 1994; Esterberg, 1994).

All in all, the 1960s were a most remarkable decade, unlike any other in American history. Perhaps because many participants are now, three decades later, professors of sociology, a number of follow-up studies are now available (Kimmel, 1989; Fendrich, 1993; Marwell et al., 1989; Dunham and Bengtson, 1989; McAdam, 1992; Jamison and Eyerman, 1994). In general, the women and men who took part in 1960s protests as college students are more likely than their nonactivist peers to have remained politically involved and to have less conventional family and work histories. It is difficult to tell whether the same impulses that led to youthful activism remained strong in adulthood or whether the experience of student protests shaped the rest of their lives.

Countermovement Activism

Because each of the 1960s social movements involved a profound challenge to established values and authority, each eventually produced organized resistance. From the point of view of the resisters, theirs are the authentic social movements, and feminists, homosexuals, and civil rights advocates are seen as countermovement protesters.

Student protest was the easiest to control because of constant turnover in personnel, the fact that school is in session only part of the year, students' vulnerability to pressure from parents, and the willingness of authorities to use force. Civil rights demonstrators were met by tear gas, police dogs, cattle prods, jail sentences, and ultimately, lynching and assassination. Antiwar protesters were attacked by club-wielding "hardhats." Women's rights advocates, however, were most often confronted with ridicule and harassment, while the anti-nuclear forces had to compete against powerful business interests.

In general, violence by countermovement activists was less effective than was their ability to manipulate the law and the media (Barkan, 1984). One exception has been the rising level of violence in anti-abortion protests, in which five people have been murdered in the past three years. Throughout the country, family planning clinics have been bombed, clinic staff assaulted, and clients harassed on the streets and in their homes. This type of extremism is found whenever an issue is framed as a moral crusade, one that permits no compromise with the "forces of darkness"—a position that tends to attract young socially isolated working-class men who find an ideological home in the fundamentalist subculture with its emphasis on absolute good and absolute evil (Blanchard and Prewitt, 1993).

Despite the strength of the backlash movements, the major social movements of the 1960s and early 1970s mobilized sufficient resources to achieve important and lasting goals. The structure of *de jure* segregation was dismantled; women's rights have been partially secured; the war in Vietnam was ended; and support for homosexual rights remains relatively high, even in the face of fear over AIDS.

Out of the interplay of movement and counter-movement come some gains, some failures, and much unfinished business. Latent and unforeseen consequences emerge over time; battles can be won but wars lost; short-term successes activate backlash forces; and countermovement tactics, in turn, produce changes in the movement's strategies.

As an example of this interplay, let us examine briefly the history of the Civil Rights Movement and the current backlash represented by the rise of white supremacy groups.

The Civil Rights Movement (CRM)

Many of you were born after the major events of the 1960s, and you have grown up in a society greatly altered by the legacy of the Civil Rights Movement. Yet it was only a generation ago that it was against the law in many states for white and black children to attend the same school, eat at the same restaurants, or swim on the same beaches. Interracial marriage was forbidden, and African-American voting was constrained by poll taxes, tests, and outright violence. Most residential areas were completely segregated, and public services such as water and electricity were often denied to minority householders.

EMERGENCE OF THE CIVIL RIGHTS MOVEMENT: 1955–1965. As degrading as conditions were for American Blacks in the late 1950s, they, too, had been able to profit from expanding educational and economic opportunities in the industrial North (McAdam, 1982). Local communities had accumulated the resources necessary to support collective protest: leadership (largely through the church), a growing middle-class, and networks of students in primarily minority colleges in the South (Morris, 1984). Thus, by 1955, all the preconditions for a social movement mobilization were present: feelings of injustice, a sense that protest would be effective, a communications network, and a community base of support (Fitzgerald, 1988). In addition, the old Southern power elite was being replaced by a new business class more interested in attracting Northern businesses than maintaining racial segregation (Bloom, 1987).

Finally, the legal groundwork for the CRM was established in 1954 when the Supreme Court decided that legally segregated schools violated the equal protection clause of the Fourteenth Amendment. By extension, no "separate but equal" facilities could meet the constitutional test, and various African-American groups began to challenge segregation in the South.

The first protest activities were not, as commonly believed, spontaneous outbreaks of the most deprived, but were carefully rehearsed test cases. Rosa Parks acted intentionally when, in 1955, in Montgomery, Alabama, she refused to give up her seat to a white man and move to the back of the bus. The con-

One of the major events of the 1960s was the Civil Rights Movement that emerged at a time when it was illegal for whites and blacks to attend the same schools, eat in the same restaurant, swim at the same beaches, or marry one another. In March 1965, Dr. Martin Luther King, Jr. (shown in the center with his wife, Coretta Scott King) led thousands of civil rights demonstrators on a peaceful 50-mile march from Selma to Montgomery, Alabama.

ductor obliged her by calling in the police, and the black community responded by a well-organized boycott of the buses and local businesses that ended when the courts ruled that segregated transportation systems were unconstitutional. Similarly, the students who defied the law and sat down at the "whites only" lunch counter at a Woolworth's store in Greensboro, North Carolina, in 1960, were part of a growing network of activists, trained by local organizers.

Throughout this period, the leadership of African-American women, through their clubs and churches, was invaluable to sustaining the CRM, although they rarely received attention from the media or the movement's male leaders (Barnett, 1993). But the experience would be empowering, and black women in the South would never again be so hidden and overlooked.

The local protests drew the attention of the national media and aroused a supportive audience throughout the country, but only in 1957 did the federal government respond when U.S. marshals and troops were sent to enforce school integration in Little Rock, Arkansas. And only in the mid-1960s, when President Lyndon Johnson committed to the full powers of the presidency to the task, was comprehensive civil rights legislation enacted by Congress—a full century after the Emancipation Proclamation.

By this time, the protests had mobilized the great mass of African Americans as well as large numbers of white supporters. Several volunteers in the South—both whites and blacks—were assaulted and murdered, and many others spent time in local jails. Each new incident only enlarged the size of further demonstrations and the amount of media attention. Public opinion grew steadily more favorable, and funding from mainstream churches and foundations flowed

into the more "moderate" civil rights organizations (Jenkins and Eckert, 1986). Although this help from the white establishment was important, the movement's own strengths were the primary keys to success (Morris, 1993).

GOALS AND TACTICS.   From the beginning, the goal of the CRM was simple and reformist: to extend the protections of the U. S. Constitution to all Americans. To maintain the moral high ground, movement leaders, especially the Rev. Martin Luther King, Jr., chose to adopt the strategy of nonviolent civil disobedience. Civil disobedience, as perfected by Mahatma Gandhi in India, involves a peaceful refusal to obey an "unjust" law. When protesters refuse to move and authorities are provoked to violence, the moral virtue of the movement is highlighted in contrast to the brutality of authorities. The most massive—and peaceful—civil rights march took place in Washington, D. C. in 1963, and is best remembered as the occasion for Dr. King's "I Have a Dream" speech. But this high point came after one full decade of organizing at the local level.

ORGANIZATIONAL DILEMMAS.   Five years later, in 1968, the CRM was greatly weakened by the assassination of Dr. King, who had been the charismatic focus of the different segments of the movement. As Max Weber would have predicted, charisma must be routinized, i.e., embodied in a nuts-and-bolts organization, if it is to survive the sudden loss of its leader. No one, with the exception perhaps of Jesse Jackson in the 1980s, has been able to unify the various factions within the CRM or appeal to nonminority voters.

Urban riots in the late 1960s provided a rationale for withdrawal of sympathy and material support on the part of many whites. During the 1970s, civil

ALDON MORRIS

The Civil Rights Movement: Personal Commitments and Accounts

Aldon Morris is a Professor and Chair of Sociology at Northwestern University. His book The Origins of the Civil Rights Movement *was co-winner of the 1986 American Sociological Association Award for the best book in sociology. He is also a co-editor, with Dr. Carol Mueller, of* Frontiers in Social Movement Theory (*Yale University, 1992*). *Currently he is doing a comparative analysis of the Northern and Southern Civil Rights Movements. Morris is past president of the Association of Black Sociologists and a consultant for the television documentary "Eyes on the Prize."*

Human societies and interactions have always fascinated me. I seldom take social reality for granted. The fact of cultural variability is nothing less than amazing. The ways in which societies survive, change, engage in conflict, build structures of inequality, generate culture, and create human liberation movements are complex and difficult to understand. On the interpersonal level, individuals interact with each other and with their own consciousness, in ways that make them laugh, cry, be angry, reflective, and even embarrassed.

The wonderful task of the sociologist is to study and generate knowledge at both the societal and interpersonal levels. Which aspect of the human drama a sociologist studies and writes about is heavily conditioned by that person's own life experiences. It is no accident that I study social movements in general and the United States Civil Rights Movement (CRM) in particular. My

decision to study social movements is directly linked to the fact that I grew up as a member of an oppressed and exploited racial group. As a young African American, I quickly came to realize that racial discrimination and inequality had devastating consequences for members of my community. This was a problem that worried me because I could see no way to change this wretched situation.

Then, as if by magic, the Civil Rights Movement exploded on the American scene. All of a sudden African Americans, along with some whites, were marching for racial justice by the thousands and being cursed, beaten, jailed, and even killed for their dignified protest against racial injustice.

I saw the Civil Rights Movement as a force capable of transforming race relations in the United States. Even as attack dogs were lunging at demonstrators throughout the South during the 1960s, I decided that my first research objective would be a major study of the CRM.

My research answered a number of sociological questions. First, I discovered that the CRM did not arise suddenly or spontaneously. To the contrary, there had always been a black movement for change in this country and several protest streams converged in the 1960s to produce a dynamic and powerful movement for change. Sociologically, then, movements are usually part of an ongoing struggle rather than a spontaneous occurrence. Second, I found that ordinary people working through grassroots community organizations constituted the real power behind the movement. Thus, the actions of ordinary people can bring about important societal change. Third, my research demonstrated how social movements can function as vehicles of social change. Fourth, my research challenged the common view that northern white lib-

erals financed the modern Civil Rights Movement. Rather, the overwhelming majority of local struggles were actually financed by the African-American community itself. In the words of Frederick Douglass, "He who could be free must himself strike the first blow." Thus, oppressed people can act to free themselves.

Fifth, my research makes it clear that African-American women were also crucial to the rise and success of the Civil Rights Movement. This should not be surprising, because African-American women have always been in the forefront of the black liberation struggle. Throughout their history, African-American women have had to assume work roles outside the home and household, as well as in the church and community. Building on this rich tradition of activism, they played pivotal roles in keeping the movement strong and focused.

The Civil Rights Movement successfully challenged legally enforced racial segregation and secured voting rights in the South. Moreover, this movement changed American politics forever. It provided a model for all oppressed groups to follow. Thus, the modern women's, student's, farmworkers', Native Americans', and the physically challenged movements all drew their inspiration and many of their tactics from the Civil Rights Movement. In addition, the CRM served as a training ground for activists in other social change movements. The CRM also influenced democratic movements abroad including those in South Africa, the Near East, and China. But this powerful movement failed to eliminate economic inequality between the races—a task for the next major social movement.

Meanwhile, the human drama continues to unfold in all its magnificence. Sociologists will never find themselves without opportunities to exercise the sociological imagination.

SUGGESTED READINGS

Choing, Dennis. *Collective Action and the Civil Rights Movement.* Chicago: University of Chicago Press, 1991. The collective action model is applied to the Civil Rights Movement of the 1960s.

Hiltermann, Joost R. *Behind the Intifada: Labor and Women's Movement in the Occupied Territories.* Princeton: Princeton University Press, 1991. An important case study of mass mobilization and the organizational efforts responsible for the success of the society-wide mobilization among Palestineans in Israel.

Lofland, John. *Polite Protestors: The American Peace Movement of the 1980s.* Syracuse, NY: Syracuse University Press, 1993. The "nuclear freeze" movement of the 1980s mobilized millions of ordinary Americans in a variety of subgroups to bring pressure on the government to halt or scale down the development of nuclear weapons. Lofland traces the many subgroups and activities that made up the broader movement, until success in the form of arms control and nuclear weapons treaties left them without clear targets.

McCartney, John T. *Black Power Ideologies: An Essay in African-American Political Thought.* Philadelphia: Temple University Press, 1992. The concept of black power is explored in this book that clarifies the Black Power movement of the 1960s.

Morgan, Edward P. *The Sixties Experience: Hard Lessons about Modern America.* Philadelphia: Temple University Press, 1991. A useful summary of the social movements of the 1960s expressed from the standpoint that the democratic vision of the sixties cannot succeed within the constraints of American institutions.

Turner, Patricia A. *I Heard It through the Grapevine: Rumor in African-American Culture.* Beverly, CA: University of California Press, 1993. An extremely readable symbolic interactionist approach to the study of rumors and urban legends in contemporary African-American communities. The author shows how such folklore is rooted in the black experience and makes sense—however exaggerated—within the minority culture.

Wasserstrom, Jeffrey N. and Elizabeth Perry, eds. *Popular Protest and Political Culture in Modern China.* Boulder: Westview press, 1992. An edited volume that looks at the sources and long-lasting effects of the Tiananmen Square student protest.

Wickham-Crowley, Timothy P. *Guerrillas and the Revolution in Latin America: A Comparative Study of Insurgents and Regimes Since 1956.* Princeton: Princeton University Press, 1991. A comparative analysis of Latin American revolutions that presents an integrated theory of guerrilla/peasant warfare and the elements necessary for a successful revolution.

APPENDIX
Studying Sociology

As a college student you face a wide number of choices regarding course offerings at your school—some are required, others are electives. Whether the introductory sociology course at your school is required or an elective, the authors of this book fully believe that what you learn as a sociology student will help you with other courses, in making work and career decisions, and in your personal affairs. Studying sociology is learning about social life.

Professors Edward Kain and Ann Sundgren are two outstanding teachers of sociology. They have been recognized both by their students and other sociologists for their contributions to the field of sociology, and both have had long-standing interests in how to teach introductory courses in sociology in an interesting and useful manner. They are only two among the many sociologists who have a serious commitment to quality undergraduate teaching. Their vignettes offer considerable wisdom about the usefulness of sociology for your education and your life.

SOCIOLOGY AND THE LIBERAL ARTS

Edward L. Kain

Edward L. Kain (Ph.D., University of North Carolina at Chapel Hill) is Professor of Sociology at Southwestern University in Georgetown, Texas. As a member of the Teaching Resources Group of the American Sociological Association, he has led nearly two dozen national and regional teaching workshops. He was the recipient of the Alumni Distinguished Teaching Award at Cornell University. He is the author of The Myth of Family Decline: Understanding Families in a World of Rapid Social Change *(Lexington, 1990), has published a number of articles on family change, and is currently editing a reader in family sociology with Mark Rank, in addition to contributing chapters to a number of books on the family. Currently he serves on the Committee on International Sociology and the Task Force on Participation of the American Sociological Association.*

L ike most people, I did not go to college planning to become a sociologist. My first year at Alma College, a small liberal arts school in Michigan, was spent as a music major. Because the liberal arts curriculum required all students to take courses in a variety of areas, I took introductory sociology during my second semester. My sociological journey had begun.

Growing up the youngest of three boys in a farm family, I had developed a solid set of Midwestern American values. Benjamin Franklin would have been proud of the belief system upon which my family was based—"early to bed and early to rise, makes a man, healthy, wealthy, and wise." I truly believed that in the United States, with hard work and enough perseverance, anyone could grow up to be President. After all, "everyone is created equal."

That first course in sociology challenged my values. I'd never noticed that all the Presidents had been men; all had been white; all, except one, had been Protestant; none had ever been divorced (until Ronald Reagan) and only one had never been married. It was also pretty clear that their social class background did not represent the full spectrum of the United States, despite stories of Lincoln's log cabin origins.

At first I dug in my heels and fought. I challenged the research showing that one-half of one percent of the U.S. population controlled over a third of the wealth in this country. I was skeptical when studies reported that African Americans were much more likely to be given the death penalty for the same crimes that brought relatively short prison terms for whites. When women in the class complained that a college education would yield them less pay in the labor market than men who dropped out of high school, I suspected sour grapes.

Then one day we got to the topic of mortality. The professor pointed out that men from lower-income backgrounds were much more likely to fight on the front lines and die during wartime. He asked how many in the class had known someone who died in Vietnam, and I was one of the few who raised my hand. I was dumbfounded. Two of my best friends had died within the past three years, and my brother's closest childhood buddy had been killed right before I came to college. I'd never thought of myself as poor, but in this upper-middle-class private school, the differences between my life and that of many of my classmates became strikingly clear. The lightbulbs began to go on, and, no matter how hard I tried, it was impossible to turn them off. Sociology helped me to see the patterns. It helped me to contrast ideal and real culture, and separate ideological myths from the reality of social structure.

Growing up in the Vietnam era shaped my sociological imagination in other ways as well. My brothers and I had very different experiences because of the few years that separated us by age. My oldest brother had a very low draft number, and, because of his religious beliefs, he was a conscientious objector who did alternate service in Canada. My middle brother had a number of friends who went to Vietnam, and he took a strong "love it or leave it" approach. Because I was in a slightly younger cohort, the war had much less effect on my life. By the time I was a senior in college, the draft no longer existed. That experience made me acutely aware of the importance of historical circumstances in shaping individual lives and helped me appreciate C. Wright Mills's claim that sociology must help us understand the linkages between history and biography, and that "all sociology worthy of the name is 'historical sociology'."

During my junior year, I worked with a faculty member on a National Science Foundation research project. My love of research blossomed, and a commitment to working relationships between faculty and students in which they jointly search for the answers to sociological questions began to develop.

In many ways, graduate school and then teaching at Cornell were an interlude. They were preparation for what I wanted to do. I am now back in a liberal arts setting, teaching and working on research with undergraduates. If I can help ignite the sociological imagination within them, then I have been successful.

Beyond the classroom, I have found sociology to be very satisfying as well. During the summer of 1988 I had the opportunity to work at the national headquarters of the American Medical Association, helping to develop their national policy on HIV and AIDS. For the past decade, I have been part of the Teaching Resources Group of the American Sociological Association, and, in that capacity, I have led national and regional teaching workshops across the country. It has been a pleasure working toward the improvement of teaching with colleagues from many types of settings.

My primary interest as a teacher and a researcher is in the broad area of social change and families. My first book on families and social change, The Myth of Family Decline, illustrates many of the lessons I learned back in that first sociology course two decades ago. Our ideology about families is often sharply at odds with the reality of family life. Images of family life in past times do not fit the information that we have about families a century ago. For example, children today are actually less likely to grow up in single-parent families than

they were a century ago. Similarly, more people celebrate their fortieth anniversary in their first marriages today than was the case at the turn of the century. Both of these statements are true because of the rapid decline in death rates since 1900. Popular wisdom is that single parenthood is a recent phenomenon, and that high divorce rates mean that fewer and fewer people have long marriages. In reality, however, increases in divorce rates have not matched the decline in death rates.

Sociology helps us see the world in a new way. It points to the gap between cultural ideals and social realities. It delineates the patterns of social behavior and gives us tools for better understanding the world around us. The sociological imagination makes us better citizens in a changing global society.

SOCIOLOGY IN COMMUNITY COLLEGES

Ann S. Sundgren

Ann S. Sundgren is a professor of sociology at Tacoma Community College, having received a Ph.D. from the University of Washington. She has held many elective offices, among them Chair of the Committee on Committees and Chair of the Section on Undergraduate Education in the American Sociological Association, and was recently elected Vice President of the Pacific Sociological Association. She has served on the editorial board of Teaching Sociology *as a member of the American Sociological Association's Teaching Services Program and has been a recipient of the faculty Excellence Award at Tacoma Community College.*

When I was growing up, my biggest dream was to go to college to become a veterinarian. But I am a member of a generation that grew into womanhood before the new feminism freed us from some widely-held beliefs that women are innately dependent and intellectually limited. Deterred from veterinary medicine by the belief that "girls can't be vets," but encouraged by my working-class parents to get as much an education as possible, I entered the university planning to major in languages and imagining myself as a foreign diplomat, flying around the world with a briefcase of secret documents handcuffed to my wrist!

Toward the end of my sophomore year, I took a course in introductory sociology. I wish I could tell you that I immediately recognized it as a turning point in my life, but in all honesty it seemed hopelessly boring to me. However, there must have been something there that sparked an interest, for the next quarter I took a course in criminology; the social theory was fascinating and the research methodology and data were like putting together the most intricate puzzle imaginable. I began to see my world through a new set of lenses. I went on to take courses on sociological theory, demography, social psychology—and each one opened a new world to me. All the other courses required for the Bachelor's degree took on new meaning as well, for now I was filtering them all through the sociological perspective.

Yet once I had decided to major in sociology I hadn't the foggiest idea what I would do after graduation. I had never had a woman instructor to serve as a role model, and I had had to work at tedious jobs throughout my undergraduate years since student loans, financial aid, and work-study programs were not then available. I didn't really know what sociologists did, except that if they were very smart white men they could teach and do research at universities!

Finally, with a Bachelor's degree in hand, I did what most of you will do. I went looking for a job that I hoped would offer the promise of a real career. I felt fortunate when I got a job at a large manufacturing firm. But after a year of impatiently waiting to be given more responsibility than typing and filing memos, I decided that maybe a Master's degree would be the ticket to professional success.

Graduate school was a revelation. The sociological perspective became crystal clear. I saw for the first time how social forces influence our actions and our attitudes, how social standards must be viewed from an historical perspective, and how understanding oneself cannot be accomplished by mere introspection, but must be approached with a clear view of one's place in time, a view that will show us how cultural values affect our personal choices, and how patterns and processes in our society can constrain us as well as provide us with opportunities we might never have imagined.

Immersed in my studies, having a wonderful time in study sessions with my classmates, serving as a research associate for one of my professors, I still had no real vision of my future. Then, one day during Christmas vacation, one of the senior faculty members in the department asked if I would like to teach an evening class in introductory sociology, a class which was scheduled to begin in one week. And *that* was the event that marked the course of my professional life as a sociologist.

My first teaching experience was about 90% fear and 10% fun. I had not yet completed my Master's degree, had never spoken in front of an audience, had never taken a course in how to teach, and had long since forgotten what introductory sociology

was all about. I prepared sixteen pages of typewritten notes for my first lecture, got through them in twenty horrifying minutes, and dismissed the class early! But it was a beginning, and before the term was over I had decided that teaching undergraduate sociology would be my career. Despite the distaste I had had for the introductory sociology course I took as a college sophomore, that course became, and still remains, my favorite course to teach.

I began teaching at Tacoma Community College shortly after earning the Master's degree and long before I finished work on the Ph.D. And except for some visiting teaching opportunities at the University of Washington, that is where I have stayed. My students range in age from 17 to nearly 70, most hold jobs while they attend college, many are raising a family, often alone, and it is not uncommon to have a child sitting in class next to his/her parent. Some are international students, tied to a distant family and community with high expectations for their success. Most of my students, like you, take introductory sociology without knowing what sociology is, and they will leave, like you, to pursue other interests and course requirements for careers. But I am confident that they will take something with them that will forever enrich their lives and inform the choices they make. So will you.

I'm telling you this because I know that many of you are struggling to find your place, just as I did. Your lives are different than mine, different than anyone else's, and yet all of you are likely to be wondering what you will do, how you will live, what obstacles you will face and what opportunities will be available to you. Today, in our rapidly changing world it is more important than ever before to understand the social forces that will affect you. And sociology can be a powerful force of understanding.

Your first course in sociology can be the most exciting course you will ever take. You will learn about the great theories of society and they will help you develop a new view of the world and of your place in it. You will begin to understand yourself as you've never done before as you study the impact of cultural and social norms, of social class and group membership, on your own values and actions. You will see how conformity and deviance are socially defined, how prejudices and racism are closely linked to historical views of human behavior and to current economic realities. You will learn about your family and interpersonal relationships and how your actions toward others elicit the behavior they direct toward you. You will begin to see how your expectations, realistic or not, have the ability to create your view of reality. And most of all, you will be able to use the sociological perspective to make informed choices about your life, your career, your community, and your power to be an instrument of social change.

Now that you have a better idea about the benefits of studying sociology at the undergraduate level, you may want to get additional information about studying sociology at the graduate level and may consider sociology as a potential field of employment. A number of useful pamphlets and publications are available from the American Sociological Association (ASA) located at 1722 N Street, N.W., Washington, D.C. 20036-2981. The telephone number is (202) 833-3410.

Among the pamphlets that may be purchased from the ASA are

1. *Embarking upon a Career with an Undergraduate Degree in Sociology* by Janet Mancini Billson and Bettina J. Huber. ($10.00) A useful guide to a successful job search designed for undergraduate sociological students.
2. *Employment Patterns in Sociology: Recent Trends and Future Prospects* by Bettina J. Huber. ($10.00) Describes and analyzes employment trends into the year 2000, including opportunities for B.A. and M.A. sociology graduates and the implications of trends for job opportunities.
3. *Mastering the Job Market with a Graduate Degree in Sociology* by Janet Mancini Billson and Bettina J. Huber. ($10.00) Provides guidelines for graduate students seeking employment in both academic and applied settings.
4. *How to Join the Federal Workforce and Advance Your Career* by Abbott L. Ferriss. ($5.00) Describes the different roles sociologists take in governmental organizations and includes salary levels and qualifications.
5. *Sociologists in the Corporate World: Academic, Research, and Practice Roles in Business and Industry* by Delbert C. Miller. ($12.50) A helpful guide to the varied positions sociologists hold in corporations.
6. *The Profession of Sociology* by David F. Mitchell and the late James K. Skipper. ($13.50) Outlines the many roles of an academic sociologist, including research, teaching, publishing, participating in professional associations, and working in the community on social issues.

7. *Graduate Programs in Applied Sociology and Sociological Practice* by Jeanne Ballantine, Carla Howery, and Brian F. Pendelton. ($12.50) A listing of departments offering applied/practice concentrations or courses at the graduate level. (Prices quoted are for non-members and are current as of Spring 1995.)

Single copies of the following are free from the ASA if you send a self-addressed, stamped envelope.

1. *The Sociology Major as Preparation for Careers in Business and Organizations* by Delbert C. Miller.
2. *Maintaining Competence in the Federal Workplace in the 1990s and Beyond* by Abbott L. Ferriss.
3. *Careers in Sociology.*
4. *Majoring in Sociology: A Guide for Students.* A revised version.

There are many regional and state sociological associations that have special student membership fees and hold annual meetings. Undergraduates can usually attend free of charge. Ask your professor or call the ASA for the association in your area.

Finally, your instructor in this course is a potential source of rich information about research, assistantships and career possibilities in sociology. We are quite certain that she or he will be flattered that you are considering further study in the field of sociology. The Chair of the Sociology or Social Science Department at your college is another good resource. You can also contact the authors at the following addresses, and we will be glad to try and help you. Professor Peter J. Stein, Department of Sociology, William Paterson College, Wayne, New Jersey, 07470; Professor Beth Hess, Department of Social Science, County College of Morris, Randolph Township, New Jersey; or write to Karen Hansen, Sociology Editor at Allyn and Bacon, Paramount Publishing Education Group, 160 Gould Street, Needham Heights, Massachusetts, 02194-2310.

Glossary

Absolute deprivation is a lack of the basic necessities of survival. (Ch. 23, p. 556)

Absolute numbers are an actual head count of people, births, deaths, and so forth. (Ch. 20, p. 476)

Accommodation occurs when members of a minority are aware of the norms and values of the dominant culture but do not replace traditional ways of life with new ones. (Ch. 11, p. 252)

Acculturation, or cultural assimilation, occurs when minority members adopt the dominant culture and participate in the economy, schools, and so on, but are refused entry into intimate social groupings. (Ch. 11, p. 252)

Achieved statuses are positions based on choice, merit, or effort. (Ch. 4, p. 76)

Acting crowds have some goals beyond expression of emotion: they desire to take action. (Ch. 23, p. 549)

Acupuncture is an ancient Chinese technique for relieving pain and reducing addiction by manipulating fine needles into designated parts of the body. (Ch. 18, p.441)

Affective factors refer to feelings and emotions. (Ch. 5, p. 113)

Age norms are social expectations of persons of a given age. (Ch. 7, p. 146)

Age stratification refers to inequality of both people and roles in terms of control over valued resources on the basis of chronological age. (Ch. 7, p. 146)

An **age structure** of a population is based on the number of persons in each age category. (Ch. 7, p. 149)

The **age structure of roles** refers to the statuses open to persons of a given age. (Ch. 7)

Agents of change occupy statuses through which they influence the direction of change. (Ch. 19, p. 456)

Agents of socialization are individuals and organizations responsible for transmitting the culture. (Ch. 5, p. 105)

Agribusiness is a type of farming in which a few high-tech corporations produce most of the food consumed domestically and abroad. (Ch. 21)

Alienation is the feeling of powerlessness, normlessness, and being cut off from the product of one's labor, from other people, and from oneself. (Ch. 13, p. 310)

The **all-volunteer force (AVF)** is composed of people who enter the military as a full-time career. (Ch. 14, p. 345)

Amalgamation is the gradual process of loss of minority group traits through social acceptance and intermarriage. (Ch. 11 p. 253)

Amenities are cultural niceties, such as symphony orchestras, expensive restaurants, and elegant shops. (Ch. 21, p. 513)

American civil religion is a common faith that the nation is divinely blessed, has a mission in the world, and is guided by ethical standards of good citizenship. (Ch. 16, p. 389)

The **American ethos** is a set of core values guiding the beliefs and behaviors of Americans. (Ch. 3, p. 67)

Anomie refers to situations in which norms are absent, unclear, or confusing. (Ch. 4, p. 81)

Anticipatory socialization involves rehearsing before assuming a role. (Ch. 5, p. 101)

Apartheid refers specifically to the South African policy of segregation and political and economic discrimination against people of color within that country. (Ch. 9, p. 212)

Artifacts, or material culture, consist of tools and other human-made objects. (Ch. 3, p. 53)

Age is an **ascribed characteristic** that determines people's social location. (Ch. 7, p. 145)

Ascribed statuses are positions occupied based on relatively unchangeable characteristics over which a person has little control, such as sex, age, and race. (Ch. 4 p. 76)

Assimilation, or **structural assimilation,** occurs when minority group status is no longer a barrier to full integration into the dominant group. (Ch. 11, p. 252)

Authority refers to socially legitimated power. (Chs. 9, 14, pp. 195, 327)

Automation is the replacing of workers with machines. (Ch. 13, p. 311)

Backstage interaction is free of the constraints of public performance. (Ch. 4, p. 88)

Behaviorism concentrates on the study of observable activity as opposed to reported or inferred mental and emotional processes. (Ch. 5, p. 117)

A **belief system** is a set of shared ideas about the meaning of life. (Ch. 16, p. 377)

The *berdaches* of Native American tribes were treated as a third sex, neither fully male nor female. (Ch. 8, p. 179)

Biological determinism is based on the belief that genetic factors explain differences in human behavior. (Ch. 1, p. 23)

A **birth cohort** consists of people born during a specified time period. (Chs. 7, 20, pp. 147, 484)

Bisexuality involves the ability to enjoy sexual relations with both males and females.

Blended families consist of a husband and wife, children of previous marriages, and any children from the new marital union. (Ch. 12, p. 289)

Blockbusting involves generating feelings of panic in stable, white neighborhoods when real estate agents sell or rent to African Americans and then urge neighboring homeowners to sell before property values decline. (Ch. 21, p. 516)

Born again means having an experience that changes one's life through the acceptance of the Lord. (Ch. 16, p. 396)

Boundaries, which may be formal or informal, differentiate group members from non-members. (Ch. 4, p. 83)

Boundary maintenance refers to the ways subcultures/subgroups protect themselves from outsiders. (Ch. 3, p. 65)

Boundary setting occurs when shared norms set the limits of acceptable behavior. (Ch. 6, p. 126)

The **bureaucracy** is a formal organization characterized by rationality and efficiency, so that large-scale administrative tasks can be accomplished. (Ch. 4, p. 91)

Capital punishment is another term for the death penalty. (Ch. 17, p. 418)

Case studies are in-depth descriptions of the social world of particular subgroups. (Ch. 2, p. 35)

Caste systems are based on ascription, with minimal movement across stratum boundaries. (Ch. 9, p. 212)

A **casual crowd** is an accidental gathering of people. (Ch. 23, p. 549)

Censorship involves the selective withholding of information. (Ch. 14, p. 331)

A **census** is an inventory of an entire population at a given moment. (Ch. 20, p. 476)

Charismatic authority is based on some extraordinary quality of the leader or the leader's ideas. (Ch. 14, p. 327)

Chiropractic is the treatment of disease through manipulation of the body, especially the spine. (Ch. 18, p. 440)

The Christian Coalition is a politically sophisticated grassroots movement with the same agenda and following as the New Christian Right (NCR). (Ch. 16, p. 395)

Christian Science healers combat poor health and other problems by using the powers of the mind and spirit. (Ch. 18, p. 441)

Civil disobedience involves peaceful refusal to obey unjust laws in the name of a higher morality. (Ch. 23)

Civil liberties are the rights to speak, publish, and assemble. (Ch. 14, p. 331)

Class awareness refers to the recognition that differences in income, occupational prestige, and life-style are reflections of one's own class position. (Ch. 9, p. 202)

Class consciousness occurs when class awareness becomes the central organizing point of self-definition and political action. (Ch. 9, p. 202)

Class immobility occurs when class status is reproduced from one generation to another. (Ch. 9, p. 215)

Coercion is the use of force to induce compliance. (Ch. 4, p. 89)

Cognitive factors refer to how people think and process information. (Ch. 5, p. 113)

Cognitive development refers to change over time in how people understand and organize their experience. (Ch. 5, p. 116)

Cognitive structures shape how the mind processes information. (Ch. 10, p. 228)

Cohabitation occurs when unmarried people share living quarters. (Ch. 12, p. 292)

Cohort flow refers to the movement of people born in a given time period across their life course. (Ch. 19, p. 455)

Collective behavior refers to actions outside established patterns and social structures in response to social change and uncertainty. (Ch. 23, p. 546)

A **collectivity** is a set of people that can be as unconnected as an aggregate or as closely linked as a group. (Ch. 1, p. 6)

"Coming out" refers to the public acknowledgment of one's homosexual identity. (Ch. 8, p. 183)

American cities before 1850 were **commercial cities**, organized around craft manufacturing, commerce, transportation, or politics. (Ch. 21, p. 509)

Commuter marriages occur when husband and wife work in different cities and typically maintain separate households. (Ch. 12, p. 294)

Comparable worth, or **pay equity**, means that people who occupy jobs requiring similar skills and supervisory responsibility and are carried out under similar conditions should receive similar wages. (Ch. 10, p. 238)

Comparative studies compare social patterns across different societies or time periods. (Ch. 2, p. 38)

Competition is the result of situations defined as ones in which scarce resources are unequally distributed. (Ch. 4, p. 89)

Compromise involves cooperation to reduce the all-or-nothing results of competition. (Ch. 4, p. 89)

Concentration occurs when a large number of people settle in a relatively small space. (Ch. 21, p. 506)

Conflict occurs when groups try to destroy or disable their opponents. (Ch. 4, p. 89)

A **conflict approach** to criminal justice assumes that laws serve the interests of the dominant social strata. (Ch. 17, p. 402)

Conflict theory examines disagreement, hostility, and struggles over power and resources in a group. (Ch. 1, p. 16)

The **conflict view of social change** focuses on recurring and lasting sources of tension and struggle among individuals and groups within a society. (Ch. 19, p. 463)

Confrontations test the limits of acceptable behavior. (Ch. 6, p. 126)

Conglomerates exist when one company owns controlling shares in a variety of commercial areas. (Ch. 13, p. 307)

Conspicuous consumption is the open display of wastefulness designed to impress others. (Ch. 3, p. 69)

Constants are characteristics that do not change from one person or time to another. (Ch. 2, p. 31)

Content analysis counts the number of references to a given item in a sample of publications. (Ch. 2, p. 39)

Contingencies refer to possibilities that open or close opportunities for change. (Ch. 6, p. 136)

A **conventional crowd** is composed of people who are gathered as spectators, audiences, or participants at events governed by established norms. (Ch. 23, p. 549)

Cooperation is the sharing of resources to gain a common goal. (Ch. 4, p. 89)

Cooperative learning occurs when students pool talents and help one another. (Ch. 15, p. 364)

Co-optation occurs when members of a dissenting group are absorbed by the dominant group. (Ch. 4, p. 89)

The **core sector** of the economy consists of major industries, large investments in plants and equipment, unionized labor, monopolies, and high profits. (Ch. 13, p. 315)

Corporate culture refers to the beliefs, values, and norms that define the organization. (Ch. 13, p. 322)

Corporations are formal organizations that are legal actors in their own right. (Ch. 13, p. 321)

Correlation refers to how change in one variable is associated with change in another variable. (Ch. 2, p. 31)

Countercultures represent alternative life-styles for those not conforming to the dominant culture. (Ch. 3, p. 67)

A **countermovement** is a set of opinions and beliefs within the population that is opposed to the goals of a social movement. (Ch. 23, p. 555)

Crazes involve a desire to have something that everyone else appears to be enjoying. (Ch. 23, p. 547)

Cross-media ownership occurs when one company controls a variety of media outlets in a single market.

Cross-sectional studies take place at one time only. (Ch. 2, p. 33)

A **crowd** is a temporary gathering of people brought together by a common concern or activity. (Ch. 23, p. 549)

Cults and **New Religious Movements (NRMs)** have developed outside the mainstream religions, compete with them for members, and have attracted attention as a result of members' unusual behavior and fear generated among members' families. (Ch. 16, p. 396)

Cultural capital refers to a style of talking and thinking, as well as to knowledge of music, art, and literature, that prepares individuals for membership in the dominant strata. (Ch. 15, p. 355)

Cultural, or **ideological, hegemony** refers to control over the production of values and norms by those in power. (Ch. 3, p. 69)

Cultural heterogeneity refers to populations having many subgroups who differ in language, race, religion, national origin, and culture. (Ch. 11, p. 248)

Cultural homogeneity refers to populations whose members share a similarity in language, race, religion, national origin, and a common culture. (Ch. 11, p. 248)

The **cultural pluralism** model emphasizes the special contributions of each minority group to the diversity of American society. (Ch. 11, p. 251)

Cultural relativism involves an effort to understand the world as seen by members of other societies. (Ch. 3, p. 61)

Cultural universals are basic elements found in all cultures. (Ch. 3, p. 59)

Cultural variability reflects the variety of customs, beliefs, and artifacts devised by humans to meet universal needs. (Ch. 3, p. 59)

Culture is the map for living of a collectivity whose members share a given territory and language, feel responsible for one another, and recognize their common identity. (Ch. 3, p. 53)

Culture contact occurs as people from different societies meet and learn about one another's beliefs, artifacts, and social structure. (Ch. 19, p. 453)

Culture lag refers to the tendency of parts of the social structure to change at different rates after a new technology is introduced. (Ch. 19, p. 456)

Cumulative social change is the long-range historical trend toward the increasing complexity of social life and interaction. (Ch. 19, p. 464)

Cyclical theories of social change are based on the view that society resembles a living organism going through phases of growth and decline. (Ch. 19, p. 462)

Date rape is nonconsenting sexual intercourse in the dating context. (Ch. 8, p. 186)

De facto segregation is not necessarily supported by law but does in fact occur. (Ch. 11, p. 252)

De jure segregation is created by laws. (Ch. 11, p. 252)

Deferred gratification is the postponing of current pleasure to achieve future goals. (Ch. 9, p. 216)

Definition of the situation is the process by which people interpret and evaluate the social context to select appropriate attitudes and behavior. (Ch. 4, p. 80)

Deindividualization is the process of removing a person's civilian identities. (Ch. 5, p. 111)

Deinstitutionalization refers to the release of mental patients into the community. (Ch. 6, p. 142)

Delinquent and **criminal subcultures** originate in the differences between hopes for legitimate success and limited opportunity for achievement. (Ch. 6, p. 132)

Under **democratic,** or **welfare, socialism,** goods and services may be privately produced, but the distribution of essential services is centrally controlled. (Ch. 13, p. 309)

Demographers are sociologists who study population trends. (Ch. 20, p. 476)

Demographic transition refers to the historical shift from populations kept in balance by both high birth and death rates to populations stabilized by low fertility and mortality. (Ch. 20, p. 479)

Demography is the study of populations. (Ch. 20, p. 476)

Demonstrations are temporary but highly organized acting crowds with a clearly defined goal. (Ch. 23, p. 552)

A **dependency ratio** compares the number of children and elderly to the number of working age. (Ch. 20, p. 484)

Dependent variables are influenced by independent variables. (Ch. 2, p. 32)

Desocialization is learning to give up a role. (Ch. 5, p. 119)

Deviant behavior refers to behavior that departs from approved, expected, and generally held norms. (Ch. 6, p. 122)

The **deviant career** refers to a journey of stages from one deviant status to another. (Ch. 6, p. 136)

A **deviant subculture** is a group or network providing acceptance of deviant behavior. (Ch. 6, p. 136)

The **dialectical model** views social change as the outcome of a struggle between opposing forces. (Ch. 19, p. 463)

The **differential association** model states that deviant behavior is learned in primary groups and involves the same learning processes as nondeviant behavior. (Ch. 6, p. 132)

Diffusion refers to the process by which culture traits are spread from one society to another. (Ch. 19, p. 453)

Discrimination is the practice of treating people unequally. (Ch. 11, p. 256)

The **disenchantment of the world** occurs as science replaces faith and fantasy. (Ch. 1, p. 12)

Division of labor is the separation of work into distinct parts, each of which is performed by an individual or a group of people. (Ch. 13)

Domestic partners include homosexual and nonmarried heterosexual couples who in some U.S. cities enjoy some of the same legal rights as married couples. (Ch. 8, p. 184)

A **dominant group** exercises control over societal resources. (Ch. 11, p. 247)

The **dramaturgical model** views role partners as actors who perform roles as series of minidramas. (Ch. 4, p. 88)

The **dramaturgical view** sees social interaction as a series of minidramas. (Ch. 1, p. 19)

Dual economy refers to the existence of two separate types of employing firms: core and peripheral. (Ch. 13, p. 315)

In **dual-career** families or couples, both partners have a career. (Ch. 12, p. 294)

In **dual-earner** families or couples, both partners are in the labor force. (Ch. 12, p. 293)

The **dyad,** a two-person group, is typified by intimacy, joint responsibility, and great opportunity for total involvement or conflict. (Ch. 4, p. 87)

Dysfunctional patterns reduce the capacity of a system to adapt and survive. (Ch. 1, p. 15)

Violations by **eccentrics** are not regarded as disruptive nor threatening to the social order. (Ch. 6, p. 137)

Ecological differentiation occurs with decentralization, when specific activities become associated with a given geographical area, such as the financial or theater district. (Ch. 21, p. 506)

Ecological invasion occurs when a differentiated area is invaded by new activities and new populations. (Ch. 21, p. 506)

Ecologists are scientists who study the adaptation of populations to their environment. (Ch. 20, p. 489)

An **economic system** consists of the norms and activities regulating the production, distribution, and consumption of goods and services. (Ch. 13, p. 302)

An **ecumenopolis** is a linking of overlapping urban and suburban areas across nations. (Ch. 21, p. 519)

Egalitarianism refers to reduced power differences between husbands and wives and between parents and children. (Ch. 12, p. 283)

Ego defenses protect the self-image. (Ch. 5, p. 113)

Ego development involves the possibility of change and growth across the life course. (Ch. 5, p. 114)

Ego identity refers to a sense of continuity and sameness in the self-concept across time and situations. (Ch. 5, p. 115)

An **elite culture** consists of items consumed and sponsored by the wealthy. (Ch. 22, p. 524)

The **emotional contagion model** focuses on how the intensity of crowds develops. (Ch. 23, p. 552)

Empirical referents are items that can be measured and counted. (Ch. 2, p. 29)

Employer discrimination is the tendency to treat employees differently on the basis of sex or race or other characteristics. (Ch. 10, p. 237)

The **empty nest** stage of the family cycle occurs when all the children are out of the house and the parents are alone together again. (Ch. 12, p. 284)

Environmental events include those produced by nature and by people. (Ch. 19, p. 453)

The **Environmental Justice Movement** is a culturally diverse grass-roots effort to change the way in which decisions that affect the quality of life are made. (Ch. 20, p. 495)

Environmental racism occurs when toxins are stored in communities that are inhabited primarily by people of color, who have little political or economic power. (Ch. 20, p. 493)

Epidemiology is the study of the patterns of occurrence of illness in a population. (Ch. 18, p. 427)

Erotic identity is based on the object of sexual attraction—persons of the opposite or same sex. (Ch. 8, p. 168)

Ethnicity refers to cultural identity derived from a common ancestry and place of origin. (Ch. 11, p. 249)

Ethnocentrism is the belief that one's own culture is the best and therefore the standard by which other cultures are consequently judged. (Ch. 3, p. 60)

Ethnomethodology involves probing beneath the "taken-for-granted" reality. (Ch. 1, p. 20)

Evaluation studies involve testing different versions of social programs. (Ch. 2, p. 42)

Evangelical refers to an emphasis on the personal witnessing of God's presence coupled with an obligation to spread the Word. (Ch. 16, p. 396)

The **evolutionary progress theory** assumes that humankind has progressed from the savagery of simple societies to the high culture of current Europe. (Ch. 19, p. 462)

Exchange and **rational-choice** theories adopt an essentially economic model of cost and benefit to explain people's behaviors. (Ch. 1, p. 22)

Experiments come closest to the scientific ideal of control over variables. (Ch. 2, p. 40)

An **expressive relationship** is valued in its own right, as an end in itself. (Ch. 4, p. 82)

An **expressive crowd** shows strong feelings with outbursts of emotion. (Ch. 23, p. 549)

Expressive roles are oriented toward the expression of group tension and emotion. (Ch. 4, p. 88)

The **extended family** is a relatively large unit composed of several related households, most often involving three or more generations. (Ch. 12, p. 278)

A **fad** is a short-lived but widely copied outburst of unexpected and often playful behavior. (Ch. 23, p. 547)

Familism is a pattern of family closeness, traditionalism, and male dominance. (Ch. 12, p. 290)

The **family system** reflects society's solutions to certain basic issues such as controlling sexuality and pairing people off for reproduction. (Ch. 12, p. 275)

Fashions are more enduring, widespread, and socially important than fads. (Ch. 23, p. 547)

A **fear of crime** keeps people from taking part in community activities and undermines group unity. (Ch. 17)

Feeling rules shape how, when, with whom, and where emotions are expressed. (Ch. 4, p. 90)

Feminist sociology directs attention to women's experience and to the importance of gender as an element of social structure. (Ch. 1, p. 22)

The **feminization of poverty** refers to the fact that a majority of the adult poor are women. (Ch. 9, p. 207)

Field experiments are conducted in the real world. (Ch. 2, p. 41)

Folkways are approved standards of behavior passed on from one generation to the next. (Ch. 3, p. 63)

Foraging involves picking readily available foods for immediate consumption. (Ch. 3, p. 52)

Formal agents of social control occupy statuses specifically charged with norm enforcement. (Ch. 6, p. 128)

Formal, or complex, **organizations** are social structures characterized by impersonality, ranked positions, large size, relative complexity, and long duration. (Ch. 4, p. 91)

Frame analysis refers to the rules governing everyday encounters that also exist apart from specific interactions. (Ch. 1, p. 20)

Free-enterprise capitalism is an economic system with minimal public ownership or controls. (Ch. 13, p. 306)

Frontstage interaction occurs in full view of the public. (Ch. 4, p. 88)

Functional analysis examines the relationship between the parts and the whole of a social system. (Ch. 1, p. 14)

Functional disorders refer to the inability to meet normative expectations. (Ch. 6, p. 139)

Fundamentalism is a rigidly traditional set of beliefs that sees the world as divided into clear-cut forces for good or for evil. (Ch. 16, pp. 388, 394)

Gatekeepers regulate the entry of patients into different kinds of treatments. (Ch. 6, p. 140)

Gathering involves transporting, storing, and preserving readily available foods. (Ch. 3, p. 52)

Along with other civil rights movements, the **Gay Rights Movement** emerged in the 1960s; it attempted to extend full rights of citizenship to all homosexuals. (Ch. 8, p. 183)

Gemeinschaft refers to small, traditional communities, characterized by primary-group relationships and intergenerational stability. (Ch. 4, p. 83)

Gender identity is a sense of being feminine or masculine. (Ch. 8, p. 168)

The **gender wage gap** refers to the discrepancy between average earnings of women and men. (Ch. 10, p. 236)

Gendered inequality refers to differences between men and women in the distribution of power, prestige, and property. (Ch. 10, p. 222)

The **generalized other** reflects societal standards of acceptable behavior in roles. (Ch. 5, p. 109)

Genocide is the systematic, intentional killing of an entire population. (Ch. 14, p. 332)

A **genre** is a specific type of artistic style. (Ch. 22, p. 533)

Gentrification refers to the migration of middle- and upper-income people into urban centers, their displacement of lower-income residents, and renovation of existing housing. (Ch. 21, p. 518)

Gesellschaft refers to contractual relationships, wherein social bonds are voluntary, based on rational self-interest, and characterized by instrumental behavior. (Ch. 4, p. 83)

A **gesture** is a symbol whose meaning is shared by group members. (Ch. 5, p. 109)

Glass ceiling blocks the way to the very top for women and minorities. (Ch. 10, p. 232)

A **global city** is focused on international trade and commerce. (Ch. 21, p. 510)

Goal displacement occurs when movement goals are displaced by the goal of maintaining formal structures; when complexities and regulations of bureaucracies upstage the stated goals of the organization. (Chs. 4, 23, pp. 93, 558)

Goal displacement in bureaucracy occurs when maintaining the structure replaces the stated goals of the organization. (Ch. 4, p. 93)

A **group** is characterized by a distinctive set of relationships, interdependence, a feeling that members' behavior is relevant, and a sense of membership. (Ch. 4, p. 81)

Head Start is a federally funded preschool program for disadvantaged children that provides learning experiences and social services to the family. (Ch. 15, p. 357)

The **health maintenance organization (HMO)** is based on prepayment for health care by patients who agree to use member physicians and hospitals. (Ch. 18, p. 444)

The **health promotion** movement perpetuates the belief that good health is an individual responsibility in order to sell their products. (Ch. 18, p. 433)

Heterogamy is the practice of selecting a mate with different social background characteristics. (Ch. 12, p. 281)

The **hidden curriculum** refers to what is learned, such as ethnocentrism and respect for authority, but is not part of the official curriculum. (Ch. 15, p. 354)

Historical societies have left written records. (Ch. 3, p. 56)

Historical records such as documents, papers, and letters identify relationships among variables over time and space. (Ch. 2, p. 38)

Homogamy is the practice of selecting a mate with similar social background characteristics. (Ch. 12, p. 281)

Homophobia refers to intense fear of homosexuals. (Ch. 8, p. 179)

Homosexual relations involve persons of the same sex. (Ch. 8, p. 178)

Homosexual subcultures offer protection and support for gay males and lesbians. (Ch. 8, p. 179)

Hospital ownership is either for-profit (proprietary) private, non-profit private, or public. (Ch. 18, p. 441)

Humanist sociology is based on the belief that sociologists must become actively involved in social change. (Ch. 1, p. 21)

Hypotheses are specific statements derived from a theory about relationships among variables. (Ch. 2, p. 31)

The **"I"** is the creative spontaneous part of the self, whereas the **"me"** consists of the internalized attitudes of others. (Ch. 5, p. 111)

Ideal culture reflects the highest virtues and standards of a society. (Ch. 3, p. 62)

Ideal types are theoretical models that exaggerate distinctive features. (Ch. 4, p. 83)

Ideological hegemony refers to control over production of cultural symbols. (Ch. 9, p. 193)

In vitro **fertilization** is a procedure in which an egg is fertilized outside the mother's body and then replanted in the womb. (Ch. 8, p. 176)

The **incest taboo** forbids sexual relations between people defined as relatives. (Ch. 12, p. 276)

The **incidence rate** of disease is the number of new cases of a disease within a population during a stated time period. (Ch. 18, p. 428)

The American education system is **inclusive**, or open, to almost all children of given ages. (Ch. 15, p. 357)

Independent variables have the greatest impact, come first in the chain of events, are relatively fixed, and/or affect dependent variables. (Ch. 2, p. 32)

Index crimes include the violent crimes of murder, forcible rape, robbery, and aggravated assault. (Ch. 17, p. 405)

In **individual practice associations (IPAs)**, physicians accept patients under a prepayment arrangement but can also accept fee-for-service reimbursement. (Ch. 18, p. 444)

The large **industrial city** was dominated by factories, railroads, and slums. (Ch. 21, p. 509)

Industrial suburban cities developed in vacant areas outside central cities for economic, political, and labor-related reasons. (Ch. 21, p. 509)

Influence is the ability to persuade others to follow one's will. (Ch. 9, p. 195)

Informal controls include expressions of approval and affection by significant others. (Ch. 6, p. 128)

Informal primary groups develop within bureaucracies as a buffer against impersonal relationships. (Ch. 4, p. 94)

In-groups are primary or secondary groups to which a person belongs. (Ch. 4, p. 83)

The **inner-directed** person's behavior is governed by an internal mechanism typical of industrial society. (Ch. 19, p. 472)

Innovation refers to the introduction of a new item of culture through discovery or invention. (Ch. 19, p. 455)

Institutional spheres are major areas of social activity. (Ch. 1, p. 14)

Institutionalization is the process whereby a given adaptation becomes an established pattern. (Ch. 13, p. 302)

Institutionalization of a social movement occurs when its beliefs are accepted and its goals are embodied in stable organizations. (Ch. 23, p. 557)

In the context of hospitalization, **institutionalization** refers to the commitment of mental patients to asylums or mental hospitals. (Ch. 6, p. 141)

Institutionalized racism is systematic discrimination of a racial or ethnic group that is built into social structures. (Ch. 11, p. 257)

Instrumental behavior is a means to some other goal. (Ch. 4, p. 83)

Instrumental roles are oriented toward specific goals. (Ch. 4, p. 88)

Interaction processes refer to ways in which partners agree on their goals, negotiate behavior, and distribute resources. (Ch. 4, p. 88)

Interactive dimensions of social networks include frequency of contact, strength of bonds, and duration. (Ch. 4, p. 87)

An **interest group** develops when members of a public seek others with similar feelings about an issue. (Ch. 23, p. 549)

Intergenerational mobility involves status change between parents and their children. (Ch. 9, p. 212)

Intergenerational, or career mobility refers to status changes over an individuals' lifetime. (Ch. 9, p. 212)

Interlocking corporate directorates involve the same individuals sitting on several boards of directors. (Ch. 13, p. 307)

Internal colonialism is the practice of treating native populations as if they were colonies. (Ch. 11, p. 261)

Interpretive sociology focuses on processes by which people make sense of daily life. (Ch. 1, p. 17)

Intragenerational or career mobility involves status changes during a person's own lifetime. (Ch. 9)

Involuntary childlessness refers to the inability to conceive. (Ch. 12, p. 292)

Jargons are special languages of subgroups/subcultures. (Ch. 3, p. 65)

Job autonomy involves making decisions about the timing and sequence of tasks; exercising judgment, and having an impact on the outcome. (Ch. 13, p. 311)

Key informants are carefully selected cases providing information on processes not easily visible but having general application. (Ch. 2, p. 35)

Kinesics is the study of nonverbal communication. (Ch. 3, p. 54)

Labeling refers to the process by which action becomes defined as deviant. (Ch. 6 , p. 136)

Latent functions are unexpected and unintended consequences. (Ch. 1, p. 14)

Laws are norms that govern behavior considered essential to group survival. (Chs. 3, 17, pp. 63, 402)

Legal-rational, or bureaucratic, authority is based on laws that limit the power of office holders. (Ch. 14, p. 328)

Life expectancy refers to the average number of years a person can expect to live. (Chs. 7, 18, pp. 147, 428)

The **life span** refers to the oldest age to which it is possible to live. (Ch. 7, p. 163)

Longitudinal studies follow a group of respondents over time. (Ch. 2, p. 33)

The **looking-glass self** suggests that we see ourselves reflected back in the reactions of others. (Ch. 5, p. 108)

Macrosociology focuses on society as a whole or on social systems at a high level of abstraction. (Ch. 1, p. 16)

Magic refers to behavior designed to manipulate unseen forces. (Ch. 16, p. 384)

Magnet schools are designed to attract students by offering specialized educational programs. (Ch. 15, p. 370)

Mainstreaming integrates disabled pupils into regular classes. (Ch. 15, p. 371)

Male and **female** refer to biological sex. **Feminine** and **masculine** are social constructions. (Ch. 10, p. 222)

Mandatory sentencing requires judges to impose specific prison terms rather than use their discretion. (Ch. 17, p. 413)

Manifest functions are open, stated, and intended goals. (Ch. 1, p. 14)

Marginality is the experience of being caught between two different cultures. (Ch. 11, p. 252)

In a **market system**, the value of goods and services is determined by supply and demand factors. (Ch. 13, p. 305)

In the **Marxist model** revolutionary situations occur whenever class divisions lead to widespread inequality and increased poverty among the masses. (Ch. 19, p. 461)

A **mass culture** is made up of those elements of popular culture that forge common values in a heterogeneous society and are produced and distributed through the mass media. (Ch. 22, p. 523)

Mass hysteria involves uncontrollable reactions to anxiety, most of which can be traced to stresses or strains in the social environment. (Ch. 23, p. 546)

Mass media refers to the print media and electronic media, which are agents of communication in a mass society. (Ch. 22, p. 527)

A **master status** has the greatest impact on a person's self-identity and appearance to others. (Ch. 4, p. 76)

Materialism refers to a desire for owning and consuming goods and services. (Ch. 3, p. 69)

Matrifocal refers to families centered on the woman. (Ch. 12, p. 291)

The **mean** is an average. (Ch. 2, p. 44)

Measures of central tendency are single numbers that summarize an entire set of data. (Ch. 2, p. 43)

The **median** is the midpoint of an entire set of cases. (Ch. 2, p. 44)

Mediation refers to the use of a third party to resolve issues. (Ch. 4, p. 89)

Medicaid is a federally funded, state-administered program for reimbursing providers of health care to the very poor. (Ch. 18, p. 443)

Medicalization occurs when forms of behavior once tolerated as unusual become defined as medical problems requiring active intervention. (Ch. 18, p. 437)

Medicare is a federally administered insurance program, funded by workers' and employers' contributions, to reimburse providers for certain services given to older patients. (Ch. 18, p. 443)

A **megalopolis** consists of overlapping metropolitan areas with many social, economic, and transportation links. (Ch. 21, p. 509)

The **melting pot** model of integration assumes that immigrants will lose their ethnic uniqueness through exposure to the dominant American culture. (Ch. 11, p. 250)

Mentors are teachers who act as guides and sponsors. (Ch. 5, p. 106)

A **meritocracy** is a hierarchy of talent, in which rewards are based on one's abilities. (Chs. 9, 15, pp. 193, 354)

A **metropolitan area** houses a large population center plus any surrounding communities strongly connected to that center socially and economically. (Ch. 21, p. 509)

Microsociology focuses on smaller units of social systems, such as face-to-face interactions. (Ch. 1, p. 17)

Migration is the movement of people out of or into a society. (Ch. 20, p. 482)

Migration statistics measure the population flow within a society as well as the movement in or out of it. (Ch. 20, p. 478)

Militarism refers to a social emphasis on military ideals and a glorification of war. (Ch. 14, p. 346)

Militarization occurs when an entire society is mobilized around militaristic goals. (Ch. 14, p. 346)

The **military-industrial complex** consists of a large permanent military establishment combined with an immense armament industry. (Ch. 14, p. 348)

Minority group status involves visible traits, differential treatment, shared identity, and self-image. (Ch. 11, p. 247)

A **mob** is an emotionally aroused crowd, often engaged in violent or disruptive acts. (Ch. 23, p. 550)

Mobilization involves the weakening of existing patterns of economic and social structures and psychological commitments, making people receptive for socialization to new patterns. (Ch. 19, p. 466)

The **mode** is the single most common category of cases. (Ch. 2, p. 44)

Mode of subsistence refers how a group adapts to its environment through the production and distribution of goods and services. (Chs. 3, 13, pp. 56, 302)

Modeling is the copying of characteristics of admired people. (Ch. 5, p. 101)

Modernization involves a global process of change whereby industrialization and urbanization are spread to nonindustrial societies, leading to the development of a world economy. (Chs. 16, 19, pp. 386, 464)

Money laundering refers to techniques for transforming "dirty" money into "clean" income. (Ch. 17, p. 414)

Monopolization refers to the tendency for a company to acquire exclusive control of a commodity or service in a particular market. (Ch. 13, p. 307)

Moral entrepreneurs define what is virtuous and combat the forces of evil. (Ch. 6, p. 126)

Moral reasoning involves the application of standards of fairness and justice. (Ch. 5, p. 116)

Mores are norms that cover moral and ethical behavior. (Ch. 3, p. 63)

Multiculturalism brings together people representing many traditions, religions, and racial types. (Ch. 11, p. 272)

Multinational corporations are firms with branches and factories in many countries and whose ownership is not linked to one nation. (Ch. 13, p. 308)

The **multiple nuclei model** describes cities in which several specialized centers emerge. (Ch. 21, p. 506)

The *National Crime Victimization Survey* (**NCVS**) collects self-reported experiences of victimization from U.S. households. (Ch. 17, p. 405)

Nationalism is a consciousness of shared identity among the members of a political distinct territory and provides a strong attachment. (Ch. 19, p. 465)

The **nation-state** is an overarching political unit that emerged as a consequence of modernization in complex societies. (Chs. 14, 19, pp. 329, 465)

Nativistic revivals arise when a culture is disintegrating under the impact of profound change. (Ch. 16, p. 386)

Natural experiments involve measuring the same population before and after a natural event that is assumed to change the situation. (Ch. 2, p. 42)

Negative sanctions convey disapproval of role performance. (Ch. 5, p. 101)

The **neoevolutionary model** traces changes in cultural and societal complexity without making value judgments about the superiority of one society over another. (Ch. 19, p. 462)

Net worth consists of the value of all assets less all debts. (Ch. 9, p. 196)

The **New Age Movement** (**NAM**) includes an array of beliefs seeking to understand the universe through contact with the supernatural, psychic healing, reincarnation, and similar mystical experiences. (Ch. 16, p. 398)

The **New Christian Right** (**NCR**) was formed by a combination of fundamentalist leaders and extremely conservative political action groups. (Ch. 16, p. 395)

Nonprofit organizations form a voluntary sector of the economy, typically involved in charitable work. (Ch. 4, p. 94)

The **nuclear family** is a unit composed of a married couple and their dependent children. (Ch. 12, p. 278)

Objective techniques of data gathering require the observer to be distanced from the object of study. (Ch. 2, p. 28)

Official data are collected by government agencies. (Ch. 2, p. 38)

Oligarchy is the rule of the many by the few. (Ch. 14, p. 334)

Open class systems allow individuals and groups to cross class boundaries. (Ch. 9, p. 212)

Operationalizing the variables involves translating an abstraction into something observable. (Ch. 2, p. 33)

Organic disorders result from disease or malfunction of the brain or nervous system. (Ch. 6, p. 139)

Organizational crimes are illegal activities taken by a corporation or its officers for the corporation's advantage. (Ch. 17)

Osteopathy, a treatment of disease that originally emphasized bones and muscles, has become very similar to mainstream medicine. (Ch. 18, p. 440)

The **other-directed** person, typical of the postindustrial society, constantly reacts and adapts to the expectations of others. (Ch. 19, p. 472)

Out-groups are primary or secondary groups to which others belong. (Ch. 4, p. 83)

Overpopulation refers to an imbalance between the number of people and the ability of the society to support them. (Ch. 20, p. 479)

Panics are actions caused by the need to escape perceived threats and fears. (Ch. 23, p. 546)

Parochial schools are private schools operated by religious organizations. (Ch. 15, p. 358)

In **participant observation**, the researcher becomes part of the interaction under study. (Ch. 2, p. 36)

The **pathological model** of disease focuses on biological symptoms and abnormal functioning in the organism. (Ch. 18, p. 436)

Patriarchy refers to male dominance. (Ch. 10, p. 224)

Patriotic crimes involve actions taken outside legitimate channels in the name of achieving important national goals. (Ch. 17, p. 411)

Peers are equals and an important source of information and socialization. (Ch. 5, p. 106)

A **percentage** indicates how many of a given item there are in every 100 cases. (Ch. 2, p. 42)

The **peripheral sector** of the economy consists of smaller, competitive low-profit firms employing low-pay, nonunion manual workers. (Ch. 13, p. 315)

Personal agency is the ability to have an effect on one's own environment (Ch. 4, p. 73).

Personal troubles are private problems experienced directly by an individual. (Ch. 1, p. 4)

Philanthropy refers to charitable giving. (Ch. 13, p. 323)

Plea bargaining is a negotiation between the prosecution and the accused to reduce the charges if the defendant pleads guilty. (Ch. 17, p. 418)

The **pluralist model** assumes there are many different and competing bases of power, with no one group dominating the others. (Ch. 14, p. 342)

Political action committees (PACs) are special organizations that collect funds to support causes and candidates. (Ch. 14, p. 336)

Political socialization includes the influences and experiences that determine one's political orientation. (Ch. 14, p. 339)

Polygamy creates extended households composed of a woman or man with more than one marriage partner at the same time. (Ch. 12, p. 278)

Popular culture consists of products designed for mass consumption during leisure time. (Ch. 22, p. 522)

Population projections are estimates of future growth or decline of a nation, state, or other geographic area. (Ch. 20, p. 478)

A **population pyramid** is a graphic representation of the age and sex distribution of a society's population. (Chs. 7, 20, pp. 147, 484)

Population shifts include major changes in birth or death rates or migration. (Ch. 19, p. 455)

Populism refers to grass-roots social movements in America that combine antibusiness sentiment with intolerance of racial, religious, and ethnic minorities. (Ch. 23)

Pornography refers to sexually detailed pictures and stories. (Ch. 8, p. 187)

Positive sanctions indicate approval of role performance. (Ch. 5, p. 101)

Positivism is based on the idea that science can be value free and objective. (Ch. 1, p. 10)

A **postindustrial era** is marked by a shift from manufacturing to the rapid development of information technology and services. (Ch. 19, p. 466)

Postindustrial society is characterized by an expanding service sector and the importance of knowledge. (Ch. 13, p. 309)

Postmodernism views all reality as constructed by language. (Ch. 19, p. 24)

The **poverty level** represents the minimum income needed to feed, house, and clothe household members. (Ch. 9, p. 206)

Power is the ability of achieving one's goals regardless of the wishes of others. (Chs. 9, 14, pp. 192, 327)

The **power-elite model** assumes that decision making is concentrated in the hands of a few similarly socialized people. (Ch. 14)

The **preferred provider organization (PPO)** is based on an agreement between health care providers and third-party payers to provide health care at a discount. (Ch. 18, p. 444)

Prejudice occurs when members of a racial, ethnic. or religious group are assumed to have a single set of favorable or unfavorable characteristics. (Ch. 11, p. 254)

Preliterate societies do not have a written language. (Ch. 3, p. 56)

Preparatory schools are private schools developed primarily to prepare children of well-off parents for entry into elite colleges. (Ch. 15, p. 359)

Prescriptive norms dictate what is expected. (Ch. 6, p. 122)

Prestige refers to the respect given by others. (Ch. 9, p. 192)

The **prevalence rate** of disease is the number of all the known cases of a disease in a population, regardless of when they began. (Ch. 18, p. 428)

Priestly functions deal with specific traditions of the faith, supporting the existing structure of power. (Ch. 16, p. 386)

Primary deviation refers to violations of norms that can be normalized by making excuses and explanations to oneself. (Ch. 6, p. 136)

A **primary group** is a group in which members have intimate personal ties with one another. (Ch. 4, p. 82)

The **principle of legitimacy**, or social fatherhood, identifies one man as responsible for the protection of a woman and her children and placement in the social system. (Ch. 12, p. 276)

Principled challenges are deliberate attempts to confront the norm setters. (Ch. 6, p. 128)

Private interests refer to property held by individuals, families, or corporations. (Ch. 13, p. 306)

Probability refers to the statistical likelihood of a given event. (Ch. 1, p. 8)

Probation allows a felon to remain in the community under close supervision. (Ch. 17, p. 423)

The **production of culture** involves markets, industries, distribution chains, organizations, and other systems that determine what is produced and offered to the public. (Ch. 22, p. 524)

The conflict perspective is concerned with who has control over the **production of popular culture**. (Ch. 22, p. 527)

Profane behaviors and objects are not holy but rather earthly and understandable. (Ch. 16, p. 384)

A **profession** is an occupation requiring lengthy training and in which practitioners control entry and monitor performance. (Ch. 9, p. 195)

The **professional model** of health care delivery is based on physician's control of health care. (Ch. 18, p. 443)

Propaganda involves the selective release of information favorable to those in power. (Ch. 14, p. 331)

Property refers to wealth owned. (Ch. 9, p. 192)

Property crimes such as burglary, larceny, and theft are much more prevalent than crimes against people. (Ch. 17, p. 406)

The **prophet** is a charismatic figure, witnessing a revelation calling for a new order. (Ch. 16, p. 386)

Proscriptive norms govern forbidden conduct. (Ch. 6, p. 122)

The **prosecutor, defense attorney,** and the **judge** are the three major parties in the criminal justice system, each representing different interests. (Ch. 17, p. 417)

The **prospective payment system** is based on fixed payment diagnosis-related groups (DRGs) rather than "reasonable costs." (Ch. 18, p. 447)

Psychology explains behavior in terms of a person's mental and emotional states. (Ch. 1, p. 4)

Public agencies are institutions, such as governments, that represent the society as a whole. (Ch. 13, p. 306)

Public issues are factors outside one's personal control and are caused by crises in the larger system. (Ch. 1, p. 4)

Publics are mass audiences of people who share a similar response to an issue. (Ch. 23, p. 548)

Qualitative research relies primarily on interpretive description rather than statistics. (Ch. 2, p. 30)

Quality circles are teams of employees and managers who meet to discuss how to improve their work performance. (Ch. 13, p. 312)

The **quality of life** of a population is measured by indices such as life expectancy, health, education, and income. (Ch. 19, p. 470)

Quantitative research uses the features of scientific objectivity, including complex statistical techniques. (Ch. 2, p. 30)

Race is a social construction influenced by the meanings assigned by a given society. (Ch. 11, p. 249)

Random sampling occurs when all possible respondents have an equal chance of being chosen. (Ch. 2, p. 33)

Rateables are properties that can be taxed by a city government. (Ch. 21, p. 515)

Rates are the number of times a given event occurs in a population, on a base other than 100. (Ch. 2, p. 42)

A **ratio** compares one subpopulation to another. (Ch. 2, p. 43)

Rational-choice theory assumes that criminals weigh costs and benefits of committing crimes. (Ch. 17, p. 404)

Real culture refers to actual beliefs and behavior. (Ch. 3, p. 62)

A **recidivist** is a repeat offender. (Ch. 17, p. 422)

Through **reciprocal socialization** children modify their parents' view of the world. (Ch. 5, p. 106)

Redlining occurs when banks refuse to give loans and mortgages to people or businesses in certain areas of a city. (Ch. 21, p. 515)

Reductionism involves reducing social life to individual behavior or biology. (Ch. 1, p. 23)

A **reference group** exerts a strong influence on one's identity, norms, and values. (Ch. 4, p. 86)

Reform movements seek changes within the existing social system. (Ch. 23, p. 556)

Rehabilitation means restoration to a former state. (Ch. 17, p. 423)

Reification is the logical fallacy of treating an abstract concept as a concrete object. (Ch. 1, p. 8)

Relative deprivation occurs when people feel unfairly treated in comparison to others thought to be their equals. (Ch. 23, p. 557)

Relative numbers are rates, ratios, and percentages that allow us to compare different societies or the same society at different historical periods. (Ch. 20, p. 476)

Reliability refers to whether the measuring instrument yields the same results on repeated trials. (Ch. 2, p. 29)

Religion is a belief system based on the concept of a divine power guiding human destiny and directed toward the supernatural: a shared set of beliefs, rituals, and worship. (Chs. 11, 16, pp. 249, 377)

Religious roles involve supervision of sacred objects, places, and ceremonies. (Ch. 16, p. 384)

Replication involves repeating a specific study often with different types of respondents in various settings and at other times. (Ch. 2, p. 30)

Psychological **repression** involves placing unacceptable impulses below the level of consciousness. (Ch. 5, p. 113)

Political **repression** involves the forceful denial of civil liberties. (Ch. 14, p. 332)

Agents in **repressive** control systems have extensive powers to detect and control many behaviors. (Ch. 6, p. 128)

Much mental illness is defined as **residual deviance** because normative expectations are more ambiguous. (Ch. 6, p. 138)

Resistance movements are designed to stop change and to restore traditional values and norms. (Ch. 23, p. 556)

Resocialization is learning important new norms and values. (Ch. 5, p. 119)

The **resource mobilization model** stresses the supports available to protesters, as well as the tactics used by social control agents. (Ch. 23, p. 553)

Restrained control systems use less intense control over fewer behaviors. (Ch. 6, p. 128)

The **revolution of rising expectations** refers to the gap between expected benefits and actual gains. (Ch. 23, p. 556)

Revolutionary events occur along a continuum of magnitude of political change. (Ch. 19, p. 459)

Revolutionary movements call for radical structural and value change in the society. (Ch. 23, p. 556)

A **revolutionary outcome** occurs when the opposition party in a revolutionary situation wins. (Ch. 19, p. 459)

A **revolutionary situation** exists when two or more political units claim control over the state, their interest cannot be resolved, and the opposition party receives support from the population. (Ch. 19, p. 459)

Riots are usually less spontaneous than mob actions and tend to involve more people over longer periods of time. (Ch. 23, p. 550)

Rites of passage are ceremonies marking important transitions form one age status to another. (Ch. 7, p. 145)

Ritualized release of hostility occurs when hostility is expressed under controlled situations. (Ch. 4, p. 90)

Rituals are culturally patterned ways of expressing central values and recurring concerns. (Ch. 3, p. 64)

Role is the expected behaviors associated with a particular status. (Ch. 4, p. 77)

Role conflict results from the competing and conflicting demands stemming from a role set. (Ch. 4, p. 79)

Role distance is the space placed between the self and the self-in-the-role. (Ch. 5, p. 111)

Role overload occurs when the total number of statuses and role sets overwhelm all activity. (Ch. 4, p. 80)

A **role set** is a collection of roles associated with a given status. (Ch. 4, p. 77)

Role slack occurs when capabilities are underdemanded as in adolescence. (Ch. 7, p. 154)

Role strain results from situations in which a single status calls for incompatible behaviors; when demands on time and energy exceeds one's capacity to meet them. (Chs. 4, 7, pp. 80, 155)

The **role structure** of a population consists of the number of roles available to persons of a given age. (Ch. 7, p. 146)

The **romantic love syndrome** involves the selection of a mate on the basis of love rather than on kin-based needs. (Ch. 12, p. 280)

The **routine-activity**, or **life-style/opportunity, approach** assumes that criminals will target situations that offer the maximum rewards at the least risk. (Ch. 17, p. 404)

The **routinization of charisma** occurs when the prophet's beliefs are institutionalized and transformed into a worldly organization. (Ch. 16, p. 386)

The **rule of reciprocity** obligates the receiver of a gift to return something of equivalent value. (Chs. 12, 13, pp. 276, 305)

Rumors are unconfirmed stories passed from one person to another. (Ch. 23, p. 548)

Sacred behaviors and objects are invested with holy, divine, mystical, or supernatural force. (Ch. 16, p. 384)

Some deviance serves as a **safety valve,** allowing controlled expressions. (Ch. 6, p. 126)

A **sample** is a selection from the entire population of interest. (Ch. 2, p. 33)

Sample surveys provide updated information at low cost within a short time. (Ch. 20, p. 477)

Sanctions refer to reactions that convey approval or disapproval of behavior. (Ch. 3, p. 63)

Scapegoating occurs when someone else is blamed for one's own misfortune. (Ch. 11, p. 255)

The **scientific method** consists of objective observations, precise measurement, and full disclosure of results. (Ch. 2, p. 29)

Secondary analysis involves the use of data collected by others. (Ch. 2, p. 38)

Secondary deviation refers to how one deals with the problems of being identified as a deviant. (Ch. 6, p. 136)

Secondary groups are characterized by few emotional ties and by limited interaction. (Ch. 4, p. 82)

Sectarian conflict refers to interreligious strife. (Ch. 16, p. 381)

The **sector model** organizes land use areas horizontally from the core of a city rather than circularly. (Ch. 21, p. 505)

Secular humanism is a belief system that assumes that people can solve their problems without divine intervention. (Ch. 16, p. 383)

A **secular ideology** is a belief system based on worldly rather than supernatural forces. (Ch. 16)

Secularization is the shift in focus from the next world and unquestioned faith to this world and reason, science, and technology. (Ch. 16, p. 386)

Segregation refers to isolating a minority from contact with other members of the society. (Ch. 11, p. 251)

Self-help groups allow people to derive strength from one another in face-to-face interaction. (Chs. 4, 14, pp. 95, 342)

Self-identity is an organization of perceptions about who and what kind of person one is. (Ch. 5, p. 107)

Service work refers to providing assistance and/or information. (Ch. 13, p. 303)

Sex identity is a definition of the self as female or male. (Ch. 8, p. 168)

Sex segregation occurs when women or men are concentrated in a given occupation or in particular jobs within an occupation. (Ch. 10, p. 236)

Sexual harassment involves unwelcome sexual advances that affect a person's chance of employment or promotion or that negatively influence one's working or school environment. (Ch. 8, p. 188)

Sexual scripts allow individuals to organize their perceptions and experiences in order to behave appropriately in particular situations. (Ch. 8, p. 169)

The **sick role** is a set of rights and obligations attached to the status of being ill. (Ch. 18, p. 436)

Significant others are persons whose affection and approval are particularly desired. (Ch. 5, p. 109)

The **Skinner box** is a completely controlled environment. (Ch. 5, p. 118)

Social, or **cultural, anthropology** is the study of total communities, typically nonmodern societies or unique subgroups in modern societies. (Ch. 1, p. 3)

Social change is the process through which values, norms, institutions, stratification systems, social relationships, and self-identities are altered over time. (Ch. 19, p. 452)

Social control refers to planned and unplanned processes to enforce conformity. (Ch. 6, p. 128)

The **social control model** highlights the bonds that reinforce law-abiding activity. (Ch. 17, p. 403)

Social differentiation involves a shift from ascribed tribal and family roles to specialized achieved roles. (Ch. 19, p. 466)

Social facts are patterned regularities that describe the collectivity. (Ch. 1, p. 7)

A **social hierarchy** is a set of ranked statuses. (Ch. 9, p. 192)

Social integration refers to the degree to which a person is part of a larger group. (Ch. 1, p. 8)

Social mobility is the movement of persons and groups within the stratification system. (Ch. 9, p. 212)

A **social movement** is a set of opinions and beliefs in favor of major change in social institutions and the stratification hierarchy. (Ch. 23, p. 555)

A **social movement industry** is created when several organizations join forces around the same goal. (Ch. 23, p. 555)

Social movement organizations are specific formal organizations that channel discontent into concrete actions. (Ch. 23, p. 555)

A **social network** offers support to individuals through social ties to others. (Ch. 4, p. 87)

Social norms are rules of behavior. (Ch. 3, p. 62)

Social statistics refer to official records and systematic observations from which social facts can be deduced. (Ch. 1, p. 12)

Social stratification refers to the unequal distribution of power, prestige, and property. (Ch. 9, p. 194)

Social structure refers to a collective reality that exists apart from individuals, constructing the context in which people interact. (Ch. 4, p. 73)

A **social system** is an arrangement of relationships existing apart from the specific people involved. (Ch. 4, p. 74)

Socialism is an economic system in which the means of production are collectively owned and the distribution of goods and services is guided by public needs. (Ch. 13, p. 308)

A **socialist economic system** is marked by central planning of production and distribution by the government. (Ch. 13, p. 306)

Socialization is the lifelong process whereby one internalizes culture and develops a sense of self. (Ch. 5, p. 99)

Sociobiology is the study of the inheritance of genetically determined behaviors. (Ch. 1, p. 23)

Socioeconomic status (SES) is a measure based on a combination of income, occupational prestige, and education. (Ch. 9)

A **sociogram** identifies interaction patterns in studying group structure. (Ch. 4)

The **sociological perspective** focuses on the totality of social life, the context of social interaction, meaning as a social product, the collectivity, and interaction among individuals. (Ch. 1, p. 6)

Sociology is the study of human behavior as shaped by collective life. (Ch. 1, p. 2)

The **sociology of emotions** demonstrates that emotions are socially constructed, exchanged, and maintained. (Ch. 4, p. 90)

The **sociology of knowledge** is the study of the way in which the production of knowledge is shaped by the social context of thinkers. (Ch. 1, p. 10)

The **split,** or **segmented, labor market** is differentiated by race and gender, core workers being white men and peripheral workers being primarily women and minorities. (Ch. 13, p. 315)

Sports are a form of structured behavior with values, norms, statuses, and roles, linked to other institutional spheres and stratification hierarchies. (Ch. 22, p. 536)

Stacking involves placing white athletes in positions that involve more responsibility and control than the positions largely occupied by minority students. (Ch. 22, p. 542)

The **statistical model** of disease defines health or illness in terms of the average of a population. (Ch. 18, p. 437)

Statistics are numerical techniques for the classification and analysis of data. (Ch. 2, p. 42)

A **status** is a position in a social system and is characterized by certain rights and obligations. (Ch. 4, p. 75)

Status attainment research traces the paths by which people reach their ultimate position in the stratification system. (Ch. 9)

Status consistency occurs when a person occupies a similar position across different hierarchies. (Ch. 9, p. 218)

Status inconsistency refers to occupying different positions in different hierarchies. (Ch. 9, p. 218)

A **status offense** is an act that would not be a crime if committed by an adult. (Ch. 17, p. 415)

A **status set** consists of all the statuses occupied by a person. (Ch. 4, p. 76)

Status symbols are outward signs of social rank. (Ch. 9, p. 218)

Statutory rape occurs when sexual intercourse takes place with people under age 15 or 16, whether willingly or not. (Ch. 8, p. 186)

Stereotyping is the tendency to generalize favorable or unfavorable traits from one person to an entire population. (Ch. 11, p. 254)

Stigma refers to a moral blemish that is attached to the characteristic defined as deviant. (Ch. 6, p. 136)

Street crimes are actions that directly threaten people or property. (Ch. 17, p. 404)

Structural dimensions include density, diversity, and size of social networks. (Ch. 4, p. 87)

Structural or **demand, mobility** refers to societal-level factors affecting mobility rates. (Ch. 9, p 214)

Subcultures consist of variations in values, beliefs, norms, and behavior among societal subgroups. (Ch. 3, p. 65)

Subjective knowledge derives from an individual's own frame of reference. (Ch. 2, p. 28)

Subjective reality is developed through social interaction and refers to the ideas and feelings we have about ourselves and the world. (Ch. 1, p. 8)

A **suburb** is closely linked to a metropolitan area socially and economically, but it is politically independent. (Ch. 21, p. 511)

Suburbanization resulted from the expansion of the highway system, the spread of housing developments, and the dispersion of industry. (Ch. 21, p. 512)

Succession is the replacement of one activity or population for another in a differentiated area. (Ch. 21, p. 508)

Surrogacy is the situation in which one woman agrees to bear a child for another woman. (Ch. 8, p. 177)

Surveys or **polls** yield information from a large group of respondents. (Ch. 2, p. 34)

A **symbol** is a sound, object, or event that is given meaning by members of a group. (Ch. 3, p. 53)

Symbolic interaction views social systems as products of interaction and the meanings that people give to their situations. (Ch. 1, p. 17)

Systems of stratification rank some individuals and groups as more deserving than others. (Ch. 9, p. 192)

Tables consist of rows and columns of figures arranged to clarify relationships among variables. (Ch. 2, p. 45)

The term **taste cultures** is used to give validity to various forms of popular culture without implying value judgments. (Ch. 22, p. 527)

A **theocracy** is a religious dictatorship. (Ch. 16, p. 381)

A **theory** is a set of logically related statements that attempt to explain an entire class of events. (Ch. 1, p. 9)

Tokenism refers to the appointment or promotion of one or two "outsiders" to high positions. (Ch. 10, p. 232)

Total institutions , such as prisons and jails, control and monitor all aspects of inmates' lives. (Ch. 17, p. 423)

In **totalitarian regimes,** the government attempts to exercise total control over society and its members. (Ch. 14, p. 330)

Traditional authority is based on custom and the force of habit. (Ch. 14, p. 327)

The **tradition-directed** person's behavior is governed by customs. (Ch. 19, p. 472)

Transcendence is the escape from everyday life through union with a divine power. (Ch. 16, p. 383)

Age is a **transitional status** as people move from one age category to another. (Ch. 7, p. 145)

The **triad,** a three-person group, is more stable than a dyad, and has a more complex division of labor. (Ch. 4, p. 87)

The **triple melting pot** model of integration suggests that ethnic differences were melting within but not across religious categories. (Ch. 11, p. 251)

The **underground economy** is an informal labor force in which the independent contractor is paid in cash to avoid reporting taxable income. (Ch. 13, p. 319)

Uniform Crime Reports (UCR) are compiled by the FBI from city, state, and county police information. (Ch. 17, p. 405)

Urban ecology refers to the fit between people and land use in the urban setting. (Ch. 21, p. 556)

Urban legends are items of modern folklore involving rumors that resonate to deeply held fears and anxieties regarding aspects of modern life beyond personal control. (Ch. 23, p. 548)

A city, town or village with 2500 or more inhabitants is considered **urban.** (Ch. 21, p. 509)

Urbanism refers to the way of life in cities, which emphasizes individualistic norms and styles of behavior. (Ch. 21, p. 501)

An **urbanized area** consists of one or more places and surrounding territory with a population of at least 50,000. (Ch. 21, p. 509)

Utopian movements seek an ideal society for true believers. (Ch. 23, p. 509)

Validation of self requires assurance that one is who one claims to be. (Ch. 5, p. 100)

Validity refers to whether the measuring instrument measures what it was designed to. (Ch. 2, p. 29)

The **value-added model** specifies six conditions that are necessary and sufficient to produce collective behavior. (Ch. 23, p. 553)

Value consensus refers to an underlying agreement about the goals of a group or collectivity. (Ch. 1, p. 14)

Value neutrality, the claim that a researcher can be free of personal bias and judgment, is a foundation of the scientific method in the social sciences. (Ch. 2, p. 46)

Values are the central beliefs of a culture that provide a standard by which norms are judged. (Ch. 3, p. 64)

Variables are factors that differ from one person or collectivity to another or that change over time. (Ch. 2, p. 31)

Verstehen is the ability to see the world as it might be experienced by others. (Ch. 1, p. 13)

Victimless crimes violate moral standards, but those involved are willing participants. (Ch. 17, p. 411)

A **virtual self** awaits us in each role we perform. (Ch. 5, p. 111)

Vital statistics are records of births, deaths, divorces, and marriages collected at the state level. (Ch. 20, p. 478)

Voluntary childlessness refers to the decision to remain child free. (Ch. 12, p. 292)

The **voucher system** allows families to spend a given sum of tax money for any type of schooling available. (Ch. 15)

Warfare and **invasion** occur when one group's or nation's territory is overrun and controlled by another. (Ch. 19, p. 453)

Welfare, or **state, capitalism** refers to free markets existing within limits designed to ensure social stability. (Ch. 13, p. 306)

White-collar crimes are illegal activities committed by individuals of high status, usually by nonviolent means, in the course of their employment, for their own benefit. (Ch. 17, p. 409)

The **Wife as Senior Partner (WaSP)** model involves a family organized around the wife's career. (Ch. 12, p. 294)

The **work ethic** refers to a set of beliefs that emerged in western Europe in the sixteenth century and are associated with the rise of modern capitalism. (Ch. 3, p. 68)

Workfare programs are designed to prepare welfare recipients for permanent positions in the labor force. (Ch. 9, p. 209)

Workplace democracy occurs when the workers become the managers and often the owners. (Ch. 13, p. 312)

The **world social system** involves increased cooperation and trade across national boundaries and a rapid spread of information and technology, culture contact, flows of money, and large-scale migration of refugees and workers. (Ch. 19, p. 468)

Yuppie stands for young upwardly mobile professional. (Ch. 14, p. 341)

Zero population growth (ZPG) occurs when fertility reaches the replacement level of the 2.1 offspring required to replace the parental couple. (Ch. 20, p. 479)

Bibliography

Abowitz, Deborah A. "Sociopolitical Participation and the Significance of Social Context: A Model of Competing Interests and Obligations." *Social Science Quarterly* 71 (1990): 543-566.

Abramovits, Mimi, and Frances Fox Pivan. "Scapegoating Women on Welfare." *New York Times*, September 2, 1993: A23.

Abu-Lughod, Lila. *Writing Women's Worlds: Bedouin Stories.* Berkeley, CA: University of California Press, 1992.

Acker, Joan. "Thinking About Wages: The Gendered Wage Gap in Swedish Banks." *Gender & Society* 5 (1991): 390-417.

Acock, Alan C., and K. Jill Kiecolt. "Is It Family Structure or Socioeconomic Status? Family Structure during Adolescence and Adult Adjustment." *Social Forces* 68 (1989): 553-571.

Acock, Alan C., and Theodore Fuller. "The Attitude-Behavior Relationship and Parental Influence: Circular Mobility in Thailand." *Social Forces* 62 (4) (1984): 973-994.

Acosta-Belén, Edna, and Christine Bose. "From Structural Subordination to Empowerment: Women and Development in Third World Contexts." *Gender & Society* 4 (1990): 299-320.

Acton, J.E.E.D. "The History of Freedom in Antiquity," (1878). In *Selected Writings of Lord Acton*, Vol. 1. Indianapolis, IN: Liberty Fund, 1985.

Adam, Barry D. *The Rise of a Gay and Lesbian Movement.* Boston: Twayne, 1987.

Adams, Frank, and David Ellerman. "The Many Roads to Worker Ownership in America." *Social Policy* (Winter 1989): 12-18.

Aday, David P., Jr. *Social Control at the Margins: Toward a General Understanding of Deviance.* Belmont, CA: Wadsworth, 1989.

Aday, Lu Ann. *At Risk in America: The Health and Health Care Needs of Vulnerable Populations in the United States.* San Francisco: Jossey-Bass, 1993.

Addelson, Kathryn Pyne. "Some Moral Issues in Public Problems of Reproduction." *Social Problems* 37 (1990): 1-17.

Adler, Patricia A., and Peter Adler. *Backboards and Blackboards: College Athletes and Role Engulfment.* New York: Columbia University Press, 1991.

Adler, Patricia A., and Peter Adler. "Countercultures." In Edgar F. Borgatta and Marie L. Borgatta (Eds.), *Encyclopedia of Sociology*, Vol. 1, pp. 328-332. New York: Macmillan, 1992.

Adler, Patricia A., Steven J. Kless, and Peter Adler. "Socialization to Gender Roles: Popularity among Elementary School Boys and Girls." *Sociology of Education* 65 (1992): 169-187.

Adorno, Theodor E., Elsie Frenkel-Brunswick, David Levinson, and R.N. Sanford. *The Authoritarian Personality.* New York: Harper, 1950.

Afary, Janet. "From Radical Democracy to Militant Islam: The Iranian Women's Movement in the 20th Century." Paper presented at the XII World Congress of Sociology, Bielefeld, Germany, July, 1994.

Afshari, Reza. "The Poet and the Prophet: The Iconoclasm of The Satanic Verses." *Humanity & Society* 14 (1990): 419-427.

Aging International "National Perspectives on Age Bias." XX (3)(1993), pp. 46-50.

Aguirre, B. E., E. L. Quarantelli, and Jorge L. Mendoza. "The Collective Behavior of Fads: The Characteristics, Effects, and Career of Streaking." *American Sociological Review* 53 (1988): 569-584.

Ahlberg, Beth Miana. *Women, Sexuality, and the Changing Social Order: The Impact of Government Policies on Reproductive Behavior in Kenya.* Philadelphia: Gordon and Breach, 1991.

Ahlberg, Dennis A., and Carol J. DeVita. "New Realities of the American Family." *Population Bulletin* 47 (2) August, 1992.

Ahmed, Leila. *Women and Gender in Islam: Historical Roots of a Modern Debate.* New Haven, CT: Yale University Press, 1992.

Ahn, Namkee. "Teenage Childbearing and High School Completion: Accounting for Individual Heterogeneity." *Family Planning Perspectives* 26 (1994): 17-21.

Aho, James A. *The Politics of Righteousness: Idaho Christian Patriotism.* Seattle, WA: University of Washington Press, 1990.

Akers, Ronald L. *Deviant Behavior: A Social Learning Approach*, 3rd ed. Belmont, CA: Wadsworth, 1985.

Akiyama, H., and Antonucci, T. "Sex Differences in Friendship over the Life Course." Paper presented at the 1993 annual meetings of the Gerontological Society of America, New Orleans, LA, November 1993.

Alan Guttmacher Institute. *Sex and America's Teenagers.* New York: AGI, 1994.

Alasuutari, Pertti. *Desire and Craving: A Cultural Theory of Alcoholism.* Albany, NY: State University of New York Press, 1992.

Alba, Richard D. *Ethnic Identity: The Transformation of White America.* New Haven, CT: Yale University Press, 1990.

Alba, Richard D., and John R. Logan. "Minority Proximity to Whites in Suburbs: An Individual-Level Analysis of Segregation." *American Journal of Sociology*, Vol. 98, No. 6, May 1993.

Alexander, Jeffrey, and Paul Colomy. "Neofunctionalism: Reconstructing a Theoretical Tradition." In George Ritzer (Ed.), *Frontiers of Social Theory: The New Synthesis*, pp. 33-67. New York: Columbia University Press, 1990.

Alexander, Karl L., Doris R. Entwisle, and Maxine S. Thompson. "School Performance, Status Relations, and the Structure of Sentiment: Bringing the Teacher Back In." *American Sociological Review* 52 (1987): 665-682.

Alfano, Peter. "Academic Elite Using Sports Too." *New York Times*, February 15, 1989.

Allen, Walter R., Edgar G. Epps, and Nesha Z. Haniff. *College in Black and White: African American Students in Predominantly White and in Historically Black Public Universities.* Albany, NY: State University of New York Press, 1991.

Allport, Gordon, and L. Postman. *The Psychology of Rumor.* New York: Henry Holt, 1947.

Alstone, Nan Marie, and Sara S. McLanahan. "Family Structure, Parental Practices, and High School Completion." *American Sociological Review* 56 (1991): 309-320.

Altbach, Philip G., and Lionel S. Lewis. "Reforming Higher Education: A Modest Proposal." *Thought & Action* 9 (1994): 31-40.

Althauser, Robert P. "Paradox in Popular Religion: The Limits of Instrumental Faith." *Social Forces* 69 (1990): 585-602.

Althauser, Robert P., and Michael Wallace (Eds.). *Research in Social Stratification and Mobility*, Vol. 10. Greenwich, CT: JAI Press, 1991.

Altman, Billy. "Country Just Ain't What it Used to Be." *New York Times*, January 31, 1993.

Alwin, Duane F., Ronald L. Cohen, and Theodore M. Newcomb. *Political Attitudes Over the Life Span: The Bennington Women after Fifty Years.* Madison, WI: University of Wisconsin Press, 1991.

Alwin, Duane F., and Jon A. Krosnick. "Aging, Cohorts, and the Stability of Sociopolitical Orientations over the Life Span." *American Journal of Sociology* 97 (1991): 169-195.

Amato, Paul R. "Personality and Social Network Involvement as Predictors of Helping Behavior in Everyday Life." *Social Psychology Quarterly* 53 (1990): 31-43.

Amato, Paul R., and Bruce Keith. "Separation from a Parent during Childhood and Adult Socioeconomic Attainment." *Social Forces* 70 (1991): 187-206.

Amenta, Edwin, Kathleen Dunleavy, and Mary Bernstein. "Stolen Thunder? Huey Long's 'Share Our Wealth,' Political Mediation, and the Second New Deal." *American Sociological Review* 59 (1994); 678-702.

American Bar Association. "Bill of Rights Survey." Washington, DC: ABA, 1991.

American Council on Education. *The American Freshman: National Norms for Fall 1993.* New York: ACE, 1994.

American Hospital Association. *AHA Hospital Statistics: 1992-93 Edition.* Washington, DC: AHA, 1992.

American Humanist Association. *Humanism is the Best Way of Life.* Amherst, NY: AHA, 1988.

American Legislative Exchange Council. *The Report Card on American Education.* New York: ALEC,1994.

American Psychiatric Association. *Diagnostic and Statistical Manual III-R.* Washington, DC: American Psychiatric Association, 1987.

Ammerman, Nancy Tatom. *Southern Baptists Observed: Multiple Perspectives on a Changing Religion.* Knoxville, TN: University of Tennessee Press, 1993.

Anderson, Benedict. *Imagined Communities: Reflections on the Origin and Spread of Nationalism.* Chicago: University of Chicago Press, 1993.

Anderson, Elijah. *Streetwise: Race, Class, and Change in an Urban Community.* Chicago: University of Chicago Press, 1990.

Anderson, Kay J. *Vancouver's Chinatown: Racial Discourse in Canada, 1875-1980.* Montreal, CAN: McGill-Queen's University Press, 1991.

Andes, Nancy. "Social Class and Gender: An Empirical Evaluation of Occupational Stratification." *Gender & Society* 6 (1992): 231-251.

Andrews, Edmund L. "'Flintstones' and Shows Like It Aren't 'Educational,' U.S. Says." *New York Times*, March 4, 1993.

Aneshensel, Carol S., Leonard I. Pearlin, and Roberleigh H. Schuler. "Stress, Role Captivity, and the Cessation of Caregiving." *Journal of Health and Social Behavior* 34 (1993b): 54-70.

Angel, Ronald J., and Jacqueline L. Angel. *Painful Inheritance: Health and the New Generation of Fatherless Families.* Madison, WI: University of Wisconsin Press, 1993.

Angier, Natalie. "The Purpose of Playful Frolics: Training for Adulthood." *The New York Times* October 20, 1992, C1 ff.

Anleu, Sharyn R. "Surrogacy: For Love But Not for Money?" *Gender & Society* 6 (1992): 30-48.

Ansari, Maboud. *The Making of the Iranian Community in America.* New York: Pardis Press, 1992.

Ansari, Maboud. "Ibn Khaldun: The Father of the Conflict School of Sociology." Unpublished manuscript, William Paterson College, 1993.

Antilla, Susan. "'I Want' Now Gets." *New York Times*, April 4, 1993, Section 4-A, p. 17.

Antilla, Susan. "Cramming for Kindergarten." *New York Times Education Supplement*, January 9, 1994:34-36.

Apple, Michael W. *Official Knowledge: Democratic Education in a Conservative Age.* New York: Routledge, 1993.

Appleyard, Bryan. *Understanding the Present: Science and the Soul of Modern Man.* New York: Doubleday, 1993.

Arendell, Terry. "Women and the Economics of Divorce in the Contemporary United States." *Signs* 13 (1987): 121-135.

Arendell, Terry. "Fathers After Divorce: A Masculinist Discourse of Divorce." Paper presented at the annual meeting of the American Sociological Association. Miami Beach, FL: August 1993.

Aries, Phillipe. *Centuries of Childhood: A Social History of Family Life.* New York: Knopf, 1962.

Armstrong, L. *And They Call It Help: The Psychiatric Policing of America's Children.* Reading MA: Addison Wesley, 1993.

Aronoff, Marilyn, and Valerie Gunter. "Defining Disaster: Local Constructions for Recovery in the Aftermath of Chemical Contamination." *Social Problems* 39 (1992): 354-65.

Aronowitz, Stanley. *The Politics of Identity: Class, Culture, Social Movements.* New York: Routledge, 1992.

Asch, Solomon. "Studies of Independence and Conformity: A Minority of One against a Unanimous Majority." *Psychological Monographs* 70 (1956): 1-70.

Aseltine, Robert H., Jr., and Ronald C. Kessler. "Marital Disruption and Depression in a Community Sample." *Journal of Health and Social Behavior* 34 (1993): 237-251.

Ash, Timothy Garton. "Eastern Europe: The Year of Truth." *New York Review of Books* XXXVII (2) (February 15, 1990): 17-22.

Ashe, Arthur R., Jr. *A Hard Road to Glory: A History of the African-American Athlete*, Vols. 1-3. New York: Warner, 1988.

Asher, Robert, and Charles Stephenson (Eds.). *Labor Divided: Race and Ethnicity in United States Labor Struggles, 1835-1960.* Albany, NY: State University of New York Press, 1990.

Atkinson, Maxine P., and Jacqueline Boles. "WASP (Wives as Senior Partners)." *Journal of Marriage and the Family* 46 (1984): 861-870.

Auletta, Ken. *Three Blind Mice: How the Networks Lost Their Way.* New York: Random House, 1991.

Avison, William R., and Donna D. McAlpine. "Gender Differences in Symptoms of Depression Among Adolescents." *Journal of Health and Social Behavior*, 33 (1992): 77-96.

Axinn, William G., and Arland Thornton. "Mothers, Children, and Cohabitation: The Intergenerational Effects of Attitudes and Behavior." *American Sociological Review* 58 (1993): 233-246.

Baca Zinn, Maxine. "Family, Feminism, and Race in America." *Gender & Society* 4 (1990):

Bachman, Ronet. *Death and Violence on the Reservation: Homicide, Family Violence, and Suicide in American Indian Populations.* New York: Auburn House, 1992.

Bachman, Ronet. *Violence Against Women: A National Crime Victimization Survey Report.* Washington, DC: U.S. Department of Justice, 1994.

Bachrach, Christine A., and Marjorie C. Horn. "Sexual Activity among US Women of Reproductive Age." *American Journal of Public Health* 78 (1988): 320-321.

Bachrach, Christine A., Kathy Sheperd Stolley, and Kathryn A. London. "Relinquishment of Premarital Births: Evidence from National Survey Data." *Family Planning Perspectives* 24 (1992): 27-32.

Back, Kurt W. *Family Planning and Population Control: The Challenges of a Successful Movement.* Boston: Twayne, 1989.

Backhaus, Tara N., Peter B. Belden, and Thomas J. Espenshade. *AIDS and Thailand's Future Population Growth.* Princeton, NJ: Office of Population Research, Princeton University, 1994.

Baer, Hans A., and Merril Singer. *African-American Religion in the Twentieth Century: Varieties of Protest and Accommodation.* Knoxville, TN: University of Tennessee Press, 1992.

Bagdikian, Ben H. *The Media Monopoly.* 4th ed. Boston: Beacon Press, 1993.

Bailey, J. Michael, and Richard Pillard. "Are Some People Born Gay?" *New York Times.* December 17, 1991, p. A21.

Bailey, J. Michael, and Richard C. Pillard. "Heritable Factors Influence Sexual Orientation in Women." *Archives of General Psychiatry* 50 (1993):217-223.

Bailey, Kenneth D. "Ethical Dilemmas in Social Problems Research:A Theoretical Framework." *American Sociologist* 19 (1988): 121-137.

Bailey, William C. "Murder, Capital Punishment, and Television: Execution Publicity and Homicide Rates." *American Sociological Review* 55 (1990): 628-633.

Bainbridge, William Sims. "Explaining Church Member Rate." *Social Forces* 68 (1990): 1287-1296.

Bakalian, Anny. *Armenian-Americans: From Being to Feeling Armenian.* New Brunswick, NJ: Transaction, 1993.

Bakanic, Eunice, Clark McPhail, and Rita J. Simon. "The Manuscript Review and Decision-Making Process." *American Sociological Review*, 52 (1987): 631-642.

Baker, David P., and Deborah Perkins Jones. "Creating Gender Equality: Cross-national Gender Stratification and Mathematical Performance." *Sociology of Education* 66 (1993): 91-103.

Baker, Scott. "Reflection, Doubt, and the Place of Rhetoric in Postmodern Social Theory." *Sociological Theory* 8 (1990): 232-245.

Baker, Wayne E., and Robert R. Faulkner. "The Social Organization of Conspiracy: Illegal Networks in the Heavy Electrical Equipment Industry." *American Sociological Review* 58 (1993): 837-860.

Baldassare, Mark. *Trouble in Paradise: The Suburban Transformation in America.* New York: Columbia University Press, 1986.

Baldwin, John D. *George Herbert Mead: A Unifying Theory for Sociology.* Newbury Park, CA: Sage, 1986.

Balkwell, James W. "Ethnic Inequality and the Rate of Homicide." *Social Forces* 69 (1990): 53-70.

Baltzell, E. Digby. *The Protestant Establishment: Aristocracy and Caste in America.* New York: Random House, 1964.

Baltzell, E. Digby, and Howard G. Schneiderman. "Social Class in the Oval Office." *Society* (September/October 1988): 42-49.

Banac, Ivo (Ed.). *Eastern Europe in Revolution*. Ithaca: Cornell University Press, 1992.

Bane, Mary Jo., and David T. Ellwood. *Welfare Realities: From Rhetoric to Reform*. Cambridge, MA: Harvard University Press, 1994.

Barak, Gregg (Ed.). *Crimes by the Capitalist State: An Introduction to State Criminality*. Albany, NY: State University of New York Press, 1991.

Barkan, Steven E. "Legal Control of the Southern Civil Rights Movement." *American Sociological Review* 49(4) (1984): 552–565.

Barkan, Steven E., Steven F. Cohn, and William H. Whitaker. "Commitment across the Miles: Ideological and Microstructural Sources of Membership Support in a National Antihunger Organizations." *Social Problems* 40 (1993): 362–373.

Barkun, Michael. *Religion and the Racist Right: The Origins of the Christian Identity Movement*. Chapel Hill, NC: University of North Carolina Press, 1994.

Barlett, Donald L., and James B. Steele. *America: Who Really Pays the Taxes?* New York: Simon & Schuster, 1994.

Barnet, Richard J., and John Cavanagh. *Global Dreams: Imperial Corporations and the New World Order*. New York: Simon and Schuster, 1994.

Barnett, Bernice McNair. "Invisible Southern Black Women in the Civil Rights Movement: The Triple Constraints of Gender, Race, and Class." *Gender & Society* 7 (1993): 162–182.

Barnett, Rosilind C. "Home-to-Work Spillover Revisited: A Study of Full-Time Employed Women in Dual-Earner Couples." *Journal of Marriage and the Family* 56 (1994): 647–656.

Barnhart, Joe Edward. *The Southern Baptist Holy War*. Austin: Texas Monthly Press, 1987.

Baron, Ava (Ed.). *Work Engendered: Toward a New History of American Labor*. Ithaca, NY: Cornell University Press, 1991.

Baron, James N., Brian S. Mittman, and Andrew E. Newman. "Targets of Opportunity: Organizational and Environmental Determinants of Gender Integration within the California Civil Service, 1979–1985." *American Journal of Sociology* 96 (1991): 1362–1401.

Barrett, Michele, and Anne Philips. *Destabilizing Theory: Contemporary Feminist Debates*. Stanford: Stanford University Press, 1992.

Barringer, Felicity. "Rural America is Growing Slightly, Population Studies Show." *New York Times*, Tuesday, May 25, 1993.

Bart, Pauline B., and Eileen Geil Moran (Eds.). *Violence Against Women: The Bloody Footprints*. Newbury Park, CA: Sage, 1993.

Barthel, Diane. *Putting on Appearances: Gender and Advertising*. Philadelphia: Temple University Press, 1988.

Bates, Timothy. "Social Resources Generated by Group Support Networks May Not Be Beneficial to Asian Immigrant-Owned Small Business." *Social Forces* 72 (1994): 671–689.

Bauer, John R. "Patterns of Voter Participation in the American States." *Social Science Quarterly* 71 (1990): 824–834.

Baxter, Janeen. "Is Husband's Class Enough? Class Location and Class Identity in the United States, Sweden, Norway, and Australia." *American Sociological Review* 59 (1994): 220–235.

Bayat, Assef. *Work, Politics, and Power: An International Perspective on Workers' Control and Self-Management*. New York: Monthly Review Press, 1991.

Bearman, Peter S. "The Social Structure of Suicide." *Sociological Forum* 6 (1991): 501–524.

Becker, Howard S. *Outsiders: Studies in the Sociology of Deviance*. New York: Free Press, 1963.

Becker, Howard S., and Michael M. McCall (Eds.). *Symbolic Interaction and Cultural Studies*. Chicago: University of Chicago Press, 1990.

Becker, Marshall H. "A Medical Sociologist Looks at Health Promotion." *Journal of Health and Social Behavior* 34 (1993) 1–6.

Beckett, Katherine. "Setting the Public Agenda: 'Street Crime' and Drug Use in American Politics." *Social Problems* 41 (1994): 425–447.

Beeghley, Leonard. *Living Poorly in America*. New York: Praeger, 1983.

Beeghley, Leonard. "Social Class and Political Participation." *Sociological Forum* 1 (1986): 496–513.

Beeghley, Leonard, and Debra Van Ausdale. "Status of Women Faculty in Graduate Departments: 1973 and 1988." *Footnotes*. Washington, DC: American Sociological Association, December 1990, p. 3.

Beeghley, Leonard, E. Wilbur Bock, and John K. Cochran. "Religious Change and Alcohol Use: An Application of Reference Group and Socialization Theory." *Sociological Forum* 5 (1990): 261–278.

Beisel, Nicola. "Morals Versus Art: Censorship, the Politics of Interpretation, and the Victorian Nude." *American Sociological Review* 58 (1993): 145–162.

Belkin, Lisa. "Fairness Debated in Quick Transplant." *New York Times*, June 16, 1993.

Bell, Daniel. (1960) "The End of Ideology in the West: An Epilogue." In *The End of Ideology: On the Exhaustion of Political Ideas in the Fifties*. New York: Free Press, 1965.

Bell, Daniel. *The Coming of Post-Industrial Society: A Venture in Social Forecasting*. New York: Basic Books, 1973.

Bell, Daniel. "Socialism and Planning: Beyond the Soviet Economic Crisis," *Dissent* Winter 1991: 50–54.

Bell, Derrick. *Faces at the Bottom of the Well: The Permanence of Racism*. New York: Basic Books, 1992.

Bell, Michael M. "The Fruit of Difference: The Rural-Urban Continuum as a System of Identity" *Rural Sociology* 57 (1), 1992, pp. 65–82.

Bellah, Robert N. *The Broken Covenant: American Civil Religion in a Time Trial*. New York: Seabury Press, 1975.

Bellas, Marcia L. "The Effects of Marital Status and Wives' Employment on the Salaries of Faculty Men: The (House) Wife Bonus." *Gender & Society* 6 (1992): 609–622.

Bellas, Marcia L. "Comparable Worth in Academia: The Effects on Faculty Salaries of the Sex Composition and Labor-Market Conditions of Academic Disciplines." *American* Sociological Review 59 (1994): 807–821.

Bem, Sandra Lipsitz. *The Lenses of Gender: Transforming the Debate on Sexual Inequality*. New Haven, CT: Yale University Press, 1993.

Ben-Yehuda, Nachman. *The Politics and Morality of Deviance: Moral Panics, Drug Abuse, Deviant Science, and Reversed Stigmatization*. Albany, NY: State University of New York Press, 1990.

Benavot, Aaron, Yun-Kyung Cha, David Kamens, John W. Meyer, and Suk-Ying Wong. "Knowledge for the Masses: World Models and National Curricula, 1920–1986." *American Sociological Review* 56 (1991): 85–100.

Benedict, Helen. *Virgin or Vamp: How the Press Covers Sex Crimes*. New York: Oxford, 1992.

Benedict, Ruth. *Patterns of Culture*. Boston: Houghton Mifflin, 1934.

Benedict, Ruth. *The Chrysanthemum and the Sword*. Boston: Houghton Mifflin, 1946.

Benford, Robert D. "Frame Disputes within the Nuclear Disarmament Movement." *Social Forces* 71 (1993): 677–701.

Bengtson, Vern L., and W. Andrew Achenbaum (Eds.). *The Changing Contract Across Generations*. New York: Aldine de Gruyter, 1993.

Bennett, Neil G., Ann Klimas Blanc, and David E. Bloom. "Commitment and the Modern Union: Assessing the Link Between Premarital Cohabitation and Subsequent Marital Stability." *American Sociological Review* 53 (1988): 127–138.

Bennett, Richard R. "Routine Activities: A Cross-National Assessment of a Criminological Perspective." *Social Forces* 70 (1991): 147–163.

Berezin, Mabel. "Cultural Form and Political Meaning: State-subsidized Theater, Ideology, and the Language of Style in Fascist Italy." *American Journal of Sociology* 99 (1994): 1237–1286.

Berger, Bennett M. "Utopia and Its Environment." *Society*, January/February 1988, pp. 37–41.

Berger, Joseph, Robert Z. Norman, James W. Balkwell, and Roy F. Smith. "Status Inconsistency in Task Situations: A Test of Four

Status Processing Principles." *American Sociological Review* 57 (1992): 843–855.

Berger, Peter L. *A Far Glory: The Quest for Faith in an Age of Credulity*. New York: The Free Press, 1992.

Berger, Peter L., and Thomas Luckmann. *The Social Construction of Reality*. Garden City, NY: Doubleday, 1966.

Berger, Ronald, Patricia Searles, and Charles Cottle. *Feminism and Pornography*. New York: Praeger, 1991.

Berheide, Catherine White. "Women Still 'Stuck' in Low-Level Jobs." *Women in Public Service* 3 (1992): 1–4.

Berk, Richard A., Alec Campbell, Ruth Klap, and Bruce Western. "The Deterrent Effect of Arrest in Incidents of Domestic Violence: A Baysian Analysis of Four Field Experiments." *American Sociological Review* 57 (1992): 698–708.

Berke, Richard L. "Christian Right Defies Categories." *New York Times*, July 22, 1994a.

Berke, Richard L. "Religious-Right Candidates Gain as G.O.P. Turnout Rises." *New York Times*, November 12, 1994c.

Berman, Marshall. "Close to the Edge: Reflections on Rap." *Tikkun* 8 (1993): 13–18.

Bernard, Thomas J. *The Cycle of Juvenile Justice*. New York: Oxford University Press, 1992.

Bernstein, Basil. *The Structuring of Pedagogic Discourse: Vol. 4: Class, Codes, and Control*. New York: Routledge, 1990.

Bernstein, M., and D. Adler (Eds.). *Understanding American Economic Decline*. New York: Cambridge University Press, 1994.

Bernstein, Richard. "A Growing Islamic Presence: Balancing Sacred and Secular." *New York Times*, May 2, 1993.

Berry, Gordon LaVern, and Joy Keiko Asamen. *Black Students: Psychosocial Issues and Academic Achievement*. Newbury Park, CA: Sage, 1989.

Berry, Jason. *Lead Us Not Into Temptation: Catholic Priests and the Sexual Abuse of Children*. New York: Doubleday, 1992.

Berryman, Sue E. *Who Serves? The Persistent Myth of the Underclass Army*. Boulder, CO: Westview Press, 1988.

Besser, Terry L. "The Commitment of Japanese Workers and U.S. Workers: A Reassessment of the Literature." *American Sociological Review* 58 (1993): 873–881.

Best, Joel. *Threatened Children: Rhetoric and Concern about Child Victims*. Chicago: University of Chicago Press, 1990.

Beveridge, Andrew A. "Observing Racial Segregation and Neighborhood Change in the New York Metropolitan Area." Paper presented at the annual meeting of the Eastern Sociological Society, Baltimore, MD, March 1994.

Bharadwaj, Lakshmi K. "Human Ecology and the Environment." In Edgar F. Borgatta and Marie L. Borgatta (Eds.), *Encyclopedia of Sociology* (1992):848–867.

Biblarz, Timothy J., and Adrian E. Raftery. "The Effects of Family Disruption on Social Mobility." *American Sociological Review* 58 (1993): 97–109.

Bickerton, Derek. *Languages and Species*. Chicago: University of Chicago Press, 1991.

Bielby, William T., and Denise D. Bielby. "Family Ties: Balancing Commitment to Work and Family in Dual Earner Households." *American Sociological Review* 54 (1989): 776–789.

Bielby, William T., and Denise S. Bielby. "I Will Follow Him: Family Ties, Gender-Role Beliefs, and Reluctance to Relocate for a Better Job." *American Journal of Sociology* 97 (1992): 1241–1267.

Bielby, William T., and Denise D. Bielby. "'All Hits Are Flukes:' Institutionalized Decision Making and the Rhetoric of Network Prime-Time Program Development." *American Journal of Sociology* 99 (1994): 1287–1313.

Biesty, Patrick. "If It's Fun, Is It Play? A Meadian Analysis." In Bernard Mergen (Ed.), *Cultural Dimensions of Play, Games, and Sport*, pp. 61–72. Champaign, IL: Human Kinetics, 1986.

Billings, Dwight B. "Religion as Opposition: A Gramscian Analysis." *American Journal of Sociology* 96 (1990): 1–31.

Billingsley, Andrew. *Climbing Jacob's Ladder: The Enduring Legacy of African-American Families*. New York: Simon & Schuster, 1993.

Billy, John O. G., and David E. Moore. "A Multilevel Analysis of Marital and Nonmarital fertility in the U.S." *Social Forces* 70 (1992): 977–1011.

Billy, John O. G., Korey Tanfer, William R. Grady, and Daniel H. Klepinger. "The Sexual Behavior of Men in the United States." *Family Planning Perspectives* 25 (1993): 52–60.

Binder, Amy. "Constructing Racial Rhetoric: Media Depictions of Harm in Heavy Metal and Rap Music." *American Sociological Review* 58 (1993): 753–767.

Birdwhistle, Ray. *Kinesics and Context*. Philadelphia: University of Pennsylvania Press, 1970.

Birenbaum, Arnold. *Putting Health Care on the National Agenda*. Westport, CT: Praeger, 1993.

Bittner, Egon. *Aspects of Police Work*. Boston: Northeastern University Press, 1990.

Bjornberg, Ulla (Ed.). *European Parents in the 1990s: Contradictions and Comparisons*. New Brunswick, NJ: Transaction, 1992.

Blackwood, E. "Sexuality and Gender in Certain Native American Tribes." *Signs* 10 (1984): 127–142.

Blair, Samson Lee. "The Sex-Typing of Childrens' Household Labor." Paper presented at the Annual Meeting of the American Sociological Association, Cincinnati, Ohio, August, 1991.

Blake, Judith. *Family Size and Achievement*. Berkeley, CA: University of California Press, 1989.

Blalock, Hubert M., Jr. "The Real and Unrealized Contributions of Quantitative Sociology." *American Sociological Review* 54 (1989): 447–460.

Blanchard, Dallas A., and Terry J. Prewitt. *Religious Violence and Abortion: The Gideon Project*. Gainsville, FL: University Press of Florida, 1993.

Blau, Joel. *The Visible Poor: Homelessness in the United States*. New York: Oxford University Press, 1992.

Blau, Judith R. "High Culture as Mass Culture." *Society*, May-June 1986, pp. 65–69.

Blau, Judith R., and Peter M. Blau. "The Cost of Inequality: Metropolitan Structure and Violent Crime." *American Sociological Review* 47 (1982): 114–129.

Blau, Judith R., and Gordana Rabrenovic. "Interorganizational Relations of Nonprofit Organizations: An Exploratory Study." *Sociological Forum* 6 (1991): 327–343.

Blau, Peter. *Exchange and Power in Social Life*. New York: John Wiley & Sons, 1964.

Blauner, Robert. *Alienation and Freedom: The Factory Worker and His Industry*. Chicago: University of Chicago Press, 1964.

Blee, Kathleen M. *Women of the Klan: Racism and Gender in the 1920s*. Berkeley, CA: University of California Press, 1991.

Block, Fred. *Postindustrial Possibilities: A Critique of Economic Discourse*. Berkeley, CA: University of California Press, 1990.

Bloom, Jack M. *Class, Race, and the Civil Rights Movement: The Changing Political Economy of Southern Racism*. Bloomington: Indiana University Press, 1987.

Bluestone, Barry, and Irving Bluestone. *Negotiating the Future: A Labor Perspective on American Business*. New York: Basic Books, 1992.

Blum, Debra E. "College Sports' L-Word." *Chronicle of Higher Education*, March 9, 1994: A35.

Blumberg, Leonard U., with William L. Pittman. *Beware the First Drink! The Washington Temperance Movement and Alcoholics Anonymous*. Seattle, WA: Glen Abbey, 1991.

Blumberg, Rae Lesser. *Women and the Wealth of Nations: Theory and Research on Gender and Global Development*. New York: Praeger, 1989.

Blumberg, Rae Lesser. *Gender, Family, and the Economy: The Triple Overlap*. Newbury Park, CA: Sage, 1991.

Blumer, Herbert. "Collective Behavior." In Alfred McLung Lee (Ed.), *New Outlines of the Principles of Sociology*. New York: Barnes & Noble, 1951.

Blumer, Herbert. *Symbolic Interactionism*. Englewood Cliffs, NJ: Prentice-Hall, 1969.

Blumer, Herbert. "Social Movements." In R. Serge Denisoff (Ed.), *The Sociology of Dissent*, pp. 74-90. New York: Harcourt Brace Jovanovich, 1974.

Blumer, Herbert. *Industrialization as an Agent of Social Change: A Critical Analysis*. New York: Aldine de Gruyter, 1990.

Bobo, Lawrence. "Social Responsibility, Individuality, and Redistributive Policies." *Sociological Forum* 6 (1991): 71-92.

Bobo, Lawrence, and James R. Kleugel. "Opposition to Race-Targeting: Self-Interest, Stratification Ideology, or Racial Attitudes?" *American Sociological Review* 58 (1993): 443-464.

Boden, Deirdre, and Don H. Zimmerman (Eds.). *Talk and Social Structure: Studies in Ethnomethodology and Conversation*. Berkeley: University of California Press, 1991.

Bogart, Leo. *The American Media System and Its Commercial Culture*. New York: Gannett Foundation Media Center, 1991.

Boisjoly, Johanne, and Greg J. Duncan. "Job Losses among Hispanics in the Recent Recession." *Monthly Labor Review* 117, No.6 (1994): 16-23.

Bologh, Roslyn Wallach. *Love or Greatness: Max Weber and Masculine Thinking—A Feminist Inquiry*. Boston: Unwin Hyman, 1990.

Bookman, Ann, and Sandra Morgen (Eds.). *Women and the Politics of Empowerment*. Philadelphia: Temple University Press, 1988.

Booth, Alan, and Paul Amato. "Divorce and Psychological Stress." *Journal of Health and Social Behavior* 32 (1991): 396-407.

Booth, Alan, and James M. Dabbs, Jr. "Testosterone and Men's Marriages." *Social Forces* 72 (1993): 463-477.

Bordo, Susan. *Unbearable Weight: Feminism, Western Culture, and the Body*. Berkeley, CA: University of California Press, 1993.

Borofsky, Gerald L., Gary E. Stollak, and Lawrence A. Messe. "Sex Differences in Bystander Reactions to Physical Assault." *Journal of Experimental Social Psychology* 7 (1971): 313-318.

Bose, Christine E. "Dual Spheres." In Beth B. Hess and Myra Marx Ferree (Eds.), *Analyzing Gender: A Handbook of Social Science Research*. Newbury Park, CA: Sage, 1987, pp. 267-285.

Boswell, Terry, and William J. Dixon. "Dependency and Rebellion: A Cross-National Analysis." *American Sociological Review* 55 (1990): 540-559.

Botev, Nikolai. "Where East Meets West: Ethnic Intermarriage in the Former Yugoslavia, 1962 to 1998." *American Sociological Review* 59 (1994): 461-480.

Bourdieu, Pierre. *Distinction: A Social Critique of the Judgement of Taste*. Cambridge, MA: Harvard University Press, 1984.

Bourdieu, Pierre, and Jean-Claude Passeron. *Reproduction in Education, Society, and Culture*. Newbury Park, CA: Sage, 1977.

Bourque, Linda B. *Defining Rape*. Durham, NC: Duke University Press, 1989.

Bowditch, Christine. "Getting Rid of Troublemakers: High School Disciplinary Procedures and the Production of Dropouts." *Social Problems* 40 (1993): 493-509.

Bowen, Gary L., and Dennis K. Orthner (Eds.). *The Organization Family: Work and Family Linkages in the U.S. Military*. New York: Praeger, 1989.

Bradley, Karen, and Diana Khor. "Toward an Integration of Theory and Research on the Status of Women." *Gender & Society* 7 (1993): 347-378.

Braun, Denny. *The Rich Get Richer: The Rise of Income Inequality in the United States and the World*. Chicago: Nelson-Hall, 1990.

Braungart, Richard G., and Margaret M. Braungart. "Life-Course and Generational Politics." *Annual Review of Sociology* 12 (1986): 205-231.

Braverman, Harry. *Labor and Monopoly Capital*. New York: Monthly Review Press, 1974.

Brazell, Jan F., and Alan C. Acock. "Influence of Attitudes, Significant Others, and Aspirations on How Adolescents Intend to Resolve a Premarital Pregnancy." *Journal of Marriage and the Family* 50 (1988): 413-425.

Brewster, Karin L. "Race Differences in Sexual Activity Among Adolescent Women: The Role of Neighborhood Characteristics." *American Sociological Review* 59 (1994): 408-424.

Brewster, Karin L., John O. G. Billy, and William R. Grady. "Social Context and Adolescent Behavior: The Impact of Community on the Transition to Sexual Activity." *Social Forces* 71 (1993): 713-740.

Bridges, George S. "Deviance Theories." In Edgar F. Borgatta and Marie L. Borgatta (Eds.), *Encyclopedia of Sociology*, pp. 476-487. New York: Macmillan, 1992.

Bridges, William P., and Robert L. Nelson. "Markets in Hierarchies: Organizational and Market Influences on Gender Inequality in a State Pay System." *American Journal of Sociology* 95 (1989): 616-658.

Brines, Julie. "Economic Dependency, Gender, and the Division of Labor at Home." *American Journal of Sociology* 100 (1994): 652-688.

Brint, Steven G., and Jerome Karabel. *The Diverted Dream: Community Colleges and the Promise of Educational Opportunity in America, 1900-1985*. New York: Oxford University Press, 1991.

Brinton, Mary C. *Women and the Economic Miracle: Gender and Work in Postwar Japan*. Berkeley, CA: University of California Press, 1992.

Brison, Karen J. *Just Talk: Gossip, Meetings, and Power in a Papua New Guinea Village*. Berkeley, CA: University of California Press, 1992.

Britt, Chester L. "Crime and Unemployment Among Youths in the United States, 1958-1990." *American Journal of Economics and Sociology* 53 (1994): 99-109.

Brod, Harry (Ed.). *The Making of Masculinities—The New Men's Studies*. Boston: Allen & Unwin, 1987.

Brody, David. "The Breakdown of Labor's Social Contract: Historical Reflections, Future Prospects." *Dissent* Winter 1992: 32-41.

Broman, Clifford L., William S. Hoffman, and V. Lee Hamilton. "Impact of mental Health Services Use on Subsequent Mental Health of Autoworkers." *Journal of Health and Social Behavior* 35 (1994): 80-94.

Brooke, James. "Pragmatic Protestants Win Catholic Converts in Brazil." *New York Times*, July 4, 1993a.

Brooke, James. "A Soldier Turned Politician Wants to Give Brazil Back to Army Rule." *New York Times*, July 25, 1993b.

Brooke, James. "A City of Blonds Builds Walls: Migrants Keep Out." *New York Times*, May 4, 1994.

Brooks-Gunn, Jeanne, Greg J. Duncan, Pamela Kato Klebanov, and Naomi Sealand. "Do Neighborhoods Influence Child and Adolescent Development?" *American Journal of Sociology* 99 (1993): 353-395.

Broschart, Kay. "After the Fall: The Impact of Democratization and Economic Restructuring on Women in the Former Soviet Union." Hollins College, 1993.

Brown, Judith K., and Virginia Kerns. *In Her Prime: A New View of Middle-Aged Women*. South Hadley, MA: Bergin & Garvey, 1985.

Brown, Lester R., Hal Kane, and Ed Ayres. *Vital Signs 1994: The Trends That Are Shaping Our Future*. New York: W.W. Norton and Company, 1994.

Brown, Lyn Mikel, and Carol Gilligan. *Meeting at the Crossroads: Women's Psychology and Girls' Development*. Cambridge, MA: Harvard University Press, 1992.

Brown, M. Craig, and Barbara D. Warner. "Immigrants, Urban Politics, and Policing in 1900." *American Sociological Review* 57 (1992): 293-305.

Brown, Richard Harvey. "Cultural Representation and Ideological Domination." *Social Forces* 71 (1993): 657-676.

Brown, Tim, and Peter Xenos. "AIDS in Asia: The Gathering Storm." *Asia Pacific Issues* 16 (1994).

Brown, Victoria Bissell. "Golden girls: female socialization among the middle class of Los Angeles, 1880-1910." In Elliott West and Paula Petrik (Eds.), *Small Worlds: Children and Adolescents in America, 1850-1950*. Lawrence KS: University Press of Kansas, 1992.

Bruderl, Josef, Peter Preisendorfer, and Rolf Ziegler. "Survival Chances of Newly Founded Business Organizations," *American Sociological Review* 57 (1992): 227-242.

Brunvand, Jan Harold. *The Mexican Pet: More 'New' Urban Legends*. New York: Norton, 1986.

Brush, Lisa D. "Violent Acts and Injurious Outcomes in Married Couples: Methodological Issues in the National Survey of Families and Households." *Gender & Society* 4 (1990): 56-67.

Bruyn, Severyn T. *A Future for the American Economy: The Social Market.* Stanford, CA: Stanford University Press, 1991.

Bryant, Bunyan, and Paul Mohai (Eds.). *Race and the Incidence of Environmental Hazards: A Time for Discourse.* Boulder, CO: Westview Press, 1992.

Bryk, Anthony, Valerie E. Lee, and Peter B. Holland. *Catholic Schools and the Common Good.* Cambridge, MA: Harvard University Press, 1993.

Buchbinder, Georgeda, and Roy A. Rappaport. "Fertility and Death Among the Maring." In P. Brown and G. Buchbinder (Eds.) *Man and Woman in the New Guinea Highlands*, pp. 13-35. Washington, DC: American Anthropological Association, 1976.

Buford, Bill. "The Hate Behind the Game." *New York Times*, June 15, 1994.

Bullard, Robert D. "Anatomy of Environmental Racism." In Richard Hofrichter (Ed.), *Toxic Struggles: The Theory and Practice of Environmental Justice.* Philadelphia: New Society Publishers, 1993.

Bullough, Vern L. and Bonnie Bullough. *Cross Dressing, Sex, and Gender.* Philadelphia, PA: University of Pennsylvania Press, 1993.

Burawoy, Michael. "The End of Sovietology and the Renaissance of Modernization Theory." *Contemporary Sociology* 21 (1992): 774-785.

Burawoy, Michael, and Pavel Krotov. "The Soviet Transition from Socialism to Capitalism: Worker Control and Economic Bargaining in the Wood Industry," *American Sociological Review* 57 (1992): 16-38.

Burgess, Ernest W. "The Growth of the City." In Robert E. Park, Ernest W. Burgess, and R. D. McKenzie (Eds.), *The City.* Chicago: University of Chicago Press, 1925.

Burke, Peter J. "Gender Identity, Sex, and School Performance." *Social Psychology Quarterly* 52 (1989): 159-169.

Burkitt, Ian. *Social Selves: Theories of the Social Formation of Personality.* London: Sage, 1991.

Burr, Chandler. "Homosexuality and Biology." *The Atlantic* 271 (3), March 1993: 47-65.

Burris, Beverly H. *Technocracy at Work.* Albany, NY: State University of New York Press, 1994.

Burrows, William E., and Robert Windrem. *Critical Mass: The Dangerous Race for Superweapons in a Fragmenting World.* New York: Simon and Schuster, 1994.

Bursik, Robert J., and Harold G. Grasmick. *Neighborhoods and Crime: The Dimensions of Effective Community Control.* New York: Lexington, 1993.

Burstein, Paul, and Susan Pitchford. "Social-Scientific and Legal Challenges to Education and Test Requirements in Employment." *Social Problems* 37 (1990): 243-257.

Burtless, Gary (Ed.). *A Future of Lousy Jobs? The Changing Structure of U.S. Wages.* Washington, DC: The Brookings Institution, 1990.

Burton, C. Emory. *The Poverty Debate: Politics and the Poor in America.* Westport, CT: Praeger, 1992.

Burton, James G. *The Pentagon Wars: Reformers Challenge the Old Guard.* Annapolis, MD: Naval Institute Press, 1993.

Business Week. "Executive Pay...But You Wouldn't Know It." April 26, 1993: 56-58.

Butler, Edgar R. *Urban Sociology: A Systematic Approach.* New York: Harper & Row, 1976.

Butsch, Richard (Ed.). *For Fun and Profit: The Transformation of Leisure into Consumption.* Philadelphia, PA: Temple University Press, 1990.

Byne, William. "The Biological Evidence Challenged." *Scientific American* May, 1994: 50-55.

Cable, Sherry, and Michael Benson. "Acting Locally: Environmental Injustice and the Emergence of Grass-roots Environmental Organizations." *Social Problems* 40 (1993): 464-477.

Cable, Sherry, Edward J. Walsh, and Rex H. Warland. "Differential Paths to Political Activism: Comparisons of Four Mobilization Processes After the Three-Mile Island Accident." *Social Forces* 66 (1988): 951-969.

Cabrera, Mario. "Land and Poverty." *Noticias de Guatemala*, February/March, 1993: 6-8.

Cage, Mary Crystal. "Graduation Rates of American Indians and Blacks Improve, Lag Behind Others." *Chronicle of Higher Education* May 26, 1993: A29.

Cain, Glen G., and Douglas A. Wissoker. "A Reanalysis of Marital Stability in the Seattle-Denver Income-Maintenance Experiment." *American Journal of Sociology* 95 (1990): 1235-1269.

Calasanti, Toni M., and Carol A. Bailey. "Gender Inequality and the Division of Household Labor in the United States and Sweden: A Socialist-Feminist Approach." *Social Problems* 38 (1991): 34-53.

Calavita, Kitty, and Henry N. Pontell. "'Other People's Money' Revisited: Collective Embezzlement in the Savings and Loan and Insurance Industries." *Social Problems* 38(1) (1991): 94-112.

Callero, Peter, and Judith A. Howard. "Biases of the Scientific Discourse on Human Sexuality: Toward a Sociology of Sexuality." In Kathleen McKinney and Susan Sprecher (Eds.), *Human Sexuality: The Social and Interpersonal Context.* Norwood, NJ: Ablex, 1989.

Cancian, Francesca M. *Love In America: Gender and Self-Development.* New York: Cambridge University Press, 1987.

Cancian, Francesca M. "Feminist Science: Methodologies That Challenge Inequality." *Gender & Society* 6 (1992): 623-642.

Canterella, Eva. *Bisexuality in the Ancient World.* New Haven, CT: Yale University Press, 1992.

Carlson, Susan M. "Trends in Race/Sex Occupational Inequality: Conceptual and Measurement Issues." *Social Problems* 39 (1992): 268-290.

Carnegie Corporation. *Starting Points: Meeting the Needs of Our Youngest Children.* New York: Carnegie Corporation, 1994.

Carrier, James G. *Social Class and the Construction of Inequality in American Education.* New York: Greenwood, 1986.

Carrier, James G. "Gifts, Commodities, and Social Relations: A Maussian View of Exchange." *Sociological Forum* 6 (1991): 119-136.

Carter, Bill. "Advertisers Less Skittish About Explicit Programs." *New York Times*, December 7, 1992.

Carter, Deborah, and Reginald Wilson. *College Enrollment Trends for Mid- and Low-Income Black and Hispanic Youth.* Washington, DC: American Council on Education, 1990.

Carter, Gregg Lee. "Hispanic Rioting During the Civil Rights Era." *Sociological Forum* 7 (1992): 301-322.

Carter, Lewis F. *Charisma and Control in Rajneeshpuram: The Role of Shared Values in the Creation of a Community.* New York: Cambridge University Press, 1990.

Casey, Timothy J. "Childhood Poverty and Public Transfers in International Perspective." New York: Center on Social Welfare Policy and Law, 1991.

Casper, Lynne M., Sara S. McLanahan, and Irwin Garfinkel. "The Gender-Poverty Gap: What We Can Learn From Other Countries." *American Sociological Review* 59 (1994): 594-605.

Castillo, Dennis. "Origins of the Priest Shortage 1942-62." *America* 167 (1992): 302-305.

Catalano, Ralph, David Dooley, Georgeanna Wilson, and Richard Hough. "Job Loss and Alcohol Abuse: A Test Using Data from the Epidemiologic Catchment Area Project." *Journal of Health and Social Behavior* 34 (1993): 215-225.

Catsambis, Sophia. "The Path to Math: Gender and Racial-Ethnic Differences in Mathematics Participation from Middle School to High School." *Sociology of Education* 67 (1994): 199-215.

Cavender, Gray, and Paul Knepper. "Strange Interlude: An Analysis of Juvenile Parole Revocation Decision Making." *Social Problems* 39 (1992): 387-399.

Celis, William 3d. "40 Years After Brown, Segregation Persists." *New York Times,* May 18, 1994.

Center for the American Women and Politics. "Women in Elective Office 1989." Eagleton Institute of Politics, Rutgers University, New Brunswick, NJ, 1994.

Center for Population Options. *Teenage Pregnancy and Too-Early Childbearing: Public Costs, Personal Consequences.* Washington, DC: Center for Population Options, 1992.

Cerulo, Karen A. "Sociopolitical Control and the Structure of National Symbols." *Social Forces* 68 (1989): 76–99.

Cerulo, Karen A. "Symbols and the World System: National Anthems and Flags." *Sociological Forum* 8 (1993): 243–271.

Chafetz, Janet Saltzman. *Gender Equity: An Integrated Theory of Stability and Change.* Newbury Park, CA: Sage, 1990.

Chalk, Frank, and Kurt Jonassohn. *The History and Sociology of Genocide.* New Haven, CT: Yale University Press, 1990.

Chambliss, William J. "Policing the Ghetto Underclass: The Politics of Law and Law Enforcement." *Social Problems* 41 (1994): 177–194.

Champion, Dean J., and G. Larry Mays. *Transferring Juveniles to Criminal Courts: Trends and Implications for Juvenile Justice.* New York: Praeger, 1991.

Chancer, Lynn S. *Sadomasochism in Everyday Life: The Dynamics of Power and Powerlessness.* New Brunswick, NJ: Rutgers University Press, 1992.

Chang, Patricia Mei Yin. "Beyond the Clan: A Re-Analysis of the Empirical Evidence." In Durkheim's *The Elementary Forms of the Religious Life. Sociological Theory* 7 (1989): 64–69.

Chappell, Neena L., and Harold L. Orbach. "Socialization in Old Age: A Meadian Perspective." In Victor W. Marshall (Ed.), *Later Life: The Social Psychology of Aging,* pp. 75–106. Beverly Hills: Sage 1986.

Charmaz, Kathy. *Good Days, Bad Days: The Self in Chronic Illness and Time.* New Brunswick, NJ: Rutgers University Press, 1991.

Chase-Dunn, Christopher, and Thomas D. Hall. "Comparing World Systems: Concepts and Working Hypotheses." *Social Forces,* Vol. 70, No. 4, June 1993.

Chass, Murray. "Yankees Write the Biggest Check When Paying Their Major Leaguers." *New York Times,* April 6, 1994.

Chaves, Mark. "Secularization as Declining Religious Authority." *Social Forces* 72 (1994): 749–774.

Chayko, Mary. "How You 'Act Your Age' When You Watch TV." *Sociological Forum* 8 (1993): 573–593.

Cherlin, A. J., F. F. Furstenberg, Jr., P. L. Chase-Lansdale, K. E. Kiernan, P. K. Robins, D. R. Morrison, and J. O. Teitler. "Longitudinal Studies of the Effects of Divorce on Children in Great Britain and the United States." *Science,* June 7, 1991: 1386–1389.

Chesney-Lind, Meda. "Girls, Gangs, and Violence: Anatomy of a Backlash." *Humanity & Society* 17 (1993): 321–344.

Chew, Kenneth S.Y. "The Demographic Erosion of Political Support for Public Education: A Suburban Case Study." *Sociology of Education* 65 (1992): 280–292.

Children's Defense Fund. *The State of America's Children, 1994.* Washington, DC: Children's Defense Fund, 1994.

Chin, Ko-lin. *Chinese Subculture and Criminality: Non-Traditional Crime Groups in America.* Westport, CT: Greenwood Press, 1990.

Chinoy, Ely. *Automobile Workers and the American Dream.* New York: Doubleday, 1955.

Chiricos, Theodore G., and Miriam A. DeLone. "Labor Surplus and Punishment: A Review and Assessment of Theory and Evidence." *Social Problems* 39 (1992) 421–446.

Chodorow, Nancy. *Femininities, Masculinities, Sexualities: Freud and Beyond.* Lexington, KY: University Press of Kentucky, 1994.

Chronicle of Higher Education. "Alcohol Abuse by Students is Found Most Severe on Campuses in Northeast." May 26, 1993: A-28.

Chronicle of Higher Education. "Top Players Produce Up to $1 Million in Revenue for Their Universities." April 13, 1994a: A33–34.

Chubb, John E., and Terry M. Moe. *Politics, Markets, and American Schools.* Washington, DC: Brookings Institute, 1989.

Chubin, Daryl E., and Edward J. Hackett. *Peerless Science: Peer Review and U.S. Science Policy.* Albany, New York: State University of New York Press, 1990.

Churchill, Ward. "Radioactive Colonization: A Hidden Holocaust in Native America." Unpublished paper, 1992.

Chynoweth, Judith K., and Michael D. Campbell. "Towards a Rural Family Policy." Family Resource Coalition Report, Volume 11, Number 1, 1992.

Clancy, Carolyn M., and Peter Franks. "Physician Gender Bias in Clinical Decision-Making: Screening for Cancer in Primary Care." *Medical Care* 31 (1993): 213–218.

Clark, E. Culpepper. *The Schoolhouse Door: Segregation's Last Stand at the University of Alabama.* New York: Oxford University Press, 1993.

Clark, Janet. "Getting There: Women in Political Office." *Annals of the American Academy of Political and Social Science,* 515 (May 1991): 63–76.

Clark, Rebecca L., Jeffrey S. Passel, Wendy Zimmerman, and Michael Fix. *Fiscal Impacts of Undocumented Aliens: Selected Estimates for Seven States.* Washington, DC: Urban Institute, 1994.

Clark, Roger. "Multinational Corporate Investment and Women's Participation in Higher Education in Noncore Nations." *Sociology of Education* 65 (1992): 37–47.

Clark, Roger, Rachel Lennon, and Leanna Morris. "Of Caldecotts and Kings: Gendered Images in Recent American Children's Books by Black and Non-Black Illustrators." *Gender & Society* 7 (1993): 227–245.

Clark, Roger, Thomas W. Ramsey, and Emily Steir Adler. "Culture, Gender, and Labor Force Participation: A Cross-National Study." *Gender & Society* 5 (1991): 47–66.

Clarke, Lee. *Acceptable Risk? Making Decisions in a Toxic Environment,* Berkeley: University of California Press, 1989.

Clarke, Lee. "Technological Risks and Society." In Edgar F. Borgatta and Marie L. Borgatta (Eds.), *Encyclopedia of Sociology* (4) (1992): 2159–2163.

Clausen, John A. *American Lives: Looking Back at the Children of the Great Depression.* New York: Free Press, 1993.

Clawson, Dan, and Alan Neustadtl. "Interlocks, PACs, and Corporate Conservatism." *American Journal of Sociology* 94 (1989): 749–773.

Clawson, Dan, Alan Neustadtl, and Denise Scott. *Money Talks: Corporate PACs and Political Influence.* New York: Basic Books, 1992.

Clayman, Steven E. "Booing: The Anatomy of a Disaffiliative Response." *American Sociological Review* 58 (1993): 110–130.

Clear, Todd R. *Harm in American Penology: Offenders, Victims, and Their Communities.* New Brunswick: Rutgers University Press, 1994.

Clegg, Stewart R. *Modern Organizations: Organization Studies in the Postmodern World.* Newbury Park, CA: Sage, 1990.

Clinard, Marshall B., and Peter C. Yeager. *Corporate Crime.* New York: Free Press, 1980.

Clotfelter, Charles T. (Ed.). *Who Benefits from the Nonprofit Sector?* Chicago, IL: University of Chicago Press, 1992.

Cloward, Richard A., and Lloyd E. Ohlin. *Delinquency and Opportunity.* New York: Free Press, 1960.

Cloward, Richard A., and Frances Fox Piven. *Regulating the Poor: The Functions of Public Welfare,* 2nd ed. New York: Pantheon, 1993.

Clymer, Adam. "Abortion Foes Say Poll Backs Curb on Advice." *New York Times* June 25, 1991.

Coakley, Jay. "Burnout Among Adolescent Athletes: A Personal Failure or Social Problems?" *Sociology of Sport Journal* 9 (1992): 271–285.

Coakley, Jay. *Sport in Society.* 5th ed. St. Louis, MO: Moseby, 1994.

Coates, Vary T. "The Potential Impact of Robotics." *The Futurist,* February 1983, pp. 28–32.

Cobble, Dorothy Sue (Ed.). *Women and Unions: Forging a Partnership.* Ithaca, NY: ILR Press, 1993.

Cohen, Albert K. *Delinquent Boys.* New York: Free Press, 1955.

Cohen, David. "Notes on a Grecian Yearn: Pederasty in Thebes and Sparta." *New York Times,* March 31, 1993.

Cohen, Elizabeth, Rachel A. Lotan, and Chaub Leechor. "Can Classrooms Learn?" *Sociology of Education* 62 (1989): 75–94.

Cohen, Susan A., and Cory L. Richards. "The Ciaro Consensus: Population, Development, and Women. *Family Planning Perspectives* 26 (1994): 272–277.

Cohn, Samuel. *The Process of Occupational Sex-Typing: The Feminization of Clerical Work in Great Britain.* Philadelphia: Temple University Press, 1985.

Cole, Robert E. *Strategies for Learning: Small Group Activities in American, Japanese, and Swedish Industry.* Berkeley, CA: University of California Press, 1989.

Coleman, James S. "Recent Trends in School Integration." *Educational Researcher* 4 (1975): 3-12.

Coleman, James S. "Open Forum." *ASA Footnotes,* January 1989, pp. 4-5.

Coleman, James S. *Equality and Achievement in Education.* Boulder, CO: Westview Press, 1990.

Coleman, James S. "Rational Choice Theory." In Edgar F. Borgatta and Marie L. Borgatta (Eds.), *Encyclopedia of Sociology,* pp. 1619-1624. New York: Macmillan, 1992.

Coleman, James S. "The Rational Reconstruction of Society." *American Sociological Review* 58 (1993): 1-15.

Coleman, James S., Elihu Katz, and Herbert Menzel. "The Diffusion of Innovation Among Physicians." *Sociometry* 20 (1957): 253-269.

Coles, Gerald. *The Learning Mystique: A Critical Look at "Learning Disabilities."* New York: Pantheon, 1987.

The College Board. "Annual Report on Tuition, Room and Board at American Colleges and Universities." New York: The College Board, 1994a.

The College Board. *1994 Profile of SAT and Achievement Test Takers.* Princeton, NJ: Educational Testing Service, 1994b.

Collins, Patricia Hill. *Black Feminist Thought: Knowledge, Consciousness, and the Politics of Empowerment.* Boston: Unwin Hyman, 1990.

Collins, Randall. *Theoretical Sociology.* San Diego, CA: Harcourt Brace Jovanovich, 1988.

Collinson, David L. *Managing the Shopfloor: Subjectivity, Masculinity, and Workplace Culture.* New York: Walter de Gruyter, 1992.

Coltrane, Scott. "Father-Child Relationships and the Status of Women: A Cross-Cultural Study." *American Journal of Sociology* 93 (1988): 1060-1095.

Coltrane, Scott. "The Micropolitics of Gender in Nonindustrial Societies." *Gender & Society* 6 (1992): 86-107.

Coltrane, Scott. "Engendering Families: Equity and Obligation in Family Work." Paper presented at the XII World Congress of Sociology, Bielefeld, Germany, July 1994.

Coltrane, Scott, and Neal Hickman. "The Rhetoric of Rights and Needs: Moral Discourse in the Reform of Child Custody and Child Support Laws." *Social Problems* 39 (1992): 400-420.

Congressional Budget Office. *1992 Green Book.* Washington, DC: Committee on Ways and Means, U.S. House of Representatives, 1992.

Connell, R. W. *Gender and Power: Society, the Person, and Sexual Politics.* Stanford, CA: Stanford University Press, 1987.

Connell, R. W. "A Whole New World: Remaking Masculinity in the Context of the Environmental Movement." *Gender & Society* 4 (1990): 452-478.

Connell, R. W. "A Very Straight Gay: Masculinity, Homosexual Experience, and the Dynamics of Gender." *American Sociological Review* 57 (1992): 735-751.

Cook, Alice H. *The Most Difficult Revolution: Women and Trade Unions.* Ithaca, NY: ILR Press, 1992.

Cook, Karen Schweers, and Margaret Levi (Eds.). *The Limits of Rationality.* Chicago: University of Chicago Press, 1991.

Cook, Phillip J. "The Demand and Supply of Criminal Opportunities." In Michael Tony and Norval Morris (Eds.), *Crime and Justice: An Annual Review of Research,* pp. 1-27. Chicago, IL: University of Chicago Press, 1986.

Cookson, Peter W., Jr. *Contested Ground: School Choice and the Struggle For the Soul of American Education.* New Haven, CT: Yale University Press, 1993.

Cookson, Peter W., Jr., and Caroline Hodges Persell. *Preparing for Power: America's Elite Boarding Schools.* New York: Basic Books, 1985.

Cooley, Charles Horton. *Social Organization: A Study of the Larger Mind.* New York: Scribners, 1909.

Coontz, Stephanie. *The Way We Never Were: American Families and the Nostalgia Trap.* New York: Basic Books, 1992.

Coppens, Yves. "East Side Story: The Origin of Humankind." *Scientific American,* May 1994: 88-95.

Corcoran, Mary. "Background, Earnings, and the American Dream." *Contemporary Sociology* 21 (1992): 603-608.

Cordes, Colleen. "NIH to Develop Guidelines for Research Agreements that Universities Sign with Private Companies.: *Chronicle of Higher Education,* June 23, 1993: A-21.

Corman, Hope, and Theodore Joyce. "Urban Crime Control: Violent Crimes in New York City." *Social Science Quarterly* 71 (1990): 567-584.

Cornfield, Daniel B. *Becoming a Mighty Voice: Conflict and Change in the United Furniture Workers of America.* New York: Russell Sage, 1989.

Cornwall, Marie. "The Determinants of Religious Behavior: A Theoretical Model and Empirical Test." *Social Forces* 68 (1989): 572-592.

Corsaro, William A. "Interpretive Reproduction in Children's Peer Cultures." *Social Psychology Quarterly* 55 (1992): 160-170.

Corsaro, William A., and Thomas A. Rizzo. "*Discussion* and Friendship: Socialization Processes in the Peer Culture of Italian Nursery School Children." *American Sociological Review* 53 (1988): 879-894.

Cortese, Anthony J. *Ethnic Ethics: The Restructuring of Moral Theory.* Albany, NY: State University of New York Press, 1990.

Coser, Rose Laub. *In Defense of Modernity: Role Complexity and Individual Autonomy.* Stanford: Stanford University Press, 1991.

Costa, Paul T., Jr., Alan B. Zonderman, Robert R. McGrae, Joan Cornoni-Huntley, Ben Z. Locke, and Helen E. Barbano. "Longitudinal Analysis of Psychological Well-Being in a National Sample: Stability of Mean Levels." *Journal of Gerontology* 42 (1987): 50-55.

Coupland, Douglas. "A Mythical Medical Monster." *New York Times,* September 1, 1993.

Coverdill, James E. "The Dual Economy and Sex Differences in Earnings." *Social Forces* 66 (1988): 970-993.

Craig, Steve (Ed.). *Men, Masculinity, and the Media.* Newbury Park, CA: Sage, 1992.

Crane, Diana. *The Production of Culture: Media and the Urban Arts.* Newbury Park, CA: Sage, 1992.

Crane, Jonathan. "The Epidemic Theory of Ghettos and Neighborhood Effects on Dropping Out and Teenage Childbearing." *American Journal of Sociology* 96 (1991): 1226-1259.

Crippen, Timothy. "Old and New Gods in the Modern World: Toward a Theory of Religious Transformation." *Social Forces* 67 (1988): 316-336.

Crispell, Diane. "The Brave New World of Men." *American Demographics,* January 1922: 38-43.

Crosset, Todd W., Mark A. McDonald, and Jeffrey R. Benedict. "Male Student-Athletes Reported for Sexual Assault: A Survey of Campus Police Departments and Judicial Affairs Officers." Paper presented at the annual meeting of the North American Society for Sports Sociology, Savannah, GA., November, 1944.

Cruz, Jon D. "Resentment and Vengeance in American Popular Culture: The Morton Downey, Jr. Show and Conservative Populism." In Clinton R. Sanders (Ed.), *Marginal Conventions: Popular Culture, Mass Media, and Social Deviance.* Bowling Green, OH: The Popular Press, 1990.

Cummings, Scott, and Daniel Monti (Eds.). *Gangs: The Origins and Impact of Contemporary Youth Gangs in the United States.* Albany, NY: State University of New York Press, 1993.

Cunningham, William C., John J. Strauchs, and Clifford W. Van Meter. "Private Security: Patterns and Trends." *Research in Brief.* Washington, DC: National Institute of Justice, August 1991.

Currie, Elliott. "Crimes Without Criminals: Witchcraft and Its Control in Medieval Europe." *Law and Society Review* 3 (1968): 7-32.

Currie, Elliott. "Crime in the Market Society: From Bad to Worse in the Nineties." *Dissent* Spring 1991: 254-259.

Currie, Elliott. *Reckoning: Drugs, the Cities and the American Future.* New York: Hill & Wang, 1993.

Curry, Timothy Jon. "Fraternal Bonding in the Locker Room: A Profeminist Analysis of Talk About Competition and Women." *Sociology of Sport Journal* 8 (1991): 119-135.

Curry, Timothy Jon. "A Little Pain Never Hurt Anyone: Athletic Career Socialization and the Normalization of Sports Injury." *Symbolic Interaction* 16 (1993): 273-290.

Curtis, Richard F. "Household and Family in Theory on Inequality." *American Sociological Review* 51 (1986): 168-183.

Dabbs, James M., Jr. "Testosterone and Occupational Achievement." *Social Forces* 70 (1992): 813-824.

Dallek, Geraldine. "Hospital Care for Profit." *Society* 23(5) (1986): 54-59.

Dalton, Russell J., and Manfred Kuechler (Eds.). *Challenging the Political Order: New Social and Political Movements in Western Democracies.* New York: Oxford University Press, 1991.

Daniels, Cynthia R. *At Women's Expense: State Power and the Politics of Fetal Rights.* Cambridge, MA: Harvard University Press, 1993.

D'Antonio, William V., James D. Davidson, Dean R. Hoge, and Ruth A. Wallace. *American Catholic Laity in a Changing Church.* Kansas City, MO: Sheed & Ward, 1989.

Darden, Joe T., Harriett Orcutt Duleep, and George C. Galster. "Civil Rights in Metropolitan America." *Journal of Urban Affairs*, Vol 14, Number 3/4, pp. 469-496, 1992.

Daula, Thomas, D. Alton Smith, and Roy Nord. "Inequality in the Military: Fact or Fiction?" *American Sociological Review* 55 (1990): 714-718.

Dauphanais, Pat Dewey, Steven E. Barkan, and Steven F. Cohn. "Predictors of Rank-and-File Feminist Activism: Evidence from the 1983 General Social Survey." *Social Problems* 39 (1992): 332-344.

David, Helene. "Canada's Labor Market: older workers need not apply." *Aging International XX* (3)(1993), pp. 21-25.

Davidman, Lynn. *Tradition in a Rootless World: Women Turn to Orthodox Judaism.* Berkeley, CA: University of California Press, 1991.

Davis, D. L., and R. G. Whitten. "The Cross-Cultural Study of Human Sexuality." *Annual Review of Anthropology* 16 (1987): 69-98.

Davis, F. James. *Who Is Black? One Nation's Definition.* University Park, PA: Pennsylvania State University Press, 1991.

Davis, Fred. *Fashion, Culture, and Identity.* Chicago, IL: University of Chicago Press, 1992.

Davis, Gerald F., Kristina A. Diekmann, and Catherine H. Tinsley. "The Decline and Fall of the Conglomerate Firm in the 1980s: The Deinstitutionalization of an Organizational Form." *American Sociological Review* 59 (1994): 547-570.

Davis, James A., and Tom Smith. *General Social Survey Cumulative File, 1972-1982.* Ann Arbor, MI: Inter-University Consortium for Political and Social Research, 1984.

Davis, Kingsley. "Final Note on a Case of Extreme Isolation." *American Journal of Sociology* 456 (January 1940): 554-565.

Davis, Kingsley, and Wilbert E. Moore. "Some Principles of Stratification." *American Sociological Review* 10 (April 1945): 242-247.

Davis, Maradee A., John M. Neuhaus, Deborah J. Moritz, and Mark R. Segal. "Living Arrangements and Survival Among Middle-Aged and Older Adults in the NHANES I Epidemiologic Follow-up Study." *American Journal of Public Health*, 7 (1991).

Davis, Melissa G., Richard J. Lundman, and Ramiro Martinez, Jr. "Private Corporate Justice: Store Police, Shoplifters, and Civil Recovery." *Social Problems* 38 (1991): 395-409.

Dayan, Daniel, and Elihu Katz. *Media Events: The Live Broadcasting of History.* Cambridge, MA: Harvard University Press, 1992.

Dean, Alfred, Bohdan Kolody, and Patricia Wood. "Effects of Social Support from Various Sources on Depression in Elderly Persons." *Journal of Health and Social Behavior* 31 (1990): 148-161.

Deegan, Mary Jo. *American Ritual Dramas: Social Rules and Cultural Meanings.* New York: Greenwood Press, 1989.

Deegan, Mary Jo (Ed.). *Women in Sociology: A Bio-Bibliographical Sourcebook.* Westport, CA: Greenwood Press, 1991.

Dees, Morris. "Young, Gullible and Taught to Hate." *New York Times*, August 25, 1993.

DeKeseredy, Walter S., and Martin D. Schwartz. "Theories of Male Peer Support and Woman Abuse: Strengths, Limitations, and Recommendations for Further Development." Paper presented at the Annual Meeting of the Society for the Study of Social Problems, Miami Beach, Fl, August 1993.

Delaney, Kevin J. *Strategic Bankruptcy: How Corporations and Creditors Use Chapter 11 to Their Advantage.* Berkeley: University of California Press, 1992.

Demerath, N.J., III, and Rhys H. Williams. *A Bridging of Faith: Religion and Politics in a New England City.* Princeton, NJ: Princeton University Press, 1992.

D'Emilio, John, and Estelle B. Freedman. *Intimate Matters: A History of Sexuality in America.* New York: Harper & Row, 1988.

Demos, John. "Old Age in Early New England." In John Demos and Spence Boocock (Eds.), *Turning Points: Historical and Sociological Essays on the Family*, Vol. 84, pp. 284-287. Chicago: University of Chicago Press, 1978.

Denisoff, R. Serge, and Ralph Wahrman. *An Introduction to Sociology.* 3rd ed. New York: Macmillan, 1983.

Denno, Deborah W. *Biology and Violence: Birth to Adulthood.* Cambridge, ENG: Cambridge University Press, 1990.

Denzin, Norman K. *Symbolic Interaction and Cultural Studies: The Politics of Interpretation.* Cambridge, MA: Blackwell, 1992.

DePalma, Anthony. "Rare in Ivy League: Women Who Work As Full Professors." *New York Times*, January 24, 1993.

DeParle, Jason. "States' Eagerness to Experiment on Welfare Jars Administration." *New York Times* April 14, 1994: 1 ff.

Derksen, Linda, and John Gartrell. "The Social Context of Recycling." *American Sociological Review* 58 (June): 434-442, 1993.

Desai, Sonalde, and Linda J. Waite. "Women's Employment During Pregnancy and After the First Birth: Occupational Characteristics and Work Commitment." *American Sociological Review* 56 (1991): 551-566.

de Toqueville, Alexis. *Democracy in America* (1830). New York: Mentor Books, 1956.

DeVault, Marjorie L. "Talking and Listening from Women's Standpoint: Feminist Strategies for Interviewing and Analysis." *Social Problems* 37 (1990): 96-116.

DeVault, Marjorie L. *Feeding the Family: The Social Organization of Caring as Gendered Work.* Chicago: University of Chicago Press, 1991.

Devine, Joel A., Mark Plunkett, and James D. Wright. "The Chronicity of Poverty: Evidence from the PSID, 1968-1987." *Social Forces* 70 (1992): 787-812.

Devine, Theresa J. "Characteristics of Self-Employed Women in the United States." *Monthly Labor Review* 117 (1994): 20-34.

de Waal, Frans. *Peacemaking Among Primates.* Cambridge, MA: Harvard University Press, 1989.

Dewart, Janet (Ed.). *State of Black America*, Vol. 15. New York: National Urban League, 1991.

De Witt, Paula M. "Breaking Up Is Hard to Do." *American Demographics*, October 1992: 52-59.

Diamond Jared. *The Third Chimpanzee: The Evolution and Future of the Human Animal.* New York: HarperCollins, 1992.

Dietz, Henry, Jerrold Elkin, and Maurice Roumani, (Eds.). *Ethnicity, Integration, and the Military.* Boulder, CO: Westview, 1991.

DiIulio, John J., Jr. "Save the Children." *New York Times*, November 13, 1993: 23.

DiMaggio, Paul. "Cultural Capital and School Success: The Impact of Status Culture Participation on the Grades of U.S. High School Students." *American Sociological Review* 47 (1982a): 189-201.

DiMaggio, Paul. "Cultural Entrepreneurship in Nineteenth- Century Boston: The Creation of an Organizational Base for High Culture in America." *Media, Culture, and Society* 4 (1982b): 33-50.

Diprete, Thomas A. "The Upgrading and Downgrading of Occupations: Status Redefinition vs. Deskilling as Alternative Theories of Change." *Social Forces* 66 (1988): 725-746.

DiPrete, Thomas A. "Industrial Restructuring and the Mobility Response of American Workers in the 1980s." *American Sociological Review* 58 (1993): 74–96.

Diprete, Thomas A., and David B. Grusky. "Structure and Trend in the Process of Stratification for American Men and Women." *American Journal of Sociology* 96 (1990): 107–143.

Dobratz, Betty A., and Stephanie Shanks-Meile. "The Contemporary Ku Klux Klan and the American Nazi Party: A Comparison to American Populism at the Turn of the Century." *Humanity & Society* 12 (1988): 20–50.

Doherty, William J., and Thomas L. Campbell. *Families and Health.* Newbury Park, CA: Sage, 1988.

Domhoff, G. William. *Who Rules America Now?: A View for the '80s.* Englewood Cliffs, NJ: Prentice-Hall, 1983.

Domhoff, G. William. *The Power Elite and the State: How Policy Is Made in America.* New York: Aldine de Gruyter, 1990.

Doob, Anthony N. "Deviance: Society's Side Show." *Psychology Today* 5 (October 1971): 47–51, 113.

Dorn, Nicholas, Karim Murji, and Nigel South. *Traffickers: Drug Markets and Law Enforcement.* London, ENG: Routledge, 1992.

Dougherty, Kevin. "Educational Policy-Making and the Relative Autonomy of the State: The Case of Occupational Education in the Community College." *Sociological Forum* 3 (1988): 400–432.

Dougherty, Kevin, and Floyd M. Hammack. "Educational Organization." In Edgar F. Borgatta and Marie L. Borgatta (Eds.), *Encyclopedia of Sociology*, pp. 535–541. New York: Macmillan, 1992.

Douglas, Jack, and John M. Johnson (Eds.). *Business and Professional Deviance.* Philadelphia: Lippincott, 1978.

Douglas, Jack, and Frances Chaput Waksler. *The Sociology of Deviance: An Introduction.* Boston: Little, Brown, 1982.

Douglas, Susan J. *Where the Girls Are: Growing Up Female with the Mass Media.* New York: Random House, 1994.

Doxiadas, Constantine A. "Ecumenopolis: World City of Tomorrow." *Impact of Science on Society* 19, 1969.

Dreier, Peter, and John Atlas. "The Scandal of Mansion Subsidies." *Dissent*, Winter, 1992: 93–94.

Dronkers, Jaap. "Educational Reform in the Netherlands: Did It Change the Impact of Parental Occupation and Education?" *Sociology of Education* 66 (1993): 262–277.

Drury, Elizabeth. "Older Workers in the European Community: Pervasive Discrimination, Little Awareness." *Aging International*, XX (3) (1993): 12–16.

Duberman, Martin B. *Stonewall.* New York: Dutton, 1993.

Duberman, Martin B., Martha Vicinus, and George Chauncey, Jr. (Eds.). *Hidden from History: Reclaiming the Gay and Lesbian Past.* New York: New American Library, 1989.

Dubin, Seven C. *Arresting Images: Impolitic Art and Uncivil Actions.* New York: Routledge, 1992.

DuBois, W.E.B. *The Souls of Black Folk* (1903). New York: Blue Heron Press, 1953.

Dunaway, David King. "Music As Political Communication in the United States." In James Lull (Ed.), *Popular Music and Communication*, pp. 36–52. Newbury Park, CA: Sage, 1987.

Duncan, Cynthia (Ed.). *Rural Poverty in America.* Westport, CT: Auburn House, 1992.

Duncan, Greg J. "Welfare Can Fuel Upward Mobility." Ann Arbor, MI: University of Michigan. *ISR Newsletter* 18 (1994): 6.

Duncan, Greg J., Timothy M. Smeeding, and Willard Rodgers. "The Incredible Shrinking Middle Class." *American Demographics*, May 1992: 34–38.

Duneier, Mitchell. *Slim's Table: Race, Respectability, and Masculinity.* Chicago: University of Chicago Press, 1992.

Dunham, Charlotte Chorn, and Vern L. Bengtson. "Married with Children: Protest and the Timing of Family Life Course Events." Paper presented at the 84th annual meeting of the American Sociological Association. San Francisco, August 1989.

Durkheim, Emile. *The Division of Labor in Society* (1893). New York: Free Press, 1964.

Durkheim, Emile. *The Rules of Sociological Method* (1895). New York: Free Press, 1958.

Durkheim, Emile. *Suicide* (1897). Translated by John A. Spaulding and George Simpson, Glencoe, IL: Free Press, 1951.

Durkheim, Emile (1912). *The Elementary Forms of the Religious Life.* New York: Collier Books, 1961.

Durning, Alan Thein. "Supporting Indigenous Peoples." In Lester R. Brown, *State of the World.* New York: W.W. Norton and Company, 1993.

Dworkin, Ronald. "Is Clinton's Health Plan Fair?" *New York Review of Books*, January 13, 1994: 20–25.

Easterlin, Richard A. *Birth and Fortune.* Chicago, IL: University of Chicago Press, 1987.

Easterlin, Richard A. "The Economic Impact of Prospective Population Changes in Advanced Industrial Countries: An Historical Perspective." *Journal of Gerontology* 46 (1991): 299–309.

Ebaugh, Helen Rose. "Patriarchal Bargains and Latent Avenues of Social Mobility: Nuns in the Roman Catholic Church." *Gender & Society* 7 (1993): 400–414.

Eccles, Jaquelynne. "Does Junior High Itself Create Those 'Monsters'?" *Institute for Social Research Newsletter* 18 (1994): 10.

Eckberg, Douglas Lee. "The Physicians' Anti-Abortion Campaign and the Social Bases of Moral Reform Participation." *Social Forces* 67 (1988): 378–397.

Eckert, Penelope. *Jocks and Burnouts: Social Categories and Identities in High School.* New York: Teachers College Press, 1989.

Edelman, Murray J. *Constructing the Political Spectacle.* Chicago: University of Chicago Press, 1988.

Edin, Kathryn. "Surviving the Welfare System: How AFDC Recipients Make Ends Meet in Chicago." *Social Problems* 38 (1991): 462–470.

Edwards, Harry. *Sociology of Sport.* Homewood, IL: Dorsey, 1973.

Egan, Timothy. "Less Risk for Officers, Nationwide Data Show." *New York Times*, April 25, 1991.

Egan, Timothy. "The Great Alaska Debate: Can Oil and Wilderness Mix?" *New York Times Magazine*, August 4, 1991b.

Egan, Timothy. "Montana's Sky and Its Hopes are Left Bare After Logging." *New York Times,* October 19, 1993.

Egolf, Brenda, Judith Lasker, Stewart Wolf, and Louise Potvin. "The Roseto Effect: A 50-Year Comparison of Mortality Rates." *American Journal of Public Health* 82 (1992): 1089–1092.

Ehrenreich, Barbara. "Making Sense of la Difference." *Time*, January 10, 1992: 51.

Eitzen, D. Stanley, and George H. Sage (Eds.). *Sociology of North American Sport.* 5th ed. Dubuque, IA: W.C. Brown, 1993.

Elder, Glen H., Jr. "Time, Human Agency, and Social Change: Perspectives on the Life Course." *Social Psychology* Quarterly 57 (1994): 4–15.

Eller, Cynthia. *Living in the Lap of the Goddess: The Feminist Spirituality Movement in America.* New York: Crossroad Press, 1993.

Ellickson, Robert C. *Order without Law: How Neighbors Settle Disputes.* Cambridge, MA: Harvard University Press, 1991.

Ellison, Christopher G. "Are Religious People Nice People? Evidence from the National Survey of Black Americans." *Social Forces* 71 (1992): 411–430.

Ellison, Christopher G. "Religious Involvement and Self-Perception among Black Americans." *Social Forces* 71 (1993): 1027–1055.

Ellison, Christopher G., and David A. Gay. "Black Political Participation Revisited: A Test of Compensatory, Ethnic Community, and Public Arena Models." *Social Science Quarterly* 70 (1989): 101–119.

Ellison, Christopher G., and Marc A. Musick. "Southern Intolerance: A Fundamentalist Effect?" *Social Forces* 72 (1993): 379–398.

Ellison, Christopher G., and Darren E. Sherkat. "Conservative Protestantism and Support for Corporal Punishment." *American Sociological Review* 58 (1993): 131–144.

Employee Benefit Research Institute. *The Role of the Health Care Sector in the U.S. Economy.* Washington, DC: EBRI, 1993.

Employee Benefit Research Institute. *Sources of Health Insurance and Characteristics of the Uninsured: Analysis of the March 1993 Current Population Survey.* Washington, DC: EBRI, 1994.

England, Paula. "From Status Attainment to Segregation and Devaluation." *Contemporary Sociology* 21 (1992a): 643–647.

England, Paula. *Comparable Worth: Theories and Evidence.* New York: Aldine de Gruyter, 1992b.

England, Paula, Melissa S. Herbert, Barbara Stanek Kilbourne, Lori L. Reid, and Lori McCreary Megdal. "The Gendered Valuation of Occupations and Skills: Earnings in 1980 Census Occupations." *Social Forces* 73 (1994): 65–99.

England, Paula, and Barbara Stanek Kilbourne. "Markets, Marriages, and Other Mates: The Problem of Power." In Roger Friedland and Sandy Robertson (Eds.), *Beyond the Marketplace: Rethinking Society and Economy.* New York: Aldine de Gruyter, 1989.

Enloe, Cynthia. *The Morning After: Sexual Politics at the End of the Cold War.* Berkeley, CA: University of California Press, 1993.

Ennis, Philip H. *The Seventh Stream: The Emergence of Rocknroll in American Popular Music.* Amherst, MA: University Press of Massachusetts, 1993.

Ensel, Walter M., and Nan Lin. "The Life Stress Paradigm and Psychological Distress." *Journal of Health and Social Behavior* 32 (1991): 321–341.

Ensminger, Margaret E., and Anita L. Slusarcick. "Paths to High School Graduation or Dropout: A Longitudinal Study of a First-Grade Cohort." *Sociology of Education* 65 (1992): 95–113.

Entwisle, Doris R., and Karl Alexander. "Winter Setback: The Racial Composition of Schools and Learning to Read." *American Sociological Review* 59 (1994): 446–460.

Entwisle, Doris R., Karl L. Alexander, and Linda Steffel Olson. "The Gender Gap in Math: Its Possible Origins in Neighborhood Effects." *American Sociological Review* 59 (1994): 822–838.

Epstein, Daniel Mark. *Sister Aimee: The Life of Aimée Semple McPherson.* New York: Harcourt Brace Jovanovich, 1993.

Erickson, P. I., and A. J. Rapkin. "Unwanted Sexual Experiences Among Middle and High School Youth." *Journal of Adolescent Health* 12 (1991): 319–24.

Erikson, Erik H. "Identity and the Life Cycle." *Psychological Issues* (1). New York: International Universities Press, 1959.

Erikson, Kai. *The Wayward Puritans.* New York: John Wiley & Sons, 1966.

Erikson, Kai. *Everything in Its Path: Destruction of Community in the Buffalo Creek Flood.* New York: Simon & Schuster, 1976.

Erikson, Kai. *A New Species of Trouble: Explorations in Disaster, Trauma, and Community.* New York: W.W. Norton, 1994.

Erikson, Kai, and Steven P. Vallas (Eds.). *The Nature of Work: Sociological Perspectives.* New Haven, CT: Yale University Press, 1990.

Erikson, Robert, and John H. Goldthorpe. *The Constant Flux: A Study of Class Mobility in Industrial Societies.* Oxford, ENG: Clarendon Press, 1992.

Erikson, Victoria. *Speaking in the Dark and Hearing Voices: Toward a Feminist Social Theory of Religion.* Philadelphia, PA: Fortress Press, 1992.

Espanshade, Thomas J., and Wenzhen Ye. "Differential Fertility Within an Ethnic Minority: The Effect of 'Trying Harder' Among Chinese-American Women." *Social Problems* 41 (1994): 97–113.

Esposito, John L. *Islamic Threat: Myth or Reality?* New York: Oxford University Press, 1992.

Esterberg, Kristin G. "From Accommodation to Liberation: A Social Movement Analysis of Lesbians in the Homophile Movement." *Gender & Society* 8 (1994): 424–443.

Estes, Carroll L., Charlene Harrington, and Solomon Davis. "Medical-Industrial Complex." In Edgar F. Borgatta and Marie L. Borgatta (Eds.), *Encyclopedia of Sociology,* pp. 1243–1254 . New York: Macmillan, 1992.

Etzkowitz, Henry. "Entrepreneurial Science in the Academy: A Case of the Transformation of Norms." *Social Problems* 36 (1989): 14–29.

Etzkowitz, Henry. "Inventions." In Edgar Borgatta and Marie L. Borgatta, *Encyclopedia of Sociology,* pp. 1001–1005. New York: Macmillan Publishing Co., 1992.

Evans, M. D. R., Jonathan Kelley, and Tamas Kolosi. "Images of Class: Public Perceptions in Hungary and Australia." *American Sociological Review* 57 (1992): 461–482.

Exter, Thomas G. "Workforce 2005." *American Demographics* (May, 1992): 59.

Eyer, Diane E. *Mother-Infant Bonding: A Scientific Fiction.* New Haven, CT: Yale University Press, 1992.

Eyerman, Ron, and Andrew Jamison. *Social Movements: A Cognitive Approach.* University Park, PA: The Pennsylvania State University Press, 1991.

Falls, Anne Floden. "Technology Expands the Reach of Family Services in Rural South Dakota." *Family Resource Coalition Report,* No. 1, 1992, p. 20.

Faludi, Susan. *Backlash: The Undeclared War Against American Women.* New York: Crown, 1991.

Farkas, George, Robert P. Grobe, Daniel Sheehan, and Yuan Shuan. "Cultural Resources and School Success: Gender, Ethnicity, and Poverty Groups Within an Urban School District." *American Sociological Review* 55 (1990): 127–142.

Farley, Reynolds, Charlotte Steeh, Maria Krysan, Tara Jackson, and Keith Reeves. "Stereotypes and Segregation: Neighborhoods in the Detroit Area." *American Journal of Sociology* 100 (1994): 750–780.

Farnsworth, Clyde H. "Experiment in Worker Ownership Shows a Profit." *New York Times,* August 14, 1993a.

Farnsworth, Clyde H. "Americans Filching Free Health Care in Canada." *New York Times,* December 20, 1993b.

Fass, Paula S. *Outside In: Minorities and the Transformation of AmericanEducation.* New York: Oxford University Press, 1989.

Fausto-Sterling. "How Many Sexes Are There?" *New York Times,* March 12, 1993.

Fay, Robert E., Charles F. Turner, Albert D. Klassen, and John H. Gagnon. "Prevalence and Patterns of Same-Gender Sexual Contact Among Men." *Science* 243 (1989): 338–343.

Feagin, Joe R., and Clairece Booker Feagin. *Social Problems: A Critical Power Conflict Approach,* 4th ed. Prentice-Hall, 1994.

Feagin, Joe R., and Nikitah Imani. "Racial Barriers and African American Entrepreneurship: An Exploratory Study." *Social Problems* 41 (1994): 562–584.

Feagin, Joe R., Anthony M. Orum, and Gideon Sjoberg (Eds.). *A Case for the Case Study.* Chapel Hill: University of North Carolina Press, 1991.

Feagin, Joe R., and Melvin P. Sikes. *Living with Racism: The Black Middle-Class Experience.* Boston: Beacon, 1994.

Feder, Barnaby J. "Struggle to Survive in Town that Steel Forgot." *New York Times,* May 13, 1993.

Federal Bureau of Investigation. *Uniform Crime Reports,* December, 1994.

Fein, Helen (Ed.). *Genocide Watch.* New Haven, CT: Yale University Press, 1992.

Feinberg, William E., and Norris R. Johnson. "Outside Agitators and Crowds: Results from a Computer Simulation Model." *Social Forces* 67 (1988): 398–423.

Feldberg, Roslyn, and Evelyn Nakano Glenn. "Technology and Work Degradation: Effects of Office Automation on Women Clerical Workers." In Joan Rosthschild (Ed.), *Women, Technology and Innovation.* New York: Pergamon, 1982.

Felson, Richard B., Allen E. Liska, Scott J. South, and Thomas L. McNulty. "The Subculture of Violence and Delinquency: Individual vs. School Context Effects." *Social Forces* 73 (1994): 155–173.

Fendrich, James Max. *Ideal Citizens: The Legacy of the Civil Rights Movement.* Albany, NY: State University of New York Press, 1993.

Fernandez, Marilyn, Kichiro Iwamoto, and Bernadette Muscat. "Dependency and Severity of Abuse: Impact on Women's Persistence in Utilizing the Court System as Protection Against Domestic Violence." Paper presented at the annual meeting of the American Sociological Association, Los Angeles, CA, August 1994.

Fernandez-Kelly, Maria Patricia, and Anna M. Garcia. "Power Surrendered, Power Restored: The Politics of Work and Family Among Hispanic Garment Workers in California and Florida," pp. 130–152. In Louise Tilly and Patricia Guerin (Eds.), *Women, Social Change, and Politics.* New York: Russell Sage, 1990.

Ferner, Anthony, and Richard Hyman (Eds). *Industrial Relations in the New Europe*. Oxford, ENG: Blackwell, 1992.

Ferraro, Kathleen J. "Policing Women Battering." *Social Problems* 36 (1989): 61–74.

Ferree, Myra Marx. "Beyond Separate Spheres: Feminism and Family Research." *Journal of Marriage and the Family* 52 (1990): 866–884.

Ferree, Myra Marx. "The Political Context of Rationality: Rational Choice Theory and Resource Mobilization." In Aldon D. Morris and Carol McClurg Mueller (Eds.), *Frontiers of Social Movement Theory*, pp. 29–52. New Haven, CT: Yale University Press, 1992.

Ferree, Myra Marx, and Beth B. Hess. *Controversy and Coalition: The New Feminist Movement Across Three Decades of Change*. Revised ed. New York: Twayne, 1994.

Fiala, Robert. "Postindustrial Society." In Edgar F. Borgatta and Marie L. Borgatta (Eds.). *Encyclopedia of Sociology*, pp. 1512–1522. New York: Macmillan 1992.

Fielding, Stephen L. "Changing Medical Practice and Medical Malpractice Claims." *Social Problems* 42 (1995): 38–52.

Fine, Gary Alan. *With the Boys: Little League Baseball and Preadolescent Culture*. Chicago: University of Chicago Press, 1987.

Fine, Gary Alan. "The Culture of Production: Aesthetic Choices and Constraints in Culinary Work." *American Journal of Sociology* 97 (1992a): 1268–1294.

Fine, Gary Alan. *Manufacturing Tales: Sex and Money in Contemporary Legends*. Knoxville, TN: University of Tennessee Press, 1992b.

Fingerhut, Lois, Cheryl Jones, and Diane M. Makuc. "Firearms and Motor Vehicle Injury Mortality—Variations by State, Race, and Ethnicity: United States 1990-1991." *Advance Data* 242. Hyattsville, MD: National Center for Health Statistics, January 1994.

Finke, Roger, and Rodney Stark. *The Churching of America, 1776–1990*. New Brunswick, NJ: Rutgers University Press, 1992.

Finkelstein, JoAnne. *Dining Out: A Sociology of Modern Manners*. New York: New York University Press, 1989.

Finn, Peter, and Andrea K. Newlyn. "Miami's 'Drug Court': A Different Approach." *National Institute of Justice*. Washington, DC: Office of Justice Programs, 1993.

Finney, Henry C. "Mediating Claims to Artistry: Social Stratification in a Local Visual Arts Community." *Sociological Forum* 8 (1993) 403–431.

Fiorentine, Robert. "Men, Women, and the Premed Persistence Gap: A Normative Alternatives Approach." *American Journal of Sociology* 92 (1987): 1118–1139.

Fiorentine, Robert, and Stephen Cole. "Why Fewer Women Become Physicians: Explaining the Premed Persistence Gap." *Sociological Forum* 7 (1992): 469–496.

Firebaugh, Glenn. "Growth Effects of Foreign and Domestic Investment." *American Journal of Sociology*. Vol. 98, No. 1, July, 1992.

Firebaugh, Glenn, and Frank D. Beck. "Does Economic Growth Benefit the Masses? Growth, Dependence, and Welfare in the Third World." *American Sociological Review* 59 (1994): 631–653.

Firth, Simon. "The Industrialization of Popular Music." In James Lull (Ed.), *Popular Music and Communication*, Newbury Park, CA: Sage, 1987, pp. 53–77.

Fischer, Claude S. *The Urban Experience*. 2nd ed. New York: Harcourt Brace Jovanovich, 1984.

Fischer, Claude S. *America Calling: A Social History of the Telephone to 1940*. Berkeley, CA: University of California Press, 1992.

Fish, Virginia Kemp. "Hull House: Pioneer in Urban Research during Its Creative Years." *History of Sociology* 6 (1985): 33–54.

Fishman, Mark. *Manufacturing the News*. Austin: University of Texas Press, 1980.

Fitzgerald, Charlotte D. "The Anatomy of a Movement: Danville, Virginia, as a Case History." *Humanity & Society* 12 (1988): 254–265.

Fitzpatrick, Kevin M., and William C. Yoels. "Policy, School Structure, and Sociodemographic Effects on Statewide High School Dropout Rates." *Sociology of Education* 65 (1992): 76–93.

Fitzpatrick, Peter. *The Mythology of Modern Law*. London, ENG: Routledge, 1992.

Fizel, John L., and Randall W. Bennett. "The Impact of College Football Telecasts on College Football Attendance." *Social Science Quarterly* 70 (1989): 980–988.

Flanagan, William G. *Contemporary Urban Sociology*. Cambridge, ENG: Cambridge University Press, 1993.

Flavin, Christopher and Nicholas Lenssen. "Reshaping the Power Industry." In Lester R. Brown (Ed.), *State of the World 1994*. New York: W.W. Norton, 1994, pp. 61–80.

Fligstein, Neil. *The Transformation of Corporate Control*. Cambridge, MA: Harvard University Press, 1990.

Flora, Cornelia B. "International Development Policies and Women." Briefing paper prepared for Conference on Social Change in a Feminist Direction, February, 1992, Minneapolis, MN.

Flora, Cornelia B., and James A. Christenson. *Rural Policies for the 1990s*. Boulder, CO: Westview Press, 1992.

Florida, Richard, and Martin Kenney. "Transplanted Organizations: The Transfer of Japanese Industrial Organization to the U.S." *American Sociological Review* 56 (1991): 381–398.

Flynn, Kevin, and Gary Gerhardt. *The Silent Brotherhood: Inside America's Racist Underground*. New York: Free Press, 1989.

Fonow, Mary M., Laurel Richardson, and Virginia A. Wemmerus. "Feminist Rape Education: Does It Work?" *Gender & Society* 6 (1992): 108–121.

Forrest, Jacqueline Darroch, and Susheela Singh. "The Sexual and Reproductive Behavior of American Women, 1982–1988." *Family Planning Perspectives* 22 (1990): 206–214.

Foshee, Vangie, and Karl E. Bauman. "Parental and Peer Characteristics as Modifiers of the Bond-Behavior Relationship: An Elaboration of Control Theory." *Journal of Health and Social Behavior* 33 (1992): 66–76.

Fosset, Mark A., and Jill Kiecolt. "A Methodological Review of the Sex Ratio: Alternatives for Comparative Research." *Journal of Marriage and the Family* 53 (1991): 941–957.

Foster, John L. "Bureaucratic Rigidity Revisited." *Social Science Quarterly* 71 (1990): 223–238.

Foucault, Michel. *The History of Sexuality*, Vol. 1: An Introduction. New York: Pantheon, 1978.

Fox, Bonnie J. "Selling the Mechanized Household: 70 Years of Ads in *Ladies Home Journal*," *Gender & Society* 4 (1990): 25–40.

Fox, Mary Frank. "Women, Men, and the Social Organization of Science—Doctoral Education and Beyond." Paper presented at the 63rd Annual Meeting of the Eastern Sociological Society, March 1993, Boston, MA.

France, Anatole. *The Red Lily* (1894). New York: Modern Library, 1917.

Franklin, Benjamin. *Poor Richard's Almanac* (1784). New York: David McKay, 1970.

Franklin, Clyde W. II. "'Hey, Home—Yo, Bro:' Friendship Among Black Men." In Peter M. Nardi (Ed.), *Men's Friendships*, pp. 201–214. Newbury Park, CA: Sage, 1992.

Franks, Peter, Carolyn M. Clancy, and Marthe R. Gold. "Health Insurance and Mortality: Evidence from a National Cohort." *Journal of the American Medical Association* 270 (1993): 737–741.

Free, Marvin D. "Another Look at the Relationship Between the Home and Juvenile Delinquency." Paper presented at the annual meeting of the Society for the Study of Social Problems, Cincinnati, OH, August 1991.

Freedman, Samuel G. *Upon This Rock: The Miracles of a Black Church*. New York: HarperCollins, 1993.

Freedman, Vicki A. "Kin and Nursing Home Length of Stay: A Backward Recurrence Time Approach." *Journal of Health and Social Behavior* 34 (1993): 138–152.

Freire, Paulo. *The Politics of Education: Culture, Power, and Liberation*. Translated by Donald Macedo. South Hadley, MA: Bergin & Garvey, 1985.

French, Howard W. "In Nicaragua, No Peace, and Nostalgia for Somoza." *New York Times,* July 27, 1993.

Freud, Sigmund. *Observations on Transference-Love* (1915). Vol. 12 of the *Complete Psychological Works of Sigmund Freud,* pp. 169-170. London: Hogarth, 1958.

Freud, Sigmund. *Civilization and Its Discontents* (1930). Translated by James Strachey. New York: W. W. Norton, 1962.

Freudenburg, William R. "Addictive Economies: Extractive Industries and Vulnerable Localities in a Changing World Economy." *Rural Sociology* 57(3), 1992, pp. 305-332.

Freudenberg, William R. "Risk and Recrecancy: Weber, the Division of Labor, and the Rationality of Risk Perceptions." *Social Forces* 71 (4) June 1993: 909-932.

Freudenberg, William R., and Robert Gramling. *Oil in Troubled Waters: Perception, Politics, and the Battle over Offshore Drilling.* Albany, NY: State University of New York Press, 1994.

Freudenheim, Milt. "Physicians Selling Practices to Companies as Changes Loom." *New York Times,* September 1, 1993: 1 ff.

Frey, William H. "Black College Grads, Those in Poverty Take Different Migration paths." *Population Today* 22 (1994): 1-2.

Friedlander, Daniel, and Gary Burtless. *Five Years After: The Long-Term Effects of Welfare-to-Work Programs.* New York: Russell Sage Foundation, 1995.

Friedman, Alan. *Spider's Web: The Secret History of How the White House Illegally Armed Iraq.* New York: Bantam Books, 1994.

Friedman, Berhard, Ronald J. Ozminkowski, and Zachery Taylor. "Excess Demand and Patient Selection for Heart and Liver Transplants." *Health Economics Worldwide,* 1992: 161-186.

Friedman, Lawrence M. *Crime and Punishment in American History.* New York: Basic Books, 1993.

Fritsch, Jane, with Dean Baquet. "Pleading Poverty, an Insurer Finds Its Image Is a Handicap." *New York Times,* March 31, 1993.

Fudge, Judy, and Patricia McDermott (Eds.). *Just Wages: A Feminist Assessment of Pay Equity.* Toronto, CAN: University of Toronto Press, 1991.

Fuerst, J.S., and Roy Petty. "Quiet Success: Where Managed School Integration Works." *The American Prospect* Summer 1992: 65-72.

Fugita, Stephen S., and David J. O'Brien. *Japanese American Ethnicity: The Persistence of Community.* Seattle, WA: University of Washington Press, 1991.

Fujita, Kuniko, and Richard C. Hill (Eds.). *Japanese Cities in the World Economy.* Philadelphia, PA: Temple University Press, 1993.

Fuller, Bruce. *Growing Up Modern: The Western State Builds Third-World Schools.* New York: Routledge, 1991.

Furstenberg, Frank F., Jr., and Andrew J. Cherlin. *Divided Families: What Happens to Children When Parents Part.* Cambridge, MA: Harvard University Press, 1991.

Gagnon, John, Cathy Greenblat, and Michael Kimmel. *Human Sexualities,* 2nd ed. New York: Allyn & Bacon, 1995.

Gaines, Donna. *Teenage Wasteland: Suburbia's Dead End Kids.* New York: HarperCollins, 1992a.

Gaines, Donna. "An American Girl: Amy Fisher's Teenage Wasteland." *Village Voice,* October 13, 1992b: 32.

Galaskiewicz, Joseph. *Social Organization of an Urban Grants Economy.* San Diego, CA:Academic Press, 1985.

Galinsky, Ellen, James T. Bond, and Dana E. Freidman. *The Changing Workforce: Highlights of the National Study.* New York: Families and Work Institute, 1993.

Galinsky, Ellen, and Peter J. Stein. "Balancing Careers and Families: Research Findings and Institutional Responses." In Marsha Lakes Matyas and Lisa Baker and Rae Goodell (Eds.), *Marriage, Family and Scientific Careers: Institutional Policy Versus Research Findings.* American Association for the Advancement of Science, 1990, pp. 13-30.

Gallup Organization. "American Workers and their Jobs." Washington: National Occupational Information Coordinating Committee, 1990.

Gallup Organization. *Survey of New Age Religious Beliefs.* Princeton, NJ: December, 1991.

Gallup Organization. *The Gallup Poll Monthly,* No. 316. Princeton, NJ. January 1992.

Gallup Organization. *Gallup Youth Survey.* Princeton, NJ: 1993.

Galster, G. "Black Suburbanization: Has It Changed the Relative Location of Races?" In *Urban Affairs Quarterly,* Vol. 26, No. 4, June 1991.

Game, Ann. *Undoing the Social: Toward a Deconstructive Sociology.* Toronto Canada: University of Toronto Press, 1991.

Gamoran, Adam. "The Variable Effects of High School Tracking." *American Sociological Review* 57 (1992): 812-828.

Gamson, William A. "Commitment and Agency in Social Movements." *Sociological Forum* 6 (1991): 27-50.

Gamson, William A. "Hiroshima, the Holocaust, and the Politics of Exclusion." *American Sociological Review* 60 (1995): 1-20.

Gamson, William A., and Andre Modigliani. "Media Discourse and Public Opinion on Nuclear Power: A Constructionist Approach." *American Journal of Sociology* 95 (1989): 1-37.

Gans, Herbert. *Popular Culture and High Culture.* New York: Basic Books, 1974.

Gappa, Judith, and David W. Leslie. *The Invisible Faculty: Improving the Status of Part-Timers in Higher Education.* San Francisco, CA: Jossey-Bass, 1993.

Gardner, Howard. *To Open Minds: Chinese Clues to the Dilemma of American Education.* New York: Basic Books, 1989.

Garfinkel, Harold. *Studies in Ethnomethodology.* Englewood Cliffs, NJ: Prentice-Hall, 1967.

Gargan, Edward A. "Ultrasound Skews India's Birth Ratio." *New York Times,* December 13, 1991.

Garland, David. *Punishment and Modern Society: A Study in Social Theory.* Chicago, IL: University of Chicago Press, 1990.

Garofalo, Reebee (Ed.). *Rockin' the Boat: Mass Music and Mass Movements.* Boston, MA: South End Press, 1992.

Garreau, Joel. "Edge Cities in Profile." *American Demographics* 16:2 (1994): 24-33.

Garson, Barbara. *The Electronic Sweatshop: How Computers Are Transforming the Office of the Future into the Factory of the Past.* New York: Simon & Schuster, 1988.

Gartner, Rosemary, Kathryn Baker, and Fred C. Pampel. "Gender Stratification and the Gender Gap in Homicide Victimization." *Social Problems* 37 (1990): 593-612.

Gaventa, John, Barbara Ellen Smith, and Alex Willingham. *Communities in Economic Crisis: Appalachia and the South.* Philadelphia: Temple University Press, 1990.

Gaydosh, Louis R. "Portsiders: Left-Handed People as a Minority Group." Paper presented at the Annual Meeting of the Eastern Sociological Society, Boston, MA, March 1993.

Gaylin, Willard. *The Male Ego.* New York: Viking, 1992.

Ge, Xiaojia, Rand D. Conger, Frederick O. Lorenz, and Ronald L. Simons. "Parents' Stressful Life Events and Adolescent Depressed Mood." *Journal of Health and Social Behavior* 35 (1994): 28-44.

Gecas, Viktor, and Monica A. Seff. "Social Class and Self-Esteem: Psychological Centrality, Compensation, and the Relative Effects of Work and Home, *Social Psychology Quarterly* 53 (1990): 165-173.

Gedicks, Al. *The New Resource Wars: Native and Environmental Struggles against Multinational Corporations.* Boston, MA: South End Press, 1993.

Geertz, Clifford. *The Interpretation of Cultures.* New York: Basic Books, 1973.

Geis, Gilbert, and Paul Jesilow (Eds.). *White Collar Crime.* Newbury Park, CA: Sage, 1993.

Gendell, Murray, and Siegel, Jacob S. "Trends in Retirement Age by Sex, 1950-2005." *Monthly Labor Review,* July 1992:24.

Gentry, Curt. *J. Edgar Hoover: The Man and the Secrets.* New York: W.W. Norton, 1991.

Gergen, Kenneth. *The Saturday Self.* New York: Basic Books, 1991.

Gerhards, Jurgen, and Dieter Rucht. "Mesomobilization: Organizing and Framing in Two Protest Campaigns in West Germany." *American Journal of Sociology* 98 (1992): 555-595.

Gerlach, Michael L. *Alliance Capitalism: The Social Organization of Japanese Business*. Berkeley, CA: University of California Press, 1992.

Geronimus, A.T., and S. Korenman. "Maternal Youth or Family Background? On the Health Disadvantages of Infants with Teen Age Mothers." *American Journal of Epidemiology* 137 (1993): 213-225.

Gerson, Judith M., and Kathy Peiss. "Boundaries, Negotiation, Consciousness: Reconceptualizing Gender Relations." *Social Problems* 32(4) (1985): 317-331.

Gerson, Kathleen. *No Man's Land: Men's Changing Commitments to Family and Work*. New York: Basic Books, 1993.

Gerstel, Naomi, and Sally Gallagher. "Caring for Kith and Kin: Gender, Employment, and the Privatization of Care." *Social Problems* 41 (1994): 519-539.

Gerstel, Naomi, and Harriet Gross. *Commuter Marriage: A Study of Work and Family*. New York: Guilford Press, 1984.

Gesler, Wilbert M., and Thomas C. Ricketts (Eds.). *Health in Rural North America: The Geography of Health Care Services and Delivery*. New Brunswick, NJ: Rutgers University Press, 1992.

Geyer, Felix, and Walter R. Heinz (Eds.). *Alienation, Society and the Individual: Continuity and Change in Theory and Research*. New Brunswick, NJ: Transaction, 1992.

Gibbons, Don C. *Society, Crime and Criminal Behavior*, 5th ed. Englewood Cliffs, NJ: Prentice-Hall, 1987.

Gibson, James William. *Warrior Dreams: Paramilitary Culture in Post-Vietnam America*. New York: Hill and Wang, 1994.

Giddens, Anthony. *The Consequences of Modernity*. Stanford: Stanford University Press, 1990.

Giddens, Anthony. *The Transformation of Intimacy: Sexuality, Love, and Eroticism in Modern Societies*. Stanford, CA: Stanford University Press, 1992.

Gilbert, Jess, and Carolyn Howe. "Beyond 'State vs. Society': Theories of the State and New Deal Agricultural Policies." *American Sociological Review* 56 (1991): 204-220.

Gilkes, Cheryl Townsend. "Together and in Harness': Women's Traditions in the Sanctified Church." *Signs* 10(4) (1985): 678-699.

Gilligan, Carol. *In a Different Voice: Psychological Theory and Women's Development*. Cambridge, MA: Harvard University Press, 1982.

Gilligan, Carol, Janice Victoria Ward, and Jill McLean Taylor. *Mapping the Moral Domain: A Contribution of Women's Thinking to Psychological Theory and Education*. Cambridge, MA: Harvard University Press, 1989.

Gilmore, David D. *Manhood in the Making: Cultural Concepts of Masculinity*. New Haven, CT: Yale University Press, 1990.

Gilmore, Samuel. "Tradition and Novelty in Concert Programming: Bringing the Artist Back Into Cultural Analysis." *Sociological Forum* 8 (1993): 221-242.

Gimbutas, Marija. *The Civilization of the Goddess*. San Francisco: Harper & Row, 1991.

Girard, Chris. "Age, Gender, and Suicide: A Cross-National Analysis." *American Sociological Review* 58 (1993): 553-574.

Gitlin, Todd. "On Thrills and Kills." *Dissent* (Spring 1991): 245-248.

Gittleman, Maury. "Earnings in the 1980s: An Occupational Perspective." *Monthly Labor Review* 117 (1994): 16-27.

Giuffre, Patti A., and Christine L. Williams. "Boundary Lines: Labeling Sexual Harassment in Restaurants." *Gender & Society* 8 (1994): 378-401.

Glass, Jennifer, Vern L. Bengtson, and Charlotte Chorn Dunham. "Attitude Similarity in Three-Generation Families: Socialization, Status Inheritance, or Reciprocal Influence?" *American Sociological Review* 51 (1986): 685-698.

Glass, Jennifer, and Valerie Camarigg. "Gender, Parenthood, and Job-Family Compatibility." *American Journal of Sociology* 98 (1992): 131-151.

Glassman, Ronald M. *Democracy and Despotism in Primitive Society*. Port Washington, NY: Kennicott Press, 1986.

Glazer, Nona Y. *Women's Paid and Unpaid Labor: The Work Transfer in Health Care and Retailing*. Philadelphia, PA: Temple University Press, 1993.

Glenn, Norval D. "What Does Family Mean?" *American Demographics*, June 1992: 30-37.

Glenn, Norval D. "Television Watching, Newspaper Reading, and Cohort Differences in Verbal Ability." *Sociology of Education* 67 (1994): 216-230.

Gober, Patricia. "Americans on the Move." *Population Bulletin* 48:3, 1993.

Gober, Patricia, and Carl Haub. "U.S. Migration: South Retains Its Magnetism; Midwest Rallies." *Population Today*, 22:1 (1994): 4-5.

Goethals, Gregor T. *The TV Ritual: Worship at the Video Altar*. Boston: Beacon Press, 1981.

Goffman, Erving. *The Presentation of Self in Everyday Life*. Garden City, NY: Doubleday, 1959.

Goffman, Erving. *Asylums*. Garden City, NY: Doubleday, 1961.

Goffman, Erving. "The Interaction Order." *American Sociological Review* 48 (1983): 1-17.

Golden, Tim. "Was Illness at Bridges in the Minds of Workers?" *New York Times*, March 12, 1990.

Goldman, Ari L. "For Some Catholic Girls, Dreams of Serving at Altar Are No Longer Just Dreams." *New York Times*, June 23, 1993.

Goldschieder, Frances K., and Calvin Goldscheider. "Gender Roles, Marriage, and Residential Independence." *Sociological Forum* 7 (1992): 679-696.

Goldscheider, Francis K., and Calvin Goldscheider. "Leaving and Returning Home in 20th Century America." *Population Bulletin* 48, No. 4, 1994.

Goldscheider, Frances K., and Linda J. Waite. *New Families, No Families? The Transformation of the American Home*. Berkeley, CA: University of California Press, 1991.

Goldsmith, William, and Edward J. Blakely. *Separate Societies: Poverty and Inequality in U.S. Cities*. Philadelphia: Temple University Press, 1992.

Goldsteen, Raymond L., and John K. Schorr. *Demanding Democracy after Three Mile Island*. Gainesville, FL: University of Florida Press, 1991.

Goldstein, Josh. *Soft Money, Real Dollars: Soft Money in the 1992 Elections*. Washington, DC: Center for Responsive Politics, 1993.

Goldstein, Michael S. *The Health Movement: Promoting Fitness in America*. New York: Twayne, 1992.

Goldstone, Jack A. *Revolution and Rebellion in the Early Modern World*. Berkeley: University of California Press, 1991.

Goleman, Daniel. "Anatomy of a Rumor: It Flies on Fear." *New York Times*, June 4, 1991a.

Goleman, Daniel. "New Studies Map the Mind of the Rapist." *New York Times*, December 10, 1991b.

Goleman, Daniel. "New Storm Brews on Whether Crime Has Roots in Genes." *The New York Times*, September 15, 1992.

Goode, William J. "The Theoretical Importance of Love." *American Sociological Review* 24(1) (February 1959): 38-47.

Goode, William J. *World Revolution and Family Patterns*. New York: Free Press, 1963.

Goode, William J. *World Changes in Divorce Patterns*. New Haven, CT: Yale University Press, 1993.

Goodgame, Dan. "Welfare for the Well-Off." *Time*, February 22, 1993: 36-38.

Goodman, Gail. "The Profile of Ritualistic and Religion Related Abuse Allegations Reported to Clinical Psychologists in the United States." Paper presented at the annual meeting of the American Psychological Association, San Francisco, CA, August 1994.

Goodman, Walter. "Re Somalia: How Much Did TV Shape Policy?" *New York Times*, December 8, 1992.

Goodman, Walter. "'Tabloid' Charge Rocks Network News." *New York Times*, February 13, 1994.

Gordon, Diana R. *The Justice Juggernaut: Fighting Street Crime, Controlling Citizens*. New Brunswick, NJ: Rutgers University Press, 1992.

Gorer, Geoffrey, "Themes in Japanese Culture." *Transactions of the New York Academy of Sciences.* 1945: 5-25.

Gorham, Gary A. "The Growing Problem of Low Earnings in Rural America." In Duncan, Cynthia M. (Ed.), *Rural Poverty in America.* Westport, CT: Auburn House, 1992.

Gottdiener, M. "Hegemony and Mass Culture: A Semiotic Approach." *American Journal of Sociology* 90(4) (1985): 979-1001.

Gottfredson, Michael R., and Travis Hirschi. *A General Theory of Crime.* Palo Alto, CA: Stanford University Press, 1990.

Gottfried, Heidi. "Mechanisms of Control in the Temporary Help Service Industry." *Sociological Forum* 6 (1991): 699-713.

Gottlieb, Robert. *Forcing the Spring: The Transformation of the American Environmental Movement.* New York: Island Press, 1994.

Gould, Roger V. "Collective Action and Network Structure." *American Sociological Review* 58 (1993): 182-196.

Gove, Walter. "The Effect of Age and Gender on Deviant Behavior: A Biopsychological Perspective." In A. Rossi (Ed.). *Gender and the Life Course.* New York: Aldine de Gruyter, 1985.

Gracey, Harry L. "Learning the Student Role: Kindergarten as Academic Boot Camp." In Dennis H. Wrong and Harry Gracey (Eds.), *Readings in Introductory Sociology,* 3rd ed., pp. 243-253. New York: Macmillan, 1977.

Graham, Ellen. "Sprawling Bureaucracy Eats Up Most Profits of Girl Scout Cookies". *The Wall Street Journal,* May 13, 1993, pp. A1 and A7.

Graham, John W. *Small Change: The Economics of Child Support.* New Haven, CT: Yale University Press, 1993.

Gramsci, Antonio. *The Modern Prince and Other Writings.* New York: International Publishers, 1959.

Gramsci, Antonio. *Prison Notebooks: Selections.* Quintin Moore and Geoffrey N. Smith (trans.). New York: International Publishers, 1971.

Grandjean, Burke D., and Jill E. Fuller. "Work and Religion in the Neolithic Revolution." Paper presented at the 86th Annual Meeting of the American Sociological Association, Cincinnati, Ohio, August 1993.

Granfield, Robert, and Thomas Koenig. "The Fate of Elite Idealism: Accommodation and Ideological Work at Harvard Law School." *Social Problems* 39 (1992): 315-331.

Granovetter, Mark. "The Strength of Weak Ties." *American Journal of Sociology.* Vol. 78, No. 6 (May 1973): 1360-80.

Grant, Gerald. *The World We Created at Hamilton High.* Cambridge, MA: Harvard University Press, 1988.

Grant, Linda, Kathryn B. Ward, and Xue Lan Rong. "Is There an Association between Gender and Methods in Sociological Research?" *American Sociological Review* 52 (1987): 856-862.

Grant, Nicole J. *The Selling of Contraception: The Dalkon Shield Case, Sexuality, and Women's Autonomy.* Athens, OH: University of Ohio Press, 1992.

Grasmick, Harold G., Linda Patterson Wilcox, and Sharon R. Bird. "The Effects of Religious Fundamentalism and Religiosity on Preference for Traditional Family Norms." *Sociological Inquiry* 60 (1990): 352-369.

Grauerholz, Elizabeth, and Mary A. Korelewski. *Sexual Coercion: A Sourcebook on Its Nature, Causes, and Prevention.* Lexington, MA: Lexington Books, 1991.

Grauerholz, Elizabeth, and Bernice Pescosolido. "Gender Representation in Children's Literature." *Gender & Society* 3 (1989): 113-125.

Greeley, Andrew M. "Books in Review." *Society.* May/June 1990: 103-105.

Greeley, Andrew M. "How Serious is the Problem of Sexual Abuse by Clergy?" *America* 168 (1993a): 6-10.

Green, Richard. *Sexual Science and the Law.* Cambridge, MA: Harvard University Press, 1993.

Greenberg, Edward S. *Workplace Democracy: The Political Effects of Participation.* Ithaca, NY: Cornell University Press, 1986.

Greenfield, Liah. "Professional Ideologies and Patterns of 'Gatekeeping': Evaluation and Judgment within Two Art Worlds." *Social Forces* 66 (1988): 903-925.

Greenfield, Liah. *Nationalism: Five Roads to Modernity.* Cambridge, MA: Harvard University Press, 1992.

Greeno, Catherine G., and Eleanor E. Maccoby. "How Different is 'The Different Voice'?" *Signs* 11(2) (1986): 310-316.

Greif, Geoffry L., Albert DeMaris, and Jane C. Hood. "Balancing Work and Single Fatherhood." In Jane C. Hood (Ed.), *Men, Work, and Family,* pp. 176-194. Newbury Park, CA: Sage, 1993.

Greil, Arthur L. *Not Yet Pregnant: Infertile Couples in Contemporary America.* New Brunswick, NJ: Rutgers University Press, 1991.

Greisman, Harvey Clark. "Freedom From the Press: Repressive Tolerance and Its Origins." *Humanity & Society* 11 (1987): 287-301.

Grembowski, Davis, Donald Patrick, Paula Diehr, Mary Durham, Shirley Beresford, Erica Kay, and Julia Hecht. "Self-Efficacy and Health Behavior Among Older Adults." *Journal of Health and Social Behavior* 34 (1993): 89-104.

Grenier, Guillermo. *Inhuman Relations: Quality Circles and Anti-Unionism in American Industry.* Philadelphia: Temple University Press, 1988.

Greven, Philip. *Spare the Rod: The Religious Roots of Punishment and the Psychological Impact of Physical Abuse.* New York: Knopf, 1991.

Grigsby, Jill S. "Women Change Places." *American Demographics* November 1992: 46-50.

Grimes, Michael D. *Class in Twentieth-Century American Sociology.* New York: Praeger, 1991.

Grimshaw, Allan D. (Ed.). "Special Issue: Needed Sociological Research on Issues of War and Peace." *Sociological Forum* 7 (1), 1992.

Grissmer, David, Sheila Kirby, Mark Berends, and Stephanie Williamson. *Student Achievement and the Changing American Family.* Santa Monica, CA: The Rand Corporation, 1994.

Griswold, Robert L. *Fatherhood in America: A History.* New York: Basic Books, 1993.

Griswold, Wendy. "The Writing on the Mud Wall: Nigerian Novels and the Imaginary Village." *American Sociological Review* 57 (1992): 709-724.

Grob, Gerald N. *From Asylum to Community: Mental Health Policy in Modern America.* Princeton, NJ: Princeton University Press, 1991.

Groce, Stephen B., and Margaret Cooper. "Just Me and the Boys? Women in Local-Level Rock and Roll." *Gender & Society* 4 (1990): 220-229.

Grogger, Jeff, and Stephen Bronars. "The Socioeconomic Consequences of Teenage Childbearing: Findings from a Natural Experiment." *Family Planning Perspectives* 25 (1993): 156-161, 174.

Gross, Jane. "Divorced, Middle-Aged and Happy: Women, Especially, Adjust to the 90s." *New York Times,* December 7, 1992.

Gunther, Barrie. *Dimensions of Television Violence.* New York: St. Martin's Press, 1985.

Guralnik, Jack M., Kenneth C. Land, Daniel Blazer, Gerda G. Fillenbaum, and Laurence G. Branch. "Educational Status and Active Life Expectancy Among Older Blacks and Whites." *New England Journal of Medicine* 329 (1993): 110-116.

Guterbock, Thomas M., and Bruce London. "Race, Political Orientation, and Participation: An Empirical Test of Four Competing Theories." *American Sociological Review* 48 (1983): 439-453.

Gutierrez, Ramon A. *When Jesus Came, the Corn Mothers Went Away.* Stanford, CA: Stanford University Press, 1991.

Gutis, Philip. "New Albany Audits Collect $28 Million from 12 Tax Cheats." *New York Times,* February 8, 1989.

Gutmann, David. *Reclaimed Powers: Toward a New Psychology of Men and Women in Later Life.* New York: Basic Books, 1987.

Guttentag, Marcia, and Paul F. Secord. *Too Many Women: The Sex Ratio Question.* Beverly Hills, CA: Sage, 1983.

Guttmann, Allen. *From Ritual to Record: The Nature of Modern Sports.* New York: Columbia University Press, 1978.

Haas, Linda. *Equal Parenthood and Social Policy: A Study of Parental Leave in Sweden.* Albany, NY: State University of New York Press, 1992.

Haber, Carole, and Brian Gratton. *Old Age and the Search for Security: An American Social History.* Bloomington, IN: Indiana University Press, 1994.

Hadaway, C. Kirk, Penny Long Marler, and Mark Chaves. "What the Polls Don't Show: A Closer Look at U.S. Church Attendance." *American Sociological Review* 58 (1993):741-752.

Hadden, Jeffrey K. "Toward Desacralizing Secularization Theory." *Social Forces* 65 (1987): 587-611.

Hadden, Jeffrey K. "The Rise and Fall of American Televangelism." *Annals of the American Academy of Political and Social Science* 527 (May 1993): 113-130.

Hagan, John. "The Gender Stratification of Income Inequality Among Lawyers." *Social Forces* 68 (1990): 835-855.

Hagan, John. *Structural Criminology.* New Brunswick, N.J.: Rutgers University Press, 1989.

Hagan, John, A. R. Gillis, and John Simpson. "The Power of Control in Sociological Theories of Delinquency." In Freda Adler and William S. Laufer (Eds.), *New Directions in Criminological Theory,* Vol. 4, pp. 381-389. New Brunswick, NJ: Transaction, 1993.

Hagan, John, and B. Wheaton. "The Search for Adolescent Role Exits and the Transition to Adulthood." *Social Forces,* 71 (1993): 955-980.

Hage, Jerald, Paul D. Collins, Frank Hull, and Jay Teachman. "The Impact of Knowledge in the Survival of American Manufacturing Plants." *Social Forces* 72 (1993): 223-246.

Hagedorn, John M. "Gangs, Neighborhoods, and Public Policy." *Social Problems* 38 (1991): 529-542.

Hagen, Jan L., and Irene Lurie. *Implementing JOBS: Initial State Choices.* Albany, NY: Nelson A. Rockefeller Institute of Government, State University of New York, 1992.

Haines, Herb. "Flawed Executions, the Anti-Death Penalty Movement, and the Politics of Capital Punishment." *Social Problems* 39 (1992): 125-238.

Haj, Samira. "Palestinian Women and Patriarchal Relations." *Signs* 17 (1992): 761-778.

Hall, Edward. *The Silent Language.* Garden City, NY: Doubleday, 1959.

Hall, Elaine J. "Waitering/Waitressing: Engendering the Work of Table Servers." *Gender and Society.* 7 (1993): 329-346.

Hall, G. S. *Adolescence.* Vols 1 and 2. New York: Appleton-Century-Crofts, 1904.

Hallinan, Maureen T. "School Differences in Tracking Effects on Achievement." *Social Forces* 72 (1994): 799-820.

Halper, Thomas. "Rationing Health Care on the Basis of Age: Is This the Future of American Health Care?" *Aging International* XX(3)(1993):3-6.

Hamilton, V. Lee, Clifford L. Broman, William S. Hoffman, and Deborah S. Renner. "Hard Times and Vulnerable People: Initial Effects of Plant Closing on Autoworkers' Mental Health." *Journal of Health and Social Behavior* 31 (1990): 123-140.

Hammond, Philip E. *Religion and Personal Autonomy: The Third Disestablishment in America.* Columbia, SC: University of South Carolina Press, 1992.

Hammond, Philip E., and Kee Warner. "Religion and Ethnicity in Late-Twentieth Century America." *Annals of the Academy of Political and Social Sciences* 527 (1993): 55-66.

Hancock, M. Donald, John Logue, and Bernt Schiller (Eds.). *Managing Modern Capitalism: Industrial Renewal and Workplace Democracy in the United States and Western Europe.* New York: Praeger, 1991.

Haney, Craig, and Philip G. Zimbardo. "It's Tough to Tell a High School from a Prison." *Psychology Today,* June 1975, p. 25.

Hannan, Michael T., and John Freeman. *Organizational Ecology.* Cambridge, MA: Harvard University Press, 1989.

Hannan, Michael T., and Nancy Brandon Tuma. "A Reassessment of the Effect of Income Maintenance on Marital Dissolution in the Seattle-Denver Experiment." *American Journal of Sociology* 95 (1990): 1270-1298.

Hanson, F. Allan. *Testing Testing: Social Consequences of the Examined Life.* Berkeley, CA: University of California Press, 1993.

Hanson, Sandra L. "Lost Talent: Unrealized Aspirations and Expectations among U.S. Youth." *Sociology of Education* 67 (1994): 159-183.

Hardin, Garrett. "The Tragedy of the Commons." *Science* 162 (1968): 1243-1248.20

Harding, Sandra (Ed.). *The "Racial" Economy of Science.* Bloomington, IN: Indiana University Press, 1993.

Harlow, Caroline W. *Female Victims of Violent Crime.* U.S. Department of Justice, NCJ-126826, January, 1991.

Harootyan, R. A., R. Vorek, and Karl Kronebusch. "Direct and Indirect Transfers Across the Generations: Prevalence and Monetary Value." Paper delivered at the 1993 annual meetings of the Gerontological Society of America, November 1993, New Orleans, LA.

Harris, Kathleen Mullan. "Work and Welfare among Single Mothers in Poverty." *American Journal of Sociology* 99 (1993): 317-352.

Harris, Lis. "O Guru, Guru, Guru." *New Yorker* November 14, 1994: 92-109.

Harris, Marvin. *Good to Eat: Riddles of Food and Culture.* New York: Simon & Schuster, 1985a.

Harris, Marvin. *Culture, People, Nature: An Introduction to General Anthropology,* 4th ed. New York: Harper & Row, 1985b.

Harris, Marvin, Josildeth Gomes Consorte, Joseph Lang, and Bryan Byrne. "Who Are the Whites? Imposed Census Categories and the Racial Demography of Brazil." *Social Forces* 72 (1993): 451-462.

Harris, Norma. "Employees Are Paying More for Health Benefits." *Business and Health* 11 (1993): 32-39.

Harrison, Bennett. *Lean and Mean: The Changing Landscape of Corporate Power in the Age of Flexibility.* New York: Basic Books, 1994.

Hart, Stephen. *What Does the Lord Require? How American Christians Think about Economic Justice.* New York: Oxford University Press, 1992.

Harvey, David L. *Potter Addition: Poverty, Family and Kinship in a Heartland Community.* New York: Aldine de Gruyter, 1993.

Hathaway, Dale A. *Can Workers Have a Voice? The Politics of Deindustrialization in Pittsburgh.* University Park, PA: The Pennsylvania State University Press, 1993.

Haub, Carl. "Russia's New Revolution: A Demographic Baby Bust." *Population Today* 22, No. 4 (1994): 1-2.

Hauser, Robert M., and Douglas K. Anderson. "Post-High School Plans and Aspirations of Black and White High School Seniors: 1978-1986." *Sociology of Education* 64 (1991): 263-277.

Hausknecht, Murray. "Patriotic Crime: Iran-Contra." *Dissent* Spring, 1992: 245-249.

Haveman, Heather A., and Lisa E. Cohen. "The Ecological Dynamics of Careers: The Impact of Organizational Founding, Dissolution, and Merger on Job Mobility." *American Journal of Sociology* 100 (1994): 104-152.

Haviland, William A. *Cultural Anthropology,* 7th ed. New York: Harcourt Brace, Jovanovich, 1993.

Hawes, Joseph. *The Children's Rights Movement: A History of Advocacy and Protection.* New York: Twayne, 1991.

Hawk, Maureen Norton. "The Treatment of Chemically Dependent Mothers." Paper presented at conference on "Social Change in Feminist Directions," Minneapolis, MN, February, 1992.

Hawley, John Stratton (Ed.). *Fundamentalism and Gender.* New York: Oxford University Press, 1994.

Hay, Iain. *Money, Medicine, and Malpractice in American Society.* New York: Praeger, 1992.

Hayghe, Howard V. "Are Women Leaving the Labor Force?" *Monthly Labor Review* 117 (1994): 37-39.

Hayghe, Howard V., and Suzanne M. Bianchi. "Married Mothers' Work Patterns: The Job-Family Compromise." *Monthly Labor Review* 117, No. 6 (1994): 24–30.

Haynes, Stephen E., and David Jacobs. "Macroeconomics, Economic Stratification, and Partisanship: A Longitudinal Analysis of Contingent Shifts in Political Identification." *American Journal of Sociology* 100 (1994): 70–103.

Headland, Thomas N., and Lawrence A. Reid. "Hunter-Gatherers and Their Neighbors from Prehistory to the Present." *Current Anthropology* 30 (1989): 43–66.

Hearn, Frank. *Reason and Freedom in Sociological Thought.* Boston: Allen & Unwin, 1985.

Hearn, Jeff, Deborah L. Sheppard, Peta Tancred Sheriff, and Gibson Burrell (Eds.). *The Sexuality of Organizations.* Newbury Park, CA: Safe, 1989.

Hedges, Chris. "Mobilizing Against Pop Music and Other Horrors." *New York Times,* July 21, 1993.

Hedges, Larry V., Rob Greenwald, and Richard V. Laine. "Does Money Matter? A Meta-Analysis of Studies of the Effects of Differential School Inputs on Student Outcomes." *Educational Research* 23 (1994): 5–14.

Heilman, Samuel. *Defenders of the Faith: Inside Ultra-Orthodox Jewry.* New York: Schocken, 1991.

Heimer, Karen, and Ross L. Matsueda. "Role-Taking, Role Commitment, and Delinquency: A Theory of Differential Social Control." *American Sociological Review* 59 (1994): 365–390.

Henig, Jeffrey R. "Choice in Public Schools: An Analysis of Transfer Requests among Magnet Schools." *Social Science Quarterly* 71 (1990): 68–82.

Hennenberger, Melinda. "For Some, Rituals of Abuse Replace Youthful Courtship." *New York Times,* July 11, 1993.

Henshaw, Stanley K., and Jennifer Van Vort. "Abortion Services in the United States, 1991 and 1992." *Family Planning Perspectives* 26 (1994): 100–106.

Herberg, Will. *Protestant, Catholic, Jew.* Garden City, NY: Doubleday, 1960.

Herdt, Gilbert H. (Ed.). *Ritualized Homosexuality in Melanesia.* Berkeley: University of California Press, 1984.

Herdt, Gilbert H. *The Sambia: Ritual and Gender in New Guinea.* New York: Holt, Rinehart & Winston, 1987.

Herdt, Gilbert H. (Ed.). *Gay Culture in America: Essays from the Field.* Boston: Beacon Press, 1992.

Herek, Gregory M., and Kevin T. Berrill. *Hate Crime: Confronting Violence Against Lesbians and Gay Men.* Newbury Park, CA: Sage, 1992.

Heritage, John. *Garfinkel and Ethnomethodology.* Cambridge, MA: Polity, 1984.

Hernandez, Donald J. *America's Children: Resources from Family, Government, and the Economy.* New York: Russell Sage Foundation, 1993.

Herrnstein, Richard J., and Charles Murray. *The Bell Curve: The Reshaping of American Life by Differences in Intelligence.* New York: The Free Press, 1994.

Hertz, Rosanna. *More Equal Than Others: Women and Men in Dual-Career Marriages.* Berkeley: University of California Press, 1986.

Hertz, Rosanna. "Guarding Against Women? Responses of Military Men and Their Wives to Gender Integration." Paper presented at the 86th Annual Meeting of the American Sociological Association, Cincinnati, Ohio, August, 1991.

Hess, Beth B. "Beyond Dichotomy: Drawing Distinctions and Embracing Differences." *Sociological Forum,* 5 (1990): 75–94.

Hess, Beth B., and Elizabeth Markson. *Growing Old in America,* 4th ed. New Brunswick, NJ: Transaction, 1991.

Hess, David J. *Science in the New Age: The Paranormal, Its Defenders and Debunkers, and American Culture.* Madison, WI: University of Wisconsin Press, 1993.

Hewitt, John P. *Dilemmas of the American Self.* Philadelphia: Temple University Press, 1990.

Higgens, Paul C. *Making Disability: Exploring the Social Transformation of Human Variation.* Springfield, IL: Charles C. Thomas, 1992.

Higginbotham, Evelyn Brooks. *Righteous Discontent: The Women's Movement in the Black Baptist Church, 1880–1920.* Cambridge, MA: Harvard University Press, 1993.

Hilchey, Tim. "2 Studies Report Heart Care Lag for Blacks." *New York Times,* August 26, 1993.

Hill, Richard J. "Potential Expansion of the Academic Job Market: Opportunities for Sociologists." *American Sociologist* 20 (1989): 144–153.

Hilts, Philip J. "Health Chief Assails Deal Between U.S. Research Lab and Swiss Company." *New York Times,* March 12, 1993.

Hindelang, Michael, Michael Gottfredson, and James Garofalo. *Victims of Personal Crime: An Empirical Foundation for a Theory of Personal Victimization.* Cambridge, MA: Ballinger, 1978.

Hinrichs, Karl, William Roche, and Carmen Sirianni (Eds.). *Working Time in Transition: The Political Economy of Working Hours in Industrial Nations.* Philadelphia, PA: Temple University Press, 1991.

Hirsch, Eric L. "Sacrifice for the Cause: Group Processes, Recruitment, and Commitment in a Student Social Movement." *American Sociological Review* 55 (1990): 243–254.

Hochschild, Arlie Russell. *The Managed Heart: Commercialization of Human Feelings.* Berkeley: University of California Press, 1983.

Hochschild, Arlie Russell, with Anne Machung. *The Second Shift: Working Parents and the Revolution at Home.* New York: Viking, 1989.

Hodge, Bob, and David Tripp. *Children and Television.* Stanford, CA: Stanford University Press, 1986.

Hodson, Randy, Dusko Sekulic, and Garth Massey. "National Tolerance in the Former Yugoslavia." *American Journal of Sociology* 99 (1994): 1534–1558.

Hoecker-Drysdale, Susan. *Harriet Martineau: First Woman Sociologist.* New York: Berk, 1992.

Hoerr, John. "Solidaritas at Harvard: Organizing in a Different Voice," *The American Prospect* Summer 1993: 67–82.

Hoffer, Thomas B., and Adam Gamoran. "Effects of Instructional Differences Among Ability Groups." Paper presented at the 88th annual meeting of the American Sociological Association, Miami Beach, August, 1993.

Hofferth, Sandra L., Joan R. Kahn, and Wendy Baldwin. "Premarital Sexual Activity among U.S. Teenage Women Over the Past Three Decades." *Family Planning Perspectives* 19 (1987): 46–53.

Hofrichter, Richard. (Ed.) *Toxic Struggles: The Theory and Practice of Environmental Justice.* Philadelphia: New Society Publishers, 1993.

Hogan, Dennis P., David J. Eggebeen, and Clifford C. Clogg. "The Structure of Intergenerational Exchanges in American Families." *American Journal of Sociology* 98 (1993): 1428–1458.

Hogan, Dennis P., Ling-Xin Hao, and William L. Parish. "Race, Kin Networks, and Assistance to Mother-Headed Families." *Social Forces* 68 (1990): 797–812.

Holmes, Steven A. "Gay Rights Advocates Brace for Ballot Fights." *New York Times* January 12, 1994: 17.

Holstein, James A. *Court-Ordered Insanity: Interpretive Practice and Involuntary Commitment.* New York: Aldine de Gruyter, 1993.

Holusha, John. "Industry Is Learning to Love Agility." *New York Times,* June 25, 1994.

Homans, George C. *Social Behavior: Its Elementary Forms.* New York: Harcourt Brace Jovanovich, 1961.

Homer-Dixon, Thomas F., Jeffrey H. Boutwell, and George W. Rathjens. "Environmental Change and Violent Conflict." *Scientific American,* January 1993: 38–43.

Honan, William H. "Cost of 4-year Degree Passes $100,000 Mark." *New York Times,* May 4, 1994.

Hondagneu-Sotelo, Pierrette. "Overcoming Patriarchal Constraints: The Reconstruction of Gender Relations Among Mexican Immigrant Women and Men." *Gender & Society* 6 (1992): 393-415.

Hondagneu-Sotelo, Pierrette. "Regulating the Unregulated?: Domestic Workers' Social Networks." *Social Problems* 41 (1994): 50-64.

Hood, Jane C. "'Let's Get a Girl:' Male Bonding Rituals in America." In Michael S. Kimmel and Michael A. Messner (Eds.), *Men's Lives*, 2nd ed., pp. 363-369. New York: Macmillan, 1992.

Hood, Jane C. (Ed.). *Men, Work, and Family.* Newbury Park, CA: Sage , 1993.

Hooks, Gregory. *Forging the Military-Industrial Complex: World War II's Battle of the Potomac.* Urbana, IL: University of Illinois Press, 1991.

Hooks, Gregory. "Regional Processes in the Hegemonic Nation: Political, Economic, and Military Influences on the Use of Geographic Space." *American Sociological Review* 59 (1994): 746-772.

Hope, Christine A., and Ronald G. Stover. "Gender Status, Monotheism, and Social Complexity." *Social Forces* 65 (1987): 1132-1138.

Hopper, Joseph. "Oppositional Identities and Rhetoric in Divorce." *Qualitative Sociology* 16 (1993): 135-142.

Horwitt, Sanford D. *Let Them Call Me Rebel: Saul Alinsky-His Life and Legacy.* New York: Knopf, 1989.

House Ways and Means Committee. "Report on AFDC Program." Cited in Robin Toner, "New Politics of Welfare Focuses on Its Flaws." *New York Times,* July 15, 1992.

Hout, Michael, and Andrew M. Greeley. "The Center Doesn't Hold: Church Attendance in the United States, 1940-1984." *American Sociological Review* 52 (1987): 325-345.

Howard, Judith A., and Peter L. Callero. *The Self-Society Dynamic: Cognition, Emotion, and Action.* New York: Cambridge University Press, 1991.

Howard, Michael C. *Contemporary Cultural Anthropology,* 2nd ed. Boston: Little Brown, 1986.

Howe, Carolyn. *Political Ideology and Class Formation: A Study of the Middle Class.* Westport, CT: Praeger, 1992.

Hubbard, Ruth. "False Genetic Markers." *New York Times*, August 2, 1993.

Huber, Joan. "Macro-Micro Links in Gender Stratification." *American Sociological Review* 55 (1990): 1-10.

Huber, Joan (Ed.). *Macro-Micro Linkages in Sociology.* Newbury Park, CA: Sage, 1991.

Huddle, Donald L. "A Growing Burden." *New York Times,* September 3, 1993.

Hudgins, John L. "The Segmentation of Southern Sociology? Social Research at Historically Black Colleges and Universities." *Social Forces* 72 (1994): 885-983.

Huff, Ronald C. (Ed.). *Gangs in America: Diffusion, Diversity, and Public Policy.* Newbury Park, CA: Sage, 1990.

Hughes, James W., and Todd Zimmerman. "The American Dream is Alive." *American Demographics* 15: 8 (1993): 32-37.

Hummer, Robert A. "Racial Differences in Infant Mortality in the U.S.: An Examination of Social and Health Determinants." *Social Forces* 72 (1993): 529-554.

Hunt, Geoffrey, Stephanie Riegel, Tomas Morales, and Dan Waldorf. "Changes in Prison Culture: Prison Gangs and the Case of the 'Pepsi Generation.'" *Social Problems* 40 (1993): 398-409.

Hunter, Andrea G., and James Earl Davis. "Constructing Gender: An Exploration of Afro-American Men's Conceptualization of Gender." *Gender & Society* 6 (1992): 464-479.

Hunter, James Davison. *Evangelicism: The Coming Generation.* Chicago: University of Chicago Press, 1987.

Hurst, Jeremy, and Jean-Pierre Poullier. "Paths to Health Reform." *The OECD Observer* 179 (Dec. 1992/Jan. 1993): 4-7.

Hurtado, Aida, Patricia Gurin, and Timothy Peng. "Social Identities—A Framework for Studying the Adaptations of Immigrants and Ethnics: The Adaptations of Mexicans in the United States." *Social Problems* 41 (1994): 129-151.

Hurwich, Cecelia. "Still Vital After All These Years: Older Women and Personal Growth." *Aging International* XX (3) (1993), pp. 53-57.

Hyllegard, David, and David E. Lavin. "Higher Education and Challenging Work: Open Admissions and Ethnic and Gender Differences in Job Complexity." *Sociological Forum* 7 (1992): 239-260.

Hyman, Herbert H. "The Psychology of Status." *Archives of Psychology* 37 (1942): 15.

Hyman, Irwin. *Reading, Writing, and the Hickory Stick: The Appalling Story of the Physical and Psychological Abuse in American Schools.* New York: Free Press, 1990.

Iannaccone, Laurence R. "Why Strict Churches Are Strong." *American Journal of Sociology* 99 (1994): 1180-1211.

Iannaccone, Laurence R., and Carrie A. Miles. "Dealing with Social Change: The Mormon Church's Response to Change in Women's Roles." *Social Forces* 68 (1990): 1231-1250.

Inciardi, James A. (Ed.). *The Drug Legalization Debate.* Newbury Park, CA: Sage, 1991.

Inciardi, James A., Ruth Horowitz, and Anne P. Pottieger. *Street Kids, Street Drugs, Street Crime: An Examination of Drug Use and Serious Delinquency in Miami.* Belmont, CA: Wadsworth, 1993.

Inglehart, Ronald. *Culture Shift in Advanced Industrial Society.* Princeton: Princeton University Press, 1990.

International Labor Organization. *Report on Women and Unions in the United States and Canada.* New York: ILO, 1993.

Inter-Parliamentary Union. *Women in Parliaments*: Third Annual Report. Geneva, Switzerland, 1994.

Ishida, Hiroshi. *Social Mobility in Contemporary Japan: Educational Credentials, Class and the Labour Market in a Cross-National Perspective.* Stanford, CA: Stanford University Press, 1993.

Ishida, Hiroshi, John H. Goldthorpe, and Robert Erikson. "Intergenerational Class Mobility in Postwar Japan." *American Journal of Sociology* 96 (1991): 954-992.

Iyengar, Shanto. *Is Anyone Responsible? How Television Frames Political Issues.* Chicago, II.: Chicago University Press, 1991.

Jackman, Mary R. *The Velvet Glove: Paternalism and Conflict in Gender, Class, and Race Relations.* Berkeley, CA: University of California Press, 1994.

Jackson, Pamela Irving. *Minority Group Threat, Crime, and Policing: Social Context and Social Control.* New York: Praeger, 1989.

Jacobs, Jerry A., David Karen, and Katherine McClelland. "The Dynamics of Young Men's Career Aspirations." *Sociological Forum* 6 (1991): 609-639.

Jacobs, Jerry A., and Ronnie J. Steinberg. "Compensating Differentials and the Male-Female Wage Gap: Evidence from the New York State Comparable Worth Study." *Social Forces* 69 (1990): 439-468.

Jacobson, Jodi. *Gender Bias: Roadblock to Sustainable Development.* Washington, DC: Worldwatch, 1992.

Jaffee, David. "The Political Economy of Job Loss in the United States, 1970-1980." *Social Problems* 33 (1986): 297-315.

Jamison, Andrew, and Ron Eyerman. *Seeds of the Sixties.* Berkeley, CA: University of California Press, 1994.

Jansen, Sue Curry. *Censorship: The Knot That Binds Power and Knowledge.* New York: Oxford University Press, 1988.

Jarrett, Robin L. "Living Poor: Family Life Among Single Parent, African-American Women." *Social Problems* 41 (1994): 30-49.

Jasper, James M., and Dorothy Nelkin. *The Animal Rights Crusade: The Growth of a Moral Protest.* New York: Free Press, 1992.

Jasper, James M., and Jane Poulsen. "Fighting Back: Vulnerabilities, Blunders, and the Countermobilization by the Targets in Three Animal Rights Campaigns." *Sociological Forum* 8 (1993): 639-657.

Jasso, Guillermina, and Mark R. Rosensweig. *The New Chosen People: Immigrants in the United States.* New York: Russell Sage, 1990.

Jay, Nancy. *Throughout Your Generations Forever: Sacrifice, Religion, and Paternity.* Chicago, IL: University of Chicago Press, 1992.

Jeffords, Susan. *The Remasculinization of America: Gender and the Vietnam War.* Bloomington, IN: Indiana University Press, 1989.

Jeffreys-Jones, Rhodri. *The CIA and American Democracy.* New Haven, CT: Yale University Press, 1989.

Jelen, Ted G. *The Political Mobilization of Religious Beliefs.* New York: Praeger, 1991.

Jenkins, J. Craig, and Craig M. Eckert. "Channeling Black Insurgency: Elite Patronage and Professional Social Movement Organizations in the Development of the Black Movement." *American Sociological Review* (1986): 812-829.

Jenkins, Philip. *Intimate Enemies: Moral Panics in Contemporary Great Britain.* Hawthorne, New York: Aldine de Gruyter, 1992.

Jenness, Valerie. "From Sex as Sin to Sex as Work: COYOTE and the Reorganization of Prostitution as a Social Problem." *Social Problems* 37(3) (August 1990): 403-420.

Jenness, Valerie. "Social Movement Growth, Domain Expansion, and Framing Processes." *Social Problems* 42 (1995): 145-170.

Jennings, M. Kent, and Gregory B. Markus. "Yuppie Politics." *ISR Newsletter*, Spring/Summer 1986, pp. 5-7.

Jensen, Gary F. "Power-Control vs. Social-Control Theories of Common Delinquency: A Comparative Analysis." In Freda Adler and William S. Laufer (Eds.), *New Directions In Criminological Theory*, Vol. 4, pp. 363-380. New Brunswick, NJ: Transaction, 1993.

Jesilow, Paul, Henry M. Pontell, and Gilbert Geis. *Prescription for Profit: How Doctors Defraud Medicaid.* Berkeley, CA: University of California Press, 1993.

Jewell, K. Sue. *From Mammy to Miss America and Beyond: Cultural Images and the Shaping of U.S. Social Policy.* New York: Routledge, 1993.

Jhally, Sut, and Justin Lewis. *Enlightened Racism: The Cosby Show, Audiences, and the Myth of the American Dream.* Boulder, CO: Westview Press, 1992.

Jodelet, Denise. *Madness and Social Representations: Living with the Mad in One French Community.* Berkeley, CA: University of California Press, 1992.

Johnson, Benton, Dean Hoge, and Donald Luidens. "Vanishing Boundaries: The Religion of Protestant Baby Boomers." New York: Lily Endowment, 1992.

Johnson, Dirk. "Colorado Klansman Refines Message for the 90's." *New York Times*, February 23, 1992.

Johnson, Dirk. "Indians' Casino Money Pumps Up the Volume." *New York Times*, September 1, 1993a.

Johnson, Dirk. "As Mormon Church Grows, So Does Dissent from Feminists and Scholars." *New York Times*, October 2, 1993b.

Johnson, Norris R. "Panic at 'The Who Concert Stampede': An Empirical Assessment." *Social Problems* 34 (1987): 362-373.

Johnson, Stephen D., and Joseph B. Tamney (Eds.). *The Political Role of Religion in the United States.* Boulder, CO: Westview Press, 1986.

Johnson, Timothy P., James G. Hougland, Jr., and Richard R.Clayton. "Obtaining Reports of Sensitive Behavior: A Comparison of Substance Use Reports from Telephone and Face-to-Face Interviews." *Social Science Quarterly* 70 (1989): 174-183.

Johnston, Les. *The Rebirth of Private Policing.* New York: Routledge, 1992.

Jones, Anthony, Walter D. Connor, and David E. Powell (Eds.). *Soviet Social Problems.* Boulder, CO: Westview Press, 1991.

Jones, Elsie F., Jaqueline Darroch Forrest, Noreen Goldman, Stanley K. Hensaw, Richard Lincoln, Jeannie I. Rosoff, Charles E. Westoff, and Dierdre Wulf. *Teenage Pregnancy in Industrialized Countries.* New Haven, CT: Yale University Press, 1987.

Joseph, Nathan. *Uniforms and Nonuniforms: Communication Through Clothing.* Westport, CT: Greenwood, 1986.

Judd, Dennis R. "Segregation Forever?" *The Nation*, December 9, 1991.

Judkins, D. R., W. D. Mosher, and S. Botman. "National Survey of Family Growth: Design, Estimation, and Inference." *National Center for Health Statistics*, Series 2, No. 109, 1991.

Juergensmeyer, Mark. *The New Cold War? Religious Nationalism Confronts the Secular State.* Berkeley, CA: University of California Press, 1993.

Kagan, Jerome. *Galen's Prophecy: Temperament in Human Nature.* New York: Basic Books, 1994.

Kahn, J. R., and K. E. Anderson. "Intergenerational Patterns of Teenage Fertility." *Demography* 29 (1992): 39-41.

Kahn, Katherine L., Marjorie L. Pearson, Ellen R. Harrison, Katherine A. Desmond, William H. Rogers, Lisa V. Rubenstein, Robert H. Brook, and Emmet B. Keeler. "Health Care for Black and Poor Hospitalized Medicare Patients." *Journal of the American Medical Association* 271 (1994): 1169-1174.

Kalish, Susan. "Twentysomething Group Evades Easy Labels." *Population Today*, vol 20, No. 11 (1992), pp. 1-2.

Kalish, Susan. "Sexual Behavior and STDs: Men at Risk." *Population Today* 21 (1993): 3.

Kalmijn, Matthijs. "Status Homogamy in the United States." *American Journal of Sociology* 97 (1991a): 496-523.

Kalmijn, Matthijs. "Shifting Boundaries: Trends in Religious and Educational Homogamy." *American Sociological Review* 56 (1991b): 786-800.

Kalmijn, Matthijs. "Trends in Black-White Intermarriage." *Social Forces* 72 (1993): 119-146.

Kalmijn, Matthijs. "Mother's Occupational Status and Children's Schooling." *American Sociological Review* 59 (1994a): 257-275.

Kalmijn, Matthijs. "Assortive Mating by Cultural and Economic Occupational Status." *American Journal of Sociology* 100 (1994b): 422-452.

Kalmus, Debra, P.B. Nemerow, and U. Bauer. "Short-term Consequences of Parenting Versus Adoption Among Unmarried Women." *Journal of Marriage and the Family* 54 (1992): 80.

Kamo, Yoshinori. "A Note on Elderly Living Arrangements in Japan and the United States." In Beth B. Hess and Elizabeth W. Markson (Eds.), *Growing Old in America*, 4th ed., pp. 457-463. New Brunswick, NJ: Transaction, 1991.

Kane, Emily W., and Laura Sanchez. "Family Status and Criticism of Gender Inequality at Home and Work." *Social Forces* 72 (1994): 1079-1102.

Kane, John, and Lawrence M. Spitzman. "Race, Financial Aid Awards and College Attendance: Parents and Geography Matter." *American Journal of Economics and Sociology* 53 (1994): 85-97.

Kanter, Rosabeth Moss. *Commitment and Community.* Cambridge, MA: Harvard University Press, 1972.

Kanter, Rosabeth Moss. *Men and Women of the Corporation.* New York: Basic Books, 1977.

Kanter, Rosabeth Moss, Barry A. Stein, and Todd D. Jick. *The Challenge of Organizational Change: How Companies Experience It, and Leaders Guide It.* New York: Free Press, 1992.

Kaplan, E. Ann. *Rocking Round the Clock: Music Television, Postmodernism, and Consumer Culture.* New York: Methuen, 1987.

Kaplan, Laurence (Ed.). *Fundamentalism in Comparative Perspective.* Amherst, MA: University of Massachusetts Press, 1992.

Karen, David. "'Achievement' and 'Ascription' in Admission to an Elite College: A Political-Organizational Analysis." *Sociological Forum* 6 (1991): 349-380.

Karp, David A., Gregory P. Stone, and William C. Yoels. *Being Urban: A Sociology of City Life.* 2nd ed. New York: Praeger Publishers, 1991.

Kasarda, John D., and Allan M. Parnell (Eds.). *Third World Cities: Problems, Policies, and Prospects.* Newbury Park: Sage, 1993.

Kasinitz, Philip. *Caribbean New York: Black Immigrants and the Politics of Race.* Ithaca, NY: Cornell University Press, 1992.

Katsillis, John, and J. Michael Armer. "Education and Mobility." In Edgar F. Borgatta and Marie L. Borgatta (Eds.), *Encyclopedia of Sociology*, pp. 541-544. New York: Macmillan, 1992.

Kaufman, Debra. *Rachel's Daughters: Newly Orthodox Jewish Women*. New Brunswick, NJ: Rutgers University Press, 1991.

Kean, Patricia. "Temps Perdus: The Woes of the Part-Time Professoriate." *Lingua Franca*, March/April 1994: 49-54.

Keith, Verna M., and Cedric Herring. "Skin Tone and Stratification in the Black Community." *American Journal of Sociology* 97 (1991): 760-778.

Keller, Bill. "Misfits of Peace: Is This the End of the Bushmen," *New York Times*, May 10, 1993.

Kellerman, Arthur L., Frederick P. Rivara, Norman B. Rushforth, Joyce G. Banton, Donald T. Reay, Jerry T. Francisco, Ana B. Locci, Janice Prodzinski, Bela B. Hackman, and Grant Somes. "Gun Ownership as a Risk Factor for Homicide in the Home." *New England Journal of Medicine* 329 (1993): 1084-1091.

Kelley, Jonathan, and M.D.R. Evans. "The Legitimation of Inequality: Occupational Earnings in Nine Nations." *American Journal of Sociology* 99 (1993): 75-125.

Kelley, Maryellen. "New Process Technology, Job Design, and Work Organization: A Contingency Model." *American Sociological Review* 55 (1990): 191-208.

Kelley, Maryellen, and Nennett Harrison. "Unions, Technology, and Labor Management Cooperation," in *Unions, and Economic Competitiveness*. Armonk, NY: M.E. Sharpe, 1992.

Kelly, Dierdre M. *Last Chance High: How Girls and Boys Drop in and out of Alternative Schools*. New Haven, CT: Yale University Press, 1993.

Kemper, Theodore K. *Social Structure and Testosterone*. New Brunswick, NJ: Rutgers University Press, 1990.

Kempf, Kimberly L. "The Empirical Status of Hirschi's Control Theory." In Freda Adler and William S. Laufer (Eds.), *New Directions in Criminological Theory*, Vol. 4, pp. 143-186. New Brunswick, NJ: Transaction, 1993.

Kennedy, Elizabeth L., and Madeline D. Davis. *Boots of Leather, Slippers of Gold*. New York: Routledge, 1993.

Kennedy, Robert E. *Life Choices: Applying Sociology*, 2nd ed. New York: Holt, Rinehart & Winston, 1989.

Kennickell, Arthur B., and R.L. Woodburn. "Estimation of Household Net Worth: Evidence from the 1989 Survey of Consumer Finances." Board of Governors, Federal Reserve System, April 1992.

Kephart, William M., and William W. Zellner. *Extraordinary Groups*, 5th ed. New York: St. Martin's Press, 1993.

Kerckhoff, Alan C. "On the Social Psychology of Social Mobility Processes." *Social Forces* 68 (1989): 17-25.

Kerckhoff, Alan C. *Diverging Pathways: Social Structure and Career Deflections*. New York: Cambridge University Press, 1993.

Kerns, Virginia. *Women and the Ancestors*. Urbana, IL: University of Illinois Press, 1992.

Kerr, Peter. "National Study Finds Insurance Industry Bias." *New York Times*, February 5, 1993.

Kertzer, David I. *Ritual, Politics, and Power*. New Haven, CT: Yale University Press, 1988.

Kertzer, David I., and Dennis P. Hogan. "Family Structure, Individual Lives, and Societal Change." In Matilda White Riley (Ed.), *Social Structure and Human Lives*, Vol. 1, pp. 83-100. Newbury Park, CA: Sage, 1988.

Kessler, Ronald C., and William J. Magee. "Childhood Family Violence and Adult Recurrent Depression." *Journal of Health and Social Behavior* 35 (1994): 13-27.

Kessler, R. C., K. A. McGonagle, S.Y. Zhao, C. B. Nelson, M. Hughes, S. Eshelman, H. U. Wittchen, and K. S. Kendler. "Lifetime and 12-Month Prevalence of DSM-III-R Psychiatric Disorders in the United States—Results from the National Comorbidity Survey." *Archives of General Psychiatry* 51 (1994): 3-99.

Ketterlinus, R. D., et al. "Adolescent Nonsexual and Sex-Related Problem Behaviors." *Journal of Adolescent Research* 7 (1992): 431.

Keysar, Ariela, Barry A. Kosmin, Nava Lerer, and Egon Meyer. "Exogamy in First Marriages and Remarriages: An Analysis of Mate Selection in First and Second Marriages Among American Jews in the 1990s, and Its Theoretical Implications." *Contemporary Jewry* 12 (1991): 45-66.

Kiecolt, K. Jill. "Stress and the Decision to Change Oneself: A Theoretical Model." *Social Psychology Quarterly* 57 (1994): 49-63.

Kilborn, Peter T. "For Hispanic Immigrants, A Higher Job-Injury Risk." *New York Times*, February 18, 1992: 1 ff.

Kilborn, Peter T. "New Jobs Lack the Old Security In a Time of 'Disposable' Workers." *New York Times,* March 15, 1993.

Kilborn, Peter T. "The Boss Only Wants What's Best for You." *New York Times*, May 8, 1994.

Kilbourne, Barbara, Paula England, George Farkas. Kurt Beron, and Dorothy Weir. "Returns to Skill, Compensating Differentials, and Gender Bias: Effects of Occupational Characteristics on the Wages of White Women and Men." *American Journal of Sociology* 100 (1994): 689-719.

Kilbourne, Barbara, Paula England, and Kurt Beron. "Effects of Individual, Occupational, and Industrial Characteristics on Earnings: Intersections of Race and Gender." *Social Forces* 72 (1994): 1149-1176.

Kilgore, Sally B. "The Organizational Context of Tracking in Schools." *American Sociological Review* 56 (1991): 189-203.

Kimmel, Michael S. "The Sixties Without Metaphor." *Society*, March/April 1989: 77-84.

Kimmel, Michael S. *Men Confront Pornography*. New York: Crown, 1990.

Kimmel, Michael. *Against the Tide: "Pro-feminist Men" in the United States, 1776-1990: A Documentary History*. Boston, MA: Beacon Press, 1992.

Kimmel, Michael S., and Michael A. Messner (Eds.). *Men's Lives*, 2nd ed. New York: Macmillan, 1993.

Kimmel, Michael. *Manhood: The American Quest*. New York: Harper Collins, 1994.

Kinder, Douglas Clark in William O. Walker, III (Ed.). *Drug Control Policy: Essays in Historical and Comparative Perspective*. University Park, PA: The Pennsylvania State University Press, 1992.

King, Mary C. "Occupational Segregation by Race and Sex, 1940-1988." *Monthly Labor Review*, April 1992: 30-38.

Kingston, Paul W. "Sociology of Education." In Edgar F. Borgatta and Marie L. Borgatta (Eds.), *Encyclopedia of Sociology*, pp. 2022-2026. New York: Macmillan, 1992.

Kingston, Paul W., and Lionel Lewis (Eds.). *The High-Status Track: Studies of Elite Schools and Stratification*. Albany, NY: State University of New York Press, 1990.

Kingston, Paul W., and Steven L. Nock. "Time Together among Dual-Earner Couples." *American Sociological Review* 52 (1987): 391-400.

Kinney, David A. "From Nerds to Normals: The Recovery of Identity Among Adolescents from Middle School to High School." *Sociology of Education* 66 (1993): 21-40.

Kinsey, Alfred C., Wardell Pomeroy, and Clyde Martin. *Sexual Behavior in the Human Male*. Philadelphia: Saunders, 1948.

Kinsey, Alfred C., Wardell Pomeroy, Clyde Martin, and Paul H. Gebhard. *Sexual Behavior in the Human Female*. Philadelphia: Saunders, 1953.

Kirk, Stuart A., and Herb Kutchins. *The Selling of D.S.M.* New York: Aldine de Gruyter, 1992.

Kirp, David L. "Tales from the Bright Side: The Surprising Success of America's Biggest Community College." *Lingua Franca* February/March 1992: 20-26.

Kishor, Sunita. "'May God Give Sons To All': Gender and Child Mortality in India." *American Sociological Review* 58 (1993): 247-256.

Kitcher, Philip. *Vaulting Ambition: Sociobiology and the Quest for Human Nature*. Cambridge, MA: MIT Press, 1985.

Kitson, Gay C., and William M. Holmes. *Portrait of Divorce: Adjustment to Marital Breakdown*. New York: Guilford, 1992.

Kitzinger, Celia. *The Social Construction of Lesbianism.* Newbury Park, CA: Sage, 1988.

Klandermans, Bert. "A Theoretical Framework for Comparisons of Social Movement Participation." *Sociological Forum* 8 (1993): 383-402.

Klandermans, Bert, and Dirk Oegema. "Potentials, Networks, Motivations, and Barriers: Steps Toward Participation in Social Movements." *American Sociological Review* 52 (1987): 519-531.

Klanwatch Annual Report. Montgomery, AL: Southern Poverty Law Center, February 1993.

Kleck, Gary. *Point Blank: Guns and Violence in America.* Hawthorne, NY: Aldine de Gruyter, 1991.

Kleidman, Robert. "Volunteer Activism and Professionalism in Social Movement Organizations." *Social Problems* 41 (1994): 257-276.

Klein, Alan M. *Little Big Men: Bodybuilding Subculture and Gender Construction.* Albany, NY: State University of New York Press, 1993.

Kluckhohn, Clyde, and Henry A. Murray (Eds.). *Personality in Nature, Society and Culture.* New York: Alfred A. Knopf, 1948.

Kluegel, James R. "Macro-economic Problems. Beliefs about the Poor and Attitudes Toward Welfare Spending." *Social Problems* 34 (1987): 82-99.

Kluegel, James R., and Lawrence Bobo. "Dimensions of Whites' Beliefs About the Black-White Socioeconomic Gap." In P.M. Sniderman, P. Tetlock, and E. Carmines (Eds.), *Race and Politics in American Society.* Palo Alto, CA: Stanford University Press, 1994.

Kluegel, James R., and Eliot R. Smith. *Beliefs About Inequality: Americans' Views of What Is and What Ought to Be.* Hawthorne, NY: Aldine de Gruyter, 1986.

Kluger, Richard. *Simple Justice.* New York: Vintage, 1994.

Knoke, David. *Political Networks: The Structural Perspective.* New York: Cambridge University Press, 1990.

Knottnerus, J. David. "Status Attainment Research and Its Image of Society." *American Sociological Review* 52 (1987): 113-121.

Knouse, Stephen B., Paul Rosenfeld, and Amy L. Culbertson (Eds.). *Hispanics in the Workplace.* Newbury Park, CA: Sage, 1992.

Koenig, Frederick. *Rumor in the Marketplace: The Social Psychology of Commercial Hearsay.* Dover, MA: Auburn House, 1985.

Kohlberg, Lawrence. *The Philosophy of Moral Development.* Vol. 1. *Essays on Moral Development.* New York: Harper & Row, 1981.

Kohn, Alfie. *Punished By Rewards.* Boston: Houghton-Mifflin, 1993.

Kohn, Melvin L. "Bureaucratic Men: A Portrait and an Interpretation." *American Sociological Review* 36 (June 1971): 461-474.

Kohn, Melvin L. Atsushi Naoi, Carrie Schoenbach, Carmi Schooler, and Kazimierz M. Slomczynski. "Position in the Class Structure and Psychological Functioning in the United States, Japan, and Poland." *American Journal of Sociology* 95 (1990): 964-1008.

Kohn, Melvin L., and Kazimierz M. Slomczynski. *Social Structure and Self-Direction: A Comparative Analysis of the United States and Poland.* Cambridge, MA: Blackwell, 1990.

Kohn, Richard H. "Upstarts in Uniform." *The National Interest,* April 10, 1994.

Kolbert, Elizabeth. "Sexual Harassment at Work is Pervasive, Survey Suggests." *New York Times,* October 11, 1991.

Kolchin, Peter. *American Slavery, 1619-1877.* New York: Hill & Wang, 1993.

Kondo, Anja. "Contraceptive Knowledge and Behavior Among Dutch Teenagers." Paper presented at the annual meeting of the Eastern Sociological Society, Providence, RI (April 1991).

Koopmans, Ruud. "The Dynamics of Protest Waves: West Germany, 1965-1989." *American Sociological Review* 58 (1993): 637-658.

Korczyk, Sophie. *Gender Issues in Employer Pensions Policy.* Washington, DC: Employee Benefits Research Institute, 1993.

Korman, Abraham K. *The Outsiders: Jews and Corporate America.* Lexington, MA: Lexington Books, 1989.

Korn/Ferry International. *Decade of the Executive Woman.* New York: Korn/Ferry International, 1993.

Kornai, Janos. *The Socialist System: The Political Economy of Communism.* Princeton, NJ: Princeton University Press, 1992.

Korzeniewicz, Roberto P., and Kimberley Awbrey. "Democratic Transitions and the Semiperiphery of the World-Economy." *Sociological Forum* 7 (1992): 609-640.

Kosmin, Barry A., and Seymour P. Lachman. *One Nation Under God: Religion in Contemporary American Society.* New York: Harmony Books, 1993.

Koss, M. P. "Hidden Rape: Incidence, Prevalence, and Descriptive Characteristics of Sexual Aggression and Victimization in a National Sample of College Students." In Anne W. Burgess (Ed.), *Sexual Assault.* Vol. 2. New York: Garland, 1988.

Kost, Kathryn, and Jacqueline D. Forrest. "American Women's Sexual Behavior and Exposure to Risk of Sexually Transmitted Diseases." *Family Planning Perspectives* 24 (1992): 244-254.

Kotlikoff, Laurence. "The Economic Impact of the Demographic Transition: Problems and Prospects." In *Aging of the U. S. Population: Economic and Environmental Implications. Proceedings of an Invitational Workshop.* Washington, DC: American Association of Retired Persons, 1992.

Kowalewski, David. "Core Intervention and Periphery Revolution, 1821-1985." *American Journal of Sociology* 97 (1991): 70-95.

Kraus, Linda A., Mark H. Davis, Doris Bazzini, Mary Church, and Clare M. Kirchman. "Personal and Social Influences on Loneliness: The Mediating Effect of Social Provisions." *Social Psychology Quarterly* 56 (1) (1993): 37-53.

Krause, Paul. *The Battle for Homestead, 1880-1892: Politics, Culture, and Steel.* Pittsburgh, PA: University of Pittsburgh Press, 1992.

Krauss, Celene. "Community Struggles and the Shaping of Democratic Consciousness." *Sociological Forum* 4 (1989): 227-239.

Krauss, Celene. "Women and Toxic Waste Protests: Race, Class and Gender as Resources of Resistance." *Qualitative Sociology,* Vol. 16, No. 3, 1993.

Krauss, Clifford. "U.S., Aware of Killings, Kept Ties to Salvadoran Rightists, Papers Suggest." *New York Times* November 9, 1993: A9.

Kravanja, Mario E. "Greeting Cards and Emotional Culture: Mixed Feelings on Father's Day." Paper presented at the Annual Meeting of the American Sociological Society, Miami Beach, FL., August, 1993.

Kreft, Ita G.G. "Using Multilevel Analysis to Assess School Effectiveness: A Study of Dutch Secondary Schools." *Sociology of Education* 66 (1993): 104-129.

Krimerman, Len, and Frank Lindenfeld (Eds.). *When Workers Decide: Workplace Democracy Takes Root in North America.* New York: New Society, 1992.

Krisberg, Barry, and James F. Austin. *Reinventing Juvenile Justice.* Newbury Park, CA: Sage, 1993.

Kristof, Nicholas D. "For Lucky Students, It's All Work, Work, Work." *New York Times,* May 1, 1993.

Krugman, Paul R. "The Right, the Rich, and the Facts: Deconstructing the Income Distribution Debate." *The American Prospect* 11 (1992): 20-31.

Krull, Catherine, and Frank Trovato. "The Quiet Revolution and the Sex Differential in Quebec's Suicide Rates: 1931-1986." *Social Forces* 72 (1994): 1121-1147.

Kruttschnitt, Candace, Jane D. McLeod, and Maud Dornfeld. "The Economic Environment of Child Abuse." *Social Problems* 41 (1994): 299-315.

Krymkowski, Daniel H., and Tadeusz K. Krauze. "Occupational Mobility in the Year 2000: Projections for American Men and Women." *Social Forces* 71 (1992): 145-157.

Krysan, Maria, and William V. D'Antonio. "Voluntary Associations." In Edgar F. Borgatta and Marie L. Borgatta (Eds.), *Encyclopedia of Sociology,* pp. 2231-2234. New York: Macmillan, 1992.

Ku, Leighton C., Freya L. Sonenstein, and Joseph H. Pleck. "Young Men's Risk Behaviors for HIV Infection and Sexually Transmitted

Diseases, 1988 through 1991." *American Journal of Public Health* 83 (1993): 1609–1615.

Kuhl, Patricia K., Karen A. Williams, Francisco Lacerda, Kenneth N. Stevens, and Bjorn Lindblom. "Linguistic Experience Alters Phonetic Perception in Infants by 6 Months of Age." *Science* 225 (1992): 606–608.

Kuhn, Thomas S. *The Structure of Scientific Revolutions.* Chicago: University of Chicago Press, 1962.

Kunda, Gideon. *Engineering Culture: Control and Commitment in a High-Tech Corporation.* Philadelphia: Temple University Press, 1992.

Kupers, Terry A. *Revisioning Men's Lives: Gender, Intimacy and Power.* New York: Guilford, 1993.

Kurz, Demie. "Social Science Perspectives on Wife Abuse: Current Debates and Future Directions." *Gender & Society* 3 (1989): 489–505.

Kurzweil, Edith. *The Freudians: A Comparative Perspective.* New Haven: Yale University Press, 1990.

Kushner, Roland. "Motivation, Structure, and Governance: Lessons from the Non-Profit Field." Unpublished manuscript, May 1993.

Kuwahara, Yasue. "Power to the People, Y'All: Rap Music, Resistance, and Black College Students." *Humanity & Society* 16 (1992): 54–70.

Labaton, Stephen. "Benefits are Refused More Often to Disabled Blacks, Study Finds." *New York Times,* May 11, 1992.

Lachman, Richard. "Graffiti as Career and Ideology." *American Journal of Sociology* 94 (1988): 229–250.

Ladd, Anthony E. "Sociology, Humanism, and the Environmental Crossroads." *Humanity & Society* 18 (1994): 49–60.

LaFollette, Marcel C. *Stealing into Print: Fraud, Plagiarism, and Misconduct in Scientific Publishing.* Berkeley, CA: University of California Press, 1992.

Lagemann, Ellen Condliffe. *The Politics of Knowledge: The Carnegie Corporation, Philanthropy, and Public Policy.* Middletown, CT: Wesleyan University Press, 1989.

Lakoff, Robin Tolmach. *Talking Power: The Politics of Language in Our Lives.* New York: Basic Books, 1990.

Lamb, Michael, Kathleen J. Sternberg, Carl-Philip Hwang, and Anders G. Broberg. *Child Care in Context: Cross-Cultural Perspectives.* Hillsdale, NJ: Lawrence Erlbaum Associates, 1992.

Lamont, Michele. *Money, Morals, and Manners: The Culture of the French and American Upper-Middle Class.* Chicago, IL: University of Chicago Press, 1992.

Lamphere, Louise (Ed.). *Structuring Diversity: Ethnographic Perspectives on the New Immigration.* Chicago, IL: University of Chicago Press, 1992.

Land, Kenneth, Glenn Deane, and Judith R. Blau. "Religious Pluralism and Church Membership: A Spatial Diffusion Model." *American Sociological Review* 56 (1991): 237–249.

Lang, Eric. "Role Conflict." In Edgar F. Borgatta and Marie L. Borgatta (Eds.), *Encyclopedia of Sociology,* pp. 1676–1679. New York: Macmillan, 1992.

Lang, Gladys Engel, and Kurt Lang. "Recognition and Renown: The Survival of Artistic Reputation." *American Journal of Sociology* 94 (1988): 79–109.

Lang, Gladys Engel, and Kurt Lang. "Mass Media Research." In Edgar F. Borgatta and Marie L. Borgatta (Eds.), *Encyclopedia of Sociology,* pp. 1206–1211. New York: Macmillan, 1992.

Lapchick, Richard E., and Jeffrey R. Benedict. *1994 Racial Report Card.* Boston, MA: Northeastern University Center for the Study of Sport and Society, 1994.

Laqueur, Thomas. *Making Sex: Body and Gender from the Greeks to Freud.* Cambridge, MA: Harvard University Press, 1990.

Lareau, Annette. *Home Advantages: Social Class and Parental Intervention in Elementary Education.* Philadelphia, PA: Falmer Press, 1989.

LaRossa, Ralph, and Jane H. Wolf. "On Qualitative Family Research." *Journal of Marriage and the Family* 47(3)(1985): 531–541.

Larson, Jan. "Dad's a Deadbeat." *American Demographics* July, 1992: 39.

Laslett, Barbara. "Unfeeling Knowledge: Emotion and Objectivity in the History of Sociology." *Sociological Forum* 5 (1990): 413–434.

Laumann, Edward O., John H. Gagnon, Robert T. Michael, and Stuart Michaels. *The Social Organization of Sexuality: Sexual Practices in the United States.* Chicago, IL: University of Chicago Press, 1994.

Lauristan, Janet L. "Explaining Race and Gender Differences in Adolescent Sexual Behavior." *Social Forces* 72 (1994): 859–884.

Lavely, William. "Industrialization and Household Complexity in Rural Taiwan." *Social Forces* 69 (1990): 235–251.

Lawler, Edward J., and Samuel B. Bacharach. "Comparison of Dependence and Punitive Forms of Power." *Social Forces* 66 (1987): 446–462.

Lawson, Carol. "Toys: Girls Still Apply Makeup, Boys Fight Wars." *New York Times,* June 15, 1989.

Leach, Edmund. *Political Systems of Highland Burma.* Boston: Beacon Press, 1965.

Leahy, Terry. "Taking Up a Position: Discourses of Femininity and Adolescence in the Context of Man/Girl Relationships." *Gender & Society* 8 (1994) 48–72.

LeBlanc, Allen J. "Examining AIDS-related Knowledge Among Adults in the U.S." *Journal of Health and Social Behavior* 34 (1993): 23–36.

LeBon, Gustave. *The Crowd: A Study of the Popular Mind (1895).* New York: Viking, 1960.

LeCompte, Margaret D., and Anthony Gary Dworkin. *Giving Up on School: Student Dropouts and Teacher Burnouts.* Newbury Park, CA: Sage, 1991.

Lederman, Douglas. "Blacks make Up Large Proportion of Scholarship Athletes, Yet Their Overall Enrollment Lags at Division I Colleges." *Chronicle of Higher Education,* June 17, 1992: A1 ff.

Lederman, Douglas. "43% of Male Basketball Players Earned Degrees Within 6 Years." *Chronicle of Higher Education,* May 26, 1993a: A32.

Lederman, Douglas. "Abide by U.S. Sex-Bias Laws, NCAA Panel Urges Colleges." *Chronicle of Higher Education,* May 26, 1993b: A31.

Lee, Ching Kwan. "Familial Hegemony: Gender and Production Politics on Hong Kong's Electronic Shopfloor." *Gender & Society* 7 (1993): 529–547.

Lee, Gary R. "Comparative Perspectives." In Marvin B. Sussman and Suzanne K. Steinmetz (Eds.), *Handbook of Marriage and the Family,* pp. 59–80. New York: Plenum, 1987.

Lee, Raymond M. *Doing Research on Sensitive Topics.* Newbury Park, CA: Sage, 1993.

Lee, Valerie E., and Anthony S. Bryk. "A Multilevel Model of the School Distribution of High School Achievement." *Sociology of Education* 62 (1989): 172–192.

Lee, Valerie E., and Kenneth A. Frank. "Students' Characteristics that Facilitate the Transfer from Two-Year to Four-Year Colleges." *Sociology of Education* 63 (1990): 178–193.

Lee, Valerie E., Helen M. Marks, and Tina Byrd. "Sexism in Single-Sex and Coeducational Independent Secondary School Classrooms." *Sociology of Education* 67 (1994): 92–120.

Lee, Valerie E., and Julia B. Smith. "Effects of School Restructuring on the Achievement and Engagement of Middle-grade Students." *Sociology of Education* 66 (1993): 164–187.

Lehman, Edward C. "Localism and Sexism: A Replication and Extension." *Social Science Quarterly* 71 (1990): 184–195.

Lehrer, Evelyn L., and Carmel U. Chiswick. "The Religious Composition of Unions: It's Role as a Determinant of Marital Stability." Paper presented at the annual meeting of the Population Association of America, Denver, CO: April, 1992.

Leidner, Robin. "Serving Hamburgers and Selling Insurance: Gender, Work, and Identity in Interactive Service Jobs." *Gender & Society* 5 (1991): 154–177.

Leigh, Wilhelmina A., and James B. Stewart (Eds.). *The Housing Status of Black Americans.* New Brunswick: Transaction Publisher, 1992.

Leisure Trends. "Analysis of Gallup Data." Glastonbury, CT: 1992.

Leland, John. "Our Bodies, Our Sales: Girl Groups: Can You Grind in Your Videos and Still Be a Feminist." *Newsweek*, January 31, 1994: 56-5

Lemert, Charles. "The End of Ideology, Really." *Sociological Theory* 9 (1991): 164-172.

Lemert, Edwin M. *Human Deviance, Social Problems, and Social Control*, 2nd ed. Englewood Cliffs, NJ: Prentice-Hall, 1972.

Lemke, Christiane, and Gary Marks (Eds.). *The Crisis of Socialism in Europe*. Durham, NC: Duke University Press, 1992.

Lempert, Richard, and Karl Monsma. "Cultural Differences and Discrimination: Samoans Before a Public Housing Eviction Board." *American Sociological Review* 59 (1994): 890-910.

Lennon, Mary Clare, and Sarah Rosenfield. "Women and Mental Health: The Interaction of Job and Family Conditions." *Journal of Health and Social Behavior* 33 (1992): 316-327.

Lenski, Gerhard. *Power and Privilege: A Theory of Social Stratification*. New York: McGraw-Hill, 1966.

Lenski, Gerhard. "Rethinking Macrosocial Theory." *American Sociological Review* 53 (1985): 163-171.

Lenski, Gerhard, and Jean Lenski. *Human Societies*, 6th ed. New York: McGraw-Hill, 1991.

Lepowsky, Maria. *Fruit of the Motherland: Gender in an Egalitarian Society*. New York: Columbia University Press, 1994.

Lerner, Richard M. *Final Solutions: Biology, Prejudice, and Genocide*. University Park: The Pennsylvania State University Press, 1992.

Leslie, Stuart W. *The Cold War and American Science: The Military-Industrial-Academic Complex at M.I.T. and Stanford*. New York: Columbia University Press, 1993.

LeVay, Simon, and Dean H. Hamer. "Evidence for a Biological Influence in Male Homosexuality." *Scientific American*, May 1994: 45-49.

Lever, Janet. *Soccer Madness*. Chicago: University of Chicago Press, 1983.

Levi-Strauss, Claude. *Elementary Structures of Kinship*. Boston: Beacon Press, 1969.

Levine, Lawrence E. *Highbrow, Lowbrow: The Emergence of Cultural Hierarchy in America*. Cambridge, MA: Harvard University Press, 1988.

Levine, Robert. "Waiting is a Power Game." *Psychology Today*, April 1987, pp. 24-33.

Levy, Frank S., and Richard C. Michel. *The Economic Future of American Families: Income and Wealth Trends*. Washington, DC: Urban Institute Press, 1991.

Lewin, Tamar. "Study Points to Increase in Tolerance of Ethnicity." *New York Times*, January 8, 1992.

Lewis, Lionel S. "Working at Leisure." *Society* 19 (July–August 1982): 27-32.

Lewis, Lisa A. *Gender Politics and MTV: Voicing the Difference*. Philadelphia, PA: Temple University Press, 1990.

Lewis, Oscar. *Four Families: Mexican Case Studies in the Culture of Poverty*. New York: Basic Books, 1959.

Lichter, Daniel T. "Delayed Marriage, Marital Homogamy, and the Mate Selection Process among White Women." *Social Science Quarterly* 71 (1990): 802-811.

Lichter, Daniel T., and David J. Eggebeen. "Rich Kids, Poor Kids: Changing Income Inequality among American Children." *Social Forces* 73 (1993): 761-780.

Lichter, Daniel T., Diane K. McLaughlin, George Kephart, and David J. Landry. "Race and the Retreat from Marriage." *American Sociological Review* 57 (1992): 781-799.

Lieberson, Stanley, and Mary C. Waters. "The Ethnic Responses of Whites: What Causes Their Instability, Simplification, and Inconsistency?" *Social Forces* 72 (1993): 421-450.

Liebman, Robert C., and Robert Wuthnow (Eds.). *The New Christian Right: Mobilization and Legitimation*. New York: Aldine, 1983.

Liebow, Elliot. *Tell Them Who I Am: The Lives of Homeless Women*. New York: Free Press, 1993.

Light, Donald. "Life, Death, and the Insurance Companies." *New England Journal of Medicine* 330 (1994): 496-450.

Light, Stephen C. "The Severity of Assaults on Prison Officers: A Contextual Study." *Social Science Quarterly* 71 (1990): 266-284.

Lin, Nan. *The Struggle for Tienanmen: Anatomy of the 1989 Mass Movement*. Westport: Praeger, 1992.

Lin, Nan, and Yanjie Bian. "Getting Ahead in Urban China." *American Journal of Sociobiology* 97 (1991): 657-688.

Lin, Nan, and Walter M. Ensel. "Life Stress and Health: Stressors' and Resources." *American Sociological Review* 54 (June 1989): 382-399.

Lincoln, C. Eric, and Lawrence H. Mamiya. *The Black Church in the African American Experience*. Durham, NC: Duke University Press, 1990.

Lincoln, James R., and Arne L. Kalleberg. *Culture Control and Commitment: A Study of Work Organization and Work Attitudes in the United States and Japan*. Cambridge, MA: Cambridge University Press, 1990.

Lindorff, Dave. *Marketplace Medicine: The Rise of the For-Profit Chains*. New York: Bantam, 1992.

Ling, Pete J. *America and the Automobile: Technology, Reform, and Social Change*. Manchester, England: Manchester University Press, 1990.

Link, Bruce G., Howard Andrews, and Francis T. Cullen. "The Violent and Illegal Behavior of Mental Patients Reconsidered." *American Sociological Review* 57 (1992):275-292.

Link, Bruce G., Mary Clare Lennon, and Bruce P. Dohrenwend. "Socioeconomic Status and Depression: The Role of Occupations Involving Direction, Control, and Planning." *American Journal of Sociology* 98 (1993): 1351-1387.

Link, Bruce G., Jerrold Mirotznik, and Francis T. Cullen. "The Effectiveness of Stigma Coping Orientations: Can Negative Consequences of Mental Illness Labeling Be Avoided?" *Journal of Health and Social Behavior* 32(1991): 302-320.

Linner, Birgitta, with Richard J. Litell. *Sex and Society in Sweden*. New York: Pantheon, 1967.

Linton, Ralph. *The Study of Man*. New York: Appleton-Century, 1936.

Lipsyte, Robert. "There Goes the Street, There Goes the Team." *New York Times*, June 11, 1993.

Lipsyte, Robert. "In Memoriam..." *New York Times*, September 15, 1994.

Liska, Allen (Ed.). *Social Threat and Social Control*. Albany, NY: State University of New York Press, 1992.

Liska, Allen E., and William Baccaglini. "Feeling Safe by Comparison." *Social Problems* 37 (1990): 360-374.

Liska, Allen E., and Jiang Yu. "Specifying and Testing the Threat Hypothesis; Police Use of Deadly Force." In Allen E. Liska (Ed.), *Social Threat and Social Control*, pp. 53-70. Albany, NY: State University of New York, 1992.

Lofland, John, and Sam Marullo (Eds.). *Peace Movement Dynamics*. New Brunswick, NJ: Rutgers University Press, 1990.

Logan, Charles H. *Private Prisons: Pros and Cons*. New York: Oxford University Press, 1990.

Logan, John R. "Suburbanization." In Edgar F. Borgatta and Marie L. Borgatta (Eds.), *Encyclopedia of Sociology* (4) (1992): 2104-2111.

Logan, John R., Richard D. Alba, and Thomas L. McNulty. "Ethnic Economies in Metropolitan Regions: Miami and Beyond." *Social Forces* 72 (1994): 691-724.

London, Bruce. "School Enrollment Rates and Trends, Gender, and Fertility: A Cross-National Analysis." *Sociology of Education* 65 (1992): 306-316.

Long, J. Scott. "Measures of Sex Differences in Scientific Productivity." *Social Forces* 71 (1992): 159-178.

Lopata, Helena Znaniecka. *Widows, Volume 2: North America*. Durham, NC: Duke University Press, 1987.

Lopata, Helena Znaniecka. "The Interweave of Public and Private: Women's Challenge to American Society." *Journal of Marriage and the Family* 55 (1993): 176-190.

Lopes, Paul D. "Innovation and Diversity in the Popular Music Industry." *American Sociological Review* 57 (1992): 56-71.

Lopreato, Joseph. "From Social Evolutionism to Biocultural Evolutionism." *Sociolgoical Forum* 5 (1990): 187-212.

Lorber, Judith. "Believing is Seeing: Biology as Ideology." *Gender & Society* 7 (1993): 568-581.

Lorber, Judith. *Paradoxes of Gender*. New Haven, CT: Yale University Press, 1994.

Lorber, Judith, and Susan A. Farrell. *The Social Construction of Gender*. Newbury Park, CA: Sage, 1991.

Lorence, Jon, and Jeylan Mortimer. "Work Experience and Political Orientation: A Panel Study." *Social Forces* 58 (1979): 651-676.

Loscocco, Karyn A., and Joyce Robinson. "Barriers to Women's Small-Business Success in the United States." *Gender & Society* 5 (1991): 511-532.

Loscocco, Karyn A., and Glenna Spitze. "Working Conditions, Social Support, and the Well-Being of Female and Male Factory Workers." *Journal of Health and Social Behavior* 31(1990): 313-327.

Loseke, Donileen. *The Battered Woman and Shelters: The Social Construction of Wife Abuse*. Albany, NY: State University of New York Press, 1992.

Losh, Susan. "Cohort and Gender Attitude Change: Further Shifts in Public Opinion." Paper presented at the 83rd annual meeting of the American Sociological Association, Atlanta, 1988.

Lott, Juanita Tamayo, and Judy C. Felt. "Studying the Pan-Asian Community." *Population Today* 19 (2), 1991: 6-8.

Lotz, Roy E. *Crime and the American Press*. New York: Praeger, 1991.

Louis Harris Research. *Taking America's Pulse*. Washington, DC: National Conference of Christians and Jews, 1994.

Lozano, Beverly. *The Invisible Work Force: Transforming American Business with Outside and Home-Based Workers*. New York: Free Press, 1989.

Lumsden, Charles J., and Edward O. Wilson. *Genes, Mind, Culture: The Coevolutionary Process*. Cambridge, MA: Harvard University Press, 1981.

Luske, Bruce. *Mirrors of Madness: Patrolling the Psychic Borders*. New York: Aldine de Gruyter, 1990.

Luster, Tom, and Stephen A. Small. "Factors Associated with Sexual Risk-Taking Behaviors Among Adolescents." *Journal of Marriage and the Family* 56 (1994): 622-632.

Lutz, Wolfgang. "The Future of World Population." *Population Bulletin* 49 (1994), Washington, DC: Population Reference Bureau.

Luxemberg, Rosa. (1899) *Selected Political Writings of Rosa Luxemberg*. New York: Monthly Review Press, 1971.

Lynd, Robert S., and Helen Merrell Lynd. *Middletown: A Study in American Culture*. San Diego, CA: Harcourt, 1929.

Lynott, Patricia Passuth, and Barbara J. Logue. "The Hurried Child: the Myth of Lost Childhood in Contemporary American Society." *Sociological Forum* 8 (3) (1993): 471-491.

Lyons, Paul. *Class of '66 Living in Suburban Middle America*. Philadelphia, PA: Temple University Press, 1994.

Lyson, Thomas A., and William W. Falk. *Forgotten Places: Uneven Development in Rural America*. Lawrence: University Press of Kansas, 1993.

MacArthur, John R. *Second Front: Censorship and Propaganda in the Gulf War*. New York: Hill & Wang, 1993.

MacCorquodale, Patricia, and Gary Jensen. "Women in the Law: Partners or Tokens?" *Gender & Society* 7 (1993): 582-593.

MacIntosh, Donald, and David Whitson. *The Game Planners: Transforming Canada's Sport System*. Montreal: McGill-Queen's University Press, 1990.

MacKensie, R. D. "The Scope of Human Ecology." *Publications of the American Sociological Society* 20 (1925).

MacKenzie, Donald. *Inventing Accuracy: A Historical Sociology of Nuclear Missile Guidance*. Cambridge, MA: MIT Press, 1990.

MacKenzie, Doris Layton, James W. Shaw, and Voncile B. Gowdy. "An Evaluation of Shock Incarceration in Louisiana." *Research in Brief*. Washington, DC: National Institute of Justice, June 1993.

MacKinnon, Catherine. *Only Words*. Cambridge, MA: Harvard University Press, 1993.

MacShane, Denis. "Do Europeans Do It Better?," *The American Prospect*, Summer 1993: 88-95.

Magrass, Yale R. "The Boy Scouts, the Outdoors, and Empire." *Humanity and Society* 10 (February 1986): 37-57.

Majors, Richard, and Janet Mancini Billson. *Cool Pose: The Dilemmas of Black Manhood in America*. New York: Lexington, 1992.

Makinson, Larry. *PACs in Profile: Spending Patterns in the 1992 Elections*. Washington, DC: Center for Responsive Politics, 1993.

Males, Mike. "Adult Liaison in the 'Epidemic' of 'Teenage' Births, Pregnancy, and Venereal Disease." *Journal of Sex Research* 29 (1992): 525-545.

Malinowski, Bronislaw. *Argonauts of the Western Pacific*. New York: Dutton, 1922/1955.

Malinowski, Bronislaw. "The Principle of Legitimacy: Parenthood, The Basis of Social Structure." In Rose Laub Coser (Ed.), *The Family: Its Structure and Functions* (1929). New York: St. Martin's Press, 1964.

Mandell, Nancy, Patricia A. Adler, and Peter Adler (Eds.). *Sociological Studies of Child Development* (vol. 3), Greenwich, CT: JAI Press, 1990.

Manegold, Catherine S. "Study Warns of Growing Underclass of the Unskilled." *New York Times,* June 3, 1994.

Mann, Coramae Richey. *Unequal Justice: A Question of Color*. Bloomington, IN: Indiana University Press, 1993.

Mannheim, Karl. *Ideology and Utopia*. New York: Harcourt, 1936.

Marcus, Eric. *Making History: The Struggle for Gay and Lesbian Equal Rights*. New York: HarperCollins, 1992.

Margolick, David. "A Mixed Marriage's 25th Anniversary." *New York Times,* June 12, 1992.

Margolin, Leslie. "Deviance on Record: Techniques for Labeling Child Abusers in Official Records." *Social Problems* 39 (1992): 58-70.

Margolin, Leslie. "Goodness Personified: The Emergence of Gifted Children." *Social Problems* 40 (1993): 510-532.

Margolis, Diane Rothbard. "Women's Movements Around the World." *Gender & Society* 7 (1993): 379-399.

Marks, Gary, and Larry Diamond (Eds.). *Reexamining Democracy: Essays in Honor of Seymour Martin Lipset*. Newbury Park, CA: Sage, 1992.

Marks, Stephen R. "Intimacy in the Public Realm: The Case of Co-Workers." *Social Forces* 72 (1994): 843-858.

Markson, Elizabeth W., Margaret Kelly-Hayes, Spencer V. Wilking, Albert Belanger, and Brian Carpenter. "Depressive Symptoms Among the Framingham Cohort." Paper presented at the annual meeting of the American Sociological Association, Pittsburgh, PA, August 1992.

Markusen, Ann, Peter Hall, Scott Campbell, and Sabina Dietrick. *The Rise of the Gunbelt: The Military Remapping of Industrial America*. New York: Oxford University Press, 1991.

Marrett, Cora B. "Corporate Organizations. In Edgar F. Borgatta and Marie L. Borgatta (Eds.), *The Encyclopedia of Sociology*, pp. 310-315. New York: Macmillan, 1992.

Marriott, Michel. "Fervid Debate on Gambling: Disease or Moral Weakness?" *New York Times,* November 21, 1992.

Marsden, George M. *Understanding Fundamentalism and Evangelicism*. Grand Rapids, MI: William B. Eerdmans, 1991.

Marsden, Peter V., and Jeanne S. Hurlbert. "Social Resources and Mobility Outcomes: Replication and Extension." *Social Forces* 66 (1988): 1038-1059.

Marshall, Alfred. *Principles of Economics* (1890). New York: Macmillan, 1961.

Marshall, Donald S., and R. Suggs (Eds.). *Human Sexual Behavior*. Englewood Cliffs, NJ: Prentice-Hall, 1971.

Marshall, Jonathan in William O. Walker, III (Ed.). *Drug Control Policy: Essays in Historical and Comparative Perspective*. University Park: The Pennsylvania State University Press, 1992.

Marshall, Victor W., and Carolyn J. Rosenthal. "Aging and Later Life." In R. Hagedorn (Ed.), *Sociology*, 5th ed. Toronto: Holt, Rhinehart and Winston, 1994.

Marsiglio, William. "Adolescent Males' Orientation Toward Paternity and Contraception." *Family Planning Perspectives* 25 (1993): 22-31.

Martin, David. *Tongues of Fire: The Explosion of Protestantism in Latin America*. Oxford, ENG: Basil Blackwell, 1990.

Martin, Joanne. *Cultures in Organizations: Three Perspectives*. New York: Oxford University Press, 1992.

Martin, Karin A. "Gender and Sexuality: Medical Opinion on Sexuality." *Gender & Society* 7 (1993): 246-260.

Martin, Kay, and Voorhies, Barbara. *Female of the Species*. New York: Columbia University Press, 1975.

Martin, Patricia Yancey, and Roberta A. Hummer. "Fraternities and Rape on Campus." *Gender & Society* 3 (1989): 457-473.

Martin, Susan E. "'Outsider Within' the Station House: The Impact of Race and Gender on Black Women Police." *Social Problems* 41 (1994): 383-400.

Martineau, Harriet. *Society in America*. New York: Saunders and Otley, 1837.

Martorella, Rosanne. *Corporate Art*. New Brunswick, NJ: Rutgers University Press, 1990.

Marty, Martin E., and R. Scott Appleby (Eds.). *Fundamentalism and the State*. Chicago: University of Chicago Press, 1993.

Marullo, Sam. "Political, Institutional, and Bureaucratic Fuel for the Arms Race." *Sociological Forum* 7 (1) 1992: 29-44.

Marwell, Gerald, N. J. Demerath, III, and Michael T. Aiken. "The Present Lives of 1960s Civil Rights Activists: The Dreamers Turn Forty." Paper presented at the 84th annual meeting of the American Sociological Association, San Francisco, August 1989.

Marwell, Gerald, and Pamela Oliver. *The Critical Mass in Collective Action*. New York: Cambridge University Press, 1993.

Marx, Gary. "The Iron Fist and the Velvet Glove: Totalitarian Potentials Within Democratic Structures." In James F. Short, Jr. *The Social Fabric: Dimensions and Issues*, pp. 135-162. Newbury Park: Sage, 1986.

Marx, Karl, and Friedrich Engels. *The German Ideology* (1846). New York: International Publishers, 1976.

Marx, Karl. "Contribution to the Critique of Hegel's Philosophy of Law." (1844) In *Karl Marx and Fredrick Engels: Collected Works, Vol. 3*. New York: International Publishers, 1975.

Maryanski, Alexandra, and Jonathan H. Turner. *The Social Cage: Human Nature and the Evolution of Society*. Stanford, CA: Stanford University Press, 1992.

Mason, Karen Oppenheim. "The Status of Women: Conceptual and Methodological Issues in Demographic Studies." *Sociological Forum* 1 (1986): 284-300.

Mason, Karen Oppenheim, and Yu-Hsia Lu. "Attitudes Toward Women's Familial Roles: Changes in the United States, 1977-1985." *Gender & Society* 2 (1988): 39-57.

Massey, Douglas S., and Nancy A. Denton. *American Apartheid: Segregation and the Making of the Underclass*. Cambridge, MA: Harvard University Press, 1993.

Massey, Douglas S., Andrew B. Gross, and Kumiko Shibuya. "Migration, Segregation, and the Geographic Concentration of Poverty." *American Sociological Review* 59 (1994): 425-445.

Mathisen, James A. "A Further Look at 'Common Sense' in Introductory Sociology." *Teaching Sociology* 17 (1989): 307-315.

Matsueda, Ross L. "The Dynamics of Moral Belief and Minor Deviance." *Social Forces* 68 (1989): 428-457.

Matsueda, Ross L. "Reflected Appraisals, Parental Labeling,and Delinquency: Specifying a Symbolic Interactionist Theory." *American Journal of Sociology* 97 (1992): 1577-1611.

Matsueda, Ross L., and Karen Heimer. "Race, Family Structure,and Delinquency: A Test of Differential Association and Social Control Theories." *American Sociological Review* 52 (1987): 826-840.

Maume, David J., Jr. "Child-Care Expenditures and Women's Employment Turnover." *Social Forces* 70 (1991): 495-508.

Maume, David J., Jr., and Karen R. Mullin. "Men's Participation in Child Care and Women's Work Attachment." *Social Problems* 40 (1993): 533-546.

Maurer, Suzanne B., and Richard E. Ratcliff. "Looking for Where the Buck Stops: In Search of Capitalist Investors Among Wealthy Americans." Paper presented at the annual meeting of the Eastern Sociological Society, Baltimore, March 1989.

Mauss, Marcel (1925). *The Gift: Forms and Functions of Exchange in Archaic Societies*. New York: Norton, 1967.

Mazer, Donald B., and Elizabeth F. Percival. "Students' Experiences of Sexual Harassment at a Small University." *Sex Roles* 20 (1989): 1-22.

Mazur, Allan. "Signs of Status in Bridal Portraits." *Sociological Forum* 8 (1993): 273-284.

Mazur, Allan, Alan Booth, and James M. Dabbs, Jr. "Testosterone and Chess Competition." *Social Psychology Quarterly* 55 (1992): 70-77.

McAdam, Doug. *Political Process and the Development of Black Insurgency, 1930-1970*. Chicago: University of Chicago Press, 1982.

McAdam, Doug. *Freedom Summer*. New York: Oxford University Press, 1988.

McAdam, Doug. "Gender as a Mediator of Activist Experience: The Case ofFreedom Summer." *American Journal of Sociology* 97 (1992): 1211-1240.

McAdoo, Harriette Pipes (Ed.). *Family Ethnicity: Strength in Diversity*. Thousand Oaks, CA: Sage, 1993.

McCammon, Holly J. "From Repressive Intervention to Integrative Prevention: The U.S. State's Legal Management of Labor Militance, 1881-1978," *Social Forces* 71 (1993): 569-601.

McCammon, Holly J. "Disorganizing and Reorganizing Conflict: Outcomes of the State's Legal Regulation of the Strike since the Wagner Act." *Social Forces* 72 (1994): 1011-1049.

McCarthy, Bill, and John Hagan. "Mean Streets: The Theoretical Significance of Situational Delinquency among Homeless Youth." *American Journal of Sociology* 98 (1992): 597-627.

McCarthy, John D., and Dean R. Hoge. "The Social Construction of School Punishment: Racial Disadvantage Out of Universalistic Process." *Social Forces* 65 (1987): 1101-1119.

McCarthy, Kathleen D. *Women's Culture: American Philanthropy and Art, 1830-1930*. Chicago, IL: University of Chicago Press, 1991.

McChesney, Robert. *Telecommunications, Mass Media, and Democracy: The Battle for Control of U.S. Broadcasting, 1928-1935*. New York: Oxford University Press, 1994.

McClary, Susan. *Feminine Endings: Music, Gender, and Sexuality*. Minneapolis, MN: University of Minnesota Press, 1991.

McClelland, Katherine. "Cumulative Disadvantage Among the Highly Ambitious." *Sociology of Education* 63 (1990): 102-121.

McCormack, Marie C., and Jean Brooks-Gunn, and associates. "The Health and Developmental Status of Very-Low Birth-Weight Children at School Age." *Journal of the American Medical Association* 267 (1992): 22)4-2210.

McCormack, Thelma (Ed.). *Censorship and Libel: The Chilling Effect*. Greenwich, CT: JAI Press, 1990.

McFalls, Joseph A., Jr. "Population: A Lively Introduction." *Population Bulletin* 46 (2) (October, 1991), Washington, DC: Population Reference Bureau.

McGoldrick, Monica, and Randy Gerson. *Genograms in Family Assessment*. New York: Norton, 1985.

McGuire, Gail M., and Barbara F. Reskin. "Authority Hierarchies at Work." *Gender & Society* 7 (1993); 487-506.

McGuire, Meredith B. "Health and Spirituality as Contemporary Concerns." *Annals of the American Academy of Political and Social Science* 527 (May 1993): 144-154.

McIlwee, Judith S., and J. Gregg Robinson. *Women in Engineering: Gender, Power, and Workplace Culture*. Albany, NY: State University of New York Press, 1992.

McKenzie, Nancy F. *Beyond Crisis: Confronting Health Care in the U.S.* New York: Meridian, 1994.

McLanahan, Sara, and Gary Sandefur. *Growing Up With a Single Parent.* Cambridge, MA: Harvard, 1994.

McLeod, Jane D. "Childhood Parental Loss and Adult Depression." *Journal of Health and Social Behavior* 32 (1991): 205–220.

McNall, Scott G. *Road to Rebellion: Class Formation and Kansas Populism, 1865–1900.* Chicago: University of Chicago Press, 1988.

McPhail, Clark. *The Myth of the Madding Crowd.* Hawthorne, NY: Aldine de Gruyter, 1991.

Mead, G. H. *Mind, Self, and Society.* Chicago: University of Chicago Press, 1934.

Mead, Lawrence M. *The New Politics of Poverty: The Nonworking Poor in America.* New York: Basic Books, 1992.

Mead, Margaret. *Coming of Age in Samoa.* New York: Morrow, 1928.

Mechanic, David. "Correcting Misconceptions in Mental Health Policy." *Milbank Quarterly* (2) (1986): 203–230.

Medvedev, Grigori. *The Truth About Chernobyl.* New York: Basic Books, 1991.

Mehan, Hugh. "Understanding Inequality in Schools: The Contribution of Interpretive Studies." *Sociology of Education* 65 (1992): 1–20.

Meier, Barry. "Doctors' Investments in Home Care Grow, Raising Fears of Ethical Swamp." *New York Times*, March 19, 1993.

Melendez, Edwin, Clara Rodriguez, and Janis Barry Figuera (Eds.). *Hispanics in the Labor Force: Issues and Policies.* New York: Plenum, 1991.

Menaghan, Elizabeth G. "Role Changes and Psychological Well-Being: Variations in Effects by Gender and Role Repertoire." *Social Forces* 67 (1989): 693–714.

Mensch, D., and Denise Kandel. "Drug Use as a Risk Factor for Premarital Teen Pregnancy and Abortion in a National Sample of Young White Women." *Demography* 29 (1992): 409–416.

Mercer, Jane. *Labeling the Mentally Retarded.* Berkeley: University of California Press, 1973.

Merlo, Joan M., and Kathleen M. Smith. "The Portrayal of Gender Roles in Television Advertising: A Decade of Stereotyping." Paper presented at the annual meeting of the Society for the Study of Social Problems, Los Angeles, CA, August, 1994.

Merton, Robert K. *On the Shoulders of Giants: A Shandean Postscript* (1965). San Diego, CA: Harcourt, 1985.

Merton, Robert K. "Manifest and Latent Functions." In *Social Theory and Social Structure*, (Rev. Ed.) New York: Free Press, 1968.

Merton, Robert K. "The Matthew Effect in Science." In Norman W. Storer (Ed.), *The Sociology of Science: Theoretical and Empirical Investigations.* Chicago: University of Chicago Press, 1973.

Messeri, Peter, Merril Silverstein, and Eugene Litwak. "Choosing Optimal Support Groups: A Review and Reformulation." *Journal of Health and Social Behavior* 34 (1993): 122–137.

Messerschmidt, James W. *Masculinities and Crime.* Lanham, MD: Rowman and Littlefield, 1993.

Messner, Michael A. *Power at Play: Sports and the Problem of Masculinity.* Boston: Beacon Press, 1992.

Messner, Michael A., Margaret Carlisle Duncan, and Kerry Jensen. "Separating the Men from the Girls: The Gendered Language of Televised Sports." *Gender & Society* 7 (1993): 121–135.

Messner, Michael A., and Donald F. Sabo. *Sex, Violence, and Power in Sports: Rethinking Masculinity.* Trumansburg, NY: Crossing Press, 1994.

Messner, Steven F. "Television Violence and Violent Crime: An Aggregate Analysis." *Social Problems* 33(3) (1986): 218–235.

Messner, Steven F. "Socio-Cultural Determinants of Female Homicide Victimization and Offending: A State-Level Analysis of Gender Equality, Pornography, and Cultural Support for Violence." Paper presented at the Annual Meeting of the Eastern Sociological Society, April 1991, Providence, RI.

Messner, Steven F., and Judith R. Blau. "Routine Leisure Activities and Rates of Crimes: A Macrolevel Analysis." *Social Forces* 65 (1987): 1035–1052.

Messner, Steven F., and Scott J. South. "Interracial Homicide: A Macrostructural-Opportunity Perspective." *Sociological Forum* 7 (1992): 517–536.

Metz, Mary Haywood. *Different by Design: The Context and Character of Three Magnet Schools.* New York: Routledge & Kegan Paul, 1986.

Meyer, David S. "Institutionalizing Dissent: The United States Structure of Political Opportunity and the End of the Nuclear Freeze Movement." *Sociological Forum* 8 (1993): 157–180.

Meyer, David S., and Nancy Whittier. "Social Movement Spillover." *Social Problems* 41 (1994): 277–298.

Meyer, Madonna Harrington. "Gender, Race, and the Distribution of Social Assistance: Medicaid Use Among the Frail Elderly." *Gender & Society* 8 (1994): 8–28.

Michels, Robert. *Political Parties* (1911). Translated by Eden and Cedar Paul, New York: Collier, 1962.

Mickelson, Roslyn Arlin. "Why Does Jane Read and Write So Well? The Anomaly of Women's Achievement." *Sociology of Education* 62 (1989): 47–63.

Miethe, Terance D., Michael Hughes, and David McDowall. "Social Change and Crime Rates: An Evaluation of Alternative Theoretical Approaches." *Social Forces* 70 (1991): 165–185.

Miles, Stephen, and Alison August. "Courts, Gender, and the Right to Die." *Law, Medicine, and Health Care*, July 1990:

Milgram, Stanley. *Obedience to Authority.* New York: Harper & Row, 1974.

Mill, John Stuart. *The Subjection of Women* (1969). Toronto, CAN: University of Toronto Press, 1984.

Miller, Alan S. "Are Self-Proclaimed Conservatives Really Conservative? Trends in Attitudes and Self-Identification among the Young." *Social Forces* 71 (1992a): 195–210.

Miller, Alan S. "Predicting Nonconventional Religious Affiliation in Tokyo: A Control Theory Application." *Social Forces* 71 (1992b): 397–410.

Miller, David J., and Michael Herson (Eds.). *Research Fraud in the Behavioral and Biomedical Sciences.* New York: John Wiley & Sons, 1992.

Miller, Eleanor M. *Street Women.* Philadelphia: Temple University Press, 1986.

Miller, Gale. *Enforcing the Work Ethic: Rhetoric and Everyday Life in a Work Incentive Program.* Albany, NY: State University of New York, 1991.

Miller, Jerome G. *Last One Over the Wall: The Massachusetts Experiment in Closing Reform Schools.* Columbus, OH: Ohio State University Press, 1991.

Mills, Albert J., and Peta Tancred (Eds.). *Gendering Organizational Analysis.* Newbury Park, CA: Sage, 1992.

Mills, C. Wright. *The Power Elite.* New York: Oxford University Press, 1956.

Mills, C. Wright. *The Sociological Imagination.* New York: Oxford University Press, 1959.

Milner, Murray, Jr. "Theories of Inequality: An Overview and a Strategy for Synthesis." *Social Forces* 65 (1987): 1053–1089.

Milofsky, Carl. *Community Organizations: Studies in Resource Mobilization and Exchange.* New York: Oxford University Press, 1988.

Miner, Horace. "Body Ritual Among the Nacirema." *American Anthropologist* 58 (June 1956): 503–507.

Minkoff, Debra C. "The Organization of Survival: Women's and Racial-Ethnic Voluntarist and Activist Organizations, 1955–1985." *Social Forces* 71 (1993): 887–908.

Mintz, Beth, and Michael Schwartz. *The Power Structure of American Business.* Chicago: University of Chicago Press, 1985.

Mirowsky, John, and Catherine E. Ross. "Psychiatric Diagnosis as Reified Measurement." *Journal of Health and Social Behavior* 30 (1989): 11–25.

Mirowsky, John, and Catherine E. Ross. "Age and Depression." *Journal of Health and Social Behavior* 33 (1992): 187–205.

Mishel, Lawrence, and Paula B. Voos (Eds.). *Unions and Economic Competitiveness.* Armonk, NY: M.E. Sharpe, 1992.

Misztal, Bronislaw, and Anson Shupe (Eds.). *Religion and Politics in Comparative Perspective: Revival of Religious Fundamentalism in East and West.* Westport, CT: Praeger, 1992.

Mitchell, Neil J. *The Generous Corporation: A Political Analysis of Economic Power.* New Haven, CT: Yale University Press, 1989.

Mizruchi, Mark S. *The Structure of Corporate Political Action: Interfirm Relations and Their Consequences.* Cambridge, MA: Harvard University Press, 1992.

Moaddel, Mansoor. *Class, Politics, and Ideology in the Iranian Revolution.* New York: Columbia University Press, 1993.

Moaddel, Mansoor. "Political Conflict in the World Economy: A Cross-National Analysis of Modernization and World-System Theories." *American Sociological Review* 59 (1994): 276-303.

Moen, Phyllis. *Women's Two Roles: A Contemporary Dilemma.* Westport, CT: Greenwood, 1992.

Moghadam, Valentine M. (Ed.). *Women and Identity Politics.* Boulder, CO: Westview Press, 1993.

Moghadam, Valentine M. (Ed.). *Gender and National Identity: Women and Politics in Muslim Societies.* London, ENG: Zed Press, 1994.

Molm, Linda D. "An Experimental Analysis of Imbalance in Punishment Power." *Social Forces* 68 (1989): 178-203.

Molotch, Harvey. "The Restroom and Equal Opportunity." *Sociological Forum* 3 (1988): 128-132.

Monaghan, Peter. "Free After 6 Months: Sociologist Who Refused to Testify Is Released." *Chronicle of Higher Education,* November 11, 1993.

Monk-Turner, Elizabeth. "The Occupational Achievements of Community and Four-Year College Entrants." *American Sociological Review* 55 (1990): 719-725.

Montgomery, Kathryn C. *Target: Prime Time. Advocacy Groups and the Struggle Over Entertainment Television.* New York: Oxford University Press, 1989.

Monti, Daniel J. *A Semblance of Justice: St. Louis School Desegregation and Order in Urban America.* Columbia: University of Missouri Press, 1985.

Moore, Kristin A., and Nancy O. Snyder. "Cognitive Attainment Among Firstborn Children of Adolescent Mothers." *American Sociological Review* 56 (1991): 612-624.

Moore, Thomas S. "The Nature and Unequal Incidence of Job Displacement Costs." *Social Problems* 37 (1990): 230-242.

Moore, Timothy E. "Subliminal Delusion." *Psychology Today* July, 1985: 10-11.

Morales, Rebecca, and Frank Bonilla (Eds.). *Latinos in a Changing U.S. Economy: Comparative Perspectives on Growing Inequality.* Newbury Park, CA: Sage, 1993.

Morantz-Sanchez, Regina Markell. *Women Physicians in American Medicine.* New York: Oxford University Press, 1985.

Morgan, Leslie. *After Marriage Ends. Economic Consequences for Midlife Women.* Newbury Park, CA: Sage, 1991.

Morgan Quinto. *Crime State Rankings 1994.* Lawrence, KS: Morgan Quinto Corporation, 1994.

Morgan, S. Philip, Diane N. Lye, and Gretchen A. Condran. "Sons, Daughters, and the Risk of Marital Disruption." *American Journal of Sociology* 94 (1988): 110-129.

Morgan, S. Phillip, Antonio McDaniel, Andrew T. Miller, and Samuel H. Preston. "Racial Differences in Household and Family Structure at the Turn of the Century." *American Journal of Sociology* 98 (1993): 798-828.

Morin, Richard. "Polling—In Black and White." *Washington Post,* November 5, 1989.

Morris, Aldon D. *The Origins of the Civil Rights Movement: Black Communities Organizing for Change.* New York: Free Press, 1984.

Morris, Aldon D. "Birmingham Confrontation Reconsidered: An Analysis of the Dynamics and Tactics of Mobilization." *American Sociological Review* 58 (1993): 621-636.

Morris, Aldon D., and Carol McClurg Mueller (Eds.). *Frontiers in Social Movement Theory.* New Haven, CT: Yale University Press, 1992.

Morris, Martina, Annette D. Bernhardt, and Mark S. Handcock. "Economic Inequality: New Methods for New Trends." *American Sociological Review* 59 (1994): 205-219.

Morrison, Minion K. C. *Black Political Mobilization: Leadership, Power and Mass Behavior.* Albany: State University of New York Press, 1987.

Morrissey, Marietta. "Exploring Social Distance in Race and Ethnic Relations Courses." *Teaching Sociology* 20 (1992): 121-124.

Morrow, Lance. "The Temping of America," *Time* March 29, 1993: 40-41.

Mortimer, Jeylan T., and Jon Lorence. "Satisfaction and Involvement: Disentangling a Deceptively Simple Relationship." *Social Psychology Quarterly* 52 (1989): 249-265.

Mosher, Clayton, and John Hagan. "Constituting Class and Crime in Upper Canada: The Sentencing of Narcotics Offenders, circa 1908-1953." *Social Forces* 72 (1994): 613-641.

Mosher, William D., and William F. Pratt. "AIDS-Related Behavior Among Women 15-44 Years of Age: United States, 1988 and 1990." *Advance Data,* No. 239, December 1993. Hyattsville, MD: U.S. Department of Health and Human Services.

Moskos, Charles C. *A Call to Civic Service: National Service for Country and Community.* New York: Free Press, 1988.

Mott, Frank L. *Nationwide Study of Day Care,* reported in *USA Today,* August 12, 1991.

Mott, Frank L., and Joyce C. Abma. "Contemporary Jewish Fertility: Does Religion Make a Difference?" *Contemporary Jewry* 13 (1992): 74-94.

Mouseley, Judith A., Mary Rice, and Karen Tregenza. "Integration of Students with Disabilities into Regular Schools: Policy in Use." *Disability, Handicap & Society* 8 (1993): 59-64.

Moyers, Bill. "The Mystery of Chi." Program on Public Broadcasting System, February, 1993.

Moynihan, Daniel Patrick. *The Negro Family: The Case for National Action.* Washington, DC: U.S. Department of Labor, 1965.

Mukerji, Chandra. *From Graven Images: Patterns of Modern Materialism.* New York: Columbia University Press, 1983.

Mule, Pat, and Diane Barthel. "The Return to the Veil: Individual Autonomy vs. Social Esteem." *Sociological Forum* 7 (1992): 323-332.

Mulkey, Lynn M., Robert L. Crain, and Alexander J.C. Harrington. "One-Parent Households and Achievement: Economic and Behavioral Explanations of a Small Effect." *Sociology of Education* 65 (1992): 48-65.

Murphy, Patrick, John Williams, and Eric Dunning. *Football on Trial: Spectator Violence and Development in the Football World.* New York: Routledge, 1990.

Murray, Gerald. "Population Pressure, Land Tenure, and Voodoo: The Economics of Haitian Peasant Ritual." In Eric Ross (Ed.), *Beyond the Myths of Culture: Essays in Cultural Materialism,* pp. 295-321. New York: Academic Press, 1980.

Nadelman, Ethan A. "America's Drug Problem: A Case for Decriminalization." *Dissent,* Spring 1992: 205-212.

Nagel, Joane. "Constructing Ethnicity: Creating and Recreating Ethnic Identity and Culture." *Social Problems* 41 (1994): 152-176.

Naisbitt, John. *Megatrends: Ten New Directions Transforming Our Lives.* New York: Warner Books, 1982.

Nanda, Serena. *Cultural Anthropology,* 2nd ed. Belmont, CA: Wadsworth, 1984.

Naoi, Michiko, and Carmi Schooler. "Psychological Consequences of Occupational Conditions among Japanese Wives." *Social Psychological Quarterly* 53 (1990): 100-116.

Nardi, Peter M. "Sex, Friendship, and Gender Roles Among Gay Men." In Peter M. Nardi (Ed.), *Men's Friendships,* pp. 173-185. Newbury Park, CA: Sage, 1992.

Nasaw, David. *Going Out: The Rise and Fall of Public Amusements.* New York: Basic, 1994.

Nathanson, Constance A. *Dangerous Passage: The Social Control of Sexuality in Women's Adolescence.* Philadelphia, PA: Temple University Press, 1992.

National Federation News. *Sports Participation Survey 1990-91.* National Federation, Kansas City, MO: 1991.

National Research Council. *Women in Science and Engineering: Increasing Their Numbers in the 1990s.* Washington, DC: National Academy Press, 1992.

National Science Foundation. "The Influence of Testing on Teaching Math and Science in Grades 4-12." Washington, DC: NSF, October 1992.

National Victim Center. *National Women's Study.* Washington, DC: April 24, 1992.

Natriello, Gary, Aaron M. Pallas, and Karl Alexander. "On the Right Track? Curriculum and Academic Achievement." *Sociology of Education* 62 (1989): 109-118.

Nauta, Andre. "That They All May Be One: Can Denominations Die?" Paper presented at the 88th Annual Meeting of the American Sociological Association, Miami, Florida, August, 1993.

Neal, Marie Augusta. *A Report on the National Profile of the Third Sisters' Survey.* Boston, MA: Emanuel College, 1991.

Neckerman, Kathryn M., and Joleen Kirschenman. "Hiring Strategies, Racial Bias, and Inner-City Workers." *Social Problems* 38 (1991): 433-452.

Nee, Victor. "Social Inequalities in Reforming State Socialism: Between Redistribution and Markets in China." *American Sociological Review* 56 (1991): 267-282.

Nee, Victor, Jimmy M. Sanders, and Scott Sernau. "Job Transitions in an Immigrant Metropolis: Ethnic Boundaries and the Mixed Economy." *American Sociological Review* 59 (1994): 849- 872.

Neitz, Mary Jo. *Charisma and Community: A Study of Religious Commitment within the Charismatic Revival.* New Brunswick, NJ: Transaction Press, 1987.

Neitz, Mary Jo. "Inequality and Difference: Feminist Research in the Sociology of Religion." In William Swatos (Ed.), *A Future for Religion: New Paradigms for Social Analysis,* pp. 165-184. Newbury Park, CA: Sage, 1993.

Nelson, Elizabeth. Personal Communication. 1993.

Nelson, Mariah Burton. *The Stronger Women Get, the More Men Love Football: Sexism and the American Culture of Sports.* New York: Harcourt Brace, 1994.

Neugarten, Bernice L., and Gunhild Hagestad. "Age and the Life Course." In Robert H. Binstock and Ethel Shanas (Eds.), *Handbook of Aging and the Social Sciences,* 2nd ed. New York: Van Nostrand, 1983.

Neuman, W. Russell. *The Future of the Mass Audience.* New York: Cambridge University Press, 1991.

Neuman, W. Russell, Marion R. Just, and Ann N. Crigler. *Common Knowledge: News and the Construction of Political Meaning.* Chicago, IL: University of Chicago Press, 1992.

New York Times/CBS News Poll. "How the Public Views Gay Issues." *New York Times,* March 5, 1993.

New York Times/CBS News Poll. "Americans and Crime." *New York Times,* January 1, 1994a.

New York Times/CBS News Poll. "The Nation's Changing Concerns." *New York Times,* May 10, 1994b.

New York Times/CBS News Poll. "American Catholics: A Church Divided." *New York Times,* June 1, 1994c.

New York Times/CBS News Poll "Teenagers and Sex Roles." *New York Times,* July 11, 1994d.

New York Times. "Survey Finds Whites Retain Stereotypes of Minority Groups." January, 1991.

New York Times. "Women in Combat: How Other Nations Rank." May 2, 1993a.

New York Times. "2 Germans Tell Court They Joined Neo-Nazis Only for Friendship." May 18, 1993b.

New York Times. "Despite U.S. Campaign, A Boom in Pornography." July 4, 1993c.

New York Times. "Portrait of the Electorate: Who Voted For Whom in 1994." November 13, 1994.

Newcomb, Theodore M. *Personality and Social Change: Attitude Formation in a Student Community.* Dryden, CT: Holt, Rinehart, Winston, 1943.

Newcomb, Theodore M., Kathryn E. Koening, Richard Flacks, and Donald P. Warwick. *Persistence and Change: Bennington College and Its Students After Twenty-Five Years.* New York: John Wiley & Sons, 1967.

Newman, Katherine S. *Declining Fortunes: The Withering of the American Dream.* New York: Basic Books, 1993.

Newman, Maria. "Charismatic Movement Gains Among Catholics." *New York Times,* March 1, 1993.

Newman, Maria. "Women's Colleges Find a New Popularity." *New York Times,* January 15, 1994.

Newsweek. March 29, 1993: p. 54.

Noble, Barbara Presley. "Making a Case for Family Programs." *New York Times,* May 2, 1993.

Nock, Steven L. *The Costs of Privacy: Surveillance and Reputation in America.* New York: Aldine de Gruyter, 1993.

Nydegger, Corinne N. "Family Ties of the Aged in Cross-Cultural Perspective." In Beth B. Hess and Elizabeth W. Markson (Eds.), *Growing Old in America,* 4th ed. New Brunswick, NJ: Transaction Press, 1991.

Nyden, Philip W. *Steelworkers Rank-and-File: The Political Economy of a Union Reform Movement.* New York: Praeger, 1984.

Nyden, Philip W., and Wim Wiebel. *Challenging Uneven Development: An Urban Agenda for the 1990s.* New Brunswick, NJ: Rutgers University Press, 1991.

Oakes, Jeannie. "More than Misapplied Technology: A Normative and Political Response to Hallinan on Tracking." *Sociology of Education* 67 (1994): 84-88.

O'Connell, Martin. *Where's Papa? Fathers' Role in Child Care.* Washington, DC: Population Reference Bureau, 1993.

Odendahl, Teresa. *Charity Begins at Home: Generosity and Self-Interest Among the Philanthropic Elite.* New York: Basic Books, 1990.

Ofshe, Richard, and Margaret Singer. "Attacks on Peripheral versus Central Elements of Self and the Impact of Thought Reforming Techniques." *Cultic Studies Journal* 3 (1986): 3-24.

Ogbu, John. "Cultural Boundaries and Minority Youth Orientation Toward Work Preparation." In David Stern and Dorothy Eichorn (Eds.), *Adolescence and Work: Influences of Social Structure, Labor Markets, and Culture.* Hillsdale, NJ: Lawrence Erlbaum Associates, 1989, pp. 101-140.

O'Hare, William P. "America's Minorities - The Demographics of Diversity." *Population Bulletin* 47 (4), 1992.

O'Hare, William P., and William H. Frey. "Booming, Suburban, and Black." *American Demographics,* September, 1992.

O'Kane, James M. *The Crooked Ladder: Gangsters, Ethnicity, and the American Dream.* New Brunswick, NJ: Transaction, 1992.

Oliver, Pamela. "'If You Don't Do It, Nobody Else Will: Active and Token Contributors to Local Collective Action." *American Sociological Review* 49 (1984): 601-610.

Olneck, Michael R., and Ki-Seok Kim. "High School Completion and Men's Incomes: An Apparent Anomaly." *Sociology of Education* 62 (1989): 193-207.

Olshansky, S. Jay. "Estimating the Upper Limits to Human Longevity." *Population Today* 20 (1992): 6-8.

Olson, Daniel V.A., and Jackson W. Carroll. "Religiously Based Politics: Religious Elites and the Public." *Social Forces* 70 (1992) 765-786.

Olson, Mancur, Jr. *The Logic of Collective Action.* Cambridge, MA: Harvard University Press, 1965.

Olsson, Sven E. *Social Policy and Welfare State in Sweden.* Lund, Sweden: Arkiv, 1990.

Olzak, Susan. "Labor Unrest, Immigration, and Ethnic Conflict in Urban America." *American Journal of Sociology* 94 (1989): 1303-1333.

Olzak, Susan. *The Dynamics of Ethnic Competition and Conflict.* Stanford, CA: Stanford University Press, 1992.

Olzak, Susan, Suzanne Shanahan, and Elizabeth West. "School Desegregation, Interracial Exposure, and Antibusing Activity in Contemporary Urban America." *American Journal of Sociology* 100 (1994): 196-241.

Omi, Michael, and Howard Winant. *Racial Formation in the United States from the 1960s to the 1980s.* New York: Routledge & Kegan Paul, 1987.

Omran, Abdel R., and Farazaneh Roudi. "The Middle East Population Puzzle," *Population Bulletin* 48 (1)(1993). Washington, DC: Population Reference Bureau.

Oplinger, Jon. *The Politics of Demonology: The European Witch Craze and the Mass Production of Deviance.* Selinsgrove, PA: Susquehanna University Press, 1990.

Opp, Karl-Dieter. *The Rationality of Political Protest: A Comparative Analysis of Rational Choice Theory.* Boulder, CO: Westview, 1989.

Opp, Karl-Deiter, and Christine Gern. "Dissident Groups, Personal Networks and Spontaneous Cooperation: The East German Revolution of 1989." *American Sociological Review* 58 (1993): 659-680.

Opp, Karl-Dieter, and Wolfgang Roehl. "Repression, Micromobilization, and Political Protest." *Social Forces* 69 (1990): 521-547.

O'Rand, Angela M., and Vicky M. MacLean. "Labor Markets, Pension Rule Structure, and Retirement Benefits for Long-Term Employees." Social Forces 65 (1986): 134-141.

Orbell, John M., and Robyn M. Dawes. "Social Welfare, Cooperators' Advantage, and the Option of Not Playing the Game." *American Sociological Review* 58 (1993): 787-800.

Orcutt, James D. "Beyond the 'Exotic and the Pathologic': Alcohol Problems, Norm Qualities, and Sociological Theories of Deviance." In Paul M. Roman (Ed.), *Alcohol: The Development of Sociological Perspectives on Use and Abuse.* New Brunswick, NJ: Rutgers Center of Alcohol Studies, 1991, pp. 145-173.

Orcutt, James D., and J. Blake Turner. "Shocking Numbers and Graphic Accounts: Quantified Images of Drug Problems in the Print Media." *Social Problems* 40 (1993): 190-206.

Oren, Dan A. *Joining the Club: A History of Jews and Yale.* New Haven, CT: Yale University Press, 1985.

Orenstein, Peggy. *Schoolgirls: Young Women, Self-Esteem, and the Confidence Gap.* New York: American Association of University Women, 1994.

Orfield, Gary, and Carole Ashkinaze. *The Closing Door: Conservative Policy and Black Opportunity.* Chicago, IL: University of Chicago Press, 1991.

Orfield, Gary, with Sara Schley, Diane Glass, and Sean Reardon. *The Growth of Segregation in American Schools: Changing Patterns of Separation and Poverty Since 1968.* Alexandria, VA: National School Boards Association, 1993.

Orloff, Ann Shola. "Gender and the Social Rights of Citizenship: The Comparative Analysis of Gender Relations and Welfare States." *American Sociological Review* 58 (1993): 303-328.

Ortiz, Vilma. "Language Background and Literacy Among Hispanic Young Adults." *Social Problems* 36 (1989): 149-164.

Ostrander, Susan. *Women of the Upper Class.* Philadelphia: Temple University Press, 1984.

Overlooked Opinions. *Survey of Gay Americans.* Chicago, 1992.

Pace, Eric. "Women's Cults of Antiquity: The Veil Rises." *New York Times,* April 30, 1985.

Padgett, John F. "Review of Galaskiewicz." *Contemporary Sociology* 15 (1986): 818-821.

Palen, J. John. *The Urban World.* 4th ed. New York: McGraw-Hill, 1992.

Paloma, Margaret M. *The Assemblies of God at the Crossroads: Charisma and Institutional Dilemmas.* Knoxville, TN: University of Tennessee Press, 1989.

Pampel, Fred C., and Melissa Hardy. "Status Maintenance and Change during Old Age." *Social Forces* 73 (1994): 289-314.

Pappas, Gregory, Susan Queen, Wilbur Hadden, and Gail Fisher. "The Increasing Disparity in Mortality Between Socioeconomic Groups in the United States, 1960 and 1986." *New England Journal of Medicine* 329 (1994): 103-109.

Parcel, Toby L., and Elizabeth G. Menaghan. "Early Parental Work, Family Social Capital, and Early Childhood Outcomes." *American Journal of Sociology* 99 (1994a): 972-1009.

Parcel, Toby L., and Elizabeth G. Menaghan. *Parents' Jobs and Children's Lives.* New York: Aldine De Gruyter, 1994b.

Parenti, Michael. *Inventing Reality: The Politics of the Mass Media.* New York: St. Martins, 1985.

Park, Robert E. "Human Migration and the Marginal Man." *American Journal of Sociology* 32 (1928): 881-893.

Park, Robert E., and Ernest W. Burgess. *Introduction to the Science of Sociology.* Chicago: University of Chicago Press, 1921.

Park, Robert E., Ernest W. Burgess, and Roderick D. McKenzie (Eds.). *The City.* Chicago: University of Chicago Press, 1924.

Parkinson, C. Northcote. *Parkinson's Law* (1957). Boston: Houghton Mifflin, 1980.

Parnell, Allan M., Gray Swicegood, and Gillian Stevens. "Nonmarital Pregnancies and Marriage in the United States." *Social Forces* 73 (1994): 263-287.

Parrillo, Vincent N. *Strangers to These Shores: Race and Ethnic Relations in the United States,* 4th ed. New York: Macmillan, 1994a.

Parrillo, Vincent N. "Diversity in America: A Sociohistorical Analysis." *Sociological Forum* 9 (1994): 523-546

Parsa, Misagh. "Theories of Collective Action and the Iranian Revolution." *Sociological Forum* 3 (1988): 44-71.

Parsons, Talcott. *The Social System.* New York: Free Press, 1951.

Parsons, Talcott. "The American Family: Its Relations to Personality and the Social Structure." In Talcott Parsons and Robert F. Bales (Eds.), *Family Socialization and Interaction Process,* pp. 3-21. Glencoe, IL: Free Press, 1955.

Parsons, Talcott. "Definitions of Health and Illness in the Light of American Values and Social Structure." In E. Gartley Jaco, (Ed.), *Patients, Physicians, and Illness.* New York: Free Press, 1972: 100.

Pascarella, Ernest T., and Partik T. Terenzini. *How College Affects Students: Findings and Insights from Twenty Years of Research.* San Francisco, CA: Jossey-Bass, 1991.

Passell, Peter. "Like a New Drug, Social Programs Are Put to the Test." *New York Times,* March 9, 1993, p. C1 ff.

Pate, Antony M., and Edwin E. Hamilton. "Formal and Informal Deterrents to Domestic Violence: The Dade County Spouse Assault Experiment." *American Sociological Review* 57 (1992): 691-697.

Patterson, Charlotte J. "Children of Gay and Lesbian Parents." *Child Development* 63 (1992): 1025-1042.

Pavalko, Eliza K., Glen H. Elder, Jr., and Elizabeth C. Clipp. "Worklives and Longevity: Insights for a Life Course Perspective." *Journal of Health and Social Behavior* 34 (1993): 363-380.

Pavetti, LaDonna A. *The Dynamics of Welfare and Work: Exploring the Process By Which Young Women Work Their Way Off Welfare.* Cambridge, MA: Harvard University, John F. Kennedy School of Government, 1994.

Peak, Lois. *Learning to Go to School in Japan: The Transition from Home to Preschool Life.* Berkeley, CA: University of California Press, 1991.

Pear, Robert. "Report Says Energy Dept. Collects Information on Some Americans." *New York Times,* June 14, 1992: 37.

Pear, Robert. "Fewer Are Insured for Medical Care." *New York Times,* December 15, 1993: A24.

Pearce, Diana M. "Toil and Trouble: Women Workers and Unemployment Compensation." *Signs* 10 (1985): 439-459.

Pearce, Diana M. "On the Edge: Marginal Women Workers and Employment Policy." In Christine Bose and Glenna Spitze (Eds.), *Ingredients for Women's Employment Policy,* pp. 197-210. Albany: State University of New York Press, 1987.

Pearlin, L. I., J. T. Mullan, S. J. Semple, and M. M. Skaff. "Caregiving and the Stress Process: An Overview of Concepts and Their Measures." *Gerontologist,* 30 (1990): 583-594.

Pearlin, Leonard, and Clarice Radebaugh. "Age and Stress: Processes and Problems." In Beth B. Hess and Elizabeth W. Markson (Eds.), *Growing Old in America,* 4th ed., pp. 293-308. New Brunswick, NJ: Transaction Press, 1991.

Pease, John. "Sense of the Commoners." *American Sociologist* (November 1981): 257-271.

Peiss, Kathy. *Cheap Amusements: Working Women and Leisure in New York City, 1880 to 1920.* Philadelphia, PA: Temple University Press, 1985.

Pepinsky, Harold E. "Norwegian and Polish Lessons for Keeping Down Prison Populations." *Humanity & Society* 17 (1993): 70-89.

Pepinsky, Harold E., and Richard Quinney (Eds.). *Criminology as Peacemaking.* Bloomington, IN: Indiana University Press, 1993.

Perfecto, Ivette, and Baldemar Velasquez, "Farm Workers: Among the Least Protected." *EPA Journal* 18 (March/April 1992): 13-14.

Perman, Lauri, and Beth Stevens. "Industrial Segregation and the Gender Distribution of Fringe Benefits." *Gender & Society* 3 (1989): 388-404.

Perrow, Charles. *Normal Accidents: Living With High Risk Systems.* New York: Basic, 1984.

Perrucci, Carolyn C., Robert Perrucci, Dena B. Targ, and Harry R. Targ. *Plant Closings: International Context and Social Costs.* New York: Aldine de Gruyter, 1988.

Persell, Caroline Hodges, Sophia Catsambis, and Peter W. Cookson, Jr. "Differential Asset Conversion: Class and Gendered Pathways to Selective Colleges." *Sociology of Education* 65 (1992): 208-225.

Pescosolido, Bernice A. "Beyond Rational Choice: The Social Dynamics of How People Seek Help." *American Journal of Sociology* 97 (1992): 1096-1138.

Pescosolido, Bernice, and Sharon Georgianna. "Durkheim, Suicide, and Religion: Toward a Network Theory of Suicide." *American Sociological Review* 54 (1989): 33-48.

Peshkin, Alan. *God's Choice: The Total World of a Fundamentalist Christian School.* Chicago: University of Chicago Press, 1986.

Peshkin, Alan. *The Color of Strangers, the Color of Friends: The Play of Ethnicity in School and Community.* Chicago, IL: University of Chicago Press, 1991.

Pessen, Edward. *The Log Cabin Myth: The Social Background of the Presidents.* New Haven, CT: Yale University Press, 1984.

Peter, Lawrence, and R. Hull. *The Peter Principle.* New York: Morrow, 1969.

Peterson, Ruth D., and Lauren J. Krivo. "Racial Segregation and Black Urban Homicide." *Social Forces* 71 (1993): 1001-1026.

Petranek, Charles F. "Recruitment and Commitment." *Society*, January/February 1988, pp. 48-51.

Pettito, L.A. and P.F. Marenette. "Babbling in the Manual Mode: Evidence for the Ontogeny of Language." *Science* 251 (1991): 1493-1496.

Pfaff, William. *The Wrath of Nations: Civilization and the Furies of Nationalism.* New York: Simon & Schuster, 1993.

Pfeffer, Max J. "Low-Wage Employment and Ghetto Poverty: A Comparison of African-American and Cambodian Day-Haul Farm Workers in Philadelphia." *Social Problems* 41 (1994): 2-29.

Phelan, Thomas James. "From the Attic of the *American Journal of Sociology*: Unusual Contributions to American Sociology, 1895-1935." *Sociological Forum* 4 (1989): 71-86.

Philipson, C. *Capitalism and the Construction of Old Age.* London: Macmillan, 1982.

Phillips, David P. "The Behavioral Impact of Violence in the Mass Media: A Review of the Evidence from Laboratory and Nonlaboratory Investigation." *Sociology and Social Research* 66 (1982): 387-398.

Phillips, David P., Katherine Lesyna, and Daniel J. Paight. "Suicide and the Media." In Ronald W. Maris et al. (Eds.), *Assessment and Prediction of Suicide.* New York: Guilford, 1991.

Piette, John D., Vincent More, and Kenneth Mayer. "The Effects of Immune Status and Race on Health Service Use Among People With HIV Disease." *American Journal of Public Health* 83 (1993): 51-514.

Pihl, R.O., Jordan Peterson, and Peter Finn. "Inherited Predisposition to Alcoholism: Characteristics of Sons of Male Alcoholics." *Journal of Abnormal Psychology* 99 (1990):291-301.

Piirto, Rebecca. "New Women's Revolution." *American Demographics* (April 1991): 6.

Pincus, Fred L. "Vocational Education: More False Promises." In L. Stephen Zwerling (Ed.), *The Community College and Its Critics*, pp. 41-52. San Francisco: Jossy-Bass, 1986.

Pinderhughes, Howard. "The Anatomy of Racially Motivated Violence in New York City: A Case Study of Youth in Southern Brooklyn." *Social Problems* 40 (1993): 478-492.

Pinderhughes, Raquel Orvyn, and Joan Moore. *In the Barrios: Latinos and the Underclass Debate.* New York: Russell Sage, 1993.

Pittman, David J., and Helene R. White. *Society, Culture, and Drinking Patterns Reexamined.* New Brunswick, NJ: Rutgers Center on Alcohol, 1991.

Pitts, Victoria L., and Martin Schwartz. "Promoting Self-Blame in Hidden Rape Cases." *Humanity & Society* 17 (1993): 383-398.

Piven, Frances Fox (Ed.). *Labor Parties in Postindustrial Societies.* New York: Oxford University Press, 1992.

Plaskow, Judith. "Lesbian and Gay Rights: Asking the Right Questions." *Tikkun* March/April 1994: 31-32.

Plato. *Republic* (353BCE). New York: Modern Library, 1982.

Pleck, Joseph. *Family Supportive Employer Policies and Men's Participation.* Washington, DC: U.S. Government Printing Office, U.S. Department of Labor, Women's Bureau, 1989.

Pleck, Joseph H. "Are 'Family-Supportive' Employer Policies Relevant to Men?" In Jane C. Hood (Ed.), *Men, Work, and Family*, pp. 217-237. Newbury Park, CA: Sage, 1993.

Plotnick, Robert D. "The Effects of Attitudes on Teenage Premarital Pregnancy and Its Resolution." *American Sociological Review* 57 (1992): 800-811.

Poincaré, Jules Henri. *Science and Method* (1908). New York: Dover, 1952.

Pollak, Lauren Harte, and Peggy A. Thoits. "Processes in Emotional Socialization." *Social Psychology Quarterly* 52 (March 1989): 22-34.

Pollard, Kevin M. "Population Stabilization No Longer in Sight for U.S." *Population Today* 22 (1994): 1-2.

Pollock-Byrne, Jocelyn M. *Women, Prisons, and Crime.* Pacific Grove, CA: Brooks/Cole, 1990.

Pont, Sue-ling. "Preferential Policies and Secondary School Attainment in Peninsular Malaysia." *Sociology of Education* 66 (1993): 245-261.

Population Reference Bureau, Inc. *1994 World Population Data Sheet.* Washington, DC: Population Reference Bureau, 1994.

Portes, Alejandro, and Ruben C. Rumbaut. *Immigrant America: A Portrait.* Berkeley, CA: University of California Press, 1990.

Portes, Alejandro, and Alex Stepick. *City on the Edge: The Transformation of Miami.* Berkeley: University of California Press, 1993.

Post, David. "Educational Stratification, School Expansion, and Public Policy in Hong Kong. *Sociology of Education* 67 (1994): 121-138.

Poston, Dudley L., and Toni Falbo. "Academic Performance and Personality Traits of Chinese Children: 'Onlies' versus Others." *American Journal of Sociology* 96 (1990): 433-451.

Potuchek, Jean L. "'Sure Men and Women Should Be Equal, But...': Men and Gender Consciousness." Paper presented at the annual meeting of the Eastern Sociological Society, March 1993, Boston, MA.

Powell, Brian, and Lala Carr Steelman. "The Liability of Having Brothers." *Sociology of Education* 62 (1989): 134-147.

Power, Margaret. *The Egalitarians—Human and Chimpanzee: An Anthropological View of Social Organization.* New York: Cambridge University Press, 1991.

Powers, Ann. "No Longer Rock's Playthings." *New York Times*, February 14, 1993a.

Powers, Ann. "Here Come the Nerds, Again." *New York Times*, March 7, 1993b.

Pozanski, Kazimierz Z. (Ed.). *Constructing Capitalism: The Reemergence of Civil Society and Liberal Economy in the post-Communist World.* Boulder, CO: Westview, 1992.

Press, Andrea L. *Women Watching Television: Gender, Class, and Generation in the American Television Experience.* Philadelphia, PA: University of Pennsylvania Press, 1991.

Presser, Harriet B. "Employment Schedules Among Dual-Earner Spouses and the Division of Household Labor by Gender." *American Sociological Review* 59 (1994): 348-364.

Pressman, Harvey, and Alan Gartner. "The New Racism in Education." *Social Policy* 17 (Summer 1986): 11-15.

Preston, James. *Mother Worship: Themes and Variations.* Chapel Hill: University of North Carolina Press, 1983.

Preston, S. H. "Children and the Elderly in the U.S." *Scientific American*, 250 (6) (1984): 44-49.

Price, Jerome. *The Antinuclear Movement.* Boston: Twayne, 1982.

Prichard, Frederick N., and Jerold M. Starr. "Skinheads in New Orleans: An Inside View." *Humanity & Society* 18 (1994): 18-35.

Productive Aging News. "Referrals to Diagnostic Imaging Facilities by Owners and Nonowners, 1990, Florida, Medicare." November-December 1993: 3.

Protess, David L., Fay Lomax Cook, Jack C. Doppelt, James S. Ettema, Margaret T. Gordon, Donna R. Leff, and Peter Miller. *The Journalism of Outrage: Investigative Reporting and Agenda Building in America.* New York: Guilford, 1991.

Puette, William J. *Through Jaundiced Eyes: How the Media View Organized Labor.* Ithaca, NY: ILR Press, 1992.

Pyke, Karen D. "Women's Employment As a Gift or a Burden? Marital Power Across Marriage, Divorce, and Remarriage." *Gender & Society* 8 (1994): 73-91.

Qian, Zhenchao, and Samuel H. Preston. "Changes in American Marriage, 1972 to 1987: Availability and Forces of Attraction by Age and Education." *American Sociological Review* 58 (1993): 482-495.

Quadagno, Jill. "Race, Class, and Gender in the U.S. Welfare State: Nixon's Failed Family Assistance Plan." *American Sociological Review* 55 (1990): 11-18.

Quadagno, Jill. "Social Movements and State Transformation: Labor Unions and Racial Conflict in the War on Poverty." *American Sociological Review* 57 (1992): 616-634.

Quinn, Joseph F., and Timothy M. Smeeding. "The Present and Future Economic Well-Being of the Aged." In Richard V. Burkhauser and Dallas L. Salisbury, *Pensions in a Changing Economy.* Washington, DC: Employee Benefit Research Institute, 1993.

Quinney, Richard. *Class, State, and Crime: On the Theory and Practice of Criminal Justice.* New York: David McKay, 1977.

Quinonez, Lora Ann, and Mary Daniel Turner. *The Transformation of American Catholic Sisters.* Philadelphia, PA: Temple University Press, 1992.

Quint, Michael. "Anti-Black Bias Still Found in Mortgage Applications." *New York Times,* October 2, 1992.

Rabow, Jerome, Michael D. Newcomb, Martin A. Monto, and Anthony C. R. Hernandez. "Altruism in Drunk Driving Situations: Personal and Situational Factors in Intervention." *Social Psychology Quarterly* 53 (1990): 199-213.

Rachlin, Allan. "Ideological Hegemony and the News: A Comparison of Presentations of Strikes by Polish Solidarity and United States Postal Employees." Paper presented at the 56th annual meeting of the Eastern Sociological Society, New York, April 1986.

Raftery, Adrian E., and Michael Hout. "Maximally Maintained Inequality: Expansion, Reform, and Opportunity in Irish Education, 1921-75." *Sociology of Education* 66 (1993): 41-62.

Ragin, Charles C. (Ed.). *Issues and Alternatives in Comparable Social Research.* New York: E.J. Brill, 1991.

Ragin, Charles C., and Howard S. Becker (Eds.). *What Is a Case? Exploring the Foundations of Social Inquiry.* New York: Cambridge University Press, 1992.

Rakow, Lana F. *Gender on the Line: Women, the Telephone, and Community Life.* Urbana, IL: University of Illinois Press, 1992.

Ramirez, Anthony. "Privatizing America's Prisons, Slowly." *New York Times,* August 14, 1994.

Rank, Mark R. "Fertility among Women on Welfare: Incidence and Determinants." *American Sociological Review* 54 (1989): 296-304.

Rapping, Elayne. *Mediations: Forays into the Culture and Gender Wars.* Boston, MA: South End Press, 1994.

Raschke, Carl. *Painted Black.* New York: HarperCollins, 1990.

Rath, Julia Wally. "Adult Converts to Catholicism among African-American parents of Children in Catholic Schools." Paper presented at the 88th Annual Meeting of the American Sociological Association, Miami, Florida, August, 1993.

Rathje, William, and Cullen Murphy. *Rubbish! The Archeology of Garbage.* New York: HarperCollins, 1992.

Ray, Carol Axtell, and Roslyn Arlin Mickelson. "Corporate Leaders, Resistant Youth, and School Reform in Sunbelt City: The Political Economy of Education." *Social Problems* 37 (1990): 178-190.

Ray, Carol Axtell, and Roslyn Arlin Mickelson. "Restructuring Students for Restructured Work: The Economy, School Reform, and Non-college-bound Youths." *Sociology of Education* 66 (1993): 1-20.

Raymond, Janice G. *The Transsexual Empire: The Making of the She-Male,* 2nd ed. Williston, VT: Teachers College Press, 1994.

Redfield, Robert. "The Folk Society." *American Journal of Sociology* 52(4) (January 1947): 293-308.

Reed, Ralph, Jr. "The Religious Right Reaches Out." *New York Times,* August 22, 1993: E15.

Reilly, Mary Ellen, Bernice Lott, Donna Caldwell, and Luisa DeLuca. "Tolerance for Sexual Harassment Related to Self-Reported Sexual Victimization." *Gender & Society* 6 (1992): 122-128.

Reinharz, Shulamit. "Patriarchal Pontifications." *Society* 23 (1986): 23-28.

Reinharz, Shulamit, with Lynn Davidman. *Feminist Methods in Social Research.* New York: Oxford University Press, 1992.

Reinharz, Shulamit. *A Contextualized Chronology of Women's Sociological Work.* Women's Studies Program Working Papers Series, Brandeis University, Waltham, MA. 1993.

Reinisch, June M., Stephanie A, Sanders, Craig A. Hill, and Mary Ziemba-Davis. "High Risk Sexual Behavior Among Heterosexual Undergraduates at a Midwestern University." *Family Planning Perspectives* 24 (1992): 116-122.

Reskin, Barbara, and Irene Padovic. *Women and Men at Work.* Thousand Oaks, CA: Pine Forge, 1994.

Reskin, Barbara F., and Patricia A. Roos. *Job Queues, Gender Queues: Explaining Women's Inroads into Male Occupations.* Philadelphia, PA: Temple University Press, 1990.

Reynolds, Peter C. "Imposing a Corporate Culture." *Psychology Today,* March 1987: 33-38.

Rhim, Soon Man. "Untouchables in Japan: the Barakumin in Tokyo" paper presented at the Annual Meeting of the Eastern Sociological Society, 1993.

Rhim, Soon Man. "The Propagation of Christianity and the Paekchong Communities." In Chin Ki Su (Ed.), *The Liberation Movement for Korean Social Status.* Osaka, Japan: Buraku Liberation Research Institute, 1994, pp. 45-75.

Richardson, Bill. "More Power to the Tribes." *New York Times,* July 7, 1993.

Richardson, James T. "Battling for Legitimacy: Psychotherapy and the New Religions in America." Paper presented at the annual meeting of the Pacific Sociological Society, 1989.

Richardson, James T., Joel Best, and David G. Bromley (Eds.). *The Satanism Scare.* New York: Aldine de Gruyter, 1991.

Richardson, Laurel. "The Changing Door Ceremony: Some Notes on the Operation of Sex Roles in Everyday Life." *Urban Life and Culture* 2(4) (January 1974): 506-515.

Richardson, Lynda. "Minority Students Languish In Special Education System." *New York Times,* April 6, 1994.

Riche, Martha Farnsworth. "The Riche Report." *Population Today,* December 1993: 3.

Ridgeway, Cecilia L. "Structure, Action, and Social Psychology." *Social Psychology Quarterly* 57 (1994): 161-162.

Riedel, Marc. *Stranger Violence: A Theoretical Inquiry.* New York: Garland, 1993.

Riesman, David. *The Lonely Crowd.* New Haven, CT: Yale University Press, 1950.

Riforgiato, Leonard R. "What Really Happened at Salem." *The ECCSSA Journal* 7 (1993): 31–42.

Rigdon, Joan E. "Three Decades After the Equal Pay Act, Women's Wages Remain Far From Parity." *Wall Street Journal*, June 9, 1993: 1 ff.

Riley, Matilda White. "Aging and Social Change." In M. W. Riley (Ed.), *Aging from Birth to Death.* Boulder, CO: Westview, 1982.

Riley, Matilda White, Marilyn Johnson, and Anne Foner. *Aging and Society.* Vol. 3. *A Sociology of Age Stratification.* New York: Russell Sage, 1972.

Ringheim, Karin. *At Risk of Homelessness: The Roles of Income and Rent.* New York: Praeger, 1990.

Riordan, Cornelius. *Girls and Boys in School: Together or Separate?* New York: Teacher's College Press, 1990.

Risman, Barbara J. "Intimate Relationships from a Microstructural Perspective: Men Who Mother." *Gender & Society* 1 (1987): 6–32.

Risman, Barbara J., and Myra Marx Ferree. "Comment on Coleman's 'Rational Reconstruction of Society.'" *American Sociological Review*, 1995 (forthcoming).

Risman, Barbara J., and Pepper Schwartz. "Sociological Research on Male and Female Homosexuality." *Annual Review of Sociology* 14 (1988): 125–147.

Risman, Barbara J., and Pepper Schwartz. *Gender in Intimate Relationships: A Microstructural Approach.* Belmont, CA: Wadsworth, 1989.

Ritzer, George (Ed.). *Frontiers of Social Theory.* New York: Columbia University Press, 1990.

Ritzer, George. "The Recent History and Emerging Reality of American Sociological Theory: A Metatheoretical Interpretation." *Sociological Forum* 6 (1991): 269–287.

Ritzman, Rosemary L., and Donald Tomaskovic-Devey. "Life Chances and Support for Equality and Equity As Normative and Counternormative Distribution Rules." *Social Forces* 70 (1992).

Roach, Sharon L. "Men and Women Lawyers in In-House Legal Departments." *Gender & Society* 4 (1991): 207–219.

Robbins, Cynthia, and Steven S. Martin. "Gender, Styles of Deviance, and Drinking Problems." *Journal of Health and Social Behavior* 34 (1993): 302–321.

Robey, Bryant, Shea O. Rutstein, and Leo Morris. "The Fertility Decline in Developing Countries." *Scientific American*, December 1993: 60–70.20

Robinson, Robert V. "Structural Change and Class Mobility in Capitalist Societies." *Social Forces* 63 (1984): 51–57.

Rochon, Thomas R., and Daniel A. Mazmanian. "Social Movements and the Policy Process." *Annals of the American Academy of Political and Social Science* 528 (July 1993): 75–88.

Rockett, Ian H. R. "Population and Health: An Introduction to Epidemiology." *Population Bulletin* 49, No. 3, 1994.

Roebuck, Julian B., and Mark Hickson, III. *The Southern Redneck: A Phenomenological Class Study.* New York: Praeger, 1982.

Roemer, John. "Market Socialism: A Blueprint," *Dissent,* Fall 1991: 562–575.

Rohner, Ronald P., and Evelyn C. Rohner. *The Kwakiutl Indians of British Columbia.* NewYork: Holt, Rinehart & Winston, 1970.

Rohter, Larry. "From 6 New Benefactors, 425 College Dreams." *New York Times,* June 21, 1986, p. B1 ff.

Rojek, Chris (Ed.). *Leisure for Leisure: Critical Essays.* New York: Routledge, 1989.

Romero, Mary. *Maid in the U.S.A.* New York: Routledge, 1992.

Roof, Wade Clark. *A Generation of Seekers: The Spiritual Journeys of the Baby Boom Generation.* San Francisco, CA: HarperCollins, 1993.

Rose, Douglas (Ed.). *The Emergence of David Duke and the Politics of Race.* Chapel Hill, NC: University of North Carolina Press, 1992.

Rose, Peter I., Myron Glazer, and Penina Migdal Glazer. "In Controlled Environments: Four Cases of Intensive Resocialization." In Peter I. Rose (Ed.), *Socialization and the Life Cycle*, pp. 320–338. New York: St. Martin's Press, 1979.

Rose, Susan D. "Gender, Education and the New Christian Right." *Society*, January/February 1989, pp. 59–66.

Rosen, Ellen Israel. *Bitter Choices: Blue Collar Women in and out of Work.* Chicago: University of Chicago Press, 1987.

Rosenbaum, Emily. "The Constraints on Minority Housing Choices, New York City 1978-1987." *Social Forces* 72 (1994): 725–747.

Rosenberg, Janet, William R. F. Phillips, and Harry Perlstadt. "Now That We Are Here: Discrimination, Disparagement, and Sexual Harassment." *Gender & Society* 7 (1993): 415–433.

Rosenberg, Morris. "Self-Objectification: Relevance for the Species and for Society. "*Sociological Forum* 3 (1988): 548–565.

Rosenberg, Morris, and Howard B. Kaplan (Eds.) *Social Psychology of the Self-Concept.* Arlington Heights, IL: Harlan Davidson, 1982.

Rosenblum, Gerald, and Barbara Rubin Rosenblum. "Segmented Labor Markets in Institutions of Higher Education." *Sociology of Education* 63 (1990): 151–164.

Rosenfeld, Jeffrey. "The Intergenerational Wealth Study: An Update." Paper presented at the 62nd Annual Meeting of the Eastern Sociological Society, Arlington, VA., April, 1992.

Rosenfeld, Richard, and Steven F. Messner. "The Social Sources of Homicide in Different Types of Societies." *Sociological Forum* 6 (1991): 51–70.

Rosenfield, Sarah. "The Costs of Sharing: Wives' Employment and Husbands' Mental Health." *Journal of Health and Social Behavior* 33 (1992): 213–225.

Rosenhan, D. L. "Being Sane in Insane Places." *Science* 179(19) (January 1973): 250–258.

Rosenthal, Marilynn M., and Marcel Frankel. *Health Care Systems and Their Patients : An International Perspective.* Boulder, CO: Westview, 1992.

Rosenthal, Rob. "Homelessness and Isolation." Paper presented at the annual meeting of the Eastern Sociological Society, Baltimore, MD, March 1994.

Rosenthal, Robert, and Lenore Jacobson. *Pygmalion in the Classroom.* New York: Holt, Rinehart, and Winston, 1968.

Rosenzweig, Roy. *Eight Hours for What We Will: Workers and Leisure in an Industrial City, 1870-1920.* Cambridge, England: Cambridge University Press, 1983.

Ross, Alex. "Generation Exit." *The New Yorker*, April 25, 1994: 102–106.

Ross, Andrew. *No Respect: Intellectuals and Popular Culture.* New York: Routledge, 1989.

Ross, Catherine E. "Overweight and Depression." *Journal of Health and Social Behavior* 35 (1994): 63–78.

Ross, Catherine E., and John Mirowsky. "Households, Employment, and Sense of Control." *Social Psychology Quarterly* 55 (1992): 217–235.

Ross, Dorothy. *The Origins of American Social Science.* New York: Cambridge University Press, 1991.

Ross, H. Laurence. *Confronting Drunk Driving: Social Policy for Saving Lives.* New Haven, CT: Yale University Press, 1992.

Rossi, Alice. "A Biosocial Perspective on Parenting." *Daedalus*: 106 (1987): 1–31.

Rossi, Peter, James D. Wright, Gene A. Fisher, and Georgianna Willis. "The Urban Homeless: Estimating Composition and Size." *Science* 235 (March 13, 1987): 1336–1341.

Rothenbuhler, Eric W. "Commercial Radio and Popular Music: Processes of Selection and Factors of Influence." In James Lull (Ed.), *Popular Music and Communication*, pp. 78–95. Newbury Park, CA: Sage, 1987.

Rothfeder, Jeffrey. *Privacy for Sale: How Computerization Has Made Everyone's Private Life an Open Secret.* New York: Simon & Schuster, 1992.

Rothman, Barbara Katz. *Recreating Motherhood: Ideology and Technology in a Patriarchal Society.* New York: W. W. Norton, 1989.

Rothman, Sheila M. *Living in the Shadow of Death: Tuberculosis and the Social Experience of Illness in American History*. New York: Basic Books, 1994.

Rothman, Stanley, and Robert Lerner. "Television and the Communications Revolution." *Society*, November/December 1988, pp. 64-70.

Rothschild, Joyce, and J. Allen Whitt. *The Cooperative Workplace: Potentials and Dilemmas of Organizational Democracy and Participation*. New York: Cambridge University Press, 1987.

Rothstein, Richard. "The Myth of Public School Failure." *The American Prospect*, Spring 1993: 20-34.

Rouse, Timothy P., and N. Prabha Unnithan. "Comparative Ideologies and Alcoholism: The Protestant and Proletarian Ethics." *Social Problems* 40 (1993): 213-218.

Rubenstein, James M. *The Changing U.S. Auto Industry: A Geographical Analysis*. New York: Routledge, 1992.

Rubin, Herbert J. "There Aren't Going to Be Any Bakeries Here If There Is No Money to Afford Jellyrolls: The Organic Theory of Community Development." *Social Problems* 41 (1994): 401-424.

Rubin, Jeffrey Z., Frank J. Provenzano, and Zella Luria. "The Eye of the Beholder: Parents' Views on Sex of Newborns." In Juanita H. Williams (Ed.), *Psychology of Women*, pp. 134-141. New York: W. W. Norton, 1979.

Rubin, L., and B. Borgers. "Sexual Harassment in Universities During the 1980s." *Sex Roles* 23 (1990): 397-411.

Rubinstein, Ruth P. *Dress Codes: Meanings and Messages in American Society*. Boulder, CO: Westview Press, 1994.

Rueschemeyer, Dietrich, Evelyne Huber Stephens, and John D. Stephens. *Capitalist Development and Democracy*. Chicago: University of Chicago Press, 1992.

Rueschemeyer, Marilyn (Ed.). *Women in the Politics of Postcommunist Eastern Europe*. Armonk, NY: M.E. Sharpe, 1994.

Rule, James B. "Rationality and Nonrationality in Militant Collective Action." *Sociological Theory* 7 (1989): 145-160.

Rule, James B., and Peter Brantley. "Computerized Surveillance in the Workplace: Forms and Distribution." *Sociological Forum* 7 (1992): 405-423.

Rumbaut, Rubén G. "Origins and Destinies: Immigration to the United States Since World War II." *Sociological Forum* 9 (1994): 583-621.

Rumberger, Russell, Rita Ghatak, Gary Poulos, Philip L. Ritter, and Sanford M. Dornbusch. "Family Influences on Dropout Behavior in One California High School." *Sociology of Education* 63 (1990): 283-299.

Rummel, R.J. "Megamurders." *Society*, September/October 1992: 47-52.

Rural Sociological Task Force on Persistent Rural Poverty. *Persistent Poverty in Rural America*. Boulder, CO: Westview Press, 1993.

Russell, Diana E. H. *Making Violence Sexy: Feminist Views on Pornography*. New York: Teachers College Press, 1993.

Russell, Raymond. "Sharing the Wealth." *Society* 27 (January/February 1990): 239-257.

Russo, Nancy F., and K.L. Zierk. "Abortion, Childbearing, and Women's Well-Being." *Professional Psychology: Research and Practice* 23 (1992): 269 ff.

Ryan, Barbara. "Ideological Purity and Feminism: The U.S. Woman's Movement from 1966 to 1975." *Gender & Society* 3 (1989): 239-257.

Ryan, John. *The Production of Culture in the Music Industry: The ASCAP-BMI Controversy*. Lanham, MD: University Press of America, 1985.

Ryan, John, and Deborah A. Sim. "When Art Becomes News: Portrayals of Art and Artists on Network Television News." *Social Forces* 68 (1990): 869-889.

Rydell, C. Peter, and Susan S. Everingham. *Controlling Cocaine: Supply and Demand*. Santa Monica, CA: Rand Corporation, 1994.

Rymer, Rus. *Genie: An Abused Child's Flight From Silence*. New York: HarperCollins, 1993.

Ryscavage, Paul. "Gender-Related Shifts in the Distribution of Wages." *Monthly Labor Review* 117 (1994):3-16.

Sachar, Howard M. *A History of the Jews in America*. New York: Alfred A. Knopf, 1992.

Sack, Kevin. "Welfare Experiment Showing Signs of Success." *New York Times*, June 11, 1992.

Sacks, Karen Brodkin. *Caring by the Hour: Women, Work, and Organizing at Duke Medical Center*. Urbana: University of Illinois Press, 1988.

Sadker, Myra, and David Sadker. *Failing at Fairness: How America's Schools Cheat Girls*. New York: Charles Scribner's Sons, 1994.

Saferstein, Barry. "Interaction and Ideology at Work: A Case of Constructing and Constraining Television Violence." *Social Problems* 41 (1994): 316-344.

Sagan, Scott D. *The Limits of Safety: Organizations, Accidents, and Nuclear Weapons*. Princeton, NJ: Princeton University Press, 1993.

Sage, George H. "Sports Cartels." In D. Stanley Eitzen and George H. Sage (Eds.), *Sociology of North American Sport*, pp. 169-178. 5th ed. Dubuque, IA: W.C. Brown, 1993.

St. John, Craig, and David Rowe. "Adolescent Background and Fertility Norms: Implications for Racial Differences in Early Childbearing." *Social Science Quarterly* 71 (1990): 152-162.

Sakamoto, Arthur, and Meichu D. Chen. "Inequality and Attainment in a Dual Labor Market." *American Sociological Review* 56 (1991): 295-30.

Sampson, Robert J., and John H. Laub. *Crime in the Making: Pathways and Turning Points through Life*. Cambridge, MA: Harvard University Press, 1993.

Sanchez, Laura. "Women's Power and the Gendered Division of Domestic Labor in the Third World." *Gender & Society* 7 (1993): 434-459.

Sanchirico, Andrew. "The Importance of Small-Business Ownership in Chinese American Educational Achievement." *Sociology of Education* 64 (1991): 293-304.

Sanday, Peggy Reeves. *Fraternity Gang Rape: Sex, Brotherhood, and Privilege on Campus*. New York: New York University Press, 1990.

Sandefur, Gary D., Sara McLanahan, and Roger A. Wojtkiewicz. "The Effects of Parental Marital Status during Adolescence on High School Graduation." *Social Forces* 71 (1992): 103-121.

Sanders, Joseph. "Law and Legal Systems." In Edgar F. Borgatta and Marie L. Borgatta (Eds.), *Encyclopedia of Sociology*, pp. 1067-1075. New York: Macmillan, 1992.

Sanderson, Stephen K. *Social Evolutionism: A Cultural History*. Cambridge, MA: Blackwell, 1990.

Sandier, Simone. "Health Services Utilization and Physician Income Trends." *Health Care Financing Review*, Annual Supplement 1989: 33-48.

Sanger, David E. "Layoffs and Factory Closings Shaking the Japanese Psyche." *New York Times*, March 3, 1993.

Sanger, David E. "Job-Seeking Women in Japan Finding More Discrimination." *New York Times*, June 27, 1994.

Santiago, Anna M. "Comments from the Special Collection Editor: Global Perspectives on Social Problems—Current Issues and Debates." *Social Problems* 40 (1993): 207-211.

Sasaki, Masamichi, and Tatsuzo Suzuki. "Changes in Religious Commitment in the United States, Holland, and Japan." *American Journal of Sociology* 92 (1987): 1055-1076.

Sassen, Saskia. "Japan's Economy Turns Hollow." *New York Times*, April 11, 1992.

Sassen, Saskia. *The Global City: New York, London, Tokyo*. Princeton, NJ: Princeton University Press, 1993.

Sato, Ikuya. *Kamikaze Biker: Parody and Anomy in Affluent Japan*. Chicago, IL: University of Chicago Press, 1991.

Satow, Roberta. "New Yorkers in the Countryside: Status Conflict and Social Change." *Journal of Contemporary Ethnography* 22 (1993): 227-258.

Saunders, Janice M. "Relating Social Structural Abstractions to Sociological Research." *Teaching Sociology* 19 (1991): 270-271.

Savelsberg, Joachim J. "Knowledge, Domination, and Criminal Punishment." *American Journal of Sociology* 99 (1994): 911-943.

Sayle, Murray. "How to Marry a Mikado." *The New Yorker*, May 10, 1993: 43-52.

Scarce, Ric. "Letter." *ASA Footnotes*, Fall, 1993.

Schaie, K. Werner. "The Course of Adult Development." *American Psychologist* 49 (1994): 304-314.

Schaler, Jeffrey A. "Drugs and Free Will." *Society* September/October 1991: 42-49.

Scheff, Thomas J. *Being Mentally Ill: A Sociological Theory.* Chicago: Aldine, 1966.

Scheff, Thomas J. "Shame and Conformity: The Difference-Emotion System." *American Sociological Review* 53 (June 1988): 395-406.

Scheff, Thomas J., and Suzanne M. Retzinger. *Emotions and Violence: Shame and Rage in Destructive Conflicts.* Lexington, Mass: Lexington Books, 1991.

Schmalz, Jeffrey. "Poll Finds an Even Split on Homosexuality's Cause." *New York Times*, March 5, 1993.

Schmemann, Serge. "Religion Returns to Russia, With a Vengeance." *New York Times,* July 28, 1993.

Schmitt, Eric. "Military Struggling to Stem and Increase in Family Violence." *New York Times,* May 23, 1994.

Schnaiberg, Allan, and Sheldon Goldenberg. "From Empty Nest to Crowded Nest; The Dynamics of Incompletely-Launched Young Adults." *Social Problems* 36 (1989): 251-269.

Schnaiberg, Allan, and Kenneth Alan Gould. *Environment and Society: The Enduring Conflict.* New York: St. Martin's Press, 1994.

Schneider, Barbara, and James S. Coleman (Eds.). *Parents, Their Children, and Schools.* Boulder, CO: Westview Press, 1993.

Schoen, Robert, John Wooldredge, and Barbara Thomas. "Ethnic and Educational Effects on Marriage Choice." *Social Science Quarterly* 70 (1989): 617-630.

Schoenborn, Charlotte A., Shannon L. Marsh, and Ann M. Hardy. "AIDS Knowledge and Attitudes for 1992," *Advance Data* Number 243. U.S. Department of Health and Human Services, National Center for Health Statistics. Hyattsville, MD, 1994.

Schoenherr, Richard A., and Lawrence A. Young. *Full Pews and Empty Altars: Demographics of the Priest Shortage in United States Catholic Dioceses.* Madison, WI: University of Wisconsin Press, 1993.

Schor, Juliet B. *The Overworked American: The Unexpected Decline of Leisure.* New York: Basic Books, 1992.

Schroer, Todd. "The Emergence of Skinhead Subcultures in the United States, Great Britain, and the World." Paper presented at the annual meeting of the Society for the Study of Social Problems, Miami Beach, Florida, August, 1993.

Schudson, Michael. *Watergate in American Memory: How We Remember, Forget, and Reconstruct the Past.* New York: Basic Books, 1992.

Schulenberg, John, Jerald G. Backman, Patrick M. O'Malley, and Lloyd D. Johnston. "High School Educational Success and Subsequent Substance Use: A Panel Analysis Following Adolescents into Young Adulthood." *Journal of Health and Social Behavior* 35 (1994): 45-62.

Schuman, Howard, and Jacqueline Scott. "Generations and Collective Memories." *American Sociological Review* 54 (1989): 359-381.

Schutt, Russell K. "Craft Unions and Minorities: Determinants of Change in Admission Practices." *Social Problems* 34 (1987): 388-400.

Schwabe, Annette, and Beth Rushing. "Effects of National Health Care Structure on Women's Health." Paper presented at the annual meeting of the Society for the Study of Social Problems, Los Angeles, CA, August, 1994.

Schwalbe, Michael L., and Clifford L. Staples. "Gender Differences in Sources of Self-Esteem." *Social Psychology Quarterly* 54 (1991): 158-168.

Schwartz, Ira M. and Associates. *Combatting Juvenile Crime: What the Public Really Wants.* Ann Arbor, MI: Center for the Study of Youth Policy, 1992.

Schwartz, Michael (Ed.). *The Structure of Power in America: The Corporate Elite as a Ruling Class.* New York: Holmes & Meier, 1987.

Schwartz, Pepper. *Peer Marriage: How Love Between Equals Really Works.* New York: Free Press, 1994.

Schwartz, Sharon, Bruce G. Link, Bruce P. Dohrenwend, Guedalia Naveh, Itzhak Levav, and Patrick Shrout. "Separating Class and Ethnic Prejudice: A Study of North African and European Jews in Israel." *Social Psychology Quarterly* 54 (1991): 287-298.

Schwartz, William A., and Charles Derber, with Gordon Fellman, William Gamson, Morris S. Schwartz, and Patrick W. Withen. *The Nuclear Seduction: Why the Arms Race Doesn't Matter—And What Does.* Berkeley, CA: University of California Press, 1990.

Schwarz, John E., and Thomas J. Volgy. *The Forgotten Americans.* New York: W.W. Norton, 1992.

Schweinhardt. L.J., H.V. Barnes, and D.P. Weikart. *Significant Benefits: The High/Scope Perry PreSchool Study Through Age 27.* Ypsilanti, MI: High/Scope Press, 1993.

Scimecca, Joseph A. *Society and Freedom: An Introduction to Humanist Sociology.* Chicago, IL: Nelson Hall, 1995.

Scott, James C. *Domination and the Arts of Resistance: Hidden Transcripts.* New Haven, CT: Yale University Press, 1990.

Scott, Richard I., and Cheryl A. Wehler. "Insufficiency of Food and Insufficiency of Income: A Reexamination of the Federal Poverty Index." Paper presented at the annual meeting of the Society for the Study of Social Problems, Pittsburgh, PA, August, 1992.

Scott, Wilbur J., and Sandra Carson Stanley (Eds.). *Gays and Lesbians in the Military: Issues, Concerns, and Contrasts.* New York: Aldine de Gruyter, 1994.

Scoville, James G. (Ed.). *Status Influences in the Third World Labor Markets: Caste, Gender, and Custom.* New York: Walter de Gruyter, 1991.

Scritchfield, Shirley A., and Julie A. Maskar. "Gender Traditionality and Perceptions of Date Rape." Paper presented at the 84th annual meeting of the American Sociological Association, San Francisco, August 1989.

Scully, Diana. *Understanding Sexual Violence: A Study of Convicted Rapists.* Boston: Unwin Hyman, 1990.

Scully, Diana. *Men Who Control Women's Health: The Miseducation of Obstetrician-Gynecologists.* Willeston, VT: Teacher's College Press, 1994.

Sebold, Hans. "Adolescents' Shifting Orientation Toward Parents and Peers: A Curvilinear Trend Over Recent Decades." *Journal of Marriage and the Family*, February 1986, pp. 5-13.

Seccombe, Karen, and Leonard Beeghley. "Gender and Medical Insurance: A Test of Human Capital Theory." *Gender & Society* 6 (1992): 283-300.

Seeman, Melvin. "The Signals of '68: Alienation in Pre-Crisis France." *American Sociological Review* 37 (3) (1972): 385-402.

Segal, David R. *Recruiting for Uncle Sam: Citizenship and Military Manpower Policy.* Lawrence: University Press of Kansas, 1989.

Segal, Lynne, and Mary McIntosh (Eds.). *Sex Exposed: Sexuality and the Pornography Debate.* New Brunswick, NJ: Rutgers University Press, 1993.

Segal, Lynne. *Slow Motion: Changing Masculinities, Changing Men.* New Brunswick, NJ: Rutgers University Press, 1990.

Segal, Mady Wechsler. "The Social Construction of Women's Roles: Past, Present, and Future." Forthcoming in *Gender & Society* 1995.

Segura, Denise A. "Chicanas in White Collar Jobs: Gender/ Race-Ethnic Dilemmas and Affirmations." Paper presented at the Annual Meeting of the American Sociological Association, Miami, Florida, August 1993.

Segura, Denise A., and Jennifer L. Pierce. "Chicana/o Family Structure and Gender Personality: Chodorow, Familism, and Psychoanalytic Sociology Revisited." *Signs* 19 (1993): 162-191.

Seidman, Steven. "The End of Sociological Theory: The Postmodern Hope." *Sociological Theory* 9 (1991): 131-146.

Seidman, Steven. *Embattled Eros: Sexual Politics and Ethics in Contemporary America.* New York: Routledge, 1992.

Selby, Henry A., Arthur D. Murphy, and Stephen A. Lorenzen, with Ignacio Cabrera, Aida Castenada, and Ignacio Ruiz Love. *The Mexican Urban Household: Organizing for Self Defense.* Austin, TX: University of Texas Press, 1990.

Selk, Randall L., James A. Wells, and David Wypij. "Prevalence of Homosexual Behavior and Attraction in the United States, United Kingdom, and France: Results of Population-Based Studies." *Archives of Sexual Behavior* 24 (1995): forthcoming.

Seltzer, Judith A., and Debra Kalmuss. "Socialization and Stress Explanations for Spouse Abuse." *Social Forces* 67 (1988): 473-491.

Sen, Amartya. "More Than 100 Million Women Are Missing." *New York Review of Books,* December 20, 1990: 61-66.

Sen, Amartya. "Indian State Cuts Population Without Coercion." *New York Times,* January 4, 1994.

Sesser, Stan. "Reporter at Large: Logging in the Rain Forest." *The New Yorker,* May 27, 1991: 42-67.

Shanley, Mary Lyndon. "Surrogate Mothering and Women's Freedom: A Critique of Contracts for Human Reproduction." *Signs* 18 (1993): 618-639.

Shapiro, Susan P. "Collaring the Crime, Not the Criminal: Reconsidering the Concept of White-Collar Crime." *American Sociological Review* 55 (1990): 346-365.

Shavit, Yossi. "Segregation, Tracking, and the Educational Attainment of Minorities: Arabs and Oriental Jews in Israel." *American Sociological Review* 55 (1990): 115-126.

Shavit, Yossi, and Hans-Peter Blossfeld (Eds.). *Persistent Inequality: Changing Educational Attainment in Thirteen Countries.* Boulder, CO: Westview Press, 1993.

Shavit, Yossi, and Jennifer L. Pierce. "Sibship Size and Educational Attainment in Nuclear and Extended Families: Arabs and Jews in Israel." *American Sociological Review* 56 (1991): 321-330.

Sheehan, Helen E. *Toxic Circles: Environmental Hazards from the Workplace into the Community.* New Brunswick, NJ: Rutgers University Press, 1993.

Shelton, Beth Anne, and Juanita Firestone. "Household Labor Time and the Gender Gap in Earnings." *Gender & Society* 3 (1989): 105-112.

Shenon, Philip. "Saipan Sweatshops Are No American Dream." *New York Times,* July 18, 1993.

Shenon, Philip. "In Isolation, Papua New Guinea Falls Prey to Foreign Bulldozers." *New York Times,* June 5, 1994.

Sheperd, John. *Music as Social Text.* Cambridge, MA: Polity Press, 1991.

Sher, Kenneth J. *Children of Alcoholics: A Critical Appraisal of Theory and Research.* Chicago, IL: University of Chicago Press, 1991.

Sherif, M., O. Harvey, B. White, W. Hood, and C. Sherif. *Intergroup Conflict and Cooperation: The Robber's Cave Experiment.* Norman, OK: University of Oklahoma, 1961.

Sherkat, Darren E., and T. Jean Blocker. "The Political Development of Sixties' Activists: Identifying the Influence of Class, Gender, and Socialization on Protest Participation." *Social Forces* 72 (1994): 821-842.

Sherkat, Darren E., and Christopher G. Ellison. "The Politics of Black Religious Change: Disaffiliation from Black Mainline Denominations." *Social Forces* 70 (1991): 431-454.

Sherman, Arloz. "Children's Defense Fund Reports on Children in Rural America." *Family Resource Coalition Report,* No. 1, 1992, pp. 2-3.

Sherman, Lawrence W., Douglas A. Smith, with Janell D. Schmidt and Dennis P. Rogan. "Crime, Punishment, and Stake in Conformity: Legal and Informal Control of Domestic Violence." *American Sociological Review* 57 (1992): 680-690.

Sherman, Suzanne. *Lesbian and Gay Marriage: Private Commitments, Public Ceremonies.* Philadelphia, PA: Temple University Press, 1992.

Shibamoto, Janet S. "Japanese Sociolinguistics." *American Review of Anthropology* 16 (1987): 261-278.

Shils, Edward A. "Primary Groups in the American Army." In Robert K. Merton and Paul Lazarsfeld (Eds.), *Continuities in Social Research.* Glencoe, IL: Free Press, 1950.

Shilts, Randy. *Conduct Unbecoming: Lesbians and Gays in the U.S. Military, Vietnam to the Persian Gulf.* New York: St. Martin's Press, 1993.

Shively, JoEllen. "Cowboys and Indians: Perceptions of Western Films Among American Indians and Anglos." *American Sociological Review* 57 (1992): 725-734.

Shorter, Edward. *From Paralysis to Fatigue: A History of Psychosomatic Illness in the Modern Era.* New York: Free Press, 1991.

Shostak, Arthur. *Robust Unionism.* Ithaca, NY: ILR Press, 1990.

Shupe, Anson. "Pitchmen of the Satan Scare." *The Wall Street Journal,* March 9, 1990: A12.

Shweder, Richard A. "What Do Men Want? A Reading List for the Male Identity Crisis." *New York Times Book Review,* January 9, 1994: 3ff.

Sieber, Sam. *Fatal Remedies.* New York: Plenum, 1981.

Sigelman, Lee, and Susan Welch. "The Contact Hypothesis Revisited: Black-White Interaction and Positive Racial Attitudes." *Social Forces* 71 (1993): 781-795.

Silver, Hilary. "Homework and Domestic Work." *Sociological Forum* 8 (1993): 181-204.

Silver, Hilary, and Frances Goldscheider. "Flexible Work and Housework: Work and Family Constraints on Women's Domestic Labor." *Social Forces* 72 (1994): 1103-1119.

Silvestri, George T. "Occupational Employment: Wide Variations in Growth." *Monthly Labor Review* 116 (November 1993): 58-86.

Simmel, Georg. (1902) *The Sociology of Georg Simmel.* Translated by Kurt H. Wolff. New York:Free Press, 1950.

Simon, Robin W. "Parental Role Strains, Salience of Parental Identity, and Gender Differences in Psychological Distress." *Journal of Health and Social Behavior* 33 (1992): 25-35.

Simon, William, and John H. Gagnon. "Sexual Scripts: Permanence and Change." *Archives of Sexual Behavior* 15 (1986): 97-120.

Simonds, Wendy. *Women and Self-Help Culture: Reading Between the Lines.* New Brunswick, NJ: Rutgers University Press, 1992.

Simpson, Ida Harper, David Stark, and Robert A. Jackson. "Class Identification Processes of Married Working Men and Women." *American Sociological Review* 53 (1988): 284-293.

Singh, Jitendra V. (Ed.). *Organizational Evolution: New Directions.* Newbury Park, CA: Sage, 1990.

Skocpol, Theda. *States and Social Revolutions: A Comparative Analysis of France, Russia, and China.* Cambridge: Cambridge University Press, 1979.

Skocpol, Theda. *Protecting Soldiers and Mothers: The Political Origins of Social Policy in the United States.* Cambridge, MA: Harvard University Press, 1993.

Skolnick, Arlene. *Embattled Paradise: The American Family in an Age of Uncertainty.* New York, Basic Books, 1991.

Skolnick, Arlene. *The Intimate Environment,* 5th ed. New York: HarperCollins, 1992.

Skolnick, Jerome H., and James J. Fyfe. *Above the Law: Police and the Excessive Use of Force.* New York: Free Press, 1993.

Slater, Philip E. "On Social Regression." *American Sociological Review* 28 (1963): 339-364.

Sloane, Leonard. "Orwellian Dream Come True: A Badge That Pinpoints You." *New York Times,* September 12, 1992: 11.

Smelser, Neil J. "Toward a General Theory of Social Change." In Neil J. Smelser (Ed.), *Essays in Sociological Explanation.* Englewood Cliffs, NJ: Prentice-Hall, 1968.

Smith, Christopher E. *Courts and the Poor.* Chicago, IL: Nelson-Hall, 1991.

Smith, David A., and Douglas R. White. "Structure and Dynamics of the Global Economy: Network Analysis of International Trade, 1965-1980." *Social Forces,* 1992.

Smith, Michael D. "Enhancing the Quality of Survey Data on Violence Against Women." *Gender & Society* 8 (1994): 109-127.

Smith, Richard A. "Creating Stable Racially Integrated Communities: A Review." *Journal of Urban Affairs*. Vol. 15 Number 2, 1993, pp. 115-140.

Smith, Steven Rathgeb, and Michael Lipsky. *Nonprofits for Hire: The Welfare State in the Age of Contracting*. Cambridge, MA: Harvard University Press, 1993.

Smith, Thomas Ewin. "Academic Achievement and Teaching Younger Siblings." *Social Psychology Quarterly* 53 (1990): 352-363.

Smith, Thomas Ewin. "Gender Differences in the Scientific Achievement of Adolescents: Effects of Age and Parental Separation." *Social Forces* 71 (1992): 469-484.

Smith, Timothy K. "Players Charge NFL With Trying End Run On Disability Benefits." *Wall Street Journal,* December 7, 1992.

Smith, Tom W. "Sexual and Reproductive Morality." In Richard Niemi, John Mueller, and Tom W. Smith (Eds.), *Trends in Public Opinion: A Compendium of Survey Data*. Westport, CT: Greenwood, 1989.

Smith, Tom W. *General Social Survey*. Chicago: National Opinion Research Center, October, 1993.

Smith-Lovin, Lynn, and Charles Brody. "Interruptions in Group Discussions: The Effects of Gender and Group Composition." *American Sociological Review* 54 (1989): 424-435.

Smock, Pamela J. "Gender and the Short-Run Economic Consequences of Marital Disruption." *Social Forces* 73 (1994): 243-262.

Smock, Pamela J., and Franklin D. Wilson. "Desegregation and the Stability of White Enrollments: A School-Level Analysis, 1968-84." *Sociology of Education* 64 (1991): 278-292.

Smothers, Ronald. "For Black Farmers, Extinction Seems to Be Near." *New York Times*, August 3, 1992, p. A10.

Snarey, John. "A Question of Morality." *Psychological Bulletin* 97 (1987): 202-232.

Snarey, John. *How Fathers Care For the Next Generation: A Four-Decade Study*. Cambridge, MA: Harvard University Press, 1993.

Snider, Laureen. *Bad Business: Corporate Crime in Canada*. Scarborough, CN: Nelson Canada, 1993.

Snipp, C. Matthew. *American Indians: The First of This Land*. New York: Russell Sage Foundation, 1989.

Snow, David A., and Leon Anderson. *Down on Their Luck: A Study of Homeless Street People*. Berkeley: University of California Press, 1993.

Snyder, Eldon E., and Ronald Ammons. "Baseball's Emotion Work: Getting Psyched to Play." *Qualitative Sociology* 16 (1993):111-132.

Sobol, Richard B. *Bending the Law: The Story of the Dalkon Shield Bankruptcy*. Chicago, IL: University of Chicago Press, 1991.

Social Policy. "Myles Horton and the Highlander Folk School." Winter, 1991.

Sokoloff, Natalie J. *Black Women and White Women in the Professions: Occupational Segregation by Race and Gender, 1960-1980*. New York: Routledge, 1992.

Solomon, Norman. "The Media Protest Too Much." *New York Times*, May 21, 1991, p. A-31.

Sommers, Paul M. "An Empirical Note on Salaries in Major League Baseball." *Social Science Quarterly* 71 (1990): 861-867.

Sorensen, Annemette, and Sara McLanahan. "Married Women's Economic Dependency, 1940-1980." *American Journal of Sociology* 93 (1987): 659-687.

Sorokin, Pitirim A. *Social and Cultural Dynamics*. New York: American Book, 1941.

Sosin, Michael R. "Homelessness and Vulnerable Meal Program Users: A Comparison Study." *Social Problems*, Vol. 39:2, May, 1992, pp. 170-188.

Soule, Sarah A. "Populism and Black Lynching in Georgia, 1890-1900." *Social Forces* 71 (1992): 431-449.

South, Scott J., and Richard B. Felson. "The Racial Patterning of Rape." *Social Forces* 69 (1990): 71-93.

South, Scott J., and Kim M. Lloyd. "Marriage Opportunities and Family Formation: Further Implications of Unbalanced Sex Ratios." *Journal of Marriage and the Family* 54 (1992): 440-451.

South, Scott J., and Glenna Spitze. "Determinants of Divorce Over the Marital Life Course." *American Sociological Review* 51 (1986): 583-590.

South, Scott J., and Glenna Spitze. "Housework in Marital and Non-marital Households." *American Sociological Review* 59 (1994) 327-347.

Spade, Joan Z. "Occupational Structure and Men's and Women's Parental Values." Paper presented at the 78th annual meeting of the American Sociological Association, Detroit, August 1983.

Spade, Joan Z. "Wives' and Husbands' Perceptions of Why Wives Work." *Gender & Society* 8 (1994): 170-188.

Spain, Daphne. *Gendered Spaces*. Chapel Hill, NC: University of North Carolina Press, 1992.

Spalter-Roth, Roberta M., and Heidi I. Hartmann. "The Clinton Round: An Analysis of the Impact of Current Proposals to 'Free' Single Mothers from Welfare Dependence." Paper presented at the annual meeting of the American Sociological Association, Los Angeles, CA, August, 1994.

Specter, Michael. "Soaring Unemployment is Spreading Fear in Russia." *New York Times*, May 8, 1994a.

Specter, Michael. "New Moscow Mob Terror: Car Bombs." *New York Times*, June 10, 1994b.

Spence, Gerry. *With Justice for None: Destroying an American Myth*. New York: Times Books, 1989.

Spencer, Herbert. *The Social Organism*. London: Greenwood, 1860.

Spencer, Martin E. "The Imperfect Empiricism of the Social Sciences." *Sociological Forum* 2 (1987): 331-372.

Spengler, Oswald. *The Decline and Fall of the West*. New York: Alfred A. Knopf, 1928.

Sperber, Murray A. *College Sports, Inc.: The Athletic Department vs. the University*. New York: Henry Holt & Co., 1990.

Spickard, Paul R. *Mixed Blood: Intermarriage and Ethnic Identity in Twentieth-Century America*. Madison, WI: University of Wisconsin Press, 1991.

Sprague, Joey. "Gender, Class, and Political Thinking." *Research in Political Sociology*, 5 (1991): 111-139.

Sprague, Joey, and Mary Zimmerman. "Overcoming Dualisms: A Feminist Agenda for Sociological Methodology." In Paula England (Ed.), *Theory on Gender/Feminism on Theory*, pp. 255-280. New York: Aldine de Gruyter, 1992.

Spring, Jim. "Nine Ways to Play." *American Demographics*, May 1992: 26-33.

Squires, Gregory D., William Velez, and Karl E. Taeuber. "Insurance Redlining, Agency Location, and the Process of Urban Disinvestment." *Urban Affairs Quarterly*, Vol. 26, No. 4, June, 1991.

Stack, Steven. "Publicized Executions and Homicide: 1950-1980." *American Sociological Review* 52 (1987a): 532-540.

Stack, Steven. "Celebrities and Suicide: A Taxonomy and Analysis, 1948-1983." *American Sociological Review* 52 (1987b): 401-412.

Stack, Steven, and Jim Gundlach. "The Effect of Country Music on Suicide." *Social Forces* 71 (1992): 211-218.

Stage, F. K., and D. R. Hossler. "Differences in Family Influences on College Attendance Plans for Male and Female Ninth Graders." Paper presented at the annual meeting of the American Educational Research Association, New Orleans, 1988.

Staggenborg, Suzanne. "The Consequences of Professionalization and Formalization in the Pro-Choice Movement." *American Sociological Review* 53 (1988): 586-606.

Staples, Brent. "Bottom-Up the System." *Social Policy* 19 (1989): 34-38.

Starr, Paul. *The Transformation of American Medicine*. New York: Basic Books, 1982.

Staudohar, Paul D., and James A. Mangan (Eds.). *The Business of Professional Sports*. Urbana, IL: University of Illinois Press, 1991.

Steelman, Lala Carr, and Brian Powell. "Doing the Right Thing: Race and Parental Locus of Responsibility for Funding College." *Sociology of Education* 66 (1993): 223-24

Stein, Arlene. "Three Models of Sexuality: Drives, Identities, and Practices." *Sociological Theory* 7 (1989): 1–13.

Stein, Peter J. "The Diverse World of Single Adults." In James M. Henslin (Ed.) *Marriage and Family in the Modern World.* New York: Macmillan, 1989.

Stein, Peter J. *The Work and Family Experiences of Two Earner Families and Corporate Policy.* Center for Research and Education in the Workplace, Working Paper #9. Philadelphia: University of Pennsylvania Press, 1989.

Stein, Peter J., and Steven Hoffman. "Sports and Male Role Strain." In Donald Sabo and Ross Runfola (Eds.), *Jock: Sports and Male Identity*, pp. 53–74. Englewood Cliffs, NJ: Prentice-Hall, 1980.

Steinberg, Ronnie J. "Social Construction of Skill: Gender, Power, and Comparable Worth." *Work and Occupations* 17 (1990): 449–482.

Steinberg, Stephen. *The Ethnic Myth.* New York: Atheneum, 1981.

Stepan-Norris, Judith, and Maurice Zeitlin. "'Red' Unions and 'Bourgeois' Contracts?" *American Journal of Sociology* 96 (1991): 1151–1200.

Stephen, Elizabeth H., Vicki A. Freedman, and Jennifer Hess, Paper presented at the annual meeting of the Population Association of America, Denver, CO, 1992, cited in *Numbers News,* June 1992:5.

Sterngold, James. "Life In a Box: Japanese Question Fruits of Success." *New York Times,* January 2, 1994.

Stevens, Gillian. "Propinquity and Educational Homogamy." *Sociological Forum* 6 (1991): 715–726.

Stevens, Gillian, Dawn Owens, and Eric Schaefer. "Physical Attractiveness and Education in Marriage Choices." *Social Psychology Quarterly* 53 (1990): 62–70.

Stevenson, David Lee, and David P. Baker. "Shadow Education and Allocation in Formal Schooling: Transition to University in Japan." *American Journal of Sociology* 97 (1992): 1639–1657.

Stinchcombe, Arthur L. *Information and Organizations.* Berkeley, CA: University of California Press, 1990.

Stokes, Joseph P., and David J. McKirnan. "Estimating the Prevalence of Homosexual Behavior." *Family Planning Perspectives* 25 (1993): 184–5.

Stoll, David. *Is Latin America Turning Protestant? The Politics of Evangelical Growth.* Berkeley, CA: University of California Press, 1990.

Stoller, E. P. "Exchange Patterns in the Informal Support Networks of the Elderly: The Impact of Reciprocity on Morale." *Journal of Marriage and the Family* 47 (1985): 335–342.

Stoller, E. P., and K. L. Pugliesi. "Informal Networks of Community-Based Elderly: Changes in Composition Over Time." *Research on Aging* 10 (4) (1988), 499–516.

Stolzenberg, Ross M. "Educational Continuation by College Graduates." *American Journal of Sociology* 99 (1994): 1042-1077.

Stombler, Mindy. "'Buddies' or 'Slutties': The Collective Reputation of Fraternity Little Sisters." *Gender & Society* 8 (1994): 297–323.

Stone, Elizabeth. *Black Sheep and Kissing Cousins: How Our Family Stories Shape Us.* New York: Penguin Books, 1988.

Stouffer, Samuel, et al. *The American Soldier: Combat and Its Aftermath—Social Studies in Social Psychology in World War II,* Vol. 2. Princeton, NJ: Princeton University Press, 1949.

Straus, Murray A. "Sociological Research and Social Policy: The Case of Family Violence." *Sociological Forum* 7 (1992): 211–237.

Straus, Murray A., and Richard J. Gelles. *Physical Violence in American Families: Risk Factors and Adaptations to Violence in 8,145 Families.* New Brunswick, NJ: Transaction, 1989.

Straus, Murray A., and Holley S. Gimpel. "Corporal Punishment by Parents and Economic Achievement: A Theoretical Model and Some Preliminary Empirical Data." Paper presented at the annual meeting of the American Sociological Association, Pittsburgh, PA, August, 1992.

Street, Debra. "Maintaining the Status Quo: The Impact of Old Age Interest Groups on the Medicare Catastrophic Coverage Act of 1988." *Social Problems* 40 (1993): 431–444.

Strum, Charles. "Schools' Tracks and Democracy." *New York Times* April 1, 1993: B1.

Strum, Shirley C. *Almost Human: A Journey into the World of Baboons.* New York: Random House, 1988.

Subotnik, Rose R. *Developing Variations: Style and Ideology in Western Music.* Minneapolis, MN: University of Minnesota Press, 1991.

Suchman, Mark C., and Donna P. Eyre. "Military Procurement as Rational Myth: Notes on the Social Construction of Weapons Proliferation." *Sociological Forum* 7 (1992): 137–161.

Suffian, Abu Jafar Mohammad. "A Multivariate Analysis of the Determinants of Urban Quality of Life in the World's Largest Metropolitan Areas." in *Urban Studies,* Vol. 30, No. 8, 1993.

Summers, Anita (Ed.). *Urban Change in the United States and Western Europe: Comparative Analysis and Policy.* Washington, DC: Urban Institute, 1993.

Sumner, William Graham. *Folkways* (1906). Boston: Ginn, 1940.

Sutherland, Edwin H. *Principles of Criminology.* Philadelphia: Lippincott, 1939.

Sutton, John R. "The Political Economy of Madness: The Expansion of the Asylum in Progressive America." *American Sociological Review* 56 (1991): 665–678.

Svikis, Dace S., Matt McGue, and Roy W. Pickens. "Sex and Age Effects on the Inheritance of Alcohol Problems: A Twin Study." *Journal of Abnormal Psychology* 101 (1992):3-18.

Swanson, Guy E. *Ego Defenses and the Legitimation of Behavior.* New York: Cambridge University Press, 1988.

Swazey, Judith P., Melissa S. Anderson, and Karen Seashore Louis. "Ethical Problems in Academic Research." *American Scientist* 81 (1993): 542–553.

Sweeney, Paul. "Corporate Giving Goes Creative." *New York Times,* May 15, 1994.

Sweeney, Terrance. *A Church Divided: The Vatican versus American Catholics.* Buffalo, NY: Prometheus Books, 1992.

Swidler, Ann. "Culture in Action: Symbols and Strategies." *American Sociological Review* 51 (April 1986): 273–286.

Szasz, Thomas. *A Lexicon of Lunacy: Metaphoric Malady, Moral Responsibility, and Psychiatry.* New Brunswick, NJ: Transaction, 1993.

Szelenyi, Szonja. "Economic Subsystems and the Occupational Structure: A Comparison of Hungary and the United States." *Sociological Forum* 7 (1992): 563–586.

Tagliabue, John. "The New Hitler Youth Are Troubling Germany." *New York Times,* May 15, 1993.

Takeuchi, David T., Khanh-Van T. Bui, and Lauren Kim. "The Referral of Minority Adolescents to Community Health Centers." *Journal of Health and Social Behavior* 34(1993): 153–164.

Tamney, Joseph B. *The Resilience of Christianity in the Modern World.* Albany, NY: State University of New York Press, 1992.

Tate, Katherine. *From Protest to Politics: The New Black Voters in American Elections.* New York: Russell Sage Foundation and Cambridge: Harvard University Press, 1993.

Taylor, Carl S. *Girls, Gangs, Women, and Drugs.* East Lansing, MI; Michigan State University Press, 1993.

Taylor, Howard F. "Intelligence." In Edgar F. Borgatta and Marie L. Borgatta (Eds.), *Encyclopedia of Sociology*, pp. 941–949. New York: Macmillan, 1992.

Taylor, John. "Party Palace: The High Life at the Gilded Metropolitan Museum." *New York Times,* January 9, 1989.

Taylor, Patrica A., Burke D. Grandjean, and Niko Tos. "Work Satisfaction Under Yugoslav Self-Management: On Participation, Authority, and Ownership." *Social Forces* 65 (1987):1020-1034.

Taylor, Philip, and Alan Walker. "Dealing with Age Discrimination in England: The Merits of Education vs. Legislation." *Aging International,* XX (1993): 36–40.

Taylor, Ralph B., and Jeanette Covington. "Community Structural Change and Fear of Crime." *Social Problems* 40 (1993): 374–397.

Teachman, Jay D. "Contributions to Children by Divorced Fathers." *Social Problems* 38 (1991): 358–371.

Teitelbaum, Michael S., and Sharon Stanton Russell. "Fertility, International Migration, and Development." In Robert Casson (Ed.), *Population and Development: Old Debates, New Conclusions.* Washington, DC: Overseas Development Council, 1994.

Teixiera, Ruy. *The Disappearing American Voter.* Washington, DC: Brookings Institute, 1992.

Teixeira, Ruy, and Paul Swain. "Education and Training Policy: Skill Upgrading Options for the Rural Workforce." In David McGranahan (Ed.), *Education and Rural Development Strategies for the 1990's.* Washington, D.C.: Economic Research Service, 1991.

Telles, Edward E. "Residential Segregation by Skin Color in Brazil." *American Sociological Review* 57 (1992): 186-197.

Telles, Edward E., and Edward Murguia. "Phenotypic Discrimination and Income Differences among Mexican Americans." *Social Science Quarterly* 71(4) (1990): 682-696.

Testa, Mark, and Marilyn Krogh. "The Effect of Employment on Marriage among Black Males in Inner City Chicago." University of Chicago, unpublished manuscript, 1989.

Tetlock, Philip E., Jo L. Husbands, Robert Jervis, Paul C. Stern, and Charles Tilly (Eds.). *Behavior, Society, and Nuclear War,* Vol. 1 and 2. New York: Oxford University Press, 1989 and 1991.

Theberge, Nancy. "The Construction of Gender in Sport: Women, Coaching, and the Naturalization of Difference." *Social Problems* 40 (1993): 301-313.

Theilman, John, and Al Wilhite. *Discrimination and Congressional Campaign Contributions.* New York: Praeger, 1991.

Theoharis, Athan (Ed.). *From the Secret Files of J. Edgart Hoover.* Chicago, Univesity of Chicago Press, 1991.

Thoits, Peggy. "The Sociology of Emotions." *Annual Review of Sociology* 15 (1989): 317-342.

Thomas, Melvin E. "Race, Class, and Personal Income: An Empirical Test of the Declining Significance of Race Thesis, 1968-1988." *Social Problems* 40 (1993): 328-342.

Thomas, Melvin E., Cedric Herring, and Hayward Derrick Horton. "Discrimination Over the Life Course: A Synthetic Cohort Analysis of Earnings Differences Between Black and White Males, 1940-1990." *Social Problems* 41 (1994): 608-628.

Thomas, William I. *The Unadjusted Girl.* Boston: Little Brown, 1923.

Thomas, William I., and Dorothy Swain Thomas. *The Child in America: Behavior Problems and Programs.* New York: Knopf, 1928.

Thomas, William I., and Florian Znaniecki. *The Polish Peasant in Europe and America* (1918-1919). Edited and abridged by Eli Zaretsky. Urbana, IL: University of Illinois Press, 1984.

Thompson, Becky Wangsgaard. "'Way Outa No Way': Eating Problems among African-American, Latina, and White Women." *Gender & Society* 6 (1992): 546-561.

Thompson, Maxine Seaborn, Karl L. Alexander, and Doris R. Entwisle. "Household Composition, Parental Expectations, and School Achievement." *Social Forces* 67 (1988): 424-4

Thompson, Maxine Seaborn, and Margaret E. Ensminger. "Psychological Well-Being Among Mothers with School Age Children: Evolving Family Structures." *Social Forces* 67 (1989): 715-730.

Thomson, Elizabeth, Thomas L. Hanson, and Sara A. McLanahan. "Family Structure and Child Well-Being: Economic Resources vs. Parental Behaviors." *Social Forces* 73 (1994): 221-242.

Thomson, Irene Taviss. "Individualism and Conformity in the 1950s vs. the 1980s." *Sociological Forum* 7 (1992): 497-514.

Thorne, Barrie. *Gender Play: Girls and Boys in School.* New Brunswick, NJ: Rutgers University Press, 1993.

Thornton, Arland, William G. Axinn, and Daniel H. Hill. "Reciprocal Effects of Religiosity, Cohabitation, and Marriage." *American Journal of Sociology* 98 (1992): 628-651.

Thornton, Russell. *American Indian Holocaust and Survival: A Population History Since 1492.* Norman: University of Oklahoma Press, 1987.

Tiano, Susan. *Patriarchy on the Line: Labor, Gender, and Ideology in the Mexican Maquilla Industry.* Philadelphia, PA: Temple University Press, 1994.

Tien, H. Yuan, Zhang Tianlu, Ping Yu, Li Jingneng, and Liang Zhongtang. "China's Demographic Dilemmas." *Population Bulletin,* Vol. 47 No. 1, June 1992.

Tienda, Marta, Katherine M. Donato, and Hector Cordero-Guzman. "Schooling, Color, and the Labor Force Activity of Women." *Social Forces* 71 (1992): 365-395.

Tilly, Charles. *From Mobilization to Revolution.* Reading, MA: Addison-Wesley, 1978.

Tilly, Charles. *European Revolutions, 1492-1992.* Cambridge, MA: Blackwell, 1993.

Time. "Cover Story: Sizing Up the Sexes." January 20, 1992: 42-52.

Time, August 23, 1993b: 30.

Time. "Vox Pop." June 27, 1994: 26.

Tobin, Joseph J., David Y. H. Wu, and Dana H. Davidson. *Preschool in Three Cultures: Japan, China, and the United States.* New Haven, CT: Yale University Press, 1989.

Tolman, Deborah L. "Doing Desire: Adolescent Girls' Struggles for/with Sexuality." *Gender & Society* 8 (1994): 324-342.

Tomaskovic-Devey, Donald. "The Gender and Race Composition of Jobs and the Male/Female, White/Black Pay Gaps." *Social Forces* 72 (1993): 45-76.

Tönnies, Ferdinand. *Gemeinschaft und Gesellschaft.* (1887) Loomis, Charles P., translator. *Community and Society.* East Lansing, MI: Michigan State University Press, 1957.

Treaster, Joseph B. "Study Finds More Drug Use But Less Concern About It." *New York Times,* July 21, 1994.

Trent, James W. "Educating for Abstinence: Teen Pregnancy Prevention in the Reagan-Bush Years." Paper presented at the annual meeting of the Society for the Study of Social Problems, Miami, FL, August 1993.

Trent, James W. *Inventing the Feeble Mind: A History of Mental Retardation in the United States.* Berkeley, CA: University of California Press, 1994.

Trice, Harrison M., and Janice M. Beyer. *The Cultures of Work Organizations.* Englewood Cliffs, NJ: Prentice-Hall, 1993.

Troiden, Richard R. *Gay and Lesbian Identity: A Sociological Analysis.* Dix Hills, NY: General Hall, 1988.

Trovato, Frank, and Rita Vos. "Married Female Labor Force Participation and Suicide in Canada, 1971 and 1981." *Sociological Forum* 7 (1992): 661-677.

Tuchman, Gaye. *Making News: A Study in the Construction of Reality.* New York: Free Press, 1978.

Tumin, Melvin. "Some Principles of Stratification: A Critical Analysis." *American Sociological Review* 18 (Aug. 1953): 387-393.

Tunnell, Kenneth D. *Choosing Crime: The Criminal Calculus of Property Offenders.* Chicago, IL: Nelson-Hall, 1992.

Tunstall, Jeremy, and Michael Palmer. *Media Moguls.* London, ENG: Routledge, 1991.

Turk, Austin T. "A Proposed Resolution of Key Issues in the Political Sociology of Law." In Freda Adler and William S. Laufer (Eds.), *New Directions in Criminological Theory,* Vol. 4, pp. 23-44. New Brunswick, NJ: Transaction, 1993.

Turnbull, Colin. *The Mountain People.* New York: Simon & Schuster, 1972.

Turner, Ralph H., and Lewis M. Killian. *Collective Behavior,* 3rd ed. Englewood Cliffs, N.J.: Prentice-Hall, 1987.

Turner, R. Jay, Blair Wheaton, and Donald A. Lloyd. "The Epidemiology of Social Stress." *American Sociological Review* 60 (1995): 104-125.

Turner, Stephen Park, and Jonathan H. Turner. *The Impossible Science: An Institutional Analysis of American Sociology.* Newbury Park, CA: Sage, 1990.

Tyler, Patrick E. "China Migrants: Economic Engine, Social Burden." *New York Times,* June 19, 1994.

Tyree, Andrea, and Rebecca Hicks. "Sex and the Second Moment of Prestige Distributions." *Social Forces* 66 (1988): 1028-1037.

Uchitelle, Louis. "Temporary Workers Are on the Increase in Nation's Factories," *New York Times,* July 6, 1993.

Udry, J. Richard, and John O. G. Billy. "Initiation of Coitus in Early Adolescence." *American Sociological Review* 52 (1987): 841-855.

Uehara, Edwina. "Dual Exchange Theory, Social Networks, and Informal Social Support." *American Journal of Sociology* 96 (1990): 521-557.

United Nations. *Report on the World Situation, 1993.* New York: United Nations Publications,1993.

United Nations. *Human Development Report, 1994.* New York: United Nations Development Program, 1994.

U.S. Bureau of the Census. *Historical Statistics of the United States: Colonial Times to 1970.* Washington, DC: U.S. Government Printing Office, 1975.

U.S. Bureau of the Census. *We, The Asian and Pacific Islander Americans.* Washington, DC: U.S. Government Printing Office, 1988, p. 2.

U.S. Bureau of the Census. "Marriage, Divorce, and Remarriage in the 1990s." *Current Population Reports,* P23-180. Washington, DC: U.S. Government Printing Office, 1992.

U.S. Bureau of the Census. "Populations Projections of the United States, by Age, Sex, Race, and Hispanic Origin: 1992 to 2050." *Current Population Reports,* P25-1092. Washington, DC: U.S. Government Printing Office, 1992.

U.S. Bureau of the Census. "Voting and Registration in the Election of November 1992." *Current Population Reports,* P20-466. Washington, DC: U.S. Government Printing Office, 1993.

U.S. Bureau of the Census. "Household and Family Characteristics: March 1992." *Current Population Reports,* P20-467. Washington, DC: U.S. Government Printing Office, 1993.

U.S. Bureau of the Census. Fertility of American Women: June 1992. *Current Population Reports,* P20-470. Washington, DC: U.S. Government Printing Office, 1993.

U.S. Bureau of the Census. "The Black Population in the United States: March 1992." *Current Population Reports,* P20-471. Washington, DC: U.S. Government Printing Office, 1993.

U.S. Bureau of the Census. "Population Projections of the United States, by Age, Sex, Race, and Hispanic Origin: 1993 to 2050." *Current Population Reports,* P25-1104. Washington, DC: U.S. Government Printing Office, November 1993.

U.S. Bureau of the Census. "Money Income of Households, Families, and Persons in the United States: 1992." *Current Population Reports,* P60-184. Washington, DC: U.S. Government Printing Office, 1993.

U.S. Bureau of the Census. "Poverty in the United States: 1992." *Current Population Reports,* P60-185. Washington, DC: U.S. Government Printing Office, 1993.

U.S. Bureau of the Census. "Americans with Disabilities: 1991-92: Data From the Survey of Income and Program Participation." *Current Population Reports,* P70-33. Washington, DC: U.S. Government Printing Office, December, 1993.

U.S. Bureau of the Census. *Aging in Eastern Europe and the Former Soviet Union.* P95/93-1. Washington, DC: U.S. Government Printing Office, 1993.

U.S. Bureau of the Census. *Housing Characteristics of Rural Households.* H121/93-5. Washington, DC: U.S. Government Printing Office, 1993.

U.S. Bureau of the Census. "Geographical Mobility: March 1992 to March 1993." *Current Population Reports,* P20-481. Washington, DC: U.S. Government Printing Office, 1994.

U.S. Bureau of the Census. "The Hispanic Population in the United States: March 1993." *Current Population Reports,* P20-475. Washington, DC: U.S. Government Printing Office, 1994.

U.S. Bureau of the Census. "Educational Attainment in the United States: March 1993 and 1992." *Current Population Reports,* P20-476. Washington, DC: U.S. Government Printing Office, 1994.

U.S. Bureau of the Census. "Marital Status and Living Arrangements: March 1993." *Current Population Reports,* P20-478. Washington, DC: U.S. Government Printing Office, 1994.

U.S. Bureau of the Census. "School Enrollment—Social and Economic Characteristics of Students: October 1993." *Current Pop-ulation Reports* P20-479. Washington, DC: U.S. Government Printing Office, 1994.

U.S. Bureau of the Census. "Population Projections for States by Age, Sex, Race, and Hispanic Origin: 1993 to 2020." *Current Population Reports,* P25-1111. Washington, DC: U.S. Government Printing Office, 1994.

U.S. Bureau of the Census. "Projections of the Voting Age Population, for States, November 1994." *Current Population Reports* P25-1117. Washington. DC: U.S. Government Printing Office, 1994.

U.S. Bureau of the Census. "Income, Poverty, and the Valuation of Noncash Benefits, 1993." *Current Population Reports* P60-188. Washington, DC: U.S. Government Printing Office, 1994.

U.S. Bureau of the Census. "Household Wealth and Asset Ownership: 1991." *Current Population Reports,* P70-34. Washington, DC: U.S. Government Printing Office, 1994.

U.S. Bureau of the Census. "Who's Minding the Kids?" *Current Population Reports,* P70-36. Washington, DC: U.S. Government Printing Office, 1994.

U.S. Bureau of the Census. "The Earnings Ladder." *Statistical Brief* 94-3. Washington, DC: U.S. Government Printing Office, 1994.

U.S. Bureau of the Census. *America's Racial and Ethnic Groups: Their Housing in the Nineties.* H121/94-3. Washington, DC: U.S. Government Printing Office, 1994.

U.S. Bureau of the Census. "Health Insurance Coverage—Who Had a Lapse Between 1990 and 1992." *Statistical Brief* 94-6. Washington, DC: U.S. Government Printing Office, 1994.

U.S. Bureau of the Census, Center for International Research. *World Population Profile: 1994.* Washington, DC: U.S. Government Printing Office, 1994.

U.S. Bureau of the Census. *Statistical Abstract of the United States 1994.* Washington, DC: U.S. Department of Commerce, 1994.

U.S. Department of Education. *Adult Literacy in America, 1993: First Look At Results of the National Adult Literacy Survey.* National Center for Education Statistics. Washington, DC: U.S. Government Printing Office, 1993.

U.S. Department of Education. National Center for Education Statistics. *The Condition of Education 1993.* Washington, DC: U.S. Government Printing Office, 1994.

U.S. Department of Health and Human Services. "Advance Report of Final Divorce Statistics, 1988." *Monthly Vital Statistics Report,* 39 (12) (Supplement 2). Hyattsville, MD: National Center for Health Statistics, 1991.

U.S. Department of Health and Human Services. "Serious Mental Illness and Disability in the Adult Household Population: United States, 1989." *Advance Data* 218. Hyattsville, MD: National Center for Health Statistics, 1992.

U.S. Department of Health and Human Services. "Annual Summary of Births, Marriages, Divorces, and Deaths: United States, 1993." *Monthly Vital Statistics Report* 42 (13). Hyattsville, MD: National Center for Health Statistics, 1994a.

U.S. Department of Health and Human Services. National Center for Health Statistics. "Advance Report of Final Natality Statistics, 1992." *Monthly Vital Statistics Report,* 42 (5) (Supplement). Hyattsville, MD: National Center for Health Statistics, 1994b.

U.S. Department of Health and Human Services. "Advance Report of Final Mortality Statistics, 1992." *Monthly Vital Statistics Report* 43 (6) (Supplement). Hyattsville, MD: National Center for Health Statistics, 1994c.

U.S. Department of Justice. Bureau of Justice Statistics. *Criminal Victimization of Women, 1973-87.* Washington, DC: U.S. Government Printing Office, 1991.

U.S. Department of Justice. Bureau of Justice Statistics. *Recidivism of Felons on Probation, 1986-89.* Washington, DC: U.S. Government Printing Office, 1992.

U.S. Department of Justice, Bureau of Justice Statistics. *Murder in Large Urban Counties, 1988.* Washington, DC: U.S. Government Printing Office, 1993a.

U.S. Department of Justice. Bureau of Justice Statistics. *Tracking Offenders Through The Criminal Justice System: All Felons, 1988.* Washington, DC: U.S. Government Printing Office, 1993b.

U.S. Department of Justice. Bureau of Justice Statistics. *Crime and the Nation's Households, 1992.* Washington, DC: U.S. Government Printing Office, 1993c.

U.S. Department of Justice. Bureau of Justice Statistics. *Violence Against Women.* Washington, DC: U.S. Government Printing Office, 1994a.

U.S. Department of Justice. Bureau of Justice Statistics. *Criminal Victimization in the United States, 1992.* Washington, DC: U.S. Government Printing Office, 1994b.

U.S. Department of Justice. Bureau of Justice Statistics. *Women in Prison.* Washington, DC: U.S. Government Printing Office, 1994c.

U.S. Department of Justice. Bureau of Justice Statistics. *Guns and Crime: Handgun Victimization, Firearm Self-Defense and Firearm Theft.* Washington, DC: U.S. Government Printing Office, 1994d.

U.S. Department of Justice. Bureau of Justice Statistics. *Child Rape Victims, 1992.* Washington, DC: U.S. Government Printing Office, 1994e.

U.S. Department of Justice. Bureau of Justice Statistics. *Prisoners in 1993.* Washington, DC: U.S. Government Printing Office, 1994f.

U.S. Department of Justice. Bureau of Justice Statistics. *Murder in Families.* Washington, DC: U.S. Government Printing Office, 1994g.

U.S. Department of Justice. Bureau of Justice Statistics. *Sourcebook of Criminal Justice Statistics—1993.* Washington, DC: U.S. Government Printing Office, 1994h.

U.S. Department of Justice. Bureau of Justice Statistics. *Correctional Populations in the United States, 1992.* Washington, DC: U.S. Government Printing Office, 1994i.

U.S. Department of Labor. Bureau of Labor Statistics. *Employment and Earnings,* January 1993. Washington, DC: U.S. Government Printing Office, 1993a.

U.S. Department of Labor. *Consumer Expenditures in 1992.* Washington, DC: Bureau of Labor Statistics, 1993b.

U.S. Department of Labor. *Occupational Outlook Handbook 1994-1995.* Washington, DC: Bureau of Labor Statistics, 1994a.

U.S. Department of Labor. *Employment and Earnings, July 1994.* Washington, DC: U.S. Government Printing Office, 1994b.

U.S. Department of Labor. Women's Bureau. *Working Women Count.* Washington, DC: U.S. Government Printing Office, 1994c.

U.S. Department of Labor. Bureau of Labor Statistics. "Part-time Work: A Choice or a Response." *Issues in Labor Statistics.* Washington, DC: U.S. Government Printing Office, October, 1994d.

U.S. Department of the Treasury. Office of Tax Analysis. *Annual Report.* Washington, DC: 1990.

U.S. News and World Report. "Inside the Ivy League." April 12, 1993: 55-60.

Update. "News to Use." *Update: North Shore Elder Services.* Danvers, MA: North Shore Elder Services, Fall 1993: p. 1.

Useem, Bert, and Peter Kimball. *States of Siege: U.S. Prison Riots 1971-1986.* New York: Oxford University Press, 1989.

Useem, Elizabeth L. "Middle Schools and Math Groups: Parents' Involvement in Children's Placement." *Sociology of Education* 65 (1992): 263-279.

Useem, Michael. *Executive Defense: Shareholder Power and Corporate Reorganization.* Cambridge, MA: Harvard University Press, 1993.

Vallas, Steven Peter. "The Labor Process as a Source of Class Consciousness: A Critical Examination." *Sociological Forum* 2 (1987): 237-256.

Vallas, Steven Peter. *Power in the Workplace: The Politics of Production at AT&T.* Albany, NY: State University of New York Press, 1993.

Valocchi, Steve. "The Unemployed Workers Movement of the 1930s: A Reexamination of the Pivan and Cloward Thesis." *Social Problems* 37 (1990): 191-205.

Valocchi, Steve. "External Resources and the Unemployed Councils of the 1930s: Evaluating Six Propositions from Social Movement Theory." *Sociological Forum* 8 (1993): 451-470.

Valocchi, Steve. "The Racial Basis of Capitalism and the State, and the Impact of the New Deal on African Americans." *Social Problems* 41 (1994): 347-362.

van den Berghe, Pierre. "Why Most Sociologists Don't (and Won't) Think Evolutionarily." *Sociological Forum* 5 (1990): 173-186.

Van de Walle, Etienne, and John Knodel. "Europe's Fertility Transition: New Evidence and Lessons for Today's Developing World." *Population Today* 34 (6) (1980).

Van Gennep, Arnold. *The Rites of Passage* (1909). Chicago: University of Chicago Press, 1960.

Vanfossen, Beth, Merrill J. Melnick, and Donald Sabo. "Social Mobility Opportunities Through Sports Participation, By Race and Gender." Paper presented at the 84th annual meeting of the American Sociological Association, San Francisco, August 1989.

Vanneman, Reeve, and Lynn Weber Cannon. *The American Perception of Class.* Philadelphia: Temple University Press, 1987.

Vannoy-Hiller, Dana, and William W. Philliber. *Equal Partners: Successful Women in Marriage.* Newbury Park, CA: Sage, 1989.

Veblen, Thorstein. *The Theory of the Leisure Class.* New York: Macmillan, 1899.

Ventura, Stephanie, Selma Taffel, William D. Mosher, and Stanley Henshaw. "Trends in Pregnancies and Pregnancy Rates, United States, 1980-1988." National Center for Disease Control, *Monthly Vital Statistics Report,* 41 (6), November, 1992.

Verbrugge, Lois M. "The Twain Meet: Empirical Explanations of Sex Differences in Health and Mortality." *Journal of Health and Social Behavior* 30 (1989): 282-304.

Verhovek, Sam Howe. "Albany Goal: Giving Women Restroom 'Parity' With Men." *New York Times,* June 13, 1989.

Verhovek, Sam Howe. "Medical Incompetence: A Whispered Factor in Rising Costs." *New York Times,* April 9, 1994.

Vidal de Haymes, Maria R., and Keith M. Kilty. "Latino and Anglo Families: The Question of Difference." Paper presented at the annual meeting of the Society for the Study of Social Problems, Los Angeles, CA, August, 1994.

Villemez, Wayne J., and William P. Bridges. "When Bigger Is Better: Differences in the Individual-Level Effect of Firm and Establishment Size." *American Sociological Review* 53 (1988): 237-255.

Visser, Margaret. *The Rituals of Dinner: The Origins, Evolution, Eccentricities, and Meaning of Table Manners.* New York: Grove Weidenfeld, 1991.

Voigt, Lydia. "Crime in the Context of Cultural Turmoil and Social Upheaval: Is Russia Experiencing a Crime Wave?" Paper presented at the annual meeting of the American Sociological Association, Miami Beach, FL: August 1993.

Voltaire (1732). *On the Presbyterians.* Indianapolis, IN: Bobbs-Merrill, 1961.

Voydanoff, Patricia. *Work and Family Life.* Newbury Park, CA: Sage, 1987.

Wachs, Eleanor. *Crime-Victim Stories: New York City's Urban Folklore.* Bloomington: Indiana University Press, 1988.

Wacquant, Loic J. D. "Heuristic Models in Marxian Theory." *Social Forces* 64(1)(1985): 17-45.

Wadsworth, M. E. J. *The Imprint of Time: Childhood, History, and Adult Life.* New York: Clarendon Press, 1991.

Wagner, David. *Checkerboard Square: Culture and Resistance in a Homeless Community.* Boulder, CO: Westview Press, 1993.

Wagner, David, and Marcia B. Cohen. "The Power of the People: Homeless Protesters in the Aftermath of Social Movement Participation." *Social Problems* 38 (1991): 543-558.

Wagner-Pacifici, Robin, and Barry Schwartz. "The Vietnam Veterans Memorial: Commemorating a Difficult Past." *American Journal of Sociology* 97 (1991): 376-420.

Waite, Linda J., and Lee A. Lillard. "Children and Marital Disruption." *American Journal of Sociology* 96 (1991): 930-953.

Waite, Thomas L. "Those Who Rejected Vows Find New Roles in Church." *New York Times,* February 27, 1989, p. B1.

Waits, William B. *The Modern Christmas in America: A Cultural History of Gift-Giving.* New York: New York University Press, 1993.

Wakefield, Neville. *Postmodernism: The Twilight of the Real.* London, England: Pluto Press, 1990.

Walder, Andrew G. "Property Rights and Stratification in Socialist Redistributive Economies," *American Sociological Review* 57 (1992): 524-539.

Waldrop, Judith. "The Demographics of Decision-Making," *American Demographics,* June 1993: 26-32.

Walford, G. "Educational Choice and Equity in Great Britain." *Educational Policy* 6 (1992): 123-138.

Walker, Henry A., Larry Rogers, and Morris Zelditch, Jr. "Legitimacy and Collective Action." *Social Forces* 67 (1988): 216-228.

Walker, Karen. "Men, Women, and Friendship: What They Say, What They Do." *Gender & Society* 8 (1994): 246-265.

Walker, William O., III (Ed.). *Drug Control Policy: Essays in Historical and Comparative Perspective*. University Park, PA: The Pennsylvania State University Press, 1992.

Walkowitz, Judith R. *City of Dreadful Delight: Narratives of Sexual Danger in Late-Victorian London*. Chicago, IL: University of Chicago Press, 1992.

Wallace, Ruth A. *They Call Her Pastor: A New Role for Catholic Woman*. Albany, NY: State University of New York Press, 1992.

Waller, Willard. "The Rating and Dating Complex." *American Sociological Review* 2 (October 1937): 727-734.

Wallerstein, Immanuel. *Geopolitics and Geoculture: Essays on the Changing World-System*. Cambridge, MA: Cambridge University Press, 1991.

Walser, Robert. *Running with the Devil: Power, Gender, and Madness in Heavy Metal Music*. Hanover, CT: Wesleyan University Press of New England, 1993.

Walsh, Edward J. "The Role of Target Vulnerabilities in High-Technology Protest Movements: The Nuclear Establishment at Three Mile Island." *Sociological Forum* 1(2) (1986): 199-218.

Walsh, Edward J., and Marylee C. Taylor. "Occupational Correlates of Multidimensional Self-esteem: Comparisons Among Garbage Collectors, Bartenders, Professors, and Other Workers." *Sociology and Social Research* 66 (1982): 252-268.

Walsh, Jennifer R., and Stacy Rowe. "On the Streets: Mobility Paths of the Urban Homeless." *City and Society*, 6 (1992): 26-40.

Walters, Pamela Barnhouse. "Contemporary School Reform: Tensions Between Democratization of Choice and Educational Inequality." Paper presented at the 88th annual meeting of the American Sociological Association, Miami Beach, August, 1993.

Walters, Pamela Barnhouse, and David R. James. "Schooling for Some: Child Labor and School Enrollment of Black and White Children in the Early Twentieth-Century South." *American Sociological Review* 57 (1992): 635-650.

Walters, Pamela Barnhouse, and Philip J. O'Connell. "The Family Economy, Work, and Educational Participation in the United States, 1890-1940." *American Journal of Sociology* 93 (1988): 1116-1152.

Wandersman, Abraham, Paul Florin, Robert Friedmann, and Ron Meier. "Who Participates, Who Does Not, and Why? An Analysis of Voluntary Neighborhood Organizations in the United States and Israel." *Sociological Forum* 2 (1987): 534-555.

Ward, Kathryn (Ed.). *Women Workers and Global Restructuring*. Ithaca, NY: Cornell University Press, 1990.

Warner, R. Stephen. *New Wine in Old Wineskins: Evangelicals and Liberals in a Small-Town Church*. Berkeley: University of California Press, 1988.

Warner, R. Stephen. "Work in Progress toward a New Paradigm for the Sociological Study of Religion in the United States." *American Journal of Sociology* 98 (1993): 1044-1093.

Warner, Rebecca L., Gary R. Lee, and Janet Lee. "Social Organization, Spousal Resources, and Marital Power: A Crosscultural Study." *Journal of Marriage and the Family* 48 (1986): 121-128.

Warr, Mark. "Parents, Peers, and Delinquency." *Social Forces* 72 (1993): 247-264.

Warrick, Louise, Jon B. Christianson, Judy Walruff, and Paul C. Cook. "Educational Outcomes in Teenage Pregnancy and Parenting Programs: Results from a Demonstration." *Family Planning Perspectives* 25 (1993): 148-155.

Wasserman, Harvey. "Duck & Cover Up." *The Nation*, January 31, 1994: 113-114.

Wasserstrom, Jeffrey N., and Elizabeth J. Perry (Eds.). *Popular Protest and Political Culture in Modern China: Learning from 1989*. Boulder, C0: Westview Press, 1992.

Waters, Mary C. *Ethnic Options: Choosing Identities in America*. Berkeley, CA: University of California Press, 1990.

Waxman, Chaim. "Whither American Jewry?" *Society* 28 (1) (1990): 34-41.

Waxman, Chaim. "Are America's Jews Experiencing a Religious Revival?" *Qualitative Sociology* 15 (1992): 203-211.

Weakliem, David L. "Relative Wages and the Radical Theory of Economic Segmentation." *American Sociological Review* 55 (1990): 574-590.

Weber, Max. "Bureaucracy" (1915). In Hans H. Gerth and C. Wright Mills (Eds.), *From Max Weber: Essays in Sociology*, pp. 196-244. New York: Oxford University Press, 1946.

Weber, Max. *Economy and Society* (1922). New York: Bedminster Press, 1968.

Weber, Max. *The Social Psychology of the World Religions*. New York: Oxford University Press, 1922-23.

Weber, Max (1923). *The City*. D. Martendale and G. Neuwirth (trans.), New York: The Free Press, 1958.

Weber, Peter. "Safeguarding Oceans." In Lester R. Brown et al., *State of the World 1993*, pp. 42-60. New York: W.W. Norton, 1993.

Webster, Barbara, and Michael S. McCampbell. "International Money Laundering: Research and Investigation Join Forces." *Research in Brief*. Washington, DC: National Institute of Justice, 1992.

Weeks, John R. *Population: An Introduction to Concepts and Issues*. Belmont, CA: Wadsworth Publishing Company, 1992.

Wegener, Bernd. "Job Mobility and Social Ties: Social Resources, Prior Job, and Status Attainment." *American Sociological Review* 56 (1991): 60-71.

Weibel-Orlando, Joan. *Indian Country, L.A.: Maintaining Ethnic Community in Complex Society*. Urbana, IL: University of Illinois Press, 1991.

Weinberg, Martin S. "Sexual Modesty and the Nudist Camp." In Earl Rubington and Martin S. Weinberg (Eds.), *Deviance: The Interactionist Perspective*, pp. 271-279. New York: Macmillan, 1968.

Weinberg, Martin S., Colin J. Williams, and Douglas W. Pryor. *Dual Attraction: Understanding Bisexuality*. New York: Oxford University Press, 1994.

Weiner, Tim. "Bills Would Slash the Number of U.S. Secrets." *New York Times*, March 3, 1994.

Weinstein, Deena. *Heavy Metal: A Cultural Sociology*. New York: Lexington Books, 1991.

Weinstein, Deena. "The Discourse of Terror: Heavy Metal as Other." paper presented at the Annual Meeting of the Society for the Study of Social Problems, Pittsburgh, PA: August, 1992.

Weinstein, Jack B. "The War on Drugs is Self-Defeating." *New York Times* July 8, 1993.

Weisberger, Adam. "Marginality and Its Directions." *Sociological Forum* 7 (1992): 425-46.

Weisburd, David, Stanton Wheeler, Elin Waring, and Nancy Bode. *Crimes of the Middle Class: White-Collar Offenders in the Federal Courts*. New Haven, CT: Yale University Press, 1991.

Weiss, Michael J. *Latitudes and Attitudes: An Atlas of American Taste*. Boston, MA: Little, Brown & Co., 1994.

Weitz, Rose, and Deborah A. Sullivan. "The Politics of Childbirth: The Reemergence of Midwifery in Arizona." *Social Problems* 33 (1986): 163-175.

Weitzman, Lenore J., Deborah Eifler, Elizabeth Hokado, and Catherine Ross. "Sex Role Socialization in Picture Books for Pre-School Children." *American Journal of Sociology* 77 (1972): 1125-1150.

Weitzman, Lenore J., and Mavis McLean (Eds.). *Economic Consequences of Divorce: The International Perspective.* New York: Oxford University Press, 1992.

Welch, Susan, and Lee Sigelman. "A Black Gender Gap?" *Social Science Quarterly* 70 (1989): 120–133.

Wellman, Barry, and Scot Wortley. "Different Strokes from Different Folks: Community Ties and Social Support." *American Journal of Sociology* 96 (1990): 558–588.

Wells, L. Edward, and Joseph H. Rankin. "Families and Delinquency: A Meta-Analysis of the Impact of Broken Homes." *Social Problems* 38 (1991): 71–90.

Wenk, Deeann, and Patricia Garrett. "Having a Baby: Some Predictions of Maternal Employment Around Childbirth." *Gender & Society* 6 (1992): 49–65.

West, Candace, and Angela Garcia. "Conversational Shift Work: A Study of Topical Transitions Between Women and Men." *Social Problems* 35 (1988): 551–575.

West, Elliott, and Paula Petrik (Eds.). *Small Worlds: Children and Adolescents in America, 1850–1950.* Lawrence, KS: University Press of Kansas, 1992.

Western, Bruce. "Postwar Unionization in Eighteen Advanced Capitalist Countries," *American Sociological Review* 58 (1993): 266–282.

Western, Mark. "Class Structure and Intergenerational Mobility: A Comparative Analysis of Nation and Gender." *Social Forces* 73 (1994): 101–134.

Western, Mark, and Erik Olin Wright. "The Permeability of Class Boundaries to Intergenerational Mobility Among Men in the United States, Canada, Norway, and Sweden." *American Sociological Review* 59 (1994): 606–629.

Weston, Kath. *Families We Choose: Lesbians, Gays, Kinship.* New York: Columbia University Press, 1991.

Wexler, Philip, Warren Crichlow, June Kern, and Rebecca Martusewicz. *Becoming Somebody: Toward a Social Psychology of School.* Washington, DC: Falmer Press, 1992.

Wharton, Amy S. "Gender Segregation in Private-Sector, Public-Sector, and Self-Employed Occupations, 1950–1981." *Social Science Quarterly* 70 (1989): 923–940.

Wharton, Carol S. "Finding Time For the 'Second Shift': The Impact of Flexible Work Schedules on Women's Double Days." *Gender & Society* 8 (1994): 189–205.

White, L., and J. Edwards. "Emptying the Nest and Parental Well-Being: Evidence from National Panel Data." *American Sociological Review* 55, (1990): 235–242.

White, Merry. *The Material Child: Coming of Age in Japan and America.* New York: Free Press, 1993.

White, Michael D. "Conscription and the Size of Armed Forces." *Social Science Quarterly* 70 (1989): 772–781.

White, Michael J., Ann E. Biddlecom, and Shenyang Guo. "Immigration, Naturalization, and Residential Assimilation Among Asian-Americans in 1980." *Social Forces* 72 (1993): 93–117.

White, Rob. *No Space of Their Own: Young People and Social Control in Australia.* Cambridge, ENG: Cambridge University Press, 1990.

Whyte, William Foote. *Street Corner Society: The Social Structure of an Italian Slum* (1943). Chicago: University of Chicago Press, 1984.

Whyte, William Foote. *Social Theory for Action: How Individuals and Organizations Learn to Change.* Newbury Park, CA: Sage, 1991.

Whyte, William Foote, and Kathleen King Whyte. *Making Mondragon: The Growth and Dynamics of the Workers Cooperative Complex.* Ithaca, NY: ILR Press, 1988.

Wiatrowski, William J. "Employee Benefits for Union and Nonunion Workers." *Monthly Labor Review* 117 (February, 1994): 34–38.

Widom, Kathy Spatz. *The Cycle of Violence.* Washington, DC: National Institute of Justice, October 1992.

Wilcox, Clyde. *God's Warriors: The Christian Right in Twentieth Century America.* Baltimore, MD: Johns Hopkins University Press, 1992.

Wilford, John Noble. "Among the Dying Species Are Lost Tribes of Mankind." *New York Times*, January 2, 1994.

Wilkie, Janet Riblett. "Changes in U.S. Men's Attitudes Toward the Provider Role, 1972–1989." *Gender & Society* 7 (1993): 261–279.

Wilkinson, Doris Y. "Afro-American Women and Their Families." *Marriage and Family Review* 7 (1984): 125–142.

Wilkinson, Doris Y. "Ethnicity." In Marvin B. Sussman and Suzanne K. Steinmetz (Eds.), *Handbook of Marriage and the Family*, pp. 183–210. New York: Plenum, 1987.

Wilkinson, Doris, Maxine Baca-Zinn, and Esther Ngan-Ling Chow (Eds.). "Race, Class, and Gender." *Gender & Society* 6, No. 3 (1992).

Williams, Christine L. "The Glass Escalator: Hidden Advantages for Men in the 'Female' Professions." *Social Problems* 39 (1992): 253–267.

Williams, Christine L., and E. Joel Heikes. "The Importance of Researcher's Gender in the In-depth Interview: Evidence from Two Case Studies of Male Nurses." *Gender & Society* 7 (1993): 280–291.

Williams, David R., David T. Takeuchi, and Russell K. Adair. "Marital Status and Psychiatric Disorders Among Blacks and Whites." *Journal of Health and Social Behavior* 33 (1992): 140–157.

Williams, Richard. *Hierarchical Structures and Social Value: The Creation of Black and Irish Identities in the United States.* New York: Cambridge University Press, 1990.

Williams, Robin, Jr. *American Society: A Sociological Interpretation*, 3rd ed. New York: Alfred A. Knopf, 1970.

Williams, Tannis MacBeth (Ed.). *The Impact of Television: A Natural Experiment in Three Communities.* Orlando, FL: Academic Press, 1986.

Williams, Walter L. *The Spirit and the Flesh: Sexual Diversity in America Indian Culture.* Boston: Beacon, 1986.

Williamson, John B., and Fred C. Pampel. *Old-Age Security in Comparative Perspective.* New York: Oxford University Press, 1993.

Willie, Charles V., and Inabeth Miller. *Social Goals and Educational Reform: American Schools in the Twentieth Century.* Wesport, CT: Greenwood Press, 1988.

Wilmsen, Steven K. *Silverado: Neil Bush and the Savings & Loan Scandal.* Washington, DC: National Press Books, 1993.

Wilson, Bryan R. *The Social Dimensions of Sectarianism: Sects and the New Religious Movements in Contemporary Society.* New York: Oxford University Press, 1990.

Wilson, James Q. *The Moral Sense.* New York: The Free Press, 1993.

Wilson, John. *Playing by the Rules: Sport, Society, and the State.* Dayton, OH: Wayne State University Press, 1994.

Wilson, John, and Sharon Sandomirsky. "Religious Affiliation and the Family." *Sociological Forum* 6 (1991): 289–309.

Wilson, Kenneth L., and Janet P. Boldizar. "Gender Segregation in Higher Education: Effects of Aspirations, Mathematics Achievement, and Income." *Sociology of Education* 63 (1990): 62–74.

Wilson, Thomas C. "Urbanism and Kinship Bonds: A Test of Four Generalizations." *Social Forces* 71 (1993): 703–712.

Wilson, William Julius. "Studying Inner City Social Dislocations: The Challenge of Public Agenda Research." *American Sociological Review* 56 (1991): 1–14.

Wilson, William Julius. "The Urban Experience of African-Americans." Paper presented at the annual meetings of the American Sociological Association, Miami, FL., August 1993.

Wimberley, Dale W., and Rosario Bello. "Effects of Foreign Investment, Exports, and Economic Growth on Third World Food Consumption." *Social Forces* 70 (1992): 895–921.

Wirth, Louis. "Urbanism as a Way of Life." *American Journal of Sociology* 44:1–24, 1938.

Wolf, James G. (Ed.). *Gay Priests.* New York: Harper & Row, 1989.

Wolf, Naomi. *The Beauty Myth: How Images of Beauty Are Used Against Women*. New York: Morrow, 1991.

Wolfe, Alan. *The Human Difference: Animals, Computers, and the Necessity of Social Science*. Berkeley: University of California Press, 1993.

Wolff, Edwin N. "The Changing Inequality of Wealth." *American Economic Review* 82 (1992): 552-558.

Wolff, Janet. *Feminine Sentences: Essays on Women and Culture*. Berkeley, CA: University of California Press, 1990.

Woliver, Laura R. *From Outrage to Action: The Politics of Grass-Roots Dissent*. Urbana, IL: University of Illinois Press, 1993.

Womack, Mari. "Why Athletes Need Ritual: A Study of Magic Among Professional Athletes." In Shirl J. Hoffman (Ed.), *Sport and Religion*, pp. 200-220. Champaign, IL: Human Kinetics, 1992.

Wong, Sandra L. "Evaluating the Content of Textbooks: Public Interests and Professional Authority." *Sociology of Education* 64 (1991): 11-18.

Wood, Charles H., and Peggy A. Lovell. "Racial Inequality and Child Mortality in Brazil." *Social Forces* 70 (1992): 703-724.

Wood, Peter B., and Barrett A. Lee. "Is Neighborhood Racial Succession Inevitable?" *Urban Affairs Quarterly*, 26 (4), June 1993: 26-40.

Woody, Bette. *Black Women in the Workplace: Impacts of Structural Change in the Economy*. New York: Greenwood Press, 1992.

World Almanac and Book of Facts. New York: Pharas, 1993.

World Health Organization. *Report on Global Progress on AIDS*. Geneva, Switzerland: WHO, 1994.

Woroby, J. L., and R. Angel. "Functional Capacity and Living Arrangements of Unmarried Elderly Persons." *Journal of Gerontology* 45 (1990a): 95-101.

Woroby, J. L., and R. Angel. "Poverty and Health: Older Minority Women and the Rise of the Female-Headed Household." *Journal of Health and Social Behavior* 31 (1990b): 370-383.

Wright, Erik Olin. *Classes*. London: New Left Press, 1985.

Wright, Erik Olin, Andrew Levine, and Elliott Sober. *Reconstructing Marxism*. London: Verso, 1992a.

Wright, Erik Olin, Karen Shire, Shu-Ling Hwang, Maureen Dolan, and Janeen Baxter. "The Non-Effects of Class on the Gender Division of Labor in the Home: A Comparative Study of Sweden and the United States." *Gender & Society* 6 (1992b): 252-282.

Wright, Rosemary, and Jerry A. Jacobs. "Male Flight from Computer Work: A New Look at Occupational Resegregation and Ghettoization." *American Sociological Review* 59 (1994): 511-536.

Wright, Sam. *Crowds and Riots: A Study in Social Organization*. Beverly Hills, CA: Sage, 1978.

Wright, Stuart A. "Reconceptualizing Cult Coercion and Withdrawal: A Comparative Analysis of Divorce and Apostasy." *Social Forces* 70 (1991): 125-145.

Wrong, Dennis. "The Oversocialized Conception of Man in Modern Sociology." *American Sociological Review* 26 (1961): 183-193.

Wrong, Dennis. *The Problem of Order: What Unites and Divides Society*. New York: Free Press, 1994.

Wu, Laurence L., and Brian C. Martinson. "Family Structure and the Risk of Premarital Birth." *American Sociological Review* 58 (1993): 21-232.

Wurtzel, Elizabeth. "Popular Music: Girl Trouble." *The New Yorker*, June 29, 1992a: 63-70.

Wurtzel, Elizabeth. "Popular Music: Fight the Power." *The New Yorker*, September 28, 1992b: 110-113.

Wuthnow, Robert. *The Restructuring of American Religion: Society and Faith Since World War II*. Princeton, NJ: Princeton University Press, 1988.

Wuthnow, Robert. *Communities of Discourse: Ideology and Social Structure in the Reformation*. Cambridge, MA: Harvard University Press, 1989.

Wuthnow, Robert (Ed.) *Between States and Markets: The Voluntary Sector in Comparative Perspective*. Princeton: Princeton University Press, 1991.

Wuthnow, Robert. *Christianity in the 21st Century*. New York: Oxford University Press, 1993.

Wuthnow, Robert. *Sharing the Journey: Support Groups and America's New Quest for Community*. New York: Free Press, 1994.

Wyatt, Gail Elizabeth, Stefanie Doyle Peters, and Donald Guthrie. "Kinsey Revisited. Part I. Comparisons of the Sexual Socialization and Sexual Behavior of White Women Over 33 Years." *Archives of Sexual Behavior* 17 (1988): 201-239.

Xu, Wu, and Ann Leffler. "Gender and Race Effects on Occupational Prestige, Segregation, and Earnings." *Gender & Society* 6 (1992): 376-392.

Yanagishita, Machiko, and Landis MacKellar. "Homicide in the United States: Who's At Risk." *Population Today* 23, No. 2. (1995): 1-2.

Yankelovich Clancy and Shulman. "Survey on Attitudes Toward Sex and Reproduction for *Time* and *Cable News Network*." New York, June 1992.

Yankelovich Partners. "Measuring the Gay Market." Westport, CT: Yankelovich Partners, 1994.

Yarrow, Andrew L. "Not in My Back Yard and Its Repercussions: An Effort to Keep a Woman and 10 Children Out Results in a Lawsuit." *New York Times*, October 4, 1992.

Yearbook of American and Canadian Churches. New York: National Council of Churches, 1994.

Yedidia, Michael J., Judith K. Barr, and Carolyn Berry. "Physicians' Attitudes Toward AIDS at Different Career Stages: A Comparison of Internists and Surgeons." *Journal of Health and Social Behavior* 34 (1993): 272-284.

Yee, B. W. K. "Gender and Family Issues in Minority Groups." *Generations*, XIV (1990): 39-42.

Yinger, J. Milton. "A Structural Examination of Religion." *Journal for the Scientific Study of Religion* 6 (1969): 88-99.

Yinger, J. Milton. *Countercultures*. New York: Free Press, 1982.

Yoder, Janice D. "Rethinking Tokenism: Looking Beyond Numbers." *Gender & Society* 5 (1991): 178-192.

Young, Frank W., and Thomas A. Lyson. "Branch Plants and Poverty in the American South." *Sociological Forum* 8 (1993): 433-450.

Young, Laura M., and Brian Powell. "The Effects of Obesity on the Clinical Judgments of Mental Health Professionals." *Journal of Health and Social Behavior* 26 (September 1985): 233-246.

Young, Robert L. "Race, Conceptions of Crime and Justice, and Support for the Death Penalty." *Social Psychology Quarterly* 54 (1991): 67-75.

Young, T. R. *The Drama of Social Life: Essays in Post-Modern Social Psychology*. New Brunswick, NJ: Transaction, 1990.

Yuval Davis, Nira. "Front and Rear: The Sexual Division of Labor in the Israeli Army." *Feminist Studies* 11 (1985): 649-676.

Zabin, Laurie S., Marilyn B Hirsch, Mark R. Emerson, and Elizabeth Raymond. "To Whom Do Inner-City Minors Talk About Their Pregnancies? Adolescents' Communications with Parents and Parent Surrogates." *Family Planning Perspectives* 24 (1992): 148-152.

Zablocki, Benjamin. *Alienation and Charisma: A Study of Contemporary American Communes*. New York: Free Press, 1980.

Zahn-Wexler, C., M. Radke-Yarrow, E. Wagner, and M. Chapman. "Development of Concern for Others." *Developmental Psychology* 29 (1992): 126-136.

Zald, Mayer N., and Roberta Ash. "Social Movement Organizations." In Barry McLaughlin (Ed.), *Studies in Social Movements*, pp. 461-485. New York: Free Press, 1969.

Zald, Mayer N., and John D. McCarthy (Eds.). *Social Movements in an Organizational Society*. New Brunswick, NJ: Transaction Press, 1987.

Zaslavskaya, Tatyana. *The Second Socialist Revolution.* Blooming-ton, IN: Indiana UniversityPress, 1990.

Zeitlin, Maurice. *The Large Corporation and Contemporary Classes.* New Brunswick, NJ: Rutgers University Press, 1989.

Zelizer, Viviana A. *The Social Meaning of Money.* New York: Basic Books, 1994a.

Zelizer, Viviana A. *Pricing the Priceless Child.* New York: Basic Books, 2nd. ed. 1994b.

Zerubavel, Eviatar. *The Seven Day Circle: The History and Mean-ing of the Week.* New York: Free Press, 1985.

Zerubavel, Eviatar. *The Fine Line: Making Distinctions in Every-day Life.* New York: The Free Press, 1991.

Zey, Mary. *Banking on Fraud: Drexel, Junk Bonds, and Buyouts.* New York: Aldine de Gruyter, 1993.

Zhou, Min. *Chinatown: The Socioeconomic Potential of an Urban Enclave.* Philadelphia, PA: Temple University Press, 1992.

Zhou, Min, and John R. Logan. "In and Out of Chinatown: Residen-tial Mobility and Segregation of New York City's Chinese." *So-cial Forces* 70 (1991): 387-407.

Zhou, Xuegaung. "Unorganized Interests and Collective Action in China." *American Sociological Review* 58 (1993): 54-73.

Zigler, Edward, and Susan Muenchow. *Head Start: The Inside Story of America's Most Successful Educational Experiment.* New York: Basic Books, 1993.

Zimbalist, Andrew. *Baseball and Billions.* New York: Basic Books, 1992.

Zimbardo, Philip, Curtis W. Banks, Craig Haney, and David Jaffe. "The Mind Is a Formidable Jailer." *New York Times*, April 8, 1973.

Zimmer, Lynn. "Tokenism and Women in the Workplace: The Lim-its of Gender-Neutral Theory." *Social Problems* 35 (1988): 64-77.

Zimring, Franklin E., and Gordon Hawkins. *The Search for Ratio-nal Drug Control.* New York: Cambridge University Press, 1992.

Zipp, John F. "Social Class and Social Liberalism." *Sociological Forum* 1 (1986): 301-329.

Zipp, John F. "Government Employment and Black-White Earnings Inequality, 1980-1990." *Social Problems* 41 (1994): 363-382.

Zippay, Allison. *From Middle Income to Poor: Downward Mobil-ity among Displaced Steel Workers.* New York: Praeger, 1991.

Zola, Irving. "Medicine as an Institution of Social Control." In Peter Conrad and Rochelle Kern (Eds.), *The Sociology of Health and Illness.* pp. 398-408. New York: St. Martin's Press, 1990.

Zuboff, Shoshana. *In the Age of the Smart Machine: The Future of Work and Power.* NewYork: Basic Books, 1988.

Zuravin, Susan J. "Unplanned Childbearing and Family Size: Their Relationship to Child Neglect and Abuse." *Family Planning Perspectives* 23 (1991): 155-160.

Zwerling, Craig, and Hilary Silver. "Race and Job Dismissals in a Federal Bureaucracy." *American Sociological Review* 57 (1992): 651-660.

Author Index

Subject Index

Credits

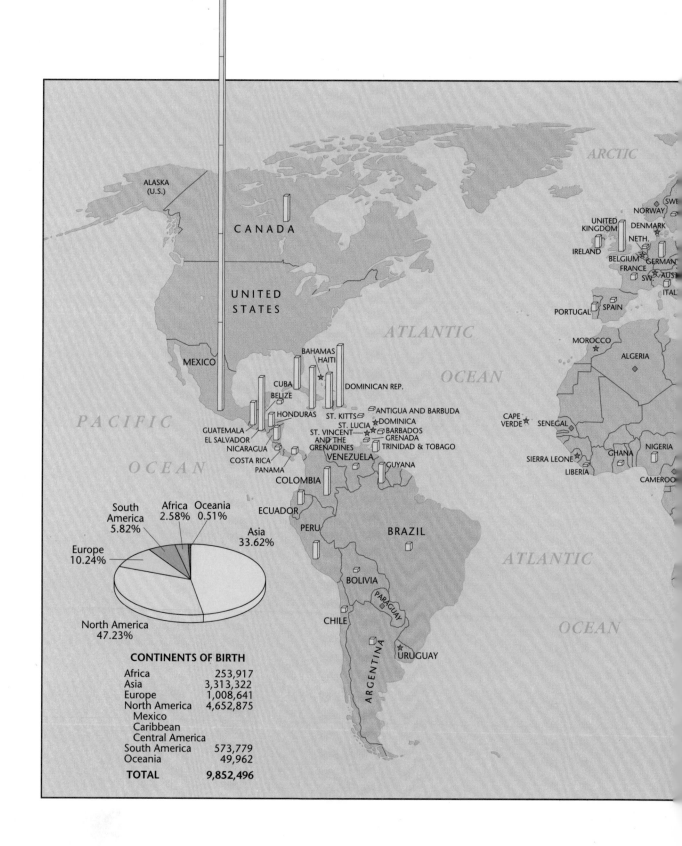

South
America
5.82%

Africa
2.58%

Oceania
0.51%

Asia
33.62%

Europe
10.24%

North America
47.23%

CONTINENTS OF BIRTH

Africa	253,917
Asia	3,313,322
Europe	1,008,641
North America	4,652,875
Mexico	
Caribbean	
Central America	
South America	573,779
Oceania	49,962
TOTAL	**9,852,496**